The WORLD

A BRIEF HISTORY

Combined Volume

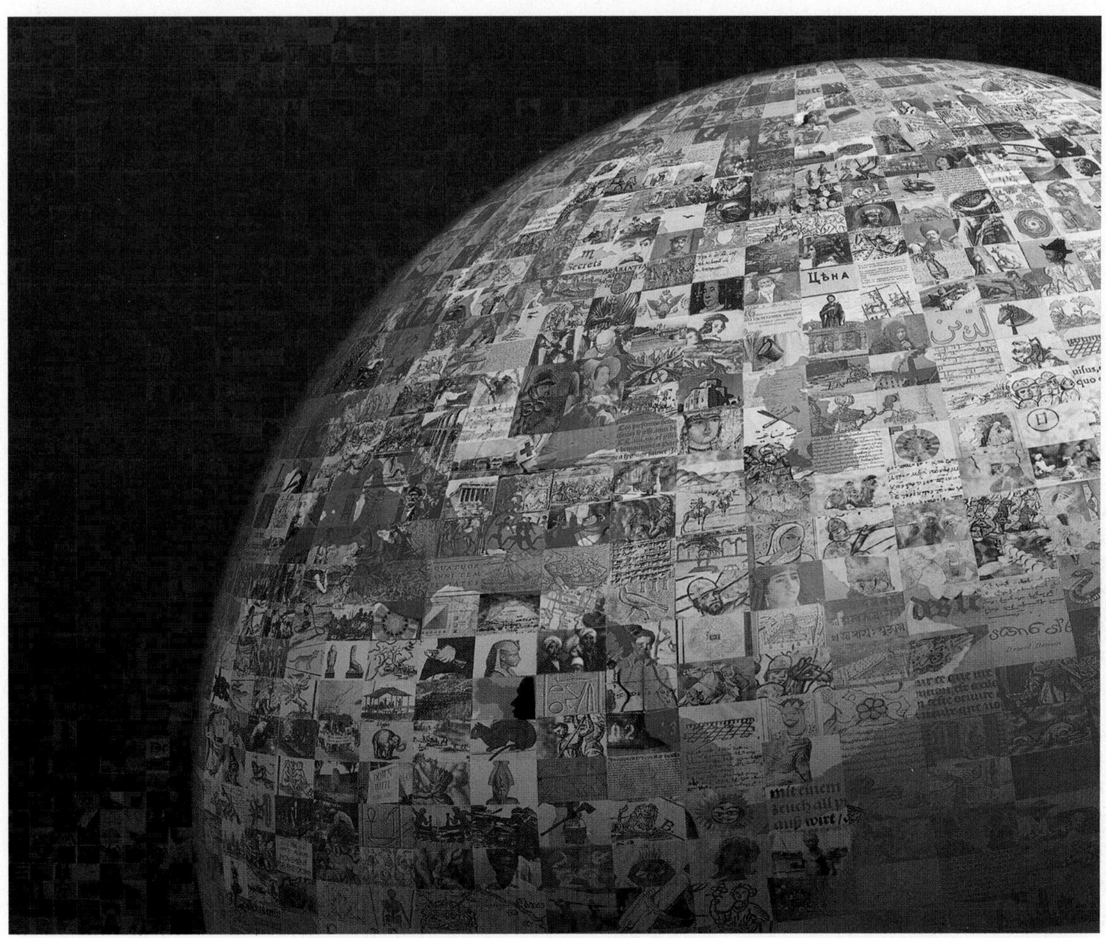

FELIPE FERNÁNDEZ-ARMESTO

Tufts University

Upper Saddle River, NJ 07458

Maps by

Dorling Kindersley

Library of Congress Cataloging-in-Publication Data

Fernández-Armesto, Felipe.
The world: a brief history / Felipe Fernández-Armesto.
p. cm.
Condensed version of: The world : history. c2007.
Includes bibliographical references and index.
ISBN 0-13-600921-2
1. Civilization--History. 2. World history. 3. Human ecology. I. Title.
CB151.F48 2008
909—dc22 2007029895

Executive Editor: Charles Cavaliere
Editorial Assistants: Maureen Diana, Lauren Aylward
Editor in Chief, Development: Rochelle Diogenes
Senior Development Editor: Gerald Lombardi
Senior Media Editor: Deborah O'Connell
Multimedia Specialist: Alison Lorber
Assistant Editor: Mayda C. Bosco
Director of Marketing: Brandy Dawson
Senior Marketing Manager: Kate Mitchell
Marketing Assistant: Jennifer Lang
Senior Managing Editor: Mary Carnis
Production Project Manager: Kathy Sleys
Operations Supervisor: Mary Ann Gloriande
Senior Art Director: Maria Lange
Cover Design: Maria Lange
Interior Design: Maria Lange/Kathy Mrozek
Design Support: Rob Aleman
Map Program Management: Gail Cocker-Bogusz, Scott Garrison
Cover Illustration: Corrin Skidds
Manager, Rights and Permissions: Zina Arabia
Manager, Visual Research: Beth Brenzel
AV Project Manager: Mirella Signoretto
Image Permission Coordinator: Craig A. Jones
Photo Researcher: Emma Brown
Composition/Full-Service Project Management: Frank Weihenig, Prepare, Inc.
Printer/Binder: Courier Companies, Inc.
Cover Printer: Phoenix Color Corporation

DK Maps designed and produced by DK Education, a division of Dorling Kindersley Limited, 80 Strand London WC2R 0RL. DK and the DK logo are registered trademarks of Dorling Kindersley Limited.

Credits and acknowledgments borrowed from other sources and reproduced, with permission, in this textbook appear on appropriate page within text or on page C-1.

Pearson Education Ltd.
Pearson Education Australia PTY, Ltd.
Pearson Education Singapore, Pte. Ltd.
Pearson Education North Asia Ltd.
Pearson Education, Canada, Ltd.
Pearson Educación de Mexico, S.A. de C.V.
Pearson Education–Japan
Pearson Education Malaysia, Pte. Ltd.

10 9 8 7
ISBN 13: 978-0-13-600921-4
ISBN 10: 0-13-600921-2

BRIEF CONTENTS

PART 1 Foragers and Farmers, to 5000 B.C.E. 2

1 Out of the Ice: Peopling the Earth 4
2 Out of the Mud: Farming and Herding After the Ice Age 26

PART 2 Farmers and Builders, 5000 to 500 B.C.E. 48

3 The Great River Valleys: Accelerating Change and Developing States 50
4 A Succession of Civilizations: Ambition and Instability 74
5 Rebuilding the World: Recoveries, New Initiatives, and Their Limits 96

PART 3 The Axial Age, from 500 B.C.E. to 100 C.E. 122

6 The Great Schools 124
7 The Great Empires 150

PART 4 Fitful Transitions, from the Third Century to the Tenth Century 178

8 Postimperial Worlds: Problems of Empires in Eurasia and Africa, ca. 200 to ca. 700 C.E. 180
9 The Rise of World Religions: Christianity, Islam, and Buddhism 210
10 Remaking the World: Innovation and Renewal on Environmental Frontiers in the Late First Millennium 236

PART 5 Contacts and Conflicts, 1000 C.E. to 1200 C.E. 260

11 Contending with Isolation, ca. 1000–1200 262
12 The Nomadic Frontiers: The Islamic World, Byzantium, and China, ca. 1000–1200 286

PART 6 The Crucible: The Eurasian Crises of the Thirteenth and Fourteenth Centuries 312

13 The World the Mongols Made 314
14 The Revenge of Nature: Plague, Cold, and the Limits of Disaster in the Fourteenth Century 342
15 Expanding Worlds: Recovery in the Late Fourteenth and Fifteenth Centuries 374

PART 7 Convergence and Divergence to ca. 1700 408

16 Imperial Arenas: New Empires in the Sixteenth and Seventeenth Centuries 410
17 The Ecological Revolution of the Sixteenth and Seventeenth Centuries 434
18 Mental Revolutions: Religion and Science in the Sixteenth and Seventeenth Centuries 462
19 States and Societies: Political and Social Change in the Sixteenth and Seventeenth Centuries 488

PART 8 Global Enlightenments, 1700–1800 514

20 Driven by Growth: The Global Economy in the Eighteenth Century 516
21 The Age of Global Interaction: Expansion and Intersection of Eighteenth-Century Empires 538
22 The Exchange of Enlightenments: Eighteenth-Century Thought 562

PART 9 The Frustrations of Progress to ca. 1900 586

23 Replacing Muscle: the Energy Revolutions 588
24 The Social Mold: Work and Society in the Nineteenth Century 614
25 Western Dominance in the Nineteenth Century: The Westward Shift of Power and the Rise of Global Empires 638
26 The Changing State: Political Developments in the Nineteenth Century 664

PART 10 Chaos and Complexity: The World in the Twentieth Century 690

27 The Twentieth-Century Mind: Western Science and the World 692
28 World Order and Disorder: Global Politics in the Twentieth Century 718
29 The Pursuit of Utopia: Civil Society in the Twentieth Century 748
30 The Embattled Biosphere: The Twentieth-Century Environment 774

CONTENTS

MAPS xix

INTRODUCING *THE WORLD* xxii

ABOUT FELIPE FERNÁNDEZ ARMESTO xxxi

PART 1 Foragers and Farmers, to 5000 B.C.E. 2

1 Out of the Ice: Peopling the Earth 4

SO YOU THINK YOU'RE HUMAN 5
- Human Evolution 6

OUT OF AFRICA 7
- Peopling the Old World 8
- Migration, Population, and Social Change 9

THE LAST GREAT ICE AGE 13
- Ice-Age Hunters 16
- Ice-Age Art 16
- Ice-Age Culture and Society 17
- Peopling the New World 19

SURVIVAL OF THE FORAGERS 21
- ■ IN PERSPECTIVE: After the Ice 23

2 Out of the Mud: Farming and Herding After the Ice Age 26

THE PROBLEM OF AGRICULTURE 28
- Preagricultural Settlements 29
- The Disadvantages of Farming 30

HUSBANDRY IN DIFFERENT ENVIRONMENTS 30
- Herders' Environments 32
- Tillers' Environments 33

THE SPREAD OF AGRICULTURE 38
- Europe 38
- Asia 38
- The Americas 38
- ■ A CLOSER LOOK: The Fertility Goddess of Çatalhüyük 39
- Africa 42
- The Pacific Islands 42

SO WHY DID FARMING START? 42
- Population Pressure 42
- The Outcome of Abundance 42
- The Power of Politics 43
- Cult Agriculture 43
- Climatic Instability 43
- Agriculture by Accident 44
- Production as an Outgrowth of Procurement 44
- ■ IN PERSPECTIVE: Seeking Stability 45

PART 2 Farmers and Builders, 5000 to 500 B.C.E. 48

3 The Great River Valleys: Accelerating Change and Developing States 50

GROWING COMMUNITIES, DIVERGENT CULTURES 52
Intensified Settlement and Its Effects 53

THE ECOLOGY OF CIVILIZATION 55

THE GREAT FLOODPLAINS 56
The Ecology of Egypt 56
Shifting Rivers of the Indus Valley 58
Fierce Nature in Early Mesopotamia 59
The Good Earth of Early China 61

CONFIGURATIONS OF SOCIETY 62
Patterns of Settlement and Labor 62
Politics 64
The Egyptian State 64
Statecraft in Mesopotamia 65
The First Documented Chinese State 67
Ruling the Harappan World 68
The Politics of Expansion 69
Literate Culture 71
■ IN PERSPECTIVE: What Made the Great River Valleys Different? 72

4 A Succession of Civilizations: Ambition and Instability 74

THE CASE OF THE HITTITE KINGDOM 76
The Importance of Trade 77
Hittite Society and Politics 79
Fragility and Fall: The End of Hatti 81

INSTABILITY AND COLLAPSE IN THE AEGEAN 81
Cretan Civilization 82
Mycenean Civilization 83

A GENERAL CRISIS IN THE EASTERN MEDITERRANEAN WORLD? 84
The Egyptian Experience 84
The Roots of Instability 85

THE EXTINCTION OF HARAPPAN CIVILIZATION 85
The Evidence of the *Rig Veda* 86
The Environment of Stress 86

CONFLICT ON THE YELLOW RIVER 86
The Rise of Zhou 87
The Zhou Political System 87

STATE-BUILDING IN THE AMERICAS 88
Andean Examples 88

Developments in Mesoamerica 89

ASSESSING THE DAMAGE 92
The Survival of Egypt 92
■ IN PERSPECTIVE: The Fatal Flaws 94

5 Rebuilding the World: Recoveries, New Initiatives, and Their Limits 96

TRADE AND RECOVERY IN THE MIDDLE EAST 98
The Phoenician Experience 98
The Assyrian Empire 99
The Babylonian Revival 102

GREECE AND BEYOND 103
The Greek Environment 103
Greek Colonialism 104
Early Greek Society 105
The Spread of State-Building and City-Building 106
■ A CLOSER LOOK: Thracian Horseback Hero 107

EMPIRES AND RECOVERY IN CHINA AND SOUTH ASIA 109
The Zhou Decline 109
South Asia: Relocated Centers of Culture 111
The Ganges Valley 111
Building Anew in Sri Lanka 112

THE FRUSTRATIONS OF ISOLATION 113
Developments in North America 113
New Initiatives in Africa 116
■ IN PERSPECTIVE: The Framework of Recovery 119

PART 3 The Axial Age, from 500 B.C.E. to 100 C.E. 122

6 The Great Schools 124

THE THINKERS OF THE AXIAL AGE 126

THE THOUGHTS OF THE AXIAL AGE 131
Religious Thinking 132
New Political Thinking 134
Challenging Illusion 137
Mathematics 137
Reason 138
Science 139
Medicine 141
Skepticism 142

AXIAL AGE–AXIAL AREA: THE STRUCTURES OF THE AXIAL AGE 143
■ IN PERSPECTIVE: The Reach of the Sages 147

7 The Great Empires 150

ROUTES THAT DREW THE OLD WORLD TOGETHER 152
The Sea Routes of the Indian Ocean 152
Land Routes: The Silk Roads 156

THE FIRST EURASIAN EMPIRE: PERSIA 157
The Persian Heartland 157
Persian Government 159
The Persian–Greek Wars 160
The Empire of Alexander the Great 160

THE RISE OF ROME 162
The Roman Frontiers 164
Imperial Culture and Commerce 164
The Celts 166

THE BEGINNINGS OF IMPERIALISM IN INDIA 166
Government 167
Asoka and His Mental World 168

CHINESE UNITY AND IMPERIALISM 169
Unity Endangered and Saved 170
The Menace from the Steppes 171

BEYOND THE EMPIRES 172
Japan and Korea 172
The Western Eurasian Steppe 172
Mesoamerica 173
■ IN PERSPECTIVE: The Aftermath of the Axial Age 174

PART 4 Fitful Transitions, from the Third Century to the Tenth Century 178

8 Postimperial Worlds: Problems of Empires in Eurasia and Africa, ca. 200 to ca. 700 C.E. 180

THE WESTERN ROMAN EMPIRE AND ITS INVADERS 184
Changes Within the Roman Empire 185
The "Barbarian" West 188

STEPPELANDERS AND THEIR VICTIMS 189
China 189
India 191

NEW FRONTIERS IN ASIA 192
Korea 192
Funan 193

THE RISE OF ETHIOPIA 193

The Crises of the Sixth and Seventh Centuries 194
Justinian and the Eastern Roman Empire 194
The New Barbarians 195
The Arabs 196
Islam 196
The Arabs Against Persia and Rome 197
The Muslim World 197
Recovery and Its Limits in China 200
Rise of the Tang 202
Empress Wu 202
Tang Decline 202
In the Shadow of Tang: Tibet and Japan 203
Tibet 203
Japan 204
■ IN PERSPECTIVE: The Triumph of Barbarism? 206

9 The Rise of World Religions: Christianity, Islam, and Buddhism 210
Commerce and Conflict: Carriers of Creeds 212
In the Islamic World 212
In Christendom 214
In the Buddhist World 214
Trade 214
Manichaeanism and the Uighurs 215
Christianity on the Silk Roads 215
Islam on Trade Routes 216
Monarchs and Missionaries 216
Constantine 217
Ezana 218
Trdat 218
Diplomatic Conversions 218
Buddhist Politics 219
Korea 219
Japan 220
Tibet 221
India 222
The Margins of Christendom 222
Vladimir and the Rus 223
Islam and the Turks 224
Trickle Down: Christianization and Islamization 224
Religious Lives: The World of Monks and Nuns 226
Christian Monasticism 226
Buddhist Monks 227
Sufism 228

Religious Women 229
■ IN PERSPECTIVE: The Triumphs of the Potential World Religions 229

10 Remaking the World: Innovation and Renewal on Environmental Frontiers in the Late First Millennium 236

ISOLATION AND INITIATIVE: SUB-SAHARAN AFRICA AND THE AMERICAS 238
African Geography 238
American Geography 239
■ A CLOSER LOOK: Royal Bloodletting 243
The Maize Frontiers 245

THE ISLAMIC WORLD AND THE ENVIRONMENT 246

FRONTIER GROWTH IN JAPAN 248

CHINA AND SOUTHEAST ASIA 250

THE PACIFIC 253

THE EXPANSION OF CHRISTENDOM 255
■ IN PERSPECTIVE: The Limits of Divergence 257

PART 5 Contacts and Conflicts, 1000 C.E. to 1200 C.E 260

11 Contending with Isolation: ca. 1000–1200 262

AMERICAN DEVELOPMENTS: FROM THE ARCTIC TO MESOAMERICA 264
Greenland and the North 264
The North American Southwest and the Mississippi Region 266
Mesoamerica 269

AROUND THE INDIAN OCEAN: ETHIOPIA, THE KHMER, AND INDIA 270
East Africa: The Ethiopian Empire 270
Southeast Asia: The Khmer Kingdom 271
India: Economy and Culture 273
India: The Chola Kingdom 275

EURASIA'S EXTREMITIES: JAPAN AND WESTERN EUROPE 275
Japan 276
Western Europe: Economics and Politics 277
Western Europe: Religion and Culture 281
■ IN PERSPECTIVE: The Patchwork of Effects 283

12 The Nomadic Frontiers: The Islamic World, Byzantium, and China, ca. 1000–1200 286

THE ISLAMIC WORLD AND ITS NEIGHBORS 288
The Coming of the Steppelanders 288
The Crusades 289
The Invaders from the Sahara 292
■ A CLOSER LOOK: A Cordovan Ivory Jar 294
The Progress of Sufism 296

THE BYZANTINE EMPIRE AND ITS NEIGHBORS 296
Byzantium and the Barbarians 296
Basil II 297
The Era of Difficulties 298
Byzantium and the Crusaders 300
Byzantine Art and Learning 302

CHINA AND THE NORTHERN BARBARIANS 303
The End of the Tang Dynasty 303
The Rise of the Song and the Barbarian Conquests 304
Economy and Society Under the Song 306
Song Art and Learning 308
■ IN PERSPECTIVE: Cains and Abels 309

PART 6 The Crucible: The Eurasian Crises of the Thirteenth and Fourteenth Centuries 312

13 The World the Mongols Made 314

THE MONGOLS: RESHAPING EURASIA 316
The Mongol Steppe 321
■ A CLOSER LOOK: A Mongol Passport 323

THE MONGOL WORLD BEYOND THE STEPPES: THE SILK ROADS, CHINA, PERSIA, AND RUSSIA 325
China 326
Persia 329
Russia 329

THE LIMITS OF CONQUEST: MAMLUK EGYPT AND MUSLIM INDIA 330
Muslim India: The Delhi Sultanate 331

EUROPE 332
■ IN PERSPECTIVE: The Uniqueness of the Mongols 336

14 The Revenge of Nature: Plague, Cold, and the Limits of Disaster in the Fourteenth Century 342

CLIMATE CHANGE 344

THE COMING OF THE AGE OF PLAGUE 348

The Course and Impact of Plague 350

Moral and Social Effects 351

THE LIMITS OF DISASTER: BEYOND THE PLAGUE ZONE 358

India 359

Southeast Asia 360

Japan 362

Mali 363

THE PACIFIC: SOCIETIES OF ISOLATION 366

■ IN PERSPECTIVE: The Aftershock 369

15 Expanding Worlds: Recovery in the Late Fourteenth and Fifteenth Centuries 374

FRAGILE EMPIRES IN AFRICA 377

East Africa 377

West Africa 378

ECOLOGICAL IMPERIALISM IN THE AMERICAS 381

The Inca Empire 381

The Aztec Empire 382

NEW EURASIAN EMPIRES 385

The Russian Empire 385

Timurids and the Ottoman Empire 386

THE LIMITATIONS OF CHINESE IMPERIALISM 391

THE BEGINNINGS OF OCEANIC IMPERIALISM 395

THE EUROPEAN OUTLOOK: PROBLEMS AND PROMISE 399

■ IN PERSPECTIVE: Beyond Empires 403

PART 7 Convergence and Divergence to ca. 1700 408

16 Imperial Arenas: New Empires in the Sixteenth and Seventeenth Centuries 410

MARITIME EMPIRES: PORTUGAL, JAPAN, AND THE DUTCH 412

The Portuguese Example 414

Asian Examples 416

The Dutch Connection 419

LAND EMPIRES: RUSSIA, CHINA, MUGHAL INDIA, AND THE OTTOMANS 422
China 423
The Mughal Example in India 423
The Ottomans 424
NEW LAND EMPIRES IN THE AMERICAS 426
Making the New Empires Work 429
THE GLOBAL BALANCE OF TRADE 430
■ IN PERSPECTIVE: The Impact of the Americas 431

17 The Ecological Revolution of the Sixteenth and Seventeenth Centuries 434

THE ECOLOGICAL EXCHANGE: PLANTS AND ANIMALS 436
Maize, Sweet Potatoes, and Potatoes 436
Weeds, Grasses, and Livestock 437
Cane Sugar 440
Coffee, Tea, and Chocolate 440
Patterns of Ecological Exchange 441
THE MICROBIAL EXCHANGE 442
Demographic Collapse in the New World 442
Plague and New Diseases in Eurasia 443
LABOR: HUMAN TRANSPLANTATIONS 444
WILD FRONTIERS: ENCROACHING SETTLEMENT 446
Northern and Central Asia: The Waning of Steppeland Imperialism 446
Pastoral Imperialism in Africa and the Americas 448
IMPERIALISM AND SETTLEMENT IN EUROPE AND ASIA 449
China 449
India 451
NEW EXPLOITATION IN THE AMERICAS 451
The Spanish Empire 451
Brazil 454
British North America 455
HOME FRONTS IN EUROPE AND ASIA 456
New Energy Sources 456
Land Reclamation 456
FRONTIERS OF THE HUNT 457
■ IN PERSPECTIVE: Evolution Redirected 459

18 Mental Revolutions: Religion and Science in the Sixteenth and Seventeenth Centuries 462

CHRISTIANITY IN CHRISTENDOM 464
CHRISTIANITY BEYOND CHRISTENDOM: THE LIMITS OF SUCCESS 467

THE MISSIONARY WORLDS OF BUDDHISM AND ISLAM 469
China and Japan 469
The Mongols 470
Islam 471

THE RESULTING MIX: GLOBAL RELIGIOUS DIVERSITY—AMERICAN AND INDIAN EXAMPLES 474
Black America 474
■ A CLOSER LOOK: The Cult Image of St. Elesbaan 475
White America 476
India 477

THE RENAISSANCE "DISCOVERY OF THE WORLD" 478

THE RISE OF WESTERN SCIENCE 480

WESTERN SCIENCE IN THE EAST 483
■ IN PERSPECTIVE: The Scales of Thought 485

19 States and Societies: Political and Social Change in the Sixteenth and Seventeenth Centuries 488

POLITICAL CHANGE IN EUROPE 490

WESTERN POLITICAL THOUGHT 492

WESTERN SOCIETY 493

THE OTTOMANS 495

MUGHAL INDIA AND SAFAVID PERSIA 498

CHINA 501
Chinese Politics 501
Chinese Society 502

TOKUGAWA JAPAN 504

THE NEW WORLD OF THE AMERICAS 505

AFRICA 509
■ IN PERSPECTIVE: Centuries of Upheaval 511

PART 8 Global Enlightenments, 1700–1800 514

20 Driven by Growth: The Global Economy in the Eighteenth Century 516

POPULATION TRENDS 518
Urbanization 519
Explanations 519
Medicine 522
The Ecology of Disease 523

ECONOMIC TRENDS: CHINA, INDIA, AND THE OTTOMAN EMPIRE 524
China 524
India 526
The Ottoman Empire and Its Environs 528
THE WEST'S PRODUCTIVITY LEAP 528
The Scientific Background 529
The British Example 529
THE EXPANSION OF RESOURCES 532
Global Gardening 532
■ IN PERSPECTIVE: New Europes, New Departures 536

21 The Age of Global Interaction: Expansion and Intersection of Eighteenth-Century Empires 538
ASIAN IMPERIALISM IN ARREST OR DECLINE: CHINA, PERSIA, AND THE OTTOMANS 540
China 541
The Asian Context 542
Persia and the Ottoman Empire 543
IMPERIAL REVERSAL IN INDIA: MUGHAL ECLIPSE AND BRITISH RISE TO POWER 544
THE DUTCH EAST INDIES 547
AFRICA, THE AMERICAS, AND THE SLAVE TRADE 548
LAND EMPIRES OF THE NEW WORLD 554
The Araucanos and the Sioux 554
Portugal in Brazil 554
Spanish America 555
Creole Mentalities 555
Toward Independence 556
■ IN PERSPECTIVE: The Rims of Empires 558

22 The Exchange of Enlightenments: Eighteenth-Century Thought 562
THE CHARACTER OF THE ENLIGHTENMENT 564
THE ENLIGHTENMENT IN GLOBAL CONTEXT 565
The Chinese Example 566
Japan 567
India 567
The Islamic World 567
THE ENLIGHTENMENT'S EFFECTS IN ASIA 568
The Enlightenment and China 568
Western Science in Japan 569
■ A CLOSER LOOK: A Meeting of China, Japan, and the West 570
Korea and Southeast Asia 571

The Ottomans 571

THE ENLIGHTENMENT IN EUROPE 572
The Belief in Progress 572
New Economic Thought 573
Social Equality 573
Anticlericalism 574

THE CRISIS OF THE ENLIGHTENMENT: RELIGION AND ROMANTICISM 575
Religious Revival 575
The Cult of Nature and Romanticism 576
Rousseau and the General Will 577
Pacific Discoveries 578
Wild Children 579
The Huron as Noble Savage 579

THE FRENCH REVOLUTION AND NAPOLEON 580
Background to the Revolution 580
Revolutionary Radicalism 581
Napoleon 581
■ IN PERSPECTIVE: The Afterglow of Enlightenment 583

PART 9 The Frustrations of Progress to ca. 1900 586

23 Replacing Muscle: The Energy Revolutions 588

GLOBAL DEMOGRAPHICS: THE WORLD'S POPULATION RISES 589

FOOD: TRANSITION TO ABUNDANCE 590

ENERGY FOR POWER: MILITARIZATION AND INDUSTRIALIZATION 596
Militarization 596
Industrialization 597

INDUSTRIALIZING EUROPE 601

INDUSTRY IN THE AMERICAS 604

JAPAN INDUSTRIALIZES 605

CHINA AND INDUSTRIALIZATION 607

INDIA AND EGYPT 608
■ IN PERSPECTIVE: Why the West? 610

24 The Social Mold: Work and Society in the Nineteenth Century 614

THE INDUSTRIALIZED ENVIRONMENT 616
Palaces of Work: The Rise of Factories 616
Critics of Industrialization: Gold from the Sewers 618

URBANIZATION 620

Beyond Industry: Agriculture and Mining 621

Changing Labor Regimes 624
Slavery and the Slave Trade 624
Female and Child Labor 628
Free Migrants 629

Hunters and Pastoralists 630

Elites Transformed 631
■ IN PERSPECTIVE: Cultural Exchange—Enhanced Pace, New Directions 635

25 Western Dominance in the Nineteenth Century: The Westward Shift of Power and the Rise of Global Empires 638

The Opium Wars 640

The White Empires: Rise and Resistance 641

Methods of Imperial Rule 648
■ A CLOSER LOOK: An Ethiopian View of the Battle of Adowa 649

Business Imperialism 652

Imperialism in the "New Europes" 655

Empires Elsewhere: Japan, Russia, and the United States 656

Rationales of Empire 658
Doctrines of Superiority 658
The Civilizing Mission 660
■ IN PERSPECTIVE: The Reach of Empires 661

26 The Changing State: Political Developments in the Nineteenth Century 664

Nationalism 666
Nationalism in Europe 666
The Case of the Jews 668
Nationalism Beyond Europe 669

Constitutionalism 672

Centralization, Militarization, and Bureaucratization 673
In and Around the Industrializing World 673
Beyond the Industrializing World 676

Religion and Politics 680

New Forms of Political Radicalism 681
Steps Toward Democracy 681
The Expansion of the Public Sphere 683

Western Social Thought 684
■ IN PERSPECTIVE: Global State-Building 686

PART 10 Chaos and Complexity: The World in the Twentieth Century 690

27 The Twentieth-Century Mind: Western Science and the World 692

WESTERN SCIENCE ASCENDANT 694
- China 695
- India 698
- The Wider World 698

THE TRANSFORMATION OF WESTERN SCIENCE 700
- Physics 700
- Human Sciences 702
- Anthropology and Psychology 705
- Philosophy and Linguistics 707

THE MIRROR OF SCIENCE: ART 709

THE TURN OF THE WORLD 714
- ■ IN PERSPECTIVE: Science, Challenging and Challenged 714

28 World Order and Disorder: Global Politics in the Twentieth Century 718

THE WORLD WAR ERA, 1914–1945 720
- The First World War 720
- Postwar Disillusionment 724
- The Shift to Ideological Conflicts 726
- The Second World War 729

THE COLD WAR ERA, 1945–1991 731
- Superpower Confrontation 731
- ■ A CLOSER LOOK: Reporting Our Harvest to Chairman Mao 736

DECOLONIZATION 738

THE NEW WORLD ORDER 742
- The European Union 743
- ■ IN PERSPECTIVE: The Anvil of War 744

29 The Pursuit of Utopia: Civil Society in the Twentieth Century 748

THE CONTEXT OF ATROCITIES 749

THE ENCROACHING STATE 750

UNPLANNING UTOPIA: THE TURN TOWARD INDIVIDUALISM 754

COUNTER-COLONIZATION AND SOCIAL CHANGE 757

GLOBALIZATION AND THE WORLD ECONOMY 762

CULTURE AND GLOBALIZATION 766

SECULARISM AND RELIGIOUS REVIVAL 767

■ IN PERSPECTIVE: The Century of Paradox 770

30 The Embattled Biosphere: The Twentieth-Century Environment 774

FUEL RESOURCES 778

FOOD OUTPUT 780

URBANIZATION 784

THE CRISIS OF CONSERVATION 785

THE UNMANAGEABLE ENVIRONMENT: CLIMATE AND DISEASE 787

■ IN PERSPECTIVE: The Environmental Dilemma 792

GLOSSARY G-1

A NOTE ON DATES AND SPELLING **DS-1**

NOTES N-1

CREDITS C-1

INDEX I-1

PRIMARY SOURCE: DOCUMENTS IN GLOBAL HISTORY **DVD-1**

* Indicates Interactive Map Explorations

*1.1 Early Human Migration, 150,000–40,000 years ago **10**

1.2 The Ice Age **15**

1.3 The Peopling of the New World, 13,000–8,000 B.C.E. **20**

2.1 Preagricultural Settlements in the Middle East **29**

2.2 Original Tillers' Environments, Early Crop Sites, and the Spread of Agriculture **40**

3.1 Intensified Settlements in Western Eurasia, 5,000–2,000 B.C.E. **55**

3.2 Ancient Egypt **58**

3.3 Harappan Civilization **59**

*3.4 Early Mesopotamia **60**

3.5 Early China **61**

*4.1 Trade in Anatolia and Mesopotamia, ca. 2000–1200 B.C.E. **78**

4.2 The Eastern Mediterranean, ca. 2000–1200 B.C.E. **83**

4.3 State-Building in the Americas, ca. 1500–1000 B.C.E. **90**

5.1 The Middle East and the Mediterranean, ca. 1000–500 B.C.E. **101**

5.2 China and South Asia, ca. 750 B.C.E. **110**

5.3 World Geography and Communication/Cultural Exchange **114**

*5.4 Africa, ca. 1000–500 B.C.E. **117**

6.1 The Axial Age **129**

6.2 The World According to Eratosthenes **140**

*7.1 Eurasian Trade, ca. 500 B.C.E.–100 C.E. **154**

7.2 The Empire of Alexander the Great **161**

7.3 The Roman World **163**

7.4 The Reign of Asoka, ca. 268–223 B.C.E. **167**

7.5 Monte Albán and Teotihuacán **173**

*8.1 The Maya and Teotihuacán **183**

8.2 The Western Roman Empire and Its Invaders **187**

8.3 Steppelanders and Asian Kingdoms, ca. 300–700 C.E. **190**

*8.4 The Muslim World, ca. 756 **198**

8.5 Tang China, Tibet, and Japan, ca. 750 C.E. **201**

9.1 The Rise of World Religions to 1000 C.E. **213**

9.2 The Christian World, ca. 1000 C.E. **230**; The Muslim World, ca. 1000 C.E.; The Spread of Buddhism to 1000 C.E. **231**

10.1 African Geography **239**

10.2 Mesoamerica and the Andes, 300 C.E. to 1000 C.E. **240**

10.3 Transmission of New Crops to the Islamic World, ca. 1000 **247**

10.4 China, Japan, and Southeast Asia, ca. 1000 **252**

*11.1 Thule Inuit and Norse Migrations to ca. 1200 **265**

11.2 North America and Mesoamerica to ca. 1200 **267**

11.3 The Indian Ocean: From Ethiopia to Cambodia, ca. 1000–1200 **274**

12.1 The Middle East and the Mediterranean, ca. 900–1100 **290**

12.2 The Almoravids and the Almohads **295**

12.3 Byzantium and Its Neighbors, ca. 1050 **299**

12.4 Song Empire, ca. 1150 **305**

*13.1 Mongol Compaigns of the Thirteenth Century **319**

13.2 European Travelers of the Mongol Roads, 1245–1295 **322**

13.3 The Travels of Rabban Bar Sauma, 1275–1288 **327**

13.4 The Delhi Sultanate **332**

13.5 Latin Christendom, 1200–1300 **334**

13.6 Grassland Environments Compared **339**

14.1 Climate Change in the Fourteenth Century **347**

*14.2 The Black Death, 1320–1355 **352**; The Travels of Ibn Battuta **353**

14.3 Jews in Medieval Europe and the Middle East, 1100–1400 **355**

14.4 South and Southeast Asia, ca. 1350 **359**

14.5 Japan, ca. 1350 **363**

*14.6 The Kingdom of Mali, ca. 1350 **364**

14.7 Societies of the Pacific, ca. 1400 **368**

14.8 The Ottoman State, ca. 1400 **370**

15.1 Great Zimbabwe **377**

15.2 Major African States, 1400–1500 **380**

15.3 The Aztec and Inca Empires, ca. 1500; The Valley of Mexico **383**

15.4 The Russian Empire, ca. 1505 **387**

15.5 Timur and the Ottomans, ca. 1370–1500 **389**

15.6 Ming China and the Voyages of Zheng He **393**

***15.7** Winds and Ocean Currents Worldwide **396**

15.8 European Oceanic Exploration up to 1500 **400**

16.1 Maritime Imperialism in the Indian and Pacific Oceans, 1500–1700 **416**

16.2 Eurasian Land Empires of the Sixteenth and Seventeenth Centuries **422**

16.3 Land Empires in the Americas, ca. 1700 **427**

17.1 Ecological, Microbial Exchanges, 1500–1700; Genetic Sameness **439**

17.2 Imperialism and Settlement in Eurasia, 1600–1725 **447**

17.3 Land Exploitation in the Americas Up to ca. 1725 **453**

18.1 The Spread of Christianity, Islam, and Buddhism in Asia by 1750 **471**

18.2 The Spread of Islam in Africa, ca. 1700 **473**

19.1 The Dominions of Charles V **491**

19.2 The Spanish Monarchy in 1600 **492**

19.3 The Safavid Empire, 1501–1736 **500**

19.4 Tokugawa Japan **504**

***19.5** Maroon Communities in the Americas, 1500–1800 **508**

19.6 West and West-Central Africa, ca. 1750 **510**

20.1 World Population Growth, 1500–1800 **520;** The Growth of London in the Eighteenth Century **521**

20.2 China in the Late Eighteenth Century **525**

20.3 Industrial Britain, ca. 1800 **531**

21.1 Wahhabi Expansion **544**

21.2 The Marathas **545**

21.3 European Expansion in South and Southeast Asia, ca. 1800 **546**

***21.4** The World Slave Trade, ca. 1800 **550**

21.5 The Sokoto Fulani Kingdom, ca. 1820 **553**

21.6 The Americas in 1828 **559**

22.1 The Shape of the Earth **565**

22.2 Napoleon's Empire, ca. 1799–1815 **582**

23.1 World Population Growth, ca. 1700–1900 **592**

23.2 Industrialization, Technology, and Food Manufacturing in the Nineteenth Century **595**

23.3 The Industrialization of Europe by 1914 **602**

23.4 The Politics of Cotton **609**

24.1 The Growth of Manchester, England 1840–1900 **620**

24.2 The Movement of Indentured Labor in the Late Nineteenth Century **627**

***24.3** Ethnic Neigborhoods in Manhattan, ca. 1920 **632;** World Migration 1860–1920 **633**

25.1 Foreign Imperialism in East and Southeast Asia, 1840–1910 **642**

***25.2** The Imperial World, 1900 **644**

25.3 The Scramble for Africa **654**

25.4 Russian and Japanese Expansion, 1868–1918 **657**

26.1 The Peoples of Europe; Nationalities Within the Habsburg Empire **667**

***26.2** Examples of Resistance to European and United States Imperialism, 1880–1920 **669**

26.3 Revolts in the Qing Empire, 1850–1901 **675**

26.4 Muslim Reform Movements in Africa and Arabia in the Nineteenth Century **679**

27.1 Spread of Western Scientific Learning, 1866–1961 **696**

28.1 Europe, the Middle East, and North Africa in 1914 and 1923 **722**

28.2 World War II **730**

28.3 The Alliances of the Cold War **733**

28.4 Decolonization Since World War II **740**

29.1 Genocides and Atrocities, 1900–Present; The Holocaust **752**

29.2 Percentage of Noncitizen Population, ca. 2005 **758**

***29.3** International Trade Flows, ca. 2004 **764**

30.1 World Population, 2003 **777**

30.2 Comparative World Wealth, ca. 2004 **778**

***30.3** Population in Urban Areas, ca. 2005 **785**

***30.4** Deforestation Worldwide, ca. 2005 **786**

30.5 Life Expectancy, ca. 2005 **790**

30.6 HIV in Africa **792**

By the standards of astronauts, say, or science fiction writers, historians seem timid, unadventurous creatures who are only interested in one puny species—our species, the human species—on one tiny planet—our planet, Earth. But Earth is special. So far, we know of nowhere else in the cosmos where so much has happened and is happening today. By galactic standards, global history is a small story—but it's a good one.

Humans, moreover, compared with other animals, seem outward looking. Our concerns range over the universe and beyond it, to unseen worlds, vividly imagined or mysteriously revealed. Not just everything we do but also everything that occurs to our minds is part of our history and, therefore, part of this book, including science and art, fun and philosophy, speculations and dreams. We continually generate stories—new stories—at an amazing rate.

But the present passes instantly into the past. The present is always over, transformed into history. And the past is always with us, tugging at our memories, shaping our thoughts, launching and limiting our lives. So human history may seem narrowly self-interested, but it focuses on a riveting subject that is also our favorite subject—ourselves.

THE WAY OF HUMANKIND

Though the story of this book is a human story, it can never be merely human because, in isolation, humankind does not make perfect sense. Humans are animals, and to understand ourselves thoroughly and to know what, if anything, makes us unique, we have to compare ourselves with other animals. As with other animals, we are best studied in our habitats. We cannot begin to comprehend our own history except in context. Our story is inseparable from the climates where it takes place and the other life-forms that we depend on or compete with. All the elaborate culture we produce generates new, intimate relationships with the environment we refashion and the life-forms we exploit.

We are exceptionally ambitious compared to other animals, consciously remodeling environments to suit ourselves. We turn prairies into wheat lands, deserts into gardens, and gardens into deserts. We fell forests where we find them and plant them where none exist; we dam rivers, wall seas, cultivate plants, extinguish some species, and call others into being by selective breeding. Sometimes we smother terrain with environments we build for ourselves. Yet nothing we do liberates us from nature. As we shall see, one of the paradoxes of the human story is that the more we change the environment, the more vulnerable we become to ecological lurches and unpredictable disasters. Failure to establish a balance between exploitation and conservation has often left civilizations in ruins. History becomes a path picked across the wreckage. This does not mean that the environment determines our behavior or our lives, but it does set the framework in which we act.

We are an exceptionally successful species in terms of our ability to survive in a wide range of diverse climates and landscapes—more so than just about any other creatures, except for the microbes we carry around with us. But even we are still explorers of our planet, still trying to change it. Indeed, we have barely begun to change planet Earth, though, as we shall see, some human societies have devoted the last 10,000 years to trying to do it. We call ourselves masters, or, more modestly, caretakers of creation, but about 90 percent of the biosphere is too far underwater or too deep below the Earth for us to inhabit with the technology we have at present: These are environments that humans have only recently begun to invade and that we still do not dominate.

If we humans are peculiarly ambitious creatures, who are always intruding in the life of the planet, we are also odd compared to other animals in the way we generate change among ourselves. We are an unpredictable, unstable species. Lots of other animals live social lives and construct societies. But those societies are remarkably stable compared to ours. As far as we know, ants and elephants have the same lifeways and the same kinds of relationships that they have had since their species first appeared. That is not to say animals never change their cultures. One of the fascinating discoveries in primatology is that apes and monkeys develop cultural differences from one another, even between groups living in similar and sometimes adjacent environments. In West Africa, chimpanzees have developed a termite-catching technology. They "fish" with stripped branches that they plunge into termite nests but do not use tools to break open nuts. Chimps in a neighboring region ignore the termites but are experts in nut cracking, using rocks like hammers and anvils. In Sumatra in Indonesia, orangutans play a game—jumping from falling tress—that is unknown to their cousins in nearby Borneo. In East Africa, some male baboons control harems while others have one mate after another. In some chimpanzee societies, hunting and meat eating seem to have increased dramatically in recent times.

These are amazing facts, but the societies of nonhuman animals still change little compared with ours. So, alongside the theme of human interaction with the rest of nature is another great theme of our history: the ways our societies have changed, grown apart from one another, reestablished contact, and influenced one another in their turn.

THE WAY OF THIS BOOK

This book, then, interweaves two stories—of our interactions with nature and with each other. The environment-centered story is about humans distancing themselves from the rest of nature and searching for a balance between constructive and destructive exploitation. The culture-centered story is of how human cultures have influenced each other but also been different from each other. Both stories have been going on for thousands of years. We do not know whether they will end in triumph or disaster.

No one book can cover all of world history, and the fabric of this book is woven from carefully selected strands. Readers will see these at every turn, twisted together into yarn, stretched into stories. Human-focused historical ecology—the environmental theme—will drive readers back, again and again, to the same concepts: food, shelter, disease, energy, technology, art. (The last is a vital category for historians, not only because it is part of our interface with the rest of the world, but also because it forms a record of how we see reality and of how we see it change.) In the global story of human interactions—the cultural theme—we return constantly to the ways people make contact with each another: migration, trade, war, imperialism, pilgrimage, gift exchange, diplomacy, travel—and to their social frameworks: the economic and political arenas, the human groups and groupings, the states and civilizations, the sexes and generations, the classes and clusters of identity. In both stories, ideas and imagination play key roles, because most—perhaps all—of the changes we make happen first in our heads. We observe the world as it is, imagine it differently, and try to fend off our fears and realize our hopes.

The stories that stretch before us are full of human experience. "The stork feeds on snakes," said the ancient Greek sage Agathon, "the pig on acorns, and history on human lives." To build up our picture of human societies and ecosystems of the past we have to start with the evidence people have left. Then we reassemble it bit by bit, with the help of imagination disciplined by the sources. Anyone reading a history book needs to remember that interpreting evidence is a challenge—half burden and half opportunity. The subject matter of history is not the past directly because the past is never available to our senses. We have only the evidence about it. This makes history an art, not a science, a disciplined art like that of poetry disciplined by rhyme and meter, or a novel disciplined by character and plot, or a play disciplined by the limitations of stagecraft.

For a book like this, the sources set the limits of my imagination. Sometimes, these are concrete clues to what people really did—footprints of their wanderings, debris of their meals, fragments of their technologies, wreckage of their homes, traces of diseases in their bones. Usually, however, the sources reflect at best, not the way things were but the way people wished to represent them in their arts, crafts, and writings. Most sources—in short—are evidence of what happened only in the minds of those who made them. This means, in turn, that our picture of what went on in the world beyond human minds is always tentative and open to reinterpretation. The historian's job is not—cannot be—to say what the past was like, but rather, what it felt like to live in it, because that is what the evidence tends to reveal.

One of the most admirable historians of the twentieth century, R. G. Collingwood, who was also a professor of philosophy at Oxford, said that "all history is intellectual history." He was right. History—even the environmental and cultural history that is the subject of this book—is largely about what people perceived rather than what they really saw, what they thought or felt rather than what happened outwardly, what they represented rather than what was real. The nineteenth-century philosopher Arthur Schopenhauer, one of the most pessimistic thinkers ever, who drew on Hindu and Buddhist writings for his inspiration, said that history's only subject was "humankind's oppressive, muddlesome dream." He thought it made history pointless. I think it makes it intriguing.

Because the evidence is always incomplete, history is less a matter of describing or narrating or question-answering than it is of problem-posing. No one reading this book should expect to be instructed in straightforward facts or to acquire proven knowledge. The thrill of history is asking the right question, not getting the right answer. Most of the time, we can only hope to identify interesting problems that stimulate debate. And we have to accept that the debate is worthwhile for its own sake, even if we have insufficient knowledge to reach conclusions.

Historians do not even agree about which questions to ask. Some—including me—are interested in huge philosophical questions, such as how does history happen? What makes change? Is it random or subject to scientific laws? Do impersonal forces beyond human control—environmental factors or economics or some world force called fate, evolution, God, or progress—determine it? Or is change the externalization of ideas that people project onto the world? And if it's a mixture of all or some of these, what's the balance?

Some historians ask questions about how human societies function. How and why do societies grow and fragment and take different forms? How do people get power over others? How and why do revolutions happen and states and civilizations rise and fall?

Other historians like to pose problems about the present. How did we get into the mess we're in? Can we trace the causes of our problems back into the past and, if so, how far? Why do we have a globally connected world without global governance? Why is peace always precarious? Why does ecological overkill menace our environment? Having accounted—or failed to account—for the present, some historians like to focus on the future. They demand lessons from history about how to change our behavior or cope with recurrences of past difficulties. Others, again, search to make sense of the past, to find a way to characterize or narrate it that makes us feel we understand it.

Yet others—the majority, and again including me—like to study the past for its own sake and try to identify the questions that mattered to people at the time they first asked them. This does not mean that the sort of history found in this book is useless (although I do not necessarily think it would be a bad thing if it were). For to penetrate the minds of people of the past—especially the remote past of cultures other than your own—you have to make a supreme effort of understanding. The effort enhances life by sharpening responses to the streetscapes and landscapes, art and artifacts, laws and letters we have inherited from the past. And understanding is what we need most today in our multicultural societies and multi-civilizational world.

HOW THIS BOOK IS ARRANGED

After finding the time, accumulating the knowledge, posing the questions, stiffening the muscles, and summoning the blood, the big problem for the writer of a global history textbook is organizing the material. The big problem for the reader is navigating it. It is tempting to divide the world into regions or cultures or even—as I did in a previous book—into biomes and devote successive chapters to each. You could call that "world history," if you genuinely managed to cover the world. But "global history" is different: an attempt to see the planet whole, as if from an immense, astral height, and discern themes that truly transcend geographical and cultural boundaries. In this book, therefore, I try to look at every continent in just about every chapter (there are a couple of chapters that, for reasons described in their place, focus only on part of the world). Each chapter concentrates on themes from the two great global stories: how human societies diverge and converge, and how they interact with the rest of nature.

Because history is a story, in which the order of events matters, the chapters are arranged chronologically. There are 30 chapters—one for each week in a typical U.S. academic year (though of course, every reader or group of readers will go at their own pace)—and ten parts. I hope there is plenty to surprise readers without making the parts perversely defiant of the "periods" historians conventionally speak of. Part I runs roughly from 150,000 to 20,000 years ago, and, on the whole, the periods covered get shorter as sources accumulate, cultures diverge, data multiply, and readers' interests quicken. Of course, no one should be misled into thinking the parts are more than devices of convenience. Events that happened in, say, 1850, are in a different part of this book from those that happened in, say, 1750. But the story is continuous, and the parts could be recrafted to start and end at different moments.

At every stage, some parts of the world are more prominent than others, because they are more influential, more populous, more world-shaping. For much of the book, China occupies relatively more space, because China has, for much of the past, been immensely rich in globally influential initiatives. In the coverage of the last couple of centuries, Europe and the United States get a lot of attention: this is not "Eurocentrism" or "Westocentrism" (if there is such a word), but an honest reflection of how history happened. But I have tried not to neglect the peoples and parts of the world that historians usually undervalue: poor and peripheral communities, the margins and frontiers of the world, are often where world-changing events happen—the fault lines of civilizations, which radiate seismic effects.

HOW THIS BOOK HELPS STUDENTS

Pedagogy that Focuses and Enriches

The pedagogical features in *The World* help students engage with the narrative, provide reinforcement for learning, and enrich their study of world history.

Focus Questions open each chapter and encourage students to think critically while they read.

An Extensive and Integrated Map Program, created by Dorling Kindersley, one of the world's leading cartographic publishers, provides clear and innovative perspectives on both the larger themes and the particular events of world history.

Compelling Visual Sources, tightly coordinated with the text, include images never before published and captions that stimulate inquiry.

A Closer Look sections provide in-depth visual analysis of a specific cultural artifact. Detailed notes draw the viewer into close contact with the object.

Making Connections tables throughout the text offer visual summaries of important concepts. Instead of simply listing facts, these tools help students see connections that span across regions.

In-text Pronunciation Guides, embedded directly in the narrative, provide phonetic spellings for terms that may be unfamiliar to students.

Key Terms are defined in the Glossary and set in boldface type in the text

In Perspective sections end each chapter and ask students to consider the fundamental questions of a time period in world history.

HOW THIS BOOK SUPPORTS TEACHERS AND STUDENTS

An Extensive Teaching and Learning Package

The supplement package has been carefully crafted to enhance the instructor's classroom teaching experience and to provide students with resources that enrich the learning process.

Extensively revised and updated, the **Primary Source: Documents in Global History DVD** is both an immense collection of textual and visual documents in world history and an indispensable tool for working with sources. Extensively developed with the guidance of historians and teachers, the revised and updated DVD-ROM version includes over 800 sources in world history—from cave art to satellite images of the Earth from space. More sources from Africa, Latin America, and Southeast Asia have been added to this revised and updated DVD-ROM version. All sources are accompanied by headnotes and focus questions, and they are searchable by topic or region. The DVD comes with all new copies of *The World*. A stand-alone version can be purchased separately (0-13-178938-4).

myhistorylab www.myhistorylab.com With the best of Prentice Hall's multimedia solutions in one easy-to-use place, MyHistoryLab for *The World: A Brief History* offers students and instructors a state-of-the-art, interactive solution for world history. Organized by the main subtopics of *The World*, and delivered within a course-management platform (WebCT or Blackboard), or as a website, MyHistoryLab supplements and enriches the classroom experience and can form the basis for an online course.

www.prenhall.com/armesto The open-access companion website for *The World* includes study questions, flash cards, and interactive maps.

The **Instructor's Resource DVD** offers class presentation resources, including all of the maps and many of the illustrations from the text, PowerPoint presentations, and Classroom-Response System presentations.

The **Instructor's Guide to Teaching the World** provides everything instructors need to incorporate *The World: A Brief History* into their courses. An extensive Test-Item File, sample syllabi from users of *The World: A Brief History*, and teaching notes authored by David Ringrose, University of California, San Diego, enrich the utility of the Guide.

CourseSmart Learn Smart. Choose Smart. **CourseSmart Textbooks Online** is an exciting new *choice* for students looking to save money. As an alternative to purchasing the print textbook, students can *subscribe* to the same content online and save up to 50% off the suggested list price of the print text. With a CourseSmart eTextbook, students can search the text, make notes online, print out reading assignments that incorporate lecture notes, and bookmark important passages for later review. For more information, or to subscribe to the CourseSmart eTextbook, visit www.coursesmart.com.

Study on the go with **VangoNotes**. VangoNotes is a digital audio study guide for *The World: A Brief History* that can be downloaded to an mp3 player. Students can study wherever they are or whatever they are doing by listening to the key concepts they need to know for each chapter of *The World.*

VangoNotes are **flexible**; students can download all the material directly to their mp3 players, or only the chapters they need. www.vangonotes.com

Study Guide, Volumes I and II, includes practice tests, essay questions, and map exercises.

Titles from the renowned **Penguin Classics** series can be bundled with *The World: A Brief History* for a nominal charge. Please contact your Pearson Arts and Sciences sales representative for details.

The Prentice Hall Atlas in World History, Second Edition includes over 100 full-color maps in world history, drawn by Dorling Kindersley, one of the world's most respected cartographic publishers. Copies of the *Atlas* can be bundled with *The World* for a nominal charge. Contact your Pearson Arts and Sciences sales representative for details.

DEVELOPING *THE WORLD*

Developing a project like *The World* required the input and counsel of hundreds of individuals. We thank all those who shared their time and effort to make *The World* a better book.

Reviewers

Donald R. Abbott, San Diego Mesa College
Wayne Ackerson, Salisbury University
Roger Adelson, Arizona State University
Alfred J. Andrea, University of Vermont (Emeritus)
David G. Atwill, Pennsylvania State University
Mauricio Borrero, St. John's University
Leonard Blussé, Harvard University
John Brackett, University of Cincinnati
Gayle K. Brunelle, California State University—Fullerton
Fred Burkhard, Maryland University College
Antoinette Burton, University of Illinois
Jorge Cañizares-Esguerra, University of Texas—Austin
Elaine Carey, St. John's University
Tim Carmichael, College of Charleston
Douglas Chambers, University of Southern Mississippi
Nupur Chaudhuri, Texas Southern University
David Christian, San Diego State University
Duane Corpis, Georgia State University
Dale Crandall-Bear, Solano Community College
Touraj Daryaee, California State University—Fullerton
Jeffrey M. Diamond, College of Charleston
Brian Fagan, University of California—Santa Barbara
Nancy Fitch, California State University—Fullerton
Alison Fletcher, Kent State University
Patricia Gajda, The University of Texas at Tyler
Richard Golden, University of North Texas
Stephen S. Gosch, University of Wisconsin—Eau Claire
Jonathan Grant, Florida State University
Mary Halavais, Sonoma State University
Shah M. Hanifi, James Madison University
Russell A. Hart, Hawaii Pacific University
Phyllis G. Jestice, University of Southern Mississippi
Amy J. Johnson, Berry College
Deborah Smith Johnston, Lexington High School
Eric A. Jones, Northern Illinois University
Ravi Kalia, City College of New York
David M. Kalivas, Middlesex Community College
Frank Karpiel, College of Charleston
David Kenley, Marshall University
Andrew J. Kirkendall, Texas A&M University
Dennis Laumann, The University of Memphis
Donald Leech, University of Minnesota
Jennifer M. Lloyd, SUNY—Brockport
Aran MacKinnon, University of West Georgia
Moria Maguire, University of Arkansas—Little Rock
Susan Maneck, Jackson State University

Anthony Martin, Wellesley College
Dorothea Martin, Appalachian State University
Adam McKeown, Columbia University
Ian McNeely, University of Oregon
Margaret E. Menninger, Texas State University—San Marcos
Stephen Morillo, Wabash College
William Morison, Grand Valley State University
Laura Neitzel, Brookdale Community College
Kenneth J. Orosz, University of Maine—Farmington
Michael Pavkovic, Hawaii Pacific University
Kenneth Pomeranz, University of California—Irvine
Phyllis E. Pobst, Arkansas State University
Sara B. Pritchard, Montana State University
Norman Raiford, Greenville Technical College
Stephen Rapp, Georgia State University
Vera Blinn Reber, Shippensburg University
Matthew Redinger, Montana State University—Billings
Matthew Restall, Pennsylvania State University
Jonathan Reynolds, Arkansas State University
Richard Rice, University of Tennessee—Chattanooga
Peter Rietbergen, Catholic University (Nijmegen)
David Ringrose, University of California—San Diego
Patricia Romero, Towson University
Morris Rossabi, Queens College
David G. Rowley, University of Wisconsin—Platteville
Sharlene Sayegh, California State University—Long Beach
William Schell, Murray State University
Linda Bregstein Scherr, Mercer County Community College
Patricia Seed, University of California, Irvine
Lawrence Sondhaus, University of Indianapolis
Richard Steigmann-Gall, Kent State University
John Thornton, Boston University
Ann Tschetter, University of Nebraska—Lincoln
Deborah Vess, Georgia College & State University
Stephen Vinson, SUNY—New Paltz
Joanna Waley-Cohen, New York University
Anne M. Will, Skagit Valley College
John Wills, University of Southern California
Theodore Jun Yoo, University of Hawaii—Manoa

ACKNOWLEDGMENTS

Without being intrusive, I have tried not to suppress my presence—my voice, my views—in the text, because no book is objective, other than by pretense, and the reader is entitled to get to know the writer's foibles and failures. In overcoming mine, I have had a lot of help (though there are sure still to be errors and shortcomings through my fault alone). Textbooks are teamwork, and I have learned an immense amount from my friends and helpers at Pearson Prentice Hall, especially my editors, Charles Cavaliere and Gerald Lombardi, whose indefatigability and forbearance made the book better at every turn. I also thank the picture researcher Emma Brown and the members of the production and cartographic sections of the team who performed Herculean labors: Mary Carnis, managing editor; Kathleen Sleys, production project manager; Frank Weihenig, production editor; Marianne Gloriande, print buyer; Maria Lang, designer; Alison Lorber, media editor; and Maureen Diana, editorial assistant. Finally, Kate Mitchell has once again crafted a superb marketing campaign.

I could not have gotten through the work without the help and support of my wonderful colleagues at Queen Mary, University of London; the Institute of Historical Research, University of London; and the History Department of Tufts University. I owe special thanks to the many scholars who share and still share their knowledge of global history at the Pearson Prentice Hall Seminar Series in Global History, which now meets at Tufts University. David Ringrose of University of California, San Diego, was a constant guide, whose interest never flagged and whose wisdom never failed. Many colleagues and counterparts advised me on their fields of expertise or performed heroic self-sacrifice in putting all of the many pieces of the book together: Natia Chakvetadze, Shannon Corliss, Maria Guarascio,

Anita Castro, Conchita Ordonez, Sandra Garcia, Maria Garcia, Ernest Tucker (United States Naval Academy), David Way (British Library), Antony Eastmond (Courtland Institute), Morris Rossabi (Columbia University), David Atwill and Jade Atwill (Pennsylvania State University), Stephen Morillo (Wabash College), Peter Carey (Oxford University), Jim Mallory (Queens University, Belfast), Matthew Restall (Pennsylvania State University), Roderick Whitfield (School of Oriental and African Studies, University of London), Barry Powell (University of Wisconsin), Leonard Blussé (Harvard University), Guolong Lai (University of Florida), and Jai Kabaranda, my former graduate student at Queen Mary, as well as the many good people whose assistance I may have failed to acknowledge.

In making this abridged version of the original book, I have been able to make some small changes as well as many cuts. Readers inspired most of these, and I am especially grateful to the universities that gave me a chance to talk to teachers and students who have used or were going to use the book: Colorado State University; Jackson State University; Northern Kentucky University; Pennsylvania State University; Salem State University; the U.S. Air Force Academy; the US Naval Academy; the University at Buffalo (SUNY); the Ohio State University; the University of Arkansas, Little Rock; and the University of Memphis. I also learned a lot from the comments and feedback from subscribers to the H-World listserv. They are too numerous to name, but I owe special debts for self-sacrificingly generous help to Jack Betterly, Jerry Green, David Kalivas, and Peter Wozniak. I am also indebted to seminar-goers at the Boston Global History Consortium's Global History Seminar at Tufts University. But it has taken a long time to produce the book, and much of the good advice I've had, which came too late or required too much re-thinking for the time available, will only be reflected in future editions, if I am lucky enough to have any.

Felipe Fernández-Armesto
Tufts University
Fall 2007

About Felipe Fernández-Armesto

Felipe Fernández-Armesto holds the Prince of Asturias chair of Spanish Civilization at Tufts University where he also directs the Pearson Prentice Hall Seminar Series in Global History. Fernández-Armesto is a visiting professor of Global Environmental History at Queen Mary College, University of London, and is on the editorial board of the History of Cartography for the University of Chicago Press, the editorial committee of Studies in Overseas History (Leiden University), and the *Journal of Global History*. He has also served on the Council of the Hakluyt Society and was Chairman of Trustees of the PEN Literary Foundation. Recent awards include a Premio Nacional de Investigación (Sociedad Geográfica Española) in 2003, a fellowship at the Netherlands Institute of Advanced Study in the Humanities and Social Sciences, and a Union Pacific Visiting Professorship at the University of Minnesota (1999–2000). He won the Caird Medal of the National Maritime Museum in 1995 and the John Carter Brown Medal in 1999. In 2008, Fernández-Armesto will give the keynote address at the annual meeting of the World History Association.

The author, coauthor, or editor of over 25 books and numerous papers and scholarly articles, Fernández-Armesto's work has been translated into 24 languages. His books include *Before Columbus; The Times Illustrated History of Europe; Columbus; Millennium: A History of the Last Thousand Years* (the subject of a ten-part series on CNN); *Civilizations: Culture, Ambition, and the Transformation of Nature; Near a Thousand Tables; The Americas; Humankind: A Brief History; Ideas that Changed the World; The Times Atlas of World Exploration;* and *The Times Guide to the Peoples of Europe*. Two recent works are *Amerigo: The Man Who Gave His Name to America* and *Pathfinders: A Global History of Exploration* (which was awarded the World History Association Book Prize for 2006).

The WORLD

A BRIEF HISTORY

Combined Volume

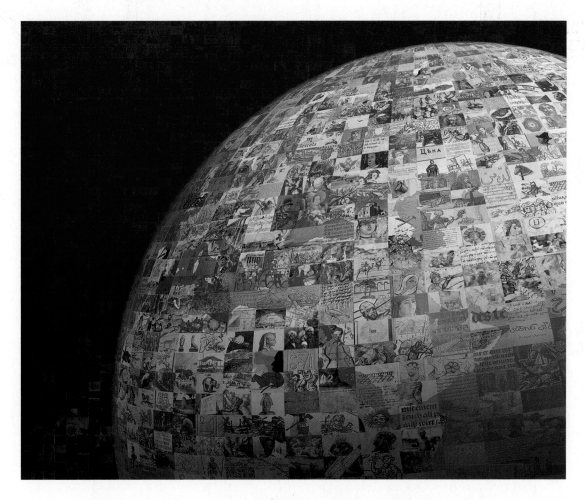

FELIPE FERNÁNDEZ-ARMESTO

Tufts University

PART

One

Foragers and Farmers, to 5000 B.C.E.

CHAPTER 1 Out of the Ice: Peopling the Earth 4

CHAPTER 2 Out of the Mud: Farming and Herding After the Ice Age 26

Early art? Early science? Or both? In 2001, the discovery in South Africa of a stone carved 70,000 years ago showed that humans have used symbols for at least that long. These shapes, engraved in ochre, a soft reddish-brown stone that was a valuable, magical substance at the time, have been interpreted as a device to aid in counting or as a kind of calendar.

ENVIRONMENT

1.75 million to 1.25 million years ago
Homo erectus migrations out of East Africa

6 million years ago
Evolution of hominids/early humans

CULTURE

since 3 million years ago
Stone tools

150,000 to 20,000 years ago
Most recent Ice Age

since 20,000 years ago
Global warming

since ca. 10,000 years ago
Agriculture

since ca. 150,000 years ago
Homo sapiens

150,000 years ago
Fire, fire-hardened wood spears

since at least 100,000 years ago
Art, ritual, religion; first migrations out of Africa

since 20,000 years ago
Bow and arrow

CHAPTER 1 Out of the Ice: Peopling the Earth

The Spanish painter Francisco Goya painted these nightmare-visions in the mid-1820s on slivers of ivory, with novel techniques, burying the background in lamp-black, scratching the ivory to produce strange effects of light. He captured the fascinated unease with which human beings eye each other.

Francisco Goya y Lucientes, Spanish, 1746–1828. Boy Staring at an Apparition *(1824–1825) Carbon Black and watercolor on ivory (Black wash heightened with vermilion and brown) 6.03 × 6.03 cm (2 3/8 × 2 3/8 in.) Museum of Fine Arts, Boston. Gift of Eleanor I. Arxiu Mas.*

IN THIS CHAPTER

SO YOU THINK YOU'RE HUMAN
Human Evolution
OUT OF AFRICA
Peopling the Old World
Migration, Population, and Social Change
THE LAST GREAT ICE AGE
Ice-Age Hunters
Ice-Age Art
Ice-Age Culture and Society
Peopling the New World
SURVIVAL OF THE FORAGERS
IN PERSPECTIVE: After the Ice

In exile in France in the 1820s, in the last years of his tortured, haunted life, Francisco Goya (1746–1828) etched nightmares—frightening faces stripped of every sane and civilized quality. The most abstract image captured the truth about how we understand human nature. A little boy, half bewildered, half fascinated, stares up at a baffling blur, recognizable as a human face because it inspires us with distinctive emotions: attraction, empathy, unease. But we perceive it unclearly. We think we know what it means to be human, but if anyone asks us to define humankind, we cannot do it. Or at least we cannot do it satisfactorily.

FRANCE

SO YOU THINK YOU'RE HUMAN

We can call humankind a species, but species are just categories for grouping together closely related life forms, with boundaries that are fuzzy and subject to change. There is no standard of how closely related you have to be to a fellow creature to be classed in the same species, or among species of the same sort, or, as biologists say, "genus." DNA evidence reveals that all the people we now recognize as human had a common ancestor who lived in Africa, probably more than 150,000 years ago. If we go back 5 to 7 million years, we share ancestors with chimpanzees. Double the length of time, and the fossils reveal ancestors whom we share with other great apes. Further back, the flow of evolution erodes the differences between our ancestors and other creatures. If we accept the theory of **evolution**—and, in outline, it does present a true account of how life forms change—we cannot find any transforming moment in the past when humankind began. Species so like ourselves preceded us in the evolutionary record that, if we were to meet them today, we should probably embrace some of them as fellow humans, and puzzle over how to treat others.

Even today, there are nonhuman species—especially among the apes—whose humanlike qualities so impress people who work and live with them that they seem morally indistinguishable from humans and should, according to some biologists and philosophers, be included in the same genus and even the same moral community as ourselves, with similar rights. In terms of the sort of cultures they have, emotions they reveal, societies they form, and behaviors they adopt, chimpanzees share many characteristics with the fellow apes we call humans. To a lesser extent, gorillas

FOCUS questions

- WHERE IN the evolutionary record do humans begin?
- WHAT CAUSED the rapid population growth of *Homo sapiens*?
- WHY WAS the Ice Age a time of abundance?
- WHAT DOES its art tell us about Ice-Age society?
- WHEN DID *Homo sapiens* migrate to North and South America?
- HOW DID human life change when the Ice Age ended?

and orangutans are also like us. All of us apes use tools, learn from each other, practice altruism and deceit, like to play, detest boredom, and seem self-aware. Our bodies and our behaviors are so like those of chimpanzees that the physiologist and historian Jared Diamond has suggested we reclassify our species as a kind of chimp. Our relationship with other animals could come full circle. In the often-filmed story of *The Island of Dr. Moreau*, H. G. Wells (1866–1946) fantasized about a scientist who strove to produce perfect creatures by surgically combining human characteristics with those of other animals. Today, in theory, genetic engineering can produce such hybrids, prompting us to wonder at what point a hybrid would become human. The first big question for this chapter, then, is where in the evolutionary record does it make sense to talk about humans? When does the story of humankind begin?

Human Evolution

Paleoanthropologists—the specialists responsible for answering or, at least, asking the question about which species are human—give conflicting responses. The usual place to look is among creatures sufficiently like us to be classified, according to the present consensus, in the same genus as ourselves: the genus called "Homo" from the Latin word that means "human." A creature known as *Homo habilis* ("handy"), about 2.5 million years ago, chipped hand axes from stones. In calling this species the first humans, scholars defined humans as toolmakers—a now old-fashioned, indeed, discredited concept. *Habilis* also had a larger brain than earlier predecessors, but this is of doubtful significance. Ours is not the biggest-brained species in the evolutionary record. At one time, anthropologists backed a later species, *Homo erectus* ("standing upright"), of about 1.5 million years ago, as the first human, largely because they admired the flint tools and weapons that species carved. From finds over 800,000 years ago, a variant (or, perhaps, a different species) called *Homo ergaster* ("workman") appeared who later—at one site at least—stacked the bones of the dead. But reverence for the dead is not uniquely human, either. All these creatures, and others like them, have had champions who have claimed them as the first humans. Clearly, these instances of backing one set of ancestors over another reflect subjective criteria: supposed resemblance to ourselves. We are like the bereaved of some horrible disaster, scanning the remains of the dead for signs to prompt our recognition.

Species that occurred earlier than those we class under the heading "Homo," or who resembled us less, have tended to get labeled with names that sound less human. Anthropologists used to call them "pithecanthropoi"—literally, ape-men. Current terminology favors "**australopithecines**" ("southern ape-like creatures"), or "paranthropoi" ("next to humans"), as if they were identifiably nonhuman or prehuman. But in 1974, the archaeologist Dan Johansen made a discovery that blew away all notions of a clear dividing line. He spotted the bones of an australopithecine sticking out of the mud in Hadar in Ethiopia in East Africa. He dug her up and called her "Lucy" after the title of a Beatles song he happened to play that night in camp. Lucy had died over 3 million years ago. She was only about three feet tall, but she and her kind turned out to have characteristics that were thought to belong exclusively to later species of *Homo*. They walked on two legs and lived in family groups. Johansen discovered tools 2.5 million years old near the site the following year. In 1977, he found two-legged footprints, dating back 3.7 million years. Finds with similar characteristics may date as far back as 6 million years ago.

As evolution slowly grinds out species, who's human? Who's to say? It is tempting to reserve the term *human* for ourselves—members of the species we call **Homo sapiens.** Literally, the term *sapiens* means "wise," a grandiose name that betrays the foolishness of self-ascribed wisdom, for other species also have embarrassingly strong claims to "wisdom." One example is *Homo neanderthalensis,* who vanished only 30,000 years ago, and coexisted with our own ancestors for something like 100,000 years. Neanderthals had distinctive vocal tracts but could have interacted with *Homo sapiens* by nonverbal communication, just as we do today to talk with apes and even with humans whose spoken language we do not understand.

In most other respects, the two species of *Homo* were alike. **Neanderthals** were as big as *sapiens* and had a similar appearance; their brains were also similar but, on average, slightly larger. They followed the same hunting, foraging ways of life in overlapping habitats. They made the same kinds of tools our ancestors made, lived in the same types of society, ate the same foods, and had many of the same customs and rites. They cared for their old and sick and buried their dead with signs of honor that suggest a sense of religion. They also seem to have expected an afterlife, burying bears' jaws with their dead, as if to protect them and perhaps—though the evidence is uncertain—strewing flowers on some graves as if to help, honor, or adorn the deceased. Yet some paleoanthropologists seem determined to deny Neanderthals the name of humans—using arguments startlingly, frighteningly reminiscent of those that nineteenth-century scientific racism employed to deny full humanity to black people, claiming, for instance, that they were inferior and doomed to extinction. Evidence of Neanderthals' attainments is explained away. Assemblages of ritual objects found at their graves, detractors say, must be "tricks of evidence," deposited accidently by streams, winds, or animals.

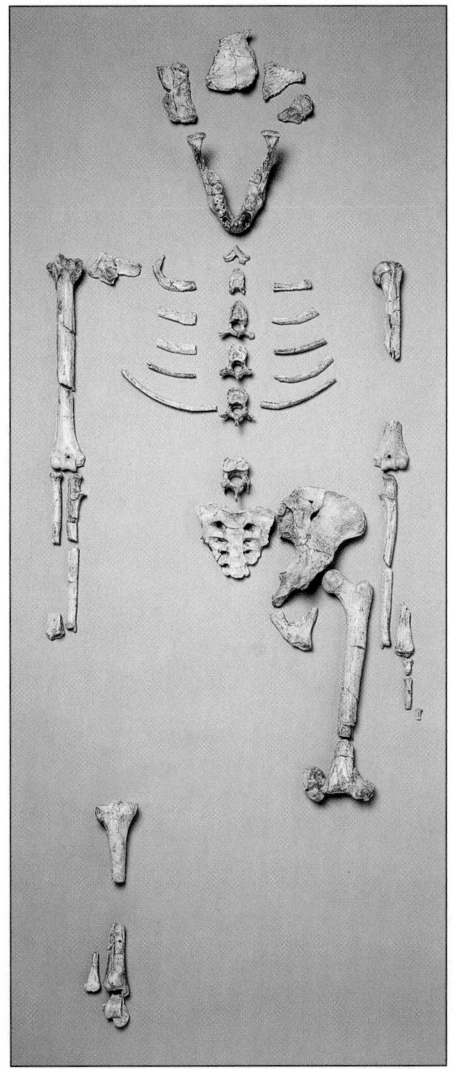

Lucy. The bones shown here aren't connected to each other, but modern imaginations have reconstructed the 3-million-year-old skeleton known as "Lucy," as human or nearly so. Lucy walked on two legs and was closer to humans, in evolutionary terms, than any non-human creature that exists today.

Paleoanthropologists continue to dig up specimens that challenge believers in human uniqueness. In October 2004, excavators published news of a stunning find in southeast Asia on the island of Flores in Indonesia, which included the remains of a woman whose teeth, when they found her, were mashed to pulp, her bones rotted and soggy. She died 18,000 years ago. She was dwarfishly tiny. Her brain was barely as big as a chimpanzee's. But she had the power to subvert anthropological orthodoxy. *Homo floresiensis,* as her finders called her, proved that big brains do not make their possessors superior to other creatures. To judge from adjacent finds, these "hobbits," as the press dubbed them, had tools typical of early *Homo sapiens,* despite chimp-sized brains in imp-sized bodies. *Floresiensis* almost certainly made those tools. In known cases where nonhuman creatures lie alongside *sapiens*-made tools, *sapiens* ate them. But the remains of *floresiensis* showed no signs of butchering.

OUT OF AFRICA

Since no clear-cut line separates human from nonhuman species, we might rationally start our story with our last common ancestor. We all have a chemical component in our cells that a mother in East Africa passed on to her daughters over 150,000 years ago. We nickname her Eve after the first woman in Genesis. Of course, she was neither our first ancestor nor the only woman of her day. By the

Stone tools. Paleoanthropologists have long used stone tool-making technologies to classify hominid cultures, because these artifacts have survived in relatively large numbers. The chopper on the left, of a pattern that dates from over 2 million years ago, was made by striking cobblestones against each other. Chimpanzees can be taught to make similar tools. The more elegant axe-blade in the center is of a kind that predominated over much of the world between about 1.5 million and 150,000 years ago. Though the size, shape, and presumably function of these tools varied, as the examples on the right show, the technology was surprisingly uniform around the world. No bone tools, for example, from the period survive.

best available estimates, there were perhaps 20,000 individuals of the species *Homo sapiens* at the time, all living in the same region. In 2003, archaeological evidence of Eve's world turned up in Herto, in Ethiopia. Three skulls about 160,000 years old had been stripped of flesh and polished, which suggests that the culture they belonged to practiced some death-linked ritual. The remains of a butchered hippopotamus lay nearby. We can begin to picture not only the appearance of the African Eve—we can do that by looking in a mirror—but also something of her way of life or, at least, life at a time close to her own.

Eve's home of mixed grassland and woodland was no Eden, but it suited our ancestors. Compared with competitor species, they had—as we still have—feeble bodies, weak senses of sight, smell, and hearing, poor digestions, and unthreatening teeth and claws. But they could make up for their deficiency as climbers by standing erect to look around them. Their profuse sweat kept them cool during long chases. With relatively accurate throwing-arms, they could ward off rival predators. With fire, they could manage grazing for the animals they hunted with fire-hardened spears and butchered with sharpened stones.

Peopling the Old World

From beginnings in East Africa, Eve's people spread over the world (see Map 1.1). But why? Why did they want to move? How did they adapt to new environments? Most species stay in the environments that suit them best. Even human migrants seek familiar surroundings or try to reproduce the feel of home by transporting their animals and transplanting their crops.

Yet *Homo sapiens* penetrated challengingly different environments: deep forests, where grassland habits were of limited use; cold climates, to which humans were physically ill suited; deserts and seas, which demanded technologies they had not yet developed. These new habitats bred unfamiliar diseases. Yet people kept on moving, through them and into them, with speed, range, and purpose unmatched in the dispersals of other creatures.

We can reconstruct routes, though the archaeological evidence is patchy, by measuring differences in blood type, genetic makeup, and

Early Human Migration

(All dates are approximate)	
150,000 years ago	Hypothetical African Eve (*H. sapiens*)
100,000 years ago	*H. sapiens* migrates out of Africa to Middle East
67,000 years ago	*H. sapiens* in China
60,000 years ago	*H. sapiens* reestablishes colony in Middle East
50,000 years ago	*H. sapiens* in Australia
40,000 years ago	*H. sapiens* in Europe
15,000 years ago	*H. sapiens* in the Americas

language among populations in different parts of the world. The greater the differences, the longer the ancestors of the people concerned are likely to have been out of touch with the rest of humankind. This is inexact science, because people are rarely isolated for long. There are, moreover, no agreed ways to measure the differences among languages. Still, for what it is worth, the best-informed research puts *Homo sapiens* in the Middle East by about 100,000 years ago. The colony failed, but new migrants reestablished it about 60,000 years ago. Settlement then proceeded along the coasts of Africa and Asia, probably by sea. The earliest agreed-upon archaeological evidence of *Homo sapiens* in China is about 67,000 years old (although some digs have yielded puzzlingly earlier dates for remains that seem like those of *Homo sapiens*).

The first colonizers of Australia arrived over 50,000 years ago in boats. At that time, water already separated what are now Australia and New Guinea from Asia. *Homo sapiens* reached Europe only a little later. Northern Asia and America—isolated by impenetrable screens of cold —were probably colonized much later. The most generally accepted archaeological evidence indicates the New World was settled no earlier than about 15,000 years ago.

If these dates are correct, the expansion of *Homo sapiens* implies remarkable population growth. Though we have no idea—beyond guesswork—of the actual numbers that migrated, we can estimate a figure in millions by the end of the process. A handful of Eve's children had multiplied to the point where they could colonize most of the habitable Old World in less than 100,000 years. But was the increase in population cause or effect of the migrations? And how did it relate to the other changes migration brought? Migrating groups were doubly dynamic: not just mobile, but also subject to huge social changes—divisive and violent, but also with constructive ways of organizing their lives. Migration, moreover, affected their understanding of the world and the way they interacted with the species they competed with, preyed on, and outlasted.

Migration, Population, and Social Change

As far as we know, everyone at the time lived by foraging and moved on foot. Because mothers cannot easily carry more than one or two infants, large numbers of children are unsuited to foraging life. Consequently, foragers limit opportunities to breed by strictly regulating who can mate with whom. Their main contraceptive method is a long period of lactation. Breast-feeding mothers are relatively infertile. The demographic growth that peopled the Earth is surprising, therefore, because it breaks the normal pattern of population stability in foraging communities. So how can we explain it?

Creatures like us, with short guts, weak jaws, blunt teeth, and only one stomach each, can chew and digest limited energy sources. So any increase in the range and amount of food available was a major evolutionary advantage. Cooking with fire probably helped, because it made food easier to digest. So did improved hunting technologies: drive lanes and corrals to herd animals for killing, and fire-hardened spears. The dating is debated, but all these developments were in place by the start of the migrations.

Whether or not new technologies empowered humans to migrate, perhaps new stresses drove them on, such as food shortages or ecological disasters. But no evidence supports this or fits with the evidence of rising population. In every other case we know of, in all species, population falls when food sources shrink. Another possible source of stress is warfare, for plague, famine, and natural disaster tend to

MAP 1.1

Early Human Migration 150,000–40,000 years ago

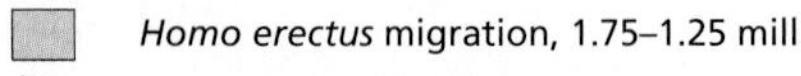

- *Homo erectus* migration, 1.75–1.25 million years ago
- *Homo sapiens* migration, 150,000–40,000 years ago
- possible coastal migrations
- *Homo erectus* site
- *Homo sapiens* site
- Neanderthal site
- *Homo Floresiensis* site
- ancient coastline
- ancient lake

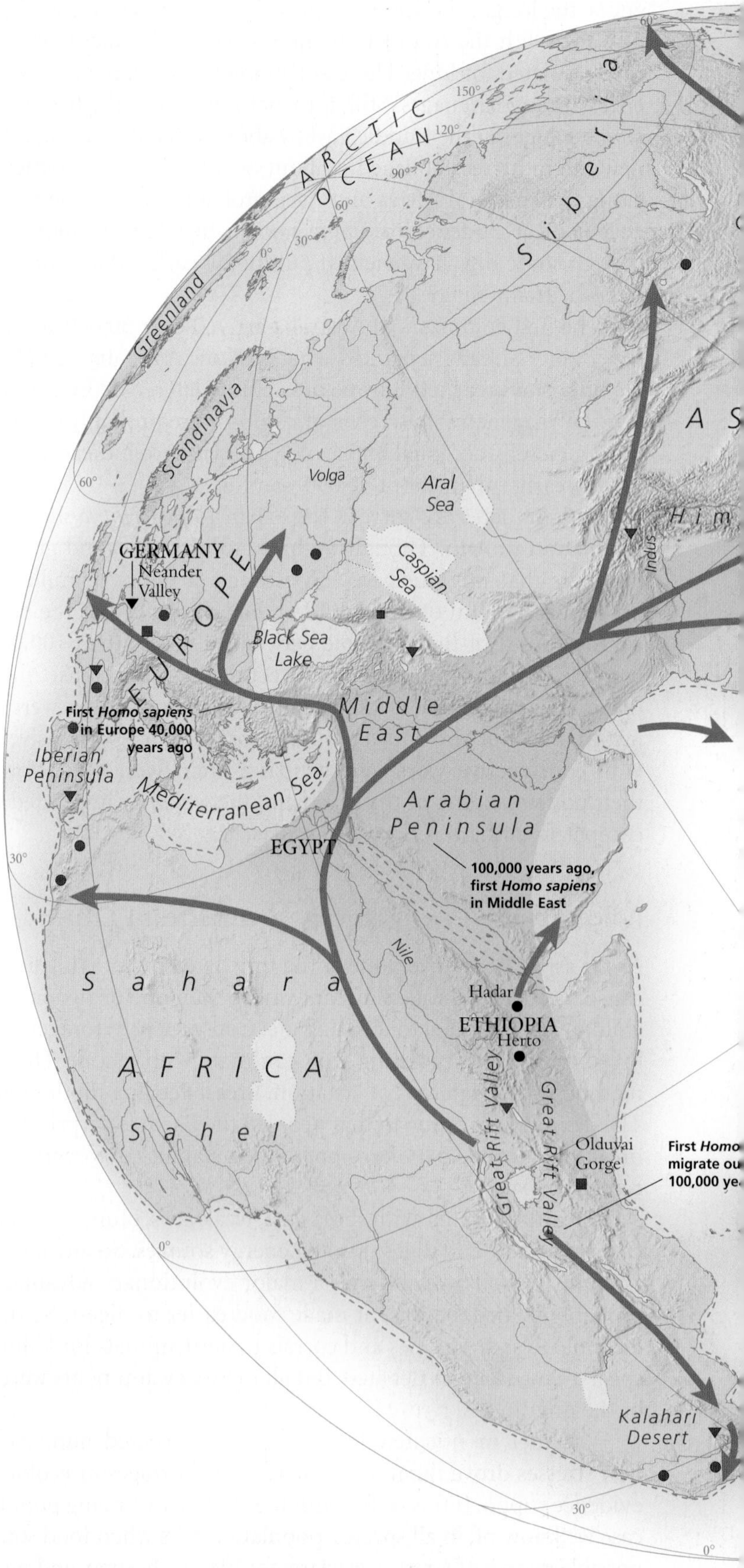

MAP EXPLORATION

www.prenhall.com/armesto_maps

150,000 years ago: earliest evidence of Homo sapiens in East Africa
60,000 years ago: reestablishment of Homo sapiens in Middle East
50,000 years ago: first Homo sapiens in Australia
120,000 y.a.
90,000 y.a.
60,000 y.a.
30,000 y.a
100,000 years ago: first Homo sapiens migrate out of Africa
67,000 years ago: first Homo sapiens in China
40,000 years ago: first Homo sapiens in Europe
PACIFIC OCEAN
Japan
Zhoukhoudian
67,000 years ago–earliest evidence of Homo sapiens in China
Yellow River
Yangtze
CHINA
Philippine Islands
New Guinea
Southeast Asia
Mekong
Borneo
Flores
India
Sumatra
INDONESIA
First colonizers in Australia 50,000 years ago
Australia
INDIAN OCEAN
Madagascar
Scale varies with perspective
13,340 km (8290 miles)
20,040 km (12,450 miles)

Margaret Mead, from "Warfare Is Only an Invention—Not a Biological Necessity"

inhibit human action, whereas war spurs new responses. One of the most fascinating problems of history is how and when war started. According to one school of thought, war is natural. The commander of British forces in the Second World War, Bernard Montgomery (1887–1976), referred to a book on *The Life of the Ant* when people challenged him to justify war. Evolution, he meant, implanted aggressive and violent instincts in humans as it did in other animals. Romantics defend the opposite point of view. Human nature is essentially peaceful until competition corrupts it. War, according to Margaret Mead, the great liberal anthropologist of the 1920s and 1930s, was not a biological necessity but an invention that began or, at least, entered a new, more systematic phase, when settled communities started to fight one another to control land and resources. Indeed, the earliest archaeological proof we have of large-scale warfare—including the savage massacre of women and children—is a battle fought at Jebel Sahaba, near the modern border of Egypt and Sudan, about 11,000 years ago, when agriculture was in its infancy.

Yet organized warfare must really be much older. In the 1970s, the primatologist Jane Goodall observed warfare among chimpanzee communities in the forests of West Africa. When chimpanzee splinter groups secede from their societies, their former fellows try to kill them. Similar conflicts may have made early human splinter groups migrate to safety. It is an intriguing possibility, but, even if it were to prove correct, it poses other problems. What stresses could have caused people to divide and fight each other 100,000 years ago? Rising population again? Or are we driven back to more speculation about increasing competition for supposedly diminishing food stocks, or even to assertions about innate animal aggression?

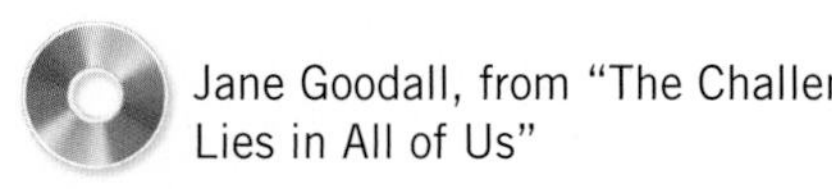

Jane Goodall, from "The Challenge Lies in All of Us"

In societies of increasing violence, men have enhanced roles. Among all primates, including humans, greater competitiveness in mating makes males, on average, bigger and stronger than females. In consequence, alpha males rule, or at least boss, most ape societies. Human males usually seem to bond more closely with each other, or form more or stronger alliances, than females. This, too, is useful in competitive circumstances, such as those of war and politics. Yet women are, in at least one respect, more valuable in most societies than men for a society can dispense with most of its men and still reproduce. That is why societies more commonly risk men in war than women. Women, moreover, are more easily mistaken as sacred because of the obvious correspondences between the cycles of their bodies and the rhythms of the heavens. Menstruation and the cycle of female fertility match the phases of the moon.

So how did male domination come to be normal in human societies? One theory ascribes it to a deliberate, collective power-seeking strategy by males, inspired by dislike of women or resentment or envy or a desire to get control of the most elementary of resources—the means of reproducing the species. By analogy with chimpanzees, a rival theory suggests that male dominance is a consequence of hunting, which, in the few chimpanzee groups known to practice it, is an almost exclusively male activity. Hunting increases male dominance in chimpanzee society because the hunters distribute the meat, in almost ritual fashion. Females line up and, in effect, beg for morsels. Female chimps often exchange sex for food, especially meat. By contrast, among bonobos, who are like chimps but are strictly plant eating, both sexes share foraging, and females tend to be socially equal or even dominant. Hunting, however, seems to be a recent development in chimpanzee society and to have followed and strengthened male dominance—not caused it.

Chimp agression. Humans obviously share aggressive individual tendencies with other apes. The American naturalist Jane Goodall discovered that chimpanzees organize conflicts with other groups of chimpanzees: They practice warfare, in other words. This seems to support what some philosophers and psychologists long suspected: that war is a "natural" activity, or, if it is an effect of culture, that it arose early in the history of culture.

MAKING CONNECTIONS

THE FIRST POPULATION BOOM: REASONS FOR POPULATION GROWTH

Fire-managed grazing of animals; driving lanes; corrals →	*control over food supply*
Throwing-arms; fire-hardened spears → improved hunting →	*improved diet*
Cooking with fire → improved taste and digestibility →	*increase in range of available foods*
Sexual economic specialization → hunting and gathering →	*women liberated for childbearing*

Without evidence to the contrary, it is unwise to assume that early in the migration period either sex monopolized political power. Still, migrating groups must have developed ways to liberate more women for childbirth or increase the fertile period of women's lives. Otherwise, population would have stagnated. Improved nutrition helped. Was there also some redistribution of economic activities, with men taking on more food-supplying roles?

As far as we know, in the earliest kind of sexual economic specialization, men did most of the hunting, while women did most of the gathering. Women's work seems to have been more productive in terms of calorific value per unit of energy expended. But we do not know when this specialization started or how rigid or widespread it was. In any case, the balance between hunted and gathered foods in the diets of the migrants varied with the environment. In known cases, hunters supplied about a third of the nutrition. The migrations, and the accompanying demographic changes, would have been impossible without both hunting and gathering.

The peopling of the Earth was such a long-lasting phenomenon that we can safely presume it had multiple causes operating in different combinations in different places and at different times. Then, too, some migrations were surely one-of-a-kind events. We can imagine, for instance, the first boat people who colonized Australia as the drop-outs of more than 50,000 years ago, opting out of a changing world to settle a new continent, where they could maintain a traditional way of life. In general, if people moved into new environments, they must have been drawn by an abundance of new resources elsewhere, not driven by a shortage of resources in their old homes. The era of opportunity coincided with, and was perhaps caused by, new trends in global climate.

THE LAST GREAT ICE AGE

Whatever caused it, the peopling of the world spanned the most convulsive period of climatic change that *Homo sapiens* experienced before our own times. The cooling and warming phases of the planet are regular occurrences, and one or the other is always going on. Every 100,000 years or so, a distortion in the Earth's orbit tugs the Northern Hemisphere away from the sun. On more frequent cycles, the Earth tilts and wobbles on its axis. When these phenomena coincide, temperatures change dramatically. Ice ages set in. A great cooling began about 150,000 years ago. The great migrations almost coincided with this, as if humans actively sought the cold (see Map 1.2).

PACIFIC OCEAN
NORTH AMERICA
Rocky Mountains
Beringia
Cordilleran Ice Sheet
Vancouver
Laurentide Ice Sheet
Hudson Bay
Greenland
Mississippi
Chicago
Ohio
Toronto
Boston
Reykjavik
Iceland
see inset
Caribbean Sea
Andes
SOUTH AMERICA
Amazon
BRAZIL
ATLANTIC OCEAN
Great Britain
North Afr
Sah
Niger
Equator
Tropic of Cancer
SWEDEN
Stockholm
RUSSIA
Volga
Sungir
Moscow
Star Carr
YORKSHIRE
Skateholm
Maininskaya
London
GERMANY
Oder
UKRAINE
Vogelherd
Dolni Vestonice
FRANCE
CZECH REP.
Willendorf
Laussel
DORDOGNE
Brassempouy
Chauvet
Carpathian Mountains
Black Sea Lake
SPAIN
500 km
500 miles

PACIFIC OCEAN
INDIAN OCEAN
Yellow Sea
South China Sea
Bay of Bengal
Arabian Sea
Caspian Sea
Black Sea
SOUTHEAST ASIA
AUSTRALIA
Arnhem Land
Kenniff Cave
Siberia
EURASIA
AFRICA
Himalayas
Yellow
Yangtze
Mekong
Ganges
Indus
Tigris
Euphrates
Danube
Anatolia
Nile
Madagascar
NAMIBIA
Kalahari Desert
San
SOUTH AFRICA
LESOTHO
Lion Cave
Arctic Circle
Tropic of Cancer
Equator
Tropic of Capricorn
1,000 km
1,000 miles
scale varies with perspective
MAP 1.2
The Ice Age
extent of ice cover 20,000 years ago
extent of ice cover 12,000 years ago
tundra
tundra and coniferous forests
steppe
modern-city
foraging settlement described on page 22
Ice-Age sites
San native people
ancient coastlines
ancient lake

Ice-Age Hunters

The severity of the Ice Age is unimaginable, but it was not an entirely hostile world. For the hunters who inhabited the vast **tundra** that covered much of Eurasia, the edge of the ice was the best place to be. Over thousands of years of cold, many mammals had adapted by efficiently storing their own body fat—and that was the hunters' target. Dietary fat has a bad reputation today, but for most of history, most people have eagerly sought it. Relatively speaking, animal fat is the world's most energy-abundant source of food.

Marshall Sahlins, "The Original Affluent Society," from *Stone-Age Economics*

In some of the vast Ice-Age tundra, concentrations of small, easily trapped arctic hare could supply human populations. More commonly, however, hunters favored species they could kill in large numbers by driving them over cliffs or into bogs or lakes. The bones of 10,000 Ice-Age horses lie at the foot of a cliff in France, and remains of a hundred mammoths have turned up in pits in Central Europe. About 20,000 years ago, the invention of the bow and arrow revolutionized killing technology for smaller prey. While stocks lasted, there was a fat bonanza, achieved with relatively modest effort.

It is rash to suppose that Ice-Age communities were small, limited to 30 or 50 people, like modern hunter–gatherers. Today, hunter–gatherers survive only in regions of great scarcity, where the modern world has driven them. Back then, community size varied according to the available resources; we can rarely put a figure to a group because only partial traces of Ice-Age dwellings have survived.

Venus of Laussel. An image of a woman carved in relief on a cave wall in central France more than 20,000 years ago reveals much about Ice-Age life: esteem for big hips and body fat, the love of revelry suggested by the uplifted drinking-horn, the involvement of women in presumably sacred activity, and the existence of accomplished, specialized artists.

For Ice-Age artists, fat was beautiful. One of the oldest artworks in the world is the Venus of Willendorf—a plump little carving of a fat female, 30,000 years old and named for the place in Germany where she was found. Critics have interpreted her as a goddess, ruler, or since she could be pregnant, a fertility symbol. Her slightly more recent look-alike, the Venus of Laussel, carved on a cave wall in France, evidently got fat the way most of us do: by enjoyment and indulgence. She raises a horn, which must contain food or drink.

Ice-Age people, on average, were better nourished than most later populations. Only modern industrialized societies surpass their intake of 3,000 calories a day. The nature of the plant foods they gathered—few starchy grains, relatively large amounts of wild vegetation—and the high ascorbic acid content of animal organ meats provided more vitamin C than an average American gets today. Abundant game guaranteed **Ice-Age affluence.** High levels of nutrition and long days of leisure, unequalled in most subsequent societies, meant people had time to observe nature and think about what they saw. The art of the era shows the sublime results. Like all good jokes, *The Flintstones*—the popular television cartoon series about a modern Stone-Age family—contains a kernel of truth. "Cave people" were like us, with the same kinds of minds and many of the same kinds of thoughts.

Ice-Age Art

In the depths of the Ice Age, a resourceful way of life took shape. We know most about Europe—especially southwest France and northern Spain, where extensive art has survived because it was made in deep caves evidently chosen because they were inaccessible. About 50 cave complexes contain thousands of paintings, mostly of animals.

Only now are the effects of tourism, too many respiratory systems, too many camera flashes, damaging these works in their once-secret caverns. Examples of sculptures, carvings, and other art objects are scattered across Europe, from the Atlantic to the Ural Mountains.

Footprints and handprints probably inspired the art, but what was it for? It surely told stories and had magical, ritual uses, as a way to reach a spirit-world inside or beyond the earth's depths or the cave walls. Some animal images are slashed or punctured many times over, as if in symbolic sacrifice. A good case has been made for seeing the cave paintings as aids to track prey. Hoof-prints, dung, seasonal habits, and favorite foods of the beasts are among the artists' standard stock of images.

The Ice Age

(All dates are approximate)	
150,000 years ago	Earth cools; last great Ice Age begins
18,000 years ago	Peak of Ice Age—farthest extent of ice cap
18,000 years ago	Warming of the Earth begins
16,000–8,000 years ago	Temperatures fluctuate; glaciers retreat; coastlines form
15,000–20,000 years ago	World emerges from Ice Age

Their technology was simple: a palette of red, brown, and yellow ochre (OH-ker), mixed with animal fat, and applied with wood, bone, and hair. Even the earliest works appeal instantly to modern sensibilities. The looks and litheness of the animal portraits spring from the rock walls, products of practiced hands and inherited learning. Carvings exhibit similar elegance—ivory sculptures of 30,000-year-old arched-necked horses from south Germany; female portraits from France and Moravia, over 20,000 years old; clay models of bears, dogs, and women fired 27,000 years ago in Russia.

Cave art (Lascaux)

Outside Europe, what little we know of the peoples of the time suggests that they created equally skillful work. Four painted rock slabs from Namibia in southwest Africa are about 26,000 years old, almost as old as any art in Europe, and bear similar animal images. The earliest paintings that decorate rocks in northernmost Australia show faint traces of long-extinct giant kangaroos and scary snakes. A clue to the very idea of representing life in art fades today from a rock face in Kenniff, Australia, where stencils of human hands and tools were made 20,000 years ago. But most of the evidence has been lost, weathered away on exposed rock faces, perished with the bodies or hides on which it was painted, or scattered by wind from the earth where it was scratched.

Ice-Age Culture and Society

The discovery of so much comparable art, of comparable age, in such widely separated parts of the world suggests an important and often overlooked fact. The Ice Age was the last great era of what we would now call a kind of **globalization.** That is, key elements of culture were the same all over the inhabited world. People practiced the same hunter–gatherer economy with similar kinds of technology, ate similar kinds of food, enjoyed similar levels of **material culture,** and—as far as we can tell—had similar religious practices.

The material culture—concrete objects people create—that many archeological digs yield offers clues to what goes on in the mind. A simple test establishes that fact. We can make informed inferences about people's religion, or politics, or their attitudes toward nature and society, or their values in general, by looking at what they eat, how they

Cave art. Until they died out—victims of competition with and exploitation by settler communities—in the early twentieth century, the Southern Bushmen of South Africa made cave paintings similar to those their ancestors made more than 20,000 years ago. On rock surfaces and cave walls, shamans painted their visions of the creatures of the spirit-world, glimpsed in states of ecstasy on imaginary journeys beyond the ordinarily accessible world.

dress, and how they decorate their homes. For instance, the people who hunted mammoths to extinction 20,000 years ago on the Ice-Age steppes of what is now southern Russia built dome-shaped dwellings of mammoth bones on a circular plan 12 or 15 feet in diameter that seem sublime triumphs of the imagination. They are reconstructions of mammoth nature, humanly reimagined, perhaps to acquire the beast's strength or to conjure power over the species. Ordinary, everyday activities went on inside these extraordinary dwellings—sleeping, eating, and all the routines of family life—in communities, on average, of fewer than 100 people. But no dwelling is purely practical. Your house reflects your ideas about your place in the world.

Thanks to the clues material culture yields, we can make confident assertions about other aspects of Ice-Age people's lives: their symbolic systems, their magic, and the kind of social and political units they lived in. Although Ice-Age people had nothing we recognize as writing, they did have highly expressive symbols, which we can only struggle to translate. Realistic drawings made 20,000 to 30,000 years ago show recurring gestures and postures. Moreover, they often include what seem to be numbers, signified by dots and notches. Other marks, which we can no long interpret, are undeniably systematic. One widely occurring mark that looks like a P may be a symbol for female because it resembles the curves of a woman's body. What looks as if it might be a calendar was made 30,000 years ago in France. It is a flat bone inscribed with crescents and circles that may record phases of the moon.

Clues to spiritual lives appear in traces of red ochre, the earliest substance that seems to have had a role in ritual. The oldest known ochre mine in the world, about 42,000 years old, is at Lion Cave in what is now Lesotho in southern Africa. The vivid, lurid color was applied in burials, perhaps as a precious offering, perhaps to imitate blood and reinvest the dead with life. The speculation that people might also have used ochre to paint their living bodies is hard to resist.

Those who controlled ritual wielded power. In paintings and carvings, we can glimpse the Ice-Age elite. Animal masks—antlered or lionlike—transform the wearer. From anthropological studies, we know such disguises are normally efforts to communicate with the dead or with the gods. Bringing messages from other worlds is the role of a **shaman** (SHAH-mehn), an intermediary between humans and spirits or gods. The shaman may seek a state of ecstasy induced by drugs or dancing or drumming, to see and hear visions normally inaccessible to the senses. He becomes the medium through which spirits talk to this world. Among the Chukchi hunters of northern Siberia, whose way of life and environment are similar to Ice-Age peoples', the shaman's experience is represented as a journey to consult the spirits in a realm that only the dead can normally enter. The shaman may adopt an animal disguise to acquire the animal's speed or strength or identify with an animal ancestor. Shamans' roles can be an awesome source of authority. They can challenge alpha males. Like other religions, shamanism involves spiritual insight, which people of both sexes, various levels of intellect, and all kinds of physique can acquire. It can replace the strong with the seer and the sage. By choosing elites who had the gift of communicating with spirits, Ice-Age societies could escape the oppression of the physically powerful or those privileged by birth.

Shaman. In many societies, communication with the spirit-world remains the responsibility of the specialists whom anthropologists call shamans. Typically, they garb and paint or disguise themselves to resemble spirits or the animals deemed to have privileged access to realms beyond human sense. The shamans then "journey" to the spirits or ancestors in trances induced by dancing, drumming, or drugs. Shamans often acquire social influence and political authority as healers, prophets, and arbitrators.

Although we cannot be sure about the nature of the Ice-Age power class, we know it existed because of glaring inequalities in how Ice-Age people were buried. In a cemetery near Moscow, dated about 24,000 years ago, the highest-status person seems, at first glance, to have been an elderly man. His burial goods include a cap sewn with fox's teeth and about 20 ivory bracelets. Nearby, however, two boys of about eight or ten years old have even more spectacular ornaments. As well as ivory bracelets and necklaces and fox-tooth buttons, the boys have animal carvings and beautifully wrought weapons, including spears of mammoth ivory, each over six feet long. About 3,500 finely worked ivory beads had been drizzled over the head, torso, and limbs of each boy. Here was a society that marked leaders for greatness from boyhood and therefore, perhaps, from birth.

In our attempt to understand where power lay in Ice-Age societies, the final bits of evidence are crumbs from rich people's tables, fragments of feasts. Archaeologists have found ashes from large-scale cooking and the calcified debris of food at sites in northern Spain, perhaps from as long as 23,000 years ago. The tally sticks that survive from the same region in the same period may also have been records of expenditure on feasts. What were such feasts for? By analogy with modern hunting peoples, the most likely reason was alliance-making between communities. They were probably not male-bonding occasions, as some scholars think, because they are close to major dwelling sites where women and children would be present. Instead, from the moment of its emergence, the idea of the feast had practical consequences: to build and strengthen societies and enhance the power of those who organized the feasts and controlled the food.

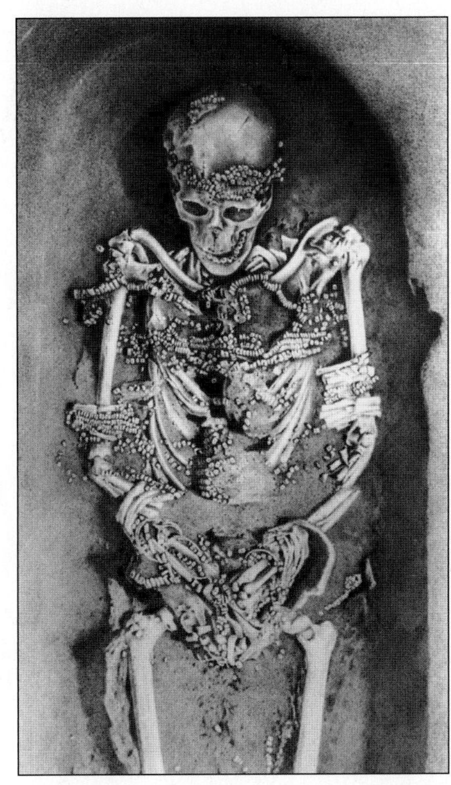

Sunghir burial. A profusion of beads distinguishes the graves of people of high status at Sunghir in Russia, from about 24,000 years ago. The distribution of signs of wealth in burials suggests that even in the Ice Age inequalities were rife and that status could be inherited.

Peopling the New World

The New World was the last part of the planet *Homo sapiens* peopled, but it is not easy to say exactly when or by whom. According to the formerly dominant theory, a gap opened between glaciers toward the end of the Ice Age. A race of hunters crossed the land link between North America and Asia, where the Bering Strait now flows, where no human hunter had ever trod before. The invaders found abundance so great and animals so unwary that they ate enormously and multiplied greatly. They spread rapidly over the hemisphere, hunting great game to extinction as they went. The story appealed to an unsophisticated form of U.S. patriotism. The Clovis people, as these hunters were dubbed after an early archaeological site in New Mexico, seemed to resemble modern American pioneers. They exhibited quick-fire locomotion, hustle and bustle, technical prowess, big appetites, irrepressible strength, enormous cultural reach, and a talent for reforging the environment.

Clovis points

By comparison, the truth about the peopling of the hemisphere is disappointingly undramatic. These first great American superheroes—like most of their successors—did not really exist. Although archeologists have excavated too few sites for a complete and reliable picture to emerge, a new theory dominates. We have evidence of early human settlement scattered from the Yukon to Uruguay and from near the Bering Strait to the edge of the Beagle Channel, over so long a period, in so many different geological layers, and with such a vast range of cultural diversity that one conclusion is inescapable. Colonists came at different times, bringing different cultures with them (see Map 1.3).

No generally accepted evidence dates any inhabited sites in the American hemisphere earlier than about 13,000 B.C.E. The first arrivals came when glaciers covered much of North America. They stuck close to the cold, where the game was fattest. They followed corridors between walls of ice or along narrow shores away from glaciers. Other arrivals came by sea and continued to come after the land bridge was submerged. Around 10,000 years ago, a catastrophic cluster of extinctions wiped out the mammoth, mastodon, horse, giant sloth, saber-toothed tiger, and at least 35 other large species in the Americas. New hunting techniques and

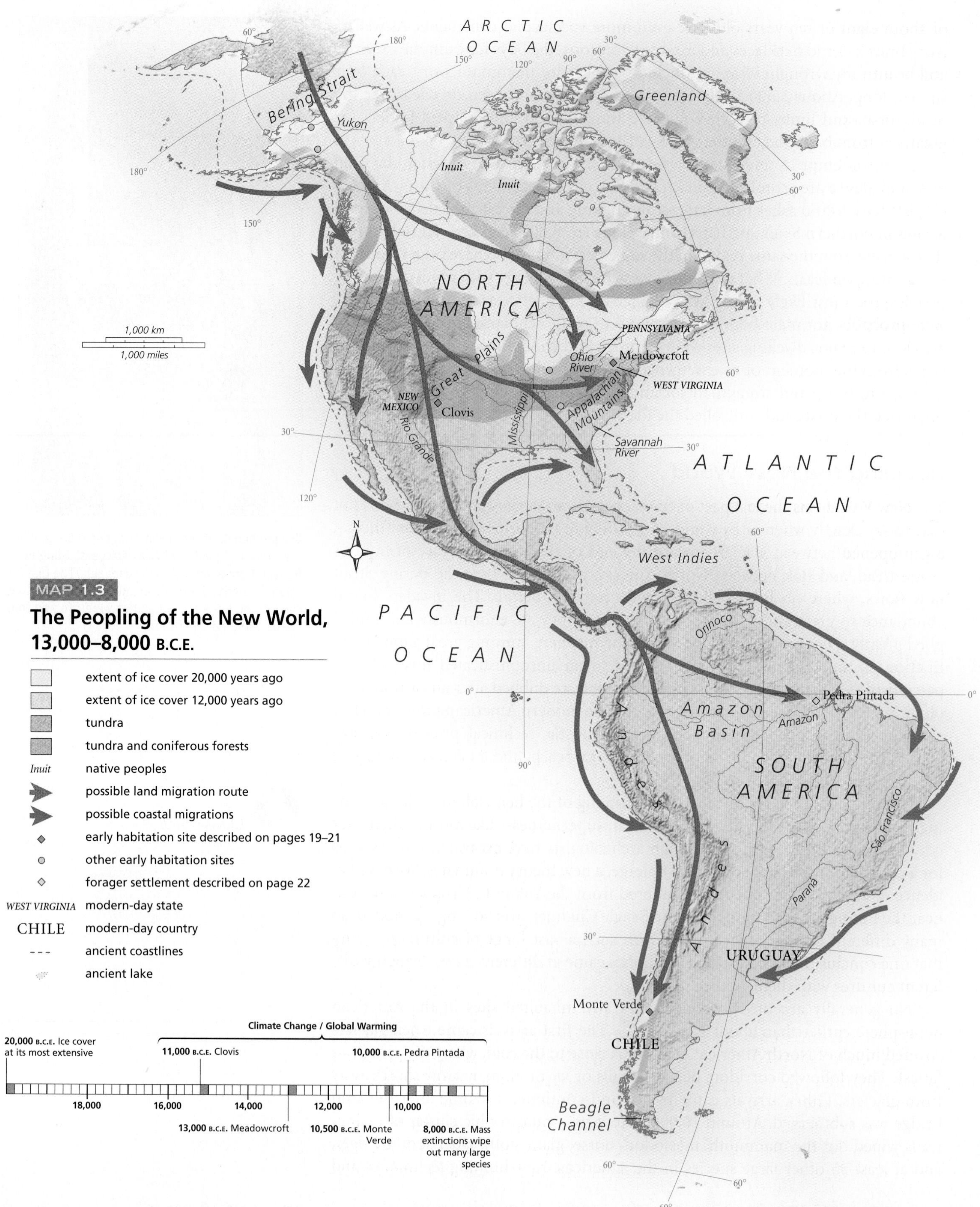
ARCTIC OCEAN
Greenland
Bering Strait
Yukon
Inuit
Inuit
NORTH AMERICA
Great Plains
PENNSYLVANIA
Ohio River
Meadowcroft
WEST VIRGINIA
Appalachian Mountains
Mississippi
NEW MEXICO
Clovis
Rio Grande
Savannah River
ATLANTIC OCEAN
PACIFIC OCEAN
West Indies
Orinoco
Pedra Pintada
Amazon Basin
Amazon
SOUTH AMERICA
Andes
São Francisco
Paraná
URUGUAY
Monte Verde
CHILE
Beagle Channel
1,000 km
1,000 miles
N
extent of ice cover 20,000 years ago
extent of ice cover 12,000 years ago
tundra
tundra and coniferous forests
Inuit native peoples
possible land migration route
possible coastal migrations
early habitation site described on pages 19–21
other early habitation sites
forager settlement described on page 22
WEST VIRGINIA modern-day state
CHILE modern-day country
ancient coastlines
ancient lake
Climate Change / Global Warming
20,000 B.C.E. Ice cover at its most extensive
11,000 B.C.E. Clovis
10,000 B.C.E. Pedra Pintada
18,000
16,000
14,000
12,000
10,000
13,000 B.C.E. Meadowcroft
10,500 B.C.E. Monte Verde
8,000 B.C.E. Mass extinctions wipe out many large species

MAP 1.3

The Peopling of the New World, 13,000–8,000 B.C.E.

perhaps new hunting peoples were probably partly responsible. But we can only explain the events in the context of vast climatic changes that affected habitats and the ecology on which these animals depended.

Many supposedly early sites of human habitation have proved to be delusions of overenthusiastic archaeologists—false, or, at best, unconvincing. A few sites, however, offer strong evidence of the antiquity and range of settlement. Most are in the eastern United States—a long way from Asia. It must have taken a long time for these people to get there from the vicinity of the modern Bering Strait. In the mid-1970s, 15,000-year-old basketwork and tools made with fine flints emerged from deep under the discarded beer cans that topped a dig at Meadowcroft, on the Ohio River, near the border of Pennsylvania and West Virginia. Archaeologists are investigating similar sites between the Ohio and Savannah Rivers. Later in the 1970s, excavations at Monte Verde in southern Chile revealed a 20-foot-long, wooden, hide-covered dwelling preserved in a peat bog for about 12,500 years. Nearby were a big mastodon-butchery and a space devoted to making tools. The inhabitants brought salt and seaweed from the coast, 40 miles away, and medicinal herbs from mountains equally far in the opposite direction. Half-chewed lumps of seaweed show the eaters' dental bites; a boy's footprints survive in the clay lining of a pit. If Meadowcroft is a long way from the colonizers' entry point near the Bering Strait, southern Chile is a world away again—almost as far as you can get in the Western Hemisphere. How long would it have taken the settlers of Monte Verde to cross the hemisphere, over vast distances and through many different environments, each demanding new forms of adaptation? Most specialists think it must have taken thousands of years. The question of the date of the first peopling of the New World therefore remains open.

SURVIVAL OF THE FORAGERS

As the ice cap retreated and the great herds shifted with it, many human communities opted to follow. Archeology has unearthed traces of their routes. Along the way, in what is now northern Germany, about 12,000 years ago, people sacrificed reindeer by weighting them with stones sewn into their stomachs and drowning them in a lake. About 1,000 years later, hunters as far north as Yorkshire in England found an environment as abundant as the cave artists' had been. Not only was it filled with tundra-loving species such as red deer, elk, and aurochs—huge, shaggy wild cattle—but also with wild boar in surroundings that were becoming patchily wooded.

At Skateholm in Sweden, about 8,000 years ago, hunters founded the largest known settlement of the era. It was a winter camp in an area where the 87 different edible animal species roamed. The people trapped river-fish, netted sea-birds, harpooned seals and dolphin, stuck pigs, and drove deer into pits or ponds. In summer, they moved farther north. They lie today in graves decorated with beads and ochre and filled with the spoils of their careers, including antlers and boar's tusks. Their burly dogs are buried nearby, sometimes with more signs of honor than humans were given, for hunting prowess and skill in war determined status. Many of the human dead bear wounds from man-made weapons. Women have only a third as many wounds as the men: evidence of sexual specialization.

The most persistently faithful followers of the ice were the North American Inuit. About 4,000 years ago, they invented the blubber-filled soapstone lamp. Now they could follow big game beyond the tundra and into the darkness of an arctic

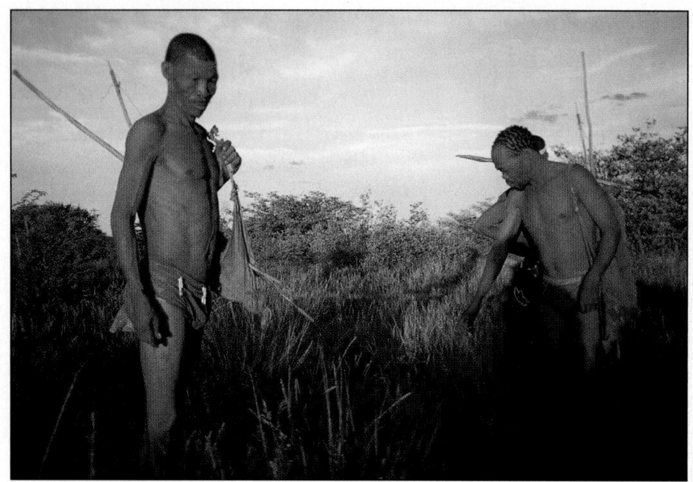

Bushmen. Though now obliged to adopt a mixed economy, supported in part by farming and donations of food, the San or Bushmen of southern Africa have been among the most conservative of the world's peoples. They maintained their foraging way of life, essentially unchanged, for millennia—despite neighbors' attempts to exterminate them. This record of survival contrasts with the rapid turnover of more ambitious civilizations that radically modify their environments, usually with disastrous results.

winter. They could track the musk ox to the shore of the ocean and the caribou on its winter migrations, when its fur is thickest and its fat most plentiful. This way of life persisted until the late twentieth century, although the people who first practiced it have disappeared. Migrants from the Arctic Ocean replaced them 1,000 years ago.

Climate change trapped other foraging peoples in environments where they had to develop new ways of life. Some of these environments offered new kinds of abundance. Here were life-filled rivers, lakes, and broad-leaved forests, rich in acorns (nutritious food for humans with enough time to fine-grind them). New World prairies held apparently inexhaustible stocks of bison. Between unstable periods of climate change around 12,000 years ago, foragers even colonized dense, tropical forests in southeast Asia and in the New World at Pedra Pintada in Brazil where the Amazon River now flows. This is a region where foragers today have to struggle to find foods they can digest, but it seems to have been more environmentally diverse toward the end of the Ice Age.

Some societies perpetuated their foraging life in hot, arid deserts, as different from the best hunting grounds of the Ice Age as it is possible to imagine. This required two forms of adaptation. First, thinly dispersed populations had to create collaborative networks. Such interdependence explains why peoples who live in ecologically shaky homelands often require people to marry outside the group and why they regard hospitality to strangers as a sacred obligation. Second, poor environments demanded that inhabitants develop what we might call orally transmitted science. For only with accurate and extensive knowledge of their habitat can people survive in harsh environments.

The San or Bushmen of southern Africa's Kalahari Desert illustrate the difficulties and solutions. Their domain has shrunk in the last few centuries, as Bantu farmers, Khoi herdsmen, and white invaders have overrun much of their former territory. But their heartland was already dry at the time of the San's first occupancy, about 14,000 years ago. The increased rainfall that usually followed the retreat of the ice hardly fell here. There are underground rivers but few permanent water holes. The people watch for rare signs of rain and hurry to gather the vegetation that accompanies it. The scrubland plant foods, including water-bearing tubers and a kind of cactus, supply 30 percent of their sustenance. The rest comes from game, which grazes on tough desert shrubs that humans cannot digest. To kill large game is almost impossible with a Bushman's bow. He wounds the beast with a poisoned barb and follows it at a run for many miles until it drops from exhaustion and the effects of the drug, before butchering the heavy animal and dragging it home. Bushmen who persist with this demanding way of life to this day are pursuing a commitment that has grown out of generations of invested emotion. As difficult as it may be for us to understand, the San would find it heart-wrenching to change their way of life for the mere sake of efficiency, convenience, or material gain.

In one sense, the world's food supply still depends on foraging. The amount of food from hunting actually increased in the twentieth century, which may go down in history not only as the last age of hunting but also as the greatest. World over today, we practice a highly specialized, mechanized, and unusual form of hunting—deep-sea trawling. Fish farming is likely to replace it in the future, but in any case, deep-sea fishing is a historical throwback.

IN PERSPECTIVE: After the Ice

In the post–Ice-Age world, little by little, over thousands of years, most societies abandoned foraging and adopted farming or herding to get their food. Among peoples who still live close to the ice cap, the Inuit remain faithful to their hunting tradition in North America. Most of their Old World counterparts, however, have long abandoned it. In Eurasia, though some hunting cultures still cling to the old ways at the eastern end of Siberia, the peoples on the western Arctic rim—the Sami (or Lapplanders) of Scandinavia and their neighbors, the Samoyeds and Nenets—adopted reindeer herding over 1,000 years ago. The Ice-Age way of life, if not over, is drawing to a close. Hunting is now thought of as a primitive way to get food, long abandoned except as an aristocratic or supposedly manly sport.

The disappearance of foraging seems a remarkable turnaround for a predator-species such as *Homo sapiens*. There was a time before hunting, when our ancestors were scavengers, but for hundreds of thousands, perhaps millions, of years, foraging was reliable and rewarding. It fed people through every change of climate. Its practitioners spread over the world and adapted successfully to every kind of habitat. Humans dominated every ecosystem they entered. They achieved startling increases in their numbers, which we struggle to explain. They founded more varied societies than any other species (though the differences among these societies were slight compared to later periods). They had art-rich cultures with traditions of learning and symbolic systems to record information. They had their own social elites, political customs, ambitious magic, and practical methods to exploit their environment.

Our next task is to ask why, after the achievements recounted in this chapter, did people abandon the foraging life? Renouncing the hunt and pursuing new ways of life after the Ice Age are among the most far-reaching and mysterious transformations of the human past. If the puzzle of why *Homo sapiens* spread over the Earth is the first great question in our history, the problem of why foragers became farmers is the second.

CHRONOLOGY

(All dates are approximate)

Over 3 million years ago	Lucy
2–1 million years ago	*Homo erectus* migrates from East Africa to Africa and Eurasia
100,000 years ago	*Homo sapiens* migrates out of Africa
67,000 years ago	*Homo sapiens* in Asia
50,000 years ago	*Homo sapiens* colonizes Australia and New Guinea
	Homo sapiens reaches Europe
30,000 years ago	Last Neanderthals vanish
20,000–15,000 B.C.E.	World emerges from the Ice Age
20,000 B.C.E.	Invention of the bow and arrow
13,000 B.C.E.	*Homo sapiens* in the Americas

PROBLEMS AND PARALLELS

1. When does the story of humankind begin? Is it possible to define what it means to be human?
2. How do Neanderthals and *Homo floresiensis* challenge definitions of *Homo sapiens?*
3. Why did *Homo sapiens* migrate out of Africa? How did migration change people's relationships with each other and with their environment?
4. Why did the population of *Homo sapiens* increase so rapidly?
5. Which stresses could have caused early peoples to divide and fight each other? Which theories have been put forward for how war started?
6. How did male domination come to be normal in human societies? What impact did sexual economic specialization have on early societies?
7. Why was the Ice Age a time of affluence? What role did shamans play in Ice-Age society?
8. Why has the foraging life persisted today?

DOCUMENTS IN GLOBAL HISTORY

- Margaret Mead, from "Warfare Is Only an Invention—Not a Biological Necessity"
- Jane Goodall, from "The Challenge Lies in All of Us"
- Marshall Sahlins, "The Original Affluent Society," from *Stone-Age Economics*
- Cave art (Lascaux)
- Cave art (Chauvet)
- Clovis points

Please see the Primary Source DVD for additional sources related to this chapter.

READ ON

F. Fernández-Armesto, *Humankind: A Brief History* (2004) traces debates over the boundaries of the concept of humankind. Jared Diamond's book on the human overlap with apes is *The Third Chimpanzee* (1992). The works of F. de Waal, especially *The Ape and the Sushi Master* (2001), and those of J. Goodall, especially *The Chimpanzees of Gombe* (1986), are fundamental for understanding the issues. B. Sykes, *The Seven Daughters of Eve* (2001), is the best introduction to the use of DNA in paleoanthropology. C. Stringer and C. Gamble, *In Search of the Neanderthals* (1995), is an interesting review of human engagement with Neanderthal remains. The classic novel by W. Golding, *The Inheritors* (1963), is an imaginative attempt to envisage Neanderthal life.

Good general introductions to human evolution include R. G. Klein, *The Human Career* (1999), and I. Tattersall, *The Fossil Trail* (1997). C. Gamble, *Timewalkers: The Prehistory of Global Colonization* (1994), is an excellent account of the migrations. On fire, J. Goudsblom, *Fire and Civilization* (1993), is a classic, which the author has kept up-to-date in recent editions. R. Wrangham's views appeared in "The Raw and the Stolen," *Current Anthropology*, vol. xl (1999), 567–594. On war, K. Lorenz, *On Aggression* (1966), and R. Ardrey, *The Territorial Imperative* (1997), are controversial classics. J. Haas, ed., *The Anthropology of War* (1990) and L. H. Keeley, *War Before Civilization* (1997), survey the evidence.

On sex roles, G. Lerner, *The Creation of Patriarchy* (1987), and E. Martin, *The Woman in the Body: A Cultural Analysis of Reproduction* (1992), set the terms of debate. J. Peterson, *Sexual Revolutions* (2002), is an invaluable short survey.

On the conditions of Ice-Age life, M. D. Sahlins, *Stone Age Economics* (1972), is a stimulating classic. T. D. Price and J. A. Brown, eds., *Prehistoric Hunter-Gatherers* (1985) is an important collection of studies. On the art, the most illuminating works include S. J. Mithen, *Thoughtful Foragers* (1990), and J. D. Lewis-Williams, *Discovering Southern African Rock Art* (1990).

On the peopling of the New World, the challenging and readable work of J. Adovasio, *Before America* (2004), makes a stimulating starting point. S. Mithen, *After the Ice* (2004) is an engaging and imaginative introduction to the post–Ice-Age world.

The material on the San, L. van der Post's much maligned classic, *The Lost World of the Kalahari* (1977) is a thrilling read. For up-to-date studies, see L. Marshall, *The !Kung of Nyae Nyae* (1976), and E. Wilmsen, *Land Filled with Flies* (1989).

CHAPTER 2 Out of the Mud: Farming and Herding After the Ice Age

In environments that have no plants that humans can digest, herding is a life-giving option: Animals and humans live in mutual dependence. Humans protect the flocks from predators; their livestock convert grasses and shrubs into meat and milk. But, as with the Somali herdsmen pictured here, herders' lives are often precarious in marginal environments, because domesticated animals host disease-bearing organisms that can infect humans. Typically, herding cultures cope with restricted diets by developing a tolerance to digest dairy foods after infancy.

IN THIS CHAPTER

THE PROBLEM OF AGRICULTURE
Preagricultural Settlements
The Disadvantages of Farming

HUSBANDRY IN DIFFERENT ENVIRONMENTS
Herders' Environments
Tillers' Environments

THE SPREAD OF AGRICULTURE
Europe
Asia
The Americas
Africa
The Pacific Islands

SO WHY DID FARMING START?
Population Pressure
The Outcome of Abundance
The Power of Politics
Cult Agriculture
Climatic Instability
Agriculture by Accident
Production as an Outgrowth of Procurement

IN PERSPECTIVE: Seeking Stability

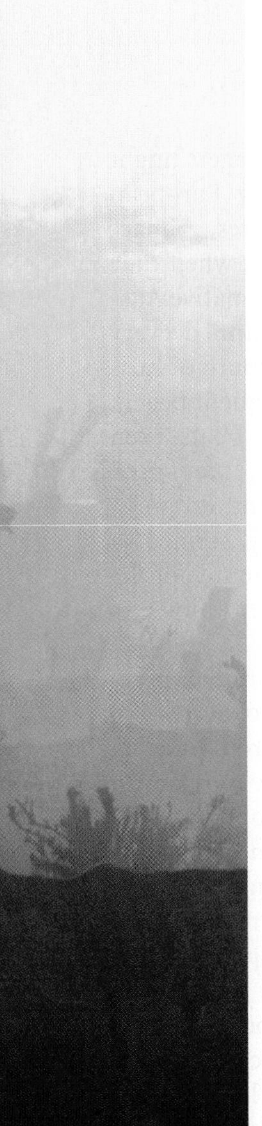

In August 1770, Captain James Cook, charting the Pacific Ocean for Britain's Royal Navy, paused at an island off the north coast of Australia. He named it Possession Island, for to Cook's mind, it was waiting to be grabbed. The natives had left no marks of possession on its soil. Plants they could have domesticated—"fruits proper for the support of man"—grew wild. The people, Cook wrote, "know nothing of cultivation. ... It seems strange."

AUSTRALIA

He was puzzling over one of the most perplexing problems of history—the difference between foragers and farmers, food procurers and food producers. To most people, in most societies, for most of the time, food is and always has been the most important thing in the world. Changes in how we eat are among history's big changes. The biggest of all came after the Ice Age, as the world warmed: **husbandry**—breeding animals and cultivating crops—began to replace hunting and gathering.

Together, farming and herding revolutionized humans' place in their ecosystems. Instead of merely depending on other life forms to sustain us, we forged a new relationship of interdependence with species we eat. We rely on them for food; they rely on us for their reproduction. Husbandry was the first human challenge to evolution. Instead of evolving species through **natural selection**, farming and herding proceed by what might be called unnatural selection—sorting and selecting by human hands, for human needs, according to human agendas.

Herding and tilling also changed human societies. By feeding people on a vastly greater scale, agriculture allowed societies to get hugely bigger than ever before. We can only guess at the absolute figures, but in areas where farming has replaced foraging in modern times, population has increased fifty- or even a hundredfold. Larger populations demanded new forms of control of labor and food distribution, which, in turn, nurtured strong states and powerful elites.

Society became more volatile and, apparently, less stable. In almost every case, for reasons we still do not understand, when people begin to practice agriculture, the pace of change quickens immeasurably and cumulatively. States and civilizations do not seem to last for long. Societies that we think of as being most evolved turn out to be least fitted for survival. Compared with the relative stability of forager communities, societies that depend on agriculture are prone to lurch and collapse. History becomes a path picked among their ruins.

FOCUS questions

- WHY ARE settled foragers better off than farmers?
- WHAT KINDS of environments are suited to herding?
- WHAT KINDS of environments were suited to early agriculture?
- WHERE DID farming start, and what were the first crops?
- GIVEN THE disadvantages, why did people farm?

Still, for Captain Cook, and for most people who have thought about it, it was strange that people who had the opportunity to practice agriculture should not take advantage of it. The advantages of agriculture seem so obvious. The farmer can select the best specimens of edible crops and creatures, collect them in the most convenient places and pastures, crossbreed livestock, and hybridize plants to improve size, yield, or flavor. By these methods, farming societies build up large populations. Usually they go on to create cities and develop ever more complex technologies. To Cook and his contemporaries in Europe, who believed that progress was inevitable and that the same kind of changes are bound to happen everywhere, peoples who clung to foraging seemed baffling.

James Cook, from *Captain Cook's Journal During His First Voyage Round the World*

THE PROBLEM OF AGRICULTURE

Cook and others at the time saw only two explanations for why foragers might reject agriculture: They were either stupid or subhuman. Early European painters in Australia depicted indigenous people as apelike creatures, grimacing oddly and crawling in trees. Colonists ignored the natives, or, when they got in the way, often hunted them down—as they would beasts. But native Australians rejected more than agriculture. In some areas, they shunned every technical convenience. On the island of Tasmania, in the extreme south of Australia, where the natives became extinct soon after European settlement began, they seemed to have forgotten every art of their ancestors: bows, boats, even how to kindle fire. In Arnhem Land, in the extreme north, they used boomerangs to make music but no longer as weapons for the hunt. Progress, which the European discoverers of Australia believed in fervently, seemed to have gone into reverse. Australia was not only on the exact opposite side of the world from England, but also it was a topsy-turvy place where everything was upside down.

We can, however, be certain that if natives rejected agriculture or other practices Europeans considered progressive, it must have been for good reasons. Native Australians did not lack the knowledge necessary to switch from foraging to farming had they so wished. When they gathered wild yams or the root known as nardoo, they ensured that enough of the plant remained in the ground to grow back. In many regions, too, they used fire to control the grazing grounds of kangaroos and concentrate them for hunting, a common technique among herders to manage pasture and among tillers to renew the soil. Along the Murray and Darling Rivers, aborigines even watered and weeded wild crops and policed their boundaries against human and animal predators. They could have planted and irrigated crops, farmed the grubs they liked to eat, penned kangaroos, and even tried to domesticate them. In the far north of Australia, aboriginal communities traded with the farming cultures of New Guinea. So they could have learned agriculture from outsiders.

If the aborigines did not farm, it must have been because they were doing well without it. Similar cases all over the world support this conclusion. Where wild foods are abundant, there is no incentive to domesticate them. Of course, people often adopt practices that do them no good. We can concede this general principle, but, case by case, we still want to know why.

The rice fields of Bali in Indonesia are among the most productive in the world, using varieties of rice and techniques for farming it that are about 1,000 years old. Irrigation channels, maintained and administered by farmers' cooperatives, distribute water evenly among the terraces. Though originally a lowland crop, favoring swampy conditions, rice adapts perfectly to upland environments and to terrace farming.

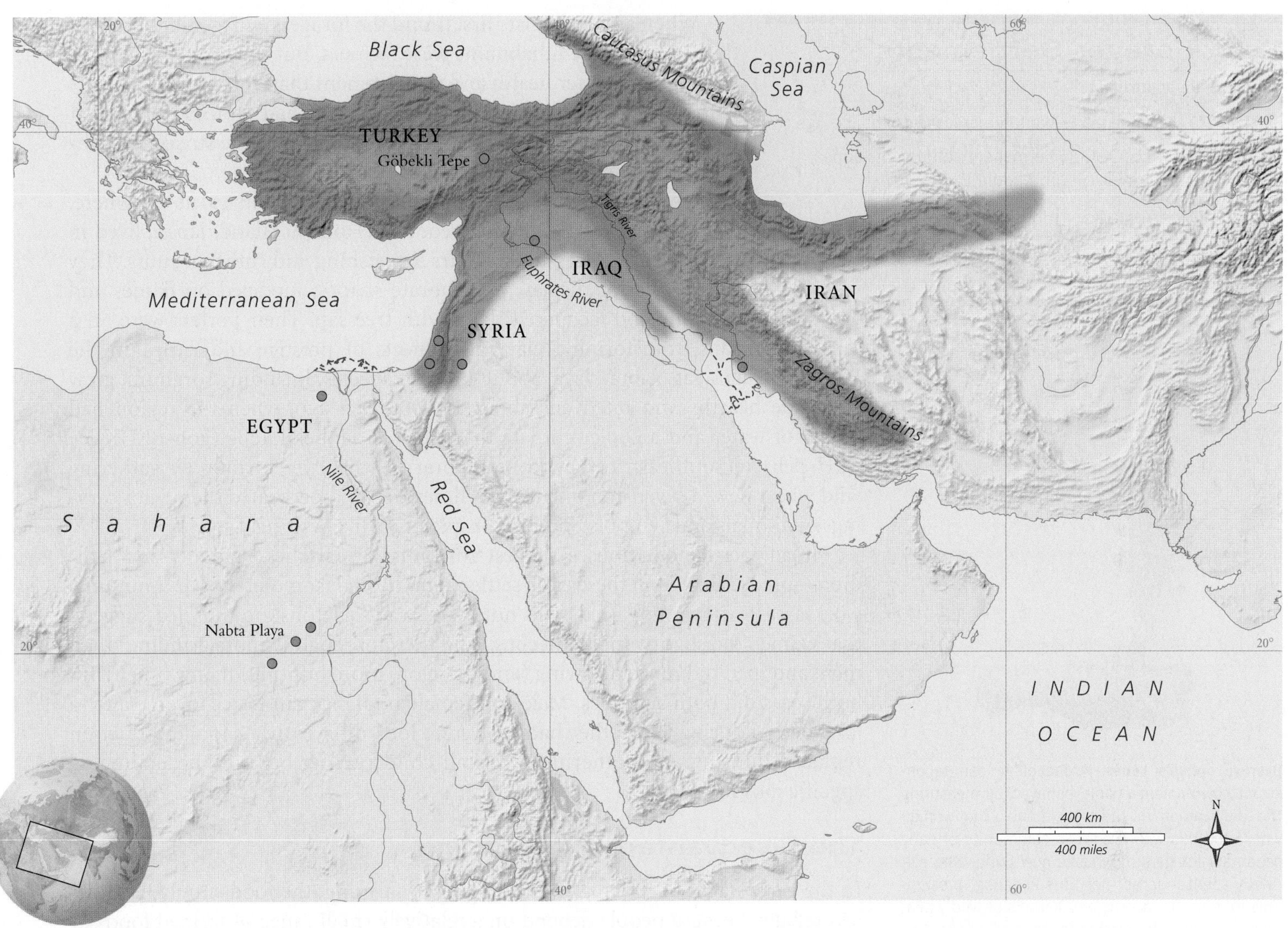

MAP 2.1

Preagricultural Settlements in the Middle East

forest
grassland
TURKEY modern-day country
preagricultural settlement
ancient coastlines

Preagricultural Settlements

Under some conditions, people can settle in one place without the trouble of farming. Archaeological evidence from the Middle East shows this. After the Ice Age, a frontier zone between forest and grassland stretched across the eastern shore of the Mediterranean and what are now Iran, eastern Turkey, and Iraq (see Map 2.1). Forests were full of nuts, which gatherers ground into flour. Grasslands bred vast quantities of wild grass with edible seeds. These foods could all be warehoused between harvests and had the additional advantage of maturing at different times. Dense herds of gazelle provided more nutrition for hunters to bring home. Food was so plentiful that foragers did not have to move around much to find it.

By about 14,000 to 15,000 years ago, permanent settlements arose throughout the region: clusters of dwellings made of wood on stone foundations, or cut from soft stone and roofed with reeds. Villages had distinctive habits, which almost amounted to badges of identity. Some favored gazelle toe bones for jewelry; some preferred fox teeth and partridge legs. Villagers married within their own communities, as inherited physical characteristics show: People were relatively short in some villages or had distinctive palates in others. They cut plans of their fields on limestone slabs, which suggests that they had a sense of possession that Captain Cook would have recognized.

Early Forager Settlements

(All dates are approximate)	
15,000 years ago	World emerges from the Ice Age
14,000–15,000 years ago	Permanent settlements appear in Middle East
13,000 years ago	Honshu Island, Japan
10,000 years ago	Nabta Playa, Egypt; Göbekli Tepe, Turkey

When archaeologists first found the foragers' villages in the 1930s, they assumed the inhabitants were farmers. But their remains, on the whole, show better health and nourishment than the farming peoples who followed. A diet rich in seeds and nuts had ground down their teeth, but—unlike the farmers—they had none of the streaked tooth-enamel common among the under-nourished.

Similar evidence of preagricultural settlements exists elsewhere. The Jomon (JOHM-mehn) people of Honshu Island, Japan, lived in permanent villages 13,000 years ago, fishing and gathering nuts. They made pots for display, in elaborate shapes, modeled on flames and serpents and lacquered them with tree sap. Their potters were, in a sense, magicians, transforming clay into objects of prestige and ritual. In the Egyptian Sahara, at Nabta Playa, about 40 plant species, including sorghum, grew alongside hearths and pit ovens about 10,000 years ago, when the region had plenty of water and a cooler climate than now. At Göbekli Tepe (goh-BEHK-lee TEH-peh) in southeast Turkey, contemporaries who lived mainly by gathering wild wheat hewed seven-ton pillars from limestone and decorated them with carvings of animals and symbols that look suspiciously like writing.

Overuse deforms bones. Archaeology can reconstruct how ancient people behaved by measuring the deformities in their skeletons. The woman whose toe this was lived in a community of early sedentary foragers in what is now Syria. She evidently spent much of her time kneeling, presumably to grind the acorns and kernels of wild wheat on which her people relied for food.

Small, permanent houses suggest that nuclear families—parents and children—predominated in these early settlements, though some sites have communal work areas for grinding seeds and nuts. The way skeletons are muscled suggests that women did slightly more kneeling (and therefore slightly more grinding) than men, and men did more throwing (and therefore more hunting) than women. But both sexes did both activities. Male and female bodies began to reconverge after a long period during which they had evolved to look differently. As food production replaced hunting and gathering, war and child rearing became the main sex-specific jobs in society.

The Disadvantages of Farming

In the early stages of moving from foraging to farming, the food supply becomes less reliable because people depend on a relatively small range of farmed foods or even on a single species. Communities become vulnerable to ecological disasters. Famine is more likely as diet narrows. When people have to plant and grow food as well as gather it, they use more energy to get the same amount of nourishment (although domesticated foods, once harvested, tend to be easier to process for eating). The need to organize labor encourages inequalities and exploitation. Concentrations of domesticated animals spread disease, such as smallpox, measles, rubella, chicken pox, influenza, and tuberculosis.

So the problem is really the opposite of what Cook supposed. Farmers' behavior, not foragers', is strange. Husbandry in some ways makes life worse. No one has put the problem better than the historian of agronomy, Jack L. Harlan: "The question must be raised: Why farm? ... Why work harder for food less nutritious and a supply more capricious? Why invite famine, plague, pestilence and crowded living conditions?"[1]

HUSBANDRY IN DIFFERENT ENVIRONMENTS

The most obvious contrast in environments is between **herders** and **tillers.** Herding developed where plants were too sparse or indigestible to sustain human life, but animals could convert these plants into meat—an energy source that people can access by eating the animals. In some places, roamed by crea-

MAKING CONNECTIONS

FORAGERS AND FARMERS COMPARED

FORAGERS	FARMERS
Food procurers hunt and gather	**Food producers** husbandry (breed animals, cultivate crops)
Fit into nature little environmental impact	**Change nature** herders: some environmental impact tillers: massive environmental impact
Manage the landscape	**Nature remade and reimagined**
Dependence on wild animals and plants	**Interdependence between humans, plants, and animals** animals and plants exploited and domesticated
Stable food supply nomadic foragers move in response to environmental change	**Unstable food supply** small range of farmed foods increases vulnerability to ecological disasters, change of climate
Stable population • relatively little labor needed • population control available, mainly by managed lactation	**Expanding population** • breeding livestock and cultivating plants lead to increased food supply • increased population • concentrations of domesticated animals spread disease
Stable society • kinship and age fix individual's place in society • sexes usually share labor by specializing in different economic tasks	**Radically changed, unstable society** • need to control labor and food distribution leads to social inequalities • work shared between the sexes, increased reliance on female labor • strong states develop with powerful elites, complex technologies

tures with herd instinct, people could manage herds instead of hunting them. Breeding enhanced qualities that evolution did not necessarily favor, such as docility; size; and yield of meat, milk, eggs, and fat. But herds, on the whole, kept to traditional patterns of migration, and people continued to accompany them—driving the beasts, now, rather than following them. Domesticated animals remained recognizably the heirs of their wild ancestors, and the landscapes through which they traveled did not change much, except that the herds' feeding and manure probably encouraged the grasses they ate to flourish at the expense of other plant species.

In other environments, tilling develops where the soil is suitable or enough ecological diversity exists to sustain plant husbandry or mixed farming of plants and animals. In the long run, tillage of the soil changed the world more than any previous innovation by Homo sapiens. From postglacial mud, people coaxed what we now call "**civilization**"—a way of life based on radically modifying the environment. Instead of merely trying to manage the landscape nature provided, farmers recarved it with fields and boundaries, ditches and irrigation canals. They stamped the land with a new look, a geometrical order. Agriculture enabled humans to see the world in a new way—to imagine that magic and science had the power to change nature. Such power, in turn, changed people's sense of where they fit into the panorama of life on Earth. Now they could become lords or, in more modest moments or cultures, stewards of creation.

Jack Harlan, from *Crops and Man*

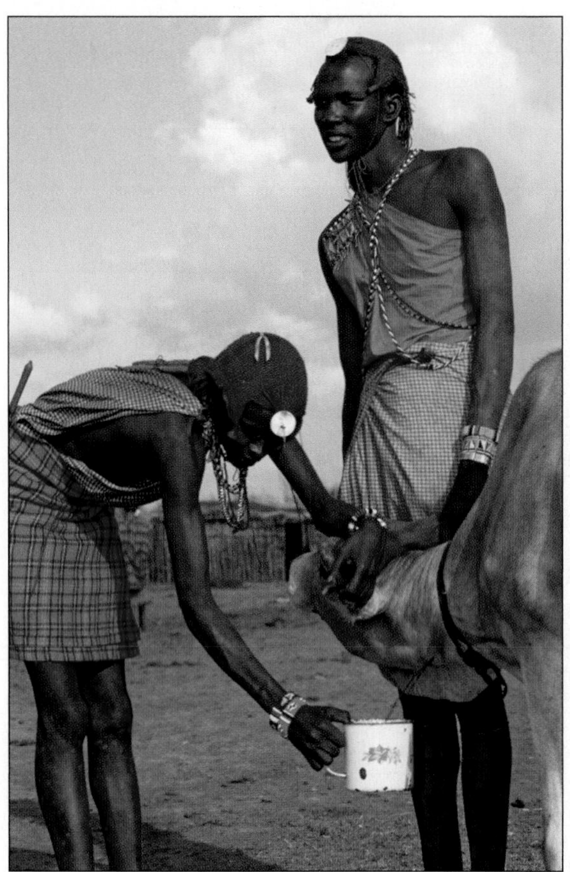

Masai. Humans need vitamin C, but the meat and dairy products from herds do not supply much of it. So people in herding cultures eat half-digested plants from animals' stomachs and organ meats, such as the liver, in which vitamin C tends to get concentrated. Fresh blood—drawn here from the veins of a calf by Masai women in Kenya—is also a useful source of the vitamin. Drinking blood confers an added advantage: Nomads can draw it from their animals "on the hoof," without slaughtering them or halting the migrations of their flocks.

Herders' Environments

In tundra and evergreen forests, where cold shortens the growing season, too little humanly digestible plant food thrives to keep large communities alive. People can remain foragers—and primarily hunters, seeking the fat-rich species typical of such zones—like the Inuit in the North American Arctic, who hunt seal and walrus, or they can become herders, like the Sami and Samoyeds of northern Europe and northwest Asia, who live off reindeer.

Similarly, the soils of the world's vast grasslands—known as prairie in North America, pampa in South America, steppe in Eurasia, and the **Sahel** (sah-HEHL) in Africa—have, for most of history, been unfavorable for tillage. Though there are favorable patches, the sod is mostly too difficult to turn without a steel plow. The peoples of the Eurasian and African grasslands were probably herding by about 5000 B.C.E. Native American grassland dwellers of the New World, on the other hand, retained a foraging way of life because available species—bison, various types of antelope—were more abundant for the hunt and less suitable for herding.

For those who choose it, herding has three special consequences.

First, it imposes a mobile life. The proportion of the population who follow the herds—and, in some cases, it is the entire population—cannot settle in permanent villages. Herder peoples can build on a large scale. The Scythians, for instance, people of the western Asian **steppe** who first domesticated the horse and invented the wheel and axle about 6,000 to 7,000 years ago, built impressive stone structures. But these were underground tombs, dwellings for the dead, while the living inhabited temporary camps. Some herding societies in Asia and Africa have become rich enough to found cities for elites or for specialist craftsmen or miners. In the thirteenth century C.E., a city of this type, Karakorum in Mongolia, was one of the most admired in the world. On the whole, however, herding does not favor cities or the kind of culture that cities nourish, such as monumental buildings, large-scale institutions for education and the arts, and industrial technology.

Second, since herders breed from animals that naturally share their grassland habitats, their herds consist of such creatures as cattle, sheep, horses, goats—milk-yielding stock. To get the full benefit from their animals, herding peoples have to eat dairy products. To modern, milk-fed Americans, this may sound normal. But it required a modification of human evolution. Most people, in most parts of the world, do not naturally produce lactase, the substance that enables them to digest milk, after infancy. They respond to dairy products with distaste or even intolerance.

Third, the herders' diet, relying heavily on meat, milk, and blood, lacks variety compared to diets in more ecologically diverse environments. If you eat organ meats, drink animal blood, and prepare dairy products to harness beneficial bacteria, you can get everything the human body needs, including adequate vitamin C, but herding peoples, although they often express contempt for farmers, prize cultivated plants and import them at great cost or take them as tribute or booty. They also value products of tree-rich environments, such as timber, silk, linen, and cotton.

So conflict arose not from herders' hatred of farmers' culture but from a desire to share its benefits. On the other hand, farmers have not normally had to depend on herding cultures for meat or dairy products. Typically, they can farm their own animals, feeding them on the waste or surplus of their crops or by grazing them between their areas of tillage or at higher altitudes above their fields. Therefore, in herder–settler warfare, the herders have typically been aggressive and the settlers defensive, until about 300 years ago or so, when the war technology of sedentary societies left herding societies unable to compete.

Tillers' Environments

The first prerequisite for farming was soil loose enough for a dibble—a pointed stick for poking holes in the ground—to work. At first, this was the only technology available. Where the sod had to be cut or turned—where, for instance, the soil was heavy, or dense, or sticky—agriculture had to wait for the more advanced technology of the spade and the plow.

Equally necessary for agriculture were water to grow the crop, sun to ripen it, and nourishment for the soil. Farming can exhaust even the richest soils. Flooding and layering with silt or dredging and dressing new topsoil is needed to replace nutrients. Alternatively, farmers can add fertilizer, such as ash from burned wood, leaf mold from forest clearings, or dung, from bird colonies or domesticated animals.

Three broad types of environment suited early agriculture: swampy wetlands, uplands, and alluvial plains, where flooding rivers or lakes renew the topsoil. (Cleared woodlands and irrigated drylands are also suitable for agriculture, but as far as we know, farming never originated in these environments. Rather, outsiders brought it to these areas from someplace else.) Each of the three types developed with peculiar characteristics and specialized crops.

SWAMPLAND Swamp is no longer much in demand for farming. Nowadays, in the Western world, if we want to turn bog into farmland we drain it. But it had advantages early on. Swamp soil is rich, moist, and easy to work with simple technology. At least one staple grows well in waterlogged land—rice. We still do not know where or when rice was first cultivated, or even whether any of these wetland varieties preceded the dryland rice that has gradually become more popular around the world. Most evidence, however, suggests that people were producing rice on the lower Ganges River in India and in parts of southeast Asia some 8,000 years ago, and in paddies in the Yangtze River valley in China not long afterward.

Where rice is unavailable, swampland cultivators can adapt the land for other crops by dredging earth, making mounds for planting and ditches for water-dwelling creatures and plants. In the western highlands of New Guinea, the first agriculture we know of started fully 9,000 years ago in boggy valley bottoms. Drains, ditches, and mounds still exist in the Kuk swamp there. More extensive earthworks were in place by 6000 B.C.E. The crops have vanished—biodegraded into nothingness—but the first farmers probably planted **taro**, the most easily cultivated, indigenous native root. Modern varieties of taro exhibit signs of long domestication. A diverse group of plants—sago, nuts, and native bananas, yams, and other tubers—was probably added early. At some much disputed point, pigs arrived.

Variety of crops made New Guinea's agriculture sustainable. Variety may also help explain why farming remained a small-scale enterprise there. New Guinea never generated the big states and cities that grew up where the range of crops was narrower and agriculture more fragile. It may sound paradoxical that the most advantageous crop range produces the most modest results, but it makes sense. One of the pressures that drives farming peoples to expand their territory is fear that a crop will fail. The more territory you control, the more surplus you

MAKING CONNECTIONS

HERDERS AND TILLERS COMPARED

HERDERS	TILLERS
Environment	**Environment**
tundra, evergreen forests of northern Eurasia, grasslands, uplands	swampy wetlands, alluvial plains, temporal forests, irrigated deserts, some uplands
Way of life	**Way of life**
mobile	settled
Diet	**Diet**
reliance on meat, milk, and blood, sometimes supplemented by cultivated plants from tillers	reliance on cultivated plants, supplemented by meat and dairy from their own animals
Culture	**Culture**
does not favor development of cities, large-scale institutions, industry	tends to become urban, with large-scale institutions, industry

desire for goods from farming cultures, need for extensive grazing land

possessive attitude to land

mutual incomprehension and demonization

violence between herders and tillers

can warehouse, the more manpower you command, and the more productive your fields. Moreover, if you farm an environment with a narrow range of food sources, you can diversify only by conquering other people's habitats. The history of New Guinea has been as violent as that of other parts of the world, but its wars have always been local and the resulting territorial adjustments small. Empire-building was unknown on the island until European colonizers got there in the late nineteenth century.

We know of no other swamps that people adapted so early, but many later civilizations arose from similar sorts of ooze. We do not know much about the origins of agriculture among **Bantu** speaking peoples in West Africa, but it is more likely to have begun in the swamp than in the forest. Swampland is suited to the native yams on which Bantu farming first relied. Waterlogged land is also the favorite habitat of the other mainstay of Bantu tradition, the *oil palm*. The earliest archaeological evidence of farming based on yams and oil palms dates from about 5,000 years ago in swampy valley bottoms of Cameroon, above the forest level.

Swampland also contributed to agriculture along the Amazon River in South America 4,000 or 5,000 years ago. At first, the crops were probably richly diverse, supplemented by farming turtles and mollusks. Later, however, from about

500 C.E., farmers increasingly focused on bitter manioc, also known as cassava or yucca, which has the great advantage of being poisonous to predators. Human consumers can process the poison out. Olmec civilization, which, as we shall see in Chapter 3, was enormously influential in the history of **Mesoamerica**, was founded in swamps thick with mangrove trees about 3,000 years ago.

UPLANDS Like swamplands, regions of high altitude are not places that people today consider good for farming. There are three reasons for this: First, as altitude increases, cold and the scorching effects of solar radiation in the thin atmosphere diminish the variety of viable plants. Second, slopes erode (although relatively rich soils then collect in valleys). Finally, slopes in general are hard to work with plows. Still, this does not stop people who do not use plows from farming them, and in highlands suitable for plant foods, plant husbandry or mixed farming did develop.

The Andes Highlands usually contain many different microclimates at various altitudes and in valleys where sun and rain can vary tremendously within a short space. Some of the world's earliest farming, therefore, happened at surprisingly high altitudes. Evidence of mixed farming survives from between about 12,000 and 7,000 years ago near Lake Titicaca, 13,000 feet up in the Andes Mountains of South America. Here, in the cave of Pachamachay, bones of domesticated llamas cover those of hunted species. The domesticated animals fed on quinoa (kee-NOH-ah), a hardy grain that grows at high altitudes thanks to a bitter, soapy coating that cuts out solar radiation. The llamas ingested the leafy part and deposited the seeds in their manure. Their corrals therefore became nurseries for a food fit for humans to grow and eat.

The earliest known experiments in domesticating the potato probably occurred at about the same time in the same area—between 12,000 and 7,000 years ago. Potatoes were ideal for mountain agriculture. Some naturally occurring varieties grow at altitudes of up to 14,000 feet. Eaten in sufficient quantities, moreover, potatoes provide everything the human body needs to survive. High-altitude varieties have a hidden advantage. Whereas wild lowland potatoes are poisonous and need careful processing to become edible, the concentration of poison in potatoes diminishes the higher you climb. There is an obvious evolutionary reason for this. The poison is there to deter predators, which are most numerous at low altitudes.

The potato gave Andean mountain dwellers the same capacity to support large populations as peoples of the valleys and plains, where a parallel story began in the central coastal region of what is now Peru. There, around 10,000 years ago, farmers grew sweet potato tubers, perhaps the New World's earliest farmed crop. Andean history became a story of highland–lowland warfare, punctuated by the rise and fall of mountain-based empires.

Mesoamerica The Mesoamerican highlands, which are less high and less steep than those of the Andes, produced their own kind of highland-adapted food: a trinity of *maize*, *beans*, and *squash*. This combination grows well together and when eaten together provides almost complete nutrition. The earliest surviving specimens of cultivated maize are 6,000 years old, developed from a wild grass known as teosinte (TEE-eh-SIN-tee), which is still found in central Mexico, along with the wild ancestors of domesticated beans. Botanists estimate that people domesticated beans about 9,000 years ago (see Figure 2.1). The earliest domesticated squashes date from about the same period. The fact that their wild ancestors have disappeared suggests that farming here might have started with squashes when gatherers of wild beans and grains needed to provide food for times of drought. Squash grows well during arid spells severe enough to wither teosinte and blight beans.

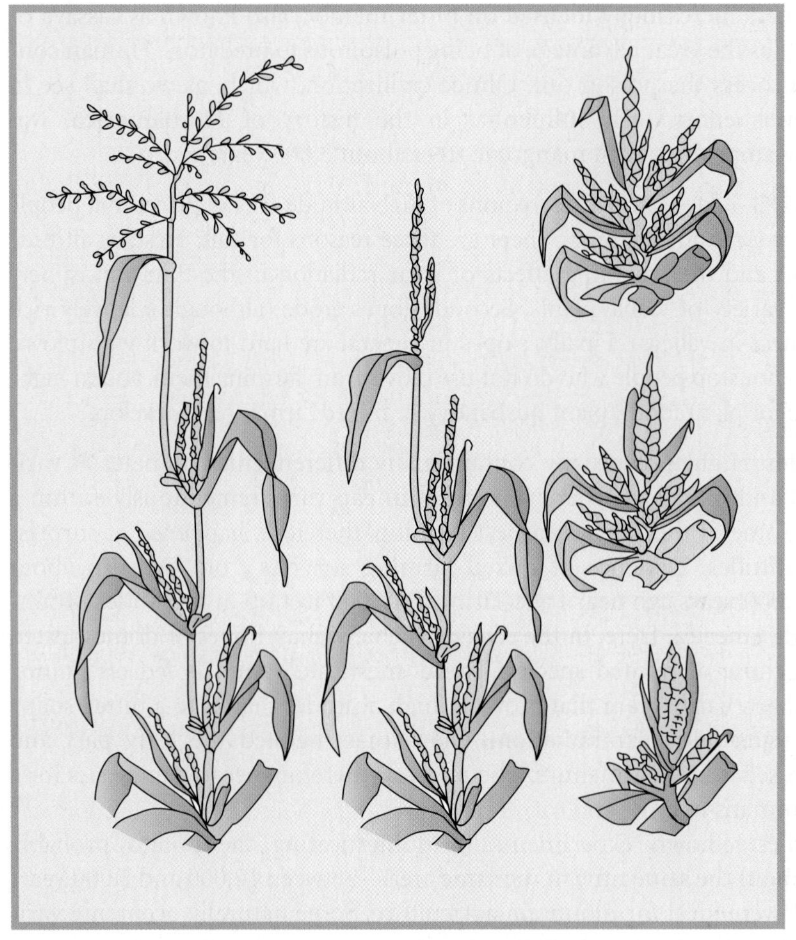

FIGURE 2.1 TEOSINTE AND MAIZE. The form of teosinte from which early farmers in Mesoamerica developed maize no longer exists. But the diagram illustrates the stages through which Mesoamericans may have bred teosinte into maize, until they developed the characteristic thick, densely packed cobs familiar today. Unlike teosinte, maize cannot germinate without human help.
Permission of The University of Michigan Museum of Anthropology.

The Old World The Old World had no potatoes, quinoa, or maize for highland farmers to work with. The hardiest staples available in most of Eurasia and Africa were *rye* and *barley*. Surprisingly, however, people in lowlands first domesticated both of them in what are now Jordan and Syria, probably about 10,000 years ago. Rye germinates at just a couple degrees above freezing, but its drawbacks made it more popular as a winter crop in wheat-growing lowlands than as a mountain staple. Its yield is lower, and it is less nutritious than other grains. Rye is also extremely vulnerable to fungus infection. Barley did not fulfill its potential to be an Old World equivalent of quinoa or potatoes until the sixth century C.E., when it became the staple food in Tibet.

Teff—the staple grain of early Ethiopian civilization—remains unique to the region, where it is still harvested regularly. But, as the picture shows, it more closely resembles wild grasses than modern high-yielding food grains. The starchy ears are tiny and require much labor to mill. So, like many traditional staples, teff faces the threat of extinction today from the competition of commercial hybrids or genetically modified varieties, promoted by powerful corporations.

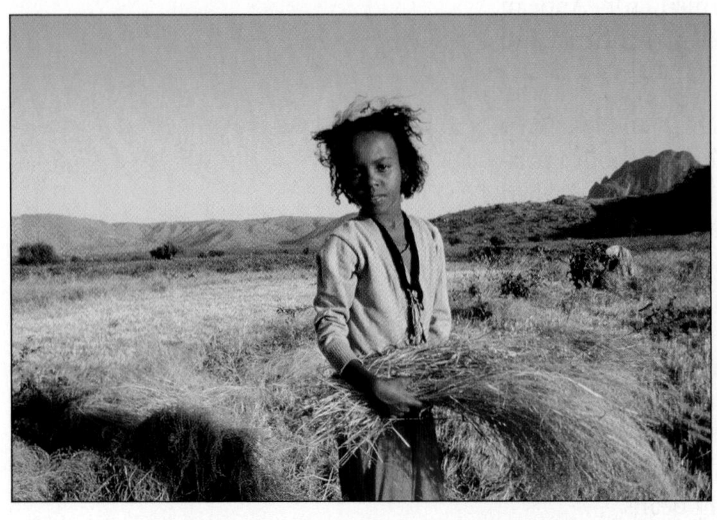

The only other Old World grain with similar potential was Ethiopia's indigenous grass called *teff*. Though its tiny grains make teff laborious to cultivate and process, it was suited to the region's fertile soil and temperate climate above 7,200 feet. Although farmers in Ethiopia cultivated teff at least 5,000 years ago, they never had to rely on it absolutely. Some varieties of *millet*—the name of a huge range of grasses whose seeds humans can digest—had superior yields. Over time, millet displaced teff, which never became a major staple outside Ethiopia.

ALLUVIAL PLAINS Although swamps and rain-fed highlands have produced spectacularly successful agriculture, farmers get the best help from nature in alluvial plains, where river-borne or lake-borne mud renews the topsoil. If people can channel the floods to keep crops from being swept away on these plains, sediment restores nutrients and compensates for lack of rain. Alluvial soils in arid climates sustained, as we shall see in the next chapter, some of the world's most productive economies until late in the second millennium B.C.E. *Wheat* and barley grew in the black earth that lines Egypt's Nile River, the floodplains of the lower Tigris and Euphrates Rivers in what is now Iraq, and the Indus River in what is now Pakistan. People first farmed millet on alluvial soils in a cooler, moister climate in China, in the crook of the Yellow River and the Guanzhong (gwang-joe) basin around 7,000 years ago. And in the warm, moist climate of Indochina in what is now Cambodia, three crops of rice a year grew on soil that the annual counterflow of the Mekong River created. The Mekong becomes so torrential that the delta—where the river enters the sea—cannot funnel its flow, and water is forced back upriver.

Jericho skull. No one knows why people in Jericho, in the eighth millennium B.C.E., kept skulls, painted them with plaster, and inserted cowrie shells into the eye sockets. But these decorated skulls have, in a sense, helped the dead to survive. Some of the skulls even show traces of painted hair and mustaches.
Ashmolean Museum, Oxford, England, U.K.

Smaller patches of alluvium, deposited by floods, nourished the world's earliest known fully farming economies. Among the first was Jericho on the Jordan River in modern Israel. Today, the Jordan valley is crusted with salt and sodium. Ten thousand years ago, however, Jericho overlooked an alluvial fan that trickling streams washed down from the hills, filling the river as it crept south from the Sea of Galilee. The river Jordan was thick with silt. The banks it deposited formed the biblical "jungle of Jericho," from where lions raided the sheepfolds. Here, rich wheat fields created the landscape the Bible called "the garden of the Lord." Desert people, such as the Israelites were tempted to conquer it.

In much the same period, between about 9,000 and 11,000 years ago, farming towns also appeared in Anatolia in Turkey. Çatalhüyük (chah-tahl-hoo-YOOK), the most spectacular of them, stood on an alluvial plain that the river Çarsamba flooded. Nourished by wheat and beans, the people filled an urban area of 32 acres. Walkways across flat roofs, not streets as we define them, linked a honeycomb of dwellings. You can still see where the occupants swept their rubbish—chips of bone and shiny, black flakes of volcanic glass called obsidian—into their hearths.

By exchanging craft products—weapons, metalwork, and pots—for primary materials such as cowrie shells from the Red Sea, timber from the Taurus Mountains in Anatolia, and copper from beyond the Tigris, the inhabitants of Çatalhüyük became rich by the standards of the time. Archeologists have unearthed fine blades, obsidian mirrors, and products of the copper-smelting technology that these people developed.

Yet the inhabitants of Çatalhüyük never got safely beyond the mercy of nature. They worshipped images of its strength: bulls with monstrous horns and protruding tongues, crouching leopards who guard goddesses leaning on grain bins, fuming volcanoes, giant boar with laughing jaws and bristling backs. This is surely farmer's art, animated by fear. Most people died in their late twenties or early thirties. Their corpses were ritually fed to vultures and jackals—as surviving paintings show—before their bones were buried in communal graves. Catalhüyük became doomed as the waters that supplied it dried up. But it lasted for nearly 2,000 years, remarkable longevity by the standards of later cities. Along with Jericho and other settlements of the era, it showed how farming, despite its short-term disadvantages and the sacrifices it demanded, could sustain life through hard times.

THE SPREAD OF AGRICULTURE

The development of food production was not a unique occurrence—a one-of-a-kind accident or a stroke of genius. Rather, farming was an ordinary and fairly frequent process that could therefore be open to a variety of explanations. Scholars used to suppose that it was so extraordinary it must have begun in some particular spot and that **diffusion** spread it from there—carried by migrants or conquerors, or transmitted by trade, or imitated. The last 40 years of research have shown, on the contrary, that the transition to food production happened over and over again, in a range of regions and a variety of environments, with different foodstuffs and different techniques (see Map 2.2). Nevertheless, connections between neighboring regions were unquestionably important in spreading husbandry. Some crops were undoubtedly transferred from the places they originated to other regions.

Europe

It seems likely (though disputed) that migrants from Asia colonized Europe. They brought their farming materials and knowledge with them, as well as their **Indo-European languages**, from which most of Europe's present languages descend. Colonization was a gradual process, beginning about 6,000 years ago. Early farmers may have cleared some land, but probably did not undertake large-scale deforestation. Well-documented cases from other forest environments suggest that early agriculturists in Europe found trees useful and even revered them. So large-scale deforestation more likely occurred naturally, perhaps through tree diseases.

Asia

Similar migrations probably spread farming to parts of Central Asia south of the steppeland. The farming that developed in alluvial environments in Anatolia and the Jordan valley colonized or converted every viable part of the region by 8,000 or 9,000 years ago, crossing the Zagros Mountains (in what is now Iran) and, by about 6,000 years ago, spreading comprehensive irrigation systems between oases in southern Turkmenistan, which had a moister climate than it has now. In southern Pakistan remnants of domestic barley and wheat in mud bricks and the bones of domestic goats confirm the presence of agriculture about 9,000 years ago. This is also the site of the world's earliest surviving cotton thread, strung through a copper bead about 7,500 years ago. In the Indian subcontinent, the sudden emergence of well-built villages in the same period was probably the result of outside influence.

The Americas

In much of North America, maize spread northward from its birthplace in central Mexico. The process took thousands of years and demanded the development of new varieties as the crop crossed climate zones. The best estimate puts maize farming in the southwestern United States about 3,000 years ago. Meanwhile, some North American peoples began to farm sunflowers and sumpweed for their edible seeds and roots. In South America, the idea of agriculture spread from, or across, the high Andes, through the upper Amazon basin.

A CLOSER LOOK

THE FERTILITY GODDESS OF ÇATALHÜYÜK

In recent times, the so-called "fertility goddess" or "Earth Mother" of Çatalhüyük has become a cult-object for feminists, who make pilgrimages to the site. But what her image was for, and what it represents, are unknown.

Her seated position and uptilted head seem to suggest authority, as do the predatory felines that guard the throne, as if in obedience to someone able to command nature.

Her bulbous breasts and exaggerated sex organs suggest the importance of fertility to the society in which this image was crafted.

The folds of fat around her joints suggest a degree of obesity amounting to clinical pathology or physical deformity. Most human societies, for most of history, have admired body fat on both men and women.

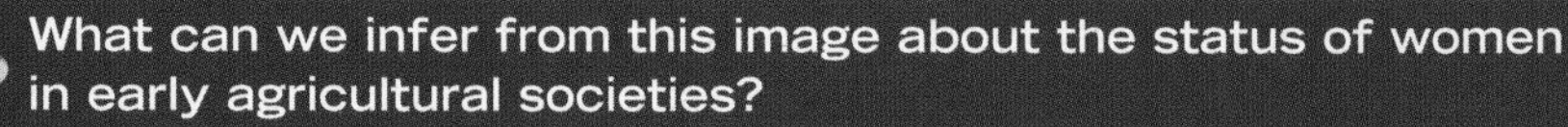
What can we infer from this image about the status of women in early agricultural societies?

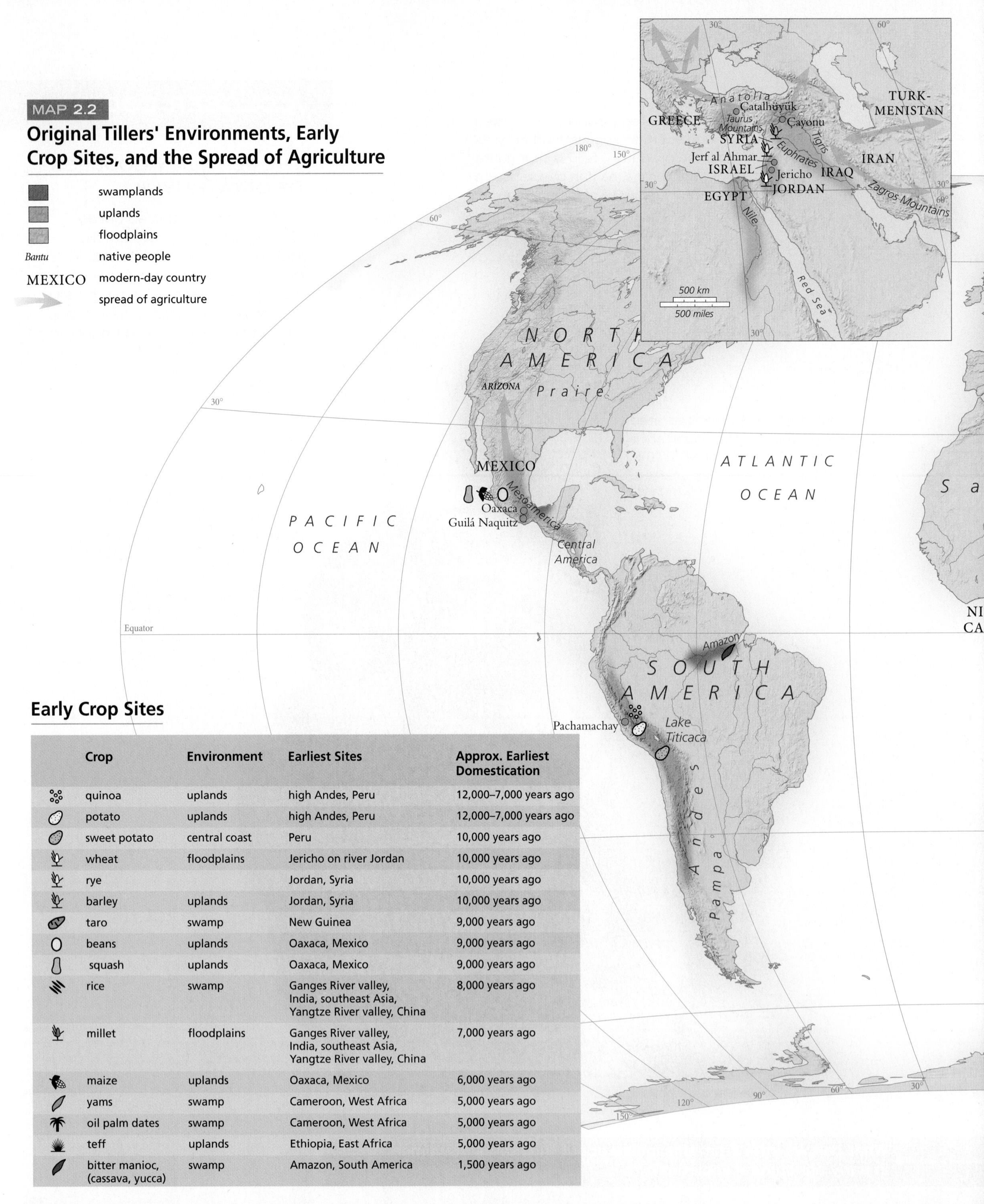

MAP 2.2

Original Tillers' Environments, Early Crop Sites, and the Spread of Agriculture

Early Crop Sites

Crop	Environment	Earliest Sites	Approx. Earliest Domestication
quinoa	uplands	high Andes, Peru	12,000–7,000 years ago
potato	uplands	high Andes, Peru	12,000–7,000 years ago
sweet potato	central coast	Peru	10,000 years ago
wheat	floodplains	Jericho on river Jordan	10,000 years ago
rye		Jordan, Syria	10,000 years ago
barley	uplands	Jordan, Syria	10,000 years ago
taro	swamp	New Guinea	9,000 years ago
beans	uplands	Oaxaca, Mexico	9,000 years ago
squash	uplands	Oaxaca, Mexico	9,000 years ago
rice	swamp	Ganges River valley, India, southeast Asia, Yangtze River valley, China	8,000 years ago
millet	floodplains	Ganges River valley, India, southeast Asia, Yangtze River valley, China	7,000 years ago
maize	uplands	Oaxaca, Mexico	6,000 years ago
yams	swamp	Cameroon, West Africa	5,000 years ago
oil palm dates	swamp	Cameroon, West Africa	5,000 years ago
teff	uplands	Ethiopia, East Africa	5,000 years ago
bitter manioc, (cassava, yucca)	swamp	Amazon, South America	1,500 years ago

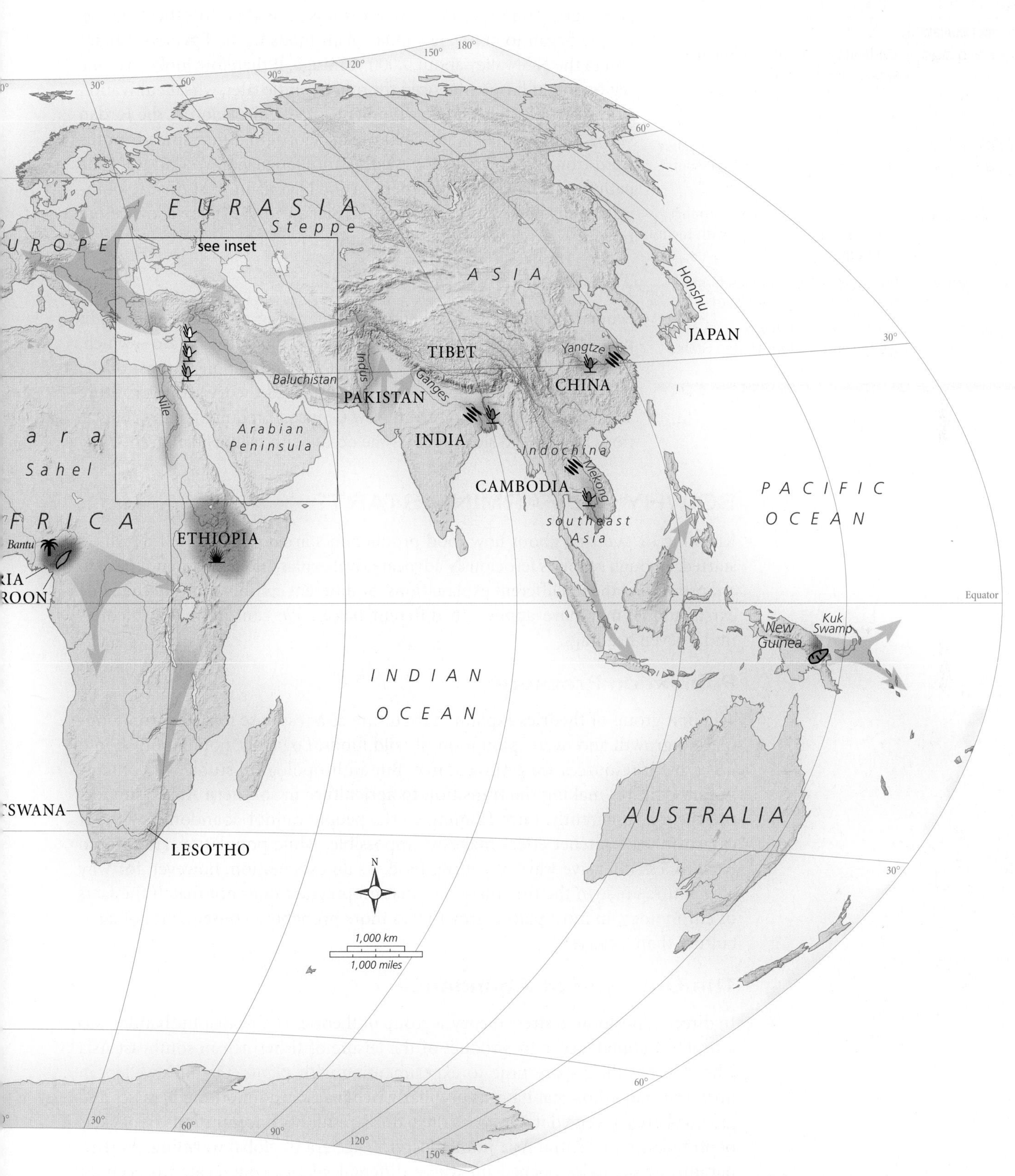
E U R A S I A
Steppe
U R O P E
see inset
A S I A
Honshu
JAPAN
Yangtze
TIBET
CHINA
Indus
Baluchistan
Ganges
PAKISTAN
Nile
INDIA
Arabian Peninsula
a r a
Sahel
Indochina
Mekong
CAMBODIA
P A C I F I C
O C E A N
southeast Asia
F R I C A
ETHIOPIA
Bantu
RIA
ROON
Equator
Kuk Swamp
New Guinea
I N D I A N
O C E A N
AUSTRALIA
TSWANA
LESOTHO
N
1,000 km
1,000 miles

The Spread of Agriculture

(All dates are approximate)	
9,000 years ago	Evidence of agriculture in Indian subcontinent; farming spreads by diffusion in the Egyptian Sahara and Nile valley
8,000–9,000 years ago	Farming spreads from Jordan valley and Anatolia to central Asia, south of the steppe
6,000 years ago	Migrants from Asia bring farming materials and knowledge with them to Europe
4,500–5,000 years ago	Bantu expansion spreads farming from West Africa southward
3,000 years ago	Maize moves northward from Mexico to southwestern United States

Africa

How agriculture spread in Africa is less clear than in other regions. People began to cultivate similar plant foods in the Egyptian Sahara and in the Nile valley about 9,000 years ago. It therefore looks as if one region might have influenced the other. A little later, wheat cultivation along the Nile followed developments of a similar kind in the Jordan valley. Between 4,500 and 5,000 years ago, agriculture spread southward from West Africa along with Bantu languages. We can trace the path from what are now Cameroon and Nigeria in West Africa, southward and then eastward across the Sahara to the Nile valley, before turning south again.

The Pacific Islands

Scholars debate when agriculture originated in the Pacific Islands. In particular, we do not know how or when the sweet potato—which, together with the pig, is the basis of food production in most of the region—got there. The most widely respected theory sees agriculture as the result of diffusion from New Guinea. It required many adaptations as it spread slowly across the ocean with seaborne migrants.

SO WHY DID FARMING START?

Knowing or guessing about how food production started does not tell us why it started. Though scholars ferociously advocate rival explanations, we do not have to choose among them. Different explanations, or different combinations of the same explanations, may have applied in different places. We can group the theories under seven headings.

Population Pressure

The first group of theories explains agriculture as a response to stress from population growth and overexploitation of wild foods. Logically, population should not grow if resources are getting scarce. But anthropological studies of contemporary cultures making the transition to agriculture in southern Africa support the theory. Apparently, once farming starts, people cannot abandon it without catastrophe. A ratchet effect makes it impossible, while population rises, to go back to less intensive ways of getting food. As an explanation, however, for why agriculture arose in the first place, population pressure does not match the facts of chronology. In most places, growth was more probably a consequence of agriculture than a cause.

The Outcome of Abundance

In direct opposition to stress theory, a group of theories claims that husbandry was a result of abundance, a by-product of the leisure of fishermen in southeast Asia who devoted their spare time to experimenting with plants. Or hill dwellers in northern Iraq, whose habitat was peculiarly rich in easily domesticated grasses and grazing herds, invented it. Or it was the natural result of concentrations of pockets of abundance in Central Asia in the post–Ice-Age era of global warming. As temperatures rose, oases opened up where different species congregated peacefully. Humans discovered they could domesticate animals that would otherwise be rivals, enemies, or prey. Abundance theory may explain why agriculture developed in some key areas, but not why, in good times, people would want to change how they got their food and take on extra work.

The Power of Politics

Stress theory and abundance theory may apply to why agriculture arose in different areas, but they cannot be true simultaneously. Therefore, beyond the food supply, it is worth considering possible political or social or religious influences on food strategies. After all, food not only sustains the body. It also confers power and prestige. It can symbolize identity and generate rituals. In hierarchically organized societies, elites nearly always demand more food than they can eat, not just to ensure their security but also to show off their wealth by squandering their waste.

In a society where leaders buy allegiance with food, competitive feasting can generate huge increases in demand, even if population is static and supplies are secure. Societies bound by feasting will always favor intensive agriculture and massive storage. Even in societies with looser forms of leadership or with collective decision making, feasting can be a powerful incentive to boost food production and storage, by force if necessary. Feasting can celebrate collective identity or cement relations with other communities. Then, too, people could process most of the early domesticated plants into intoxicating drinks. If farming began as a way to generate surpluses for feasts, alcohol must have had a special role.

Cult Agriculture

Religion may well have been the inspiration for farming. Planting may have originated as a fertility rite, or irrigation as libation, or enclosure as an act of reverence for a sacred plant. To plow or dibble and sow and irrigate can carry profound meaning. They can be rites of birth and nurture of the god on whom you are going to feed. In exchange for labor—a kind of sacrifice—the god provides nourishment. Most cultures represent the power to make food grow as a divine gift or curse or a secret that a hero stole from the gods. People have domesticated animals for use in sacrifice and prophecy as well as for food. Many societies cultivate plants that play a part at the altar rather than at the table. Examples include incense, ecstatic or hallucinatory drugs, the sacrificial corn of some high Andean communities, and wheat, which, in orthodox Christian traditions, is the only permitted grain for the Eucharist. And if religion inspired agriculture, alcohol as a drink that can induce ecstasy might have had a special appeal. In short, where crops are gods, farming is worship.

Cult agriculture. Chimú goldsmiths (Chapter 14) produced this ceremonial dish, which depicts the succession of the seasons, presided over by the central figure of the maize god, and offerings of the characteristic starches of the Peruvian lowlands—maize, cassava, sweet potatoes. By the time this object was made, however, around 1200 C.E., maize varieties had been adapted for varied environments, including uplands and temperate climates.

Climatic Instability

Global warming, as we saw in Chapter 1, presented some foragers with thousands of years of abundance. But warming is unpredictable. Sometimes it intensifies, causing drought; sometimes it goes into temporary reverse, causing little ice ages. Its effects are uneven. In the agrarian heartland of the Middle East, for example, warming squeezed the environment of nut-bearing trees but favored some grasses. The forest receded dramatically as the climate got drier and hotter between about 13,000 and 11,000 years ago. The new conditions encouraged people to rely more and more on grains for food and perhaps try to increase the amount of edible wheat. Gatherers who knew the habits of their plants tended them more carefully. It was, perhaps, a conservative, even a conservationist strategy: a way to keep old food stocks and lifestyles going under the impact of climate change.

Agriculture by Accident

In the nineteenth century, the most popular theory of how farming started attributed it to accident. One can hardly open a nineteenth-century book on the subject without encountering the myth of the primitive forager, usually a woman, discovering agriculture by observing how seeds, dropped by accident, germinated on fertilized soil. The father of the theory of evolution Charles Darwin (1809–1882; see Chapter 25), himself, thought something similar:

> The savage inhabitants of each land, having found out by many and hard trials what plants were useful ... would after a time take the first step in cultivation by planting them near their usual abodes. ... The next step in cultivation, and this would require but little forethought, would be to sow the seeds of useful plants; and as the soil near the hovels of the natives would often be in some degree manured, improved varieties would sooner or later arise.[2]

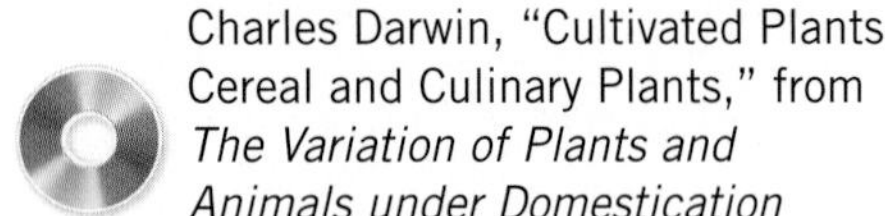
Charles Darwin, "Cultivated Plants: Cereal and Culinary Plants," from *The Variation of Plants and Animals under Domestication*

Darwin makes accident interact with human action. But historians are never satisfied to fall back on what would or might have happened (though this may be necessary to help understand remote or poorly documented periods). We want to know—and it is the historian's job to try to tell us—what really did happen. Assuming that anything a "savage" does requires "little forethought" does not fit with what we now know of human nature. Cleverness occurs at every period of history and in every type of society—in New Guinea as well as in New York, in antiquity as well as in modernity.

Production as an Outgrowth of Procurement

Still, the accident theory may be right in one respect. Early practitioners may not have consciously thought of food production as a different strategy from foraging. It makes sense, for instance, to see herding as a natural development of some hunting techniques, such as improving a species by culling weak or old animals, managing grazing by setting fires, driving herds down lanes to a place of slaughter, or corralling them for the kill. Similarly, farming and gathering might have been parts of a single continuous attempt to manage food sources. It is hard to tell where one leaves off and the other begins. The Papago Native Americans of Arizona drift in and out of an agrarian way of life as the weather permits, using patches of surface water to grow fast-maturing beans.

Einkorn is one of the few wild grasses that yield kernels that human stomachs can digest. It was a principal food source for the early sedentary foraging cultures of the Middle East, and one of the first species farmers adopted. But its grains are hard to separate from their tough husks, which helps explain why farmers strove to produce new varieties of grain by selection and hybridization.

The archaeological evidence has begun to yield clues to how gatherer communities of southwestern Asia transformed themselves into farming communities after the Ice Age. Grasses on the whole are naturally too indigestible to be human food. But the region produced wild barley and two kinds of wheat—einkorn (EYEN-korn) and emmer (EH-mehr). Archaeologists have found ground fragments of these grains from 14,000 to 15,000 years ago. The kernels are hard to free from their tough, inedible covering, so people who ate large amounts of them may have had an incentive to try to breed varieties that were easier to process. At first, the gatherers beat sheaves of wheat with sticks where they grew and collected edible seeds in baskets as they fell. As time went on, they cut stalks with flint sickles, which meant that fewer seeds fell when the wheat was harvested. This new method suggests that people were selecting preferred seeds for replanting. Modern experiments show that this process could produce a self-propagating species within 20 years. Alternatively, the new method itself might have encouraged changes in the species because heavier, larger seeds would be more likely to fall to the ground at the point of harvesting. Eventually, new varieties would emerge, but the process would be slower.

Even earlier, humans used a similar process with snails and other mollusks, which are an efficient food, self-packaged in a shell for carrying and cooking. People can isolate aquatic varieties, such as mussels and clams, in a pool, or enclose a snail-rich spot with a ditch. Moreover, snails are grazers and do not need to be fed with foods that humans would otherwise eat themselves. They can be herded without the use of fire, any special equipment, personal danger, or the need to train leashed animals or dogs to help. By culling small or undesirable types by hand, the early snail farmers could soon enjoy the benefits of selective breeding. Shell mounds from the late Ice Age or soon thereafter contain varieties of snails that are bigger on average than today's, so it looks as if the snail eaters were already selecting for size. Sometimes large-scale consumption of mollusks preceded that of foods that the more elaborate technologies of the hunt obtained. In southern Greece, a huge dump of snail shells nearly 13,000 years old was topped first by red deer bones with some snail shells, and then, nearly 4,000 years later, by tuna bones.

CHRONOLOGY

(All dates are approximate)

15,000 B.C.E.	End of Ice Age
14,000–13,000 B.C.E.	First permanent settlements in Middle East
11,000 B.C.E.	Appearance of Jomon culture, Japan
10,000–5000 B.C.E.	Mixed farming and potato cultivation develop (South America)
9000–7000 B.C.E.	Farming towns appear in Anatolia and Egypt
8000 B.C.E.	Rye and barley cultivation in Jordan and Syria; farming spreads from Jordan and Anatolia to Central Asia
7000 B.C.E.	"Trinity" of maize, beans, and squash develops in Mesoamerica; farming spreads in Egyptian Sahara and Nile valley; evidence of agriculture in Indian subcontinent; earliest evidence of agriculture in New Guinea
6000 B.C.E.	Rice cultivation in India, southeast Asia, and China
4000 B.C.E.	Scythians domesticate the horse and invent wheel and axle; Indo-European languages spread as migrants from Asia colonize Europe; millet farmed in Yellow River valley, China
5000–2000 B.C.E.	River valley civilizations flourish
3000 B.C.E.	Teff cultivated in Ethiopia; Bantu languages and agriculture begin to spread southward from West Africa; earliest specimens of cultivated maize (Mexico)
1000 B.C.E.	Maize cultivation moves northward from Mexico to southwestern United States

IN PERSPECTIVE: Seeking Stability

Gathering, hunting, herding, and tillage, which our conventional chronologies usually place one after the other, were complementary techniques to obtain food. They developed together, over thousands of years, in a period of relatively intense climatic change. The warming, drying effects of the post–Ice-Age world multiplied opportunities and incentives for people to experiment with food strategies in changing environments. The naturalist David Rindos described early farming as a case of human–plant symbiosis, in which species developed together in mutual dependence, and—in part at least—evolved together: an unconscious relationship, until some foodstuffs needed human help to survive and reproduce. For instance, maize seeds would not fall to the ground unless a human removed the husks.

David Rindos, from "Symbiosis, Instability, and the Origins and Spread of Agriculture: A New Model"

Some food procurers and early food producers were surprisingly alike: Their settlements, art, religious cults, even foods (although obtained by different means) were often of the same order. The similarities suggest that the transition to agriculture was an attempt to stabilize a world convulsed by climatic instability—a way to cope with environmental change that was happening too fast and to preserve ancient traditions. In other words, the peoples who switched to herding or farming and those who clung to hunting and gathering shared a common, conservative mentality. Both wanted to keep what they had.

Perhaps, then, we should stop thinking of the beginnings of food production as a revolution, the overthrow of an existing state of affairs and its replacement by an entirely different one. Rather, we should think of it as a **climacteric** (kleye-MAK-tehr-ihk)—a long period of critical change in a world poised between different possible outcomes. Indeed, the concept of climacteric can be a useful way to understand change throughout the rest of this book as we confront other so-called revolutions that were really uncertain, slow, and sometimes unconscious transitions.

If early farmers' motivations were conservative, in most cases they failed. On the contrary, they inaugurated the spectacular changes and challenges that are the subject of the next chapter.

PROBLEMS AND PARALLELS

1. How was husbandry, with its emphasis on "unnatural selection," the first human challenge to evolution?
2. What are the disadvantages of farming compared to foraging?
3. How did agriculture affect the pace of change in human society? Why were agricultural settlements less stable than foraging communities?
4. What are the relative benefits of farming and herding? Why was violence between farmers and herders common until recently?
5. What were the prerequisites for early agriculture? Why were alluvial plains the most hospitable environment for early agricultural communities?
6. Why did farming start at different places and at different times around the world? What are some of the rival theories advocated by scholars?
7. Why is the beginning of food production more of a climacteric than a revolution?

- James Cook, from *Captain Cook's Journal During His First Voyage Round the World*
- Jack Harlan, from *Crops and Man*
- Charles Darwin, "Cultivated Plants: Cereal and Culinary Plants," from *The Variation of Plants and Animals under Domestication*
- David Rindos, from "Symbiosis, Instability, and the Origins and Spread of Agriculture: A New Model"

Please see the Primary Source DVD for additional sources related to this chapter.

READ ON

The lines of the argument are laid down in F. Fernández-Armesto, *Near a Thousand Tables* (2002). The method of classifying events in environmental categories comes from F. Fernández-Armesto, *Civilizations* (2001). Indispensable for the study of the origins of the agriculture are J. R. Harlan, *Crops and Man* (1992); B. D. Smith, *The Emergence of Agriculture* (1998); D. Rindos, *The Origins of Agriculture* (1987); and D. R. Harris, ed., *The Origins and Spread of Agriculture and Pastoralism in Eurasia* (1996). K. F. Kiple and K. C. Ornelas, eds., *The Cambridge World History of Food* (2000) is an enormous compendium.

I. G. Simmons, *Changing the Face of the Earth: Culture, Environment, History* (1989) is a superb introduction to global environmental history, as is B. De Vries and J. Goudsblom, eds., *Mappae Mundi: Humans and Their Habitats in a Long-Term Socio-Ecological Perspective* (2004).

The quotation from Darwin comes from his work of 1868, *The Variation of Animals and Plants under Domestication*.

On feasts, M. Dietler and B. Hayden, *Feasts: Archaeological and Ethnographic Perspective on Food, Politics, and Power* (2001) is an important collection of essays. M. Jones, *Feasts* (2007) is now the best study, with invaluable insights on early agriculture.

O. Bar-Yosef and A. Gopher, eds., *The Natufian Culture in the Levant* (1991) is outstanding. On Çatalhüyük, up-to-date information is in M. Özdogan and N. Basgelen, eds., *The Neolithic in Turkey: The Cradle of Civilization* (1999), and I. Hodder, *Towards a Reflexive Method in Archaeology* (2000), but the classic J. Mellaart, *Çatal Huyuk* (1967) is more accessible. On Jericho, the classic work is by Kenyon, *Digging up Jericho; The Results of Jericho Excavations* (1957).

PART

Two

Farmers and Builders, 5000 to 500 B.C.E.

CHAPTER 3 The Great River Valleys: Accelerating Change and Developing States 50

CHAPTER 4 A Succession of Civilizations: Ambition and Instability 74

CHAPTER 5 Rebuilding the World: Recoveries, New Initiatives, and Their Limits 96

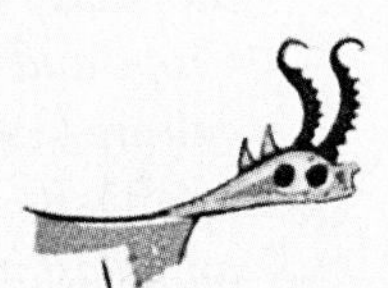

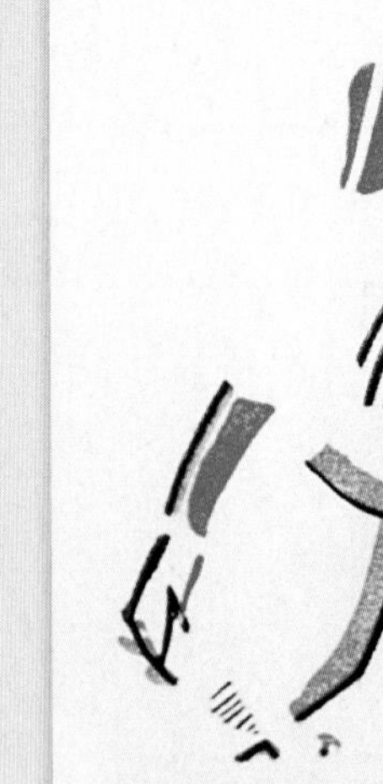

One of the world's earliest surviving paintings on plaster was found at Tel-Eilat Ghasuul in Jordan. It dates to about 4500 B.C.E., but the meaning of most of the images it depicts—veiled faces, a gazelle and other creatures, a hand apparently emerging from a sleeve—are too faded and fragmentary to decipher. The star-shaped diagram, however, seems to depict a vision of the Earth or the universe. The colors, markings, and forms are geometrically arranged to suggest an ordered array of mountains, plains, skies, and waters, within an enclosed world, from which alternating light and darkness radiate.

ENVIRONMENT

ca. 4500 B.C.E.
Irrigation

ca. 3500 B.C.E.
Horses domesticated

since 5000 B.C.E.
Intensive agriculture, bronze metallurgy: Tigris-Euphrates, Nile, Indus, Yellow Rivers

CULTURE

since ca. 3500 B.C.E.
Complex, hierarchical societies and states

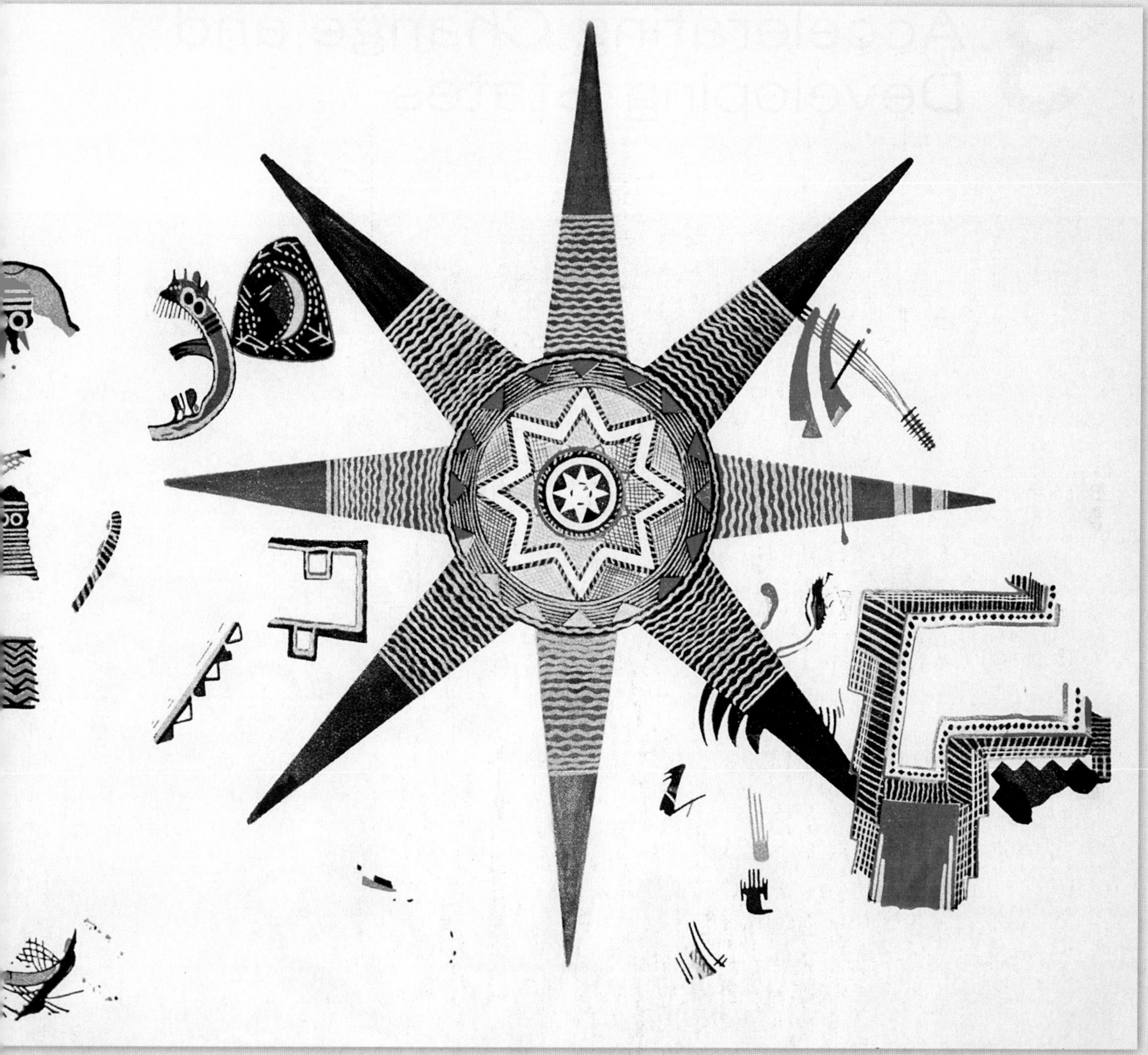

ca. 3000–1000 B.C.E.
Continued warming

ca. 1200–800 B.C.E.
Widespread environmental crises

ca. 1800 B.C.E.
Spread of iron technology

ca. 3200 B.C.E.
Writing

ca. 2000 B.C.E.
Epic of Gilgamesh

ca. 1000 B.C.E.
Mediterranean maritime colonialism begins

CHAPTER 3 The Great River Valleys: Accelerating Change and Developing States

Nebamun's tomb from about 1500 B.C.E. shows the Egyptian vizier hunting in the lush Nile delta, abundant in fish below his reed-built boat, prolific in the bird- and insect-life flushed from the blue thickets at his approach. He grabs birds by the handful and wields a snake like a whip.
© Copyright The British Museum

IN THIS CHAPTER

GROWING COMMUNITIES, DIVERGENT CULTURES
Intensified Settlement and Its Effects
THE ECOLOGY OF CIVILIZATION
THE GREAT FLOODPLAINS
The Ecology of Egypt
Shifting Rivers of the Indus Valley
Fierce Nature in Early Mesopotamia
The Good Earth of Early China
CONFIGURATIONS OF SOCIETY
Patterns of Settlement and Labor
Politics
The Egyptian State
Statecraft in Mesopotamia
The First Documented Chinese State
Ruling the Harappan World
The Politics of Expansion
Literate Culture
IN PERSPECTIVE: **What Made the Great River Valleys Different?**

GREAT RIVER VALLEYS

Witnesses in court swear to tell "the whole truth." This would be a risky oath for a historian to take because we see the past only in glimpses and patches. Sometimes-contrasting, sometimes-contradictory sources confuse or distract us. To get close to the whole picture, we have to shift perspective, dodging and slipping between rival viewpoints. With every shift, we get a bit more of the picture—like glimpsing the depths of a forest, between the leaves and the trees.

The boldest possible perspective shift is imaginary, to envision history from a viewpoint outside it—perhaps from an enormous distance of time and space, and ask how it might look to a visitors from a remote future in another world. They would have an enviable advantage: objectivity, which we, who are entangled in our history, can never attain. Today, globalization is spreading uniform ways of life across the world, but galactic observers could see that, since agriculture started, the main theme of our past has been increasingly rapid cultural divergence. Compared with foragers, herders and tillers generated more change of all kinds. More spectacular, however, were the differences that separated farming cultures from each other.

Some of them came to occupy vast zones, feed huge populations, and sustain spectacular material achievements—including cities, monumental arts, and world-changing technologies. Other farmers' societies remained relatively small and static. This does not mean they were backward or primitive. Their modest scale and relative isolation kept them stable. These were peoples who succeeded in adapting to climate change without subjecting their societies to social and political convulsions, which were often part of the price other peoples paid for material achievements that seem impressive to us. The big problem we need to look at in this chapter, then, is what made the difference?

It is also worth asking whether within these diverse societies we can detect any common patterns. This is a long-standing quest for historians and, especially, for sociologists, who look for models that they can use to describe and predict how societies change. At a simple level, intensified agriculture clearly unlocks a potential pattern. More food makes it possible to sustain larger populations, to concentrate them in bigger settlements, and to divert more manpower into nonagricultural activities. But intensification also requires organization, and, broadly speaking, the more intensive the farming, the more organized it has to be. It calls for someone—or some group—with power to divide land, marshal labor, and regulate the distribution of water and—if necessary—fertilizer. Surplus production needs to be guarded in case crops fail or natural disasters strike. A legal elite is necessary to resolve the frequent disputes that arise in thickly settled communities, where people have to compete for resources. So, intensively farmed areas all tend to develop similar political institutions and personnel, including bureaucrats and enforcers.

FOCUS questions

- WHY DID intensified agriculture lead to cultural differences?
- WHERE DID the first great river valley civilizations develop?
- HOW CAN we account for the similarities and differences in political institutions, social structure, and ways of life in the four great river valleys?
- HOW DID the river valley states expand?
- IS WRITING a defining characteristic of civilization?
- WHY IS cultural divergence one of the main themes of human history since the beginning of agriculture?

These effects are the themes of this chapter, which focuses on the most conspicuous examples, in regions with common environmental features. The next chapter follows the crises, catastrophes, and transformations large-scale farming societies faced up to the end of the second millennium B.C.E. Chapter 5 covers the recovery or renewal of ambitious states and cultural experiments after the crises had passed.

GROWING COMMUNITIES, DIVERGENT CULTURES

Most of the communities that early agriculture fed resembled the forager settlements that preceded them. They were small and did not change much over time. Lack of evidence means that we mostly have to infer what we think we know about them. So with no reason to think otherwise, we assume that early farming societies in New Guinea, North America, along the Amazon River in South America, and among the Bantu people in West Africa were like those in most of the rest of the world. They were extended family businesses where everyone in the community felt tied to everyone else by kinship. Elsewhere, owing to greater resources or to the enlivening effects of cross-cultural contacts through migration or trade, different patterns prevailed. Communities became territorially defined. Economic obligations, not kinship, shaped allegiance. Chiefs or economic elites monopolized or controlled the distribution of food.

Scholars have tried to divide subsequent change in societies of this type into sequences or stages of growth—chiefdoms become states, towns become cities. But these are relative terms, and no hard-and-fast lines divide them. At most, differences are a matter of degree. For instance, we think of chiefdoms as having fewer institutions of government than states. In chiefdoms, the chief and a few counselors handle all the business of government. In a state, those functions get split among groups of specialists in, say, administering justice, handling revenue, or conducting war. In practice, however, we know of no community that does not delegate at least some power, and no state where the responsibilities of different government departments do not merge or overlap.

Similarly, the difference between a small city and a big town or a small town and a big village is a matter of judgment. Some of the characteristics we traditionally associate with particular lifeways turn out, in the light of present knowledge, to provide little or no help for defining the societies in which they occur. Metallurgy, pottery, and weaving, for example, exist among herding and foraging peoples, as well as in settled communities.

However, where many people settle together, predictable changes usually follow. As markets grow, settlements acquire more craftsmen, who engage in more specialized trades and who organize into more and larger units. As they get bigger, settlements and politically linked or united groups of settlements also expand the number of government functions. Where once there was just a chief and his counselors, now there are aides, advisers, officials, and administrators.

Densely settled communities also tend to divide their populations into more categories. This usually happens in two ways. On the one hand, as society gets bigger, people seek groups within it of manageable size, with whom to identify and to whom to appeal for help in times of need. On the other hand, rulers organize subjects into categories according to the needs of the state, which include collective labor, taxation, and war. The categories get more numerous and varied as opportunities for economic specialization multiply and as more districts or quarters appear in growing settlements. In some cases, these categories resemble what, in our society, we call classes, that is, groups arrayed horizontally, one above or below another according to power, privilege, or prosperity. For most of history, however, it is misleading to speak of classes. Societies were more usually organized vertically into groups of people of widely varying rank and wealth, linked by some form of common allegiance. They might feel bound by a place of origin, or a locality or neighborhood, or a common ancestor, or a god, or a rite, or a family, or a sense of identity arising from shared belief in some myth (see Figure 3.1).

So, if we want to try to trace the early history of cultural divergence, we should look for certain sorts of changes, namely, intensified settlement, population concentrated in relatively large settlements, multiplying social categories and functions of government, emergence of chiefs and fledgling states, and increasingly diversified and specialized economic activity. Between 5000 and 3000 B.C.E., we can detect these changes in widely separated places around the world. We can take a few examples in a selective tour through cultures launched into divergent futures.

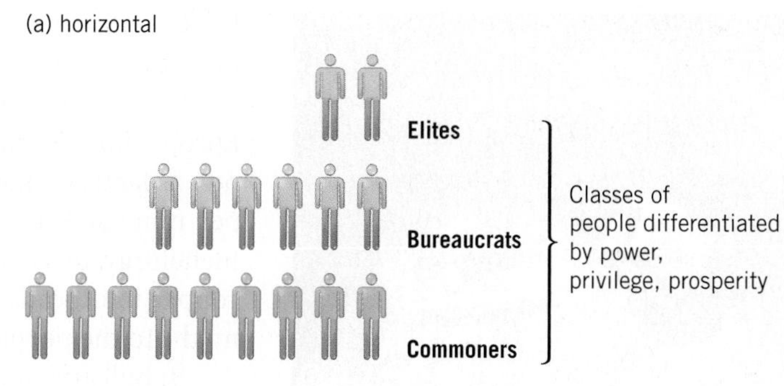

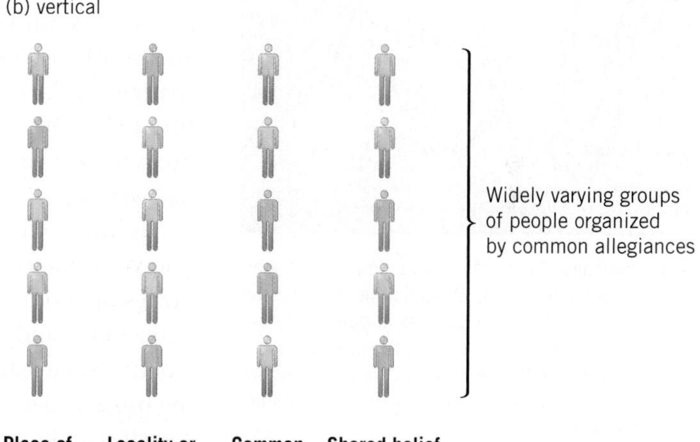

FIGURE 3.1 HORIZONTAL AND VERTICAL ORGANIZATIONS OF SOCIETY

Intensified Settlement and Its Effects

In the New World, Mesoamerica and Central America remained a region of small villages. We can document monumental cities and large states there only from about 2000 B.C.E. In North America, agriculture barely appeared. By contrast, at the base of the high Andes in South America, archaeology has unearthed early evidence of many different social rankings, economic specializations, and grossly unequal concentrations of wealth and power.

In about 3500 B.C.E., large farming settlements began to appear on alluvial plains in coastal Peru, north of present-day Lima, and especially in the Supe Valley, which has over 30 archaeological sites. The most impressive was Aspero, where by the mid–third millennium B.C.E. 17 mounds supported half a dozen platforms and various terraces, with large, complex dwellings and storehouses. The platforms were built up with loads of rubble in uniform containers, which suggests that a system existed to measure the labor of different groups of workers. An infant's grave gives us a glimpse into the society and perhaps the politics of the time. Under a grinding stone he lies painted with red ochre, wrapped in textiles, and scattered with hundreds of beads. This is evidence of heritable wealth and, perhaps, power in an economy dependent on grain where a flour-making tool literally marked the difference between life and death.

Covering over 32 acres, Aspero must have had a big population—uniquely big by the standards of the Americas at the time. There were, however, many settlements of between two and three thousand people. They were trading centers where people exchanged the products of different ecosystems—marine shells, mountain

Trade enriches. Gold-laden graves in a 6,000-year-old cemetery at Varna, Bulgaria, lie by an inlet beside a wood-built village that is quite different from mud-walled settlements in the interior, where the graves are under the houses. The Varna culture vanished—overwhelmed perhaps by horse-tamers from the nearby steppes.

foods, and featherwork made from the brightly colored birds that lived in the forests east of the Andes.

Comparable developments occurred across Eurasia (see Map 3.1). In Eastern Europe, for instance, innovations in technology and government emerged, without, as far as we know, any influence from outside the region. Europe's oldest copper mine at Rudna Glava in modern Serbia made the region a center of early metallurgy. In Tisza in what is now Hungary, over 7,000 years ago, smelters worked copper into beads and small tools—magic that made smiths powerful figures of myth. To the people who left offerings, the mines were the dwellings of gods.

In Bulgaria of the same period, trenches and palisades surrounded settlements, with gateways exactly aligned at the points of the compass, as in later Roman army camps. Here prospectors traded gold for the products of agriculture. No place in prehistoric Europe gleams more astonishingly than Varna on the Black Sea, where a chief was buried clutching a gold-handled axe, with his penis sheathed in gold, and nearly 1,000 gold ornaments, including hundreds of discs that must have spangled a dazzling coat. This single grave contained more than three pounds of fine gold. Other graves were symbolic, containing earthenware masks without human remains. At Tartaria in Romania, markings on clay tablets look uncannily like writing.

A little to the east, also around 5000 B.C.E., in what is now Ukraine, the earliest known domesticators of horses filled their garbage dumps with horse bones. In graves of about 3500 B.C.E., as if for use in an afterlife, lie covered wagons, arched with hoops and designed to be pulled by oxen, rumbling on vast wheels of solid wood: evidence that rich and powerful chiefdoms could carry out ambitious building projects despite a herding way of life that required constant mobility. Few other societies in the world were rich enough to bury objects of such size and value. Central Eurasia became a birthplace for early transportation technology. For instance, the earliest recognizable chariot dates from early 2000 B.C.E., in the southern Ural Mountains that divide Europe from Asia.

Meanwhile, monumental building projects, on a scale only agriculture could sustain and only a state could organize, were under way in the Mediterranean. The remains of the first large stone dwellings known anywhere in the world are on the island of Malta, which lies between Sicily and North Africa. Here, at least half a dozen temple complexes arose in the fourth and third millennia B.C.E. They were built of limestone around spacious courts shaped like clover leaves. The biggest temple is almost 70 feet wide under a 30-foot wall. Inside one building was a colossal, big-hipped goddess attended by sleeping beauties—small female models scattered around her. There were altars and wall carvings—some in spirals, some with deer and bulls—and thousands of bodies piled in communal graves. We wonder how Malta's soil, so poor and dry, could sustain a population large and leisured enough to build so lavishly.

Even on Europe's Atlantic edge, in the fourth millennium B.C.E., luxury objects could find a market and monumental buildings arose. Some of the earliest signs of the slow-grinding social changes lie among the bones of aristocrats in individual graves with the possessions that defined their status and suggest their way of life—weapons of war and drinking cups that once held liquor or poured offerings to the gods. Then come the graves of chiefs, buried under enormous standing stones, near stone circles probably designed to resemble glades that preceded them as places of worship. In the Orkney Islands, for instance, off the north coast of Scotland, settled about 5,500 years ago, an elaborate tomb at Maes Howe lies close to a temple building, filled with light on midsummer's day. Nearby stone circles hint on

Stonehenge

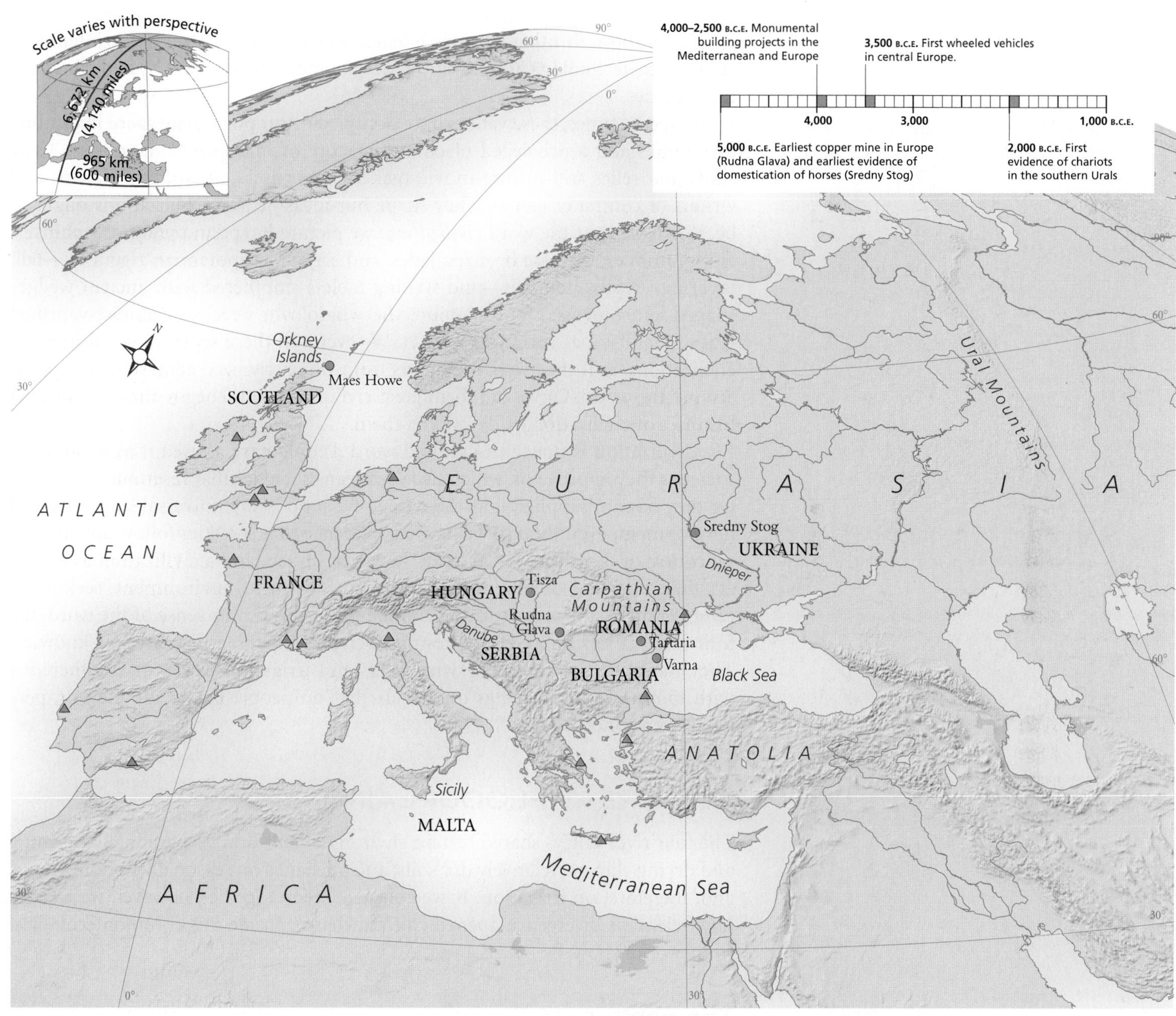

MAP 3.1

Intensified Settlements in Western Eurasia, 5,000–2,000 B.C.E.

a smaller scale at attempts to monitor the Sun and, perhaps, control nature by magic. A stone-built village to the west has hearths and fitted furniture still in place. It is tempting to imagine this as a far-flung colonial station, preserving the styles and habits of a distant home in southwest Britain and northwest France, where the big tombs and stone circles are found.

THE ECOLOGY OF CIVILIZATION

In this world of increasing diversification, four river valleys stand out in terms of scale: the middle and lower Nile in Egypt; the Indus and the now dried-up Saraswati (sah-rah-SWAH-tee) (mainly in what is now Pakistan); the Tigris and Euphrates in what is now Iraq; and the Yellow River in China. Between 5000 and 2000 B.C.E., people in these regions exploited more land and changed at a faster pace than those in other regions. Change was measured in terms of intensified agriculture, technological innovation, development of state power, and construction of cities.

In recent times, these valleys have occupied disproportionate space in our history books and a privileged place in our store of images and memories. Their ruins and relics still inspire movie makers, advertisers, artists, toy makers, and writers of computer games. They shape our ideas of what civilizations ought to be. When we hear the word *civilization*, we picture Egyptian pyramids, sphinxes, and mummies; Chinese bronzes, jades, and clays; Mesopotamian ziggurats—tall, tapering, steplike temples—and writing tablets smothered with ancient wedge-shaped letter forms. Or we conjure the windblown wrecks of almost-vanished cities in landscapes turning to desert. We even call these seminal—or nursery—civilizations, as if they were seed plots from which civilized achievements spread around the world. Or we call them great civilizations, and begin our conventional histories of civilization by describing them.

Civilization is now a discredited word. People have abused it as a name for societies they approve of, which usually means societies that resemble their own. Or they have misapplied it as the name of a supposedly universal stage of social development, even though we have no evidence that societies follow any universal course of development. We can, however, understand a civilization as a society that, for good or ill, engages ambitiously with its environment, seeking to remodel the rest of nature to suit human purposes. In this sense of the word, the four river valleys housed societies more civilized than earlier cases we know of. They modified the landscape with fields and irrigation works or smothered it with monumental buildings on a scale that no people before attained or, perhaps, even conceived.

THE GREAT FLOODPLAINS

The four river valleys shared certain environmental features: a gradually warming and drying climate; relatively dry soils; and a reliance on seasonally flooding rivers and, therefore, on irrigation. If we consider them, together, however, we can see how relentless divergence opened cultural chasms inside this common ecological framework.

The Ecology of Egypt

In the north, where the Nile empties into the Mediterranean, distinctive food sources and useful plants complemented what farmers could grow in the irrigated lands to the south. In the delta's teeming marshlands, birds, animals, fish, and plants clustered for the gatherer and hunter. A painter showed Nebamun—a scribe and counter of grain who lived probably about 3,500 years ago—hunting in a land "full of everything good—its ponds with fish and its lakes with birds. Its meadows are verdant; its banks bear dates; its melons are abundant." Fish fed on lotus-flowers. Thickets of rushes and papyrus provided rope and writing paper.

Most of Egypt, however, lay above the delta. The Nile flows from south to north, from the highlands of Ethiopia in Central Africa to the Mediterranean, and where the ground breaks from higher altitudes or where the riverbed narrows, dangerous rapids hinder navigation. Soil samples reveal the history of climate change. By about 4,000 years ago, the valley was already a land of "black" earth between "red" earths. Floods fed the fertile, alluvial black strip along the Nile; slowly drying red desert lay

Making bread. Some of the activities portrayed in ancient Egyptian tomb-offerings seem humdrum. Beer-making or—as in this example, nearly 3,000 years old—bread-making, are among the most common scenes. But these were magical activities that turned barely edible grains into mind-expanding drinks and a life-sustaining staple food.

on either side. Hunting scenes painted at Memphis, Egypt's first capital, in the Nile delta, showed game lands turning to scrub, sand, and bare rock. Rain became rare, a divine gift, according to a pious king's prayer to the Sun, dropped from "a Nile in heaven." Thirst was called "the taste of death." Other lands had rain, as an Egyptian priest told a Greek traveler, "Whereas in our country water never falls on fields from above, it all wells up from below."

The Nile turns green with algae in early summer, then red with tropical earth in August. In September and October, if all goes well, the river floods and spreads the dark, rich silt thinly over the earth. Between floods, the nitrogen content of the soil decreases by two-thirds in the top six inches. But the annually renewed topsoil grew some of the densest concentrations of wheat in the ancient world. If the flood is too high, the land drowns. If the level of the river falls below about 18 feet, drought follows. In one of the oldest surviving documents of Egyptian history, probably of about 2500 B.C.E., a king reveals a dream. The river failed to flood because the people neglected the gods who ruled beyond the rapids, where the waters came from. Still, compared to the other river valleys of the period, the Nile flood waters were—and still are—exceptionally regular and, therefore, easy to exploit.

The economy guaranteed basic nutrition for a large population, not individual abundance. Most people lived on bread and grainy, nutritious beer in amounts only modestly above subsistence level. A surplus generated trade, which made up for the country's lack of timber and aromatic plants for perfumes and incense. The wall carvings of a memorial to Queen Hatshepsut, who reigned around 3,500 years ago, reveal vast stores of grain and live cattle unloaded in the land of Punt, at the far end of the

Food aid. Egypt exported surplus food across the Red Sea in exchange for the luxury aromatics, especially incense, of the land of Punt, whose queen, depicted in a painting perhaps 3,500 years old, appears comically—or realistically?—obese. Like modern Westerners, but unlike most people in most cultures, the Egyptians esteemed thin body shapes.

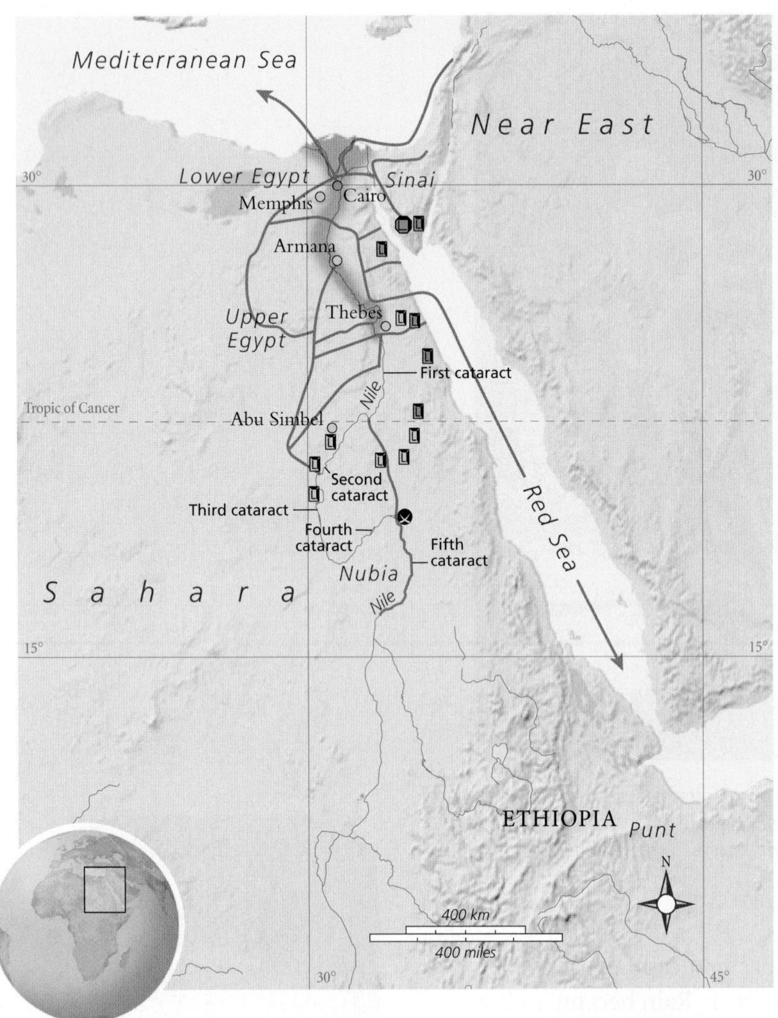

MAP 3.2

Ancient Egypt

Red Sea in East Africa, in exchange for scented trees to grace a temple garden and exotic animals for the Egyptian royal zoo. Most of the courtly luxuries that today's Western museum goers see in exhibits on ancient Egypt came from trade, raids, and conquest. Gold and ivory, for example, came from Nubia, an African kingdom beyond the cataracts, and copper and turquoise came from Sinai, a region of desert uplands that link Egypt to the Near East (see Map 3.2).

Shifting Rivers of the Indus Valley

In the Indus valley, the sparse remains of the society called Harappan, after one of its earliest excavated cities, lie beyond historians' reach. The rising water table has drowned evidence of the earliest phases, and scholars have not been able to decipher the writing system. Here the Indus and Saraswati Rivers were more powerful and capricious than the Nile, changing course and cutting new channels that might deprive settlements of water supplies. Ultimately, perhaps, they were fatally unpredictable, for Egypt lasted thousands of years longer. When the Indus altered course and the Saraswati dried up, Harappan cities dwindled to faint traces in the dust.

But three to five thousand years ago, the Indus floodplain was broader than the Nile's. The Indus and Saraswati flooded twice a year—first with the spring snowmelt when the rivers rose, and then in summer when warm air, rising in Central Asia, sucks moisture in from the sea. As a result, farmers here could grow two crops annually. The basic patterns were the same as in Egypt. Wheat and barley grew on rainless, irrigated soil, and cattle grazed on marginal grassland. No region was as rich as the Nile delta, but Harappa had a coastal outpost at the seaport of Lothal, on the Indian Ocean, in a land of rice and millet (see Map 3.3).

The Harappan heartland had few valuables of its own. As in Egypt, the basis of its wealth was the surplus of its agriculture. Around 2000 B.C.E., the

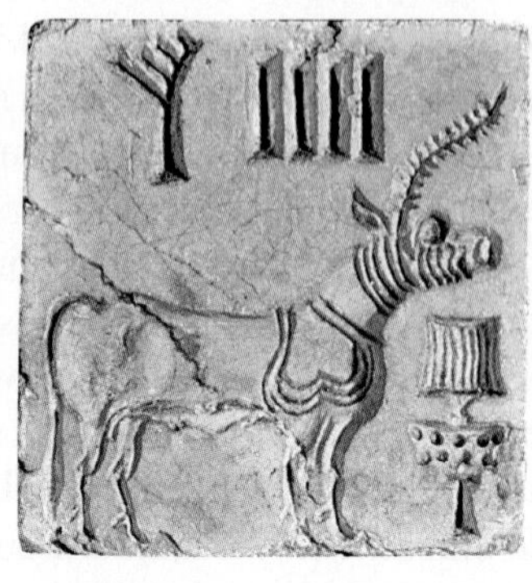

Harappan seals. In the last couple of centuries, scholarly code-crackers have worked out how to read most of the world's ancient scripts. But the writing on Harappan seals remains elusive. The seals seem to depict visions and monsters—but the messages they conveyed were probably of routine merchants, data-stock-taking, and prices. In most cases that we know of, writing was first devised to record information too uninteresting for people to confide to memory.

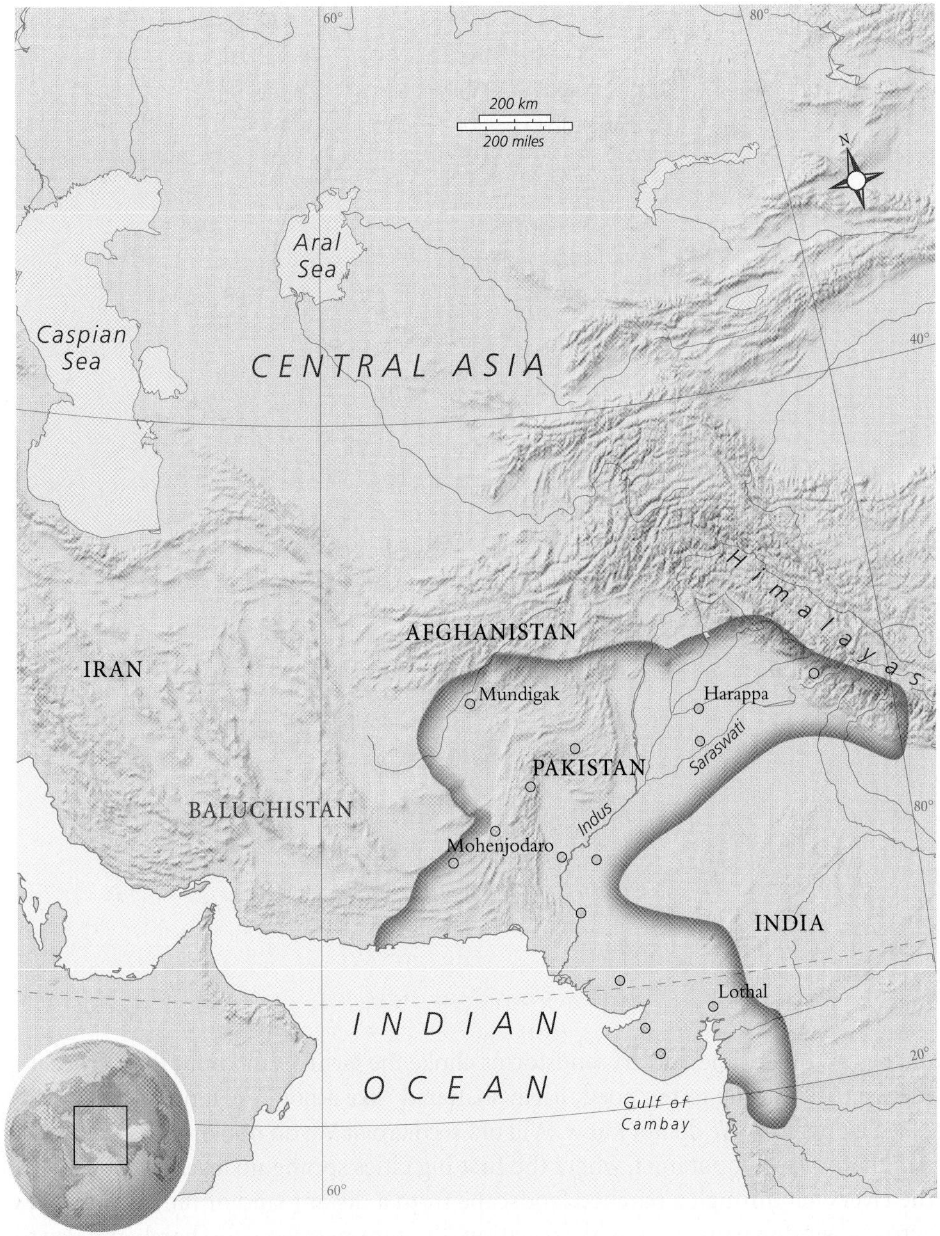

MAP 3.3

Harappan Civilization

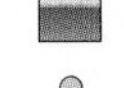 extent of Harappan culture

○ Harappan site

INDIA modern-day country

Harappan-culture area was the biggest in the world, stretching over half a million square miles. This was, perhaps, evidence of weakness rather than strength. Territorial expansion was the Harrapan solution to feeding its increasingly dense population in the heartland, and no society can keep expanding forever.

Most surviving Harappan art is engraved on seals used to mark trading goods. These little masterpieces capture how people of the time saw their world. Some show naturalistic representations of animals, feasting tigers, and elegant bulls. Violations of realism, however, are more characteristic and include jokey elephants and rhinoceroses. Perplexing scenes, probably from Harappan mythology, include magical transformations of human into tiger, starfish into unicorn, horned serpent into tree.

Fierce Nature in Early Mesopotamia

The Nile and the Indus spill and recede according to a reasonably predictable rhythm, but the Tigris and Euphrates flood at any time, washing away dikes, overflowing

MAP 3.4

Early Mesopotamia

- fertile crescent
- place described on pages 60–66
- IRAN modern-day country
- ancient coastlines
- ancient irrigation and water works
- trade route
- ziggurat

www.prenhall.com/armesto_maps

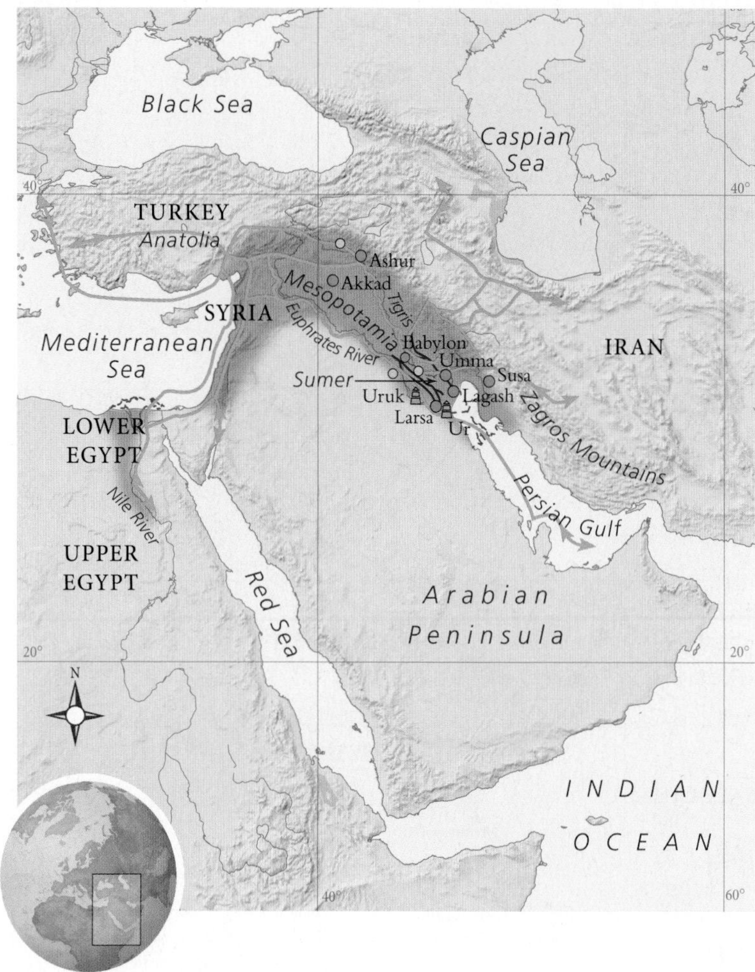

ditches. At other times, desert sandstorms choke the farmers and bury their crops. In the wind, according to the poets, earth shattered "like a pot." "Will new seed grow?" asked a proverb. "We do not know. Will old seed grow? We do not know."

In lower Mesopotamia, where the first big cities sprang up around 3000 B.C.E., the rivers fell through a parched landscape from a distant land of rain, like trickles across a windowpane. Even with irrigation, the summers were too harsh and dry to produce food for the early cities, which had to rely on winter crops of wheat and barley, onions, chickpeas, and sesame. Rain fell then more often than it does today, but it was largely confined to winter when ferocious storms made the sky flare with sheet lightning. "Ordered by the storm-god in hate," according to a poet, "it wears away the country." The floods that created the life-giving alluvial soils were also life-threateningly capricious. Unleashed in early summer by mountain rains, rivers could swell and sweep away crops (see Map 3.4).

Meanwhile, earth and water, the benign forces that combined to create the alluvial soil, were also celebrated in verse. The goddess Nintu personified Earth—zealous, jealous mother, yielding nourishment, suckling infants, guarding embryos. Water, to awaken the land's fertility, was a male god, Enki, empowered "to clear the pure mouths of the Tigris and Euphrates, to make greenery plentiful, to make dense the clouds, to grant water in abundance to all ploughlands, to make corn lift its head in furrows and to make pasture abound in the desert." But Nintu and Enki were subordinate deities, at the beck and call of storm and flood.

The ferocity of the climate demanded hardy plants, so Mesopotamia produced much more barley than wheat. Exhausting digging raised dwellings above the flood and diverted and conserved water. The people who lived along the lower stretches of the river depicted themselves in their art as dome-headed, potbellied lovers of music, feasts, and war. But they were necessarily resourceful people who made ships in a country with no timber, worked masterpieces in bronze in a part of the world where no metal could be found, built fabulous cities without stone by baking mud into bricks, and dammed rivers as the Marsh Arabs of southern Iraq do to this day—with brushwood, reeds, and earth.

The Good Earth of Early China

Mesopotamia and Harappa traded with each other. Mesopotamia and Egypt were close to each other and in constant touch. The map shows, however, that long distances and physical barriers surrounded China's Yellow River valley (see Map 3.5). Nevertheless, perhaps in part because the environment was similar, developments here unfolded in familiar ways.

The Yellow River collects rain in the mountains of Shaanxi province, where rapid thaws bring torrents of water. Where it disgorges, the stream broadens suddenly and periodically overflows. Here the climate has been getting steadily drier for thousands of years. The region today is torrid in summer, icy in winter, stung

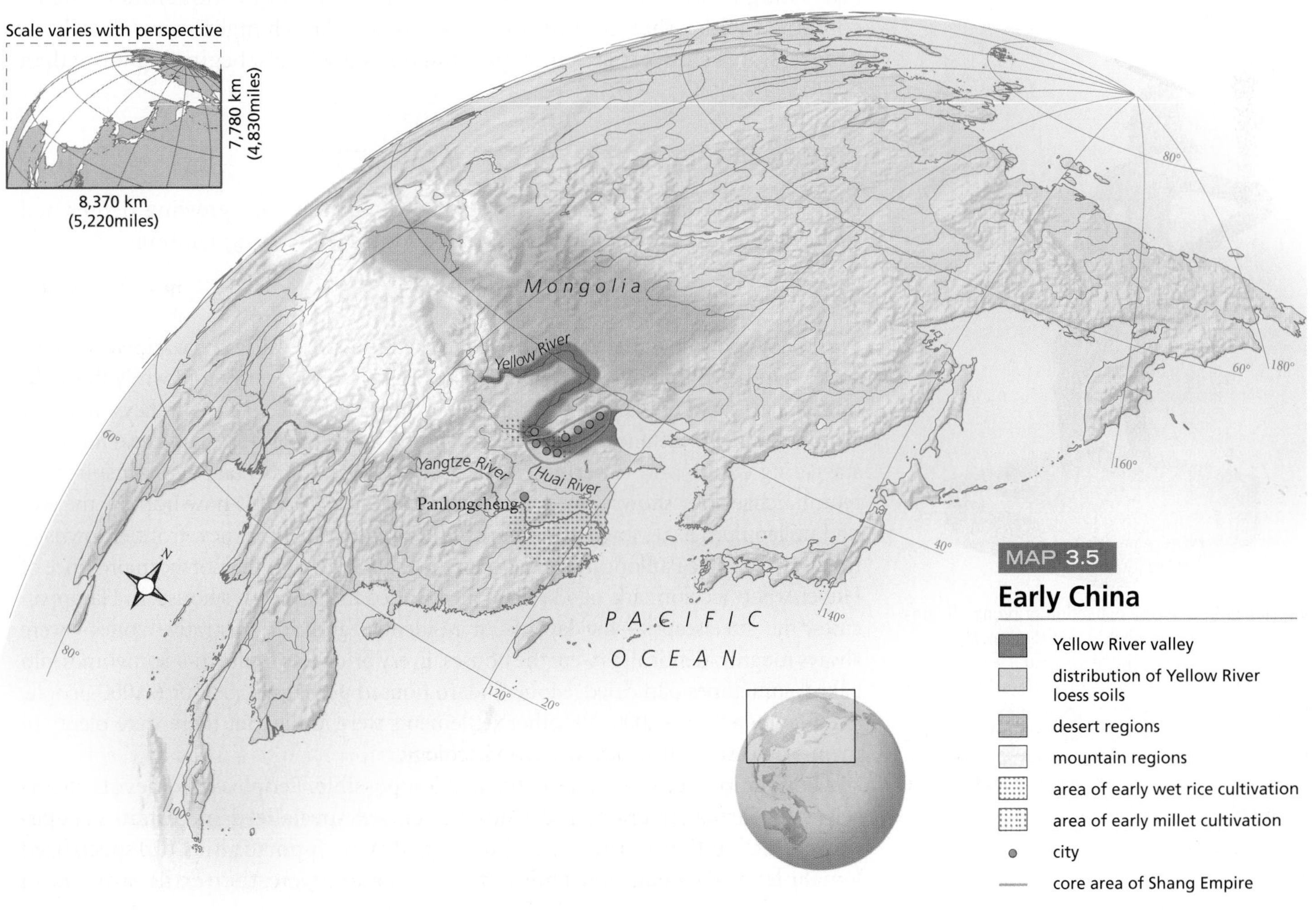

MAP 3.5

Early China

by chill, gritty winds, and rasped by rivers full of ice. The winds blow dust from the Mongolian desert over the land, creating the crumbly, yellow earth that gives the river its name. This soil is almost sterile if it is not watered, but the fierce, unpredictable flood coaxes it into amazing fertility. The river needs careful management, with dikes to stem the flood, ditches to channel it, and artificial basins to conserve water against drought.

When farmers first began to till them, these lands were a sort of savanna, where grasslands mixed with woodland. Three or four thousand years ago, water buffalo were still plentiful, together with other creatures of marsh and forest. In the *Shi Jing*, a collection of ancient songs, poets rhapsodize about the toil of clearing weeds, brush, and roots. "Why in days of old did they do this task? So that we might plant our grain, our millet, so that our millet might be abundant." During the Shang dynasty, between about 3000 and 1000 B.C.E., millet sustained what were perhaps already the densest populations in the world and kept armies of tens of thousands of warriors in the field. The earliest known cultivators cleared the ground with fire before dibbling and sowing. They harvested each cluster of ears by hand and threshed seeds by rubbing between hands and feet. Crop rotation secured the best yields. Eventually soya beans provided the alternating crop, but it is not clear when soya cultivation began.

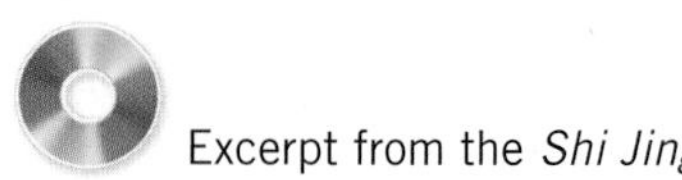
Excerpt from the *Shi Jing*

Even at its wettest, the Yellow River valley could not sustain a rice-eating civilization. Rice could become a staple only when people colonized new areas. Later poets recalled expansion from the Yellow River southward as a process of conquest, grasping at the Yangtze River. But conquest makes more interesting myths than colonization does. Colonists and conquerors probably combined with other communities, where similar changes were already in progress, in a slow process of expansion on many levels, beginning more than 3,500 years ago.

CONFIGURATIONS OF SOCIETY

All four valleys faced the same problems—population was growing denser and society becoming more complex. Yet they adopted contrasting solutions.

Patterns of Settlement and Labor

We do not know how many people lived in the great river-valley civilizations, but they surely numbered millions. In Egypt, the people were spread fairly uniformly throughout the narrow floodplain of the Nile. Cities strewed the other three valleys. In lower Mesopotamia for instance, Ur, Abraham's home in the bible story, had royal tombs of staggering wealth and towering ziggurats, built over 4,000 years ago—inspired, as recent archaeology shows—by even earlier structures in what is now Iran. By the second millennium B.C.E. towns also marked the growth of China: new frontier towns—modest places like Panlongcheng, or Curled Dragon Town, in the northern province of Hubei, where a colonnade of 43 pillars surrounded the governor's house. In Harappan cities, the streetscapes—the layouts of residential and administrative zones—were always roughly identical, as were the houses. Every brick was uniform—sometimes kiln baked, sometimes pan dried. Mohenjodaro housed perhaps 50,000 or 60,000 people, and Harappa over 30,000. No other settlements were as big, but there were plenty of them—at least 1,500 are known to archaeology.

Dancing girl. One of a collection of bronze figures known as "dancing girls" unearthed at Mohenjodaro. Their sinuous shapes, sensual appeal, and provocative poses suggest to some scholars that they may portray temple prostitutes. They are modeled with a freedom that contrasts with the formality and rigidity of the handful of representations of male figures that survive from the same civilization (see page 68).
Dancing girl. Bronze statuette from Mohenjo Daro. Indus Valley Civilization. National Museum, New Delhi, India. Borromeo/Art Resource, NY

Population density made specialization possible. People could devote themselves to particular crafts and trades. Each sex specialized in certain occupations. Outside the home, urban life created new opportunities for specialized female labor. Women and children, for instance, were the textile workers in

MAKING CONNECTIONS

THE ECOLOGY OF CIVILIZATIONS

REGION →	ENVIRONMENTAL DIVERSITY →	PRIMARY MODIFICATION →	ECONOMIC CONSEQUENCES →
Egypt (Nile River)	Delta: marshlands, ponds, lakes; upriver: "black earth," alluvial plain created from regular floods from central African headwaters; bordered by Sahara Desert, with scattered oasis	Exploitation of lush delta flooded alluvial plain with irrigation	Everyday abundance of basic commodities (wheat, barley, cattle) leads to population increase, regional trade
Indus (Indus, Saraswati Rivers)	Wide alluvial floodplain, frequent changing river courses, varied climate—coastal outposts, hot interior, upriver Himalayan headwaters; flooding twice a year from spring snowmelt and monsoon rains	Widespread irrigation of rainless upriver regions; grazing on grasslands, marsh areas	Agricultural surplus with two harvests a year; rapid population growth, urbanization
Mesopotamia (Tigris, Euphrates Rivers)	Delta: marshlands, ponds, lakes, waterways; upriver alluvial plains flooded irregularly; harsh summer sandstorms, intense heat; winter floods, rainstorms; lack of forests, stone	Irrigation; dependence on winter crops: barley, wheat, onions, chickpeas; intensive plowing; digging of dikes and ditches to divert and store water	Widespread cultivation of grains leads to regional trade; use of mud brick for housing, temples
China (Yellow River)	Unpredictable river floods surrounding areas creating loess soil—basis of agriculture; probably more rainfall than the other three regions	Dikes, irrigation canals control flooding; creation of basins to conserve water; early exploitation of savanna grasslands, buffalo, and other animals; farming based on millet, later supplanted by soya	Gradual expansion/colonization southward toward rice-growing region of Yangtze River

Ashur, a large city in northern Mesopotamia, and probably wove cotton in Harappan cities. Moreover, women were not necessarily excluded from power. These societies employed them as rulers, prophetesses, and priestesses and included them as subjects of art. Yet art also depicted women in servile roles. For instance, pouting, languid bronze dancing girls—or are they temple prostitutes?—figure among the few artworks excavated from Harappan cities of the second millennium B.C.E. Mesopotamian law codes and Chinese texts show people increasingly inheriting status from their fathers rather than their mothers, and depict women's talents increasingly focused on the family home and child rearing. This is understandable because population increase created more domestic work, while increasingly ambitious agriculture and construction were more efficiently entrusted to males. Concentrating on domestic life, however, gave women opportunities to exercise informal power. Surviving texts show some of the consequences. Women could initiate divorce, recover their property, and, sometimes, win additional compensation on divorce. A wife, says the Egyptian *Book of Instructions*, "is a profitable field. Do not contend with her at law and keep her from gaining control."

Ptahhotep, from the Egyptian *Book of Instructions*

Politics

All four river valley societies shared, in one respect, a type of environment suited to tyranny, or, at least, to strong states exercising minute control over subjects' lives. Even without agriculture, people could have no security of life without collective action to manage the floods. Even foragers would need ditches and dikes to protect wild foodstuffs and defend dwellings. The importance of collectively managing the floods helps account for the obvious resemblances between the political systems of all these regions. All practiced divine or sacred kingship; all had rigid social hierarchies; all placed the lives and labor of the inhabitants at the disposal of the state. The mace head of an Egyptian king of the fourth millennium B.C.E. shows him digging a canal. Proverbially, a just judge was "a dam for the sufferer, guarding lest he drown." A corrupt one was "a flowing lake."

We can see how one irrigation system worked, in Larsa in Mesopotamia, from the archive of a contractor named Lu-igisa, which has survived from around 2000 B.C.E. His job was to survey land for canal building, organize the laborers and their pay and provisions, and supervise the digging and the dredging of accumulated silt. Procuring labor was the key task—5,400 workers to dig a canal and 1,800 on one occasion for emergency repairs. In return, he had the potentially profitable job of controlling the opening and closing of the locks that released or shut off the water supplies. Failure was fatal. "What is my sin," he complained when he was fired, "that the king took my canal from me?"

The Egyptian State

In Egypt, defying nature meant more than refashioning the landscape. Above all, it meant stockpiling against disaster, to safeguard humans from the invisible forces that let loose the floods. A temple at Abu Simbel had storehouses big enough to feed 20,000 people for a year. The taxation yields proudly painted on the walls of a high official's tomb are an illustrated menu for feeding an empire: sacks of barley, piles of cakes and nuts, hundreds of head of livestock. The state as stockpiler existed, it seems, not to redistribute goods but for famine relief.

Methods of collecting and storing grain were as vital as the systems of flood control, precisely because the extent of the flood could vary from one year to the next. The biblical story of Joseph, an Israelite who became a pharaoh's chief official and saved Egypt from starvation, recalls "seven lean years" at one stretch. Such bad times were part of folk memories, as were spells when "every man ate his children." A tomb scene from the city of Amarna shows a storehouse with only six rows of stacked victuals, including grain sacks and heaps of dried fish, laid on shelves supported on brick pillars. A strong state was an inseparable part of this kind of farsightedness. Grain had to be taxed under compulsion, transported under guard, and kept under watch.

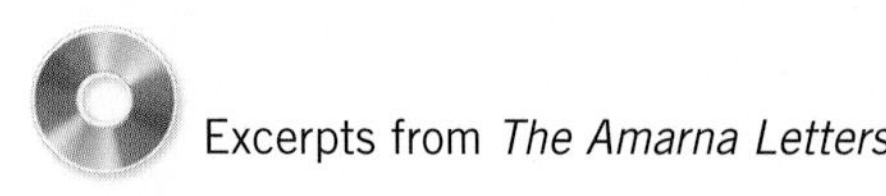

If pharaohs were highly glorified storekeepers, what did the Egyptians mean when they said their king was a god? Furthermore, how could pharaohs bear the names and exercise the functions of many gods, each with a separate identity? A possible aid to understanding is the Egyptian habit of making images. The image "was" the god only when the god inhabited the image. The pharaoh's person could provide a similar opportunity for a god to take up residence. In a letter from around 1350 B.C.E., pharaoh is "my Sun-god" and the ruler of a city in Palestine "thy servant and the dirt whereon thou dost tread." Some 400 years earlier, a father, Sehetep-ib-Re, wrote advice to his children—"a counsel of eternity and a manner

Weighing the soul. About 4,500 years ago, Egyptian sensibilities changed. Instead of showing the afterlife as a prolongation of life in this world, tomb-painters began to concentrate on morally symbolic scenes, in which gods interrogate the dead and weigh their good against their evil deeds.
Michael Holford

of living aright." The king is the Sun-god, but he is more. "He illumines Egypt more than the sun, he makes the land greener than does the Nile."

In Egypt the law remained in the mouth of the divine pharaoh, and the need to put it in writing was never strong. Instead, religion defined a moral code that the state could not easily modify or subvert. The evidence comes from Egyptian tombs. Early grave goods include the cherished possessions and everyday belongings of this world, suggesting that the next world would reproduce the inequalities and lifestyles of this one. At an uncertain date, however, a new idea of the afterlife emerged. This world was called into existence to correct the imbalances of the one we know. It is particularly well documented in ancient Egyptian sources that most of the elite seem to have changed their attitude to the afterlife around 2000 B.C.E. Earlier tombs are antechambers to a life for which the world was practical training. Tombs built later are places of interrogation after a moral preparation for the next life.

Wall paintings from the later tombs show the gods weighing the souls of the dead. Typically, the deceased's heart lies in one scale, and a feather symbolizing truth lies in the other. The jackal-headed god of the underworld, Anubis, supervises the scales. The examined soul renounces a long list of sins that concentrate on three areas: sacrilege, sexual perversion, and the abuse of power against the weak. Then the good deeds appear: obedience to human laws and divine will, acts of mercy, offerings to the gods and the spirits of ancestors, bread to the hungry, clothing to the naked, "and a ferry for him who was marooned." The reward of the good is a new life in the company of Osiris, the sometime ruler of the universe. For those who fail the test, the punishment is extinction.

Statecraft in Mesopotamia

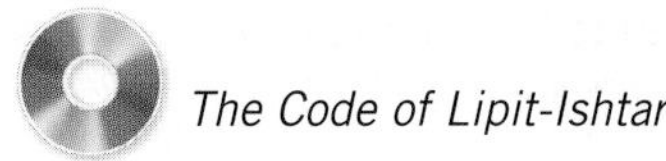
The Code of Lipit-Ishtar

Unlike Egypt, a single state under a single ruler, Mesopotamia was divided into numerous small rival kingdoms, each based on a single city. In Mesopotamia, kings were not gods, which is probably why the earliest known law codes come from there. The codes of Ur from the third millennium B.C.E. are fragmentary—essentially, lists of fines. But the code of King Lipit-Ishtar of Sumer and Akkad, around 2000 B.C.E., is clearly an attempt to regulate the entire society. It explains that the laws were divinely inspired. Their purpose was to make "children support the father and the father children, ... abolish enmity and rebellion, cast out weeping and lamentation ... bring righteousness and truth and give well-being."

Gilgamesh, king of Uruk, hero of the world's earliest known work of imaginative literature, shown in a relief more than 3,000 years old, kills the Bull of Heaven. The bull was a personification of drought. It was part of a king's job to mastermind irrigation.
Royal Museums of Art and History, Brussels, Belgium. Copyright IRPA-KIK, Brussels, Belgium

Hammurabi, ruler of Babylon in the first half of the 1700s B.C.E., gets undue credit because his code happens to survive intact, having been carried off as a war trophy to Persia. It is engraved in stone and shows the king receiving the text from the hands of a god. It was clearly intended to substitute for the physical presence and utterance of the ruler. "Let any oppressed man who has a cause come into the presence of the statue of me, the king of justice, and then read carefully my inscribed stone, and give heed to my precious words. May my stone make his case clear to him." These were not laws as we know them, handed down by tradition or enacted to restrain the ruler's power. Rather, they were means to perpetuate royal commands. Obedience was severely enforced in Mesopotamia—to the vizier in the fields, the father in the household, the king in everything. "The king's word is right," says a representative text, "his word, like a god's, cannot be changed."

Even if we had no written evidence to confirm it, royal power would gleam from the luxurious artifacts that filled rulers' tombs, evidence of the realm's wealth: a gilded harp carved in the form of a ram; dice and gaming boards of inlaid shell and polished stone; lively animals sculpted in gold and silver; tapering vessels of gold, and golden cups modeled on ostrich eggs. The stunning collections of jewelry seem to have religious themes, as if each had a distinct ritual function.

In Mesopotamian carvings, the king is commonly the biggest figure in any scene that includes him. He drinks. He receives supplicants who petition his help and citizens and ambassadors who pay him tribute. He presides over armies and processions of chariots drawn by wild asses. He carries bricks to build cities and temples, purifying them with fire and consecrating them with oil. To form the first brick from the mud was the king's exclusive right, and bricks from the state kilns were stamped with royal names. Royal seals make plain why this was. They show gods building the world up out of mud. They mix it, carry it up ladders, and fling mud bricks up to the men who set them layer by layer. The transformation of mud into city was royal magic.

Oracles—means of supposed access to knowing the future—told kings what to do. Augurers were the hereditary interpreters of oracles. They read the will of the gods in the livers of sacrificed sheep, the drift of incense, and, above all, in the movements of heavenly bodies. Their predictions of royal victory, danger, anger, and recovery from sickness fill surviving records. Religion, however, did not necessarily limit royal power. Kings firmly controlled the oracles and sometimes slept in temples to induce prophetic dreams, especially during a crisis, such as the failure of the floods. Of course, the predictions they reported may have merely legitimated the policies they had already decided to follow.

Yet these rulers were there to serve the people: to mediate with the gods on behalf of the whole society, to organize the collective effort of tillage and irrigation, to warehouse food against hard times, and to redistribute it for the common good.

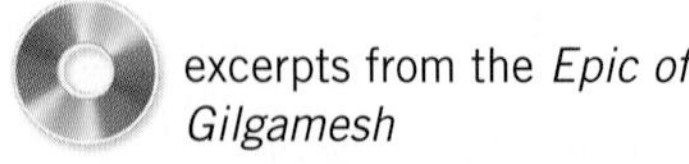
excerpts from the *Epic of Gilgamesh*

The most famous relic of ancient Mesopotamian literature, the *Epic of Gilgamesh*, sheds further light on the nature of leadership. There was a real Gilgamesh, or at least a king of that name who ruled the city of Uruk, probably around 2700 B.C.E. The poem quotes a proverbial saying about him: "Who has ever ruled with power like his?" In the surviving versions, written down, perhaps about 1800 B.C.E., the same natural forces that molded the Mesopotamian environment shaped the story. When Gilgamesh, the hero of the poem, confronts a monster who breathes fire and plague, the gods blind the attacker with a scorching wind. When Gilgamesh explores the Ocean of Death to find the secret of immortality, he encounters the only family to have survived a primeval flood. The disaster, wrought by divine whim, had destroyed the rest of the human race and even left the gods themselves "cowering like dogs crouched against a wall."

The First Documented Chinese State

Tan-fu the Duke, from the *Shi Jing*

The earliest recorded kingship traditions of China resemble those of Egypt and Mesopotamia, with the same connection between royal status and the management of food and water. The legendary engineer-emperor Yu the Great was praised for having "mastered the waters and caused them to flow in great channels." Early folk poetry describes a period of city building after his time, so fast "that the drums could not keep pace." The legendary ruler Tan-fu supervised builders of houses and temples, as they "lashed the boards and erected the frames."

The earliest China we know of was a unitary state. The dynasty known as Shang dominated the Yellow River valley for most of the second millennium B.C.E. Diviners, whose job was to detect the gods' messages, heated animal bones and turtle shells to breaking point and read the gods' answers to questions along the lines of the cracks. Scribes transcribed the answers onto the fragments, so the bones tell of the lives and duties of kings. The king was most often engaged in war and sometimes in diplomacy and marriage, which later emperors called "extending my favor." To soldiers, "our prince's own concerns" rolled them "from misery to misery" and gave them homes "like tigers and buffaloes . . . in desolate wilds." The court treasury held millet, turtle shells, and oracle bones in tribute.

Above all, the king was a mediator with the gods, performing sacrifices, preparing for and conducting oracle readings, breaking the soil, praying for rain, founding towns. He spent half his time hunting—presumably as a way to entertain counselors and ambassadors, train horsemen, and supplement the table. Scholars claim to detect an increasingly businesslike tone in the oracles. References to dreams and sickness diminish as time goes on; the style becomes more terse and the tone more optimistic. Sometimes the bones reveal revolutions in the conduct of rites from reign to reign, evidence that kings fought tradition and tried to give the world a stamp of their own. Tsu Jia, for instance, a king of the late second millennium B.C.E., discontinued sacrifices to mythical ancestors, mountains, and rivers and increased those to historical figures. Beyond reasonable doubt, he was modifying the practices of the longest-lived and most renowned of his dynasty, Wu Ding (woo-ding).

The chronology is uncertain, but Wu Ding must have ruled about 1400 B.C.E. He was remembered 1,000 years later as a conqueror and glorious hunter. One of his 64 consorts was buried in the richest known tomb of the period, with her human servants, dogs, horses, hundreds of bronzes and jades, and thousands of cowrie shells, which were used as money. Although there is room for confusion because of the habit of calling different people by the same name, court records probably identify her correctly. Wu Ding repeatedly consulted the oracles about her childbeds and sickbeds. She was one of his three principal wives and an active participant in politics. She had a domain of her own and could mobilize 3,000 warriors.

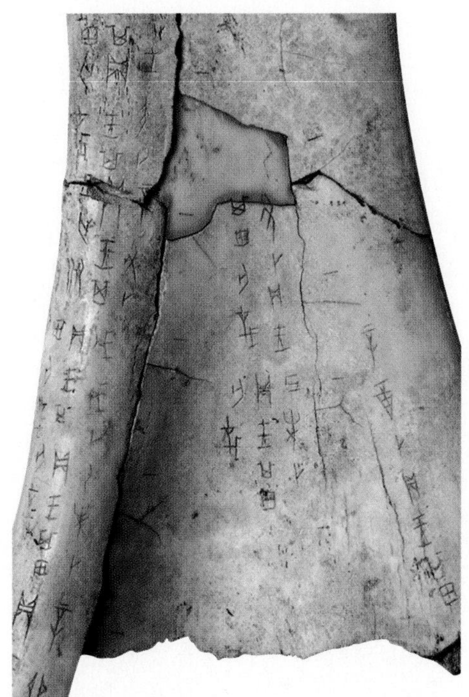

Oracle bones in China in the second millennium B.C.E. were heated until they cracked. Specialist diviners—shamans at first, later royal appointees—read the future along the lines of the cracks, scratching their interpretations into the bone. Most predictions were formal and even banal. This example says characteristically, "If the king hunts, there will be no disaster."

As mediator with the gods, the king was a substitute for the shaman, the middleman between humans and gods, eliciting the "sharp-eared, keen-eyed" wisdom of ghosts and spirits and restoring contact with heaven after disordered times. By taking over the divination of bones and turtle shells, the king transferred to the state the most important political functions of magic and religion—foretelling the future and

The Great River Valleys

(All dates are approximate)

5000 B.C.E.	Beginning of intense agriculture in great river valleys; use of plows widespread in Mesopotamia
3000 B.C.E.	Menes unites Upper and Lower Egypt; large cities appear in lower Mesopotamia (Sumer)
2500 B.C.E.	Sargon of Akkad conquers Sumer; cities of Harappa and Mohenjodaro flourish
2000–1000 B.C.E.	Shang dynasty (China)
2250–2000 B.C.E.	Ziggurat of Ur
2000 B.C.E.	Law code of Lipit-Ishtar (Mesopotamia); concept of afterlife becomes more moralistic in Egypt
1800 B.C.E.	*Epic of Gilgamesh* written down
1700 B.C.E.	Law code of Hammurabi
1500 B.C.E.	Reading of oracle bones becomes secularized in China; beginning of gradual expansion of Yellow River valley southward toward Yangtze

interpreting the will of the spirits. The king became the guardian of a secular bureaucracy—a slowly developing corps of court historians, who could acquire experience on which predictions could be based more reliably than on the shamans' supposed insights.

At this stage, the Chinese viewed kingship in practical terms—how well the ruler looked after his subjects' well-being. Shang rulers claimed to have come to power as executors of divine justice against an earlier—doubtless mythical—dynasty, the Xia (SHEE-ah), whose last representative had forfeited his right to rule by "neglecting husbandry": failing, that is, in his duty to look after the realm as a farmer cares for his fields. The earliest scholars' texts that describe the emergence of China probably reflect traditional propaganda fairly accurately. They depict kind, generous rulers who fostered the arts of peace. The Yellow Emperor, a mythical figure, was credited with inventing the carriage, the boat, the bronze mirror, the cooking pot, the crossbow, "and a kind of football." Poems and popular legends, however, reveal more of the bloody business of kingship, which inherited ancient clan leaders' rights of life and death. An axe engraved with the emblems of the executioner—hungry smiles and devouring teeth—signified the original term for rulership. "Bring your tongues under the rule of law," says a late Shang ruler in an approving poet's lines, "lest punishment come upon you when repentance will be of no avail."

Wealth and warfare were inseparable essentials of kingship. Tombs of Shang rulers around 1500 B.C.E. display the nature of their power: thousands of strings of cowrie shells, bronze axes and chariots, lacquerware, and hundreds of intricately carved treasures of jade and bone. The greatest treasures were bronzes of unparalleled quality, cast in ceramic molds. Bronze making was the supreme art of Shang China, and its products were a privilege of rank. Thousands of human sacrifices, buried with kings to serve them in the next world or to sanctify their tombs were—to those who buried them—among the cheapest sacrifices.

Ruling the Harappan World

In the Harappan world, the extraordinary consistency in urban layout and building design did not necessarily arise from political unity. Hierarchically ordered dwelling spaces hint at a class or even a more rigid caste structure. In a class system, individuals can rise or fall through the ranks of society. In a caste system they are stuck with the status with which they are born. In Harappan cities, the extensive communal quarters must have had something to do with the organization of manpower—soldiers, perhaps, or slaves, or scholars. Huge warehouses suggest a system to distribute food. The waste-disposal system looks like a masterpiece of urban planning, with clay pipes laid under the streets. The uniform bricks must have come from state kilns and pans. The imposing citadels or fortresses enclosed spaces that might have had an elite function, like the spacious bathing tank at Mohenjodaro. Harappan sites, however, have no rich graves, and the absence of kingly quarters or regal furnishings tempts us to imagine Harappan societies as republics or theocracies.

Normally, for a society like Harappa's, whose writings we cannot read, archaeological evidence tells us what little we know. We would hope to learn something from works of art, but no pictorial art has survived, and Harappan artists seem to have produced little sculpture, except on a small scale in clay and bronze. One extraordinary figure from Mohenjodaro, of great seriousness, with almond eyes and rigidly fluted beard, wears a headband with what looks like the setting for a gem. He has a rich garment slung over one shoulder and extends what is left of his arm in what must have been a symbolic or ritual gesture. He has been called a priest-king or a philosopher-king, but these romantic terms are valueless. With no context for interpreting him, we can only describe him.

The Politics of Expansion

Although just about everything in Harappan politics remains mysterious, the reach of the culture seems so vast it is hard to imagine how it can have spread so far, into a range of different environments, except by force of arms. A sense of what the Harappan frontier was like—expanding and violent—grips you when you see the garrisons that reached toward the interior of Asia, in unirrigatable deserts and siltless hills. In what is now northern Afghanistan, lapis lazuli and copper were traded at oasis settlements that reached westward toward the Caspian Sea. Mundigak, a fortified trading center, was equipped to house entire caravans. Today, behind formidable walls with square bastions, the wreck of a great citadel lunges over the landscape, baring rows of deep, round columns at its flank, like the ribs of a huge, squat beast crouched to guard the routes of commerce.

In Egypt, Mesopotamia, and China, the sources are ample enough to reveal how states grew by conquest. In Egypt, the Nile was the spine that supported a unitary state. More than the source of life-giving mud, the river was a highway through a long, thin land. Culture and trade could flow freely from the coast to the cataracts. Models and paintings of river craft are among the most common decorations of tombs. At Thebes, you can still see painted scenes of grain-laden barges, and others with oil jars and bundles of fodder, docking by the marketplace.

The river was politically unifying, too. Pharoahs took the river route for inspection tours of the kingdom, mooring at royal docks with brick shrines and exercise yards for chariots. Egypt was an empire shaped like the fans Egyptians used to rake and beat their wheat—the long staff of the Nile linked to the spread of the delta where the river meets the Mediterranean. Mythology preserved the

MAKING CONNECTIONS

POLITICS AND STATE POWER IN GREAT RIVER VALLEY SOCIETIES

STATE →	LEADER & SYMBOLIC ROLE →	METHOD OF UNIFICATION →	RULER'S MEANS OF CONTROL →
Egypt	Pharaoh (herdsman) sometimes functions as god	Organizing labor to manage floods; distributing food; use of Nile River as highway to unify, control	Pharaoh's commands, policies function as law, regarded as divine
Mesopotamia city-states	Kings/royals meditate, lead worship, receive oracles	Organizing labor; distributing food; competition with other city-states	Earliest law codes; rituals performed by oracles guide decision making
China	Emperor/engineer, builder, hunter, takes on shamans' role in receiving prophecies	Organizing dike building, irrigation; use of Yellow River as highway to unify and control	Ritual divination using oracle bones—foretelling future, interpreting will of spirits
Harappa	Uncertain if singular ruler or priests dominated ruling class	Harnessing river, irrigation; distributing food; engineering and construction of complex urban systems	Unknown; widespread standardization of measurements and trade point to coordination/leadership

memory of a prehistoric Egypt divided into an upriver South Kingdom, or Upper Egypt, and Lower Egypt, occupying the delta region. Pharaohs wore a double crown to recall this past. Egypt's traditional lists of dynasties began with Menes, who supposedly conquered the delta from his own kingdom in the south around 3000 B.C.E. He united the kingdoms and founded Memphis, his capital, at the point on the Nile where Upper and Lower Egypt joined, a little to the south of modern Cairo.

Conveyance by river was one of the features this world had in common with heaven. To accompany the immortals as they were ferried across the sky, the pharaoh Cheops was provided with transport. In one pit adjoining his pyramid lies the barge that carried his body to the burial place. Egyptologists are currently excavating an adjoining pit, where his celestial boat is buried. In this sailing vessel, he would navigate the darkness, joining the fleet that bore the Sun back to life every night.

In retrospect, the unity of Egypt seems "natural"—river shaped. Mesopotamia was not so easy to unify. Competition was probably the driving force behind Mesopotamian city-states. Inscriptions addressed to their cities' patron gods are full of victories against rivals, each one's propaganda contradicting the others. Around 2000 B.C.E., the most boastful author of inscriptions, Lugal Zagesi, king of the city of Umma in Sumer, claimed more. The supreme god, Enlil, "put all the lands at his feet and from east to west made them subject to him" from the Persian Gulf to the Mediterranean.

This was almost certainly just a boast. Left to themselves, the warring Sumerian city-states could never have united for long. Around 2500 B.C.E., however, invaders from northern Mesopotamia forced political change. The conquering king, Sargon of Akkad, was one of the great empire builders of antiquity. His armies poured downriver and made him King of Sumer and Akkad. "Mighty mountains with axes of bronze I conquered," he declared and dared kings who came after him to do the same. His armies were said to have reached Syria and Iran.

Such a vast empire could not last. After a century or two, native Sumerian forces expelled Sargon's successors. Nevertheless, his achievement set a new pattern—an imperial direction—for the political history of the region. City-states sought to expand by conquering each other. For a time, Lagash, a northern neighbor of Ur, dominated Sumer. One of its kings was the subject of 27 surviving images. We have no better index of any ruler's power. But around 2100 B.C.E., Ur displaced Lagash. The new capital began to acquire the look for which it is renowned, with showy ziggurats and daunting walls. Within a few years more, tribute, recorded on clay tablets, was reaching Ur from as far away as the Iranian highlands and the Lebanese coast. A 4,000-year-old box—the soundbox of a harp, perhaps—gorgeously depicts the cycle of royal life in imperial Ur—victory, tribute-gathering, and celebration. Thereafter, leadership in the region shifted among rival centers, but it always remained in the south.

In China, itineraries for royal travel dating around 1500 B.C.E. reveal a different political geography. Kings constantly rattled up and down the great vertical artery of the realm, the eastern arm of the Yellow River, and frenziedly did the round of towns and estates to the south, as far as the river Huai. Occasionally, they touched the northernmost reach of the Yangtze River. This was a telltale sign. Shang civilization was expanding south from its heartlands on the middle Yellow River, growing into a regionally dominant superstate. Gradually, the worlds of Chinese culture and politics absorbed the Yangtze valley. The result was a unique state containing complementary environments: the millet-growing lands of the Yellow River, the rice fields of the Yangtze. The new ecology of China helped protect it against ecological disaster in either zone. It also formed the basis of the astonishingly resilient and productive state seen in subsequent Chinese history. The consequences will be apparent throughout the remainder of this book. For most of the rest of our story, China wields disproportionate power and influence.

Moreover, the broadening of China's frontiers stimulated rulers' ambitions. They became boundless. Religion and philosophy conspired. The sky was a compelling deity: vast and pregnant with gifts—of light and warmth and rain—and bristling with threats of storm and fire and flood. A state that touched its limits would fulfill a kind of "manifest destiny"—a reflection of divine order. Comparing the state to the cosmos prompted rulers to seek a dominion as boundless as the sky's. The Chinese came to see imperial rule over the world as divinely ordained. Emperors treated the whole world as rightfully or potentially subject to them. By the time of the Zhou, the dynasty that succeeded the Shang, the phrase **mandate of heaven** came into use to express these doctrines.

The concept of the mandate of heaven spread to neighboring peoples. On the Eurasian steppes, the immense flatlands and vast skies encouraged similar thinking. We have no documentation for the ambitions of the steppe dynasties until much later. But, as we shall see, steppelanders with conquest in mind repeatedly challenged empires around the edges of Eurasia in the first millennium B.C.E. It is probably fair to say that for hundreds, perhaps thousands, of years the concept of a right to rule the world drove imperialism in Eurasia.

Literate Culture

It used to be thought—some people still think—that one reason the early Egyptians, Mesopotamians, Chinese, and Harappans qualified as "civilized" was because they were the first to use symbolic methods to record information and pass it on to future generations.

Mesopotamians devised the wedge shapes of the writing known as **cuneiform** to be easily incised, or cut, in the clay tablets used to keep records. The hieroglyphs of the earliest Egyptian texts and the symbols carved on Chinese oracle bones were **logograms**, stylized pictures that provoked mental associations with ideas they were intended to represent or with the sounds of their spoken names. The surviving Harappan texts marked the cord or sacks of merchants' goods. Archaeologists have retrieved many of them from heaps of discarded produce.

So, these civilizations all developed useful and expressive writing systems. For three reasons, however, we can no longer claim that writing was a special and defining feature that made these the first civilizations. First, writing systems originated independently in widely separated parts of the world and were far more varied than traditional scholarship has supposed. Notched sticks and knotted strings can be forms of writing as much as letters on a page or in an inscription. Some writing systems were much older than the civilizations of the river valleys.

Second, it is not clear why we should consider writing special compared to information-retrieval systems based on memory. The earliest writing systems were usually employed for trivia—merchants' price lists, tax collectors' memoranda, potters' marks, and similar jottings. Real art—the great creative poems and myths, like the *Epic of Gilgamesh*—were too sacred for writing to taint and too memorable for such a crude method of transmission. Instead, for centuries, people memorized them and transmitted them orally from one generation to the next.

Finally, how much information does a system have to be able to convey before we can call it writing? Will knotted strings or notched sticks do? Surviving Shang oracle bones of the second millennium B.C.E. bear the ancestral language of modern Chinese. Yet a symbolic system of recording information appears on pottery more than 2,000 years older from Banpo in the Yellow River region. The symbols might be numerals and potters' marks. They do not seem to be connected sentences because the symbols are simple and used one at a time. So is this writing or something else unworthy of the name? Turtle shells recently discovered at Wuyang (woo-yahng) in China, which are thousands of years older, bear marks that we can only explain as part of a system of symbolic representation.

Early writing. In almost all known cases, writing was devised to record neither wisdom nor art, but only tedious data, such as prices and tax returns. This clay tablet from a collection at the Library of Congress is written in Sumerian and concerns the wages paid to named supervisors of day laborers. It dates to 2039 B.C.E.

Instead of restricting our definition of writing, we ought to feel awe at the adventure of combining isolated symbols to tell stories and make arguments. But familiarity disperses awe. Some cultures may have taken thousands of years to make this leap, even while they used writing systems for other purposes, such as labels, oracles, bureaucracy, and magic charms.

IN PERSPECTIVE: What Made the Great River Valleys Different?

Still, the fact remains that, thanks in part to writing, the civilizations of the four great river valleys—or, at least, the three whose writings we can decipher—are, to us, the best known of their time. For that reason, not because of their supposed influence on other peoples, they fairly occupy so much space in books like this one. Studying their written works helps us identify at least two reasons for the cultural divergence of the era, of which they are extreme examples. First, in part, divergence was environmentally conditioned. That is, the greater or more diverse the resource base, the bigger and more durable the society it feeds. The great river valleys were large, continuous areas of fertile, easily worked soil, and for farming societies, exploitable land is the most basic resource of all. Environmental diversity gave the river valley peoples extra resources, compared with civilizations in less privileged regions. Egypt had the Nile delta at hand. In the Yellow River and Yangtze valleys, China had two complementary ecological systems. Mesopotamia had a hinterland of pastures, and Mesopotamia and Harappa had access to each other by sea.

Second, interactions matter. Societies learn from each other, compete with each other, and exchange culture with each other. The more societies are in touch with other societies, the more these activities occur. By contrast, isolation retards. Egypt was in touch with Mesopotamia and Mesopotamia with Harappa. China's relative isolation perhaps helps explain its late start in some of the common processes of change that these societies all experienced. All these societies enclosed, within their own bounds, relatively large zones of exchange. But all were remarkably self-contained. As we shall see in the next chapter, however, travel and trade were increasingly important. These were the means of communicating the cultures from the great river valleys to other regions, some of which were less environmentally fortunate. Invasions and migrations, too, were—and still are—effective forms of interaction because they shift many people around, and people carry their culture with them.

The grandeur of the great river valley civilizations raises questions about their sustainability. Their wealth and productivity excited envy from outsiders and invited attack. Continued population growth demanded ever more intensive exploitation of the environment. At the same time, climates and ecosystems continued to change. The vast collective efforts required for irrigation, storage, and monumental building left huge classes of people oppressed and resentful of elites. As a result of these and other stresses, beginning around 1500 B.C.E., transformation or collapse threatened all these societies. Meanwhile, peoples in less easily exploitable environments found the will and means to reproduce, challenge, or exceed the achievements of these four civilizations. The question of how well they succeeded is the focus of the next chapter.

CHRONOLOGY

(All dates are approximate)

5000–2000 B.C.E.	Four great river valley civilizations develop: Middle and Lower Nile, Egypt; Indus and Saraswati Rivers; Tigris and Euphrates Rivers, Mesopotamia; Yellow River, China
3000 B.C.E.	Menes unites Upper and Lower Egypt
2500 B.C.E.	Cities of Harappa and Mohenjodaro flourish; Sargon of Akkad conquers Sumer
2250–2000 B.C.E.	Ziggurat of Ur built
2000–1000 B.C.E.	Shang dynasty, China
1800 B.C.E.	*Epic of Gilgamesh* written down
1700 B.C.E.	Law code of Hammurabi

Because they all made use of bronze, nineteenth-century archaeology—classifying societies according to their characteristic technology—called the era of the great river valley civilizations the Bronze Age. In the late second millennium B.C.E., the crises that afflicted them seemed to herald transition to an "Iron Age." Such labels no longer seem appropriate. Though there were bronze-using and iron-making societies, there was never an "age" of either. Some societies in Africa never used bronze. Many societies never took up iron. Few employed iron to make tools and weapons until well into the first millennium B.C.E. Although bronze making came to have an important place in the economies and art of many Eurasian peoples during the second millennium B.C.E., other societies achieved similar standards of material culture and developed comparable states without it. In any case, there are aspects of civilization—ways of thinking and feeling and behaving—more deeply influential than technology, "more lasting"—as a Roman poet said of his poems—"than bronze," and therefore more worthy of attention.

PROBLEMS AND PARALLELS

1. How did the distinctive ecological differences of the four great river valleys affect their economic activity?
2. How did environmental transformations caused by humans (such as irrigation) affect the great river valley civilizations, both positively and negatively?
3. What was the connection between religion and political leadership in Egypt, Mesopotamia, and China? What is the evidence for these relationships?
4. What methods did rulers use to expand their states in China, Mesopotamia, the Indus valley, and Egypt? How did each area's environment affect this expansion?
5. What do the writing systems of China, Mesopotamia, Indus valley, and Egypt tell us about each society's politics, religion, and economy?
6. Why are the ways a civilization thought, felt, and behaved not adequately conveyed by labels such as "Bronze Age"?

DOCUMENTS IN GLOBAL HISTORY

- Stonehenge
- Excerpts from the *Shi Jing*
- Ptahhotep, from the Egyptian *Book of Instructions*
- Excerpts from *The Amarna Letters*
- *The Code of Lipit-Ishtar*
- excerpts from the *Epic of Gilgamesh*
- Tan-fu the Duke, from the *Shi Jing*

Please see the Primary Source DVD for additional sources related to this chapter.

READ ON

R. L. Burger, *Chavín and the Origins of Andean Civilization* (1993) is an excellent introduction to the Peruvian material. H. Silverman, ed., *Andean Archaeology* (2004) contains some important recent research.

L. Nikolova, *The Balkans in Later Prehistory* (1999) is authoritative on the southeastern European sites. C. Renfrew, ed., *Problems in European Prehistory* (1979) includes some vital contributions. D. V. Clarke, *Skara Brae* (1983) is a useful pamphlet on those of the Orkneys. For the vexed question of the "rise" of "civilization," K. Wittfogel, *Oriental Despotism* (1967) is the now almost universally repudiated classic on the subject. K. W. Butzer, *Early Hydraulic Civilization in Egypt* (1976) is a pioneering classic on the ecological dimensions. B. J. Kemp, *Ancient Egypt* (1989) is an excellent introduction.

G. Algaze, *The Uruk World System* (1993) is an important study of the origins of Mesopotamian civilization.

K. C. Chang, *Art, Myth and Ritual* (1983) and *Shang Civilization* (1980) are indispensable on China. E. L. Shaughnessy, *Sources of Western Zhou History* (1992) is immeasurably illuminating.

B. and R. Allchin, *The Rise of Civilization in India and Pakistan* (1982) is particularly useful for Harappa, on which the studies collected by G. Possehl, ed., *Harappan Civilization* (1993) are an important supplement.

CHAPTER 4 A Succession of Civilizations: Ambition and Instability

One measure of the influence of the Hittites is the durability of their art. This relief, from Carchemish in Phoenicia, dates from at least two centuries after the Hittite empire collapsed but continues to reflect Hittite conventions and values. The winged sun was a symbol other regional empires adopted.

IN THIS CHAPTER

THE CASE OF THE HITTITE KINGDOM
The Importance of Trade
Hittite Society and Politics
Fragility and Fall: The End of Hatti

INSTABILITY AND COLLAPSE IN THE AEGEAN
Cretan Civilization
Mycenean Civilization

A GENERAL CRISIS IN THE EASTERN MEDITERRANEAN WORLD?
The Egyptian Experience
The Roots of Instability

THE EXTINCTION OF HARAPPAN CIVILIZATION
The Evidence of the *Rig Veda*
The Environment of Stress

CONFLICT ON THE YELLOW RIVER
The Rise of Zhou
The Zhou Political System

STATE-BUILDING IN THE AMERICAS
Andean Examples
Developments in Mesoamerica

ASSESSING THE DAMAGE
The Survival of Egypt

IN PERSPECTIVE: **The Fatal Flaws**

For a moment, the scribe thought the king was dead. He ruled a line under his notes.

HATTI

They formed a grim, faltering record of an old man's regrets: his hatred of his treacherous sister—"a serpent" who "bellows like an ox"; the faithlessness of his adopted heir—"an abomination ... without compassion"; the disloyalty of relatives—"heedless of the word of the king." The dying monarch railed against his daughter, too. "She incited the whole land to rebellion." Rebels taunted him, "There is no son for your father's throne. A servant will sit on it."

With his last bit of strength, Hattusili, the great king of the Hittites, ruler of the land of Hatti, south of the Black Sea, and of an empire that touched upper Mesopotamia and the Mediterranean, sought to keep a grasp on power beyond the grave. With no suitable adult to succeed him, he decided that his infant grandson must be the next king. The administrators of the kingdom must protect the child and prepare him for manhood, reading to him every month his grandfather's testament, with its warnings against disloyalty and its exhortations to mercy, piety, and forgiveness.

Around the deathbed in the city of Kussara, in a room gleaming with lapis lazuli and gold, the assembled warriors and officials contemplated an insecure future. But the king was not yet dead. He stirred, striving to speak. The scribe, straining to catch the royal words, scratched hurried characters onto his clay tablet. A woman's name fell from the king's lips: Hastayar. Who was she? Wife or concubine, sorceress or daughter? No one now knows. But she was at the bedside, consulting with the old women who were the court's prophetesses, even as the king's life ebbed. With Hattusili's last breath came these final words: "Is she even now interrogating the soothsayers? ... Do not forsake me. Interrogate me! I will give you words as a sign. Wash me well. Hold me to your breast. Keep me from the earth."

FOCUS questions

- WHY WERE the Hittite, Cretan, and Mycenean states more fragile than the great river valley civilizations?
- WHAT FUNDAMENTAL problems to their survival did all large ancient civilizations face?
- WHY DID Harappan civilization disappear?
- WHAT WERE the continuities between the Shang and the Zhou in China?
- WHERE DID the first states arise in the New World?
- WHY WAS Egypt able to survive when other ancient civilizations collapsed around 1000 B.C.E.?

Hattusili dictated this deathbed testament in about 1600 B.C.E. It is the most intimate and lively document to survive from its time, our only glimpse of a king with his guard down, disclosing his own personality. It also reveals the nature and problems of a state at this time: the all-importance of the person of a king, the sacred nature of his word, the ill-defined rules of succession, the power and jealousies of military and administrative elites, an intelligence system that relied on soothsayers, and an atmosphere of danger and insecurity. In short, it was a political environment made to be volatile.

In the Hittite kingdom, we see the great themes of the second millennium B.C.E. First, features that characterized the great river valley civilizations of the previous chapter began to emerge in other environments. These features included intensive agriculture, densely distributed populations, stratified societies (with higher and lower classes), large cities, and states often seeking to build empires. Second, the number of complex states—those with large-scale systems to organize production, control distribution, and regulate life—rapidly increased. These new states also developed a great variety of political institutions and ways to structure society and organize economic activity. Finally, accelerating change claimed victims. By about 1000 B.C.E., war, natural disaster, environmental overexploitation, and social and political disintegration had strained or shattered most of the big states and civilizations that had emerged from the transition to agriculture.

Students of history often dislike this period, with its bewildering succession of empires and civilizations that rise and fall, sometimes with baffling speed. Textbook pages resemble a bad TV soap opera—crowded with action, empty of explanation, with too many characters and too few insights into their behavior. To make sense of the millennium between 2000 and 1000 B.C.E., we need to understand the problems associated with accelerating change. This was a period of climacteric: an era of critical change that extinguished some civilizations, changed others, and might have wiped all of them out. The question for this chapter, then, is, why were some ambitions in the world of around 3,000 years ago realized and others were not? What made the difference between success and failure for states and civilizations?

THE CASE OF THE HITTITE KINGDOM

Anatolia (an-a-TOH-lee-ah), where Hattusili's kingdom took shape, seems an unlikely place to found a large state. Most of it suffered alternating seasonal extremes that scorched and froze crops. Rainfall was, and still is, less than 20 inches a year. (Western Europe and North America receive two or three times more.) Desert stretched between cultivatable patches.

Yet from the central part of this region, between about 1800 and 1500 B.C.E., the people who called themselves children of Hatti—Hittites—drew thousands of such patches and millions of people into a single network of production and distribution, under a common allegiance and built a state we can call an empire. It had palace complexes, storehouses, towns, and armies. And all were comparable in scale with those of the river-valley peoples of the last chapter. Egyptian pharaohs treated Hittite kings as equals. When one pharaoh died without heirs, his widow sent to the king of Hatti for "one of your sons to be my husband, for I will never take a servant of mine and make him my husband." We can picture the Hittites with the help of images they have left us of themselves: hook-nosed, short-headed, and arrayed for war. But how did their state and empire happen in such a hostile environment?

The Importance of Trade

Hatti became a regional power through enrichment by trade. In the second millennium B.C.E., new potential trading partners arose as the economic center of gravity in Mesopotamia gradually shifted upriver. Changes in the course of the Tigris and Euphrates Rivers stranded formerly important cities. Accumulations of silt kept merchants offshore. Wars at the far end of the Persian Gulf and the disappearance of some of the great cities of the Indus valley probably disrupted commerce in the Arabian Sea and Persian Gulf. New opportunities, meanwhile, arose in the north as economic development created new markets, or expanded old ones, in Syria, the Iranian highlands, and Anatolia (see Map 4.1).

For instance, the archives of Ebla, an independent city-state in Syria, reveal exchanges with Mesopotamia. Ebla's commerce was a state monopoly. Its merchants were ambassadors. A dozen foreign cities delivered gold, silver, copper, and textiles to its markets and treasury. Its royal granary stored enough food for 18 million meals. The most complete surviving record of a tour of inspection of the state warehouses names 12 kinds of wheat, abundant wine and cooking oil, and more than 80,000 sheep. The city's ceramic seals, ivory figurines, and metalwork reached the courts of chiefs in central Anatolia.

With the shift of economic activity from Lower to Upper Mesopotamia and beyond, networks of traders spread, east and north, from growing upriver cities such as Ashur on the Tigris and Mari on the Euphrates. Thousands of documents—16,000 in Ebla, 17,000 in Mari—describe wealthy private merchants underwritten by the state and stateless middlemen who served as deal makers. Trade forges social obligations, establishes new relationships of power, and legitimates old ones. Merchant-diplomats carried gifts between palaces. The king of the city of Ugarit (OOH-gahr-riht) rewarded an official called Tamkaru for this kind of work with a grant of land in the mid-1200s B.C.E. Leaders who accumulated imported luxuries or who were tough enough to tax passing trade could reinvest in more goods or buy the allegiance of other chiefs. They might build palace centers like those of Mesopotamia and Egypt to redistribute goods.

Business had its human side. The royal family of Ashur had a farm at a frontier trading post on the routes to Anatolia and the Mediterranean. Over 1,000 people lived there—migrants from Ashur, exiled foreigners, prisoners of war. The steward, permanently frustrated by impractical orders, frustrated the king in turn, who wrote: "What is this, that whatever I tell you, you fail to do as I say?" The supply of beer and tableware to entertain passing embassies provoked many quarrels. So did the problems of enforcing tolls on luxuries.

Anitta, king of Kanes, early in the second millennium had "a throne of iron and a sceptre of iron." Iron was new, originating in this region but still rare and soft, smelted at a temperature only slightly higher than that required for copper. The technique of

Ebla's palace walls in the mid–third millennium B.C.E. were 40 or 50 feet high. The ceremonial court in the foreground was 165 feet long. The holes show where pillars supported the roof. Akkadian invaders destroyed the palace around 2300 B.C.E. but left intact the precious archives that recorded the range of trade with Mesopotamia, Anatolia, and Egypt.

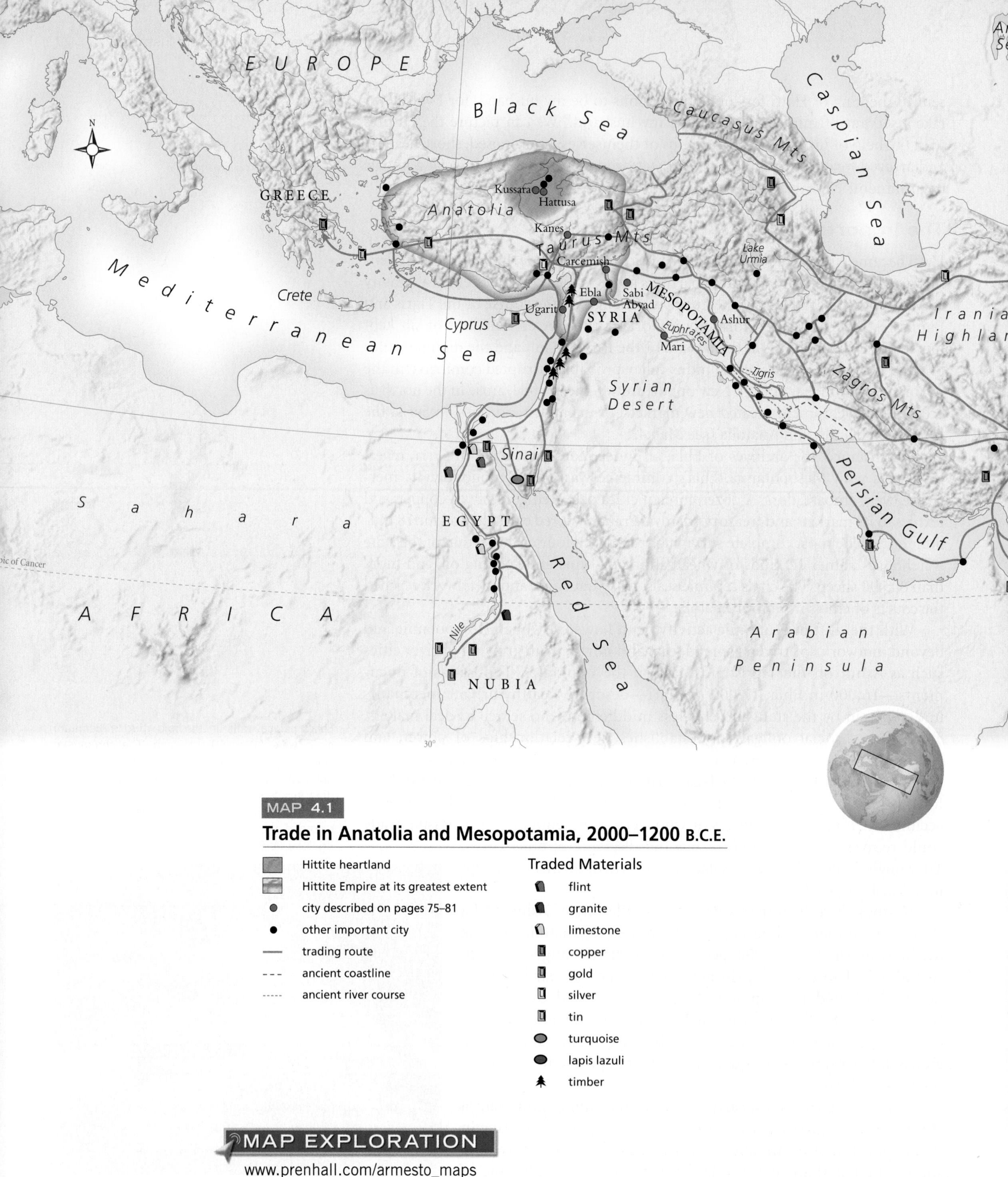

MAP 4.1
Trade in Anatolia and Mesopotamia, 2000–1200 B.C.E.

MAP EXPLORATION
www.prenhall.com/armesto_maps

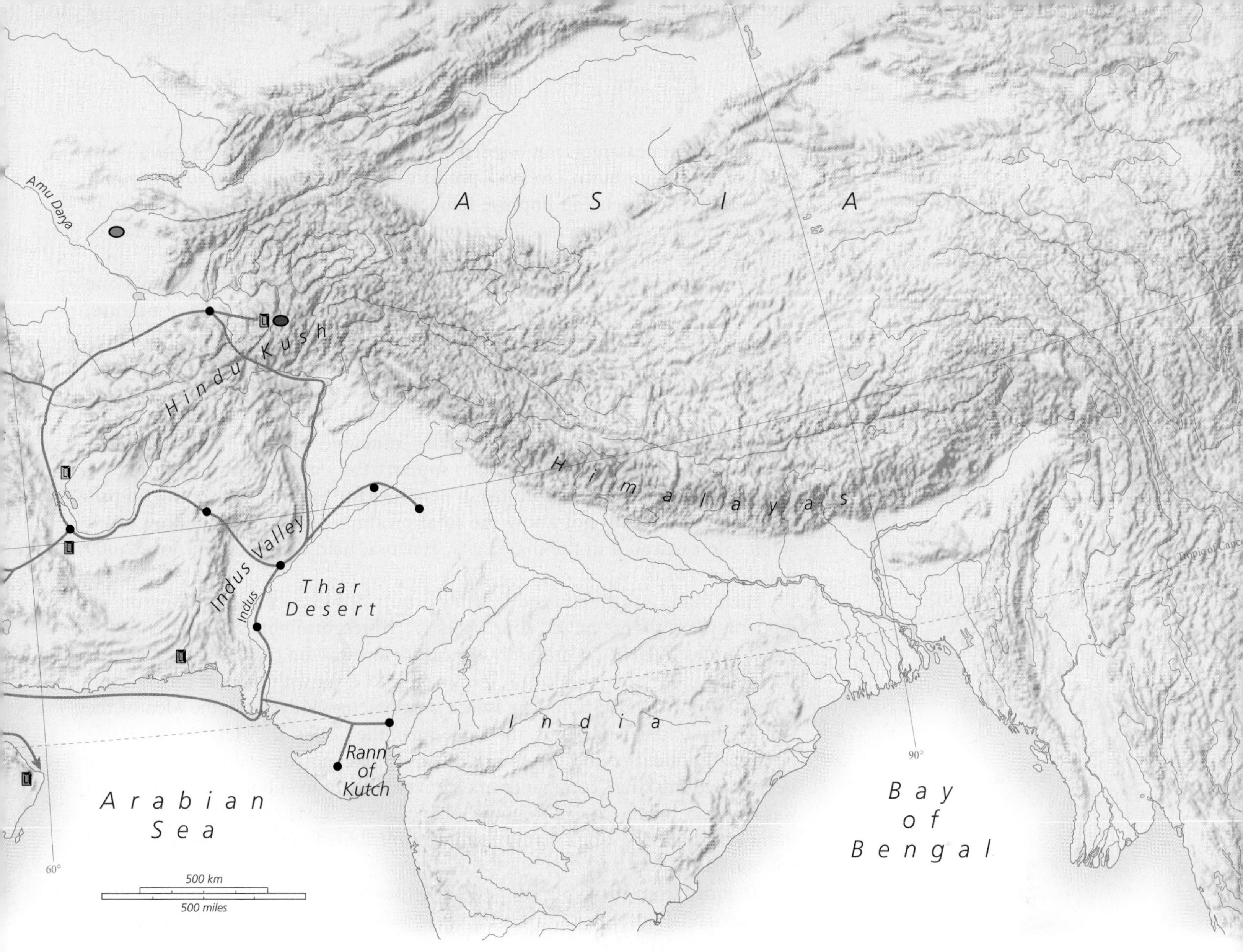

combining it with carbon to make it hard was unreliable. Bronze remained the metal of choice for weapons and agricultural tools. One of the towns Anitta saw as a rival was Kussara, the hometown of the dynasty that later founded the kingdom of Hatti. According to one of his inscriptions, he demolished the place and cursed it, so that it might never arise again. The curse failed. His example, however, inspired the Hittites and showed them how trade and conquest could build a state.

Hittite Society and Politics

The Hittite kingdom brought farmers and herders into a single state and economic system. This was how to make the most of the rugged Anatolian environment, with its small concentrations of cultivatable soil surrounded by marginal grazing land. Herders' wool combined with small farmers' food production. Such mixed farming by independent peasants—not bonded or enslaved workers or wage earners—was of the highest importance. Livestock produce fertilizer to help feed growing populations. Milk-rich diets can improve human fertility. The consequences are more opportunity for economic specialization, urbanization, and the mobilization of manpower for war.

Hittite Land Deed

The surviving inventory of the estate of a typical Hittite peasant lists one house for his family of five, three dozen head of livestock, one acre of pasture, and three and a half acres of vineyard, with 42 pomegranate and 40 apple trees. The pasture must have been for his eight oxen. His goats, hardier animals, presumably foraged where they could. Farmers like these were the manpower that, for a time, made Hatti invincible. Children worked the farms during military campaigns, which usually coincided with sowing and harvest. Peasants were willing, presumably, to support the state that in turn protected them, for Hittite law laid down harsh penalties for theft or trespassing on private property. We do not know the total productivity of the economy, but a single silo excavated in the major city, Hattusa, held enough grain for 32,000 people for a year.

Hatti's king was the sun god's earthly deputy. Subjects called him "My sun," as modern monarchs are called "Your Majesty." His responsibilities were war, justice, and relations with the gods. Hardly any case at law was too trivial to be referred to the king, although, in practice, professional clerks dealt with most of them. A vast household surrounded him: "the Palace servants, the Bodyguard, the Men of the Golden Spear, the Cupbearers, the Table-men, the Cooks, the Heralds, the Stable boys, the Captains of the Thousand." It was a bureaucratic court, where writing perpetuated the king's commands and conveyed them to subordinates. The court was vast, too, because it had to house a huge harem. Royal concubines were rivets of the kingdom. The king's many daughters contributed to the harems of allies and tributaries.

To judge from surviving law codes, Hittites observed many apparently arbitrary sexual taboos. Intercourse with pigs or sheep was punishable by death, but not cases involving horses or mules. Hittites evidently measured the civilization of other societies by the severity of their incest laws. Their own code forbade intercourse between siblings or cousins. Any sexual act, however, was polluting in some degree and had to be cleansed by bathing before prayer. If we knew more about Hittite religion, we might understand their morality better. Strong sexual taboos are usually found in "dualist" religions, alongside belief in the eternal struggle of forces of good and evil or spirit and matter. Hittite attitudes toward sex contrasted with those in Mesopotamia, where—in what seems to have been a more typical pattern—sex was in some sense sacred, and temples employed prostitutes.

Hittite Soldiers' Oath

In some ways, Hatti was a man's world, with the masculine attitudes and values typical of a war state. The oath army officers took indicates this:

> Do you see here a woman's garments? We have them for the oath. Whoever breaks these oaths and does the king harm, let the oaths change him from a man to a woman! Let them change his soldiers into women, and let them dress in the fashion of women and cover their heads with a length of cloth! Let them break the bows, arrows and clubs in their hands and let them take up instead the distaff and the looking-glass!

Women, however, exercised power. Old women acted as diviners at court. Others, lower down the social scale, were curers, waving sacrificial piglets over the victims of curses, with the cry, "Just as this pig shall not see the sky ..., so let the curse not see the sacrificers!"

The Hittites

(All dates are approximate)	
1800–1500 B.C.E.	Hatti develops into an empire
1300 B.C.E.	Plague strikes Hatti
1210 B.C.E.	Last recorded mention of Hatti

Fragility and Fall: The End of Hatti

The Hittite state was formidable in war. It had to be. Its domestic economy was fragile and its homeland poor in key resources. It needed to grow. Conquests were the only way to guarantee food for an increasing population and tin to make bronze weapons. But even successful conflicts can weaken a state by overextending its power and disrupting its trade. Growth butts against immovable limits. In Hatti's case, those limits were the frontiers of Egypt and Mesopotamia.

The Hittite kingdom suffered from other weaknesses. As with all communities that made the transition to agriculture, it was vulnerable to famine and disease. Around 1300 B.C.E., King Mursili II reproached the gods for a plague: "Now no one reaps or sows your fields, for all are dead! The mill-women who used to make the bread of the gods are dead!" A couple of generations later, there was reputedly "no grain in Hatti," when Puduhepa—a formidable royal spouse—wrote to Egypt demanding some as part of the dowry of her daughter. For one of the last Hittite kings, Tudhaliya IV, an order not to detain a grain ship bound for his country was "a matter of life and death." Nomadic prowlers from the hinterlands were another common hazard. People the Hittites called Kaska invaded repeatedly to grab booty or extort protection. On at least one of their raids, they robbed the royal court.

In the last few decades of the 1300s B.C.E., the Hittite state was in decline. Hatti lost southern provinces to an expanding kingdom in Upper Mesopotamia. The oaths the king demanded from his subordinates have an air of desperation: "if nobody is left to yoke the horses . . ., you must show even more support . . . . If . . . the chariot-driver jumps down from the chariot, and the valet flees the chamber, and not even a dog is left, . . . your support for your king must be all the greater." Among the last documents the court issued are complaints that subject kings were neglecting tribute or diplomatic courtesies. After 1210 B.C.E., the Hittite kingdom disappeared from the record.

INSTABILITY AND COLLAPSE IN THE AEGEAN

The Hittite story is a case study of the problems of global history in the second millennium B.C.E. It demonstrates how agrarian communities became consolidated into states, elevated into empires, and how most of them failed to survive past 1000 B.C.E. Echoes, parallels, and connected cases occurred in many regions near the experiments in civilization building that we discussed in the last chapter.

The civilization scholars call Minoan or Cretan, for instance, took shape in the second millennium on the large Mediterranean island of Crete, which lies between what are now Greece and Turkey. Nearby in the southern Peloponnese, the peninsula that forms the southern part of Greece, the civilization we call Mycenean emerged. Both have inspired Western imaginations. Europeans and Americans view Crete and Mycenae as part of their history, assuming that they can trace the civilization of classical Greece—and therefore of the Western world—to these glamorous, spendthrift cultures of 3,500 years ago. That now seems doubtful. Crete and Mycenae were almost as mysterious to the Greeks as they are to us, and almost as remote. Still, they are worth studying for their own sake and the light they cast on their times.

Crystal vase. Under the elite apartments, Cretan palaces contained workshops where craftsmen made luxuries for elite consumption and for export, such as this crystal vase, about 3,500 years old, from the palace of Zakros, and the unguents and perfumes that vessels like this contained.

Cretan Civilization

Crete is big enough to be self-sustaining, but mountains cover two-thirds of it leaving little land to cultivate amid devastating droughts and earthquakes. But wall paintings from around 2000 B.C.E., when the first palace-storehouses arose there, show fields of grain, vines, and orchards of olives, almonds, and quince. Forests of honey and venison surround gardens of flowers. The seas seem full of dolphin and octopus, under skies where partridge and brightly colored birds fly.

This lavish world was carved from a tough environment, harsh soil, and dangerous seas. And it depended on two despotic methods to control an unpredictable food supply: organized agriculture, embracing, as in Hatti, both farming and herding, and state-regulated trade. The function of the palace as storehouse was a vital part of the system. The greatest palace complex on the island, Knossos, covers more than 40,000 square feet. When it lay in ruins, visitors from Greece who saw its galleries and corridors imagined an enormous maze, built to house a monster who fed on human sacrifices. In fact, the labyrinth was an immense storage area for clay jars, 12 feet high, filled with wool, wine, cooking oil, and grain, some still in place.

Stone chests, lined with lead to protect the foodstuffs they contained, were like strongboxes in a central bank waiting to be distributed or traded. Cretan ships brought ivory and ostrich eggs from Africa and baboons from Egypt. Craft workshops inside the palaces added value to imports by spinning and weaving fine garments, delicately painting stone jars, and hammering gold and bronze into jewels and chariots. Palace records suggest a staff of 4,300 people.

Yet Knossos and buildings like it were also dwellings of an elite who lived in luxury. Squat columns with tops like fat pumpkins supported majestic staircases. Pillars were lacquered red, and the wall paintings glowed with a wonderful sky blue—scenes of feasting, gossiping, playing, and bull leaping. At Zakros, a site that was never plundered, you can see marble-veined chalices, stone storage jars, and a box of cosmetic ointment with an elegant little handle in the form of a reclining greyhound.

Lesser dwellings, grouped in towns, were tiny imitations of the palace. Many had columns, balconies, and upper-storey galleries. In the houses of more prosperous inhabitants, colorful, delicate pottery, stone vases ground into seductively sinuous shapes, and elaborately painted baths survive in large numbers. Yet at lower levels of society, there was little surplus for luxury or time for leisure. Few people lived beyond their early forties. If the purpose of the state was to recycle food, its efficiency was limited. Skeletons show that the common people lived near the margin of malnutrition.

The cities' environment was destructive. On the nearby island of Thera, which a volcanic eruption blew apart around 1500 B.C.E., ash and rock buried the lavish city of Akrotiri. Knossos and similar palaces along the coasts of Crete were all rebuilt once or twice on an increasingly generous scale, after unknown causes, possibly earthquakes, destroyed them.

Fortifications—evidence of internal warfare—began to appear. At the time of the last rebuilding of Knossos, generally dated around 1400 B.C.E., a major change in culture occurred. The archives began to be written in an early form of Greek. By this time, the fate of Crete seems to have become closely entangled with another Aegean civilization—the Mycenean.

Mycenean Civilization

The fortified cities and gold-rich royal tombs of the Mycenean civilization began to appear early in the 1500s B.C.E. States in the region already had kings who made war, hunted lions, and inhabited palace-storehouses similar to those of Crete. At Pylos, one of the largest Mycenean palaces, clay tablets list the vital and tiresome routines of numerous palace officials: levying taxes, checking that the landowner class observed its social obligations, mobilizing resources for public works, and gathering raw materials for manufacture and trade. Workshops turned out bronzeware and perfumed oils for export to Egypt and the Hittite empire. Trade reached north as far as Scandinavia (see Map 4.2), for eastern Mediterranean elites craved Baltic amber for glowing jewels.

The essential duty of the palace bureaucrats was to equip their rulers for almost constant warfare. Palaces were heavily fortified. As well as fighting each other, the kingdoms felt the threat of the barbarian hinterland, which may, in the end, have overwhelmed them. Paintings on the walls of Pylos show warriors, in the boar's-head helmets also worn on Crete and Thera, in battle with skin-clad savages.

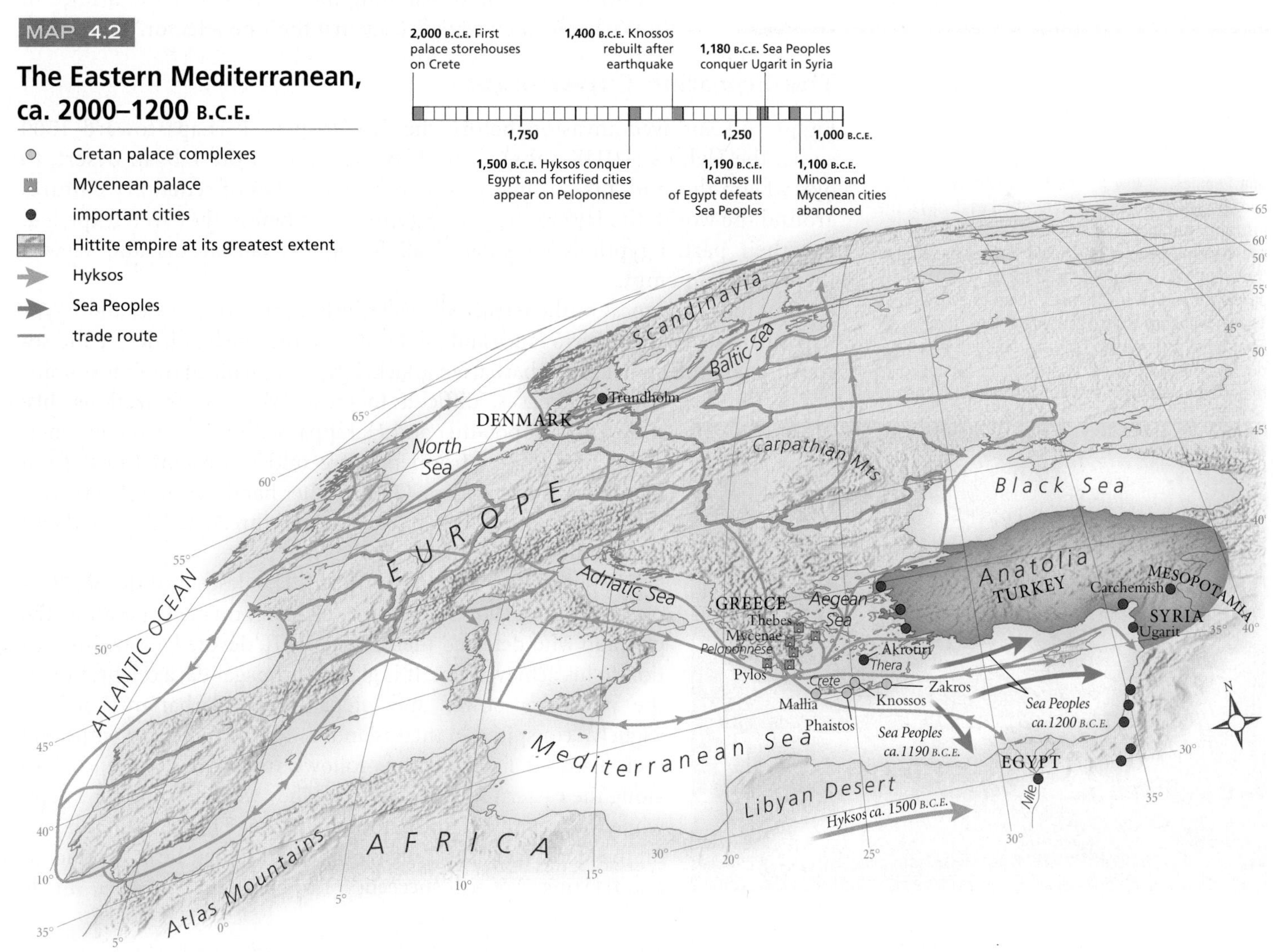

MAP 4.2 **The Eastern Mediterranean, ca. 2000–1200 B.C.E.**

Stunned by earthquakes, strained by wars, Mycenean cities followed those of Crete into abandonment by 1100 B.C.E. What is surprising is not, perhaps, that they should ultimately have perished, but that their fragile economies, sustained by elaborate and expensive methods of collecting, storing, and redistributing food, should have managed to feed the cities and support the elite culture for so long.

A GENERAL CRISIS IN THE EASTERN MEDITERRANEAN WORLD?

Although we could explain the extinction of Crete, Mycenae, and Hatti in terms of local political failures or ecological disasters, it is tempting to try to relate them to a general crisis in the eastern Mediterranean. For not only was the grandeur of the Aegean civilizations blotted out and the Hittite empire of Anatolia overwhelmed, but nearby states also reported fatal or near-fatal convulsions. The Egyptians almost succumbed to unidentified **Sea Peoples**, who exterminated numerous states and cities in the region. Meanwhile, in Upper Mesopotamia, an anguished king of Ashur prayed to Assur (AHS-soor), the city's god, "Darkness without sunshine awaits the evildoers who stretch out threatening hands to scatter the armies of Assur. Wickedly, they conspire against their benefactor."

Crete and Mycenae

(All dates are approximate)	
2000 B.C.E.	First palace-storehouses on Crete
1400 B.C.E.	Knossos (Crete) rebuilt after earthquake; early Greek language used at Knossos
1100 B.C.E.	Cretan (Minoan) and Mycenean cities abandoned

The Egyptian Experience

Egypt had survived invasion before the Sea Peoples. Perhaps toward 1500 B.C.E., the Hyksos (HIUK-sohs) arrived, sweating from the Libyan desert, to overwhelm the land. Like so many nomadic conquerors of sedentary cultures around the world, the Hyksos became Egyptianized before they were expelled. For their part, Egyptians considered all foreigners barbarians and viewed them with contempt.

But the narrowness of the fertile Nile valley was a cause of unease, and Egyptians alternated between arrogance and insecurity. On the one hand, desert and sea constituted protection against barbarian attack. Egypt was flanked by almost uninhabitable spaces, difficult to cross, whereas civilizations, like those of Mesopotamia and Harappa, with more attractive environments at their frontiers, were under constant threat from marauders and invaders. On the other hand, sea and desert were the realm of Seth, the god of chaos who threatened to overwhelm the cosmic order of life along the Nile.

Sea Peoples. "Now the northern peoples in their isles were quivering in their bodies," says the inscription that accompanies a ship-borne battle-scene of the reign of Ramses III. "They penetrated the channels of the mouths of the Nile.... They are capsized and overwhelmed where they stand.... Their weapons are scattered on the sea." Pharaohs' propaganda tended to lie or exaggerate, but the "Sea Peoples" really existed, and Egypt really escaped conquest or colonization by them.

Exposure to invasion continued. The descent of the Sea Peoples—about 1190 B.C.E.—is well documented because the pharaoh who defeated them, Ramses III, devoted a long inscription to his achievement. It is glaring propaganda, a celebration of the pharaoh's power and preparation: "Barbarians," it says vaguely, "conspired in their islands . . . . No land could withstand their arms." A list of victims follows, including Hatti and cities along the eastern Mediterranean. "They were heading for Egypt, while we prepared flame before them . . . . They laid their hands on the land as far as the edges of the Earth, their hearts confident and trusting, 'We will succeed!'" The Nile delta, however, "made like a strong wall with warships ... I was the valiant war-god, standing fast at their head. Those who came forward together on the sea, the full flame was in front of them at the river mouths, while a stockade of lances surrounded them on the shore. They were dragged in, enclosed, and prostrated on the beach, killed and made into heaps."

The Roots of Instability

The pharaoh's boasts reflect real events. Other documents confirm the existence of the Sea Peoples. For example, when the city of Ugarit in Syria fell, probably early in the twelfth century B.C.E., never to be reoccupied, messages begging for seaborne reinforcements were left unfinished. The reply from the governor of an inland trading center on the way to Hatti and Mesopotamia was typical—too little, too late: "You must remain firm. . . . Surround your towns with ramparts ..., and await the enemy with great resolution."

Ramses III, "The War Against the Sea Peoples"

The image of a general crisis brought about by barbarian invasions has appealed to Western historians influenced by a familiar episode of their own past: the decline and fall of the Roman Empire. A general crisis also fits with a popular conception of the past as a battlefield of barbarism versus civilization. However, such an idea is, at best, an oversimplification because both barbarism and civilization are relative, subjective terms.

We can best understand the intruders as a symptom of a broader phenomenon of the period: the widespread instability of populations driven by hunger and land shortages. Egyptian carvings show desperate migrants, with oxcarts full of women and children. From Mesopotamia and Anatolia comes evidence of marauders in the late thirteenth century B.C.E. But migrants probably did not cause the decline of the states they ravaged. Rather, they were among its consequences. Environmental and economic historians have scoured the evidence unsuccessfully for some sign of a deeper trauma, such as earthquakes or droughts or commercial failures, that might explain grain shortages and disrupted trade.

The causes of the crisis lay in common structural problems of the states that faltered or failed, namely, their ecological fragility and unstable, competitive politics. In this respect, the crisis was even more general, not just confined to the civilizations around the eastern Mediterranean where the Sea Peoples roamed. If we turn to trace the fate of communities elsewhere in Asia, and even to some examples in the New World, we can detect similar strains and comparable effects.

Instability in the Eastern Mediterranean

(All dates are approximate)	
1500 B.C.E.	Hyksos conquer Egypt
1200 B.C.E.	Sea Peoples attack Mesopotamia and Anatolia
1190 B.C.E.	Ramses III defeats Sea Peoples

THE EXTINCTION OF HARAPPAN CIVILIZATION

In the Indus valley, city life and intensive agriculture were in danger of collapse even when they were at their most productive. Many sites were occupied only for a few centuries. Some sites were abandoned by about 1800 B.C.E., and by 1000 B.C.E., all had dwindled to ruins. Meanwhile, in Turkmenia, on the northern flank of the Iranian plateau, relatively young but flourishing fortified settlements on the Oxus River (Amu Darya) shrank to the dimensions of villages. Some scholars believe a sudden and violent invasion was responsible, while others think of a gradual ecological disaster.

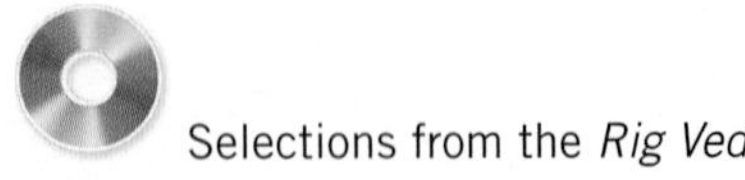
Selections from the *Rig Veda*

The Evidence of the *Rig Veda*

A collection of hymns and poems called the ***Rig Veda*** (rihg VEH-dah) inspired the invasion theory. The people who created this literature of destruction were sedentary speakers of an Indo-European language, living in what is now the Punjab, the area north of the Indus valley where northern India and Pakistan meet from about 1500 B.C.E. They were not newcomers or nomads, though strong in horses and chariots. When poets wrote down the *Rig Veda*, around 800 B.C.E., after centuries of oral transmission, it still had the power to carry hearers and readers back to a lost age of heroes.

The hymns tell of a people who wanted a world of fat and opulence, basted with butter, flowing with milk, dripping with honey. They valued boasting and drinking. Their rites of fire included burning down their enemies' dwellings. Their favorite god, Indra, was a "breaker of cities," but this was part of his generally destructive role, which included mountain smashing and serpent crushing.

Some of the cities seem already to have been in ruins when the *Rig Veda* poets beheld them. Excavators who claimed that they could read traumatic events at Mohenjodaro, in the bones of massacre victims and scorch marks on the walls, seem to have been wrong. Few of the supposed massacre victims have any wounds. Instead of a single violent event, the more likely explanation speaks of a gradual decline—a climacteric, a point at which Harappan civilization collapsed, and its cities were abandoned.

The Environment of Stress

The climate was getting drier in the Indus valley. The Saraswati River disappeared into the advancing Thar Desert. Yet not even the loss of a river adequately explains the abandonment of the cities. The Indus River is still disgorging its wonderful silt, year by year, over vast, shining fields, which would have been sufficient to maintain the urban populations. Presumably, something happened to the food supply that was connected with the drying climate or human mismanagement of environmental resources—the cattle and hinterland products that supplemented the wheat and barley of the fields.

In addition—or instead—the inhabitants apparently fled from some plague more deadly than the malaria that anthropologists have detected in buried bones. In an environment where irrigation demands standing water, mosquitos can breed. Malaria is inevitable. The people left, "expelled by the fire-god," as the *Rig Veda* says, and "migrated to a new land." This is probably an exaggeration. People stayed on or squatted in the decaying cities, inhabiting the ruins for generations. But the fall of Harappan civilization remains the most dramatic case of large-scale failure in the second millennium B.C.E. In broad terms, Harappa suffered essentially the same fate as the Hittite and eastern Mediterranean civilizations: The food distribution system outran the resource base. And when networks of power began to break down, invaders broke in.

The Collapse of Harappan Civilization

(All dates are approximate)	
1800 B.C.E.	Some Harappan cities abandoned
1000 B.C.E.	All Harappan cities in ruins
800 B.C.E.	*Rig Veda* written down

CONFLICT ON THE YELLOW RIVER

China's problems toward the end of the second millennium B.C.E. were part of what looks increasingly like a global pattern, yet different in some ways from those of Egypt or Harappa. China suffered no large-scale population loss, no wholesale abandonment of regions, no wreck of cities.

The basis of the Shang (shawng) state had always been shaky. War, rituals, and oracles are all gamblers' means of power, vulnerable to the lurches of luck. Manipulating the weather, the rains, the harvests, for instance, was part of the king's job, but in reality, of course, it was not one he could accomplish. Failure was built into his job description. It was a common problem for monarchs of the time, exposing pharaohs to blame for natural disasters, driving Hittite kings to depend on soothsayers.

The late Shang state was shrinking. Beginning about 1100 B.C.E., the names of subject, tribute-paying, and allied states gradually vanished from the oracle bones. The king's hunting grounds grew smaller. The king became the sole diviner and commander, as the numbers at his disposal fell. Former allies became enemies.

Meanwhile, just as Mesopotamian culture had been exported to Anatolia and Cretan ways of life to Mycenae, so Shang was exported beyond the Shang state. New chiefdoms were developing in less favorable environments under the influence of trade. As far away as northern Vietnam and Thailand, bronze-making techniques similar to those of China appeared at the courts of chiefs. More ominously and closer to home, right on the Shang border, a state arose in imitation and, increasingly, in rivalry: Zhou (jaow).

Bronze drum. This intricate geometric design on the face of a Vietnamese drum shows a sunburst at the center. Rulers often displayed these impressive bronze drums as emblems of their royal status.

The Rise of Zhou

The earliest Zhou sites—of the 1100s B.C.E.—are burials in the mountains of western China. This was probably not the Zhou heartland but the area they had migrated to from grazing country farther to the north. Their own legends recalled time spent "living among the barbarians." The Zhou were highland herders, an upland, upriver menace to the Shang, just as Akkad was to Sumer in Mesopotamia.

According to chronicle evidence, Shang-style turtleshell oracles had inspired the Zhou to conquest, and later Zhou rulers upheld that tradition. Chronicles composed in the third century B.C.E. tell the same story as texts hundreds of years older. If they can be believed, the Zhou "captured"—as they put it—the Shang state in a single battle in 1045 B.C.E. at Muye. They annexed it as a kind of colony and established garrisons all along the lower Yellow River to the coast. Archaeological evidence shows that they shifted the center of the empire north, to the hilly region west of where the Yellow River turns toward the sea.

The Zhou Political System

Inscriptions on bronze loving cups are the only contemporary written sources to survive from the period of Zhou supremacy, which lasted from about 1000 through the 700s B.C.E. Those who could afford them—and, of course, few could—recorded their inheritances, their legacies to their families, and, above all, the key moments in their family's relationships with the imperial house. Documenting the family's achievements was related to a belief in inherited virtue. Indeed, as an adviser to an early Zhou king put it: "there is nothing—neither wisdom nor power—that is not present at a son's birth."

The inscriptions tend to combine self-praise and self-justification. Shortly before 1000 B.C.E., for instance, a king's nephew recorded how he had been made ruler of the colony of Xing (shing). He tells us first of the royal decision to make the appointment. Then we get the circumstances: The nominee performs a rite of gratitude. He accompanies the king on a lake hunt in a ship with a red banner. The

Zhou China

1100 B.C.E.	Shang state in decline
1045 B.C.E.	Zhou overthrow Shang at Battle of Muye
1045–700 B.C.E.	Zhou supremacy

king bags a goose and gives the nominee a black axe. "In the evening, the lord was awarded many axe-men as vassals, two hundred families, and was offered the use of a chariot-team in which the king rode; bronze harness-trappings, an overcoat, a robe, cloth and slippers." The gifts apparently mattered a great deal because all such inscriptions mention them. The special clothes conferred status. The newly ennobled lord then commissioned a commemorative cup, which bore the inscription "With sons and grandsons, may he use it for ever to confer virtue, invoke blessings, and recall the order to colonize Xing."

The Zhou did not continue all Shang traditions. Despite pious declarations, they gradually abandoned divination by bone oracles. Though they extended China's cultural frontiers before their own state dissolved in its turn in the eighth century B.C.E., their leaders were not universal emperors in the mold of the Shang, ruling all the world that mattered to them. Rival states multiplied around them, and their own power tended to erode and fragment. But they originated the ideology of the **mandate of heaven**, which "raised up our little land of Zhou." All subsequent Chinese states inherited the same notion that the emperor was divinely chosen. Furthermore, all subsequent changes in rule appealed to the same claim that heaven transferred power from a decayed dynasty to one of greater virtue. The Zhou created an effective myth of the unity and continuity that dominated how the Chinese came to think of themselves. This myth is now the part of the standard Western view of China, too, as a monolithic state—massive, uniform, durable, and hungry for world dominance.

Cerro Sechín. As urban life and monumental building spread upland from the river valleys of coastal central Peru in the second millennium B.C.E., warfare and rites of human sacrifice spread with them. Walls at Cerro Sechín are carved with scenes of warriors overseeing the severed heads and cleft bodies of their victims.

STATE-BUILDING IN THE AMERICAS

On a relatively smaller scale and over a longer time span, communities in parts of the New World experimented with some of the same processes of state-building and civilization that we have seen in the Old World. Some peoples of the Andean region and in Mesoamerica were particularly ambitious in modifying their environments.

Andean Examples

About 3,500 years ago, experiments in civilization spread from alluvial areas on the Peruvian coast to less obviously favorable environments (see Map 4.3). In Cerro Sechín (SER-roh se-CHIN), only about 300 feet higher than the Supe (SOO-peh) valley in north-central Peru (see Chapter 2), an astounding settlement existed in about 1500 B.C.E. on a site of about 12 acres. On a stone platform 170 feet square, hundreds of carved warrior images slash their victims in two, exposing their entrails, or slicing off their heads in a rite of victory. By about 1200 B.C.E., nearby Sechín Alto (se-CHIN al-toh) was one of the world's great ceremonial complexes, with gigantic mounds erected to perform rituals, and monumental buildings arrayed along two boulevard-like spaces, each more than a mile long, at its heart. The biggest mound covers 30 square miles and is almost 140 feet tall.

These places, and others like them, suggest new experiments to manage the environment and coordinate food production in numerous small, hilly areas, each irrigated by a gravity canal and organized from a central seat of power. The violent carvings of Cerro Sechín show the price paid in blood to defend or enlarge them.

In the same period—in the last three centuries or so of the second millennium B.C.E.—farther up the coast, new settlements took shape around the Cupisnique (KOO-pees-nee-keh) gorge. Though the environment was similar, the physical remains suggest a different culture and different politics. Huaca de los Reyes (WA-kah deh las RAY-ess), for instance, had dozens of stucco-fronted buildings and colonnades of fat pillars, each up to 6.5 feet thick, guarded by huge, saber-toothed heads in clay. At Pampa de Caña Cruz (PAM-pah deh KAN-yah krooss), a gigantic mosaic, 170 feet long, represented a similar head, embedded in the earth, so that a viewer could only appreciate its shape from a height humans could not reach—but their gods, perhaps, could. These regions traded with nearby highlands, where building on a monumental scale followed soon afterward at sites that exhibit extraordinary cultural diversity.

Most Andean experiments in civilization were short-lived. With modest technologies, they struggled to survive in unstable environments. At irregular intervals, usually once or twice a decade, **El Niño** (el NEEN-yo)—the periodic reversal of the normal flow of Pacific currents—drenched the region in torrential rain and killed or diverted the ocean fish. Population levels outgrew food supplies, or overexploitation impoverished the soil, or envious neighbors unleashed wars.

The city of Chavín de Huantar (cha-VEEN deh wan-tar) began to emerge about 1000 B.C.E., over 3,300 feet up in the Andes. Chavín demonstrates how people could achieve prosperity and magnificence at middling altitudes. Essential prerequisites were command of trade routes and the availability of diverse foodstuffs in the microclimates of mountain environments. Gold-working technology, already at least 1,000 years old in the highlands, provided objects for luxury trade. Forest products from east of the mountains were also in demand in the lowland cities. Chavín was in the middle of these trades.

Even in the impressive world of early Andean civilizations, the sheer workmanship of Chavín stood out and attracted imitators in architecture, water management, engineering, metalwork, and ceramics. Today the ceremonial spaces, storehouses, and barrack-like dwellings inspire speculation about how this society was organized and ruled. The best clues are probably in the sculptures of humans half-transformed into jaguars, often with traces of drug-induced ecstasy. Nausea and bulging eyes contort their faces; their nostrils stream with mucus. Here is the evidence of a society ruled by shamans.

Developments in Mesoamerica

States developed in the Andes the same way they developed in the Old World—as responses to the stimulation of trade. Both followed the model described in Chapter 3: beginning with intensified agriculture, leading to population density, economic specialization, growing markets, and trade. In the Andes, the model emerged from the soil of Aspero in the Supe valley and climaxed in Chavín. In Mesoamerica, however, stunning experiments in civilization began, as far as we know, without the benefit of trade.

The culture we call Olmec (OL-mek) arose in southern Mexico in the second millennium B.C.E. (see Map 4.3). We can picture the Olmecs with help from portraits they left: heads, carved from stones and columns of basalt, each of up to 40 tons, toted or dragged over distances of up to 100 miles. Some have jaguarlike masks or almond eyes, parted lips, and sneers of cold command. Perhaps they, too, are shaman-rulers with the power of divine self-transformation, though they are never as thoroughly transformed as the coca-crazed shamans of Chavín.

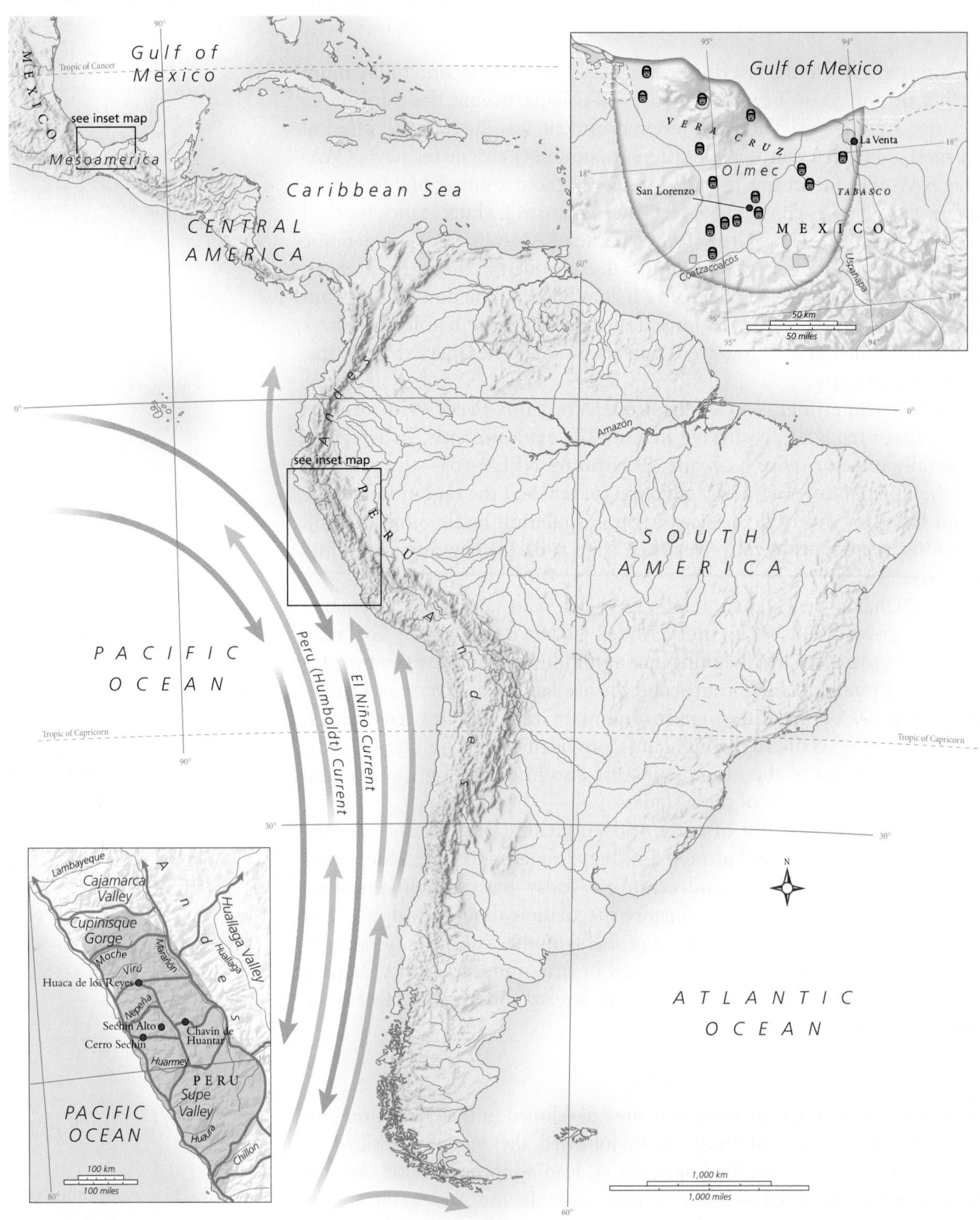

MAP 4.3

State-Building in the Americas, ca. 1500–1000 B.C.E

- Olmec cultural area
- Chavín cultural area
- normal flow of Pacific Ocean current
- El Niño current
- PERU modern-day country
- *TABASCO* state province
- Olmec sculptural site
- PERU modern-day country
- *TABASCO* state province

The swamps of southern Mexico had supported agriculture for at least 1,000 years before the first monumental art and ceremonial centers in the Olmec tradition appeared. The Olmec chose settlement sites where they could exploit a variety of environments. Marshy lakes, full of aquatic prey, were alluring to settlers. They dredged mounds for farming from the swamp and, between the mounds, coaxed canals into a grid for raising fish, turtles, and perhaps caymans.

The agricultural mounds became the model for ceremonial platforms. The earliest known ceremonial center was built around 1200 B.C.E. Two large centers soon followed, at La Venta, deep among the mangrove swamps, and at nearby San Lorenzo. By about 1000 B.C.E., San Lorenzo had substantial reservoirs and drainage systems, integrated into a plan of causeways, plazas, platforms, and mounds. At La Venta, there are early examples of the ritual spaces that fitted into these gridworks. The center was built with stones toted and rolled from more than 60 miles away. The focus of La Venta is a mound over 100 feet tall—evidently a setting for the most important rituals. One of the ceremonial courts has a mosaic pavement that resembles a jaguar mask that its creators appear to have deliberately buried. Similar buried offerings were placed under other buildings, perhaps the way some Christians bury relics from saints in the foundations and altars of churches. Although the stone buildings—those that survive—were designed for ritual life, these were cities: dense settlements clustered around the ceremonial centers.

Shaman. Masks, music, and dance often play roles in bringing about shamanic ecstasy. This ceramic flute-player from Chavín de Huántar in the Peruvian Andes, of the mid–first millennium B.C.E., wears a jaguar mask, with the bulging eyes and dilated nostrils typical of a visionary trance.

Two unsolved problems exist in connection with the Olmecs: How and why did intensive food production begin? And how and why did ambitious attempts to modify the environment begin? Monumental building requires ample food to support manpower and generate energy. Many scholars still believe that the Olmecs could have produced sufficient food by slashing forest clearings, setting fire to the stumps, and planting seeds directly in the ash. But as far as we know, no society using such methods ever prospered the way the Olmecs did. It is more likely that the transition to city-building began when the Olmecs started farming high-yielding varieties of maize. With beans and squash, maize provided complete nourishment. The three plants together were so important to Olmec life that they depicted them on gods' and chieftains' headgear.

It looks as if a determined, visionary leadership energized by shamanism drove Olmec civilization forward. An exquisite scene of what seems to be a ceremony in progress suggests the seemingly pivotal role of shamanism. Archaeologists found it buried in sand, perhaps as an offering. Carved figures with misshapen heads, suggesting that the skull was deliberately deformed, stand in a rough circle of upright stone slabs. They wear nothing but loincloths and ear ornaments. Their mouths are open, their postures relaxed. Similar figures include a were-jaguar—half jaguar, half human. Others carry torches on phallic staffs. Or else they kneel or sit in a restless posture, as if ready to be transformed from shaman into jaguar, as other works depict. For the rites these figures suggest, the Olmecs built stepped platforms—forerunners, perhaps, or maybe just early examples of the angular mounds and pyramids typical of later New World civilizations.

Rulers were buried in the sort of disguises they wore for ritual performances. They became fantastic creatures with a cayman's body and nose, a jaguar's eyes and mouth, and feathered eyebrows that evoke raised hands. They lay in pillared chambers with bloodletting tools of jade or stingray spine beside them. We can still see their images carved on thrones of basalt, where they sat to shed blood—their own and their captives'.

State-Building in the Americas

(All dates are approximate)	
1500 B.C.E.	Cerro Sechín (Peru)
1200 B.C.E.	Sechín Alto (Peru)
1000 B.C.E.	Chavín civilization emerges
1000 B.C.E.	Olmec cities of San Lorenzo and La Venta flourishing
500 B.C.E.	End of Chavín civilization
300 B.C.E.	Olmec civilization in decline

Believers in the diffusionist theory of civilization have often hailed the Olmecs as the mother civilization of the Americas. Diffusionism states, in brief, that civilization is such an extraordinary achievement that only a few gifted peoples created it. It then diffused—or spread by example and instruction—to less inventive peoples. This theory is almost certainly false. Rather, several civilizations probably emerged independently in widely separated places.

Nevertheless, Olmec influence seems to have spread widely in Mesoamerica and perhaps beyond. Numerous aspects of Olmec life became characteristic of later New World civilizations: mound building; a tendency to seek balance and symmetry in art and architecture; ambitious urban planning around angular temples and plazas; specialized elites, including chieftains commemorated in monumental art; rites of rulership involving bloodletting and human sacrifice; a religion rooted in shamanism with bloody rites of sacrifice and ecstatic performances by kings and priests; agriculture based on maize, beans, and squash.

ASSESSING THE DAMAGE

By 1000 B.C.E., failed states littered the landscape. Some of the world's spectacular empires broke up. Mysterious catastrophes cut short the histories of complex cultures. Food distribution centers controlled from palace labyrinths shut down. Trade was disrupted. Settlements and monuments were abandoned. Harappan civilization vanished, as did Crete's and Mycenae's. Hatti was obliterated.

In Mesopotamia, Akkadian armies spread their language the length of the Tigris and Euphrates. Sumerian speech dwindled from everyday use to become—like Latin in the Western world today—a purely ceremonial language. Sumer's cities crumbled. Their memory was preserved chiefly in the titles that invaders from uplands and deserts used to dignify the rule of their own kings. Ur declined to a cult center and tourist resort.

Something similar occurred in China, which succumbed to conquerors from neighboring uplands. The civilization survived, but its center of gravity was shunted upriver. As we shall see in Chapter 5, when numerous competing kingdoms in turn succeeded Zhou in the 700s B.C.E., continuity was not broken. Society and everyday life remained essentially intact. This was a pattern often repeated in Chinese history. In the New World, meanwhile, Mesoamerica and the Andean region undertook environmentally ambitious initiatives, but none showed much staying power.

The Survival of Egypt

Though there were more losers than winners after the climacteric of the second millennium B.C.E., the outstanding case of endurance was Egypt. Invasions in the late second millennium failed, and the basic productivity of the agrarian system remained intact. But even Egypt was reined in.

Nubia (NOO-bee-ah)—the region upriver of the cataracts, in what is now Sudan—disappeared from Egyptian records by 1000 B.C.E. This was a major reversal because Egypt had constantly tried to extend its empire along the Nile. The abundant ivory, the mercenaries that Nubia supplied, and the river trade that made gold in Egypt "as plentiful as the sand of the sea" had long drawn Egypt southward. Egypt originally became interested in Central Africa when the explorer Harkhuf made three expeditions around 2500 B.C.E. He brought back "incense, ebony, scented oil, tusks, arms, and all fine produce." Harkhuf's captive pygmy, "who dances divine dances from the land of the spirits..." fascinated the boy pharaoh Pepi. Writing to the explorer, the pharaoh commanded the utmost care in guarding him: "inspect him ten times a night. For my Majesty wishes to see this pygmy more than all the products of Sinai and Punt."

Contact and commerce led to the formation of a Nubian state in imitation of Egypt, beyond the second cataract. From about 2000 B.C.E. on, Egypt tried to influence or control this state, sometimes by erecting fortifications, sometimes by invasion, sometimes by pushing its own frontier southward. Pharoahs' inscriptions piled curses on the Nubians as the latter became more difficult to handle. Eventually, around 1500 B.C.E., Pharoah Tut-mose I conquered the kingdom of Kush and made Nubia a colonial territory. Egypt studded Nubia with forts and temples. The last temple, to Ramses II, at Abu Simbel, was the most crushingly monumental that Egyptians had built for 2,000 years. It has remained a symbol of power ever since. But during the reigns of his immediate successors, disastrously little flooding of the Nile, on which the success of Egyptian agriculture depended, was recorded. This was the era, toward the end of the thirteenth century B.C.E., when Egypt came closer to collapse than at any time since the invasion of the Hyksos. To abandon Nubia in the late second millennium B.C.E., after investing so much effort and emotion, shows how severe Egypt's need for retrenchment must have been.

MAKING CONNECTIONS

INSTABILITY: CONDITIONS LEADING TO DOWNFALL OF KINGDOMS 2000–1000 B.C.E.

KINGDOM AND REGION →	PRIMARY PROBLEMS →	CONSEQUENCES
Egypt	Exposure to invasion; limited areas of soil fertility; occasional grain shortages	Famines, land shortages, and sizable migrations; invasion by Sea Peoples exploits instability
Hatti—Northern Anatolia	Growth overlaps with frontiers of Egypt, Mesopotamia; overextension of power; disruption of trade through warfare; vulnerability to famine and disease in early stages of agriculture	Nomadic prowlers attack during weak periods, conquered subjects revolt
Crete—Aegean Sea	Uneven organization of labor; distribution of food; competition with other city-states; destruction of environment; little fertile soil; dangerous seas	Social inequality, internal warfare combine with nearby volcanic activity and earthquakes to force abandonment of cities, palaces
Mycenean Civilization	Barbarian raiders from north attracted by wealth of palaces; earthquakes; social inequality; internal warfare	Social inequality, internal warfare combine with nearby volcanic activity and earthquakes to force abandonment of cities, palaces
Harappa and Mohenjodaro: Indus River	Gradually drying climate; evidence of earthquakes, shifting riverbeds, disease; overuse of environmental resources	Gradual collapse of food distribution system; political control; cities and towns abandoned
Shang and Zhou Dynasties—China	Overdependence of Shang leaders on rituals, oracles, war, conquest to manipulate harvest, weather	Collapse of Shang rule; rise of Zhou state; shifting center of empire; lessened dependence on divination by bone oracles

CHRONOLOGY

(All dates are approximate)

2500 B.C.E.	Egypt expands southward
2000–1000 B.C.E.	Climacteric: critical and accelerating change; state-building in Hatti, Crete, Egypt; Shang China, the Andes, and Mesoamerica
2000 B.C.E.	Nubian state formed, emulating Egypt, Cretan civilization emerges
1800–1500 B.C.E.	Hittite kingdom flourishes
1500 B.C.E.	Mycenean civilization appears; Cerro Sechín flourishes in Andes (Peru)
1210 B.C.E.	Last record of Hatti
1190 B.C.E.	Ramses III defeats Sea Peoples
1100 B.C.E.	Cretan and Mycenean cities abandoned; Shang state in decline; Harappan cities in ruin; Chavín civilization emerges; Nubia disappears from Egyptian records
300 B.C.E.	Olmec civilization declines (Mesoamerica)

IN PERSPECTIVE: The Fatal Flaws

Paradox racked the most ambitious states of the era. They were committed to population growth, which imposed unsustainable goals of expansion on overextended frontiers. They were founded on intensified methods of production, which drove them to overexploit the environment. They concentrated large populations, making them more vulnerable to famine and disease. Enemies surrounded them, jealous of their wealth and resentful of their power. They created more enemies by inspiring rivals and imitators in their hinterlands. When their food distribution programs failed, disruptive migrations resulted. Their rulers condemned themselves to failure and rebellion because they lived a lie, manipulating unreliable oracles, negotiating with heedless gods, bargaining with hostile nature. If Harappan society was unsustainable in the silt-rich Indus valley, how realistic were the Hittite or Olmec or Cretan or Andean ambitions in much less favorable environments?

In some cases, the traditions that failed or faltered during the great climacteric reemerged elsewhere. In others, dark ages of varying duration—periods of diminished achievement, about which we have little evidence—followed the climacteric. Chavín survived for about 500 years, until about 500 B.C.E., but during the following several centuries, people in the Andes attempted nothing on a comparable scale. After the Olmec stopped building on a large scale, probably in the 300s B.C.E., they had no successors for many centuries. Squatters occupied the cities of Harappa and Mycenae. The literacy of these civilizations was lost, their writing systems forgotten. When writing resumed in these regions centuries later, the inhabitants had to invent new alphabets.

Our next problem is to penetrate that darkness and trace the displaced traditions from failed states. We want to examine the context that would produce a different world after the climacteric, post-1000 B.C.E. In the last millennium B.C.E.—thanks to an extraordinary blossoming of intellectual and spiritual life—the world was literally rethought.

PROBLEMS AND PARALLELS

1. How did the features that characterized the great river valley civilizations begin to emerge in other environments in the second millennium B.C.E.?
2. Why did the number of complex states rapidly increase during this period?
3. Why did the Hittite kingdom fall? Why did Cretan and Mycenean civilization collapse and disappear in this period, while Egypt survived?
4. What factors might account for the long-term survival of Chinese civilization and the collapse and disappearance of Harrapan/Indus valley civilization?
5. Why is the period between 2000 and 1000 B.C.E. a climacteric in global history?

DOCUMENTS IN GLOBAL HISTORY

- Hittite Land Deed
- Hittite Soldiers' Oath
- Ramses III, "The War Against the Sea Peoples"
- Selections from the *Rig Veda*

Please see the Primary Source DVD for additional sources related to this chapter.

READ ON

T. Bryce, *Life and Society in the Hittite World* (2002) is incomparable in its field. To understand the nature and importance of trade, the books of M. W. Helms, *Ulysses' Sail* (1988) and *Craft and the Kingly Ideal* (1993) are of great help. M. Heltzer, *Goods, Prices and the Organisation of Trade in Ugarit* (1978), and E. H. Cline, *Sailing the Wine-Dark Sea* (1994) are valuable studies of particular trade routes.

The best book on Crete is now O. Dickinson, *The Aegean Bronze Age* (1994). E. D. Oren, ed., *The Sea Peoples and Their World* (2000) is an important collection.

Leading works on the so-called Indo-Europeans are J. P. Mallory, *In Search of the Indo-Europeans* (1989), and C. Renfrew, *Archaeology and Language* (1987). The books listed for Chapter 3 by Shaghnessy, Posspehl, and Bulger remain important for this chapter.

Especially useful on the Olmecs are M. D. Coe, ed., *The Olmec World: Ritual and Rulership* (1996), and E. Benson and B. de la Fuente, eds., *Olmec Art of Ancient Mexico* (1996). D. O'Connor, *Ancient Nubia* (1994) is a good introductory work.

CHAPTER 5

Rebuilding the World: Recoveries, New Initiatives, and Their Limits

The elephant wall of Anuradhapura, the city in northern Sri Lanka that became a courtly center in the second half of the first millennium B.C.E., when kings endowed it with great irrigation cisterns, monumental trees, and sites of sacrifice, pilgrimage, and monastic life. The elephants guard a stupa—a dome-like spiritual dwelling place for the Buddha—built in the second century B.C.E. (See pp. 111–112.)

IN THIS CHAPTER

TRADE AND RECOVERY IN THE MIDDLE EAST
The Phoenician Experience
The Assyrian Empire
The Babylonian Revival

GREECE AND BEYOND
The Greek Environment
Greek Colonialism
Early Greek Society
The Spread of State-Building and City-Building

EMPIRES AND RECOVERY IN CHINA AND SOUTH ASIA
The Zhou Decline
South Asia: Relocated Centers of Culture
The Ganges Valley
Building Anew in Sri Lanka

THE FRUSTRATIONS OF ISOLATION
Developments in North America
New Initiatives in Africa

IN PERSPECTIVE: The Framework of Recovery

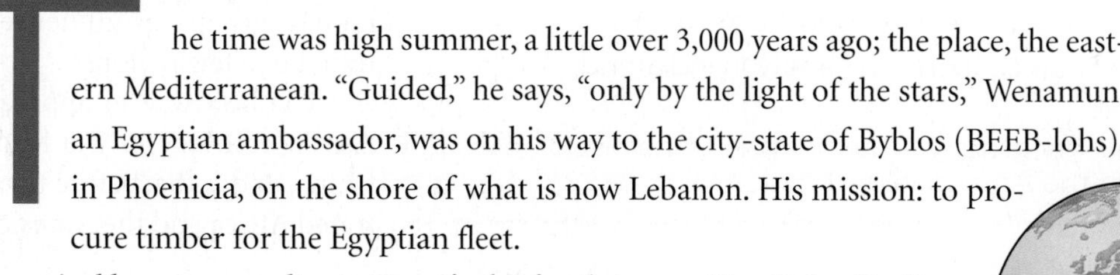

The time was high summer, a little over 3,000 years ago; the place, the eastern Mediterranean. "Guided," he says, "only by the light of the stars," Wenamun, an Egyptian ambassador, was on his way to the city-state of Byblos (BEEB-lohs), in Phoenicia, on the shore of what is now Lebanon. His mission: to procure timber for the Egyptian fleet.

PHOENICIA

On arrival he set up an altar to Egypt's chief god, Amun. King Zeker Baal kept Wenamun waiting for weeks. Then the king suddenly summoned the ambassador in the dead of night. Presumably, the summons was a negotiating ploy. Wenamun, however, reported it as a change of heart. The ambassador recorded the dialogue that followed—doctored, no doubt, but still revealing.

"I have come," Wenamun began, "for timber for the great and august ship of Amun, king of gods." He recalled that Zeker Baal's father and grandfather had sent wood to Egypt, but the king resented the implication that it was tribute.

"They did so by way of trade," he replied. "When you pay me I shall do it… I call loudly to the Lebanon which makes the heavens open, and the wood is delivered to the sea."

"Wrong!" retorted Wenamun. "There is no ship which does not belong to Amun. His also is the sea. And his is the Lebanon of which you say, 'It is mine.' Do his bidding and you will have life and health."

In the end, the Egyptians had to pay Zeker Baal's price: four jars of gold and five of silver, unspecified amounts of linen, 500 ox hides, 500 ropes, 20 sacks of lentils, 20 baskets of fish. "And they felled the timber," Wenamun wrote, "and they spent the winter at it and hauled it to the sea."

• • • • •

The Egyptian ambassador's story opens a window into a world recovering from the crises and climacteric of the late second millennium B.C.E. The confidence of a small city-state like Byblos in the face of demands from a giant like Egypt seems astounding. But increasing trade and cultural exchange inspired it.

The question for this chapter, then, is what happened between 1000 and 500 B.C.E. that led some places to recover from the failures of the second millennium? The investigation will equip us to approach a far bigger problem in the next part of this book: How do we explain the vitality and influence—the intellectual and spiritual achievements—of some groups and centers in Eurasia in the period that followed?

FOCUS questions

- WHY WAS the Phoenician alphabet so significant in world history?
- WHAT WERE the political and economic foundations of the Assyrian Empire?
- WHAT ROLES did colonization and trade play in Greek and Phoenician cultures?
- WHY DID the Zhou state decline in China?
- HOW WAS civilization built anew in India and Sri Lanka?
- HOW DID geography influence the transmission of culture in the Americas and Africa?

Equally important is the problem of why new initiatives were so rare, late, and slow beyond Eurasia. In particular, why did promising states in the Americas and sub-Saharan Africa wither instead of thrive in this period? Why, for example, was Greece's dark age after the fall of Mycenae so much shorter than the dark ages of the Andes after Chavín or Mesoamerica after the Olmecs? Why did big states and monumental cities appear later in sub-Saharan Africa than in China, India, or the Mediterranean? And why did so much historical initiative—the power of some human groups to influence others—become so concentrated in a few regions?

The best way to approach these questions is to look first at recovery in the Middle East, the Mediterranean, China, and India, before turning to see how isolation frustrated Africa and the Americas.

TRADE AND RECOVERY IN THE MIDDLE EAST

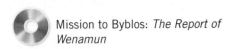

Mission to Byblos: *The Report of Wenamun*

Byblos was one of the largest city-states of Phoenicia, a maritime culture along the eastern coast of the Mediterranean (see Map 5.1), from where, beginning early in the first millennium B.C.E., traders and colonists spread. Meanwhile, however, new, land-based empires arose that grew rich as much by conquest as by trade, threatening and eventually engulfing Phoenicia.

The Phoenician Experience

In front of them, Phoenicians had waters accessible through excellent harbors. Behind them, they had forests for shipbuilding and timber exports. What they did not have was much land to farm. They turned, therefore, to industry and trade.

Their wealth was the stuff of other peoples' stories. Phoenician cities stood, as the biblical prophet Ezekiel said of Tyre, "at the entry of the sea . . . a trader for the people of many isles. Their ports ring with precious metals, exude aromas of spice, and swirl with dye-steeped textiles. But the basis of everything is shipbuilding: the timbers from Lebanon, the oak for the oars, benches of ivory, sails of Egyptian linen, and mariners and builders from the Phoenician coast."

This was a period when the only way to trade with a region that did not have its own merchant class was to colonize it. According to legend, the Phoenicians' earliest colonies were at Carthage in what is now Tunisia and at Cadiz in Spain by around 800 B.C.E., followed by Malta and Sardinia. From these bases, Phoenician navigators broke into the Atlantic and established a trading post as far away as Mogador on the northwest coast of Africa.

Where they built cities, the Phoenicians were agents of cultural exchange, borrowing from all over the eastern Mediterranean, while exporting some of their religious cults. In Carthage, newborn babies rolled from the arms of statues of their gods, Baal and Tanit, as sacrifices into sacred flames.

The colonies remained, even when the cities of Phoenicia fell to foreign raiders or rulers. In 868 B.C.E. the king of Assur (see Chapter 4) "washed his weapons in the Great Syrian Sea," and his successors continued to grab tribute from Phoenicia for over a century. Egypt-

Phoenicia

(All dates are approximate)	
1000 B.C.E.	Phoenicia trades and colonizes in the Mediterranean
800 B.C.E.	Carthage founded as a Phoenician colony
700 B.C.E.	Malta and Sardinia colonized
500 B.C.E.	Carthage seeks control of Mediterranean trade
146 B.C.E.	Carthage destroyed by the Romans

ian, Babylonian, and Persian rulers preyed on the region. By 500 B.C.E., Carthage aspired to be an imperial capital of its own, fighting to control Mediterranean trade—first with Greek cities, then with Rome. It had a fine harbor in the center of the Mediterranean and a fertile hinterland of flocks, wheat fields, vineyards, and irrigated gardens.

A Roman poet later recalled Phoenicians as "a clever people who prospered in war and peace. They excelled in writing and literature and the other arts, as well as in seamanship, naval warfare, and ruling over an empire." Their records might illuminate for us the dark age of lack of sources after the fall of Mycenae, but the Romans, who defeated Carthage in three wars and destroyed the city in 146 B.C.E., were too thorough in victory. The Phoenician language and almost the whole of Phoenician literature disappeared. Only fragments of stone inscriptions survive, along with the Phoenicians' unique gift to the world, the alphabet.

All writing systems, as far as we know, except those indebted to the Phoenician, are based on syllables, logograms, or some combination of both. In the former, each sign represents a syllable. In the second type, a sign stands for an entire word. Both methods require the user to know a large number of signs—dozens in the syllabic system and hundreds or even thousands in a logographic one. Systems in the Phoenician tradition, on the other hand, suit societies with wide literacy and cheap writing materials. The Greeks seem to have gotten the idea of an alphabet and some of the symbols from the Phoenicians. From there, the idea spread to the Romans and other European peoples who, in turn, transmitted it around the world.

The Assyrian Empire

By 1000 B.C.E., Hatti's extinction was Assur's opportunity (see Chapter 4). Kings of Assur, who were already wide-scale raiders, forged a state along the Upper Tigris. By about 750 B.C.E., Assyrian rulers were contending for more than regional power, calling themselves "Kings of the World" (see Map 5.1).

In northern Mesopotamia, the Assyrian kings replaced local rulers with governors, who ran provinces too small to mount successful rebellions. Beyond this core, Assyrian supremacy was looser, adjusted to local feeling and custom. In Babylon, for instance, the king of Assyria performed the rite of allegiance to the city god; in Gaza, near the border between modern Israel and Egypt, he was enrolled among local divinities. Elsewhere, he destroyed temples and statues of gods to demonstrate his power and then restored them to show his generosity.

An ideology of domination is obvious in the remnants of Assyria that archaeologists have dug up: in the crushing weight of palace gates, the gigantic scale of the royal beasts that guard them, and the monumental sculptures, with their endless portrayals of battles and tribute bearers. The king was not divine but heroic and intimate with gods. In portraits he kills bulls and lions and consults heaven, while winged spirits attend him. He literally entertained gods in his bedchamber. Attendants brought the statues of gods in and offered them food and libations.

Inscriptions from the reign of King Ashurbanipal (ah-shoor-BAH-nee-pahl) in the mid–seventh century B.C.E. capture the character of the Assyrian state. He was probably the most self-celebrated monarch in Mesopotamian history. While never dethroning war as the Assyrians' priority, he made a cult of literacy, looting the learning of Babylon for his library at Nineveh (NIH-neh-veh). He was proud of the canals dug and the wine pressed in his reign, the 120 layers of bricks in the foundations of his palace, the offerings he made of first fruits to "the temples of my land." A portrait survives of him picnicking with his wife under a vine and the dangling head of a slain enemy.

Winged bull. "May the guardian bull, the guardian genius, who protects the strength of my throne, always preserve my name in joy and honor until his feet move themselves from this place." An inscription left by King Esarhaddon, son of Sennacherib, explains the function of the winged bulls—usually carved with the portrait heads of kings—that guarded Assyrian gates and throne rooms.
Human-headed winged bull and winged lion (lamassu). Alabaster (gypsum); Gateway support from the Palace of Ashurnasirpal II (ruled 883–859 B.C.E.). Limestone. H: 10' 3/1/2". L: 9' 1". W: 2" 1/2". The Metropolitan Museum of Art, Gift of John D. Rockefeller, Jr., 1932. (32.143.2) Photography © 1981 The Metropolitan Museum of Art.

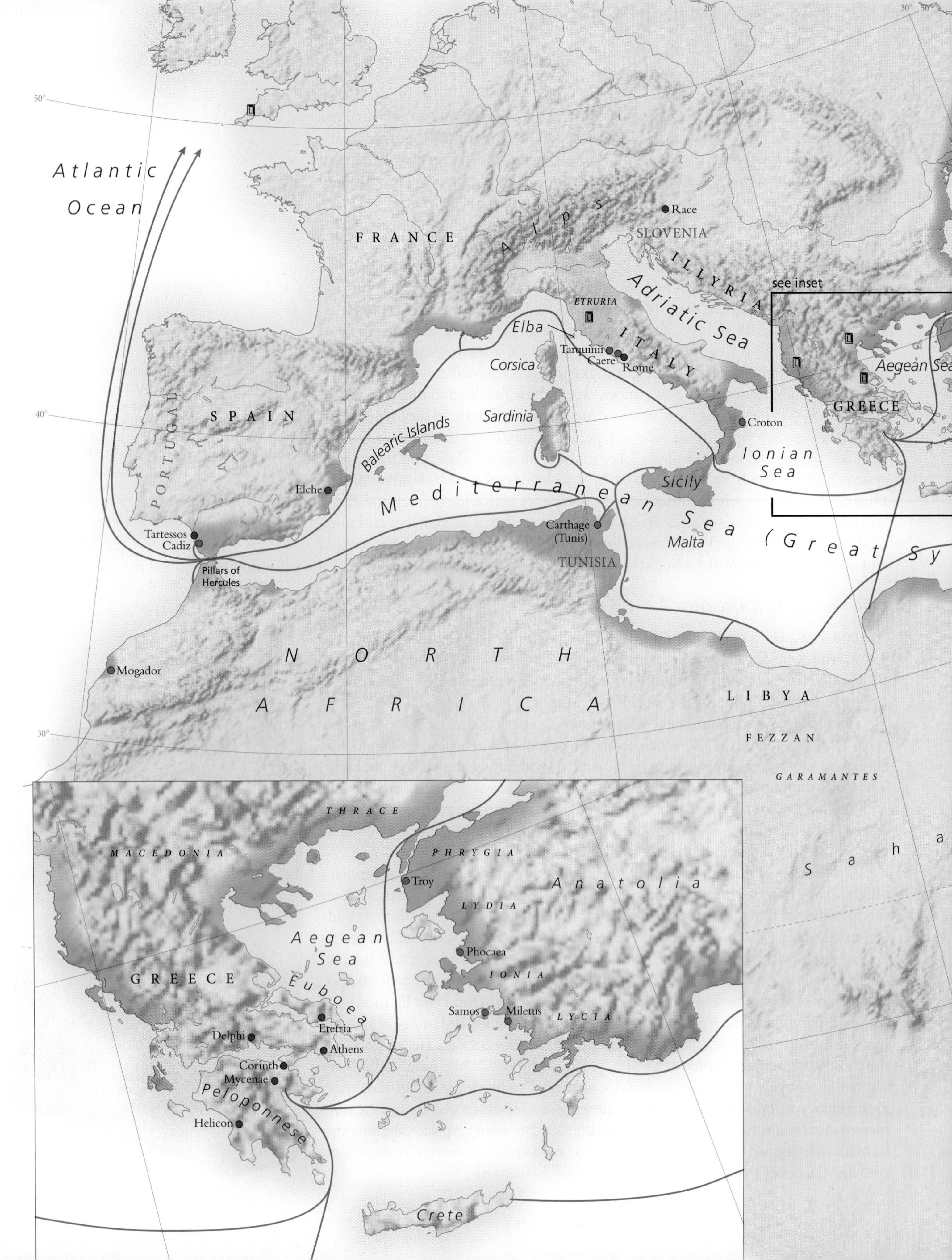

Atlantic
Ocean
FRANCE
Alps
Race
SLOVENIA
ILLYRIA
Adriatic Sea
see inset
ETRURIA
Elba
ITALY
Tarquinii
Caere
Rome
Corsica
Aegean Sea
GREECE
SPAIN
PORTUGAL
Sardinia
Balearic Islands
Croton
Ionian Sea
Sicily
Elche
Mediterranean Sea (Great Sy
Tartessos
Cadiz
Carthage (Tunis)
Malta
TUNISIA
Pillars of Hercules
Mogador
NORTH
AFRICA
LIBYA
FEZZAN
GARAMANTES
Saha
50°
40°
30°
10°
20°
30°
THRACE
MACEDONIA
PHRYGIA
Troy
Anatolia
LYDIA
Aegean Sea
Phocaea
IONIA
GREECE
Euboea
Samos
Miletus
LYCIA
Eretria
Delphi
Athens
Corinth
Mycenae
Peloponnese
Helicon
Crete

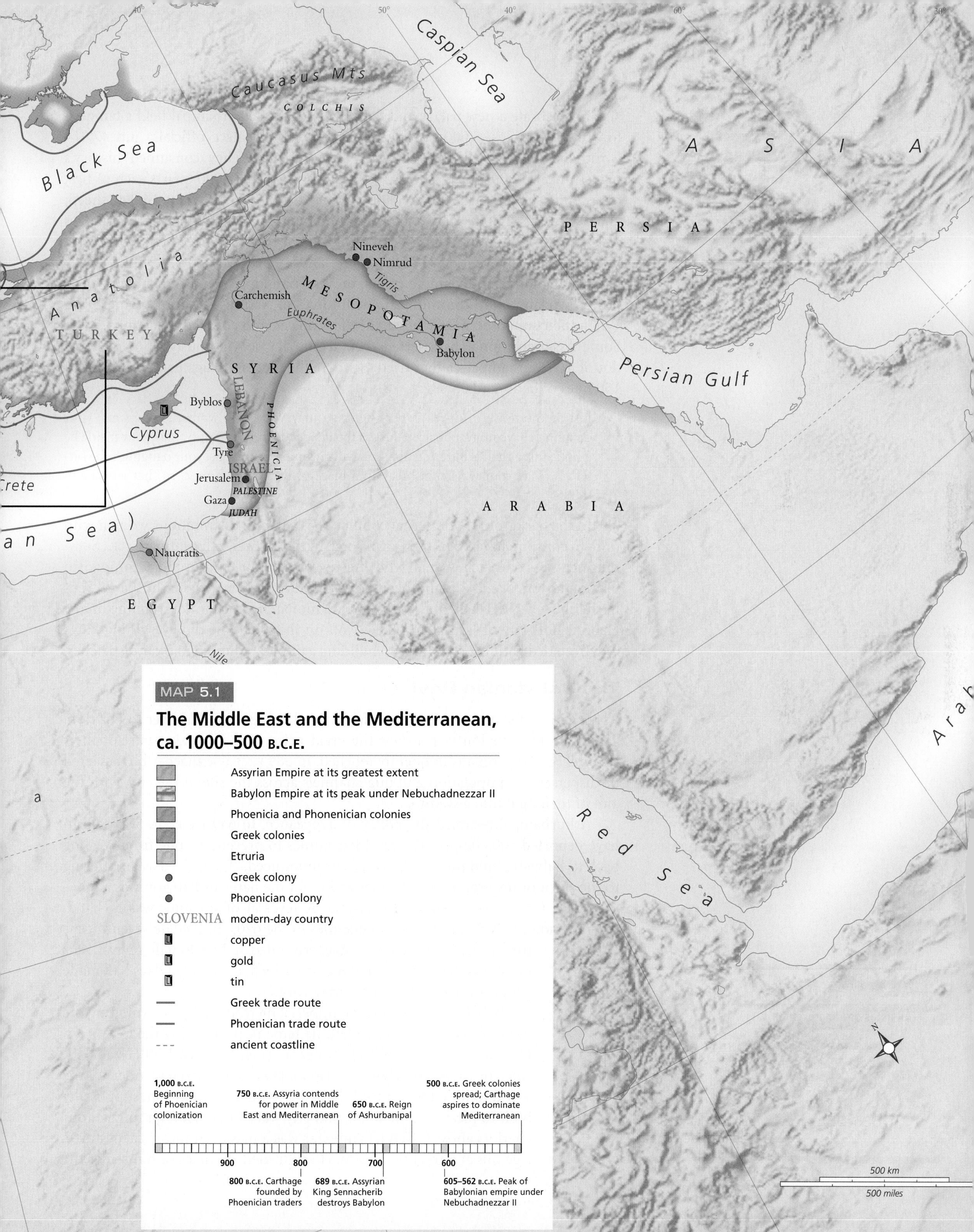
Caspian Sea
Caucasus Mts
COLCHIS
Black Sea
ASIA
PERSIA
Anatolia
TURKEY
Nineveh
Nimrud
Tigris
MESOPOTAMIA
Carchemish
Euphrates
Babylon
Persian Gulf
SYRIA
LEBANON
PHOENICIA
Byblos
Cyprus
Tyre
ISRAEL
Jerusalem
PALESTINE
Gaza
JUDAH
Crete
ARABIA
Naucratis
EGYPT
Nile
Red Sea
500 km
500 miles
MAP 5.1
The Middle East and the Mediterranean, ca. 1000–500 B.C.E.
Assyrian Empire at its greatest extent
Babylon Empire at its peak under Nebuchadnezzar II
Phoenicia and Phonenician colonies
Greek colonies
Etruria
Greek colony
Phoenician colony
SLOVENIA modern-day country
copper
gold
tin
Greek trade route
Phoenician trade route
ancient coastline
1,000 B.C.E. Beginning of Phoenician colonization
750 B.C.E. Assyria contends for power in Middle East and Mediterranean
650 B.C.E. Reign of Ashurbanipal
500 B.C.E. Greek colonies spread; Carthage aspires to dominate Mediterranean
900
800
700
600
800 B.C.E. Carthage founded by Phoenician traders
689 B.C.E. Assyrian King Sennacherib destroys Babylon
605–562 B.C.E. Peak of Babylonian empire under Nebuchadnezzar II

To celebrate a new palace and flaunt his wealth, Ashurbanipal held a banquet for 16,000 citizens, 5,000 visiting dignitaries, 1,500 palace officials, and 47,074 workmen "summoned from all over the kingdom." They consumed history's biggest meal: 10,000 jugs of beer; 10,000 skins of wine; 30,000 quarts each of figs, dates, and shelled pistachios; 1,000 each of lambs and fat oxen; 14,000 sheep; 20,000 pigeons; 10,000 eggs; 10,000 desert rats; and hundreds of deer. "For ten days I gave them food, I gave them drink, I had them bathed, I had them anointed. I honored them and sent them back to their lands in peace and joy."

Like Egyptian and Chinese rulers, the Assyrian kings sought to enhance their power by claiming to communicate with forces in Nature—a doomed enterprise. When their supposed magic failed, they lost power, and competing factions arose. Some Assyrian monarchs asserted their legitimacy so vigorously as to make us doubt it. Ashurbanipal's father tried to secure the succession against rebellion with 150 lines of oaths and curses:

> Just as the noise of doves is persistent, so may you, your women, your sons, your daughters have no rest or sleep. Just as the inside of a hole is empty, may your inside be empty. Just as gall is bitter, so may you, your women, your sons, your daughters, be bitter . ... May your waterskin break in a place of thirst and famine, so that you die of thirst.

In the background of internal conflicts was a harem of ambitious women with time to conspire in favor of their own sons. In the early eighth century B.C.E., Sammuramat was one such woman who effectively ruled the empire and accompanied her son to war. Naqia was another. She was virtual coruler with her husband, Sennacherib (seh-NAH-keh-rihb), the Assyrian monarch famed for descending on the Hebrew holy city of Jerusalem "like a wolf on the fold." She did everything kings did, from dedicating inscriptions to building a palace and receiving war dispatches.

The Babylonian Revival

As the cities of southern Mesopotamia declined, trade shifted upriver to Babylon. To Assyrians, Babylon was always the great prize, and it became part of their empire. But Babylonians frequently rebelled. In 689 B.C.E., Sennacherib massacred or dispersed the population and dug channels across the site of the city, with the aim of turning it into a swamp.

Ashurbanipal resumed the policy of vengeance. In 649 B.C.E., he was said to have deported 500,000 people from their homes to prevent anyone from stealing back to Babylon, "and those still living," he announced, "I sacrificed as an offering to the spirit of my grandfather, Sennacherib." Yet the name of Babylon was a rallying point for native resistance to Assyria. A reversal of fortunes was at hand. Overextended Assyria succumbed to enemies in the 620s. In the late seventh century B.C.E., Nabopolassar masterminded a Babylonian revival. His boast was that he "defeated Assyria, which, from olden days had made people of the land bear its heavy yoke."

Babylon now became an imperial metropolis again, exploiting the vacuum Assyria's collapse left. Its fame peaked during the long reign (605–562 B.C.E.) of Nebuchadnezzar (neh-boo-kahd-NEH-zahr) II. Ancient Greek guidebooks attributed two of the seven wonders of the world to him: the terraced "hanging" gardens of Babylon, supposedly built to please a concubine, and city walls broad enough to race four chariots abreast. Nebuchadnezzar was a master of theatrical gestures, a genius at attracting esteem. He cultivated an image of himself as the

Assyria and Babylon

(All dates are approximate)	
750 B.C.E.	Assyria becomes an empire
689 B.C.E.	Sennacherib destroys city of Babylon
620s B.C.E.	Assyrian empire falls; Ashurbanipal is last king
605–562 B.C.E.	Peak of Babylonian empire under Nebuchadnezzar II

MAKING CONNECTIONS

CONDITIONS LEADING TO RECOVERY IN MIDDLE EAST AND MEDITERRANEAN

STATE →	TYPE OF LEADERSHIP AND INITIATIVES →	EFFECTS
Phoenician city-states	Merchant elites; economy based on trade and proximity to forest, mineral, metal resources; colonization of Mediterranean	Spread of Phoenician technical knowledge, culture, and alphabet throughout Mediterranean
Assyrian Empire	Powerful king with provincial governors; cult of personality combined with ideology of domination; palace-building, other monumental architecture	Imperial state based on upper Tigris River spreads to lower Mesopotamia, Mediterranean coast
Babylonian Empire	Strong city-state asserts independence, becomes imperial center after decline of Assyrians; large-scale building projects; monumental architecture	Large metropolis becomes regional political/trade/cultural center; Babylon and Egypt battle for control of regional resources

restorer of ancient glories by rebuilding ziggurats and city walls all over Mesopotamia. On what survives of his showy works, bulls, lions, and dragons strut in glazed brick.

Whether because Nebuchadnezzar overreached himself or because his dynasty could produce no more dynamic leaders, his was Babylon's last era of greatness. In effect, Babylon and Egypt fought each other to exhaustion in their efforts to replace Assyria. Five centuries later, the Greek geographer Strabo reflected that Babylon had been "turned to waste" by the blows of invaders and the indifference of rulers. "The great city has become a great desert."

GREECE AND BEYOND

In the late second millennium B.C.E., when the Sea Peoples and other displaced communities disrupted the eastern Mediterranean and threatened Egypt (see Chapter 4), a similar upheaval took place on land. Migrants from the north swept into southern Greece, eradicating literate culture. Refugees streamed across the Aegean and Ionian Seas to Italy, Anatolia, and islands in the eastern and central Mediterranean.

The Greek Environment

By early in the first millennium B.C.E., the Mycenean palace centers were in ruins. The only stone or rubble buildings from this period that we know of in Greece were on the island of Euboea. Few iron tools were available for farming. Barley was the staple crop, laboriously cultivated. Most Greeks lived by goat farming and in thatched huts.

Industry and trade were ways to escape. In the tenth century B.C.E. Athens, Corinth, and a few other centers exported finely decorated pots and pressed olives—the only surplus farm product—for their oil. Neighboring peoples considered the Greeks' barley unfit to eat. But olive oil was exportable and came from a crop whose care was seasonal and left time for seafaring. Olives would grow in ground that grains disdained at altitudes over 2,000 feet. It had many uses. Olive oil added fat to poor diets and could be used as lamp-fuel or for cleansing the body. Olive processers invested profits in promoting trade. Commercial enterprise lined the Aegean and Ionian Seas with cities and, from the mid–eighth century B.C.E.

onward, spread over the Mediterranean and the Black Sea. The Greeks lived, they said, "around a sea, like frogs around a pond."

Hesiod, excerpt from *Works and Days*

The Greek poet Hesiod recorded a conversation that evokes the way Greece took to the sea. Perses, his younger brother, was lolling around their humble farm while Hesiod sweated at the plow. "Greece and poverty are sisters," Perses began. "How can I make money easily?" Hesiod recommended working on the land. But Perses was the type of person who asks for advice only because he wants to confirm his own opinion. He revealed what he really wanted: "to buy and sell in distant markets." "Please don't be a fool," rejoined Hesiod. "Money may be all you want in life, but it is not worth the risk of drowning. . . . Be moderate, my brother. Moderation is best in everything."

All over Greece, however, men like Perses won the arguments. Greek writers included merchants and explorers among their heroes, something unthinkable, for example, in China of the time, which valued only farmers, warriors, and scholars. In the 500s B.C.E., trade was growing so rapidly that some Greek states introduced their own coinage and designed and built new, larger types of ships.

Greek Colonialism

By Hesiod's time, iron tools improved agriculture and increased food production, which in turn led to an increase in population. But more people meant more demands on food and land. Now, not only were the Greeks a trading people, but they also became colonizers (see Map 5.1). Greek experience echoed that of Phoenicia: city-communities at home, outreach by sea, colonies abroad.

The Greeks founded colonies on the advice of gods who spoke through oracles. At Delphi, where smoke rose from deep crevices in the earth, a priestess uttered divine pronouncements from a three-legged throne cast in the form of writhing serpents. One supplicant went to the shrine to find a remedy for childlessness, with no thought of starting a colony, and received orders to found Croton in southern Italy. Others were told to colonize to escape famine. Founding colonies became so much a part of Greek life that a comic playwright speculated on the chances of founding one in the sky. "Not that we hate our city," the would-be colonists protest, "for it is a prosperous mighty city, free for all to spend their wealth in, paying fines and fees."

Olive harvest. The export of olive oil was vital to Greece's recovery from the so-called "dark ages" that followed the fall of Mycenean cities. Greece's poor soils and hot climate could not produce much else that was salable abroad. Solon, the legendary lawgiver, supposedly compelled the Athenians to grow olives. Scenes of laborious techniques to harvest olives from their trees decorate this vase by the most prolific Athenian artist of the late sixth century B.C.E., known as the Antimenes Painter.

Most colonists were outcasts, exiles, and criminals—frontiersmen forging a new society. But wherever they went, they reproduced Greek ways of life. At Naucratis in the Nile delta, for example, colonists dedicated shrines to cults from their home towns—the goddess Hera of Samos and the Sun-god Apollo of Miletus. In the sixth and fifth centuries B.C.E., offerings to Aphrodite, goddess of love, show a steady stream of Greek sex-tourists to the lively local brothels. Such sober travelers as Solon, the great lawgiver of Athens, also visited Naucratis. They came to Egypt on business or on a grand tour in search of enlightenment from a great civilization.

Meanwhile, growing contacts inspired Greek artists and thinkers. The sea washed new cultural influences back toward Greece. Unlike so many of the earlier systems that were developed to catalog merchandise or record trade transactions, the Greek alphabet was rapidly used to record creative literature and preserve epic poems that bards once recited at warriors' drinking parties. Poems attributed to the bard Homer, for instance, were written down in their surviving versions probably toward the end of the second century B.C.E. They have been revered—and imitated—ever since in the West for the brilliance with which they evoke war and seafaring. The *Iliad* tells a story of the interplay of gods and mortals during a military expedition from Mycenae to the city of Troy in what is now Turkey. The *Odyssey* recounts the wanderings of one of the heroes of the same war on his way home. The *Iliad* bristles with ships' masts. The *Odyssey* is loud with waves. Greek literature rarely strayed far from the sea.

Early Greek Society

Greeks had a remarkably uniform set of ideas about themselves—"our community of blood and language and religion and ways of life." Some of their notions were mythical, and Western tradition has multiplied the myths. We have idealized the Greeks as originators of our civilization and embodiments of all our values. However, scholars have been revising almost everything that has traditionally been said about them. The Greek gods appear no longer as personifications of virtues and vices but as unpredictable and often demonic manipulators. Their world—and the imagination of most Greeks who shared it—was run not by reason but by weird and bloody rites, goat dances, orgiastic worship, sacrifices, signs, and omens.

Aristotle, "The Creation of the Democracy in Athens"

Plutarch on education and family in Sparta

Greeks lived in relatively small communities of citizens who saw themselves living together out of choice. Political institutions took many different forms, including hereditary and elected monarchies and states with ruling elites, defined by blood or wealth. *Demokrateia* meant a state where supreme power belonged to an assembly of all citizens. But most Greeks disapproved of such an arrangement. Only privileged males were citizens. Women were excluded. So were slaves, who made up 40 percent of the population in the fifth century B.C.E. Athens. In some Greek states, citizens used bits of broken pottery as ballots on which to scrawl their votes to exile unpopular leaders. When we look at them now, we see fragments of an oppressive system that made slaves of captives, victims of women, battle fodder of men, and scapegoats of failures.

Greek women. Women collecting water from a fountain was a common subject for Greek painters of water pots. This example from the Greek colony of Vulci in Italy, where the native population esteemed women more highly than the Greeks did, follows a standard Greek pattern. It shows the women in profile, forming a line at a fountain with a lion's-head spout under a roof supported by slender columns.

Families—groups based on monogamous couples and their descendants—were the basis of society in Greek communities. When Aristotle, the greatest of Greek scholars, speculated in the fourth century B.C.E. about the origins of the state, he assumed that it arose from the voluntary alliance of families. In Athens, some of the earliest group burials known to archaeologists are in family plots. Typically, girls married at age 14 or 15 to men twice their age. So men dominated. "The Greeks," said a writer of the fourth century B.C.E., "expect their daughters to keep quiet and do woolwork."

Myth eliminated women from Athenian origins—the founders of the community supposedly sprang from the soil. Wives and daughters did not normally inherit property. They rarely appeared in public, except as emotional mourners or as priestesses in religious cults. In art of the first half of the millennium, men are shown more and more in the company only of other men, women only with other women. Women's function was to serve the community by bearing and raising children and thereby increasing manpower for production and war. In the city-state of Sparta—which Greeks always regarded as "utterly different" from other Greek states—all women had to train for motherhood, and women who died in childbirth were commemorated in the same way as heroic warriors killed in battle.

Scholars used to infer Greek values and morality from philosophical writings, but now we also look to popular plays and satires and find that the average Greek's social attitudes were different from the philosophers'. Athenian elites, for instance, tended to idealize homosexual relationships between older men and boys, but the playwrights' audiences despised them. At times, Plato (see Chapter 6) called for women to be men's equal partners, but popular literature almost always presented women as despicable. Even women who were intellectually superior to men were portrayed as dangerous or vulgar.

One of the discredited notions is of Greek "purity"—the idea that the Greeks were a self-made civilization, owing almost nothing to other cultures. To some extent, this was one of their myths of themselves: a way of differentiating themselves from foreigners. Indeed, the Greeks went beyond mere imitation when they received influences, whether from abroad or from an antiquity that they saw as their own. But they were heavily indebted to what they called Asia, which to them included Egypt, and, especially, to parts of Anatolia and the Ionian islands. Here—as we shall see in the next chapter—the learning we call Greek first appeared. Greece was open to the eastern Mediterranean, and influences from around the sea's rim fashioned Greek culture.

The Spread of State-Building and City-Building

Phoenician and Greek colonization and trade made the Mediterranean a highway of cultural exchange. Around and across its peninsulas lay a thick crust of peoples who could build up surplus resources, strong states, monumental cities, literate culture, and vibrant art (see Map 5.1). Most of them tend to get left out of books on global history, because they are ill known or underrated. But they help us see the Phoenicians and Greeks in context. They also help us understand what made the Mediterranean a potential forge of empires and fount of influence for the future. A tour is in order.

The lands of the Thracians lay along the Aegean Sea, north and east of Greece. Their written works have perished, and surviving inscriptions are indecipherable. But archaeology gives us inklings of their culture.

Because Thrace was close to trading centers of the eastern Mediterranean, its chiefs made an early start accumulating wealth and state-building. They practiced rites of fire, commemorated in spiraling incisons that swirled on their hearths. A fine example imitates a shimmering Sun. A horseback hero dominated their art. In surviving examples he wrestles a three-headed monster, leads a bear in triumph, and does battle among severed heads.

Around 500 B.C.E., energetic rulers unified the Thracian city-states into a kingdom and sought to expand their domain. These were flesh-and-blood figures whom we know from Greek sources, not mythic heroes. In 429 B.C.E., the Thracian King Sitalkes invaded Macedonia in northern Greece. There he built a palace-city of 12.5 acres, mostly of mud bricks and painted stucco. His failure to build a permanent empire marks a new period, when Thracian states squirmed to survive alongside mightier neighbors.

To the Thracians' west, along the coast of the Adriatic Sea around 500 B.C.E., lay Illyria, whose rulers and elites were buried with hoards of gold and silver and sacrifices of oxen and boar. An urn found in present-day Slovenia depicts the luxurious life of an Illyrian court. Warriors parade. Hawkers and deer hunters stalk. Dignitaries display their authority with double-headed scepters or play on pipes. Voluptuous, long-haired women feed them.

A CLOSER LOOK

THRACIAN HORSEBACK HERO

Pre-Christian fragments of Thracian art sometimes survive because Christians recycled them as building material for churches. This heroic figure on a horse was a favorite subject for Thracian artists. Goldsmiths had depicted a similar figure, known to historians as "The Master of the Animals," for centuries.

Dominating a rearing horse and calmly feeding a lion, the hero has powers of control over sometimes unconquerable and savage forces of nature. The posture of the horse has signified command in Western art and imagery ever since.

The hero's servant contributes to mastery of the horse by pulling its tail. Perhaps in an attempt to represent Alexander the Great (r. 336–323 B.C.E.) as divine, later artists copied this feature in their depictions of him.

Two women are often onlookers in pre-Christian sacred scenes from Thrace.

How does this image shed light on state-building and cultural exchange in the Mediterranean world around 500 B.C.E.?

Greece and the Mediterranean

(All dates are approximate)	
1000–900 B.C.E.	End of Greek dark ages
750 B.C.E.	Trade expands and Greek cities line the Mediterranean
500s B.C.E.	Greek colonies spread
500 B.C.E.	Thracian city-states united
500 B.C.E.	Illyrian, Garamantine, Etruscan, and Spanish civilizations thrive
100 B.C.E.	The *Iliad* and the *Odyssey* probably written down

Across the Mediterranean, in the ferociously hot and dry region of Libya called the Fezzan (feh-ZAN), lived the Garamantes. They dug nearly 1,000 miles of irrigation tunnels under the Sahara, carving out the limestone that lies between the water table and the sand. On all sides, desert surrounded their cities. The Garamantes grew wheat where they could and barley elsewhere. No records of their own survive, but early Greek descriptions call them a slave-trading elite, driving four-horse chariots. Romans depicted their tattooed and ritually scarred faces under ostrich-plume helmets.

On the north shore of the Mediterranean, stretching like a garter across central Italy, was Etruria, the land of the Etruscans. Their "loamy, fat and stoneless" soil had to be plowed nine times to make a furrow, so they needed iron mines and powerful smelting technology. Much of the region, however, lay under malarial marshes that the Etruscans drained. Their language, which their neighbors could not understand, became a soothsayers' tongue in Roman times and was then forgotten. So we cannot decipher their inscriptions.

We can, however, glimpse Etruscan culture through their arts. Theater was their specialty, but soothsaying was the skill they esteemed most, reading omens from sheep's livers and the flight of birds. These were borrowed techniques. Like the Phoenicians (and perhaps thanks to trade with them), Etruscan culture drew from all over the Mediterranean.

Etruscan cities were the earliest in Italy. The biggest, at Caere, could have accommodated 20,000 inhabitants. The layout of their tombs imitated their houses, as if to prepare for an afterlife. At Caere, a warrior lies alongside two chariots, with shields and arrows nailed to the walls. But the tomb was not made for him. Its best chamber houses a heavily bejeweled woman. Strewn around her, gold, silver, and ivory objects are marked with her name: Larthia.

Among the Etruscans, women had freedom Greeks and Romans of the time mistook for immodesty. They could go out of their homes, attend games, dine with men. In Greek art, the only women who did such things were prostitutes, but Etruscan wives routinely dined with their husbands. In one tomb, a married couple was buried under a portrait showing them reclining as companions, side by side on a couch, in the way Mediterranean elites of the time typically ate dinner. With easy affection, he draws her close, as she offers him flowers. Since mirrors and combs often display inscriptions, we can assume upper-class Etruscan women were literate.

A ceramic sarcophagus from a richly painted Etruscan burial chamber of the sixth century B.C.E. at Cerveteri in central Italy. The couple is shown together, hospitably sitting up as if to entertain visitors. They appear in death as they might have in life—reclining together at a dinner party, exchanging affection with vivid realism. The scene would be unimaginable in Greece at the time, where women were confined to subordinate roles.
Sarcophagus of a married couple on a funeral bed. Etruscan, from Cerveteri, 6th century BCE. Terracotta. Lewandowski/Ojeda. Musée Louvre, Paris, France. RMN Réunion des Musées Nationaux/Art Resource, NY

In Greek and Roman eyes, Etruscans spent too much time on grooming and dress, like characters in TV ads, and wantonly displayed their bodies, like beach cultists in modern California. Accusations that Etruscans performed sexual acts in public may be only slight exaggerations. On the wall of one tomb, a half-naked couple shares a bed. Banquet scenes show nude serving boys, as in Greece—but this may have been normal attire, or lack of it, for the young.

Beyond Etrona lay Spain, where Greeks said, "the god of riches dwells." From western Spain comes a belt decorated with a hero in combat with a lion and a huge funeral monument depicting a banquet of monsters—one with two heads, one with a forked tongue—feeding on wild boar. In another scene, a hero challenges a fire-breathing monster. The region evidently had an elite with the resources to build on a large scale and the power to inspire heroic and terrible images of authority.

From eastern Spain comes an imposing female sculpture—startling in its realism—called the Lady of Elche. Originally, she was probably enthroned in a tomb. A hollow space in her back may have held an offering to the gods or the ashes or bones of a human fellow occupant. Her luxurious dress, elaborate hairstyle, grand headdress, and enormous jewels leave no doubt of her social status or the wealth of the society that produced her.

Lady of Elche. The limestone sculpture known as the Lady of Elche evokes the splendor of Iberian civilization in the first millennium B.C.E. Carved with startling realism, she was originally enthroned and housed in a tomb, with offerings concealed in a hollow in her back. Her luxurious dress, elaborate hair, and bulging jewels were glamorously painted.

From deep inside the steamship age, it is hard to imagine how inhibiting was the strength of the eight-knot current—the "rapacious wave," a Greek poet called it—that stoppered the entrance from the Mediterranean to the Atlantic "sea of darkness." But Greek and Phoenician traders forced their way through to Tartessos, in southern Spain, where the banks of the Rio Tinto are blotched with the flow of copper-bearing ores, and miners dug deep underground galleries.

Greek tales help us reconstruct Tartessos's history. In the mid–first millennium B.C.E., King Arganthonios was said to have subsidized the city walls that protected the marketplace of Phocaea at the other end of the Mediterranean. For a transition of this kind, from pastoralism to plutocracy, trading partners were essential. But Tartessos belongs to a long tradition of civilization-building in Spain, dimly detectable in even earlier treasure hordes. Native cultures, given the resources, were capable of spontaneous economic growth.

EMPIRES AND RECOVERY IN CHINA AND SOUTH ASIA

Summaries nearly always distort. But the story of this chapter so far is of formerly marginal regions becoming—at least for a while—rich and powerful, like Phoenicia and Greece, Assyria and Babylon, and parts of the western and central Mediterranean, as if to replace the old centers of power and wealth in Lower Mesopotamia, Hatti, and Crete. This suggests problems to bear in mind when confronting what happened in China and South Asia in the same period: Were the traditions of the Shang and Zhou, in China, and of Harappa in India passed on to successors in new places? Or was the continuity of history ruptured and a new beginning made in new locations?

The Zhou Decline

The Zhou claimed that they were divinely chosen to rule the world (see Chapter 4). But as their supremacy spread, the realm became increasingly decentralized, and rituals to appease the gods became ever more elaborate: The vessels got bigger, the ceremonies larger scale, the hymns of praise to ancestors more extravagant. "Heaven's mandate is unending," intoned the court poets and congregations, with evident unease. A poet in the provinces disagreed: "Drought has become so severe,. . . glowing, burning. . . . The great mandate is about to end."

King Li (lee) ascended the throne in 857 B.C.E. Chroniclers portrayed him as self-indulgent and heedless of advice. A bronze inscription preserves Li's own version: "Although I am but a young boy, I have no leisure day or night," sacrificing to ancestors, elevating "eminent warriors" and well-recommended sages. But there was more urgent business than these ceremonial acts. In 842 B.C.E., rebels drove him from his capital, eventually installing the young heir, Xuan (shoo-ehn). For a reign of 46 years, Xuan held off the main external threat, the Western barbarians, while trying to confront natural disasters with magic.

When he died in 782 B.C.E.—reputedly murdered by the ghost of a subordinate he had unjustly executed—an earthquake hit. Following tradition, the poet blamed the disaster on the government's shortcomings. But the problems went deeper. As wealth trickled outward from trade, outlying states grew more insubordinate. In 771 B.C.E., people whom the Zhou called "Dog barbarians" drove them from their ancestral lands forever.

The Zhou moved east, to a region glorious under the Shang, but now divided among 148 Zhou relatives or nominees. Consolidation and reconfiguration reduced the number, and by the sixth century B.C.E., the former empire had been transformed into jostling states (see Map 5.2). Leadership among them was usually determined by war—and, within states, by assassination and massacre. Instability can inhibit cultural and economic development and unleash violence. Yet the consequences were, in some respects, the opposite. As we shall see in Chapter 6, politically fragmented environments fostered intellectual endeavor. Indeed, well before the turn of the mid-millennium, this fact was also evident in South Asia.

MAP 5.2

China and South Asia, ca. 750 B.C.E.

- China during Warring States Period
- barbarian incursions
- Ganges River Valley
- Sinhalese cultural area

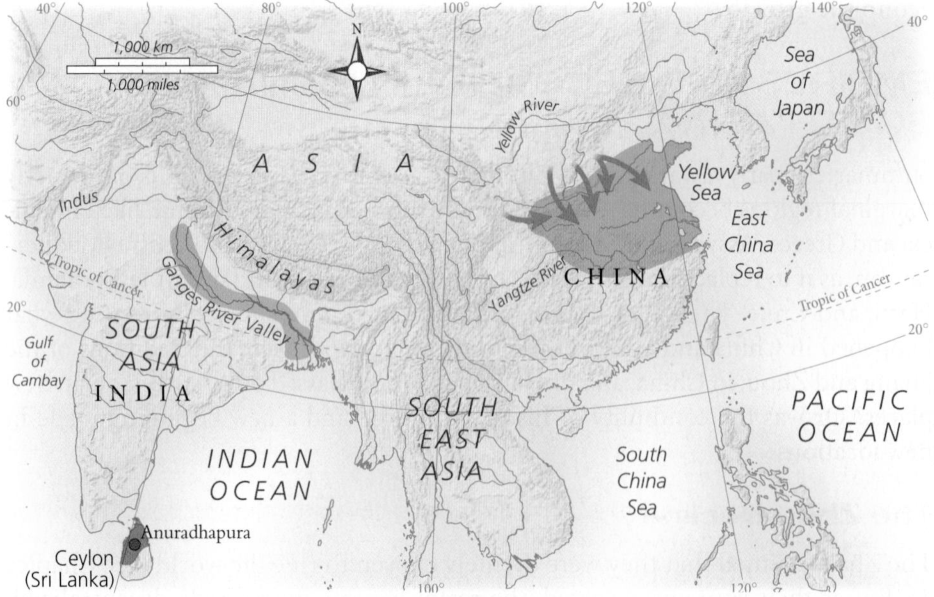

South Asia: Relocated Centers of Culture

After the erosion and disappearance of the Harappan cities, Indian history differed in an important respect from other regions of large-scale state-building and city-building. Recovery in Europe, Mesopotamia, Phoenicia, and China depended on the survival or revival of previous traditions or on stimulation by outside influences. But India provides proof that such conditions were not necessary.

Historical orthodoxy has long insisted that something of the Harappan past—migrants, culture—must have survived. Indian civilization seems to deserve a pedigree as old as the Indus cities, and those cities, in turn, deserve to have left lasting traditions. But written and archaeological sources are few, and we have no evidence of continuities or unmistakable transmissions of culture across the dark, undocumented centuries of Indian history. When civilization did reemerge in South Asia in the first millennium B.C.E., it was in the Ganges valley and the island of Sri Lanka, which was once known as Ceylon.

The Ganges Valley

After a lapse of centuries, iron axes cleared the way for farming in the Ganges valley, a different environment from the hot, dry floodplains of the Indus valley. It was a region of abundant rain and rich forests. We have no knowledge that the Ganges received colonists from Harappa at the time. The only artifacts from the region during this period are fine copperware, which no one has found in the art of the Indus people, although some decorative designs may be similar.

Later Indian cultural history does not exhibit strong evidence that Harappan culture was transplanted to the Ganges either. Only pottery fragments exist with glazes similar to Harappan wares. Moreover, the first urban sites and fortifications in the Ganges valley have none of the telltale signs of Harappan order: no seals, no weights and measures, no uniform bricks. This makes it hard to believe that the Ganges civilization could be the Harappan civilization transplanted. On the contrary, the lack of material evidence makes early Indian civilization seem even more distant from the Harappan than Greek civilization was from the Cretan and Mycenean. In only one respect does the world of the Ganges clearly resemble that of Harappa—we know all but nothing about its political and social life.

Excerpt from the Upanishads

The literature of its sages, however, survives in abundance. It is impossible to find evidence for traditional claims that the earliest texts originate from orally transmitted traditions from deep in the previous millennium. But surviving versions could have begun to be written down early in the first millennium B.C.E. The theoretical sections of these texts, the **Upanishads** (oo-PAH-nee-shadz), show the recollection of a time when teaching passed from one generation to another by word of mouth. *Upanishad* means something like "the seat close to the master."

One of the earliest Upanishads tells how the powers of nature rebelled against nature itself—how the lesser gods challenged the supreme god **Brahman** and failed. "But the fire could not burn straw without Brahman. The wind could not blow the straw away without Brahman." On its own, the story might suggest no more than a doctrine of divine omnipotence, similar to the doctrines Jews, Christians, and Muslims hold. But in the context of the other Upanishads, it seems part of a more general, mystical belief in the oneness of the universe,

India and Sri Lanka

(All dates are approximate)	
1000 B.C.E.	Civilization emerging in Ganges valley
800 B.C.E.	Upanishads probably written down
? B.C.E.	*Sinhalese* colonize Sri Lanka
500 C.E.	*Mahavamsa* probably written down

infinite and eternal. Such a "theory of everything" does not appear in the thought of earlier civilizations.

Sages of the time proclaimed two more new ideas. The first was that matter is an illusion. The world is Brahman's dream; the creation of the world was like a falling asleep. Sense organs can tell us nothing that is true. Speech is illusory since it relies on lips and tongues. Thought is illusory, since it happens in—or at least passes through—the body. Most feelings are illusory because our nerves and guts register them. We can glimpse truth only in purely spiritual visions or certain kinds of feeling, like selfless love and unspecific sadness, which do not arise from particular physical stimuli. Second, the Upanishads describe a cycle of reincarnation or rebirth. Through a series of lives virtuously lived, the soul can advance toward perfection, at which time its identity is submerged in the divine "soul of the world" known as Brahman.

These ideas are so startling and innovative that we want to know how they occurred. And who were the patrons and pupils of the sages who uttered them? Why did society value such sublimely unworldly speculations? We have no evidence on which to base answers to these questions. But ideas from about the sixth century B.C.E. to about the first century C.E. are antiquity's most influential legacy to us and the subject of our next chapter. They still inform the questions that confront our religions and philosophies and mold how we think about them.

Building Anew in Sri Lanka

South Asia's other nursery of large-scale cities and states was in Sri Lanka, off the southern tip of India, in the Indian Ocean (see Map 5.2). Here, the *Mahavamsa* (ma-ha-VAHM-sah), chronicles of the long-lived "Lion Kingdom," are deceptive documents. In surviving versions, they were written down in what Westerners think of as the sixth century C.E. to justify the ruling *Sinhalese* (sihn-hah-LEHZ) people. The chronicles begin the history of the kingdom with a credible event: colonization by seafarers from the Gulf of Cambay, on the edge of the Harappan culture area. But the Sinhalese had no known connection with the Harappans. They became large-scale builders and irrigators but produced nothing to rival the logic, creative literature, mathematics, and speculative science written down along the Ganges about 2,500 years ago.

The heartland of the early kingdom was in the relatively dry northern plateau, where annual rainfall is heavy, but long dry spells are common. Nowadays in the dry zone, rice cultivation relies on village reservoir tanks dug out of seasonal streams, dammed with earth. There is not always enough water for annual crops of rice. Even if we allow for changes in the climate, the Sinhalese colonists could not have built great cities without hydraulic ingenuity. Even before the adoption of Buddhism, which tradition dates to the third century B.C.E., Anuradhapura (an-uh-rad-POO-ra) was a large and splendid capital, with the largest artificial reservoir in the world.

So civilizations can arise without the help of either recovered traditions or stimulation from outside influences. Yet the question remains, if people in the Ganges valley and Sri Lanka could build states and cities without traditions from the past or influences from outside, why were the Americas and most of Africa relatively dormant for so long, despite the promising starts described in earlier chapters?

THE FRUSTRATIONS OF ISOLATION

North America

Civilizations developing between 1000 and 500 B.C.E.

Dorset culture—Northwest Canada to the Arctic

Poverty Point—Gulf of Mississippi

Foraging communities—Ohio River valley

San Juan and Tucson basins—Southwest United States

In discussing developments in the Americas and Africa, we have to allow for a trick of the evidence. The cultures of Eurasia churned out documents and literature, much of which we can read today. This alone accounts for their dominant place in historical tradition, compared with cultures that employed other, less accessible ways to record events and ideas. In the West, prejudice also favors Eurasian cultures over others. We pay more attention to history that seems to anticipate the way we live now. Sometimes we read into that history the origins of our own societies. Conversely, we overlook or fail to recognize history that appears too different from our own.

Compared to Eurasia, the geography of the Americas and sub-Saharan Africa discourages communication and cultural exchange (see Map 5.3). Much of Africa and Central and South America lies in the tropics, where dense rain forests make it difficult and unhealthy for any outsider attempting to cross them. Africa has relatively few rivers, and for the most part, they do not allow long-range navigation. In Eurasia, cultural exchange was rapid. It happened across zones of similar climate, with no need for either the people or the food plants and livestock they brought with them to adapt. Cultural transmission in Africa and the Americas, on the other hand, had to cross vast chasms of climate from north to south and south to north, calling for different survival strategies along the way.

Monsoonal wind systems in Asia and relatively stable weather in the Mediterranean favor navigation, whereas exposed shores and hostile winds enclose much of sub-Saharan Africa. Except in the Caribbean, the Americas have none of the narrow seas that encourage communication in parts of Europe and Asia. Even the civilizations of the Ganges and Sri Lanka, though they originated independently, could take advantage of the communications systems of maritime Asia and trans-Eurasian trade routes to link up with China and southwest Asia by land and sea.

Developments in North America

Still, there were developments beyond Eurasia. In the American far north, the Dorset culture transformed life. People there began to build semisubterranean longhouses and stone alleys for driving caribou into lakes. Their art realistically depicted all the species that shared their environment.

The critical new technology was the blubber-fueled soapstone lamp, which enabled the Dorset people to go far from home in the Arctic darkness, tracking the musk ox and caribou. No longer limited to the forest, the users of oil lamps could also hunt on the ice, where abundant fat game waited without competitors and where the climate preserved carcasses. People of the Dorset culture speared seals and harpooned walruses from kayaks on the open sea. Now that their prey was too fat to be felled by arrows, they abandoned the bow for the barbed harpoon. Ingenious notched blades stayed in the victim's flesh until it was so tired that it could be hauled in, butchered, and sped home on hand-drawn sleds with runners of walrus ivory.

Equally dramatic new ways of life developed in the same period—between the late second and mid–first millennia B.C.E.—on the lower Mississippi River and the coast of the Gulf of Mexico. The culture—called Poverty Point after the location of its biggest site in Louisiana—worked in copper and manufactured tools and jewelry. Trade goods arrived along the Mississippi, Red, and Tennessee Rivers. More

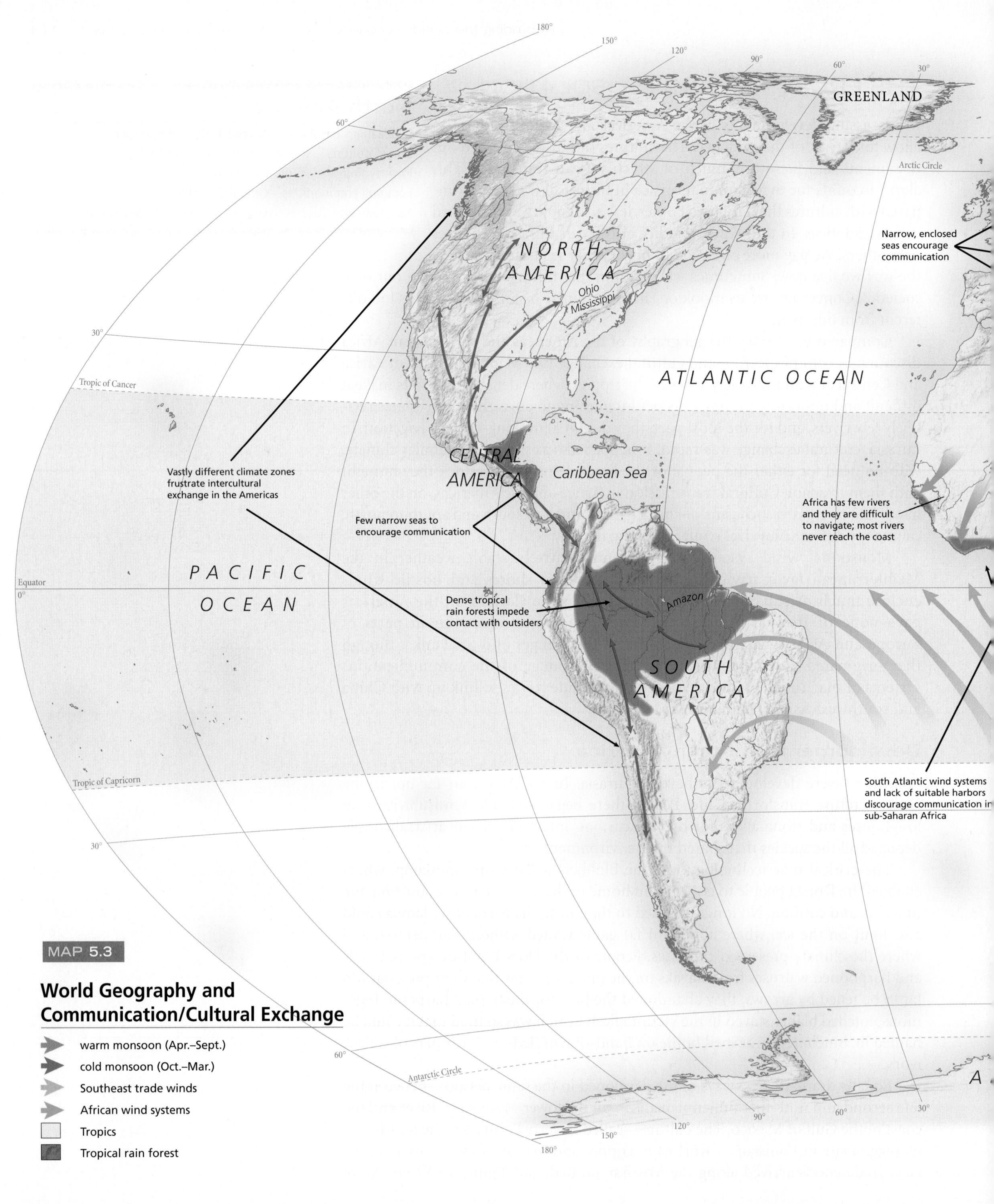

GREENLAND
Arctic Circle
NORTH AMERICA
Ohio
Mississippi
ATLANTIC OCEAN
Tropic of Cancer
CENTRAL AMERICA
Caribbean Sea
PACIFIC OCEAN
Equator
Amazon
SOUTH AMERICA
Tropic of Capricorn
Antarctic Circle
Narrow, enclosed seas encourage communication
Vastly different climate zones frustrate intercultural exchange in the Americas
Few narrow seas to encourage communication
Dense tropical rain forests impede contact with outsiders
Africa has few rivers and they are difficult to navigate; most rivers never reach the coast
South Atlantic wind systems and lack of suitable harbors discourage communication in sub-Saharan Africa
MAP 5.3
World Geography and Communication/Cultural Exchange
warm monsoon (Apr.–Sept.)
cold monsoon (Oct.–Mar.)
Southeast trade winds
African wind systems
Tropics
Tropical rain forest

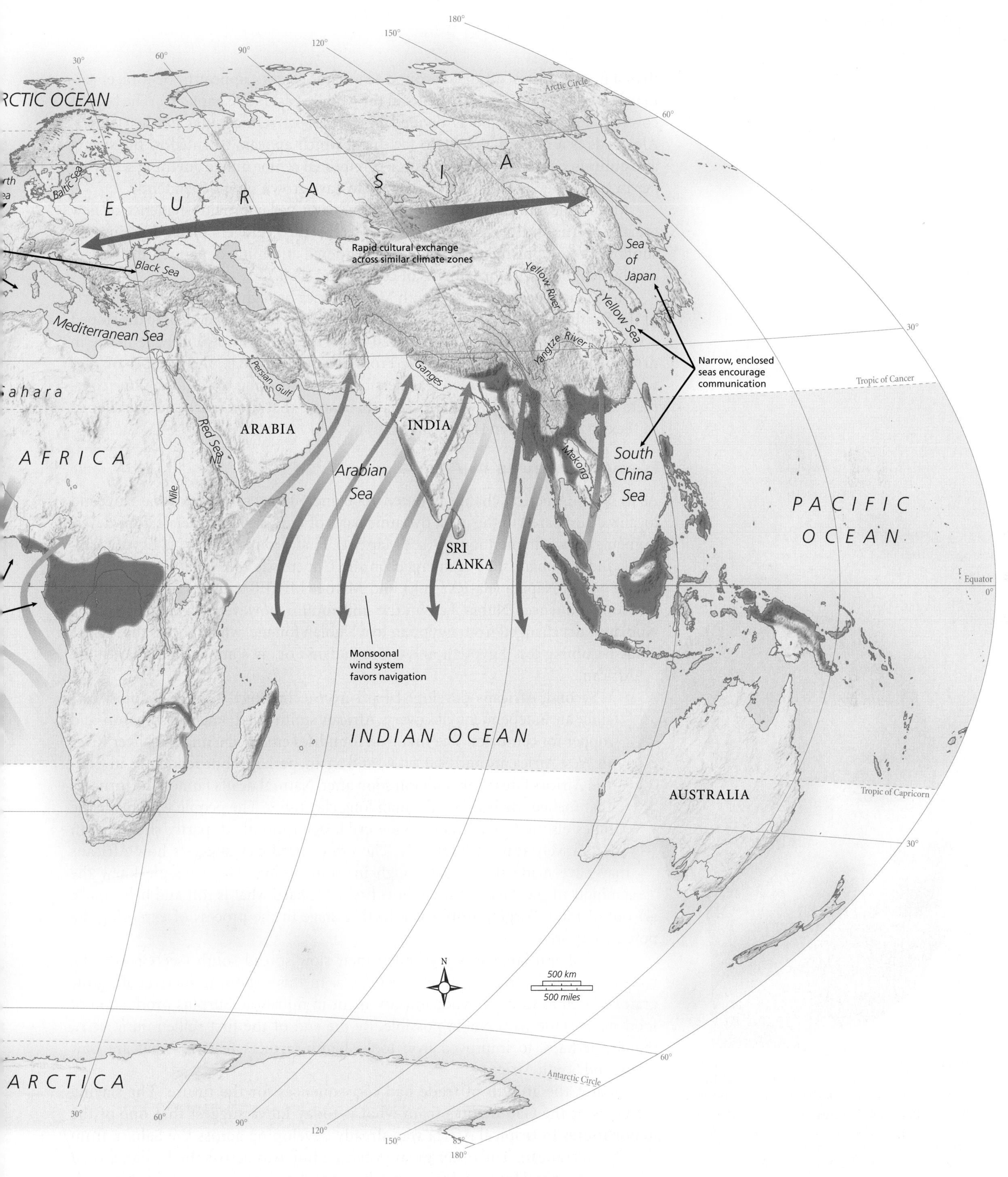
RCTIC OCEAN
E U R A S I A
Baltic Sea
Black Sea
Rapid cultural exchange
across similar climate zones
Mediterranean Sea
Sahara
Persian Gulf
Red Sea
Nile
ARABIA
AFRICA
Ganges
INDIA
Arabian
Sea
SRI
LANKA
Monsoonal
wind system
favors navigation
Yellow River
Yellow Sea
Sea
of
Japan
Yangtze River
Mekong
South
China
Sea
Narrow, enclosed
seas encourage
communication
PACIFIC
OCEAN
INDIAN OCEAN
AUSTRALIA
ARCTICA
Arctic Circle
Tropic of Cancer
Equator
Tropic of Capricorn
Antarctic Circle
N
500 km
500 miles

than a hundred sites, grouped around ten major centers, appear to be forager settlements comparable to settlements in the Middle East (see Chapter 2). The biggest covers a square mile and is divided by a series of semicircular earthen ridges. Alongside is a mound almost 70 feet high, which appears oriented to the spring and autumn equinox. The mound is a ceremonial center unlike anything seen earlier in Mesoamerica and, therefore, likely to have grown up independently.

Meanwhile, burial mounds in the Ohio River valley provide evidence of new social patterns and perhaps chiefdoms. Here, settled foragers planted grains and sunflowers to supplement the food they gathered and hunted, painted their dead, and buried them with ornaments of copper and shell.

In the same period, contact with Mesoamerica brought about changes in parts of the Southwest. In the San Juan and Tucson basins in Arizona, people developed a variety of maize that matured in 120 days. They could now cultivate maize in drier areas where squash also grew. From around 500 B.C.E., the number of sites with traces of beans increased. Farmers here were working toward the same complete system of nutrition—maize, squash, beans—that the Olmecs had developed in Mexico (see Chapter 4).

New Initiatives in Africa

As in North America, change between 1000 and 500 B.C.E. in Africa was slow and localized compared to the most dynamic parts of Eurasia. Nonetheless, four developments are worth mentioning (see Map 5.4). First, around 750 B.C.E., Egypt weakened, and a Nubian state reemerged on the Upper Nile (see Chapter 4), with its chief cities at Napata (na-PAY-tuh) and Meroe (MEHR-oh-ee). Egyptian culture had long influenced Nubia. Late in the millennium, however, the language of the Nubian court changed from Egyptian to a Nubian tongue, which shows that Nubia was becoming less Egyptian and more Sudanic or, as some scholars say, more African.

Heads sculpted from coarse-grained clay, in what is now central Nigeria, in the second half of the first millennium B.C.E., are not just fine works of art—as this example of the first century B.C.E. shows. They are also evidence of the technical accomplishments of the craftsmen who made clay tubing for the forges in which iron tools were made.

Second, Africans developed hard-iron technology. This was almost certainly an independent discovery. African smiths had smelted soft iron and copper for centuries. The first iron foundries emerged along the Niger River in West Africa around 500 B.C.E., and again, perhaps independently, in Central Africa's Great Lakes region soon after. Natural drafts fanned the furnaces that melted the iron ore through long clay tubes. The people who made the tubes also left clay heads—wide-eyed, open-mouthed, partly shaved, with decoratively scarred foreheads. The use of fired clay suggests how Africans may have made the breakthrough in iron forging. These people knew the seemingly magical uses of fire—how fire turns hard what is soft and helps make art out of mud. Forging iron was a further stage in the process of exploring the potential of fire.

Third, Bantu languages continued their slow spread south (see Chapter 1), reaching Central Africa by about 1000 B.C.E. In this region, farmers could grow grains as well as yams, a major improvement in nutrition. Surplus production of food made trade with Nubia possible. By the end of the first millennium B.C.E., thanks, perhaps, to improved iron tools, Bantu farmers reached what are now Kenya and South Africa.

Finally, the growth of trade had consequences for the future. The slaving activities of the Garamantes from what is today Libya suggest that one of the major routes to tropical Africa was already developing across the Sahara from the Mediterranean. The other great potential link was across the Indian Ocean from Asia to the Horn of Africa in what is today Somalia and Ethiopia. This

MAP 5.4

Africa, ca. 1000–500 B.C.E

- hard-iron technology, ca. 500 B.C.E
- expansion of Bantu languages
- trade route
- aromatics

MAP EXPLORATION
www.prenhall.com/armesto_maps

Africa/Southwest Arabia

(All dates are approximate)	
1000s B.C.E.	Bantu languages expanding southward
900s B.C.E.	Sabaean empire grows
750 B.C.E.	Nubian kingdom reemerges
500 B.C.E.	First iron foundries along Niger River
100s B.C.E.	Bantu languages reach South Africa

link was at least as important for the history of civilization in East Africa as the link to the Mediterranean was to Europe. We do not know when this route opened, but developments in southern Arabia provide clues about how it may have begun. Southern and southeast Arabia has fertile valleys, where seasonal streams flow from the mountains. Here, the areas that are now Oman and Bahrain forged copper goods, and Yemen produced frankincense and myrrh, aromatic resins from trees that were used in perfumes and, as biblical accounts show, for religious rituals. Some of these goods reached Mesopotamia and Harappa. But when those civilizations collapsed in the second millennium B.C.E., so did most economic development in this region.

Only Saba in southwest Arabia, closest to Africa, continued to grow. This was where the biblical Queen of Sheba supposedly came from to King Solomon in Jerusalem in the tenth century B.C.E. Numerous inscriptions survive from soon after that time. A temple outside Marib (MA-rihb), the Sabaeans' chief city, bears bronze plaques commemorating victories—scenes of warriors brandishing the severed hands of their victims. This same temple houses bronze sculptures—tribute from kings and landowners, some, evidently, personal likenesses. Piecing

MAKING CONNECTIONS

AMERICAS, AFRICA, AND EURASIAN CIVILIZATIONS: 1000–500 B.C.E.

REGION →	MEANS OF CULTURAL, ECONOMIC, POLITICAL DEVELOPMENT →	DISTINCTIVE ACHIEVEMENTS
Greece	Seaborne trade; colonization of Mediterranean basin; extensive cultural exchange	New forms of government (*demokrateia*) and communities (*poleis*, *ethne*); colonial autonomy; highly developed written literature
Zhou Dynasty/Warring States Period (China)	Centralized rule; elaborate court rituals; ancestor worship; trade and taxation; constant threat from barbarians	Political instability fosters intellectual endeavors
Ganges Valley	Highly developed spiritual literature (Vedas, Upanishads); agriculture with iron tools; little understanding of political, economic policies	First philosophies focused on doctrine of reincarnation, *maya* (matter as illusion), large-scale urban settlements, fortifications
Sri Lanka	Sophisticated water-management systems combined with urbanization	Large-scale cities, early adoption of Buddhism from neighboring India
North America	In the far north: decentralized communities, simple technologies, group hunting techniques; South/Midwest: widespread trade networks connecting to Mesoamerica, settlements	Northern regions: long-term adaptation to hostile environments, gradual depletion of wildlife; South/Midwest: forager settlements, mound building, mixed agriculture/hunting–gathering culture
Sub-Saharan Africa/southwest Arabia	Widespread trade, cultural exchange with hard-iron technology accelerating tool and weapon making, spread of Bantu language	Growth of Nubian state south of Egypt; sophisticated art, industry in Niger region; building and farming techniques spread with Bantu speakers; trade and state-building in southwest Arabia (Saba)

together the inscriptions, we see how the Sabaean state expanded at its neighbors' expense. Understanding what happened in Saba is the best way to study one of the most intriguing problems in the next part of this book—the growth of great states and great ambitions in East Africa.

CHRONOLOGY

(All dates are approximate)

1000–500 B.C.E.	Traditions and states of the late second millennium recover; Dorset culture in American far north thrives; peoples of lower Mississippi and Gulf of Mexico develop new ways of life
1000 B.C.E.	Civilization reemerges in Ganges valley; Bantu languages continue slow spread southward
800 B.C.E.	Phoenicians colonize the Mediterranean
771 B.C.E.	Zhou driven eastward from their ancestral lands
750–500 B.C.E.	Rapid expansion of Greek trading and colonization
750 B.C.E.	Egypt declines and Nubian state reemerges
605–562 B.C.E.	Peak of Babylonian Empire
500 B.C.E.	Carthage seeks control of Mediterranean trade until destroyed by Romans in 146 B.C.E.; West Africans develop and spread hard-iron technology southward
100s B.C.E.	Bantu languages reach present-day South Africa

IN PERSPECTIVE: The Framework of Recovery

The climacteric of the late second millennium B.C.E. damaged and changed the frameworks of civilization but in most cases did not break them. Recovery was possible because traditions survived—or could be revived—or because there were stimulating outside influences. In Greece and India, people forgot the art of writing and had to reinvent it from scratch centuries later. Recovery sometimes happened in new places and among new peoples. After the extinction of the Harappan world, civilization gradually emerged in India, far from the Indus. In Sri Lanka, monumental irrigation works and buildings arose. In Mesopotamia and China, the centers of activity and initiative were relocated, but, again, the continuities of tradition, which are the foundations of progress, were never entirely lost. Traditions spread through neighboring regions. Greek civilization crystallized on the edges of the Greek world, in islands and small colonies around the Ionian and Aegean Seas. Fertilized by Phoenicia and Greece, a ring of ambitious cities and states formed around the Mediterranean and Black Seas.

People continued to make ambitious attempts to modify the environment, transforming new areas. In parts of Eurasia, the pace of state-building and economic expansion quickened. The imperial experiments between 1000 and 500 B.C.E. failed to take hold, but efforts to expand borders and dominate other states became a feature of regions where change was accelerating. Political instability among competing states stimulated technological change: hotter furnaces, more iron. It also, perhaps, multiplied the opportunities of patronage for artists and intellectuals. An "age of sages" was detectable in India and would soon be apparent in other parts of Eurasia.

In the Mediterranean and what we think of as the Middle East, between 1000 and 500 B.C.E., state-building and growing trade led to imperial ambitions that eventually failed. Elsewhere, imperial projects ran out of steam or into trouble—as in China—or simply did not happen. Was this because the contenders were too well matched? Or was it because the economic environment was too undeveloped or the ecological environment too fragile? Or was it because no conqueror had found an enduring formula or a means to solidify states that were prone to failure? Whatever the problems that frustrated imperial ambitions in the first half of the millennium, states soon found ways to overcome them. The second half of the millennium was remarkabl enot only as an age of sages in Eurasia but also as an age of robust empires. A zone of connected, communicating cultures began to take shape across Eurasia and the Mediterranean, from the Pacific to the Atlantic. They nourished each other. Faint links were beginning to put parts of this central zone in touch with northern Europe and Africa. In the rest of the world, isolated cultures, still organized in kinship groups, chiefdoms, or small states, were able, at best, to develop small regional networks.

As a result, the focus of the next part of this book is on Eurasia and, in particular, the regions where sages founded well-rooted intellectual traditions that still shape the way we think: in China, India, southwest Asia, and Greece. These were homelands of huge ambitions to understand the world, change it, or conquer it. Their stories occupy the next chapters.

PROBLEMS AND PARALLELS

1. Why was the ruler of the city-state of Byblos able to stand up to a giant nation-state like Egypt?
2. Why did the Phoenician writing system play such an important role in the "recovery" of the Mediterranean world?
3. How did rulers such as Ashurbanipal and Nebuchadnezzar II enhance and extend their imperial states?
4. Why was Greek cultural influence so important for the Mediterranean world?
5. What evidence for the continuity of Harrapan/Indus valley culture exists in the civilizations of South Asia in the first millennium B.C.E.?
6. How did the interplay of cultures in the Mediterranean and Indian Ocean basins in the first millennium B.C.E. affect the development of civilizations in those areas? How did the isolation characteristic of cultures in the Americas affect the development of civilizations there?

DOCUMENTS IN GLOBAL HISTORY

- Mission to Byblos: *The Report of Wenamun*
- Hesiod, excerpt from *Works and Days*
- Aristotle, "The Creation of Democracy in Athens"
- Plutarch on Education and Family in Sparta

Please see the Primary Source DVD for additional sources related to this chapter.

READ ON

H. Goedicke, ed., *The Report of Wenamun* (1975) is a first-rate edition of the text. S. Moscati, ed., *The Phoenicians* (1968), and M. A. Aubet, *Phoenicians and the West* (1993) introduce the Phoenicians and their colonies. The standard works by H. W. F. Saggs, *The Might That Was Assyria* (1984), and *The Greatness That Was Babylon* (1962) are still valuable introductions, as is J. Oates, *Babylon* (1979). J. and D. Oates, *Nimrud* (2001) describes the palace.

S. Hornblower, *Greek World* (1983), and O. Taplin, *Greek Fire* (1989) make exciting introductions to the Greeks. J. Boardman, *The Greeks Overseas* (1964) covers Greek colonization admirably. C. Morgan, *Athletes and Oracles* (1990) is a splendid study. S. B. Pomeroy, *Goddesses, Whores, Wives, and Slaves: Women in Classical Antiquity* (1995); C. B. Patterson, *The Family in Greek History* (1998); and L. Foxhall and J. Salman, eds., *When Men Were Men* (1998), deal with women. The quotation from Hesiod on page 104 is from I. Morris and B. Powell, *The Greeks* (2006).

R. F. Hoddinott, *The Thracians* (1981); J. Wilks, *The Illyrians* (1992); C. M. Daniels, *The Garamantes of Southern Libya* (1970), and R. Harrison, *Spain at the Dawn of History* (1988) are outstanding on their respective subjects.

For the Zhou see page 110 above. On the Upanishads, J. Mascaro, *The Upanishads* (1965) is the best edition in translation; N. S. Subrahmanian, *Encyclopedia of the Upanishads* (1985) is a valuable companion.

On North America, B. Trigger and W. E. Washburn, *The Cambridge History of the Peoples of North America* (1996–2000) is an invaluable guide. B. Fagan, *Ancient North America: The Archaeology of a Continent* (1991) is a helpful introduction.

For Bantu languages in particular and the African background in general, J. Ki-Zerbo, ed., *The UNESCO General History of Africa*, i (1993) is of great value.

The Axial Age, from 500 B.C.E. to 100 C.E.

CHAPTER 6 The Great Schools 124
CHAPTER 7 The Great Empires 150

Babylonian world map The world as seen from Babylon in the mid–first millennium B.C.E. The circle represents the ocean. The towers of Babylon can be seen just inside the ring. Other cities are indicated by circles and the Tigris and Euphrates Rivers by lines.
British Museum, London, UK/Bridgeman Art Library

ENVIRONMENT

since 800 B.C.E. Trans-Mediterranean trade

since 3000 B.C.E. Steppe pastoralism

CULTURE

650–550 B.C.E. Zoroaster

ca. 623–543 B.C.E. Buddha

551–479 B.C.E. Confucius

since 300 B.C.E.
Silk Roads;
Monsoon driven Indian Ocean trade

since 100 B.C.E.
Mediterranean–Atlantic trade

ca. 550–334 B.C.E.
Persian Empire

427–347 B.C.E.
Plato

334–323 B.C.E.
Alexander's Empire

ca. 300–223 B.C.E.
Mauryan Empire

240 B.C.E.–400s C.E.
Roman Empire

221 B.C.E.–220s C.E.
Han Empire

ca. 3–33 C.E.
Jesus

CHAPTER 6 The Great Schools

The Buddha's first sermon, depicted here in a Kushanese relief of the late second or early third century C.E. The Buddha squats under a lotus tree, on a pedestal decorated with a prayer wheel. The attentive figures who stand by his pedestal among the onlookers who surround him are probably the patrons who commissioned this sculpture. Kushanese art—from the mountainous northwest of the Indian subcontinent and Afghanistan—combines influences from India, Persia, Greece, and China, demonstrating the vitality of cultural exchange across Eurasia.

Scenes from the Life of Buddha, late 2nd–early 3rd century, Kushan dynasty, Stone. Courtesy of the Freer Gallery of Art, Smithsonian Institution, Washington, D.C.

IN THIS CHAPTER

THE THINKERS OF THE AXIAL AGE

THE THOUGHTS OF THE AXIAL AGE
Religious Thinking
New Political Thinking
Challenging Illusion
Mathematics
Reason
Science
Medicine
Skepticism

AXIAL AGE–AXIAL AREA: THE STRUCTURES OF THE AXIAL AGE

IN PERSPECTIVE: The Reach of the Sages

Just over halfway through the first millennium B.C.E., a frustrated administrator in the police service set out from the small Chinese state of Lu, south of the Yellow River, on a journey in search of a worthy master. Conflicting traditions claim him as the descendant of kings and the child of a humble home. By what is said to be his own account, he was a studious child, who worked his way through his education, learning menial jobs, including grain counting and bookkeeping. He could never get ahead in the bureaucracy of Lu, perhaps because he was openly disgusted with the immorality of its politics. A book later published under his name recounts the history of his times in deadpan fashion, listing the violence and injustice of the kings and aristocrats, without any apparent moralizing. The effect heightens the reader's revulsion.

CHINA

The exile never found the ideal ruler he sought. Instead, he lived by attracting pupils and left a body of thought that still influences ideas on the conduct of politics and the duties and opportunities of daily life. For him—and for most other thinkers in an era disfigured by the disintegration of China—loyalty was the key virtue: loyalty to God, to the state, to one's family, and to the true meanings of the words one uses. Most of the world knows him today by a name that is a corruption of his honorific title: "Master Kong"—Kong Fuzi (koong foo-tzeh) in Chinese, "Confucius" in the West.

• • • • •

The importance of Confucius is a reminder of how much the world of our own day owes to the world of his—how thinkers of the time influenced the way we think now. Heroic teachers gathered disciples and handed down traditions. Typically, followers treated the founders with awestruck reverence, recast them as supermen or even gods, and clouded our knowledge of them with legends and lore. We can unpick enough evidence, however, to get tentative pictures of outstanding examples of some of them—some we even know by name—and some impression of what they taught.

These sages came up with ideas so influential as to justify a term that has become popular with scholars: the **axial age**. Different writers assign different meanings to this term. In this chapter and the next, it designates the 500 years or so, roughly up to the beginning of the Christian era. The image of an axis suits the period for three reasons. First, the areas in which the thought of the sages and their schools unfolded stretched, axis-like, across Eurasia, in regions that bordered on and influenced each other (see Map 6.1). Second, the thought of

FOCUS questions

- WHAT DO historians mean by the term *axial age*?
- WHAT WERE the main areas of axial-age thinking in Eurasia?
- WHAT WERE the most important religious ideas that developed during the axial age?
- WHAT SIMILARITIES developed among Chinese, Greek, and Indian science and medicine during the axial age?
- HOW DID political pessimists differ from optimists in their ideas about human nature and the role of government?
- WHY WAS the axial age confined to such a limited area of the world?

the period has remained central to, and supporting of, so much later thought, as its influence spread with developments described throughout the rest of this book. The religious leaders of the time founded traditions of such power that they have huge followings. The secular thinkers ran out, as if with their fingernails, grooves of logic and science in which people still think. They raised problems of human nature—and of how to devise appropriate social and political solutions—that still preoccupy us. And, third, because disciples wrote down much of their teaching, a body of texts has survived to become reference points for later study.

No one should try to study this material expecting it to be easy. We could dodge the difficulties by talking about the personalities instead of the problems of the axial age. But this chapter is designed to concentrate on what the axial-age sages thought and why they thought it—not on their lives and characters. So, after briefly outlining who the sages were and where they operated, we shall turn to the religious, political, and scientific ideas that characterized the age and made it "axial"—the shared features, which for students of global history are the most interesting.

Finally, the big problem arises: Why was there an axial age at all? Why did so much enduring thinking happen in such a relatively concentrated period? I try to explore this question, toward the end of the chapter, by investigating the networks to which the sages and their disciples belonged. The next chapter describes the political and economic contexts that surrounded, nourished, and transmitted axial-age ideas.

China, India, Greece, and southwest Asia were the linked locations in which axial thinking happened. So we also have to keep in mind the problem of why other parts of the world seem to have experienced nothing similar. If Africa, or the Americas, or the Pacific world, or western or northern Europe, or northern or Central Asia had comparable sages and schools, they left no record, and we know nothing of them. But, of course, they did produce traditions of thought that had local or regional influence, inviting us to try to understand why they have not survived and to make comparisons between the Eurasian arena of the axial age and other parts of the world.

THE THINKERS OF THE AXIAL AGE

As we saw in the last chapter, the work of thinkers of great depth and complexity was recorded earlier in India. Gradually, however, as disciples began to confide sages' secrets to writing, evidence emerged that issues similar to those already familiar in Indian sources (see Chapter 5) were attracting attention in other parts of Asia.

In what we now call Iran, the sage usually known as Zoroaster (zoh-roh-AHS-tehr) is dated to around the late seventh and early sixth centuries B.C.E. Texts ascribed to him are so partial, corrupt, and obscure that we cannot reconstruct them with confidence. As practiced by his followers, however, Zoroastrianism assumed that conflicting forces of good and evil shaped the world. The single good deity, Ahura Mazda (ah-HOO-rah MAHZ-dah), was present in fire and light;

the rites of his worshippers were connected with dawn and fire-kindling, while night and darkness were the province of Ahriman, the god of evil. Similar ideas, which dominated mainstream thinking in Iran for 1,000 years, have appeared in other Eurasian religions. Zoroastrian communities are still scattered around the world. For reasons we shall come to, however, Zoroaster had no comparable successor in his homeland.

In India, meanwhile, around the middle of the millennium, texts of the Veda multiplied. In particular, teachings about Brahman, handed down in the early Upanishads and described in Chapter 5, were studied and written down. Alongside this defining of Brahmanism in written texts, new thinking explored the moral implications of religious life, in a world of competing states comparable to that of China. Vardhamana Jnatrputra, for instance, whose life is traditionally assigned to the sixth or early fifth century B.C.E., is universally known as "Mahavira" (ma-ha-VEE-rah)—"the great hero." He founded **Jainism** (JAH-een-izm), a way of life designed to free the soul from evil by ascetic practices: chastity, detachment, truth, and charity. But Jainism is so demanding that it could only be practiced with full rigor in monasteries and religious communities. It never drew a following outside India.

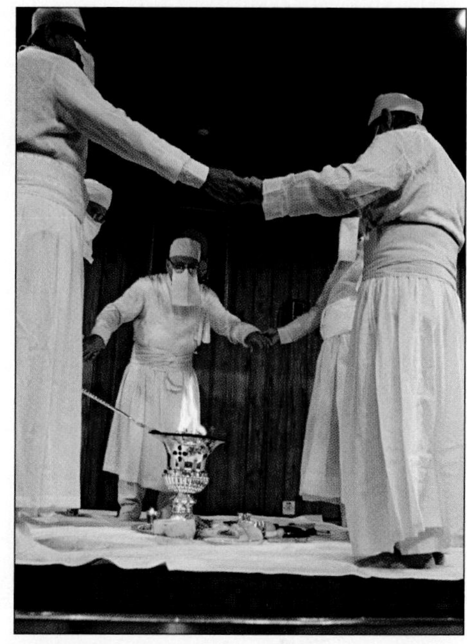

Zoroastrians. Though persecuted almost to extinction in Iran, the land of its birth, Zoroastrianism survives among exiled communities, especially in India, the United States, and Western Europe. Here Zoroastrian priests in London mark the New Year by kindling sacred light.

Siddhartha Gautama: *Identity and Nonidentity*

Gautama Siddharta (GAW-teh-mah sihd-ARTH-ah), however, who probably lived between the mid–sixth and early fourth centuries B.C.E., founded in India a religion of potentially universal appeal. Or perhaps the tradition he launched is better described as a code of life than as a religion, since Gautama himself seems never to have made any assertions about God. Rather, he prescribed practices that would liberate devotees from the troubles of this world. Gautama, whose followers called him "the Buddha" or "Enlightened One," taught that a combination of meditation, prayer, and unselfish behavior could achieve happiness. The object was escape from desire—the cause of unhappiness. For the most privileged practitioners of what came to be called Buddhism, the aim was the ultimate extinction of all sense of self in a mystical state, called **nirvana** or "extinction of the flame." Devotees gathered in monasteries to help guide each other toward this end—but individuals in worldly settings could also achieve it. Many early Buddhist stories of the attainment of enlightenment concern people in everyday occupations, including merchants and rulers. This helped create powerful constituencies for the religion. To liberate the soul from the world, either by individual self-refinement or by losing oneself in selflessness, was likely to be a long job. In the meantime, the soul could expect to be recycled by reincarnation. The distinctive element in the Buddhist view of this process was that it was ethical. A principle of justice—or at least of retribution—would govern the fate of the soul, which would be assigned a "higher" or "lower" body in each successive life according to how virtuous it had been in its previous incarnation.

Critics sometimes claim that these new religions were really forms of old magic: that the desire to "escape the world" or "extinguish the self" or achieve "union with Brahman" was, in effect, a bid for immortality, and that mystical practice was a kind of alternative medicine designed to prolong or enhance life. Or else such practices as prayer and self-denial could be seen as a bid for the charismatic power of self-transformation of the shaman (see Chapter 1), obtained without using mind-bending drugs. These analyses may have some validity. The Buddha called himself healer as well as teacher. Many legends of the era associate miracles of therapy with founders of religions. The identification of detachment from the world with the pursuit of immortality is

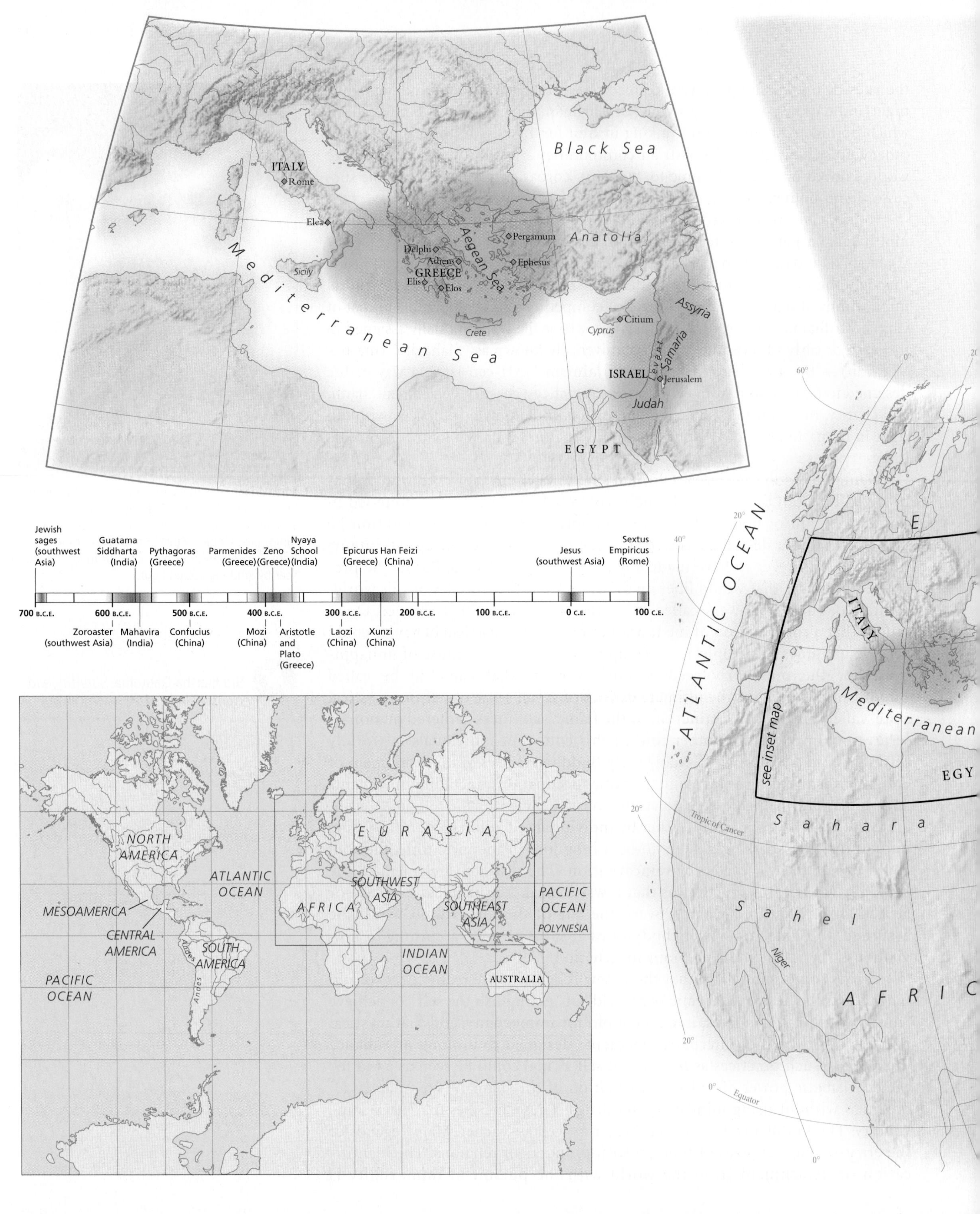

Black Sea
ITALY
Rome
Elea
Mediterranean Sea
Sicily
Delphi
Athens
GREECE
Elis
Elos
Aegean Sea
Pergamum
Anatolia
Ephesus
Crete
Cyprus
Citium
Assyria
Samaria
Levant
ISRAEL
Jerusalem
Judah
EGYPT
Jewish sages (southwest Asia)
Guatama Siddharta (India)
Pythagoras (Greece)
Parmenides (Greece)
Zeno (Greece)
Nyaya School (India)
Epicurus (Greece)
Han Feizi (China)
Jesus (southwest Asia)
Sextus Empiricus (Rome)
700 B.C.E.
600 B.C.E.
500 B.C.E.
400 B.C.E.
300 B.C.E.
200 B.C.E.
100 B.C.E.
0 C.E.
100 C.E.
Zoroaster (southwest Asia)
Mahavira (India)
Confucius (China)
Mozi (China)
Aristotle and Plato (Greece)
Laozi (China)
Xunzi (China)
NORTH AMERICA
ATLANTIC OCEAN
EURASIA
SOUTHWEST ASIA
AFRICA
SOUTHEAST ASIA
PACIFIC OCEAN
POLYNESIA
MESOAMERICA
CENTRAL AMERICA
SOUTH AMERICA
Andes
INDIAN OCEAN
AUSTRALIA
PACIFIC OCEAN
ATLANTIC OCEAN
ITALY
Mediterranean
see inset map
EGY
Tropic of Cancer
Sahara
Sahel
Niger
AFRIC
Equator

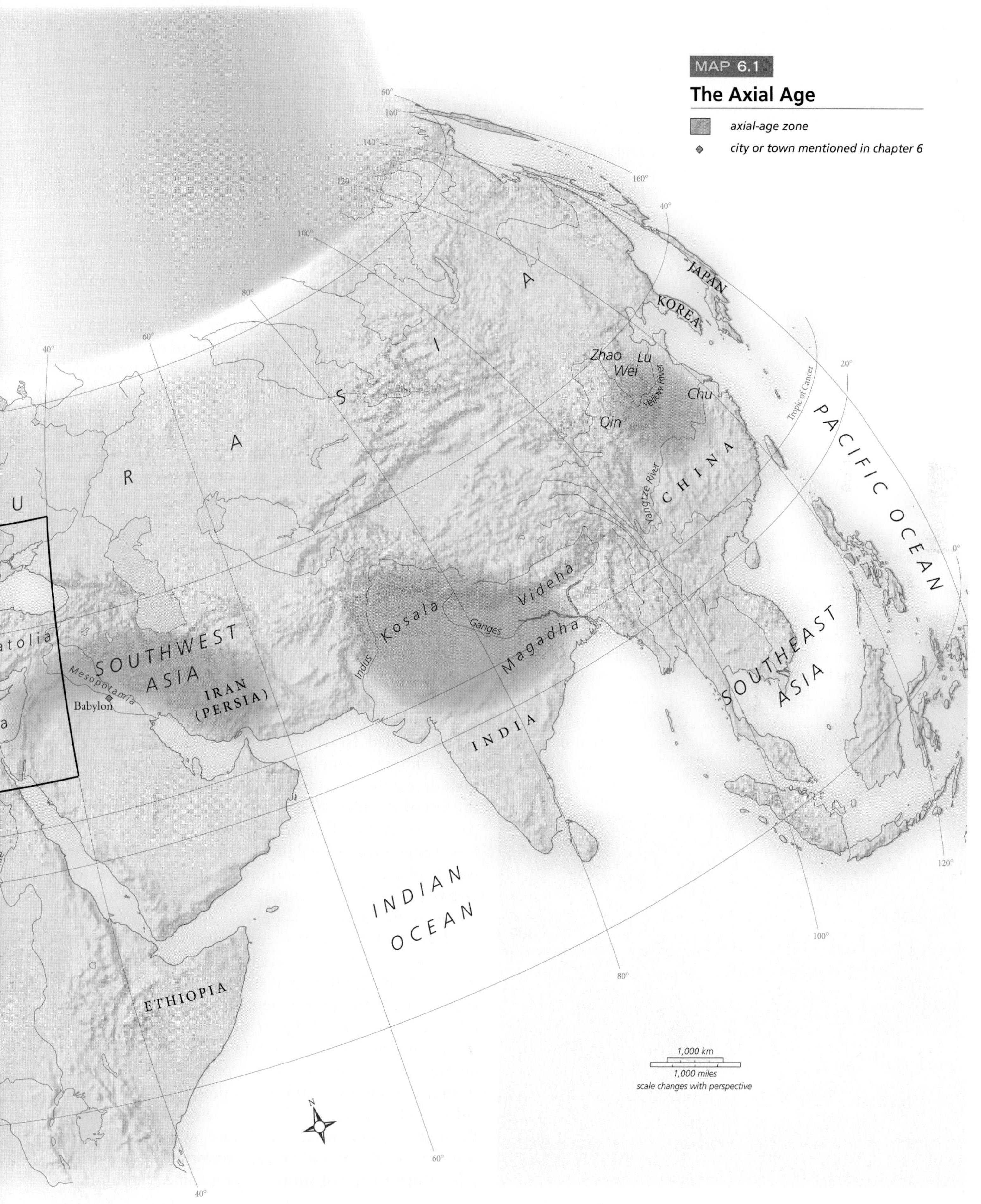
MAP 6.1
The Axial Age
axial-age zone
city or town mentioned in chapter 6
E U R A S I A
JAPAN
KOREA
Zhao
Lu
Wei
Yellow River
Chu
Qin
CHINA
Yangtze River
Tropic of Cancer
PACIFIC OCEAN
Videha
Kosala
Ganges
Magadha
Indus
SOUTHWEST ASIA
IRAN (PERSIA)
Anatolia
Mesopotamia
Babylon
INDIA
SOUTHEAST ASIA
INDIAN OCEAN
ETHIOPIA
1,000 km
1,000 miles
scale changes with perspective
N

explicit, for instance, in writings attributed to Laozi (low-tzeh), probably a fourth-century B.C.E. figure, who founded **Daoism** (daow-ihzm) in China. Amid the insecurities of life among the warring states described in the last chapter, he recommended disengagement to give the Daoist power over suffering—power like that of water, which erodes even when it seems to yield: "There is nothing more soft and weak; for attacking the hard and strong there is nothing better."

Laozi, from the *Tao Te Ching*

Yet, the new religions were genuinely new. They upheld the effectiveness of moral practice, alongside rituals, as ways to adjust humans' relationship with nature or with the divine: not just sacrificing offerings fittingly to God or gods, but also modifying how people behaved toward each other. They attracted followers with programs of individual moral progress, rather than with rites to appease nature. In other words, they were emerging as religions of salvation, not just of survival. They promised the perfection of the human capacity for goodness, or "deliverance from evil"—attainable in this world or, if not, by transfer to another world after death, or by a transformation of this world at the end of time.

Traditions developed during the axial age among Jews also showed a drift in this direction. This relatively small and politically insignificant people of southwest Asia's Mediterranean coastal region demands attention because of the enormous long-term influence of some Jewish thinking. The Jews inhabited the war zone described in the last chapter. Traditionally, in the attempt to retrieve the facts of early Jewish history, scholars have relied on supposedly historical narratives in the Bible, the sacred writings of the Jews. But archaeological investigation has made this history increasingly difficult to confirm. So any account has to be tentative.

Like most people, the Jews seem to have started with a religion tailored toward worldly ends, worshipping a tribal deity who promised material success and victory. Their sacred writings, however, tell a story of disillusionment: of defeats and dispossessions by their enemies. From the eighth century B.C.E., Egyptian, Assyrian, and Babylonian inscriptions confirm that Jews inhabited two kingdoms called Israel and Judah, which fought each other and fell victim to neighboring empires. Large-scale deportations—including a massive forced migration to Babylon after the fall of the Jews' holy city of Jerusalem in the 580s B.C.E.—incited a "diaspora mentality": exiles' sense of loss, resignation, nostalgia, defeat, and hope. "By the waters of Babylon," as psalmists put it, "we lay down and wept. . . . If I ever forget Jerusalem, let my tongue cleave to my mouth."

Exile of the Jews. "The king of Assyria carried the Israelites away to Assyria." This relief from the palace of the invading king seems to illustrate the scene described in the biblical Book of Kings (II.18:11), as soldiers take prisoners from the fortress of Lachish, which the Assyrians captured in 701 B.C.E. The Bible says that the Hebrew king then "stripped the gold from the doors of the Temple of the Lord" in an attempt to buy off the invaders.

Judean exiles carrying provisions. Detail of the Assyrian conquest of the Jewish fortified town of Lachish (battle 701 B.C.). Part of a relief from the palace of Sennacherib at Nineveh, Mesopotamia (Iraq). Erich Lessing/Art Resource, N.Y.

Instead of turning the Jews against their deity, their disasters inspired them to see him as the only true God, beside whom all other gods were false. Sufferings were trials of faith and punishments for sin—especially for failures to acknowledge God's uniqueness. God promised deliverance, if not in this life, then in the afterlife, or at the end of history, or, at best, in a remote future, as a reward for fidelity to prescribed rituals and rules of life, known as "the Law." Jews differed among themselves about what deliverance would mean. For some, it would be individual immortality; for some, relief from a sense of sinfulness; for some, the elimination of evil from the world; for some, national independence; for some, an empire over their enemies.

The last great teacher of the age—the greatest, in terms of the scale of his influence—was the Jew we usually call Jesus, who died in or about 33 C.E. To the secular historian, Jesus is best understood as an independent-minded Jewish rabbi, with a radical message. Indeed, some of his followers saw him as the culmination of Jewish tradition, embodying, renewing, and even replacing it. The name *Christ*, which his followers gave him, is a corruption of a Greek attempt to translate the Hebrew term *ha-mashiad*, or **Messiah**, meaning "the anointed," which Jews used to designate the king they hoped for at the end of history to bring heaven to earth. Jesus' message was uncompromising. The Jewish priesthood should be purged of corruption, the temple at Jerusalem "cleansed" of money-making practices. More controversially, some of his followers understood him to claim that humans could not gain divine favor by appealing to a kind of bargain with God—the "covenant" of Jewish tradition. God freely gave or withheld his favor, or grace. According to Jewish doctrine, God responded to obedience to laws and rules. But Jesus' followers preferred to think that, however righteously we behave, we remain dependent on God's grace. No subsequent figure was so influential until Muhammad, the founder of Islam, who died six centuries later, and none thereafter for at least 1,000 years.

The religious teachings of the sages were highlights in a world teeming with other new religions, most of which have not survived. In a period when no one recognized a hard-and-fast distinction between religion and secular life, spiritual ferment stimulated intellectual innovation. It is still hard to say, for instance, whether Confucius founded a religion. After all, he ordered rites of veneration of gods and ancestors but disclaimed interest in worlds other than our own. The many other schools of the axial age in China shared similar priorities but mixed what we would now think of as secular and religious thinking. Confucius's opponent, Mozi (moh-tzeh), is a case in point. He taught a philosophy of **universal love**, on secular grounds, 400 years before Jesus' religious version.

Other innovators formulated ideas that belong in what we would now classify as secular thought. Greek sages, for instance, whose work overlapped with that of the founders of new religions in Asia, taught techniques for telling good from evil and truth from falsehood that we still use. The towering figures were two teachers of the fourth century B.C.E.: Aristotle, a physician's son from northern Greece, who was, perhaps, the most purely secular thinker of the age, and his teacher, the Athenian aristocrat, Plato. Aristotle left work on science, logic, politics, and literature unequalled in the West for centuries, while Western philosophy is often jokingly dismissed as "footnotes to Plato." Logicians, scientific observers, and experimenters in China paralleled these achievements, as did thinkers in India of the school known as Nyaya, who shared confidence in reason and the urge to analyze it, resolving arguments step by step.

THE THOUGHTS OF THE AXIAL AGE

There is no easy way to analyze the thinking of the axial age. Textbook writers usually divide the subject by regions, because scholars tend to specialize in regions. This method, however, conceals the fact that an almost continuous zone across Eurasia stretching from China, through India, southwest Asia, and the Mediterranean Levant, to Greece linked these regions together (see Map 6.1).

A thematic approach, of the kind attempted over the next few pages, helps reveal connections and contrasts. We start with religious ideas, bearing in mind the now-familiar warning that religion and secular life were overlapping categories for most thinkers at the time.

Religious Thinking

Of new thoughts of God formulated or developed in the axial age, three proved especially influential in global history: the idea of a divine creator, responsible for everything else in the universe; the idea of a single God, uniquely divine, or divine in a unique way; and the idea of an involved God, engaged in the life of the world.

CREATION Gods and spirits are hard to imagine. It is even harder to imagine nothing. But the idea of nothing enabled thinkers to understand nature in a new way. For once you have got your head around the concept of nothing, you can imagine creation from nothing.

Before the axial age, creation narratives, as far as we know, were not really about creation, but were explanations of how the universe came to be the way it is. Ancient Egyptian creation myths tell of a creator transforming chaos into a world endowed with time: but the chaos was there for him to mold. The eternal being whom early Indian writings call Brahman created the world out of himself, "as a spider spins its web." "How could it be so," sneered one text of the Upanishads, "that being was produced from non-being?" Most Greek philosophers agreed. Plato's creator-god did not start from nothing but rearranged what was there. Buddhists saw no beginning to the universe and no need for a creator.

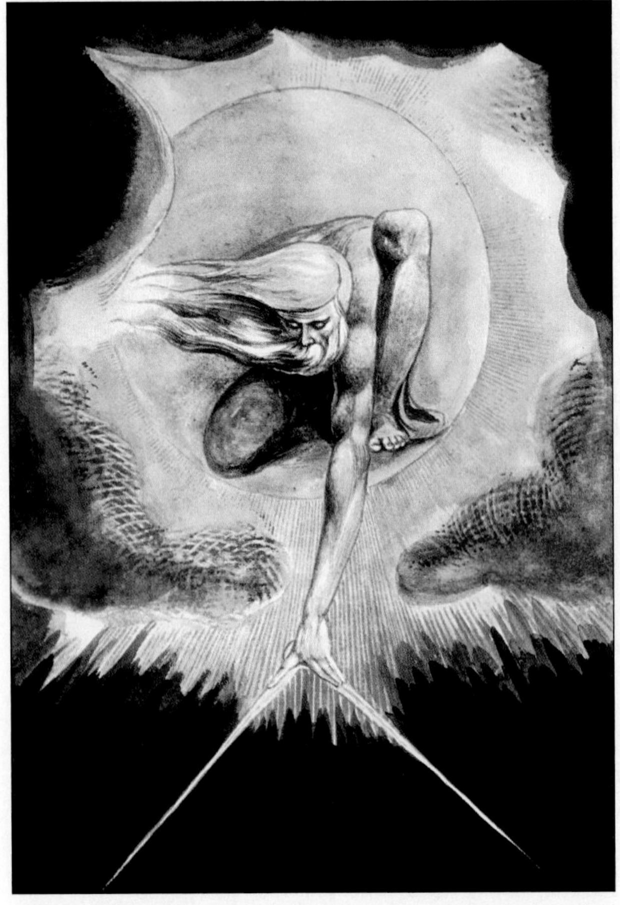

The Creator. The British poet and artist William Blake (1757–1827) was explicit; he painted visions. His version of the Creation—probably now the most famous in the world—is certainly visionary but has obvious sources. It calls the Bible to mind, as God measures "a world without form, and void." The use of rushing wind to suggest the Holy Spirit, and of sun rays to signify Jesus, are among the oldest conventions of Christian art. God's stooped posture and his dividers, flashing like lightning, recall medieval paintings of God as the architect of the cosmos (see Chapter 13).

Some ancient Greek poetry, however, described a world-beginning without prior matter. Emotion or thought was the prime mover of the universe. As the Gospel according to John put it in the late first century C.E., "In the beginning was the logos"—literally, the thought, which English translations usually render as "the word." Of all the early Christian accounts of Jesus' life, John's was the gospel Greek thought influenced most heavily. Most other Christian accounts relied heavily on traditions peculiar to Jesus' own people, the Jews, who brought an unusual philosophical twist to divine thinking: the idea of a creator who always existed but who made everything else out of nothing.

Conclusions followed. The creator was unique, for nothing else could precede creation; he was purely spiritual, since there was no matter until he made it; he was eternal—he existed, that is, outside time—since he was not himself a product of creation; he was therefore unchanging; nothing greater than he could be conceived: His power had no limits.

MONOTHEISM The idea of a unique God, who monopolizes power over nature, is now so familiar, at least in the West, that we can no longer sense how strange it is. Yet, until the first millennium B.C.E., as far as we know, most people who imagined an invisible world—beyond nature and controlling it—supposed that it was crowded with gods, the way creatures crammed nature. To systematize the world of the gods in the axial age, Greeks arrayed gods in order. Persians reduced them to two—one good, one evil. In Indian *henotheism*, a multiplicity of gods collectively represented divine unity.

For Jews, Yahweh (YAH-weh), their tribal deity, was, or became, their only God. The chronology is insecure, and we do not know whether the Jewish creation theory was cause or consequence of this development. Their writings called him "jealous"—unwilling to allow divine status to any rival. Fierce enforcement of his sole right to worship was part of the covenant in which Yahweh's favor was exchanged for obedience and veneration. "I am Yahweh your God. . . . You shall have no other gods to rival me."

Jews were not obliged to impose the Yahweh cult on others. On the contrary, for most of history, they treated it as a treasure too precious to share with non-Jews. Elsewhere, monotheism seemed unappealing. Buddhism dispensed with the need for a creator by upholding that the universe was itself infinite and everlasting. When asked about the existence of God, Buddha, in the recollection of his disciples, always answered evasively. In India, China, and Greece, the idea of a unique creator left options for polytheism: If one being inhabited eternity, why—in strict logic—might not others? Other uniqueness can be divided: You can shatter a rock, parse a statement, refract light. So maybe the uniqueness of God is of this kind. Alternatively, it could be a kind of comprehensiveness, like that of "Nature," "the Earth," or the sum of everything. God is one—any good Brahmanist would acknowledge—in the sense that everything is one. In any case, if God's power is without limits, surely he can create other gods.

Despite these arguments, three developments have conspired, in the long run, to make the God of the Jews the favorite God of much of the world. First, the Jews' own "sacred" history of sacrifices and sufferings gave a compelling example of faith. Second, a Jewish splinter group, which recognized Jesus as—so to speak—the human face of God, opened its ranks to non-Jews. Christianity built up a vigorous and sometimes aggressive tradition of trying to convert non-Christians everywhere. Thanks in part to a message adaptable to all sorts of cultural environments, it became, over nearly 2,000 years, the world's most widely diffused religion. Finally, early in the seventh century C.E., the prophet Muhammad studied Judaism and Christianity, and incorporated the Jewish understanding of God in Islam, the rival religion he founded. In its turn Islam attracted almost as many followers. Today, well over a third of the world's population subscribes to the tradition of Jewish, Christian, and Muslim monotheism (see Figure 6.1).

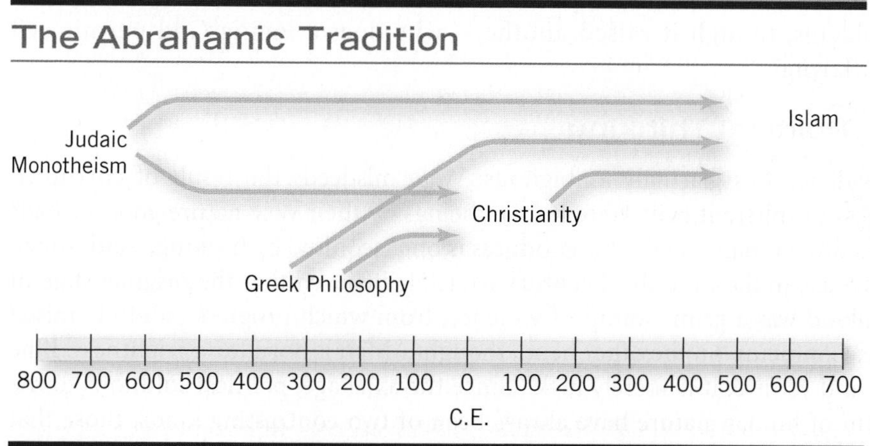

FIGURE 6.1 THE ABRAHAMIC TRADITION

DIVINE LOVE Having created, did God remain interested in creation? Most Greek thinkers of the era ignored or repudiated the suggestion. Aristotle's description of God is of a perfect being, who needs nothing else, who has no uncompleted purposes, and who feels neither sensibility nor suffering. "The benevolence of heaven" was a phrase much used in China around the midpoint of the millennium, but this seems a long way short of love. Mozi, as even his philosophical adversaries admitted, "would wear out his whole being for the benefit of humankind." But his vision of humankind bound by love was not theologically inspired. Rather, he had a romantic vision of a golden age of "Great Togetherness" in the primitive past.

The claim that God's interest is specially focused on humans seems suspiciously self-centered. Gradually, however, axial-age thinking made it believable by insisting that humankind was higher than other animals. There were dissenting traditions. Philosophers in southern Italy in the late sixth century B.C.E. taught that "All things that are born with life in them should be treated as kindred." Religious Jains' reverence for animals' souls was—and still is—so intense that they swept the ground to avoid walking on insects. But the biblical God makes "man in His own image" as the last word in creation and gives humans dominion over all other animals.

Divine love. "I am the good shepherd," said Jesus, according to the Gospel of John (10:14), "and I lay down my life for my sheep." During the persecutions that punctuated the first 300 years of the history of the Church, Christian artists interpreted the New Testament's many texts about "straying" and "lost" sheep as metaphors for the souls of martyrs, whom Jesus gathered into his fold. This third-century example shows how Christians continued the heroic and aesthetic conventions of classical sculpture.

"The Good Shepherd," marble, height: as restored 99 cm, as preserved 55 cm, head 15.5 cm. Late 3rd century A.D. Vatican Museums, Pio-Christian Museum, Inv. 28590. Courtesy of the Vatican Museums.

In the second half of the millennium, thinkers in other traditions formulated similar ideas. In the mid–fourth century B.C.E., Aristotle developed a hierarchy of living souls, in which the human soul was superior to those of plants and animals, because it had rational as well as "vegetative" and "sensitive" faculties. The Chinese formula was similar, as, for example, Xunzi (shoon-tzeh) put it early in the next century: "Man has spirits, life, and perception, and in addition the sense of justice; therefore he is the noblest of earthly beings." Humans could exploit stronger creatures because they were able to form societies and act collaboratively. Buddhism ranked humans as higher creatures than others for purposes of reincarnation. For Jews humans were lords or stewards of creation, uniquely empowered to communicate directly with God.

Late in the axial age, some Jews began to use the image of **divine love** to express this relationship—perhaps to cope with the frustrations of their history, in which they had never recovered political independence. Jesus and his followers seized on the identification of God with love. Love is a universal emotion. By making God's love embrace all humans—rather than favoring a chosen race or a righteous minority—Christianity acquired universal appeal. Creation became an act of love consistent with God's nature. This solved a lot of problems, though it raised another—why does a loving God permit evil and suffering?

New Political Thinking

The evidence was glaringly ambiguous: Were misdeeds the result of corrupted goodness or inherent evil? Were human beings by their very nature good or bad? "The nature of man is evil—his goodness is only acquired by training," said Xunzi, for instance, in the mid–third century B.C.E. He believed that the original state of humankind was a grim swamp of violence, from which progress painfully raised people. Confucius, on the other hand, thought, "Man is born for uprightness. If he lose it and yet live, it is merely luck." Since the axial age, political solutions to the problem of human nature have always been of two contrasting kinds: those that emphasize freedom, to release human goodness, and those that emphasize discipline, to restrain human wickedness.

The biblical book of Genesis contained the most widely favored compromise. God made humans good and free. The abuse of freedom made people bad. Logically, this was unpersuasive. If Adam was good, how could he use freedom for evil? To escape this trap, Genesis added a diabolical device. The serpent (or other devilish agents in other traditions) corrupted goodness from outside. This has left politics with a difficult balancing act, which no system has ever adequately accomplished, between freedom and force.

POLITICAL PESSIMISM For pessimists, the way to overcome human deficiencies was to strengthen the state. Plato was a member of an Athenian gang of intellectuals and aristocrats, who felt qualified for power and therefore resented democracy. His recommendations included censorship, repression, militarism, regimentation, rigid class structure, extreme collectivism, selective breeding of superior human beings, and deliberate deception of the people by the state. Political power should be concentrated in a self-electing class of philosopher-rulers called **Guardians.**

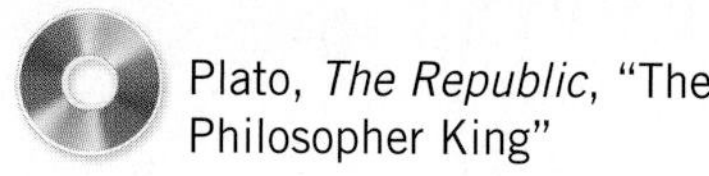
Plato, *The Republic*, "The Philosopher King"

Their qualification for office would be intellectual superiority, guaranteed by a mixture of heredity and education, which would make them selfless in their private lives and godlike in their ability to see what was good for the citizens. They would achieve Plato's declared objective: "the greatest happiness of the whole, and not that of any one class." He wrote so persuasively that this reasoning has continued to appeal to state builders ever since. "There will be no end to the troubles of states, or indeed, of humanity," he claimed, "until philosophers become kings in this world, or till those we now call kings and rulers really and truly become philosophers." His Guardians, however, became the inspiration and the intellectual ancestors of elites, aristocracies, party hacks, and self-appointed supermen whose justification for tyrannizing others has always been that they know best.

Chinese counterparts exceeded the severity even of Plato's thinking. For most of the time, they were in the minority: The consensus among the sages was that the ruler should be bound by law (a point in which Aristotle, at the other end of Eurasia, agreed). Confucius even said that ethics should override obedience to the law. In the fourth century B.C.E., however, a school of thought in China known as the **Legalists** denounced ethics as a "gnawing worm" that would destroy the state. Society required only obedience. Law and order were worth tyranny and injustice.

This was a new twist in the history of thinking about law. The explanation lies in the terror of the times. Legalist doctrine was born in a time of civil disaster and has tended to resurface in bad times ever since. Legalists laughed off earlier sages' belief in the innate goodness of people. The best penalties were the most severe: cutting off heads, slicing or ripping people in half, roasting them alive. As well as in the worship of order, ancient Chinese Legalism anticipated modern fascism, for instance, in advocating and glorifying war, recommending economic self-sufficiency for the state, denouncing capitalism, praising agriculture, and insisting on the need to suppress individualism in the interests of state unity.

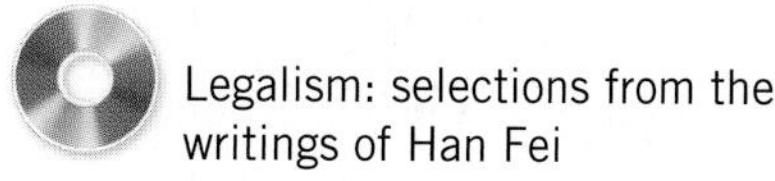
Legalism: selections from the writings of Han Fei

POLITICAL OPTIMISM But most sages of the axial age were optimists. They thought human nature was essentially good. Hence, the political doctrines of Confucianism, which demanded that the state should liberate subjects to fulfill their potential. Hence, too, the democracy Greek sages advocated, which entrusted citizens (though not, of course, women or slaves) with a voice in political affairs.

Chinese thinkers applied similarly individualistic doctrines, but they did not question monarchy. The state was meant to reflect the universe. Its unity could not be compromised. All that could be expected was that the ruler should consult the

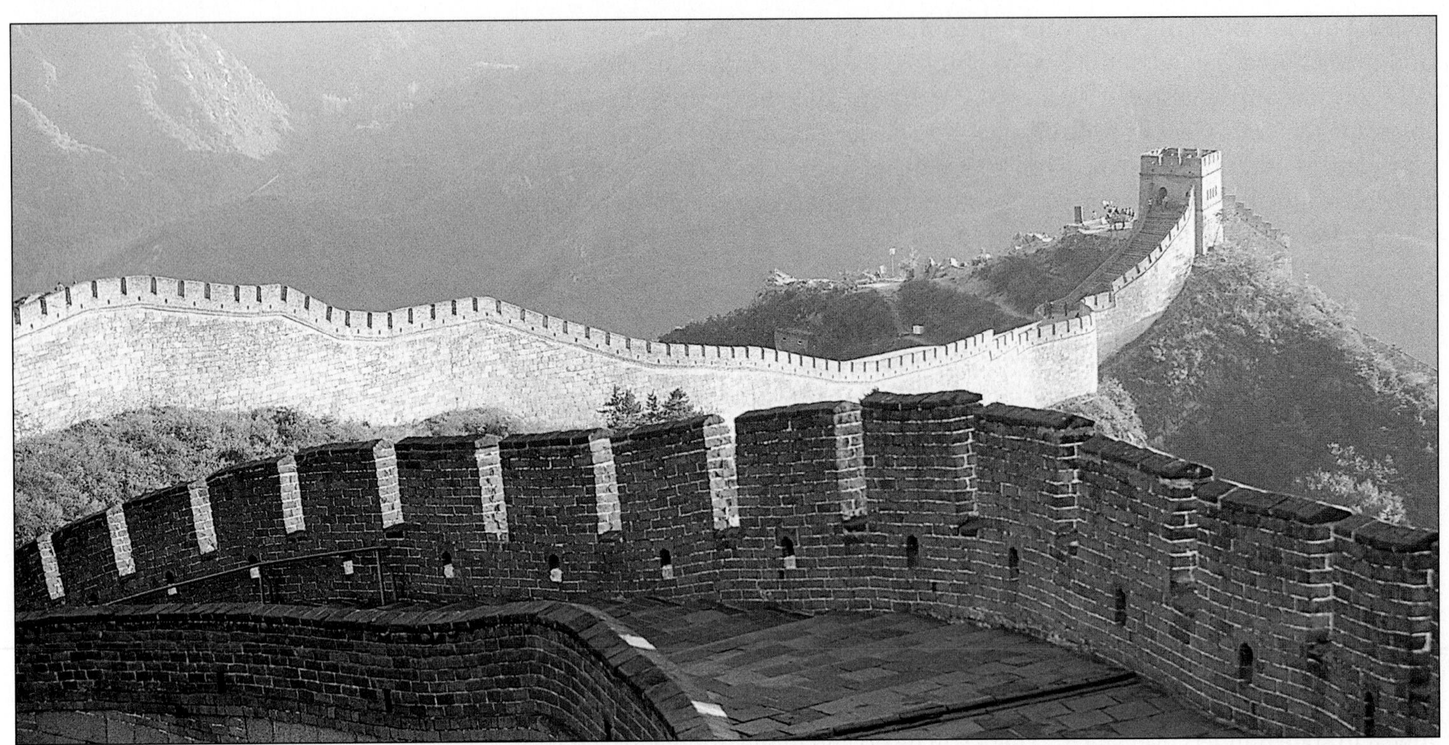

The Great Wall of China. Legend assigns the Great Wall of China to the Warring States period in the third century B.C.E. In fact, it took centuries to build and was often rebuilt thereafter. Little of the surviving workmanship, which stretches for some 4,000 miles, is more than 500 years old. Chinese culture now extends way beyond it, but the wall has an important place in the formation of Chinese identity—defining the supposed boundary of the non-Chinese world, displaying the ambition and achievement of Chinese civilization.

people's interests and views and should face the subjects' right to rebel against tyranny. "Heaven sees according as the people see," said Mencius, Confucianism's outstanding spokesman. "Heaven hears according as the people hear." This was a reminder to the ruler, not a recipe for republicanism. Nor does Indian literature of the time mention popular institutions. But some Indian states did have elites hundreds or thousands strong that ruled as a group, electing leaders for fixed terms among themselves.

Meanwhile, in Greece, a variety of political experiments unfolded, including republican, aristocratic, and even democratic systems. Aristotle made a masterly survey of them in the fourth century B.C.E. He thought monarchy was the best system in theory, but not in practice, because it was impossible to ensure that the best man would always be the ruler. More practical was aristocratic government, in which a manageable number of superior men administered the state. But it tended to generate into the self-interested rule of the wealthy or permanent power for an hereditary clique. Democracy could lead to demagogues and mob rule. The best system was a carefully crafted mixture in which aristocracy predominated, under the rule of law. Broadly speaking, this was embodied in the Roman state of the second half of the millennium (see Chapter 8), which became, in turn, the model for most republican survivals and revivals in Western history. Even when, toward the end of the axial age, Rome abandoned republican government and restored what was in effect a monarchical system, Romans still spoke of their state as a republic and the emperor as merely the chief magistrate.

In politics, Jesus preached a subtle sort of subversion. A new commandment to "love one another," he claimed, could replace virtually all laws. The Kingdom of Heaven was more important than the empire of Rome. In one of history's great ironic jokes, Jesus advised fellow Jews, in effect, to despise or even ignore the state: "Render unto Caesar that which is Caesar's and unto God that which is God's." All Jews at the time would have understood what this meant, for everything, to them, was God's.

For society at large, Jesus was equally dangerous, welcoming social outcasts—prostitutes, tax collectors, "sinners," and heretics. He favored the weak against the strong: children, women, the lame, the blind, and beggars—the "meek," who, he promised, "shall inherit the earth." In view of the radical nature of this bias, it is unsurprising that Jewish and Roman authorities combined to put him to death. His followers then turned from political activism to spiritual preparation for personal salvation.

Challenging Illusion

New thinking about reason and reality, and the relationship between them, flourished alongside or within the work of the religious leaders. Perhaps the most startling feature that united the thought of the axial age across Eurasia was the sages' struggle against illusion—their effort to see beyond appearances to underlying realities. "People dwelling in a cavern," said Plato, "see only the shadows ... that the fire throws onto the wall of their cave." Senses deceive. We are mental cave dwellers. How can we see out of our cave?

Mathematics

The question inspired innovations in mathematics. Indian sages discovered in numbers a limitless universe. Jain speculators about the age of the cosmos invoked mind-bogglingly big numbers, partly to demonstrate how impossible it was to attain the infinite. Workers in arithmetic discovered unreachable numbers: ratios that could never be exactly determined, but that seemed to underpin the universe—π, for instance (22 divided by 7), which determined the size of a circle, or the complex ratio that Greek mathematicians called the "Golden Number" (roughly 1.618) and seemed to represent perfection of proportion. The invention of geometry showed how the mind can reach realities that the senses obscure or warp: a perfect circle, a line without magnitude. Reality can be invisible, untouchable, and yet accessible to reason.

A figure of enormous importance in unfolding these mysteries (for that is what they were to people at the time) was Pythagoras. His life spanned the Greek world. He was born on an island in the Aegean, around the mid–sixth century B.C.E., but spent most of his teaching life in southern Italy. He attracted stories—he communed with the gods; he had a golden thighbone; he was not a mere man but a unique being, between human and divine.

He was the first thinker, as far as we know, to formulate the idea that numbers are real. They are obviously ways we have of classifying objects—two flowers, five flies. But Pythagoras thought that two and five really exist, quite apart from the objects they enumerate. They would still exist, even if there were nothing to count. He went further. Numbers are the basis on which the cosmos is constructed. "All things are numbers," was his way of putting it. Numbers determine shapes and structures—we still speak of "squares" and "cubes"—and numerical proportions underlie all relationships. Geometry, Pythagoras thought, is the architecture of the universe.

Not everyone was equally enthusiastic about the cult of numbers. "I sought the truth in measures and numbers," said Confucius in a text, which, though he probably did not really write it, reflects the prejudices of the third-century B.C.E. Daoist who compiled it, "but after five years I still hadn't found it." Still, the exploration of numbers was widespread among axial-age sages. **Rationalism**—the doctrine that unaided reason can elicit truth and solve the world's problems—was among the results.

Reason

The first pure rationalist we know by name was Parmenides, who was from a Greek colony of southern Italy in the early fifth century B.C.E. He started with geometry. If you believe geometrical figures are real, you believe in the truth of a supersensible world—for a perfect triangle, for instance, is like God: No one has ever seen one, though crude man-made approximations are commonplace. The only triangles we know about are those in our thoughts. Parmenides therefore suggested that the same might be true of everything else.

In some ways, the consequences are impressive. If, say, a pink rose is real by virtue of being a thought rather than a sensible object, then a black rose is equally real. The nonexistence of anything is an incoherent concept. Few of Parmenides's followers were willing to go that far, but reason did seem able to open secret caverns in the mind, where truths lay. "Fire is not hot. Eyes do not see": These were the numbing, blinding paradoxes of the fourth-century B.C.E. Chinese philosopher Hui Shih (hway-sheh)—who wrote five cartloads of books. They show that data act directly on the mind, which processes them before they become sensations. Thought does not have to arise from experience. For a true rationalist, the best laboratory is the mind, and the best experiments are thoughts.

In partial consequence, rationalism became an escapist's alternative to reality. Parmenides, for instance, thought he could prove that change was illusory and differences deceptive, and that only the unchanging and eternal were real. One of his successors, Zeno of Elea, invented famous paradoxes to demonstrate this: An arrow in flight always occupies a space equal to its size; therefore, it is always at rest. You can never complete a journey because you always have to cross half the remaining distance first. Matter is indivisible because "if a rod is shortened every day by half its length, it will still have something left after ten thousand generations."

Early in the second half of the millennium, teachers in India, Greece, and China proposed rules for the correct use of reason. Practical issues probably underpinned these movements. For pleading in courts, arguing between embassies, persuading enemies, and praising rulers, it was important to make arguments watertight. Logic was a fascinating by-product of these practical needs.

The Nyaya school

The most rigorous and systematic exposition was Aristotle's, strapping common sense into intelligible rules. He was the best-ever analyst of how reason works, in as much as it works at all. According to Aristotle, we can break valid arguments down into phases, called **syllogisms**, in which we can infer a necessary conclusion from two premises that prior demonstration or agreement have established to be true. If the premises are "All men are mortal" and "Socrates is a man," it follows that "Socrates is mortal."

At roughly the same time in India, the Nyaya school of commentators on ancient texts analyzed logical processes in five-stage breakdowns. Their conception, however, was in one fundamental way different from Aristotle's. They claimed reason was a kind of extraordinary perception that God conferred. Nor were they strictly rationalists, for they believed meaning did not arise in the mind. God, tradition, or consensus conferred it on the object of thought.

Science

Meanwhile, another route through the thought of the axial age led to science. As with the exploration of reason, the starting point was distrust of the senses. As a Daoist text of the third century B.C.E. points out, some metals seem soft but can combine to form harder ones; lacquer feels liquid but can be made dry by the application of another liquid. First appearances are deceptive. The science of the axial age sought to penetrate the veil and expose underlying truths. "Truth," said Democritus around the turn of the fifth and fourth centuries B.C.E., "lies in the depths." Although no strictly scientific texts from India survive from this period, the Upanishads contain similar warnings about the unreliability of appearances (see Chapter 5).

The idea of a distinction between what is natural and what is supernatural was, as far as we can tell, new. Previously, science seemed sacred, medicine magical. The earliest clear evidence of a shift in thinking is Chinese. In 679 B.C.E. the sage Shen Xu (shahn shoo) taught that ghosts were the products of the fears and guilt of those who see them. Confucius deterred followers from thinking "about the dead until you know the living." Confucians professed interest in human affairs—politics and practical morality—and indifference to the rest of nature. But as far as they did delve into nature studies, it was to dig out what they regarded as superstition: claims that inanimate substances had feelings and wills, that spirits inhabit all matter, or that the natural world is responsive to human sin or goodness. "The fact," says a Confucian text of about 239 B.C., "that water leaves the mountains is not due to any dislike on the part of the water but is the effect of height. The wheat has no desire to grow or be gathered into granaries." "Natural" causes displaced magic.

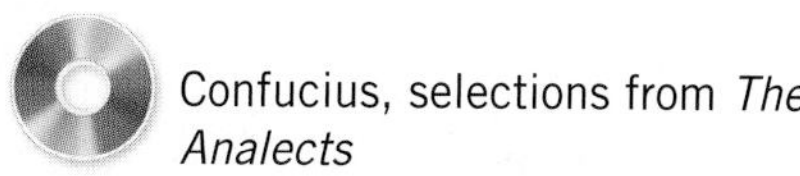
Confucius, selections from *The Analects*

In Greece, the origins of science were inseparable from magic, nature worship, and shamanistic attempts to penetrate the mysteries of unseen worlds. For science to thrive in a world that most people believed gods and sprites and demons still

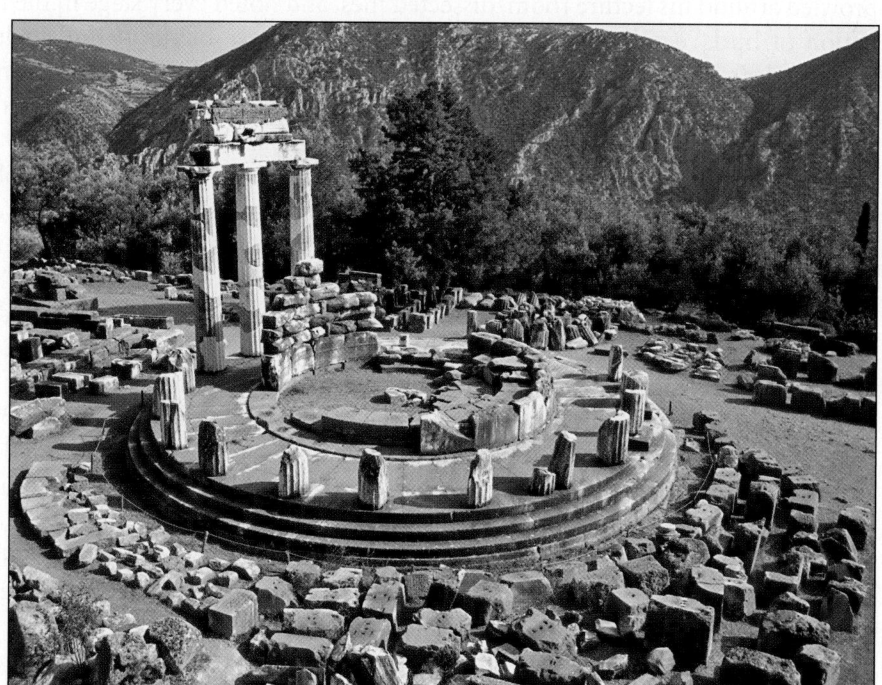

Delphi. Around Mount Parnassus, north of Athens, Greeks found or founded many shrines consecrated to Earth and Nature, as well as the most famous oracular site, at Delphi, where priestesses uttered obscure prophecies, supposedly under the influence of hallucinogenic fumes that rose from a fissure in the ground. Nearby, the circular sanctum known as the Tholos was built in the fourth century B.C.E., at or near the place where the Greeks' predecessors had located the navel of the Mother-Goddess or, as we might now say, the center of the Earth.

MAP 6.2

The World According to Eratosthenes

Eratosthenes (ca. 275–195 B.C.E.) directed the Library of Alexandria and made a remarkably accurate estimate of the size of the globe. His world map has not survived but a version can be reconstructed from ancient descriptions.

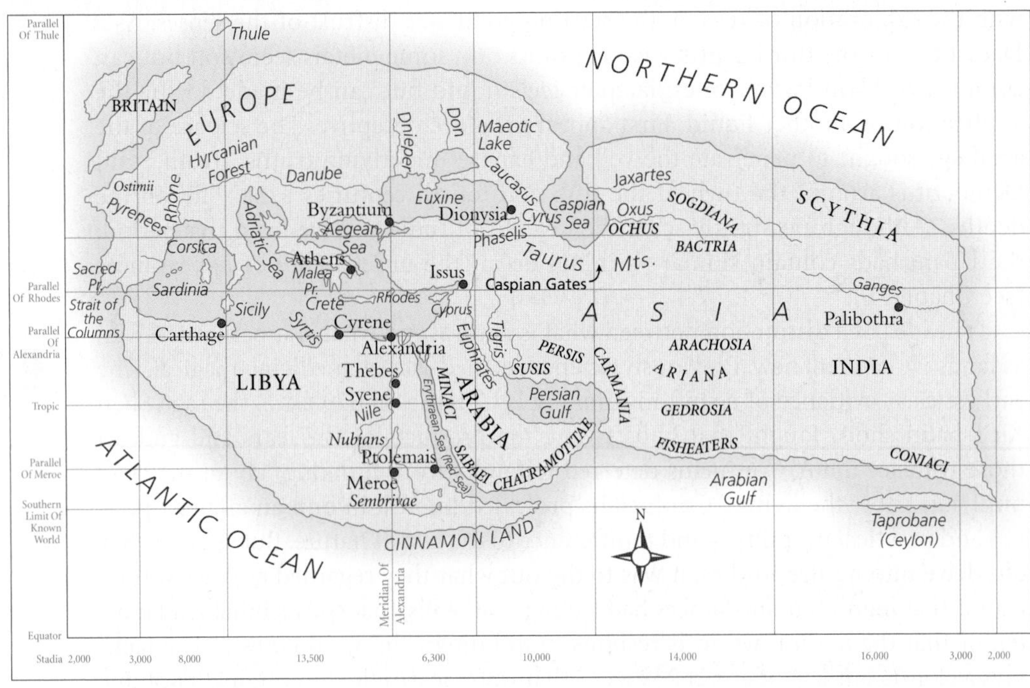

ruled, a method was needed to observe nature systematically, order the information, and test the resulting hypotheses. Aristotle was the best representative of Greek science in its maturity. "We must have facts," he said and proceeded to gather them in enormous quantities. Like the perfect example of a "nutty professor," he prowled around his lecture room, dissected flies, and noted every stage in the incubation of birds' eggs. Other highlights of Greek science of the period included Archimedes's discovery of the mechanics of leverage in the mid–third century B.C.E., and, slightly later, the work of Eratosthenes, who produced an almost exactly accurate calculation of the size of the planet (see Map 6.2).

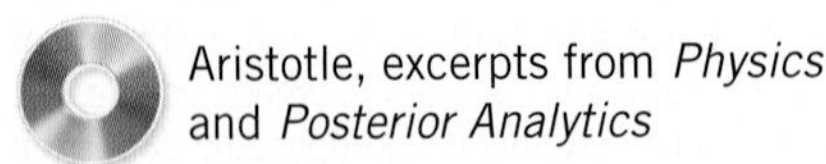
Aristotle, excerpts from *Physics* and *Posterior Analytics*

Chinese practical science—systematic investigation of nature through observation and experiment—probably arose, in parallel with that of Greece, from Daoist doctrines of nature. Habits of observation and experiment developed from magical and omen-seeking practices of early Daoism. The Daoist word for a "temple" means *watchtower*—a platform from which to observe the natural world and launch naturalistic explanations of its phenomena. Daoism has, in Confucian eyes, a reputation for magical mumbo-jumbo because its priests practice strange ceremonies, many of which seem indebted to the magical fallacy that nature responds to human ritual. But Daoism also teaches that Nature—to the one who would control it—is like any other beast to be tamed or foe to be dominated—it must be known first.

So Daoism encouraged scientific practice: observation, description, classification, and experiment. In second-century B.C.E. China, for instance, Daoist legend told of Yi (yee) the archer, who on sage advice sought the medicine of immortality away in the west, when the weed that would confer it was growing outside his door.

Daoist texts often have amusing dialogues between craftsmen who know their work and rationalists who persuade them to do it in a different way, with ruinous results. Grand theory is discouraged as an intrusion of reason into the workings of wisdom, which can be attained only by gaining knowledge. Chinese science has always been weak on theory, strong on technology.

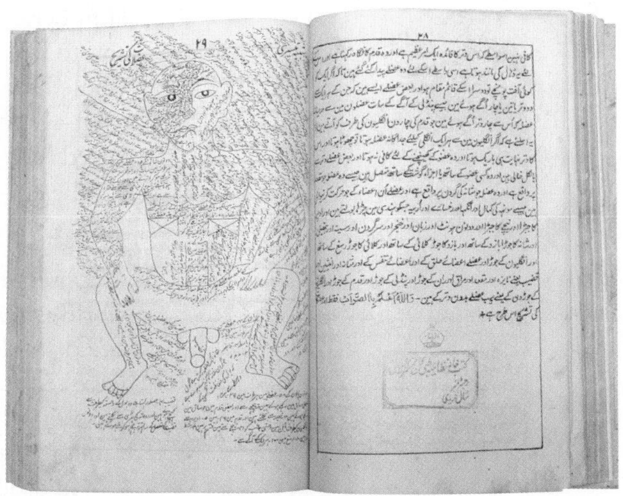

Ayurvedic medicine. This medical textbook, first published in 1593, and based on *The Canon of Medicine* written by the great Muslim scholar Avicenna early in the eleventh century, is still used by students at the Unani Medical College in Hyderabad, India. Ayurvedic treatments are usually herbal, although diet and exercise are also important remedies. The illustration and text shown here concern the muscles of the human body.

Medicine

Controversy followed between magic and medicine—or was it just between rival forms of magic? Illness, like any abnormal state, including madness, could be the result of possession or infestation by a spirit, a "demon"—to recycle a commonly used word for it. Or some diseases could have material causes, others spiritual. Or all could be a mixture of the two. Or sickness could be a divine affliction earned by sin.

In Greece in the late fifth century B.C.E., a secular school known as the Hippocratics tried to monopolize the medical profession, at the expense of rival healers who were attached to temples. The Hippocratics thought that health was essentially a state of balance among four substances in human bodies: blood, phlegm, and black and yellow bile. Adjust the balance, and you alter the patient's state of health. This condemned patients in the West for centuries to treatment mainly by diet, vomiting, laxatives, and bloodletting. The theory was wrong—but it was genuinely scientific, based on observation of substances the body expels in pain or sickness.

A treatise sometimes attributed to Hippocrates himself—supposed founder of the school—advocates a naturalistic explanation for epilepsy, which many people at the time assumed to be a form of divine possession. The test is: Find a goat exhibiting the same symptoms that a human epileptic does. "If you cut open the head, you will find that the brain is ... full of fluid and smells foul, convincing proof that the disease and not the deity is harming the body." The method sounds bizarre, but the conclusion is impressive. "Personally," the Hippocratic writer went on, "I believe that human bodies cannot be polluted by a god." A similar shift of business into the hands of secular medical specialists occurred in China. Xunzi, who died in 235 B.C.E., scorned a man who "having got rheumatism from dampness beats a drum and boils a suckling pig as an offering to the spirits." Result: "a worn-out drum and a lost pig, but he will not have the happiness of recovering from sickness." Religious explanations of disease remained. But the Hippocratics and their Chinese counterparts started a presumption that has gained ground ever since: Nothing needs to be explained in divine terms. The physical world is all there is.

These changes had close parallels in India. In the earliest known Indian work of medicine, the Arthaveda (ahr-thah-VEH-dah), which dates from the early first millennium B.C.E., diseases and demons are more or less identical and are treated with charms or drugs. From the sixth century B.C.E. onward, however, we see evidence of professional medical training and literature. Work largely complete by the second century C.E. summarizes these medical teachings. Writings attributed to Susutra, who probably lived in the sixth century B.C.E., concern surgery; writings attributed to Charaka (which may be the name of a school rather than a person) concentrate exclusively on diet and drugs. A saying attributed to Charaka is strikingly similar to the morals of the Greek

Axial-Age Science and Medicine

Sixth century B.C.E.	Susutra (India)
Late fifth century B.C.E.	Hippocrates (Greece)
ca. 250 B.C.E.	Archimedes (Greece)
d. 235 B.C.E.	Xunzi (China)
ca. 200 B.C.E.	Eratosthenes (Greece)

Hippocrates: "If you want your treatment to succeed, to earn wealth, to gain fame, and to win heaven hereafter ... seek the good of all living creatures, strive with your whole heart to cure the sick." The similarities among Indian, Greek, and Chinese axial-age medicine are so remarkable that historians often assume that they influenced each other. There is, however, no direct evidence for this influence.

Skepticism

A consequence of the rise of a scientific point of view was the suspicion that the world is purposeless. In particular, this line of thinking challenged another axial-age orthodoxy: If the world was purposeless, it was not made for humans, who were reduced to insignificance. What Aristotle called the "Final Cause"—the purpose of a thing, which explains its nature—becomes incoherent. The world is a random event.

In around 200 B.C.E., this was such a dangerous idea that a skeptical Chinese treatise, the *Liezi* (lee-ay-tzeh), avoided direct advocacy of it by putting it into the mouth of a small boy, who challenged a pious host for praising the divine bounty that provided good things for his table. "Mosquitoes suck human blood, wolves devour human flesh but we do not therefore assert that Heaven created man for their benefit." The greatest-ever exponent of a purposeless cosmos was the Chinese philosopher of the first century C.E., Wangchong (wahng-chohng). Humans, he said, live "like lice in the folds of a garment. When fleas buzz in your ear, you do not hear them: How could God even hear men, let alone concede their wishes?" Some materialist thinkers still assert that the whole notion of purpose is superstitious and that asking why the world exists or why it is as it is is pointless.

In a world without purpose, there is no need for God. The name of the Greek philosopher Epicurus, who died in 270 B.C.E., has become unfairly associated with the pursuit of physical pleasure—which he certainly recommended, albeit with restraint. A far more important element of his thought was his interpretation of the atomic theory. In a world of atoms and voids, there is no room for "spirits." Since atoms are subject to "random swerves," there can be no fate. Since atoms are perishable, and everything is composed of them, there can be no immortal soul. Gods, if they exist at all, inhabit an imaginary world from which "we have nothing to hope and nothing to fear." Epicurus's arguments were formidable, and materialists and atheists kept returning to them. At about the end of the first century C.E., the Roman writer Sextus Empiricus suggested, like a modern Marxist, that "some shrewd man invented fear of the gods" as a means of social control. The doctrines of an all-powerful and all-knowing god were devised to suppress freedom of conscience. "If they say that God controls everything, they make him the author of evil," he concluded. "We express no belief and avoid the evil of the dogmatisers."

In revulsion from the big, unanswerable questions about the nature of reality, skeptical thinkers and their schools refocused philosophy on practical issues. One of the great anecdote-inspiring characters of ancient Greece was Pyrrho of Elis, who accompanied Alexander the Great's invasion of India in 327–324 B.C.E. (see Chapter 7) and imitated the indifference of the naked sages he met there. On board ship on the way home, he admired and shared the calm response of a pig to a storm. Since, he argued, you can find equally good reasons on both sides of any argument, the only wise course is to stop thinking and judge by appearances. More effective was the argument that all reasoning starts from assumptions; so none of it is secure. Mozi had developed a similar insight in China around the beginning of the fourth century B.C.E. Most problems were matters of doubt. "As for what we now know, is it not mostly derived from past experience?"

Later Greek philosophy focused on the best practical choices for personal happiness or for the good of society. **Stoicism**, for instance, is the outstanding example, both for the coherence of Stoic ideas and for the scale of their influence. Stoicism appealed to the Roman elite and through them had an enormous effect on Christianity. First taught in the school that Zeno of Citium founded in Athens in the late fourth century B.C.E., Stoicism started from the insight that nature is morally neutral—only human acts are good or evil. The wise man therefore achieves happiness by accepting misfortune. Further Stoic prescriptions—fatalism and indifference as remedies for pain—were similar to teachings preached at about the same period at the far end of Eurasia, especially by Buddha and his followers, or Laozi and his. People have sought the "happiness priority" in so many contrasting ways that it is hard to generalize about its overall effect on the history of the world. Stoicism, however, was certainly its most effective manifestation in the West. It has supplied, in effect, the source of the guiding principles of the ethics of most Western elites ever since it emerged.

Skeptics and Stoics

Fourth century B.C.E.	Pyrrho of Elis (Greece)
Late fourth century B.C.E.	Zeno of Citium (Greece)
d. 270 B.C.E.	Epicurus (Greece)
First century C.E.	Wangchong (China)
First century C.E.	Sextus Empiricus (Rome)

AXIAL AGE–AXIAL AREA: THE STRUCTURES OF THE AXIAL AGE

Monotheism, republicanism, Legalism, rationalism, logic, science (including scientific medicine), skepticism, the most enduring religions and ethical systems—the tally of new thinking in the axial age looks impressive by any standards, but especially because of its legacy to us. Why was this period so productive? Why was it confined to so few societies around the globe?

The structures that underpinned the work of the axial-age thinkers were important for making it happen. The schools and sages formed four obvious and sometimes overlapping categories. First, there were professional intellectuals, who sold their services as teachers, usually to candidates for professional or public office, but perhaps also to those who sought happiness or immortality or, at least, health. A second class sought the patronage of rulers or positions as political advisers. Many sages belonged to both these groups. Aristotle, for instance, taught in Athens but also served as a royal tutor to the prince who later became Alexander the Great (see Chapter 7). Confucius eked out life as a teacher, but not for want of a calling to serve states. A third category was made up of prophets or holy men, who emerged from ascetic lives with inspired messages for society. A fourth was composed of charismatic leaders with visions to share with and, if possible, impose on their peoples.

Most sages fitted into networks. Though lonely, hermitlike existence was an ideal that many of them recommended, affected, and even sought, few, if any, of these sages were genuinely isolated thinkers. They usually depended on contacts. Networks stimulated innovation, nourished competition, fertilized ideas, and gave emotional support. Plato wrote all his works as dialogues and conversations—which make the function of the network visible. The Confucian Mencius, the Daoist Zhuangzi (jwahng-tzeh), and Hui Shi, the analyst of language, competed and debated. Plato's teacher, Socrates, was in contact and conflict with all the Greek schools of his day, attacking those known as Sophists for allegedly putting the elegance of an argument as more important than its truth. Epicurus

The Academy of Athens. Romans continued to admire the philosophy of classical Greece. The Acropolis of Athens is recognizable in the background of this mosaic, preserved in the ruins of Pompeii. The columns and gardens recall what the setting of Plato's Academy at Athens was really like.

and Zeno of Citium established schools in Athens within a few years of each other toward the end of the fourth century B.C.E.

Formal institutions of education played their part in defining networks and stimulating competition. We know little of how they functioned, but the Academy of Athens, founded in 380 B.C.E., had a garden and lodgings for students, which Plato purchased. Members took meals in common and contributed to costs according to their means. Master–pupil relationships created traditional or what we might call cross-generational networks. Socrates taught Plato, who taught Aristotle. Traditions of this sort can get rigid, but clever pupils often innovate by reacting against their masters' teaching (something all textbook writers should bear in mind) and set up chains of revisionism from one generation to the next. Confucius was a critic of the establishment of his day. Mohists, similarly, opposed Confucians. A succession of masters as well as a series of conflicts linked Mozi to Confucius. Han Feizi (hawn fay-tzeh), a Confucian pupil, founded the Legalist school in reaction to his teacher, Xunzi (see Figure 6.2).

Disciples confided masters' works to writing. The Upanishads were probably transmitted orally before they were finally written down. Socrates wrote nothing. Jesus wrote nothing himself that has survived—only, as far as we know, a few words scratched in the dust. Buddha's teachings were too sacred—his first disciples thought—to confide to writing and had eventually to be retrieved from memories when it was finally decided to write them down. Does this mean that the axial age is a trick of the evidence? That the ideas of its sages became so influential only because they were eventually written down? Not entirely, but it does mean that its thoughts have come down to us in a way that other regions and other periods did not have or did not use.

Some thinkers of the axial age were rich men. Plato could endow his own school with his own money. Buddha and Mahavira, the founder of Jainism, were princes.

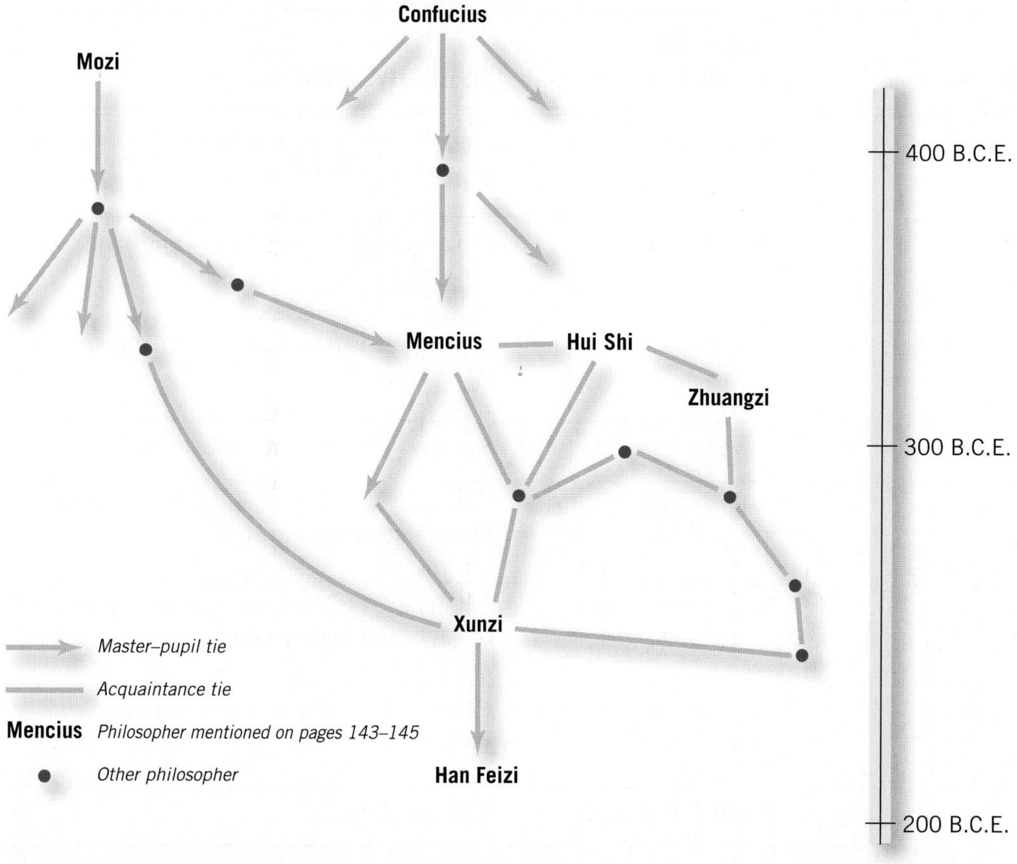

FIGURE 6.2 NETWORK OF CHINESE PHILOSOPHERS, 400–200 B.C.E.
Adapted from R. Collins, *The Sociology of Philosophies* (Cambridge, MA: Belknap Press, 1998) p. 55.

Usually, however, intellectuals need patrons or employers to survive. The politically fragmented worlds of axial-age Greece, China, and India had plenty of potential patrons. A wandering scholar like Confucius might not retain a patron for long—but he could turn to others. This made for independence of thought and liberated political philosophy to criticize rulers. Every subsequent age has successfully adapted Confucius's message, but he addressed it to his own time. Hence his emphasis on the renewal of tradition, the resumption of sacred rites, the restoration of land and property to their rightful owners. Of course, royal patrons are rarely disinterested. In mid–fourth century B.C.E. China, Mencius found his patron, the King of Wei, interested only in schemes to improve military efficiency. Also at the court of Wei, Hui Shi turned his talent for argument to negotiations with other states.

To patronize sages became a source of princely prestige. In China the prince of Zhao allegedly had 1,000 scholars at his court toward the mid–third century B.C.E. The state of Chu supported the followers of Mozi against the Confucians. Qin, supposedly a "barbarian" kingdom on the edge of the Chinese culture area, was home to thousands of scholars. When its ruler burned books in the 220s B.C.E., it was less perhaps an act against learning than a gesture of partisanship on behalf of thinkers he favored.

MAKING CONNECTIONS

THINKERS AND THOUGHTS OF THE AXIAL AGE

REGION →	SAGE / THINKER AND TIME PERIOD →	PHILOSPHY/ RELIGION →	DISTINCTIVE IDEAS
Southwest Asia	Jewish sages, ca. 700–500 B.C.E.	Judaism	Monotheism; trials of faith; punishments for sin; covenant with God
Southwest Asia	Zoroaster, ca. 600 B.C.E.	Zoroastrianism	Eternal conflict between good and evil (dualism)
India	Gautama Siddharta, ca. 560 B.C.E.	Buddhism	Meditation; karma; Four Noble Truths; escaping desire
India	Mahavira, ca. 559 B.C.E.	Jainism	Sanctity of life; nonviolence (*ahimsa*)
Greece	Pythagoras, ca. 550 B.C.E.	Mathematics	Geometrical and mathematical ideas; ratios; ideas that numbers are real
China	Confucius, ca. 500 B.C.E.	Secular philosophy	Loyalty to God, state, and family; importance of ethics and right conduct
Greece	Parmenides, ca. 425 B.C.E.	Rationalism	Objects of thought are more real than sense perception
China	Mozi, ca. 400 B.C.E.	Secular philosophy	Universal love
Greece	Zeno, ca. 390 B.C.E.	Stoicism	Nature is morally neutral; happiness achieved by accepting misfortune
Greece	Aristotle and Plato, ca. 380 B.C.E.	Secular philosophy	Logic; science; political thought
India	Nyaya school, 350 B.C.E.	Rationalism	Logic; reason as an extraordinary perception conferred by God
China	Laozi, ca. 300 B.C.E.	Daoism	Detachment from world; quest for immortality
Greece	Epicurus, ca. 280 B.C.E.	Skepticism	Centrality of matter; soul is not immortal; if God exists he is indifferent to human affairs
China	Xunzi, ca. 250 B.C.E.	Secular philosophy	Human goodness can be attained through progress and freedom
China	Han Feizi, ca. 225 B.C.E.	Legalism	Only good is the good of the state; law and order more important than tyranny and injustice
Southwest Asia	Jesus, ca. 30 C.E.	Christianity	Importance of faith, divine love

In India, too, among the states that shared the Ganges valley, similar rivalries and opportunities existed. The Veda contains fragments of sages' dialogues with kings, in which the kings sometimes outargued the sages. Buddhism relied on rulers' patronage in the kingdoms of Kosala and Magadha. Mahavira was related to the rulers of Videha, where his doctrines enjoyed official favor. His followers debated with Buddhists for supremacy in Magadha. As we shall see in the next chapter, political unification and large-scale imperialism did not promote intellectual productivity. One reason why Zoroaster had no comparably influential successors in Persia is probably because Persia rapidly became an imperial power. In China, India, and Greece the axial age waned as empires grew at the expense of small states, even though the empires themselves spread axial-age ideas.

In some places, popular support also nourished the intellectuals. Sages and holy men are useful to the public in times of political dissolution. Their wisdom and objectivity make them sought after to arbitrate between neighbors or to take the place of absent justice. Public interest is apparent in the multiplicity of schools and the willingness of pupils to seek the benefit of masters' expertise. Learned writings attracted readers. Democritus, an exponent of atomic theory in the early fourth century B.C.E., was credited with 60 books. Heraclitus, one of the first generation of Greek sages, refused to take on pupils. But he nonetheless deposited his writings in the famous temple of the goddess Artemis at Ephesus on the western coast of Anatolia— in effect, his local public library.

CHRONOLOGY

(All dates are approximate)

600 B.C.E.–100 C.E.	Teachers and their disciples influence thinking all across Eurasia
	Spread of Zoroastrianism for next 1,000 years primarily in present-day Iran
	Teachings about Brahman begin to be written down; Buddhism develops in India
	Confucianism, Daoism, and Legalism spread in China
	Legacy of Plato and Aristotle to Western philosophy
	Proponents of secular medicine (Susutra in India, Hippocrates in Greece, and Xunzi in China)
580 B.C.E.	Forced migration of Jews from Jerusalem to Babylon creates a "diaspora mentality," influential up to present times
33 C.E.	Jesus and spread of Christianity over the next two millennia

IN PERSPECTIVE: The Reach of the Sages

Although the new thinking of the axial age was confined to parts of Asia and Europe, it was a worldwide story because of how axial-age thinking later spread and shaped thoughts and feelings in every clime and continent. Empires that are the subject of the next chapter helped to spread it. Trade and colonization, which can be traced at intervals throughout the rest of this book, spread axial thought across the planet. The Roman Empire carried Greek science and philosophy into Western Europe. Buddhism became a state ideology in the first empire to cover almost all of India. The Chinese Empire became a growing arena in which Buddhism, as well as native Chinese thought, spread within and across China's widening borders. Japan's and Korea's intellectual traditions developed from Chinese-inspired starting points. Migration and trade bore Indian thinking into southeast Asia. Christianity fused Jewish and Greek intellectual traditions and spread them—ultimately—all over the world. Islam shared much of the same heritage and spread it almost as far. Buddhism is the third, in terms of numbers of followers, of the three World Religions of today. Alongside Christianity and Islam, both of which developed after the axial age, it has spread over many different countries and cultures, whereas most religions tend to remain specific to their cultures of origin. We do not fully understand the reasons for Buddhist success in this respect, but we shall trace its history in this book. But the scale of demands Buddhism makes on its followers is well suited to a variety of walks of life.

As a result of the spread of the work of the sages and their schools, the thought of the modern world has a familiar ring to a student of the axial age. It seems astonishing that today, after all the technical and material progress of the last 2,000 years, we should remain so dependent on the thought of such a distant era and have added so little to it. We debate the same issues about the nature of reality, using the same tools of logic and science. We struggle with the same problems about the relationship of this world to others, and most of us still follow religious traditions founded by axial-age sages. We search for a balance between the same kinds of optimistic and pessimistic assessments of human nature that people of the axial age identified, and we seek resolutions of similar conflicts of political ideas that arise as a result. To a remarkable extent, we express ourselves in terms the ancient sages taught.

Although the sages and schools of the axial age were confined to Eurasia, comparisons with other parts of the world help us understand how cultural contacts shape and spread what people think and believe. Over and over again, readers of this book will see and will have seen, for example, how ways of thought and life and worship radiated outward from kernel regions: from Mesoamerica, for example, into North and Central America; or from parts of the Andes along the coasts and mountain chains of South America and across the Amazon valley; or from the Ethiopian highlands into surrounding areas; or from centers on the Niger River in West Africa into the Sahel and the forest; or from western Polynesia deep into the Pacific. But the relatively isolating geography of the Americas, sub-Saharan Africa, and the Pacific worked against the kinds of comparatively intense exchange that were possible across Eurasia.

It is impossible to trace to their outer limits the networks that bound the axial-age sages. But the similarities between their thoughts across Eurasia suggest that long-range cultural exchanges must have been going on among them. This was perhaps the critical difference that made Eurasian societies relatively prolific in a period when we know of no comparable achievements in intellectual life anywhere else in the world. Our next task is therefore to look not only at the changing political frameworks of the axial age, but also at the evidence of the spread and strength of long-range cultural contacts in the world of the time.

PROBLEMS AND PARALLELS

1. What were the similarities among the ideas of the great sages of the axial age? How do they influence the way we think now?
2. How did the idea of divine love alter humankind's relationship with God and the world?
3. How did religious ideas affect political thought in the axial age? Why were most axial-age sages optimists rather than pessimists?
4. How did axial-age science investigate nature? How did axial-age medicine distinguish itself from magic?
5. What roles did networks, schools, and patrons play in spreading axial-age thinking?
6. What comparisons can be made between the axial age and the way culture radiates outward from kernel regions in other parts of the world?

DOCUMENTS IN GLOBAL HISTORY

- Siddhartha Gautama: *Identity and Nonidentity*
- Laozi, from the *Tao Te Ching*
- Plato, *The Republic*, "The Philosopher King"
- Legalism, selections from the writings of Han Fei
- The Nyaya school
- Confucius, selections from *The Analects*
- *Aristotle*, excerpts from *Physics* and *Posterior Analytics*

Please see the Primary Source DVD for additional sources related to this chapter.

READ ON

The Analects of Confucius is the best work with which to begin study of the sage. Many editions are available: R. Dawson, *Confucius* (1982) is perhaps the best general introductory account of the subject. E. L. Shaughnessy, *Before Confucius* (1997) gives the background to the thought of the period of the Hundred Schools. T. De Bary, ed., *Sources of Chinese Tradition* (2000) is an excellent introductory anthology of extracts from key texts. J. Needham, *Science and Civilisation in China* (1961), i and ii, with vol. vii by C. Habsmeier, set Chinese thought—not only on science—in global context, stressing the priority of Chinese achievement in antiquity and the Middle Ages. N. Sivin, *Medicine, Philosophy and Religion in Ancient China* (1996) collects essays on the links between Dao and science. For Chinese political thought, see S. DeGrazia, *Masters of Chinese Political Thought* (1973) for a selection of texts and B. I. Schwartz, *The World of Thought in Ancient China* (1985), for a critical guide.

R. Zaehner, *The Dawn and Twilight of Zoroastrianism* (2003) is an unsurpassed classic. R. Gotshalk, *The Beginnings of Philosophy in India* (1998) can be recommended on the Upanishads; for texts, E. Deutsch, *A Source Book of Vedanta* (1971) has a good selection. A. T. Embree, ed., *Sources of Indian Tradition* (1988) collects some useful texts. R. Gombrich, ed., *The World of Buddhism* (1991) is a superb introduction to its subject, especially good on Buddhist monasticism. K. H. Potter, ed., *Encyclopedia of Indian Philosophies* (1994), 6 vols., is a comprehensive guide to Indian thought.

On the Jewish and Jesusian concept of God, K. Armstrong, *A History of God* (1993), and J. Miles, *God: A Biography* (1995) are suggestive and instructive; the revisionist M. S. Smith, *Origins of Biblical Monotheism* (2001) can also be recommended. C. S. Lewis, *The Four Loves* is a classic work contrasting the Jesusian notion of divine love with other traditions. The version in *The New Jerusalem Bible* is the most reliable modern translation of the gospels and has manageable and instructive notes. On Jesus, G. Vermes, *Jesus the Jew* (1973) is provocative, enlightening, and gripping. C. P. Thiede and M. D'ancona, *The Jesus Papyrus* (1997) too, offers an invigorating challenge to conventional thinking. M. Staniforth, trans., *Early Jesusian Writings* (1968) collects some of the texts that did not make it into the Bible.

W. K. C. Guthrie, *A History of Greek Philosophy* (1962) is a model of scholarship; the sixth and last volume, *Aristotle: An Encounter* is also an intensely personal and fascinating study of the single most important thinker in the history of Western thought. A. A. Long, *Hellenistic Philosophy* (1974) takes up the story where Guthrie leaves off. The classic work by E. R. Dodds, *The Greeks and the Irrational* (1957) remains a valuable corrective to conventional thinking. O. Taplin, *Greek Fire* (1990) is an accessible and up-to-date study of ancient Greek thought. M. L. West, *The East Face of Helicon* (1997) settles the controversy about where Greek ideas "originally" came from. R. Collins, *The Sociology of Philosophies* (1998) makes an important contribution to tracing the connections that made schools of thinkers and forged the contacts between them.

CHAPTER 7 The Great Empires

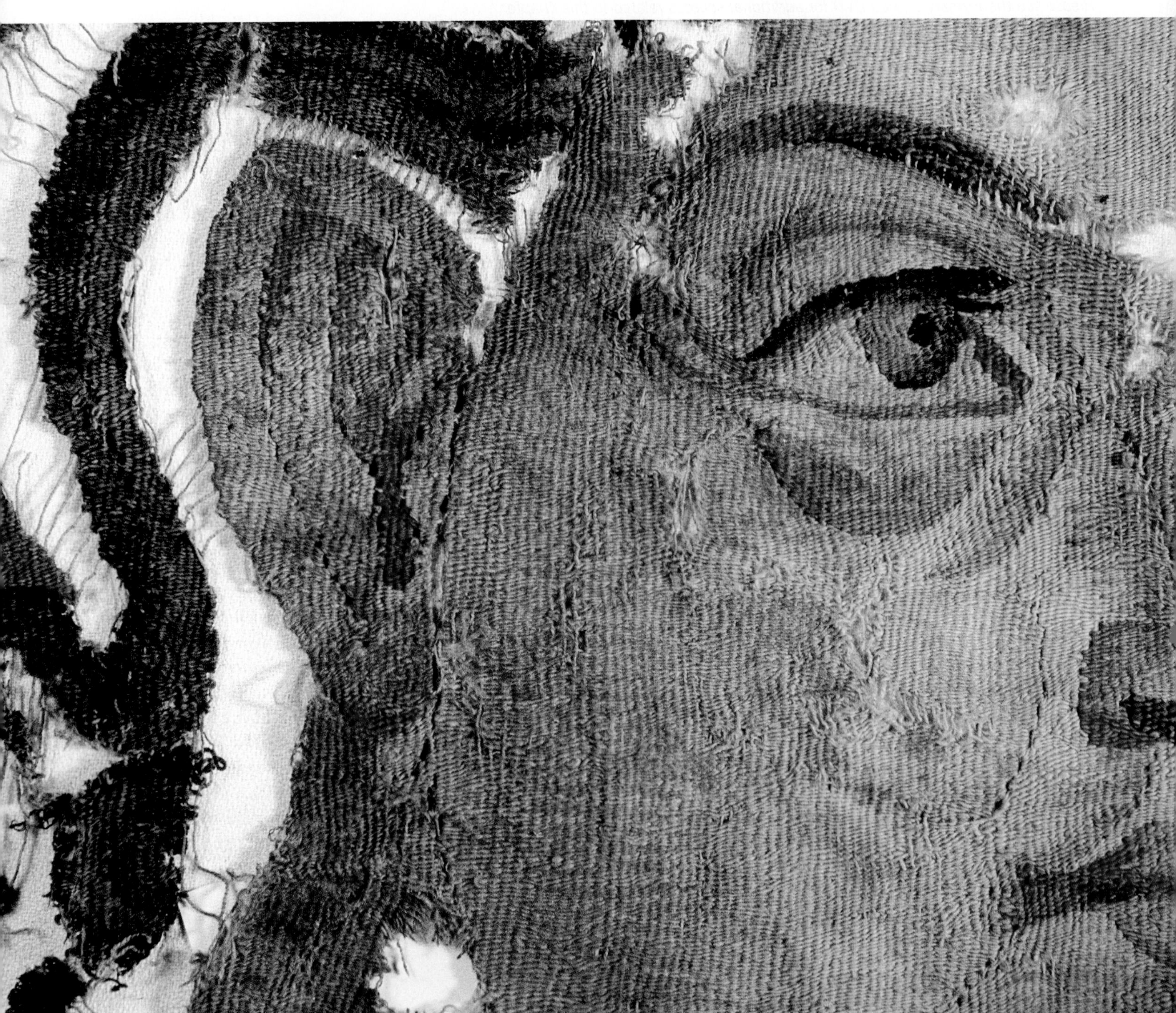

China and Rome on the Silk Roads. A face with Caucasian features on a woolen weaving from the first or second century C.E. is evidence that the Chinese and the Romans were linked by trade. The cloth was discovered in a grave on the Silk Roads in Xinjiang. The face was stitched into a pair of pants and woven in a style not used by the Chinese.

IN THIS CHAPTER

ROUTES THAT DREW THE OLD WORLD TOGETHER
The Sea Routes of the Indian Ocean
Land Routes: The Silk Roads

THE FIRST EURASIAN EMPIRE: PERSIA
The Persian Heartland
Persian Government
The Persian–Greek Wars
The Empire of Alexander the Great

THE RISE OF ROME
The Roman Frontiers
Imperial Culture and Commerce
The Celts

THE BEGINNINGS OF IMPERIALISM IN INDIA
Government
Asoka and His Mental World

CHINESE UNITY AND IMPERIALISM
Unity Endangered and Saved
The Menace from the Steppes

BEYOND THE EMPIRES
Japan and Korea
The Western Eurasian Steppe
Mesoamerica

IN PERSPECTIVE: The Aftermath of the Axial Age

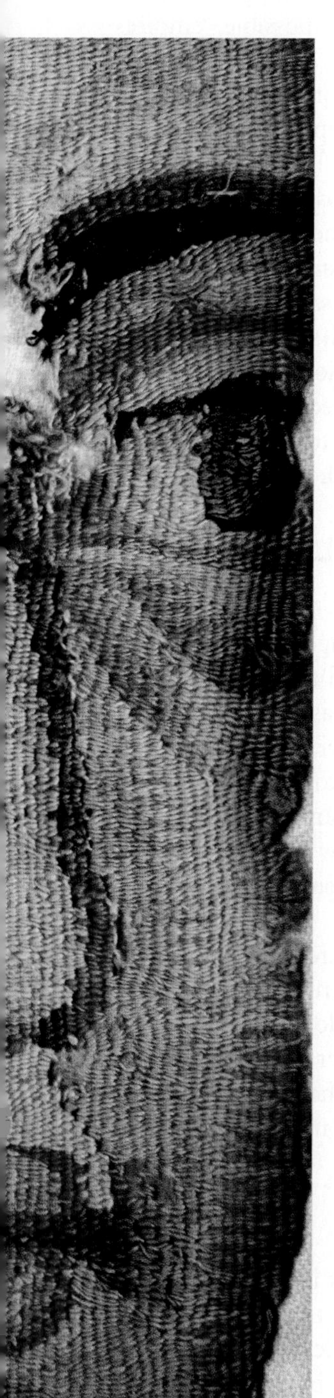

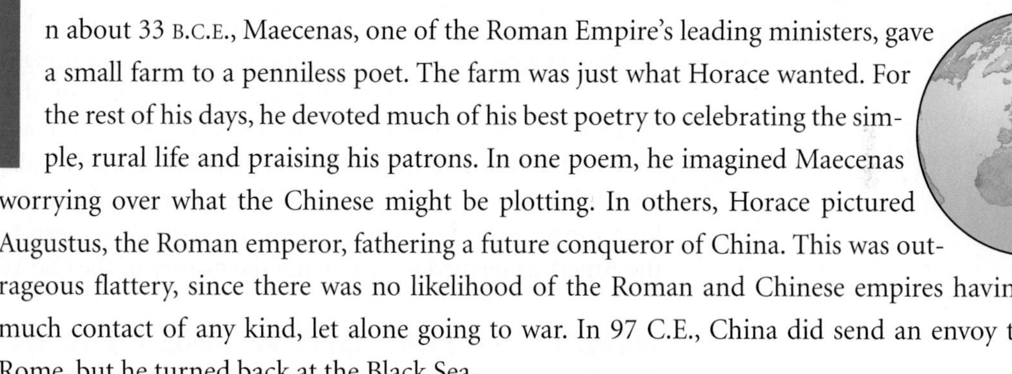

In about 33 B.C.E., Maecenas, one of the Roman Empire's leading ministers, gave a small farm to a penniless poet. The farm was just what Horace wanted. For the rest of his days, he devoted much of his best poetry to celebrating the simple, rural life and praising his patrons. In one poem, he imagined Maecenas worrying over what the Chinese might be plotting. In others, Horace pictured Augustus, the Roman emperor, fathering a future conqueror of China. This was outrageous flattery, since there was no likelihood of the Roman and Chinese empires having much contact of any kind, let alone going to war. In 97 C.E., China did send an envoy to Rome, but he turned back at the Black Sea.

That was as close as the Roman and Chinese empires ever came to direct mutual dealings. But that Horace was aware of China, and realized that events at the far end of Eurasia could affect Roman interests, shows how the world was, as we say now, getting smaller, as land trade routes opened communications across Eurasia; traffic grew along the existing maritime routes of the Indian Ocean, and, finally, sea travel began to connect the Mediterranean with northern Europe's Atlantic shores. The trade routes of the Phoenician and Greek trailblazers described in Chapter 5 led north from the Strait of Gibraltar to the tin-producing British Isles. Their colonies were staging posts in the making of a new economy—helping goods, people, and ideas cross or get around the watershed that divides Mediterranean from Atlantic Europe.

Not only did travelers and trade expand communications, but also the need for big armies and the growth of commerce created a demand for stronger, bigger states—empires that included many political communities in common allegiance. The new empires of the period took shape first in southwest Asia, then around the Mediterranean, and finally in China and India. They established common frontiers or frontier zones of conflict and culture exchange. Around them, chiefs, enriched by trade, turned into kings.

FOCUS questions

- WHY WERE trade routes so important to axial-age empires?
- HOW DID the Persian Empire benefit its inhabitants?
- HOW WAS Rome able to conquer and rule a vast empire?
- HOW DID Asoka seek to unify his empire?
- WHAT WAS the significance of the Han dynasty for China?
- WHERE DID the first potentially imperial states arise in the Americas?

The empires spilled people, technology, and means of life into frontier areas that had been little populated. Cultivated crops and domesticated livestock transformed previously undisturbed ecosystems. At an increasing rate, neighbors who had lived by hunting and foraging for wild plants adopted agriculture, following the empires' example. Those who continued to resist change were cast as enemies and savages. In the great grasslands, the steppes of central Eurasia, where tilling the soil was impossible, empires formed with a different sort of economy, based on herding livestock. A pattern began that lasted for some 2,000 years of violence between these nomad empires that lived by herding and the sedentary farmers who lived near them.

Meanwhile, beyond the routes that connected Eurasian empires, foragers and small-scale farmers survived. They could minimize risk by minimizing change. Most of them took this option. In parts of the New World, however, experiments in embracing change and attempting to control it continued. Large-scale interventions in the environment and imaginative adaptations of human society took forms that were familiar from Eurasia. Agriculture led to urbanization, long-range commerce, and eventually imperialism. Seen from today's perspective, the Americas seemed to be reliving the history of the Old World.

ROUTES THAT DREW THE OLD WORLD TOGETHER

As a general rule in history, bigger states mean more exchange over longer distances. In part, this is simply because they facilitate trade and travel within their own expanding borders; in part, because they generate increasing contacts with each other through commerce, diplomacy, and war. To understand the cultural exchanges of the period—how and why they happened and to what extent—we therefore have to understand the political framework: where and how new states formed; how their horizons broadened; what were the new institutions—the mechanisms for conveying commands and exacting obedience—that enabled them to function over unprecedented distances.

State-building and the development of communications are mutually dependent processes. Routes of commerce are the lifelines of empires: pumping them with resources, equipping them with new ideas and technologies, laying down tracks for their armies to follow. We must begin, therefore, by drawing in the long-range causeways of the period: the sea lanes and land routes that crossed Eurasia, making possible the cultural exchanges of the axial age and the new political developments in the empires the routes linked (see Map 7.1).

The Sea Routes of the Indian Ocean

The world maps Indian geographers of the axial age drew look like the product of stay-at-home minds. Four—then, from the second century B.C.E. onward, seven—continents radiate from a mountainous core. Around concentric rings of rock flow seven seas, made up respectively, of salt, sugarcane juice, wine, butter, curds, milk, and water.

Real observations, however, underlay the metaphors of the maps. The world was grouped around the great Himalaya Mountains and the triangular, petal-like form of India, with the island of Sri Lanka falling from it like a dewdrop. The ocean was divided into separate seas, some imaginary or little known, but others representing real routes to frequented destinations and commercial centers. The Sea of Milk, for instance, corresponds roughly to what we now call the Arabian Sea, and led to Arabia and Persia. The Sea of Butter led to Ethiopia.

Stories of Indian seafaring from late in the first millennium B.C.E. appear in the *Jatakas*, collected tales of Buddhahood—guides to how to become enlightened. Here, piloting a ship "by knowledge of the stars" is a godlike gift. The Buddha saves sailors from cannibalistic goblin-seductresses in Sri Lanka. He puts together an unsinkable vessel for a pious explorer. A merchant advised by an enlightened sage buys a ship on credit and sells the cargo at a profit of 200,000 gold pieces. A guardian-deity saves shipwreck victims who have combined commerce with pilgrimage "or are endowed with virtue or worship their parents." Similar legends appear in Persian sources, like the story of Jamshid, a hero who is both king and shipbuilder and who crosses oceans "from region to region with great speed."

Accounts of real voyages back these stories. Toward the end of the sixth century B.C.E., Darius I—an emperor enthusiastic for exploration—ruled Persia. He ordered a reconnaissance of the Indian Ocean from the northern tip of the Red Sea, around Arabia, to the mouth of the Indus River in northern India. A canal built from Suez on the Red Sea to the Nile indicates there must have been traffic for it to serve, traffic that the canal increased.

What Indian mapmakers called the Seas of Milk and Butter were, to Greek merchants, "the Erythraean Sea," from which traders brought back aromatics—especially frankincense and myrrh—and an Arabian cinnamon substitute called cassia. Important ports for long-range trade lined Arabia's shores. At Gerrha, for instance, merchants unloaded Indian manufactures. Nearby, Thaj also served as a good place to warehouse imports. Egyptian merchants endowed temples in south Arabia with incense in the third century B.C.E.

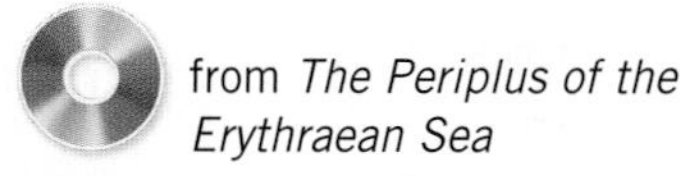
from *The Periplus of the Erythraean Sea*

The reason for the long seafaring, sea-daring tradition of the Indian Ocean lies in the regularity of the monsoonal wind system. Above the equator, northeasterlies prevail in winter, but when winter ends, the winds reverse direction. For most of the rest of the year, they blow steadily from the south and west, sucked toward the Asian landmass as air warms and rises over the continent. By timing voyages to take advantage of these predictable changes, navigators could be confident of a fair wind out and a fair wind home.

MAKING CONNECTIONS

THE DYNAMICS OF EMPIRE

ENVIRONMENT →	SOCIETY →	ECONOMY →	COMMERCE →	POLITICS
Cultivated crops and livestock transform ecosystems across Eurasia	Foragers adopt agriculture	Urbanization leads to increased trade over longer distances	Increased contact between regions leads to conflict, war, diplomacy, and cultural exchanges	Increased commerce, conflicts, numerous routes of communication provide opportunities for stronger, bigger states that can manage many political communities more efficiently

MAP 7.1
Eurasian Trade, ca. 500 B.C.E.–100 C.E.
trade route
Silk Roads
TURKEY modern-day country
desert
steppe
Wind Systems
northeast trade winds
westerlies
monsoon winds April–September
monsoon winds October –March
Trade Goods
amber
silver
gold
grain
horses
incense
ivory
olive oil
precious stones
silk
slaves
spices
timber
tin
tortoise shell
wine
BRITISH ISLES
Baltic Sea
GERMANY
Rhine
HUNGARY
E U R
Rome
Strait of Gibraltar
Black Sea
Caspian Sea
Athens
TURKEY
MESOPOTAMIA
Zagros
Susa
PERS
Mediterranean Sea
Suez
LEVANT
EGYPT
Thaj
Persian G.
Gerrha
Arabian Desert
ARABIA
Sahara
Red Sea
Saba
Sea of Butter
AFRICA
ETHIOPIA
ATLANTIC OCEAN
Tropic of Cancer
Equator
MAP EXPLORATION
www.prenhall.com/armesto_maps

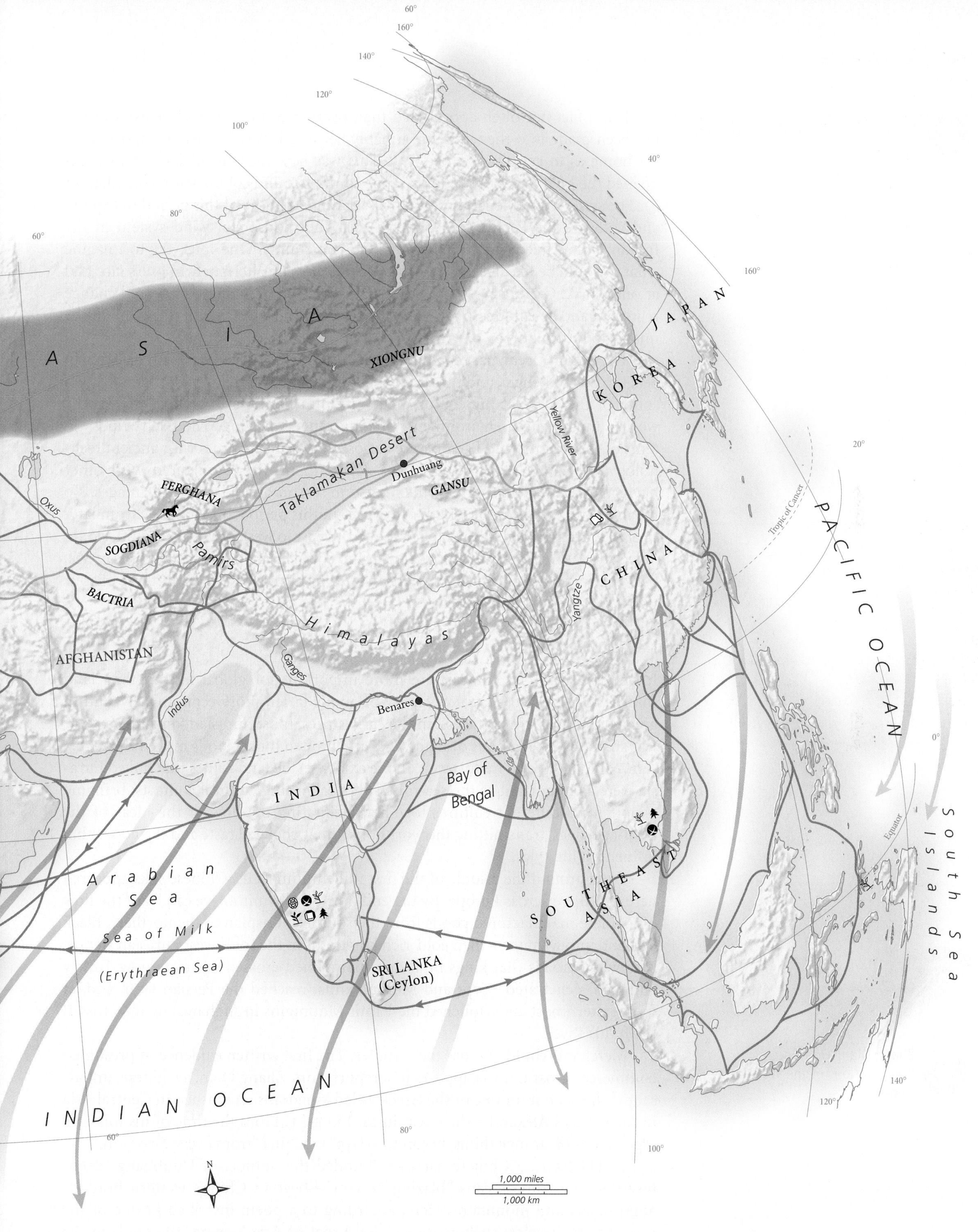
A S I A
XIONGNU
JAPAN
KOREA
Yellow River
Taklamakan Desert
Dunhuang
GANSU
FERGHANA
Oxus
SOGDIANA
Pamirs
BACTRIA
AFGHANISTAN
Himalayas
CHINA
Yangtze
PACIFIC OCEAN
Tropic of Cancer
Ganges
Indus
Benares
INDIA
Bay of Bengal
Arabian Sea
Sea of Milk
(Erythraean Sea)
SRI LANKA (Ceylon)
SOUTHEAST ASIA
South Sea Islands
Equator
INDIAN OCEAN
N
1,000 miles
1,000 km

Agatharchides of Knidos describes Saba

It is a fact not often appreciated that, overwhelmingly, maritime exploration has been made into the wind, presumably because it was at least as important to get home as to get to anywhere new. This was how the Phoenicians and Greeks opened the Mediterranean to long-range commerce and colonization (see Chapter 5). The same strategy enabled South Sea Island navigators of this period to explore and colonize the Pacific (see Chapter 10). The monsoonal wind system in the Indian Ocean freed navigators from such constraints. One must try to imagine what it would be like, feeling the wind, year after year, alternately in one's face and at one's back. Gradually, would-be seafarers realized how the wind would change regularly, and so could risk an outward voyage without fearing that they might be unable to return home.

The Indian Ocean has many hazards. Storms wrack it, especially in the Arabian Sea, the Bay of Bengal, and the deadly belt of bad weather below about ten degrees south of the equator. But the predictability of a homeward wind made this the world's most benign environment for long-range voyaging. The fixed-wind systems of the Atlantic and Pacific were almost impossible to cross with ancient technology. We know of no round trips across them. Even compared with other navigable seas, the reliability of the monsoon season offered other advantages. No reliable sources record the length of voyages in this period, but, to judge from later statistics, a trans-Mediterranean journey from east to west, against the wind, would take 50 to 70 days. With the monsoon, a ship could cross the entire Erythraean Sea, between India and a port on the Persian Gulf or near the Red Sea, in three or four weeks in either direction.

Land Routes: The Silk Roads

In the long run, sea routes were more important for global history than land routes. They carried a greater variety of goods faster, more economically, and in greater amounts. Nevertheless, in the early stages, most Eurasian long-range trade was small scale—in goods of high value and limited bulk. Goods moved through a series of markets and middlemen. In the axial age, the land routes that linked Eurasia were as important as the sea routes in establishing cultural contacts: bringing people from different cultures together, facilitating the flow of the ideas of the axial-age sages, transmitting the works of art that changed taste and the goods that influenced lifestyles.

From around the middle of the first millennium B.C.E., Chinese silks appeared here and there across Europe. By the end of the millennium, we can trace the flow of Chinese manufactured goods from the southern Caspian to the northern Black Sea, and into what were then gold-rich kingdoms in the southwest Eurasian steppe. Meanwhile, roads that kings built and maintained crossed what are now Turkey and Iran, penetrated Egypt and Mesopotamia, reached the Persian Gulf, and, at their easternmost ends, touched the Pamir Mountains in Afghanistan and crossed the Indus River.

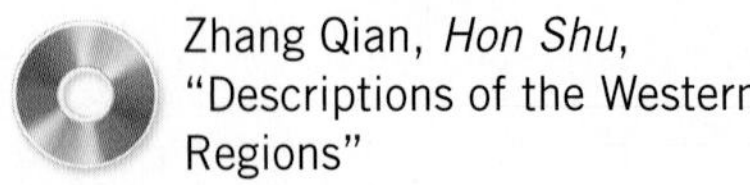
Zhang Qian, *Hon Shu*, "Descriptions of the Western Regions"

Merchants could also use these routes. The first written evidence of presumed commerce across Eurasia appears in a report from Zhang Qian, a Chinese ambassador who set out for one of the Greek-ruled kingdoms established in Central Asia in the wake of Alexander the Great in ca. 139 B.C.E. From the time of his mission, "specimens of strange things began to arrive" in China "from every direction."

In 111 B.C.E., a Chinese garrison founded the outpost of Dunhuang (deen-hwang)—the name means "blazing beacon"—beyond China's western borders, amid desert and mountains. Here, according to a poem inscribed in one of the caves where travelers sheltered, was "the throat of Asia," where "the roads to the western ocean" converged like veins in the neck. We now call them the **Silk Roads.** They led to the markets of Central Asia and linked up with routes that branched into Tibet, or doubled back toward India, or continued westward across the Iranian plateau.

China and the Silk Roads	
ca. 500 B.C.E.	Chinese silks appear in Europe
ca. 139 B.C.E.	Zhang Qian sets out for Bactria
111 B.C.E.	Chinese found Dunhuang
102 B.C.E.	Chinese invade Ferghana

From Dunhuang, the Silk Roads skirted the Taklamakan (tahk-lah-mah-KAHN) Desert, clinging to the edges, where water drains from the surrounding mountains, haunted, in Chinese accounts, by screaming demon drummers—personifications of the ferocious winds. The desert deterred even bandits, and the mountains offered protection from the predatory nomads who lived beyond them.

A few years after the founding of Dunhuang, a Chinese army, reputedly of 60,000 men, traveled to secure the mountain passes at the western end and to force the horse breeders of Central Asia to trade. A painted cave shows the general, Wudi (woo-dee), kneeling before the "golden men"—idols taken, or perhaps mistaken, for Buddhas—that Chinese forces seized. In ca. 102 B.C.E., the Chinese invaded Ferghana and obtained 30,000 horses in tribute. Meanwhile, caravans from China reached Persia, and Chinese trade goods became common along the eastern Mediterranean.

Heavenly horse. Chinese artists have favored horses as subjects in almost every period but never more than during the Han dynasty (206 B.C.E.–220 C.E.), when an intense effort to import fine horses from Central Asia enriched China's equine bloodstock. More than for their utility, horses inspired artists—as in this example from Wuwei (Gansu province) of the second century C.E.—as symbols of the fleeting, ever-changing nature of human life.
The Art Archive/Picture Desk, Inc./Kobal Collection

Trade across Eurasia exposed great disparities in wealth between East and West. These differences helped to shape the history of that region over the next 2,000 years. Already in the first century C.E., the Roman geographer, Pliny, worried about it. The Roman world produced little that its trading partners wanted, whereas the silks of China and the spices and incense of Arabia and the Indian Ocean were much in demand in Rome. The only way people in Europe could pay for them was in cash—gold or, more commonly, silver. Nowadays, we would call this an adverse **balance of trade**—the value of Europe's imports from Asia far surpassed the value of its exports. The problems of financing it, by finding enough silver and ultimately of overcoming and reversing it by finding and supplying goods Asians wanted to buy, became a major theme of the history of the West and, in the long run, as we shall see, of the world.

THE FIRST EURASIAN EMPIRE: PERSIA

Iran commanded a central position in the developing trade across Eurasia, linking Central Asian markets to those of southwest Asia and the Mediterranean. So—in view of the way trade and empire are mutually nourishing—it is not surprising that the first of the great empires of the axial age originated here.

In earlier periods, Akkadians and Assyrians had carried the traditions of lowland Mesopotamia north into their hills, like booty. Now conquerors from the adjoining and even higher tableland used the same traditions to create a new state. This state became the biggest the world had yet known: the Persian Empire.

The Persian Heartland

Its heartland consisted of scatterings of good soil and precious water in a vast, arid plateau. Ragae, with its brackish streams and sweet wells, overlooked the Zagros (ZAH-grohs) Mountains. Hamadan lay in a valley watered with springs, known for good fruit and inferior wheat. Fars was the richest area in ancient times. Water from the Zayinda Rud enriched the plain of Isfahan (IHS-fah-hahn). Rivers—including the Tigris and Euphrates—laced the southwest. Here, at the old trading city of Susa, on the border of the Mesopotamian world, the

MAKING CONNECTIONS

TRADE ROUTES AND THEIR CONNECTIONS

LONG-RANGE ROUTES →	ADVANTAGES →	GEOGRAPHICAL SCOPE →	COMMERCE AND EXCHANGE →	POLITICAL SYSTEMS
Sea Route: Indian Ocean	Changeable, predictable monsoon winds lead to reliable schedules; great variety and amount of goods can be carried via ship (emporium trading); seaborne trade usually faster than land routes	East Africa, Arabia, India, southeast Asia; canal between Red Sea and Nile River eventually connects to Mediterranean	Aromatics (incense), spices, gold, and "thousands of other things" (including wild animals)	African kingdoms, Indian empires and kingdoms, Arabian tribal chiefdoms, Mediterranean empires
Land Route: Silk Roads across Eurasia	Less investment needed to embark on small-scale trading expeditions; more cultural contacts between vastly different peoples; widespread trade of high-value items	China, Bactria, Sogdiana, Persia, Mesopotamia, Anatolia, Caspian/Black Sea, Mediterranean	Spices, silk, gold, silver, cloth, horses, aromatics	Imperial China, Central Asian kingdoms, Egypt, nomadic tribes of Middle East, Persian Empire, Roman Empire, Mediterranean city-states
Sea Route: Mediterranean	Relatively high population densities along the coastal Mediterranean provides more opportunities for trade, numerous ports; shorter distances, calmer waters than vast Indian Ocean routes	Europe, North Africa, southwest Asia, Black Sea, with Red Sea–Nile canal connections to Arabia, Indian Ocean route	Grain, wine, olive oil, timber, metals	Greek city-states/colonies, Egypt, North African city-states, Roman Empire

Persians established the capital of their state. Generally, between mountains and deserts, lay narrow strips of good pasture and land, watered by seasonal streams that could be irrigated for farming. Like the old Hittite Empire (see Chapter 4), Persia was another alliance of farmers and flocks. Hymns that are among the earliest sources for Iranian history praise herders and husbandmen as followers of truth and pronounce their nomadic enemies "adherents of lies, who uproot crops and waste livestock," which would be better employed fertilizing farmland. Farming communities' depictions of bull sacrifice show spurting blood transformed into sprouting wheat.

The founding of the Persian Empire is traditionally credited to Cyrus the Great, a general from Fars. Toward the mid–sixth century B.C.E., he launched a coup to take over one of the biggest successor-states of Assyria, the kingdom of the Medes. His subsequent campaigns stretched from Palestine to Afghanistan. His power reached almost the farthest limits the Persian Empire would ever attain. His inscriptions call him simply, "I, Cyrus, the Achaemenid" (ah-KEE-meh-nihd)—the name of the family to which he belonged. But he headed a conquest state, poor in resources, with a need to keep growing. The Persian Empire gradually adopted the

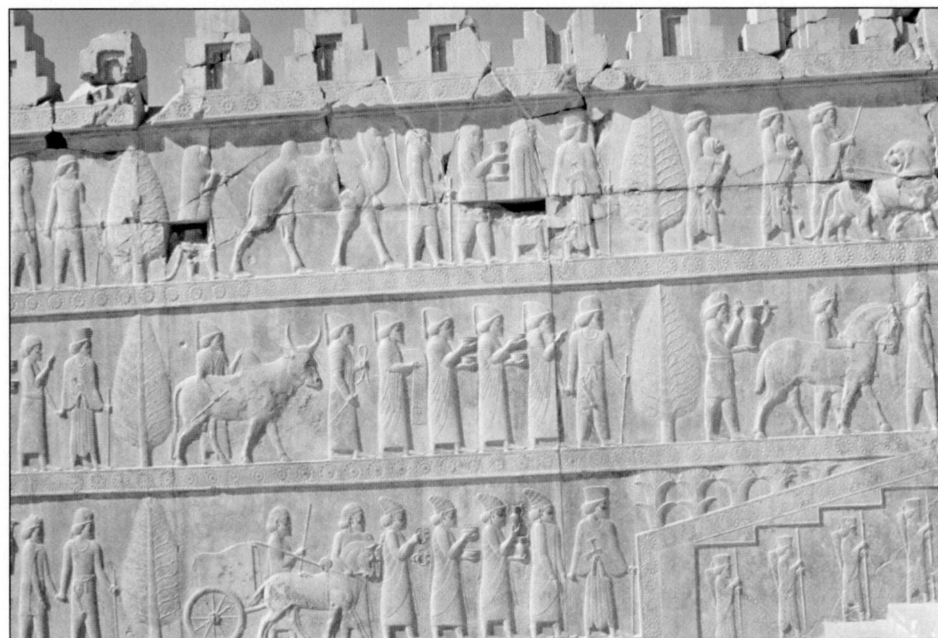

Persepolis. Reliefs that line the approach to the audience chamber of the ruler of Persia at Persepolis show exactly what went on there: reception of tribute, submission of ambassadors. The figures look uniform at first, but their various styles of beards, headgear, and robes indicate the diversity of the lands from which they came and, therefore, the range of the Great King's power.

Old World–conquering ambitions of Sargon of Akkad (see Chapter 3) and the Assyrians but with a difference: The Persians put these ambitions into practice.

The empire joined two regions—Mesopotamian and Persian—that mountains had formerly divided. At its greatest extent, it reached the Aegean coast, Egypt, and India beyond the Indus River. It relied on long-range trade and needed to invest in communications. By early in the fifth century B.C.E., nearly 1,700 miles of road from Susa to Sardis crossed the empire. Royal armies tramped them at a rate of 19 miles a day, and "Nothing mortal," it was said, "travels as fast as the royal messengers." The road was also a channel for tribute. Carvings at the imperial city of Persepolis, founded around the end of the sixth century B.C.E., show ivory, gold, and exotic animals arriving at the court of the ruler of Persia.

Persian Government

Persia was more than a robber empire. The empire provided a canal linking the Nile to the Red Sea and irrigation works on the Oxus and the Karun Rivers. Forts beyond the Caucasus Mountains kept steppe nomads at bay. At Jerusalem, Cyrus the Great undertook to rebuild the temple that symbolized the city's sanctity for the Jews. The gesture was typical of the way Persian rulers conciliated the subjects they acquired. In gratitude, the biblical prophet Isaiah hailed Cyrus as God's anointed.

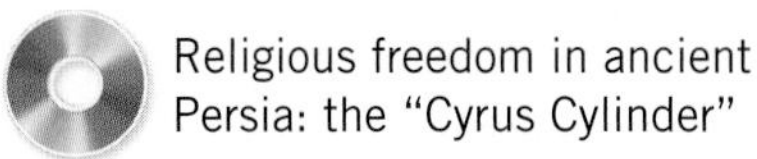

Religious freedom in ancient Persia: the "Cyrus Cylinder"

Greeks accused Persians of treating their kings like gods, in the Egyptian manner, but this charge was unjust. Persian kings were not gods, but their right to rule was god given. The other practices that Greeks found peculiar were the Persian love of luxury—a criticism excused, perhaps, by envy—and their respect for women. Surviving Achaemenid ration lists—the records of wages and payments in kind that court personnel received—assign professions by sex. These show that royal attendants could be of either sex and that women could supervise mixed groups of men and women and earn higher wages than men. It was not, however, a society of sexual equality. Scribes had to be male, while servers of rations—the lowest category by pay—had to be female. Mothers got extra rations for the birth of boys. Nevertheless, women could

Rise and Fall of the Persian Empire

Sixth century B.C.E.	Cyrus the Great founds Achaemenid dynasty
Early fifth century B.C.E.	Completion of royal road from Susa to Sardis
490 and 480 B.C.E.	Unsuccessful efforts to conquer Greece
334 B.C.E.	Alexander conquers Persian Empire

hold property in their own right. This gave them a political role as what, in modern American politics, would be called "campaign funders"—backers and patrons of men who sought power. Greek sources, exaggerating the amount of power women enjoyed as a result, blamed every lurch of palace politics on female willfulness. For Greeks, who barred women from political life in their own communities, saw them as dangerous agents of chaos in other cultures' states.

The Persian–Greek Wars

Greeks who lived on and beyond the western edge of the Persian Empire were in a giant's shadow. They needed to find ways to cope with insecurity and defeat fear. In about 500 B.C.E., the ruler of Miletus, a Greek colony on the shore of western Anatolia, had a map of the world that showed two roughly equal areas—an exaggeratedly large Europe at the top, like a protruding lip over Asia and Africa crammed into the lower half. The agenda was clear. Asia was reduced to a manageable conquest.

The map looked brash but concealed unease. Rumors claimed that the Persians wanted to conquer Europe because "its trees were too fine for anyone but the Great King to possess." More likely, the empire was committed to expanding because it needed tribute from subject-lands to support it. In any event, the Greeks saw the Persians as a threat but did not feel threatened enough to stop feuding with each other even when the Persians prepared to invade Greece. The oracle of Delphi (Chapter 5) even advised submitting to Persian rule, with its reputation for efficiency, generosity, and respect for trade. In the wars that followed, Greek unity occurred only in dire moments of Persian invasion. Persia, after testing the difficulties of conquering Greece in unsuccessful invasions in 490 and 480 B.C.E., was generally content to keep these enemies divided, while prioritizing Persian rule over rich, soft Egypt.

The sea became the effective frontier between the Greek and Persian worlds. A Persian decree of 387 B.C.E. sums it up: The king "deems it right that the cities in Asia be his . . . The other Greek cities, both small and great, shall be independent," while most of the Greek colonies on the islands of the Aegean were divided between Persia and Athens. This was an indication that Athens—best resourced of the Greek cities because it controlled silver mines—had imperial ambitions of its own, which many Greek states found more menacing than those of Persia.

The Empire of Alexander the Great

Not even Athens could assert long-term hegemony in Greece. Macedon, however, could. Macedon is an example of a now familiar fact: On the edges of civilizations, chiefdoms developed into states. This northern kingdom had what to southern Greeks was a barbarian background, but Greece profoundly influenced its culture. Increasingly, in the fourth century B.C.E., Macedonians saw themselves as Greeks. Aristotle (see Chapter 6) served as a tutor to the royal court.

In 338 B.C.E., King Philip of Macedon imposed unity by force on the Greeks and revived the idea of conquering Persia. When he was assassinated—allegedly by a Persian-backed conspiracy—two years later, his 19-year-old son, Alexander, inherited his father's ambitions. For Philip, attacking Persia was probably intended to focus his uneasily united realm on an external enemy. Alexander's motivation, however, has baffled historians. Was he seeking to vindicate his dead father? Or to reenact legendary romances of Greek campaigns in Asia, which filled his head from his boyhood reading? Or was he full of insatiable ambition to leave "no world unconquered" as some early biographers claimed? Did he have humdrum economic aims? He certainly showed interest in opening up Indian Ocean trade or seizing control of its routes. He ordered reconnaissance by sea of the routes between India, Persia, and Arabia and began, just before his death, to plan the conquest of Arabia.

Probably, his ambitions grew with his success. Alexander destroyed the Persian Empire at lightning speed in three years' campaigns from 334 B.C.E. (see Map 7.2). When the last Persian emperor died at his own officers' hands, perhaps because he had decided to abandon resistance, Alexander proclaimed himself "Great King." His success seems inexplicable except in terms of the interconnected skill and luck of the battlefield. The Persian Empire was essentially strong, well run, and easily governed. Alexander took it over intact, maintained its methods of control, and divided it among his subordinates.

Success and flattering omens convinced him that he enjoyed divine favor—perhaps, even, that he was divine. His methods became increasingly arbitrary, his character increasingly unpredictable. He dealt with disloyalty first by judicial murder, then assassination, then slaughter by his own hand, then arbitrary executions. In the last years of his life, his control slipped. He failed to impose Persian rituals of homage on his Greek and Macedonian followers who felt that it was demeaning to prostrate themselves before a mere mortal, even if he was a king. He sought conquests beyond Persia's frontiers, but his troops became insubordinate, and he had to halt his invasion of India, shortly after crossing the Indus. Characteristically,

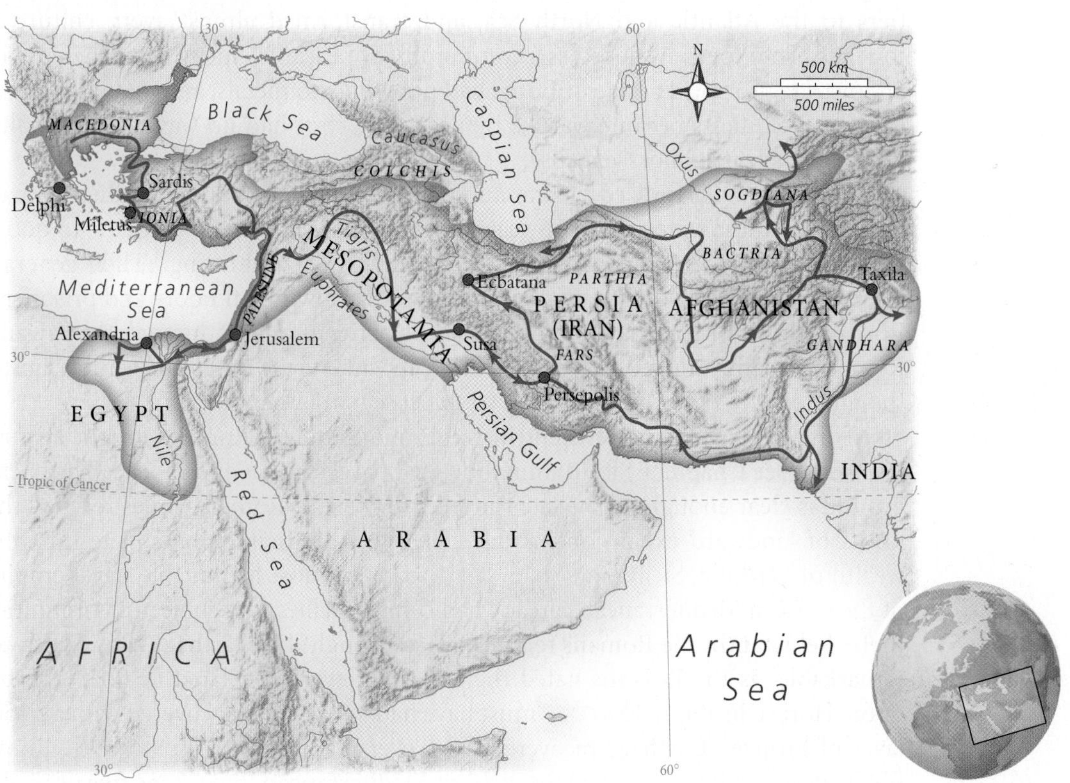

MAP 7.2

The Empire of Alexander the Great

 Empire of Alexander at its greatest extent

→ route of Alexander the Great

Alexander saved face by pretending he had submitted not to the demands of his men, but to warnings from the gods. He had just set the conquest of Arabia as his next objective when he fell dead at age 32, from unknown causes, after a drinking bout—the favorite Macedonian form of excess.

It was what modern publicists might call "a great career move." He became the world's most written-about hero. Epic romancers embroidered his life with wonder stories of his uncontainable prowess. They credited him with exploring the depths of the ocean and ascending to heaven in a chariot drawn by ravens. An epic poem celebrated him in Malay. Kings in India, Ethiopia, and Scotland named themselves after him.

His empire did not outlast him. But long-term, long-range cultural exchanges throve in the states among which it fragmented. On the frontiers of India, the kingdom of Gandhara combined Buddhist religion and Greek-style art. In Alexandria, the city Alexander founded at the Nile Delta, Greek and Egyptian traditions fused. Through the kingdoms of Bactria and Sogdiana, the trade of the Silk Roads funneled. A Persian rump state, Parthia, arose in the Iranian heartland. A power vacuum arose in the eastern Mediterranean that none of Alexander's many imitators could fill. The eventual beneficiary was Rome.

THE RISE OF ROME

One of the great unsolved puzzles of history is how a small city-state of obscure origins and limited manpower conquered the Mediterranean, extended its frontiers to the Atlantic and North Sea, and transformed almost every culture it touched. The Romans started as a community of peasants, huddling for defense in an unstrategic spot. The site of Rome had poor soil, no metals, and no outlet to the sea. Its inhabitants became warlike by necessity. They had no way to gain wealth except at their neighbors' expense.

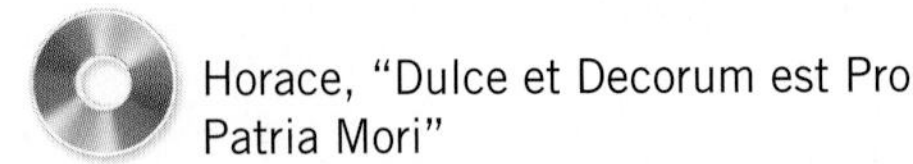
Horace, "Dulce et Decorum est Pro Patria Mori"

The Romans organized for war and made victory their supreme value. Roman citizens owed the state at least 16 years of military service. They learned—to quote Horace again—that "to die for the fatherland is sweet and fitting." Their generals celebrated victories in triumphal public parades, showing off booty and prisoners. Roman education emphasized the virtues of patience and endurance. As a result, Rome was well equipped to tough out defeats. Like those other great imperialists, the nineteenth-century British, they could "lose battles but win wars."

This was particularly evident in the Punic Wars the Romans fought against Carthage (see Chapter 5) for domination of the western Mediterranean. The background is clear enough. In the late third century B.C.E., Roman armies reached the limits of landward expansion in Italy. They turned their aggression toward the wealth of Sardinia, Sicily, and Spain. Carthage, the most formidable naval empire of the western Mediterranean, already had colonies, allies, and subject-communities there. Reluctantly, the Romans took to the sea to fight the Carthaginians. This was remarkable, as the Romans hated the sea. "Whoever first dared to float a ship," wrote Horace in about 30 B.C.E., "must have had a heart of oak covered with a triple layer of bronze." Carthage recovered from every defeat, until in 146 B.C.E. Rome finally destroyed it and turned the western Mediterranean into a zone free of rivals. Historians generally regard these wars as the crucial episode in the ascent of Rome.

Meanwhile, Rome also engaged the major powers of the eastern Mediterranean. Macedon was annexed to Rome in 148 B.C.E., after 50 years of intermittent wars. The rich kingdom of Pergamum in Anatolia was next. When its last king died, he willed his kingdom to the Roman people in 133 B.C.E. Then came Syria and Palestine. When Rome annexed Egypt in 30 B.C.E., it controlled virtually all the shores of the Mediterranean (see Map 7.3).

North Sea
ATLANTIC OCEAN
Celts
IRELAND
BRITAIN
Celts
London
Germans
Cologne
Elbe
Igei
Rhine
Germans
Danube
UKRAINE
RUSSIA
Don
Dnieper
Sarmatians
Scythians
Steppes
Scythians
Caucasus
Colchis
Crimea
Black Sea
Vix
FRANCE
Gaul
SWITZERLAND
Celts
HUNGARY
Dacia
Danube
Celts
Duero
Numancia
Conimbriga
PORTUGAL
SPAIN
Italica
Rome
ITALY
Sardinia
Sicily
Carthage
MACEDONIA
GREECE
Athens
Crete
Celts
Anatolia
Pergamum
PARTHIAN EMPIRE
SYRIA
Cyprus
Levant
PALESTINE
Alexandria
Fayyum
EGYPT
ARABIA
Red Sea
Mediterranean Sea
AFRICA
500 km
500 miles
N
extent of Roman Empire ca. 120 C.E.
Parthian Empire ca. 120 C.E.
Celts peoples
Fayyum place described on pages 160–166
maritime trade routes
wine
olive oil
garum (fish sauce)
honey
slaves
horses
wool
flax/linen
murex (purple dye)
marble
timber
gold
tin
copper
290 B.C.E.: Rome reaches limits of landward expansion in Italy
148 B.C.E.: Rome annexes Macedon
30 B.C.E.: Augustus becomes first emperor of Rome
43 C.E.: Rome invades Britain
400 B.C.E.
300 B.C.E.
200 B.C.E.
100 B.C.E.
1 C.E.
100 C.E.
200 C.E.
264 B.C.E.: Outbreak of first war between Rome and Carthage
146 B.C.E.: Rome destroys Carthage in final war
51 B.C.E.: Conquest of Gaul completed by Julius Caesar
27 B.C.E.: Rome annexes Egypt
106 C.E.: Conquest of Dacia completed

MAP 7.3
The Roman World

Tombstone of a Roman Soldier. The Roman Empire shifted people across vast distances. This tombstone in Cologne, Germany, records a veteran soldier, Marcus Valerius Celerinus, who married and settled locally after his legion was transferred to Germany from his home in southern Spain, late in the first century C.E. His wife, Marcia Procula, sits in a subordinate position, ready to serve him from a basket of fruit. The inscription proclaims the image "from life" of Marcus, naming his tribe, his citizenship of his birthplace in Spain, and his status as a veteran of the Tenth Legion. Marcus reclines to dine, the way a Roman gentleman would. At his elbow is his slave. A table with wine cups and a wine jar stand beside him.

The Roman Frontiers

The Roman Empire was an empire of coasts, with the sea as it central axis. It therefore exposed long, vulnerable frontiers to landward. On the African and Levantine shores, Roman territory seemed protected by deserts. The European flank, however, despite 100 years of further conquests, never seemed secure. There was no reliable barrier against attack. An endless quest for security led beyond the Mediterranean to the Rhine and the Danube Rivers. In the first and early second centuries C.E., Rome subdued Dacia, where deadly womenfolk were said to torture prisoners. The result was an even longer and more irrational frontier.

Roman expeditions also invaded Germany as far as the Elbe River, but the Germans seemed too barbaric to absorb. They were "wild creatures" incapable of laws or civilized arts, according to Velleius, a Roman cavalry officer who fought them around 4 B.C.E. Julius Caesar (d. 44 B.C.E.), whose methodical generalship extended the empire to the Rhine, regarded that river as the limit of civilization. So Rome abandoned the Germans to their own devices. This was probably a mistake. Almost all speakers of Germanic languages beyond Switzerland and the Rhineland were left outside the empire, seething with resentment and vengefulness at their exclusion from the wealth they associated with Rome. If Rome had absorbed them and the other sedentary peoples beyond its frontiers, as China did at the other end of Eurasia, the Roman Empire might have proved as durable as China's. The sedentary peoples China absorbed on its frontiers guarded the Chinese Empire against nomadic outsiders.

Imperial Culture and Commerce

Retired soldiers—Latin-speaking and schooled in allegiance to Rome—helped spread a common culture across the empire, settling in lands where they had been stationed, marrying local women. On his tombstone in Cologne, in the Rhineland, the image of a retired veteran from southern Spain reclines; his wife and son serve food and wine from an elegant, claw-footed table. A tombstone in northern Britain commemorates a 16-year-old boy from Roman Syria.

Roman culture was so well known in Britain that mints in the third century C.E. could stamp coins with references to the poetry of Virgil—the epic poet who, in the reign of Augustus (r. 27 B.C.E.–14 C.E.), celebrated Rome's foundation myth. Everywhere, the empire promoted the same classical style for buildings and urban planning: symmetrical, harmonious, based on Greek architecture. The artistic traditions of subject-peoples became provincial styles. For instance, the last monuments of the funerary art of the pharaohs are the Fayyum portraits, which stare from the surfaces of burial caskets in Roman Egypt. They are recognizably in an ancient Egyptian tradition, yet faces as realistic and sensitive as these might be found in portraits anywhere in the Roman Empire.

Engineering was the Romans' ultimate art. They discovered how to make cement, which made unprecedented feats of building possible. Everywhere the empire reached, Romans invested in infrastructure, building roads, sewers, and aqueducts. Amphitheatres, temples, city walls, public baths, and monumental gates were erected at public expense, alongside the temples that civic-minded patrons usually endowed. The buildings serviced new cities, built in Rome's image, where there were none before, or enlarged and embellished cities that already existed. The biggest courthouse in the empire was in London, the widest street in Italica, a Roman city in southwest Spain. Colonists in Conimbriga, on the coast of Portugal, rebuilt their town center in the first century C.E. to resemble Rome's. Trade as well as war shipped elements of common culture around the empire. Rome exported Mediterranean amenities—villas, cities, mosaics—to the provinces, or forced Mediterranean crops like wine grapes and olive trees to grow in unlikely climates.

As industries became geographically specialized, trade and new commercial relationships crisscrossed the empire. In the first century C.E., merchants from the Duero valley in Spain were buried in Hungary. Greek potters made huge jars to transport wine from Spain to southern France. In southwest Spain, huge evaporators survive from the factories where garum—the empire's favorite fish sauce—was made from tuna and mackerel. The lives of cloth merchants from northeast France are engraved on a tomb at Igel, on the frontier of Germany. They conveyed bales of cloth by road and river and sold it in elegant shops, lavishing their profits on banquets to lord it over their farming neighbors.

Of course, as the empire grew, political institutions changed. When Rome was a small city-republic, two annually elected chief executives, called consuls, shared power between themselves, subject to checks by the assembly of nobles and notables known as the senate, and by the tribunes, representatives of the common citizens. Increasingly, as the state expanded, in the emergencies of war, power was confided to individuals called dictators, who were expected to relinquish control when the emergency was over. In the second half of the first century B.C.E., this system finally broke down in struggles between rival contenders for sole power. In 27 B.C.E., all parties accepted Augustus, who had emerged as victor from the civil wars, as head of state for life, with the right to name his successor.

Fayyum portrait. When Egypt became a Roman province in 30 B.C.E., burial practices remained the same: Mummies were encased in painted caskets. But the style of painting that depicted the deceased gradually took on Roman conventions of portraiture, as in this lovely example of a young woman from the mid–second century C.E.

Effectively, henceforth, Rome was a monarchy, though Romans, schooled in republicanism, hated to use the word. Part of the consequence of Roman distaste for kings was that the rules of succession to supreme power were never perfectly defined. Augustus called himself *princeps*—a word roughly equivalent to "chief" in English. Gradually, however, "emperor" took over as the name people normally used to designate the ruler. The Latin term—*imperator*—originally meant an army commander, and the army, or parts of the army, often in rivalry with each other, increasingly dethroned and elected emperors.

Pliny the Elder, from *The Natural History*

Unified command and sustained leadership helped to make the growing empire manageable, but the problem remained of melding such diverse and widespread peoples into a single state. A common sense of belonging spread, as Rome granted Roman citizenship to subject-communities. Envoys from allies on the Atlantic and Black Sea came to Rome to hang offerings in the temple of Jupiter, "greatest and best" of Rome's guardian gods. Yet this was by no means a uniform empire. It was so big that it could only work by permitting the provinces to retain their local customs and religious practices. At one level it was a federation of cities, at another a federation of peoples. Everywhere, Rome ruled with the collaboration—sometimes enforced—of established elites. Spanish notables with barbarous names followed Roman law in legal decisions that they ordered to be carved in bronze. Hebrew princes and Germanic chiefs ruled as imperial delegates. Celts were Rome's partners in the west, Greeks in the east, where Greek rather than Latin was the most widespread common tongue and served at most levels as the language of government.

Roman Expansion

ca. 290 B.C.E.	Rome reaches limit of expansion in Italy
148 B.C.E.	Rome annexes Macedon
146 B.C.E.	Rome destroys Carthage
133 B.C.E.	Pergamum added to Roman Empire
30 B.C.E.	Rome annexes Egypt
106 C.E	Conquest of Dacia completed

Celtic conspicuous consumption. This wine vessel, buried with the queen or princess to whom it belonged in the mid–first millennium B.C.E., was as tall as she was. Too big and heavy to handle, it was just for show. Like the wine it contained, it was imported from the Mediterranean. Greek soldiers and chariots decorate the rim. Serpent-haired Gorgons form handles, inside which lions climb—all symbolizing the owner's power.

The Celts

Celts dominated Western Europe by the mid–first millennium B.C.E. They occupied present-day France, Britain, Ireland, and most of Spain. Their settlements were widespread in Central Europe and even reached Anatolia. Everywhere they lived in numerous chiefdoms and small states. What united them was language. They all spoke mutually intelligible versions of a single tongue.

Stories about the Celts made Roman gooseflesh ripple. They hunted human heads and hung them on their saddles. They stitched sacrifice victims for burning inside wicker images of gods. They had a reputation for drunkenness. A 35-year-old Celtic hostess in central France was buried with a Greek wine vessel so large that it had to be imported in sections and assembled on arrival. The Celts' courage was also renowned. Roman sculpture shows them dead or dying but never giving up.

Despite their fierce and undisciplined reputation, the Celts had a way of life that Romans recognized as civilized. They were supposedly suspicious of writing wisdom down, but many inscriptions survive, including laws, administrative records, and a calendar to foretell the future. There were modest Celtic towns in France and Spain. The town of Numancia, which was rich in iron, was a minor metropolis by Celtic standards. Covering almost 1,800 square feet, it was arranged in neat streets up to 21 feet wide. The dwellings of Numancia were of mud and thatch on a rubble base, but the inhabitants enjoyed fresh water and sanitary drainage.

By the time Rome seriously began to wage war on them—early in the last quarter of the second century B.C.E.—the Celts of what is now France had a society Romans acknowledged as like their own: no longer organized along tribal lines but according to wealth, prowess, and ancestry. Nobility was measured in livestock, not land. Peasants paid their rents in calves, pigs, and grain. After ferocious initial resistance to Roman conquest, Celts usually accepted Romanization and became enthusiastic collaborators in the Roman Empire. Generally, they welcomed the enriching economic consequences of the peace the Romans enforced.

THE BEGINNINGS OF IMPERIALISM IN INDIA

Meanwhile, beyond the eastern frontiers of Persia, in India, Alexander's threat seems to have had an immediately galvanizing effect. When one of his generals recrossed the Indus in 305 B.C.E., he found the states of the Ganges valley confederated under a leader from the delta region, Candragupta (chahn-drah-GOOP-tah). The sources are hazy, however, until the next reign, that of Asoka (ah-SHOH-kah), which began in the 260s B.C.E. The *Arthasastra* (ahr-SHAS-trah) describes the political world of Asoka. More importantly, his thoughts and deeds come to life in the decrees and self-reflective ruminations he had inscribed on pillars and rock faces. If it were not such an awful pun, one would say that the rock inscriptions are hard evidence.

Excerpts from the *Arthasastra*, "The Duties of Government Superintendents"

The sources show, first, the extraordinarily long reach of Asoka's power (see Map 7.4). Second, the evidence reveals an expanding realm, constantly reforging environments. "The king shall populate the countryside," says the *Arthasastra*, "by creating villages on virgin land or by reviving abandoned village sites. . . . Like a barren cow, a kingdom without people yields nothing."

The same source describes two main types of environment—one rainy and the other requiring irrigation—and specifies suitable crops for both: rice, millet, wheat, barley, six sorts of beans, four types of oil seeds, various vegetables, herbs,

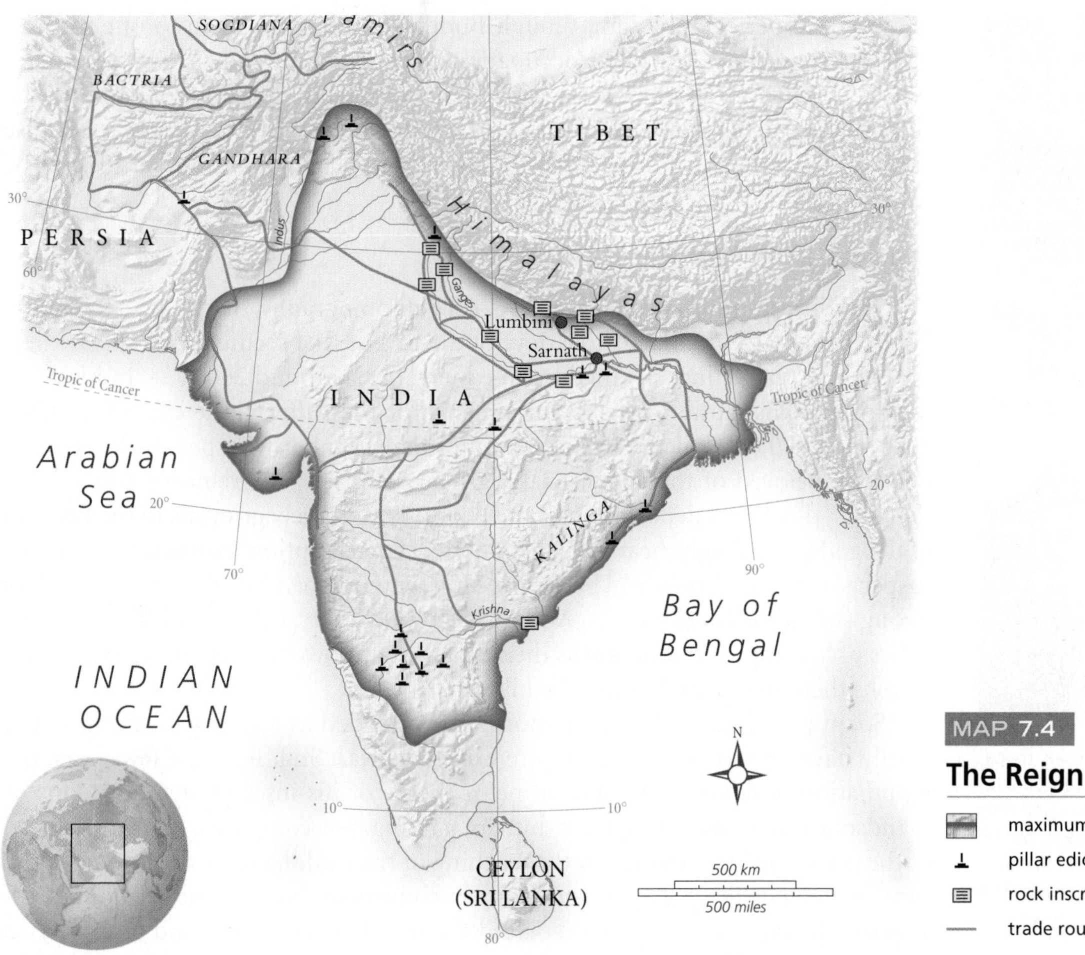

MAP 7.4

The Reign of Asoka, ca. 268–223 B.C.E.

maximum extent of Asoka's empire
pillar edict of Asoka
rock inscription of Asoka
trade route

and spices. The king is responsible for irrigation and should encourage others to irrigate by exempting them from the water tax. Pasture, mines, and forests (for obtaining war elephants) are all worthy objects of conquest. Roads are emphasized, with signposts and wells at nine-mile intervals. Regulating trade—including coinage, weights, and measures—and processing the raw materials of royal lands are also part of the ruler's job.

Government

Methods and means of government reflected central control. Peasants paid a quarter of their produce in tax, apparently directly to the king. Army leaders received pay in cash, rather than being given a share of royal power, as was customary in later Indian states. Asoka's inscriptions portray a hands-on ruler. He "received reports at all times"—in his harem or gardens, his carriage, or his barns, where he inspected his livestock. "And whatever I order by word of mouth, whether it concerns a donation or proclamation or whatever urgent matter is entrusted by my officers, if there is any dispute or deliberation about it at the Council, it is to be reported to me immediately."

The *Arthasastra* expresses an ideology of universal rule and uniform justice. It is hard to know, however, what this meant in practice. India was already becoming a **caste** society, where social rank was inherited, unchangeable, and made sacred by religious sanctions. Brahmanical literature (see Chapter 5) treated women as if

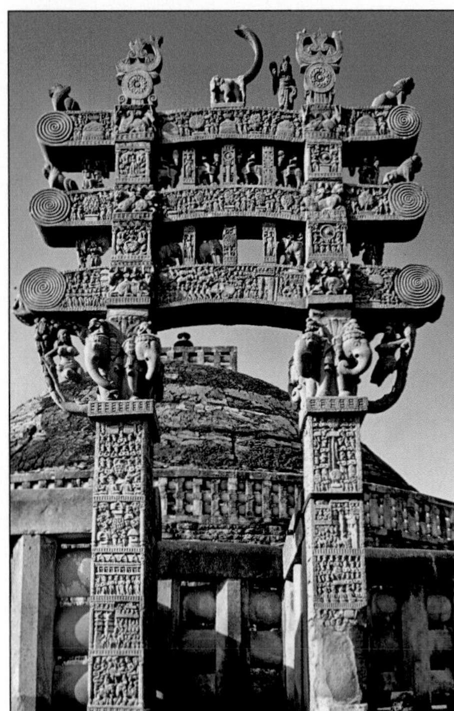

The stupa of Sanchi. The Emperor Asoka (r. ca. 272–223 B.C.E.) built the first shrine at Sanchi, near Bhopal in India, to honor a place made holy by the footprints of the Buddha. Enriched by the donations of pilgrims, it was adorned by dozens of elaborate structures over thousands of years. The northern gateway, shown here, is elaborately carved with scenes of legends of the Buddha's life and with tales of exemplary charity.

they were imperfectly human, though Buddhism admitted them to one form of high status as nuns. Few other occupations were open to them. There were state-run weaving shops for unmarriageable women, including retired prostitutes, the elderly, and the deformed. The king had female bodyguards, but this was because women's social exclusion made them trustworthy: They had nothing to gain by rebelling.

Asoka and His Mental World

The rock inscriptions are, in a sense, Asoka's autobiography, disclosing an extraordinary personal story of spiritual development. The first secure date in his reign is the conquest of Kalinga, a kingdom in eastern India around 260 B.C.E. In his commemorative inscription, he expresses regret for the suffering he caused: 150,000 deportees, 100,000 killed, "and many times that number who perished." He goes on: "The Beloved of the gods [meaning Asoka himself] felt remorse, for . . . the slaughter, death and deportation of the people is extremely grievous to the Beloved of the gods, and weighs heavily on his mind." The inscription then gets to what one suspects is the real point: "The Beloved of the gods believes that one who does wrong should be forgiven. . . . And the Beloved of the gods conciliates the forest tribes of his empire, but he warns them that he has power even in his remorse, and he asks them to repent, lest they be killed."

So, in part at least, Asoka's remorse was intended as a warning, and he could hardly have won such a large empire except by war. Still, within a few years, the repudiation of conquest became a major theme of his inscriptions. "Any sons or grandsons I may have should not think of gaining new conquests. . . . The Beloved of the gods considers victory by the teaching of the Buddha to be the foremost victory." Asoka put the policy of conquest-by-conversion into practice, sending missionaries to the kingdoms that replaced the old Persian Empire and to Sri Lanka (see Chapter 5). His descendants, he hoped, would adhere to this policy "until the end of the world."

How are we to explain Asoka's extraordinary behavior? His realm was expanding into areas where city life was only starting or, in northwest India, only reviving after the disappearance of the Harappan civilization. In the absence of existing bureaucracies, Asoka had to resort to the one disciplined, literate group available: the Buddhist clergy. This was the period when Buddhist scriptures were being recorded. Asoka recruited the scribes to his service, decreeing that monks, nuns, and his lay subjects should hear the scriptures frequently and meditate upon them.

These words are the telltale trace of Asoka's bargain with the clergy, probably made in the tenth year of his reign, 258 B.C.E. About this time, too, he made a much-publicized pilgrimage to the scene of the Buddha's enlightenment. In a further inscription, he claimed he had made society holy—where "gods mingle with men"—for the first time in India.

As the Buddhist clergy became more powerful, however, the monks' rivalry for the gifts of the pious and their theological disputes threatened the peace of the realm. So Asoka forbade them to speak ill of one another. "Concord is to be recommended, that men may hear one another's principles and obey them." Asoka's alliance with religion was the shape of things to come. As we shall see, it became a practice of kings all over the world, bringing common problems and advantages.

The language of Buddhism also infused Asoka's declarations of policy: "All men are my children. . . . There is no better work than promoting the welfare of the whole world." The disadvantaged were specifically included—slaves and servants, women and prisoners. Officials toured the empire to instruct people in

The Reign of Asoka

ca. 268–232 B.C.E.	Reign of Asoka
260 B.C.E.	Conquest of Kalinga
258 B.C.E.	Conversion to Buddhism
ca. 200 B.C.E.	Breakup of Asoka's empire

Asoka's version of Buddhist ethics: family loyalty, piety for holy men, mercy toward living creatures, and personal austerity. He made such tours himself, taking more pleasure in distributing alms and consulting holy men, he said, than in all other pleasures. These activities replaced hunting, formerly a royal obligation, now banned.

Toward the end of Asoka's reign, it appeared that his enlightenment was beginning to damage the empire. He tightened laws on the treatment of animals, forbidding the slaughter of young livestock and animals that were nursing their young. Fishless days were imposed. "Chaff, which contains living things must not be set on fire. Forests must not be burned to kill living things, or without good reason. An animal must not be fed with another animal." Gelding and branding were restricted. These decrees must have caused outrage and threatened livelihoods. The emperor's pride in the 25 amnesties he granted to imprisoned criminals can hardly have endeared him to their victims. His condemnation of all rituals as trivial and useless compared with a life in accordance with Buddhist doctrine alienated ordinary people. Perhaps worst of all, his policy against conquests meant the empire could not expand and turned the violence of the military classes inward.

Excerpts from *The Edicts of Asoka*

Only 25 years after Asoka's death in 232 B.C.E., his empire (which historians call the Mauryan Empire) broke up into separate states. But state-forming, environment-modifying habits had spread throughout India. The economic infrastructure—the routes of commerce, the enhanced range of resources—was not invulnerable. But the Mauryan infrastructure was unforgettable and it could usually be repaired or reconstructed, if necessary, after future wars and environmental disasters.

CHINESE UNITY AND IMPERIALISM

Even after 500 years of division among warring states, the ideal of imperial unity remained in China. Real unity, however, required force. Of all the warring states, Qin was the most marginal, occupying relatively infertile uplands, far from the rice-growing regions. The intelligentsia of most other states considered its people imperfectly civilized.

Toward the mid-third century B.C.E., Qin began what, in retrospect, looks like a systematic strategy of rejecting the very idea of empire. In 256 B.C.E., its ruler discontinued all imperial rites, in effect dissolving the empire. Ten years later, a new king of Qin, Shi Huangdi (shee hwang-dee), declared that having been dismantled, the empire could be replaced. Over the next 25 years, he systematically isolated and conquered rival kingdoms and declared himself "First Emperor" of a new monarchy. "If," he declared, "the whole empire has suffered, . . . it is because there were nobles and kings." In other words, with himself as sole ruler, a unified China would enjoy peace and prosperity.

Our picture of his reign comes from histories compiled one or two generations later. They are distorted partly by the awe Shi Huangdi inspired and partly by revulsion from his oppressive rule. They were based not on what he actually did, but on the sometimes unrealistic ambitions his decrees reveal. To judge by these sources, he aimed to break the aristocracy, abolish slavery, outlaw inheritance practices that concentrated wealth in noble hands, and replace the power of kings and lords with a uniform system of civil and military districts under his own appointees. He ordered the burning of hundreds of people he considered disloyal and, reputedly, of thousands of books. Only useful technical manuals and the writings of the Legalist

Terracotta warriors. Though his life and reign were short, everything else about Shi Huangdi (r. 221–210 B.C.E.), the Qin ruler who conquered China, was on a monumental scale. The size and magnificence of his tomb, guarded by an army of terracotta warriors, echoes the grandeur of his engineering works and the scope of his ambitions and uncompromising reforms.

school (see Chapter 6) were allowed. Uniformity was the keynote of the new state. Laws, coinage, measurements, script, even axle lengths of carts had to be the same all over the kingdom. Unauthorized weapons were melted down.

Shi Huangdi's demonic energy is obvious in everything he attempted. He mobilized 700,000 laborers to build a network of roads and canals. He knocked the Great Wall of China together out of older fortifications, as protection against nomad attacks. When he died in 210 B.C.E., he was buried with thousands of life-size clay models of soldiers and servants—each with different facial and body features—to accompany him into the next life. He was a showman of power on a huge scale—which is usually a sign of insecurity. His empire was too fragile to last, but sweeping away the warring states made it easier for his successors to rebuild an enduring Chinese Empire.

Unity Endangered and Saved

The first instinct of the rebels who overthrew his feeble son in 207 B.C.E. was to restore the system of the Warring States period. The result was chaotic warfare, with one of the rebel leaders, Liu Bang (lee-oh bahng), emerging victorious over all the others. He put in place a carefully tempered version of Shi Huangdi's system. Restored kings had small territories within military districts. Peasants owed the state two years' military service plus one month's labor a year, which must have seemed lenient compared to Shi Huangdi's demands.

Legalism remained the dominant political philosophy. Liu Bang put most of his former allies to death and showed contempt for Confucianism. In the long run, however, only Confucian scholars and officials could supply the literate administrators that a growing state needed. Gradually, especially in the 50-year reign of Han Wudi (hawn woo-dee), beginning in 141 B.C.E., Confucianism became the state ideology again.

Liu Bang called his dynasty "Han" after the portion of the country he received in the carving up of Shi Huangdi's realm. In the period of expansion that began in the late second century B.C.E., Han China became the essential China that we see on maps of later eras. Chinese began to call themselves Han.

The return of peaceful conditions under the Han dynasty stimulated a population explosion. The population of 20 million in Shi Huangdi's day probably tripled by the end of the millennium. In part, the huge increase was also probably a consequence of the increased size and environmental diversity of the state. Rice-growing and millet-growing regions could again exchange supplies in each other's bad times. The government coped with disasters, such as drought, famine, or earthquakes, by massive frontier colonization programs and redistributing population on a large scale. Forced migrations peopled newly conquered provinces in the southeast at the same time that settlers were encouraged to migrate south toward the Huai valley. These movements shifted the distribution of population, making the Yangtze River the main axis of China. Meanwhile, in the north in 120 B.C.E., 700,000 families were moved into a new conquest beyond the province of Shaanxi, which famine had devastated.

The Qin and the Han

ca. 256 B.C.E.	Ruler of Qin discontinues imperial rites
ca. 247 B.C.E.	Shi Huangdi becomes ruler of Qin state; beginning of Qin expansion
214 B.C.E.	Construction of Great Wall begins
210 B.C.E.	Death of Shi Huangdi
206 B.C.E.	Beginning of Han dynasty
141 B.C.E.	Han Wudi becomes Han emperor
ca. 139 B.C.E.	Embassy of Zhang Qian to Central Asia
220 C.E.	Collapse of Han Dynasty

The Han dynasty lasted from 206 B.C.E. to 220 C.E., despite a succession system that bred palace conspiracies. Succession was determined by designating a principal wife to be the mother of each emperor's heir. This gave empresses' families a unique opportunity to profit from the emperor's favor. But the advantage rarely lasted more than two generations—less, if the empress failed to produce a future emperor. Consequently, every empress's family was tempted to seize power for itself—and most tried. In these circumstances, a dynasty that survived a long time was a triumph against the odds.

The Menace from the Steppes

The other main problem China faced in this period emerged from the steppelands, north of the Great Wall and the Silk Roads. The region had a bad reputation. Its climate was inhospitable, its soil unworkable, its native herdsmen savage. In some ways, however, it was a good place to start building an empire. It bred plenty of horses and men accustomed to the saddle. Its people were voracious because they were poor. It was a vast, flat tract of land, with few geographical obstacles to the creation of a large state. Because the steppeland fringed the Silk Roads, leaders of steppelander bands could conduct raids, amass treasure, and use their wealth to build up large followings.

Chinese booty, ransom, and protection money enriched war chiefs who became wealthy enough to extend their followings beyond their own kin. According to Chinese evidence, compiled much later—which is all we have—the first great stepplander state emerged late in the third century B.C.E., among people the Chinese called Xiongnu (shee-ohng-noo). The leader styled himself "Son of Heaven," which was a Chinese imperial title and therefore suggests Chinese influence. His warriors hunted heads—exhibiting scalps from their bridles, making enemies' skulls into cups. The basis of their success in war was their skill in mounted archery. Sheep, horses, cattle, and camels were the mainstay of their economy—guaranteeing the advantages of mixed pastoralism, with milk yields of different species of animals peaking at different times. In about 176 B.C.E., they conquered Gansu (gohn-soo), at the western end of the Great Wall, and became a serious, constant nuisance to China.

The Han and the Xiongnu

Third century B.C.E.	First Xiongnu state emerges
ca. 176 B.C.E.	Xiongnu conquers Gansu
127–120 B.C.E.	Chinese mount successful operations against the Xiongnu

Confucian doctrine advocated what we would now call appeasement: "Your Majesty has but to manifest your virtue towards them and extend your favors to cover them, and the northern Barbarians will undoubtedly come of their own accord to pay you tribute at the wall." This policy was not as feeble as it sounds. Many neighboring peoples genuinely felt the "peaceful attraction" of Chinese rule, and Chinese culture absorbed huge numbers of subject-peoples. The Xiongnu, however, were unresponsive to such methods.

In the late second century B.C.E., Han efforts to recruit allies against them failed. But in the 120s B.C.E., the Chinese mounted a series of successful operations. The fortification of the Silk Roads followed. For a while around the turn of the millennium, the Xiongnu even abandoned hostilities. Thereafter, weakened by civil wars, they succumbed to celebrated campaigns in the late first century C.E., while pressure accumulated from neighbors to the north and east, who, in their turn, were beginning to move toward statehood.

BEYOND THE EMPIRES

At the Edge of Empires

Seventh century B.C.E.	First written evidence of the Scythians
ca. 500 B.C.E.	Silla, Paekche, and Koguryo states dominate Korea
Fourth century B.C.E.	Yayoi culture emerges in Japan
ca. 200 B.C.E.	Sarmatians displace Scythians

The edges of empires bred states. The Xiongnu were not the only example of economic and political development in China's shadow. Large-scale state formation also occurred in the same period in Japan and Korea, under Chinese influence, and at the other end of Eurasia, among the Scythians and Sarmatians, pastoral peoples whose lands bordered the Roman and Persian Empires.

Japan and Korea

In the fourth century B.C.E., a rice-growing, bronze-using culture known to archaeologists as Yayoi emerged in Japan. It gradually developed into a state system, under the stimulus of contacts with China. According to Chinese records, in about 200 C.E., one of the Japanese states, Yamatai, conquered the others, under the rule of a female shaman. When she died, 1,000 attendants were burned at her burial. This is the first inkling we have of a unified Japanese state.

Korean states developed faster. The Chinese were in touch with three Korean states—Silla, Paekche, and Koguryo. The Chinese sources are so vague, and the archaeological evidence so scanty, that historians can say nothing reliable about the political history of these realms. But their rulers were buried in impressive tombs, and grave goods reveal something of the nature of power and trade: iron weapons, gold diadems and chains, bronze ornaments that imitate Chinese work.

A gold cup of the mid–first millennium B.C.E. shows why Scythian art was admired in the classical world. Despite the Scythians' fierce reputation, their goldwork usually shows peaceful images of camp life, vividly depicted, such as this scene in which one warrior binds another's leg.

The Western Eurasian Steppe

Meanwhile, at the other end of the Eurasian steppe, in Ukraine and southern Russia, states formed among the pastoral peoples known as Scythians and Sarmatians. Scythian states formed in and around Crimea (creye-MEE-ah), a peninsula that juts into the Black Sea, where Greek trader-colonies lived. Here was the Scythian center of Neapolis, a ruler's court covering 40 acres and surrounded by a stone wall. Sarmatian royal courts throve beyond the rivers Dneiper and Don.

On one level, Greek writers sensed this pastoral, nomadic world was alien, wild, and menacing. The fifth-century B.C.E. Greek historian, Herodotus, told of a legendary traveler who undertook a mysterious, dreamlike journey to their land, beyond the river Don in modern Ukraine. On another level, the nomads were familiar trading partners. Greek craftsmen depicted them in everyday scenes, milking ewes or stitching their sheepskin cloaks. Greek and Celtic trade goods filled princely graves in the last half of the first millennium B.C.E.

Much of this art was produced under the patronage of Scythian and Sarmatian princes and is echoed in their own goldsmiths' work. A gold cup, for instance, from a royal tomb near the Black Sea shows bearded warriors in tunics and leggings at peace or, at least, between wars. They tend one another's wounds, fix their teeth, mend their bowstrings, and tell campfire tales. A Sarmatian queen of the first century C.E. stares, in Greek clothes and hairstyle, from the center of a gold crown. When we look at their art, we can never be sure whether these people were happy in their own traditions or envious of the sedentary empires—probably a bit of both.

Mesoamerica

Far more remarkable than these cases of state-building by peoples on the edges of existing empires are independent but comparable developments that began in this period in Mesoamerica (see Map 7.5). Chiefdom-formation and state-building had a long history in the Americas, but every innovation had been blocked or

MAP 7.5

Monte Albán and Teotihuacán

- Monte Albán
- Teotihuacán
- ○ settlement
- ● place mentioned on page 174
- *OAXACA* modern province

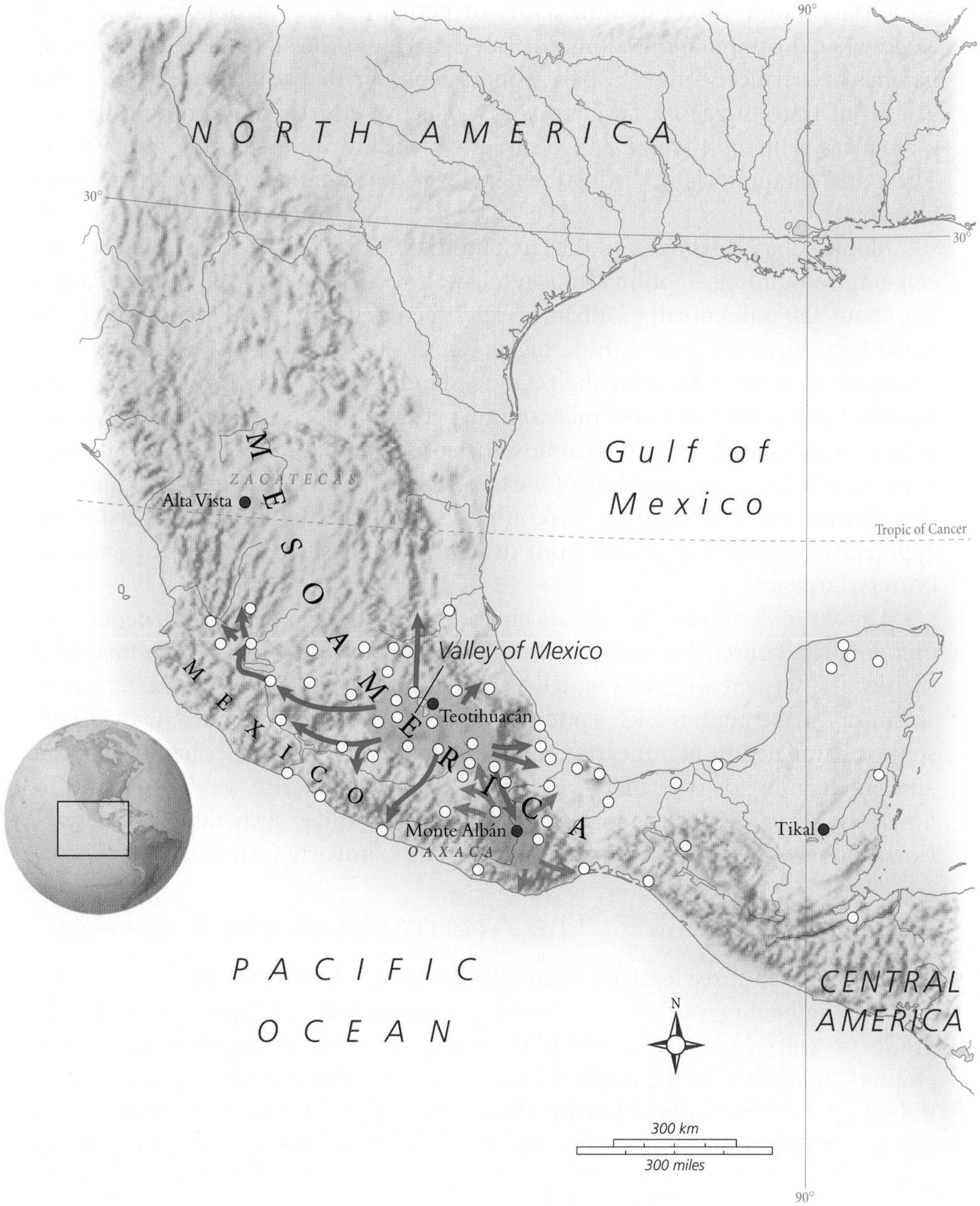

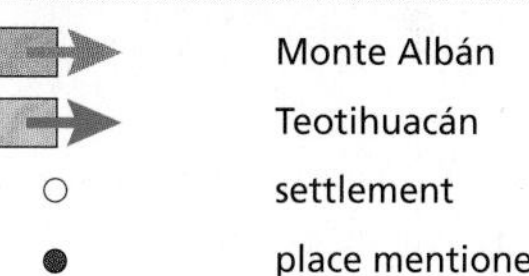

frustrated. The geography and vast climate zones of the Americas discouraged communication and cultural change (see Chapter 5).

Now, at least two centers sprang into what might fairly be called a potentially imperial role. Monte Albán (MON-tay al-BAHN) in Oaxaca was the first. In a period of social differentiation early in the millennium, the region had deer-fed elite, buried in stone-lined graves with jade-bead lip studs and earrings. Population growth accompanied their supremacy, with increasing exploitation of irrigation and the spread of settlement into areas of sparse rainfall. Around the mid-millennium, ever-larger settlements appeared, with ritual mounds and the first engraved picture-writing, or glyphs. We do not know how to read this writing, and the inscriptions are all short—perhaps only names and dates. From about the same time and place, we have the first evidence of what the ritual platforms were for: a carving of a human sacrifice, with blood streaming from a chest sliced open to pluck out the heart.

Not long after this, Monte Albán began to draw in population from surrounding settlements. It was a natural fortress, enhanced by defensive walls. From a modest village, Monte Albán became a city of perhaps 20,000 people by about 200 B.C.E., when the population stabilized. Faded carvings proclaim its warlike values in parades of sacrifice victims. A palace and a reservoir that could have held 20,000 gallons of water suggest a familiar story: collective effort under strong rule. The main plaza contains 40 huge carved stones—probably of the second century B.C.E. These are "conquest slabs," listing the names of subject-cities and the tribute these cities had to pay.

Monte Albán casts light on the later and more spectacular case of Mesoamerican empire-building. Teotihuacán (tay-oh-wah-tee-KAHN), in the valley of Mexico, about 450 miles north of Albán, was destined to be a far greater metropolis. At 6,000 feet above sea level, a little higher than Monte Albán, its agriculture was based on what were by then the region's standard products: maize, beans, and squash. Around the end of the millennium, perhaps as the result of a war, a migration as sudden as Albán's shifted almost the entire population of the valley of Mexico to Teotihuacán. The building of the towering Sun Pyramid began. By about 150 C.E., 20 monumental pyramids were in place. The other buildings included some apparently for housing people from distant lowland sites: ambassadors, tribute bearers, hostages.

The art of Teotihuacán suggests an ecologically fragile way of life, dependent on rainfall and unreliable gods to deliver fertile soil and crops. The artists imagined the sky as a serpent whose sweat fell as rain and fed the plant life of Earth, where sacrificers in serpent masks scattered blood from hands lacerated with cactus spikes or impaled human hearts on bones. Yet the city and the reach of its trade and power grew for over 350 years. At its peak, Teotihuacán was big enough to house well over 100,000 people. Carvings over 625 miles away depicted its warriors, and its trade goods and tribute came from a similarly wide area.

IN PERSPECTIVE: The Aftermath of the Axial Age

The axial age left three legacies: a remarkably durable heritage of ideas, less secure though lengthening routes for trade and cultural exchange in Eurasia, and a fragile group of empires. In some ways, these legacies seemed interdependent. The empires added little to the intellectual achievements that preceded them, but they did safeguard, enshrine, and nurture them. The Romans, for example, adopted and fostered Greek learning. Persian emperors adopted Zoroastrian rites. Asoka

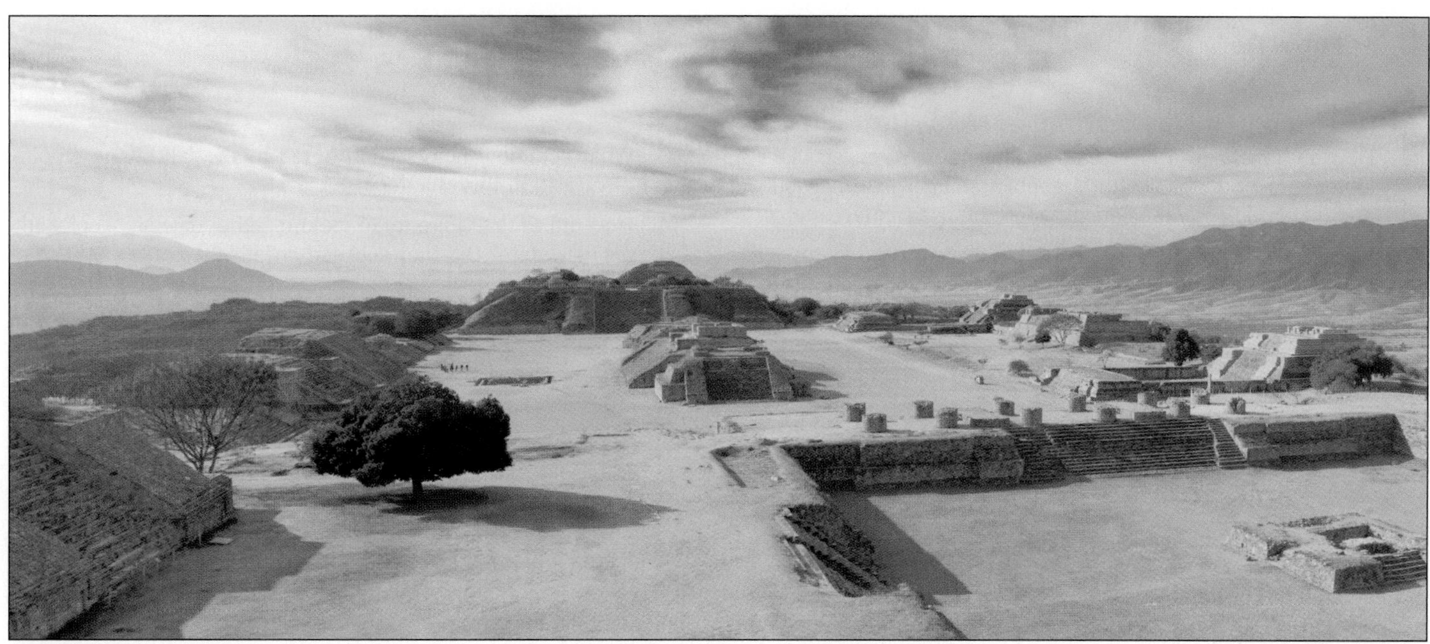

Monte Albán. The builders of Monte Albán (Oaxaca, Mexico) reshaped the 1,500-foot-high mound on which it stands to fit their idea of how a city should be: 50 acres of terraces supporting temples, palaces, and garrisons. This was truly an imperial metropolis, decorated with gaudy, gory slabs depicting dismembered captives.

became the patron of Buddhism in India. The Han rehabilitated Confucianism. The empires developed sea and land communications in Eurasia. The road-building programs, the Chinese effort to scout and fortify the Silk Roads, and the interest Alexander and his Persian predecessors took in Indian Ocean navigation all demonstrate that.

The collapse of the Persian Empire and the rapid unraveling of Asoka's empire showed that the world was not yet safe for large-scale imperialism. But the pattern of state-building seems to have been irresistible. New states on the edges of the existing Eurasian empires—and, as we shall see in the next chapter, in parts of Africa where contacts with Eurasia were multiplying—suggest this pattern. The New World resembled a "parallel universe" where, despite the environmental differences, histories similar to those of parts of Eurasia and Africa were beginning to unfold.

CHRONOLOGY

Seventh century B.C.E.	First written evidence of the Scythians
Sixth century B.C.E.	Cyrus the Great founds Persian Empire
Fifth century B.C.E.	1,700 miles of road cross Persian Empire
	Chinese silks appear in Europe
	Silla, Paekche, and Koguryo states dominate Korea
Fourth century B.C.E.	Yayoi culture emerges in Japan
334 B.C.E.	Alexander conquers Persian Empire
Third century B.C.E.	Roman Empire expands beyond Italy
	First Xiongnu state emerges north of China
ca. 268–232 B.C.E.	Reign of Asoka (India)
206 B.C.E.	Beginning of Han dynasty in China
200 B.C.E.	Population of Monte Albán reaches 20,000 (Mesoamerica)
127–120 B.C.E.	Chinese mount successful operations against the Xiongnu
27 B.C.E.	Augustus becomes first emperor of Rome
ca. 150 C.E.	Teotihuacán at peak of its influence (Mesoamerica)
220 C.E.	Collapse of the Han dynasty

PROBLEMS AND PARALLELS

1. How do travel and trade create a demand for stronger, bigger states? How do cross-cultural contacts, larger road networks, and increased communication benefit or disadvantage states?
2. What were the advantages and disadvantages of sea routes versus land routes for commerce and communication in the ancient world?
3. What common factors contributed to the fall of the empires discussed in this chapter?
4. How did each empire try to meld together diverse peoples into a single state? Did they succeed or fail?

DOCUMENTS IN GLOBAL HISTORY

- from the *Periplus of the Erythraean Sea*
- Agatharchides of Knidos describes Saba
- Zhang Qian, *Hon Shu*, "Descriptions of the Western Regions"
- Religious freedom in ancient Persia: the "Cyrus Cylinder"
- Horace, "Dulce et Decorum est Pro Patria Mori"
- Pliny the Elder, from *The Natural History*
- Excerpts from the *Arthasastra*, "The Duties of Government Superintendents"
- Excerpts from *The Edicts of Asoka*

Please see the Primary Source DVD for additional sources related to this chapter.

READ ON

For Indian maps, J. B. Harley and D. Woodward, eds., *History of Cartography* (1987), vol. ii is fundamental. L. Feer, *A Study of the Jatakas* (1963) is a good introduction to those texts. The texts I cite on the Erythraean Sea are easy to consult in L. Casson, ed., *The Periplus of the Erythraean Sea* (1989), and S. Burstein, ed., *Agatharchides of Cnidos: On the Erythraean Sea* (1989). P. Horden and N. Purcell, *The Corrupting Sea* (2000), and D. Abulafia, ed., *The Mediterranean in History* (2003) are the best histories of the Mediterranean; for the link to the Atlantic, see B. Cunliffe, *Facing the Ocean* (2001). On the Indian Ocean, M. Pearson, *The Indian Ocean* (2003) is a masterly survey; the demanding work of K. Chaudhuri, *Asia before Europe* (1991) repays the effort it requires.

On the Silk Roads, the outstanding book is now the British Library exhibition catalog edited by S. Whitfield, *The Silk Roads* (2004). On Dunhuang, see R. Whitfield et al., eds., *Cave Temples of Dunhuang* (2000). J. Mirsky, *The Great Chinese Travelers* (1976), collects extracts from key texts, including the journey of Zhang Qian.

On the Persian Empire, *The Cambridge History of Iran* (1993) is unbeatable. On women, I follow M. Brosius, *Women in Ancient Persia* (1998). On the Persian Wars, P. Green, *The Greco-Persian Wars* (1996) is authoritative. S. Hornblower, *The Athenian Empire* (2000) is a superb study. The same author's *The Greek World* (1983) provides the backdrop down to the time of Alexander, on whom R. Lane Fox, *Alexander the Great* (1973) is both scholarly and irresistibly readable. My remarks on Alexander's legacy are indebted to G. Cary, *The Medieval Alexander* (1967), which is a wonderful book.

On the Romans, T. Cornell, *The Beginnings of Rome* (1995) takes the story down to the Punic Wars. A. Goldsworthy, *The Fall of Carthage* (2004) is a history of those wars. R. Syme, *The Roman Revolution* (1939) is a classic of abiding interest and importance, centered on the rise of Augustus and a monarchical system of government. The best study of Virgil is probably R. Jenkyns, *Virgil's Experience* (1999).

For Celtic history, N. K. Chadwick, *The Celts* (1971), remains standard. H. D. Rankin, *Celts and the Classical World* (1987) is particularly interesting on Greek and Roman images. M. J. Green, *Celtic Art* (1997) is a good introduction.

On India in this period, F. R. Allchin, ed., *The Archaeology of Early Historic South Asia* (1995) is fundamental. R. Thapar, *Asoka and the Decline of the Mauryas* (1961) is insightful and close to the sources. R. McKeon and N. A. Nikam, *The Edicts of Asoka* (1959) analyzes these important sources.

For the Qin-Han revolution D. Twitchett and M. Loewe, eds., *The Cambridge History of China* (1986) is invaluable. Li Xueqin, *Eastern Zhou and Qin Civilizations* (1985) is excellent on the background. For the Xiongnu, as for all steppeland history, the classic work of R. Grousset, *The Empire of the Steppes* (1970) remains fundamental.

For Japan and Korea, *The Cambridge History of Japan* (1993) is inescapably useful. W. Hong, *Paekche of Korea and the Origins of Yamato Japan* (1994) is helpful on the links between the two regions. K. Mizoguchi, *An Archaeological History of Japan* (2002) surveys the archaeological evidence.

The Scythians and Sarmatians have inspired much good work. Useful introductions are supplied in T. Talbot Rice, *The Scythians* (1957); E. Phillips, *The Royal Hordes* (1965); and T. Sulimirski, *The Sarmatians* (1970). On Mesoamerica, J. A. Hendon and R. A. Joyce, *Mesoamerican Archaeology* (2004) has the most up-to-date account.

For Monte Albán, R. E. Blanton, *Monte Albán* (1978) is the standard work. For Teotihuacán, important works include J. C. Berlo, ed., *Art, Ideology and the City of Teotihuacán* (1993), and R. Storey, *Life and Death in the Ancient City of Teotihuacán* (1992).

PART Four

Fitful Transitions, from the Third Century to the Tenth Century

CHAPTER 8 Postimperial Worlds: Problems of Empires in Eurasia and Africa, ca. 200 to ca. 700 C.E. 180

CHAPTER 9 The Rise of World Religions: Christianity, Islam, and Buddhism 210

CHAPTER 10 Remaking the World: Innovation and Renewal on Environmental Frontiers in the Late First Millennium 236

The world map of Beatus of Liebana. The eighth-century Spanish monk, Beatus of Liebana, illustrated his Commentary on the last book of the Bible with a world map. Almost all those who later made copies of his work produced versions of their own maps. In this one, from 1109, the picture of Adam, Eve, and the serpent indicates the presumed location of the Garden of Eden, at the extreme limit of the East. Europe is the disproportionately large, nearly square shape at the lower left. ▶

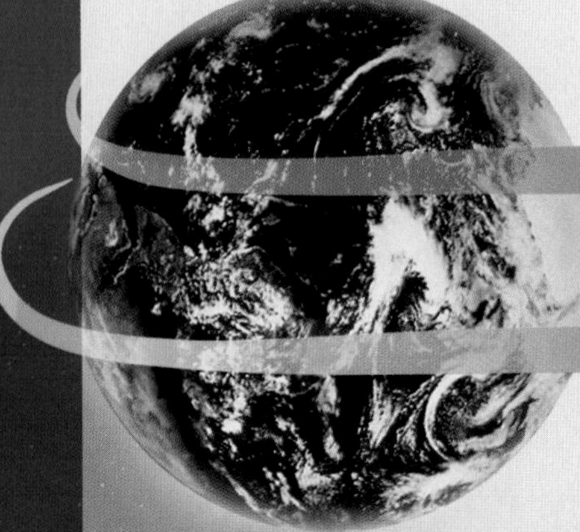

ENVIRONMENT

200–400
Spread of maize cultivation into North America

CULTURE

220
Breakup of Han Empire

200s on
Spread of Buddhism to east Asia

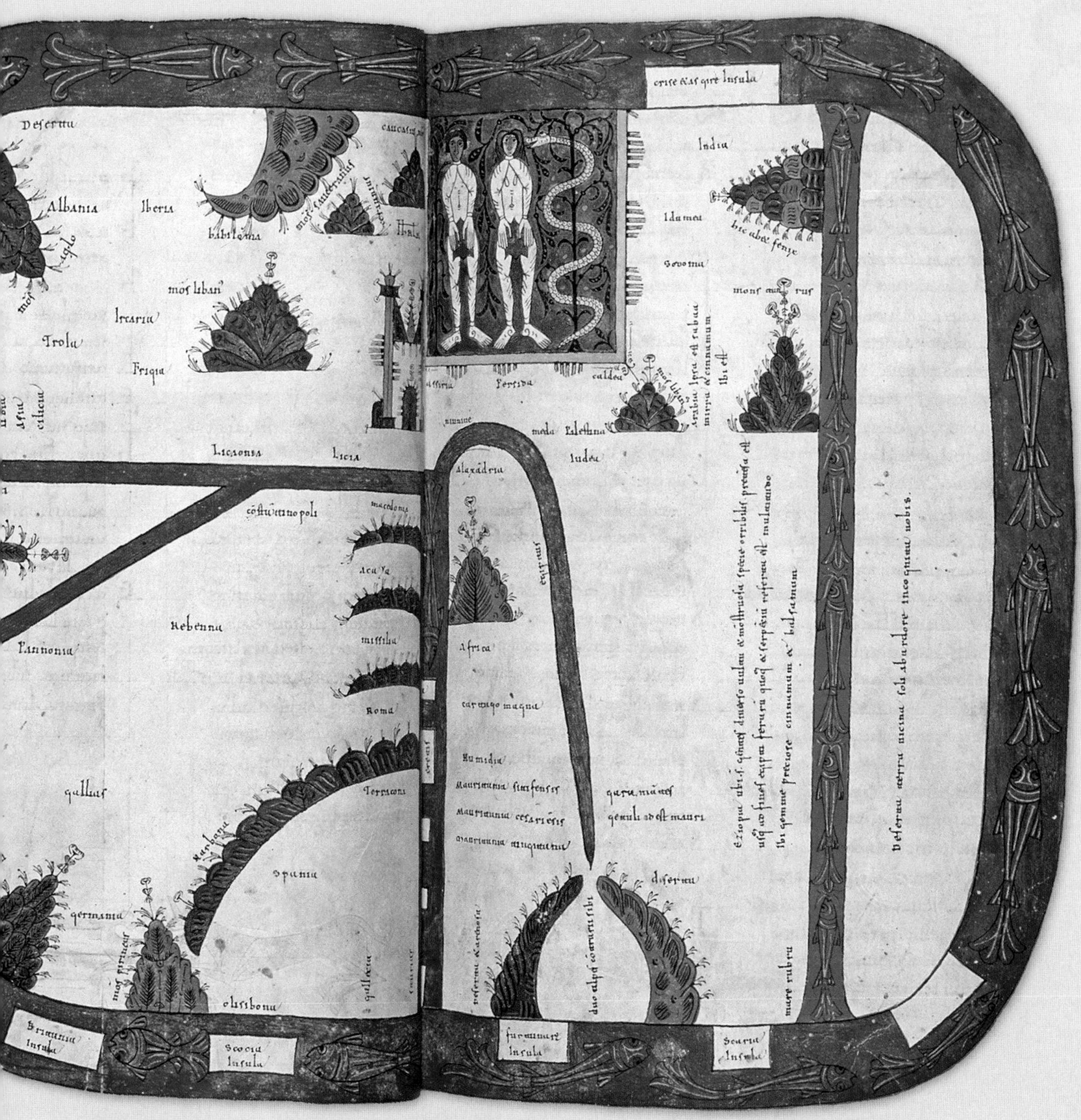

mid–500s
Plague in Arabia and eastern Mediterranean

600–800
Growing trans-Saharan trade; Polynesian diaspora

800–1000
"Internal colonization" in China, Japan, western Europe

300s on
Spread of Christianity in Roman world

400s
Breakup of Roman Empire

630 on
Rise and spread of Islam

CHAPTER 8 Postimperial Worlds: Problems of Empires in Eurasia and Africa, ca. 200 to ca. 700 C.E.

Detail from a Mayan vase, early sixth century c.e. The color scheme of red on a gold background is characteristic of ceramics from Tikal, while the bird-like symbols with forked, blood-sucking tongues on the bottom row have similarities with glyphs from Teohituacán.

IN THIS CHAPTER

THE WESTERN ROMAN EMPIRE AND ITS INVADERS
Changes Within the Roman Empire
The "Barbarian" West

STEPPELANDERS AND THEIR VICTIMS
China
India

NEW FRONTIERS IN ASIA
Korea
Funan

THE RISE OF ETHIOPIA

THE CRISES OF THE SIXTH AND SEVENTH CENTURIES

JUSTINIAN AND THE EASTERN ROMAN EMPIRE

THE NEW BARBARIANS

THE ARABS
Islam
The Arabs Against Persia and Rome

THE MUSLIM WORLD

RECOVERY AND ITS LIMITS IN CHINA
Rise of the Tang
Empress Wu
Tang Decline

IN THE SHADOW OF TANG: TIBET AND JAPAN
Tibet
Japan

IN PERSPECTIVE: The Triumph of Barbarism?

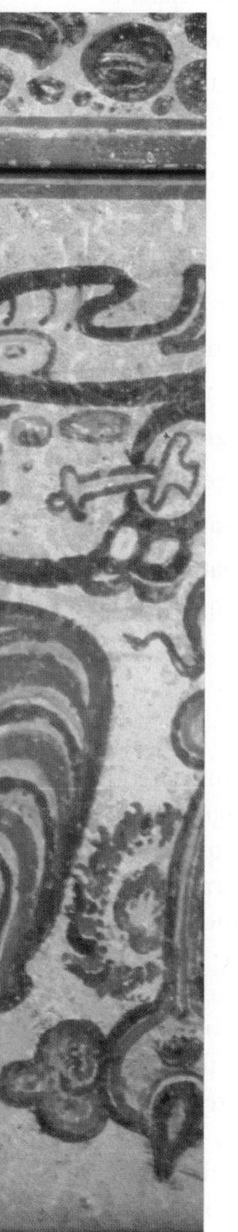

They arrived in January 378, soon after the beginning of the rains, in the tropical lowlands of what is now eastern Guatemala. They came from Teotihuacán, 7,500 feet high in the mountain-ringed valley of central Mexico, across hundreds of miles of mountains and forests, to the land of the Maya, whose environment, culture, and language were different from their own. The Maya called the leader of the group Siyaj K'ak (SEE-ah kah-AK), meaning "fire born," and added a nickname, "The Great Man from the West." But why had he come?

MESOAMERICA

His destination was Tikal (tee-KAHL), where limestone temples and gaudily painted rooftop reliefs rose above dense forest. Tikal was one of the oldest and largest of the many city-states among which the Maya world was divided. Its population at the time was perhaps over 30,000. But while Tikal was a giant by Maya standards, Teotihuacán was probably more than three times its size: no mere city-state, moreover, but the nerve center of an empire that covered the valley of Mexico and spilled into neighboring regions. Teotihuacáno influence and tribute gathering probed further still.

Relations between Tikal and Teotihuacán were important for both cities, because of the complementary ecologies of their regions (see Map 8.1). The Maya supplied Mexico with products unavailable in the highlands, including the plumage of forest birds for ornament, rubber for the ball games the elites of the region favored, cacao, jade, and incense. But visitors like Siyaj K'ak were rare, or even, perhaps, unprecedented. As they approached, day by day, along the river now called San Pedro Mártir, the communities they passed through handed on the news to neighbors down the line. What were the newcomers' intentions? Were they invaders or invitees? Envoys or adventurers? Were they mercenaries, perhaps, or a marriage party? Had they come to arbitrate disputes or to exploit them for their own purposes?

FOCUS questions

- WHY DID Teotihuacán rise and decline as an imperial state?
- WHY DID the Roman Empire collapse in the west but survive in the east?
- WHY WAS China better adapted for long-term survival than Rome and India?
- WHAT WERE the bases for Ethiopia's prosperity?
- WHY WERE the Arabs able to conquer such a vast empire so quickly?
- HOW DID the Muslims treat conquered peoples?
- HOW DID states in Korea, Tibet, and Japan develop?

The inscriptions that record the events are too fragmentary to answer these questions. But they tell a suggestive story. When Siyaj K'ak reached Tikal on January 31, his arrival precipitated a revolution. On that very day, if the inscriptions can be taken literally, the life of the city's ruler, Chak Tok Ich'aak (chak tek eech-AH-AK) (or "Great Jaguar Paw," as historians used to call him), came to an end. He "entered the water," as the Maya said, after a reign of 18 years, ending the supremacy of a royal line that had supplied 13 kings. The monuments of his dynasty were shattered into fragments or defaced and buried: slabs of stone on which images of kings were carved, with commemorations of the wars they fought, captives they took, astronomical observations they recorded, and sacrifices they offered to the gods—sometimes of their own blood, sometimes of the lives of their captives.

Siyaj K'ak installed new rulers not only in Tikal but also in other, smaller cities in the region over the next few years. The supremacy of Teotihuacán, or at least of Teotihuacános, was part of the new order. A rash of new cities was founded from Tikal, though they seem quickly, in most cases, to have asserted or exercised independence. It would exceed the evidence to speak of the birth of a new regional state or the foundation of a new province of the empire of Teotihuacán. But we can confidently assert that contacts across Mesoamerica were growing, that state formation was quickening and spreading, and that a complex political pattern was emerging: jealous Maya cities, competing and combining, with elites often drawn or sponsored from central Mexico.

• • • • •

Tikal

The influence and power of Teotihuacán were close to their maximum. Teotihuacános founded colonies wherever the city needed supplies. Chingú (cheen-GOO), near the later site of Tula (TOO-lah), was one, where lime was exported for Teotihuacán's gigantic building projects. San Ignacio in Morelos was another, supplying avocados, cacao, and cotton, which would not grow in the highlands but was vital for everyday clothing and the quilted armor warriors favored.

In part, pressure of population drove this expansion. Teotihuacán probably produced or attracted more people than it could contain. In any case, to sustain a growing city, Teotihuacán needed a growing empire. The basic foodstuffs the city consumed—maize and beans—were part of the ecosystem of its own region. But the concentration of population that had to be fed was enormous by the standards of preindustrial cities anywhere in the world and probably required extra supplies from farther away. The cotton and the luxuries and ritual objects on which elite life depended had to come from other climes. Teotihuacán had its own mines of obsidian—the black volcanic glass of which the cutting blades of tools and weapons were made. But it had no other resources to export. It had to be a military state.

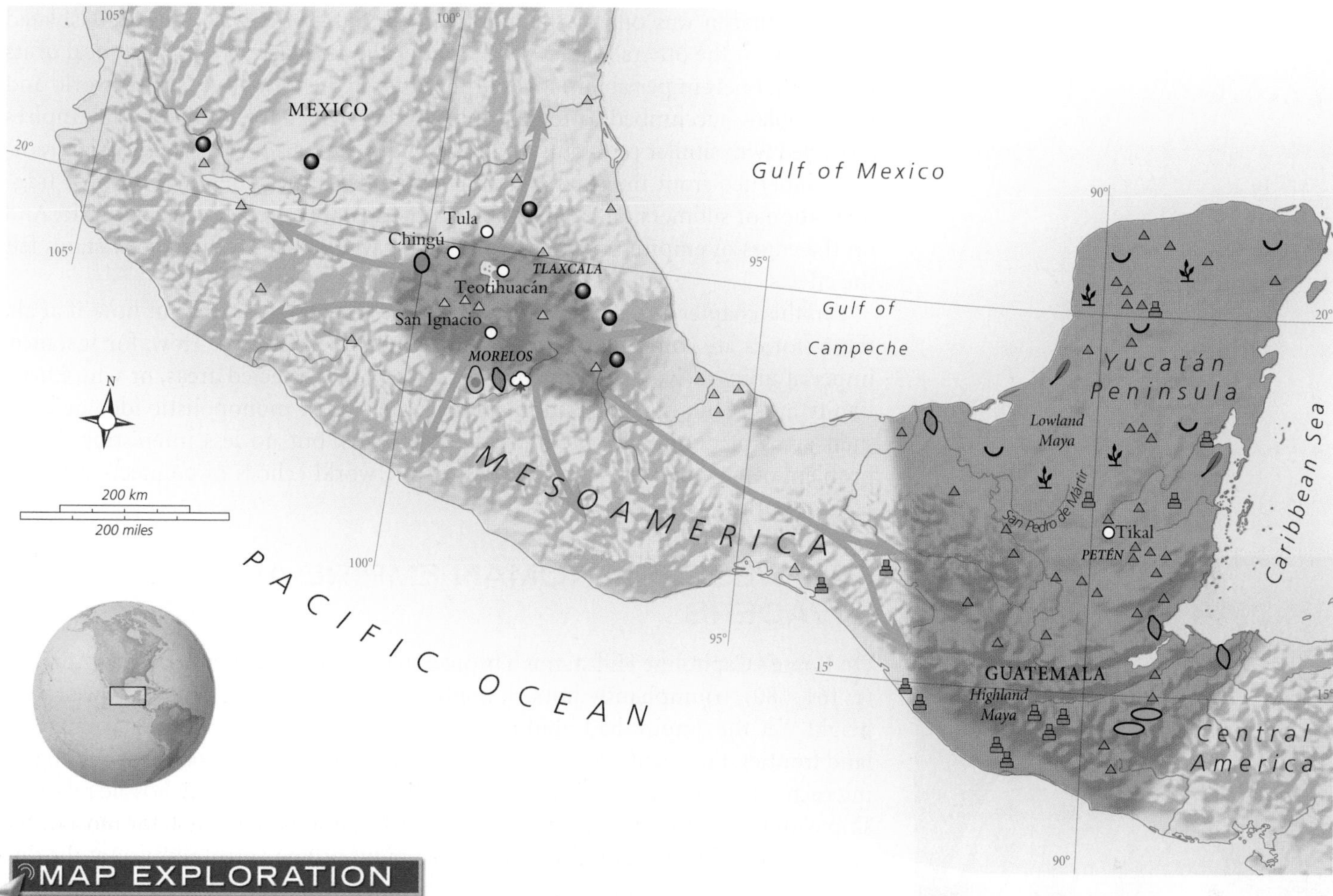

MAP EXPLORATION
www.prenhall.com/armesto_maps

MAP 8.1

The Maya and Teotihuacán

- Maya
- Teotihuacán and directions of influence
- Mayan temple
- important Mayan site
- important Teotihuacán site
- obsidian mine
- MEXICO modern-day country
- *PETÉN* modern-day province or region
- city described or mentioned on pages 181–184

Products Supplied from Maya to Teotihuacán

- cacao
- incense
- jade
- plumage
- rubber

Products Supplied to Teotihaucán from Neighboring Colonies

- avocado
- cacao
- cotton
- lime

We do not know how the state was organized. Unlike the Maya, the Teotihuacános produced no art depicting kings and, as far as we know, no chronicles of royal activities. Some curious features, however, show up in the archaeological record. During the fourth century, many families were shifted from small dwellings into large compounds, as if the city were being divided among rival, or potentially rival, focuses of allegiance. From the mid–fifth century, there are signs of internal instability. One of the most lavish temples was demolished. Thick, high internal walls divided different quarters of the city from each other. New building gradually ceased. Meanwhile, Teotihuacáno influence over distant areas withered. At an uncertain date, probably around the mid–eighth century, a traumatic event ended Teotihuacán's greatness. Fire wrecked the center of the city, and much of the population fled. Teotihuacán remained a city of perhaps 30,000 people, but it never again displayed imperial trappings or ambition. It is hard to resist the impression that the empire had overreached itself. No single city or empire of comparable dimensions replaced Teotihuacán. But people in Mesoamerica remembered it, conserved its influence, and tried to imitate it, as they entered a period of kaleidoscopic change, in which small, well-matched states fought among themselves without ever settling into an enduring pattern.

Teotihuacán was one of the world's most out-of-the-way empires—isolated from most of the others that arose in or after the axial age. Yet it was typical of its time. Other new imperial initiatives of the era—in the formative Islamic world and in Ethiopia—succumbed to remarkably similar challenges. Even the old empires struggled with similar problems. In Rome, India, China, and Persia, imperial traditions inherited from the axial age were extinguished or suffered periods of fragmentation or submersion by invaders whom the natives regarded as barbaric. And on the edges of empires in transformation, as well as within them, new states felt the effects.

In this chapter and the next two, we have to face the questions of how, if at all, these stories are connected, and why their outcomes differed. How, for instance, imperial unity revived in China but not in the other affected areas, or why Christianity and Islam, but not Buddhism, became almost monopolistic ideologies in their areas of dominance. Less pressing, perhaps, but no less interesting, is the problem of how the history of the rest of the world echoes or connects with the fates of Eurasia's empires.

THE WESTERN ROMAN EMPIRE AND ITS INVADERS

The philosopher at war. *The Meditations* of the Emperor Marcus Aurelius (r. 161–180) were written in military camps while he was campaigning against the barbarians on the empire's northern frontiers. His statue atop the Capitol at Rome has always symbolized dynamism and power, not only because of the commanding gesture of the emperor, but also because of the power his horse displays with its flared nostrils and stamping hoof.

Marcus Aurelius, from *The Meditations*

On Rome's Capitoline Hill stands a bronze statue of the Emeperor Marcus Aurelius (r. 161–180), triumphantly horsed, holding a globe, wielding Roman power at its height. Yet the empire had abiding problems: sprawling size; a long, vulnerable land frontier; the unruly behavior of politicized soldiery, with Roman armies fighting each other to make and unmake emperors; the uneasy, usually hostile relationship with Persia. Two new dangers were increasingly apparent. First, for most of the elite, Christianity seemed subversive. To the pious, Rome's greatness was at the disposal of the gods. To the practical, Roman unity depended on politically charged cults of the divine emperor and patron-gods of Rome. Second, Germanic peoples beyond the empire's borders in Europe coveted Roman wealth. The prosperity gap was like that between "North and South," on a global level, today—inspiring fear in the prosperous and envy in the poor.

Marcus Aurelius anticipated ways in which the empire would cope with these problems for the next three centuries. He sensed the need to divide government, making his adoptive brother coemperor and delegating to him responsibility for the eastern frontier. This sort of division was to be a recurrent formula for saving the state from crisis. He repudiated fancy theories in favor of practical ethics (see Chapter 6). His was a dark world, glinting with campfire light, as he fought to keep the Danube frontier secure. He snatched moments on campaign to write his *Meditations* in Greek, which was the common language of the eastern half of the empire and the prestige language favored for philosophy. "Renew yourself," he wrote in a memo to himself, "but keep it brief and basic."

In combination with threats from Persia and the convulsions of Roman politics, Germanic invasions in the third century almost dissolved the empire. In the late fourth century, the struggle to keep out the immigrants became hopeless. They came usually in relatively small, mobile war parties, numbering hundreds or at most a few thousand, composed of men detached from their traditional kinship structures by loyalty to a "ring giver"—a warlord who could buy allegiance with booty, protection money, ransom, extortion, or mercenary service. Trinkets of war-band service survive in burial sites: armbands set with jewels or onyx or inscribed with reminders of loyalty, rings bulging with garnets.

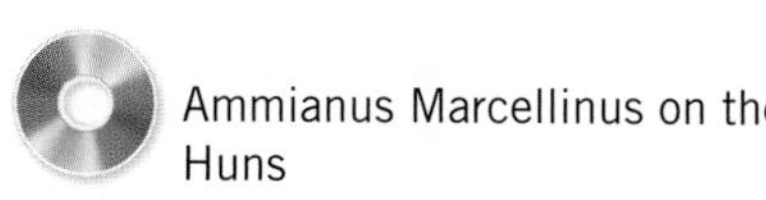
Ammianus Marcellinus on the Huns

The biggest bands of migrants, numbering tens of thousands at a time, and traveling with women and children, were driven by stresses that arose in the Eurasian steppelands. Here, the mid and late fourth century was a traumatic time, when war, hunger, plague, exceptional cold, or some combination of such events induced unprecedented mobility, conflict, and confusion. The Roman historian and retired soldier, Ammianus Marcellinus, reported a conversation with some Huns, reputedly the most ferocious of the steppeland peoples of the time. "Ask," he said, "who they are and whence they came—and they cannot tell you." Fear of the Huns glistens between the lines of every account: fear of their monstrous appearance, which Roman writers suspected must be produced by self-deformation; fear of their mounted archery; fear of their merciless treatment of enemies. Late in the fourth century, the Huns broke out of their heartlands in the depths of Asia—perhaps on the northeast borders of China, where many scholars identify them with the people the Chinese called Xiongnu (see Chapter 7). A kind of ricochet effect set in, as peoples collided and cannoned off each other, like balls on a pool table. Or perhaps all the turbulence of peoples, Germans and steppelanders alike, was the result of common problems: cold weather, shrinking pastures; or new sources of wealth, such as trade and booty, enriching new classes and disrupting the traditional stability of the societies concerned. Whatever the reasons, in the late fourth and early fifth centuries, displaced communities lined up for admission into the enticing empires of Rome, Persia, China, and India.

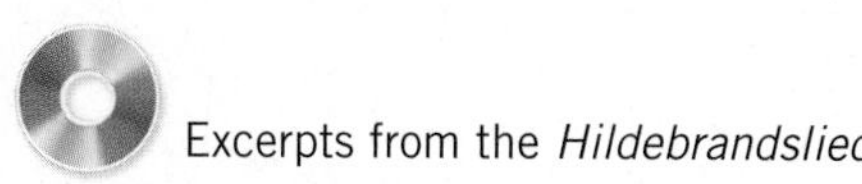
Excerpts from the *Hildebrandslied*

The hardest part of the story to appreciate is what it felt like for those who took part. Inklings emerge from the earliest surviving poem in what is recognizably German: the *Hildebrandslied*, the story of a family split in the conflicts of the fifth century. Hildebrand's wife was left "in misery"; his baby grew into his battlefield adversary. The boy, raised in ignorance of his father's identity, unwittingly rejected his present of gold and jewels, "which the King of the Huns had given him." Only the first few lines survive of the terrible climax, in which father and son fight to the death. The story shows the chaotic, divisive effects of the migrations, the interdependence of the worlds of Germans and Huns.

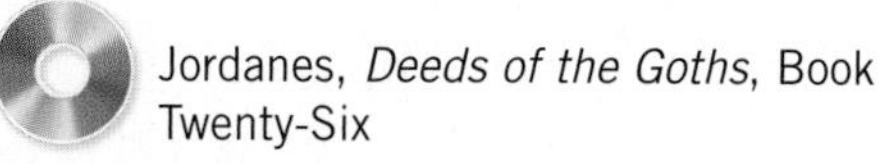
Jordanes, *Deeds of the Goths*, Book Twenty-Six

Germans were not nomadic by custom but, according to their own earliest historian, Jordanes, who wrote in the sixth century, were "driven to wander in a prolonged search for lands to cultivate." In 376, for instance, a reputed 200,000 Visigothic refugees were admitted into the Roman Empire. But the Romans then left them to starve, provoking a terrible revenge at the battle of Adrianople in 378 when a Roman emperor died along with most of his army. From 395 to 418, the Visigoths undertook a destructive march across the empire. In 410, they sacked Rome, inspiring speculations about the end of the world among shocked subjects of the empire, before settling as paid "guests" and, in effect, the masters of the local population in southern France and northern Spain. Other Germanic peoples found the Visigoths' example irresistible. Rome's frontier with the Germans was becoming indefensible (see Map 8.2).

Changes Within the Roman Empire

Meanwhile, the center of power in the dwindling empire shifted eastward into the mostly Greek-speaking zone, where barbarian incursions were more limited. In 323, the Emperor Constantine elevated a dauntingly defensible small garrison town into Constantinople, an imperial capital.

From here, in the fourth and fifth centuries, the emperors were able to keep invaders out of most of the eastern provinces or limit immigration to manageable

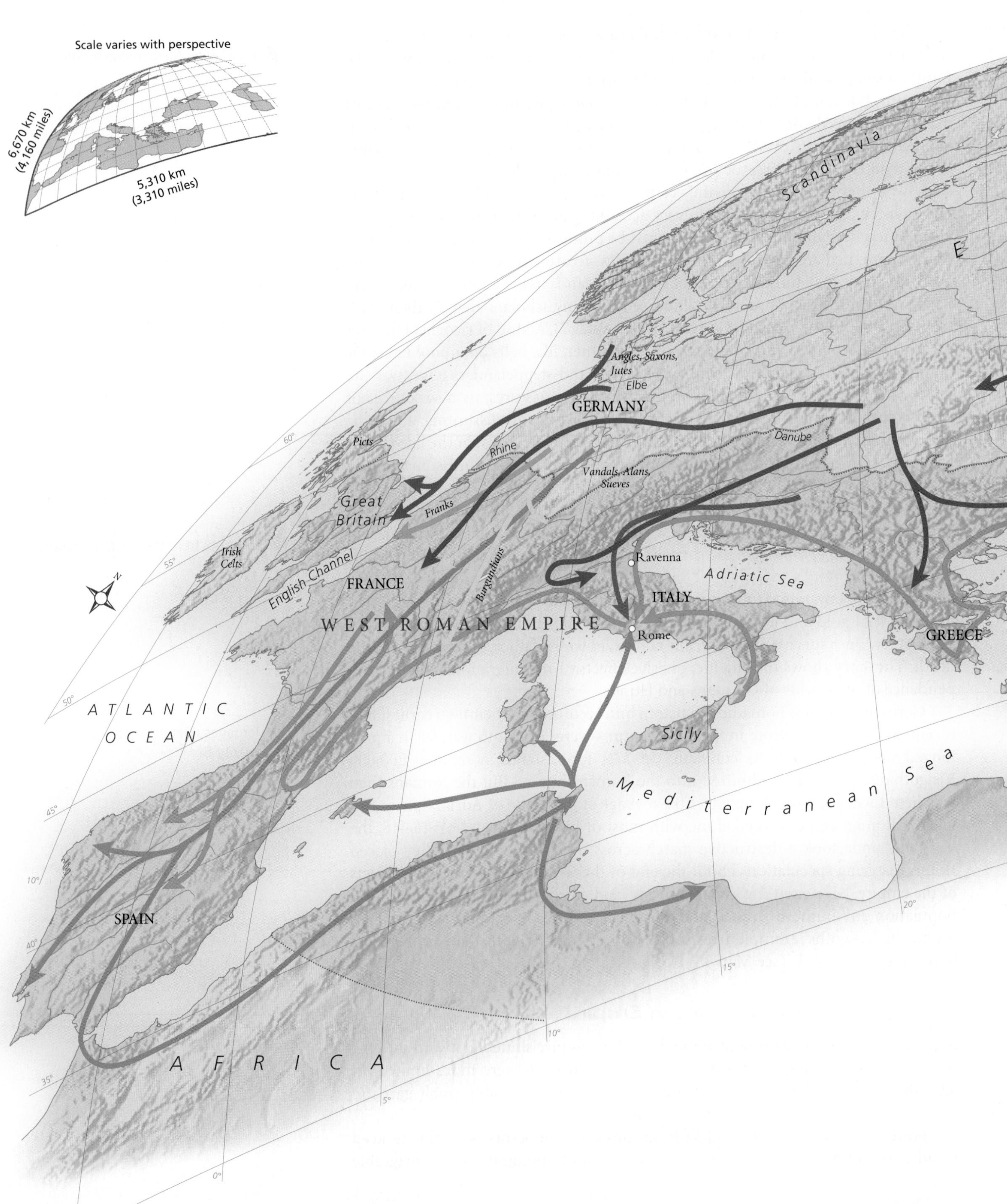

Scale varies with perspective
6,670 km
(4,160 miles)
5,310 km
(3,310 miles)
Scandinavia
E
Angles, Saxons, Jutes
Elbe
GERMANY
Danube
Picts
Rhine
Vandals, Alans, Sueves
Great Britain
Franks
Irish Celts
English Channel
Burgundians
FRANCE
Ravenna
Adriatic Sea
ITALY
WEST ROMAN EMPIRE
Rome
GREECE
ATLANTIC OCEAN
Sicily
Mediterranean Sea
SPAIN
AFRICA

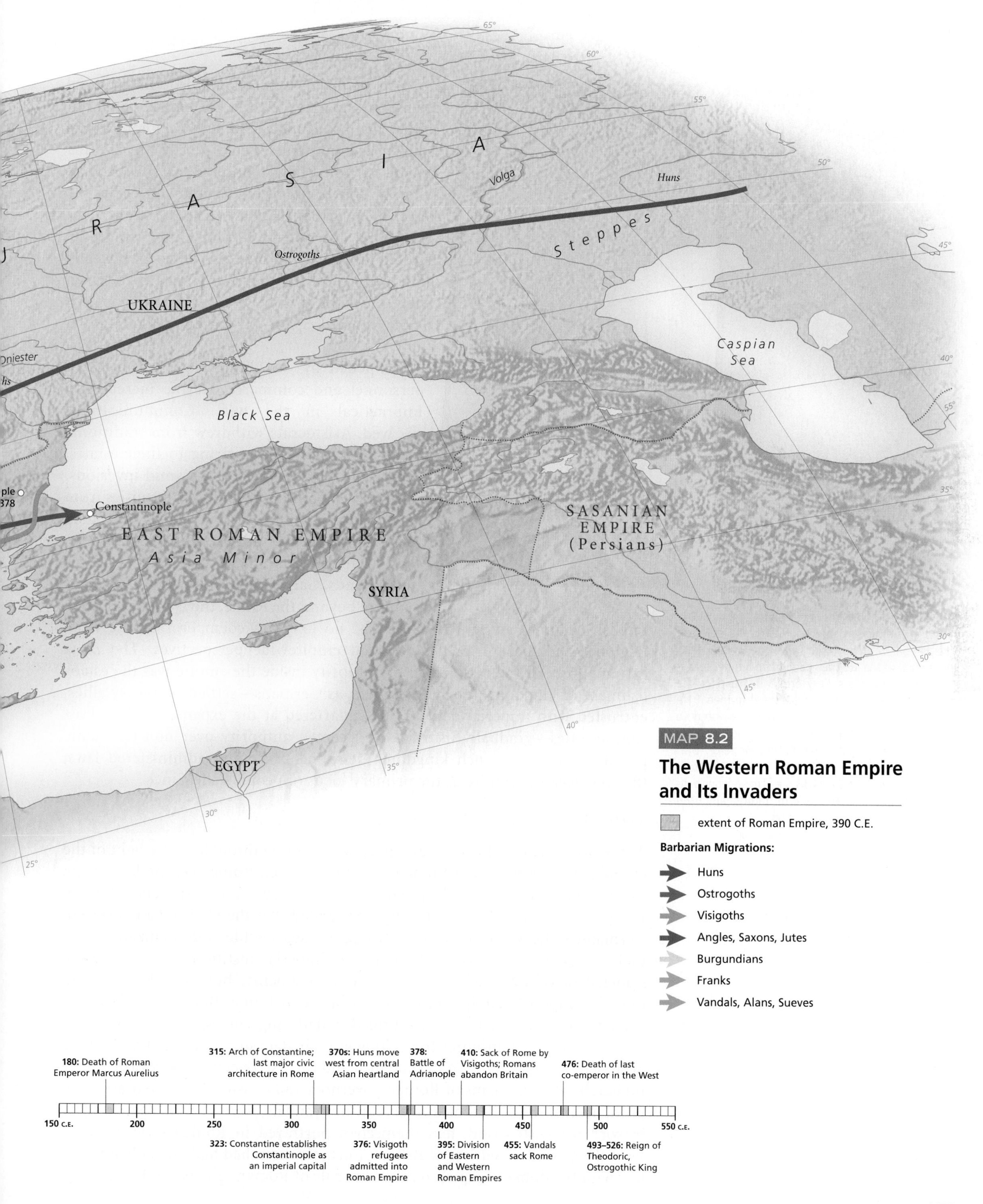

R
A
S
I
A
Volga
Huns
Steppes
Ostrogoths
UKRAINE
Dniester
Caspian Sea
Black Sea
Constantinople
378
EAST ROMAN EMPIRE
Asia Minor
SASANIAN EMPIRE (Persians)
SYRIA
EGYPT
65°
60°
55°
50°
45°
40°
35°
30°
25°
extent of Roman Empire, 390 C.E.
Barbarian Migrations:
Huns
Ostrogoths
Visigoths
Angles, Saxons, Jutes
Burgundians
Franks
Vandals, Alans, Sueves
180: Death of Roman Emperor Marcus Aurelius
315: Arch of Constantine; last major civic architecture in Rome
370s: Huns move west from central Asian heartland
378: Battle of Adrianople
410: Sack of Rome by Visigoths; Romans abandon Britain
476: Death of last co-emperor in the West
150 C.E.
200
250
300
350
400
450
500
550 C.E.
323: Constantine establishes Constantinople as an imperial capital
376: Visigoth refugees admitted into Roman Empire
395: Division of Eastern and Western Roman Empires
455: Vandals sack Rome
493–526: Reign of Theodoric, Ostrogothic King

MAP 8.2

The Western Roman Empire and Its Invaders

Stilicho. The late Roman Empire increasingly relied on immigrant mercenaries for its defense. The Vandal Stilicho (right) was one of the best, defending—as a Roman poet of the time said—"all within the sun's fiery orbit" in trust for the emperors of Rome. "All virtues meet in thee." He married an emperor's niece and maneuvered to make his son, Eucherius, also shown here, emperor. His daughter married an emperor. But, falsely accused of treachery, he loyally gave himself up for execution in 408 C.E. These ivory panels are examples of an art form traditionally used to commemorate Roman consuls.

proportions or to numbers needed for imperial defense. In the west, however, the empire could not control the incursions. Supplies and reinforcements from Constantinople could easily reach the provinces from Italy's Adriatic coast eastward, whereas the western Mediterranean lay beyond the terrible navigational bottlenecks between Italy, Sicily, and North Africa. The Rhine was easily crossed—especially in the cold winters of the early fifth century, when the river often froze. From there, invaders usually swung through northern France toward Spain, or turned south to reach Italy.

Impeded by war, long-range exchanges of personnel and commerce became increasingly impractical in the west. Communications decayed. Aristocrats withdrew from traditional civic responsibilities—retiring to their estates, struggling to keep them going amid invasions. Bishops replaced bureaucrats. In localities from which imperial authority vanished, holy men took on the jobs of judges. Almost everywhere, barbarian experts in warfare took military commands. Garrisons withdrew from outposts of empire beyond the Rhine, the Danube, and the English Channel. After 476, there was no longer a coemperor in the west. Regional and local priorities replaced empirewide perspectives. The most extreme form of the dissolution of authority inside the empire was the establishment of kingdoms led by foreigners, as Germans—settled as uneasy allies, entrusted with imperial defense, and quartered at the expense of their host communities—gradually usurped or accepted authority over non-Germanic populations. Where such kingdoms delivered peace and administered laws, they replaced the empire as the primary focus of people's allegiance.

The "Barbarian" West

At the time, writers of history and prophesy, peering through the twilight of the empire, could not believe Roman history was over. Rome was the last of the world monarchies the Bible foretold. Its end would mean the end of time. Everyone, including barbarian kings, pretended that the empire had survived. Germanic settlers were all, in varying degrees, susceptible to Romanization, and their kings usually showed deference to imperial institutions. A Visigothic leader, Athawulf, vowed "to extirpate the Roman name," but ended by marrying into the imperial family and collaborating with Rome. Burgundian kings in what is now eastern France continued a flattering correspondence with the emperors in Constantinople for as long as their state survived. The Franks, who occupied most of France in the late fifth and early sixth centuries, adorned their monarchs with emblems of Roman governors and consuls. No barbarians were proof against the appeal of Roman culture. Vandals, whose name has become a byword for destruction, had themselves portrayed in Roman-style mosaics. Even the Germanic settlers of Britain, most of whom had had virtually no contact with the Roman Empire, recalled the rule of Roman "giants" in their poetry.

Yet the limits of barbarian identification with Rome were of enormous importance. The notion of Roman citizenship gradually dissolved. Although the barbarians envied Roman civilization, most of them hankered after their own identities and—not surprisingly amid the dislocation of the times—clung to their roots. Many groups tried to differentiate themselves by upholding, at least for a time, unorthodox versions of Christianity. Some of their scholars and kings took almost as much interest in preserving their own traditional literature as in retaining or rescuing the works of classical and Christian writers. Law codes of barbarian kingdoms prescribed different rules for Germans and Romans.

The realm of the Ostrogothic king, Theodoric, was typically hybrid. He ruled Italy from 493 to 526. A church wall in his courtly center at Ravenna displays his palace, with throne room of gold, curtained like a sanctuary. His tomb is the burial mound of a Germanic king but is also in the style the Roman aristocracy of his era favored. Boethius, his chief minister, who was a Roman senator, not a Goth, worked hard to Romanize him, clinging to the old order, banking on the domestication of barbarian invaders. Imprisoned by Theodoric for his Roman partialities, he wrote *The Consolation of Philosophy*, fusing the Stoical value system of happiness with the Christian tradition of deference to God. Happiness and God, Boethius argued, were identical.

The Collapse of Empire in the West

162–180	Reign of Emperor Marcus Aurelius, high point of Roman Empire
Third and fourth centuries	Germanic migrants enter empire in increasing numbers
323	Founding of Constantinople
378	Battle of Adrianople, Roman emperor killed
Late fourth century	Huns break out of Central Asia
410	Visigoths sack Rome
476	End of empire in the west

Pliny the Elder, from the *Natural History*

STEPPELANDERS AND THEIR VICTIMS

Because Germanic peoples lined the zone between Rome's frontier and the Eurasian plains, steppeland peoples like the Huns made relatively few and brief forays into the Roman Empire. Empires centered in China, Persia, and India, by contrast, had to cope with the steppelanders directly (see Map 8.3). In some ways, invading herdsmen were easier to deal with than the Germans who were used to settled agriculture. Their techniques of warfare were less flexible, ill equipped for mountain terrain on the frontiers of Persia or India, or amid rice paddies in China. When successful as conquerors, the steppelanders were usually easier to wean from their cultural traditions than the Germans, assimilating to Chinese or, in some cases, to Indian ways within a few generations.

China

China's empire, moreover, was better adapted for survival than Rome's. Thanks to China's roughly round shape, centrally retained armies could get quickly to any point on its frontiers. No invaders threatened the long sea coast. Subject-peoples tended to embrace Chinese identity with surprising enthusiasm. Above all, size, productivity, and technical inventiveness made China self-sufficient, if necessary. No adverse balance of trade, such as Rome endured, drained wealth out of the empire. China's internal market was huge—more internal trade meant more wealth.

But, like Rome, China under the Han dynasty never solved the most basic problem of imperial government: how to secure the succession of emperors. Factionalism and rebelliousness bred in imperial households. To offset the danger, emperors relied ever more heavily on **eunuchs**, whom Roman emperors, too, regarded as perfect servants, and whose inability to father families of their own

"A Parthian shot" now means a cutting parting remark—so-called from the tactics Parthian mounted archers used in defending their homeland in what is now Iran and Iraq against the Romans. Retreating, or pretending to retreat, they turned in their saddles to shoot at their pursuers. Steppelander armies copied or developed this technique on their own. This 2,000-year-old Chinese design shows a Turkic warrior wielding a double-curve bow, constructed to be compact but with high tensile strength for use on horseback.

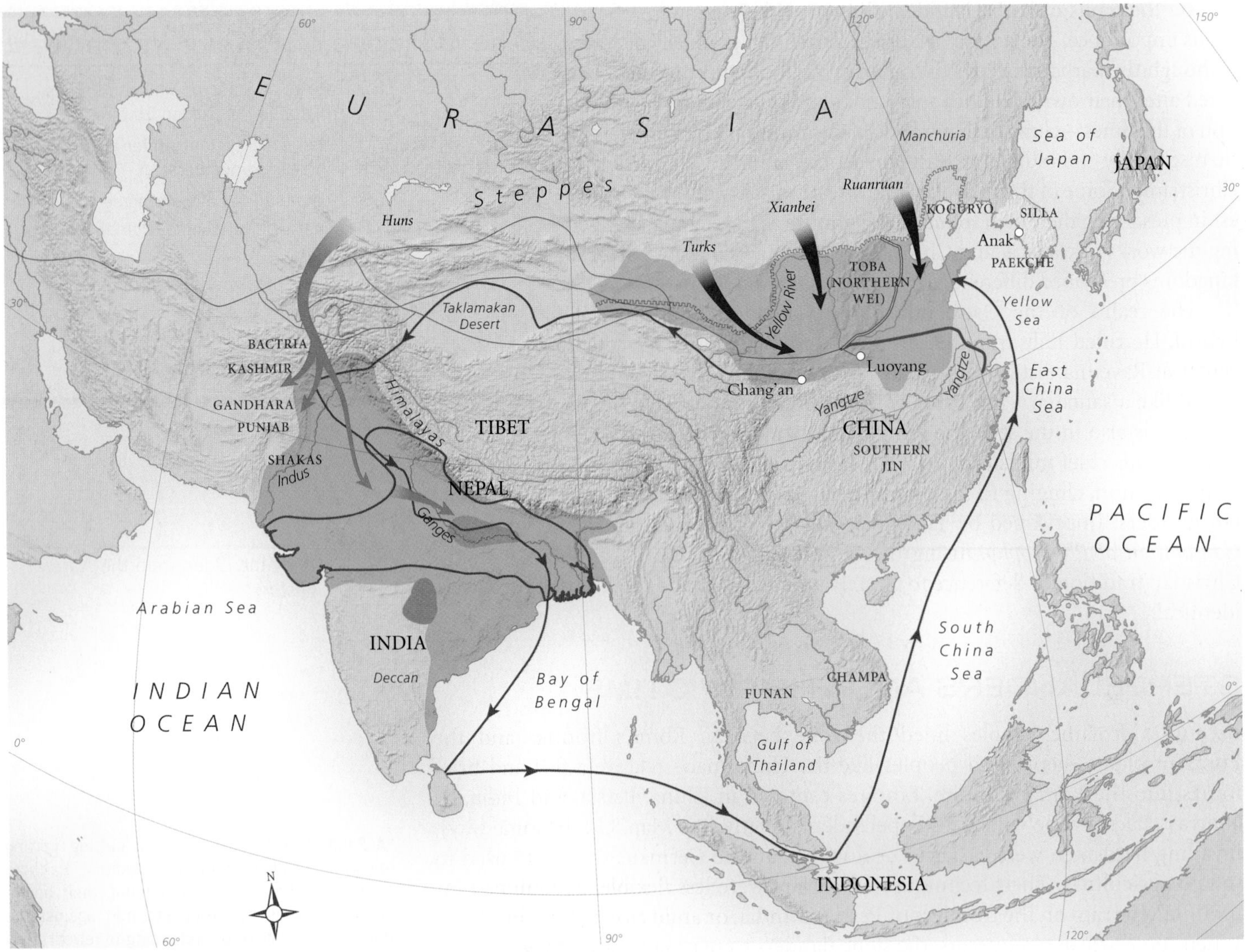

MAP 8.3

Steppelanders and Asian Kingdoms, ca. 300–700 C.E.

- farthest extent of Toba Wei, ca. 500 C.E.
- kingdom of Candra Gupta I
- farthest extent of Gupta dynasty, ca. 500 C.E.
- Vakataka dynasty
- Harsha's empire, ca. 650 C.E.
- Hun invasions
- Steppeland migrants into China
- Journey of Faxian, 405–411 C.E.
- Great Wall
- Grand Canal
- Silk Roads
- *Xianbei* people

Scale varies with perspective

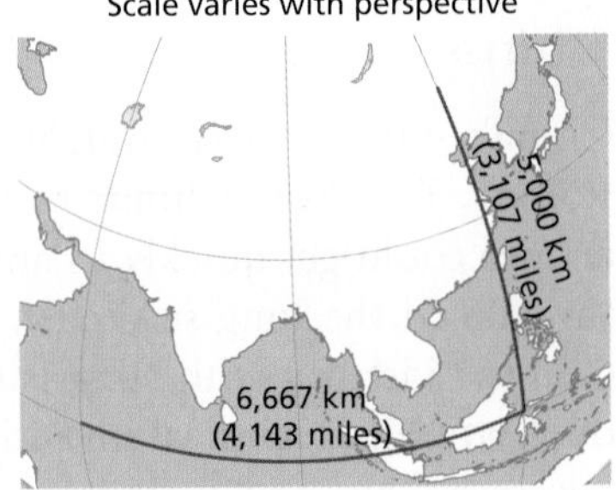

made them proof against dynastic ambitions. The long-term result was to create another faction and a new focus of resentment, as eunuchs usurped control over the succession. As in Rome, armies in China contended for the power to make and unmake emperors. Rivalry between armies and eunuchs precipitated civil war in 184, when Chang Chueh (chahng joo-ay), a wandering medic, whose plague rem-

MAKING CONNECTIONS

CHINA AND ROME COMPARED

	CHINA	ROME
Geography	Round shape ensures that centrally located armies can get quickly to any point on frontier. Numerous rivers and canals facilitate communication	Long land frontier and narrow sea lanes impede movement of troops and information
Culture	Subject peoples embrace Chinese identity; barbarian immigrants adopt Chinese customs and language	Germanic peoples beyond empire's borders covet Roman wealth. "North–South" prosperity gap leads to envy and hostility. Limited identification by barbarians with Rome.
Economy	Size, productivity, and technical inventiveness lead to self-sufficiency	Adverse balance of trade drains wealth out of the empire

edy made him a popular hero, proclaimed rebellion against eunuch rule. The army emerged ascendant from nearly 40 years of war that followed.

In 220, the last Han emperor was forced to abdicate in favor of a new, army-backed dynasty, known as Jin. But the former patterns of politics resumed. Civil war became chronic, made worse by emperors' efforts to divide their responsibilities along lines similar to those Rome adopted, giving members of the imperial family regions to run. Steppeland migrants and marauders played increasingly important roles in the wars. Contenders for disputed succession called in rival barbarian armies. In 304, the leader of one of these armies proclaimed himself emperor, and his son drove the Jin south, into the Yangtze valley. The old capital, Chang'an (chahng-ahn), filled with "weeds and thorns." Northern China became a kaleidoscope of kingdoms and self-styled empires, continually reshaken by warlords, adventurers, and Turkic and Mongol migrants. Toward the end of the fifth century, the ruler of the ascendant barbarians, the Xianbei (shee-on-bay), introduced Chinese rites, including the state cult of Confucius. But the state he founded fragmented in its turn. The old aristocracy resisted Chinese values, while the court practiced Chinese-style cycles of factionalism, family rifts, and civil wars.

India

Although the invasion routes into India from the steppes look formidable on the map, they were poorly guarded (see Map 8.3). In the fourth century, a ruler of Maghada who called himself Candra Gupta (CHAN-drah GOOP-tah), after a hero of the time of Alexander the Great, attempted to restore the unity of the Indian subcontinent. His dynasty, the Guptas, never established as wide a dominion as that of Asoka (see Chapter 7), but they did weaken the states of India's northwest frontier. The Huns who began to infiltrate India around 415 were, presumably, part of the fallout of the same catastrophes that spilled steppelanders into the Roman and Chinese Empires.

The morale of the population favored the invaders. Writers generally agreed that they were living in the *Kaliyuga*, the age of decline. A play written by Kalidasa—who probably lived in the fourth century—depicted alienated classes in a morally corrupt state, where officials practised torture and extortion on accused innocents. It was

The End of Dynasties in China and India

220	Last Han emperor forced to abdicate
304	Contenders for Chinese throne call in barbarian armies
415	Huns begin to infiltrate India
ca. 467	Demise of Gupta Empire

hard for the empire's poorest subjects to identify with a system that perpetuated their poverty by making social rank inherited. According to Faxian (faw-shee-ahn), a Chinese Buddhist pilgrim in India in 405–411, the "untouchables" of the lowest caste had to sound a clapper in the street to warn against their polluting presence.

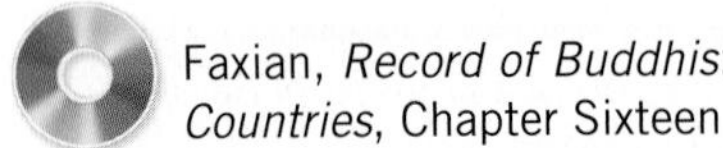
Faxian, *Record of Buddhist Countries*, Chapter Sixteen

The loose-knit Gupta political system, which covered most of India as far south as the Deccan, showed little resilience. The decline of the empire is conventionally dated from 467—less than a decade before the last emperor in Rome was forced to abdicate. Subsequent Gupta emperors are barely known, except by name, from contemporary sources. Yet within another 50 years or so, the Hunnic realm seems to have become one Indian state among many. Indian unity—such as it was—dissolved among a multitude of principalities in the north and a few relatively large, unstable kingdoms in the south.

NEW FRONTIERS IN ASIA

For the Chinese and Gupta Empires, the barbarian invasions inaugurated times of troubles, but it was a time of opportunity for developing states on their frontiers, where imperial power might otherwise have inhibited or repressed development. An early Gupta inscription mentions developing states around the frontiers: the Shaka dynasty in western India and the Vakatakas, whose daughters the Guptas took in marriage in the Deccan. The conditions favored similar effects in other parts of Asia.

Korean crown. Before Buddhism became rooted there in the sixth century C.E., Korean rulers were buried with fabulous treasures. This crown, with antler-like ornaments, is from one of the many royal burial mounds of the kingdom of Silla. It shows the influence of Chinese and Central Asian goldsmiths' work.

Korea

Refugees from China, for instance, fled from the nomad invaders in search of tamer barbarians, to whom to offer their services as technicians or sages. Dong Shou—to take a case in point—was a scholar who escaped from the Xianbei in 337, and took refuge in neighboring Koguryo (koh-goo-ryuh), an emerging state in what is now southeastern Manchuria and northern Korea. After a prosperous career, he was buried at Anak, amid wall paintings that document the history of Koguryo at the time. Buddhist and Daoist emblems mingle with scenes of the life of the kingdom: proudly displayed images of prosperity and strength, including irrigation works, rice production, people and horses eating, and a procession of well-armored soldiers. While China dissolved, Koguryo expanded. A memorial of King Kwanggaet'o, erected at the time of his death in 413, credits him with the conquest of 64 walled towns and 1,400 villages. Continuing prosperity—the result of the introduction of ox-drawn plows and irrigation for rice fields—can be measured in the results of the census the Chinese took when they eventually conquered Koguryo in 667–668. The country had 176 walled cities and 697,000 families. Unlike other communities whom the Chinese considered barbarians, however, Korean states had, by then, too much self-pride and too long a history of achievement to adopt Chinese identity.

Meanwhile, similar histories unfolded in the southern Korean kingdoms of Silla (shil-lah) and Paekche (pak-jay). Although the iron trade contributed to the enrichment of these states, they were agrarian kingdoms whose wealth was in manpower. They fought one another to gain population. Paekche paid a ransom of 1,000 households, for instance, when raiders from Koguryo occupied its capital. Silla resolutely followed Chinese models of state-building. In 520, King Pophung began to give positions of power and social prestige to Confucian scholars. The kingdom, however, also had a caste system of its own. Many positions were open only to those ranked as possessing "sacred bone"—the rank of the royal family—and "true bone," the birthright of the courtly elite. (This distinction disappeared after 653, when a true bone became king.) Silla unified the Korean peninsula in over 100 years of warfare from the mid–sixth century.

Funan

Meanwhile, the turbulence of central Eurasia, which periodically disrupted the Silk Roads, favored states along the maritime route across Eurasia, beside monsoonal seas. Chinese travelers' accounts give us glimpses into their world. Funan occupied a stretch of territory wrapped around the coast of the Gulf of Thailand. Chinese officials singled it out as a possible tributary or trading partner in the third century. Its culture was almost certainly borrowed from India. By Chinese reports, it was a repository of learning, rich enough to levy taxes in "gold, silver, pearls and perfumes." Its success depended on its role as a middleman in Chinese trade with Indonesia and the Bay of Bengal.

THE RISE OF ETHIOPIA

The most remarkable state favored by growing commerce across monsoonal seas was Ethiopia, a country at the limit of the Indian Ocean network. The right balance between accessibility and isolation was the key to Ethiopia's success. High altitude made the emergent state defensible and guaranteed it a temperate climate in tropical latitudes. Axum (AHK-soom), the capital, was around 7,200 feet up.

Outsiders saw Axum as a trading state, where all the exotic goods of Africa awaited: rhino horn, hippo hides, ivory and obsidian, tortoise shell, monkeys, slaves. Objects manufactured in China and Greece found their way to Axumite tombs. The frequent use of Greek in inscriptions, alongside the native language, indicates a cosmopolitan community. Ethiopian products could reach the outside world through the Mediterranean via Roman and later Byzantine Egypt and with the Indian Ocean via the Red Sea. The highlands could dominate the long Rift valley land route to the south, to lands rich in gold, aromatics, slaves, and ivory.

Stela of Axum. Until the rulers of Ethiopia adopted Christianity in the mid–fourth century, they invested huge amounts of capital and labor to create gigantic stelae—still the biggest structures made of single blocks of stone anywhere in the world. The largest examples—which reach well over 100 feet high—stood on ground long used for burials and probably marked important tombs. They have the skyscraper-like form of towering buildings. This art form climaxed in the early fourth century, just before Ethiopian priorities switched to church building, and the last stelae were left to topple or perhaps were never even hoisted into position.

But the corridor from the Ethiopian highlands to the sea is long and leads to dangerous waters. For the people of Axum, intent on their farming, trade was a sideline. They stamped ears of wheat on their coins. The highlands were fertile enough to produce two or three crops a year. Food mentioned in inscriptions includes wheat, beer, wine, honey, meat, butter, vegetable oils, and the world's first recorded coffee.

The material remains of the culture include finely worked ivory, metalwork, and huge, cubical tombs lined with brick arches. Three enormous stone pillars, each of a single slab of locally quarried granite, towered over the city. The largest was 160 feet tall and weighed nearly 500 tons—bigger than any other monolith ever made. Depictions of many-storied buildings or figures of hawks and crocodiles adorned the pillars. According to a Greek visitor's description, the central plaza of the city had a four-towered palace and thrones of pure marble, smothered with inscriptions, and statues of gold, silver, and bronze.

Inscriptions from early in the fourth century recorded what people at the time regarded as the key events of politics: numbers of captives; plunder in livestock; oaths of submission; doles of bread, meat, and wine granted to captives; their punitive relocation in distant parts of the empire; thank offerings for gods who bestowed victory—native gods at first, then, from the 340s, the Christian God. The ambitions of the kings seemed to tug across the strait to Arabia (see Chapter 5). Early in the sixth century, King Kaleb launched an expedition to conquer southern Arabia, much of which the Ethiopians occupied for most of the rest of the century.

The Rise of Ethiopia

340s	Spread of Christianity in Ethiopia
Early sixth century	King Kaleb begins conquest of southern Arabia
530s	Environmental crisis undermines control of south Arabia

THE CRISES OF THE SIXTH AND SEVENTH CENTURIES

Ethiopian control of south Arabia probably faltered because of an environmental crisis in the 530s. Plague played a part in the collapse of the irrigation states of southern Arabia and drove migrants northward, some seeking refuge in Roman-controlled Syria, others swelling the cities of Mecca and Medina. Twice during the Ethiopian occupation, the great dam at Marib broke. The losses of irrigation water were so traumatic that they became a major theme for poets' laments.

These disasters roughly coincided with other, more widespread catastrophes. In 535, the skies of the Northern Hemisphere darkened. A massive volcanic eruption in Indonesia split Java from Sumatra and spewed ash into the atmosphere. Thanks to the diminished sunlight, temperatures fell. The new conditions suited some disease-bearing microorganisms. A plague-bearing bacillus ravaged Constantinople. A disease that resembled smallpox devastated Japan. Even in central Mexico graves contain evidence of a severe decline in health toward the mid–sixth century. In the same period, the Eurasian steppes overspilled anew, impelling horseborne warbands into Europe: refugees, perhaps, from plague. Historians still debate how far these events are connected and whether a single volcanic explosion can account for them. Still, the sixth century marked a low point from which reformers could launch revivals of endangered traditions and rally weakened states.

In India, for instance, early in the seventh century, Harsha, king of Thanesar, tried to fill in the political fissures and reconstruct an empire (see Map 8.3). He devoted his reign of 41 years to the reunification of most of the Ganges basin. Rulers in Punjab, Kashmir, and Nepal paid him tribute. He made tireless tours of his realm, collecting tribute, giving alms, dispensing judgments. But even in the biography Harsha himself commissioned, practical compromises with kingly ideals are evident. The book describes the poor, gathering fragments of grain left after the king's camp has moved on. The king's elephants trample the hovels of peasants who can defend themselves only by hurling clods of earth. Harsha's dominion was an improvised conquest, and his achievement did not survive him. He had, however, more successful counterparts in China and Rome.

JUSTINIAN AND THE EASTERN ROMAN EMPIRE

Though the eastern Roman Empire remained a single state, it, too, was transformed. In the perceptions of its leaders, it remained "Roman," even after 476, when the emperors no longer had any power in Rome itself. Nowadays, however, historians prefer the term *Byzantine Empire* from "Byzantium" (bih-ZAN-tee-uhm), the former name of Constantinople. From the sixth or seventh centuries onward, use of Latin—always restricted in the eastern provinces to fairly high levels of administration—dwindled. Most invaders were defeated, turned away, bought off, or deflected by diplomacy, but migrants seeped through the frontiers.

Justinian (r. 527–565) was the last emperor to adopt a grand strategy of imperial reunification, giving equal importance to recovery in the west and defense and expansion in the east. He aimed to be a restorer but was more suited to be a revolutionary—"a born meddler and disturber," a chronicler who knew him called him. As the heir of a peasant-turned-soldier whom the army had elected to rule, he enjoyed thumbing his nose at established elites. He infuriated bishops with his

Theodora. According to court gossip, Theodora (ca. 500–548), wife of the Roman Emperor Justinian (r. 527–565), was a former prostitute of insatiable sexual appetite. But the propagandist who portrayed her in mosaic, in the church of San Vitale at Ravenna, depicted her as a sacred figure, towering over priests and nobles and equal in stature to her husband. She approaches the altar arrayed in jewels—a convention used in the art of the time to personify the Church—bearing a gift of communion wine to be converted miraculously into the blood of Christ.

attempts to reconcile conflicting theological opinions. His tax policies made the rich howl with anguish. He was a great lawgiver who had himself depicted as the biblical Moses and yet broke all the rules himself. Typically, Justinian outraged straitlaced courtiers by choosing a notoriously dissolute actress named Theodora to be his empress. He relied on her strength and intellect. She was the counselor of every policy and the troubleshooter of every crisis. In the famous mosaic portrait of her in the church of San Vitale at Ravenna in Italy, she wears jewels of triumph and a cloak embroidered with images of kingship and wisdom.

Prologue of the *Corpus Juris Civilis*

Justinian had the ill-disciplined energy of all insomniacs as he paced the palace corridors at night "like a ghost," as hostile courtiers said. He thought big. His projects included importing silk from China and allying with Arabs and Ethiopians against Persia. He built Constantinople's cathedral to be the biggest church in the world and, when it fell down, built it again. His reconquests from barbarian kingdoms reunited most of the Mediterranean world. Buildings he erected stretched from Morocco to the Persian frontier. He left his partially restored empire impoverished but enlarged. The robust performance of the eastern empire under Justinian seems impressive compared with the more radical transformation of the empire in the west. In particular, the eastern empire survived the new wave of barbarian invasions that was about to overwhelm Rome's old enemy, Persia.

THE NEW BARBARIANS

The barbarian invasions were not yet over. The Lombards invaded Italy in 568 from the north, just in time to gather the spoils of Justinian's wars, in which Romans and Goths had exhausted each other. On a plaque made to adorn the helmet of their King Agilulf, winged figures brandish drinking horns of a traditional

Germanic court along with placards marked "Victory" of a kind carried in Roman triumphs. Agilulf's sumptuous cross—all Christian barbarian kings had something similar—is a wand of victory: a sign to conquer by. In the late seventh century, the Bulgars, another invader-people from the steppes, crossed the Danube and set up as the elite of a state that stretched from the northern Balkans almost to Constantinople. In his shrine at Arkona, on the Baltic, the four-headed deity of the Slavs was perhaps already developing the thirst for wine for which he later became notorious. During the seventh and eighth centuries, in an expansion almost undocumented and never explained, Slavs spread over most of eastern Europe from the Baltic to southern Greece. Meanwhile, in North Africa, the Berbers, upland pastoralists, mobilized camel-borne war bands to terrorize the southern Mediterranean shore. In Scandinavia, in the eighth century, warriors who fought on sleds, with prows carved with the heads of monsters, took to the sea.

THE ARABS

These all proved formidable enemies of what was left of the Roman world. But most formidable of all the loiterers on the threshold were the Arabs or, more precisely, nomadic, Arabic-speaking peoples of central Arabia. They lived astride the trade routes of the peninsula, between Romanized communities and city-states in the north, and the maritime-oriented kingdoms of the seaboard. In the seventh century, they were transformed from a regional nuisance into a dynamic force. The preceding period in Arabia has a bad press—represented as chaotic and morally clueless, until the prophet Muhammad brought peace and justice in the 620s and early 630s. But the contrast between the periods before and after the Prophet's arrival may be too sharply drawn.

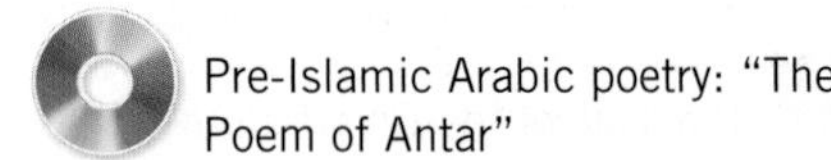

The few glimpses the sources give us suggest that Arab society was already demographically robust, militarily effective, and—at least in its poetry—artistically creative. "Poetry, horses, and numbers of people" were the standards by which different communities measured their rival merits. It is true, however, that Arabia was politically divided and riven by internal wars among tribes.

The tribes had also come to depend on war: raiding the Byzantine, Persian, and Arab cities that were scattered around the edges of the region and milking their trade. In one respect the transformation of these Arabs resembled that of other nomadic peoples mobilized for war by social change. As trade and banditry concentrated wealth, new styles of leadership dislocated the traditional, kinship-based structures of society and created an opportunity for a single, charismatic leader to unite an overwhelming force. In the Arabs' case, however, Muhammad's distinctive character marked him out from all other such leaders. His impact changed every aspect of life it touched. The Prophet taught a religion that was as rigorously monotheistic as Judaism, as humane and potentially as universal as Christianity, as traditional as paganism, and—for its time—more practical than any of them. More than a religion, Islam—literally "submission" to God—was also a way of life and a blueprint for society, complete with a demanding but unusually practical moral code, a set of rules of personal discipline, and the outline of a code of civil law.

Islam

A belief dear to Islamic scholars represents Muhammad as God's mouthpiece and therefore, in human terms, utterly original. His teachings crackle and snap with the noise of a break with the past. He picked up Jewish concepts: monotheism, providence, history ruled by God. The inspiration of Islam combined elements borrowed from Judaism and Christianity with a measure of respect for some of the traditional rites and teachings of pagan traditions in Arabia.

Muhammad claimed to have received his teaching from God, through the Archangel Gabriel, who revealed divine words into his ear. The resulting **Quran** (kuh-RAHN) was so persuasive that hundreds of millions of people believe him to this day. By the time of his death, Muhammad had equipped his followers with a dynamic social organization, a sense of unique access to God, and a conviction that war against nonbelievers was just and sanctified. Warriors were promised an afterlife in a paradise where sensual pleasures were like those of this world—lush gardens, young women. Muhammad's legacy gave Muslims (those who "submit" to God's message) administrative and ideological advantages against potential enemies. Yet the opportunity for the Arabs to become an imperial people arose as much, perhaps, from the weakness of the Byzantine and, especially, the Persian Empires as from the dynamics of their own society.

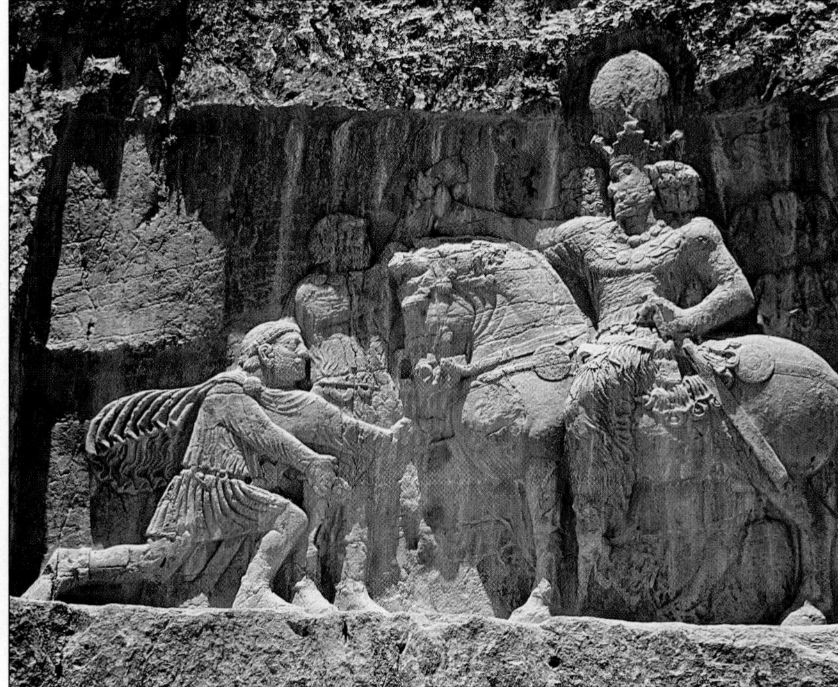

Sasanian victory. Huge rock carvings were traditional media of propaganda for Persian kings. None celebrates a more spectacular victory than that of Shapur I (r. 241–272) at the battle of Edessa in 260 C.E., when he took the Roman Emperor Valerian captive. The sculptor captured Valerian in another sense by showing him bending the knee in submission, while his cloak billows in the wind. The realism of the art enhances its symbolic significance, suggested by Shapur's huge crown, bulging physique, imperious gestures, and the stamp of his horse's hoof.

The Arabs Against Persia and Rome

Of the old Eurasian empires, Persia's was the most successful in fending off steppeland turbulence. The Sasanians, Persia's ruling dynasty from 226, however, concentrated their power in the most defensible part of the empire, in the highlands of Fars and in and beyond the Zagros Mountains. A commanding position in the world, along trade routes that linked the Mediterranean to the Indian Ocean and the Silk Roads, gave them the resources to maintain their traditional hostility to Rome—symbolized in a rock carving of 260, where the Roman emperor, Valerian, grovels at the feet of Persian captors. Yet mutual respect tempered Persia's wars against Rome. Each empire recognized the other as civilized, while condemning all other neighbors as barbarians. In the 380s, Rome and Persia responded to the barbarian menace by making peace.

The peace lasted throughout the steppeland turbulence of the fifth century, but at the beginning of the sixth century, as other dangers seemed to recede, war between Romans and Persians resumed with lethal intent—like a sparring partnership that turns deadly. By the time of the Arab conquests, the two giant empires had worn each other out. Mountains had protected Persia from northern steppeland invaders—but the Arab frontier to the southwest was flat. The Muslim Arabs absorbed the Persian Empire in its entirety in a series of campaigns from the late 630s to the early 650s. Syria, Palestine, Egypt, and North Africa—Rome's wealthiest and most populous provinces—fell to Arab or Arab-led armies by the early eighth century.

THE MUSLIM WORLD

The Muslims' conquests functioned like a single empire, gradually spreading Islam, the Arabic language, and a common Muslim identity and introducing more or less uniform principles of law and government. (See Map 8.4.) Flexibility brought

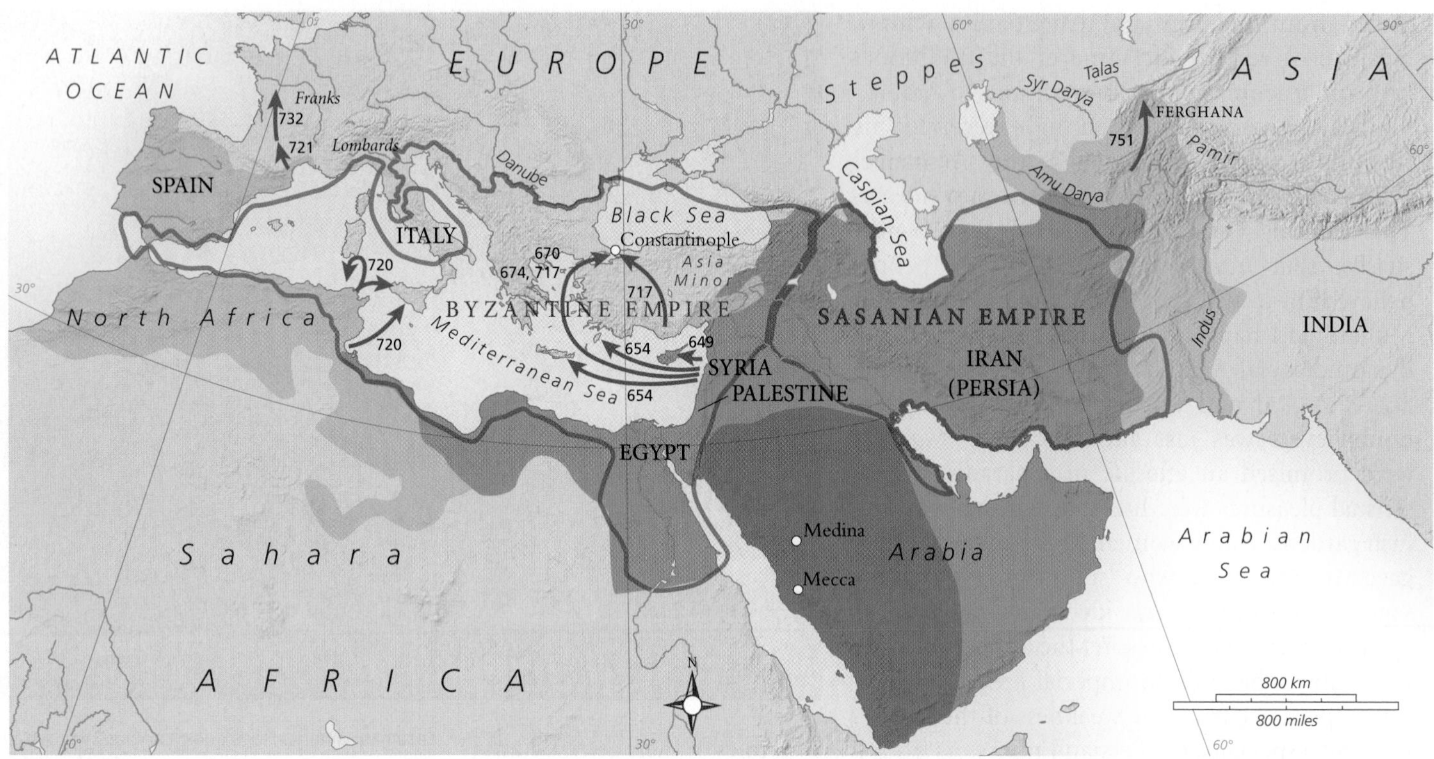

MAP 8.4

The Muslim World, ca. 756

- Muslim-ruled lands by 634
- Muslim-ruled lands by 656
- Muslim-ruled lands by 756
- Muslim invasions, with dates
- Byzantine Empire ca. 610
- Sasanian Empire ca. 610

MAP EXPLORATION
www.prenhall.com/armesto_maps

success. Although Arabs and descendants of the Prophet's own tribe enjoyed social privileges, every male Muslim could share a sense of belonging to an imperial elite. Although women were repressed, they at least had important rights: to initiate divorce (albeit under stricter conditions than those that applied to men); to own property and retain it after divorce; to conduct business in their own right. Christians and Jews, though vulnerable to periodic persecution and compelled to pay extra taxes, were normally allowed to worship in their own way. So, at first, were the Zoroastrians of Persia, who, though despised as pagans, were too numerous to alienate. Although other forms of paganism were forbidden, many traditional shrines and pilgrimages were resanctified as suitable for Muslim devotion.

But the Islamic world was too big to remain a single empire. And the precepts Muhammad left his followers at his death were not intended for a large state. For his followers, he was both prophet and ruler. Whereas Jesus invited individuals to respond to God's grace, Muhammad, more straightforwardly, called them to obey God's laws. Whereas Moses legislated for a chosen people, the Jews, and Jesus preached a "kingdom not of this world," Muhammad aimed at a code of behavior covering every department of life. He failed, however, to leave a code that was anything like comprehensive. So schools of jurisprudence set out to fill in the gaps by inferring Muhammad's principles from such laws as he did make in his lifetime, applying them more generally and, in some cases, adding insights from reason, common sense, or custom. The **Sharia**—literally, the desert-dweller's "way to water"—was both a religious discipline and a law code for the state. The principles of law were unchangeable: revealed to the masters of the eighth and ninth centuries, whose interpretations of Muhammad's tradition were regarded as divinely guided. The reconciliation of the various schools' opinions, however, has always allowed some opportunities for development.

Excerpts from the Quran

MAKING CONNECTIONS

EMPIRES IN TRANSFORMATION

EMPIRE/ REGION →	EXTERNAL ENEMIES →	INTERNAL WEAKNESSES →	STRENGTHS →	SURVIVAL STRATEGIES →	SUCCESSOR STATE
Teotihuacán/ Mesoamerica	Resentful tributary city-states	Overpopulation; reliance on imports; limited resources to export	Widely emulated culture; extensive trade network	Continual expansion to sustain population growth; installing friendly rulers in neighboring regions	—
Roman/ Mediterranean	Germanic border peoples; Huns from Eurasian steppes; Persians	Sprawling, vulnerable land frontiers; politicized military; Christian threat to paganism; internal disorder; mass migrations; uncertain succession of leadership; adverse balance of trade	Occasional strong leaders; strong military tradition; eastern provinces easily defended and supplied	Division of leadership responsibility under Marcus Aurelius (162); division of empire after Constantine (d. 337); transfer of capital to Constantinople	Byzantine Empire in east; Germanic and barbarian kingdoms in west
Han/China	Steppeland raiders and migrants	Uncertain succession of leadership; feuding imperial factions; warlords	Circular shape facilitates movement of troops and information; Chinese culture imitated by barbarians; strong internal economy	Use of eunuchs for administration; promotion of Chinese customs and language among barbarians	Jin dynasty followed by civil war and political fragmentation
Gupta/India	Huns	Cultural pessimism (age of Kaliyuga); poor defenses; inequality fostered by caste system; corrupt bureaucracy	Several strong leaders (Candra Gupta)	Differing layers of local authority linked together	Hunnic states and other principalities; kingdom of Harsha
Sasanian/ Persia	Romans; nomadic Arabs	Exhaustion after continuous wars with Rome	Commanding geographic position; strong defenses; effective diplomacy	Concentrating power in most defensible areas; diplomacy with Rome	Islamic caliphate

One consequence of the way Islam developed was that where Jesus had proclaimed a sharp distinction between the secular and the spiritual, Muslims acknowledged no difference. The supreme Islamic authority, the **caliph** (KAY-lihf)—literally, the "successor" of the Prophet—was, Christians said, both pope and emperor. The problem of identifying who was caliph split Islam between rival

Islamic Expansion

570–632	Life of Muhammad
630–early 650s	Muslim conquest of Iraq, Syria, Palestine, Egypt, Persian Empire
ca. 700	Muslim conquest of North Africa
ca. 715	Muslim conquest of Spain
751	Battle of Talas; Arabs defeat Chinese

claimants and incompatible methods of choosing a caliph within a generation of Muhammad's death. The major division that eventually developed was between **Shia** (SHEE-ah) (meaning "party"), which regarded the caliphate as the prerogative of Muhammad's nephew, Ali, and his heirs, and **Sunni** (SOO-nee) (meaning "tradition"), which maintained that the Muslim community could designate any member of Muhammad's tribe to hold the office. The rift has never healed, and although Sunnism became the dominant tradition in the Islamic world, schisms multiplied and, with them, internal conflicts, rival caliphates, and secessionist states.

For as long as unity prevailed, the limits of Arab expansion show both its explosive nature and its reliance on mobilizing the resources and manpower of conquered or converted communities to make further conquests. When Arab expansion began to run out of impetus, in the second decade of the eighth century, armies owing allegiance to the successors of Muhammad, under Arab generalship, were operating in northern Spain. More or less at the same time, they were destroying Zoroastrian temples in Central Asia and a Buddhist shrine in northern India. At its northeast extremity, the Arab effort even touched the outermost frontier of Chinese imperialism, west of the Pamir Mountains, where, in the first half of the eighth century, local rulers played off the Chinese against the Arabs to maximize their own power. In 751, Chinese and Arab armies met in direct conflict for the first and last time, on the banks of the Talas River. The result was victory for the Arabs and their Turkic allies. After this, China withdrew permanently behind the Pamirs, and most of Central Asia became securely part of the world of Islam.

RECOVERY AND ITS LIMITS IN CHINA

At home, China faced familiar problems, with only internal conflicts to weaken it and only the well-known threat from the steppelands to hold at bay. China's recovery from the crisis of the sixth century started later than Rome's under Justinian but lasted longer. A professional soldier, Yang Jian (yahng jhee-en; r. 581–605) proclaimed himself emperor, put to death 59 princes of the dynasty he had formerly served, and launched a strategy to re-create the empire (see Map 8.5). It proved remarkably easy. As a Chinese who had proved that he could master barbarians on the battlefield, Yang Jian was an attractive candidate for the throne.

Conscious of his lack of traditional credentials except success, the new emperor looked to Buddhism to legitimize his rule and to Legalism (see Chapter 6) for practical guidance in government. Law, he said, should "suit the times." In other words, there were no sacred, everlasting, or universal principles. He vowed "to replace mercy with justice"—and demonstrated his commitment by endorsing the condemnation of his own son to death for embezzlement. He affected contempt for Confucian bookworms and controlled the court by violent displays of temper. His workaholic and frugal ways—he rationed the palace women's cosmetics—were the characteristics that most impressed observers.

Yang Jian's brutal, strong-arm methods were appropriate to a time of reunification by force. In 605 his successor Yangdi reverted to tradition, announcing the revival of clemency, Confucian learning, and "ancient standards." The great triumph of his reign was the reintegration of the Yellow River and Yantgze valleys by an improved and extensive canal system, the Grand Canal. This was the kind of project that ought to have identified the dynasty with the "ancient

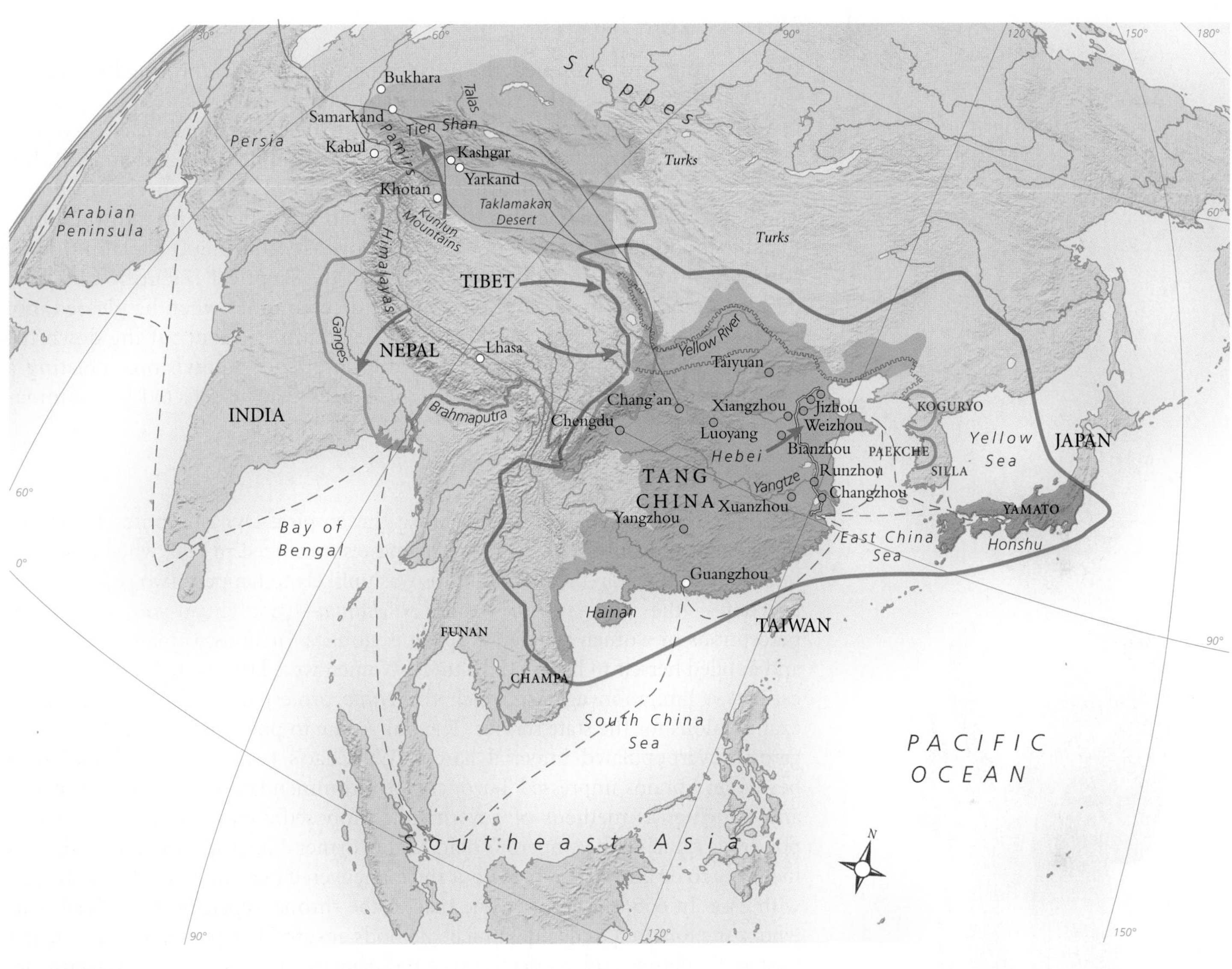

MAP 8.5

Tang China, Tibet, and Japan, ca. 750 C.E.

- Tang Empire at its greatest extent
- areas of temporary Tang control
- Yamato state
- approximate extent of Chinese cultural influence
- Tibetan Empire ca. 750 C.E.
- Tibetan invasions
- Silk Roads
- Great Wall
- Grand Canal
- maritime trade routes
- city with over 300,000 inhabitants
- other major city

Scale varies with perspective

8,392 km (5,214 miles)

3,333 km (2,071 miles)

virtue" Confucians prized. It was in the tradition of the great engineering emperors of legend, back to Yu the Great (see Chapter 3). The regime, however, forfeited this potential goodwill by the forced labor and taxes the canal-building demanded. An attempt to conquer Korea was ruinous and unsuccessful—the usual prelude to a political revolution.

Rise of the Tang

In 617, as the throne toppled, the most respected family in the kingdom, the Li, led a rebellion. Li Yuan (lee yoo-ehn), head of the family, was well connected in the army and secured neutrality or support from nomad princes. The reconquest of the country from rival rebels was not complete until about 624, but the exhaustion and disenchantment of the country favored a period of peace. The new dynasty, which called itself Tang (tahng), relied at first on this comfortable mood. The second emperor of the dynasty, Taizong (teye-tzong), took an interventionist, reformist line. He favored the skeptical, scientific tradition, derided omens and magic potions, and held ceremonies when he pleased, not when seers told him to. He rationalized the administration, cutting down the numbers of posts and administrative divisions and subdivisions, creating a new, handpicked bureaucracy for the provinces that he selected by examination, and simplified the law codes.

Empress Wu

Taizong's reforms did much to stabilize the empire. Dynastic crises no longer threatened to dissolve the state. A grueling test occurred in 690, when a woman seized the throne. On the face of it, this was unlikely to happen. Two collections of anecdotes—the *Nüjie* (noo-jay) and *Nüchunyu*—(noo-chuan-yoo) dominated perceptions of women as idle and promiscuous: a virtuous woman got up early and applied herself to household chores. Women were largely excluded from education—a limitation against which the *Nüjie* protested—and barred from the examinations for the state service. The only route to power was through the dangerous, overpopulated imperial harem. Wu Zhao's (woo jow) combination of beauty and brains impressed Taizong. Her recommendation of torture, brutality, and slaughter as methods of government supposedly amused him. She sought power by seducing the emperor's heir. As the former emperor's concubine, she was ineligible to be the next empress, but she maneuvered her way around that obstacle with ease. In 655, she married the heir to the throne, replacing his official wife, whom she tortured to death. Similar methods ensured her ascendancy during her husband's lifetime and as effective regent during the next two reigns. To secure her own elevation to the rank of emperor, she mustered every disaffected faction. The Buddhist clergy were her agents, proclaiming her as an incarnation of God, circulating propaganda on her behalf around the empire. Urged by 60,000 petitioners, she became emperor—literally, because she did not rule as an empress but used the masculine title emperor.

Tang Decline

These extraordinary and—to most people at the time—unnatural events hardly disturbed the continuity of the Tang and provoked no serious attempts at provincial succession of the kind that had been routine under previous dynasties. Resentment accumulated, however, under the less resolute rule of Wu's successors. In the

Lady-in-waiting. Though the politics of Tang China could be turbulent, they never disturbed the serenity of the arts of the imperial court. Women were frequently depicted. Many images of women as servants or, as in this example, as imperial ladies-in-waiting have survived because they were often placed as offerings in tombs. But portraits of female artisans—especially silk-makers—poets, students, equestrians, and matriarchs are also common, showing that, in an era that produced a female emperor, many occupations and roles were open to women.
Dagli Orti/Picture Desk, Inc./Kobal Collection

mid–eighth century, the defenses of the empire were beginning to look shaky as defeats by nomads became increasingly frequent. A frontier general, An Lushan (ahn loo-shawn), was selected as scapegoat. He had therefore little recourse except to rebel. The ensuing civil war confirmed the militarization of society, which, owing to the demands of frontier wars, was already happening anyway: 750,000 men were under arms in the 750s. Governors became virtually autonomous rulers of their provinces. About a quarter to a third of the empire was effectively outside imperial control. Peasants lived, it was said, "without a penny to their name."

Recovery and Its Limits in China

581	Yang Jian proclaims himself emperor (Sui dynasty)
605	Yangdi becomes emperor
609	Grand Canal completed
617	Yangdi deposed; rebellion ensues
618	Li Yuan begins reconquest of China from rival rebels; beginning of Tang dynasty
626	Beginning of reign of Taizong, second Tang emperor
690	Wu Zhao (Empress Wu) seizes throne
755–763	Rebellion of An Lushan
822	Province of Hebei effectively independent

To "bring the provinces under the rule of law" was now the watchword. "Only then can proper order be restored to the realm." Tax reforms in 782 decreed a single, uniform system throughout the empire. In practice, local authorities were left to fulfill quotas. Emperors took the initiative against the autonomous provinces and even began to restore control of provincial armed forces to the central government. But they failed to control the most wayward province, Hebei (huh-bay), which was effectively independent by 822. Meanwhile the provinces that remained supposedly subject to direct imperial control gained power at the expense of a central government that the efforts at recovery had impoverished. Governors enjoyed long tenures, levied unauthorized taxes, appointed local nominees to administrative positions, and acquired ever-larger revenues and retinues. Central government recovered some taxpayers. There were 2.5 million registered households in 807, 5 million in 839. This was still little more than half the figure attained before An Lushan's revolt. Imperial power became confined to the Yangtze valley.

Dezong, on the art of government

IN THE SHADOW OF TANG: TIBET AND JAPAN

In the shadow of Tang China, some promising states emerged. Tibet and Japan provide contrasting examples (see Map 8.5).

Tibet

At the time of the presumed beginnings of the first Tibetan state in the sixth century, the Chinese spoke of Tibetans in the conventional language used for barbarians, as pastoralists who "sleep in unclean places and never wash or comb their hair." In the river valleys of Tibet, however, sedentary agriculture was possible. An agricultural transformation in the fifth century brought barley to these areas as a staple crop. Once a cereal food was available in large amounts, the advantages of a cold climate for storage helped to create food surpluses. A land from which small numbers of nomads eked a precarious living now became a breeding ground of armies that could march on far campaigns with "ten thousand" sheep and horses in their supply trains.

Chinese descriptions of Tibetans

Before the seventh century, divine monarchs ruled Tibet, "descended," according to early poems, "from mid-sky, seven stories high," and aspiring to rule "all under heaven." Like other divine kings, they were liable to be sacrificed when their usefulness expired. At an unknown date in the sixth century, kings who ruled until they died a natural death replaced this system. Long reigns, with stability and continuity, were now possible. The first king known from more than fragmentary mentions was Songtsen Gampo. His reign, from about 627 to 650, marked an unprecedented leap in Tibetan power. China bought him off with a Chinese bride in 640. Preserved among a cache of documents in a

The Rise and Decline of Tibet

Fifth century	Barley introduced as a staple crop
627–650	Reign of Songtsen Gampo
Early ninth century	Beginning of Tibetan decline

The Potala Palace, towering above the valley of Lhasa, stands on the supposed site of the palace of the kings of Tibet in the seventh and eighth centuries. The present construction, however, began to rise in the mid–seventeenth century. The building is designed to suggest mystical power—cloud-shrouded, hard of ascent, overwhelming.

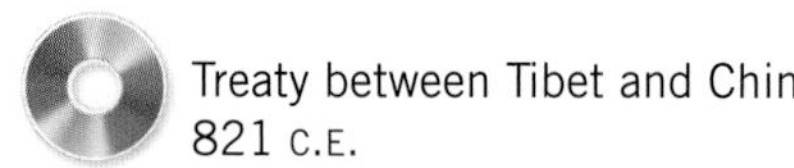

Treaty between Tibet and China, 821 C.E.

cave on the Silk Road is the oath of allegiance he exacted: "Never will we disobey any command the king may give." In practice, however, in most of the communities he conquered, he simply levied tribute, rather than practicing direct rule or close supervision.

Tibetan aggression continued for most of the next 250 years. Tibetan armies conquered Nepal and invaded Central Asia. A pillar at Lhasa, the Tibetan capital, erected before 750, records campaigns deep inside China. In 821 a Chinese ambassador described the Tibetan war camp, where shamans in tiger skins banged drums before a tent "hung with gold ornaments in the form of dragons, tigers and leopards." Inside, in a turban "the color of morning clouds," the king watched as chiefs signed the treaty with China in blood.

The kings' tastes were increasingly cosmopolitan. Ten of them, including Songtsen Gampo, lie under small mounds at Phyongrgyas, where "dead companions" attended them—now no longer sacrificed but appointed to guard and tend the graves without direct contact with the outside world. Pillars in Indian, Central Asian, and Chinese styles and a guardian lion modeled on a Persian original attest to the role of Tibet as a cultural crossroads. Their metal smiths' ingenuity was famous. Mechanical toys of gold dispatched as gifts to the Chinese court included a horse with moving limbs and a tiger with roaring jaws. Tibetan chain mail had an almost magical reputation for deflecting missiles. Yet even this could not protect the Tibetans from the effects of the instability of the era of Tang decline, which must have disrupted trade, while the power of the steppelanders limited Tibetan opportunities to raid or expand. In the early ninth century, Tibet suffered defeats on all fronts. Rebellions ensued. Tibet signed its last treaty as an equal with China in 823. Its last known king was assassinated in 842.

Japan

Better prospects of enduring experiments in statecraft existed on the remoter edges of Chinese cultural influence, in Japan, where the steppeland menace could not reach. Chinese culture began to arrive in Japan from Korea when a Buddhist monk became tutor at a Japanese court in about 400. The Korean kingdom of Paekche sent scholars and Buddhist scriptures. The leading state in Japan, Yamato, was a maritime kingdom, attracted by Korean and Chinese civilization, and at least as interested in expanding onto the mainland of Asia as in growing within the Japanese islands. Around 475, the king of Yamato applied to China for the rank of general and minister. He claimed his ancestors had conquered "55 kingdoms of hairy men to the east and 65 barbarian kingdoms to the west." Crossing the sea to the north, he added, they had subjugated 95 kingdoms. "The way to govern is to maintain harmony and peace, thereby establishing order." The ruler, one of the Korean advisers suggested, should "try to make farmers prosperous. . . . After he has followed this policy for three years, food and soldiers will become plentiful." From the mid–sixth century, Japan was following this sort of program, organizing royal estates, taking censuses.

Early in the seventh century, direct contact with China opened. The first Japanese embassy to China presented greetings "from the Son of Heaven in the land where the sun rises to the Son of Heaven in the land where the sun sets." The Chinese dismissed this as impertinence. Their accounts make the queen who ruled Japan at the time say, "As barbarians living in an isolated place beyond the sea, we do not know propriety and justice." It is not clear that the Japanese really saw themselves like that. They staked a claim to equality with China—and imperial rank—that subsequent Japanese regimes never abandoned.

In the 640s, the dynasty narrowly beat off a bid for the throne from a Chinese immigrant family. Reform of the administration then began in earnest. The drive to centralize by breaking up and replacing traditional power structures is reflected in a decree of 645 that blamed clan chieftains for dividing up the land, engaging in conflict, unjustly exploiting labor, and impoverishing peasants "who lack enough land to insert a needle." Landlords were forbidden "to increase, by one iota, the miseries of the weak." Indirectly, China's invasion of Korea in the 660s boosted imperial rule in Japan. Korean refugees were appointed to court rank. After victory in a civil war of 672, the ruling dynasty of Japan was unchallenged. Japan solved the problem that bedeviled the politics of other empires—devising a secure way to ensure the succession—by two means. First, women's aptitude to rule was accepted. This increased the dynasty's stock of suitable candidates for the throne. Indeed, until the 770s, when a disastrous empress inspired lasting revulsion against women rulers, most rulers were women. Second, from 749, it became normal for rulers to abdicate and watch over the transmission of power to their heirs. The system worked well until the mid–ninth century, when a single courtly family, the Fujiwara, established an effective monopoly over supply of the chief wives for successive emperors. Thereafter, in the Japanese system of government, the emperor presided over the realm, but a dynasty of court favorites or chief ministers usually did the ruler's job. The last big political development—the

MAKING CONNECTIONS

DEVELOPING FRONTIER STATES

STATE/REGION/PERIOD →	IMPERIAL NEIGHBOR →	RESOURCES/ORGANIZATION →	ACHIEVEMENTS
Koguryo, Silla, Paekche/ Korea ca. 300–500	China	Chinese religious influence—Buddhism and Daoism; Chinese migrants and technical knowledge	Complex irrigation system for rice cultivation; hundreds of walled towns; strong military
Funan/Indochina ca. 100–400	India, China	Indian cultural influences; commercial traders strategically located between India and China	Sophisticated culture; wealthy mercantile class; expansion around Gulf of Thailand
Ethiopia/Africa ca. 300–500	Rome, Byzantine Egypt	Accessible to Indian Ocean trade routes, isolated enough to be defensible; temperate climate; trade center connecting Africa to India and Arabia	Productive agriculture system—up to three crops a year; developed industry (metalwork, ivory) and large-scale urbanization
Tibet/Central Asia ca. 500–800	China, India	Development of barley as primary cereal crop for vast high-altitude plateau; food surpluses and strong military	Long-term alliance/tributary, relationship with China; stable leadership; conquest of neighboring kingdoms
Japan/East Asia ca. 400–600	China, Korea	Chinese/Korean cultural influences; strategic position for maritime trade; isolated and defensible; organization of royal estates; censuses	Long-term tributary relationship with China; gradually centralized power structure to maximize productivity; stable power structure with some women emperors

CHRONOLOGY

All dates are C.E.

220	End of Han dynasty in China
323	Founding of Constantinople
340	Spread of Christianity in Ethiopia
Third and fourth centuries	Germanic invasions of Roman Empire; Huns break out of Central Asia
ca. 375	Teotihuacán (Mesoamerica) at peak of its influence and power
Fifth century	Introduction of barley as a staple crop in Tibet
400	Beginning of Chinese influence in Japan
410	Visigoths sack Rome
415	Huns begin to infiltrate India
467	Death of last-known Gupta emperor (India)
476	End of western Roman Empire
493–526	Reign of Theodoric, Ostrogothic king
527–565	Reign of Justinian, Byzantine emperor
ca. 535	Massive volcanic eruption in Indonesia
570–632	Life of Muhammad
Seventh century	Beginning of Slav expansion in eastern Europe
609	Grand Canal completed in China
627–650	Reign of Songtsen Gampo in Tibet
630–720	Rapid Arab expansion
667–668	Chinese conquest of Koguryo (Korea)
690	Beginning of reign of Empress Wu (China)
751	Arabs defeat Chinese at battle of Talas

search for a means to harness Buddhism for state service while preserving Japan's native religion—belongs in the next chapter.

IN PERSPECTIVE: The Triumph of Barbarism?

Had Siyaj K'ak been able to continue his journey from Teotihuacán and cross the ocean to Eurasia he might have been gratified by the contrast between the stability and growth of the empire he represented and the perils that beset the empires of the Old World. In the year of his arrival, the Visigoths challenged Roman might at Adrianople. The crises that accompanied the traumas of the Eurasian steppelands and the migrations of Germanic and steppelander peoples into neighboring empires were already beginning. One measure of the instability that ensued is particularly striking. In much of Europe and India, the fifth and sixth centuries were so chaotic that record keeping collapsed, and we can no longer reconstruct a complete outline even of the most basic facts of political history—the names and chronology of kings and dynasties. By contrast, in the same period, for the Maya world Siyaj K'ak visited, we know far more about the rulers of many city-states, whose records are inscribed in stone in meticulous detail.

Yet, despite the waves of migrants and invaders that washed over Old World empires in the half millennium or so from about 200 onward and the crises they provoked, the most remarkable feature of the period is perhaps the durability of old orders. Cultural conflicts usually follow battlefield victories. And even where the so-called barbarians defeated the empires, they tended to get conquered in their turn by the cultures of their victims. The German invaders of the Roman world were partly Romanized, while the eastern Roman empire survived, centered on Constantinople. Steppeland conquerors played havoc with the political unity of India—but the cultural transformations of India happened from within. "Barbarians" disrupted China politically but did not disturb the continuity of Chinese civilization. On the contrary, when barbarians settled within China, they adjusted to Chinese ways. Indeed, Chinese civilization overspilled China into Korea, Japan, southeast Asia, and Tibet. The instability of the steppes damaged the land-bound trade of Eurasia, but the commerce of the Indian Ocean continued to grow, and the development of Ethiopia was among the consequences.

Still, despite continuities that survived the barbarians, the world was transformed. Rather than the world of empires that had dominated the densely populated belt of the axial age, it might be proper to speak of a world of civilizations. Western civilization was a hybrid—partly Germanic, partly Christian, partly Roman in heritage. The Islamic world was far more innovative, but it had, in some respects, a similar profile: with a biblical heritage, reinterpreted by Muhammad, and the learned legacies of Rome, Greece, and Persia, under an Arab elite from outside the empires, established by conquest but susceptible to the cultural influence of its victims. In both Islam and Christendom, notions of universal empire survived: the caliphate, Byzantium. But neither could maintain unity in practice, and the respective regions became arenas of states contending for the imperial legacy or ignoring it. In India, political fragmentation under the impact of barbarian invasion was more thoroughgoing, in China less so. In both, however, the invaders and immigrants were like chameleons, taking on the cultural hues of their new environments. In both, moreover, the traditional culture spread into new areas and new states, such as those of south India, and China's neighbors. So nowhere, by the eighth century, except in Ethiopia, was there any longer a civilization that was confined to a single state.

Even at the end of a chapter crowded with politics, we still have not reached the deepest transformative influences on the period. One of the traditional limitations of history textbooks is that politics, which generates most of the sources, tends to dominate the foreground. But politics is full of short-term changes, while ideas and environmental influences generate the sea changes. The next two chapters explore the religious transformations that made this world of civilizations distinct, in particular, from the empires that preceded them, and the discovery and development of resources that not only renewed the Old World, but also opened up new frontiers in other parts of the globe.

PROBLEMS AND PARALLELS

1. How were imperial traditions inherited from the axial age extinguished or fragmented by the year 500?
2. How does the history of Teotihuacán echo Eurasian developments in this period?
3. What were the differences between the ways that China and Rome dealt with steppeland migrants and invaders? Why was China more successful?
4. How did the Byzantine Empire and the barbarian kingdoms in Western Europe continue the traditions of Rome?
5. To what extent was Ethiopia able to achieve a balance between accessibility and isolation?
6. How did states develop on the edges of empires during this period?
7. Why were the Arabs able to conquer a vast empire in so short a time?
8. How was the world that recovered from the crises of the third through seventh centuries a world of civilizations?

DOCUMENTS IN GLOBAL HISTORY

- Tikal
- Marcus Aurelius, from *The Meditations*
- Ammianus Marcellinus on the Huns
- Excerpts from the *Hildebrandslied*
- Jordanes, *Deeds of the Goths*, Book Twenty-Six
- Pliny the Elder, from the *Natural History*
- Faxian, *Record of Buddhist Countries*, Chapter Sixteen
- Prologue of the *Corpus Juris Civilis*
- Pre-Islamic Arabic poetry: "The Poem of Antar"
- Excerpts from the Quran
- Dezong, on the art of government
- Chinese descriptions of Tibetans
- Treaty between Tibet and China, 821 C.E

Please see the Primary Source DVD for additional sources related to this chapter.

READ ON

Helpful information on relations between Teotihuacán and the Maya is in D. Drew, *The Lost Chronicles of the Maya Kings* (1999); R. Hassig, *War and Society in Ancient Mesoamerica* (1992); and S. Martin and N. Grube, *Chronicle of the Maya Kings and Queens* (2000), which is also a lavish compendium of facts and images. G. Braswell, *The Maya and Teotihuacán* (2003) is an important revisionist study that challenges the account of Siyaj K'ak above.

On the transformation of the Roman world, Peter Brown, *The World of Late Antiquity* (1989) is the ideal introduction—sprightly and subtle. A. H. M. Jones, *The Later Roman Empire* (1964) is a classic study of undiminished interest. J. Herrin, *The Formation of Christendom* (1987) is assured, fluent, and in touch with the sources. A. Cameron et al., eds., *The Cambridge Ancient History*, xiv (2000) is forbiddingly comprehensive and magisterial. R. Collins, *Early Medieval Europe* (1991) is a vigorous, thoughtful textbook. The classic works by F. Lot, *The End of the Ancient World and the Beginning of the Middle Ages* (2000), and by H. Pirenne, cited below, can still be recommended in combination with more recent scholarship.

There are many editions of the *Meditations of Marcus Aurelius*. On Constantine, R. Macmullen, *Constantine* (1987) is standard. Sources on his conversion are collected in M. Edwards, trans., *Constantine and Christendom* (2003). D. Bowder, *The Age of Constantine and Julian* (1978) is valuable in setting the context. M. Grant, *The Emperor Constantine* (1993) is lively and readable. R. Macmullen, *Christianity and Paganism in the Fourth to Eighth Centuries* (1997) is a valuable introduction. A. Momigliano, *The Conflict of Paganism and Christianity in the Fourth Century* (1964) is a collection of classic studies. R. Lane Fox, *Pagans and Christians* (1987), and K. Hopkins, *A World Full of Gods* (1999) are also helpful. On the transformation of the city of Rome, B. R. Ward-Perkins, *From Classical Antiquity to the Middle Ages* (1985) sets the context of urban change in Italy, while P. Llewellyn, *Rome in the Dark Ages* (1993) is a graphic account of the reemergence of Rome as the pope's capital.

W. Goffart, *Barbarians and Romans* (1980) is an introductory overview. E. A. Thompson, *A History of Attila and the Huns* (1972) is a classic study, still vital. There are many editions of the *Hildebrandslied*, but I know of no substantial critical studies in English except F. Norman, *Three Essays on the Hildebrandslied* (1973). The most useful study of the Christianity of Germanic invaders of the Roman Empire is E. A. Thompson, *The Visigoths in the Time of Ulfila* (1966). J. M. Wallace-Hadrill, *The Barbarian West* (1952) is the best possible introduction to the Germanic kingdoms; his *The Long-Haired Kings* (1962) is an absorbing collection of essays on the same subject, which should be read in conjunction with I. N. Wood, *The Merovingian Kingdoms* (1994). *The Consolation of Philosophy* is widely available in many editions. For Boethius's life and thought, J. Marenbon, *Boethius* (2003) is excellent, and H. Chadwick, *Boethius* (1981) is both authoritative and concise. S. Williams and G. Friell, *The Rome That Did Not Fall* (1999) is a helpful essay on the survival of the empire in the east. See now the revisionist, archaeologically informed survey of B. R. Ward-Perkins, *The Fall of Rome and the End of Civilization* (2005).

The steppes are covered in R. Grousset, *The Empire of the Steppes* (1970). Volume iii of *The Cambridge History of China* (1978) covers this period admirably. S. A. M. Adshead, *Tang China* (2004) provides an introduction to that dynasty. C. P. Fitzgerald, *The Empress Wu* (1955) is a captivating classic biography. R. K. Dwivdki and D. L. Vaish, *A History of the Guptas* (1985), and S. Goyal, *History and Historiography of the Age of Harsha* (1992) provide a political and cultural outline of India. W. E. Henthorn, *A History of Korea* (1971) is particularly good on this period.

On Axum, see the works of Munro-Hay and Phillipson mentioned in Chapter 9.

On Justinian, *The Secret History of Procopius* (1927) is an irresistibly engaging, albeit cruelly prejudiced, source. Balanced modern studies include J. A. S. Evans, *The Age of Justinian* (1996), and R. Browning, *Justinian and Theodora* (1971). G. Greatrex, *Rome and Persia at War* (1998) admirably covers the Persian wars of this period.

For an understanding of Byzantium in this period, A. Cameron, *Changing Cultures in Early Byzantium* (1996) is an authoritative, clear, and insightful collection. M. Grant, *From Rome to Byzantium* (1998) is a readable narrative. M. Whittow, *The Making of Orthodox Byzantium* (1996) is invaluable on the development of a distinctive religious culture. A. Cameron and J. Herrin, *Constantinople in the Early Eighth Century* (1984) is helpful. M. Angold, *Byzantium* (2001) is a good overview. W. E. Kaegi, *Byzantine Military Unrest* (1981) takes an interesting approach. On eunuchs, see K. Ringrose, *The Perfect Servant: Eunuchs and the Social Construction of Gender in Byzantium* (2003). On the Bulgars, O. Minaeva, *From Paganism to Christianity* (1996) wields fascinating artistic evidence. On Lombard Italy and its context, C. Wickham, *The Long Eighth Century* (2000) and *Early Medieval Italy* (1990) are excellent.

A. Hourani, *History of the Arab People* (2003) is probably the best overall survey of Arab history. M. A. Cook, *Muhammad* (1983) is a brief and brilliant introduction. Some of the same author's important essays are collected in *Studies in the Origins of Early Islamic Culture and Tradition* (2004). M. Cook and P. Crone, *Hagarism: The Making of the Islamic World* (1977) is a groundbreaking study. M. Hodgson, *The Venture of Islam*, 3 vols. (1974) is a marvelous classic. G. R. Hawting, *The First Dynasty of Islam* (2000) is an efficient narrative of the early caliphate. On the impact of the Arab conquests, all students should read—critically, of course—the classic—by H. Pirenne, *Mohammed and Charlemagne* (1939).

CHAPTER 9

The Rise of World Religions: Christianity, Islam, and Buddhism

Priests, officials, and bystanders (shown prostrating themselves, on the right) greet the pilgrim Xuanzang on his return to China from India, where he had traveled to find Buddhist scriptures. Pack horses bear the 75 sacred texts he had acquired to a temple on the left. Monks at the rear carry holy relics.

IN THIS CHAPTER

COMMERCE AND CONFLICT: CARRIERS OF CREEDS
In the Islamic World
In Christendom
In the Buddhist World
Trade
Manichaeanism and the Uighurs
Christianity on the Silk Roads
Islam on Trade Routes

MONARCHS AND MISSIONARIES
Constantine
Ezana
Trdat
Diplomatic Conversions
Buddhist Politics
Korea
Japan
Tibet
India
The Margins of Christendom
Vladimir and the Rus
Islam and the Turks

TRICKLE DOWN: CHRISTIANIZATION AND ISLAMIZATION

RELIGIOUS LIVES: THE WORLD OF MONKS AND NUNS
Christian Monasticism
Buddhist Monks
Sufism
Religious Women

IN PERSPECTIVE: The Triumph of the Potential World Religions

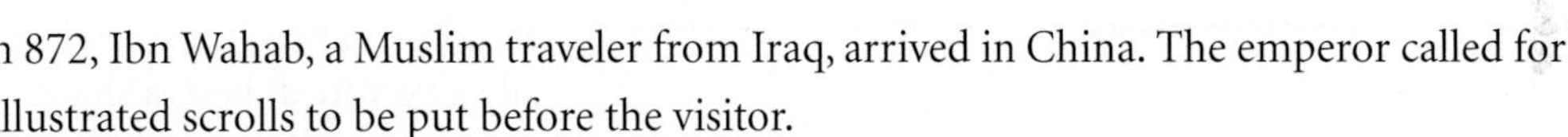

In 872, Ibn Wahab, a Muslim traveler from Iraq, arrived in China. The emperor called for illustrated scrolls to be put before the visitor.

Ibn Wahab recognized the portraits of biblical prophets and patriarchs. I said, his account continues, Here is Noah with his ark, which saved hm when the world was drowned …

At these words, the emperor laughed and said, You have identified Noah, but, as for the ark, we do not believe it. It did not reach China or India.

That is Moses with his staff, I said.

Yes, said the emperor, but he was unimportant and his people were few.

There, I said, is Jesus, surrounded by his apostles.

Yes, said the emperor. … His mission lasted only thirty months.

Then I saw the Prophet on a camel … and I was moved to tears. Why do you weep? asked the emperor.… He and his people founded a glorious empire. He did not live to see it completed, but his successors have. … I saw also other pictures, which I did not recognize. The interpreter told me that they were the prophets of China and India.

CHINA
IRAQ

• • • • •

The anecdote illustrates three themes of the time: the effectiveness of communications across Eurasia; the superiority of Chinese knowledge; and the subject of this chapter—the beginnings of the ascent of Christianity, Islam, and Buddhism to be *world religions,* with followings in all sorts of physical and cultural environments. Most religions do not spread beyond their cultures of origin. Christianity, Islam, and Buddhism were unusual. They aspired to be universal, and became global.

FOCUS questions

- WHY DID Buddhism, Christianity, and Islam become world religions?
- HOW DID commerce spread religion in parts of Eurasia and Africa?
- WHY DID missionaries seek to convert rulers and elites?
- HOW DID Christian and Muslim rulers deal with religious minorities?
- WHY WAS monasticism more important for Christianity and Buddhism than for Islam?
- WHAT ROLE did women play in the spread of world religions?
- HOW DID world religions accommodate themselves to local cultures?

Historians often claim to be interested in the past for its own sake. If we also want to understand our own world and trace the emergence of its key features, we have to confront the problem of why Christianity, Islam, and Buddhism began to acquire the global acceptance they have today. So in this chapter, we have to stay in Eurasia and Africa—in the parts where these three religions had penetrated by Ibn Wahab's time—and catch up in the next chapter with changes occurring in the meantime in other parts of the world.

There has never really been an "age of faith." Of course, there are plenty of sincere individual conversions, spiritually inspired or intellectually induced. Most people, however, in most periods, experience religion only superficially. If they do undergo real conversion or spiritual rebirth, it happens sporadically and rarely lasts long. Nor should we judge the spread of religion by the extent of people's intellectual grasp of it. If you ask most Christians or Muslims or Buddhists about the doctrines of their faiths, they will usually give you, at best, a shallow account. Their religion may not affect their ethical behavior much. Instead of understanding religion as belief, or spiritual experience, or doctrine, or ethics, we should treat it here as cultural practice, and say that a religion has "spread" where and when many people take part in its rites and identify with their fellow worshippers as members of a community. Four processes enabled Islam, Buddhism, and Christianity to take off and spread: war, trade, missionary activity, and elite—especially royal—sponsorship (see Map 9.1)

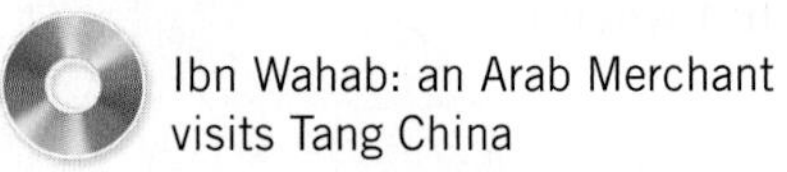

Ibn Wahab: an Arab Merchant visits Tang China

COMMERCE AND CONFLICT: CARRIERS OF CREEDS

Forcible conversion is—strictly speaking—no conversion at all. "There is no compulsion in religion," says the Quran. The Catholic Church forbids using force to spread faith. Buddhism, too, has no place for coercion. But force sometimes works.

In the Islamic World

The Arabic word **jihad** (jee-HAHD) literally means *striving*. Muhammad used the word in two contexts: first, to mean the inner struggle against evil that Muslims must wage for themselves; second, to denote real war against the enemies of Islam. These have to be genuine enemies, who "fight against you to the death." But in Muhammad's day the community he led was almost constantly at war, and Chapter Nine of the Quran seems to legitimate war against all "polytheists" and "idolaters." After the Prophet's death, his successors turned the doctrine of jihad against the "apostates" who abandoned Islam because they considered that their obligations to Muhammad had ended when he died. It was then used to proclaim successful wars of aggression.

Holy war seems an appropriate translation for "jihad": an enterprise sanctified by obedience to what are thought to be the Prophet's commands and rewarded by the promise of martyrdom. According to a saying traditionally ascribed to Muhammad, martyrs go straight to the highest rank of paradise, for "they fight," as the Quran says, "in the cause of Allah and they slay the enemy or are slain." This is

MAP 9.1

The Rise of World Religions to 1000 C.E.

- Buddhist heartland
- Shinto
- Muslim world, ca.1000 C.E.
- extent of Christianity, ca.1000 C.E.
- extent of Hinduism, ca.1000 C.E.
- spread of Mahayana Buddhism
- spread of Theravada Buddhism
- Islamic expansion
- spread of Hinduism
- Nestorian missions
- Silk Roads
- maritime routes
- *Khazars* people

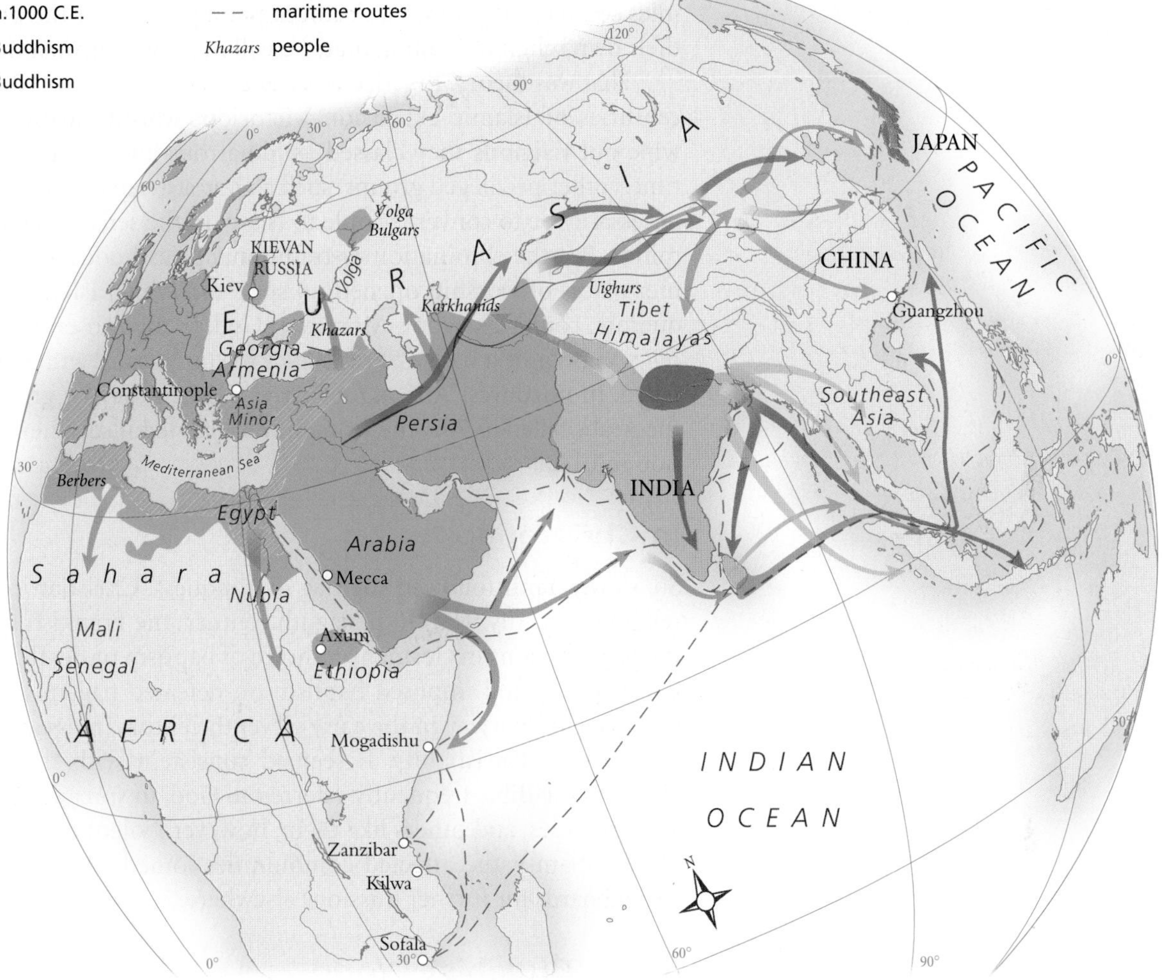

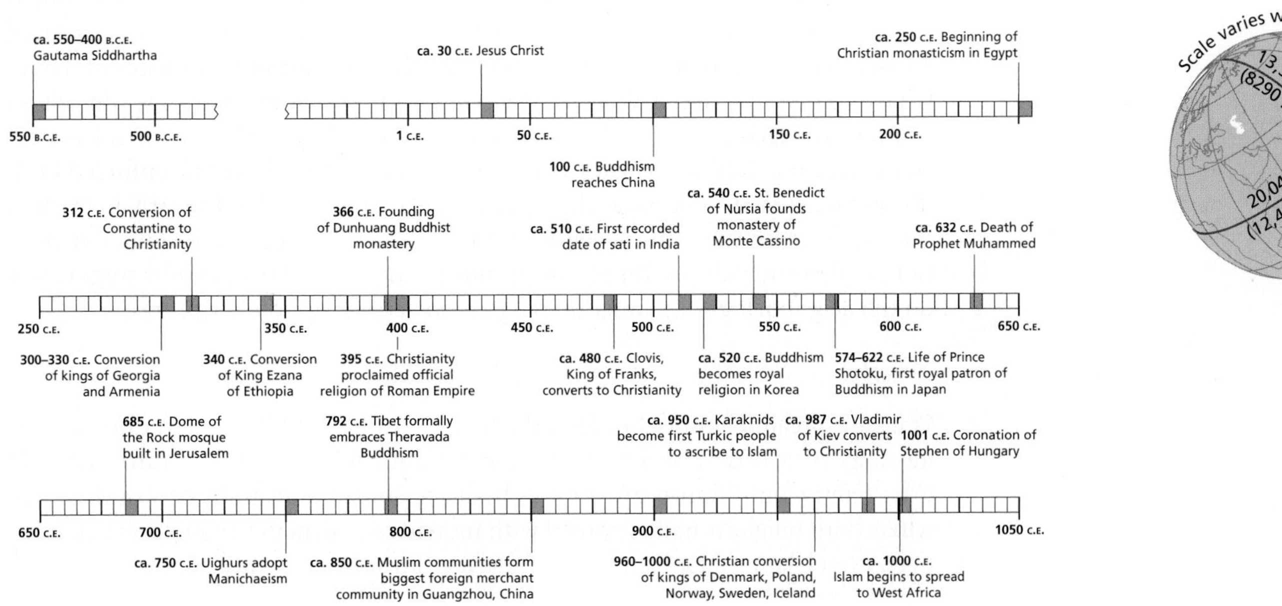

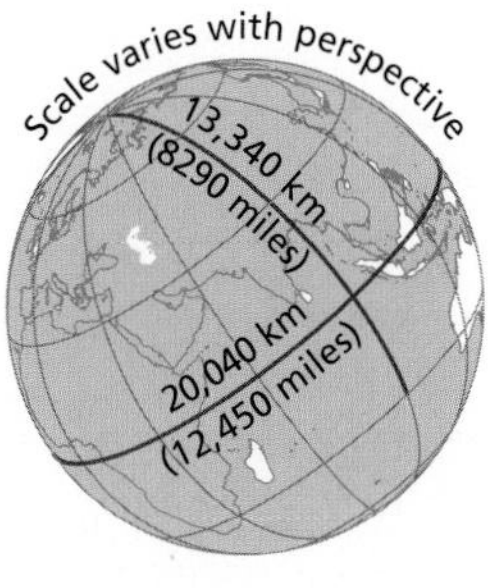

Scale varies with perspective
13,340 km (8290 miles)
20,040 km (12,450 miles)

no more bloodthirsty than many passages in the Bible and needs no more to be taken literally than Paul's injunction to Christians to "fight the good fight." But it can justify war and implies a link between war and the spread of Islam. A tenth-century Muslim jurist summed up the tradition as it had evolved by that time. Enemies could either submit to Islam or pay a poll tax for the privilege of persisting in their own religion. "Failing that, we will make war against them."

That was theory. Practice was not always so clear-cut. But in the first couple of centuries of Islamic expansion, victorious Muslim armies did normally aim to wipe out religions they classed as idolatrous and to tax Christians, Jews, and, at times, other privileged groups, such as Zoroastrians in Persia. The result would not necessarily be to convert people to Islam, in the sense of changing their hearts and minds. But the elimination of traditional priesthoods and the destruction of former places of worship opened up spaces in which Islam, the religion of the conquerors, could take root. Moreover, God seemed to endorse Islam. If traditional religion became a badge of resistance to conquest, it withered when that resistance failed. In northwest Africa, for instance, when the last great Berber revolt against the Arabs failed in 703, the woman who had led it sent her sons to receive instruction in Islam.

In Christendom

So, slowly, faith followed the flag of conquest. Christian conquerors also abused religion to justify war. In the eighth century, the Frankish king Charlemagne gave the pagan Saxons in Germany a choice of baptism or death. In the ninth, Alfred the Great of England imposed baptism on defeated pagans as a condition of peace. Olaf, king of Norway in the early eleventh century, massacred or mutilated pagans who refused Christianity. It seemed consistent with the nature of the Lord of Hosts, as the Bible frequently referred to God, to spread Christianity by war. Yet in all these cases, and others like them, however violent and arbitrary the beginnings of Christianity, the affected communities joined Christian civilization and built springboards for further missions elsewhere.

In the Buddhist World

Less well known is that much of the early spread of Buddhism relied on similar strategies by royal strongmen. As in Christendom, Buddhist rulers practiced remarkable intellectual contortions to justify the imposition by violence of a doctrine of peace and love. Asoka (see Chapter 7) was not alone in priding himself on conquests allegedly achieved "by **dharma**"—the teachings of Buddha. Asoka's near contemporary, Kaniska, King of Peshawar in what is today Pakistan, enforced Buddhism on his own subjects, as did King Vattagamani, in Sri Lanka, early in the first century B.C.E. In the mid–eleventh century C.E., when King Anuruddha (ah-non-ROOD-dah) introduced Buddhism to Burma, he showed his piety by waging war on the neighboring Mon kingdom to gain possession of holy scriptures.

Trade

War can spread religions, but after the time of Asoka, Buddhism never became the ideology of a widely successful conqueror until the sixteenth century; nor did Christianity, until European empires began to spread it around the world. Meanwhile, both religions had to spread with individual journeys beyond political frontiers. Even Islam overspilled the boundaries of Muslim conquests.

Trade was probably at least as important as war. The temples of Dunhuang are full of images of the role of the Silk Roads in spreading Buddhism. Merchants who rested at the monastery there endowed thousands of paintings that still line chambers carved from the rock. According to tradition, a Chinese monk began to hollow the caves out of the cliff face in 366. Many of the paintings portray individual merchants in acts of worship, often with their families and sometimes in the company of their ancestors. In one image, brigands, converted by a Buddhist merchant they have captured, join him in prayer. In others, merchants ransom themselves from bandits by acts of piety. In others, famous Buddhas and sages travel roads familiar to the merchants to visit Buddhist shrines in India and acquire sacred texts.

Dunhuang. The Silk Roads spread Buddhism as well as trade. Here—in a tenth-century example of the thousands of devotional paintings merchants endowed at the monastery of Dunhuang in Central Asia—a convert and his family pray at the feet of a Bodhisattva. Many Chinese converts to Buddhism retained the family values characteristic of Confucianism.

Manichaeanism and the Uighurs

Buddhism met rival religions along the Silk Roads. The Uighurs (OOEE-goors) were a pastoral, Turkic-speaking people who dominated the steppeland north of the roads for 100 years from the 740s. On service as mercenaries during the Chinese civil wars of the mid–eighth century, they picked up **Manichaeanism** (mah-nih-KEE-ahn-ih-sihm), a religion of obscure origin, probably rooted in a heretical form of Zoroastrianism (see Chapter 6). Mani (MAH-nee), its supposed founder in Persia in the third century, divided the universe into realms of spirit, which was good, and matter, which was evil. This kind of dualism was an ancient and influential idea. But although Mani relentlessly sought to spread his religion, it had never previously captured the allegiance of a state. On the contrary, Zoroastrians, Christians, Muslims, and even (in China, in 732) Buddhists persecuted it. Now, however, the Uighur ruler proclaimed himself the "emanation of Mani," and Manichaean zealots became his counselors, rather as Buddhist and Christian rulers chose clergy as advisers and bureaucrats. Indeed, a Uighur bureaucracy developed, using its own language and script. According to a ninth-century inscription, Manichaeanism transformed "a barbarous country, full of the fumes of blood into a land where the people live on vegetables, from a land of killing to a land where good deeds are fostered." Uighur monarchs endowed temples in China and sponsored the collecting of Manichaean scriptures. However, Buddhism and, to a lesser extent, Christianity ultimately replaced Manichaeanism among the Uighurs, and the creed of Mani never caught on to the same extent anywhere else.

Christianity on the Silk Roads

Christianity was only moderately successful along the Silk Roads. Relatively few Christians, especially from Western Europe, engaged in long-range trade. Among Christian peoples who did have strong vocations for commerce, the Armenians avoided trying to convert others so as not to invite persecution by non-Christian rulers. **Nestorians**—Christians named after Nestorius, Bishop of Constantinople in the fifth century, who regarded the human Jesus as merely human, quite distinct from the divine Jesus—had a network of monasteries and communities that reached China. But the Nestorians remained a thin and patchy presence across a vast area.

Camel caravan is still the most practical way to cross the Sahara, and camels still carry part of the traditional salt trade there. Like other long-range trade routes, those across the Sahara in the Middle Ages were avenues for the transfer of culture, spreading Islam, for example, from North Africa to the kingdoms of the West African Sahel and the Niger valley.

Islam on Trade Routes

If Buddhism dominated much of the Silk Roads, Islam spread almost equally effectively by trade along the sea routes of Asia and across the Sahara. Muslim merchant communities founded mosques, elected or imported preachers, and sometimes attracted local people to join them. Muhammad's commands for peaceful conversion were at least as strong as those for jihad. "Call unto the way of thy Lord with wisdom and fair exhortation," the Quran commands. According to a contemporary estimate, thousands of Muslims constituted the biggest of the foreign merchant communities that perished in Guangzhou in a rebel massacre in 879. In the same period, as East African ports became integrated into the trade routes of the Indian Ocean, they developed Muslim communities.

In West Africa, way beyond the African frontiers of the caliphates, immigration and acculturation along the Saharan trade routes prepared the way for Islamization. Arab visitors to Soninke chiefdoms and kingdoms from the ninth century noted that some people followed "the king's religion," while others were Muslims. On this frontier, Islam lacked professional missionaries. Occasionally, however, a Muslim merchant might interest a trading partner or even a pagan ruler in Islam. A late eleventh-century Arab writer tells such a story, from Malal south of the Senegal. At a time of terrible drought, a Muslim guest advised the king that if he accepted Islam, "You would bring Allah's mercy on the people of your country, and your enemies would envy you." Rain duly fell after prayers and Quranic recitations. "The king, together with his descendants and the nobility, became sincerely attached to Islam, but the common people remained pagans."

War, Trade, and Religion

366	Founding of Dunhuang
Fifth century	Nestorius, bishop of Constantinople
Seventh and eighth centuries	Rapid Islamic expansion
Mid-eighth century	Uighurs adopt Manichaeanism
Ninth century	Seaborne pilgrims begin to arrive in Mecca; Muslim merchant communities thrive in major Chinese ports
Mid-eleventh century	King Anuruddha introduces Buddhism to Burma; Islam begins to penetrate East and West Africa

MONARCHS AND MISSIONARIES

Although not much practiced by Muslims in this period, conversion of kings was one of the main strategies Buddhist and Christian missionaries employed to spread their faiths. They learned to start at the top of society because religion, like other forms of culture, tends to trickle downward, encouraged by the example the power of leaders imposes.

For Christians, in particular, the strategy of targeting elites marked a profound innovation in the history of the Church. Christianity in antiquity was branded—not altogether justly—as a "religion of slaves and women." It appealed to a low level of society and, at first, to those with a low-level education. In its earliest days, it was actually unwelcoming to persons of high status, like the rich young man in the

Gospels whom Jesus sent away grieving, or the well-to-do for whom admission to the Kingdom of God was as if through the eye of a needle. In apostolic times, converts of respectable status were few and modest: a Roman army officer; a tax collector; an Ethiopian envoy mentioned in the Acts of the Apostles; the "most excellent Theophilus," who was probably a Roman official, addressed by a gospel-writer. Over the next two to three centuries, the Church embraced people of all classes in the towns of the empire—thanks especially to Christian women, who became the evangelizers of their own husbands and children. But Christianity remained a minority religion, unable to capture the allegiance of rulers or the institutions of states. In the first half of the fourth century, however, three spectacular conversions inaugurated an era in which efforts at conversion targeted the top. The rulers of three great states adopted Christianity: the Roman Emperor Constantine, King Ezana of Ethiopia, and King Trdat (tuhr-DAHT) of Armenia.

Christian and pagan cultures were so similar and so mixed in the fourth-century Roman Empire that it is sometimes hard to tell them apart. Here an emperor, having ridden in life in triumph on an elephant, is hoisted skyward by the chariot of the sun, which pagans worshipped as a god and Christian artists used as an image for Christ. Winged spirits ascend with the emperor's soul, through the spheres of heaven, marked by the signs of the zodiac, top right, to the heavenly home of his ancestors. This is one of the last works of art that portrays a Roman emperor in a predominantly pagan setting.

Constantine

Like so many future invaders and tourists from the north, Constantine, commander of the Roman army in Britain from 306, was seduced by the feel and flavor of Mediterranean culture. The standard tale of the beginning of his conversion to Christianity is not credible. In 312, he was heading south, intent on capturing the Roman throne for himself. Approaching the decisive battle at Milvian Bridge, not far from Rome, he saw a vision that he later described as "a cross of light, superimposed on the sun"—perhaps like the cross-like clouds mountaineers have reported in the Alps, or perhaps an unusual grouping of planets, or perhaps just a dream. As Constantine already worshipped the Sun, the image appealed. The priorities reflected in the accompanying message, "In this sign, conquer!" reflected Constantine's. He was looking for a Lord of Hosts rather than a God of Love. An alternative account of the conversion may be Constantine's own. It is a stock story of revelation by grace. "I did not think that a power above could see any thoughts which I harbored in the secret places of my heart ... but Almighty God, sitting on high, has granted what I did not deserve."

Everywhere politics was so deeply implicated in royal religion that it is hard to resist skepticism about the spirituality of royal converts and the sincerity of their conversions, just as today we prudently disbelieve politicians who claim to be "born again." Bet hedging was the usual strategy. The emperor was the chief priest of the official pagan cults and was worshipped as divine. His role could not suddenly lose its traditional character. Official religion continued. Court poets and orators classified Constantine's victims in battle as divine sacrifices and his birth as a gift of the gods. One of them constructed a framework of paganism over which the emperor's Christianity could fit: "you have secret communion with the Divine Mind, which, delegating our care to lesser gods, deigns to reveal itself to you alone." Constantine continued to personify the Unconquered Sun in official portraits. The sacredness of the emperor's person, however, could now be redefined in Christian terms by calling him God's deputy on Earth and, in deserving cases, making him a saint after his death. In coins his sons issued, the hand of God guides Constantine into heaven on a chariot, like the prophet Elijah's in the Bible.

Imperial patronage profoundly affected Christianity. Constantine himself became, according to his own propaganda, "like an apostle"—settling disputes between theologians, influencing the election of bishops. During the fourth century, Christianity gradually began to displace the old cults as the official religion of the empire. Pulpits spread imperial propaganda. Millions of subjects of the empire began to go to church—without necessarily embracing, or even understanding, Christian doctrines. More than ever, learned and aristocratic classes, who had previously despised Christianity, blended its teachings with the philosophy of classical antiquity. Christian virtues blended with those of Stoicism (see Chapter 6). Christian pacifism withered as Christians supported the empire's wars.

Ezana

The adoption of Christianity at the court of Ethiopia at Axum in the 340s illustrates a similar dilemma for a war leader seeking to appropriate a religion of peace. The inscriptions of King Ezana were bloodthirsty documents, full of conquests and captives. As his reign unfolded, they remained bloody but became increasingly high-minded, full of the concept of the good of the people and service to the state. The king still waged wars but grew moralistic about justifying them. One adversary "attacked and annihilated one of our caravans, after which we took to the field." The king of neighboring Nubia (see Chapter 4) was guilty of boastfulness, raiding, violation of embassies, and refusal to negotiate. "He did not listen to me," Ezana complains, "and uttered curses." The new tone reflects the growing influence of Christian clergy.

Before the 340s, Ezana described himself as "son of Mahreb," a war god. Suddenly, he dropped the claim and waged war in the name of the "Lord of heaven and Earth" or "the Father, Son and Holy Spirit." His last monument proclaims, "I cannot speak fully of his favors, for my mouth and my spirit cannot fully express all the mercies he has done to me... He has made me the guide of my kingdom through my faith in Christ." He toppled the great stone pillars of Axum or ceased to erect them and began to build churches.

Trdat

To become Christian was to join the growing common culture—vertex of a triangle of Christian states, Ethiopia, Rome, Armenia. For Armenia, the evidence is too indistinct to yield a clear picture of what happened. A supposed letter King Trdat wrote in the late third century to an anti-Christian Roman emperor declares "loathing for Christians" and a promise to persecute them. His eventual submission to baptism supposedly arose in revulsion from the fate of 33 nuns whom he had put to death. Gregory the Illuminator—Trdat's former friend, whom he imprisoned in a pit of snakes—stirred his remorse. This looks like a theologically crafted tale of a change of heart induced by divine grace. The whole story seems loosely modeled on that of the Apostle Paul in the Bible—the persecutor turned converter. Trdat's conversion occurred sometime between 301 and 314. The latter date seems likely, as by then Constantine had begun to favor Christianity, and Trdat favored alignment with Rome against Persia.

Early Conversions to Christianity

312	Emperor Constantine of Rome
ca. 301–314	King Trdat of Armenia
340s	King Ezana of Ethiopia

Diplomatic Conversions

From *The Life of St. Nino*

In the Caucasus Mountains near Armenia, at about the same time, tradition credits an unnamed slave woman (whom later tradition called Nino) with converting the people we now know as the Georgians. Her prayers cured a queen's illness. When the king proposed to shower the slave with rewards, "She despises gold," said the queen. "The only way we can repay her is to worship divine Christ who cured me thanks to her prayers." The story sounds made up. The verifiable fact, however, is that the priests who launched the Georgian state church came from Constantine's empire. Christianity was a political option for small states striving to preserve their independence and playing Persia against Rome.

The Georgian kingdoms of Iberia and Lazica pried themselves free of Persian dominance, partly by opting for Roman support. By the early sixth century, a Roman ambassador to Lazica could hardly restrain his enthusiasm for a people who were "in no way barbarians, long association with the Romans having led them to adopt a civilized and law-abiding way of life." From 522, the kings of Lazica ceased to accept election by the emperors of Persia and chose to be invested by those of Rome.

Religious allegiances changed with political alliances. Poised between Christian and Muslim powers, the rulers of the Khazars (HAH-zahrs)—Turkic pastoralists between the Black Sea and the Caspian, who built up a state that endured for 400 years from the early seventh century—adopted, at different times, Christianity, Islam, and Judaism in their efforts to preserve their independence.

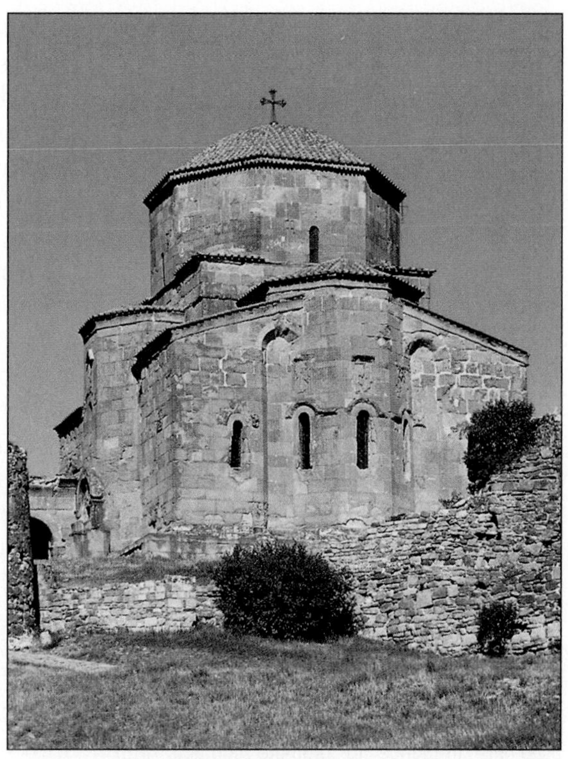

The monastery church at Jvari ("the Cross") in Georgia occupies a hilltop where St. Nino, a female evangelist traditionally credited with helping to spread Christianity in Georgia in the fourth century, is said to have paused to pray. A church on the site is documented from the seventh century, but the existing building resembles Western churches of the ninth and tenth centuries.

Buddhist Politics

Buddhist missionaries also displayed partiality for royal and imperial disciples. The Chinese emperor Ming was supposed to have introduced Buddhism as the result of a vision in the late first century. This was untrue, but it is evidence of the importance the Buddhist clergy who invented the tale attached to imperial patronage. As we saw in the last chapter, Buddhism became the favorite spiritual resource of usurpers of the Chinese throne who wanted to legitimize their rule and of monarchs who needed a propaganda machine. But no Buddhist emperor ever suspended the traditional rites and sacrifices that Chinese emperors were required to perform. Only Yang Jian in the sixth century (see Chapter 8)—a skeptic contemptuous of all religion—had the nerve to do that.

Buddhism had, moreover, to contend with Chinese belittlement of anything foreign. Indeed, the measure of Buddhism's success is that, until "Westernization" began in the late nineteenth century, it was the only movement of foreign origin ever really to catch on in China. Sporadic bursts of imperial favor enabled Buddhists to establish an enormous network of monasteries that became magnets of piety for millions of people. The scale of Buddhism's ascent appeared during one of the spasms of persecution of Buddhism in which emperors occasionally indulged. In the 820s through the 840s, thousands of monasteries were dissolved, and 250,000 monks and nuns forced back into lay life.

Korea

In the neighboring Korean kingdom of Koguryo, the rise of Buddhism began in the late fourth century, when barbarian invasions of China enriched Koguryo with refugees. Fugitive Chinese monks reconciled Buddhism with royal responsibilities under the old, indigenous religion. King Kwanggaet'o dedicated a temple with the inscription, "Believing in Buddhism, we seek prosperity." King Changsu (r. 413–491) is depicted at the tomb of his predecessor performing Buddhist as well as native rites. The rest of Korea resisted Buddhist intrusions at first, perhaps because of the importance of local religious rites as part of the ceremonial of kingship. The kings of Silla, for instance, derived prestige from their claim to have arisen from a dynasty of holy men. State formation in Korea was essentially a process of extending uniform religious rites to one community after another.

The launch of Buddhism as a royal religion in southern Korea is traditionally ascribed to the personal conversion of King Song in Paekche and King Pophung of Silla, despite noble opposition, in the 520s or 530s. Monks, like the chief minister Hyeyong in the mid–550s, became useful state servants. Won'gwang, who returned from China in 602 to head the bureaucracy, adapted dharma for political purposes. Serve your lord with loyalty and "face battle without retreating" became precepts of the faith. Having adapted to one political system in the sixth century, Korean Buddhism did so again, under new political conditions, in the tenth century, when the reform of the Korean administration along Chinese lines filled the bureaucracy with men trained in Confucianism. The scholar-administrator Ch'oe Sungno expressed the ensuing compromise well in 982: "Carrying out the teachings of Buddha is the basis for the cultivation of the self. Carrying out the teachings of Confucius is the source for regulating the state."

Japan

Japan was the scene of the most remarkable working compromise between a new, universal religion and kingly commitment to traditional paganism. The first image of the Buddha in Japan was said to have arrived as a diplomatic gift from Korea in 538. The pious efforts of the Soga clan—immigrants from China—supposedly spread the new religion around the end of the sixth century. Underlying the tale is a political saga. The traditional "way of the gods"—**Shinto** in Japanese—was the reigning dynasty's special responsibility. The Soga aimed to replace them and saw Buddhism as the path to power.

Prince Shotoku. As regent for the first reigning Japanese empress in the early seventh century, Prince Shotoku, shown here with two of his sons in a Korean painting of nearly two centuries later, used his influence to promote contacts with China, remodel the Japanese government on Chinese lines, and spread Buddhism in Japan.

A traditional anecdote captures the true lines of the debate that raged in the mid–sixth century. "All neighboring states to the west already honor Buddha," the Soga pointed out. "Is it right that Japan alone should turn her back on this religion?" But native ministers replied, "The rulers of this country have always conducted seasonal rites in honor of the many heavenly and earthly spirits of land and grain."

The search was on for a synthesis that would harness Buddhism for the state without disturbing the traditional Shinto ideology and magic of the monarchy. Prince Shotoku (574–622), the first great royal patron of Buddhism in Japan, realized the value of the Buddhist clergy as potential servants of the state. He wrote learned commentaries on Buddhist doctrine and founded monasteries. His injunctions include, "The emperor is heaven and his ministers are Earth. . . . So edicts handed down by the emperor must be scrupulously obeyed." Endorsed from the court, Buddhism flourished. The Japanese census of 624 counted 816 monks. By 690, 3,363 monks received gifts of cloth from the throne.

A reaction set in. The traditional elite feared Buddhism as a foreign menace to the imperial rites. Early eighth-century law codes banned wandering monks from "speaking falsely about misfortunes or blessings based on mysterious natural phenomena," "deluding the people," and begging without permit.

Various measures attempted to prevent monasteries from abusing their tax-exempt status.

The advances of Buddhism, however, were irresistible. A Buddhist scripture warned kings that "if they do not walk in the law, the holy men go away and violent calamities arise." In the 730s, the monk Gembo returned from China with 5,000 volumes of Buddhist scriptures and endeared himself by curing an empress's depression. In 747, 6,563 monks were ordained at a palace ceremony. Buddhist rituals originally intended in India to treat snakebites, poison, and disease were used in Japan to protect the state. The outcome was a characteristically Japanese compromise. No one in Japan, it is often said, was purely Buddhist. The traditional Shinto shrines played a part in the devotions even of monks, as they still do. Even Empress Shotoku in the 760s, whose Buddhist devotion was unsurpassed, never tried to tamper with the traditional rites.

The Introduction of Buddhism in Korea and Japan

Late fourth century	Chinese refugees introduce Buddhism in Koguryo
ca. 520–530	Kings of Paekche and Silla convert to Buddhism
538	First image of Buddha arrives in Japan
574–622	Life of Prince Shotoku, first great royal patron of Buddhism
Seventh century	Rapid expansion of Buddhism in Japan under royal patronage

Tibet

According to a legend crafted in Tibet about 500 years after the supposed event, a Chinese or Nepalese wife of King Songtsen Gampo brought Buddhism there in the sixth century. The true story was of long, slow monastic colonization. Though Songtsen Gampo probably patronized Buddhist monks and scholars, who frequented his court in the households of the Nepalese and Chinese princesses of his harem, he continued to represent himself as divine.

Even King Trisong Detsen in the second half of the eighth century, whom Buddhists hailed as a model of piety and their opponents denounced as a traitor to the traditional royal religion, depicted himself as both the divine defender of the old faith and the enlightened enthusiast of the new. In 792, he presided over a great debate between Indian and Chinese champions on the question of whose traditions better represented the Buddha's doctrine. The issue was decided in favor of the Indian traditional moral disciplines (**Theravada Buddhism,** as it is usually called), by which the soul might advance to Buddhahood by tiny incremental stages of learning and goodness, lifetime after lifetime, rather than the **Mahayana Buddhism,** argued by Chinese spokesmen, who claimed that the soul could achieve Buddhahood in one lifetime. Mahayana Buddhism, which also took root in Japan, is known as the "greater vehicle" because its proponents believe that it can carry more people to salvation than Theravada Buddhism, the "lesser vehicle."

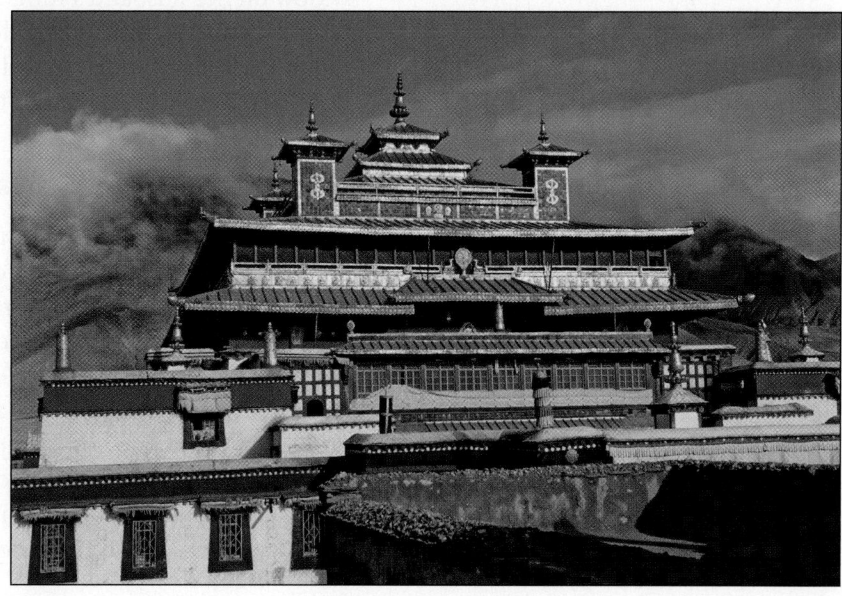

Samye monastery. The first Buddhist monastery in Tibet was reputedly founded at Samye in the valley of Lhasa. It illustrates the importance of royal patronage in bringing Buddhism to Tibet. According to legend, King Trisong Detsen in the 770s invited an Indian sage into the kingdom, who consecrated the site of the monastery after a battle with the demons who infested it.

But this debate was premature. Tibet was hardly yet a Buddhist country, nor could one tradition of Buddhism be imposed in the contexts in which Buddhism spread: missionary work and monastery founding; the spread of culture along the routes of merchant caravans; and the ebb and flow of armies, that transmitted ideas as the tide shifts pebbles.

By the time of Tibet's treaty with China in 821, Buddhism had made real progress. The treaty invoked Buddhist as well as pagan gods, and after traditional sacrifices and blood-smearing rites, the Buddhists among the treaty's negotiators withdrew for a celebration of their own. King Ralpachen was so devout that he let monks sit on his prodigiously long hair. But a reaction set in at his death in 836, and Buddhism survived in Tibet only precariously awaiting renewal by a new wave of monastic colonization. Its main rival was not the old religion but **Bon.** Of the origins of this faith, we know nothing reliable, but it was similar and heavily indebted to Buddhism. The sayings of the great Bon-po sage, Gyerspungs, closely resembled those of Buddhist masters: Existence is like a dream. "Validity is vacuity." Truth must "transcend sounds and terms and words." The main difference lay in the sages' attitude to India. Buddhists acknowledged that their teaching came from there, whereas Bon-pos traced it to a legendary land in the west, and regarded their mythical founder, Shen-rab, as the original Buddha.

India

Ironically, the effort to combine Buddhism with traditional kingship failed most conspicuously in India itself, the Buddha's homeland. In the sixth century, kingdoms multiplied in India, and kings granted revenue and property to holy men to found religious establishments, in an effort to gain their support. Kings made relatively few grants, however, to Buddhists. The circumstances of the period—the conflicts with the Huns (see Chapter 8) and the crumbling of political unity—seem to have driven popular piety back to the worship of local gods, as if the troubles of the time were proof that Buddhism had failed.

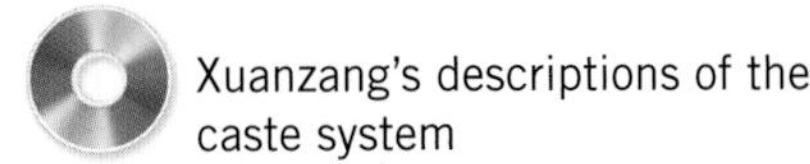
Xuanzang's descriptions of the caste system

Rites and practices associated with the traditions we now call **Hinduism** were taking hold. Indeed, some holy men set out to systematize them as an alternative to Buddhism. The development of the caste system—in which everyone has an unchangeable ritual rank, defined at birth, that determines one's place in society—indicates how Hinduism was spreading. The caste system was not yet fully defined, but according to the description of India in 630 through 645 by Xuanzang (shoo-en-tzang), the greatest Chinese Buddhist manuscript collector, butchers, fishermen, actors, executioners, and scavengers were ritually unclean and had to live outside city limits. Almost everyone acknowledged the superiority of the highest caste, the priestly Brahmans. The spread of blood sacrifice also shows that Buddhism was in retreat. Kings sacrificed horses, in defiance of Buddhist teaching, but protected cows, which Hinduism regards as sacred. The first **sati**—the burning of a widow on her husband's funeral pyre—was recorded in 510. The Palas dynasty of Bengal in the eighth to the eleventh centuries was the last nominally Buddhist reigning family in India. Most Indian kings preferred to stake their power on devotion to traditional gods rather than on Buddhism.

The Margins of Christendom

In Christendom, the *Constantinian model*, according to which conversion begins with the ruler, prevailed for most of what we think of as the Middle Ages. Almost every conversion of a nation or a people, as related in medieval sources, began with the conversion of a king. There were exceptions. Clovis, for instance, the Frankish chief who took over most of Gaul (modern France) in the 480s, gave up his claim to descent from a sea god for allegiance to the Church, which promised victories and supplied literate administrators. But conversions among the Frankish people preceded or accompanied Clovis's. In Iceland, where supposedly "democratic" decision making is generally supposed to have prevailed, the collective adoption of Christianity was resolved in the assembly of the people in 1000, but the law speaker who presided over the assembly, Thorgeirr Thorkelsson, withdrew to meditate or commune with the gods for a day and a night before lending his decisive influence to the debate. Of course, Christianity was also spread in undocumented or barely documented ways: movements of population, journeys of merchants and envoys. But missionary strategy focused on leaders as means of mobilizing peoples.

In northern and eastern Europe, a great sequence of royal conversions in the late tenth and early eleventh centuries more or less established the frontier of Christendom, beginning with Harold Bluetooth in the 960s in Denmark and Mieszko of Poland in 966. In Norway, a year or two after the king's confirmation as a Christian in 995, a popular assembly endorsed the new religion. In Sweden King Olof Skötkunung began minting coins with Christian symbols on them before 1000. He established an uninterrupted sequence of Christian rulers. The coronation of Stephen of Hungary in 1001 settled the Christian destiny of that country.

Vladimir and the Rus

No case was more significant for the future than that of Vladimir, ruler of Kiev in what is today Ukraine, in 987–988, for his adherence ensured that Christianity would be privileged among the eastern Slavs—including the Russians, who became Europe's most numerous people. Vladimir was the descendant of Scandinavians as well as Slavs, pagans on both sides (see Chapter 10). Like many great saints, he sinned with gusto. His harem was said to contain over 800 girls. Russians trace proverbs in praise of drunkenness to his invention. He left a reputation, in the words of a German chronicler, as "a cruel man and a fornicator on a huge scale."

Among his people, paganism was entrenched by terror. The horror of a human sacrifice among the Rus profoundly impressed a Muslim ambassador who witnessed it in 922. The slave girl chosen to die with her master sang songs of farewell over her last cups of liquor before ritually copulating with her executioners. An old woman called the Angel of Death then wound a cord around her neck and handed the slack to men standing on either side. Warriors beat their shields to drown the victim's screams. While the cord was tightened, the Angel of Death plunged a dagger repeatedly in and out of the girl's breast. The funeral pyre, built on a ship, was then lighted, and the fire fed until it burned to ashes.

Ibn Fadlan's journey to Russia

To replace this religion, and break the power of its priests, Vladimir needed something equally powerful. The traditional story of his emissaries' quest led first to the Bulgars, who "bow down and sit, look hither and thither like men possessed, but there is no joy in them, only sorrow and a dreadful stench. Their religion is not good. Then we went to the Germans, and we saw them celebrating many services in their churches, but we saw no beauty there. Then we went to the Greeks, and they led us to the place where they worship their God [the church of Hagia Sophia that Justinian had built in Constantinople]; and we knew not whether we were in heaven or on Earth; for on Earth there is no such vision or beauty and we do not know how to describe it. We only know that there God dwells among men."

Vladimir's decision in favor of Orthodox Christianity owed more to politics than aesthetics. Conversion was the price he paid for the hand of a Byzantine princess whom he demanded with threats. Imperial Byzantine princesses were not normally permitted to marry foreign suitors, for, according to the tenth-century emperor, Constantine VII, "just as each animal mates with its own species, so it is right that each nation should also marry and cohabit not with those of other race and tongue but of the same tribe and speech." Marriages between imperial princesses and foreign

The Spread of Christianity

ca. 500	Clovis, king of the Franks, converts to Christianity
960	Harold Bluetooth of Denmark converts
966	Conversion of King Mieszko of Poland
ca. 988	Vladmir of Kiev adopts Orthodox Christianity
ca. 997	Norway and Sweden convert to Christianity
1000	Iceland converts to Christianity
1001	Coronation of Stephen of Hungary as a Christian monarch

rulers diminished the divinely sanctioned dignity of the Byzantine monarchy and opened the way for foreign rulers to claim the Byzantine throne. Vladimir solemnly evicted his idols. The thunder god, Perun, was dragged through the dust before being flung in a river. Vladimir imposed Christianity by violence, while making it more acceptable by ordering that Christian liturgy be conducted in the Slavonic language the Rus spoke, rather than in Greek.

Islam and the Turks

The magnetism Christianity exerted on the frontiers of Christendom was paralleled in the Islamic world. Around the mid–tenth century, the Karakhanids (kah-rah-HAHN-ihds) became the first Turkic people to subscribe to Islam—apparently as a result of the favorable impression they derived from raiding Islamic territory. This was an event pregnant with consequences for the future, because the Turks would bring to the Islamic world a vital infusion of manpower and expertise in war—"the army of God, whom I have installed in the East," according to a legendary saying of the Prophet.

Islam's attraction for them is easier to express than explain. Their values were warlike. Boys were not named until they had "lopped off heads in battle." Even women were war trained and "made the enemy vomit blood." Yet some of their leaders saw attractions in Islam. In 962, Altigin (AHL-tee-geen), a Turk who had adopted Islam while serving as a slave in Persia, founded at Ghazni (GAHZ-nee) in Afghanistan a Muslim state that was to exert great influence in the future. In about 985, a Turkic chief, Seljuk (SEHL-jook), who dreamed of "ejaculating fire in all directions" and conquering the world, ruled a small state in Central Asia. His descendants supplied some of the Islamic world's most effective frontiersmen.

TRICKLE DOWN: CHRISTIANIZATION AND ISLAMIZATION

From converted rulers and conquered elites, religions trickled down to the rest of society. For Christians, for example, Constantine's patronage was an extraordinary windfall. At the time, despite the gradual accumulation of converts among the socially respectable and intellectual, Christianity had remained one among many popular eastern cults. It still bore the marks of its origins as a Jewish heresy, founded by a rabbi whose birth and death were, in the world's eyes, equally disreputable. Its scriptures were, by the sophisticated standards of the Greek schools of rhetoric and philosophy, so badly written as to embarrass all educated Christians.

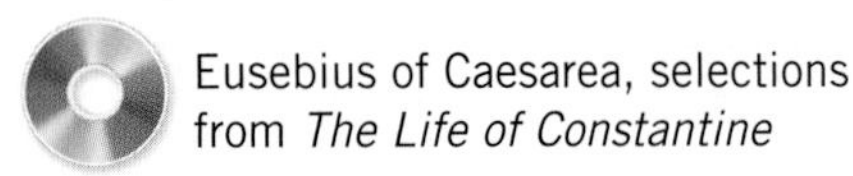

Eusebius of Caesarea, selections from *The Life of Constantine*

Now, after the conversion of Constantine, according to the fourth-century Christian historian Eusebius, "It felt as if we were imagining a picture of the kingdom of Christ and that what was happening was no reality but a dream." There were subsidies for the Church, exemptions from fiscal and military obligations for the clergy, jobs in the state service for Christians, and the assurance, from the emperor's own hand, that the worship of Christians benefited the empire.

The rise of the Church from persecution to predominance was completed in 395, when the emperor Theodosius proclaimed Christianity the official religion of the Roman Empire and reduced pagan traditions to the underprivileged status formerly imposed on Christians. From the late fourth century onward, nobility and sanctity converged. So many young aristocrats became monks that monasteries came to resemble "noblemen's clubs." Christianity guaranteed the best opportunities for promotion in the army and bureaucracy and for personal enrichment.

MAKING CONNECTIONS

FACTORS AIDING THE SPREAD OF UNIVERSAL RELIGIONS

RELIGION →	WAR →	TRADE →	MISSIONARIES →	ELITES
Buddhism	Early rulers Asoka, Kaniska, Anuruddha invoke "dharma" (teachings of Buddha) in violent conquests	Silk Roads fundamental to spreading Buddhism via traveling monks and monasteries housing merchants, pilgrims	Missionaries/pilgrims important—Xuanzang (China); conversion of kings a primary means of accelerating social acceptance	Emperor Ming (China); King Song (Korea); Prince Shotoko (Japan); Trisong Detsen (Tibet)
Christianity	Charlemagne, other rulers (Alfred the Great of England, Olaf of Norway) justify war, conquest by forcible conversion	Few long-distance Christian traders along Eurasian trade routes; Nestorians a thin and patchy presence along Silk Roads	Converting kings and elite groups a fundamental strategy	Constantine (Roman Empire); Ezana (Ethiopia);. Trdat (Armenia); Vladimir (Kiev, Russia)
Islam	Jihad justifies both interior struggle and warfare against polytheists, idolaters, apostates; continual warfare against non-Islamic neighboring states	Effectively spread via land and sea routes across Africa. Dispersal of Muslim–merchant communities throughout south and southeast Asia	Traveling merchants; conversion encouraged by specific social/political policies favoring Muslims (beneficial tax system, legal codes)	Especially important in Turkic areas (Central Asia): tenth-century leaders Altigin, Seljuk

Those who accepted it subscribed to a cultural package associated with success. Ethiopian sources are too meager for certainty, but in Armenia, too, the continuing progress of Christianity depended, at least until the Arab conquest in the eighth century, on royal and aristocratic initiatives.

To some extent, parallel considerations applied within the Islamic world. Because the Muslim conquests were vast, and the conquerors relatively few in number, Muslim rulers could not exclude non-Muslims from positions of authority. The caliph Umar (OO-mahr) I expelled non-Muslims from Arabia in 635, but without the services of Christians and Jews in the rest of the Middle East, or of Zoroastrians in Persia, the administrations of the eighth- and ninth-century caliphates would have been understaffed. Still, by favoring Muslims, discriminating against non-Muslims, and insisting on the exclusive use of Arabic as the language of administration, rulers created a climate of prejudice in favor of Islam among elites. Even mild persecution could exert considerable pressure. The caliph Umar II (r. 717–720) tried to exclude Christians and Jews from public offices. He also forbade them to build places of worship or lift their voices in prayer. They had to wear distinctive clothing and were forbidden saddles for their horses. If a Muslim killed a Christian, his penalty was only a fine. Christians could not give valid testimony against Muslims in legal cases. Later caliphs sporadically renewed persecution. In 807, Caliph Harun al-Rashid (hah-ROON ahr-rah-SHEED) ordered all churches on the frontiers of his empire demolished and reinforced the clothing laws against Christians. In the 850s, the caliph al-Mutawakkil (ahl-moo-tah-WAH-keel) ordered that Christian and Jewish graves should be level with the ground. Converts

The Dome of the Rock in Jerusalem marks the spot where, according to Muslim tradition, the Prophet Muhammad ascended to paradise. The Caliph Abd al-Malik had it built in the late seventh century, marking as sacred to Islam a city that Christians and Jews already revered. The splendor and scale of the building out-dazzled and dwarfed the nearby Church of the Holy Sepulcher and the remains of the last Jewish Temple.

to Islam, on the other hand, could rapidly ascend through the ranks of society.

For most Christian and Jewish subjects of Islamic states, the tax system—which exempted Muslims from most charges—was the focus of discrimination. Indeed, many people proclaimed themselves Muslims simply to take advantage of reduced tax rates, until Al-Hajjaj (ahl-hah-JAHL), the brutal governor of Iraq in the 690s and early 700s, reimposed the old tax levels on supposedly phoney converts.

Partly because Islam tolerated some other religions, the conquered societies were slow to become Islamized. Indeed, substantial Christian minorities have survived in Egypt, Iraq, Syria, and, especially, Lebanon to this day. Some historians have tried to measure the rate of acceptance of Islam by calculating the numbers of people who gave their children Muslim-sounding names. This method suggested to Richard W. Bulliet, its greatest exponent, that only 2.5 percent of the population of Iran were converted to Islam in the seventh century. Not until the early ninth century was the majority of the population Muslim. The remainder were Islamized during the ninth and tenth centuries. The significance of name giving is broadly cultural, in most places, rather than specifically religious. But the names people were given or adopted do help to demonstrate roughly the rate at which Islam became the dominant influence on the culture of Iran.

RELIGIOUS LIVES: THE WORLD OF MONKS AND NUNS

In Buddhism and Christianity, monasticism grew as these religions spread and, in turn, became a major cause of their success.

Christian Monasticism

As a result of the triumph of Christianity as an elite religion, the Church became the great upholder of Roman standards of learning, art, and government. This is not surprising among aristocratic bishops, whose family traditions were of power. Pope Gregory the Great (r. 590–604) organized the defenses of Rome (see Chapter 8), launched missions of spiritual reconquest to pagan parts of Western Europe, and reimposed on the western empire a kind of unity by the sheer range of his correspondence. In Visigothic Spain, Isidore of Seville (ca. 560–636) passed the learning of classical Greece and Rome on to future generations in the form of an encyclopedia.

Isidore of Seville's T-O map of the world

It was harder to domesticate the church's own barbarians—the antisocial ascetics and hermits, whose response to the problems of the world was to withdraw from them or rail at them from their caves. The monastic movement made their lives "regular," in houses of work, study, and prayer to benefit society as a whole. There is no scholarly consensus on the origins of monasticism. Christians perhaps got it from Buddhists, or maybe it arose independently as hermits and holy men clubbed together for mutual support. The earliest recorded Christian monastic communities emerged in Egypt in the second century, among ascetics seeking to imitate Jesus' period of self-exile in the desert. Of the many rules of life for monks written in the following centuries, the most influential rule in the western church was that of Benedict of Nursia.

The only certain date in his life is 542, when a king visited him at his monastery of Monte Cassino in southern Italy. Benedict started as a typical, obsessive ascetic, in a cave, where food was lowered to him while he disciplined the lusts of the flesh in a convenient thorn bush. In one of the earliest surviving illustrations of his life, the cave mouth is jagged and bloody. When he established his own community, he rededicated the pagan shrine of the Roman god Jupiter on the spot to St. Martin, the patron of poverty, who gave half his cloak to a beggar. The nearby pagan shrine of Apollo became the chapel of John Baptist, the biblical voice crying in the wilderness. These rededications disclose Benedict's program: the practice of charity in refuge from the world.

The Rule of St. Benedict

His book of rules for monks borrowed freely from others. But its superiority and universality were recognized almost at once, and there has hardly been a monastic movement or revival in the West since then that has not been based on or deeply influenced by it. The animating principles are the quest for salvation in common and the subordination of individual willfulness. Benedict banned extremes of mortification in favor of steady spiritual progress, manual labor, study, and prayer in private and in common. He devised a means to make civilization survive, for monastic study also embraced the learning of ancient Greece and Rome. Monasteries became centers for colonizing wasteland and wilderness. Monks sought "desert" frontiers to build new monasteries, and lay people followed them.

from the *Confession of St. Patrick*

Buddhist Monks

Monasticism was even more important in Buddhism than in Christianity, since most Buddhist clergy were subject to monastic discipline. In practice, Buddhist monasteries performed particular functions, especially in transmitting learning, similar to those of monasteries in Christendom. The 50,000 ancient manuscripts preserved in the library cave of Dunhuang—a precious time capsule, sealed for 800 years in the tenth century—are a measure of the importance of scholarship in Buddhist monasteries. The business of retrieving, translating, editing, and purifying the best written evidence of the Buddha's teachings turned monks into giants and heroes of learning. The first Chinese to be ordained as a Buddhist priest, for instance, in about 250, was Zhu Shixing (joo-sha-shang). He was nearly 80 years

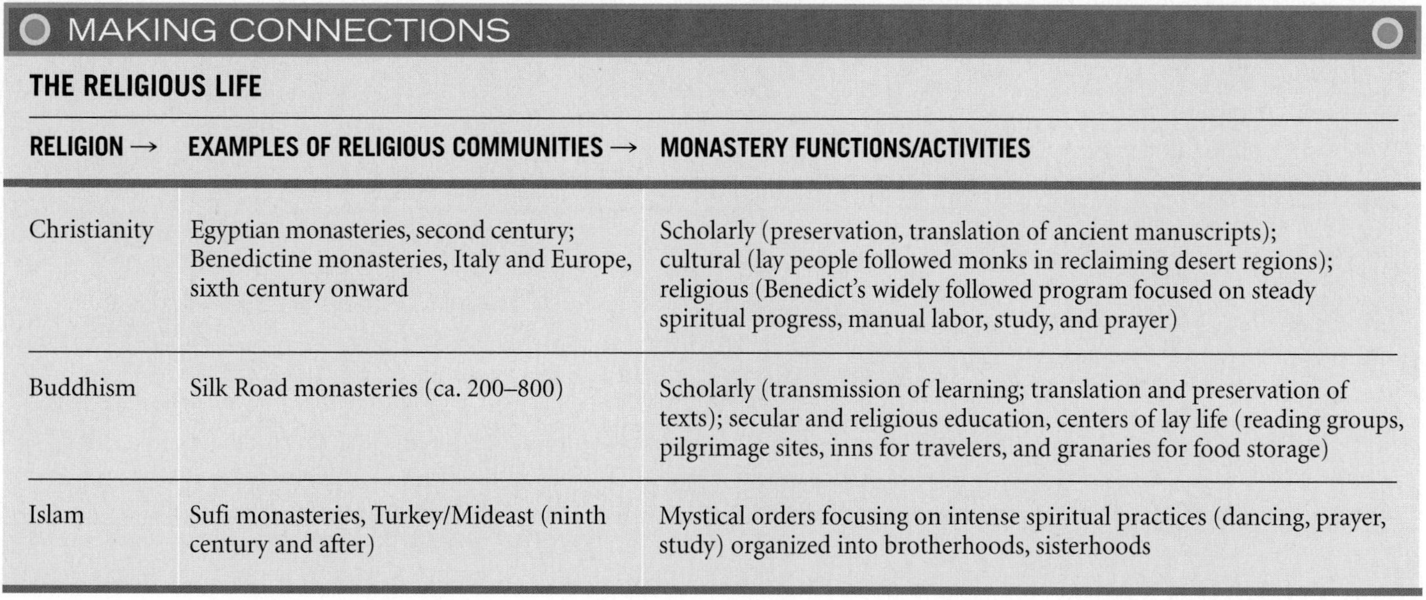

MAKING CONNECTIONS

THE RELIGIOUS LIFE

RELIGION →	EXAMPLES OF RELIGIOUS COMMUNITIES →	MONASTERY FUNCTIONS/ACTIVITIES
Christianity	Egyptian monasteries, second century; Benedictine monasteries, Italy and Europe, sixth century onward	Scholarly (preservation, translation of ancient manuscripts); cultural (lay people followed monks in reclaiming desert regions); religious (Benedict's widely followed program focused on steady spiritual progress, manual labor, study, and prayer)
Buddhism	Silk Road monasteries (ca. 200–800)	Scholarly (transmission of learning; translation and preservation of texts); secular and religious education, centers of lay life (reading groups, pilgrimage sites, inns for travelers, and granaries for food storage)
Islam	Sufi monasteries, Turkey/Mideast (ninth century and after)	Mystical orders focusing on intense spiritual practices (dancing, prayer, study) organized into brotherhoods, sisterhoods

old when he made a pilgrimage to India to procure a manuscript of the Buddha. Exhausted by the journey, he handed it to his disciples to carry to China before he died. Kumarajiva, translator into Chinese of the most famous of Buddhist scriptures, the **Lotus Sutra,** in the early fifth century, was said to be able to memorize 30,000 words a day. As in Christendom, Buddhist monastic libraries diversified into secular learning, imaginative literature, and administrative and historical records of life way beyond the monastery walls. They were centers of lay life, too, hosting reading clubs for believers, including groups of women, who would pay fines—such as a jug of wine or bowl of cereal—for failure to attend meetings. And monasteries functioned as objects of pilgrimage, inns for travelers, and granaries to store food against hard times.

Sufism

Strictly speaking, there should never have been anything like monasticism in Islam. The Quran condemns it. But Christian influence was not easy to filter out of early Islam. In the early eighth century, Hasan al-Basri quoted Jesus to support his view that asceticism is God's "training ground that his servants might learn to run to him." He advocated fasting and meditation to induce a mystical sense of identity with God. When, toward the end of the same century, the female mystic, Rabia al-Adawiyya (rah-BEE-yah ahl-dahWEE-yah), experienced a vision of Muhammad, he asked her if she loved him. "My love of God has so possessed me," she replied, "that no space is left for loving or hating any but him." Groups of devotees founded houses of common life, or, at least, schools in which they trained in mystical techniques and cultivated the tradition these thinkers established. Though fellow Mus-

The Lotus Sutra. Composed between the first century B.C.E. and the second century C.E., the *Lotus Sutra* is the most important text of Mahayana Buddhism. This printed version, from around 1000 C.E., shows the Western Paradise of the Amitabha Buddha and his court of Bodhisattvas.

lims often suspected these **Sufis** (SOO-fees) of being heretical, Sufism supplied Islam with some of its supplest thinkers and most dedicated and successful missionaries.

Early Monasticism

ca. 250	Zhu Shixing is the first Chinese to be ordained Buddhist priest
Second century	Earliest Christian monastic communities (Egypt)
Sixth century	Life of Saint Benedict
Seventh century	Abbess Hilda rules important religious establishments
Late eighth century	Rabia al-Adawiyya, Islamic Sufi mystic

Religious Women

In Christianity, Buddhism, and the Islamic world, women acquired new roles, inside the home as guardians of religious tradition for their children, and outside the home as members of religious orders. Nuns played the same role as monks in prayer and scholarship. In some places, both sexes shared the same houses of religion, often under female leadership. At Whitby in seventh-century England, the formidable Abbess Hilda ruled one of the largest and most learned religious establishments of the day. Nunneries played an important part in Buddhist life in China and Japan as schools for women. The empresses Shotoku of Japan (see Chapter 10) and Wu of China (see Chapter 8) were nuns before their ascent to power. In the Buddhist world, the nun's vocation was often a stage before returning to secular life in households where husbands had several wives and concubines. In Islam, which allowed men to have up to four wives, there was relatively little spare woman power. So female monasticism never developed, and female Sufis—though often individually influential—were rare. Only exceptionally strong-minded women like Rabia al-Adawiyya could pursue their vocations in a life of renunciation of marriage.

Rabia al-Adawiyya, "Brothers, My Peace Is in My Aloneness"

IN PERSPECTIVE: The Triumphs of the Potential World Religions

The story of this chapter has been of cultural change rather than religious conversion. Some of the conditions—violence, mass migration, enforced refugeeism, pestilence, famine, natural disaster, "culture shock," and demographic collapse—constitute, on a large scale, influences comparable to the traumas that often precede individual conversion. Yet, when we monitor the public progress of Christianity, Islam, and Buddhism, we glimpse, at best, shadows of individual religious experience. Instead, we see shrines multiplying; congregations growing; influence deepening on laws, rites, customs, and the arts.

By around 1000, all three religions had demonstrated their adaptability to different cultures and climates (see Map 9.2). Buddhism had big followings in China, Japan, Tibet, and southeast Asia and had spread into Central Asia along the Silk Roads. Christianity had a near monopoly in Western Europe and spilled east and north into Scandinavia and the Slav lands, while retaining the allegiance of communities scattered through Asia. Islam, dominant in southwest Asia and North Africa, spread by conquest, conversion, and migration among Turkic peoples and around the trade

MAP 9.2a

The Christian World, ca.1000 C.E.

- Catholic Christianity
- Orthodox Christianity
- Christian churches believing Jesus to be wholly divine (Monophysite)
- Nestorian Christianity
- area with significant Christian minorities today
- missions
- † important church or monastery
- *Saxons* people

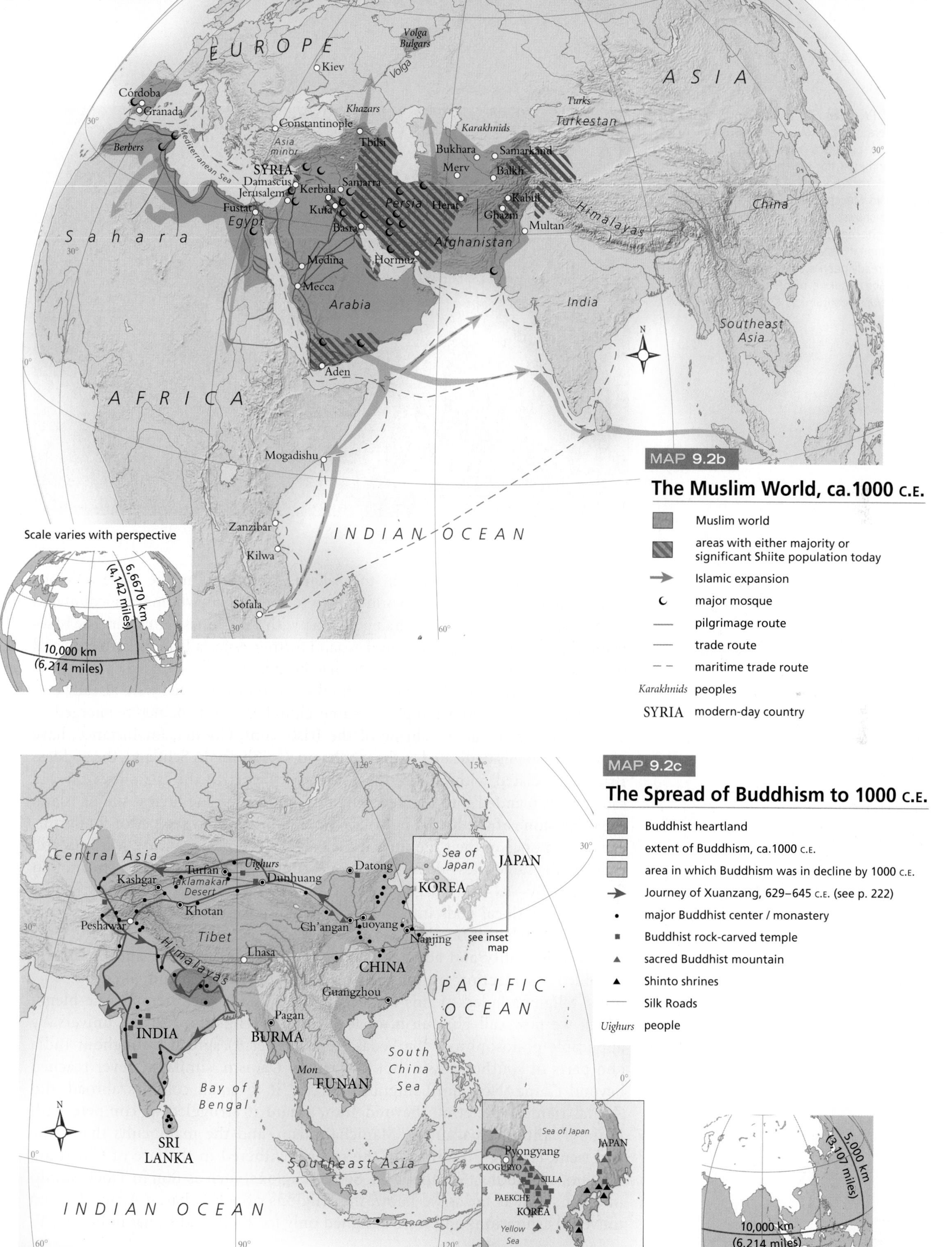

EUROPE
ASIA
AFRICA
Sahara
Arabia
Persia
Afghanistan
India
China
Southeast Asia
INDIAN OCEAN
Scale varies with perspective
6,6670 km (4,142 miles)
10,000 km (6,214 miles)
MAP 9.2b
The Muslim World, ca.1000 C.E.
Muslim world
areas with either majority or significant Shiite population today
Islamic expansion
major mosque
pilgrimage route
trade route
maritime trade route
Karakhnids peoples
SYRIA modern-day country
MAP 9.2c
The Spread of Buddhism to 1000 C.E.
Buddhist heartland
extent of Buddhism, ca.1000 C.E.
area in which Buddhism was in decline by 1000 C.E.
Journey of Xuanzang, 629–645 C.E. (see p. 222)
major Buddhist center / monastery
Buddhist rock-carved temple
sacred Buddhist mountain
Shinto shrines
Silk Roads
Uighurs people
Central Asia
Tibet
INDIA
CHINA
BURMA
FUNAN
SRI LANKA
KOREA
JAPAN
PACIFIC OCEAN
South China Sea
Bay of Bengal
Southeast Asia
INDIAN OCEAN
see inset map
5,000 km (3,107 miles)
10,000 km (6,214 miles)

The Kaaba. Promoters of new religions often had to reconsecrate pagan sites—it was easier to do that than to persuade worshippers to abandon them. Muhammad, for instance, made pilgrimage to the black rock housed in a building known as the Kaaba in Mecca compulsory for Muslims. As the picture shows, tens of thousands of pilgrims circle the site each year at the beginning of a series of annual rituals called the hajj. But the rock had already been a place of pagan pilgrimage in Arabia and a shrine of many gods for generations, perhaps centuries, before Muhammad's time.

routes of the Indian Ocean and the Sahara. Among them, the three religions seemed to have carved up the world known to Ibn Wahab, whom we encountered at the start of this chapter discussing religion with the Chinese emperor. The bases from which all three religions would expand further, especially in the sixteenth and seventeenth centuries (see Chapter 18), had been laid.

Their competitive advantages with religions they displaced were already evident. Pagan groves and temples became churches. Local deities reemerged as saints. Excavations at the shrine of the Irish saint, Gobnet, for instance, have yielded 130 anvils dedicated to the smith god, Goibhnin. In Scotland, the goddess Brigid, associated with childbirth, became St. Bride. In the Islamic world, old sacred sites blended into the new religious landscape. The holiest site of Islam, the black stone of the **Kaaba** in Mecca, where Muslims have to perform pilgrimage at least once in their lifetimes if they able, was a pagan shrine. Muslims still perform the same rites—kissing the stone, running the course of the stream that flows nearby—as their pagan predecessors did. Buddhists had no difficulty incorporating local gods into the vast Buddhist pantheon or sanctifying local shrines with relics of Buddhas.

This flexibility and adaptability made Christianity, Islam, and Buddhism suitable for projection around the world. This does not explain, of course, why other religions failed in this respect or never made the attempt. The blend, which we now call Hinduism, of local Indian religions with the universally applicable philosophy of the Vedas (see Chapter 3) spread throughout India and parts of southeast Asia, but no farther. Daoism, similarly, never reached beyond China. Nor, until migrants carried it to small colonies abroad, did Zoroastrianism penetrate beyond Iran, where it struggled to compete with Islam. Traditional paganism, Manichaeanism, and the many cults that came and went, leaving little trace in the record, withered in the face of Christian, Muslim, or Buddhist competition. Some religions, such as Bon in Tibet, Shinto in Japan, and, as far as we know, the religions of sub-Saharan Africa, had no universal aspirations and were designed only for their traditional followers. To judge from later artistic evidence, there was a good deal of exchange between the local and regional religions of Mesoamerica from the twelfth century to the sixteenth. We cannot say how much farther they might have spread had Christianity, arriving in the 1500s, not transformed the religious profile of the region. In the Americas, in sub-Saharan Africa, and in regions of which we know even less, such as Australia and the Pacific, the same reasons that inhibited the spread of other forms of culture also tended to limit the communicability of religions. There were no great, long-range avenues of communication, such as the Silk Roads and the monsoonal ocean. The kind of competition that Islam, Christianity, and Buddhism generated never took effect.

CHRONOLOGY

(All dates are C.E.)

Second century	Earliest Christian monastic communities (Egypt)
ca. 250	Zhu Shixing becomes first Chinese to be ordained as Buddhist priest
ca. 314	King Trdat of Armenia converts to Christianity
ca. 340	King Ezana of Ethiopia converts to Christianity
366	Founding of Dunhuang monastery, western China
395	Proclamation of Christianity as official religion of Roman Empire
ca. 520	Conversion of kings of Paekche and Silla to Buddhism
538	First image of Buddha arrives in Japan
Sixth century	Life of Benedict of Nursia
Seventh and eighth centuries	Rapid expansion of Islam; spread of Buddhism in Tibet
Ninth century	Seaborne Muslim pilgrims begin to arrive in Mecca
ca. 988	Vladimir of Kiev converts to Orthodox Christianity

Even as they changed the societies in which they triumphed, the new religions changed in their turn, compromising with vested interests, modifying their messages to suit mighty patrons, serving the needs of warriors and kings, even becoming organs of the state, instruments of government, means of training bureaucrats, and communicating with subjects. A further consequence of expansion was that different traditions within each of the religions lost patience or touch with each other. Christians in different parts of the world adopted different theologies. In Ethiopia, for instance, the church believed that Jesus was wholly divine, with no distinctly human person. The Nestorian Christians of the Silk Roads preached the opposite doctrine: that the human Jesus was wholly human, leaving his divine nature in heaven. Theological differences gradually drove Christians in Europe apart. After 792, most congregations in Western Europe modified the creed, the basic statement of Christian belief, to make the Holy Spirit "proceed" from "the Father and the Son" rather than "the Father" alone. Most churches in eastern Europe denounced the new wording as heresy. Different Islamic states subscribed variously to Shiism and Sunnism (see Chapter 8) and to different interpretations of Islamic law. In Buddhism divisions between followers of the Theravada and Mahayana traditions were sometimes just as bitter.

Although all these religions had started by appealing to people of modest or marginal social position, they "took off" by converting rulers and elites, who favored new religions—spiritual merits apart—because they saw advantages in doing so. The support of the church, for instance, was expensive for rulers and aristocrats. But it was worth it because it meant that God and his angels and saints became one's allies and friends. We can measure the value a typical royal convert got from the deal in the weight of gold and jewels in the votive crown that the seventh-century Spanish Visigothic king Reccesvinth hung in the sanctuary of his royal church. In return for such rich gifts, matched by comparable generosity in land, he got the prayers of the priests and monks, the services of a clerical bureaucracy, and the miraculous power of the relics of an army of martyrs. There was also a hidden advantage that no ruler could have banked on and that the next chapter must disclose. In the last three centuries of the first millennium, Islam, Buddhism, and, to a lesser extent, Christianity played vital and spectacular roles in new forms of environmental management.

PROBLEMS AND PARALLELS

1. What were the four chief ways in which world religions were spread? In which world religions did merchants play a leading role in spreading the faith?
2. What advantages did Buddhism, Christianity, and Islam enjoy over older religions?
3. How did rulers and elites use religion to consolidate and justify their power over societies?
4. Why is Japan a unique example of a world religion coexisting with a traditional native religion? Was such a working compromise possible in other areas of the world? Why or why not?
5. How did differing forms of Christianity arise on the margins of Christendom?
6. How did Christianity and Islam trickle down to the masses after the elites adopted these religions in Eurasia and Africa? How did average citizens benefit from adopting (or not adopting) these religions?
7. Why did monasticism play such a large role in the early history of Buddhism and Christianity? Why was monasticism less important in the Islamic world? What new roles did women acquire?
8. How did the triumph of Buddhism, Christianity, and Islam change the societies and cultures where they triumphed? How were they in turn changed and modified?

DOCUMENTS IN GLOBAL HISTORY

- Ibn Wahab: an Arab Merchant visits Tang China
- from *The Life of St. Nino*
- Xuanzang's descriptions of the caste system
- Ibn Fadlan's journey to Russia
- Eusebius of Caesarea, selections from *The Life of Constantine*
- Isidore of Seville's T-O map of the world
- The Rule of St. Benedict
- from *The Confession of St. Patrick*
- Rabia al-Adawiyya, "Brothers, My Peace Is in My Aloneness"

Please see the Primary Source DVD for additional sources related to this chapter.

READ ON

To understand the problems of what conversion means, A. D. Nock, *Conversion: The Old and the New in Religion from Alexander the Great to Augustine of Hippo* (1933) is an indispensable classic, and K. F. Morrison, *Understanding Conversion* (1992) is an up-to-date introduction.

On Buddhism H. Bechert and R. Gombrich, eds., *The World of Buddhism: Buddhist Monks and Nuns in Society and Culture* (1984) is a superb survey, much wider in scope than the title implies. Works that deal with the reception of Buddhism in particular cultures are E. Zürcher, *The Buddhist Conquest of China* (1959), which is a work of outstanding scholarship; K. Lal Hazra, *Royal Patronage of Buddhism in Ancient India* (1984); M. T. Kapstein, *The Tibetan Assimilation of Buddhism* (2000); and the collections of essays edited by L. R. Lancaster and C. S. Yu, *Introduction of Buddhism to Korea* (1989); *Assimilation of Buddhism in Korea* (1991); and (with K. Suh) *Buddhism in Koryo* (1996). The Cambridge History of Japan (1988) deals expertly with all aspects of Japanese history in the period, including the reception of Buddhism. The travels of Xuangzang and other Chinese monks in search of Buddhist learning are covered in J. Mirsky, *The Great Chinese Travelers* (1964).

On Manichaeanism, P. Mirecki and J. BeDuhn, *Emerging from Darkness: Studies in the Recovery of Manichaean Sources* (1997) is a fascinating insight into the development of current scholarship. C. Mackerras, *The Uighur Empire* (1972) is a masterly survey.

On the spread of Islam it is helpful to consult G. S. P. Freeman-Grenville, *Historical Atlas of Islam* (2002). For the Indian Ocean, K. Chaudhuri, *Asia before Europe* (1990) is again to be recommended, with a word of caution about the demanding nature of this work.

For Africa, T. Insoll, *The Archaeology of Islam in sub-Saharan Africa* (2003) is of great importance. M. Hiskett, *The Course of Islam in Africa* (1994) is a useful introduction. On East Africa, J. Trimingham, *Islam in East Africa* (1964), and M. Horton and J. Middleton, *The Swahili* (2000) (which is a good general history of the coastlands) can be recommended. For West Africa, M. Hiskett, T*he Development of Islam in West Africa* (1984) and J. S. Trimingham, *A History* *of Islam in West Africa* (1962) are standard. For the Turks, an interesting source from the pre-Muslim period is G. Lewis, ed., *The Book of Dede Korkut* (1974). The important work I cite on Persia is R. W. Bulliet, *Conversion to Islam in the Medieval Period: An Essay in Quantitative History* (1979).

On Christianity, W. H. C. Frend, *The Rise of Christianity* (1984); R. MacMullen, *Christianizing the Roman Empire* (1984); and R. Fletcher, *The Barbarian Conversion: From Paganism to Christianity* (1997) are fundamental and between them take the story down to the late Middle Ages. Exemplary case studies can be found in H. R. Mayr-Harting, *The Coming of Christianity to Anglo-Saxon England* (1972), J. Muldoon, ed., *Varieties of Religious Conversion in the Middle Ages* (1997), and B. Sawyer et al., eds., *The Christianization of Scandinavia* (1987).

For works on Constantine, see Chapter 8.

For the rise of Christianity in Ethiopia, S. Munro-Hay, *Aksum* (1991) is vigorous and makes much use of the stela texts; D. W. Phillipson, *Ancient Ethiopia* (2002) is a superb survey based on archaeological evidence; G. W. B. Huntingford, *The Historical Geography of Ethiopia* (1989) is a basic and classic work.

For the Caucasus, N. Garsoian, *Church and Culture in Early Medieval Armenia* (1999), and *Armenia Between Byzantium and the Sasanians* (1985) are collections of significant essays. C. Toumanoff, *Studies in Christian Caucasian History* (1963), and D. Braund, *Georgia in Antiquity* (1994) are also useful and important.

On Vladimir, F. Butler, *Enlightener of the Rus* (2000) is an interesting work, tracing the subject's historical reputation. The work of S. Franklin is fundamental.

On the origins of monasticism, G. Gould, *The Desert Fathers on Monastic Community* (1993), and W. Harmless, *Desert Christians* (2004) are highly instructive; and M. Dunn, *The Emergence of Monasticism* (2000) is a good introduction. There are many editions of *The Rule of St. Benedict.*

On Sufism, F. Meier, *Essays on Islamic Piety and Mysticism* (1999) contains many interesting pieces, while A. D. Knysh, *Islamic Mysticism* (2000) surveys the whole history of the subject efficiently. For Buddhist monasticism, the already-cited work edited by Bechert and Gombrich is excellent.

The account of human sacrifice among the Rus is from S. H. Gross and O. P. Sherbowitz, eds., *The Russian Primary Chronicle: Laurentian Text* (1953), p. 111.

CHAPTER

10 Remaking the World: Innovation and Renewal on Environmental Frontiers in the Late First Millennium

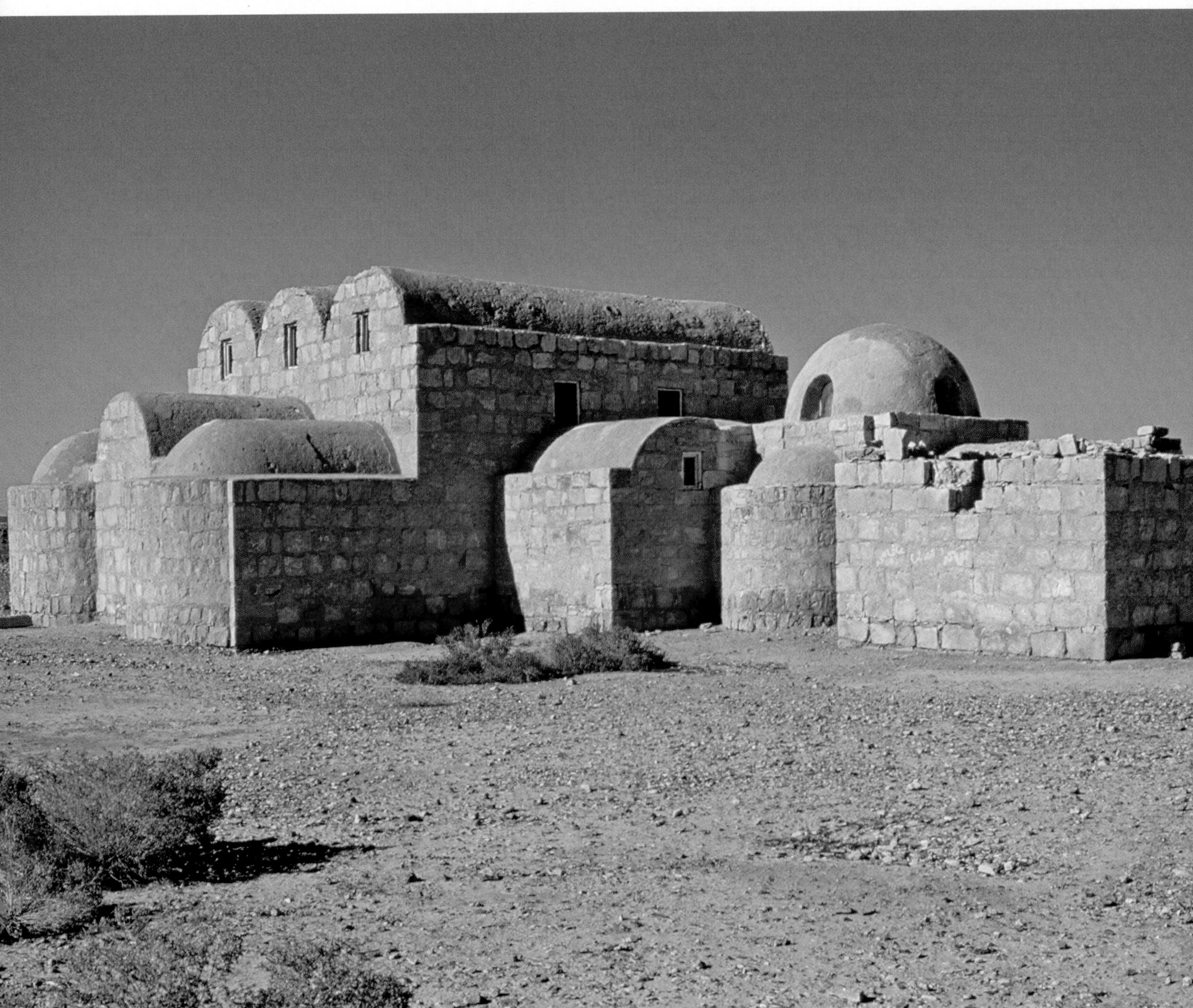

The small castle of Qusayr Amra dates from the reign of Caliph Walid I (ca. 705–715). It contains his spectacular bathhouse, lavishly decorated with paintings, including portraits of the monarchs he considered his rivals: the rulers of Byzantium, Ethiopia, Persia, and Visigothic Spain.

IN THIS CHAPTER

ISOLATION AND INITIATIVE: SUB-SAHARAN AFRICA AND THE AMERICAS
African Geography
American Geography
The Maize Frontiers

THE ISLAMIC WORLD AND THE ENVIRONMENT

FRONTIER GROWTH IN JAPAN

CHINA AND SOUTHEAST ASIA

THE PACIFIC

THE EXPANSION OF CHRISTENDOM

IN PERSPECTIVE: The Limits of Divergence

One of the oddest monuments of the early Islamic world is the bathhouse of a caliph's hunting lodge in the Jordanian desert. Here Muhammad's successor could relax unseen. He could also relax Islamic condemnations of art that depicted the human form, for Muhammad was supposed to have exempted bathhouses specifically from such bans. Mosaics smother the walls and ceilings. One wall was decorated with six portraits of failed enemies of Islam. Two of the images are too decayed to be recognizable. The others show a Visigothic king from Spain, Roman and Persian monarchs, and an Ethiopian emperor, depicted as the equal of the other great rulers of the world.

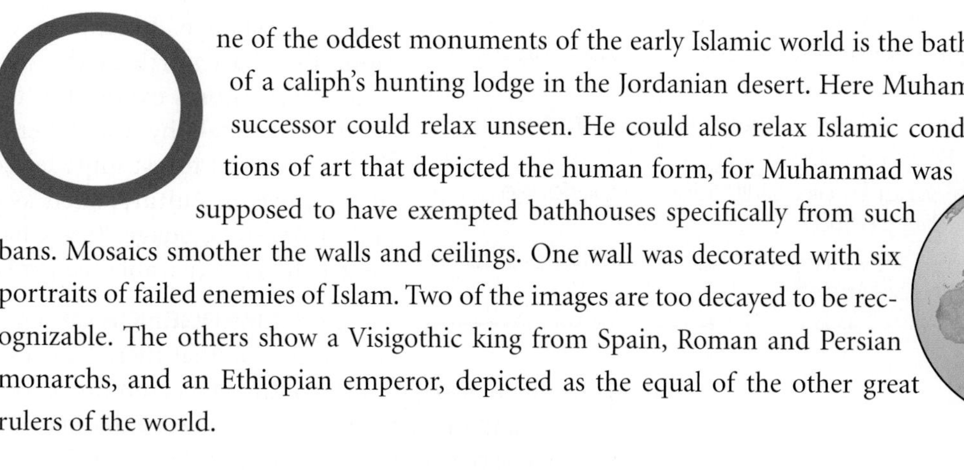

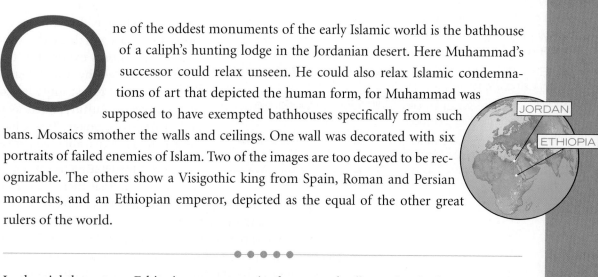

In the eighth century, Ethiopia was not yet in the state of collapse that had overcome the Roman and Persian realms, but it was in trouble. Nomadic "barbarians" infiltrated from the north. No coinage was issued. Monumental building stopped. Squatters were taking over abandoned mansions in the capital. At the port of Adulis on the Red Sea, eighth-century ash lies thickly over ruined buildings, evidence that fire had wrecked the city. By the ninth century, central political control was hard or impossible to maintain. Later writers remembered shadowy, allegedly demonic female rulers, who seized power in the tenth century. "God has become angry with us," wrote a fugitive king. "We have become wanderers. ... The heavens no longer send rain and the earth no longer gives its fruits."

Environmental influences played a big part in Ethiopia's eclipse. Trees vanished from hills overexploited for wood and charcoal. Intensive farming exhausted the soil. Heavy rains aggravated erosion. Mudslides buried buildings. Below volcanic hills, once-rich earth turned to dust. To renew the state and resume expansion, Ethiopians had to find new resources, new frontiers, new techniques.

From around 700 to 1000, states all over the world responded to similar problems. New ways to manage the environment multiplied. They constitute something like a global story—or at least, a story that spans most of the world. Outcomes, however, continued to vary, and in some regions, such as the Islamic world, China, and Japan, the innovations of the period proved more durable than in others. What we might call the **axial zone** of the world expanded. The densely populated central belt of Eurasia, stretching from China to Europe and North Africa—the region that had seen so many experiments in civilization for so long—incorporated new frontiers within it. In the Americas, sub-Saharan Africa, and the Pacific, similar but smaller zones began to take shape but remained fragile.

FOCUS questions

- HOW DID geography influence the transmission of culture in sub-Saharan Africa and the Americas?
- WHAT WERE the environmental consequences of the Islamic conquests?
- HOW DID Japan, China, and the states of southeast Asia seek to stimulate economic growth?
- HOW DID Pacific Islanders succeed in colonizing the Pacific?
- WHERE DID Christendom expand in the eighth and ninth centuries?
- WHERE—if anywhere—did civilizations experience "dark ages" in this period?
- HOW WIDESPREAD during the history of this period was ecological experiment?

ISOLATION AND INITIATIVE: SUB-SAHARAN AFRICA AND THE AMERICAS

African Geography

Geography is often said to imprison sub-Saharan peoples. While great axes of communication cross-fertilize much of the Old World, the Sahara and the Indian Ocean separate most of Africa from those highways of cultural exchange. Except on the Mediterranean and along the coast north of the Mozambique Channel in East Africa, shores exposed to the wind make communication difficult by sea. Rivers are hard to navigate. Dense, malarial forest impedes communications. Some of the flows of culture, such as the spread of farming and of Bantu languages (see Chapter 5), took centuries longer than comparable transmissions in Eurasia.

THE EMERGENCE OF GHANA AND GAO Still, it is surprising that there has never been much exchange along the obvious axis of transcontinental communication in Africa: the Sahel, the belt of grassland that links East Africa, where Ethiopian civilization took shape, to another precocious region in the Niger valley in West Africa. Here, urban life, commerce, and industry show up in the archaeological record of the third century B.C.E. onward. By the first century C.E., at Jenne-Jeno, where floods fed the soil, farmers and ironworkers grew millet and rice. The population was reputedly so dense that royal proclamations could be "called out from the top of the city's walls and transmitted by criers from one village to the next."

The region was a natural crossroads, where traders could deal in slaves, desert salt, local copper, and gold from the mines of Senegambia and the middle Volta River. Toward 1000, two states impressed Arab visitors: Ghana and Gao (gow). Ghana was in the territory of the Soninke (son-in-KAY) people, west of the middle Niger River. Its capital at Kumbi-Saleh had houses of stone and wood, and a royal compound, where a sacred snake with a sensitive snout supposedly sniffed out royal quality from among the contenders for the throne. Enriched by taxes on trade, the monarchs of Ghana and Gao attracted the reverence paid to sacred beings. Subjects prostrated themselves and covered their heads with dust. When the king of Gao ate, all business in the town was suspended, until shouts announced he had finished.

Sacred kingship spread along the Sahel. The Zaghawa of the Chad region in the late ninth century had "no towns," according to an Arab traveler's report, but "they worshipped their king as if he were Allah." In Yoruba (YOU-roo-bah) territory on the lower Niger River, evidence of divine kingship appears from the tenth century in clay portraits of men and women with elaborate headgear and hairstyles. Had contacts developed across the Sahel between West African realms and Ethiopia, rather in the way that the steppeland linked Europe to China, African history might have, in the long run, more closely resembled that of Eurasia. But the West African kingdoms remained focused on relations north across the Sahara, while Ethiopia's avenues of approach to the rest of the world led every direction but westward: north to the Nile, east to the Indian Ocean, south along the Rift valley (see Map 10.1).

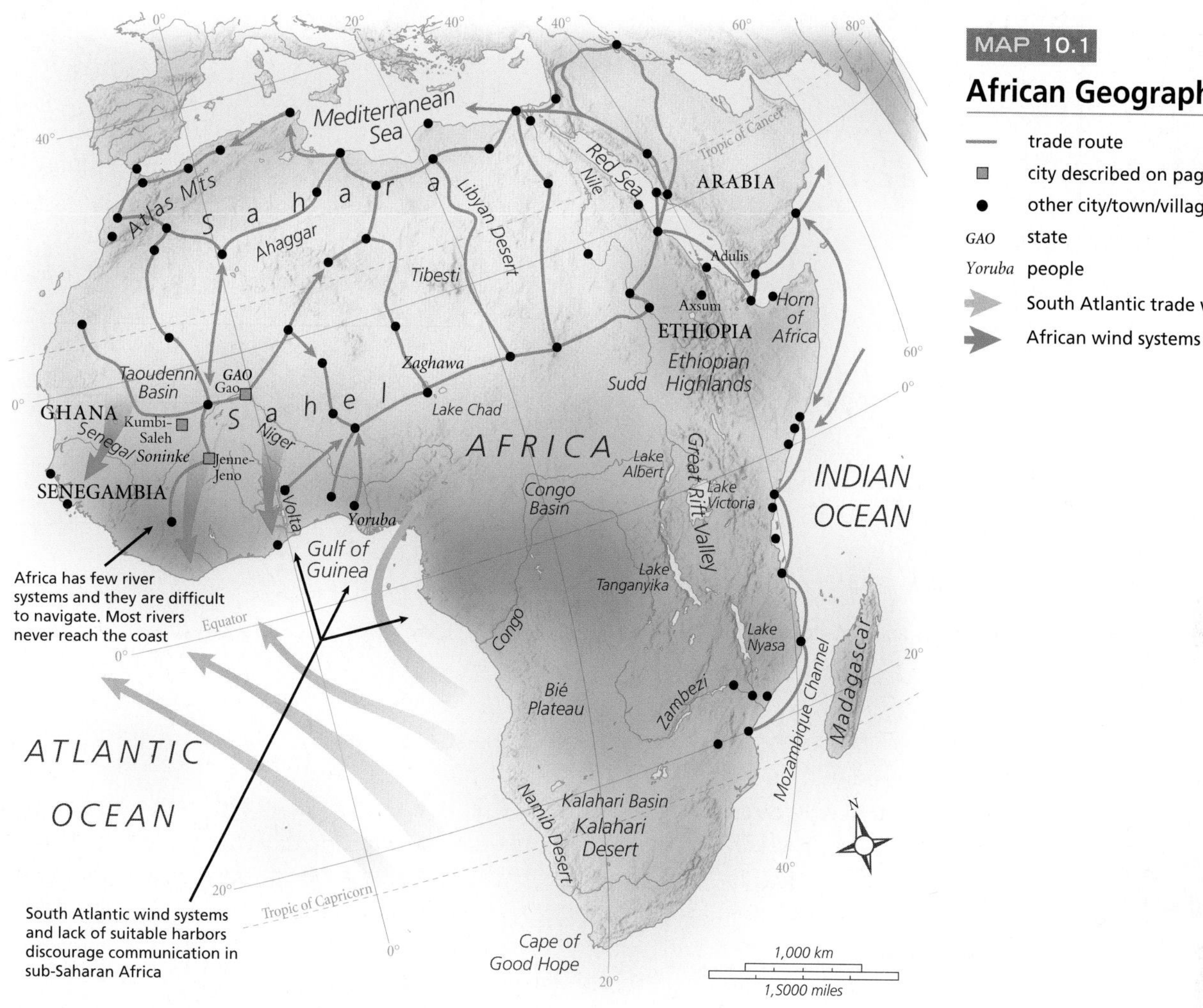

MAP 10.1

African Geography

— trade route
■ city described on pages 301–302
● other city/town/village
GAO state
Yoruba people
South Atlantic trade winds
African wind systems

American Geography

It is tempting to use similar arguments about the geography of the Americas to explain why the Old World developed differently from the New. The shape of the American hemisphere slowed diffusion of new culture and new crops, which had to travel across climate zones through the narrow, central continental funnel. Most of the great rivers flow east and west from the mountain spines that run up and down North and South America, and only the Mississippi River traverses much distance from north to south.

Still, isolation did not prevent civilizations from developing in the Andean region, in parallel with those of Mexico and Central America, taking advantage of the different ecosystems that a world of slopes and valleys, microclimates, and diverse plants and animals provided. The highlands of North America, on the other hand, housed nothing comparable. This may have been, in part, because the Andes and the Sierra Madre in Central America and Mexico are better placed than the mountains of the north: close to rain forests, seas, and swamps for maximum biological diversity.

MOCHE AND NAZCA Similarly, though North and South America both have arid deserts, the effort to civilize them encountered earlier success in the south (see Map 10.2). One of the strangest deserts in the world is in northern Peru.

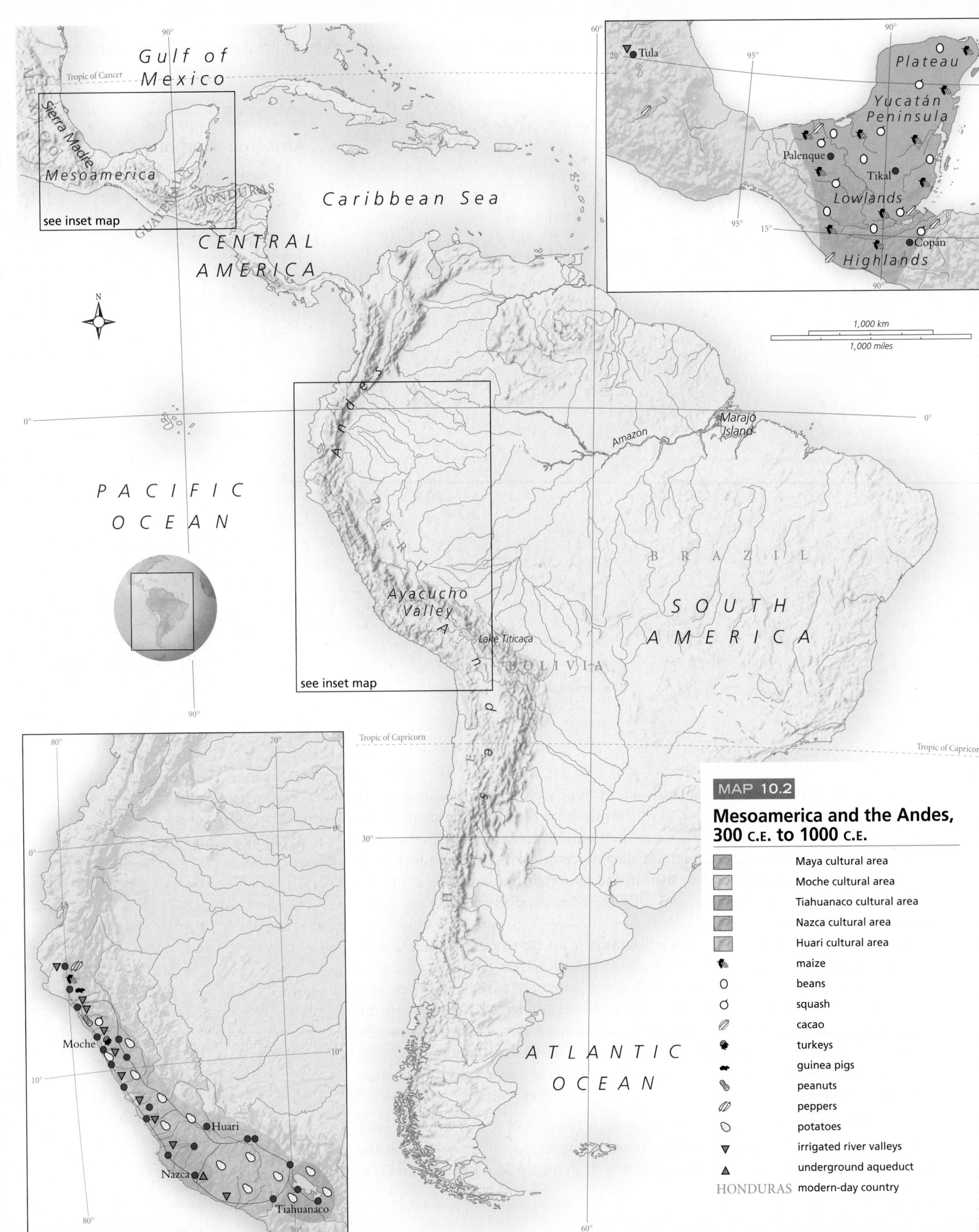
Gulf of Mexico
Tropic of Cancer
MEXICO
Sierra Madre
Mesoamerica
GUATEMALA
HONDURAS
see inset map
Caribbean Sea
CENTRAL AMERICA
N
Andes
PACIFIC OCEAN
PERU
Ayacucho Valley
Lake Titicaca
BOLIVIA
see inset map
Amazon
Marajó Island
BRAZIL
SOUTH AMERICA
Tropic of Capricorn
CHILE
ATLANTIC OCEAN
1,000 km
1,000 miles
Tula
Plateau
Yucatán Peninsula
Palenque
Tikal
Lowlands
Copán
Highlands
Moche
Huari
Nazca
Tiahuanaco
MAP 10.2
Mesoamerica and the Andes, 300 C.E. to 1000 C.E.
Maya cultural area
Moche cultural area
Tiahuanaco cultural area
Nazca cultural area
Huari cultural area
maize
beans
squash
cacao
turkeys
guinea pigs
peanuts
peppers
potatoes
irrigated river valleys
underground aqueduct
HONDURAS modern-day country

Except when El Niño drenches the land, almost no rain falls. The region is cool, although dank with ocean fog. Little grows naturally, but modest rivers create an opportunity to irrigate. The sea is at hand, with rich fishing grounds, and guano provides fertilizer to turn desert dust into cultivable soil. From the third century to the eighth, the civilization known as Moche (MOH-cheh) made this desert rich with corn, squash, peppers, potatoes, and peanuts.

Under platforms, built as stages for royal rituals, their rulers' graves lie: divine impersonators in golden masks, with earspools decorated with objects of the hunt, scepters and bells with scenes of human sacrifice, necklets with models of shrunken heads in gold or copper, and portraits of a divine sacrificer wielding his bone knife. At San José de Moro, a woman was buried with limbs encased in plates of precious metals. In 2006, archaeologists in southern Peru found another female Moche mummy with gold jewelry and weapons. Farther south, in the same period, in the even more inhospitable desert of northern Chile, the people known as the Nazca built underground aqueducts to protect irrigation water from the sun. Above ground, they created some of the most ambitious works of art in the world: stunning representations of nature—a hurtling hummingbird, a cormorant spread for flight, sinuous fish—and bold abstract lines, triangles, and spirals, scratched in the rock. Some of the images are 1,000 feet wide, too vast to be visible except from a height the artists could not reach, capable of permanently arousing the imagination.

Despite these achievements, the desert remained a fragile environment for ambitious ways of life. The Moche survived repeated droughts, which archaeologists have inferred from cores sampled from nearby mountain glaciers. El Niño events periodically drove away the fish and washed away the irrigation works. These were occurrences frequent enough for the locals to learn to live with. After the mid–eighth century, however, no mounds were built, no great artworks made, and the irrigated land dwindled. No one knows why, though most scholars speculate that the people overexploited their environment, or an unusually protracted drought may have defeated them.

ANDEAN DEVELOPMENTS The center of gravity of large-scale innovation shifted to the high Andes, though with little long-term gain in security. The city of Huari, 9,000 feet up in the Ayacucho valley in Peru, lasted as a metropolis only from the seventh century to the ninth. It had garrison buildings, dormitories for the elite, and communal kitchens, with a population of at least 20,000 clustered around it. It also seems to have had satellite towns dotted about the area.

At over 12,000 feet above sea level, potatoes fed the city of Tiahuanaco (tee-ah-wahn-AH-koh) in Bolivia because its altitude was hostile to growing grains. The tillers built stone platforms topped with clay and silt. They drew water from Lake Titicaca through channels to irrigate their mounds and protect them from violent changes of air temperature. Beds in this form stretched more than nine miles from the lakeside and could produce up to 30,000 tons of potatoes a year. By about 1000, building had ceased, and the site was becoming abandoned—again for unknown reasons, but perhaps because of overexploitation of the soil, or a shift in the balance of power. Tiahuanaco, as it gradually subsided into ruins, became a source of inspiration for all subsequent efforts to cultivate and build in the Andes.

THE MAYA No case has excited more curiosity than that of the Maya. They inhabited—their descendants still inhabit—three contrasting environments: the abrupt, volcanic highlands of Guatemala, where microclimates create diverse eco-niches at different altitudes; the dry, hilly, limestone plateau of

The Dresden codex. The Maya almanac known as the Dresden Codex contains a wealth of data on agriculture, divination, and religion. But its most remarkable contents, perhaps, are the detailed astronomical observations and predictions, especially the table recording the cycle of Venus, one page of which is shown here. The red bars and dots at bottom right are numbers, adding up to 584—the average number of days between the dates on which Venus rises with the sun. Such dates were favorable for war and sometimes foretold drought and death. The gods depicted represent, from top to bottom, the Morning Star, Venus as bringer of war, and Venus demanding sacrifice.

Yucatán (yoo-kah-THAN), the peninsula on Mexico's Caribbean coast, where agriculture depends on irrigation from pools and wells; and tropical lowlands in Central America, with dense forests of heavy seasonal rain. There is bound to be cultural diversity across such varied environments, and among these regions, the chronology of Maya civilization varied considerably. The lowlands experienced a Classic Age of monumental building and art from about the third to about the tenth centuries, whereas the plateau "peaked" later in these respects. But Maya civilization has some surprisingly uniform features.

The Maya demonstrated, in spectacular ways, common threads of Native American civilizations seen from the Olmecs onward (see Chapter 4). Maya rulers had three areas of responsibility: war, communication with the gods and the dead, and building and embellishing monumental ceremonial centers. Royal portraits, often engraved on stone and displayed in the grand plazas where their subjects assembled, show rulers in roles similar to those of professional shamans, wearing divine disguises, or engaged in rituals of bloodletting designed to induce visions. We can still confront the images of many kings. At Palenque (pa-LEHN-keh), in the rain forest of southern Mexico, the seventh-century King Pacal (pa-KAL) is depicted on his tomb—dead, but refertilizing the world. A sacred ceiba tree springs from his loins. In Copán (koh-PAN) in Honduras, the kings of the Macaw dynasty from the fifth century to the ninth, are shown communing together, as if at a celestial conference. At Tikal, when the sun is in the west and gilds the huge temple where he was buried, you can still pick out the vast outline of the fading image of King Jasaw Chan Kaui'il (ha-SA-oo chan kah-wee-EEL), molded onto the temple facade.

Politically, the Maya world was divided among city-states. They were perhaps too equally matched for imperialism to succeed. They were competitive in trade and war, which, for most of them, seem to have been almost constant. Boasts of captives sacrificed are common in the texts. Mayan art often depicts scenes of sacrifice—including torturing to death and dismemberment while the victim was still alive.

Everything the Maya thought important—everything on Earth that they thought worth recording—happened in and around the ceremonial centers. The countryside was there to support and sustain those centers. Monumental buildings housed elites and displayed rites to appease the gods and promote civic solidarity. Elite dwellings were imposing and built of stone, but the facades of some of them are adorned with carvings of humble dwellings, such as the Maya peasantry still inhabit today, built of reeds and thatch with a single stone lintel. The temples, which often doubled as tombs, always evoked the mounds on which, in the lowlands, farming was practiced: structures with vast, terracelike flights of steps, surmounted by platforms on which rituals were enacted. Typically, especially in the highlands and lowlands, false facades topped them, jutting into the sky, decorated with molded reliefs, displaying the symbols of the city, the portraits of the kings, the records of war, and the rewards of wealth. In their time, for travelers, traders, or would-be aggressors, they carried an unmistakable message of propaganda: an invitation to commerce, a deterrent against attack.

Thousands of peasants' flimsy dwellings surrounded these centers in a landscape adapted for intensive agriculture. Small fields called *milpas* were carved into highland terraces or dredged, in the lowlands, between canals that were used for

A CLOSER LOOK

ROYAL BLOODLETTING

The reign of Itzamnaaj B'alam ("Shield Jaguar") II of Yaxchilán (681–742), in what is today Mexico, produced some of the finest stone reliefs in which Maya rulers commemorated their performance of important rituals. The most common ritual was royal bloodletting, which was intended to provoke visions. During these bloodlettings, kings communicated with ancestors or gods.

The date of the ritual, shown here, was October 26, 709.

The carvings announce that the king and queen are shedding their blood.

The king wears a sacrificed captive's skull on his headdress and an emblem of the sun on his breast.

The queen draws a spiked thong through her tongue to spill her blood. A king would draw blood from his penis. Bark paper in the bowl below the monarchs absorbed the blood, which was then burned. The monarchs would inhale the smoke to induce a trance.

What does this stone relief tell us about Mayan kingship?

irrigation or fish farming. The fields were sown with the three Native American staples: maize, beans, and squash, supplemented with other foods according to region or locality. Or they were devoted to cash crops, like cacao, which was in high demand for the luxury beverage that accompanied rituals and feasts.

The Maya possessed a singular feature—it is tempting to say, a secret ingredient—because their writing system, the most expressive and complete known in the Native American world before the arrival of Europeans, did not spread to other culture areas. Much more common in lowland regions than in the plateau and highlands, these writings were carved in stone. Virtually all the writing falls into two categories: first, records of astronomical observations and priestly timekeeping—a vital area of interest in Maya efforts to communicate with the gods and appease nature; second, dynastic records, genealogies of kings, records of their conquests, sacrifices, and acts of communion with their ancestors.

Of course, all the surviving written evidence is propaganda, produced under the patronage of states. Claims and counterclaims of conquests and captures are evidence not of what the kings actually did but what they thought important. The central drama of kingship—the ritual the inscriptions most often commemorate—was the spilling of royal blood. A king would use a bone needle or spike to draw blood from his penis or scatter it from his hand. A queen might perform the ceremony by dragging a knotted thong, studded with sharp bones or spines, through a perforation in her tongue. Blotted onto bark, the blood would burn with hallucinatory drugs in an open fire. Enraptured by the fumes and by blood-loss, the monarch would succumb to a vision, characteristically depicted as a serpent rising from the smoke. The serpent was the mouthpiece of the ancestors. Their message usually justified war.

Maya civilization largely abandoned the lowlands in the ninth and tenth centuries. New building in ceremonial centers ended. Inscriptions ceased. The royal cult disappeared. Evidence vanished of rich elites and professions specialized in learning and the arts. Squatters occupied the ruins of decaying ceremonial centers. Traditional scholarship has dramatized and mystified these events as the collapse of classic Maya civilization—an echo of the decline and fall of the Eurasian civilizations of the axial age. It seems more helpful to see what happened as the displacement of the centers of the Maya world from the lowlands to the plateau. Still, it is mysterious. None of the explanations scholars suggest fit the chronology or the evidence. War is unlikely to have put an end to the lowland tradition. The Maya practiced wars so constantly that warfare must have served a useful purpose in their society. Spells of severe and prolonged drought certainly overlapped with the period of decline but do not seem to have matched it. Political revolutions—rebellions of the masses or struggles within the elite—might have overthrown the regimes. But even if there were direct evidence of such upheavals, we would still need to explain why they occurred at roughly the same time in so many states.

That elite activities ended only in one eco-zone suggests that an environmental explanation should help us understand what happened. The lowlands were always hostile to intensive agriculture and monumental building. In some ways, it is more surprising that such practices should have happened at all, and attained such impressive achievements, than that they should ultimately have failed. To sustain hundreds of cities and what were evidently dense populations, the Maya probably had to exploit their environment close to the limit of its possibilities.

Civilizations of the Americas, ca. 200–1100

ca. 200–900	Flourishing of Moche and Nazca civilizations
ca. 200–1100	Maya Classic Age (lowlands)
1000	Andean city of Tiahuanaco abandoned
ca. 1106–1200	Tula abandoned

TULA For a while, the influence and, in some degree, the power of the central Mexican empire of Teotihuacán stretched into the Maya world. Yet, as we saw in Chapter 8, Teotihuacán itself withered in the eighth and ninth centuries. This vast metropolis—once the center of a population that could probably be numbered in six figures—was never reoccupied, but became something like what we today would call a heritage site: revered and remembered by peoples who imitated its art and recalled its grandeur in their poetry. A new metropolis arose, well to the northwest, at Tula, the "garden of the gods," where blood sacrifices irrigated groves of stone pillars and ceremonial enclosures. The region already had a history of unstable settlement and, by comparison with most earlier Maya cities or with Teotihuacán, Tula did not last long. Its site was abandoned in the twelfth century, but the ruins continued to inspire experiments in urbanization.

Bird claw. Cut from a sheet of mica, this sublime representation of the claw of a hawk or eagle was buried in a chief's grave in what is now Ross County, Ohio, in about 400 C.E. Hands and birds of prey were the symbols most often placed in the graves of the region's chieftains in this period.

The Maize Frontiers

We can sum up all these New World histories of the late first millennium as efforts to open up frontiers of exploitation for intensive agriculture, state formation, and city-building—activities formerly confined to narrowly limited areas and vulnerable to periodic extinction. Hunter–gatherers, too, could engage with their environment in more productive ways. On the northwest coast of North America, houses got bigger as fishhooks got more plentiful and became more specialized. Along the northern edge of America, whale hunters were working their way along the Arctic coast, spreading new hunting and fishing techniques as they went, reaching Greenland by about 1000.

In other parts of the Americas, new crops and new technologies extended farmers' frontiers, sometimes with transforming effects. Between the Missouri and Ohio River valleys, for instance, a large trading network flourished among peoples of similar material culture from about 200 to about 400. They buried their dead with copper earrings and breastplates, clay figures and smoking pipes, and ornaments carved from flat sheets of copper ore in the shape of leaves and claws. They built tombs into mounds of elaborate design: one in Ohio is in the shape of a long, coiling serpent—identifiable from a practically unattainable height, like the artworks of the Nazca in Chile. Sometime after 500, these practices ended; as leadership of society changed, maize cultivation spread through the region, and population grew.

This was the period of the great extension of maize cultivation into regions of North America formerly inhabited almost exclusively by hunter–gatherers, displacing former power groups, coaxing chiefdoms into existence and existing chiefdoms toward statehood. Farmers brought maize and beans into the central plains and, in some places from the Dakotas to the Red River in Canada, built burial mounds and earthworks similar to those found earlier along the Ohio and Missouri Rivers. In some respects, this process looks like another case of a culture not extinguished, but changed and displaced from its former heartland. Maize farming reached the Great Basin of the North American plains, at sites where pottery and rock art were also made for the first time in this period. Beginning after 700, in the North American southwest, where maize had been long established (see Chapter 5), large dwellings of adobe or stone displaced the semiunderground houses in which people formerly sheltered. Villages got larger, building toward the urban network that emerged around 1000 and that is

MAKING CONNECTIONS

EXPANDING STATES OF THE AMERICAS, 200–900

REGION / CULTURE →	ENVIRONMENT →	POLITICAL ORGANIZATION →	ACHIEVEMENTS
South America Moche and Nazca	Desert; adjacent to Pacific Ocean; cool weather; little precipitation; abundant fish; small rivers	Communities governed by elites	Highly developed ceramics, gold/silver work; pottery; elaborate irrigation systems, some underground
Andean highlands (Huari)	Mountainous; glacier-fed streams and lakes; cultivable soil	Empire governing highlands and coast after decline of Moche; administrative centers; satellite towns	Intensive mound agriculture (potatoes); religious centers; road networks
Mesoamerica Maya	Contrasting environments: volcanic highlands of Guatemala; limestone plateau of Yucatán; tropical lowlands	City-states with rulers responsible for war, communication with gods; numerous ceremonial sites	Large-scale cities with monumental architecture; writing system and literature; long-distance trade networks; intensive agriculture, industry fueling population growth
Tula	Highlands with access to rivers, trade routes	City-states with ceremonial enclosures; use of blood sacrifice	Successor to Teotihuacán, largest city-state in Mesoamerica; monumental architecture; intensive irrigation
North America	Wide range of environments from mountains, to forests, deserts, open plains	Primarily chiefdoms, with larger-scale communities in Mississippi, Missouri, Ohio River valleys	As maize agriculture spreads, agricultural populations increase, displacing hunter–gatherer groups; large-scale mounds, tombs mark large population centers

a subject for the next chapter. Meanwhile, in the southeast, the arrival of maize and, by around the year 1000, beans fed the ancestors of the large-scale builders of the early part of the next millennium.

On Marajó Island, in the mouth of the Amazon in Brazil, although there is no evidence of new crops or techniques, people were practicing traditional agriculture with enhanced efficiency in an expanded area. Clusters of villages got denser after the middle of the first millennium, with mounds raised for ceremonies and agriculture. Here, the bones of the elite, boiled of their flesh, were buried in pots with clay representations of female genitals and gifts of beads, axes, and other valuables dependent on rank. Richly decorated burial urns grant glimpses of the creatures of their myths: turtles, scorpions, serpents, and almond-eyed humans.

THE ISLAMIC WORLD AND THE ENVIRONMENT

So cultures widely scattered around the New World showed how basic tool kits or limited new crops could have profound effects. This feature of the period was paralleled in the Old World—especially in the Islamic world. Though Islamic conquests slowed in the eighth century, an even more significant kind of expansion followed it: ecological expansion, as cultivators developed new crops and introduced them to new environments (see Map 10.3). For the desert pastoralists who bore Islam abroad, every frontier was a revelation. When, for example, the follow-

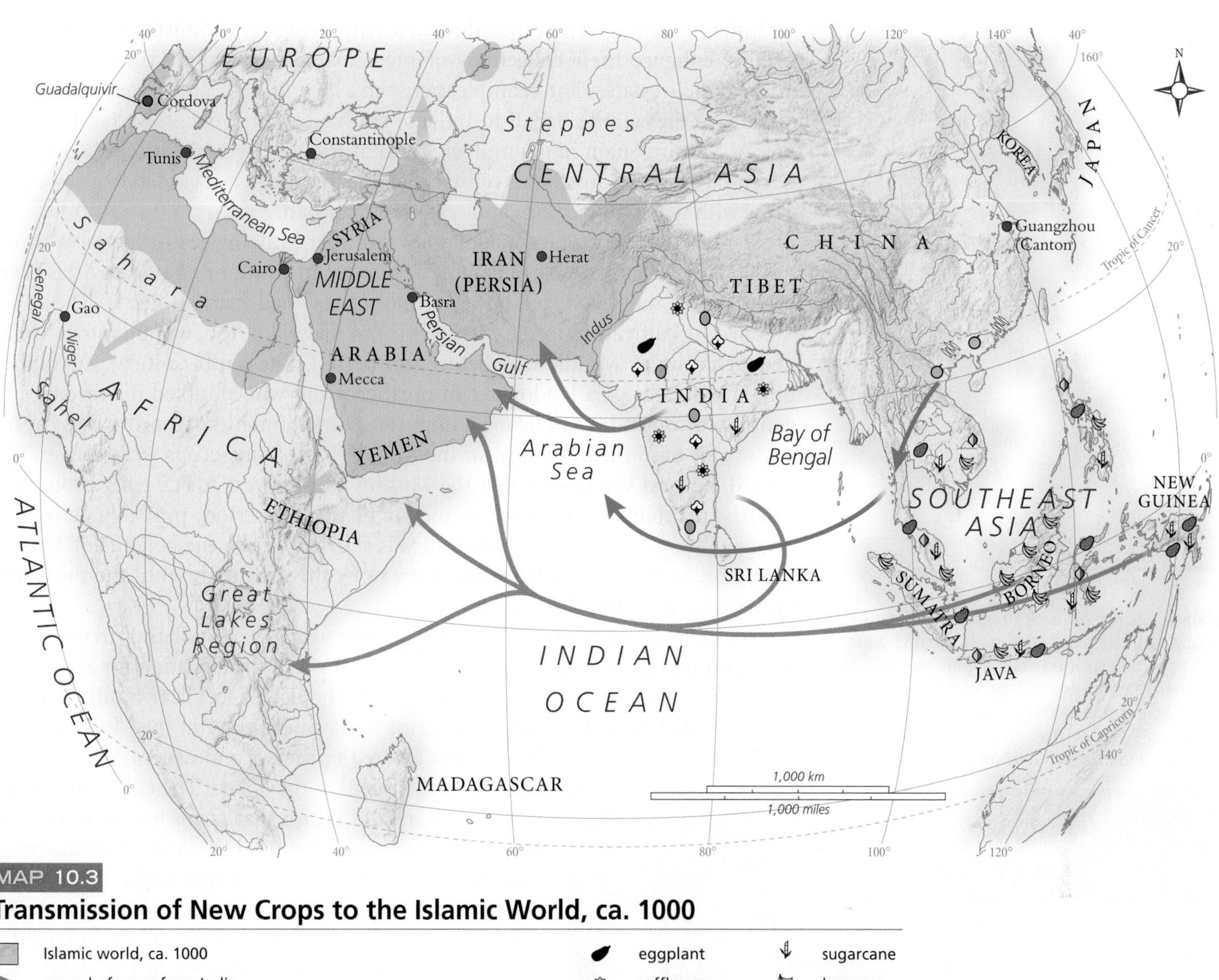

MAP 10.3

Transmission of New Crops to the Islamic World, ca. 1000

- Islamic world, ca. 1000
- spread of crops from India
- spread of crops from South and southeast Asia
- spread of crops from China (by way of southeast Asia/Indian Ocean
- Transmission of crops beyond Islamic frontier
- eggplant
- safflower
- mung bean
- cotton
- lemon/lime
- sugarcane
- bananas
- taro
- orange
- rice

ers of Muhammad captured Basra on the Persian Gulf in what is today Iraq in 637, an eyewitness reported how they found two food baskets that the retreating Persians had abandoned. They ate the basket of dates but assumed the other contained poison, until a horse ate its contents without ill effects. "And their commander said, Pronounce the name of Allah over it and eat. And they ate of it and they found it a most tasty food." It was the Arabs' first taste of rice.

The outreach of Islam was a process of discovery and renaissance in which a great array of new foods was gathered, adapted, and transplanted. The Islamic world extended over the Mediterranean, and touched Sahel, savanna, and tropical forests in sub-Saharan Africa, as well as monsoon lands in Yemen and northwest India, and regions of severe continental climate in Central Asia. The result was an unparalleled opportunity to exchange useful plants and animals among diverse environments.

Rulers encouraged new introductions, employing agronomists to manage their gardens, enhance their collections of medicinal plants, supply their tables, and improve their estates. For example, between 775 and 785, Yahya ibn Khalid led a mission on the caliph's behalf to India to study medicinal drugs. Abd al-Rahman, ruler of Muslim Spain in the mid–eighth century, sent plant collectors to Syria. By the tenth century, Cordova his capital, had, in effect, a special garden to grow exotic plants with fields for cuttings and seeds from abroad.

Plants from the tropics made a new summer growing season possible in the Middle East. Sugarcane, for instance, originated in south or southeast Asia. From India, "a reed that produced honey without bees" had reached Persia. The Arabs extended its cultivation to the Mediterranean. Eggplant, too, was unknown in the Mediterranean or Middle East before this period. The tenth-century geographer, Ibn Hawqal, tells of a landowner in northern Iraq who doubled his revenues by planting cotton and rice. The most important development to improve mass nutrition was of hard durum wheat in the Middle East. Some crops were transmitted onward, beyond the frontiers of the Muslim world. West Africa got cotton, taro, bananas, plantains, sour oranges, and limes in this period, probably across the Sahara. Christian Europe, by contrast, was slow to receive the benefits of Muslim agronomy. Spinach and hard wheat were not cultivated there until the thirteenth century, rice not until the fifteenth.

The new crops required watering during summer, stimulating irrigation by underground tunnels and wells, which led, in turn, to the adoption for agriculture of marginal land. Forest clearance increased. The use of fertilizer multiplied crop yields. Fertile land left uncultivated seems to have been rare in the Muslim world.

Watermill. Increased agricultural output caused demand for more and bigger mills to grind grain. Most have not survived, but a fine example of medieval watermill technology, pictured here, is on the Orontes River at Hama, Syria. Waterwheels on this scale also hoisted water from riverbeds to aqueducts and irrigation channels.

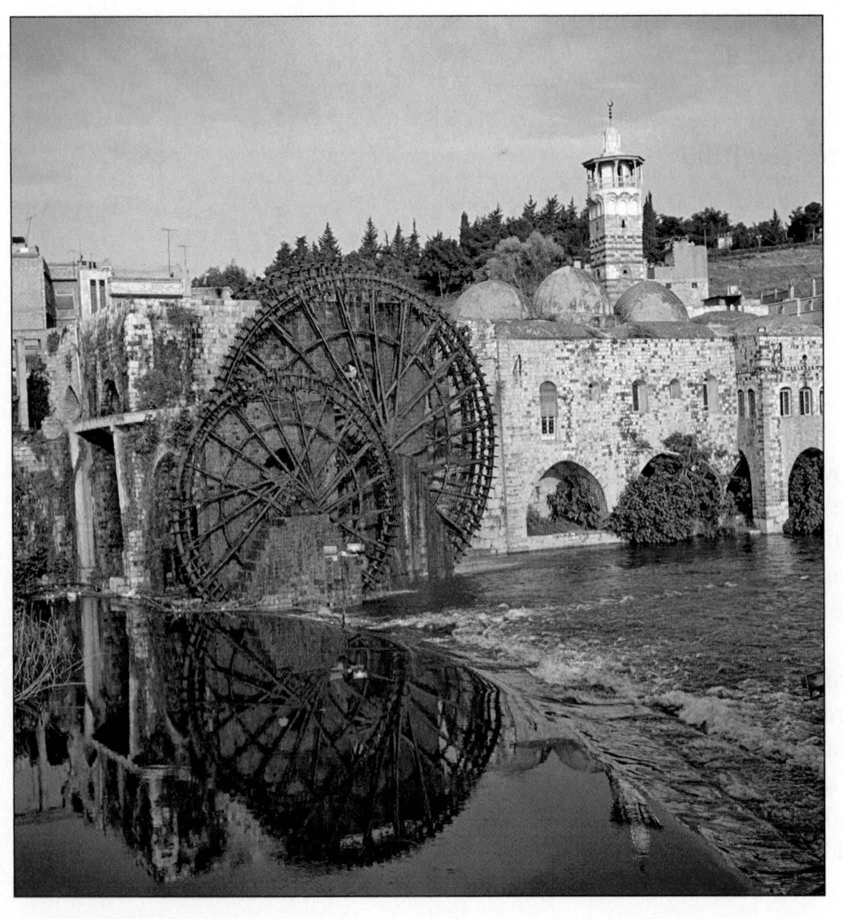

Islamic law favored farmers. Landowners could use and dispose of their land as they liked. The enforcement of a free market in land meant that farms tended to fall into the hands of owners who used them most productively. Tenants acquired farms, as conquest broke up big holdings that had stagnated under the previous regimes. Tax rates in regions under the rule of the caliphs in Baghdad (bag-DAD) were low after reforms in the late eighth century—commonly a tenth of output, with summer crops often being exempted. Villages thrived. There were 12,000 villages along the Guadalquivir (gwahd-ahl-kee-BEER) River in Muslim Spain by the tenth century. Forty-eight thousand square miles were subject to land tax in seventh-century Sawad (sah-WAD) in Syria—virtually the entire cultivable area.

FRONTIER GROWTH IN JAPAN

The vast extent of the Islamic world made this rich environmental history possible. But on a smaller scale, a similar program was possible even in relatively small and isolated Japan. Here, bureaucrats carefully totted up the hostility of the natural world. Between 806 and 1073, official records list 653 earthquakes, 134 fires, 89 cases of damage to crops, 91 epidemics, 356 supernatural warnings (including volcanic eruptions), and 367 appearances by ghosts. They recorded only 185 favorable events in the same period. In the *Nihongi* of the early eighth century, one of the earliest native Japanese chronicles, the rise of the imperial dynasty is linked with the overthrow of Susa-no-o, a god who "brought many people to an untimely end" by "making green mountains wither" and wrecking rice fields. Japanese rulers took seriously their responsibility to regulate their subjects' relations with the natural world. Unlike their counterparts in most other cultures, they did not limit themselves to acts and sacrifices intended to appease the forces of nature. From the early eighth century, they had ambitious environmental policies.

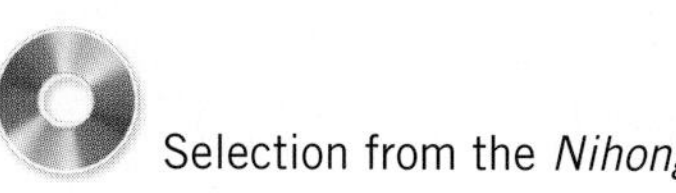

Selection from the *Nihongi*

Some growth in the yield of agriculture would have happened even without state guidance. Rice yields improved thanks to new, labor-intensive techniques in which whole communities cooperated: growing seedlings in nurseries and transplanting them to the fields. Heavy plows arrived from Korea in the fifth century. It is doubtful, however, whether they made much impact until the ninth or tenth century because Japan had little iron to make plows, and most cultivation was on wetlands. Meanwhile, barley gradually replaced millet as the country's second most important crop after rice, with some benefits for nutrition. Population was growing. Census returns show—by global standards—exceptionally large households of an average of ten persons each. Family customs helped. Young mothers commonly spent the first 5 to 15 years of married life in their parents' home, where their husbands visited them. This spread the burden of child care.

The government drive to boost food production was under way by 711, when a decree authorized aristocrats to apply to provincial governors for permission to cultivate virgin land at their own expense. The aim, according to a proclamation of 722, was to add 2.5 million acres to the area devoted to rice production. In the following year, farmers became eligible to inherit newly cultivated fields for three generations if they irrigated those fields from new ditches or ponds. In 743, farmers acquired absolute ownership of such lands.

As well as a state-sponsored, aristocratic enterprise, the conquest of new environments was a preserve of freelance holy men. The most effective of them was the Buddhist monk Gyoki. Traditionalists accused him of embezzling alms, impiously burning the bodies of the dead, and aggressively pursuing converts. But everyone approved of the way he organized his followers to perform public works—building bridges and roads, digging ponds and embankments. The state contracted Gyoki's workers to undertake official projects.

Frontier expansion at the expense of the "barbarians" of Japan's northeast Honshu island increased available land (see Map 10.4). The native Emishi (ah-MEE-shee) were described in terms that seem almost universal among imperial peoples who want to conquer, dispossess, or exterminate others. They were "fierce and wild," dangerous, lacking a recognizable political or legal system. Without chiefs, they "all rob each other. . . . In winter they lodge in holes, in summer they dwell in nests." By 796, the state had settled 9,000 colonists on Honshu to cultivate conquered lands.

By the early ninth century, the state was growing more confident about its ability to manage the environment and keep disaster at bay. After performing a successful rainmaking rite, the hermit Kukai began his song of self-praise with a conventional reflection. Nature, he said, responded to human decadence. "And thus," he continued, "even though it is time for rain to fall, the four horizons are blazing with heat." In such circumstances, the emperor intervenes. He fasts, and orders appropriate rites in all temples. "As the venerable monks chant the sacred scriptures . . . waterfalls gush forth from high peaks and soak wild animals, while rain fills the fields enough to drown water buffaloes. . . . Peasants! Do not lament any more. . . . See the storehouses, where grain piles up like islands, like mountains."

Indian land grants, 753 C.E.

CHINA AND SOUTHEAST ASIA

In Japan, as in the Islamic world, the human assault on the natural frontier had growing state power to back it. But in the same period, similar developments occurred even in politically unstable conditions in China and India. After the collapse of the Gupta empire (see Chapter 9), kingdoms in south India and the Deccan boosted their revenues, reach, and power by granting wasteland to priests, monks, and warriors to promote agriculture. In land grants recorded in forest areas acquired by conquest in the sixth century, monks and holy men are the biggest beneficiaries. This should not be seen merely—or perhaps at all—as evidence of kings' religious priorities but of monasteries' ability to transform the environment.

An inscription on copper, dated 753, shows what happened when a priest received a royal land grant. "We the inhabitants went to the boundaries which the headman of the district pointed out, circumambulated the village . . ., and planted milk-bushes and placed stones around it. . . . The donee shall enjoy the wet land and the dry land included within these four boundaries, wherever the iguana runs and the tortoise crawls, and shall be permitted to dig river channels and inundation channels." The king would receive taxes on these facilities. The inscription also reveals the full range of collective activities that community contributions supported. The settlers made and operated oil presses and looms. They dug wells. They paid taxes to support the king, the district administration, and the priestly caste out of the yield of crops, including water lilies, "the share of the potter," the price of butter and cloth. To the royal court they sent huntsmen, messengers, dancing girls, servants, fodder, cotton, molasses, "the best cow and the best bull," and "the fourth part of the trunks of old trees." Irrigation and double cropping appear in many Indian inscriptions of the following two centuries. Marginal land was coming under the plow.

In China, although the emperors of the early seventh century were unable to sustain a lasting dynasty, they did build a canal system that crisscrossed the country, stimulating the grain trade and improving irrigation. In 624, in Shaanxi province, imperial waterworks irrigated more than 80,000 acres. Meanwhile, large-scale land reclamation proceeded by drainage, as population growth and improving food supply stimulated each other. The policy of the Tang dynasty (see Chapter 8) was usually to break up large landholdings and distribute them among taxpayers. A major land reform of 737 divided great estates among their workers. This encouraged cultivation because peasants farmed their holdings more intensively than large landowners did. It was part of an ideology of imperial benevolence that also established price-regulating granaries where food stocks accumulated at government expense when prices were low for redistribution at a discount when prices were high. The resulting stocks helped cushion disaster in the plague-ravaged, famine-fraught 730s through 740s. Improved rice strains, adapted from varieties of rice that Tang armies brought back from campaigns in Vietnam, helped.

Imperial policy also stimulated the southward shift of settlement into regions, far from the threat of steppeland invasion, where rice grew, with beneficial effects on nutrition and therefore on levels of population. In 730, vagrant families were ordered to agricultural colonies under military discipline. Such proclamations often failed to produce results, but some colonies did take shape under this program, cultivating rice on the Huai River in 734. Although Confucians tended to despise Buddhism and Daoism as superstitious, monasteries were generally encouraged because they could kick start development in underexploited areas. By the mid–eighth century, a third of China's people lived in the Huai and Yangtze River valleys and, by the eleventh century, over half did. As colonization proceeded,

Chinese villages replaced aboriginal populations, which were exterminated, assimilated, or driven into marginal areas. Population figures—statistics untrustworthy anywhere at the time except in China—suggest Tang environmental policies paid off. China had about 50 million people after An Lushan's rebellion in the 750s (see Chapter 8). Its population had grown to 60 million by the year 1000.

The extension of the frontier of settlement and of rice cultivation in southern China was part of a bigger phenomenon, extending over the moist, hot, dense forests of mainland southeast Asia (see Map 10.4). In the sixth century, Chinese geographers located a state they called Chen-la in the interior of what is now Cambodia. This was the first sign we get of an important change under way in the region. Alongside the maritime states, founded on trade that lined the routes from China to India, agrarian kingdoms were growing up, based on rice production.

For centuries small chiefdoms and aspiring states had dotted the lower Mekong River valley, but in the eighth century, the people of the region, the Khmer (k-MER), began to coalesce into a single kingdom, centered at the new city of Angkor (AHNG-kor), on the north shore on the Tonle Sap—a natural reservoir of monsoonal rains. This region had no mines, no great commercial fleets, and no great industries. The wealth of the Khmer derived from a peculiar feature of the Mekong. Swollen by the monsoon, the river becomes, in effect, too heavily charged to empty into the sea through its own delta. The water begins to flow backward, flooding the plain of the Tonle Sap. The soil there is so rich that, provided the waters are well managed and channeled into reservoirs, it yields three rice crops a year. In 802, Angkor became a capital with explicitly imperial pretensions, when King Jayavarman II proclaimed himself monarch of the universe, and priests in his employ performed a ceremony nullifying all former oaths of loyalty.

Similar experiments occurred all over southeast Asia. The growth of the Viet and Cham kingdoms—the other big states that took shape in Indochina in the period—owed something to the traditional wealth of the region in ivory, rhinoceros horn, and aromatic woods, and much to the bureaucracy that arrived with Buddhism. But it was based mainly on taxes from lumber and food, as new fields replaced forests. By the year 1000, a comparable transformation was taking shape in the northwest corner of the region. Here, in the Irawaddy valley on the borders between India and Bangladesh, dry rice cultivation began to transform a near-desert. Meanwhile, offshore, maritime state building shifted toward the Indonesian islands.

Here, in the seventh century, the realm of Srivijaya (sree-vee-JEYE-ah), on the Sumatran coast, impressed the first Chinese sources to notice it. When the pilgrim I-ching (yee-jing) stopped there in 671, the capital had a community of 1,000 Buddhist monks. The court employed Hindu and Buddhist scholars. But the maharajah (mah-ha-RAH-jah), as the sources called the king of Srivijaya, was said to use magic to control the sea, with enchanted crocodiles to guard the mouth of his river.

Srivijaya's economy relied on harbor tolls and the profits of piracy. A river-linked domain behind it supplied it with soldiers and rice, because even trading states needed their own food supplies. Srivijaya had big commercial resources in the form of spices and aromatic woods, but the inhabitants still worked to expand rice production. According to a legend of the foundation of Palembang, the fathers of the city chose its site by weighing the waters of Sumatra's various rivers for silt and finding that those of the Musi would be best for irrigating rice lands. Palembang's earliest inscription, dated 685,

Population of China, 730–1000

730	Vagrant families ordered to resettle in agricultural colonies
734	Rice cultivation on the Huai River
750	China's population is 50 million
Mid-eighth century	One-third of China's population lives in the Huai and Yangtze valleys
1000	China's population is 60 million
Eleventh century	Half of China's population lives in the Huai and Yangtze valleys

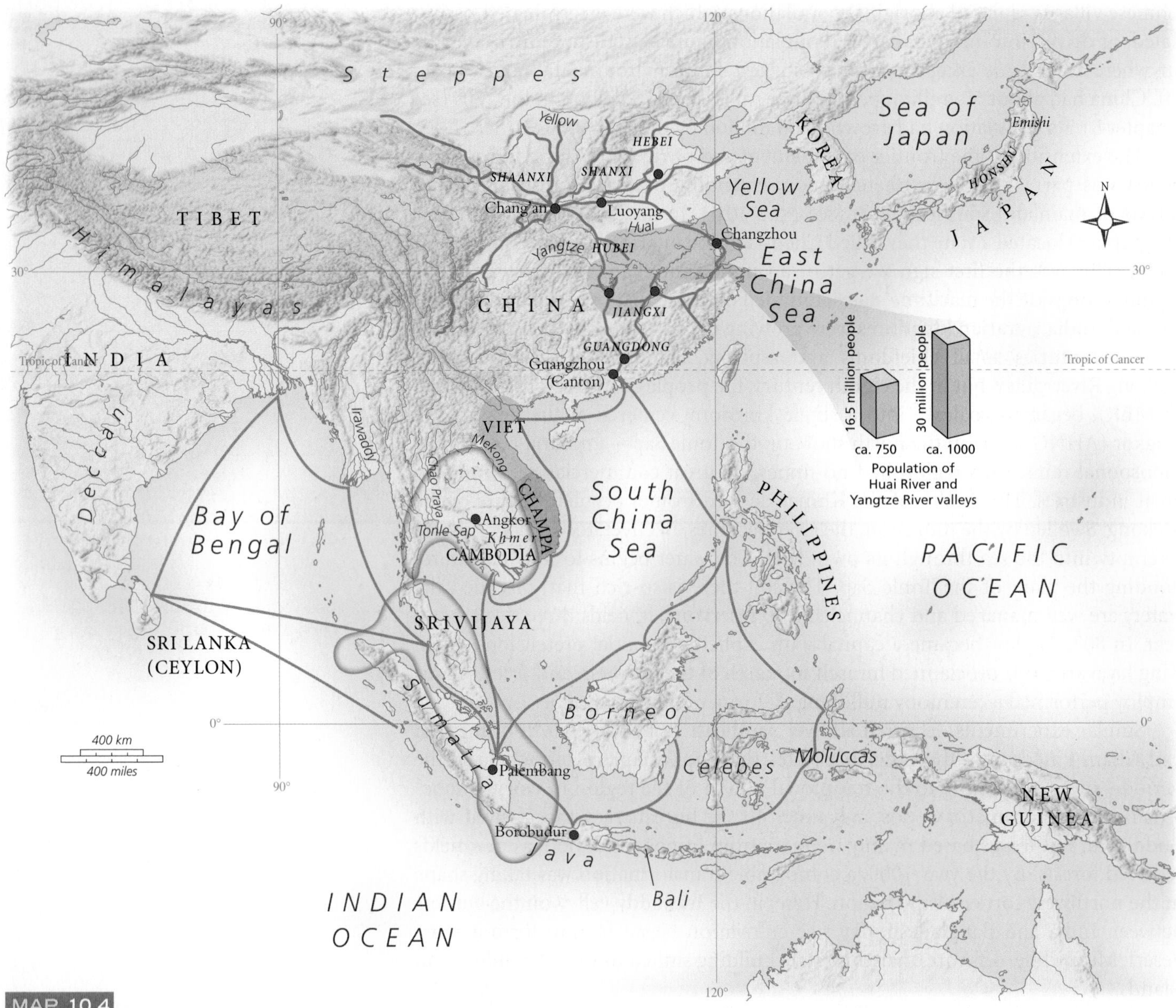

MAP 10.4

China, Japan, and Southeast Asia, ca. 1000

- Huai River and Yangtze River valley
- Champa
- Viet
- Cambodia
- Srivijaya
- maritime trade route
- canal
- *Khmer* people

expresses a king's concern that "all the clearances and gardens his people made should be full, that the cattle of all species raised by them and their bondsmen should prosper."

The capital, where even the parrots spoke four languages, attracted merchants. The maritime strength of Srivijaya was concentrated in the ragged east coast of Sumatra, with its fringe of islands and mangrove swamps, its deep bays and shelters for shipping, its natural coral-reef defenses, its abundant fish and turtles. Its greatness and survival depended on Chinese commerce, especially for its sandalwood and frankincense.

In eighth-century Java, the Sailendra dynasty rivaled Srivijaya. Their huge temple, Borobudur, seemed to proclaim their patrons' privileged access to heaven. Built of half a million blocks of stone, it arose between about 790 and 830. The maritime economy of Sailendra comes to life in the carvings. One of the most

by star. They mapped the ocean's swells—mentally or perhaps with maps made of reeds, of which later examples survive. Eighteenth-century European observers noted that Caroline and Polynesian navigators could literally feel their way around the ocean, identifying their position by the way that waves felt on their own bodies.

Polynesian Expansion

3,000–2,000 years ago	Origins of Polynesian civilization
600	"Takeoff" of Polynesian expansion
ca. 800	Settlement of Hawaii
ca. 1000	Colonization of New Zealand

By about the year 1000, the Polynesians may have gotten close to the limits of navigation accessible to them with the technology at their disposal. Oral traditions recall and presumably embellish their history. The most heroic tale is perhaps that of Hui-te-Rangiora, whose journey from Raratonga in the Cook Islands in the remote Pacific in the mid–eighth century took him through bare white rocks that towered over a monstrous sea, to a place of uninterrupted ice. Myths ascribe the discovery of New Zealand to the godlike Maui, who baited giant stingray with his own blood. A less shadowy figure is the indisputably human Kupe, who claimed that a vision of the supreme god Io guided him to New Zealand from Raratonga. Maybe, however, he just followed the migration of the long-tailed cuckoo birds. His sailing directions were: "Let the course be to the right hand of the setting sun, moon, or Venus in the second month of the year."

THE EXPANSION OF CHRISTENDOM

At the opposite end of Eurasia, in the eighth century, Christendom began to outgrow the frontiers of the Roman Empire. Here conquest was the main agent of change. Christendom developed no new crops or technologies. The heavy plow had long been in use. Rye and barley—the grains suitable for the frost-rimed, dense soils of northern Europe—were ancient crops.

Beyond Rome's farthest northern frontiers, monastic exiles took memories of antiquity into Scotland and Ireland, like the monk Columba, longing to compose his hymns "on a rocky outcrop, overlooking the coiling surface of the sea." A similar—more dangerous—enterprise flickered in Germany, where Boniface traveled from England in 719 to share the gospel with the Saxons. Boniface was martyred around 754, but the task of converting the Saxons was taken up 30 years later, from inside the most dynamic spot on the frontier of Christendom: the kingdom of the Franks.

Two events transformed its ruler, Charlemagne, into the self-styled renovator of Rome. His journey to Italy in 774 opened his eyes to ruined splendors and enabled him to gather books and scholars. From the 790s, he could afford unprecedented ambitions when he captured the treasure of invading steppelanders, the Avars. Taking advantage of the fact that Irene, an empress of dubious legitimacy, ruled in Constantinople, he now proclaimed himself successor of the ancient Roman emperors. While remaining first and foremost a Frankish king, Charlemagne affected what he thought was Roman taste. He appeared on coins in a laurel crown. His seals were stamped with slogans of imperial revival. His court writers, who must have known what he wanted to hear, compared him to Constantine and Justinian (see Chapter 8). The manuscript painters, scribes, and ivory carvers of his palace copied ancient models.

Even before Charlemagne came to the throne, the Frankish realm had incorporated lands beyond the margins of the old empire, especially along the North Sea and in central Germany. Charlemagne's conquest of Saxony in 802, which took 18 years to complete, was the first annexation of a large new

Irish cross. Outside the Roman Empire, Christianity was slow to take root in Europe—except in Scotland and Ireland. Isolation made Irish Christian art highly distinctive. This eighth-century bronze crucifix was probably made to adorn the cover of a gospel book. The artist was apparently concerned to represent scripture authentically—hence, the soldiers who pierce Jesus' side and hoist a sponge to his lips. The angels who perch on the arms of the cross display fragments of what may be intended to represent Christ's shroud, or the cloth used to wipe his face.

province in Europe by a selfconsciously "Roman" empire since the Emperor Trajan had conquered Dacia in the early second century. Saxony became a parade ground of Christendom, converted from an insecure frontier into an imperial heartland.

On Christendom's other exposed flanks, similar expansion made slow progress. In the early ninth century, Mojmir I established a Slav state patterned on Charlemagne's monarchy in Bohemia. In 864, the Bulgar Tsar Boris decided to accept Christianity and impose it on his people. The Bulgars rapidly became like the Franks, rival claimants to the mantle of Rome, under a ruler who called himself "emperor of all the Greeks and Bulgars." Yet if the Bulgar Empire was a threat to Constantinople, it was a bulwark for Christendom against pagan steppelanders from farther east.

Despite an isolated position and scant resources, Asturias in northern Spain in the ninth century successfully defended Christendom's frontier at the opposite end of the Mediterranean. Part of the sacred armory of its kings lies in Oviedo Cathedral—vessels of gold, housing relics from the saints who could have a magical effect on the battlefield. On a hill above the town, Ramiro I could look out on his kingdom from his summer palace, or receive ambassadors in a hall decorated with carvings molded after Persian silverwork from some Roman hoard. By the end of the century, the kingdom began to expand beyond the mountains that screened it to the south.

Exploitation of the shrine attributed to the Apostle James the Great at Compostela gave Asturias advantages over other Christian states in Spain—in pilgrim wealth, monastic colonization, and the chances of recruiting knightly manpower. But a frontier position generally was good for state-building. In the 890s, Wilfrid the Hairy, Count of Barcelona, conquered almost all counties around his own, south of the Pyrenees. Laborious settlement of underpopulated areas is the subject of all the documents that survive from his time. Wilfrid's story was typical of the edges of Christendom. In lands reclaimed from pagan conquest on the northern frontier, in England, Alfred the Great was securing a similar reputation as a state builder by lavish generosity to monks, the custodians of the historical record. By 924, Alfred's heirs had completed their reconquest of northern and eastern England. The extension or restoration of the frontier of Christendom was pushing Europe outward.

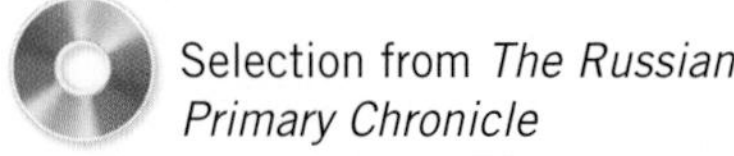

Selection from *The Russian Primary Chronicle*

At the same time, a secular political tradition was being spread even farther afield. Christianity, as we saw in the last chapter, was barely beginning to penetrate Scandinavia, which—in terms of the colonists it generated, the new lands it explored—was the most dynamic part of Europe. A letter from the northern Russian city of Novgorod is said to have reached a Viking prince in 862. "Our land," it read, "is great and rich. But there is no order in it. Come and rule us." In response, he founded the state that eventually became Russia. The story shows how territorial statehood was exported, far beyond the limits of the old Roman Empire, to northern and eastern Europe. Meanwhile, Scandinavian expansion was also going on northward, spreading the frontiers of farming and statehood within its own peninsula, and turning seaward, colonizing Iceland.

IN PERSPECTIVE: The Limits of Divergence

On the face of it, sub-Saharan Africa and the Americas seem to diverge from Eurasia and North Africa from the eighth century to the end of the millennium. In Christendom, Islam, China, southeast Asia, and the western and central Pacific, states came and went, but economies and civilizations were robust—extending frontiers, colonizing new areas, founding new states and empires, or reviving old ones. These regions seem to have bucked the patterns detected by traditional historiography: to have endured beyond periods of decline and fall. At first glance, the contrast with sub-Saharan Africa looks glaring. Ethiopia's dark age really was dark, in the sense that we know virtually nothing about it. Ghana's frustration, and the absence of any evidence of comparable state-building initiatives elsewhere, confirm the traditional picture of a region—like far northern Asia or Australia—about which historians of the period can find almost nothing to say. The myth of Maya collapse has long dominated the way we conventionally think of the Americas in this period as a hemisphere where it was more usual for civilizations to perish than to grow outward or renew themselves. This is an exaggeration—perhaps even a caricature. But there is something in it. Teotihuacán, the Moche, the Nazca, the lowland Maya, Huari, Tiahuanaco—these casualties of the era were replaced, if at all, by unstable successors.

Nevertheless, a theme that, if not quite global, genuinely embraces the Old and New Worlds underlies the apparent differences between them. Broadly stated, this was a period of unusual ecological experiment: the exploration or conquest of new environments. In some cases, new frontiers were breached by expansion into neighboring regions and already-familiar environments, like those of the Islamic world or southeast Asia or most of Christendom. In others, like the Caroline Islands or the Scandinavian expansion, apparently unprecedented adventures were launched from origins that present knowledge cannot adequately explain. In others again, as in China and Japan, internal colonization adapted and transformed previously underexploited wastelands. In others, such as the Andes, central Mexico, and the Maya world, the centers of activity were displaced to new environments—the limestone hills of Tula or Yucatán, the almost incredibly high altitude of Tiahuanaco. In others, which remain necessarily underrepresented in history books because of the absence of evidence, the business of locating resources, developing foodstuffs, and improving production techniques continued without leaving much trace in the record. In the 800s and 900s, for instance, all we have is linguistic evidence for two enormously important developments in the ecology of East Africa. An explosion of new terms shows that banana cultivation and cattle breeding spread inland from the Indian Ocean coast to the Great Lakes of Central Africa. Against this background, the history of the next three centuries, which is the subject of the next part of the book, becomes intelligible. Vibrancy and innovativeness, which became characteristic of most of these regions—and of others where

CHRONOLOGY

(All dates are C.E.)

200–400	Flourishing of mound-building culture in eastern North America
600	"Takeoff" of Polynesian expansion
750	China's population reaches 50 million
754	Martrydom of Boniface
Third through tenth centuries	Maya Classic Age
Seventh through tenth centuries	Ecological expansion of Islam
Eighth century	Government drive to boost food production in Japan
Eighth through ninth centuries	Decline of Ethiopia
790–830	Construction of Borobodur temple, Java
ca. 800	Settlement of Hawaii
ca. 802	Charlemagne completes conquest of Saxony
ca. 860	Scandinavians begin colonization of Iceland
ca. 1000	Andean city of Tiahuanaco abandoned; China's population reaches 60 million
1100s	Tula abandoned

the evidence only begins to mount up from this point onward—grew out of painstaking efforts to find new, more productive ways to exploit the environment.

The story of the last few centuries of the first millennium C.E. suggests an important point about how history happens. In the past, the search for patterns that help to explain it has driven historians to grotesque oversimplifications: seeing history as a continuous story of "progress" or decline; or representing it as a kind of swing between revolutions and counterrevolutions, or between decadence and dynamism, or between dark ages and rebirths. The reality, it seems, as we get to learn more about the past, is much more subtle and intriguing. At one level, the slow growth of compatible changes—what historians' jargon sometimes calls "structures"—gradually gave the world a new look. Simultaneously, and often with contradictory effect, random or short-term changes stimulate, impede, interrupt, or temporarily reverse those trends, and—sometimes—permanently deflect or end them. So both continuity and discontinuity tend to be visible in the story, pretty much all the time. A picture that omits either is almost certain to be distorted.

In these respects, history is like climate, in which many cycles of varying duration all seem to be going on all the time, and where random or almost-random changes frequently intervene. With increasing intensity in recent years, historians have struggled to match changes in the human record to knowledge of how these cycles and changes have interacted since the end of the Ice Age. As we are about to see, some of the most remarkable insights to have emerged from this quest illuminate worldwide changes that began—or that we can first begin to detect—around 1,000 years ago.

PROBLEMS AND PARALLELS

1. What were new ways of managing the environment during the late first millennium? How did societies exploit new resources and colonize new lands?
2. What role did geography play in impeding the diffusion of culture and crops in sub-Saharan Africa and the Americas?
3. What factors contributed to the flourishing of South American and Mesoamerican cultures and states?
4. What were the effects of environmental expansion under Islam?
5. How were monks and holy men important to the conquest of new environments and the expansion of states?
6. What was the importance of ecological experiment and the conquest of new environments in Christendom, China, southeast Asia, and the Pacific in the late first millennium?

DOCUMENTS IN GLOBAL HISTORY

- Selection from the *Nihongi*
- Indian land grants, 753 C.E.
- Nineteenth-century description of Lelu, Caroline Islands
- Selection from *The Russian Primary Chronicle*

Please see the Primary Source DVD for additional sources related to this chapter.

READ ON

The written sources on West Africa are collected in J. F. P. Hopkins and N. Levtzion, eds., *Corpus of Early Arabic Sources for West African History* (2000).

J. Diamond, *Guns, Germs, and Steel* (2003) sets out the case for the isolating effects of American geography.

On the Moche, G. Bawden, *The Moche* (1996) is standard. For the Nazca, A. F. Aveni, *Nazca: Eighth Wonder of the World* (2000) is useful. B. Fagan, *Floods, Famines, and Emperors* (1999) is a lively romp through the history of the effects of El Niño. For Tiahuanaco, A. Kolata, *Tiwanaku and Its Hinterland* (1996), 2 vols., is exhaustive. R. Keatinge, ed., *Peruvian Prehistory* (1988) collects important essays on the Andean background. On the Maya, M. Coe, *The Maya* (2005), and N. Hammond, *Ancient Maya Civilization* (1982) are the most useful overviews. The exhibition catalog by L. Schele and M. Miller, *The Blood of Kings* (1992), is important for understanding royal rituals. D. Webster, *The Fall of the Ancient Maya* (2002) is a brilliant and provocative study of the crisis of the ninth and tenth centuries. On Copán in particular, W. Fash, *Scribes, Warriors, and Kings* (1993) is a vivid and engaging study. On Tula, R. A. Diehl, *Tula* (1983) is authoritative. On Marajó and related topics, the exhibition catalog by C. McEwan et al., *Unknown Amazon* (2001), contains a wealth of exciting data.

For maize, see W. C. Gallinat, "Domestication and Diffusion of Maize," in R. I. Ford, ed., *Prehistoric Food Production in North America* (1985).

A. M. Watson, *Agricultural Innovation in the Early Islamic World* (1983) is the standard work on Islam's agrarian revolution in this period. K. W. Butzer, *Archaeology as Human Ecology* (1982) is classic, and D. W. Phillipson, *African Archaeology* (1994) is a survey by the leading living expert on Ethiopia.

The Cambridge History of Japan (1993) is unsurpassed on Japanese environmental history in this period.

R. Thapar, *Early India* (2004) and B. Chattopadhyaya, *Aspects of Rural Society and Settlements in Early Medieval India* (1990), and *The Making of Early Medieval India* (1994) are the best works to consult on environmental aspects of Indian history at the time.

M. Elvin, *The Retreat of the Elephants* (2004) is a sparkling historical study of the Chinese environment, focusing on the history of deforestation, about which there is much, too, in N. K. Menzies, "Forestry," in J. Needham, ed., *Science and Civilisation in China*, vi (2000). *The Cambridge History of China*, iii (1979) is fundamental for Chinese history generally in this period.

On Angkor, the classic by G. Coedes, *Angkor, An Introduction* (1986) remains fundamental, supplemented now by the ingenious work of E. Mannika, *Angkor Wat: Time, Space, Kingship* (1996). M. D. Coe, *Angkor and the Khmer Civilization* (2005) is of special interest from a comparative point of view, as the author is a Mayanist. On southeast Asia generally, D. G. E Hall, *A History of South-East Asia* (1981) and the same author's contribution to *The Cambridge History of South-East Asia*, i (2000) are important.

On the Pacific, important contributions are collected in P. V. Kirch and T. L. Hunt, eds., *Historical Ecology in the Pacific Islands* (1997). P. V. Kirch, *On the Road of the Winds* (2001) is immeasurably helpful. P. Bellwood, *The Polynesians* (1987) is a useful introduction. The classic by B. Malinowski, *Argonauts of the Western Pacific* (1984) can still be read for pleasure and profit.

On Christendom, useful essays are collected in the forthcoming series, edited by F. Fernández-Armesto and J. Muldoon, *The Expansion of Christendom: The Middle Ages*, especially in my volume, "The Internal Frontier." C. Wickham, *The Mountains and the City* (1988), and R. Bartlett, *The Making of Europe* (1994) are fundamental.

PART Five

Contacts and Conflicts, 1000 C.E. to 1200 C.E.

CHAPTER 11 Contending with Isolation: ca. 1000–1200 262

CHAPTER 12 The Nomadic Frontiers: The Islamic World, Byzantium, and China, ca. 1000–1200 286

The World Map of Al-Idrisi, a Muslim geographer who worked in Christian-ruled Sicily in the mid–twelfth century. He tried to follow the advice of the ancient Greek geographer, Ptolemy, and constructed his map on a grid. South is at the north. The shape of Arabia is clearly recognizable to a modern eye (upper center), as is that of Spain at the extreme right.

ENVIRONMENT

1000–1300
North Atlantic warm spell

1000–1200
Transfer of crops from south and southeast Asia to Islamic world

CULTURE

ca. 1000
Tale of Genji (Japan)

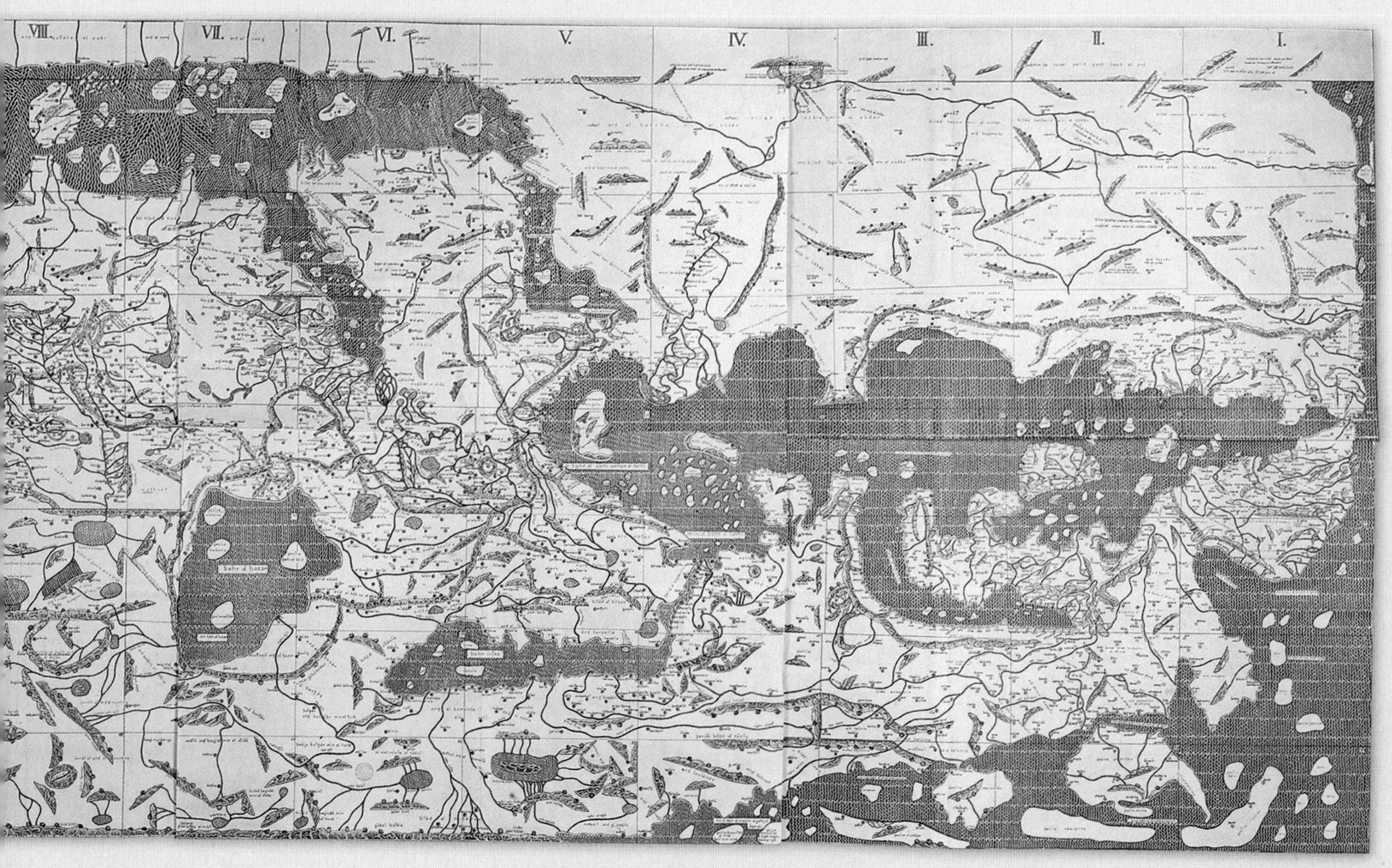

1040s–1090
Increased steppelander migrations into Middle East

ca. 1070–1122
Chola maritime expansion

900–1200
Growing population, especially in Europe and China

1098
First Crusade

ca. 1125
Angkor Wat

1000–1200
Spread of Islam to West Africa

ca. 1200
Cahokia, height of Mississippian mound building

CHAPTER 11 Contending with Isolation: ca. 1000–1200

The pilgrimages of Buddhist monks inspired Japanese stories about the ferocity of the sea. One of the most popular tales in the late twelfth and early thirteenth centuries was about Gisho, a monk who renounced the love of a beautiful woman and set sail for Korea. But in the incident depicted here, she followed him and flung herself into the sea, where, transformed into a dragon, she protected him from storms.
Tokyo National Museum, Photographer: Kanai Morio/DNP Archives.

IN THIS CHAPTER

AMERICAN DEVELOPMENTS: FROM THE ARCTIC TO MESOAMERICA
Greenland and the North
The North American Southwest and the Mississippi Region
Mesoamerica

AROUND THE INDIAN OCEAN: ETHIOPIA, THE KHMER, AND INDIA
East Africa: The Ethiopian Empire
Southeast Asia: The Khmer Kingdom
India: Economy and Culture
India: The Chola Kingdom

EURASIA'S EXTREMITIES: JAPAN AND WESTERN EUROPE
Japan
Western Europe: Economics and Politics
Western Europe: Religion and Culture

IN PERSPECTIVE: The Patchwork of Effects

The farewells lasted "all day and into the night." Aboard ship, the travelers prayed for a peaceful crossing. When the clouds cleared, before dawn, "oars pierced the moon's reflection." Winds lashed. Typhoons threatened. Pirates lurked. The voyagers appealed to the gods by flinging tokens, charms, and cupfuls of rice wine into the sea. They even sacrificed jewels and precious mirrors. It was a routine journey along the coast of Japan in the year 936. The governor of Kochi was on his way home to the capital city of Kyoto.

A journal that the governor's wife, the "Tosa lady," supposedly wrote recorded the journey. Despite dramatizations and fictional conventions, the sailing conditions she described were true to life. The coast was so strewn with dangers that sailors dared not sail at night, except to elude pirates. Unpredictable head winds kept the voyagers cowering in harbor. The journey from Tosa to the port of Osaka can hardly have covered more than 400 miles, yet it took nearly three months. Hostile seas penned in the Japanese, despite their skill in nautical technology. This fact helps to explain why, for most of their history, the Japanese have been confined in their own islands, despite considering themselves an empire.

In other parts of the world, however, long-range navigations were leaping oceans. In the time the Tosa Lady took to sail to Osaka, an Indian Ocean trader, with the benefit of the reversible wind system, could get from the Persian Gulf to Sumatra: a distance of more than 5,000 miles. One Persian captain made the journey to China and back to Persia seven times. The Japanese could only imagine such journeys. Not long after the Tosa diarist wrote, a fanciful Japanese sea story told of a ship—a "hollow tree"—blown by accident nonstop from Japan to Persia.

Pilgrim traffic to Mecca also stimulated Indian Ocean navigation, as Muslim merchant communities spread across Asia and Muslim holy men made converts. Meanwhile, beyond the range of the monsoon, migrants from what is now Indonesia crossed the ocean across the path of the southeast trade winds and colonized Madagascar, off the east coast of Africa. Meanwhile, Polynesian navigators were penetrating deep into the Pacific Ocean with the aid of some of the world's most regular long-range winds (see Chapter 10). Even more remarkably, around the year 1000, Thule Inuit from the Pacific and Norse from Scandinavia crossed the Arctic and Atlantic Oceans from opposite directions and met in Greenland.

FOCUS questions

- HOW DID geography influence the spread of culture and state-building in North America and Mesoamerica?
- WHY WAS the Indian Ocean so important for the spread of culture?
- WHY WERE the land routes across Eurasia less significant than the sea routes across the Indian Ocean?
- WHICH AREAS of India were most prosperous in the tenth and eleventh centuries and what was the basis of their prosperity?
- HOW DID their relative cultural isolation affect Japan and Western Europe during these centuries?

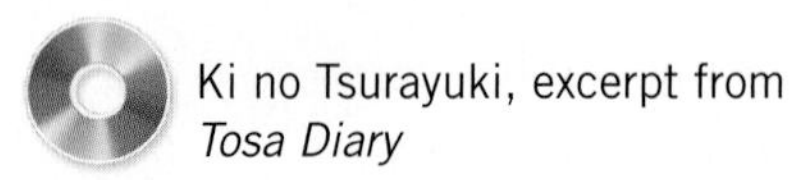
Ki no Tsurayuki, excerpt from the *Tosa Diary*

These extraordinarily long-range migrations were part of a double dynamic, as people stretched the resources available to them to explore for new resources and exploit existing opportunities in new ways. Region by region, culture by culture, in this chapter and the next, we can see people in widely separated parts of the world using similar strategies: felling forests, extending areas of cultivation and pasture, expanding into new terrain, enhancing muscle power with new technologies.

In the eleventh and twelfth centuries, these forms of expansion were widespread themes of world history, but they followed divergent courses in different regions. As was so often the case, relative isolation was usually the key to the difference between long-lasting innovation and faltering, short-lived change. Cultures that exchanged information and artifacts were relatively robust. Peoples isolated from fruitful contacts found it much harder. In the Americas, therefore, as so often before, experiments in new ways of life were arrested by checks, frustrated by failures, interrupted by discontinuities. Meanwhile, however, some parts of the Old World, where long-range contacts were easier and more frequent, experienced enduring transformations.

The new opportunities arose partly from the environmental changes of the preceding centuries, described in the last chapter. To see how people responded, we can devote this chapter to a world tour of some of the regions most affected—starting in the Americas, before turning to the shores of the Indian Ocean, including the parts of East Africa that face that ocean, and ending with the extremities of Eurasia in Japan and Western Europe. In these parts of the world, societies struggled against isolation with varying degrees of success.

In other regions of Africa and Eurasia—China, Central Asia, West Africa, the Byzantine Empire, and the Islamic world—the single most important source of new pressures for change arose from the stirrings of nomadic peoples. These are the subject of the next chapter.

AMERICAN DEVELOPMENTS: FROM THE ARCTIC TO MESOAMERICA

The history of the Americas in the eleventh and twelfth centuries is scattered with stories of new frontiers, developed by new migrations or new initiatives.

Greenland and the North

About 1,000 years ago, a relatively warm spell disturbed the lives of ice hunters along North America's Arctic edge. Taking advantage of improved conditions for hunting and navigating, migrants worked their way across the southern edge of the Arctic Ocean. The Thule (TOO-lee) Inuit, as archaeologists call them, traveled in vessels made of walrus hides stretched across wooden ribs that were so shallow they could hug the shore, and so light that the voyagers could lift them from between ice floes.

The Thule hunted at sea for whales and polar bears. They mounted their harpoons on floats made from seal bladders, which they blew up like balloons. Game

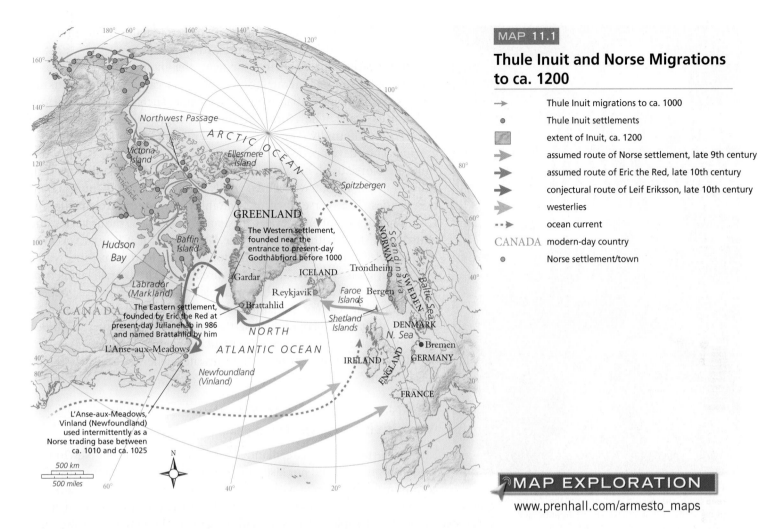

MAP 11.1

Thule Inuit and Norse Migrations to ca. 1200

- Thule Inuit migrations to ca. 1000
- Thule Inuit settlements
- extent of Inuit, ca. 1200
- assumed route of Norse settlement, late 9th century
- assumed route of Eric the Red, late 10th century
- conjectural route of Leif Eriksson, late 10th century
- westerlies
- ocean current
- CANADA modern-day country
- Norse settlement/town

MAP EXPLORATION
www.prenhall.com/armesto_maps

could then be towed home. On land, they hunted with dogs of a breed new to North America. For warfare against human enemies, they reintroduced the bow and arrow (see Chapter 1). By about 1000, they had reached Greenland and the western extremities of North America (see Map 11.1). The navigation of the Arctic was an astonishing feat, not repeated until the twentieth century.

At the same time, almost equally heroic migrations were under way in the opposite direction, toward the same destinations, across the North Atlantic. Exploitable currents helped navigators from Scandinavia cross the ocean, via Iceland, below the Arctic Circle. It seems extraordinarily daring to risk such a long journey across the open sea, without chart or compass, but the Scandinavians knew that the prevailing winds blew from the west in the latitudes they inhabited. So they could always hope to get home. The voyagers probably judged their latitude by observing the polestar with the naked eye on cloudless nights. By day, the only technical aid they had, as far as we know, was a stump of wood with a protruding stick. The shadow it cast would tell the navigator whether his latitude had changed.

Excerpt from *Speculum Principis*, "The Animal Life of Greenland and the Character of the Land in Those Regions"

Whereas the Thule Inuit were drawn by the fat-rich foods of the Arctic, the Norse—or Northmen—as the Atlantic voyagers are called, were usually escapees or exiles from poverty or restricted social opportunity. "As to your enquiry what people go to seek in Greenland and why they fare thither through such great perils," said a medieval

The Norse and Thule Inuit

900–1100	Warm spell in Arctic
ca. 986	Founding of Brattahlid
ca. 1000	Thule Inuit reach Greenland
1189–1200	Construction of cathedral at Gardar

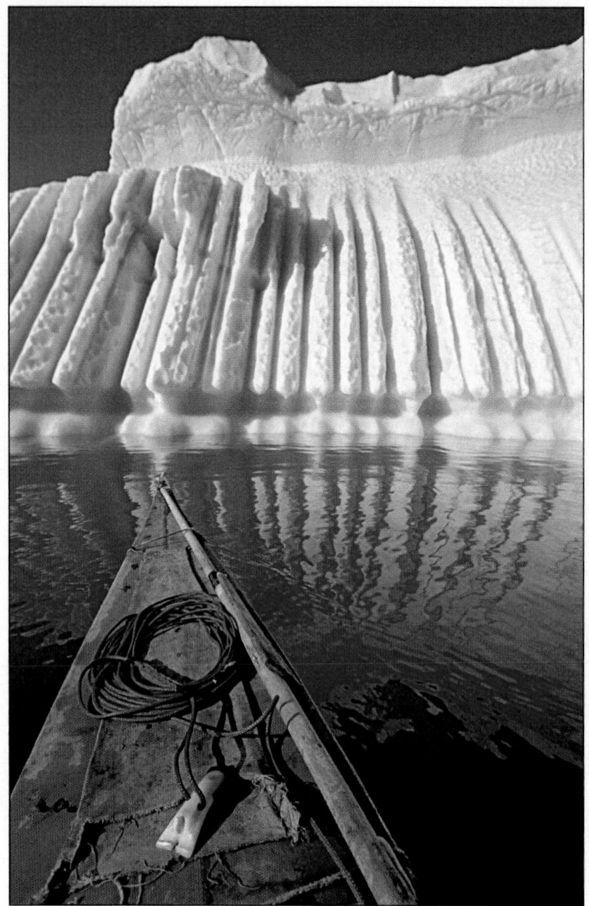

Inuit seacraft European technology was unable to make a ship that could sail around the Arctic coast of North America between the Atlantic and the Pacific until 1904. But the Thule Inuit accomplished the task with hide-covered craft by about 1000 C.E. Their boats were shallow enough to hug the shore, light enough to hoist onto the ice, and buoyant enough to avoid being crushed by ice floes.

Norwegian book, the answer is "in man's threefold nature. One motive is fame, another curiosity, and the third is lust for gain."

In the early years of their settlement, the environment, harsh as it was, had a lot to offer the newcomers: fish and game, including luxury items valuable as potential exports to Europe, such as hunting falcons and walrus ivory. The Norse, however, changed the environment of Greenland profoundly. They introduced grain and European grasses for grazing. They developed sheep whose wool was prized. The big wooden ships the Norse used, held together with iron nails, in a land with little timber or iron, must have seemed wildly extravagant to the Inuit in their skin canoes. The Norse town of Brattahlid in western Greenland—the remotest outpost of medieval Christendom—had 17 monasteries and churches of stone with bells of bronze. The cathedral at Gardar was built between 1189 and 1200, of red sandstone and molded soapstone, with a bell tower, glass windows, and three fireplaces. The largest farms supported an aristocratic way of life, with big halls in which to feast dependents. But the colony remained precarious and isolated. Adam of Bremen, a learned geographer of the late eleventh century, confided what little he knew: "Greenland is situated far out in the ocean. . . . The people there are greenish from the saltwater, whence, too, that region gets its name."

The North American Southwest and the Mississippi Region

The shore station that Greenlanders or Icelanders set up in Newfoundland in about 1000 did not last. There were not enough wealthy or settled communities in the area with which the Norse could establish trade and cultural exchange. A glance at the map of North America at the time shows similar cases, deep inland, of peoples struggling with isolation. The new way of life traveled along two routes: from the heartlands of maize in what is now Mexico, into the arid lands of the North American Southwest; and from the Gulf of Mexico into the wetlands of the Mississippi valley and the United States' Deep South. The results included the rise of cultures with similarities to predecessors in Mesoamerica (see Chapter 4), with urban life, irrigation, elaborate ceramics and shellcraft, gold and copper work, ball games, and unmistakable signs of statehood (see Map 11.2).

In parts, for instance, of what are now Colorado, New Mexico, and Arizona, evidence of a political network is spread over 57,000 square miles: from high in the drainage area of the San Juan River in the north to beyond the Little Colorado River in the south, and from the Colorado River to the Rio Grande. A system of roadways, up to 12 yards wide, radiated from a cluster of sites around the great canyon near the source of the Chaco River. Only two needs can account for such an elaborate network. Either some ritual was being enacted, demanding close ties between the places linked; or the roads were there to move armies.

The environment is parched and—one would think—unsuitable for settled life. Apart from turquoise, which became the basis of trade, natural wealth was scarce. But the region was densely settled, at least in patches. The canyon people built ambitious cities or ceremonial centers around irregular plazas, surrounded by massive outer walls. The main buildings were of stone, faced with fine masonry. Roofs were made of great timbers from pine forests in the hills—a dazzling show of wealth and power in a treeless desert. To construct the ceremonial center at Chaco Canyon, 200,000 trees were felled. We do not know what the political system was.

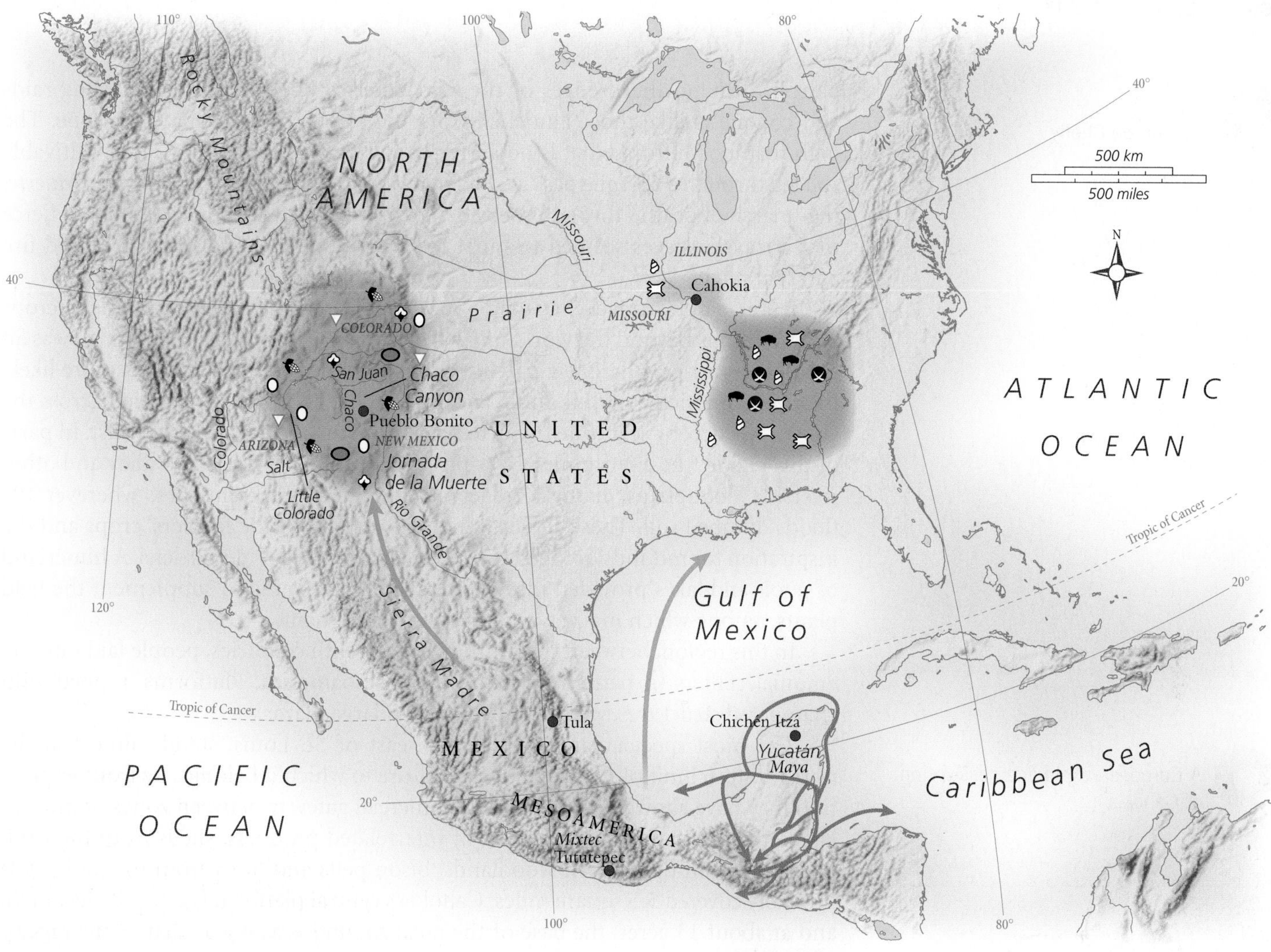

MAP 11.2

North America and Mesoamerica to ca. 1200

- canyon cultures
- major city or ceremonial center
- Mississippian cultures
- city associated with Mississippian peoples
- roads leading north from Mesoamerica
- sea route from Mesoamerica to Mississippi River valley
- Mayan trade route
- *Mixtec* peoples
- ARIZONA modern-day state

Economic Basis of Canyon People

- maize
- beans
- cotton
- irrigation
- turquoise

Mississippian Trade Goods

- seashells
- deerskins
- bison pelts
- horn

But we know it was tough. Mass executions have left piles of victims' bones, crushed, split, and picked as if at a cannibal feast.

The economic basis of this civilization was fragile. If water could be delivered to the fields, cotton, maize, and beans would grow predictably, without danger from the fluctuating temperatures that threatened at higher altitudes. Long irrigation canals did the job.

But from the twelfth century onward, the climate got drier, putting the irrigation system under constant strain. The rulers of the canyon people responded by expanding into new zones, building more ambitiously, organizing labor more ferociously. But decline, punctuated by crisis, shows through a series of periodic contractions of the culture area and reorganizations of the settlements. Meanwhile, the harsh peacekeeping methods seem to have stopped working. Settlements withdrew to defensible locations. The problems of isolation defeated or limited all attempts to revive a similar way of life until the nineteenth century.

The canyon cultures were as remote from Mesoamerican civilizations as the Norse of Greenland were from Europe. Roads north from Mesoamerica led across dangerous territory. Nomadic peoples

Canyon de Chelly

patrolled the northern edges of the Mesoamerican culture area, practicing raids and conquests, like those launched from the steppes into China or Europe. The high road north from what is now Mexico to the nearest patch of easily cultivable soil led through a 61-mile pass known in modern times as the *Jornada de la Muerte*: the "march of death," through rocky defiles and dunes where the glare was so fierce that a traveler's eyes seemed to burst from their sockets, and men "breathed fire and spat pitch."

It was hard to travel that road—harder still to transmit Mesoamerican crops and traditions beyond the world of Chaco Canyon. The prairie, though flat, was an ecological barrier, where few patches could sustain sedentary life. It is more likely that Mesoamerica's tool kit, food, and ways of life and thought traveled across the Gulf of Mexico, by seaborne trade, to reach the North American Southeast. In parts of this region, the environment was promising. In the Mississippi valley and other riverside floodplains, natural ridges accumulated over centuries, wherever the floods dumped soil. These ridges were the nurseries of the farmers' crops and the inspiration for mounds dredged from the swamps to provide gardens. A hinterland of pools and lakes provided ideal centers for fish farming to supplement the field plants, among which maize was increasingly dominant.

In this region, between the ninth and thirteenth centuries, people laid out ceremonial centers in patterns like those of Mesoamerica. Platforms, topped with chambered structures, were grouped around large plazas.

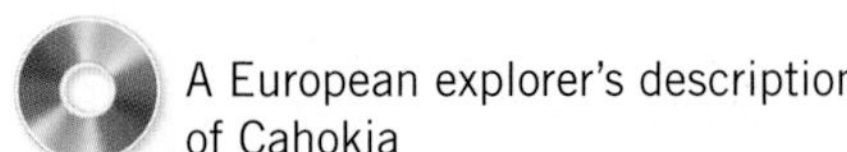
A European explorer's description of Cahokia

The most spectacular site, Cahokia, east of St. Louis, stands almost at the northwestern limit of the reach of the culture to which it belongs. Its frontier position may have allowed it to act as a commercial gateway between zones of interrelated environments and, therefore, of interrelated products: shells from the Gulf, deerskins from the eastern woodlands, bison pelts and horn from the prairies. It probably covered 5.5 square miles. Cahokia's central platform is over 100 feet high, and at about 13 acres, the base of the great mound is as big as that of the biggest Egyptian pyramid.

The city arose in the tenth century. At its height, in about 1200, Cahokia probably had about 10,000 inhabitants in its built-up area. It was the most intensely and elaborately constructed of a great arc of mound clusters from St. Louis to the easternmost edges of the Mississippi floodplain. Smaller, similar sites extend from the riverbanks to the uplands of Illinois and Missouri. Cahokia's size and air of importance tempt some scholars to think of it as something like the capital of something like a state, or, at least, a cultural center from which influence radiated.

Graves at Cahokia have given up honored dead. Their treasures included tools and adornments of copper, bones, and tortoiseshell covered in copper. One grave had gold and copper masks. Thousands of seashells from the Gulf of Mexico must have possessed the highest imaginable status in this inland place. As time went on, finely made stone arrowheads were buried in elite graves. This is a precious clue to how Cahokian culture changed but is hard to interpret. Were the arrows trophies of success in war or hunting, or simple counters of wealth? In any case, the arrows were aristocratic possessions in a society graded for status and equipped for conflict. When Cahokia lost political power in the thirteenth century, the place retained a sacred aura: Its manufactures—pots, shell work, soapstone carvings, and small axe heads—circulated for centuries after the mound dwellers died out or dispersed.

North America and Mesoamerica, 10th to 13th Centuries

Tenth century	Flourishing of canyon culture in American Southwest; founding of Cahokia in Mississippi River valley; founding of Chichén Itzá in Mesoamerica
Eleventh century	Mixtec first appear in historical record
1063–1125	Life of Eight-Deer Tiger-Claw
ca. 1100	Climate in American Southwest gets progressively drier
Eleventh–twelfth centuries	Maya intensively exploit Yucatán peninsula
ca. 1150	Canyon settlements withdraw to higher ground
1200	Cahokia population reaches 10,000
ca. 1300	Decline of upper Mississippi valley culture sites

When objects of great value are concentrated without evidence of a dwelling, grave, or warehouse, it is tempting to talk of a temple. An impressive cache of this type, found at a site southeast of Cahokia, contains carvings that give us glimpses into a mythic history or symbolic system that attached a high value to two themes: fertility and farming, and especially to maize and squash. One female figure tames a snake with multiple tails in the form of squash plants. Another female holds maize. Images and fragments from other sites repeat some of these themes: female guardians of corn and serpents, some of whom also hold dishes as if offering a sacrifice.

The people who built Cahokia inaugurated a way of life that was economically successful and artistically productive for not much more than 200 years—not bad for its place and time, but much shorter than the span major cities in Eurasia achieved. After a spell of stagnation or decline, their inhabitants deserted the upper Mississippi valley culture sites over a period of about four generations around the thirteenth and fourteenth centuries.

Yet culture of the kind that climaxed at Cahokia did not disappear. Rather, it was displaced and some of its more ambitious features—the huge mounds, the vast reach of trade—were abandoned. Mound building continued on a smaller scale, in the lower Mississippi valley and the North American Southeast. Here, traditions of burying chiefs, with rich grave goods and sometimes with large-scale sacrifices, were also maintained.

Mesoamerica

In a similar way in Mesoamerica, the collapse of the cities of the classic Maya in the ninth and tenth centuries in Central America and southern Mexico (see Chapter 10) did not end Maya civilization. Maya city life and state-building continued in a new environment on the Yucatán peninsula in eastern Mexico. Here, unlike the old lowland heartlands of the Maya, the climate was dry, and irrigation relied on pools and wells. But it was possible to reconstruct the old Maya way of life. In Yucatán, lowland tradition met links with central Mexico, which was accessible through seaborne and overland routes (see Map 11.2).

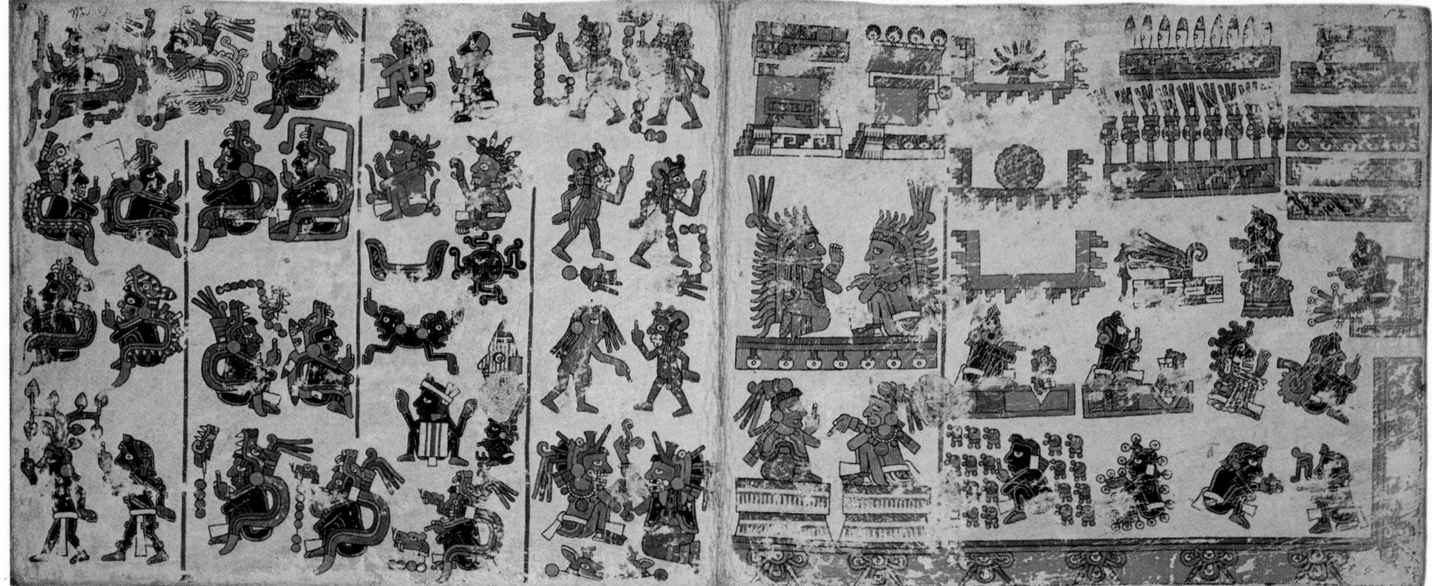

Mixtec creation myth. This Mixtec manuscript about the origins of the Earth predates the fifteenth century. Known as the Vienna Codex and painted on deerhide, it depicts Lord and Lady One-Deer, the legendary ancestors of all the Mixtec rulers, offering sacrifices to the gods of incense and tobacco.

Continuities with the former Maya world are evident in the way the buildings are arrayed in the cities of Yucatán, in layouts that reflect an abiding interest in observing the movements of the stars and planets, and in facades decorated with curl-nosed gods, the jaws of feathered serpents, or scenes of human sacrifice. The greatest Yucatán city, Chichén Itzá (chee-CHEIN eet-SAH), arose in the tenth century, at about the time the lowland Maya culture withered. If traditions recorded later are reliable, a dynasty with imperial ambitions, the Cocom, ruled in this city, and their wars dominated the region for centuries.

Yucatán was a new frontier for the Maya: a region of unprecedentedly intense exploitation in the eleventh and twelfth centuries. It was not the only such area in Mesoamerica. In the Pacific-facing regions of Mexico, beyond the Sierra Madre, the people known as Mixtec (MEESH-tahk) lived, in relatively small communities that were densely settled and famed for their elite craftsmen, especially in gold work and books made of bark. One of the greatest Mesoamerican heroes came from here: Eight-Deer Tiger-Claw (ca. 1063–1125). His activities show what was expected of a Mesoamerican king. He married frequently and had many children. He visited shrines, mediating between gods and men, offering sacrifices, consulting ancestors. He sent and received ambassadors, played the ball game against rival kings, and—above all—made war. He died as he had lived. This model of Mesoamerican kingship was defeated, sacrificed, and dismembered by his enemies—entombed with his royal symbols in an episode vividly recorded in the genealogy of the kings of two Mixtec towns, who wanted to be remembered as his descendants.

AROUND THE INDIAN OCEAN: ETHIOPIA, THE KHMER, AND INDIA

In the Americas, poor communications kept peoples apart and made it hard to exchange wealth and ideas. The Indian Ocean, by contrast, was the world's great arena of exchange, crossed by trade routes and rimmed with rich societies.

East Africa: The Ethiopian Empire

Links across the Indian Ocean lessened East Africa's isolation. By the twelfth century, important changes were occurring there. Arabic-speaking geographers recorded the names of places along the East African coast and knew of Muslim communities as far away as the island of Zanzibar. By 1200, Muslims from the Persian Gulf ruled Mogodishu in modern Somalia. Muslim geographers mentioned Mogadishu's transoceanic trade, bound for India and China, and East Africa is well marked on thirteenth-century Chinese maps.

The increased trade of coastal kingdoms and cities could affect state-building far inland. This is important, because state-building is a measurable indicator of thoroughgoing, long-term change. In twelfth-century Ethiopia, a new dynasty recovered political unity and began a modest recovery. In this land, which had now been predominantly Christian for over 700 years (see Chapter 9), a time of internal crusade began, recorded in the lives of frontier saints. On tireless pilgrimages, for instance, Takla Haymanyot made converts, dethroned idols, and chopped down "devils' trees" to build churches. An ideology of holy war seems to have taken hold.

On the Ethiopian frontier, the monastery churches of Lalibela began to emerge from the rocks: literally so, for they are hewn out of the ground. King Lalibela, after whom their location is named, and who is credited with building most of them, is known only from semilegendary sources. But the traditional tales are revealing:

After showing him what churches are like in heaven, God said to Lalibela, "It is not for the passing glory of this world that I will make you king, but that you may construct churches, like those you have seen, ... out of the bowels of the earth." Stories of angels who worked on the buildings reflect the superiority of the craftsmanship. The monks who wrote Lalibela's life story emphasized that he used wage labor to supplement angelic work. Hatred of slavery was common in the writings of Ethiopian monks.

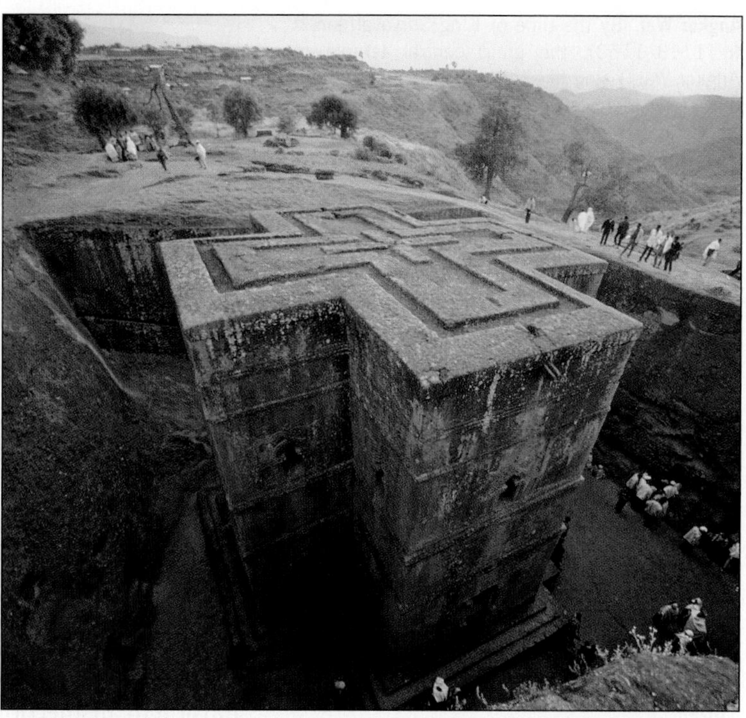

Rock-cut church. Perhaps because of its relative isolation in a mountainous region, Ethiopian civilization has always shown great originality. The political and cultural revival of Ethiopia in the late twelfth and early thirteenth centuries is associated with King Lalibela, who began to build a new sacred capital in a frontier region, where masons dug churches out of the rock. Lalibela seems to have conceived this work as a place of pilgrimage, a "New Jerusalem," and an embodiment of what he claimed was a vision of heaven.

The Zagwe (ZAHG-way), as the kings of Lalibela's dynasty were called, were frontiersmen. The elites of the central highland region around Axum despised them. Nor perhaps did the Zagwe carry total conviction when they claimed to be heirs of Solomon. Everyone knew that they were upstarts. Propaganda increasingly identified Ethiopia with the realm of the biblical Queen of Sheba, Solomon's concubine. Ethiopia was even proclaimed as "the new Israel." These claims to ancient roots favored rivals for the throne, who emerged in the second half of the thirteenth century, representing themselves as the rightful heirs of the Axumite monarchs or claimed to be descended from King Solomon. In 1270, they seized power. The state was organized for war. The monasteries of Debra Hayq and Debra Libanos, on the islands of Lake Tana, became schools of missionaries whose task was to consolidate Ethiopian power in the conquered pagan lands of Shoa and Gojam.

Ethiopia remained primarily an agrarian state, a mountain kingdom, with an ideology of defiance against neighboring states and peoples. But the multiplication of contacts across the Indian Ocean enabled Ethiopia to struggle against the effects of isolation with increasing success.

Southeast Asia: The Khmer Kingdom

At the opposite end of that ocean in southeast Asia, the same context helps to explain the wealth and power of another inland, agrarian kingdom: that of the Khmer in Cambodia. As we saw in Chapter 10, the fertility of the soil of the Khmer homeland nourishes three rice harvests a year. That productivity was the foundation of the kingdom's greatness. The rhythms of its rise, however, matched the growth of Indian Ocean trade, which opened outlets for the Khmer farmers' surplus. The ascent of the kingdom is documented in the growth and embellishment of its great city of Angkor.

The plan of the city reflects influences from India. Angkor was laid out to evoke the divine design of the world common to both Hindu and Buddhist beliefs: the central mountain or *Meru*, the mountains that ring it, the outer wall of rock, the seas flowing beyond in circle-like patterns. The royal palace built in the eleventh century centered on a tower that bore the inscription: "He thought the center of the universe was marked by Meru, and he thought it fitting to have a Meru in the center of his capital."

The architecture of the twelfth-century King Suryavarman II proclaims a new era. He had himself carved in the walls of his greatest foundation, the biggest temple in the world, Angkor Wat. Previously, monumental sculptures had only honored dead monarchs or royal ancestors. Suryavarman appears repeatedly in one of

Angkor Wat. By the time of King Suryavarman II (r. 1113–1150), the great central temple of Angkor Wat, rising like the sacred mountain Hindus and Buddhists imagined at the center of the world, already dominated the skyline of Angkor. Thanks to silt deposited by the Mekong River, intensive rice cultivation generated huge food surpluses, making possible the investment of work and wealth required to build the stupendous city.

the temple galleries, surrounded by environment-defying goods: umbrellas against the sun, fans against the humidity. A dead snake dangles from his hand, perhaps in allusion to an anecdote about his accession. He seized the throne by leaping on the royal elephant and killing his aged predecessor, like a god, who, "landing on the peak of a mountain, kills a serpent." Carvings reenact the creation of the world, as if his reign were the world's renewal. They show the cosmic tug of war between good and evil gods. Scenes of the churning of the magic potion of life from the ocean suggest that the fortunate age of the world is about to begin. According to Hindu myth, peace and unity will prevail in the new age, and the various ranks of society will willingly perform their roles.

Hindu tradition predicted that this new age would last 1,728,000 years. Suryavarman's was over by 1150. But his ambitious building programs continued, especially under King Jayavarman VII later in the century. Jayavarman surrounded Angkor with shrines and palaces, way stations, and—it was said—more than 100 hospitals. A proclamation of his public health policy reads:

> He felt the afflictions of his subjects more than his own. . . . May all the kings of Cambodia, devoted to the right, carry on my foundation, and attain for themselves and their descendants, their wives, their officials, their friends, . . . deliverance in which there will never be any sickness.[1]

The allocation of resources for the hospitals hints at both the scale and the basis of Khmer wealth. Over 80,000 tributaries provided rice, healing spices, 48,000 varieties of fever medicines, salve for hemorrhoids, and vast amounts of antiseptics, purgatives, and drugs. From no other realm of the time—not even China—do we have figures of this sort or on this scale.

Even amid all this medication, the favorite remedy for illness was prayer. In 1186, Jayavarman dedicated a temple to house an image of his mother as "the Perfection of Wisdom." Again the statistics recorded in surviving documents are dazzling for their precision—which reveals the participation of meticulous bureaucrats—and the wealth they display. The temple received tribute from over 3,000 villages. Its endowments included vessels made of gold and silver weighing more than 1,100 pounds. The records itemize thousands of precious stones, together with imported and locally produced luxury textiles. Daily provisions for a permanent establishment of 500 residents included rice, butter, milk, molasses, oil, seeds, and honey. Worshippers at the temple required annual supplies of wax, sandalwood, camphor, and clothing for the temple's 260 images of Buddhas. This is all evidence of the penetration of Cambodia by Indian Ocean trade.

The same source adds evidence on a revolution of Jayavarman's reign: the triumph of Buddhism over Hinduism as the court religion. "Doing these good deeds," the inscription concludes,

> the king with extreme devotion to his mother, made this prayer: that because of the virtue of the good deeds I have accomplished, my mother, once delivered from the ocean of transmigration, may enjoy the state of Buddhahood.[2]

Meanwhile, in the inner chamber of the gilded tower that the king added to the city, a Buddha replaced the Hindu images of previous reigns. The triumph of Buddhism in a state rooted in Hinduism was part of a broader trend. Though Buddhism dwindled in India, it spread in east, southeast, and Central Asia.

India: Economy and Culture

The strength of cultural links across the Bay of Bengal, between India and southeast Asia, is a reminder of another problem. India had long exerted influences across Eurasia: Buddhism and Hinduism; the science, logic, and technology of the Indian sages (see Chapter 6). The Indian subcontinent's central position athwart Indian Ocean trade routes guaranteed it against isolation and gave it privileged access to far-flung markets (see Map 11.3). India's long, open coasts could soak up ideas from across the oceans like the pores of a sponge.

Yet from the eleventh century, India's role in originating and recycling cultural influences began to diminish. Whereas earlier Muslim scholars had looked to India as a source of useful learning, Al Biruni, who came from Persia in the 1020s and was regarded as the most learned man of his time, found the Indian sages of his day complacent and uninterested in learning from abroad. Hindu science "presumed on the ignorance of the people."

While his picture may have been distorted by the desire to advocate the superiority of Islam over native Indian religion, there was some truth on Al Biruni's side. At least in the north—the part of India he knew—political dissolution accompanied a decline in the quality and output of works of art and learning. The large states that had filled most of the subcontinent since the early ninth century collapsed under the strain of trying to compete with each other and the impact of invaders and rebellions. Much of central and northern India was divided among competing royal dynasties that found it hard to sustain the loyalties of their followers. The rich Hindu temples of northern India became the prey of Muslim raiders from Afghanistan.

Nevertheless, though states provide the peace commerce requires—and, if the rulers are wise, the infrastructures that help trade thrive—economies can sometimes function well despite political troubles. In some parts of India, the economy was booming. Records of tribute paid to the temples in Rajasthan in northwest India reveal a lively trade in sugar, dyes, textiles, salt, areca nuts, coconuts, butter, salt, sesame oil. A ruler in Shikar in Rajasthan in 973 levied tribute in pearls, horses, "fine garments," weapons, camphor, betel nuts, sandalwood, "and endless quantities of gold and with spirited rutting elephants, huge like mountains, together with their mates." From the eleventh century, we can reconstruct merchant lineages that are astonishing, because they reveal how merchants saw

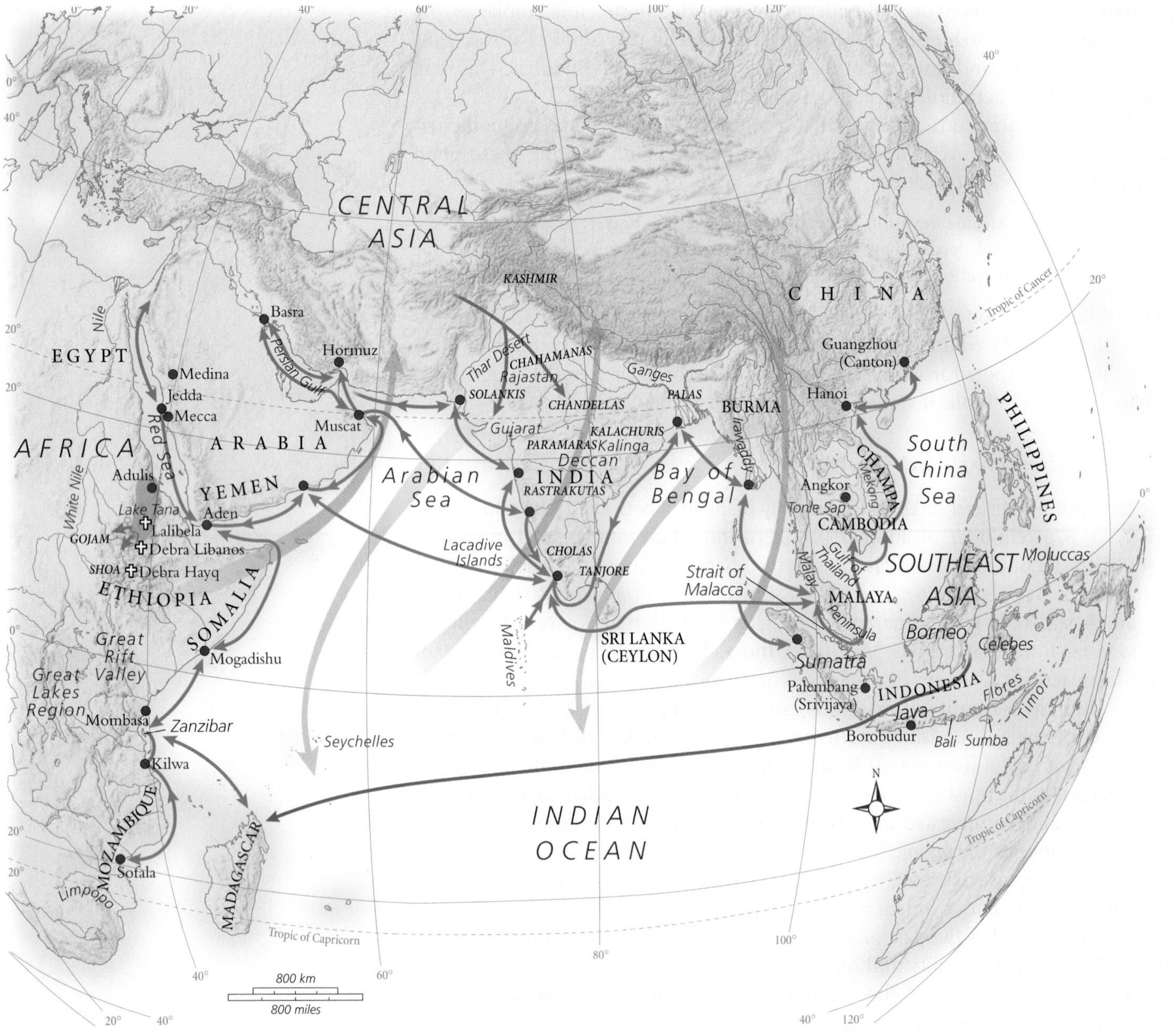

MAP 11.3

The Indian Ocean: From Ethiopia to Cambodia, ca. 1000–1200

- Zagwe dynasty, Ethiopia
- Ethiopian expansion under the Solomids
- monastery
- maritime trade route
- *CHOLAS* Indian dynasty, 9th–13th centuries
- colonization route to Madagascar
- warm monsoon (April to September)
- cold monsoon (October to March)
- Muslim raids into northern India, 11th century

themselves. The Pragvata family, for instance, considered themselves warriors in a trade war against Muslim competitors and advanced loans to rulers to fight real wars. Not only the warrior caste, says one inscription, can fight in "the shop of the battlefield." In most societies of the time, merchants would not have dared to liken themselves to the warrior elite. Clearly, the economy was doing well.

The most spectacular effect was the revival of Indian cities after a long period of relative stagnation. This effect was particularly strong in the south, where political troubles were fewer and invasions infrequent. In Karnataka in southwest India, eleventh-century inscriptions mention 78 towns—three times the number recorded for the eighth century. A grant to a temple in northern Karnataka in 1204 reveals how a city was laid out, with streets leading between white-plastered temples, bazaars, water tanks, flower gardens, and food plots, with arterial roads at the city's edges.

India: The Chola Kingdom

The Chola Kingdom	
1070–1122	Reign of Kulottunga I, proponent of seaborne imperialism
Thirteenth century	Decline of Chola

Far from the political disorder of the north, states in southern India could enjoy the strength that the wealth of the Indian Ocean made possible. The Chola kingdom was the most remarkable. Like that of the Khmer or of Ethiopia, its heartland lay away from the coasts in rice fields and pastures. The Chola labored to extend their landward frontiers and develop their landward resources by ruthless exploitation, felling forests on a gigantic scale.

The power, wealth, and ambitions of the Chola kings fused with those of the merchant communities on the coast. In the kingdom's grand ports, gold was exchanged for pearls, coral, betel nuts, cardamom, cottons, ebony, amber, incense, ivory, and rhinoceros horn. Elephants were stamped with the royal tiger emblem before being shipped out for export.

Chola merchants had private armies and a reputation "like the lion's" for "springing to the kill." The imperial itch seemed strongest in kings whose relations with merchants were closest. King Kulottunga I (r. 1070–1122), who relaxed tolls paid to the crown, imagined himself the hero of songs "sung on the further shore of the ocean by the young women of Persia." Most Chola seaborne "imperialism" was probably just raiding, though there were Chola footholds and garrisons on Sri Lanka, the Maldives, and perhaps in Malaya. Its impact, however, crippled Srivijaya in Indonesia (see Chapter 10) and enriched the temples of southern India.

Hindu temples were the allies of the Chola kings in managing the state and the biggest beneficiaries of victories in war. While the seaward drive lasted, the registers of gifts inscribed on temple walls show its effects: dazzling bestowals of exotic goods and cash, especially from about 1000 to about 1070. The treasures of the city temple of Tanjore included a crown with enough gold to buy enough oil to keep 40 lamps alight in perpetuity, and hundreds of precious gemstones and jewels, with plenty of umbrellas and fly whisks for the comfort of the worshippers at ceremonies.

The temples are the best evidence of the grandeur of the Chola Empire and the reach of its power and trade. But they also suggest why, ultimately, the Chola withdrew from overseas ventures. The temples invested heavily in land and in the revenues of farmers whom they supplied with capital to make agricultural improvements. In consequence, they may have contributed to a shift toward agriculture and land-based wealth and, therefore, to weakening Chola maritime imperialism—an enfeeblement that became marked in the thirteenth century. So, although India remained as rich as ever, some forms of Indian enterprise turned inward.

EURASIA'S EXTREMITIES: JAPAN AND WESTERN EUROPE

The Indian Ocean enclosed the main routes of communication around maritime Asia and between Asia and Africa. Of secondary importance were the land roads across Central Asia and the Sahara, which are subjects for the next chapter. For travelers on both the ocean roads and the land roads, Japan and Western Europe—the regions at the easternmost and westernmost extremities of Eurasia—were hard to get to and from. But they were close enough to the major communications routes to tap into the great exchanges of culture. During the eleventh and twelfth centuries, both areas emerged from relative isolation.

Japan

While in much of the world people struggled to overcome isolation, Japanese rulers had tried to make a virtue of it. They were fearful of losing migrants to richer regions and apprehensive of Chinese power. They had suspended diplomacy and trade with China in 838 and with Korea nearly a century later. Permission to trade abroad was hard to obtain. Even Buddhist monks had to get permission to leave the country on pilgrimage. Of course, illicit trade—or "piracy"—went on. But self-sufficiency remained government policy.

The best-known Japanese literature of the tenth and eleventh centuries is focused on a narrow, closed court society in a narrow, closed country. The fiction of Murasaki Shikibu in *The Tale of Genji*, one of the earliest realistic novels ever written, depicts a world in which the supreme values seem to be snobbery and sensitivity. Struggles for precedence dominate court life. The emperor grants his favorite cat the privileges "of a lady of middle rank." A nurse can tell from the sound of a visitor's cough to what level of the nobility he belongs. The court is everything. Even an appointment as governor of a province is a disgrace. Court literature scarcely mentions the peasants, beaten down by famine and plague, whose rice taxes sustained the aristocracy.

Murasaki portrayed the vices of a faction-ridden system. She was a spokeswoman for courtiers excluded from power by the man she hated, whose amorous advances she claimed to have turned down: the all-powerful courtier, Fujiwara no Michizane, who manipulated the political system by marrying his womenfolk into the imperial family and providing an effective bureaucracy from his own household. After three emperors died in factional struggles, he was left as regent of the empire in 1008. He exploited his opportunities so well that, according to one embittered critic, "not a speck of earth was left for the public domain." Emperors were so preoccupied with ritual duties that they could only bid for power by abdicating and attempting to control their heirs.

Morasaki Shikibu, Selections from *The Tale of Genji*

Provincial rule was left to administrators supported by retinues of hired tough guys. Despised at court for their "badly powdered faces," these local leaders wielded real power and wealth. Many of them were the descendants of imperial princes who had been sent to the provinces for want of employment at court, or who had opted for provincial careers to pursue wealth and authority. Increasingly they became warriors whose authority depended on force. As the court began to lose control of the provinces, these provincial warmongers allied in rival bands.

Genji. The earliest illustrated manuscripts of *The Tale of Genji* date from the 1120s, more than 100 years after the novel was written. But they demonstrate its enduring popularity and faithfully capture its atmosphere: the leisured opulence of the imperial palace at Heian, the learning and luxury of the court ladies, and the difficulty of leading a private life—let alone conducting the complex love affairs that the story depicts—behind frail partitions that were literally paper-thin.

In the 1070s, courtiers, temples, and merchants succeeded in opening Japan to foreign trade in their own economic interests. Trade with Korea resumed for a while as a result of the initiative of Korea's energetic King Munjon (r. 1046–1083). Direct relations between Japan and China followed. The results were dramatic: Newly rich families became players for power. The greatest profiteers were the Taira clan, who relentlessly, during the twelfth century, built up their power by acquiring provincial governorships and dominating the imperial court. In a series of civil wars, culminating in 1185, their rivals and relatives, the Minamoto clan, replaced them as imperial "protectors" or **shoguns** (shoh-GUNS). From then on the emperors never recovered real power. The renowned monk Mongaku was an adviser to successive shoguns. Invited to pray for a new shogun in 1200, he showed just what he thought of the request: "In the dwellings of those who offend, prayer is of no avail."

Japan: Official Isolation

838	Trade and diplomacy with China suspended
ca. 1000	*The Tale of Genji* written
1070s	Opening of Japan to limited foreign trade; restoration of direct relations with China
1160	Taira clan ascendant
1185	Minamoto replaces Taira as shoguns

As the diary of the Tosa Lady shows, it was hard to get around Japan's home islands—even that relatively small part of the islands the Japanese state occupied. Overseas contacts were difficult, the surrounding seas daunting. Yet Japan's isolation had never shut out Chinese cultural influence. Some of Murasaki's characters showed impatience with "Chinesified" styles, appealing to the "spirit of Japan." And popular literature did depict China as strange and exotic. But educated Japanese were aware of their dependence on China for almost all their models of learning, art, and government. Chinese was the language of the upper administration as well as of serious literature. The elite used quotations from Chinese classics to clinch arguments. Confucian ceremonies and Chinese poetry contests were among the main occupations at court. Murasaki repelled Fujiwara's unwanted attentions by capping his Chinese verses.

Western Europe: Economics and Politics

Nowhere else in the world were there long-range trade routes to match those of the Indian Ocean. But the land routes across Eurasia, from Europe to China, and across the Sahara, between the Mediterranean and the Sahel, were probably carrying increasing amounts of traffic through the eleventh and twelfth centuries. Western Europe lay at or just beyond the western and northern extremities of these land routes.

Its relative isolation always threatened the region with backwardness. The Atlantic clouded Europe's outlook to the west. The Sahara cut it off from much of Africa. Europe's frontier on the east to the great civilizations of Asia was hard to keep open across plains that hostile steppelanders patrolled or forests and vast marshlands obstructed. There was no direct access to the Indian Ocean. Western European merchants rarely went there—and, when they did, they had to undertake epic overland journeys via the Nile valley or across Arabia or what are now Turkey and Iraq.

A Muslim geographer, al-Istakhri, contemplating the world from Persia in 950, hardly noticed Western Europe at all. In his map, the West dangled feebly off the edge of the known world. Meanwhile, Latin Christians who looked out at the world in their own imaginations probably saw something like the version mapped at about the same time by the monks who drew the illustrations in the *Commentary on the Apocalypse* of Beatus of Liébana in northern Spain: Asia and Africa take up most of the space, Europe consists mainly of three peninsulas—Spain, Italy, and Greece, jutting into the Mediterranean—with a thin strip of hinterland above

A Muslim view of the world. The world, mapped by the Muslim geographer al-Istakhri in the tenth century. The map is now in the library of Leiden University in the Netherlands. Persia, the mapmaker's homeland, is in the center. Europe is the tiny triangle at the lower right. The Caspian and Aral Seas are represented as two large round blobs in the middle of Asia in the lower portion. West Africa is the landmass at the top.

them. In 1095, urging fellow Christians to new efforts against the Muslims, Pope Urban II expressed the feeling of being under siege:

> The world is not evenly divided. Of its three parts, our enemies hold Asia. . . . Africa, too, the second part of the world, has been held by our enemies for two hundred years and more. . . . Thirdly there is Europe. . . . Of this region we Christians inhabit only a small part, for who will give the name of Christians to those barbarians who live in the remote islands and seek their living on the icy ocean as if they were whales?[3]

Urban wanted Christendom to combine to redress what he saw as an imbalance of power. But disunity fragmented what political scientists call a state system with lots of interlocking territorial states. From 962, the German ruler Otto I called himself—more in hope than in reality—"Roman emperor," and tried to recover a sense of unity. When his grandson, Otto III (r. 982–1002), looked back at the reflection of himself that stared, enthroned in power, from an illustration in his gospel book, he could see lavish images of Germany, Gaul, and the Slav lands humbly bearing their tribute toward him, led by a personification of Rome. These pretensions were hollow. The empire of the Ottos did not cover much more than modern Germany.

Yet disunity can be stimulating, encouraging rival states in competition. Latin Christendom emerged as an expanding world, as it stretched between increasingly remote horizons. As we have just seen with Ethiopia, expansion does not only happen outward. There are often inward cracks and gaps to fill, slack to take up. From the eleventh to the early fourteenth centuries, a process of internal expansion, accompanied by new economic activity, was under way in Western Europe.

Settlement encroached on marginal soils and headed uphill. Forests fell. Bogs were drained. Farmers moved in. This was more than an economic enterprise: It was a sacred undertaking—reclaiming for God the terrain of paganism. The forest was alive with sprites, demons, and "wild men of the woods." The pious felled trees sacred to pagans. The most famous example is the best. Unable to sleep "on a certain night" in 1122, Abbot Suger of Saint-Denis, a monastery near Paris, rose to search the forest for 12 trees mighty enough to frame the new sanctuary he was planning for his abbey church, built—he hoped—to be full of light and "to elevate dull minds to the truth." The foresters wondered if the abbot was "quite ignorant of the fact that nothing of the kind could be found in the entire region"; but he found what he needed "with the courage of faith."

It was a representative incident in a vast project to tame little-exploited and underexploited environments. The Cistercians, one of the most dynamic new monastic orders of the period, directed their efforts into "deserts" where habitation was sparse and nature hostile. They razed woodlands and drove flocks and ox teams into wildernesses where today, all too often, the vast abbeys lie ruined in their turn. Sometimes, in their craving to escape the greedy secular society that put their souls at risk, Cistercians actually drove existing settlers away from their lands, extending the frontiers of colonization even farther as peasants imitated Cistercian practices on even more marginal lands.

Engineering came to the aid of environmental adaptation. Drainage extended the land on which people could dwell. In Holland, rapid population growth seems closely linked with the success of a project Count Floris V (r. 1256–1296) launched to reclaim waterlogged land. New embankments and canals made rivers easier to navigate. Searching out new routes and building roads and bridges were urgent tasks for which monarchs accepted some responsibility and for which—for example—Domingo de la Calzada, who built causeways and bridges for pilgrims to the shrine of St. James at Compostela in northern Spain, was made a saint.

Behind the expanding frontiers, modest technical revolutions were boosting production. Among inventions originating in Europe at this time were windmills, ground lenses, and clocks. Others, brought there thanks to improved communications across Eurasia, were paper mills, the compass, firearms, and—in the fourteenth century—the blast furnace. Large, heavy plows with curved blades enabled farmers to exploit the dense, wet soil of northern Europe. More effective harnesses enabled horses to pull the plows and take over a lot of hard work in the fields. More efficient windmills and water mills, more exact metallurgy and new products, especially in arms and glassware, extended the range of business and the flow of wealth. The advances in agriculture that began in the Islamic world toward the end of the previous millennium (see Chapter 10) spread hesitantly, across Western Europe, improving farming with new strains of wheat and—where it would grow—of rice. More varieties of beans improved nutrition and added nitrates to the soil.

Historians debate who was responsible for extending tillage and coaxing new wealth from the soil. Was it primarily the work of "free peasants"? Or did landowners force peasant dependants into greater productivity? There were many different patterns of landholding, which varied regionally and locally, and the drive to improve efficiency probably happened no matter what form landholding took. In any case, the colonization of new lands created opportunities of enrichment at all social levels. More food meant more people. The population of Europe may have doubled, from about 35 million around the year 1000, while these changes took place.

As production and population increased, so did opportunities for trade. New trade routes knitted Atlantic and Mediterranean seaboards in a single economy. This was important, because Western Europe has two natural economic zones—formed respectively along the Mediterranean and Atlantic coasts. The Strait of Gibraltar separates them, with widely different sailing conditions along the two seaboards. Inland a chain of breakwaters splits the continent, determining the flow of rivers and, therefore, the directions of exchange. Communication between these two zones was not easy. Limited access across France and the Alpine passes kept commerce alive, even when commercial navigation from sea to sea was abandoned.

New kinds of economic activity became possible in growing towns. Lübeck, founded in 1143, was the pioneer city of what became the **Hanseatic League**—a network of allied ports along the North Sea and Baltic coasts that collaborated to promote trade. Soon after, Mediterranean craft, mainly from the Italian city of Genoa, the island of Majorca, and Spain, resumed large-scale ventures along Atlantic coasts, such as had not been recorded since the Western Roman Empire collapsed in the fifth century (see Chapter 8).

Exchange across vast distances made geographical specialization and genuine industrialization possible. For instance, industries served by the trade of Genoa depended on geographical specialization. Textiles depended on concentrating wools and dyestuffs from widely separated places of origin. Food processing relied on matching fresh foodstuffs, such as herring, with salt. Shipbuilding demanded a similar marriage of raw materials—wood, iron, sailcloth, and pitch.

The results included urbanization: the revival of old cities and the building of new ones. The best way, indeed, to measure the economic progress of the period in much of Europe is by the growth of towns—ways of organizing life, which, at the time, were prized as uniquely virtuous. "The order of mankind," according to Gerald

Otto III. The workshop of the Abbey of Reichenau in Germany was one of the finest art studios in tenth- and early eleventh-century Europe, producing the Gospel book of Emperor Otto III on gilded pages. The enthroned emperor grasps the orb of the world, stamped with the cross of Christ (top). He towers over clergy and aristocracy alike, while the regions of Europe, led by Rome, shuffle humbly toward him with their tribute (bottom).

MAKING CONNECTIONS

CONTENDING WITH ISOLATION, CA. 1000–1200

REGION / PEOPLE OR KINGDOM →	OPPORTUNITIES →	EXPLOITATION STRATEGIES
Arctic/Inuit	Change in climate: warming weather allows for navigation across Canadian Arctic; introduction of new breed of pack dogs for transportation; introduction of bow and arrow	New techniques for constructing walrus-hide boats; new uses for sealskin, other animal hides for transport, hunting, food
Greenland/Norse	Warming climate; wealth of fish and game in almost uninhabited region; availability of export items such as hunting falcons, walrus ivory	Improved navigational techniques; new understanding of prevailing winds, ocean currents to improve chances of successful voyages; introduction of European grains and grasses for grazing animals; development of new breed of sheep
North American Southwest and Mississippi region/ Native Americans	Southwest: introduction of maize from Mexico; defensible canyons with water supply; growing population Mississippi: introduction of Mesoamerican "tool kit," food, way of life, thought; expanded trade routes bring deerskin, shells, bison hides, metals, and minerals	Southwest: irrigation canals to expand agriculture; many ceremonial centers; expansion into new zones; intensive organization of labor; development of multistoried residential structures Mississippi: expansion of trade routes; new forms of agriculture with maize, beans, squash, and fish farming; larger populations lead to more intensive crafts development/industry
Mesoamerica/Yucatán: Maya	Abundant forests, wildlife, coastal resources	New forms of irrigation, wells; new communities lead to expanded sea and land trade routes
East Africa/Ethiopia	Wider access to trade goods	Increased Indian Ocean trade with Arabs, Chinese, Indians helps equip Ethiopian dynasties to expand into new terrain
Southeast Asia: Khmer kingdom (Cambodia)	Growth of Indian Ocean trade opens outlets for Khmer rice surplus; wealth from trade and taxes funds Angkor Wat	Expansion of kingdom coincides with monumental temple complexes at Angkor, complete with expanded amenities for subjects—hospitals, shrines, etc.
India/Chola kingdom	Expansion of frontiers through inland raids brings additional natural resources (forests, agricultural land)	Landward strategy of clearing forests, planting crops and building large temples; coastal merchant communities merge with pirate expeditions sponsored by Chola kings to raid foreign ports
Japan	Provincial warriors break away from imperial court, open Japan to foreign trade; new wealth	Taira and other newly rich families begin to dominate imperial court, develop shogunate system of government to rule more efficiently
Western Europe	Expanding settlements into marginal agricultural areas; new engineering techniques to manage rivers, build infrastructure	Intensive land management—felling forests, draining bogs combines with Christianizing efforts to "civilize" barbarian areas; increased commerce leads to economic specialization, growth of towns and communes

of Wales in the 1180s, "progresses from the woods to the fields and from the fields to the towns and the gatherings of citizens." In Italy, the **commune**—as the citizen body was collectively called—became an institution of civic government in the late eleventh or early twelfth century. In what seems to have been a conscious reaching back to a Roman model, many Italian cities acquired "consuls" in this period. By the mid–twelfth century Otto of Freising regarded autonomous city governments as typical of northern Italy. Instead of deferring to some great protector—bishop, nobleman, or abbot—Italian cities became their own "lords" and even extended jurisdiction into the countryside. In effect, some cities were independent republics, forming alliances in defiance of, or despite, their supposed lords. Others tried unsuccessfully for the same status.

Technology and Growth in Europe

Late tenth century	Beginning of warm spell in climate
1000	Population of Europe approximately 35 million
1143	Founding of Lübeck; beginning of Hanseatic League
ca. 1200	Introduction of new technologies: heavy plows, better harnesses, windmills, water mills, ground lenses, clocks

Self-ruling city-states were most common in Italy, where, perhaps, memories of Rome remained most alive. But urban awareness and the numbers and size of towns grew over much of Europe. On the edges of Christendom, planned towns were laid out with the measuring rod and peopled by wagon trains. In Spain, the granting by monarchs of founding documents to tiny new communities marked the progress of settlement on the frontier with the Islamic world. These usually gave the inhabitants some share in judicial or administrative power. All towns of the time were small by modern standards. As few as 2,000 citizens could make a town if it had walls and a charter. "Feelings," it was said, "make the town." If the people felt urban, in other words, they were urban. Thirty thousand inhabitants was a metropolis.

For the sake of comparison, it is worth glancing at the farther edge of Christendom, beyond the reach of the Latin church, in western Russia. Here the cities of Novgorod and Pskov contended against a hostile climate beyond the grain lands on which they relied for sustenance. Famine beseiged them more often than human enemies did. Yet control of the trade routes to the river Volga made Novgorod cash rich. It never had more than a few thousand inhabitants, yet its monuments record its progress: its *kremlin* (or palace-fortress) walls and five-domed cathedral in the 1040s; in the early twelfth century, a series of buildings that the ruler paid for; and in 1207, the merchants' church of St. Paraskeva in the marketplace.

From 1136, communal government prevailed in Novgorod. The revolt of that year marks the creation of a city-state on an ancient model—a republican commune like those of Italy. The prince was deposed for reasons the rebels' proclamations specify. "Why did he not care for the common people? Why did he want to wage war? Why did he not fight bravely? And why did he prefer games and entertainments rather than state affairs? Why did he have so many gerfalcons and dogs?" Thereafter, the citizens' principle was, "If the prince is no good, throw him into the mud!"

Western Europe: Religion and Culture

Transformations in art, thought, and worship matched the dynamism of the economy and of political change. New forms of heresy, for instance, were enormously important for the future of Western Christendom. If popular heresy existed in Western Europe before the eleventh century, no one noticed it. After the year 1000, however, it emerged as a threat. A French peasant named Leutard had a vision in which bees—a symbol of supposedly sexless reproduction—entered his body through his penis. The vision drove him to renounce his wife, shatter the images of

Hell's mouth. The Archangel Michael locks the gate of hell, pictured as a monster's jaws. Note that some of the tortured souls in this thirteenth-century miniature painting are monarchs and monks, with crowns and tonsures. Whatever their wealth or social position, all Christians were equally subject to God's judgment.

Jesus and the saints in the local church, and preach universal celibacy. Among fellow peasants, he attracted a following that survived his death, albeit not for long. In 1015, the first burnings of heretics in the West for over 600 years were kindled. From then on, popular heretical movements were a continuous feature of Western European history.

Two long, slow changes seem to underlie this phenomenon. By the late eleventh century, a movement of Christian renewal and evangelizing fervor (known to historians as the Gregorian Reform, after Pope Gregory VII [r. 1073–1085], its greatest sponsor) was demanding new and exacting standards both of clerical behavior and of lay awareness of the faith, and challenging kings and noblemen for control over appointments in the church. More than a power struggle, it was a drive to purge the church of profanity.

At the same time, the evangelical fervor of the clergy was lowering its sights to include the peasantry, to whom clerics had, up to then, paid little attention. This was the result, in part, of a long build up of dissatisfaction with the shallowness with which Christianity had penetrated popular minds. Among its effects was a new or increased emphasis in saints' lives on how saints could—in today's jargon—"relate" to ordinary people by doing menial jobs. A French count, for instance, who joined a monastery in about 990, was set first to keep the hens, then the sheep, then the pigs, and was astonished at his own delight in each successive task.

On the other hand, the rise of popular dissent bears some signs of a revolution born of prosperity. Lay people were demanding more of their clergy. The really popular heresies of the eleventh and twelfth centuries were those ministered to by men of ferocious sanctity, like the preachers who called themselves "the perfect," and whose fanatical renunciation of worldly pleasures made them seem holier than the church. At the same time, the new security of life, the opportunities to gather harvests without being attacked, the leisure that increased yields from the soil gave to people, all bought time for a luxury unavailable in hard times: time to think about the Christian mysteries and develop a desire to get involved in them. At a relatively high level of education, the church could satisfy these stirrings by providing pilgrimages, private prayers, devotional reading matter, and orders of chivalry for the warrior class. Spiritually minded peasants, like Leutard's enthusiasts, could not be accommodated so easily.

In the struggle to save their souls, European laymen in the Middle Ages were at a disadvantage. The religious life opened heaven's gates; the warrior's life, stained with bloodshed, distracted by the world, closed them. The religious model suggested that obedience to rules—like those of monks and nuns—could sanctify the lay life. The first such rules or "codes of chivalry" in the twelfth century emphasized religious vows of chastity, poverty, and obedience, but lay virtues gathered prominence, redirected against deadly sins: generosity against greed, self-control against anger, loyalty against lies and lust. **Chivalry** became the prevailing disposition among the aristocracy of the age. It did not make warfare any more gentle or moral or all aristocrats good. But it did widen the range of the virtues to which aristocrats aspired.

The art of the West in the eleventh and twelfth centuries reveals a sort of cult of the commoner. Images of peasants and artisans appeared alongside saints and angels around church doorways, engaged in the economic activities that paid for this art. Here were arrayed the members of a peaceful and orderly society, with everyone in their place and doing well out of it. The new mood affected the way artists humanized heaven by evoking piercing emotions. Early in the eleventh century, the painter of the gospel book of Abbess Hilda of Merschede painted a scene of Jesus asleep in a storm on the Sea of Galilee, in which the ship leaps into life and the anxiety of the Apostles burdens their brows. The Jesus carved for Archbishop Gero of Cologne dates from before the end of the tenth century, but no modern master ever chiseled the face of the suffering Jesus with more exquisite agony: drawn lips, taut cheeks, nerveless lids, and a trickle of blood at the brow.

Romanesque art has a reputation for stylization and formality. But in this early example that Archbishop Gero of Cologne in Germany commissioned before the end of the tenth century, the artist was evidently already interested in anatomical realism and in depicting intense emotion. Instead of a remote, divine, judgmental Christ, we see the sorrow and resignation of Jesus, a suffering human being.

In art, literature, and scholarship, a sense of continuity with ancient civilization shines through. Sculptors and builders copied classical works. Abbot Suger's ideas on the beauty of light were derived from what he thought was a Greek text from the first century. The twelfth-century English historian, Geoffrey of Monmouth, claimed to trace the "British" monarchy back to characters from the ancient Greek poet Homer. Poets in England and Germany tried to write like ancient Romans. Lectures in Paris introduced students to the logic of Aristotle. Abelard (1079–1142), the most renowned teacher of the era in Paris, gave audiences the impression that there was nothing logic could not do. In his book on logic, *Sic et Non* (*Yes and No*) of 1122, he exposed the contradictions in many treasured assumptions of theology and philosophy. The twelfth-century Archbishop of Canterbury, Anselm, too, wrote about God using reason as his only guide—suppressing references to Scripture or the tradition of the church. Indeed, Anselm sought to prove the existence of God—or at least of a real being with the perfection Christianity ascribed to God—by unaided reason. Roughly, his proof says that the most perfect being we can think of must exist, since, if he did not, we should be able to think of another, more perfect being who did.

By the twelfth century, students of nature were beginning to "stand on the shoulders of giants" of antiquity and see farther than they had. In 1092, Walcher of Malvern fixed the difference in time between Italy and England by timing an eclipse. Adelard of Bath noted that light travels faster than sound. He agreed with his younger contemporary, William of Conches, that God likes to work through nature and that miraculous explanations should never be invoked when scientific ones will do. Practical observations piled up: the heights of tides, the habits of volcanoes. Carvers of capitals on pillars in churches imitated natural forms. Sculptors chiseled plants and flowers into monastery cloisters.

Abelard defends himself, from *The Letters of Abelard and Heloise*

IN PERSPECTIVE: The Patchwork of Effects

The great leap of Latin Christendom—the renaissance or rebirth in art and thought that began after the year 1000—was possible because Western Europeans found ways to cope and contend with their relative isolation. Scholars in the late tenth and eleventh centuries went to Muslim Spain to learn science, mathematics, and Arabic. Gerbert of Aurillac—the Emperor Otto III's tutor—sweated to learn mathematics in the Spanish Muslim city of Toledo. Adelard of Bath studied Arabic translations of classical Greek books, lost in the West. In the late eleventh and twelfth centuries, as we shall see in the next chapter, pilgrimages, wars, and trade took Western Europeans in unprecedented numbers eastward, to the eastern Mediterranean, and to contact with the Islamic world and Eastern Christendom at Constantinople. At the same time, the westward trickle of communications with south and east Asia probably increased along the Silk Roads.

For Japan, too, isolation might have been frustrating. But there was just enough contact with Korea and China to stoke Japanese art and learning with Chinese influences. The delicately folded poems written by Genji and his friends and

CHRONOLOGY

Tenth century	Flourishing of canyon culture in American Southwest; Chichén Itzá founded
Late tenth century	Norse reach Greenland
ca. 1000	*The Tale of Genji* (Japan); Thule Inuit reach Greenland
1000–1300	Rapid population growth in Europe and development of new technologies; Maya intensively exploit Yucatán peninsula
1000–1100	Flourishing of Chola kingdom (India)
1070s	Opening of Japan to limited foreign trade; restoration of direct relations between China and Japan
Early twelfth century	Building of Angkor Wat (Cambodia) begins
1150	Canyon settlements in American Southwest withdraw to higher ground
1200	Population of Cahokia reaches 10,000
1270	Solomids seize power in Ethiopia
1300	Decline of upper Mississippi valley culture

real-life counterparts were all in Chinese—part of an ancient renaissance, as influential as anything Europeans wrote or sculpted in imitation of antique models.

In the preindustrial world, the size of states and the scope of economies were functions of time as well as distance. Messages, armies, revenues, and cargoes took a long time to travel across broken country or, by sea, through variable winds. Around the Indian Ocean, increased traffic brought areas in East Africa and southeast Asia out of isolation and kept India rich, despite its political troubles. Despite the heroic efforts of the Norse in the Atlantic, the Thule Inuit in the Arctic, and the Polynesians in the Pacific, the wealth-creating effects of sustained transoceanic or interoceanic commerce could not yet be reproduced outside the region of the monsoons around the Indian Ocean.

Even so, India was much less influential in world history—far less productive of ideas and movements that affected the rest of the world—after 1000 than it had been before. This is only one of many ways in which India seems to have reached a "peak" of achievement. According to the best available studies, India's population was over 200 million in 1000 and fell for the rest of what we think of as the Middle Ages. The Chola kingdom was the last Indian empire to exert major influence in southeast Asia, where Hinduism began to decline—ultimately, to survive only in patches outside India itself.

In the Americas and parts of sub-Saharan Africa, the arresting effects of isolation could not be overcome. Cultural contacts between Mesoamerica and parts of North America helped, for a while, to produce spectacular experiments in building states and modifying environments. But the networks were too fragile and temporary for the effects to endure.

In the next century, the thirteenth, changes in the pattern of communications across Eurasia would heighten the differences between the Old and the New Worlds. To understand these events and their effects, we have to turn first to the other great theme of the history of the eleventh and twelfth centuries: the growing contacts and conflicts between sedentary and nomadic peoples in Eurasia and parts of Africa and their effects on the interactions of surrounding regions.

PROBLEMS AND PARALLELS

1. How did societies around the world contend with their relative isolation between 1000 and 1200?
2. How did isolation affect Greenland and the North American cultures from 1000 to 1200?
3. What roles did Cahokia play in central North America? What evidence is there that it was influenced by the civilizations of Mesoamerica?
4. How did Buddhism and Hinduism spread throughout southeast Asia? How did these religious traditions affect parts of Asia outside India?
5. How did the lands on the extremities of Eurasia (Japan and Europe) overcome their isolation and emerge with powerful political, cultural, and economic systems?
6. How did urbanization affect religious, economic, and political life in Europe between 1000 and 1200?
7. How did increased trade across the Indian Ocean affect East Africa during the eleventh century?
8. What are the benefits and drawbacks of cultural and economic isolation?

DOCUMENTS IN GLOBAL HISTORY

- Ki no Tsurayuki, excerpt from the *Tosa Diary*
- Excerpt from *Speculum Princips*, "The Animal Life of Greenland and the Character of the Land in Those Regions"
- Canyon de Chelly
- A European explorer's description of Cahokia
- Morasaki Shikibu, Selections from *The Tale of Genji*
- Abelard defends himself, from *The Letters of Abelard and Heloise*

Please see the Primary Source DVD for additional sources related to this chapter.

READ ON

A convenient version of the Tosa diary is printed in D. Keene, ed., *Anthology of Japanese Travel Literature* (1960). *The Book of the Wonders of India* is available in an edition by G. S. P. Freeman-Grenville (1984). G. R. Tibbetts, *Arab Navigation in the Indian Ocean before the Coming of the Portuguese* (2002) gives the background.

On Greenland, K. Seaver, *The Frozen Echo* (1997), is a brilliant work with contentious conclusions.

On the North American Southwest, S. Lekson et al., *Great Pueblo Architecture of Chaco Canyon* (1986) is outstanding; pages in B. G. Trigger and D. Washburn, eds., *The Cambridge History of the Native Peoples of North America*, v.1, Part I, bring it up to date. The Mississippi sites are covered in T. R. Pauketat and T. E. Emerson, *Cahokia: Domination and Ideology in the Mississippian World* (2000); T. E. Emerson and R. B. Lewis, eds., *Cahokia and the Hinterland* (2000); and T. R. Pauketat, *The Ascent of Chiefs* (1994). On the Mixtec, R. Spores, *The Mixtec Kings* (1967) cannot be bettered.

For Ethiopia under the Zagwe, some sources appear in R. B. Pankhurst, *The Royal Chronicles of Ethiopia* (1967). On Ethiopia and Angkor the works recommended for Chapter 9 are good for the period covered here.

Albiruni's *India*, ed. C. Sawyer is the classic text. M. A. Saleem Khan, *Al-Biruni's Discovery of India* (2001) attempts an interpretation. The works of Chattopadhyaya and Thapar remain fundamental for this period in India. For the Cholas, V. Dehejia, *Art of the Imperial Cholas* (1990) is a breathtaking work; B. K. Pandeya, *Temple Economy under the Cholas* (1984) is important.

V. K. Jain, *Trade and Traders in Western India* (1990) and B. Stein, *Peasant, State and Society in Medieval South India* (1994) are useful on their subjects.

There are many editions of *The Tale of Genji*. For Japan in this period, *The Cambridge History of Japan*, ii (2002) is comprehensive.

On Western Europe, R. Southern, *The Making of the Middle Ages* (1961) is a classic work, unsurpassed. R. Bartlett, *The Making of Europe* (1994) is fundamental. Classic essays on some of the topics covered here are collected in F. Fernández-Armesto and J. Mudoon, eds., *The Internal Frontier of Christendom* (Forthcoming). A useful little collection of Cistercian sources is in P. Matarasso, ed., *The Cistercian World* (1993). Abbot Suger is best approached through E. Panofsky, ed., *Abbot Suger on the Abbey Church of St Denis and Its Art Treasures* (1979). On technology, J. Gimpel, *The Medieval Machine* (1977) is superb and standard. On peasants, G. Astill and J. Langdon, eds., *Medieval Farming and Technology* (1997) provides an excellent introduction.

On heresy, M. Lambert, *Medieval Heresy* (2002) is spirited and comprehensive. A. Murray, *Reason and Society in the Middle Ages* (1978) is an ingenious work, full of insights. C. H. Haskins, *The Renaissance of the Twelfth Century* (2005) is a classic, once pioneering, now enduring. P. Lasko, *Ars Sacra* (1995) is a good introduction to the art of the period.

CHAPTER 12 The Nomadic Frontiers: The Islamic World, Byzantium, and China, ca. 1000–1200

Scenes of steppeland life in the Middle Ages. Two warriors do their washing. A shaman writhes by the campfire. Weapons are stacked. Horses graze. Starving dogs hope for scraps. A chief mends his saddle.

IN THIS CHAPTER

THE ISLAMIC WORLD AND ITS NEIGHBORS
The Coming of the Steppelanders
The Crusades
The Invaders from the Sahara
The Progress of Sufism
THE BYZANTINE EMPIRE AND ITS NEIGHBORS
Byzantium and the Barbarians
Basil II
The Era of Difficulties
Byzantium and the Crusaders
Byzantine Art and Learning
CHINA AND THE NORTHERN BARBARIANS
The End of the Tang Dynasty
The Rise of the Song and the Barbarian Conquests
Economy and Society Under the Song
Song Art and Learning
IN PERSPECTIVE: Cains and Abels

On a winter's morning in 1021, the Caliph al-Hakim, ruler of a state that stretched from Egypt to what is today Algeria, climbed to his astronomical observatory in Cairo. He intended—so his courtiers supposed—to amuse himself with the huge copper instrument he used to observe the movements of the stars. It was al-Hakim's habitual way to unwind. On this occasion, however, as far as anyone knew, he simply vanished. He was never officially heard of again. Some of his followers believe that heaven had absorbed him. He would return at the end of time. A sect in Lebanon, the Druze, still regards him as an incarnation of God.

CAIRO

To most observers, however, he was just mad: His "deeds were without reason and his dreams without interpretation." At different times, he outlawed dogs, churches, evening traffic, canal trade, and women's shoes. He expected the end of the world—which perhaps explains his personal austerity and reckless almsgiving. His main defect, in his critics' eyes, was that he was a Shiite (see Chapter 9). He saw himself as the fulfillment of Shiite belief in the divine appointment of an infallible **imam,** or holy ruler, to supplement Muhammad's teaching.

The conflict between rival caliphs, the Shiite in Cairo, and the Sunni in Baghdad, divided the Islamic world into roughly equal portions. To make matters worse, from the 920s, a third dynasty, with its court in Cordova in Spain, also claimed to be caliphs. In the tenth and eleventh centuries, Shiites seized Baghdad and humiliated the Sunni caliphs. From 1090, the Shiite sect known as the Assassins occupied Alamut—a mountain fortress in Persia—from where they launched raids and unleashed allegedly drug-crazed fanatics to execute political murders. The word *assassin* comes from "hashish."

Threads of cultural unity still linked the Islamic world: veneration of the prophet Muhammad, adherence to the Quran, the use of Arabic as the language of religion and learning, the unifying force of the pilgrimage to Mecca. Mutual obligations among Muslims were strong, even between Shiites and Sunnis. In 1070, for instance, when famine threatened Cairo, the Fatimid caliph sent his womenfolk to Sunni Baghdad to escape starvation. Islamic civilization was still the most widely dispersed civilization the world had ever seen. Muslims ruled a continuous band of territory from Spain, across North Africa, to the Arabian Sea and the Indus River, and into Central Asia (see Map 12.1).

FOCUS questions

- HOW DID the Islamic world deal with its steppeland neighbors?
- WHAT STRENGTHS did the Turks bring to the Islamic world?
- HOW DID Byzantine civilization combine religious and secular values?
- HOW DID Byzantium survive? How far can it be said to have "declined"?
- HOW DID the Crusades affect the Islamic world and Byzantium?
- HOW DID Song China deal with the northern barbarians?
- WHY DO nomads and settled peoples tend to be enemies?

Nonetheless, political disunity disturbed Muslims. Fragmentation weakened the states it created and wasted their strength in wars against each other. The strain told. In the eleventh century, the Spanish caliphate crumbled. In most of Iran and Kurdistan, minor dynasties made the rule of the caliph in Baghdad no more than symbolic. The Fatimid caliphate had reached the limits of its expansion. In Spain, southern Italy, and Anatolia, aggressive Christian states were active.

THE ISLAMIC WORLD AND ITS NEIGHBORS

Both a challenge to and the salvation of Islam came from unlikely directions: the Sahara and the steppes. The Islamic world was caught up in a sweeping Eurasian confrontation. Settled societies faced warlike, pastoral ememies from Central Asia and North Africa. Sometimes the relationship was hostile. It was always tense. In this chapter, we look in turn at the societies most affected—the Islamic world, with its western neighbors in Spain and West Africa, and then the Byzantine and Chinese Empires.

Pilgrim caravan. "I cling to journeying, I cross deserts, I loathe pride." The freedom and frequency of travel across the Muslim world are among the main themes of one of the most popular Arabic works of the thirteenth century, the *Maqamat* (or *Scales of Harmony*) of al-Hariri, which inspired some of the finest illustrated manuscripts of the time.

The Coming of the Steppelanders

The steppelands seemed full of threat, as Turkic peoples overspilled the steppeland in waves of migrants and invaders. We do not know what set them off. But once the shifts of population began, they rattled a chain reaction, with some groups pushing others ahead of them.

In 1055, Seljuk Turks seized Baghdad and turned the caliph into a client—"a parrot in a cage." In Afghanistan, Mahmud of Ghazni, the descendant of a Turkish adventurer, was the self-appointed guard of Islam, whose raids into India gathered so many captives that prices in the slave markets tumbled. Muslims called the Turks "the army of God"—not in approval but in fear. God had unleashed these ferocious pagans to punish Muslims' sins.

Just as the Arabs had destroyed the Persian Empire and the western barbarians had broken Rome, the Turks might have shattered the Islamic world. After stunning conquests, however, they stopped, converted by the culture they had conquered. Seljuk and his sons were among the early converts. The ruins of the capital they built at Konya in Anatolia show how thoroughly they abandoned pastoralism and absorbed urban habits. By the end of the twelfth century, 108 towers enclosed the city. Market gardens on the surrounding plain fed a population of perhaps 30,000. Inns accommodated merchants and their camels. But the Seljuks never entirely forgot the steppe. Their coins showed hero-horsemen with stars and haloes round their heads. Their sultans lay in tombs, shaped to recall the tents in which their ancestors dwelled. Seljuk experience was typical. No one knows how it happened, but the Islamic world transformed most of the Turkic invaders into its strength and shield.

The newly converted Turks conquered Anatolia and Armenia from Christians, Syria and Palestine from Shiites. Success in attracting, converting, and domesticating pastoral peoples—and recycling their violence in Muslim service—is one of the decisive and distinctive features of the history of the Islamic world. Its importance is apparent when one compares the Islamic record with those of other settled agricultural societies in Christendom, China, India, and Africa. Christendom usually dealt with steppelander threats by trying to fight them off or buy them off. The Magyars (MAHG-yahrs) and Bulgars, who settled in Hungary and Bulgaria respectively, were Europe's only successfully absorbed steppeland invaders. China seduced steppeland conquerors to Chinese ways of life, but was unable or unwilling to turn them permanently into a favorable fighting force. In India invading pastoralists sometimes adopted parts of Indian culture but usually remained intruders. In none of these regions did native cultures manage to harness nomad energies for wars of their own.

Early Turkish history from the *Dede Korkut*

Al-Thalibi, *Recollections of Bukhara*

The Crusades

It is worth comparing the Islamic world's response to the steppeland invaders with the fate of other intruders: the crusaders, who attacked from Christian Europe. Writers of world history usually give the Crusades a lot of attention, seeking signs of the vitality of the West—the capacity of Western Europeans to reach overseas and make war way beyond their frontiers. For the Islamic world, however, the Crusades were a minor nuisance. Crusaders were few. Their states were small and mostly short-lived. Crusaders could not be converted to Islam, but—thanks to the availability of Turkish manpower and leadership—their threat was neutralized.

The Crusading movement started as an outgrowth from pilgrimage. Increasingly in the tenth and eleventh centuries, Christians made pilgrimages as an act of penance for their sins. Pilgrimages—in theory, peaceful journeys, on which the pilgrims relied on the charity of people whose lands they crossed—became armed expeditions. Simultaneously, Christians began to adopt what had formerly been a Muslim notion: holy war. The land where Jesus' feet trod sanctified those who fought and died for it. Warriors could fulfill their vocation for violence and still be saved. "The blood of Muslims," declared a French poet in the twelfth century, "washes out sins." War for the recovery of Jerusalem would also be just, according to Christian theorists: Palestine had once been Christian land—so it was right to try to win it back.

In the 1090s, preachers whipped up collective hysteria that sent thousands of poor, ill-armed pilgrims to their deaths in an effort to get to Jerusalem. Pope Urban II (r. 1088–1099) orchestrated a relatively well-planned military expedition. It is often claimed that the crusaders were younger sons, with inadequate inheritances, and adventurers "on the make." But many crusaders were rich men with a lot to lose. The church is also often thought to have encouraged the Crusades to increase its own wealth. That was one of the effects, as crusaders left property to monasteries and churches to look after in their absence, and, once they got to the east, made grants of conquered land and treasure to religious institutions there.

The early crusaders blundered to success, capturing Jerusalem in 1099 and lining the shores of the Levant with states their own leaders ruled. Muslim divisions made these successes possible. Muslim indifference and infighting prolonged them. The crusader kingdoms got support from Italian merchant-communities, which welcomed access to trade, and, occasionally, received reinforcements from Europe.

A medieval tourist-guide. This late twelfth-century guide was made to help English pilgrims find the major tourist attractions and useful spots in and around Jerusalem. The money exchange is in the center, and the food market is to its right. The Temple of Solomon occupies the upper right quarter of the city (surrounded by circular walls), and the Golden Gate "where Jesus entered sitting on a donkey" leads to it. The cross marks Golgotha where Jesus was crucified. The Holy Sepulcher where he was buried is below it.

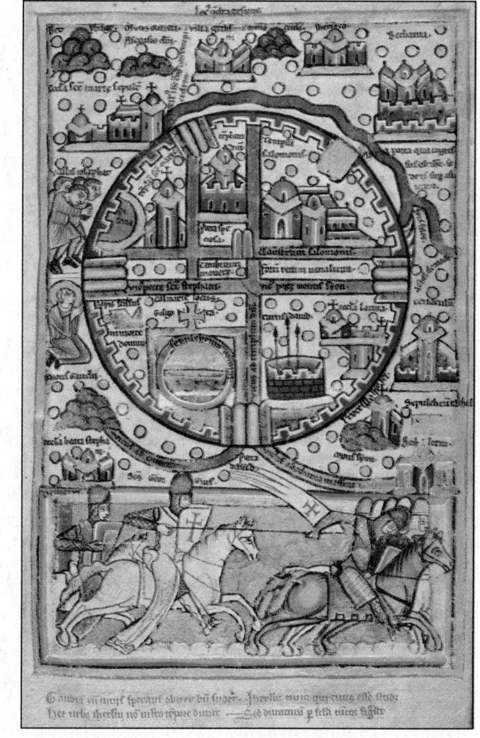

MAP 12.1

The Middle East and the Mediterranean, ca. 900–1100

- extent of caliphate, ca. 900
- area controlled by Ghaznavids, ca. 1000
- raids by Mahmud of Ghazni
- *BUWAYHIDS* Muslim dynasty with dates
- Seljuk conquests, ca.1040–1090
- Seljuk capital (from 1077)
- Assassin stronghold
- UZBEKISTAN modern-day country
- Byzantine Empire, ca. 1050
- battle
- *Karkhanids* people
- Jewish communities
- Sufi shrines, ca. 1250
- Christian communities
- caliphate of Cordova
- Fatimid dynasty

The newcomers from Europe, however, were often zealots who tended to disrupt the delicate tolerance between Christians and Muslims on which the crusader states relied for stability.

In the mid–twelfth century, Zangi (ZAN-gee)—a Turkish chief who dubbed himself "pillar of the faith"—proclaimed a *jihad* against infidels and Shiites. He and his heirs began to reconquer the lands lost to the crusaders. Saladin (SAH-lah-deen), the Kurdish soldier who seized Zangi's empire in 1170, overthrew the crusader kingdom of Jerusalem in 1187, reduced the crusader states to tiny enclaves on the coast, and beat off attempts by new crusaders to recover Jerusalem.

Yet the defeat of the crusaders was a sideshow. More important, in the long run, for the future of the Islamic world was Saladin's extinction of the Fatimid caliphate and the conquest of Egypt for Sunni Islam. Though heresy continued to disrupt Islamic uniformity, no such large or menacing Shiite state outside Iran ever again challenged Islamic solidarity. The other legacy of the Zangi and Saladin was Islamic militancy. Jihad remained a way to legitimize upstart dynasties and regimes.

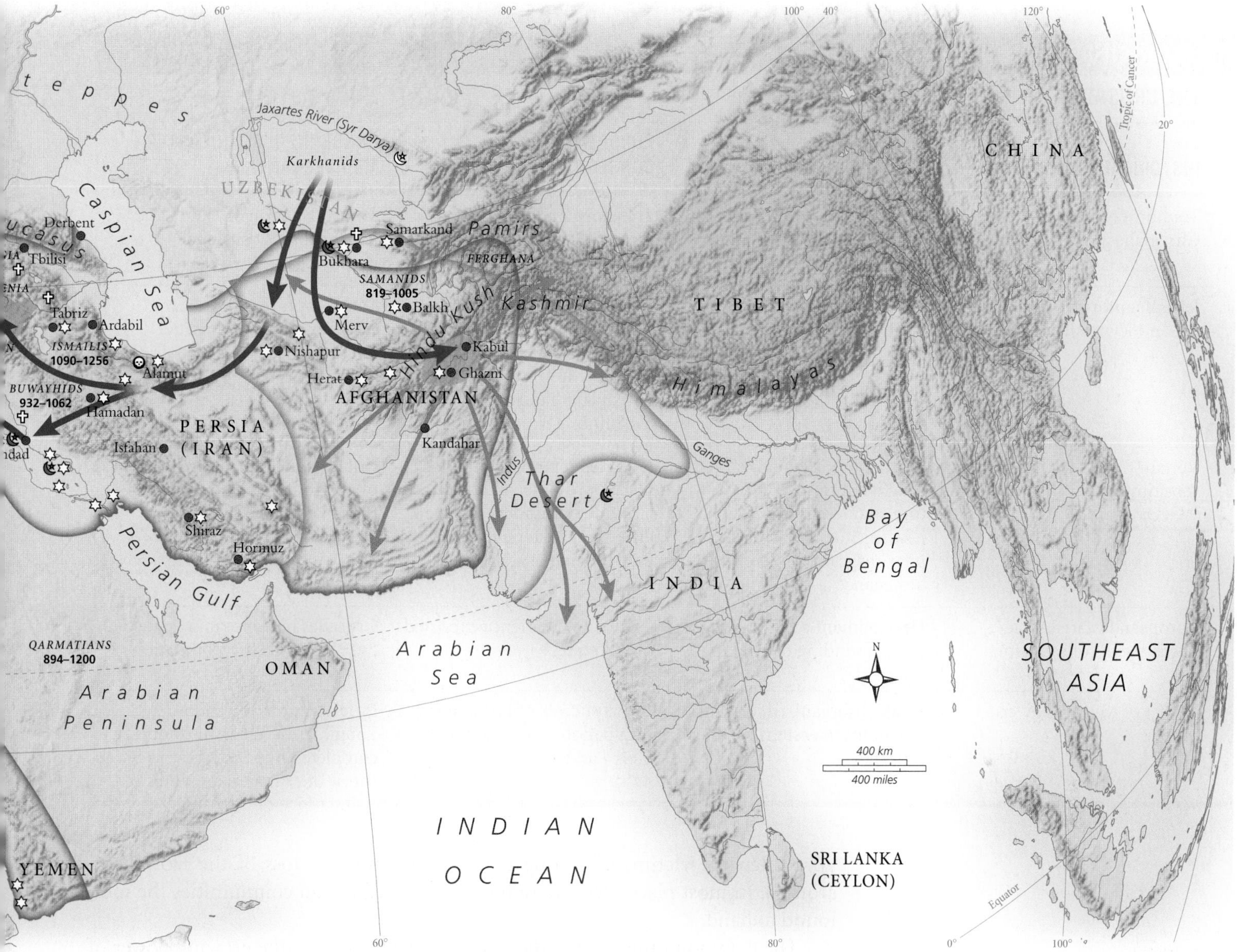

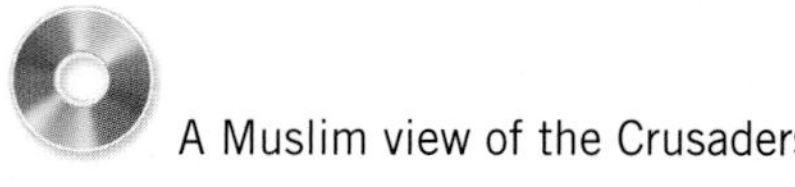
A Muslim view of the Crusaders

The Crusades, meanwhile, left an equally sad legacy. For most of the Middle Ages, Christian, Muslim, and Jewish communities in the Middle East, Egypt, and Spain lived alongside one another in relative peace. Christians and Muslims intermarried, exchanged culture, and, in some frontier zones, even worshipped at the same shrines. Christian and Muslim states often made alliances against third parties, regardless of religious affiliation. The Crusades, however, fed on religious propaganda and encouraged the two traditions to demonize each other. Crusading fervor also increased hostility in Europe between Christians and Jews, since Jews

MAKING CONNECTIONS

THE CRUSADES

HISTORICAL BACKGROUND →	CAUSE FOR ACTION →	EUROPEAN CONSEQUENCES →	CONSEQUENCES IN EASTERN MEDITERRANEAN
Tradition of pilgrimage—Christians go to Jerusalem	By 1050, increased danger, disorder, and occasional persecution in Middle East	Transformation of armed escorts; adoption of Islamic idea of holy war	Transformation of Holy Land into region of continual battle
Jerusalem formerly a Christian and Jewish land	Muslim population, kingdoms control the region	Religious leaders whip up mass movement—disorganized expeditions lead to disastrous results; Pope Urban II organizes a military expedition (First Crusade)	Quick capture of Jerusalem; creation of small "crusader kingdoms"
Roman Catholic Church most important institution in Western Europe	Church needs land, wealth to fund its clerics, infrastructure, and religious activity; new spirituality favors annual pilgrimages as a form of penance	Local bishops and papacy help coordinate, orchestrate Crusades; crusaders left property to monasteries and churches while abroad	Conquered land and treasure often granted to church institutions
European lay aristocracy needs means of salvation	Development of chivalric ethos; founding of knightly orders	Aristocratic violence exported on Crusades	Crusades become ruling elite over large Muslim population
Defeat of Muslims by crusaders	Weak, disorganized Muslim kingdoms in eastern Mediterranean	Initial success of crusaders; occupation of Jerusalem and Holy Land	Proclamation of *jihad* by Zangi, Turkic chief; reconquest completed by Saladin; overthrow of crusader kingdoms

were often the victims of rioting that laments over the loss of the Holy Land aroused. In most places, Jews were the only non-Christian communities the mob found to hand.

The common opinion that the Crusades demonstrated the growing power of Latin Christendom seems—at best—exaggerated. There was dynamism in the Western Europe of the eleventh and twelfth centuries, but most of it was expended on inward development and on expanding the frontiers. If anything, the Crusades' failure helped alert people in Europe to their backwardness and vulnerability compared to the cultures of the Near East.

The Invaders from the Sahara

On their westernmost frontier, in Spain and Portugal, Muslims badly needed new strength. Since the eighth century, Muslim rulers had held territory as far north as the Duero and Ebro River valleys. But **al-Andalus** (ahl-AHN-dah-loos), as they called it, was hard to hold together and defend. The original Muslim settlers—mostly Berbers from North Africa—were few in number, uneasily holding down large Christian populations. Internal communications relied on roads that the Romans had built centuries earlier to link widely scattered communities. Between the rivers Tagus and Duero was a vast frontier, strewn with fortifications. Wealth made al-Andalus viable: wealth gathered from the agricultural surplus of rich soils in the south and east; wealth spent on the luxuries—

ivory work, jewels, palaces, lavish gardens—for which Spanish art of the time is renowned.

In the late tenth century, a general, Almanzor (ahl-mahn-SOHR), kept the potentially mutinous armies and regional aristocracies of the Spanish "caliphate" busy with wars against the Christians. He died in 1002. In 1009, Berber mutineers sacked his headquarters, "wilder now than the maws of lions, bellowing the end of the world." The caliphate dissolved into numerous competing kingdoms. The northern Christian kingdoms took advantage. By the 1080s, the Tagus valley was in Christian hands. In alarm, some of the Spanish Muslim kingdoms called on warrior ascetics from North Africa, the Almoravids (ahl-moh-RAH-vihds), for help.

In Arabic the Almoravids' name suggests both hermits and soldiers. They emerged as an alliance of pastoral bands from the Sahara, whom firebrand preaching aroused into self-dedication to holy war from the mid–tenth century. Nomads whom the Fatimids had expelled from southern Egypt had already wrought havoc in the region. The Almoravids, however, were more numerous and effective.

When they received the summons to Spain, the Almoravids had already created a state that spanned the Sahara. In the tradition of many Saharan tribes, they had—at least at an early stage of their history—a surprisingly egalitarian attitude to women. A woman, Zaynab al-Nafzawiya, dominated: "Some said the spirits spoke to her, others that she was a witch."

In Spain, the Almoravids drove back the Christians but also swept away the rulers of the petty Muslim kingdoms, first denouncing their luxury, then seizing it for themselves. The corruption to which the Almoravids submitted in their turn became a provocation and an enticement to other religiously inspired desert pastoralists. In the 1140s, the Almoravids' empire was conquered by a new ascetic alliance, the Almohads (AHL-moh-hads)—the name means "people of the oneness of God"—who again invaded Spain from North Africa and, for a while, propped up the Islamic frontier (see Map 12.2).

These movements of desert zealots also turned south on Islam's frontier with paganism in Africa. Almoravid efforts focused on Ghana (see Chapter 10). Ghana was gold-rich, for it controlled access to trans-Saharan trade, where gold was exchanged for salt. It was also offensive to the Almoravids as the home of "sorcerers," where, according to reports, people buried their dead with gifts, "made offerings of alcohol," and kept a sacred snake in a cave. Muslims—presumably traders—had their own quarter in or near the Ghanian capital Kumbi Saleh, reportedly with a dozen mosques, but were kept apart from the royal quarter of the town. Ghana fought off Almoravid armies until 1076 when Kumbi fell, and its defenders were massacred. The northerners' political hold south of the Sahara did not last, but Islam was firmly implanted in West Africa.

In the next century, Arab writers regarded Ghana as a model Islamic state, whose king revered the true caliph in Baghdad and dispensed justice with exemplary openness. They admired his palace, with its objects of art and windows of glass; the huge gold ingot that was the symbol of his authority; the gold ring by which he tethered his horse; his silk clothes; his elephants and giraffes. This magnificence did not last. After a long period of stagnation or decline, pagan invaders destroyed Kumbi. But Islam had spread so widely by then in the Sahel that it retained its foothold south of the Sahara for the rest of the Middle Ages.

Christian and Muslim harmony. Songs in praise of the Virgin Mary, written by King Alfonso X of Castile (r. 1252–1284), could be played and enjoyed by both Christian and Muslim musicians. Both traditions upheld—and still uphold—the virginity of Jesus' mother. Food, dress, language, and even some religious practices spanned the frontier between Christian- and Muslim-ruled areas.
A Moor and a Christian playing the lute, miniature in a book of music from the 'Cantigas' of Alfonso X 'the Wise' (1221–84). 13th Century (manuscript). Monasterio de El Escorial, El Escorial, Spain/ bIndex/Bridgeman Art Library.

The Almoravids and Almohads

1076	Kumbi Saleh falls to Almoravid armies
1080s	Muslim kingdoms in al-Andalus call on Almoravids for help
1140s	Almoravid Empire falls to the Almohads

A CLOSER LOOK

A CORDOVAN IVORY JAR

Richly carved ivory jars for holding rare and costly essences, such as camphor, ambergris, and musk, show how luxurious life was in the palace of Madinat al-Zahra in Cordova in Muslim Spain in the late tenth century. This example was made for a brother of the reigning caliph.

The domed shape suggests the architecture of palaces and mosques. The missing knob would have had the form of a rich fruit, such as a pomegranate.

The inscription reads: "Blessings from God, goodwill, happiness, and prosperity to al-Mughira, son of the Commander of the Faithful, may God's mercy be upon him," with the date, 967.

The scenes depict hunters picking dates, court attendants, boys stealing eagles' eggs, and lions devouring bulls. The exact meaning of the images—if there ever was any—is lost, but all hint at royal power and well-being.

Ivory pyxis of Al–Mughira. Scene of harvesting dates. 968 CE. From Cordoba, Spain. Inv. 4068. Photo: H. Lewandowski/ Musée du Louvre/RMN Reunion des Musées Nationaux, France. Art Resource, NY.

How does this ivory jar reflect the wealth of Muslim Spain around 1000 C.E.?

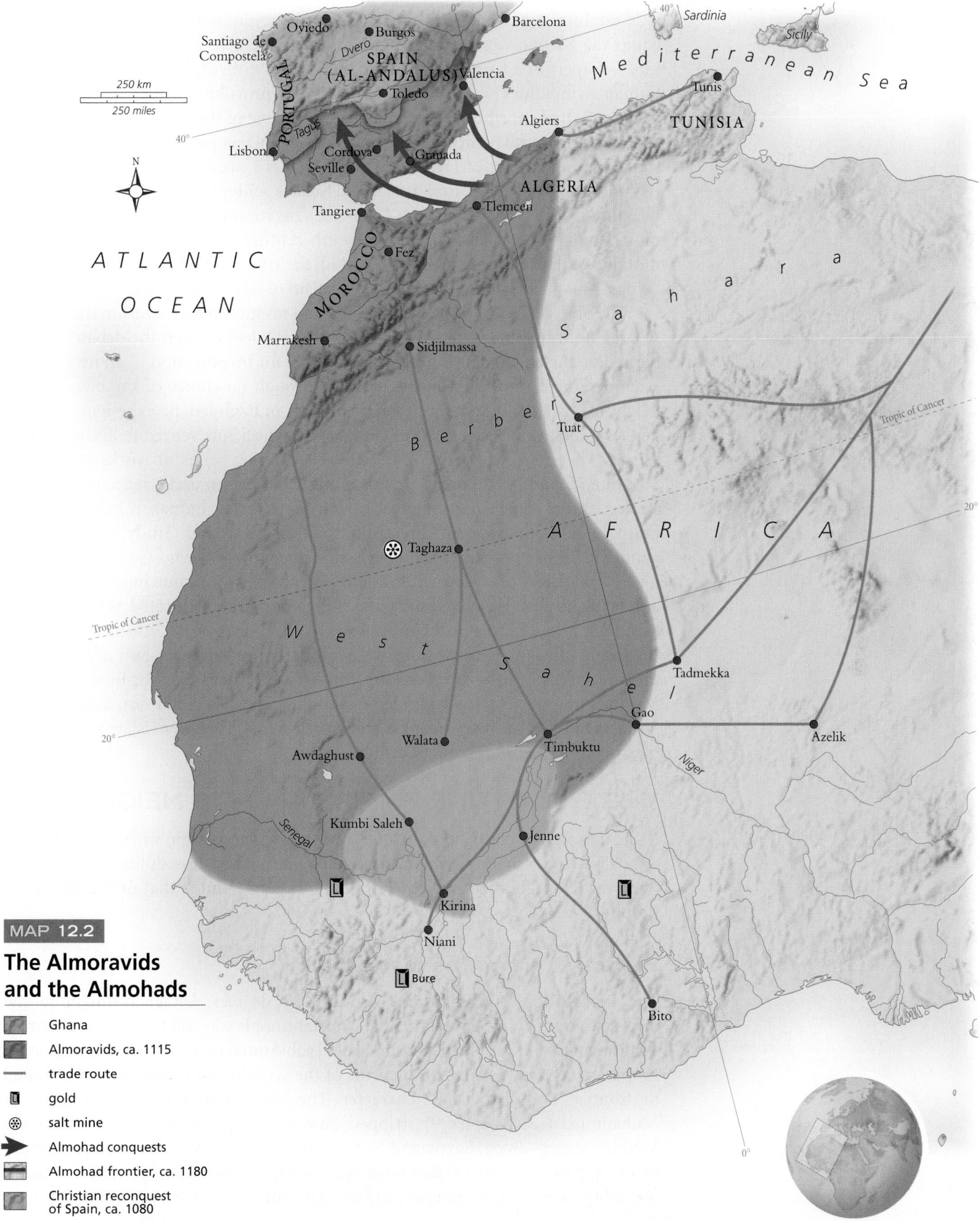
Oviedo
Burgos
Barcelona
Santiago de Compostela
Dvero
SPAIN (AL-ANDALUS)
Valencia
Toledo
PORTUGAL
Tagus
Lisbon
Cordova
Granada
Seville
Sardinia
Sicily
Mediterranean Sea
Tunis
Algiers
TUNISIA
ALGERIA
Tangier
Tlemcen
250 km
250 miles
N
ATLANTIC OCEAN
Fez
MOROCCO
Marrakesh
Sidjilmassa
Sahara
Berbers
Tuat
Tropic of Cancer
AFRICA
Taghaza
West Sahel
Tadmekka
Gao
Azelik
Walata
Timbuktu
Awdaghust
Niger
Senegal
Kumbi Saleh
Jenne
Kirina
Niani
Bure
Bito
40°
20°
0°

MAP 12.2

The Almoravids and the Almohads

Ghana
Almoravids, ca. 1115
trade route
gold
salt mine
Almohad conquests
Almohad frontier, ca. 1180
Christian reconquest of Spain, ca. 1080

The Progress of Sufism

It is doubtful whether war alone could heal the divisions among Muslims and equip the Islamic world to expand. For that, inventive intellectuals were necessary—shapers of a religion that could appeal to a diversity of cultures and engage human sympathies and sensibilities without provoking conflict. Sufism (see Chapter 9) had enormous popular appeal. But most of the Muslim elite rejected it. In the early tenth century, for instance, ordinary people revered the great spokesman of Sufism, al-Hallaj (ahl-hah-LAJ), as a saint, but the Islamic authorities put him to death, because he claimed to have achieved self-extinction and mystical union with God. Gilani (gee-LAH-nee), his successor, who became one of the most popular preachers in mid–eleventh-century Baghdad, offered a simple morality of dependence on God—based on the rule, "Expect nothing from human beings"—as an alternative to the rigid legalism of Islamic scholars.

Al-Ghazali, "On the Separation of Mathematics and Religion"

The divergence between legal-minded and mystic-minded Muslim theologians seemed unbridgeable until al-Ghazali (ahl-ga-ZA-lee) entered the debate. He was blessed or cursed with an "unquenchable thirst for investigation ... an instinct and a temperament implanted in me by God through no choice of my own." At the height of a career as a conventional theologian in Baghdad, he experienced a sudden awareness of his ignorance of God. He became a Sufi, retired to his native Persia, and, before his death in 1111, wrote a dazzling series of works reconciling Sufism and Sunni orthodoxy. He was a master of reason and science but demonstrated, to the satisfaction of most of his readers, that human minds could not grasp some truths without direct illumination from God. Study could tell you about God, but only a mystical experience can show you who God is. Al-Ghazali likened the effect of mysticism to the difference between knowing what health is and being healthy. He valued the faith of the poor and uneducated as highly as the learning of the officials of the mosques. His rehabilitation of Sufism was vital for the future of Islam. Because Sufis were indifferent to externals, Sufi mystics could tolerate cultural differences among Muslims and between Muslims and non-Muslims in a way the legal-minded Islamic intellectuals could not. Sufi habits of holiness satisfied ordinary people's craving for saints. They were Islam's most effective missionaries in subsequent centuries.

THE BYZANTINE EMPIRE AND ITS NEIGHBORS

If the pastoralists contributed to the salvation of the Islamic world, their attacks were disastrous for the non-Muslim states that proved less skillful at absorbing them or deflecting their power. A dramatic case in point is that of the Byzantine Empire.

Byzantium and the Barbarians

The Roman-ness of Byzantium dwindled by degrees. Under Justinian in the mid–sixth century, the government at Constantinople was still trying to reconstruct the Roman world (see Chapter 8) and ruled substantial parts of the Western Roman Empire as far away as Spain. But events of the seventh and eighth centuries shifted its frontiers and changed its character. The Arab expansion after the death of Muhammad (see Chapter 9) stripped away the empire's territory south of the Mediterranean—Syria, Egypt, and North Africa. Meanwhile, from the sixth century to the eighth, speakers of Slav languages slowly colonized much of the Balkans, including Greece. Arabs, Bulgars, and Russians threatened Constantinople itself.

In defense of the empire, missionaries and diplomats were as important as armies. The church virtually monopolized literacy in the areas of the Balkans and Russia where Byzantine missions were active. Missionaries invented the alphabets in which Slav languages were written. They also helped to spread statehood, legitimating strong rulers, sanctifying weak ones. Many Balkan states slipped and slid between allegiance to the Latin- and Greek-speaking churches, but for a while, thanks to missionary efforts launched from Constantinople, Moravians, Croats, and Hungarians hovered in Byzantium's orbit before finally opting for the Latin church. The greatest success for this religious diplomacy was the conversion of the rulers of much of what is now Russia (see Chapter 9). The policy was most effective when lavish gifts and the hands of Byzantine princesses, who married Bulgar khans and Russian princes, backed it. Instead of an empire like Rome's, a Byzantine "commonwealth" of Christian states was being built up—a diplomatic ring of outer defenses.

Byzantine diplomacy economized on force by intimidating visiting barbarians with elaborate ceremonials. The early tenth-century emperor, Constantine VII, laid down rules for courtly displays that were designed to embody imperial power and, in effect, to wield it. The effect designers aimed for was unashamedly theatrical. When an ambassador arrived at Constantinople in 924, the artificial roar of mechanical lions that guarded the imperial throne surprised him.

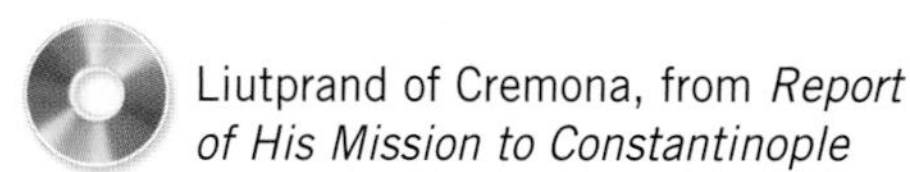
Liutprand of Cremona, from *Report of His Mission to Constantinople*

The deftness of Byzantine diplomacy, its rulers' ability to impress or intimidate surrounding "barbarians," is part of the repertoire of strategies with which all successful states managed the surge of migrations of the period. The wealth of the empire underpinned those strategies and paid for vital military backup. The Byzantine economy relied on the productivity of the peasantry of Anatolia and the trade that passed through Byzantine territory, for the empire enjoyed a privileged position where great arteries of trade converged: the Silk Roads, the Volga, the Mediterranean.

Yet the system was rickety. Wealth depended on security, which was hard to guarantee. And the effectiveness of Byzantine diplomacy had its limits. While a zone of Byzantine influence took shape in the Balkans, Russia, and the Caucasus, most steppeland peoples, and the Muslims to the east and south, were indifferent to Byzantine religion and unintimidated by Byzantine methods. Caught between Bulgars and Turks, Byzantium seemed to lie at the eye of the steppelander storm. Byzantines tended to see their predicament as a test of faith—an episode of sacred history. In 980, the miracle at Chonae first appeared in Byzantine writings: the story of how the Archangel Michael diverted a river that evil pagans had turned to threaten his church. It is tempting to read this story as an allegory for the prayed-for escape of the "Roman Empire" from destruction at barbarian hands.

The crown of King Geza I of Hungary (r. 1074–1077) received from Byzantium was not a disinterested gift, but an attempt to imply that the king was a subject of the empire and dependent on Byzantium for the legitimacy of his rule. Hungary, however, remained firmly attached to the Church of Rome and to Latin culture.

Basil II

The longed-for savior appeared from an unlikely quarter. The emperor Basil II barely survived adolescence. Usurpers allowed him to live on after his father's death until he succeeded to the throne peacefully in 976. His image appears on a page from his prayer book—heavily armed, attended by angels, while barbarians cringe at his feet. This is how he liked to see himself and wished to be remembered.

He ruled intuitively, as if coping with a constant state of emergency, enforcing his own will, administering rough justice, respecting no laws or conventions. In 996, he dealt with a landowner he saw exploiting peasants: "we had his luxurious villa razed to the ground and returned his property to the peasants, leaving him with what he had to begin with and reducing him to the peasants' level." This was an instance of a long conflict between great landowners and the throne. Emperors needed prosperous, independent peasants to provide taxes and manpower for the armies. Landowners wanted to control the peasants themselves. Aristocratic revolts and resistance to taxation were commonplace.

Basil dealt with the most troublesome of Byzantium's satellite peoples, the Bulgars, by blinding—so it was said—14,000 of their captured warriors and cowing them into submission. He incorporated Bulgaria into the empire in 1018. On the southern front, he made peace with the Arabs. In consequence, he gave the empire virtually ideal borders. In Bulgaria he followed up his terror stroke with conciliation, cooperating with the native elite, appointing a Bulgar as the local archbishop. In Greece he relied on repression, forcing the empire's religion and language on the immigrant Slavs. In Armenia, his successors lost patience with diplomacy and reconquered the region (see Map 12.3).

Force was expensive by comparison with the waiting game, bribes, and tricks of traditional Byzantine policy. Basil paid for a professional army by heavily taxing the aristocracy. When he died in 1025, his treasury was fuller than any emperor's since the sixth century. Prayers cited his name in Russia and Armenia. As late as the 1070s, a Hungarian king accepted a crown from Constantinople. The so-called crown of St. Stephen depicts the king reverencing the rulers of the Byzantine Empire.

The Era of Difficulties

Basil's legacy, however, was unsustainable. His methods of government were personal and arbitrary. The aristocracy could afford his taxes only while his power protected their lands from invaders. As Turkish migrations and invasions began to roll over Byzantine Anatolia, the revenues failed. The succession to the throne was problematic. Basil had no children, and his brother, who succeeded him, had only daughters. These were unusual circumstances: an opportunity for strong women to come to the fore. In the background, deeper social changes were under way. The family—formerly, in theory, a second-best lifestyle to monastic chastity—rose in Byzantine esteem in the tenth century. Women began to be admired for fertility as well as virginity.

In the eyes of influential classes—clergy, landowners, courtiers—eleventh-century experiments did not seem to justify the empowerment of female rulers. Princesses spent their lives confined to the palace, and though they got the same formal education as men, they were denied the opportunity to accumulate useful experience of the world. Basil's niece, Zoe, regarded the throne as a family possession and responsibility. Her "family album" is laid in mosaic in her private enclosure in the gallery of Constantinople's cathedral. Her third husband's portrait smothers that of her second, who murdered his predecessor, at Zoe's behest. Zoe outraged Constantinople's snobbish elite by adopting a workman's son as her heir—an upstart "pygmy playing Hercules," said the snobs. Zoe's sister Theodora ruled alone in 1055–1056, "shamefully" and "unnaturally"—according to her opponents—refusing to marry. These judgments lack objectivity, but show the outrage the sisters provoked among the elite.

Meanwhile, relations between the Latin- and Greek-speaking churches broke down. Differences had been growing over rites, doctrines, language, and discipline between the sees of Constantinople and Rome for centuries. Underlying the theo-

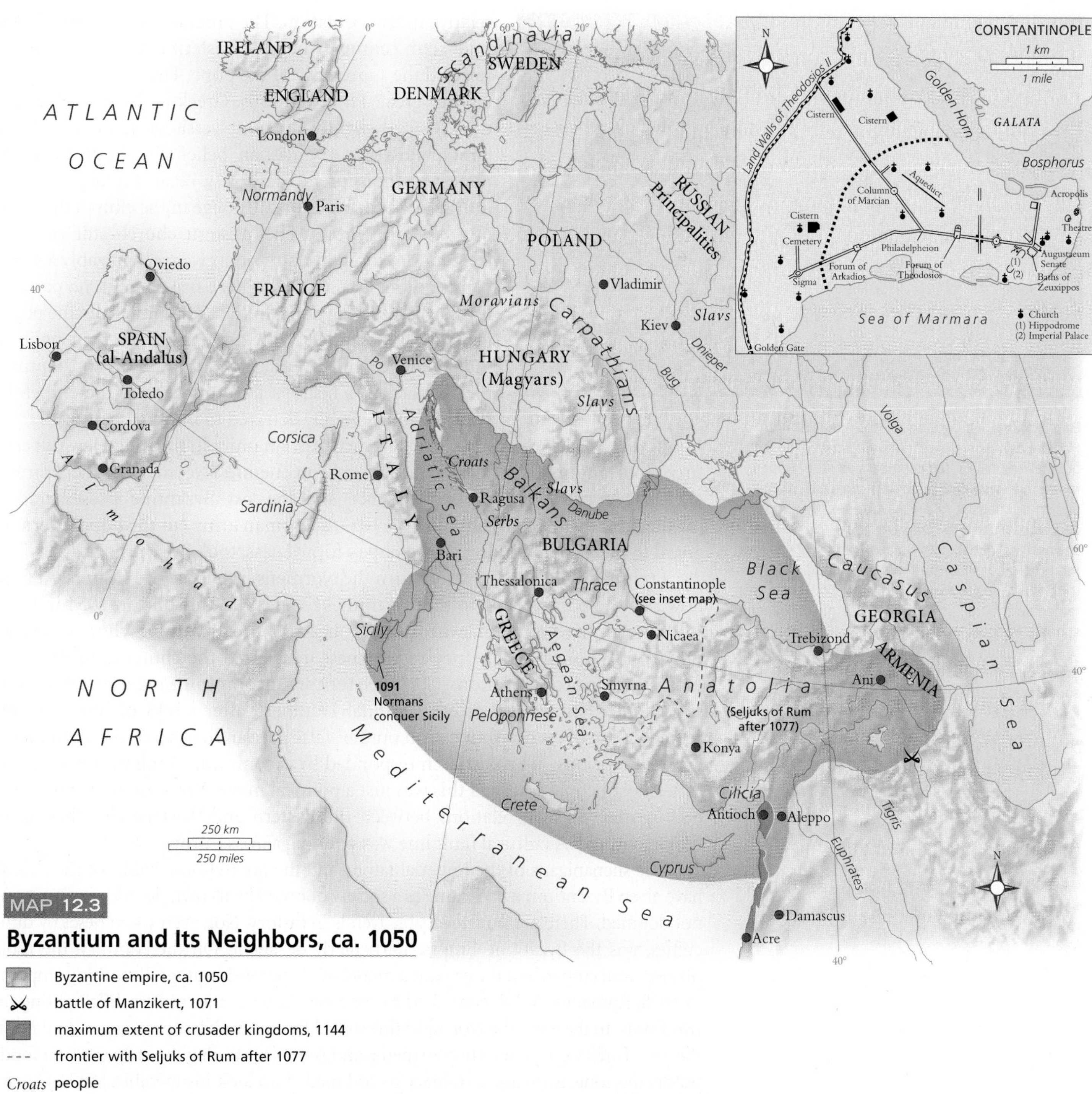

MAP 12.3

Byzantium and Its Neighbors, ca. 1050

- Byzantine empire, ca. 1050
- battle of Manzikert, 1071
- maximum extent of crusader kingdoms, 1144
- frontier with Seljuks of Rum after 1077
- *Croats* people

logical bitterness were deep cultural differences. Language was in part to blame. The Greek-speaking Byzantine Empire could not share the common culture of the Latin-speaking elites of Western and Central Europe, while few in the Latin West could speak or read Greek with fluency. Subtle theological distinctions, inexpressible in Latin, came easily in Greek.

Dogmas supposed to be universal turned out differently in the two tongues. For most people, religion is more a matter of conduct than creed. In this respect, differences between the Roman and Byzantine traditions built up over centuries of

Empress Zoe. The gallery of the great church of Hagia Sophia in Constantinople functioned as a private enclosure for members of the imperial family and was decorated with portraits of rulers and their spouses in pious attitudes. The mosaic dedicated to the Empress Zoe (980–1050) betrays the questionable complexities of her sex life. The face of Constantine IX Monomachus, her third husband, shown offering gold to Christ, was remodeled to replace the likeness of her second spouse, Michael IV, whom she had first employed to murder his predecessor, then banished to a monastery in 1041 when she tired of him. The squashed lettering above Constantine's halo to the left is clear evidence of a botched job.

relative mutual isolation. The process began as early as the mid–sixth century, when the Eastern churches resisted or rejected the supremacy of the pope. The effects were gradual but great. From the 790s, Greek and Latin congregations recited slightly different versions of the creed, the basic statement of Christian belief. By about 1000, the pope was the supreme authority regarding doctrine and liturgy and the source of patronage in the church throughout Western Europe. The Western church still enclosed tremendous local diversity, but it was recognizably a single communion. Eastern Orthodox Christians felt no particular allegiance to the pope. In the West, moreover, the popes generally maintained, with difficulty, their own political independence. In the East, the patriarchs of Constantinople, as that city's bishops were titled, were the emperor's subjects and generally deferred to imperial power.

It might have been possible to restore Christian unity in the mid–eleventh century. Constantinople and Rome faced common enemies. Norman invaders threatened the pope's political independence and the last Byzantine possessions in southern Italy and Sicily. On June 17, 1053, a Norman army cut the pope's German guard to pieces and, imploring the pope's forgiveness, took him hostage.

Eventually, the papacy would turn the Normans into its sword bearers. At first, however, the pope turned to the Byzantines for help. Meanwhile, in 1054 in Constantinople, the patriarch, who was the head of the Byzantine church, saw an opportunity to exploit the pope's weakness. He closed the churches of the city's Latin-speaking congregations. The pope sent an uncompromising mission to Constantinople. His representative, Cardinal Humbert, after weeks of bitter insults, served notice of excommunication on the "false patriarch, now for his abominable crimes notorious." The patriarch responded by excommunicating the pope. At the time, most people assumed this was just a political maneuver, soon to be rescinded or forgotten. In fact, relations between the Eastern and Western churches never fully recovered. A cultural fault line was opening across Europe.

The shenanigans of the imperial family and the quarrelsome habits of the church have given Byzantium a bad name as a society doomed by its own decadence. But it was not doomed. There are no irreversible trends in history. Nor, even when beset by difficulties, was the Byzantine Empire particularly decadent. On the contrary, the most unsuccessful emperor of the era was a model of energy and courage. Becoming emperor in 1068, Romanus IV Diogenes had to cope with aristocratic unrest while fighting on two fronts. In the west, the Normans threatened Byzantium's last possessions in Italy. In the east, Turks were penetrating Armenia and Anatolia, stealing the empire's vital food-producing zone. Romanus's military record made him look insuperable, but his generalship proved unequal to the task. In 1071, at the battle of Manzikert, the Turks forced the emperor to kiss the ground before the feet of their leader, Alp Arslan—a great-grandson of Seljuk's. Romanus was deposed by a coup. Feuding at Constantinople between aristocratic factions allowed the Turks to overrun much of Anatolia.

Byzantium and the Crusaders

In 1097, crusaders arrived at Byzantium, ostensibly to help. But by then, the Byzantines had already begun to recover the lost ground on their own. The Byzantine princess Anna Comnena considered the newcomers more of a hindrance. Superbly

Anna Comnena, from the *Alexiad*

educated in the classics, she was the official biographer of her father, the emperor. To her, the crusaders were lustful drunkards, enemies whose object was "to dethrone the emperor and capture the capital."

The tense cooperation between Byzantium and the crusaders, which characterized the First Crusade, broke down completely in the twelfth century. The crusaders failed to return to the empire most of the Byzantine territory they recaptured from the Muslims. Instead, they kept it for themselves. Byzantines were convinced of their own moral and cultural superiority over impious, greedy Westerners, while crusaders blamed "Greek treachery" for their failures. The crusades might have saved Byzantium, as the Turks saved the Islamic world. Instead, they undermined the empire.

Byzantium's difficulties multiplied. Agriculture was stagnant, despite the boom in other parts of Eurasia. The empire's hinterland beyond Constantinople was too insecure to prosper. In the twelfth century, in a reversal of earlier emperors' policy of nurturing the peasants at the landowners' expense, emperors tried to revive their rural revenues by granting control of peasant lands to great lords and encouraging monastic colonization of new lands. To some extent, this was another case of the attempt to exploit new resources, familiar in other societies of the time. The emperor Isaac II Angelus (r. 1185–1195), for instance, gave a port to a monastery that settled a site in Thrace, formerly "devoid of men and dwellings, a haunt of snakes and scorpions, just rough ground, overgrown with spreading trees." Measures like these—which so dramatically increased the farmland of Western Christendom, Ethiopia, or, as we shall see, of China—were of limited usefulness in a state whose territory was much diminished. Byzantium never recovered most of inland Anatolia from the Turks.

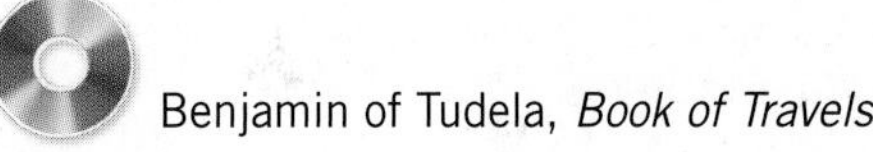
Benjamin of Tudela, *Book of Travels*

Increasingly, the empire was obliged to look to trade and industry for its wealth. There were, as a Byzantine poet observed, "big merchants" who "for large profits disdain terrors and defy seas." Self-made upstarts coveted money "as a polecat gazes at fat." The huge city of Constantinople benefited from its uniquely favorable position for trade, where Mediterranean and trans-Asian routes met. The Jewish merchant, Benjamin of Tudela, who visited in about 1170, celebrated "a busy city" with inhabitants so rich they "they look like princes" where "merchants come from every country by sea and land." With revenues of 20,000 gold pieces a year from rents, market dues, and the tolls on passing trade, "Wealth like that of Constantinople," Benjamin wrote, "is not to be found in the whole world. Here also are men learned in all the books of the Greeks, and they eat and drink, every man under his vine and his fig tree." For William of Tyre, a Latin bishop who visited at about the same time, the city seemed equally splendid on the surface. But William was more aware of underlying squalor and inequalities of wealth. "The wealthy overshadow the streets," he wrote—alluding to the mansions of the rich—"and leave dark, dirty spaces to the poor and to travelers." William's prejudices are obvious, but, precisely because he was so keen to criticize the city, we can trust his witness to its wealth.

A special relationship developed between Byzantium and Venice, a maritime republic near the northernmost point of the Adriatic Sea, where trade routes across the Alps converged with the main axis of north Italian commerce, the river Po. Venice's position on marshy, salty islands allowed little scope to accumulate wealth except by piracy, which Venetians practiced, mainly at the expense of Muslim shipping. In the ninth and tenth centuries, however, they began to build up enough capital to become major traders, channeling toward Europe a share of the valuable

Byzantium

527–565	Reign of Justinian
Sixth to eighth centuries	Colonization of Balkans by Slavs
Seventh and eighth centuries	Loss of territory as a result of Arab expansion
Ninth century	Missions to convert Balkans and Central Europe to Byzantine Christianity
1018	Bulgaria incorporated into Byzantine Empire
1054	Schism between Orthodox and Latin churches
1071	Battle of Manzikert; Byzantine army routed by Seljuk Turks
1095	Launch of First Crusade
1204	Sack of Constantinople

trade in silks and spices that was concentrated at Byzantium. Culturally, as well as economically, Venice was close to Byzantium. Though Venetians belonged to the Latin church and spoke a language derived from Latin, Byzantine models saturated their taste in art and buildings. It could not be otherwise. They knew Byzantium well, and so they had to admire it—and covet what they saw there.

Byzantium's wealth was a magnet and its weakness a motive. Toward the end of the 1190s, in Western Europe, popular enthusiasm revived for a new effort to launch a Crusade to recapture Jerusalem. The Venetians agreed to ship the crusading army out at what was to prove an unaffordable price. While the army gathered, an embassy arrived from the pretender to the Byzantine throne, Alexius IV, proposing a detour. If the crusaders put Alexius on the throne, he would help them against the Turks. Faced with their inability to pay the Venetians' bill, most of the crusaders agreed to a diversion. The Fourth Crusade, launched in 1202 to recapture Jerusalem, ended by shedding Christian blood in 1204 by capturing and sacking Constantinople and dividing most of what was left of the Byzantine Empire in Europe among the victors. Venice seized—in the words of the treaty that divided the empire—"one quarter and one half of one quarter" of Byzantine territory, achieving virtual monopoly rights in Byzantine trade and suddenly becoming an imperial power in the eastern Mediterranean. Meanwhile, in the remnants of Byzantine Anatolia, rival dynasties disputed claims to the imperial title.

Byzantine Art and Learning

Throughout the period this chapter covers, even amid the most severe difficulties of the twelfth century, Byzantium remained a beacon of learning and art. It is easy to get starry-eyed about the excellence of Byzantine culture. The most constant and careful Byzantine work in copying and analyzing the texts of classical authors and of the fathers of the Church was probably over by the tenth century. Mystics, represented by Saint Symeon the New Theologian (as he is called), who died in 1022, proposed an alternative route to learning, through divine illumination. "Orators and philosophers" could not access the wisdom of God. Painters

The Veroli casket. Classical stories with an erotic edge decorated Byzantine trinket boxes in the twelfth century. The panels visible in this picture of a famous example, the Veroli casket, finely carved in ivory, show Helen of Troy, Bellerophon with his winged horse, and the chaste Hippolytus on the right resisting the sexual advances of his wicked stepmother. Such were the subjects that entertained a rich lady's mind while she donned her jewels.

developed a tradition that abandoned realism in favor of stylized, formal figures, usually set against abstract or sketchy backgrounds, more indebted, perhaps, to the mosaics, in which Byzantine artists excelled, than to classical painting or sculpture. Most painters worked only on religious commissions and accepted the artistic vocation as a sacred obligation, aiming at work that captured the spirit of its subject and would be revered as holy in itself. Innovation happened slowly and subtly, for artists had to treat every subject strictly in accordance with tradition and church dogma.

Nonetheless, in most arts, and in learning, Byzantium preserved the classical legacy, and more. In the eleventh and twelfth centuries, it was revived in an intellectual movement comparable with the renaissance of the same period in the West (see Chapter 11). The historian and biographer Michael Psellus (1018–1078), for instance, wrote in an antique style based on classical Greek models, interpreted the meanings of ancient art, and lectured on Plato and Aristotle (see Chapter 6). Anna Comnena's historical work was saturated in knowledge of Homer, and she commissioned commentaries on neglected works of Aristotle. A renaissance of classical pagan themes in art followed in the twelfth century. The recovery of classical traditions in the West would probably have been impossible without cross-fertilization with the Islamic world and Byzantium.

CHINA AND THE NORTHERN BARBARIANS

Beyond the limits of the Turkish steppe, other steppeland peoples were even harder to deal with. Not even the Seljuks seemed able to win battles against them. Fortunately, however, for the Islamic world, none of these remoter nomads yet seemed willing to extend their conquests beyond the steppeland. Their critical relationships lay to the east, with China. We thus need a brief account of what had happened in China in the ninth and tenth centuries at this point.

The End of the Tang Dynasty

The history of China, in the 800s and 900s, looks like a series of disasters. An era of political disintegration began in the ninth century. Eunuchs controlled the succession to the imperial throne. The Xuantong (shoo-ehn-tuhng) emperor, who died in 859, never named an empress or an heir lest he be "made idle," that is, murdered. Steppelander incursions continued. In 840, in a typical incident, 10,000 Uighurs (see Chapter 9), driven from their Central Asian homeland by rival nomads, arrived on the Yellow River proposing to garrison the Chinese frontier. A new menace was the rise of banditry. In a land as densely populated as China's, every invasion, war, or natural disaster had profound environmental consequences, impoverishing many peasants and driving them to survive by any available means. In the late ninth century, bandit gangs grew into rebellious armies led by renegade members of the elite—students who had failed to pass the examinations for the civil service, Buddhist clergy forced out of monasteries the government had confiscated.

An imperial decree of 877 complained that the bandit forces "come and go just as they please." In 879, the bandit leader, Huang Chao (hwang chow), took Chang-an, the seat of the court, with effects described in one of the most striking poems of the time, the *Lament of Lady Qin*: rape, pillage, and bloodshed. Huang's successor, Zhu Wen (joo when), emerged as the most powerful man in China, effectively replacing the Tang dynasty in 907. His state fell in turn in 923 to Turkic nomads, and the Chinese Empire dissolved into "ten kingdoms."

China's situation recalls that of Western Europe, striving to maintain the ancient sense of unity and—for some rulers—even actively seeking to recover it in times of political dissolution. The Chinese predicament also parallels those of the Islamic world and Byzantium, beset by nomadic migrants and invaders. Chinese responses, as we shall see, were also similar. They tried to fend off the "barbarians" by methods akin to those of the Byzantines: diplomacy, bribery, intimidation, displays of cultural superiority. As in the Islamic world, Chinese worked to convert invaders to their own culture, usually successfully. As in all the states we have looked at, the reexploitation of internal resources—especially by converting forest to farmland—made an important contribution.

For China, however, the outcome was different from those of other comparable regions. Throughout the period this chapter covers, the reconstruction of unity never seemed perfect or stable, but unity remained an actively pursued and—as we shall see—ultimately recoverable ideal. Divisions over religion, which deepened disunity in Christendom, or in the world of al-Hakim, had no parallel in China. China survived the invaders from the steppes but surrendered much territory to them. And, unlike the Islamic world, China never wholly succeeded in turning invading warriors into a force it could use for its own expansion.

The Rise of the Song and the Barbarian Conquests

The fight for unity after the collapse of the 920s began in 960, when a mutinous army proclaimed its general as emperor. The dynasty he founded, the Song (soong), lasted until 1279, but it always had to share China's traditional territory with steppeland invaders who created empires and dynasties of their own in the north. These barbarian states adopted Chinese political ideas and bureaucratic methods and claimed the mandate of heaven—or, at least, a share in it—for themselves. But none of them were able to extend their conquests south of the Huai River, into the lands of rice paddies and dense population the Song retained.

First, from the early tenth to the early twelfth centuries, the Khitan state of Liao (lee-ow) loomed over China from Mongolia and Manchuria. In the tenth century, mainly under warrior-empresses, the Liao state acquired a southern frontier across the Yellow River valley. The Khitans remained faithful to their pastoral traditions, but they split their empire into two spheres, creating a Chinese-style, Chinese-speaking administration for their southern provinces. They began to build cities, following Chinese urban planning models, apparently to attract migrants. The Khitan Empire had its own civil service, selected on Confucian principles. In a treaty of 1004, the Song conceded equality to Liao, which became known as the Northern Kingdom, alongside the Southern Kingdom of the Song. The two states lived together in uneasy equilibrium.

Toward the end of the 1030s, a second steppeland state proclaimed itself an empire—the realm of Xia (hsia). The axis of the state was a strip of grazing land, 900 miles long, squeezed between Tibet and the southern Gobi Desert. In 1044 Xia arrogated the status of a kingdom superior to all others except Song and Liao. It had its own system of writing, its own bureaucracy, and an iron coinage much used along the Silk Roads. It also had a scholarly establishment, largely devoted to acquiring and commenting on Buddhist scriptures.

The last state builders to intrude into the region were the Jurchen (juhr-chehn), who from 1115 began to build up conquests that eventually included the whole Liao Empire and covered northern China as far as the Huai River (see Map 12.4). Their homeland was in the forests of northern Manchuria. Their traditional economy

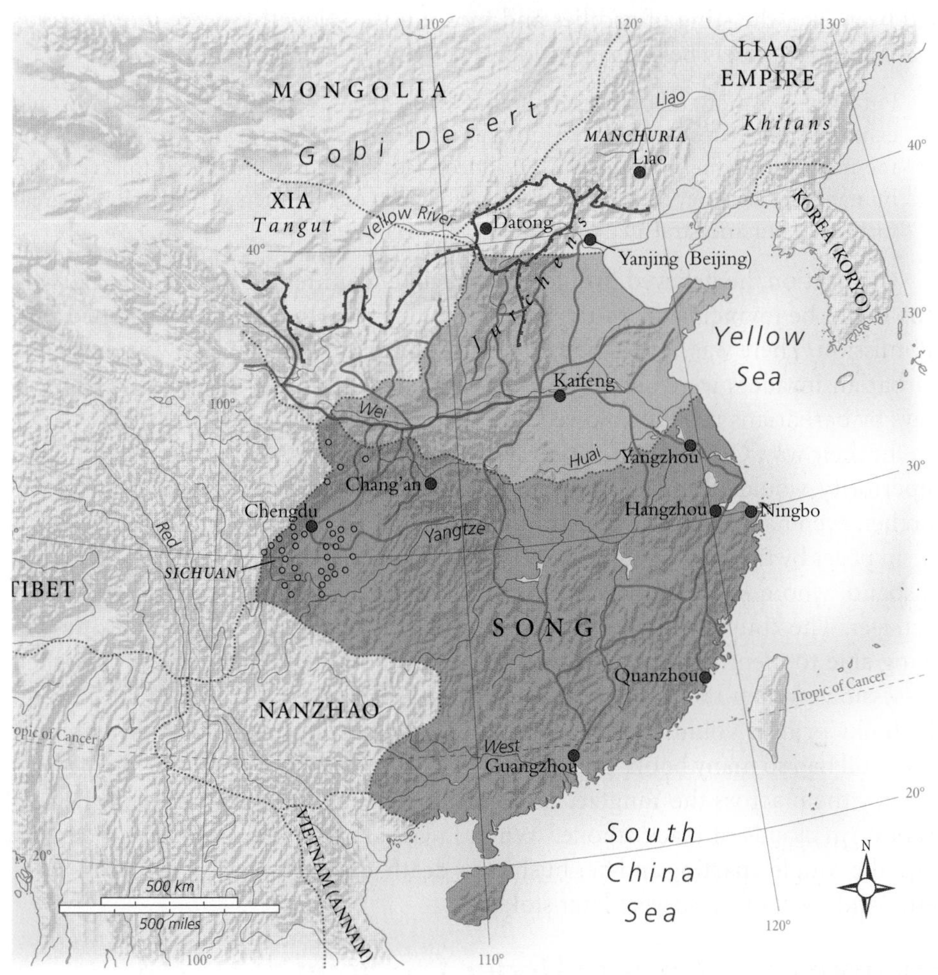

MAP 12.4

Song Empire, ca. 1150

Song empire, ca.1050

Song empire, 1127–1234

Silk Road

Great Wall

salt mine

imperial highways

Jurchens people

relied on hunting rather than herding. They were "sheer barbarians," Chinese envoys reported, "worse than wolves or tigers."

The Jurchen wars forced the Chinese to acknowledge Jurchen claims to the mandate of heaven. A treaty of 1127 imposed heavy annual tribute on the Song in silver, copper, and silk. Jurchen campaigns penetrated far into the south of China. In 1161, however, the invaders despaired of creating a river navy strong enough to dominate the Yangtze. The Song and Jurchen states learned to live with each other.

Meanwhile, the Jurchen adopted Chinese habits and traditions more fully than even the Khitans and Xia had. The Jurchen emperors were uncertain about this trend. On the one hand, they were quick to adopt Chinese bureaucracy and courtly customs themselves. On the other, they were afraid that the Jurchen would lose their warlike strength and will to dominate. The Jurchen, after all, were few in number—perhaps a few hundred thousand—compared with their more than 50 million Chinese subjects recorded in a census of 1207. Despite legislation forbidding Jurchens to adopt Chinese language or dress, distinctive Jurchen culture largely vanished.

Chinese thinkers found it hard to adjust to a world in which "barbarians" seemed their equals. On the whole, the Song accepted the reality of the new distribution of power, bribing and coaxing the foreigners into remaining quiet. One of the most supple intellects of the Song era was that of the early eleventh-century palace official, Ouyang Xiu (oh-yahng shoo). Earlier barbarian attacks, he thought, had been like "the sting of gadflies and mosquitoes." Now they were more serious and could not merely be brushed aside. He advised,

> Put away ... armor and bows, use humble words and ... generous gifts. ... Who would exhaust China's resources ... to quarrel with serpents and swine? ... Now is the moment for binding friendship. ... If indeed Heaven causes the rogues to accept our humaneness and they ... extinguish the beacons on our frontiers, which will be a great fortune to our ancestral altars.[1]

Civilization, he believed, would always win encounters with savagery. Barbarians might be invincible in battle, but in the long run, they could be shamed into submission. There was a lot to be said for this point of view. China always survived. Barbarian invaders were always seduced by culture. But the adoption of Chinese ways by barbarians usually followed bloody wars and destruction.

In their way, Ouyang Xiu's arguments simply rewrote the old script—Chinese superiority would ultimately prevail. This kind of thinking made defeat by the Jurchen even harder to bear. The traumas the victims of the wars suffered come to life in pages by the poet Li Qingzhao (lee ching-jhao): a memoir of her life with her husband, whom she had married for love when he was a student and she was a teenager. The couple played intellectual games at teatime, rivaling each other in being able to identify literary quotations. Their books were their most cherished possessions. When the Jurchen invaded in 1127, the fleeing couple "first gave up the bulky printed volumes, the albums of paintings, and the bulkiest ornaments." They still had so many books that it took 15 carts to bear them and a string of boats to ferry them across the Yangtze. Another Jurchen raid scattered more of the collection "in clouds of black smoke." When Li Qingzhao finally got beyond danger, after the couple's parting and her husband's death, only a few baskets of books were left—and most of those were later stolen.

Economy and Society Under the Song

Under pressure from the barbarian north, Song rule shrank toward the south. The Yangtze became the axis of the Song Empire. This amputation of the ancient Yellow River heartlands was bearable because population, too, had shifted southward. About 60 percent of Chinese lived in the Yangtze valley by the end of the tenth century.

Away from the steppeland frontier, Chinese expansion continued. Loss of traditional territory, combined with the growth of population, stimulated colonization in new directions. The census of 1083 reported 17,211,713 families. By 1124, the number had grown to 20,882,258. Censuses tended to underestimate numbers because tax evaders eluded the count. The Jurchen wars brought the growth of population to an end, but by then, Song China must have had well over 100 million inhabitants—perhaps about half as many again as the whole of Europe. The state had the most basic resource: labor. It needed food and space.

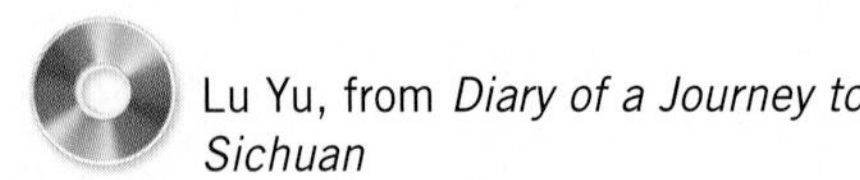

Lu Yu, from *Diary of a Journey to Sichuan*

The founder of the Song dynasty, known as the Taizu (teye-tzoo) Emperor, realized that China's new opportunities lay in a further shift to the southwest: the vast, underpopulated region of Sichuan (seh-chawn). Colonization needed peaceful conditions. So the native tribes had to be suppressed. In a heavily forested, mountainous region, where tribal chiefs had a demonic reputation, this was not easy. By repute, the wildest inhabitants were the Black Bone Yi, led by a chief the Chinese called the "Demon Master." In 1001, the Song divided the region into two administrative units called "routes." A campaign in 1014 began the pacification. In 1036, the Demon Master became a salaried state official. The "forbidden hills" of

Sichuan were stripped of forests and planted with tea and mulberries for silk production. The salt mines became resources of the Chinese Empire. A land poets formerly praised as a romantic wilderness became China's "heavenly storehouse."

Rice cultivation. In the second half of the thirteenth century, Zhen Ji illustrated poems on rice cultivation in a long series of paintings, all copied—like the poems—from twelfth-century originals. His art demonstrates the continuity of Chinese agriculture. Even after revolutionary new strains of rice were introduced in China, older varieties of the crop were still cultivated in traditional ways.

Alongside the colonization of new land, new methods of exploitation enriched China, in a process of internal expansion reminiscent of what was going on at the same time in other regions, notably in Europe and Ethiopia (see Chapter 11). Environmental change fed the growing population. Wetlands were drained. New varieties of rice arrived from Vietnam. Planting and harvesting two crops a year effectively doubled the capacity for food production in the Yangtze valley. From the 1040s, the state promoted agriculture by making loans to peasants for seed grain at favorable rates. Deforestation continued, stimulated by a tax on unharvested timber. By the end of the eleventh century, the forests around the city of Kaifeng (keye-fung) had disappeared, sacrificed to huge iron-smelting works, employing 3,000 men. In 1132, a new palace at Kaifeng was built with timber from the Qingfeng (chihng-fung) Mountains, reputedly inaccessible for centuries, like the enchanted forests of fairy tales.

Meanwhile, the money economy boomed. Song mints were always pumping out new coins—a million strings of coins a year in the early eleventh century, 6 million in 1080—and always devaluing the currency by putting less gold and silver into coins. Paper money became a state monopoly from 1043. Towns grew spectacularly. Until the Jurchen captured it, Kaifeng was not just a seat of government but a thriving place of manufacture and trade. A famous twelfth-century painting by Zhang Zeduan (jwang tzeh-dwan) depicts the bustling life of the city: craftsmen, merchants, peddlers, entertainers, shoppers, and gawking crowds; groaning grain ships bring the extra food; diners enjoy their meals in some of Kaifeng's 72 large restaurants, each of up to five pavilions, three storeys high, and connected by delicate bridges. In 1147, the poet Master Meng (mung) recalled in his *Dream of the Eastern Capital's Splendor* how in Kaifeng the entertainers' din "could be heard for miles."

Women rarely appear in Meng's verses or on Zhang's scroll. They never enjoyed the same status in China as among the pastoral cultures of the steppeland, where women were always important partners in managing the herds. Increasingly, in China, women were traded as commodities, and as young girls, their feet were tightly bound with cloth, so that they became permanently deformed, in a practice perhaps originally designed to hobble them against escape.

Despite the troubled relationship with the nomads and the loss of the northern provinces, the late Song Empire brimmed with wealth. In 1170, an official set off up the Yangtze to his job in Sichuan. He admired everything he saw: the new bridges, the flourishing commerce, the boats crowded together "like the teeth of a comb." The war readiness of 700 river galleys, with their "speed like flight," excited him. He celebrated ample signs of prosperity. Sichuan possessed enviable wealth. Two districts there had between them 22 centers of population producing annual tax revenue of between 10,000 and 50,000 strings of cash—more than any other district of the Song Empire outside the lower Yangtze. The frontier had been drawn into the empire.

Song Art and Learning

The era left an enduring intellectual and artistic legacy. To the eleventh-century elite, philosophy was the basis and business of government. On one side of the debate, Ouyang Xiu aimed to restore "the perfection of ancient times"—an ideal age "when rites and music reached everywhere." Wang Anshi (wahng ahn-sheh), who led the party on the other side of the debate, thought life was like a dream and valued "dreamlike merits" equally with practical results. He carried the notion of socially responsible government to extremes and consulted "peasants and serving girls" rather than relying on Confucian principles and ancient precedents. His policies when he was in charge of the government in the 1070s included progressive taxation, the substitution of taxes for forced labor, cheap loans for farmers, and state-owned pawnshops. Wang mistrusted Confucian confidence in China's ability to tame the steppelanders—he introduced universal conscription. To combat banditry, he organized village society in groups of ten families, so that each family was held responsible for the good behavior of the others.

Both parties supported reform of the examination system that produced the imperial officials with two objectives in mind: to encode in it an ethic of service to society, and to recruit the state's servants from as wide a range of social backgrounds as possible. The old examination tested only skill in composition, especially in verse, and in memorizing texts. The new test asked questions about ethical standards and about how the state could serve the people better. It was a conservative revolution.

While Wang's agenda shaped policy, Ouyang Xiu's dominated the intellectual mainstream. The dominant trend in philosophy for the rest of the Song era was the effort to reinterpret the Confucian classics for the readers' own times. Zhu Xi (joo shi) (1130–1200) summarized and synthesized all previous thinking on this subject. In some ways, he was what we would now call a secular humanist. He upheld the doctrine of the natural goodness of human beings. He doubted whether "there is a man in heaven judging sin" and dismissed prayer in favor of self-examination and study of the classics. Morality, he thought, was a matter of individual responsibility, not heavenly regulation. But he did accept the tradition on which the Chinese state was based: "Heaven" decreed the fortunes of society according to the merits of its rulers. Zhu's synthesis defined what subsequent ages called Confucianism.

The intellectual and economic environment of the Song Empire was favorable to the arts. There was money and enthusiasm for patronage of artists. The painting of the era has always attracted admiration, not just because it was technically excellent, but also because it specialized in scenes from the natural world. Admiration for the beauty of nature, untouched by human hands, is, perhaps, a measure of the maturity of a civilization. It is doubtful, however, whether Song artists painted nature, as modern romantics do today, for its own sake. To them, the natural world was a book of lessons about humankind. Su Dongpo (soo dohng-pwoh) (1036–1101) painted virtually nothing but bamboo, because its fragility suggested human weakness. Li Longmian (lee lung-mee-en) (1049–1106) favored gnarled trees, defying weather, as symbols of the resilience of the sages. Mi Fei (mee fay) (1051–1107) perfected the representation of mist—which is the breath of nature, with power to shape the image, like the spiritual dimension of human beings. With other Song painters, they produced some of the world's most influential, most imitated images.

Chinese night revels. A female musician entertains members of the scholar-gentry in *The Night Revels of Han Xizai,* painted in the tenth century by Gu Hongzhong. Chinese paintings rarely show men and women together in this kind of interior setting. The elaborately laid and decorated table, the porcelain ware, and the luxury and sexual appeal of female entertainment provide an intimate glimpse of courtly life during the Song dynasty.

IN PERSPECTIVE: Cains and Abels

The North African Muslim Ibn Khaldun (ihb-ihn hahl-DOON), one of the world's best historians, looking back from the late fourteenth century, saw history as a story of struggle between nomads and settled people. To some extent, he based his view on the experience of his native region in the eleventh and twelfth centuries, when, as far as he could make out, pastoralist invaders wrecked its peace and prosperity: first, Arab herders whom the Fatimids released or expelled from southern Egypt; then the Almoravids and Almohads from the Sahara. Modern historians have challenged his interpretation. The mutual disdain between tillers and herders was neither as deep nor destructive as Ibn Khaldun thought. But the tension he perceived was real. The biblical story of Cain and Abel traces the origins of human conflict to the mutual hatred and murderous rivalry of a tiller of the soil and a keeper of flocks.

Ibn Khaldun, from *The Muqaddimah*

Nomads threatened their farming neighbors in various ways. The nomadic way of life demanded immeasurably more land per head of population than the intensive agriculture that fed dense farming populations. Nomads were ill equipped for some economic activities, including mining and silk manufacture, and the production of commodities, such as tea, fruit, and grain. For these things, therefore, they depended on theft, tribute, or trade from farming communities. The nomads were better equipped for war. Horsemanship made their way of life a preparation for battle. Sedentary peoples had not yet developed firearms or fortifications good enough to tilt the balance in their own favor. The nomads tended to cherish ideologies of superiority—of jihad or of divine election for empire—that clashed with the opposite convictions of the settled peoples. Nomads could exploit farmers' lands, but agricultural communities did not yet have the technology—steel plows, mechanical harvesters—to turn the soils of the grasslands into farmland.

Yet the hostility of nomads and farmers arose less, perhaps, from conflicts of interest than from mutual misunderstanding: a clash of cultures, incompatible ways of seeing the world and coping with it. There is no moral difference between settled and nomadic lifeways. Yet each type of community tended to see the other as morally inferior. This was probably because for followers of each way of life, those of the other represented all that was alien. Their mutual descriptions were full of incomprehension and disgust.

Real differences underpinned this mutual revulsion. Pastoralist diets were, for farmers, literally stomach churning. Pastoralists relied on dairy foods, which most

MAKING CONNECTIONS

NOMADIC THREATS TO SEDENTARY PEOPLES

CHARACTERISTICS OF NOMADS	CONSEQUENCES
Nomadic way of life requires extensive land →	Constant threat of attack on sedentary peoples
Nomads ill equipped for certain economic activities and the manufacture of favored commodities →	Dependence on theft and tribute from or trade with sedentary peoples
Nomads expert horsemen →	Until development of firearms and fortifications, sedentary peoples at a disadvantage in war
Nomads cherish ideologies of superiority →	Clash between nomads and settled peoples
Nomads can easily exploit farmers' lands →	Until development of steel plows and mechanized harvesters, farmers could not exploit grasslands

CHRONOLOGY

907	End of Tang dynasty
960	Beginning of Song dynasty; conversion of Karkhanid Turks to Islam
1054	Schism between Latin and Orthodox Christianity
1071	Battle of Manzikert; end of Byzantine dominance in Anatolia
1076	Kumbi Saleh falls to Almoravid armies
1080s	Muslim kingdoms in al-Andalus call on Almoravids for help
1095	Pope Urban II calls for crusade to capture Jerusalem
1099	Jerusalem falls to crusaders
1111	Death of al-Ghazali, Sufi mystic and theologian
1140s	Almoravid Empire falls to the Almohads
1187	Crusader kingdom of Jerusalem falls to Saladin
1204	Sack of Constantinople by crusaders

farmers rejected, because after early childhood they did not naturally produce lactase—the substance that makes milk digestible. It was also normal for herders to open their animal's veins for fresh blood to drink. This practice enabled nomad armies to take nourishment without halting on the march. Nomad diets tended to be short on plant foods. So to balance their intake, nomads would usually eat the raw organ meats of dead animals, which contain relatively high levels of vitamin C, which, in other cultures, people get from fruit and vegetables. Indeed, meat processed without cooking was important in the treeless environments of the steppe and the desert, where the only cooking fuel was dried animal dung. One of the great resources of the Eurasian steppe was the fat-tailed sheep, specially bred to drag its broad tail behind it. Its fat is wonderfully soft. Even if nomads have no time to heat this fat, or no kindling with which to cook it, they can eat it raw and digest it quickly. These were all elements of a rational food strategy for the nomadic life, but they inspired denunciations of the "barbaric" customs of eaters of raw meat and drinkers of blood. The nomads responded with equal contempt. For them, the settled life was soft and corrupt. Farming involved grubbing and groveling in mud. Cities and rice paddies were cramped and unhealthy.

After successful conquests, the nomads could usually be absorbed and induced to adopt or tolerate settled ways of life; but the conquerors kept coming. The relative success of the Islamic world in absorbing and converting the invaders of the tenth and eleventh centuries was a decisive feature of the history of the period. Byzantium, by contrast, failed to tame the intruders, while Western Christendom could recruit no more pastoralists after the Magyars. China developed no strategy to cope with the nomads, except to retreat and wait for them to adopt Chinese ways. Unprecedented changes in the steppeland, however, were about to upset the balance between nomads and settled peoples and unleash the most formidable steppeland conquerors of all, the Mongols. The outcome would transform the history of Eurasia.

PROBLEMS AND PARALLELS

1. Was the Islamic world's disunity an inevitable outcome of its vast geographic expansion by 1000? What parallels, if any, are there to earlier empires?
2. What was the influence of steppeland invaders on the Islamic world? Why was the Islamic world more successful in absorbing nomads than was Christian Europe?
3. The Crusades started as an outgrowth of the tradition of pilgrimage. How was a religious process transformed into a series of violent military campaigns? What were the ultimate effects of the Crusades?
4. Did the Almoravids' and Almohads' involvement in Spain in the twelfth century ultimately hinder or help Islamic power there? Why is the conversion of Ghana to Islam ultimately of more historical significance?
5. Why did most Muslim elites and clerics reject the Sufis? Why were the Sufis more popular with ordinary Muslims than with the Islamic elite?
6. Why was it important for the Byzantines to claim to be the Roman Empire? Why was it strategically important for the rulers of Constantinople to build a Byzantine "commonwealth"? What were the consequences of the rupture in relations between Latin and Orthodox Christianity?
7. How did China under the Tang deal with nomadic invaders? Were the Chinese more or less successful than their European and Muslim contemporaries?
8. Why does the hostility between pastoralists and sedentary peoples have less to do with conflicts of interest than with a clash of cultures?

DOCUMENTS IN GLOBAL HISTORY

- Early Turkish history from the *Dede Korkut*
- Al Thalibi, *Recollections of Bukhara*
- A Muslim view of the Crusaders
- Al-Ghazali, on "On the Separation of Mathematics and Religion"
- Liutprand of Cremona, from *Report of His Mission to Constantinople*
- Anna Comnena, from the *Alexiad*
- Benjamin of Tudela, *Book of Travels*
- Lu Yu, from *Diary of a Journey to Sichuan*
- Ibn Khaldun, from *The Muqaddimah*

Please see the Primary Source DVD for additional sources related to this chapter.

READ ON

B. Lewis, *The Middle East* (1997) is a broad introductory narrative. M. S. Hodgson, *The Venture of Islam* (1977) is as always fundamental for anything in Islamic history. L. Yaacov, *State and Society in Fatimid Egypt* (1991) is an important collection of studies on the background to the caliphate of al-Hakim. T. Talbot-Rice, *The Seljuks in Asia Minor* (1960) is important for understanding the assimilation of the Turks. The *Dede Korkut* (1974) is available in an excellent edition by G. Lewis.

T. Asbridge, *The First Crusade* (2005) is a vigorous, up-to-date account. C. Tyerman, *God's War* (2006) is an efficient general introduction, as is J. Riley-Smith, *The Crusades* (2005). J. Riley-Smith, *Atlas of the Crusades* (1990) is a useful standby. K. M. Setton, ed., *A History of the Crusades* (1969) is exhaustive.

H. Kennedy, *Muslim Spain and Portugal* (1997) and R. Fletcher, *Moorish Spain* (1993) are helpful as introductions. D. Wasserstein, *The Rise and Fall of the Party Kings* (1985) deals with the dissolution of the caliphate of Cordova and its successor states. For the Spanish background, R. Fletcher, *The Quest for El Cid* (1991) is scintillating and highly readable. E. W. R. Bovill, *The Golden Trade of the Moors* (1992) and *Saharan Myth and Legend* (1959) are classic works that unfold the background to the Almoravids. N. Levtzion, *Ancient Ghana and Mali* (1980) is an authoritative and concise study. J. S. Trimingham, *The Sufi Orders in Islam* (1998) is the great classic treatment of its subject.

On Byzantium, as well as works recommended in earlier chapters, C. Mango, *Byzantium and Its Image* (1984) is particularly good on cultural aspects, and D. Obolensky, *The Phoenix: The Byzantine Commonwealth* (2000), which is particularly good on diplomacy, are helpful. B. Hill, *Imperial Women in Byzantium* (1999) is an indispensable modern study. A. J. Toynbee, *Constantine Porphyrogenitus and His World* (1973) is a timeless classic by one of the great historians of the last century. Among the texts referred to in this chapter, *The Embassy to Constantinople and Other Writings of Liutprand of Cremona*, ed. J. J. Norwich is instructive and there are many editions of the *Alexiad* of Anna Comnena and *The Itinerary of Benjamin of Tudela* (many editions). On relations with the Latin church, S. Runciman, *The Eastern Schism* (1955), though now half a century old, is concise and readable. J. J. Norwich, *A History of Venice* (1982) is a richly detailed narrative. D. E. Queller, *The Fourth Crusade* (1999) nicely blends narrative and analysis. There are many editions of the most engaging source: G. de Villehardouin, *The Conquest of Constantinople* (2006). N. Wilson, *Scribes and Scholars* (1991) is a lively account of Byzantine learning.

On Liao, J. S. Tao, *Two Sons of Heaven* (1988) is valuable; for the Jurchen, Y. S. Tao, *The Jurchen in Twelfth-Century China* (1977) is particularly good on sinicization. R. von Glahn, *The Country of Streams and Grottoes* (1988) is scholarly and well written, bringing the internal frontier of China to life. R. Egan, ed., *The Literary Works of Ou-yang Hsiu* (1984) is an invaluable source. J. T. C. Liu, *Reform in Sung China*, which originally appeared in the 1950s, has not been replaced as far as I know.

PART Six

The Crucible: The Eurasian Crises of the Thirteenth and Fourteenth Centuries

CHAPTER 13 The World the Mongols Made 314

CHAPTER 14 The Revenge of Nature: Plague, Cold, and the Limits of Disaster in the Fourteenth Century 342

CHAPTER 15 Expanding Worlds: Recovery in the Late Fourteenth and Fifteenth Centuries 374

This Korean world map, from about 1402, known as the Kangnido, is the earliest known map of the world from east Asia. It is also the oldest surviving Korean map. Based on Chinese maps from the fourteenth century, the Kangnido clearly shows Africa (with an enormous lake in the middle of the continent) and Arabia on the lower left. The Indian subcontinent, however, has been merged into a gigantic landmass that represents China. The Korean peninsula, on the upper right, is shown as much bigger than it actually is, while Japan, on the lower right, is placed much farther south than where it is actually located.

ENVIRONMENT

1300–1800
Little Ice Age

since mid-1200s
Lenses and clocks in Europe

CULTURE

1206–1360s
Mongol hegemony

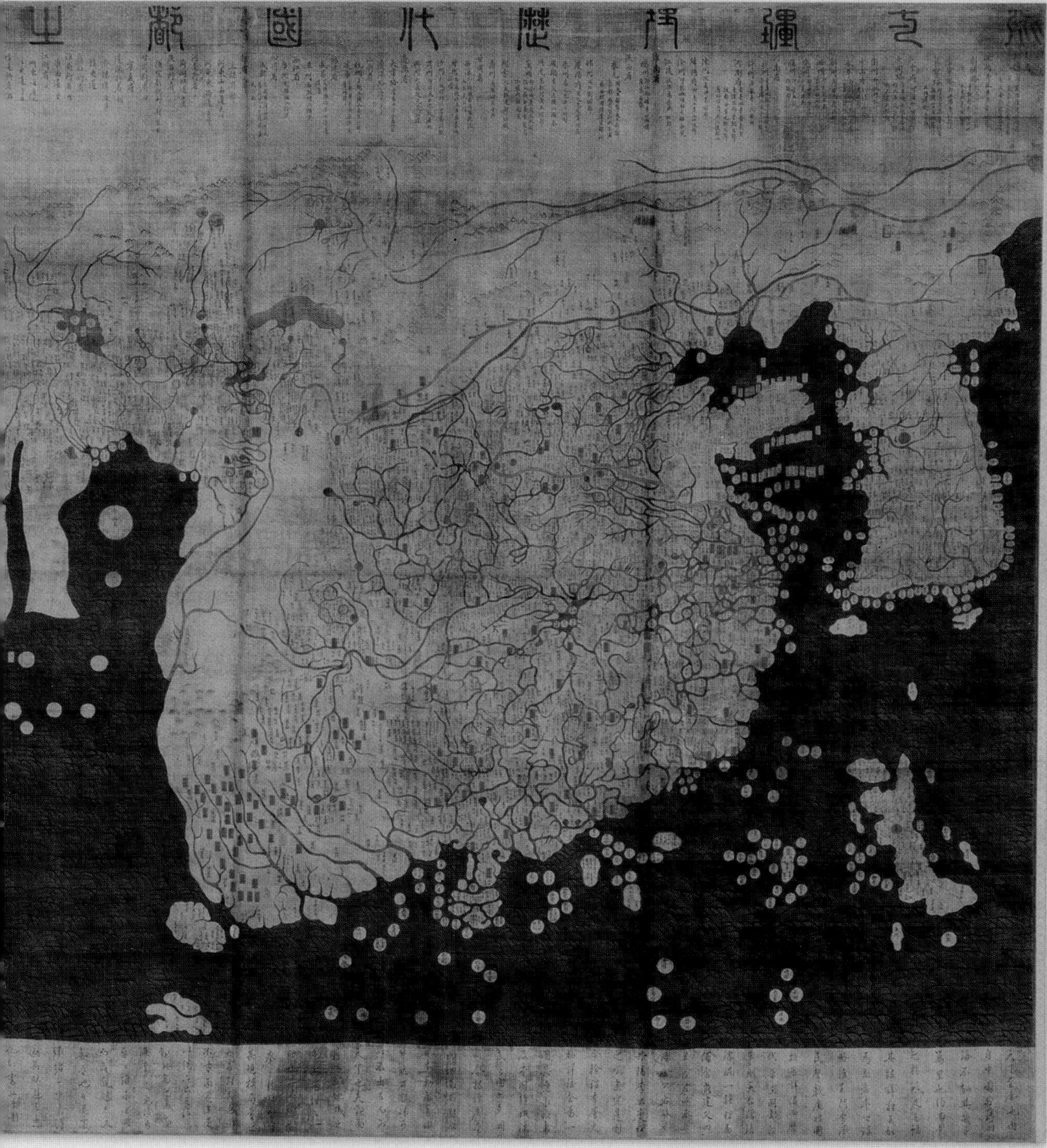

1330s–mid-1400s (and sporadically to 1700s)
Plague in Eurasia

since mid-1400s
Growth of Atlantic navigation

from 1350s
Rise of the Ottomans

1368–1644
Ming Dynasty (China)

from 1440s
Rise of Muscovy

from mid-1400s
Rise of Incas, Aztecs

Beginnings of oceanic imperialism

CHAPTER 13

The World the Mongols Made

The Mongols arrive in Georgia. Two coins from the kingdom of Georgia, minted less than two decades apart, show that the Mongols had conquered that Caucasian state. The front of the top coin, minted by Queen Rusudan of Georgia in 1230, features a bust of a bearded Jesus Christ, draped in a mantle and backed by a cross-shaped halo. The Greek abbreviations for the words "Jesus" and "Christ" flank his right and left shoulders respectively. A Georgian inscription runs along the border. The back of the coin shows inscriptions in both Georgian and Arabic. In contrast, on the bottom coin, minted by King David in 1247, a figure on horseback has replaced the image of Jesus Christ (front), while the inscription on the back of the coin is exclusively in Arabic and identifies the king as "the slave of the Great Khan."

IN THIS CHAPTER

THE MONGOLS: RESHAPING EURASIA
The Mongol Steppe

THE MONGOL WORLD BEYOND THE STEPPES: THE SILK ROADS, CHINA, PERSIA, AND RUSSIA
China
Persia
Russia

THE LIMITS OF CONQUEST: MAMLUK EGYPT AND MUSLIM INDIA
Muslim India: The Delhi Sultanate

EUROPE

IN PERSPECTIVE: The Uniqueness of the Mongols

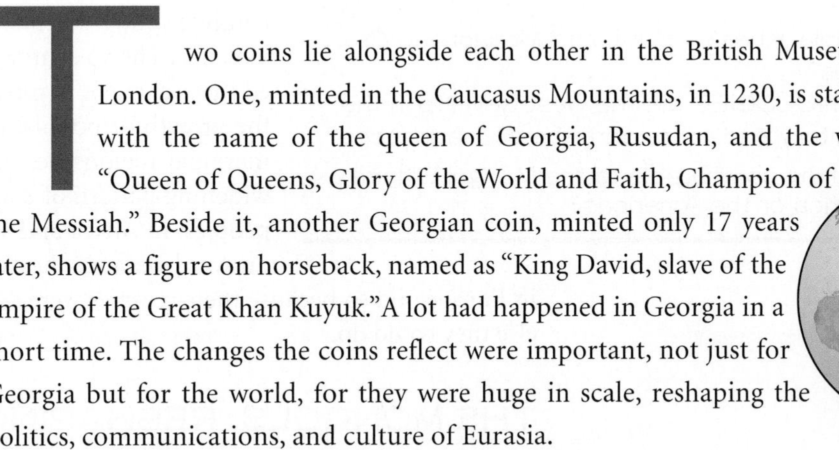

Two coins lie alongside each other in the British Museum in London. One, minted in the Caucasus Mountains, in 1230, is stamped with the name of the queen of Georgia, Rusudan, and the words, "Queen of Queens, Glory of the World and Faith, Champion of the Messiah." Beside it, another Georgian coin, minted only 17 years later, shows a figure on horseback, named as "King David, slave of the empire of the Great Khan Kuyuk." A lot had happened in Georgia in a short time. The changes the coins reflect were important, not just for Georgia but for the world, for they were huge in scale, reshaping the politics, communications, and culture of Eurasia.

Georgia, protected by its high mountains, had been remarkably successful in resisting the nomad armies of the eleventh and twelfth centuries. Though the Seljuk Turks (see Chapter 12) had briefly terrorized the kingdom and exacted tribute, the Georgians fought back. They refused to pay tribute, recovered their lost possessions, and extended their frontiers over parts of neighboring Armenia. In the early thirteenth century, Georgia was a formidable state, capable of imposing rulers as far afield as the Byzantine city of Trebizond (TREH-bih-zahnd) on the Black Sea and the Muslim city of Ahar in Azerbaijan (ah-zehr-bay-ZHAHN) on the Caspian. In the 1220s, James of Vitry, a Catholic bishop and historian of his own times, admired Georgian pilgrims he saw in Jerusalem, who "march into the holy city with banners displayed, without paying tribute to anyone, for the Muslims dare in no way molest them".

As James of Vitry noted, Georgia was "surrounded by infidels on all sides". That did not seem to matter. The Georgians even wrote to the pope promising assistance in a new crusade. Suddenly, however, in 1224, letters from Georgia arrived in Rome, withdrawing the promise. "A savage people of hellish aspect has invaded my realm," wrote Rusudan, "as voracious as wolves in their hunger for spoils, and as brave as lions." In the next decade, her letters got increasingly desperate. The Mongols were coming. The world would never be the same again.

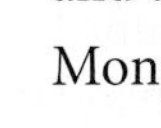

FOCUS questions

- WHY WERE the Mongols able to conquer such a vast empire?
- WHAT WERE the positive and negative effects of the Mongol conquests?
- WHY DID the Mongols fail to conquer Egypt, India, and Japan?
- HOW DID Kubilai Khan's reign blend Mongol and Chinese traditions?
- WHAT TECHNOLOGIES did the West develop in the thirteenth century and what were the consequences?
- WHY DID nothing comparable to the Mongol Empire develop in Africa or the Americas?

The effects of the events of the rest of the century refashioned Eurasia, destroying old states, creating new ones, disrupting existing communications and reforging stronger, wider-ranging links. Though at first the Mongols razed cities, destroyed crops, slaughtered elites, and depleted peoples, it looked for a while as if a safer, richer, more interconnected, more dynamic, more expanding, and more enlightened world might emerge—as if something precious were to form in an alchemist's crucible, out of conflicting ingredients, flung at random and stirred with violence. Then a century of environmental disasters arrested these changes in most of Eurasia. Catastrophes reversed the growth of populations and prosperity. But previously marginal regions began to be drawn more closely into a widening pattern of contacts and cultural exchange. Some peoples, in Africa and southeast Asia, for example, looked outward because they escaped disaster. Others, especially in Europe, did so because their reverses were so enormous that there was nothing else they could do.

THE MONGOLS: RESHAPING EURASIA

The earliest records of Mongol-speaking peoples occur in Chinese annals of the seventh century, when they emerged onto the steppes of Central Asia, from forests to the north, and became horse-borne nomads and sheepherders. In the early twelfth century, the bands or alliances they formed got bigger, and their raids against neighboring sedentary peoples became more menacing. In part, this was the effect of the growing preponderance of some Mongol groups over others. In part, it was the result of economic change.

Contact with richer neighbors enriched Mongol chiefs as mercenaries or raiders. Economic inequalities arose in a society in which blood relationships and seniority in age had formerly settled every person's position. Prowess in war enabled particular leaders to build up followers in parallel with—and sometimes in defiance of—the old social order. They called this process "crane catching"—comparing it to caging valuable birds. Successful leaders enticed or forced rival groups into submission. The process involved peoples who were not strictly Mongols, including many who spoke Turkic languages. In 1206, Temujin (TEH-moo-jeen), the most dynamic leader, proclaimed himself ruler "of all those who live in felt tents"—staking a claim to a steppe-wide empire. He was acclaimed by a title of obscure meaning that is traditionally rendered in the Roman alphabet as "Genghis Khan" (GEHN-gihs hahn).

Today, his memory is twisted between myths. When Mongolia was a communist state between 1921 and 1990, he was an almost unmentionable figure, inconsistent with the "peace-loving" image the communists tried to project. Now he is Mongolia's national hero. In his own day, he addressed different audiences with conflicting messages. To Muslims, he was sent by God to punish them for their sins. To Chinese, he was a candidate for the mandate of heaven. To Mongols, he was a giver of victory and of the treasure it brought. To monks and hermits, he stressed his own asceticism. "Heaven is weary of the inordinate luxury of China," he declared. "I have the same rags and the same food as cowherds and grooms, and I treat the soldiers as my brothers."

The violence endemic in the steppes now turned outward to challenge neighboring civilizations. Historians have been tempted to speculate about the reasons. One explanation is environmental. Temperatures in the steppe fell. People farther west on the Russian plains complained that a cold spell in the early thirteenth century caused crops to fail. So declining pastures might have driven the Mongols to expand from the steppes. Population in the region seems to have been relatively high, and the pastoral way of life demands large amounts of grazing land to feed relatively few people. So perhaps the Mongol outthrust was a consequence of having more mouths to feed. Yet the Mongols were doing what steppelanders had always sought to do: dominate and exploit sedentary peoples. The difference was that they did it with more ambition and efficiency than their predecessors.

Genghis Khan enforced or induced unity over almost the entire steppeland. A single ideology came to animate, or perhaps reflect, his program: the God-given right of the Mongols to conquer the world. Mongol-inspired sources constantly insist on an analogy between the overarching unity of the sky and God's desire for the Earth to echo that unity through submission to one ruler. This imperial vision probably grew on Genghis Khan gradually, as he felt his way from raiding, tribute gathering, and exacting ransom to constructing an empire, with permanent institutions of rule. Tradition alleges a turning point. When one of his generals proposed to exterminate 10 million Chinese subjects and convert their fields into pasture for Mongol herds, Genghis Khan realized that he could profit more by sparing the peasants and taxing them to the tune of 500,000 ounces of silver, 400,000 sacks of grain, and 80,000 bolts of silk a year.

Genghis Khan. Rashid al-Din (1247–1318) was a former Jewish rabbi, converted to Islam, who became the chief minister of the Mongol rulers of what is now Iran. His *Compendium of Chronicles* was propaganda that depicted Mongol rulers in Persian style. This is the image of Genghis Khan his successors liked to project—a lone, simple tent-dweller who was the arbitrator and lawgiver to petitioners from many nations.

The process, however, that turned him from destroyer to builder was tentative. The khan himself may have been only dimly aware of it. His initially limited ambitions are clear from the oath Mongol chiefs swore to him at his election. "If you will be our khan, we will go as your vanguard against the multitude of your enemies. All the beautiful girls and married women that we capture and all the fine horses we will bring to you." The khan acquired an unequaled reputation for lust and bloodlust. "My greatest joy," he was remembered for saying, "is to shed my enemies' blood, wring tears from their womenfolk and take their daughters for bedding." Meanwhile, he made the streets of Beijing (bay-jeeng)—according to an admittedly imaginative eyewitness—"greasy with the fat of the slain." His victims in Persia amounted, believably, to millions. Even after Genghis Khan had introduced more constructive policies, terror remained an instrument of empire. Mongol sieges routinely culminated in massacre.

Wherever Mongol armies went, their reputation preceded them. Armenian sources warned Westerners of the approach of "precursors of Antichrist ... who rush with joy to carnage as if to a wedding feast or orgy." The invaders looked like monkeys, it was said, barked like dogs, ate raw flesh, drank their horses' urine, knew no laws, and showed no mercy. Matthew Paris, the thirteenth-century English monk who, in his day, probably knew as much about the rest of the world as any of his countrymen, summed up the Mongols' image: "They are inhuman and beastly, rather monsters than men. ... And so they come, with the swiftness of lightning to the confines of Christendom, ravaging and slaughtering, striking everyone with terror and with incomparable horror."

The Rise of the Mongols

Seventh century	Earliest records of the Mongol people
Early twelfth century	Larger Mongol bands attack sedentary peoples
1206	Temujin proclaims himself khan

The Mongol conquests reached farther and lasted longer than those of any previous nomad empire (see Map 13.1). At its fullest

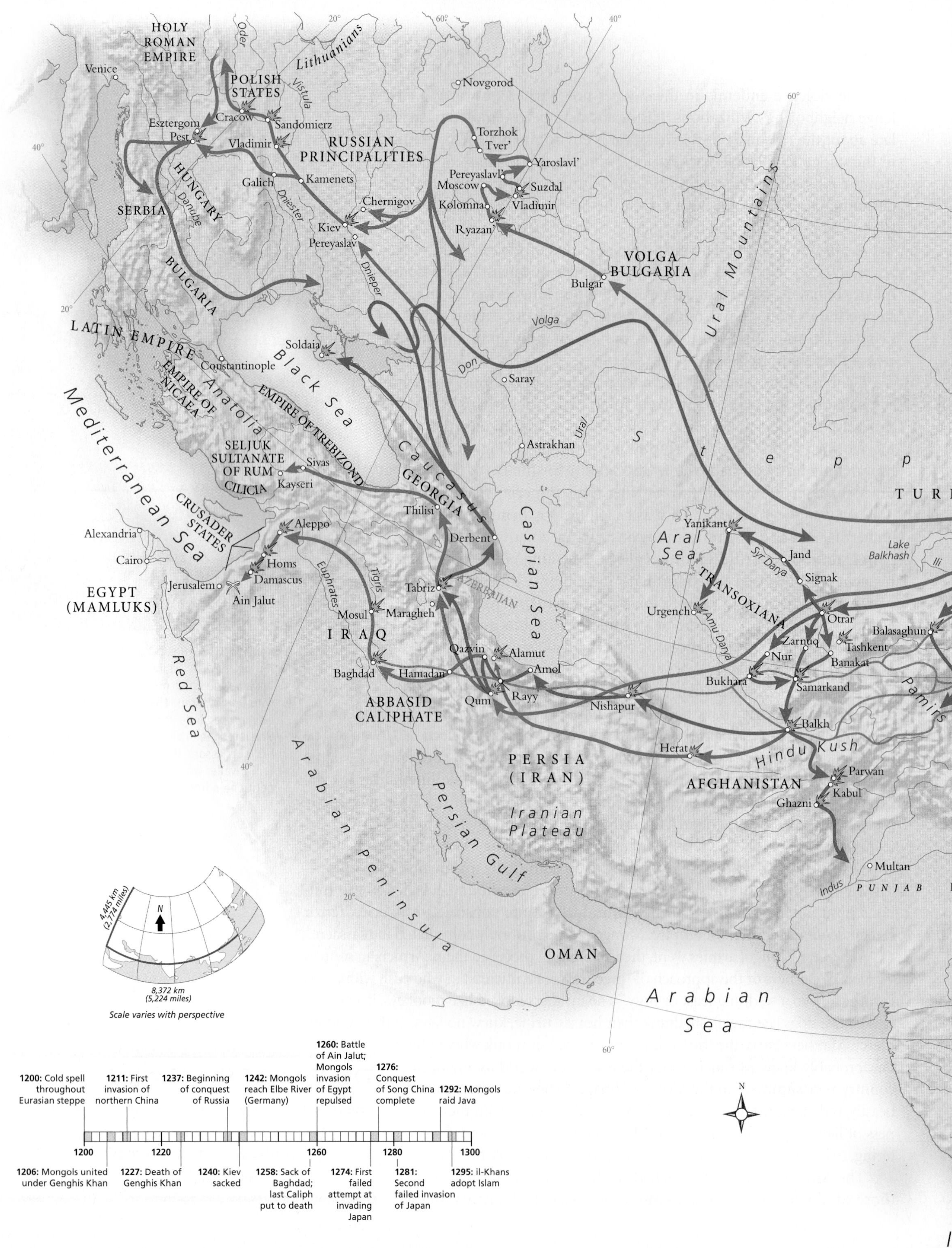

HOLY ROMAN EMPIRE
Venice
Oder
Lithuanians
POLISH STATES
Vistula
Novgorod
Cracow
Sandomierz
Esztergom
Pest
Vladimir
RUSSIAN PRINCIPALITIES
Torzhok
Tver'
Yaroslavl'
Pereyaslavl'
Moscow
Suzdal
Vladimir
Kolomna
Ryazan'
HUNGARY
Danube
Galich
Kamenets
Dniester
SERBIA
Chernigov
Kiev
Pereyaslavl
Dnieper
Ural Mountains
VOLGA BULGARIA
Bulgar
BULGARIA
Volga
LATIN EMPIRE
Soldaia
Constantinople
Black Sea
Don
Saray
EMPIRE OF NICAEA
Anatolia
EMPIRE OF TREBIZOND
Mediterranean Sea
SELJUK SULTANATE OF RUM
Sivas
Kayseri
CILICIA
Caucasus
GEORGIA
Ural
Astrakhan
Steppe
TURK
Caspian Sea
CRUSADER STATES
Tbilisi
Alexandria
Aleppo
Derbent
Yanikant
Aral Sea
Syr Darya
Jand
Lake Balkhash
Ili
Cairo
Homs
Damascus
Jerusalem
Ain Jalut
Euphrates
Tigris
Tabriz
AZERBAIJAN
TRANSOXIANA
Signak
EGYPT (MAMLUKS)
Mosul
Maragheh
Urgench
Amu Darya
Otrar
Balasaghun
IRAQ
Zarnuq
Nur
Tashkent
Banakat
Qazvin
Alamut
Amol
Bukhara
Samarkand
Pamirs
Red Sea
Baghdad
Hamadan
Qum
Rayy
Nishapur
ABBASID CALIPHATE
Balkh
Hindu Kush
Herat
PERSIA (IRAN)
AFGHANISTAN
Parwan
Kabul
Ghazni
Arabian Peninsula
Persian Gulf
Iranian Plateau
Multan
Indus
PUNJAB
OMAN
Arabian Sea
4,445 km (2,774 miles)
N
8,372 km (5,224 miles)
Scale varies with perspective
N
1200: Cold spell throughout Eurasian steppe
1211: First invasion of northern China
1237: Beginning of conquest of Russia
1242: Mongols reach Elbe River (Germany)
1260: Battle of Ain Jalut; Mongols invasion of Egypt repulsed
1276: Conquest of Song China complete
1292: Mongols raid Java
1200
1220
1260
1280
1300
1206: Mongols united under Genghis Khan
1227: Death of Genghis Khan
1240: Kiev sacked
1258: Sack of Baghdad; last Caliph put to death
1274: First failed attempt at invading Japan
1281: Second failed invasion of Japan
1295: il-Khans adopt Islam

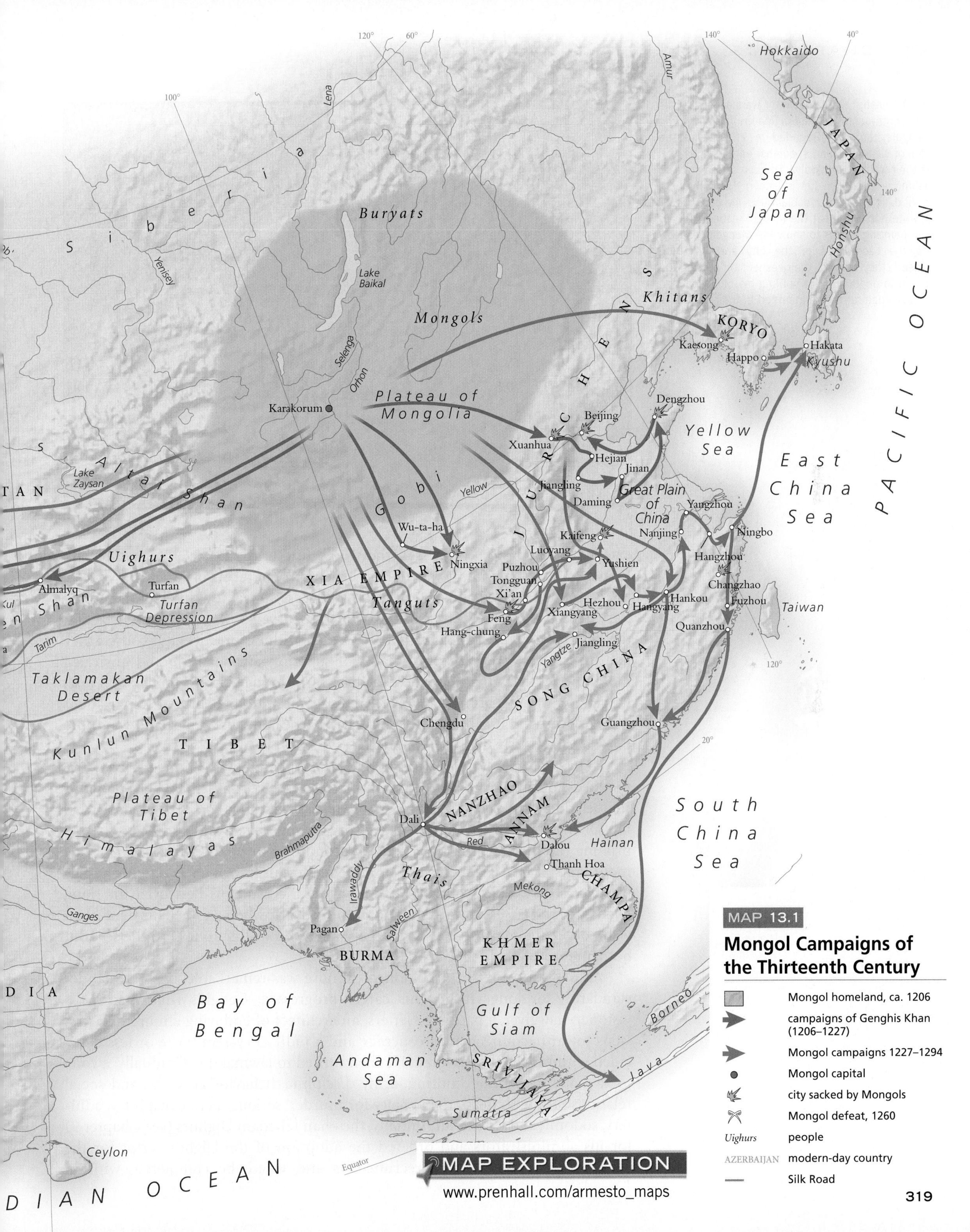
MAP 13.1
Mongol Campaigns of the Thirteenth Century
Mongol homeland, ca. 1206
campaigns of Genghis Khan (1206–1227)
Mongol campaigns 1227–1294
Mongol capital
city sacked by Mongols
Mongol defeat, 1260
Uighurs people
AZERBAIJAN modern-day country
Silk Road
Siberia
Buryats
Lake Baikal
Mongols
Khitans
KORYO
Kaesong
Happo
Hakata
Kyushu
JAPAN
Sea of Japan
Honshu
Hokkaido
PACIFIC OCEAN
Karakorum
Plateau of Mongolia
JURCHENS
Beijing
Xuanhua
Dengzhou
Yellow Sea
Hejian
Jinan
Jiangling
Daming
Great Plain of China
Yangzhou
Nanjing
Ningbo
Hangzhou
Changzhao
Fuzhou
Quanzhou
Taiwan
East China Sea
Kaifeng
Luoyang
Yushien
Puzhou
Tongguan
Xi'an
Feng
Hang-chung
Xiangyang
Hezhou
Hangyang
Hankou
Jiangling
SONG CHINA
Guangzhou
Chengdu
Gobi
Wu-ta-ha
Ningxia
XIA EMPIRE
Tanguts
Altai Shan
Lake Zaysan
Uighurs
Almalyq
Turfan
Turfan Depression
Tarim
Taklamakan Desert
Kunlun Mountains
TIBET
Plateau of Tibet
Himalayas
Brahmaputra
Dali
NANZHAO
ANNAM
Dalou
Red
Thanh Hoa
Hainan
CHAMPA
Thais
Mekong
Irawaddy
Salween
Pagan
BURMA
KHMER EMPIRE
South China Sea
Gulf of Siam
Bay of Bengal
Andaman Sea
SRIVIJAYA
Sumatra
Java
Borneo
Ganges
Ceylon
INDIAN OCEAN
Equator
Lena
Yenisey
Selenga
Orhon
Amur
Yellow
Yangtze
MAP EXPLORATION
www.prenhall.com/armesto_maps

"Exceptionally adaptable warmongers". This fourteenth-century Muslim painting shows the Mongols capturing Baghdad in 1258, with the help of siegecraft and specialist engineers as well as their traditional cavalry. The last caliph appears behind a screen in his palace in the left background. In the center background, he emerges on a white horse to meet the Mongol leader, Hülegü. The painting seems to show the Mongols respecting the sacredness of the city and its ruler. Indeed, they showed their respect by putting the caliph to death without spilling his blood—a sign of reverence for the condemned in their culture

extent, the empire encompassed the whole of Russia, Persia, China, the Silk Roads, and the steppes. It was the largest empire, in terms of territorial extent, the world had seen. Efforts to explain this success appeal to Genghis Khan's military genius, the effectiveness of the Mongols' curved bows and inventive tactics, the demoralizing psychological impact of their ruthless practices. Of course, they had the usual steppelander advantages of superior horsemanship and unrivaled mobility. It is likely that they succeeded, in part, through sheer numbers. Though we call it a Mongol army, Genghis Khan's was the widest alliance of steppelander peoples ever. And it is probable that, relatively speaking, the steppeland was more populous in his day than ever before.

Above all, the Mongols were exceptionally adaptable warmongers. They triumphed not only in cavalry country, but also in environments where previous steppelander armies had failed, pressing into service huge forces of foot soldiers, mobilizing complex logistical support, organizing siege trains and fleets, appropriating the full potential of sedentary economies to finance further wars. The mountains of Georgia could not stop them. Nor, in the long run, could the rice paddies and rivers of southern China where the Mongols destroyed the Song dynasty in the 1270s. Toward the end of the century, when another supreme khan wanted to conquer Java and Japan, they were even willing to take to the sea. But both attempts failed.

As well as for extent, the Mongol Empire was remarkable, by steppelander standards, for longevity. As his career progressed, Genghis Khan became a visionary lawgiver, a patron of letters, an architect of enduring empire. His first steps toward acquiring a bureaucracy and a judicial system more or less coincided with his election as khan. He then turned to lawmaking. Gradually, a code took shape, regulating hunting, army discipline, behavior at feasts, and social relationships, with death the penalty for murder, serious theft, conspiracy, adultery, sodomy, and witchcraft. Initially, the khan relied on Uighurs (see Chapter 9) for his administrators and ordered the adoption of the Uighur script for the Mongols' language. But he recruited as and where he conquered, without

Mongol defeat. Japanese screen painters recorded the defeat of Mongol invaders. Though the Mongols adapted successfully to every kind of terrain, they were unable to continue their conquests overseas. The "divine winds"—kamikaze, as the Japanese called them—protected Japan by making it impossible for the Mongols adequately to supply or reinforce their task force.

Copyright Museum of Imperial Collections, Sannomaru Shozo kan. Photographs through courtesy of the International Society for Educational Information, Inc.

favoritism for any community or creed. His closest ministers included Muslims, Christians, and Buddhists.

In 1219, a Chinese Daoist sage, Changchun (chahng-chwauhn), answered the khan's call for wise experts. At age 71, he undertook a three-year journey from China to meet the khan at the foot of the Hindu Kush mountains. There were sacrifices of principle he would not make. He would not travel with recruits for the imperial harem, or venture "into a land where vegetables were unavailable"—by which he meant the steppe. Yet he crossed the Gobi Desert, climbed "mountains of huge cold," and braved wildernesses where his escort smeared their horses with blood to ward off demons. Admittedly, Changchun's meeting with the khan was disappointing. The question the conqueror was most eager to put was not about the art of government, but about a potion to confer longevity on himself.

The Mongol Steppe

Still, many lettered and experienced officials from conquered states took service at the khan's court. The result was an exceptional, though short-lived, era in steppeland history: the **Mongol peace**. A European, who witnessed it in the 1240s, described it to reproach his fellow Christians with the moral superiority of their enemies: "The Mongols are the most obedient people in the world with regard to their leaders, more so even than our own clergy to their superiors. ... There are no wranglings among them, no disputes or murders." This was obviously exaggerated, but Mongol rule did make the steppeland safe for outsiders. This was new. A previously inaccessible road through the steppes opened across Eurasia north of the Silk Road. The Mongols became its highway police. Teams of Mongol horses, for instance, took the pope's ambassador, John of Piano Carpini, 3,000 miles in 106 days in 1246. Missionaries, spies, and craftsmen in search of work at the Mongol court also made the journey in an attempt to forge friendship between the Mongols and the Christian West, or, at least, to gather intelligence (see Map 13.2).

John of Piano Carpini on the Mongols

William of Rubruck, a Franciscan envoy, recorded vivid details of his mission to Genghis Khan's grandson in 1253. After taking leave of the king of France, who hoped for an alliance with the Mongols against the Muslims, William crossed the Black Sea in May and set out across the steppe by wagon, bound for Karakorum (kah-rah-KOH-ruhm), the new city in Mongolia where the khan held court. "After three days," he recorded, "we found the Mongols and I really felt as if I were entering another world."

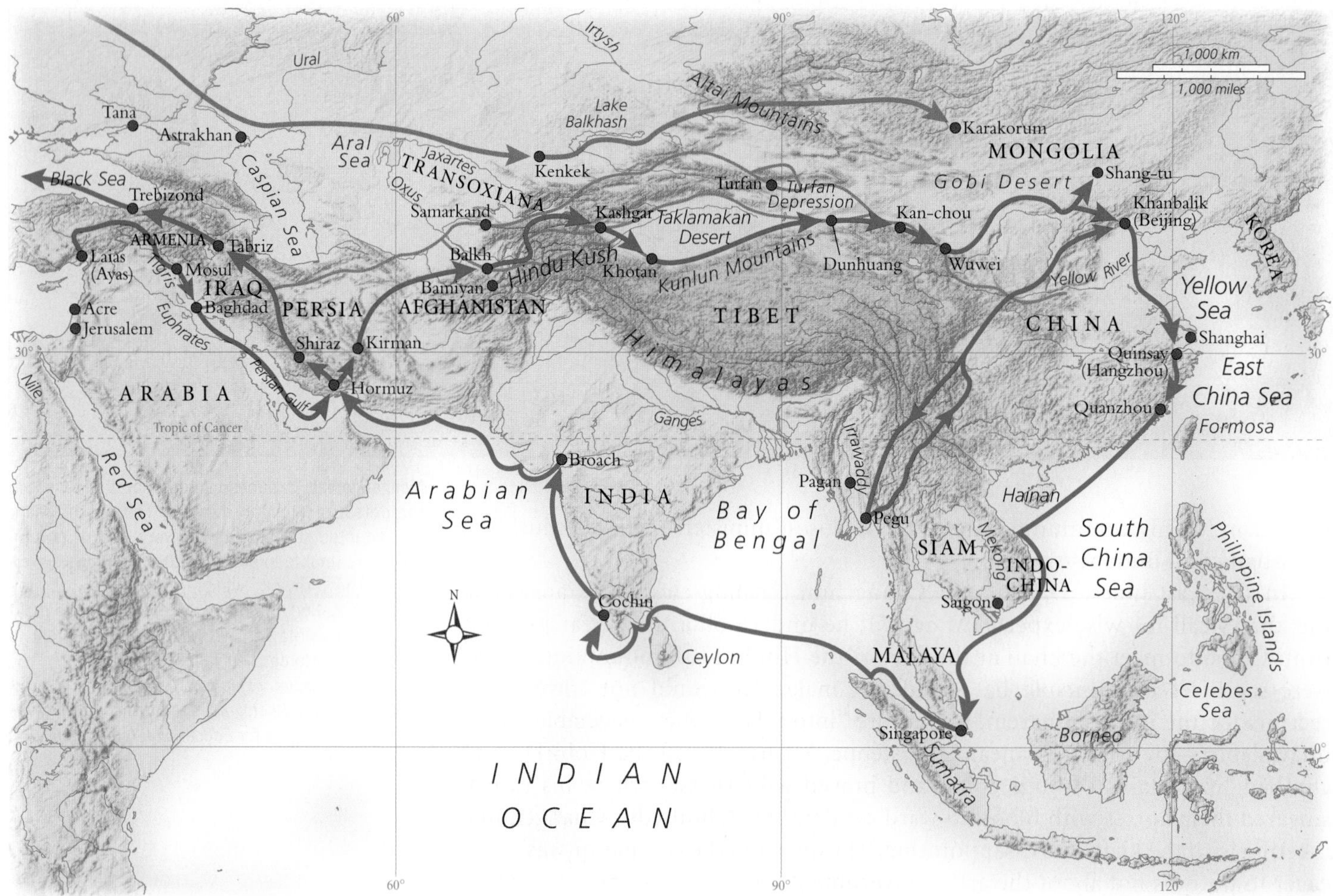

MAP 13.2

European Travelers of the Mongol Roads, 1245–1295

- John of Piano Carpini 1245–1247 and William of Rubruck 1253–1254
- Marco Polo 1271–1275
- Marco Polo 1275–1295
- Silk Road

By November, he was in Transoxiana, "famished, thirsty, frozen, and exhausted." In December, he was high in the dreaded Altai Shan, the mountains. Here he "chanted the creed, among dreadful crags, to put the demons to flight." At last, on Palm Sunday, 1254, he entered the Mongol capital.

Friar William always insisted that he was a simple missionary, but he was treated as an ambassador and behaved like a spy. And, indeed, he had more than one objective. The Mongols might adopt Christianity or at least make an alliance against common enemies in the Muslim world. On the other hand, they were potential enemies, who had invaded the fringes of Europe and might do so again. Intelligence about them was precious. William realized that the seasonal migrations of Mongol life had a scientific basis and were calculated for military efficiency. "Every commander," he noted, "according to whether he has a greater or smaller number of men under him, is familiar with the limits of his pasture lands and where he ought to graze in summer and winter, spring and autumn."

Little useful intelligence escaped William. But he also showed interest in the culture he tried unsuccessfully to convert to Christianity. His description of a Mongol tent dwelling still holds good. The layout, social space, and way of life William saw have not changed much since his day. A frame of interlaced branches stretched and converged at the top. The covering was of white felt, "and they decorate the felt with various fine designs." Up to 22 oxen hauled houses on wagons 20 feet broad.

A MONGOL PASSPORT

Although they were in use in China before the Mongols arrived, documents called *paizi*, such as the one depicted here, were used as passports to regulate communication and administration in the vast Mongol empire. Their use, the way they were designed, and the language in which they were written help us understand the massive movements of people and the rapid exchange of ideas and technology that occurred across Eurasia during the thirteenth and fourteenth centuries when Mongol rule was at its height. William of Rubruck and Marco Polo would have carried one of these passports on their return journeys from Mongol courts in Asia to Europe.

A CLOSER LOOK

This passport is made of iron. Thick silver bands on it form characters in the script that the Tibetan monk Phagspa, a close advisor to Kubilai Khan (r. 1260–1294), devised for writing the Mongol language in 1269.

Above the inscription is a handle with a silver lion mask inlaid on it that shows the influence of Tibetan and Indian art.

Most *paizi* were circular or rectangular in shape and were either fastened on an item of clothing or suspended from the neck, so that customs officers could easily see them.

The inscription reads: "By the strength of Eternal Heaven, an edict of the Emperor [Khan]. He who has no respect shall be guilty."

The Metropolitan Museum of Art, Purchase, Bequest of Dorothy Graham Bennet, 1993 (1993.256) Photograph © The Metropolitan Museum of Art.

What does this passport reveal about the Mongol peace?

Yurt. The shape and decoration of a Mongol tent dwelling—known as a *yurt* or *ger*—has not changed since William of Rubruck described those he saw in the thirteenth century. In the background of this photograph are the Pamir Mountains, which travelers westward on the Silk Roads had to cross when they emerged from the Taklamakan Desert.

Each wife of the master of the household had her own tent, where the master had a bench facing the entrance. In an inversion of Chinese rules of precedence, the women sat on the east side, the men to the right of the master, who sat at the north end. Ancestral spirits resided in felt bags arrayed around the walls. One each hung over the heads of master and mistress, with a guardian image between them. Others hung on the women's and men's sides of the tent, adorned with the udders of a cow and a mare, symbols of life for people who relied on dairy products for their diet. The household would gather to drink fermented mare's milk in the tent of the chosen wife of the night. "I should have drawn everything for you," William assured his readers, "had I known how to draw."

Shamans' trances released the spirits from the bags that held them. Frenzied drumming, dancing, and drinking induced the shamans' ecstasies. The power of speaking with the ancestors' voices gave **shamans** enormous authority in Mongol decision making, including the opportunity to interfere in making and unmaking khans. This was a point William missed. The Mongols leaders' interest in foreign religions, and their investment in the cult of heaven, were, in part at least, strategies to offset the power of the native priests.

Outside the tent, William vividly captured the nature of the terrain—so smooth that one woman could pilot 30 wagons, linked by trailing ropes. He described a way of life that reflected steppeland ecology. The Mongols had mixed flocks of various kinds of sheep and cattle. Mixed pastoralism is essential in an environment in which no other source of food is available. Different species have different cycles of lactation and fertility. Variety ensures a reliable food supply.

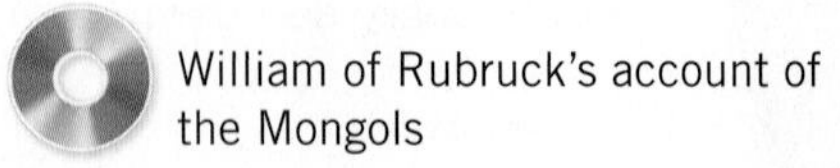

William of Rubruck's account of the Mongols

The horse was the dominant partner of life on the steppe. Mare's milk was the Mongols' summer food. By drawing blood from the living creatures, Mongols on campaign could refresh themselves without slowing the herds. This was the basis of their reputation for blood-sucking savagery among their sedentary neighbors. Fermented mare's milk was the favorite intoxicating drink. The Mongols revered drunkenness and hallowed it by rites: offerings sprinkled over the bags of ancestral spirits, or poured out toward the quarters of the globe. Drinking bouts were a nightly entertainment.

William's conversations with the habitually drunken Möngke Khan, (MOHNG-keh hahn), grandson of Genghis Khan, revealed some of the qualities that made the Mongols of his era great: tolerance, adaptability, respect for tradition. "We Mongols believe," Möngke said, "that there is but one God, in Whom we live and in Whom we die, and towards him we have an upright heart." Spreading his hand, he added, "But just as God has given different fingers to the hand, so He has given different religions to people."[1] Later in the thirteenth century, Kubilai Khan (KOO-bih-la-yee hahn), another of Genghis Khan's grandsons, expressed himself to the Venetian traveler, Marco Polo, in similar terms.

THE MONGOL WORLD BEYOND THE STEPPES: THE SILK ROADS, CHINA, PERSIA, AND RUSSIA

The steppeland route was ideal for horseborne travelers. Trading caravans, however, still favored the traditional **Silk Roads**, which crossed Eurasia to the south of the steppe through the Taklamakan (tahk-lah-mah-KAHN) Desert. These routes had developed over centuries, precisely because high mountains protected them from steppeland raiders. But the security of the Mongol peace boosted the amount of traffic the roads carried. Mongol partiality for merchants also helped. Mongols encouraged Chinese trade, uninhibited by any of the traditional Confucian prejudices against commerce as an ignoble occupation. In 1299, after the Mongol Empire had been divided among several rulers, a Persian merchant was made the ambassador of the Supreme Khan to the court of the subordinate Mongol **Il-khan** (EEL-hahn) in Persia—an elevation unthinkable under a native Chinese dynasty, which would have reserved such a post for an official educated in the Confucian classics. The khans gave low-cost loans to Chinese trading companies. Chinese goods—and with them, patterns and styles—flowed to Persian markets as never before. Chinese arts, under Mongol patronage, became more open to foreign influences.

from *The Travels of Marco Polo*

Geography still made the Silk Roads hard to travel. Marco Polo was a young Venetian who accompanied his father and uncle on a trading mission to Mongol-ruled China in the early 1270s. "They were hard put to it to complete the journey in three and a half years." The Taklamakan Desert was the great obstacle. The normal rule for caravans was the bigger, the safer. But the modest water sources of the desert could not sustain many more than 50 men at a time with their beasts. The key to exploiting the desert routes was the distribution of water, which drains inland from the surrounding mountains and finds its way below the desert floor by underground channels. It was normal to go for 30 days without finding water, though there might be an occasional salt-marsh oasis or an unreliable river. The worst danger was getting lost—"lured from the path by demon-spirits."[2] As a fourteenth-century painter at Persia's Mongol court imagined, the demons were black,

The Silk Roads. Cresques Abraham was the finest mapmaker of his day. He painted this image of a caravan on the Silk Roads in the late 1370s or early 1380s in an atlas probably commissioned for the king of France. By that date the Mongols no longer controlled the whole of the route, though the lances of an armed escort, presumably of Mongols, are visible behind the merchants. The caption says the caravan is bound for China, but it is heading in the opposite direction.

Travelers During the Mongol Peace

1245–1247	John of Piano Carpini
1253–1254	William of Rubruck
1271–1275; 1275–1295	Marco Polo
1275–1288	Rabban Bar Sauma

athletic, and ruthless, waving dismembered limbs of horses as they danced. As Friar William had seen, the Mongols recommended warding them off by smearing a horse's neck with blood.

A fourteenth-century guide included tips for Italian merchants who headed for East Asia to extend the reach of the commerce of their cities. At the port of Tana (TAH-nah), on the Black Sea, you should hire a good guide, regardless of expense. "And if the merchant likes to take a woman with him from Tana, he can do so." On departure from Tana, 25 days' supply of flour and salt fish were needed—"other things you will find in sufficiency and especially meat." The road was "safe by day and night" and protected by Mongol police. But it was important to take a close relative for company. Otherwise, should a merchant die, his property would be forfeit. The text specified rates of exchange at each stop and recommended suitable conveyances for each stage of the journey: oxcart or horse-drawn wagon to the city of Astrakhan (AHS-trah-hahn) where the Don River runs into the Caspian Sea. Thereafter camel train or pack mule was best, until you arrived at the river system of China. Silver was the currency of the road, but the Chinese authorities would exchange it for paper money, which—Westerners were assured—they could use throughout China.

from Francesco Balducci Pegolotti's *The Practice of Commerce.*

After the deserts, the next obstacles were the mountains on their rims. The Tian Shan, which screens the Taklamakan Desert, is 1,800 miles long, up to 300 miles wide, up to 24,000 feet high, and punctuated by deep depressions. Farther north, the Altai Shan mountains guard the Mongolian heartlands. "Before the days of the Mongols," wrote the bishop of the missionary diocese the Franciscans had established in China, "nobody believed that the Earth was habitable beyond these mountains, ... but by God's leave and wonderful exertion the Mongols crossed them, and ... so did I."

Europeans frequently made the journey to China. That reflects the balance of wealth and power at the time. China was rich and productive, Europe a needy backwater. We know of only one subject of the Chinese emperor who found it worthwhile to make the journey in the opposite direction. Rabban Bar Sauma (rah-BAHN bahr SAH-no-mah) was a Nestorian Christian who set out from China on a pilgrimage to Jerusalem. He got as far as Maragha in what is now Azerbaijan, the intellectual capital of the western Mongol world, with a library reputedly of 400,000 books and a new astronomical observatory. Then in 1286 he was appointed the Mongols' ambassador to the kingdoms of the Christian West, to negotiate an alliance against Muslim Egypt (see Map 13.3).

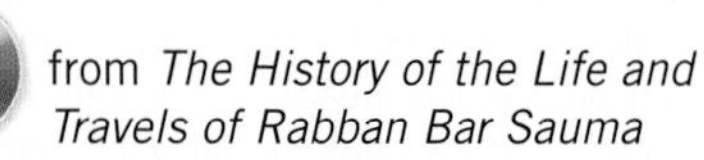

from *The History of the Life and Travels of Rabban Bar Sauma*

When he got to Rome, he was received by the cardinals who had assembled to elect a pope. In Paris, he recognized the university there as an intellectual powerhouse reminiscent of Maragha, with schools of mathematics, astronomy, medicine, and philosophy. Persian was the only language in which Bar Sauma could communicate with Western interpreters. He mistook diplomatic evasions for assent and vague expressions of Christian fellowship for doctrinal agreement. But the fact that he completed the journey at all shows how the Mongols made it possible to cross Eurasia.

China

The Mongols never ran their dominions as a centralized state. Three main areas of conquest beyond the steppeland—in China, Persia, and Russia—were added after Genghis Khan's death. All were exploited in different ways, specific to the Mongols' needs and the peculiarities of each region.

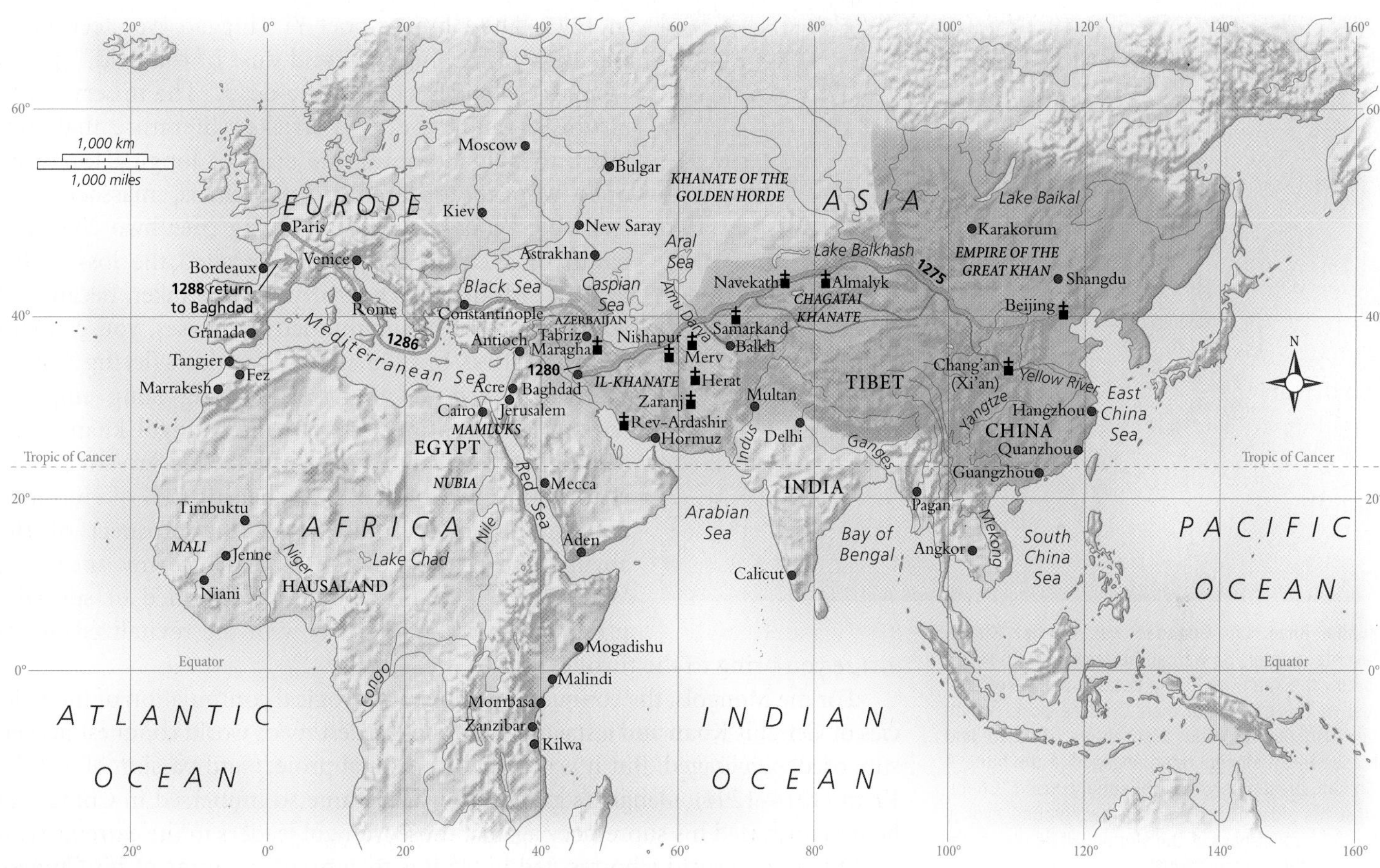

MAP 13.3

The Travels of Rabban Bar Sauma, 1275–1288

- Silk Road
- travels of Rabban Bar Sauma, 1275–1288
- Nestorian see

The conquest of Song China was long and difficult for two reasons. It was a more powerful state than any the Mongols faced elsewhere, and it was highly defensible: compact, so that its armies could maneuver on interior lines of communication, and scored by terrain inhospitable to Mongol horsemen. But, fueled by resources from the Mongols' other conquests, the conquest unfolded relentlessly bit by bit. Letters from the Chinese court seeped desperation as the Mongols closed in for the kill. In 1274, the Chinese empress mother reflected on where the blame lay.

> The empire's descent into peril is due, I regret, to the instability of our moral virtue. ... The sound of woeful lament reverberated through the countryside, yet we failed to investigate. The pall of hunger and cold enveloped the armed forces, yet we failed to console.[2]

Unlike previous steppelander invaders, the Mongols spared no resources to pursue all-out victory and hired the troops and equipment needed to subdue a country of cities, rice paddies, and rivers. Clearly, the size of the Mongols' existing empire helped. Persian engineers built the siege engines that helped overcome southern Chinese cities. The last battle was at Changzhao (chanhg-jeeow)

Kubilai Khan. Liu Guandao was Kubilai Khan's favorite painter. So we can be fairly sure that this is how the khan would like to be remembered: not just in the traditional inert Chinese pose (which Liu also painted), but also active, dressed and horsed like a Mongol ruler, engaged in the hunt. A woman, presumably his influential consort, Chabi, is at his side. The blank silk background evokes the featurelessness of the steppe, while also highlighting the human figures.

in 1275. The Chinese poet Yi Tinggao (yee teen-gow) was there, "smelling the acrid dust of the field," spying "the green irridescence of the dead." The misery could be measured in the grief-stricken literature that survives: the suicide notes, the cries of longing for loved ones who disappeared in the chaos, massacred or enslaved. Years later, Ni Bozhuang (nee bwo-chwang), bailiff of a Daoist monastery, recalled the loss of his wife: "I still do not know if you were taken because of your beauty, or if, surrounded by horses, you can still buy cosmetics." In 1276, with his advisers fleeing and his mother packed for flight, the young Song emperor wrote his abdication letter to the Mongol khan. "The **Mandate of Heaven** having shifted, your Servant chooses to change with it, ... yet my heart is full of emotions and these cannot countenance the prospect of the abrupt annihilation of the ... altars of my ancestors. Whether they be misguidedly abandoned or specially preserved intact rests solely with the revitalized moral virtue you bring to the throne."

For the Mongols, the conquest of China was a logical continuation of the policies of Genghis Khan and a stage in fulfilling the destiny of world conquest heaven supposedly envisaged. But it was also the personal project and passion of Kubilai Khan (1214–1294), Genghis's grandson, who became so immersed in China that he never asserted his supremacy against those Mongol leaders in the extreme west of the Mongol world who resisted his claims to supremacy. Some of his Chinese subjects resented Kubilai's foreign ways: the libations of fermented mare's milk with which he honored his gods, his barbarous banquets of meat, the officials he chose from outside the Confucian elite and even from outside China. Marco Polo reported that all the Chinese "hated the government of the Great Khan, because he set over them steppelanders, most of whom were Muslims, and ... it made them feel no more than slaves." In this respect, the khan indeed broke with Chinese tradition, which was to confine administrative positions to a meritocracy, whose members were selected by examination in the Confucian classics. Kubilai showed his reverence for Confucius by building a shrine in his honor, but he needed to recruit, as Genghis Khan had, from the full range of talent the Mongol Empire supplied.

Kubilai, indeed, remained a Mongol khan. In some respects, he flouted Chinese conventions. He showed traditional steppelander respect for the abilities of women, giving them court posts and, in one case, a governorship. His wife, Chabi, was one of his closest political advisers. Mongols became a privileged minority in China, ruled by their own laws, and resented for it by most Chinese. In defiance of Confucian teachings, Kubilai felt obliged to fulfill the vision of world conquest he inherited from Genghis Khan. But beyond China, he registered only fleeting success. In Java, the Mongols replaced one native prince with another, without making permanent gains. In Vietnam, the Mongols were only able to levy tribute at a rate too low to meet the cost of their campaigns there. So-called *kamikaze* winds—divine typhoons that wrecked the Mongol fleets—drove Kubilai's armies back from Japan.

While upholding Mongol traditions, Kubilai also sought to be a Chinese emperor, who performed the due rites, dressed in the Chinese manner, learned the language, patronized the arts, protected the traditions, and promoted the interests of his Chinese subjects. Marco Polo, who seems to have served him as a sort of professional storyteller, called him "the most powerful master of men, lands, and treasures there has been in the world from the time of Adam until today."

Persia

In Persia, meanwhile, the Mongol rulers were like chameleons, taking on the hues of the culture they conquered. But, as in China, they were anxious to maintain a distinct identity and to preserve their own traditions. The court tended to stay in the north, where there was grazing for the kinds of herds their followers brought with them from the steppe. The Il-khans—"subordinate rulers," so called in deference to Kubilai Khan's nominal superiority—retained nomadic habits, migrating every summer and winter to new camps. In southern Iran and Iraq, the Il-khans tended to entrust power to local dynasties, securing their loyalty by marriages with the ruling family or court nobility. In effect, this gave them hostages for the good conduct of provincial rulers.

Eventually in 1295, the Il-khans adopted Islam, after flirtations with Nestorianism and Buddhism. This marked an important departure from the tradition of religious pluralism Genghis Khan had begun and Kubilai had upheld. From the moment the Il-khan Ghazan (r. 1295–1304) became a Muslim, the state began to take on a militantly religious character, excluding the Christians, Zoroastrians, Buddhists, and Jews formerly admitted to the khan's service. Moreover, the form of Islam the Il-khans finally adopted was Shiism, the prevailing tradition in Iran. Shiites (see Chapter 9) embraced doctrines most Muslims rejected: that Muhammad's authority descended via his nephew Ali; that a divinely selected leader or imam would perfect the Prophet's message; and that in the meantime the clergy had the right to interpret Islam. The Il-khans' option ensured that Persia would be the only officially Shiite state in the Muslim world.

Il-Khan art. When Mongols converted to Islam, they did not necessarily accept all the beliefs and conventions of orthodox religion. In this fourteenth-century painting from what is now Iran, the white rooster symbolizes the Muslim call to prayer—but the rooster was also a traditional Zoroastrian symbol of dawn. The prophet Muhammad, moreover, is realistically depicted at bottom right—something most Muslim painters would regard as impious, even today. The other figures are of angels.

The religious art of the Il-khanate looked unorthodox, full of human figures, especially those of Muhammad and his nephew. Painters even copied Christian nativity scenes to produce versions of the Prophet's birth. The Il-khans' Persia, however, was not isolated from neighboring states. On the contrary, as was usual in the Mongol world, the presence of rulers descended from Genghis Khan promoted trans-Eurasian contacts and exchanges of goods, personnel, and ideas. Persia supplied China, for instance, with engineers, astronomers, and mathematicians, while Persia received Chinese porcelain and paper money, which, however, did not take root in Persia before the twentieth century. Chinese designs influenced Persian weavers, and Chinese dragons appeared on the tiles that decorated Persian buildings. Mongol rule ended in Persia in 1343 when the last Il-khan died without an heir.

Russia

Meanwhile, the Mongols who remained in their central Asian heartlands continued their traditional way of life. So did those who formed the elite in the remaining areas the heirs of Genghis Khan inherited: in Turkestan and Kashgaria in Central Asia, and the steppes of the lower Volga River. From the last of these areas, where the Mongols were known as the Golden Horde, they exercised overlordship over Russia, where they practiced a kind of imperialism different from

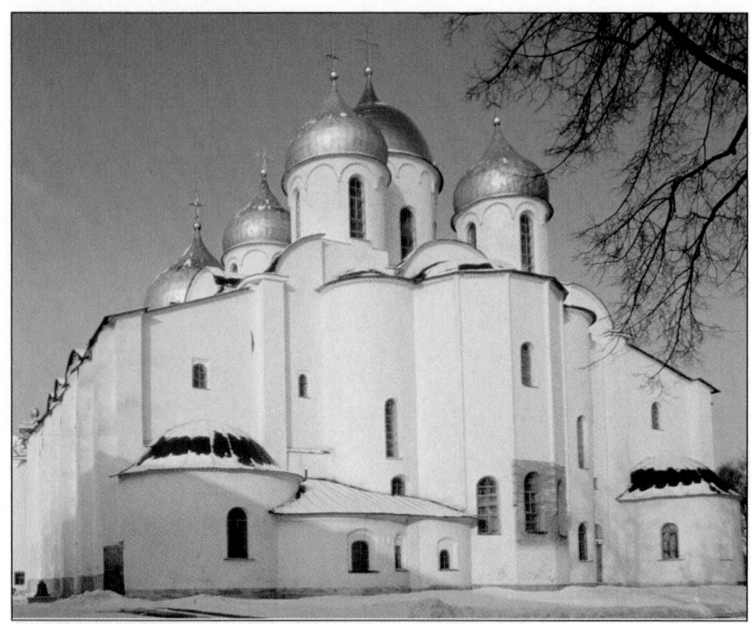

Novgorod. The cathedral of St. Sophia in Novgorod in Russia would have presented essentially the same outline in the thirteenth century that it does today. At the time, it was one of relatively few buildings in that mercantile city-state built of stone rather than wood. The tallest gilded dome shows the position of the sanctuary at the heart of the church.

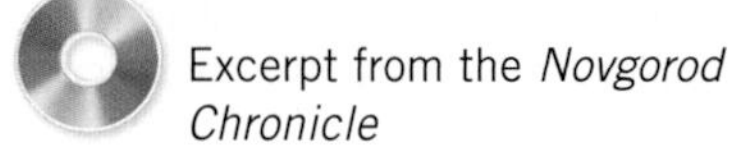

Excerpt from the *Novgorod Chronicle*

those in China and Persia. The Mongols left the Christian Russian principalities and city-states to run their own affairs. But their rulers had to receive charters from the khan's court at Saray (sah-RAY) on the lower Volga, where they had to make regular appearances, loaded with tribute and subject to ritual humiliations. The population had to pay taxes directly to Mongol-appointed tax gatherers—though as time went on, the Mongols assigned the tax gathering to native Russian princes and civic authorities.

The Russians tolerated this situation—albeit unhappily, and with many revolts—partly because the Mongols intimidated them by terror. When the Mongols took the great city of Kiev in 1240, it was said, they strewed the fields "with countless heads and bones of the dead." Partly, however, the Russians were responding to a milder Mongol policy. In most of Russia, the invaders came to exploit rather than to destroy. According to one chronicler, the Mongols spared Russia's peasants to ensure that farming would continue. Ryazan, a Russian principality on the Volga, southeast of Moscow, seems to have borne the brunt of the Mongol invasion. Yet there, if the local chronicle can be believed, "the pious Grand Prince Ingvary Ingvarevitch sat on his father's throne and renewed the land and built churches and monasteries and consoled newcomers and gathered together the people. And there was joy among the Christians whom God had saved from the godless and impious khan." Many cities escaped lightly by capitulating at once. Novgorod, that hugely rich city (see Chapter 11), which the Mongols might have coveted, they bypassed altogether.[3]

Moreover, the Russian princes were even more fearful of enemies to the west, where the Swedes, Poles, and Lithuanians had constructed strong monarchies, capable of sweeping the princes away if they ever succeed in expanding into Russian territory. Equally menacing were groups of mainly German adventurers, organized into crusading "orders" of warriors, such as the Teutonic Knights and the Brothers of the Sword, who took monastic-style vows but dedicated themselves to waging holy war against pagans and heretics. In practice, these orders were self-enriching companies of professional fighters, who built up territorial domains along the Baltic coast by conquest. Between 1242 and 1245, Russian coalitions fought off western invaders, but they could not sustain war on two fronts. The experience made them submissive to the Mongols.

THE LIMITS OF CONQUEST: MAMLUK EGYPT AND MUSLIM INDIA

In the 1200s, Egypt was in chaos because of rebellions by pastoralists from the southern desert and revolt by the slaves who formed the elite fighting force. It seems counterintuitive to arm slaves. But for most of the thirteenth century, the policy worked well for Saladin's heirs, who had ruled Egypt since 1192. The rulers' handpicked slave army, or Mamluks, came overwhelmingly from Turkic peoples that Mongol rebels displaced or captured and sold. These slaves had nowhere else to go and no future except in the Egyptian sultan's service. They were acquired young. They were trained in barracks, which became their substitutes for families and the source of their pride and sense of comradeship. The Mamluks seemed, from the ruler's point of view, ideally reliable: a dependent class. However, in the 1250s, they rebelled "like an unleashed torrent." Their own later propaganda cites the sultan's failure to reward them fairly for their services, and their outrage at the promotion of a black slave to one of the highest offices in the court.

Rise of the Mamluks

1254	Mamluks depose sultan of Egypt
1260	Mamluk army victorious at the battle of Ain Jalut in Syria
1268–1291	Mamluks overthrow last of the crusader states

In September 1260, the rebels turned back the Mongol armies at one of the decisive battles of the world at Ain Jalut (EYE-in jah-LOOT) in Syria. It was the first serious reversal the Mongols had experienced since Genghis Khan united them. And it gave the slave army's commander, Baybars (BYE-bahrs), the chance to take over Egypt and Syria. He boasted that he could play polo in Cairo and Damascus within the space of a single week. The Mamluks mopped up the last crusader states on the coast of Syria and Palestine between 1268 and 1291. In combination with the effects of the internal politics of the Mongol world, which inhibited armies from getting too far from the centers of power, the Mamluk victory kept the Mongols out of Africa.

Mamluk victory marked a further stage in the Islamization of Africa. The Mamluks levied tribute on the Christian kingdoms of Nubia (see Chapter 9). Then, in the next century, they imposed Islam there. Cairo became a normal stopping place on the pilgrimage route to Mecca for Muslim kings and dignitaries from West Africa. Islam percolated through the region of Lake Chad and in what is today Nigeria.

Muslim India: The Delhi Sultanate

After the disruptions the violent Turkic migrations of the twelfth century caused, it took a long time for a state in the mold of Mahmud's to reemerge in Ghazna (see Chapter 12). By the 1190s, however, a Muslim Turkic dynasty and people, the Ghurids (GOO-rids), had resumed the habit of raiding into Hindu India, where they levied tribute and scattered garrisons. One of their most far-flung outposts—and therefore one of the strongest—was at the city of Delhi in northern India. The adventurer Iltutmish (eel-TOOT-mihsh) took command there in 1211. He was a former slave who had risen to general and received his freedom from his Ghurid masters. He avoided war with Hindus—which was, in essence, his job—in favor of building up his own resources. In 1216 he effectively declared himself independent. Over the next 12 years, he exploited the rivalries of Muslim commanders to construct a state from the Indus River to the Bay of Bengal. Meanwhile, the effects of the Mongol conquests on Central Asia protected this new realm, which became known as the Sultanate of Delhi, against outside attack (see Map 13.4). As one of the early chroniclers of the sultanate said, "Rulers and governors, ... and many administrators and notables came to Iltutmish's court from fear of the slaughter and terror of the accursed Mongol, Genghis Khan."

There was no consistent form of administration. In most of the remoter territories, the Delhi sultan was an overlord of small, autonomous states, many of which Hindus ruled. But there was a core of lands that was the sultan's personal property, exploited to benefit his treasury and run by his administrators. Lands the sultan granted in exchange for military service ringed the core. At great

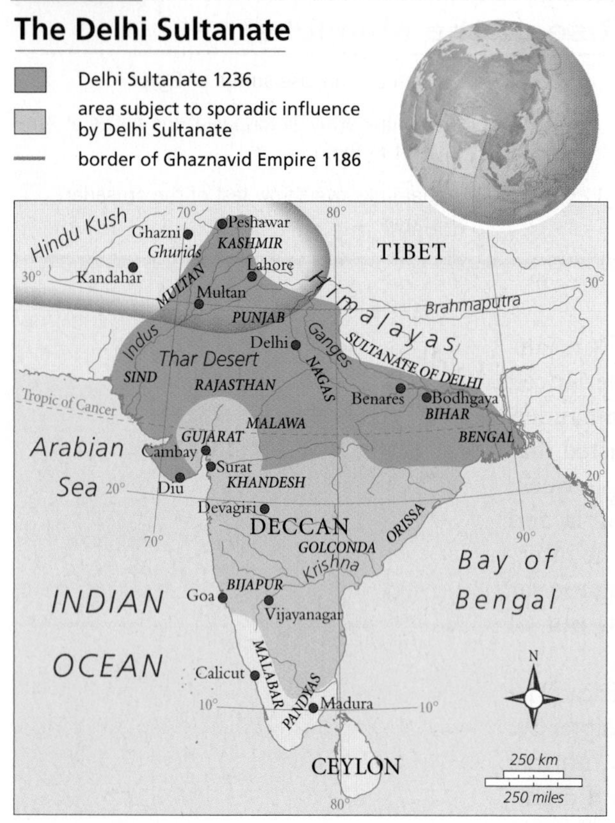

MAP 13.4
The Delhi Sultanate

oath-taking ceremonies, the aristocracy—a great diversity of freelance warriors and local rulers whom it was difficult or impossible for the sultan to dismiss—would make emotional but often short-lived declarations of loyalty.

As an ex-slave, Iltutmish was no respecter of conventional ideas of hierarchy. Denouncing his sons for incompetence, he chose his daughter, Radiyya (rah-DEE-ah), as his successor in 1236. In the steppes, women often handled big jobs. In the Islamic world, a woman ruler was a challenge to what was thought to be the natural order of the world. When, in 1250, a little before the Mamluks took over in Egypt, a woman had seized the throne there and applied to Baghdad for legitimation by the caliph, he is supposed to have replied that he could supply capable men, if no more existed in Egypt. Radiyya had to contend both with a brother who briefly ousted her—she put him to death—and male mistrust. Some of her coins emphasize claims to unique feminine virtues as "pillar of women." Others have modest inscriptions, in which all the glorious epithets are reserved for her father and the caliph in Baghdad. Her best strategy was to behave like a man. She dressed in male clothing, refused to cover her face, and "mounted horse like men, armed with bow and quiver." To conventional minds, these were provocations. Accused of taking a black slave as a lover, she was deposed in 1240 in favor of a brother. Her real offense was self-assertion. Those modest coin inscriptions suggest that power brokers in the army and the court were only willing to accept her as a figurehead, not as an active leader of men.

The sultanate had to cope not only with the turbulence of its elite but also with Hindu subjects and neighbors. Dominion by any state over the entire Indian subcontinent remained, at best, a dream. Frontier expansion was slow. Deforestation was an act of state, because, as a Muslim writer of the fourteenth century complained, "the infidels live in these forests, which for them are as good as city walls, ... so that they cannot be overcome except by strong armies of men who go into these forests and cut down those reeds." In Bengal, the eastward shift of the Ganges River made Islamization easier. Charismatic **sufis**, with tax-free grants of forest land for mosques and shrines, led the way.

For most of the thirteenth century, the Mongol menace overshadowed the sultanate. The internal politics of the dynasty of Genghis Khan caused dissensions and hesitancies that protected Delhi. Mongol dynastic disputes cut short periodic invasions. Moreover, a buffer state dissident Mongols created in Delhi's western territories absorbed most of the khans' attacks. In the 1290s, however, the buffer collapsed. By what writers in Delhi considered a miracle, the subsequent Mongol attacks failed.

EUROPE

With the scare the Mongol invasions caused and the loss of the last crusader states in Syria to the Mamluks, Latin Christendom looked vulnerable. Attempts to revitalize the crusading movement—especially by Louis IX, the king of France (r. 1226–1270) who became a model monarch for the Western world—all failed. A further reverse was the loss of Constantinople by its Latin rulers to a Byzantine revival. The Mongols destroyed or dominated most of the successor states that claimed Byzantium's legacy, but at the city of Nicaea in western Anatolia, rulers who continued to call themselves "Roman emperors" maintained the court rituals and art of Byzantine greatness. In 1261, they recaptured the old capital from the crusaders "after many failures," as Emperor Michael VIII (r. 1261–1282), admitted, "because God wished us to know that the possession of the city was a grace dependent on his bounty."

Nevertheless, Latin Christendom grew on other fronts, deep into formerly pagan worlds along the Baltic in Livonia, Estonia, Prussia, and Finland. The *Rhyming Chronicle* of the conquest of Livonia recounts with equal pleasure the destruction of native villages and the piety of forced converts. Swedish knights led by Henry of Finland (d. ca. 1160) were said to have wept over the potential converts they slew in the twelfth century.

Between the 1220s and the 1260s, Christian kingdoms seized most of the Mediterranean seaboard of Spain and the Balearic islands from Muslim rulers. Here the existing economy and population were not much disturbed. Conquests Castile and Portugal made over the same period in the Iberian southwest became a sort of wild west, of sparse settlements, tough frontiersmen, and vast cattle and sheep ranches. Meanwhile, traders of the western Mediterranean increased their commerce with northern Europe along the coasts the Spaniards conquered, through the Strait of Gibraltar (see Map 13.5). Toward the end of the century, as they became accustomed to Atlantic sailing conditions, some of them began to think of exploring the ocean for new routes and resources. In 1291, an expedition set off from the Italian city of Genoa to try to find "the regions of India by way of the ocean." The voyagers were never heard of again, but their voyage marked the beginning of a long effort by maritime communities of Western Europe to exploit the ocean at their feet.

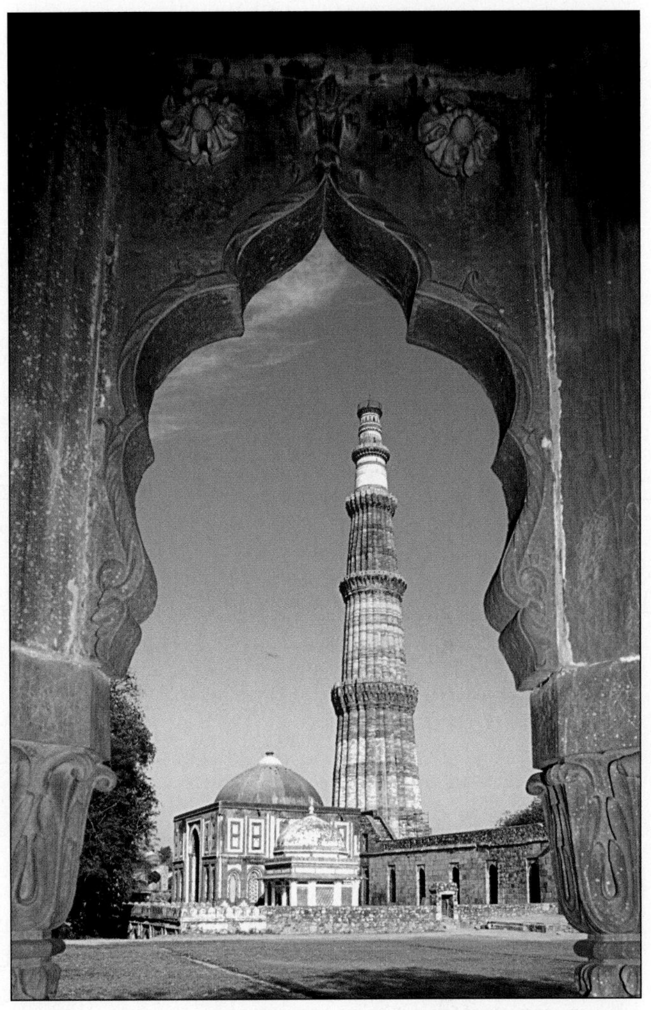

The Qutb Minar. The founder of the Ghurid dynasty began the Qutb Minar, near Delhi, as a monument to his own prowess in battle, toward the end of the twelfth century. Successors continued the project until, by the late fourteenth century, it was the tallest tower in India—much bigger than any minaret designed to hoist the call to prayer. The ridged form and decorative use of sandstone are typical of the stylistic traditions the Ghurids brought to India from Afghanistan.

The big new opportunities, however, lay to the east, from where transforming technologies reached Europe. Paper was a Chinese invention that had already reached the West through Arab intermediaries, but only in the late thirteenth century was it manufactured in Europe on a large scale. European maritime technology—a prerequisite of the prosperity borne by long-range trade and of the reach of most long-range imperialism—was especially primitive by non-European standards up to this time. Though the compass was first recorded in Europe in about 1190, the West had as yet no maritime charts. The earliest reference to such a device dates only from 1270. Gunpowder and the blast furnace were among the magical-seeming technologies that first reached Europe from China in the thirteenth and fourteenth centuries.

Meanwhile, with consequences for the future that can hardly be overestimated, Western science grew more **empirical**, more committed to observation and experiment. The cosmos came to seem measurable, portrayed between the dividers of Christ the geometer, like a ball of fluff trapped between tweezers. At the University of Paris, scholars cultivated a genuinely scientific way of understanding the world. The work of encyclopedists arrayed in precise categories everything known by experience or report. The greatest intellect of the age, Thomas Aquinas (1225–1274), compiled comprehensive schemes of faith and secular knowledge.

Thomas Aquinas, from *Summa Theologica*

MAP 13.5

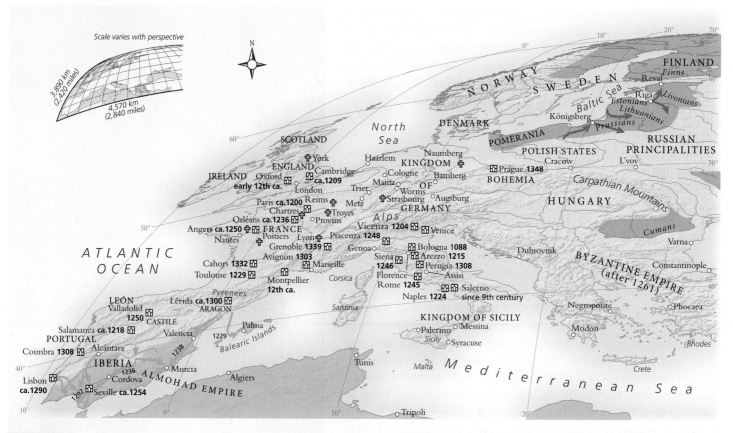

Latin Christendom, 1200–1300

- predominantly pagan lands
- reconquest of Spain in thirteenth century
- university, with date of foundation
- important churches with stained glass
- campaigns of Teutonic Knights and Sword Brothers

In the third quarter of the thirteenth century, Parisian teachers pointed out that the doctrines of the church on the creation and the nature of the soul conflicted with classical philosophy and empirical evidence. "Every disputable question," they argued, "must be determined by rational arguments." A professor at the University of Paris, Roger Bacon, said that excessive deference to authority—including ancestral wisdom, custom, and consensus—was a cause of ignorance. He insisted that scientific observations could help to validate holy writ and that medical experiments could increase knowledge and save life. He also claimed—citing the lenses with which Archimedes reputedly set fire to a Roman fleet during the siege of the Greek city of Syracuse in Sicily in 212 B.C.E.—that science could cow and convert infidels. Bacon was a Franciscan friar, a follower of Francis of Assisi (1181–1226), and his enthusiasm for science seems to have owed something to Francis's doctrine that because the world made God manifest, it was worth observing.

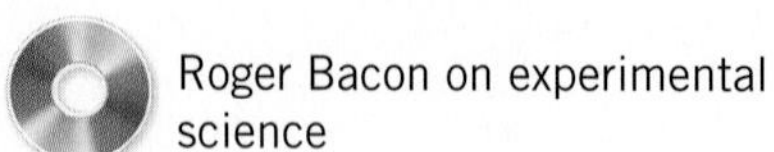
Roger Bacon on experimental science

Francis was a witness and maker of the new European imagination. He was a rich man's son inspired by Jesus' advice to renounce riches for a life of total dependence on God. In anyone less committed and charismatic, his behavior might have been considered insane or heretical. He launched his mission by stripping naked in the public square of his native city, as a sign that he was throwing himself, unprotected, on God's mercy. He relied for sustenance on what people gave him. He modeled his followers' way of life on the way he thought Jesus and the Apostles lived, refusing to accept property, sharing the alms the brethren received. For a church that relied on immense wealth to keep its operations going, these were dangerous ideas. The very notion of a religious order wandering around the world without the discipline of common life ran counter to everything the church had believed about monasticism for at least 500 years.

Francis, however, could be tamed. He had enough humility to defer to the church's discipline. Bishops who met him—including the pope himself—let him carry on. He made compromises with respectability, ordering his female followers into nunneries, and—in obedience to a vision in which Jesus told him, "Build my Church"—put his efforts into buildings of stone and mortar, as well as spiritual edification. Francis was suspicious of learning. It was a kind of possession—a compromise with poverty. It made men vain. But he accepted that education was part of the church's mission and that friars had to study to equip them to be preachers and confessors.

The Franciscans became the spearhead of the church's mission to the poor and inspired other orders of friars—clergy who combined religious vows of poverty, chastity, and obedience with work in the world. In an age of urbanization, friars could establish bonds of sympathy with the rootless masses, who had lost the familiar companionship of rural parishes. Friars, if they stayed true to their vocations, were also a valuable counter force to heretics who denounced the church for worldliness.

In his attitude to nature, Francis was representative of his time. Against heretics who condemned the world as evil, he insisted on the goodness of God's creation, which was all "bright and beautiful." Even its conflicts and cruelties were there to elicit human love. He tried to enfold the whole of nature in love. He preached to ravens and called creatures, landscapes, sun, and moon his brothers and sisters, eventually welcoming "Sister Death." He communicated his sensibilities to his followers. As a result, Franciscans were prominent in scientific thinking in the West. Love of nature made them observe it more closely and keenly and scrutinize it for good uses.

Francis of Assisi. Franciscan art patronage rewarded painters like Giotto, who were interested in creating vivid versions of sacred scenes in which the actors seemed real rather than abstract. Francis preached to the birds because humans failed to heed his message—but the image suggests, too, how the Franciscans promoted awareness of the natural world. Piety and science coincided in the observation of nature.

Francis of Assisi, selection from *Admonitions*

Franciscans also became patrons of naturalistic art. The art they commissioned for their churches drew the onlooker into sacred spaces, as if in eyewitness of the lives of Jesus and the saints. The devotion of the rosary, introduced early in the thirteenth century, encouraged the faithful to imagine sacred mysteries, while praying, with the vividness of scenes of everyday life, as if witnessed in person—looking at the world with eyes as unblinking as those of the new scientific thinkers. Considered from one point of view, the realism Western painting increasingly favored was a tribute to the enhanced prestige of the senses. To paint what one's eyes could see confered dignity on a subject not previously thought worthy of art. So art linked the science and piety of the age.

The revolutionary experiences of the West at the time—the technical progress, the innovations in art, the readjustment of notions of reality through the eyes of a new kind of science—were owed, in part, to influences transmitted along routes the Mongols maintained. None of this experimentation and imagination put Western science abreast of that of China, where observation and experiment had been

Astrolabe. The Syrian instrument maker, al-Sarraj engraved his signature on this fine astrolabe in 1230–1231. The purpose of the astrolabe is to assist in astronomy—one of the many sciences in which the Islamic world excelled at the time. By suspending the instrument at eye level and swiveling a narrow central bar until it aligned with any observed star, the user could read the star's elevation above the horizon, as well as such additional information as the latitude, the date, and even the time of day from the engraved discs.
© National Maritime Museum Picture Library, London, England. Neg. #E5555-3

continuous in scientific tradition since the first millennium B.C.E. (see Chapter 6). In two technologies, however—key technologies for their influence on world history—Western Europe came to house the world's leading centers of development and production.

The first was glassmaking. In the thirteenth century, demand for fine glassware leaped in the West because of the growing taste for using church windows made of stained glass, to illuminate sacred stories and to exhibit the wonders of creation. Glassmakers adapted their skills to meet demand for glass mirrors and optical lenses. These objects were not manufactured on a significant scale anywhere else in the world, though for centuries scholars writing in Arabic had known how to make them and use them in scientific observation. Now Western savants could make the same experiments and even improve on them.

Second, the West drew ahead in the technology of clockwork. Mechanical clocks had a long history in China and the Islamic world. But clockwork never caught on except in Europe, perhaps because it is too regular to match the movements of the heavens. It divides the day into arbitrary hours of equal length that do not match those of the sun. But this way to organize life suited Western monasteries, where, apart from the prayers prescribed for the dawn and nightfall, the services of prayer were best arranged at regular intervals, independently of the sun. For city churches in an age of urban growth, regular timekeeping was also convenient. Clockwork suited the rhythms of urban life. Civic authorities began to invest in town clocks in the thirteenth and fourteenth centuries. This was the beginning of the still-familiar Western convention of an urban skyline dominated by the town hall clock tower.

The combination of lenses and clockwork mattered because eventually—not until the seventeenth century, when telescopes were combined with accurate chronometry—it gave Western astronomers an advantage over Muslim and Chinese competitors. This in turn gave Western scientists the respect of their counterparts and secured the patronage of rulers all over the world in societies interested in astronomy either for its own sake or—more often—because of astrology.

IN PERSPECTIVE: The Uniqueness of the Mongols

Like most great revolutionaries, the Mongols started bloodily and became constructive. The Mongols came to play a unique and constructive role in the history of Eurasia. For 100 years after the initial horror of the Mongol conquests, the steppe became a highway of fast communication, helping transfer culture across two continents. Without the Mongol peace, it is hard to imagine any of the rest of world history working out as it did, for these were the roads that carried Chinese ideas and technology westward and opened up European minds to the vastness of

MAKING CONNECTIONS

EUROPEAN TRANSFORMATIONS AND INNOVATIONS, THIRTEENTH AND EARLY FOURTEENTH CENTURIES

TRADE AND TRANSPORTATION	TECHNOLOGY AND SCIENCE	POLITICS	RELIGION
Increased communication across Eurasia leads to introduction of Chinese and Arabic technology, medicine, and inventions	Imported inventions such as paper, magnetic compasses, gunpowder, and blast furnace combine with focus on empiricism	Christian kingdoms seize Muslim lands in Spain, Mediterranean islands; revival of Crusades, extension of frontier north to the Baltics, Finland, and Scandinavia	Francis and his religious order place new emphasis on observing nature, serving the poor, and renouncing wealth; increased emphasis on sacred mysteries
↓	↓	↓	↓
Increased transportation and trade links within Europe aided by new infrastructure (roads, canals); growth of towns; economic and political stability leads to larger towns and cities; more productive industry	Better maritime technology expands range of sea voyages; demand for elaborate church windows spurs glassmaking and innovation in glass lenses; clocks provide regularized timekeeping for monasteries and cities; availability of paper multiplies books and empowers states with a medium for their messages	Bigger, richer states with more scope to communicate and enforce commands; more church–state competition and conflict	Mendicants prominent in scientific thinking in West; spearhead Church's mission to poor in growing towns

the world. The importance of the Mongols' passage through world history does not stop at the frontiers of their empire. It resonated across Eurasia.

The Eurasian experience was unique. Why did nothing like it happen in Africa or the Americas? Cultural exchanges across the grasslands of prairie, pampa, and Sahel never spread far until the nineteenth century. None of those regions saw conquerors like the Mongols, able to unify the entire region and turn it into a causeway of civilizations, shuttling ideas and techniques across a continent.

In the Americas, geography was an inhibiting influence. The North American prairie is aligned on a north–south axis, across climatic zones, whereas the steppe stretches from east to west. Plants and animals can cross the steppe without encountering impenetrable environments. Seeds can survive the journey without perishing and without finding, at the end of the road, an environment too sunless or cold to thrive in. In North America, it took centuries longer to achieve exchanges on a comparable scale. As we have seen almost whenever the Americas have entered our story, transmissions of culture across latitudes are much harder to effect than those that occur within latitudes, which have relatively narrow boundaries, where climate and conditions are familiar.

Moreover, to function, an avenue of communications needs people at either end of it who want to be in touch. The Eurasian steppe was like a dumbbell, with densely populated zones and productive economies at either end of it (see Map 13.6). People in Europe, southwest Asia, and North Africa wanted the products of south, southeast, and east Asia. The suppliers of spices, drugs, fine textiles, and luxury products in the east liked having customers who paid in silver. In the Americas, there was no chance to reproduce such relationships. The concentrations of

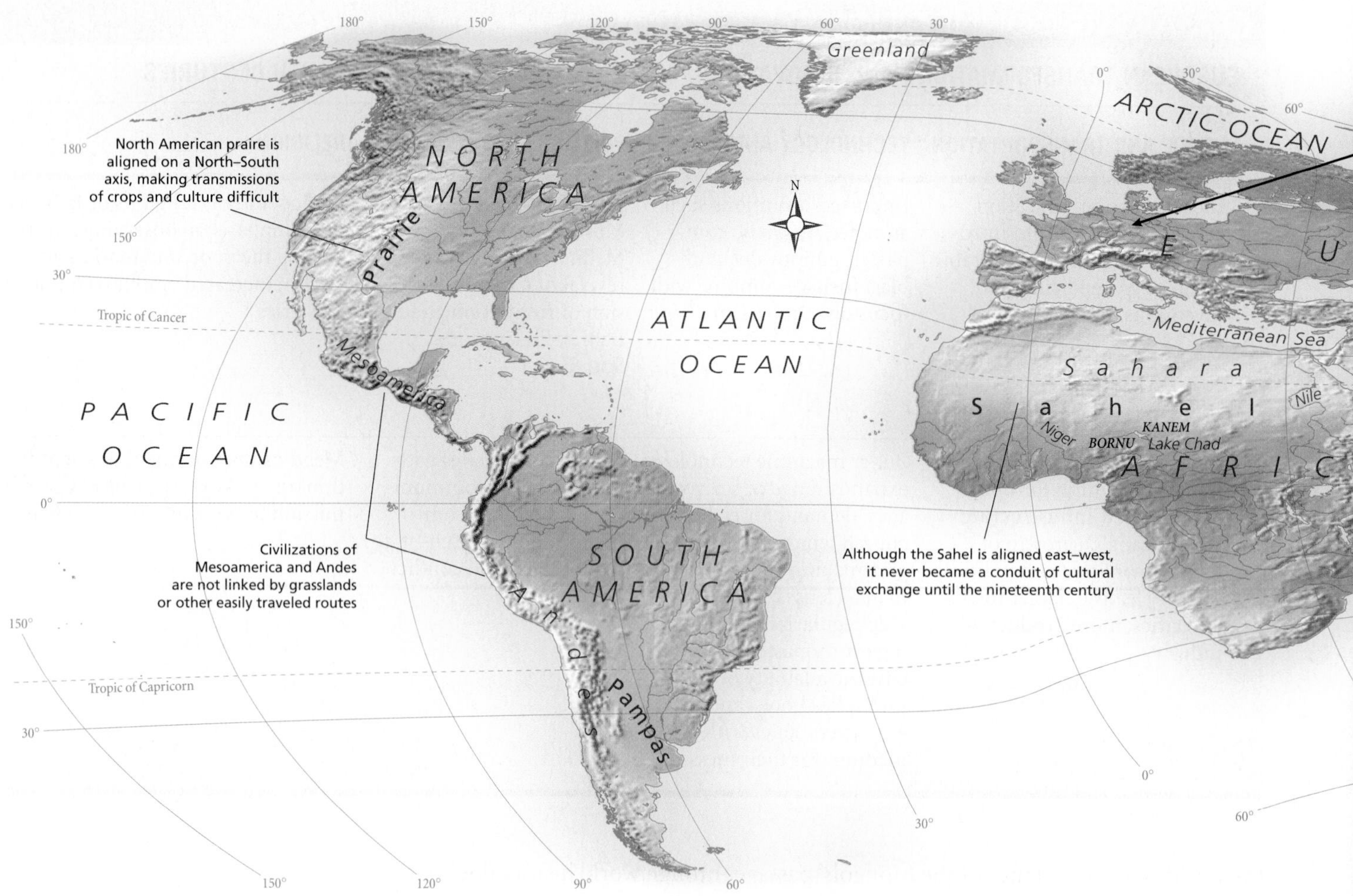
Greenland
ARCTIC OCEAN
North American praire is aligned on a North–South axis, making transmissions of crops and culture difficult
NORTH AMERICA
Prairie
ATLANTIC OCEAN
Mediterranean Sea
Sahara
Sahel
Nile
KANEM
Niger
BORNU
Lake Chad
AFRIC
Tropic of Cancer
Mesoamerica
PACIFIC OCEAN
Civilizations of Mesoamerica and Andes are not linked by grasslands or other easily traveled routes
SOUTH AMERICA
Andes
Pampas
Although the Sahel is aligned east–west, it never became a conduit of cultural exchange until the nineteenth century
Tropic of Capricorn

wealth and population were in two regions—Mesoamerica and the Andes—that neither grasslands nor any other easily traveled routes linked. Though societies in other parts of the hemisphere drew lessons, models of life, technologies, and types of food from those areas, the results (see Chapter 11) were hard to sustain because communications between these areas and outlying regions were hard to keep up. Without the horse—extinct in the Americas for 10,000 years—the chances of an imperial people arising in the prairie or the pampa to do the sort of job the Mongols did in Europe were virtually zero. (Much later, as we shall see in Chapter 21, when European invaders reintroduced the horse in the Americas in the 1500s, experiments in grassland imperialism by peoples such as the Sioux followed.)

In Africa, the constraints were different. The **Sahel** might have played a role similar to that of the steppes in Eurasian history. There was a viable corridor of communication between the Nile and Niger valleys. In theory, an imperial people might have been able to open communications across the continent between the civilizations of East Africa, which were in touch with the world of the Indian Ocean, and those of West Africa, which the trade routes of the Sahara linked to the Mediterranean. But it never happened. For long-range empire building, the Sahel was, paradoxically, too rich, compared with the Eurasian steppe. The environment of the Sahel was more diverse. Agrarian or partly agrarian states had more oppor-

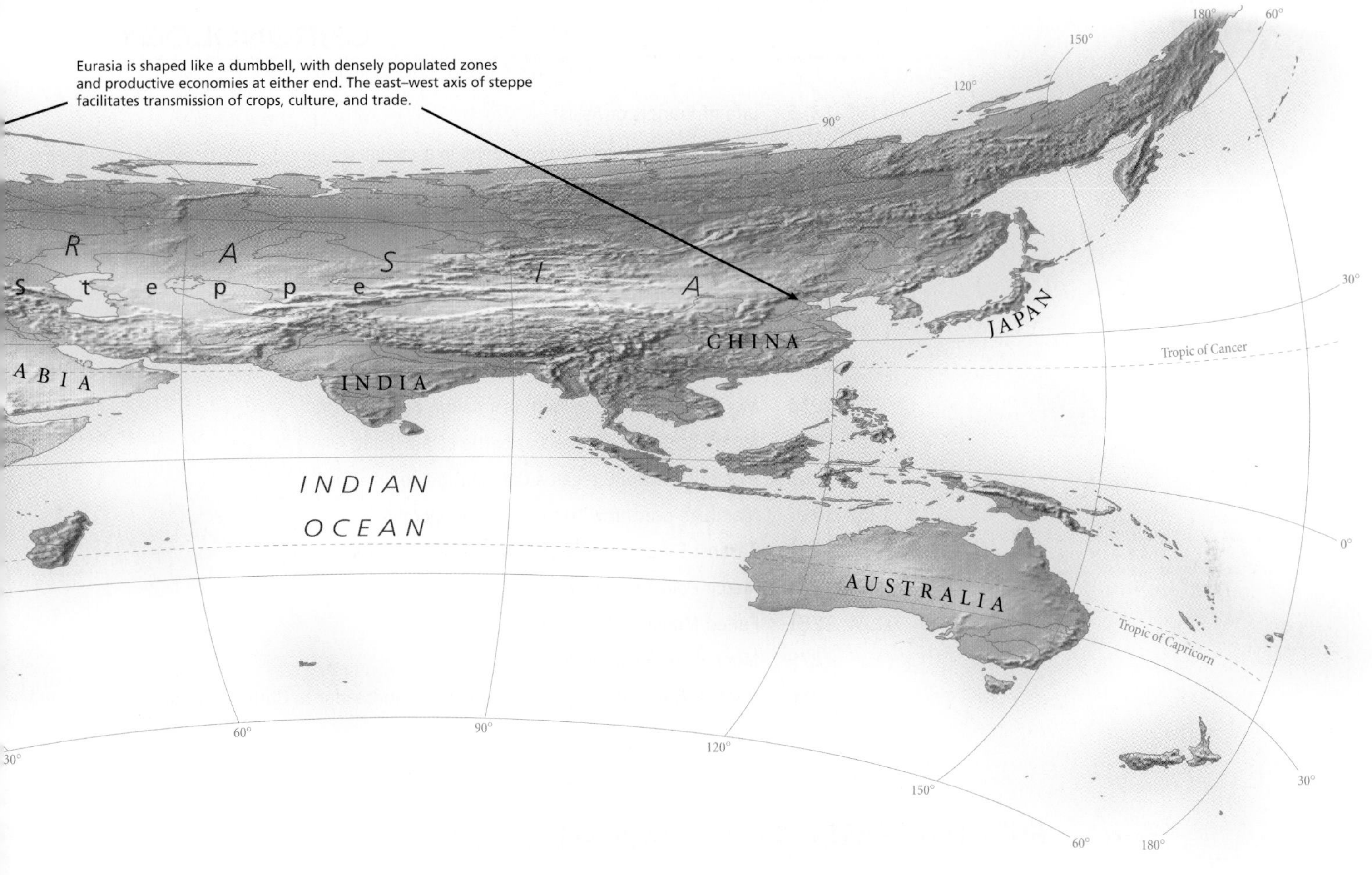

MAP 13.6
Grassland Environments Compared

tunity to develop, obstructing the formation of a Sahel-wide empire. Although pastoral peoples of the western Sahel often built up powerful empires, they always tended to run into either or both of two problems. First, as we have seen, and shall see again, invaders from the desert always challenged and sometimes crushed them (see Chapter 12).

Second, while they lasted, the empires of the Sahel never reached east of Lake Chad. Here states grew up, strong enough to resist conquest, but not strong enough to expand to imperial dimensions themselves: states like Kanem and Bornu—which were sometimes separate, sometimes united. Early Muslim visitors reviled the region for its "reed huts ... not towns" and people clad only in loincloths. But by the twelfth and thirteenth centuries, Kanem and Bornu commanded respect in Arab geography. Lakeshore floodplains for agriculture enriched them, together with the gold they obtained from selling their surplus millet. According to Arab sources, the region enclosed 12 "kingdoms" around 1300.

The Mongols, after their initial bout of extreme destructiveness, brought peace, and, in the wake of that peace, wealth and learning. But with increased travel, the steppeland also became a highway to communicate disease. The Mongol peace lasted less than 150 years. The age of plague that was about to begin would influence the history of Eurasia, and therefore of the world, for centuries.

CHRONOLOGY

1181–1226	Life of Francis of Assisi
1190	First European recorded reference to a compass
1206	Temujin proclaims himself khan
1211–1236	Reign of Iltutmish, sultan of Delhi
1225–1274	Life of Thomas Aquinas
1234	Mongols conquer Georgia
1241–1242	Mongol armies reach Elbe River, Germany
1253–1254	Mission of William of Rubruck to Mongolian court
1258	Mongols capture Baghdad, last caliph put to death
1260	Mamluks defeat Mongols at battle of Ain Jalut
1261	Byzantine Empire regains Constantinople
1268–1291	Mamluks overthrow last crusader kingdoms
1270	Earliest European reference to maritime charts
1271–1275	Marco Polo's first journey to China
1274, 1281	Failed Mongol attempts to invade Japan
1279	Mongol conquest of China completed
1286	Rabban Bar Sauma appointed Mongol ambassador to Christian West

PROBLEMS AND PARALLELS

1. How did the Mongols transform Eurasia in the thirteenth century? What techniques did the Mongols use to rule neighboring civilizations, and how successful were they?
2. How did Mongol rule affect travel and trade along the Silk Roads?
3. How did the civilizations they conquered affect the Mongols? How did Mongol culture in turn influence the civilizations they ruled?
4. Why did Egypt and India show so much vitality in the thirteenth century?
5. How did Francis of Assisi and the Franciscan order remedy some of the social problems that medieval Europe faced? What was the impact of empirical-based learning on European thinking at this time?
6. How did geography hinder the development of continent-wide empires in Africa and the Americas?

DOCUMENTS IN GLOBAL HISTORY

- John of Piano Carpini on the Mongols
- William of Rubruck's account of the Mongols
- From *The Travels of Marco Polo*
- From Francesco Balducci Pegolotti's *The Practice of Commerce*
- From *The History of the Life and Travels of Rabban Bar Sauma*
- Excerpt from the *Novgorod Chronicle*
- Thomas Aquinas, from *Summa Theologica*
- Roger Bacon on experimental science
- Francis of Assisi, selection from *Admonitions*

Please see the Primary Source DVD for additional sources related to this chapter.

READ ON

D. Morgan, *The Mongols* (1986) is the best history of the Mongols: concise, readable, reliable. R. Grousset, *The Empire of the Steppes* (1970) is a translation of the unsurpassed classic history of steppeland peoples in antiquity and the middle ages. Samuel Adshead, *Central Asia in World History* (1993) is also helpful on this period.

P. Jackson, ed., *The Travels of Friar William of Rubruck* (1990) is an outstanding and informative edition of the most vivid of sources. Extracts from sources of the same kind are in I. de Rachewitz, ed., *Papal Envoys to the Great Khan* (1971) and Dawson, ed., *Mission to Asia* (1980). A. Waley, ed., *The Secret History of the Mongols* (2002) collects some Mongol sources in lively translation.

M. Rossabi, *Voyager from Xanadu: Rabban Sauma and the First Journey from China to the West* (1992), and *Kubilai Khan* (1989) are the best books on their respective subjects. On the voyage of Chang Chun, J. Mirsky, *Chinese Travellers in the Middle Ages* (2000) translates the main texts.

On the Silk Roads, the exhibition catalog edited by S. Whitfield, *The Silk Roads* (2004) is the best work. R. Latham, ed., *The Travels of Marco Polo* (1958) is a convenient and accessible abridgement in translation.

On China, R. Davis, *Wind against the Mountain: the Crisis of Politics and Culture in Thirteenth-century China* (1996) is an outstanding account written with close reference to the sources. The exhibition catalog edited by M. Rossabi, *The Legacy of Genghis Khan* (1996) is the best guide to the art of the Ilkhanate and other Mongol successor-states. M. Ipsiroglu, *Painting and Culture of the Mongols* (1966) is indispensable.

J. A. Boyle, ed., *The History of the World Conqueror* (1997) and *The Successors of Genghis Khan* (1971) translate some of the most important sources on the Ilkhanate.

On the Mamluks, R. Irwin, *The Middle East in the Middle Ages: The Early Mamluk Sultanate* (1986) is the best account of their rise, and R. Amitai-Preiss, *Mongols and Mamluks* (2005) is superb study of the wars against the Mongols. S. A. El-Banasi, ed., *Mamluk Art* (2001) covers a wide range of revealing objects.

P. Jackson, *The Delhi Sultanate* (2003) is a splendid introduction to the subject. The best edition of Ibn Battuta is by H. W. Gibb and C. F. Beckingham for the Hakluyt Society, *The Travels of Ibn Battuta* (1956).

On the transmission of Chinese technology westward, J. Needham, *Science and Civilisation in China* (1956) is fundamental—but it is a vast work still in progress. An abridged version in two volumes—*The Shorter Science and Civilisation in China* (1980)—is available. For western science in the period, A. Crombie, *Robert Grossteste and the Origins of Experimental Science* (1971) is controversial and stimulating. D. C. Lindberg, *The Beginnings of Western Science* (1992) gives an efficient and comprehensive account.

Of many studies of St. Francis, none is entirely satisfactory, but J. H. R. Moorman, *St. Francis of Assisi* (1976) can be recommended, first, for its scholarship and brevity and, second, for its vivacity. K. B. Wolf, *The Poverty of Riches* (2003) is good on St. Francis's theology.

On glassmaking, see G. Martin and A. MacFarlane, *The Glass Bathyscape* (2003) and, on clockwork, D. Landes, *Revolution in Time: Clocks and the Making of the Modern World* (1983). On the general background of the thirteenth-century West, D. Abulafia, ed., *The New Cambridge Medieval History*, vol. 5 (1999) is as close as one can get to a comprehensive guide.

CHAPTER

14 The Revenge of Nature: Plague, Cold, and the Limits of Disaster in the Fourteenth Century

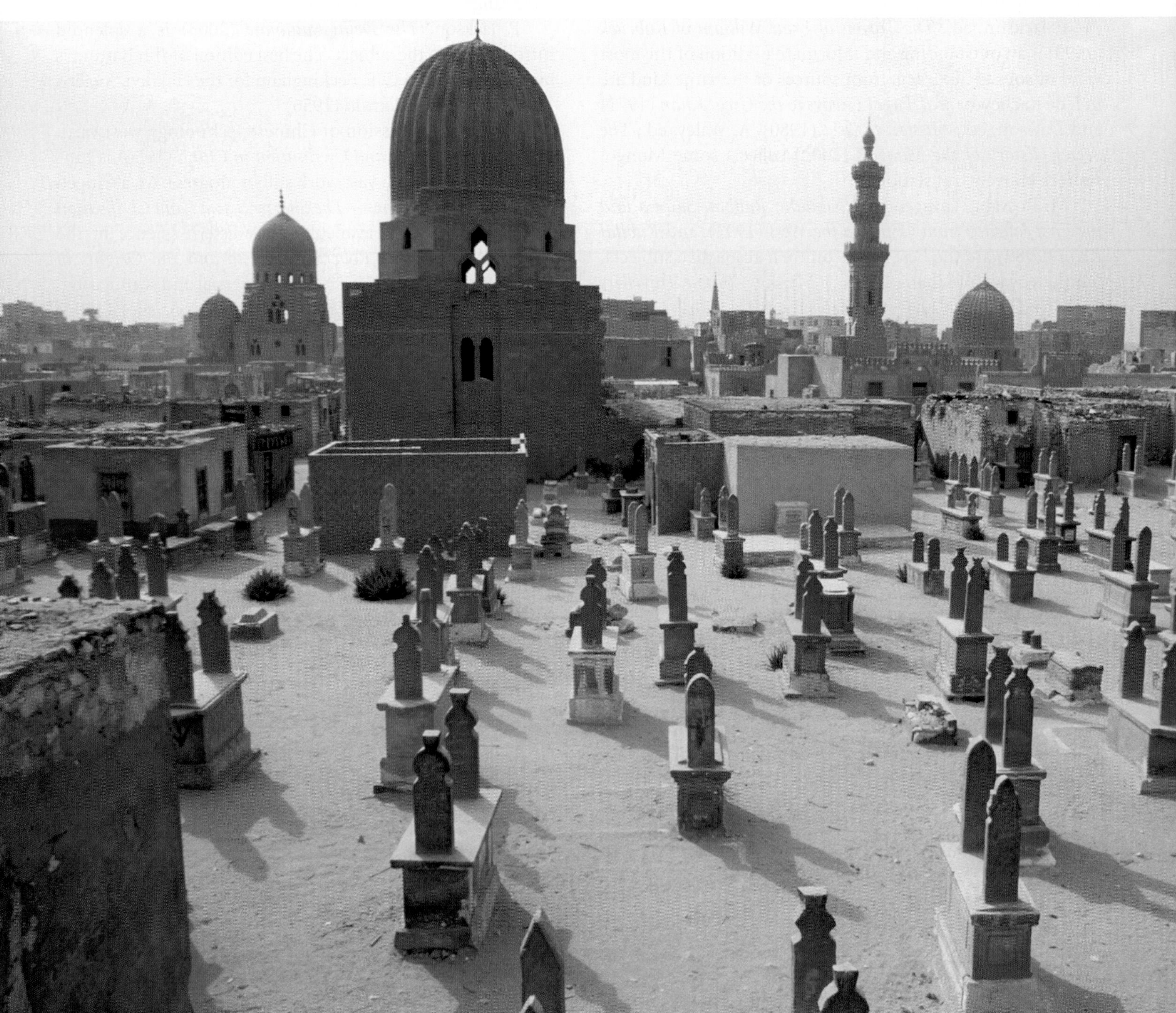

City of the dead. The fourteenth-century Arab traveler Ibn Battuta described Cairo's Southern Cemetery as "a place of peculiar sanctity" that "contains the graves of innumerable scholars and pious believers." The Mamluk domes and minarets visible here form part of the Sultaniyyah tomb complex that was built around 1360, a little over ten years after the plague known as the Black Death had struck the city.

IN THIS CHAPTER

CLIMATE CHANGE
THE COMING OF THE AGE OF PLAGUE
The Course and Impact of Plague
Moral and Social Effects
THE LIMITS OF DISASTER: BEYOND THE PLAGUE ZONE
India
Southeast Asia
Japan
Mali
THE PACIFIC: SOCIETIES OF ISOLATION
IN PERSPECTIVE: The Aftershock

"The people of Cairo are fond of pleasure and amusement," wrote Ibn Battuta (ih-bihn bah-TOO-tah), when he first visited the Egyptian city in 1325. Wanderlust had made this Muslim pilgrim the world's most traveled man. Yet he had never seen a city so big. Cairo had—he was told—12,000 water carriers, 30,000 donkey-rental businesses, and 36,000 river craft. Among sources of pleasure he noted were "boys and maids with lustrous eyes," and the gardens and buildings peerless in splendor. On his next visit in 1348, plague raged in the city and corpses were piled in its streets. "I was told that ... deaths there had risen to 21,000 a day. . . . All the sheikhs I had known were dead. May God Most High have mercy upon them!"

CAIRO

Ibn Battuta was witnessing the most devastating natural catastrophe ever to have hit Eurasia. The Black Death killed millions of people, disrupted states, and checked expansion. Under the impact of a climate that was growing colder, Eurasia's densely populated zone contracted. The growth of trade and states slowed or stopped. Cultural transmissions across the landmass diminished. Isolation from the main routes of trade and travel suddenly became an advantage.

Among the hardest-hit societies were those with the longest and most active records in challenging their environments. It was as if nature had struck back. Indeed, that was how many observers saw it: Muslim theologians argued that plague was a warning from God, "a martyrdom and a mercy" for Muslims, but "a punishment for an infidel." In China, too, conventional wisdom understood natural disasters as examples of what historian Mark Elvin calls "moral meteorology"—the corrections of heaven, unleashed to restore the balance of nature disturbed by human wickedness.

Climate and microbes resist human power. The fourteenth century was exceptional because, in parts of the world, climate change and disease coincided to menace human activities. The loss of life could be made up—eventually. The empires we shall see shaken and states overthrown in this chapter and the next were restored or replaced. The regions and classes that profited from disaster—for there were some, as there always are in every disaster—did not always retain their advantage for long. But the social shake-up that accompanied the changes had, for some of the people affected, irreversible effects. And it was impossible to undo the jarring psychological impact on societies that had accumulated self-confidence over a long period of expansion.

FOCUS questions

- HOW DID the climate change globally in the fourteenth century?
- WHICH PARTS of the world suffered most from the plagues of the fourteenth century?
- WHAT WERE the social and political effects of the plague in China, the Islamic world, and Europe?
- WHY DID some parts of the world not suffer from plague?
- HOW DID the absence of plague affect Japan, Java, India, Mali, and the cultures around the Pacific Ocean?

The best—or even, because of the evidence available, the only—way to approach the changes of the fourteenth century is to start in those parts of the Northern Hemisphere, especially in Eurasia and North Africa, where the effects of cold and plague combined. We can then turn to areas that escaped plagues or their worst consequences, in India, sub-Saharan Africa, Japan, and southeast Asia. Finally, we shall turn to far-away societies in and around the Pacific to appreciate how isolation—which usually retards change—acted as a form of quarantine against disease. As plagues affected some of the planet's previously most dynamic regions, other parts of the world leaped into the sight lines of global history.

CLIMATE CHANGE

Climate change is full of conflicting shifts. Three levels are detectable. At one level, ice ages, which periodically smother great parts of the globe, alternate with global warming, when some glacier-covered areas reemerge. We are between ice ages now. All the fluctuations of the period this book covers have happened in a relatively warm era on the planet. Meanwhile, at another level, periods of a few hundred years of relative cold and warmth alternate within eras of global warming. But even within these periods, changes in winds and currents can produce spells, lasting from 10 to 50 years or so, of warmer or cooler temperatures (see Figure 14.1). Finally, there are sudden interruptions of normal conditions—occurring irregularly and, from what we know, unpredictably—when the distribution of atmospheric pressure is disturbed for unknown reasons. This produces the notorious **El Niño** effect in the tropics and the Southern Hemisphere (see Chapter 4). In Europe, reversals of normal patterns produce longer spells, often of a decade or so, of extremely cold weather.

Short-term fluctuations are sometimes traceable to particular causes. The middle of the second decade of the fourteenth century, for instance, was a cold period all over the Northern Hemisphere, probably because the explosion of Indonesian volcanoes pumped ash into the atmosphere and clouded the sun. But the fall in temperatures was

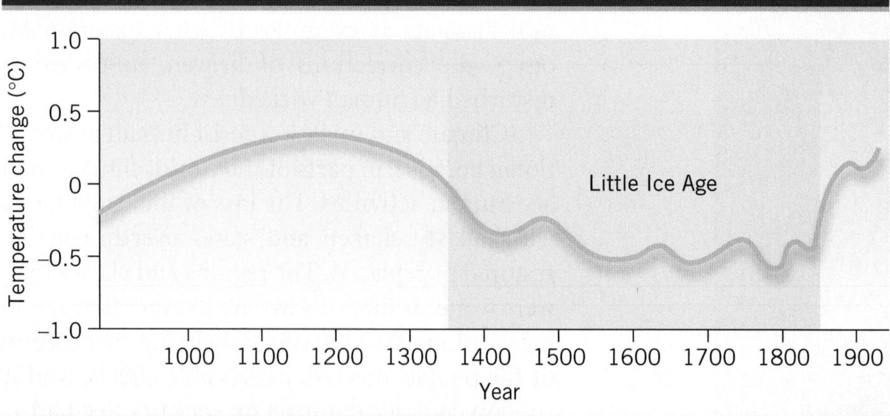

FIGURE 14.1 GLOBAL TEMPERATURE CHANGE, 1000–1900
Source: Hidore, John E., Global Enviornment Change: Its Nature and Impact, (1996). Electronically reproduced by permission of Pearson Education, Inc., Upper Saddle River, New Jersey.

not confined to a few exceptional years. It was part of a general, long-term trend that historians call the "Little Ice Age."

Broadly speaking, from about the tenth century, global temperatures had been relatively warm, with much erosion of natural environments as people converted under-exploited land for farming or grazing (see Chapter 10). Now a cool period—of fluctuating but relatively low temperatures—would last for about 500 years.

The trend began in the Arctic in the thirteenth century. The ice cap crept southward. Glaciers disrupted shipping. Mean annual temperatures in China, which had stayed above freezing from the seventh century to the eleventh, dipped below freezing from the thirteenth century until late in the eighteenth. Glacier growth suggests that North America, too, felt the cold in the fourteenth century. Other indicators for the same century include the persistence of pack ice in summer around Greenland and the disappearance of water-demanding plants from the hinterland of Lake Chad in Central Africa. This is important, because glacier growth affects precipitation. When water ices over, less of it evaporates and falls as rain.

"The Frozen Thames," 1677. The Thames River with old London Bridge in the middle distance and Southwark Cathedral on the right. People amuse themselves on the ice. Some shoot, and others skate. The Thames no longer freezes because the arches of the modern bridges across it don't impede the flow of water.

The weather of the early fourteenth century seemed hostile to people who had to endure it because temperatures were lower than previously, not because it was cold in any absolute sense (see Map 14.1). The cold was, an English poet wrote, "a new kind of affliction, ... not known for a thousand years. . . ." English uplands were abandoned. Glaciers forced Norwegian farmers into retreat.

In 1309–1310 wrote an English chronicler, "bread wrapped in straw or other covering froze and could not be eaten unless it was warmed." During the prolonged cold of 1315–1316, before the ice grew sufficiently to disrupt rainfall, heavy rains all over northern Europe wrecked crops, inflicting famine. Grain "could not ripen, nor had bread such power or essential virtue as it usually has," complained an English chronicler. During 1316, from May to October, cities in Belgium lost 5 to 10 percent of their population. Calamitous flooding and coastal erosion around the North Sea culminated in the "Great Drowning" of 1362, when the sea swallowed vast areas of Holland, Denmark, and England.

Far from the sea, cooling in the Northern Hemisphere brought droughts and famines. In Central Asia, the Mongol world began to contract. China experienced exceptionally severe winters for 36 of the fourteenth century's 100 years. Famines struck China in every year of the reign of the Shun Ti emperor (r. 1333–1368).

At about the same time, climate change seems to have helped destroy an impressive regional system of agriculture and urban life in North America, between the Gila and San Juan Rivers and around present-day Phoenix, Arizona. First the Hohokam people—as archaeologists called them—re-located, from their scattered villages, for closer collaboration in relatively few, dense settlements with huge multi-storey adobe houses. At Paquimé they huddled in a city with the traditional amenities of earlier indigenous civilizations (see Chapter 11): ball courts, carved facades for temples and palaces, wells and irrigation works, workshops for copper workers and jewelers. There was even a macaw hatchery to produce the feathers the elite coveted. It was a splendid effort, but it was clearly a response to stress. Every indicator shows severe population loss throughout the Southwest in the thirteenth and fourteenth centuries. By around 1400, even the new settlements were abandoned. Ruins remain. Casa Grande, in Pinal County, Arizona, leaves

PACIFIC OCEAN
Lack of rainfall leads to population loss throughout the American Southwest
North American glaciers increase
Rocky Mountains
Phoenix
ARIZONA
Casa Grande
Paquimé
NORTH AMERICA
MEXICO
Mississippi
Hudson Bay
Greenland
Caribbean Sea
Iceland
Persistence of pack ice in summer off coast of Greenland
Thames River freezes during the winter of 1309–1310
North Sea
ENGLAND
London
Bruges
Ypres
Cold, heavy rain and flooding destroy crops and erode coastlines in northern Europe
FRANCE
ATLANTIC OCEAN
Andes
SOUTH AMERICA
Amazon
SPAIN
MOROCCO
North Africa
Niger
Water demanding plants disappear from the Lake Chad region
Equator
Tropic of Cancer
1,000 km
1,000 miles
scale varies with perspective
N

ar ice cap begins
reep southward in
thirteenth century
PACIFIC
OCEAN
JAPAN
KOREA
Yellow Sea
Severe winters and famines strike China throughout the fourteenth century
MONGOLIA
Yellow
CHINA
South China Sea
Cooling in Northern Hemisphere reduces food abundance, forcing Mongol world to contract
Yangtze
Mekong
SOUTHEAST ASIA
INDONESIA
AUSTRALIA
EURASIA
RUSSIA
Steppes
TIBET
Himalayas
Bay of Bengal
Between 1310 and 1315 Indonesian volcanoes pump ash into the atmosphere, clouding the sun.
Ganges
Caspian Sea
Black Sea
Danube
Indus
INDIA
Anatolia
PERSIA
Tigris
Euphrates
Arabian Sea
ean Sea
ARABIA
EGYPT
INDIAN
OCEAN
Nile
RICA
Madagascar
Tropic of Cancer
Equator
Tropic of Capricorn
Arctic Circle

MAP 14.1

Climate Change in the Fourteenth Century

ice pack
polar ice pack
major volcanic eruptions
prevailing current, South Pacific (Humboldt Current)
El Niño current
ARIZONA modern-day state or country

MAKING CONNECTIONS

CLIMATE CHANGE IN EURASIA, AFRICA, AND THE AMERICAS

REGION/PERIOD →	EVIDENCE AND ENVIRONMENTAL EFFECTS →	EFFECTS ON HUMAN SOCIETY
Arctic / 1200s	Polar ice cap in Northern Hemisphere creeps southward	Glaciers disrupt shipping
North Atlantic, Arctic Ocean / 1300s	Increased evidence of falling temperatures, glaciation	Persistence of pack ice in summer around Greenland disrupts sea voyages
Central Africa / 1300s	Disappearance of water-demanding plants near Lake Chad	Lessened rainfall reduces crop yields
Europe / 1300s	Glaciers encroach in Norway; calamitous flooding and coastal erosion occur around North Sea coasts	Formerly productive agricultural land abandoned in England; famine and mortality increase dramatically throughout northern Europe; numerous coastal villages disappear in flooding
Central Asia, China / 1300s	More severe winters	Abundance of food that fueled Mongol advances runs out; Mongol world begins to contract; famines strike China from mid-1300s
American Southwest /1300s	Evidence of decreasing rainfall, water supplies	Relocation of Hohokam villages in Arizona; severe population loss throughout Southwest including Arizona, New Mexico sites

onlookers amazed at the ambition of the builders and clueless about what befell them. Scholars have speculated that the conditions that crushed the Hohokam may also have driven migrants southward to colonize central Mexico and found the state that later became the kernel of the Aztec world (see Chapter 15). But the only evidence for this is in untrustworthy legends.

THE COMING OF THE AGE OF PLAGUE

In Eurasia the cold spell coincided with the beginning of an age of plague. Starting in the 1320s, unprecedented bouts of pestilence culminated in the Black Death. Innumerable recurrences—less widespread and less intense—of similar or identical diseases remained frequent in Eurasia until the eighteenth century. The age of plague was so unusual and significant that we want to know what the disease was, where it came from, what caused it, and how much damage it did. All these questions are hard to answer.

Most attempts to write the history of disease have foundered on a false assumption: that we can recognize past visitations of identifiable diseases, known to modern medical science, from symptoms historical sources describe. For two reasons, this is an unrealistic expectation.

First, people in the past looked at disease with perceptions different from ours. The symptoms they spotted would not necessarily be those we would note, nor would they use the same sort of language to describe them. Second, diseases change. Many of the microorganisms that cause disease evolve fast because they reproduce rapidly and respond quickly to changing environments.

The plagues of the age of plague need not all have been visitations of a single disease. They may have included some diseases recognizable in today's medical handbooks. But we must be open to the likelihood that some of the diseases that devastated Eurasia in the age of plague were peculiar to that period. New pathogens are deadly, because when they strike, no one has had a chance to build up immunity to them.

Of diseases now known to medical science, bubonic plague—not, perhaps, of the same variety we know today—was most likely to have played a part in the age of plague. Bubonic plague is a rat-borne disease. When they bite, rats' fleas regurgitate the bacillus, ingested from rats' blood, into human victims, or communicate infection by defecating into their bites. In cases of septicemic plague (a systemic disease caused by pathogens in the blood), one of the first symptoms is generally death. Otherwise, swellings appear—small like Brazil nuts or big like grapefruit—over the neck and groin or behind the ears. Jitters, vomiting, dizziness, and pain might follow, often accompanied by an inability to tolerate light.

Marchione di Coppo Stefani, from *The Florentine Chronicle*

Fourteenth-century sources describe all these symptoms, together with sudden fainting, before victims, as one observer explained, "almost sleeping and with a great stench eased into death." The trouble is that during the first hundred years of the age of plague, of all the sources that describe the symptoms, fewer than one in six lists symptoms of this kind. Moreover, almost everyone at the time was convinced that plague spread by infection or contagion. Rats—the normal agent for the spread of bubonic plague—play little part in the accounts. Finally, it seems most unlikely that the frequent epidemics reported in China from the 1320s to the 1360s can have been of bubonic plague in the form now familiar to us, which, as we shall see, hit an unimmunized China in the late eighteenth century. The suddenness and virulence of the visitations suggest the arrival of a new and previously unexperienced pathogen, for the Chinese, with their long experience in farming and animal domestication, enjoyed highly developed natural immunities to the familiar diseases that breed in farming environments.

Many accounts of the Black Death include a bewildering variety of symptoms that are not associated with bubonic plague: complications in the lungs, spitting blood, headaches, extremely rapid breathing, strangely colored urine. The emphasis on lung disorders suggests a mixture of bubonic and pneumonic plague, which primarily attacks the lungs. To judge from other descriptions, outbreaks of typhus, smallpox, and various kinds of influenza coincided with some visitations of plague. In the Mediterranean, the plague usually struck in summer. In northern Europe, autumn seems to have been the deadliest season. But, looked at as a whole, the plagues of the period had no seasonal pattern and no obvious connection with any particular weather systems or atmospheric conditions. This again points to the involvement of more than one pathogen.

It seems likely that domestic animals were an essential part of the background—as carriers of disease, as a reservoir of infection, and even as sufferers. Some early plague victims were sure that their domestic animals suffered from the disease, just as they did themselves. A chronicler in the city of Florence in Italy listed "dogs, cats, chickens, oxen, donkeys, and sheep" among the sufferers, with the same symptoms as humans, including swellings in the groin and armpits. At the port of Salona on the Adriatic coast, the Black Death's first victims were "horses, oxen, sheep, and goats." The Egyptian chronicler, al-Maqrizi (ahl-mah-KREE-zee), who was among the most observant and thoughtful witnesses, believed that the disease started, like so many others, among animals before transferring to human hosts. It had spread from grazing flocks on the steppe in 1341, after which "the wind transmitted their stench around the world." He and other Muslim commentators thought wild animals caught it, too. If these sources are correct, the Black Death must have been—or included—a disease unknown today.

Plague victims. The illustrator of an early fifteenth-century German chronicle imagined the plague of Egypt—sent by God, according to the Book of Exodus in the Bible, to make Pharaoh "let my people go"—with the same symptoms as the Black Death. In the background, Moses brings plague down on Egypt by prayer. By implication, prayer and obedience to the will of God could also be remedies for plague.

An unanswered question is, *How, if at all, were changes in climate and disease patterns linked?* The plague pathogens, as we have seen, struck at different seasons and in climatically different regions of Eurasia, from cold Scandinavia and rain-drenched Western Europe to the hot, dry Middle East. The plagues were less penetrative, however, in hot, moist regions and do not seem to have reached across the Sahara to tropical Africa, even though many potential disease carriers crossed that desert to trade. It is worth bearing in mind, however, that the plague pathogens seem to have included new arrivals in the microbial world that remained active for as long as global cooling lasted.

The Course and Impact of Plague

It is easier to describe the routes by which the plague traveled (see Map 14.2). The Italian chronicler Matteo Villani said the plague came from China and Central Asia, "then through their surrounding lands and then to coastal places across the ocean." Arabic sources specify the same, or a similar, path.

The age of plague indeed seems to have started in China. But that is not the same as saying that subsequent outbreaks elsewhere were the result of communication from China, or even that they were necessarily outbreaks of the same disease or diseases. Repeated occurrences—or, perhaps, a continuous visitation—of massively lethal maladies were recorded in southwest China and central China in the early 1320s. In 1331, mortality rates in parts of northeast China that had endured five reported outbreaks of plague in the previous two decades reputedly reached 90 percent. Two years later, a plague claimed 400,000 lives in the Yangtze and Huai (hway) valleys. In 1353–1354, chroniclers reported that around two-thirds of the population perished from pestilence in eight distinct Chinese districts. Most of those areas experienced repeated bouts of disease of the same sort in the late 1350s or early 1360s.

Doubt persists, however, over whether the diseases rampant in China were the cause of—or even the same as—those found farther west. Most commentators at the time in Europe and the Middle East believed that plague, like the Mongols, was an invader from the steppeland. Many observers noted that the Mongols transmitted plague. Of course, there were multiple points of entry, as a lawyer in Italy acknowledged:

> Almost everyone who had been in the East, or in the regions to the south and north, fell victim. . . . The scale of the mortality ... persuaded ... the Chinese, Indians, Medes, Kurds, Armenians, Cilicians (sih-LEES-see-yahns), Georgians, Mesopotamians, Nubians, Ethiopians, Turks, Egyptians, Arabs, Saracens, and Greeks... that the last judgement has come.[1]

A pandemic on this scale was unprecedented. The pathogens responsible had found an eco-niche as wide as Eurasia.

Chroniclers' estimates of mortality are notoriously unreliable, but verifiable evidence bears out some of the most shocking assessments of the damage. In Barcelona on the Mediterranean coast of Spain, 60 percent of jobs in the church fell vacant. Clerical records in northern England suggest the first visitation of the plague killed 40 percent of clergy there. Clergy were members of a high-risk profession, but the laity suffered just as much. In some manors in England, up to 70 percent of tenants died. Villages in southern France lost four-fifths of their population. Towns ran out of cemetery space. The living had to pile the dead in pits with quicklime to speed decomposition and minimize rot. Half the villages of Sicily were abandoned, as were a third of those around Rome.

When the plague reached the Middle East, Ibn Battuta was there to observe it, on his way back to Cairo. Arriving in Syria in May 1348, he found that deaths in the city of Damascus reached 2,400 a day. In one town, three-quarters of the public officials had died. The plague spread along the coast of North Africa, causing—so people claimed—1,000 deaths a day at its height in Tunis. In Morocco, Ibn Battuta's own mother was among the victims.

In Central Asia, where plagues bred or where microorganisms traveled between the densely populated ends of Eurasia, Arab sources reported that many steppeland dynasties and Mongol warriors succumbed to plague. Nestorian headstones in what is now Russian Central Asia refer to plague as the cause of deaths in 1338 and 1339. In 1345 and 1346, according to Russian chronicles, pestilence devastated cities in the Mongol-ruled parts of southern Russia. Uzbek villages emptied. In 1346–1347, an official in Crimea reputedly counted 85,000 corpses.

In China, there seems little doubt that the population fell in the relevant period. The census of 1393, with adjustments demographers made to compensate for the official habit of underestimating the numbers, suggests a total population of around 80 million—compared with about 120 million in the mid–fourteenth century. The loss of people was by no means uniform. Some regions even seem to have made slight gains.

Moral and Social Effects

Natural disasters always inspire moralizing. Although the Black Death killed the vicious and the virtuous alike, it was tempting, especially for Christians, to see it as a moral agent, even a divine instrument to call the world to repentance and make people good. The plague was a leveler, attacking all sorts and conditions. For many who experienced it, the plague was a test of faith, first eliciting selfish reactions of terror and flight, profiteering and despair, then, as a Florentine chronicler observed, "people ... began to help one another, from whence many were cured."

Flagellants. In 1349, the Black Death inspired thousands of penitents to organize processions and cults of self-flagellation across Europe in an attempt to deflect God's wrath. Like many others, the Flemish chronicler whose work is depicted here denounced the flagellants for claiming that their penance was a kind of baptism, that it could wipe out sin, and that it was a sacrifice akin to Christ's death on the cross. The king of France banned flagellation, and the pope outlawed it.

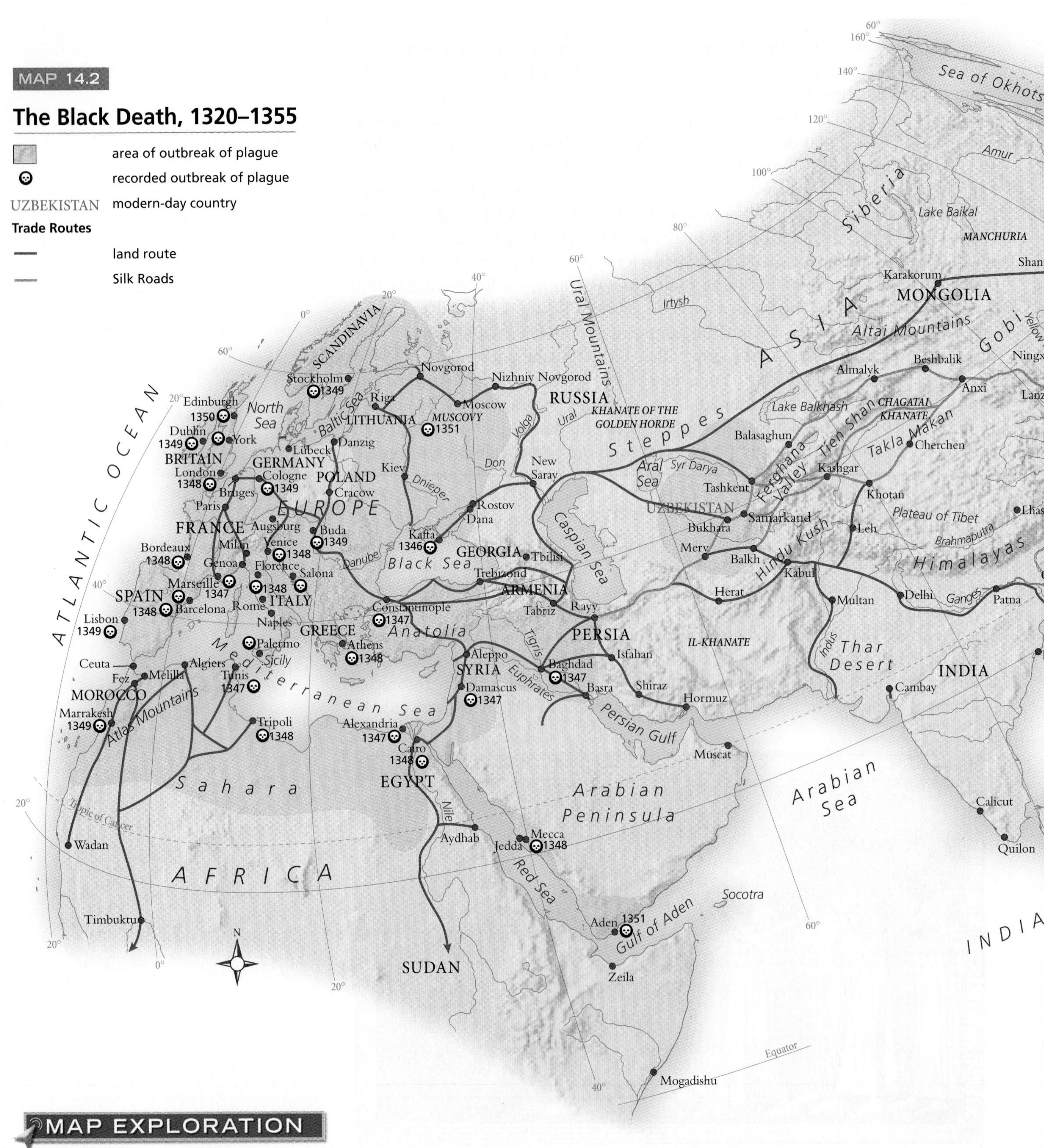

MAP EXPLORATION
www.prenhall.com/armesto_maps

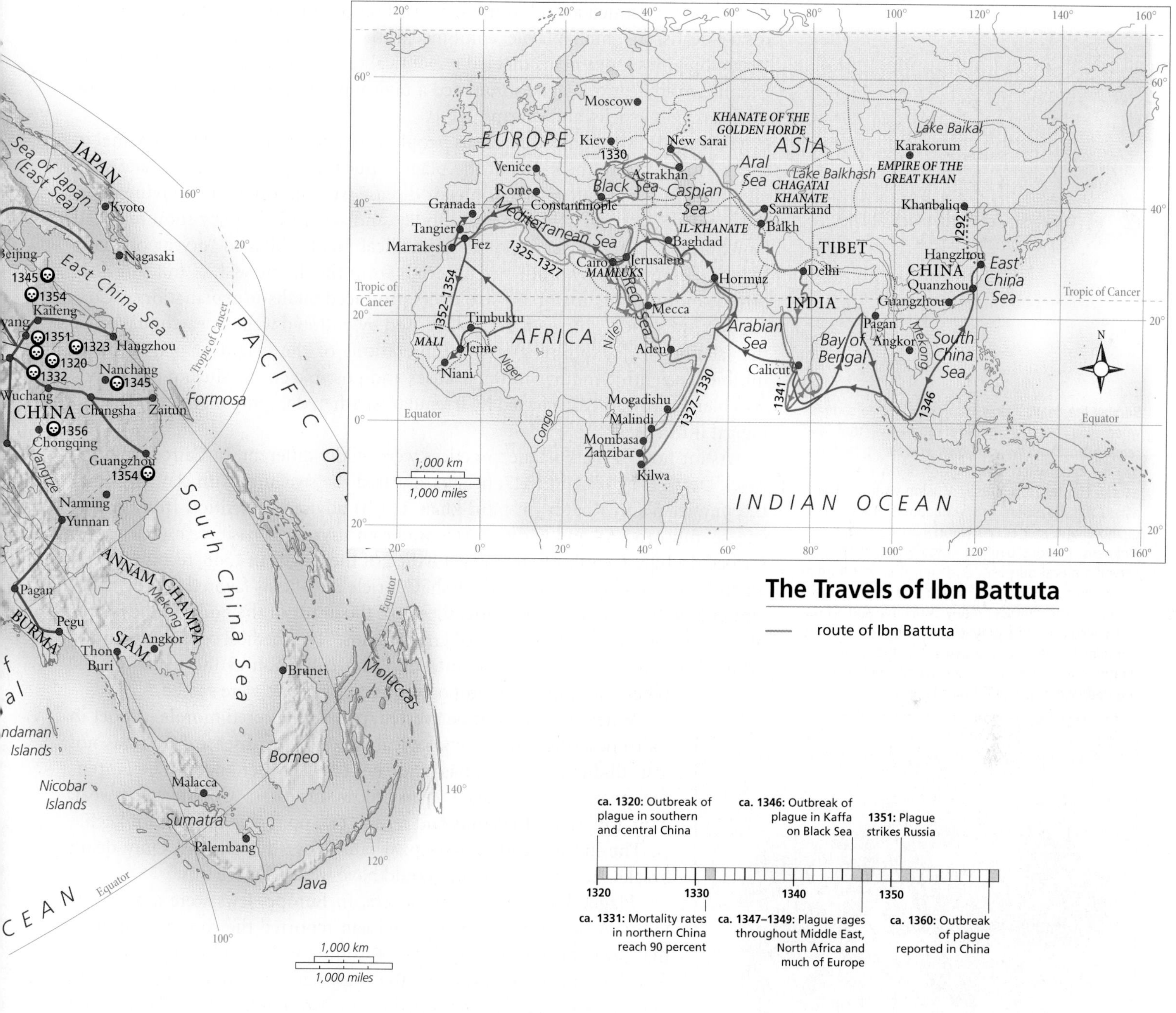

The Travels of Ibn Battuta

Dice makers, claimed an abbot in northern France, turned to the manufacture of rosary beads. In China, plague, combined with other natural disasters, helped to stir up religious movements that led to political revolution (see Chapter 15). In the Islamic world, fear of plague stimulated a revival of popular religion: summoning spirits, magical spells, and charms.

Plague also stimulated science as people searched for a cure. It was normal to speak as if sin were the cause of the plague. But most people did not take such talk literally. Moralistic explanations of disease were hardly more convincing in the fourteenth century than they are today, and scientific inquiry soon replaced lamentations. The University of Paris medical faculty blamed "a year of many fogs and damps ... any pestilence proceeds from the divine will, ... but this does not mean forsaking doctors." Astrologers produced fatalistic explanations. "Corrupt air" was widely blamed, perhaps caused by polluted wells or earthquakes. In the Islamic world, too, religious interpretations of the origin of plague never inhibited scientific inquiry into its causes and possible cures. Muslim physicians also blamed corrupt air, caused by irregular weather, decaying matter, and astrological influences.

University of Paris Medical Faculty, *Report on the Plague*

As for how to treat plague, practices were wildly different. In Cairo, when the Black Death broke out in 1347, healers smeared the swellings with clay. In Spain, the physician Ibn Khatib (ih-bihn khah-TEEB) advised abstention from grains, cheese, mushrooms, and garlic. Barley water and syrup of basil were widely prescribed. In Italy, Gentile of Foligno, who died of the plague in 1348, recommended an ancient medicine, dried snake's flesh. Gabriele de' Mussis favored bloodlettings and plasters of mallow leaves. Turks sliced off the heads of the boils on the bodies of the sick and supposedly extracted "green glands." The medical consensus among both Christians and Muslims saw infection and contagion as the main threats. Where the authorities imposed quarantine, lives were spared.

Burying the dead. "How come you feel no sadness when you bury a fellow-creature ... that you remain unready for your own graves ... that you pay no heed when warnings of death reach your ears?" The twelfth-century Muslim writer al Hariri asked this question in his Maqamat, a collection of moralistic stories. Al Hariri had no doubt that sickness, besides being a physical affliction, also served a moral purpose. God sent it to test human virtue and compassion. When the Black Death struck in the 1300s, many Muslims and Christians also saw the plague this way and tried to minister to the sick and dying. Yet the number of deaths could overwhelm the living, and many of the dead were dumped in mass graves.

Where it could not be averted, plague shattered morale. A poet in Cairo described the psychological effect of the disease: "God has not just subdued Egypt, he has made her crawl on her knees." The Florentine poet, Petrarch, raged at his fellow survivors: "Go, mortals, sweat, pant, toil, range the lands and seas to pile up riches you cannot keep. . . . The life we lead is a sleep; whatever we do, dreams. Only death breaks the sleep. ... I wish I could have woken before this."

Plague had winners and losers. In Europe, Jews were among the losers. A skeptical German Franciscan reported the common opinion that Jews started the plague by poisoning wells "and many Jews confessed as much under torture: that they had bred spiders and toads in pots and pans, and had obtained poison from overseas. . . . Throughout Germany, and in all places, they were burnt. For fear of that punishment many accepted baptism and their lives were spared." The massacres that ensued, especially in Germany, were nearly always the result of outbreaks of mob violence, which the authorities tried to restrain. In July 1348, Pope Clement VI declared the Jews innocent of the charge of well poisoning and excommunicated anyone who harmed them. In January 1349, the city council of Cologne in the Rhineland warned other cities that anti-Jewish riots could ignite popular revolt. "Accordingly we intend to forbid any harrassment of the Jews in our city because of these flying rumors, but to defend them and keep them safe, as our predecessors did—and we are convinced that you ought to do the same." But massacres continued.

Why did some Europeans victimize Jews? Jewish communities had existed all over the Mediterranean since Roman times (see Map 14.3). Like other migrants from the east, such as Greeks, Syrians, and Arabs, they were an urban and often a commercial people. The twelfth-century Jewish merchant, Benjamin of Tudela, describes their close-knit world, in which a structure of family firms and coreligionists helped Jews to trade between the Christian and Muslim worlds. An isolated reference to Jews in Cologne occurs as early as 321 C.E. when the Rhineland was part of the Roman Empire, but Mediterranean communities

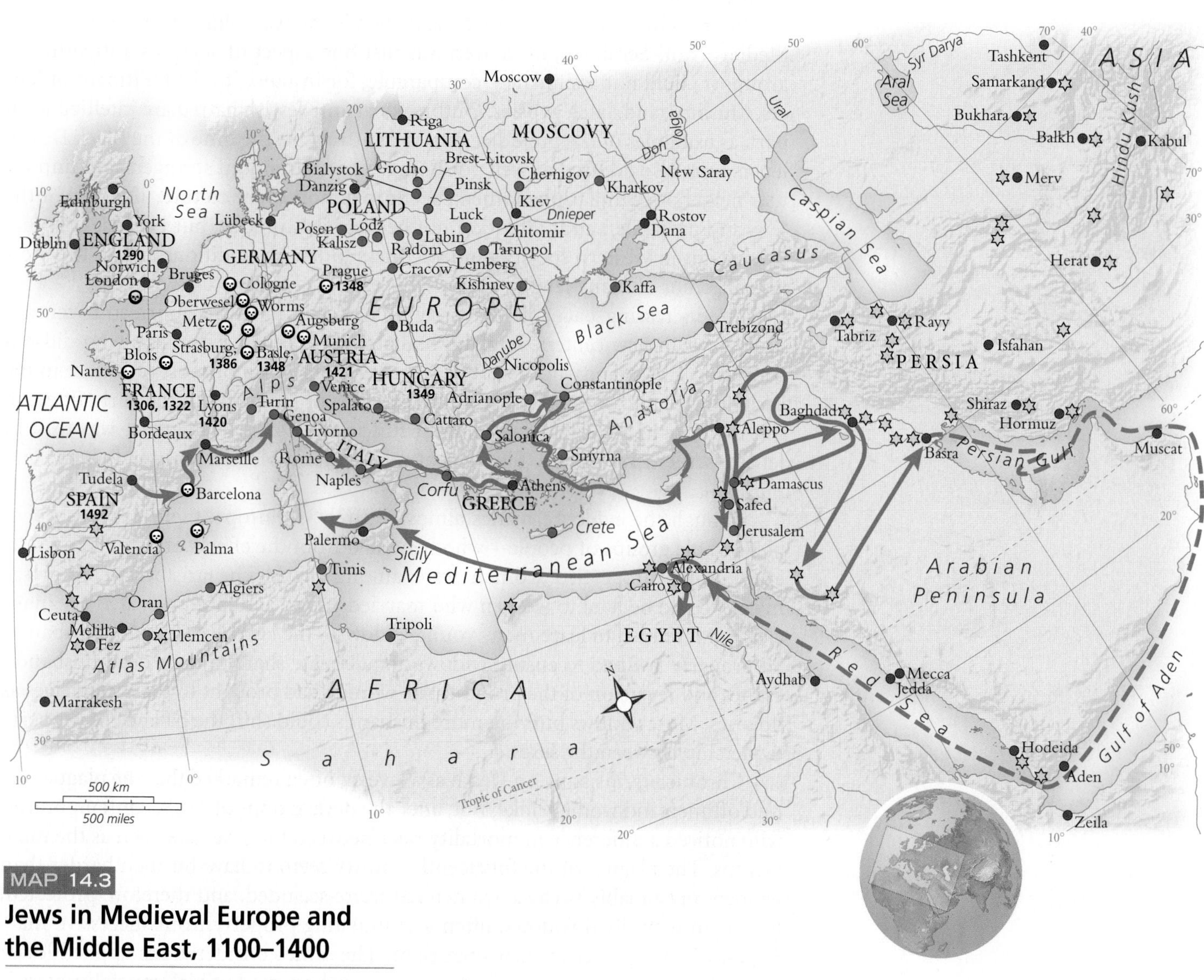

MAP 14.3

Jews in Medieval Europe and the Middle East, 1100–1400

- ● major centers of Jewish resettlement, 1200–1500
- massacres of Jews, ca. 1100–1400
- **1290** date of expulsion of Jews
- travels of Benjamin of Tuleda, ca. 1160–1173
- presumed route of Benjamin of Tuleda
- ✡ Jewish communities in Muslim world

were probably the springboard for Jewish colonization of northern European cities between the sixth and eleventh centuries.

Wherever they went, Jews were alternately privileged and persecuted: privileged, because rulers who needed productive settlers rewarded them with legal immunities; persecuted, because host communities resented intruders who were given special advantages. **Anti-Semitism** has been traced to the influence of Christianity. Indeed, medieval anti-Semitism did exploit Christian prejudices. Gospel texts could be read—as they were, for example, at the time of the First Crusade (see Chapter 12)—to saddle Jews with collective responsibility for the death of Jesus. And Holy Week, when Christians prepare to commemorate Christ's death, was at best an expensive and at worst a fatal time for Jewish communities, who had to buy security from bloody reprisals.

In the Greek world, however, anti-Semitism was older than Christianity. Medieval anti-Semitism, moreover, was just one aspect of society's antipathy for groups it could not assimilate—comparable, for instance, to the treatment of lepers, Muslims, and, later, gypsies. Outbreaks of anti-Jewish hatred are intelligible, in part, as examples of the prejudice outsiders attract. At the time of the Black Death, lepers were also accused of well poisoning. So were random strangers and unpopular neighbors. Similar phenomena occur in almost every culture. The case of the Jews in Europe demands attention not because it is unique, but because it is surprising, given Western society's indebtedness to Jewish traditions and to the individual genius of many Jews.

The increasing pace and intensity of persecution in the fourteenth century drove Jews to new centers. England had already expelled those Jews who did not convert to Christianity in 1290. The Jews were forced out of most of France in the early fourteenth century, and from many areas of Germany in the early fifteenth century. (Spain and Portugal followed suit in the 1490s.) The effect was to shift Jewish settlement toward the central and eastern Mediterranean, Poland, and Lithuania.

Though the evidence relates almost entirely to Europe, there were also people—whole groups of people—who benefited from the effects of plague. In Western Europe, propertied women were among them. The aristocratic marriage market could be fatal to women who married young and faced repeated pregnancies, but it tended to leave many young widows—the last wives of aging husbands. So property law had to ensure widows an adequate share in their dead husbands' estates and reversion of the property the women had brought to their marriages as dowries. More widows burying more husbands could shift the balance of property ownership between the sexes.

Chroniclers, insisting on Death as a leveler, often remarked that the plague carried off men and women alike. But, after the devastations of 1348, contemporaries who noticed a difference in mortality rates between the sexes saw men as the main victims. The plagues of the fourteenth century seem to have hit men harder than women, presumably because women led more secluded, and therefore protected, lives than men. Rich widows, often accumulating property from successive marriages, wielded power in their own right. The same considerations applied lower down the ranks of society. For instance, during the period of high mortality associated with cold and famine in the second decade of the fourteenth century, more than half the weddings among the peasants of the manor of Taunton in southwest England involved rich widows. After the Black Death, the lords of the manor introduced massive license fees for anyone who wanted to make such marriages, ostensibly to protect widows from predatory Romeos. In unprecedented numbers, widows became the administrators of estates. Women of leisure, education, and power played a bigger part in Western society after this. The increased prominence of women in political, literary, and religious life from the fifteenth century onward might not have been possible without the damage plague did to men.

The Wife of Bath. "Thanks be to God, who is for aye alive / Of husbands at Church door have I had five." "The Wife of Bath" was a fictional character of about 1400—shown here in a contemporary illustration to the English writer Geoffrey Chaucer's verses about her. But, like all good satire, she was representative of the society of her times: sexually shameless, irrepressibly bossy, and determined to exert "power, during all my life" over any husband "who shall be both my debtor and my slave."
"Facsimile of Ellesmere Chaucer, The Wife of Bath" 1400–1410. V & A Museum, London. Picture Desk, Inc./Kobal Collection

In Western Europe peasants, if they survived the plague, also benefited from it. In the long run, owners could only keep great properties viable after plague had scythed the labor force by splitting the proceeds with their workers, or by breaking the estates up and letting peasants farm the parcels as tenants. Instead of taking orders from the lord's agent or bailiff, tenants paid rent and could manage their landholdings as they liked. The trend toward "free" peasantries started long before the Black Death struck, because it suited landowners, too. Peasants often made the land more productive. It made economic sense to allow them to improve their holdings. In England, where the royal courts encouraged peasant freedom to weaken aristocrats' power, about half the peasants in the south of the country were already free when the plague arrived.

Lords wrote off their rights to labor services because, as a steward on an English estate admitted in 1351, "the lord's interest made it necessary." The contract peasant dependants of an English abbey renegotiated is revealing: "At the time of the mortality or pestilence which occurred in 1349, scarcely two peasants remained on the manor." They threatened to leave unless a new contract were made. Most of their former services—including plowing, weeding, carting, and preparing soil for planting—were commuted for rent "as long as it pleases the lord—and would that it might please the lord for ever," added the scribe, "since the aforesaid services were not worth very much." It is remarkable, however, that the growth of lease-holding and the relaxation of lordly controls over peasant farmers happened on a large scale in the late fourteenth and fifteenth centuries in the parts of Western Europe plague affected. In areas the Black Death bypassed—such as Poland, much of Russia, and parts of Central Europe—the opposite happened. Peasants became tied to their lords' land and subject to the landholders' jurisdiction.

Were the effects on the European peasantry duplicated in other plague-ridden lands? Certainly, the rural population became more restive and mobile in Egypt and Syria. Villages in Egypt often had their tax burdens reduced in acknowledgment of the loss of population. The cost of labor services rose as population fell, creating opportunities for economic mobility among peasants and urban workers, and stimulating a further decline in rural population levels as peasants migrated to towns. But these changes did not disturb landowners' grip on their holdings. Peasants and landowners seem to have suffered together the effects of declining rural productivity.

Moreover, most governments responded to the demographic disaster, loss of revenue, and loss of labor by raising taxes and trying to limit labor mobility. In previous centuries, ecological disasters and political oppression had often driven peasants into religious extremism or rebellion. Now, popular revolt took on a new agenda: revolutionary **millenarianism**—the doctrine that in an imminent relaunch of history, God would empower the poor. This happened independently but in strikingly similar ways, in both Europe and China. A popular preacher, who incited peasant rebels in England in 1381, expressed the doctrine of egalitarianism:

> How can the lords say or prove that they are more lords than we—save that they make us dig and till the ground so that they can squander what we produce? But it is from us and our labor that everything comes with which they maintain their pomp.[2]

Prophecies nourished revolt. Some Franciscans (see Chapter 13), with their special vocation to serve the poor, excited expectations that the end of the world was near, and that God would release riches from the Earth and eliminate inequality. In China, a similar doctrine inspired peasant rebels in the 1350s. A new Buddha would inaugurate a golden age and give his followers power over their oppressors (see Chapter 15). According to both movements, a divinely appointed hero would put a bloody end to the struggle of good and evil.

The next chapter describes the politics of the ensuing revolt. According to popular traditions, the leader of the rebellion, the founder of China's Ming dynasty, who claimed to be the prophesied hero, rose to prominence by inventing a medicine that could cure a new plague, "which killed half the people and which no known medicine could combat."

The plagues also helped transform the Mongol world. The region the Mongols dominated spanned the plague's trans-Eurasian corridors of transmission. Though the evidence comes from European observers, it is a safe assumption that Mongol manpower suffered, and that population levels in some regions from which the Mongols levied recruits and taxes also fell. The loss of China in 1368 was, of course, the Mongols' most spectacular forfeiture of power. But Mongol control also slackened in other dominions, and, on the Chinese front, it never recovered.

In general, plague-stricken societies showed more social mobility. Aristocracies, which were always subject to rapid turnover as families died out, thinned and refilled faster than ever. This seems to have applied as much to China's scholar elite, whose hold on power was not fully reasserted until the fifteenth century, as to Western European nobilities, whose composition changed. In Western Europe, the increase in the numbers of free peasants and tenants created a form of rural capitalism. Families formerly restricted to modest social ambitions could accumulate wealth and bid for higher status, buying education, business opportunities, or more land.

THE LIMITS OF DISASTER: BEYOND THE PLAGUE ZONE

How far did the plagues of the fourteenth century reach? The plague changed the history of China, Western Europe, the Middle East, and the steppeland empires. But much of Central and Eastern Europe escaped. So did areas that ought to have been vulnerable, such as southeast Asia, and the parts of West and East Africa that were in touch, via the Indian Ocean or the Saharan caravan routes, with affected regions. Relative isolation protected Japan. Apart from a pestilence in the capital Kyoto in 1342, there were no visitations of any disease on a scale resembling that of the Black Death. The principalities and city-states of central and northern Russia suffered relatively little and late—not before 1350, which is surprising in view of Russia's openness to the steppeland and close contact with the Mongols. India was relatively little affected.

Beyond the reach of the plagues—or, at least, beyond the zone of its most severe effects—the fourteenth century was an era of opportunity in Eurasia (see

Map 14.4). The Mongols were now troubled giants, from whom states in India, Japan, and southeast Asia were safe. We can look at those regions first, before turning to others where, as far as we know, the plagues never penetrated, in sub-Saharan Africa and the Pacific.

India

In India, the sultanate of Delhi profited from the Mongols' decline. Sultan Muhammad Ibn Tughluq (moo-HA-mahd ih-bihn TOOG-look) (r. 1325–1351) was the driving force of a policy of conquest that almost covered the subcontinent with campaigns. Ibn Battuta called him "of all men the most addicted to the making of gifts and the shedding of blood. His gate is never without some poor man enriched or some living man executed." Emphasis on the sultan's generosity reflects Ibn Battuta's own priorities. He was always on the lookout for rich patrons. But Ibn Tughluq's ran his court and army by balancing lavish gifts with intimidating displays of wrath.

His administration was a machine for recycling wealth. Ibn Battuta describes the regular arrival of revenue collectors from villages, casting gold coins into a golden basin: "These contributions amount in all to a vast sum which the sultan gives to anyone he pleases."

MAP 14.4

South and Southeast Asia, ca. 1350

- region where Majapahit claimed tribute
- Delhi sultanate at its greatest extent, ca. 1335
- area subject to sporadic influence by Delhi Sultanate
- main trade route
- important trade centers

Traded Goods

- pepper
- cinnamon
- sandalwood
- nutmeg
- cloves
- mace

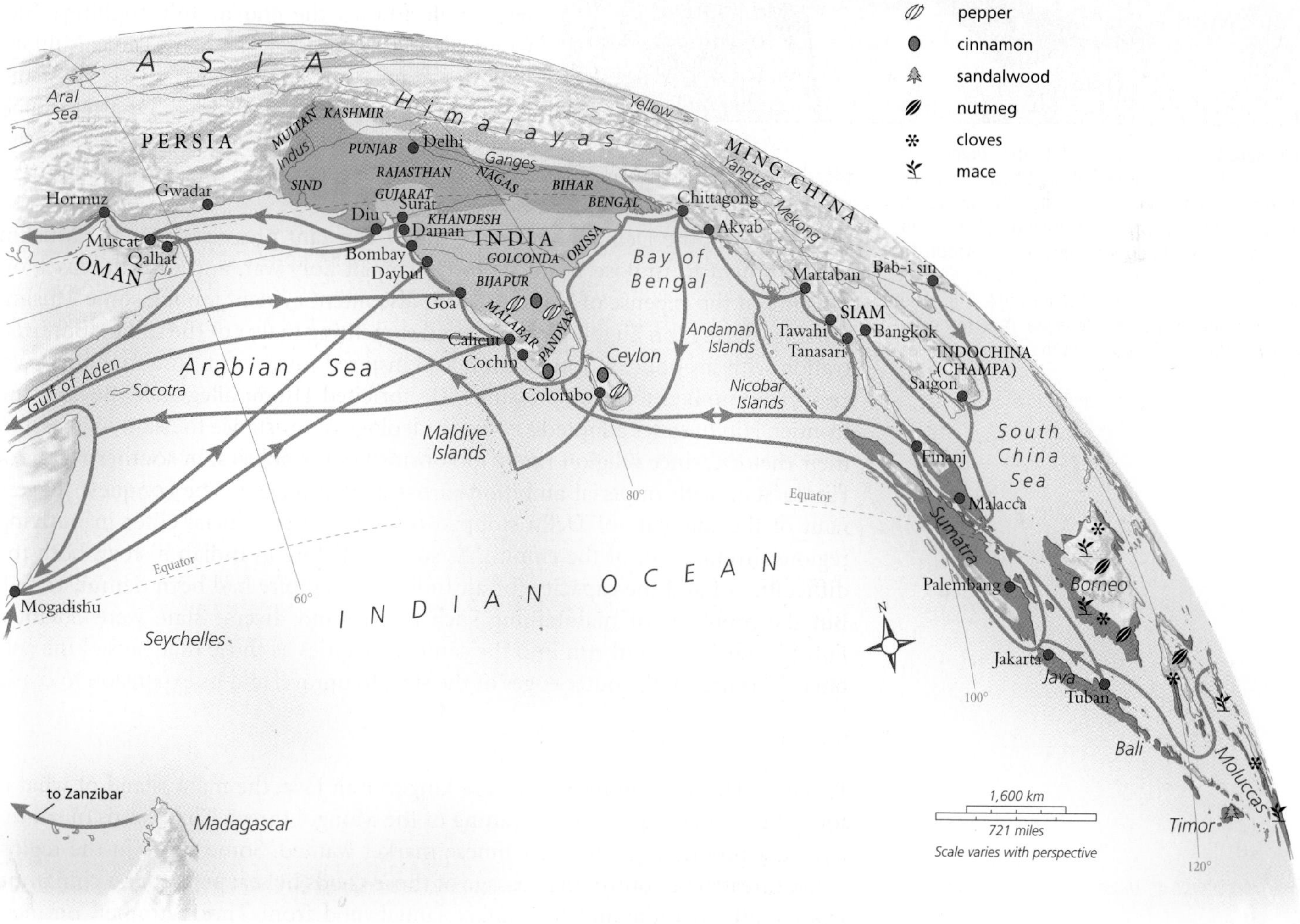

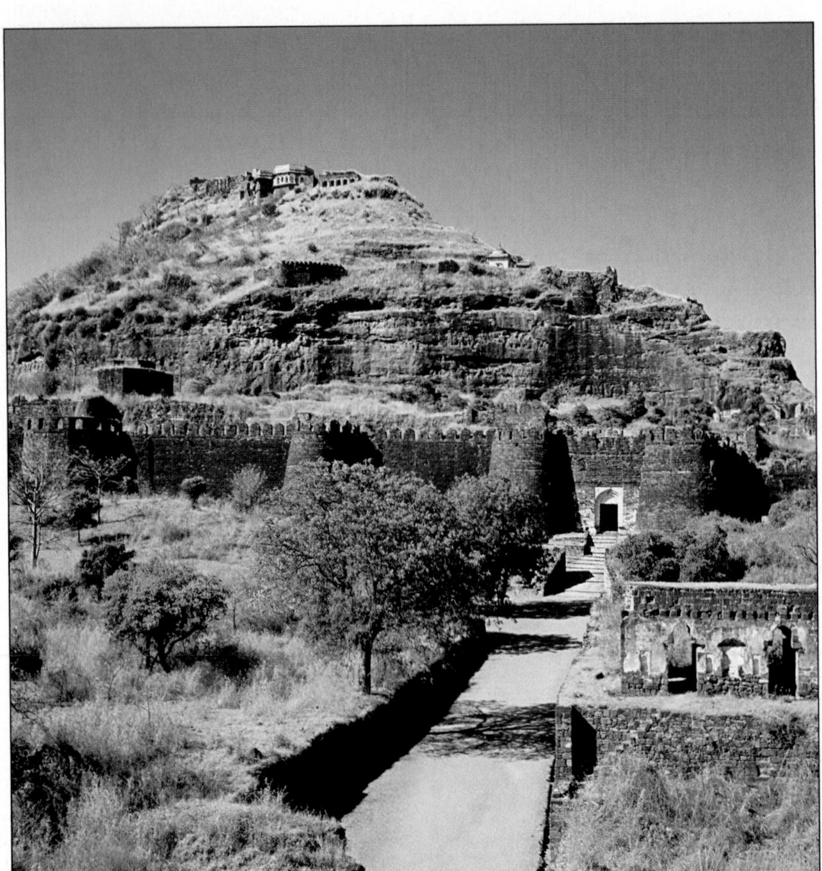

Daulatabad. The Delhi Sultan Ibn Tughluq (r. 1325–1351) transferred his court to the strongest fortress in India, which he called Daulatabad or "City of Riches," near the frontier of his campaigns against Hindu kingdoms in the south. He planned to re-locate the entire population of the city of Delhi to the surrounding slopes. The steep ascent made the place defensible. A narrow gangway was the only approach to the palace complex.

While praising the sultan's sense of justice, Ibn Battuta indicts him for the use of terror, arbitrary abuses of power, and judicial murder. "Every day there are brought to the audience hall hundreds of people, chained, beaten and fettered, and those who are for execution are executed, those for torture tortured, and those for beating beaten." On one occasion, the sultan executed 350 alleged deserters at once. A sheikh who accused him of tyranny was fed with excrement and beheaded. Twice, Ibn Tughluq expelled the classes of Muslim notables whom he suspected of disaffection from Delhi.

Ibn Tughluq's was a personal empire. His own dynamism and a policy of religious toleration held it together—the only policy workable for a Muslim elite in a largely Hindu country. But Ibn Tughluq's state was not built to last. It relied on conquest to fuel the system. The Turkic elite, who provided the muscle for revenue collection and war, demanded constant rewards. When they did not get them, they seceded from the state. This began to happen on a large scale toward the end of Ibn Tughluq's life. Conquest is, in any case, a gambler's game. Military fortunes change, and military systems, even of the most crushing superiority, can fail. Disaster struck Ibn Tughluq, for in stance, when a plague devastated his army. "The provinces withdrew their allegiance," Ibn Battuta reported, "and the outer regions broke away."

Moreover, the Delhi sultans were under constant pressure from the Muslim establishment to impose Islam by force, launch holy war, and ease the taxes on Muslims at the expense of "infidels." The discontent evident among some Muslim notables during Ibn Tughluq's reign owed something to fear of the sultan. But frustration with his policies of toleration also inspired much of it. Ibn Tughluq's successor succumbed to these pressures. He forfeited Hindu allegiance. Beyond the frontier, Hindu states adopted a counter ideology of resistance to Islam—at least in their rhetoric, since religion rarely took priority over politics. In southern India, a Hindu state with imperial ambitions arose at Vijayanagar. The conquest juggernaut of the sultanate of Delhi stopped rolling, and provincial elites in outlying regions dropped out of the empire. As so often before in Indian history, both the difficulties of and the capacity for an India-wide empire had been demonstrated. But the problems of maintaining such a large and diverse state were obvious. Future attempts would run into the same difficulties as those that caused the sultanate's control of the outer edges of the state to unravel and its expansion to cease.

Southeast Asia

Rather as Delhi did in India, a native kingdom in Java, the main island of what is today Indonesia, exploited the waning of the Mongol threat. The islands of southeast Asia produced goods the Chinese market wanted. Some states in the region could threaten or control the passage of those goods by sea: pepper and cinnamon from southern India and Sri Lanka; sandalwood from Timor; timber, nutmeg, cloves, and mace from Borneo and the Moluccas. Control of the strait between

Malaya, Java, and Sumatra was strategically vital for China-bound trade, and the shipping of Java was important for the commerce of the region. That is why Kubilai Khan focused on Java when he tried to extend his empire into southeast Asia (see Chapter 15).

The establishment of a powerful state on Java, centered on the inland city of Majapahit, was the achievement of Kertanagara, who died in 1292. Chroniclers credited him with magic powers or saintly virtues. In fact, he seems to have balanced the rituals of Buddhist, Hindu, and indigenous religions to keep a diverse array of followers together and repulse Kubilai Khan's Mongol invasion.

The king who launched Majapahit on its own imperial career in the mid–fourteenth century was Hayan Wuruk, who died in 1389. He had dazzling ambitions. We know this because one of his chief ministers wrote a poem in his praise that reveals how the king wanted people to think of him. The royal palace at Majapahit had gates of iron and a "diamond-plastered" watchtower. When Hayan Wuruk traveled, his court filled numberless carts. Through the streets of his capital, he paraded, clad in gold, borne on a throne carved with lions, to the sound of music. Ambassadors from foreign courts sang his praises.

He was both "Buddha in the body" and "Shiva incarnate"—worshipful to Buddhist and Hindu subjects alike. Hayan Wuruk's realm, according to the poet, was more famous than any country in the world except India. In reality, the kingdom occupied about half the island of Java. The king, however, aimed to make it bigger. The poet listed tributaries in many islands in what is today Indonesia, and "protectorates" in northern Malaya, Thailand, and Indochina. Even China and India, he claimed, defer to Hayan Wuruk. "Already the other continents," he boasts, "are getting ready to show obedience to the illustrious prince" and a state "renowned for its purifying power in the world."

That was all the exaggeration of propaganda. But a disinterested foreign chronicler left a description of Majapahit that confirms much of the picture:

> The empire grew prosperous. . . . There was a ceaseless coming and going of people from the territories overseas which had submitted to the king . . . . Everywhere one went there were . . . people dancing to the strains of all kinds of loud music, entertainments of all kinds . . . .[3]

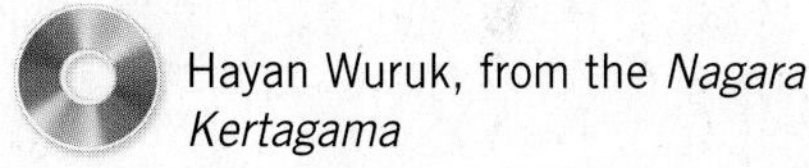

Hayan Wuruk, from the *Nagara Kertagama*

Surviving temple reliefs show what the Java of Hayan Wuruk was like. Wooden houses, perched on pillars over stone terraces, formed neat villages. Peasants grew paddy rice, or coaxed water buffalo over dry fields to break up the soil. Women did the harvesting and cooking. Orchestras accompanied masked dancers. Royal charters fill out the picture of economic activities. Industrial processes included salt making by evaporation, sugar refining, processing water-buffalo meat, oil pressing from seeds, making rice noodles, ironmaking, rattan weaving, and dyeing cloth. More sophisticated ceramics and textiles were imported from China. The same charters reveal the extension of royal power into the hinterland. They establish direct relationships between the royal court and local elites. They favor the foundations of new temples and encourage the spread of communications, the building of bridges, the commissioning of ferries, and the erection of "rest houses, pious foundations, and hospitals."

Majapahit was an expanding realm. As Mongol vigilance relaxed, Majapahit's power increased. In the 1340s, a network of ports in the hands of Majapahit garrisons spread over the islands of Bali and Sumatra. In 1377, Hayan Wuruk launched an apparently successful expedition against Palembang, the major way station on the route from India to China. A struggle was on to profit from southeast Asia's trade.

Japan

Japan, like Java, was a region the plagues spared and the Mongols failed to conquer. Here, however, as the Mongol threat receded, so did pressure to stay united. Rebels could now raise armies with increasing ease. Japan had enjoyed more than a century of stability. The warrior class had been pacified with grants of estates and their revenues. Now people at all social levels were accumulating wealth, and social status was up for grabs. Warriors began to diversify into new occupations, to sell or break up their estate rights, and to resort to violence as a way of life.

At the top of this volatile society, rival branches of the imperial family contested the throne. From 1318, the emperor Godaigo fought to exclude family competitors and take back the power the shoguns exercised in the emperor's name. He found, however, that loyalty was liable to change hands as circumstances changed. "Then was then," proclaimed a saying of the time. "Now is now: rewards are lord!"

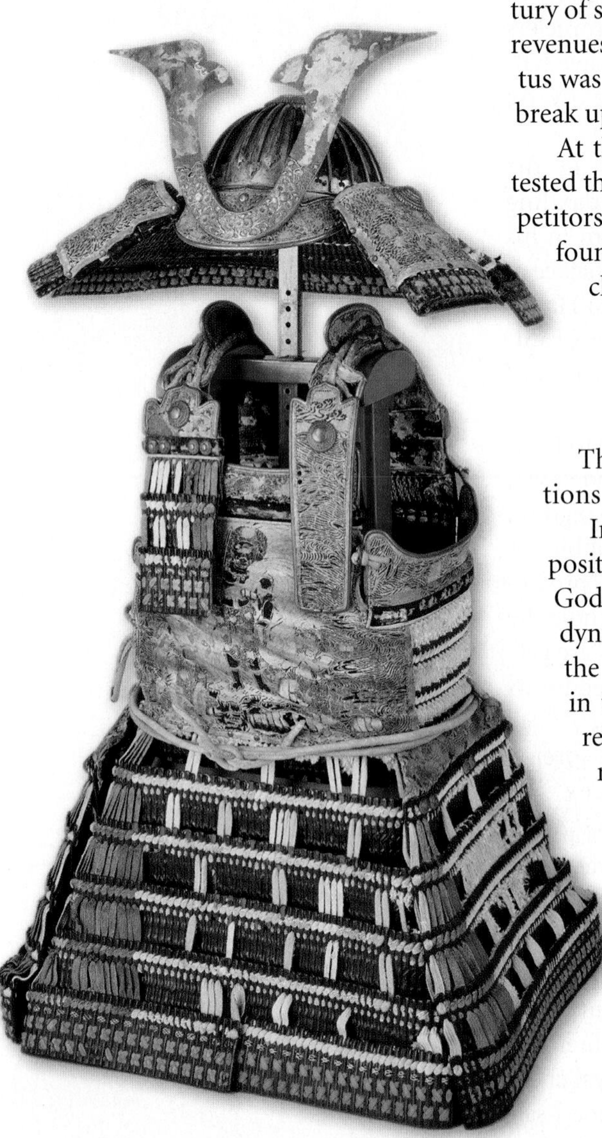

A shogun's armor. This armor is believed to have belonged to Ashikaga Takauji who was shogun from 1338 to 1358. The quality and costliness of the gilt copper breastplate and helmet mountings show that the armor could only have belonged to a person of high status such as Ashikaga Takauji. Stenciled in lacquered doeskin, an image of Fudo Myo-o—the god who personified the samurai virtues of outward ferocity and inner calm—adorns the breastplate. Silk ribbons of many colors, symbolizing the fleeting beauty of the rainbow, were used to tie up the skirts of the armor. *The Metropolitan Museum of Art, Gift of Bashford Dean, 1914 (14.100.121) Photograph © 1991 The Metropolitan Museum of Art*

Godaigo's army deserted in dissatisfaction over the rewards he could provide. "How," complained one of his officials, "can those who tend to have the outlook of a merchant be of use to the court?" The new disorder was, for some, a social revolution: the result of violations of the proper boundaries of class and rank.

In 1335, the most powerful of the warlords, Ashikaga Takauji, seized the position of **shogun** in defiance of Godaigo's wishes. In 1336, he overwhelmed Godaigo's followers at the Battle of Minato River (see Map 14.5). The Ashikaga dynasty survived as shoguns almost until the end of the century by accepting the realities of the changed world and attempting only modest interventions in the spheres of other major warlords. The Ashikaga also restored the old relationship between shogun and emperor, in which pieties disguised the real displacement of authority into the shogun's hands.

The chaos of the fourteenth century favored the rise of **Zen**, a Buddhist tradition that valued personal extinction as a part of mystical experience. A twelfth-century Japanese text defined it: "a special transmission outside the scriptures, not founded on words or letters, which allows one to penetrate the nature of things by pointing directly to the mind." Zen made progress, partly because of the influx of monks from China, escaping from the Mongols, and partly because Zen ideas suited the warriors and warlords who now ruled Japan. Discipline, self-denial, and willingness to die are martial virtues. The warriors recognized Zen monks as kindred spirits.

For the women of families of warrior and aristocratic rank, the changes of the period were oppressive. Women could attain responsible positions in the emperor's court. Hino Meishi, for instance, was in charge of the sacred imperial symbols in 1331, when the shogun tried to depose Godaigo. But changing marriage customs were unfavorable to women's personal independence. Until the fourteenth century, marriage in Japan was predominantly a private, essentially sexual relationship. Now it became increasingly formalized, as a union of two families. Wives moved into the homes of their husbands' families, instead of remaining in their own homes.

A sign of women's changed circumstances is that they stopped writing fiction and the kind of personal diaries familiar from earlier periods. Self-expression was now considered inappropriate for the female sex. Wives came to be thought of as their husbands' property. It also became common for women aristocrats to receive a life interest in a share of family property, rather than inheriting property out-

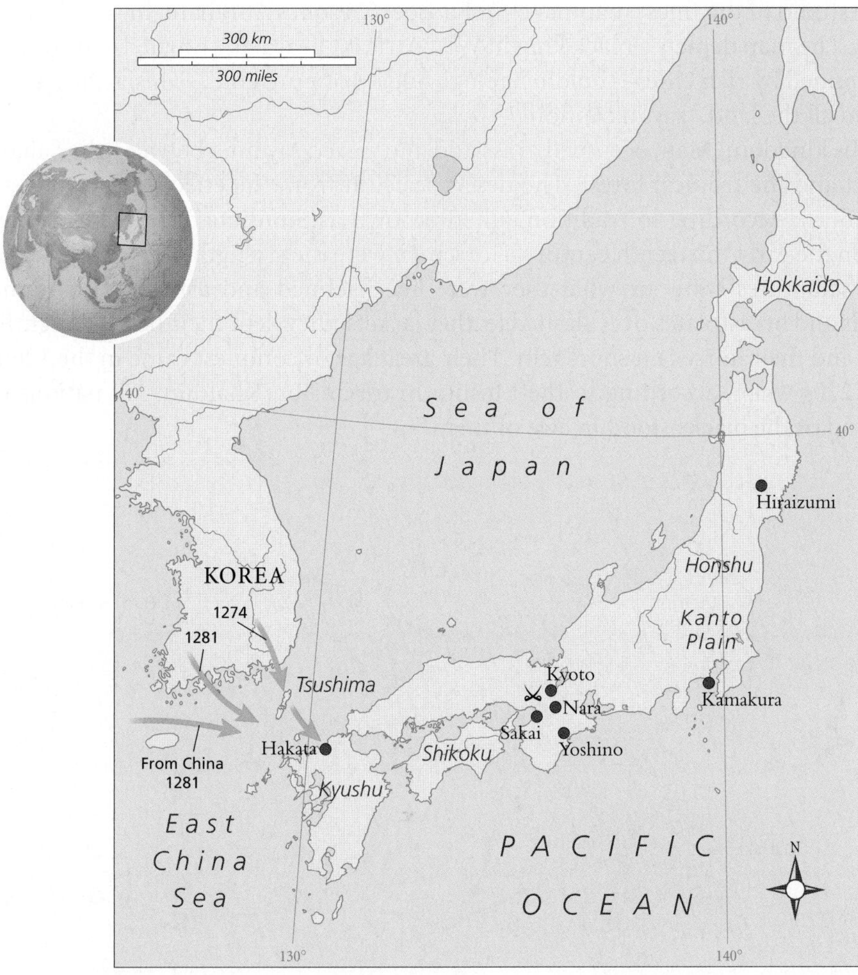

MAP 14.5

Japan, ca. 1350

Mongol invasion attempts

battle of Minato River

right. Property rights were steered toward a single male heir. Among commoners, however, this practice failed to take hold, and women held property and engaged in business in their own right.

The peasants profited from the changes that were transforming the warrior class. Relaxation of central authority freed villagers to get on with improving crop yields as they saw fit. The new regime of rewards for military service meant that the landlords were always changing—dispossessed and replaced as the fortunes of war shifted. The rapid turnover of lords, who were usually absentees, also allowed the peasants to get on with their business. There were no epidemics in the fourteenth-century countryside in Japan, and serious crop failures were rare. Nor were population growth and the extension of cultivated land interrupted. As a result of the successful exploitation of formerly marginal lands, outside the great estates, the numbers of small independent farmers multiplied, though not on anything like the scale discernible at the same time in Western Europe.

The Ashikaga Shogunate

Fourteenth century	Changing marriage customs diminish women's independence
1318	Emperor Godaigo seeks to regain imperial power
1335	Ashikaga Takauji seizes shogunate in defiance of Godaigo
1336	Last of Godaigo's supporters defeated

Mali

Just as Java and Japan seemed to grow in stature by comparison with the afflictions of China and the Mongols, parts of West Africa projected an image of abundance toward the devastated Mediterranean world. Evidence for West African prosperity is the Catalan Atlas, made in the studio of the finest mapmaker in Europe, Cresques Abraham, in the 1370s or 1380s. The map depicts a black king in West Africa—bearded, crowned, enthroned, surrounded by rich cities—holding a huge nugget of pure gold. "This is the richest king in all the land," says a caption.

His kingdom, Mali, occupied grassland and mixed savanna between the Sahara Desert and the tropical forest. The desert sealed it from the effects of plague (see Map 14.6). According to tradition, a hero known as **Sundiata** founded the kingdom in the early thirteenth century. Horsemen were the strength of its army. Terracotta sculptures show us what they were like. Helmed and armed, with round shields and breastplates over slashed leather jackets, they kept their heads haughtily tilted and their horses on short rein. Their great age of conquest came in the 1260s and 1270s when, according to the Muslim historian Ibn Khaldun, "all nations of the land of the blacks stood in awe of them."

MAP 14.6

The Kingdom of Mali, ca. 1350

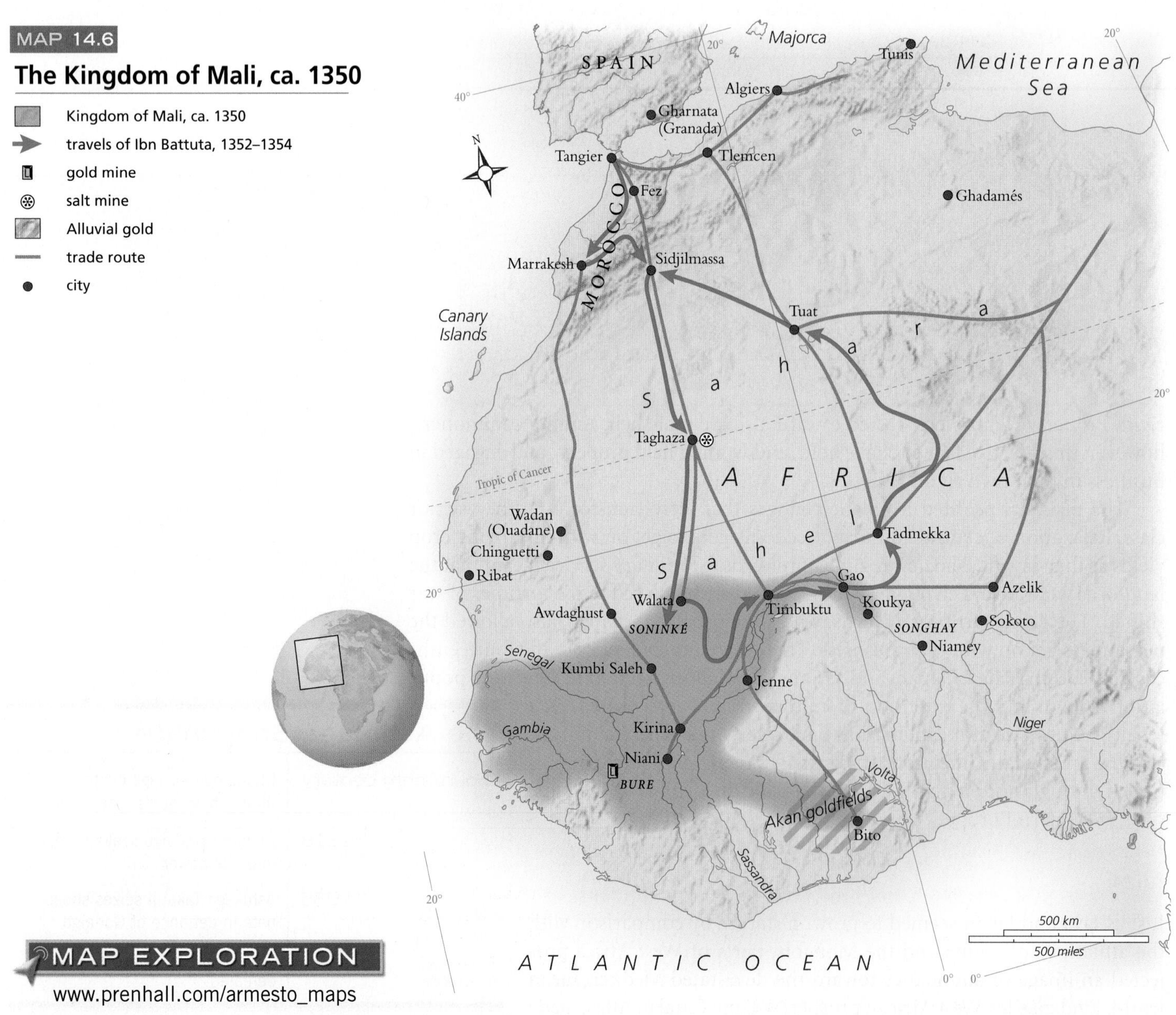

MAP EXPLORATION
www.prenhall.com/armesto_maps

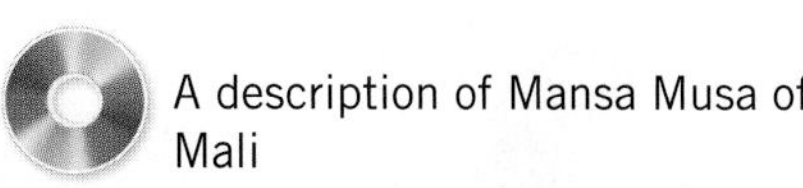
A description of Mansa Musa of Mali

The "mansas," as the kings of Mali were titled, made pilgrimages to the Muslim holy city of Mecca via Cairo. The mere fact that they dared absent themselves for the year-long journey shows how stable the state must have been. In about 1324, Mansa Musa stayed in Egypt for about three months on his way to Mecca. He gave 50,000 gold coins to the Mamluk sultan and endowed so many mosques and shrines that he caused inflation.

The location of West Africa's gold mines was a closely guarded secret, but it was probably in Bure (BOO-ray), around the upper reaches of the Niger River and the headwaters of the Gambia and Senegal Rivers. The merchants of Mali handled the gold trade but never controlled its production. The mansa took nuggets for tribute—hence, the image on Cresques Abraham's map. The gold bought salt. Mali was so rich in gold and so short of salt that the price of salt reputedly tripled or quadrupled in the kingdom's markets.

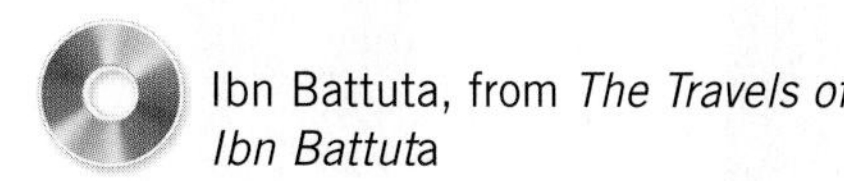
Ibn Battuta, from *The Travels of Ibn Battuta*

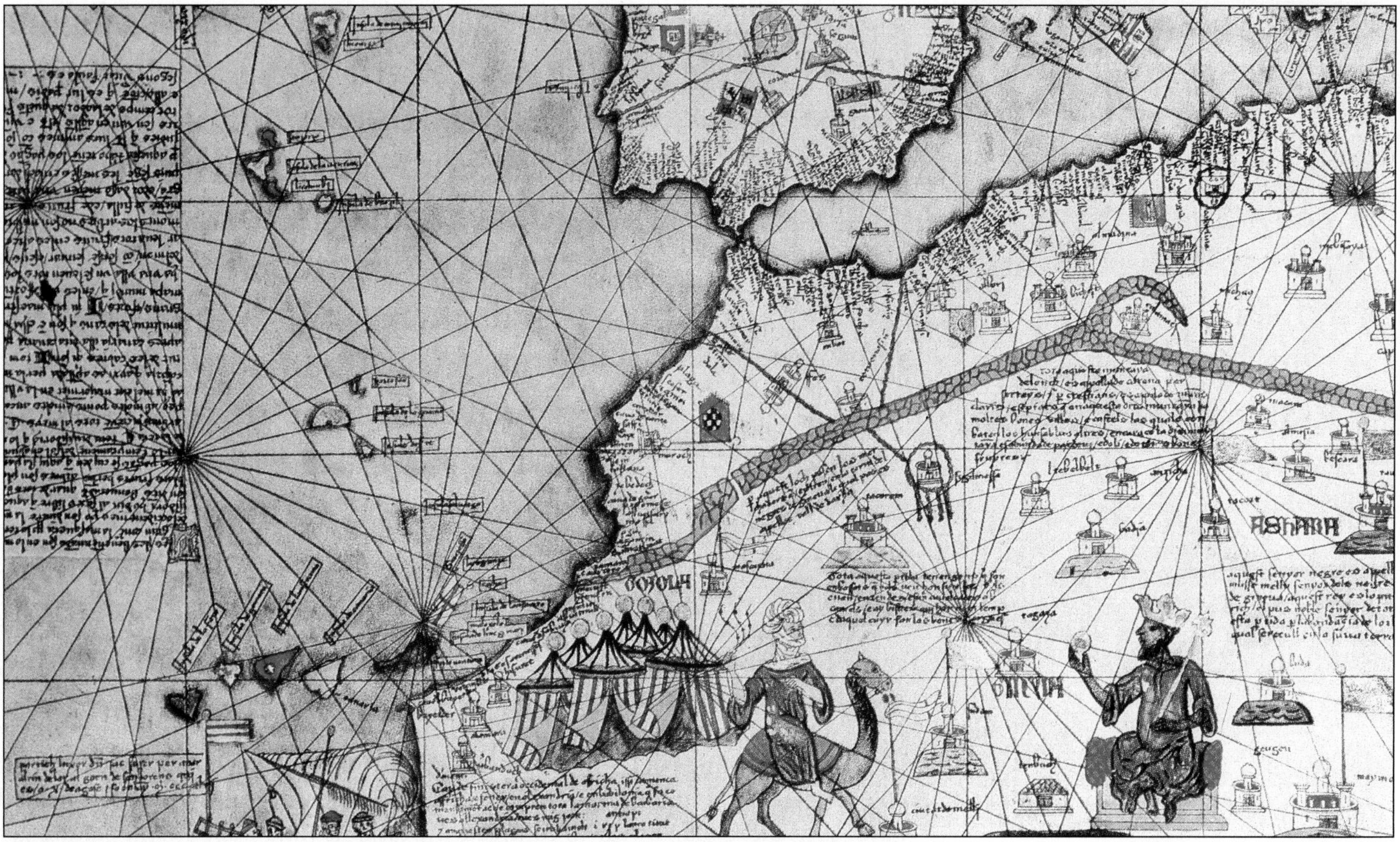

In 1352, Ibn Battuta joined a salt caravan across the Sahara. He detested the manners, food, and sexual promiscuity he found in Mali, "and their contempt for white men," but praised the "abhorrence of injustice" he found. The mansa's court impressed him and other visitors in the same period. This consensus is striking, because North African Muslim writers rarely praised black achievements. The

Mansa Musa. "Lord of the blacks of Guinea," reads the legend accompanying the portrait of Mansa Musa (r. ca. 1312–1327), the king of Mali in West Africa, on the fourteenth-century Catalan Atlas. "This lord is the richest and most noble lord of all this region owing to the abundance of gold which is gathered in this land." The Mansa's wealth was said to exceed that of all other kings. His European-style crown and ample beard are compliments bestowed by an artist who had not learned, as Europeans were to do in later centuries, to despise black African kingship.

Mansa. "All the peoples of the land of the Blacks stood in awe of them," wrote Ibn Khaldun of the mounted warriors of the mansas of Mali. Many fired-clay representations of these soldiers survive from the thirteenth to the fifteenth centuries. Nearly all show the same erect posture, proudly uptilted head, and elaborate helmets and bridles.

mansa, according to Ibn Battuta, commanded more devotion from his subjects than any other ruler in the world, though most of the court ceremonial was traditional in West Africa. The ruler, for instance, spoke only through an intermediary, for to raise his voice was beneath his dignity. Supplicants had to prostrate themselves and sprinkle dust on their heads as they addressed him. When his words were relayed to the people, guards strummed their bowstrings and everyone else hummed appreciatively. Sneezing in the mansa's presence was punishable by death. Hundreds of servants attended him with gilded staves. Poets and scholars came to serve the mansa from Muslim Spain and North Africa.

Meanwhile, the gold of West Africa inspired European efforts to get to its source. Western Europe produced only small amounts of silver, and its economies were permanently short of precious metals with which to trade. There was a longstanding adverse trade balance with more productive Silk-Road economies. To keep it going, this trade always needed infusions of cash. So, as Mali's reputation grew, the search for African gold obsessed European adventurers. But the attempts to find a sea route to Mali were hopeless. Mali was landlocked, and the African coasts had little gold until well into the fifteenth century.

THE PACIFIC: SOCIETIES OF ISOLATION

Beyond the world that escaped the Black Death lay regions contagion did not threaten. Isolation, which had arresting effects in so many cases, was a privilege in the fourteenth century. To understand this reversal of the normal pattern of global history, we need to look at some relatively isolated societies. The vastness of the Pacific—which the technology of the time could not cross—ensured that exceptionally isolated cultures lay scattered around that ocean.

For instance, Easter Island lay, at the time, more than 2,000 miles away from any other human habitation. The island covers only 64 square miles of the Pacific Ocean. It is hard to believe that the Polynesian navigators who first colonized the island, possibly over 1,500 years ago, would have stayed if they had been able to continue their journey or go home. Most of the soil is poor. Chickens and the starchy plant called taro came with the first settlers. But not much that was edible was available to them when they arrived. Migrant birds were their renewable source of food.

Yet despite the island's natural poverty and its isolation from other societies, it housed, in the fourteenth century, a people at the height of their ambition. Probably late in the first millennium, they had begun to erect monumental statues called *Moais* for reasons we can no longer determine. These stone statues resemble those other Polynesian peoples erected: tall, elongated, stylized faces. They were originally adorned with red topknots and white coral eyes. The Easter Island statues are unique compared with other Polynesian works of the same sort only because they are so big and there are so many of them—some 600 finished examples survive, most of them more than 20 feet tall.

It took communal effort to make and erect the statues, each carved from a pillar of rock weighing between 30 and 40 tons. A single extended family—say, about 400 people—joining together to provide the labor and feed the workers, would have taken more than a year to complete the task. As time went on, the statues got bigger—a clear case of competition, driving up the costs of the culture, and, perhaps, condemning it to collapse, a century or two later. So an enterprising community could buck the effects of isolation, and even turn isolation to advantage—but, in an extreme case like that of Easter Island, the effort was hard to sustain. Statue building slowed and, in the sixteenth or seventeenth century, stopped.

Moais. Monumental statue making on Easter Island was probably at its most intense in the fourteenth century. For a small population on a poorly provided and remote island, the investment of energy the practice required seems astounding. The images are similar to those of ancestor cults elsewhere in Polynesia, but they are exceptional in being carved from stone, rather than wood, huge, and numerous. Isolation apparently made Easter Island culture distinctive, but still recognizably like that of other Polynesian colonies.

New Zealand was an almost equally remote outpost of the Polynesian world (see Chapter 11), but with infinitely more resources than Easter Island. By the fourteenth century, population had increased, and hunting resources diminished as the fur seal and the moa began to get scarce. The moa was a huge, flightless bird, with eggs as big as a hundred hen's eggs, that was among early settlers' main sources of food until they hunted it to extinction.

As the balance of the way of life shifted from hunting toward farming, mobile colonies settled down. The results included stronger community identification with land and, therefore, more competition for cultivable resources. Part of the farming surplus was invested in war. From the fifteenth century, the number of places where weapons were made grew enormously. So did the number of fortified villages. War was only one of many new or newly intensive activities that favored the power of chiefs. Farming required strong centers of power to organize collective activity and regulate the distribution of food. So did new fishing technologies with gigantic nets that needed many hands to operate them.

Meanwhile, on the Pacific rim of the New World, people experimented with contrasting responses to isolation (see Map 14.7). Good evidence has survived for two different communities. One body of evidence comes from the north of the hemisphere. Probably toward the end of the fifteenth century, a mudslide at Ozette, in Washington State, buried a community of whalers and seal fishers and perfectly preserved the site. This was a hunting culture whose ways of life had not changed significantly for centuries.

MAP 14.7

Societies of the Pacific, ca.1400

area of Polynesian settlement

Economic activities and food resources

- seals
- fishing
- taro
- moa
- cotton
- migrant birds
- chickens
- pigs
- coconuts/breadfruit

PERU modern country or state

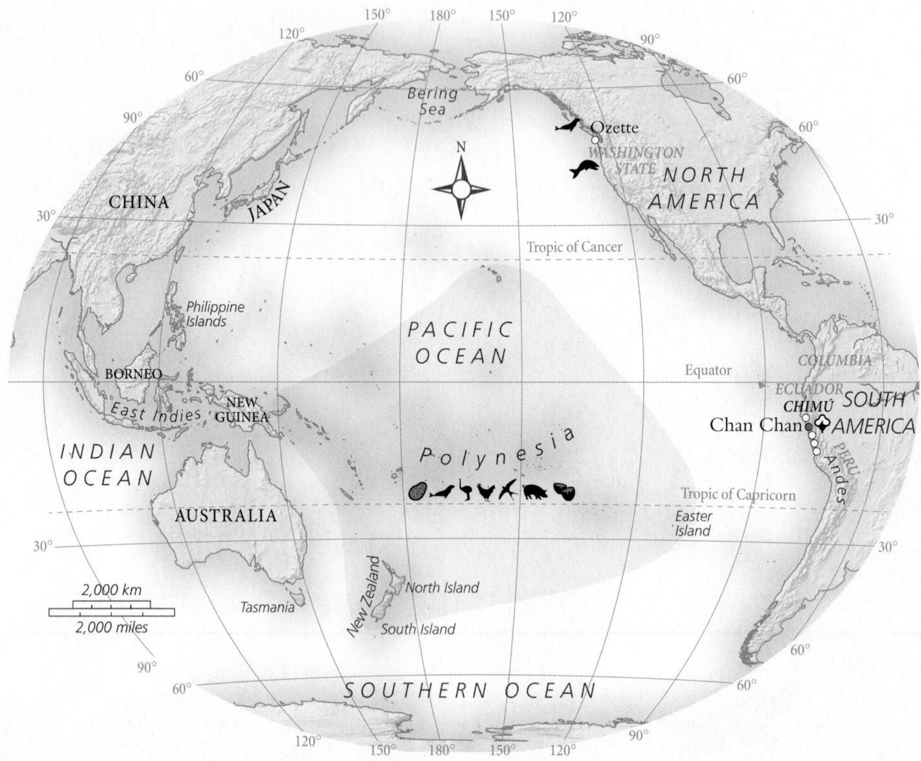

Huaca del Dragón. The date of the stacked platforms of Huaca del Dragón, near the site of Chan Chan in Peru, is much disputed, but the adobe reliefs—of which a recently restored section is depicted here—are probably of Chimú workmanship. Below a frieze of warriors, a divine feast is shown. A double-headed serpent, with a rainbow-like body surrounded by clouds, devours curl-nosed victims, framing similar scenes shown in profile. Food-storage areas were built into the structure, which seems to have been both temple and warehouse—a repository, perhaps, for food of the gods.

The victims of the mudslide lived in cedar buildings, each more than 50 feet long and 30 feet wide. Each building housed about 40 people, divided typically by partitions into half a dozen smaller family units, each with its own hearth. The Ozette people ate almost no vegetable matter except wild berries. Seals provided nearly 90 percent of their meat. For cooking, they boiled or steamed their food in watertight cedar boxes. They hunted and fished in dugouts. Whale images dominated their art, probably because the art had a magical function in bringing good fortune to the whale hunt. Their way of life was, broadly speaking, similar to that of the Thule Inuit centuries earlier (see Chapter 11).

On the Pacific's South American edge, we can trace new activity to roughly the same period. This region was less isolated than New Zealand, Easter Island, or Ozette. The coasts of what are now Peru, Ecuador, and Pacific-side Colombia were always in touch with the cultures of the high Andes and the lowlands beyond. In South America, in and around the fourteenth century, the latest experiment in state-building, intensive agriculture, and city life was under way at Chan Chan. This city was in the coastal desert region of Peru where the Moche had built complex irrigation works and prosperous cities (see Chapter 10) in defiance of a hostile environment. The methods of the Chimú (chee-MOO) people of Chan Chan were dif-

MAKING CONNECTIONS

BEYOND THE PLAGUE ZONE

REGION →	TENTATIVE REASON FOR ABSENCE OF PLAGUE →	CONSEQUENCES
Japan	Protected by relative isolation	Protected from Mongols; new threats emerge from prosperous provincial warlords; in addition, the imperial family divides into rival factions; new dynasty of shoguns emerges; Zen Buddhism expands influence
India	Unknown—although Silk Roads and sea-trade routes were adjacent	Islamic sultanate of Delhi profited from Mongols' decline, initiating policy of conquest; Turkic elite responsible for war and revenue collecting eventually secedes; problems of Hindu/Muslim relations are ever present
Southeast Asia	Unknown—trade routes from China, Europe, Africa should have made the region vulnerable	Establishment of powerful state on Java (Majapahit), to control trade with China and India, creating stable and prosperous society
Pacific	Isolation	Expansion of existing societies; new efforts at developing agricultural resources
Sub-Saharan Africa	Unclear	Control over West Africa's gold trade leads to affluence, European obsession with finding Mali

ferent. They concentrated agriculture in the environs of the city, where 30,000 people lived. Hinterland population was not much bigger than that of Chan Chan itself.

Cotton production was a major economic activity. For protein, the Chan Chan people—or, perhaps, just the elite—relied on llamas, which were farmed in corrals in and around the city. Chan Chan covered almost seven square miles. Its layout shows that the Chimú state was oppressive, with a security-obsessed elite. Fortifications protected the rulers' quarters from their own people. Warehouses were the most vital part of the state because El Niño periodically and unpredictably washed away the irrigation works. Stockpiling enabled the Chimú to recover.

The Chimú elite favored gold for their precious ornaments and ritual objects. But gold did not occur naturally in this part of Peru. Trade or tribute must have brought it to Chimú, for Chimú was evidently an expansionist state. Perhaps it had to be to boost its resources in a difficult environment. Sites of towns built in the style of Chan Chan stretch between the Sana and Supe Rivers.

IN PERSPECTIVE: The Aftershock

Ibn Khaldun left an unforgettable description of the effects of the Black Death on the Muslim world:

> Civilization shrank with the decrease of mankind. Cities and buildings were bared, roads and signposts were abandoned, villages and palaces were deserted. Tribes and dynasties were expunged. It was as if the voice of existence in the world had called out for oblivion, and the world had responded to the call.[4]

But how serious and enduring were the consequences? For Western Europe, many promising initiatives of the preceding period ended. North Atlantic navigation dwindled. The last Icelan7dic voyage to mainland America was in 1347. The Norse Greenland colonies became increasingly isolated. When a bishop's representative sailed to the more northerly of them in the 1340s, he "found nobody, either Christians or heathens. . . ." When the Greenland colony was finally extinguished in the fifteenth century, mysterious raiders of savage ferocity—presumably, the Thule Inuit with whom the Norse had long shared the island— were partly responsible. Exploration of other parts of the Atlantic virtually stopped at the time of the Black Death. In the previous half century preceding the onset of the plague, explorers from maritime communities in Western Europe had made considerable progress. Mapping of the African Atlantic had begun, with the Canary and Madeira Islands, and navigators had begun to investigate the pattern of the northeast trade winds. Few similar voyages were recorded in the second half of the fourteenth century.

Human foes supplemented the plague, famine, and cold. In the northeast, pagan Lithuanians eroded the conquests of the Teutonic Orders along the Baltic (see Chapter 13). Meanwhile, in the parts of Eastern Europe the plague spared, state-building continued, under rulers whose longevity helped bring stability. The period of the Black Death in Western Europe was spanned by the reigns of Charles the Great in Bohemia (r. 1333–1378), Casimir the Great in Poland (r. 1333–1370), and Louis the Great of Hungary (r. 1342–1382). On the whole, the effects of plague favored the state even in the West, because afflicted populations turned to monarchs as potential saviors and were willing to trust them with enhanced powers.

In the Mongol dominions, the case was different. Mongol expansion ceased. Russian principalities began to shake off Mongol control. The Mongol state in Persia fragmented, and the last Il-khan died in 1343. From the ruins of Mongol domination, a new state arose in Anatolia, ruled by a Turkish dynasty, known as the Ottomans. They gradually came to dominate Byzantium and invaded the Balkans (see Map 14.8).

MAP 14.8

The Ottoman State, ca. 1400

- Ottoman state, ca. 1400
- Byzantine Empire, ca. 1400

In China, as we shall see in the next chapter, the ecological crisis of the mid–fourteenth century contributed to the replacement of the Mongol state by the native Chinese Ming dynasty.

At a deeper level than that of the rise and fall of states and political elites, the coming of the age of plagues, made worse by unpredictable changes in climate, affected the balance of population—and therefore of power—among Eurasian civilizations. Population can recover with surprising speed from natural disasters. But recovery was harder in the wake of the Black Death because, although plagues became less ferocious, and populations built up immunity, plagues affected the same regions for centuries to come, at a rate too rapid to enumerate—more than once on average every four years, for instance, in Egypt in the two centuries following the Black Death. The population of Eurasia probably remained static during the late fourteenth century and most of the fifteenth. In the long run, it looks as if the Islamic world may have been more affected than Christendom or China, both of which seem to have recovered faster and resisted better. This can only be a tentative conclusion, because the evidence is unreliable. It does seem, however, that the populations of Christendom and China recovered to preplague levels by the end of the fifteenth century, while in Egypt, Syria and, perhaps, in other parts of the Islamic world, the recovery did not even begin until then. The increase of population thereafter was generally slower in the Islamic world than in Christendom and China until the twentieth century (see Figure 14.2). This may help to explain one of history's great shifts in wealth, power, and every kind of dynamism—away from the Islamic world. Whereas in what we call the Middle Ages, the Islamic world had contributed far more than Christendom to cultural exchange in Eurasia, and had tended to win out in conflicts with Christendom, Muslim power dwindled over the succeeding centuries. The relative eclipse of the Islamic world and the relative ascent of Europe are major themes of the age of plague and, therefore, of the next two parts of this book.

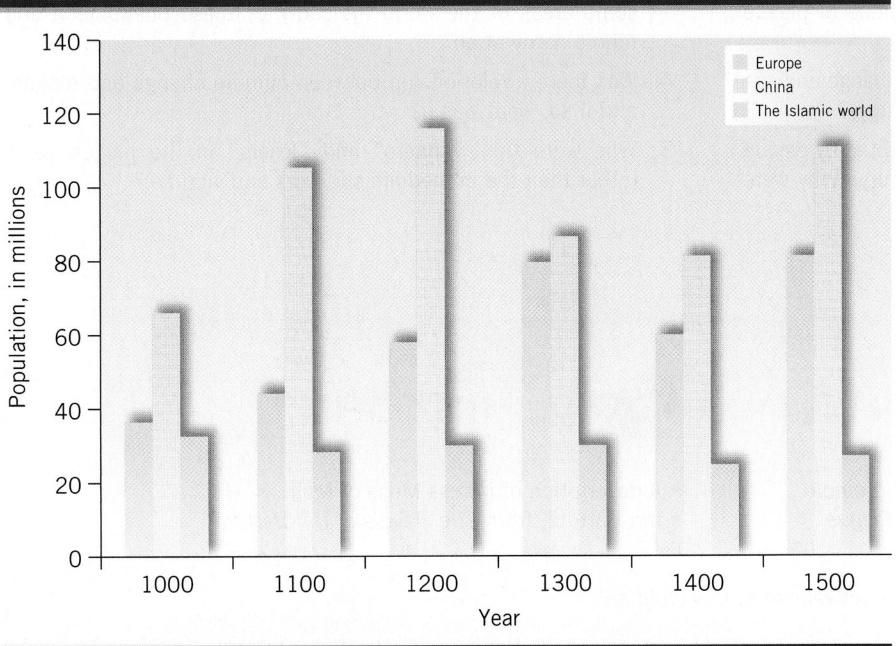

FIGURE 14.2 THE POPULATION OF EUROPE, CHINA, AND THE ISLAMIC WORLD COMPARED

CHRONOLOGY

1290	England expels Jews
Thirteenth and fourteenth centuries	Climate change in Northern Hemisphere
1315–1316	Heavy rains reported all over northern Europe
1320s	Plague epidemics in southwestern and central China
1324	Mansa Musa makes *hajj* to Mecca
1325–1351	Reign of Ibn Tughluq (India)
1326	Ottoman Turks set up capital at Bursa (western Anatolia)
1330s	Mortality rates in northeast China reach 90 percent
1335	Ashikaga Tokauji seizes shogunate (Japan)
1343	Last Il-khan dies in Persia
1346	Plague reported in Crimea (Black Sea)
1347	Last Icelandic voyage to America
1347–1349	Plague rages throughout Europe, Middle East, and North Africa
1350s	Peasant rebellions spread throughout China
1351	Plague strikes southern Russia
1352	Ibn Battuta sets off for Mali
1360	Plague reported in China
1389	Death of Hayan Wuruk (Majapahit)
1400	Settlements in American Southwest abandoned

PROBLEMS AND PARALLELS

1. How might Mongol rule have facilitated the spread of plague during the fourteenth century?
2. What were the long-term effects of the climate change and age of plagues that began during the fourteenth century?
3. What parts of the globe were most adversely affected by plague and climate change during the fourteenth century? Why were some areas of the world hit badly by these phenomena and others hardy at all?
4. Was there a relationship between climate change and plague, and if so, what was it?
5. Who were the "winners" and "losers" in the plague years (other than the immediate survivors and victims)?

DOCUMENTS IN GLOBAL HISTORY

- Marchione di Coppo Stefani, from *The Florentine Chronicle*
- University of Paris Medical Faculty, *Report on the Plague*
- Hayan Wuruk, from the *Nagara Kertagama*
- A description of Mansa Musa of Mali
- Ibn Battuta, from *The Travels of Ibn Battuta*

Please see the Primary Source DVD for additional sources related to this chapter.

READ ON

H. Lamb, *Climate, History and the Modern World* (1995) is the classic work on its subject, complemented by B. Fagan's *The Little Ice Age* (2000). Classic works—now superseded on many points—on the global history of disease are H. Zinsser, *Rats, Lice, and History* (1996), and W. H. McNeill, *Plagues and Peoples* (1998). S. Cohn, *The Black Death* (2003) is indispensable for the plagues in Europe and for the epidemiology of the Black Death. N. Cantor, *In the Wake of the Plague* (2001) has some interesting material on social effects. R. Horrox, *The Black Death* (1994) is a valuable anthology of source material. M. W. Dols, *The Black Death in the Middle East* (1977)—though corrected in some respects by Cohn's work—is invaluable on its subject. As so often, the edition by H. Gibb and C. Beckingham of *The Travels of Ibn Battuta* (1994) is an indispensable guide.

On China, the *Cambridge History of China*, multiple volumes is in preparation; meanwhile, vol. vi is of some help, and the collection of essays edited by P. J. Smith and R. von Glahn, *The Song-Yuan-Ming Transition in Chinese History* (2003) crackles with revisionism. For Europe, M. Jones, ed., *The New Cambridge Medieval History*, vi (2000) is a comprehensive survey. On the problems of the status of women, G. Duby and M. Perrot, eds., *A History of Women* (2000) is the leading work; particularly useful work on the subjects touched on in this chapter includes R. Smith, "Coping with Uncertainty: Women's Tenure of Customary Land in England," in J. Kermode, ed., *Enterprise and Individual in Fifteenth-Century England* (1997), and L. Mirrer, ed., *Upon My Husband's Death* (1992).

For Hohokam, the article by P. Crown, "The Hohokam of the American Southwest," *Journal of World History*, iv (1990) is a good introduction. G. J. Gumerman, ed., *Themes in Southwest Prehistory* (1994) contains some important contributions.

On the Jews, N. Cohn, *Europe's Inner Demons* (2001) is a controversial but gripping attempt to trace the origins of anti-Semitism. P. Johnson, *History of the Jews* (1988)—though superseded in its coverage of the early period—remains the best general history. L. Kochan, *The Jew and His History* (1985) is a good introduction.

On peasant millenarianism, N. Cohn, *The Pursuit of the Millennium* (1970) remains unsurpassed. On Japan, J. Mass, ed., *Origins of Japan's Medieval World* (1997) amounts to a fine history of the fourteenth century. The Delhi sultanate is covered in R. Majumdar, *The History and Culture of the Indian People*, iv (1951). On Java, T. Pigeaud, ed., *Java in the Fourteenth Century* (1960) is a marvelous edition of the poem I cite about Hayan Wuruk. D. G. Hall in N. Tarling, ed., *The Cambridge History of Southeast Asia*, i (1992) provides further help. On Mali, N. Levtzion, *Ancient Ghana and Mali* (1986) is highly accessible, and D. T. Niane covers the subject expertly in *UNESCO History of Africa*, iv (1998), but the classic work by E. W. R. Bovill, *The Golden Trade of the Moors* (1995), can still be read with pleasure. For the Pacific, J. van Tilburg, *Easter Island* (1995) is the only fully reliable work on that island. J. Belich, *Making Peoples* (2002) is insuperable on New Zealand. On Ozette, see R. Kirk and R. D. Dougherty, *Hunters of the Whale* (1998). On the Chimú, R. Keatinge, *Peruvian Prehistory* (1988) is standard.

CHAPTER 15

Expanding Worlds: Recovery in the Late Fourteenth and Fifteenth Centuries

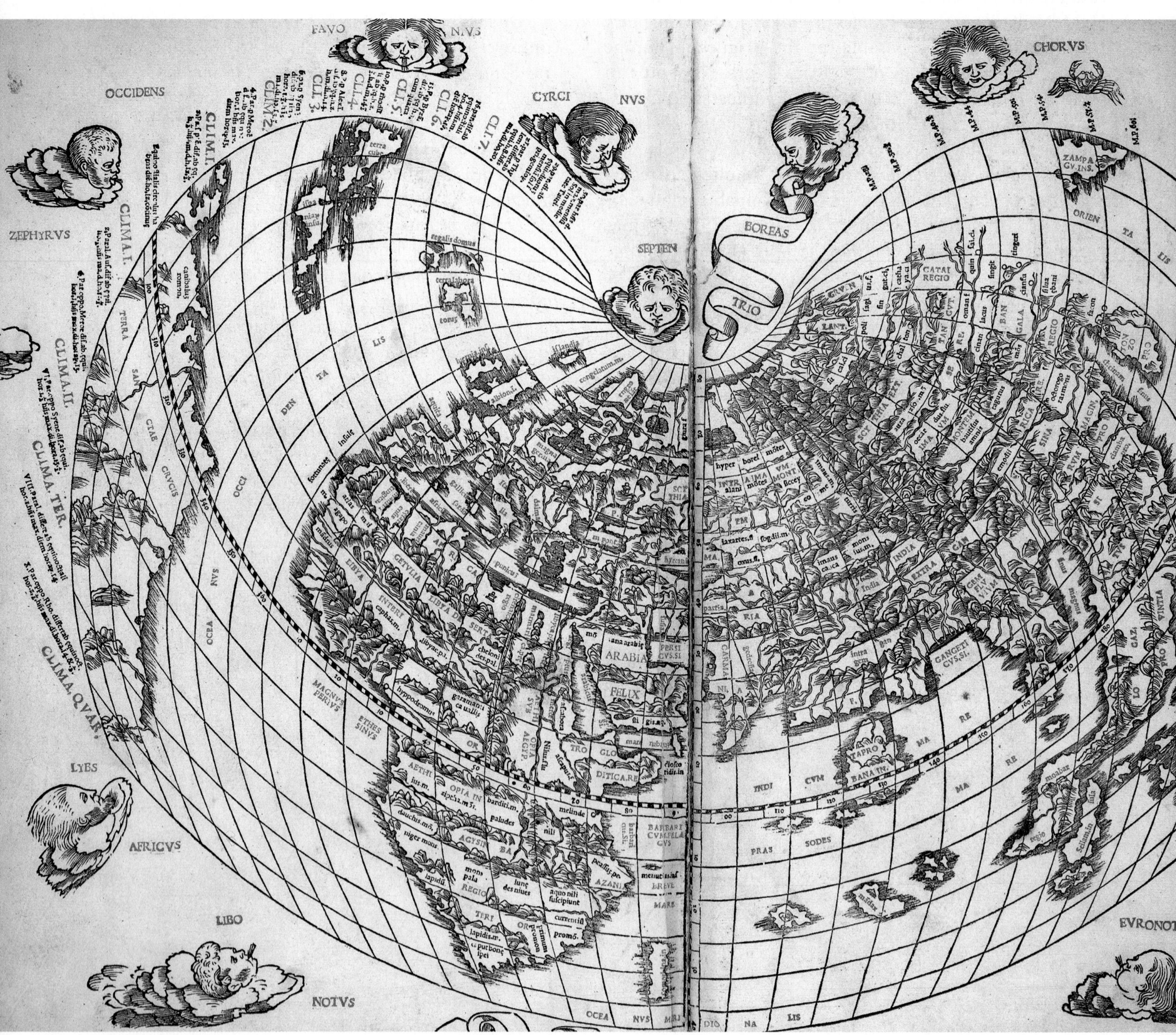

Map of the world. Published in Venice by Bernardus Sylvanus in 1511, this is the first map printed in two colors and represents the earliest period of European exploration of the New World. The islands of Cuba and Hispaniola are identified on the far left side, while Newfoundland is inaccurately shown just to the west of Ireland.

IN THIS CHAPTER

FRAGILE EMPIRES IN AFRICA
East Africa
West Africa

ECOLOGICAL IMPERIALISM IN THE AMERICAS
The Inca Empire
The Aztec Empire

NEW EURASIAN EMPIRES
The Russian Empire
Timurids and the Ottoman Empire

THE LIMITATIONS OF CHINESE IMPERIALISM

THE BEGINNINGS OF OCEANIC IMPERIALISM

THE EUROPEAN OUTLOOK: PROBLEMS AND PROMISE

IN PERSPECTIVE: Beyond Empires

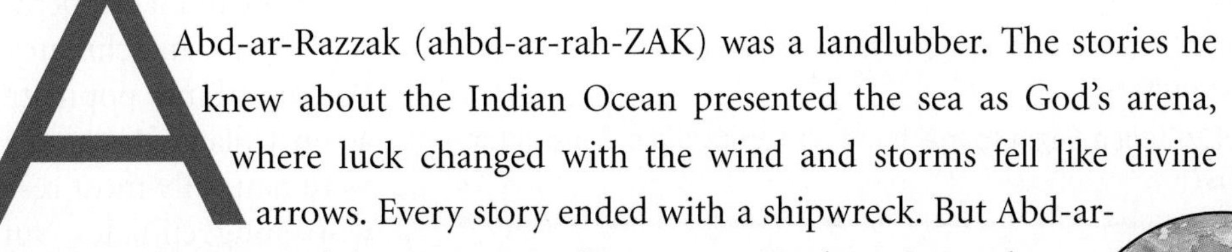

Abd-ar-Razzak (ahbd-ar-rah-ZAK) was a landlubber. The stories he knew about the Indian Ocean presented the sea as God's arena, where luck changed with the wind and storms fell like divine arrows. Every story ended with a shipwreck. But Abd-ar-Razzak could not avoid the sea. In 1417, he was appointed Persian ambassador to Vijayanagar (vee-jeh-yeh-NAH-gar), a kingdom in southern India, and there were too many hostile kingdoms between it and Persia for him to cross by land. But his ship sailed late,

INDIAN OCEAN

> so that the favorable time for departing by sea, that is to say the beginning or middle of the monsoon, was allowed to pass, and we came to the end of the monsoon, which is the season when tempests and attacks from pirates are to be dreaded.... The merchants, who were my intimate friends, cried with one voice that the time for navigation was past, and that everyone who put to sea at this season was alone responsible for his death.

Abd-ar-Razzak's predicament, however, had a positive side. The late monsoon is so fierce that ships speed before it. He made the journey in only 19 days, about two-thirds of the time one might normally expect.

● ● ● ● ●

Abd-ar-Razzak's voyage demonstrates the importance of winds in world history. Most of the planet's surface area is sea. Long-range communications have to traverse wide waters. Throughout the age of sail—for almost the entire history of travel—winds and currents limited what was possible: the routes, the rates, the mutually accessible cultures. More particularly, Abd-ar-Razzak's experience illustrates the paradox of Indian Ocean navigation in his day. The monsoon winds made travel speedy, but the ocean was stormy, unsafe, and hard to get into and out of. Access from the east was barely possible in summer, when typhoons tore into the shores. Fierce storms guarded the southern approaches. No one who knew the reputation of these waters cared to venture between about 10 and 30 degrees south and 60 or 90 degrees east during the hurricane season. Yet the Indian Ocean was the biggest and richest zone of long-range commerce in the world.

FOCUS questions

- WHY WERE some African empires able to expand on such an impressive scale during this period?
- WHAT ROLE did geographic diversity play in the Inca and Aztec Empires?
- WHAT STRONG new empires arose on the Eurasian borderlands?
- WHY DID China turn away from overseas expansion in the fifteenth century?
- WHY DID Europe begin to reach out and cross the oceans in the late 1400s?

By the end of the fifteenth century, European navigators had found a way to penetrate it. Meanwhile, the Atlantic was developing into a rival zone, with transoceanic routes ready to be exploited. Indeed, seafaring on the Atlantic would transform the world by bringing cultures that had been torn apart into contact, conflict, commerce, and cultural and ecological exchange. The divergent, isolated worlds of ancient and medieval times were coming together to form the interconnected world we inhabit today.

How did it happen? How did the world rebound from the plagues and climate changes of the fourteenth century? For one thing, populations gradually acquired immunity against plague, as susceptible people died and those who were naturally most resistant passed on their genes. As for worsening climates, survivors relocated or got used to colder, wetter conditions. To some extent, technological advance made up for—indeed, was a response to—decreased population. Across Eurasia, and in parts of Africa that were in contact with Eurasia, the long period of accelerated exchange in the Song and Mongol eras had equipped expanding economies with improved technology (see Chapter 13). In regions that escaped the catastrophes of the fourteenth century, long-term population growth strengthened states and economies. So it is not surprising that the world of the late fourteenth and fifteenth centuries was a world in recovery and resumed expansion.

From about 1460 on, in states in widely separated parts of the world, expansion speeded up, but the phenomenon was of an expanding world, not, as some historians say, of European expansion. The world did not wait passively for European outreach to transform it, as if touched by a magic wand. Other societies were already turning states into empires and cultures into civilizations. Indeed, in terms of territorial expansion and military effectiveness, some African and American empires outclassed any state in Western Europe until the sixteenth century.

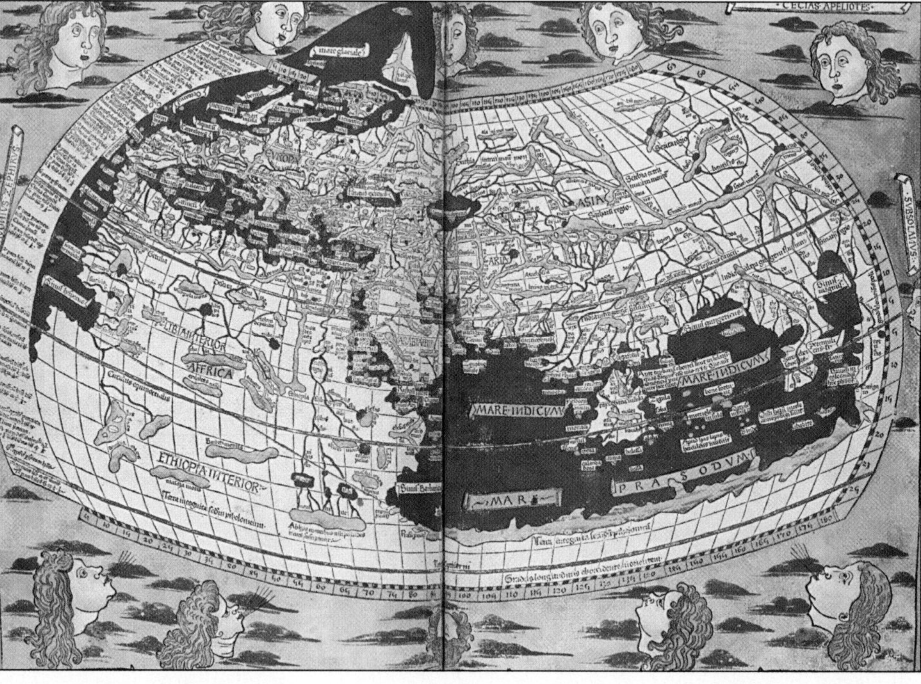

Claudius Ptolemy's Geography, written in Alexandria, Egypt, in the second century, was still the standard source for how educated Europeans saw the world in the fifteenth century. Printed editions, like this one of 1482, usually included attempts to map the world as Ptolemy described it. Common features include a grid of lines of latitude and longitude—the system Ptolemy devised for locating places in relation to one another; the exaggerated size and prominence of Sri Lanka; locating the source of the Nile in mountains beyond large lakes deep in Africa; and showing the Indian Ocean as landlocked, which undermined navigators' confidence that they could reach India and Asia by sea.

As we shall see, European expansion did have unique features—exceptional range, above all, which enabled people from parts of Western Europe to cross unprecedented distances on previously unexplored routes. But we have to see Europe in global context and acknowledge that expansion was a worldwide phenomenon. If we start in Africa and approach Europe only after looking at the Americas and following Abd-ar-Razzak's route in Asia, we can begin to make sense of the peculiar features of the history of Atlantic-side European peoples who launched empires that will take up more and more space in the rest of the book.

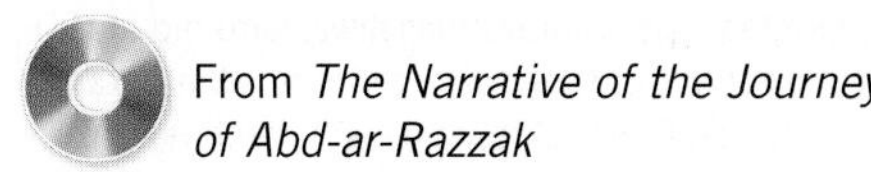

FRAGILE EMPIRES IN AFRICA

East Africa

In the late fourteenth century, Ethiopia again began to reach beyond its mountains. Monasteries became schools of missionaries whose task was to consolidate Ethiopian power in the conquered pagan lands of Shoa and Gojam (see Chapter 10). Rulers reopened outlets to the Red Sea and the Indian Ocean. By the time they recaptured the port of Massaweh in 1403, Ethiopian rule stretched into the Great Rift valley. The resulting wealth funded defense of the empire and fueled expansionist ambitions.

Although Ethiopia conquered no more territory after 1469, saints' lives tell of internal expansion. Wasteland was converted to farmland and settled by monks. When Portuguese diplomatic missions began to arrive in Ethiopia in the 1490s, "men and gold and provisions like the sands of the sea and the stars in the sky" impressed them. As we shall see in the next chapter, however, Ethiopia had probably already overreached its resources.

The Reemergence of Ethiopia

Late fourteenth century	Ethiopia expands into surrounding regions
1403	Recapture of port of Massaweh
1469	End of period of conquest
1490s	First Portuguese diplomatic missions arrive in Ethiopia

Southward from Ethiopia, at the far end of the Rift valley, lay the gold-rich Zambezi valley and the productive plateau beyond, which was rich in salt, gold, and elephants. Like Ethiopia, these areas looked toward the Indian Ocean for trade with maritime Asia, but their outlets to the sea lay below the reach of the monsoon system and, therefore, beyond the normal routes of trade. Still, adventurous merchants risked the voyage to bring goods from Asia in trade for gold and ivory.

Evidence of the effects of trade lies inland between the Zambezi and the Limpopo Rivers, where fortified, stone-built administrative centers—called **zimbabwes**—had been common for centuries. Now, in the late fourteenth and fifteenth centuries, the zimbabwes entered their greatest age. The most famous, Great Zimbabwe, included a citadel on a hill 350 feet high (see Map 15.1). Near stone buildings, the elite were buried with gold, jeweled ironwork, large copper ingots, and Chinese porcelain.

In the second quarter of the fifteenth century, the center of power shifted northward to the Zambezi valley, with the expansion of a new power. Mwene Mutapa (MWEH-nee MOO-TAH-pah), as it was called, arose during the northward migration of bands of warriors from what are now parts of Mozambique and KwaZulu-Natal. When one of their leaders conquered the middle Zambezi valley, he took the title Mwene Mutapa, or "lord of the tribute payers," a name that became extended to the state. But Mwene Mutapa never reached the ocean. Native merchants, who traded at inland fairs, had no interest in a direct outlet to the sea. They did well enough using middlemen on the coast and had no incentive for or experience of ocean trade. Like Mali (see Chapter 14), Mwene Mutapa was a landlocked empire, sustained by trade in gold and salt.

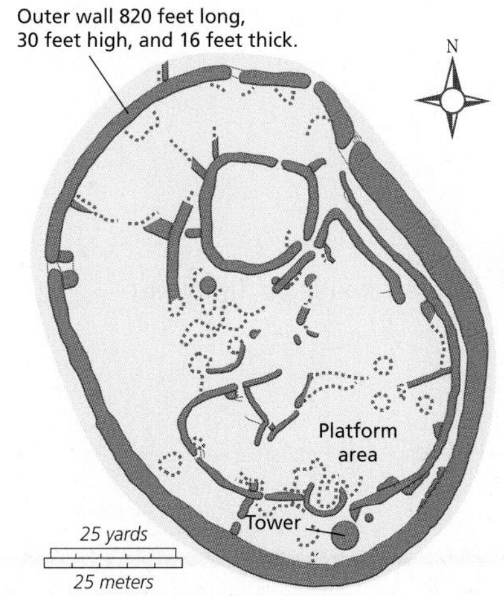

MAP 15.1

Great Zimbabwe

stone construction
walls in ruin
drain

The turreted walls of Great Zimbabwe surround a 350-foot-high hill, crowned by a formidable citadel, which housed the elite, who ate beef and were buried with gifts of gold, copper, jewels, and Chinese porcelain. Though it was the biggest of the stone-built settlements of the period, Great Zimbabwe was typical, in style and substance, of other buildings in the region south of the Zambezi River during what we think of as the late Middle Ages.

West Africa

New states emerged in West Africa, too, following the decline of Mali. Like many empires in out-of-the-way places, Mali became a victim of its relative isolation. From about 1360, a power struggle pitted the descendants of Mansa Musa against those of his brother. At about the end of the century, the Songhay (SOHNG-eye), a people from lower down the Niger River, broke away and seized Gao (gow), one of the great trading cities between the rain forest and the desert. Traders could now outflank Mali's trading monopoly. Mali was further weakened in the 1430s when invaders from the Sahara seized its northernmost towns.

Leo Africanus on Timbuktu

By the 1450s, when Portuguese expeditions made the first recorded European contact with Mali, the Mansa's power was virtually confined to the original heartland. The result was a tragedy for the history of the world, for the absence of a strong African state undermined Europeans' views of black Africans as equals. Instead of a great, rich empire, the Portuguese found Mali a ramshackle wreck. Their disappointment prejudiced them, and they wondered if black Africans had any capacity for political greatness. Though some Europeans continued to treat black Africans as equals—and the Portuguese crown, in particular, maintained the affectation that black kings were fellow monarchs on a par with those of Europe—from now on, white people in Africa could nourish convictions of superiority.

The Portuguese in West Africa and the Congo

1450s	First reported Portuguese contact with Mali
1480s	Portuguese make contact with kingdom of Kongo
1482	West African trading post of São Jorge da Mina established

Songhay became the most powerful state in the region, but it never controlled as much of the Saharan trade as Mali had. Muhammad Touray Askia, a general who used Islam to justify seizing the throne, wrenched Songhay into the Islamic mainstream in the late fifteenth century. In 1497, he undertook a pilgrimage to Mecca on a scale of magnificence calculated to echo that of Mansa Musa in 1324–1325 (see Chapter 14). Askia's ascent to power ensured that the Sahel would be predominantly Muslim. His alliance with the Muslim intelligentsia made Songhay a state "favored by God" in the eyes of religious Muslims—the class on which the state depended for administrators. By imposing peace, he increased Saharan merchants' sense of security. New canals, wells, dikes, and reservoirs scored the land. Cultivated terrain was extended, especially for rice, which had long been known in the region but never previously farmed on a large scale.

Songhay, like Mali before it, benefited from the trade routes of the Sahara that linked the Mediterranean coast to the Niger valley. The river Niger is navigable for almost its entire length, but the Atlantic's adverse winds and currents limited long-range communications by sea. The states and cultures of the tropical forest and coast in the African "bulge" were limited to regional power and wealth. Nevertheless, they have left plenty of evidence of economic expansion and of the wealth and power of their kings in the fifteenth century: the fortifications, for instance, of the city-state of Benin and the splendid metal weapons, adornments, and courtly furnishings of Benin and the Ife.

The whole African coast from Senegambia to the mouth of the Niger impressed Europeans at the time. The trading post that Portugal opened at São Jorge da Mina, on the underside of the African bulge, in 1482, appeared on maps as a fantasy city. It suited the purposes of the Portuguese monarchs to exaggerate the grandeur, but their propaganda reflected the reality of a region of rich kingdoms, commerce, and urban life.

Farther south, too, in the Congo basin, the opportunities for states to reach out by sea were limited. The Kingdom of Kongo dominated the Congo River's navigable lower reaches, probably from the mid–fourteenth century. When Portuguese explorers established contact in the 1480s, Kongo's rulers enthusiastically adopted the religion and technology of the visitors. The kingdom became host to Portuguese missionaries, craftsmen, and mercenaries. The royal residence was rebuilt in Portuguese style. The kings issued documents in Portuguese, and royal princes went to Portugal for their education. One became an archbishop, and the kings continued to have Portuguese baptismal names for centuries thereafter. Portuguese firepower gave the kings a military advantage over their neighbors. They gained territory and slaves, many of whom they sold to the Portuguese for export.

Portuguese soldier. The court art of Benin, in the Niger Delta of West Africa, preserves precious images of Portuguese visitors, as native artists saw them in the sixteenth century. The Obas, as the rulers of Benin were called, frequently asked for Portuguese military help—sometimes offering to adopt Christianity in exchange—and this Portuguese soldier, carved in ivory, is supporting the Oba's saltcellar. Salt was a precious commodity in Benin. The soldier's short spear, feathered straw hat, and sweatband are local touches, but the rest of his clothes, his beard, his sword, and his pectoral cross were exotic emblems to the African artist who carved them.

African, Nigeria, Edo peoples, court of Benin, Saltcellar: Portuguese Figure, 15th–16th century, Ivory; H. 7–1/8 in. (18.1 cm). The Metropolitan Museum of Art, Louis V. Bell and Rogers Funds, 1972. (1972.63ab) Photograph by Stan Reis. Photograph © 1984

Although Ethiopia, Mwene Mutapa, Songhay, and Kongo were all formidable regional powers, and although many small states of the West African coast expanded commercially and territorially, little of this activity was on an unprecedented scale (see Map 15.2). Ethiopia's sequence of rise and decline had been going on for centuries. Songhay was the latest in a series of empires in the Sahel. Trading states had long studded the underside of the West African bulge. Mwene Mutapa was the successor state of the builders of the zimbabwes. If there was something new out of Africa at this time, it was part of a wider phenomenon. The empires grew at impressive rates and to impressive extents because they were in touch with other phenomena of commercial and political expansion: Songhay across the Sahara, Ethiopia and Mwene Mutapa across the Indian Ocean, the coastal trading cities and Kongo with Portugal. In the Americas, however, in the late fifteenth century, even states that had to contend with isolation could expand on a new scale.

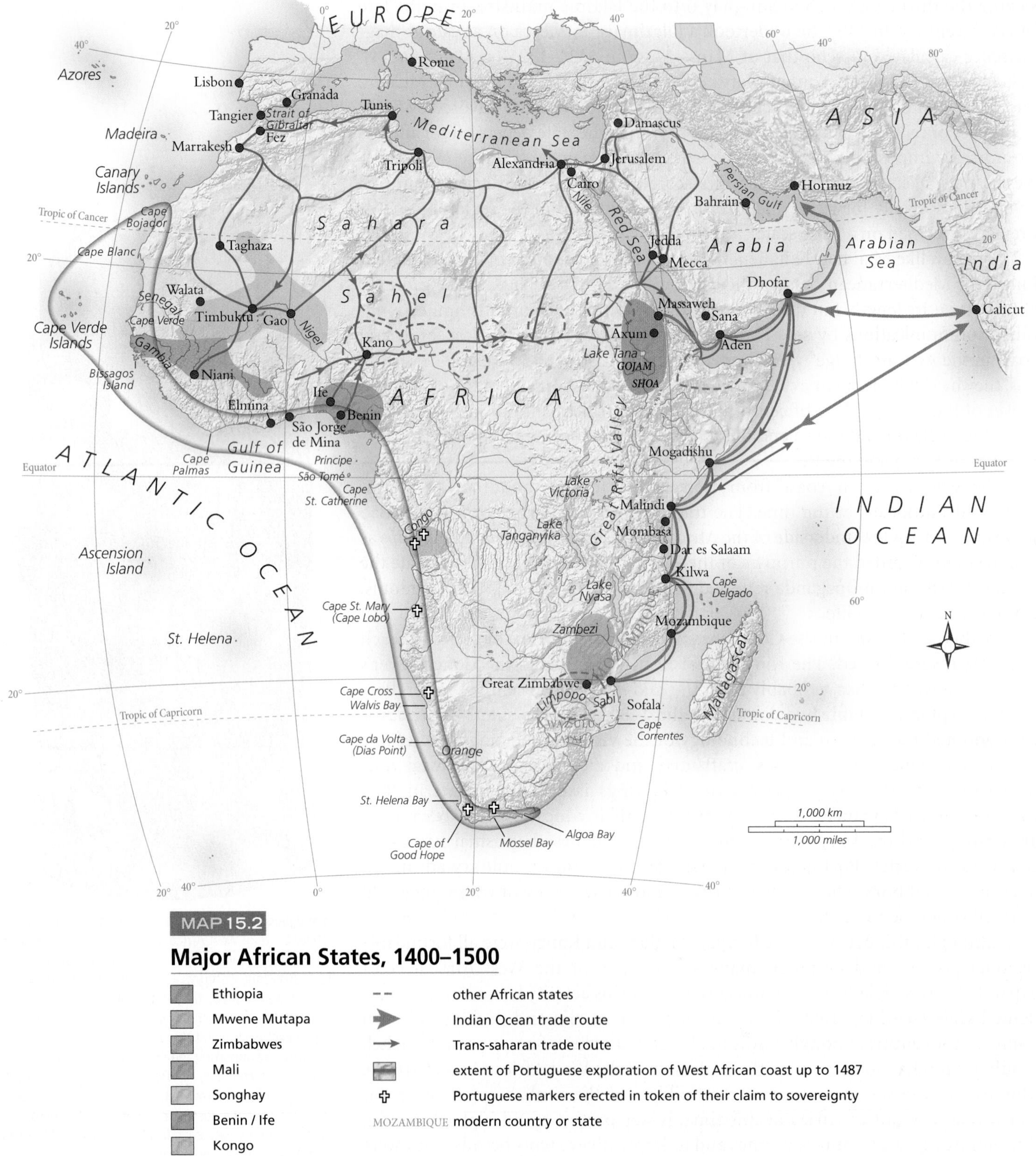

MAP 15.2

Major African States, 1400–1500

ECOLOGICAL IMPERIALISM IN THE AMERICAS

Since Alfred Crosby coined the term **ecological imperialism** in 1972, historians have used it to refer to the sweeping environmental changes European imperialists introduced in regions they colonized. The term also suits Native American empires, especially in Mesoamerica and the Andes, where the key to success in large-scale state-building lay in combining diverse regions and exploiting the complementary products of contrasting ecosystems.

The Inca Empire

In the late fifteenth century, the world's fastest-growing empire was the Inca Empire. The Incas seem to have built their empire during the reigns of three rulers in the late fifteenth and early sixteenth centuries.

Probably early in the second half of the fifteenth century, the founders of the Inca state descended from the highlands to find fertile land. They occupied Cuzco in what is today Peru, which became their biggest city, and began subjugating their neighbors. Their story was typically Andean. They gathered many diverse environments into one state to facilitate exchanging and stockpiling a wide range of products. The Incas, however, took this well-established practice to new lengths. Theirs was one of the most environmentally diverse empires of the time. It was long and thin, with the Andes forming its spine and creating valleys. Abrupt mountains multiplied microclimates, where sun, wind, and rain hit different slopes in different ways (see Figure 15.1). The Inca realm encompassed coastal lowlands and the fringes of rain forest. The tribute system was based on the exchange of products between contrasting zones, as a form of insurance against disaster. When the maize of the lowlands failed, for instance, potatoes from the highlands might still be abundant. The Inca transferred populations to new locations according to the needs of the system.

However, to maintain the state, the Inca had to acquire new territories, leading to hectic and perhaps unsustainable expansion. Moreover, their methods of subjugation were extreme. For example, they extinguished the coastal civilization of Chimú (see Chapter 14) and deported its entire population. An Inca ruler was said to have drowned 20,000 enemy warriors when he conquered the Cañaris (kan-YAR-ees). The survivors became irreconcilable opponents. Many subject-peoples harbored grievances arising from memories of massacred warriors and forced migrations. Even the Incas' allies and elites were dissatisfied. The Checa, for instance, never forgave the Inca for breaking his promise to perform ritual dances at their principal shrine in acknowledgment of their alliance. The Inca never seemed

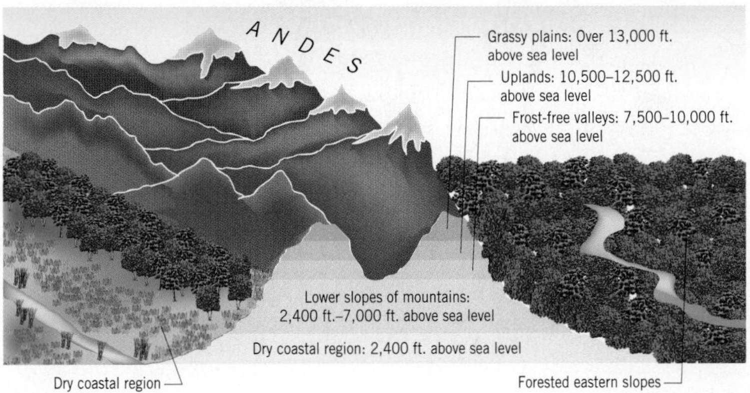

FIGURE 15.1 MICROCLIMATES OF THE ANDES. The Andean environment packs tremendous ecological diversity into a small space, with various climatic zones at different altitudes, contrasting microclimates in the valleys, and tropical forest and the ocean close at hand.

Incas and Aztecs

ca. 1325	Aztecs found city of Tenochtitlán
ca. Mid–fifteenth century	Inca begin period of conquest and expansion
ca. Late fifteenth century	Inca Empire approaches greatest extent
ca. Early sixteenth century	Aztec Empire reaches its peak

to have enough rewards to go around. The cults of dead leaders—who lay, mummified, in expensive shrines maintained by huge payrolls—existed to appease key Inca clans and factions, whose resources they boosted at the state's expense because tribute had to be diverted to meet the costs. Toward the end of the fifteenth century, the Inca Empire approached its greatest extent, from Quito (KEE-toh) in what is today Ecuador in the north to what is today Chile in the south—over 1,000 miles. But at its core, the empire was shaky.

The Aztec Empire

In the same period, rapid expansion and environmental diversity characterized Mesoamerica. Here, a dynamic state grew from the city of Tenochtitlán (teh-noch-teet-LAHN) in the valley of Mexico (and some neighboring, allied cities). Tenochtitlán stood in the middle of a lake, some 5,000 feet above sea level. There was too little cultivable soil to grow enough maize and beans to feed the city. Tenochtitlán was too high and the climate too severe for cacao and cotton. Its people, whom we have traditionally called Aztecs, had only two options: poverty or warfare. They chose the latter. At its peak, the Aztec Empire stretched from the Pánuco River in the north to what is now the Mexican-Guatemalan border on the Pacific coast and encompassed hundreds of tributary communities (see Map 15.3).

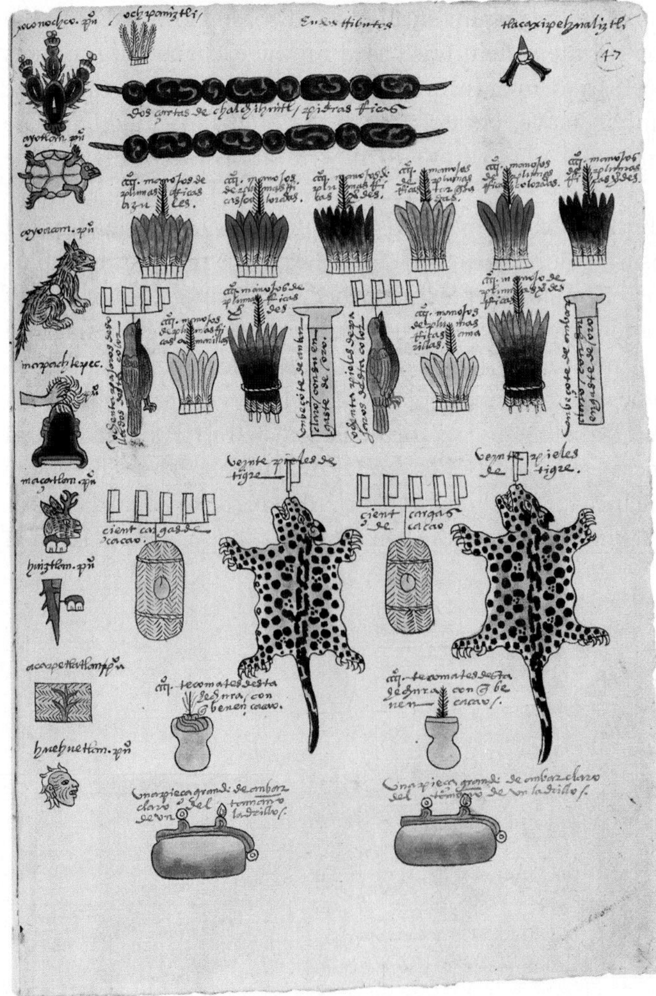

Aztec tribute. Early colonical Spanish administrators were careful to copy tribute records from the archives of the preconquest Aztec state. The records show both the complexity of the tributary networks that linked the Aztec world and the amazing environmental diversity of the regions from which tribute flowed. This folio, from the Codex Mendoza, shows the tribute due to Tenochtitlán—the Aztec capital in central Mexico—from the "hot country" near what is now the Mexican-Guatemalan border. Among the items depicted are ornamental feathers, bird skins, jaguar pelts, and jade beads.

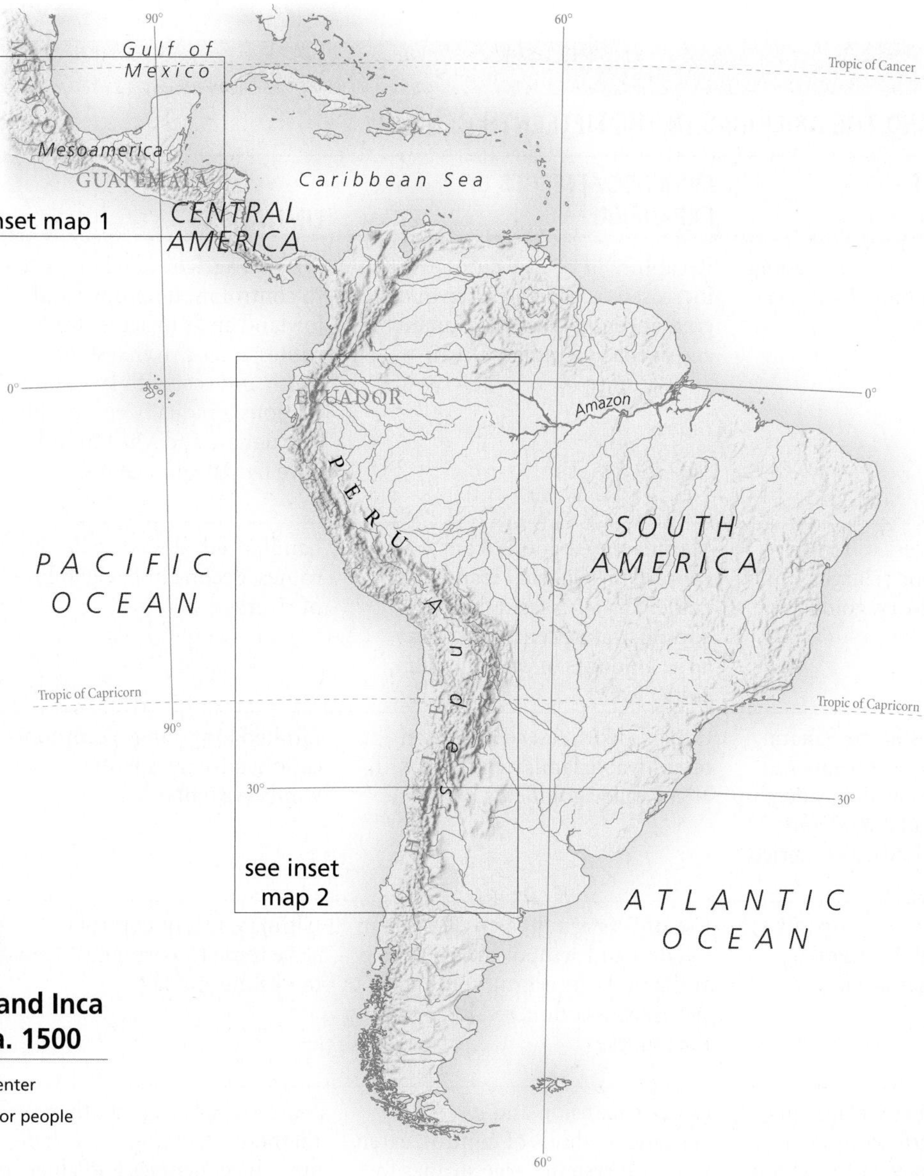

Gulf of Mexico
MEXICO
Mesoamerica
GUATEMALA
see inset map 1
CENTRAL AMERICA
Caribbean Sea
Tropic of Cancer
ECUADOR
Amazon
PERU
Andes
CHILE
SOUTH AMERICA
PACIFIC OCEAN
ATLANTIC OCEAN
Tropic of Capricorn
see inset map 2
90°
60°
0°
30°

Quito
Japurá
Tumibamba (Cuenca)
Marañón
Amazon
Juruá
PERU
Cajamarca
CHIMU
Taparaku
Huánuco Pampa
Tunsucancha
Pumpu
Tarman Jauja
Madeira
Guaporé
Lima
Pachácamac
Vilcashuaman
CHECA
Machu Picchu
Cuzco
Hatuncolla
Chucuito
Lake Titicaca
La Paz
Paria
Lake Poopó
PACIFIC OCEAN
Tupiza
Andes
Tropic of Capricorn
Catarpe
La Paya
Copiapó
Tembería del Inca
Mendoza
Santiago
Salado
Biobío
0°
30°
inset map 2

MAP 15.3

The Aztec and Inca Empires, ca. 1500

- ● Important center
- *MAYA* native state or people
- trade route
- Inca road

inset map 1

To Casas Grandes
Tropic of Cancer
90°
Tuxpan
Rio Grande de Santiago
Tampico
Tochpan (Tuxpan)
Gulf of Campeche
I. de Cozumel
HUASTEC
Atocpan
see inset map
Matiatzinco
Tlaxcata
Quiahuitztlan
MAYA
Yucatán
Tzintzuntzán
Tenochtitlán
Cholula
Cempoala
TEOTITLÁN
Tetellan
Balsas
ZAPOTEC
Xicalango
Guauhpiloayan
Ichpaatun
Gulf of Honduras
MIXTEC
Cuauhtepec
Tecuantepec (Tehuantepec)
300 km
300 miles
Tototepec (Tututepec)
Cuauhtolco
Gulf of Tehuantepec
Mezcalapa
Mapachtepec (Mapastepec)
MAYA
Ayotlan
SOCONUSCO
Xoconocho
PACIFIC OCEAN
N

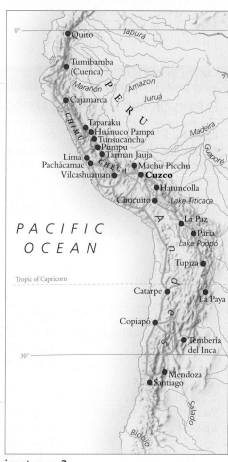

The Valley of Mexico

- ○ Aztec town or city
- aqueduct
- causeway
- dike
- marshland

inset map of Tenochtitlán

99°
89°45'
19°45'
Lake Zumpango
N
Lake Texcoco
19°30'
dyke of Netzahualcoyotl
Tenochtitlán
Lake Chalco
19°15'
15 km
15 miles

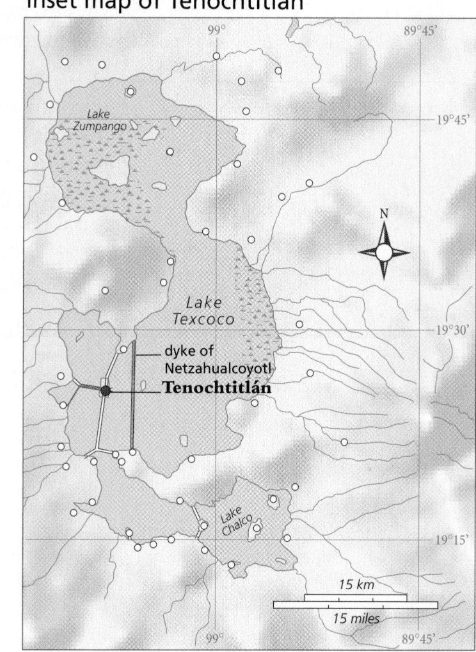

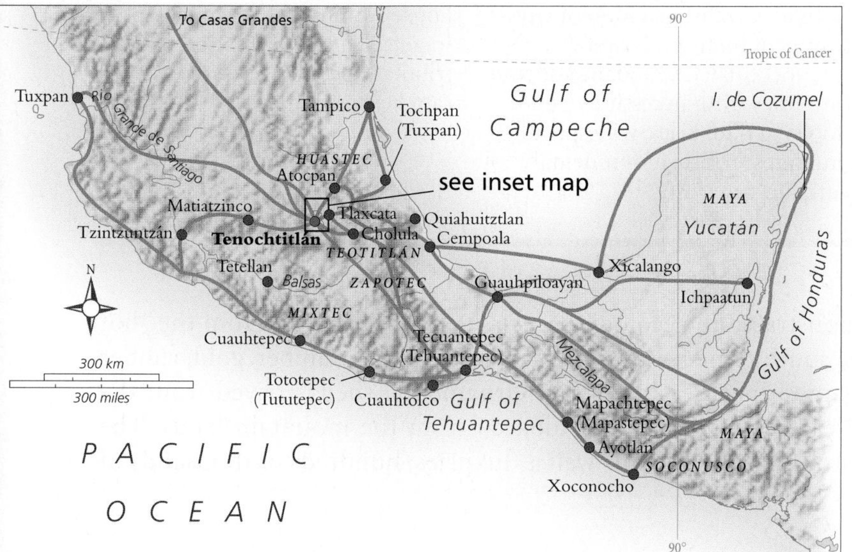

MAKING CONNECTIONS

EXPANSION AND ITS LIMITS: AFRICA AND THE AMERICAS IN THE FIFTEENTH CENTURY

REGION / STATE OR EMPIRE →	CAUSES FOR EXPANSION →	EVIDENCE / EFFECTS OF EXPANSION →	LIMITATIONS
East Africa / Ethiopia	Access to long-range trading routes to Indian Ocean via Red Sea ports	Recapture of coastal cities in 1400s, increased trade in slaves, ivory, gold, incense; creation of main access road to Indian Ocean	Limited agricultural land; need to control mountainous and lowland areas to access trade routes; major river systems to south and east with large populations; gradually encroaching Portuguese and Muslim influence by sixteenth century
East/Central Africa / Zambezi River valley, Great Zimbabwe	Difficult access to Indian Ocean seaports; large populations with ivory, gold, metal resources	Manufactured goods from Asia (porcelain, silk, etc.) traded for gold, ivory; increasingly large administrative centers in stone, large amounts of coins, jewelry, gold, etc.	Landlocked; altered trade routes; decline in navigability of rivers
West Africa / Songhay Empire	Trade routes of the Sahara, linking Mediterranean and Niger valley; astute leadership (Muhammad Askia) and alliance with Muslim clerics, scholars	Canals, dikes, reservoirs; extension of cultivable land; rich trade with Niger valley goldfields	Limited long-range communication; adverse Atlantic winds/currents
Central Africa / Kongo	Domination of Congo River; alliance with Portuguese; abundant natural resources	Use of Western firearms, Christian religion and symbols to legitimate and maintain control; trading of slaves from conquered territories to Portuguese	Ultimate loss of control over slave trade to Portuguese leads to decline and fall
South America / Inca	Diversity of environments, resources; tribute system allows exchange of products between zones	Quick expansion and use of extreme methods of control; extensive road system; large shrines for dead leaders	Mass executions and other methods of subjugation alienate subject peoples and allies
Mesoamerica / Aztecs	Environmental diversity; hundreds of tributary communities; efficient record-keeping; large array of natural resources	Intensive transformation of environment in/around capital (Tenochtitlán); abundance of commodities, both necessities (food, tools) and luxuries; widespread human sacrifice; monumental architecture	Loose administrative control; fragile alliances; alienation of tributary peoples; excessively rapid expansion

The tribute demonstrated the ecological diversity of the regions. From the "hot countries" in the south came feathers and jaguar pelts, jade, amber, gold, rubber for ritual ball games, incense, and cacao. Ornamental shells arrived from the Gulf Coast and eagles, deerskins, and tobacco from the mountain lands. The tribute system brought necessities as well as luxuries: hundreds of thousands of bushels of maize and beans every year, with hundreds of thousands of cotton garments and quilted cotton suits of armor. Finally, there was the product that best expressed Aztec power and—perhaps in Aztec minds—supplied the blood that fueled the universe: human-sacrifice victims, captured in war or tendered in tribute. In 1487, for instance, at the dedication of a temple in Tenochtitlán, thousands of captives were said to have been slaughtered at once.

Tributary networks were complex. Some communities exchanged tribute, often collecting it from some tributaries to pass part of it on to others. Tenochtitlán was at the summit of the system, but it left most communities to their own devices as long as they paid tribute. This was contrary to the interventionist politics of the Inca. According to records copied in the sixteenth century, Tenochtitlán only garrisoned or directly ruled 22 communities. But like the Incas, the Aztecs relied on fragile alliances, bore the resentment of tributary peoples, and expanded so rapidly that their reach always threatened to outrun available manpower and technology.

The founding of Tenochtitlán

The Aztecs and Incas saw themselves as continuing the traditions of earlier empires: Tula and Teotihuacán for the Aztecs, Tiahuanaco for the Incas. The reach of their power seems, however, to have exceeded anything either region had witnessed before. So how did they do it? Long-range exchanges with other cultures helped to propel empires in Eurasia and Africa into expansion, but these advantages did not apply in the Americas. They did not benefit from new technology. Nor, as far as we know, were people in either region bouncing back from anything resembling the demographic catastrophe of parts of the Old World in the previous century. There was no momentum of recovery behind the enormous extensions of Aztec and Inca power. The most likely explanation is that demographic growth crossed a critical threshold in both areas. Probably, only imperial solutions could command the resources and compel the exchanges of goods needed to sustain the growing cities in which the Aztecs and Incas lived. In any case, both empires, as we shall see in the next chapter, were short-lived. They were empires of types traditional in the region and overreached the realistic limits of their potential.

NEW EURASIAN EMPIRES

The expanding states of fifteenth-century Africa and the Americas proved relatively fragile. In the sixteenth century, European conquerors swallowed the Aztec and Inca states almost at a gulp; Ethiopia barely endured, eroded by Muslim invaders and waves of pagan, pastoralist immigrants; and Songhay fell to invaders from Morocco. Finally, though Mwene Mutapa fought off would-be conquerors from Europe, it dissolved in the 1600s into numerous petty states. It was the borderlands that straddle Europe and Asia that nurtured the really big, enduring new or resumed empires of the age, those of Turks and Russians.

The Russian Empire

The rise of a powerful Russian state was without precedent. Previously, the geography of the region produced unstable empires. Open, flat lands and scattered populations contributed to an environment in which states formed with ease but survived with difficulty. Most came and went quickly, vulnerable to external attack and internal rebellion.

In the fifteenth century, however, the rulers of Moscow established a state of imperial dimensions. Muscovy—as the early Russian Empire was called—has been exceptionally enduring. One of the features that made Muscovy different was the shape of its heartland, based on control of the Volga River, a north–south axis of trade. Earlier empires, including the Mongol, were based on the east–west axis of the steppes, which served as highways for horse-borne armies.

Muscovy's sudden take-off in the second half of the fifteenth century, when territorial conquests of neighboring peoples turned it into an imperial state, overshadowed early efforts at expansion. Indeed, when Constantinople fell to the Turks in 1453, Muscovites could see their city as, potentially, the "Third Rome," replacing Constantinople as Constantinople had replaced Rome (see Chapter 9). By the 1470s, Ivan the Great (r. 1462–1505) had absorbed most of Russia's other surviving principalities. He married a Byzantine princess, incorporated an imperial eagle into his coat of arms, forged a genealogy that traced his family back to the Roman Caesars, imported Italian technicians to fortify his palace, and dismissed an offer from the German emperor to invest him as king. "We have been sovereign in our land from our earliest forefathers," he replied, "and we hold our sovereignty from God."

During his reign, Ivan the Great more than trebled the territory he ruled—to over 240,000 square miles (see Map 15.4). His realm also took a new shape around most of the length of the Volga, uniting the fur-rich north and the cash-rich fringes of Asia. Fur was the "black gold" of the north, inducing Russians to conquest and colonization, just as gold and spices lured other European peoples to Africa and the East.

War parties gathered pelts as tribute along a northern route that missionaries pioneered in the late fourteenth century. Repeatedly from 1465, Ivan sent expeditions to the rivers Perm and Ob to levy tribute. The expedition of 1499 numbered 4,000 men, equipped with sleds drawn by reindeer and dogs. They crossed the Ob in winter, returning with 1,000 captives from the forest-dwelling peoples who hunted for the furs. Ivan's ambassador to the rich Italian duchy of Milan boasted that his master received 1,000 gold ducats' worth of tribute annually in furs—five or six times an Italian nobleman's income.

Timurids and the Ottoman Empire

In the early fifteenth century, Turkish—and therefore Muslim—expansion resumed in southern Europe and Asia, under the leadership of the Ottoman dynasty. The Mongol supremacy had shattered the reputation of Muslim armies and inspired the religious minded to withdraw from the world in a spirit of resignation. The Black Death had also battered the Islamic world. Muslims' numerical preponderance over Christians never got back to earlier levels. But, for global history, the Islamic recovery is a much bigger story than the temporary setback.

To understand recovery, we turn to one of its most brilliant Muslim observers after the Black Death, the historian Ibn Khaldun (ihb ihn-hahl-DOON). In 1377, he began to write one of the most admired works of all time on history and political philosophy, the *Muqaddimah*. Its theme was the counterpoint of herder and tiller, which Ibn Khaldun saw as the motivating force of historical change. Everywhere in his day, Islamic survival and success depended on Muslims' ability to tame the invaders from the deserts and the steppes, and turn their power to the service of Islam. Most Turkic peoples and many Mongols were converted into warriors for Islam. Consequently, Central Asia stayed Muslim, and the Indian Ocean linked mainly Muslim shores. In other words, the Silk Roads and maritime routes of Eurasia had to pass through Muslim-ruled territory. Human fuel also renewed the Islamic world's capacity to wage war and expand its frontiers.

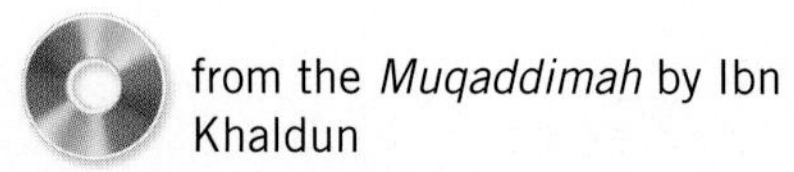

MAP 15.4

The Russian Empire, ca. 1505

Russian Empire

 routes used by fur traders

fur

The most conspicuous mobilizer of steppeland manpower in Muslim service in the late fourteenth and early fifteenth centuries was the self-proclaimed "world conqueror," Timur (tee-MOOR) the Lame. His court historian represented him as "the being nearest to perfection" and a pious devotee of holy war, but his role models were Alexander the Great (see Chapter 5) and Genghis Khan.

When Turkic nobles rebelled against their Mongol masters in his homeland, Timur emerged as their leader. By the time he died in 1406, he had conquered Iran, halted the Ottomans, invaded Syria and India, and planned the conquest of China (see Map 15.5). Wherever he went, he heaped up the skulls of citizens unwise enough to resist his sieges. But this destruction was for efficiency, not for its own sake. It made most conquests submit cheaply. His success seemed decreed by God: "Almighty God has subjugated the world to my domination, and the will of the Creator has entrusted the countries of the Earth to my power."

The day after his death, as his heirs turned on one another, his achievements seemed transitory. Even today, Timur's impact on the Islamic world is usually seen as

 A contemporary describes Timur

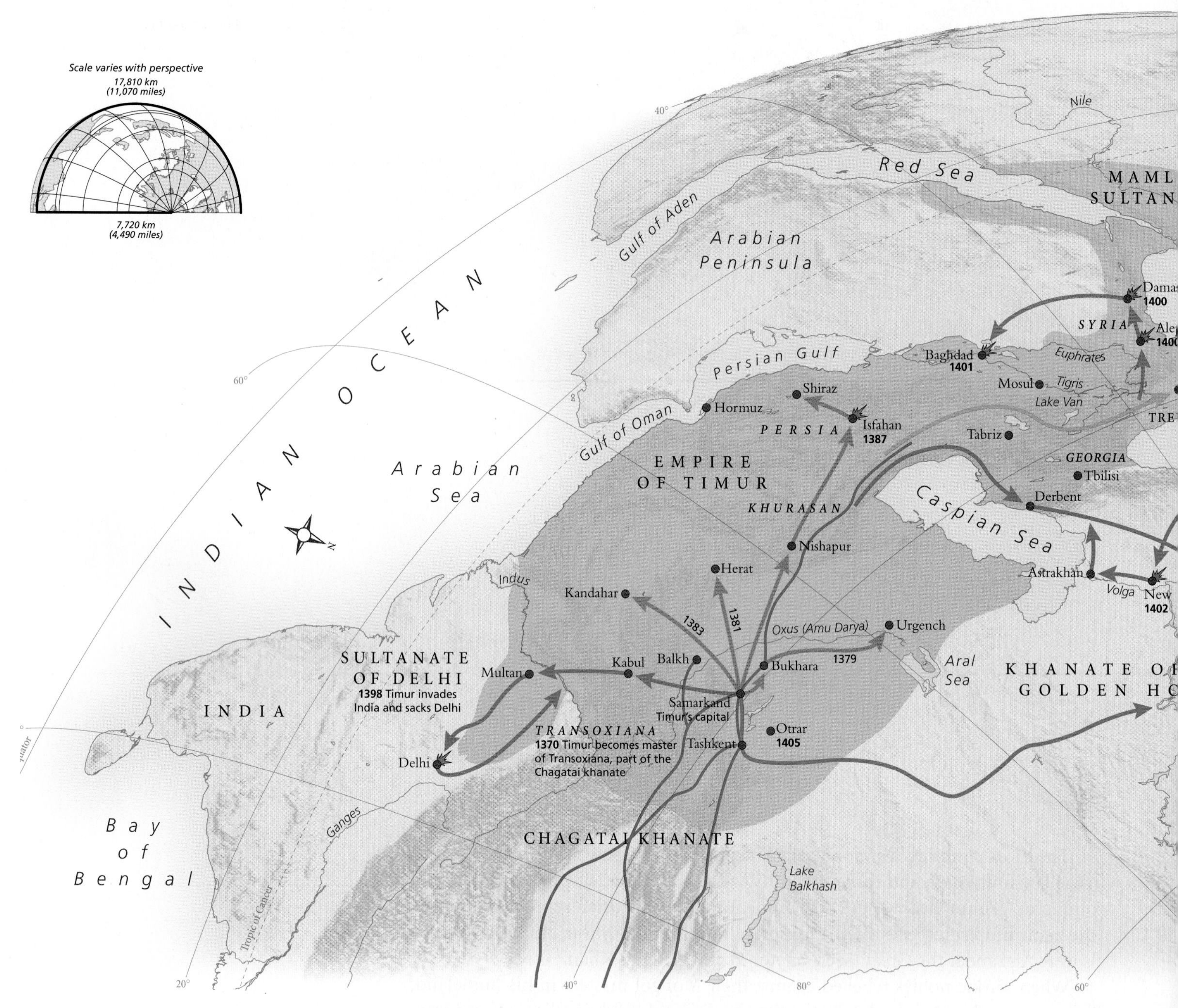

negative. His success against the Ottomans gave Christendom a reprieve. By humbling the Mongols, he encouraged Christians in Russia. By weakening the Muslim sultans of Delhi, he liberated millions of Hindus. These reflections, however, overlook his psychological legacy. He was a champion of Islamic orthodoxy and exerted great influence as a patron of Muslim education. He is also an example of the process that converted pastoralists. Having been the scourge of the Islamic world, they became its sword.

Timur was like a hurricane—his force soon spent. The Ottomans were more like a monsoon—their armies returned and receded as each season came and went, but they constantly made new conquests. The fate of the Mongols—expelled from China, retreating from Russia—shows how hard it was for a great Eurasian empire to survive in the aftermath of the Black Death, which jarred economies and felled manpower. Yet, the Ottoman Empire managed to do so.

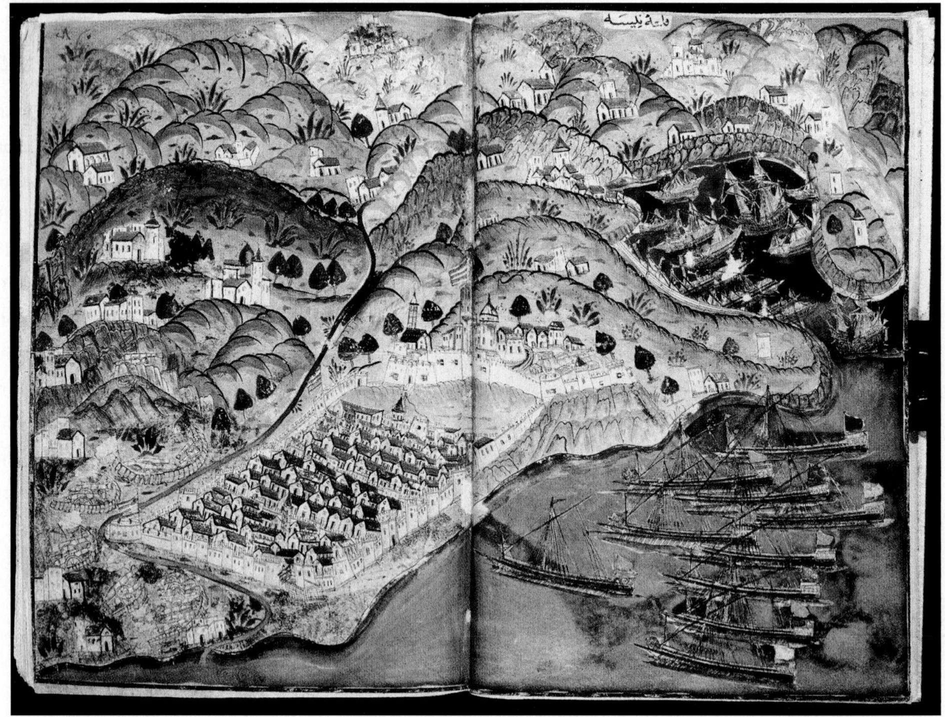

A Turkish fleet at anchor off Toulon, in southern France, in 1543, from a chronicle written to celebrate the wide-ranging campaigns of Sultan Suleiman the Magnificent (r. 1520–1566). The Ottomans were able to wage naval war in the western Mediterranean, thanks to the many harbors along the North African coast controlled by Muslim chiefs who were subjects of the sultans.

The Ottomans' great advantage was location. The heartlands of the empire were at the crossroads of some of the world's great trade routes, where the Silk Roads, the Indian Ocean routes, the Volga, the Danube, and the Mediterranean almost converged (see Map 15.5). The history of the Byzantine Empire showed the importance of holding on to this location. Byzantium flourished while it occupied these lands, faltered when its control there slackened and ceased (see Chapter 12). From their own past, the Ottomans inherited the traditions of steppeland imperialism. They were content, at first, to levy tribute and allow their tributaries to govern themselves or to exist as puppet states, manipulated according to Ottoman needs.

Gradually, they adapted to the environments they conquered, agrarian, urban, and maritime. Other empires of nomadic origins failed when required to adapt to new military technologies, but the Ottomans' readily became a gunpowder empire. Their forces could blow away cavalry or batter down city walls. They even took to the sea. In the 1390s, the sultans began to build fleets, and by the end of the fifteenth century, the Ottomans had overturned the 400-year-old Christian maritime supremacy in the Mediterranean. Never since Rome defeated Carthage (see Chapter 7) had such an unlikely candidate become a naval power.

Like other steppeland imperialists, the Ottomans mastered the art of keeping subjects of diverse religions loyal to them. They tolerated Jews, Christians, and Shiites but levied punitive taxes on these minorities. On Christians, they imposed a levy of male child slaves, who were brought up as Muslims to form the **Janissaries**, an elite corps of the armed forces, and staff the ranks of the administration. The system provided servants for the state and converts for Islam, while keeping Christian communities in submission. From the 1420s, the sultan functioned as head of two linked systems of law and justice. The first consisted of secular laws and customs that the sultan's appointees administered. The second was enshrined in the Quran and the traditions of Islamic law, with a body of experts to run it, who met in the sultan's palace.

In 1451, Mehmet (MEH-meht) II became sultan at the age of 19. His predecessors had prudently allowed self-rule to continue in the city of Constantinople and its few surviving dependencies—the last fragments of the Byzantine Empire that still proclaimed itself the heir of Rome. The Ottomans controlled what happened in Constantinople with threats and bribes. But some factions in the city were determined to challenge the Turks and formed an alliance with Western Christendom. Mehmet laid siege to Constantinople. He built huge forts to command the sea approaches to the city and fired the heaviest artillery ever made at its walls. He transported ships overland to elude Byzantine defenses. In the end, weight of numbers was decisive. The last Byzantine emperor fell fighting.

With the fall of Constantinople in 1453, Mehmet II could see his empire as a continuation of Rome. He chose Italians to paint his portrait, sculpt his medals, and write some of his propaganda. The direction of Ottoman conquests tilted toward Europe as Mehmet extended his territory into most of what are now Greece, Romania, and Bosnia, seeking to control the shores of the Adriatic and Black Seas.

THE LIMITATIONS OF CHINESE IMPERIALISM

So Ottoman imperialism in the fifteenth century resumed its former course after setbacks caused by the Black Death and the rise of Timur. An observer at the time might have predicted that China, too, would resume expansion and bid for a maritime empire. The best way to understand why such developments seemed likely—and why they were frustrated—is to look back at China's recovery from the mid–fourteenth-century plagues. Like so many decisive episodes of Chinese history, the story begins among the people on whose labor and manpower the empire depended: peasants.

The Yellow River. This pictorial map of the Yellow River is both an artistic masterpiece and a scientific source of information. Ten famous painters representing China's northern and southern schools of art worked on it. Ordered by the first emperor of the Ming Dynasty (1368–1644), the map was drawn to an exact scale and was an invaluable tool to assess the impact of the frequently flooded Yellow River. The houses in the map indicate the population of cities, with each house representing 100 families.

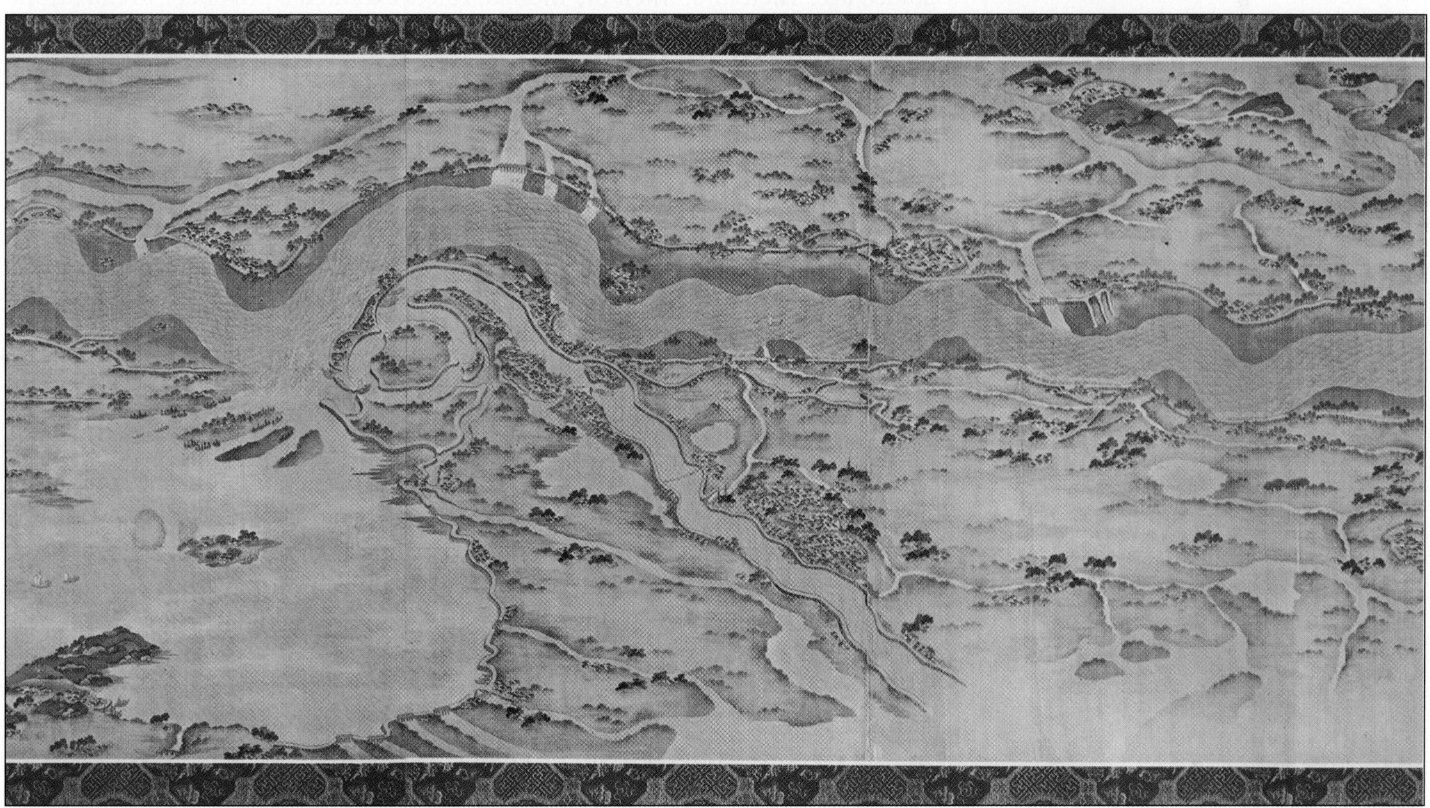

Peasants sometimes defer hope and waiting for the millennium—a fabled future, when divine intervention will either perfect the world or end it. Often, however, in times of extreme disaster, peasant movements arise to try to trigger the millennium. One of the most explosive of all such movements began among Chinese canal workers in 1350.

In mid–fourteenth-century China, peasants were the victims of the slow-grinding effects of economic misery and the survivors of environmental disasters. The plagues that began in the 1320s kept on returning. Not until well into the 1350s did the plagues begin to lose their virulence or to encounter naturally immunized populations. In 1344, the Yellow River flooded. Droughts followed. In this setting, peasants were forced to repair the Grand Canal, which carried essential food supplies from southern and central China to Beijing.

The peasants' hope of deliverance was based on a Buddhist myth. The lord Maitreya, the last of the earthly Buddhas, would come to prepare the world for extinction. Now, however, given the peasants' miserable lives, the myth acquired a political edge. Maitreya would put a triumphant end to the struggle of good against evildoers and give his followers power over their oppressors. A similar movement was current at the same time in Western Europe, where the Fraticelli, a group of Franciscans, identified with the needs of the wretched of the Earth. Fulfilling the biblical prophecy uttered by the mother of Jesus, which the prayers of the church repeated every day, a cosmic hero would put down the mighty from their seat and exalt the humble and meek.

In China, along with their desire for deliverance, peasants harbored a folk memory of the Song dynasty (see Chapter 12) and a hankering for the good times supposed to have preceded the Mongol invasions of a century before. Peasant revolts are often revolutionary in the most literal sense of the word, wanting to turn the world back, "revolve" it full circle, to an imagined or misremembered golden age. Therefore, when the Mongol rulers executed a pretender to the throne who claimed to be the heir of the Song in 1351, his followers rebelled and recruited thousands to their cause.

The leader who emerged from the rebellion was Zhu Yuanzhang (joo yoo-ehn-jhang). By the end of the 1350s, the empire in the Yangtze region had dissolved into a chaos of small states run by similar upstarts. In river warfare of reckless daring, Zhu conquered his rivals and proclaimed a new dynasty in 1368.

Zhu cleverly managed the coalition that had brought him to power. To please the Confucian establishment, he restored ancient ceremonies and the examinations for public service. He kept the military command structure. He renounced the cult of Maitreya, but only after making it clear that he had fulfilled it in his own person by adopting the name "Ming" for his dynasty. The word, which means bright, was traditionally used to describe the lord Maitreya.

Zhu had the self-educated man's contempt for academics. But he recognized that the Confucian bureaucrats had expertise he could use. He therefore kept the traditional power centers of his court in balance: the military top brass, the eunuchs who ran the imperial household, the foreign and Muslim advisers and technicians, the Buddhist and Daoist clergies, and the merchant lobby. Combined, they limited the power of the Confucian elite.

The result was a brief period when expansionist policies prevailed over Confucian caution. Zhu's son, the Yongle (yuhng-leh) emperor (r. 1402–1424), sought contact with the world beyond the empire. He meddled in the politics of China's southern neighbors in Vietnam and enticed the Japanese to trade.

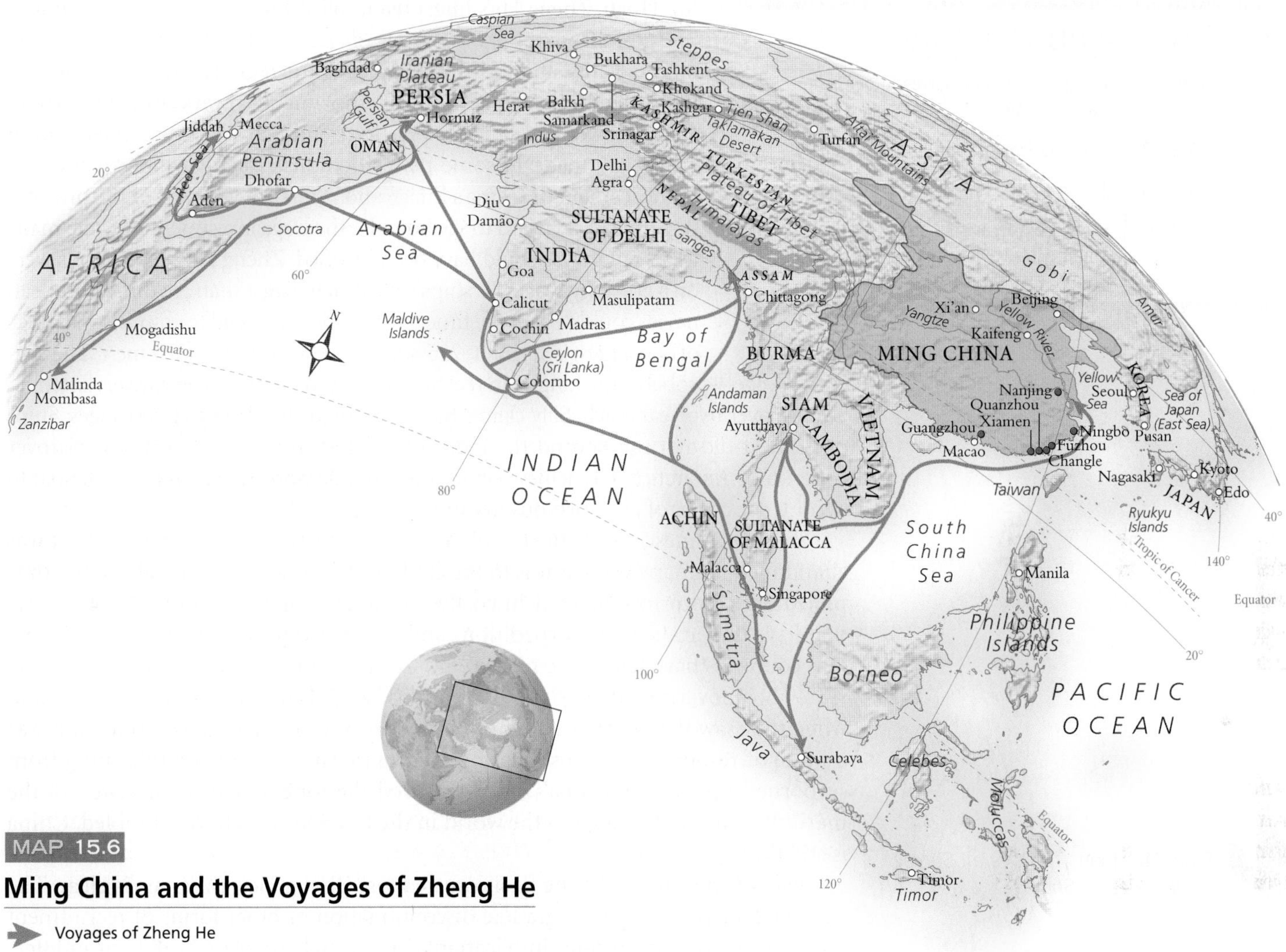

MAP 15.6

Ming China and the Voyages of Zheng He

Voyages of Zheng He

The most spectacular manifestation of the new outward-looking policy was the career of the Muslim eunuch-admiral, Zheng He (jehng heh). In 1405, he led the first of a series of naval expeditions, which was intended in part, at least, to show China's flag all over the Indian Ocean (see Map 15.6). He replaced unacceptable rulers in Java, Sumatra, and Sri Lanka, founded a puppet state on the commercially important strait of Malacca, and gathered tribute from Bengal. He displayed Chinese power as far away as Jiddah, on the Red Sea coast of Arabia and as far south as the island of Zanzibar in East Africa.

Can Zheng He's voyages be called an imperial venture? Their official purpose was to pursue a fugitive pretender to the Chinese throne—but that would not have required such vast expeditions to such distant places. The Chinese called the vessels treasure ships and emphasized what they called tribute gathering (in the more distant spots Zheng He's ships visited, what happened was more like an exchange). Commercial objectives may have been involved. Almost all the places Zheng He visited had long been important in Chinese trade. In part, the voyages were scientific missions:

The Early Ming Dynasty

1350s	Yangtze region dissolves into small warring states
1368	Zhu Yuanzhang founds Ming dynasty
1405	Zheng He leads first naval expedition
1425	Hongxi emperor succeeds to throne; Zheng He's voyages cancelled; Confucian values ascendant

Ma Huan, Zheng He's interpreter, called his own book on the subject *The Overall Survey of the Ocean's Shores*, and improved maps and data on the plants, animals, and peoples of the regions visited were among the expeditions' fruits. But flag showing is always, to some extent, about power or, at least, prestige. And the aggressive intervention Zheng He made in some places demonstrates that the extension or reinforcement of China's image and influence was part of the project.

Indeed, it is hard to see how else the huge investment the state made in his enterprise could have been justified. Zheng He's expeditions were on a crushing scale. His ships were much bigger than anything European navies could float at the time. His first fleet was said to comprise 66 junks of the largest ever built, 225 support vessels, and 27,870 men. The seventh voyage—probably the longest in reach—sailed 12,618 miles. The voyages lasted on average over two years each. Silly claims have been made for Zheng He's voyages. Ships of his fleet did not sail beyond the limits of the Indian Ocean—much less discover America or Antarctica. His achievements, however, demonstrated China's potential to become the center of an enormous maritime empire.

But the Chinese naval effort could not last. Historians have debated why it was abandoned. In many ways, it was to the credit of Chinese decision makers that they pulled back from involvement in costly adventures far from home. Most powers that have undertaken such expeditions and attempted to impose their rule on distant countries have had cause to regret it. Confucian values included giving priority to good government at home. "Barbarians" would submit to Chinese rule if and when they saw the benefits. Attempting to beat or coax them into submission was a waste of resources. By consolidating their landward empire and refraining from seaborne imperialism, China's rulers ensured the longevity of their state. All the maritime empires founded in the world in the last 500 years have crumbled. China is still there.

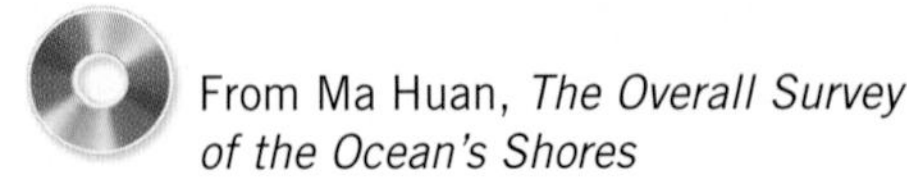
From Ma Huan, *The Overall Survey of the Ocean's Shores*

Part of the context of the decision to abort Zheng He's missions is clear. The examination system and the gradual discontinuation of other forms of recruitment for public service had serious implications. Increasingly scholars, with their indifference to expansion, and gentlemen, with their contempt for trade, governed China. In the 1420s and 1430s, the balance of power at court shifted in the bureaucrats' favor, away from the Buddhists, eunuchs, Muslims, and merchants who had supported Zheng He. When the Hongxi (huhng-jher) emperor succeeded to the throne in 1425, one of his first acts was to cancel Zheng He's next voyage. He restored Confucian office holders, whom the Yongle emperor had dismissed, and curtailed the power of other factions. In 1429, the shipbuilding budget was cut almost to extinction. The scholar-elite hated overseas adventures and the factions that favored them so much that they destroyed all Zheng He's records to obliterate his memory. Moreover, China's land frontiers became insecure as Mongol power revived. China needed to turn toward the new threat. The state never resumed overseas expansion. Trade and colonization in southeast Asia were left to merchants and migrants. China, the empire best equipped for maritime imperialism, opted out. Consequently, lesser powers, including those of Europe, were able to exploit opportunities in seas that Chinese power vacated.

By the late fifteenth century, the scholars' position seemed unshakable, and the supremacy of Confucian values could not be challenged. The Hongxi emperor aspired to Confucian perfection. He ordered the slaughter or expulsion of court magicians and exiled 1,000 Buddhist and Daoist monks. He resumed a Confucian priority: study of the penal code, which previous Ming emperors had neglected. He reintroduced the palace lectures, during which Confucian professors instructed the emperor. He endowed a library alongside the Confucian temple at the sage's birthplace in Qufu (shoo-foo) and patronized artists whose work radiated Confucian serenity.

THE BEGINNINGS OF OCEANIC IMPERIALISM

Even under the Yongle emperor, China confined its seaward reach to the monsoonal seas of maritime Asia and the Indian Ocean—seas of terrible hazards and fabulous rewards. As we have seen, the Indian Ocean was relatively easy to cross but relatively hard to enter or exit. For most of history, therefore, it was the preserve of peoples whose homes bordered it or who traveled overland—like some European and Armenian traders—to become part of its world. Moreover, all the trade was internal. Merchants took no interest in venturing far beyond the monsoon system to reach other markets or supplies.

From Europe, however, access to the Indian Ocean was well worth seeking. Merchants craved a share of the richest trades and most prosperous markets in the world, especially the spices, drugs, and aromatics that came from Sri Lanka, India, and what is now Indonesia. These products, sold to rich buyers in China, southwest Asia, and Europe, were the most profitable in the world. Many Europeans sought to find out where they came from and take part in the trades. But the journey was too long, laborious, and hazardous to generate much profit. From the Mediterranean, merchants had either to travel up the Nile and proceed by camel caravan to a Red Sea port, or negotiate a dangerous passage through the Ottoman Empire to the Persian Gulf. In either case, they obviously could not take ships with them. This was a potentially fatal limitation because Europeans had little to offer to people in the Indian Ocean basin except shipping services. Until the 1490s, Europeans were unsure whether it was possible to approach the Indian Ocean by sea at all.

Europe's only effective access by sea to the rest of the world is along its western seaboard, into the Atlantic. For the Atlantic to become Europe's highway to the rest of the world, explorers had to discover the winds that led to commercially important destinations. There were, first, the northeast trade winds, which led to the resource-rich, densely populated regions of the New World, far south of the lands the Norse reached. There was also the South Atlantic wind system, which led, by way of the southeast trade winds and the westerlies of the far south, to the Indian Ocean (see Map 15.7).

The technology to exploit the Atlantic's wind systems only gradually became available during a period of long, slow improvements to hulls, rigging, and water casks in the thirteenth, fourteenth, and fifteenth centuries. Historians have emphasized the contribution of formal science in developing maritime charts and instruments for navigating by the stars. Now it seems that these innovations were irrelevant. No practical navigator of this period in Europe seems to have used them.

Only the long accumulation of information and experience could make a breakthrough possible. Several attempts were made during the fifteenth century to explore Atlantic space, but most doomed themselves to failure by setting out in the belt of westerly winds. Presumably explorers chose this route because they wanted to be sure that they would be able to get home. Shortly after 1450, the westernmost islands of the Azores were reached. Over the next three decades, the Portuguese crown often commissioned voyages of exploration farther into the Atlantic, but none is known to have made any further progress.

Not only was exploitation of the Atlantic slow, it yielded, at first, few returns. In the 1480s, however, the situation changed, and Atlantic exploration began to

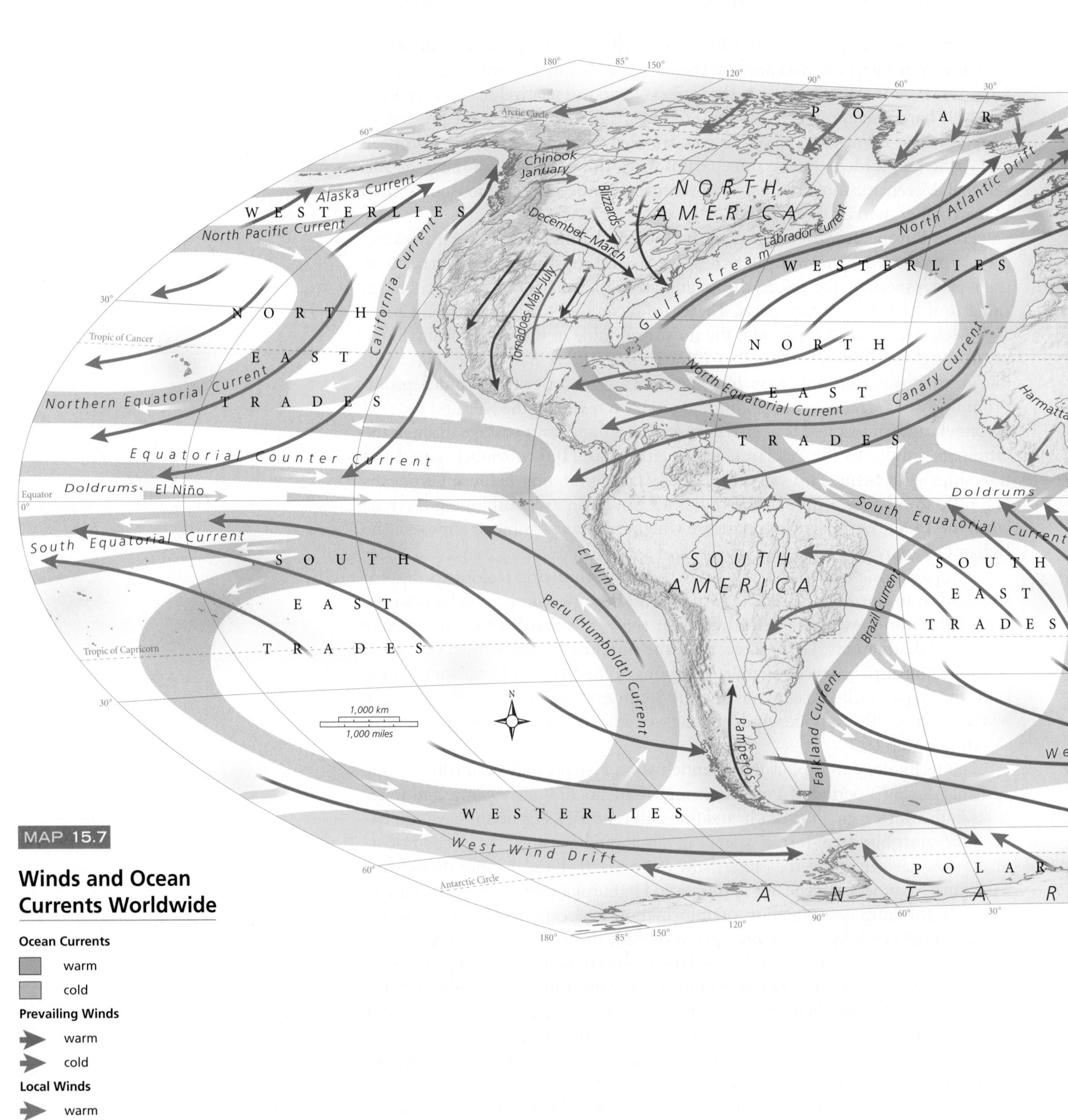

MAP 15.7

Winds and Ocean Currents Worldwide

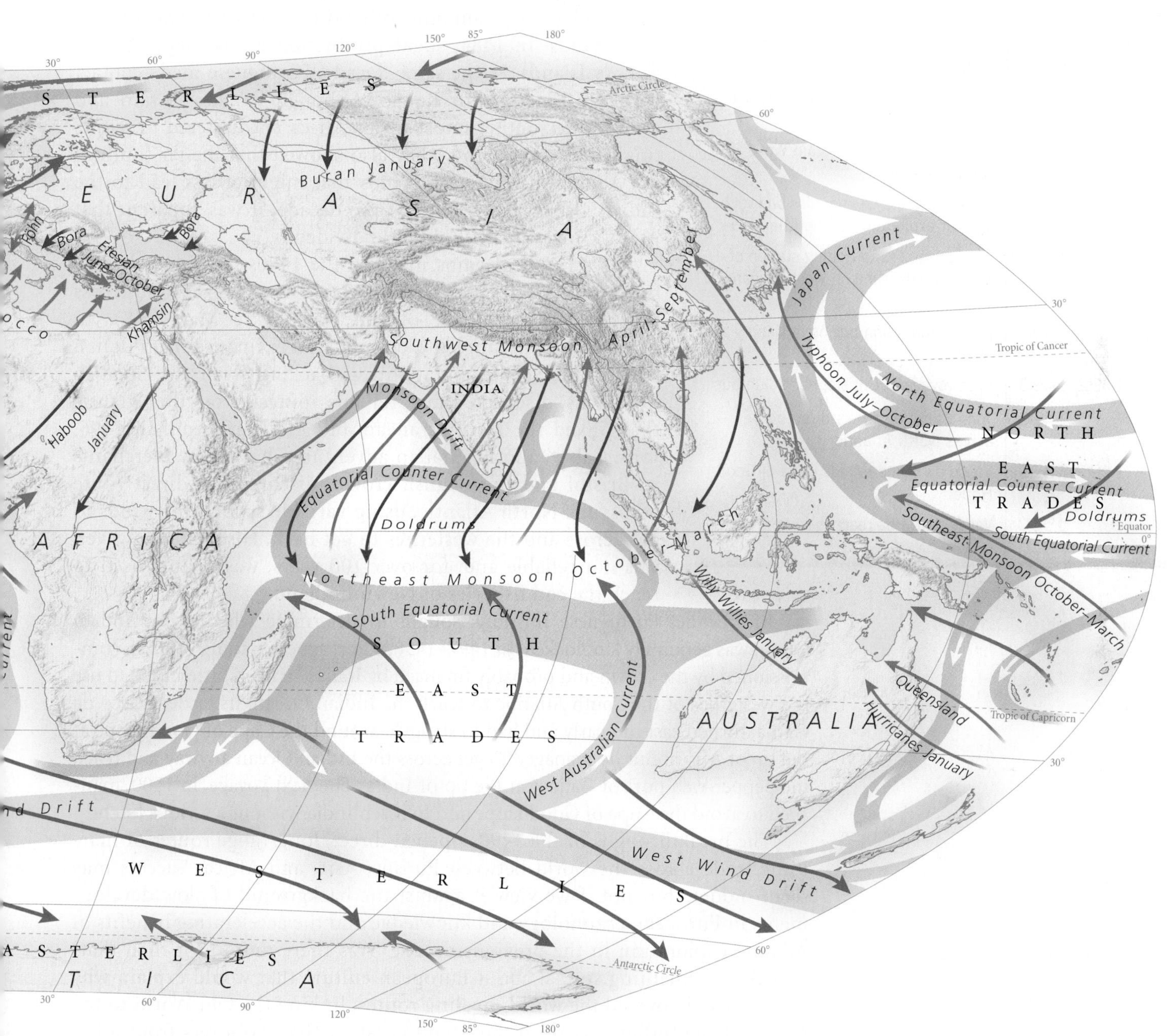

S T E R L I E S
E U R A S I A
Buran January
Föhn
Bora
Etesian June–October
Bora
Khamsin
Southwest Monsoon
April–September
INDIA
Monsoon Drift
Haboob
January
Equatorial Counter Current
Doldrums
AFRICA
Northeast Monsoon October–March
South Equatorial Current
S O U T H
E A S T
T R A D E S
West Australian Current
Willy Willies January
AUSTRALIA
Queensland
Hurricanes January
Japan Current
Typhoon July–October
North Equatorial Current
N O R T H
E A S T
T R A D E S
Equatorial Counter Current
Doldrums
South Equatorial Current
Southeast Monsoon October–March
Arctic Circle
Tropic of Cancer
Equator
Tropic of Capricorn
Antarctic Circle
West Wind Drift
W E S T E R L I E S
A S T E R L I E S
T I C A

MAP EXPLORATION
www.prenhall.com/armesto_maps

The Beginnings of European Oceanic Imperialism

Tenth and eleventh centuries	Norse explore North Atlantic
Thirteenth and fifteenth centuries	Europeans make advances in maritime technology and knowledge
1430s	Portuguese establish way stations in Azores
1440s	Portuguese begin to obtain West African slaves
1450–1480	Portuguese crown commissions voyages of exploration of the Atlantic
1482	Portuguese found trading station of Saõ Jorge da Mina on West African coast
1484	Sugar production begins in Canary Islands
1492–1493	First voyage of Christopher Columbus
1496	John Cabot discovers direct route across North Atlantic
1497–1498	Vasco da Gama rounds Cape of Good Hope
1500	Vasco da Gama reaches India

pay off. In the North Atlantic, customs records of the English port of Bristol indicate that quantities of whaling products, salt fish, and walrus ivory from the ocean increased dramatically. In West Africa, in 1482, Portuguese traders opened a new post at São Jorge da Mina that was close to goldfields in the Volta River valley. Large amounts of gold now began to reach European hands. In 1484, sugar production at last began in the Canary Islands. In the same decade, Portuguese made contact with the Kingdom of Kongo. Although voyages toward and around the southernmost tip of Africa encountered unremittingly adverse currents, they also showed that the far south of the Atlantic had westerly winds that might at last lead to the Indian Ocean. By the end of the decade, it was apparent that Atlantic investment could yield dividends.

As a result of gains made in the 1480s, the 1490s were a breakthrough-decade in Europe's efforts to reach out across the ocean to the rest of the world (see Map 15.8). In 1492–1493, Christopher Columbus, with finance from Italian bankers in Seville and political backing from the Spanish monarchs, discovered fast, reliable routes across the Atlantic that linked the Mediterranean and the Caribbean. In 1496, John Cabot, another Italian adventurer, backed by merchants in Bristol and the English crown, discovered a direct route across the North Atlantic, using variable springtime winds to get across and the westerlies to get back. His route, however, was not reliable and, for over 100 years, was mainly used to reach the cod fisheries of Newfoundland.

Meanwhile, Portuguese missions sought to determine whether the Indian Ocean was genuinely landlocked. In 1497–1498, a Portuguese trading venture, commissioned by the crown and probably financed by Italian bankers, attempted to use the westerlies of the South Atlantic to reach the Indian Ocean. Its leader, Vasco da Gama, turned east too early and had to struggle around the Cape of Good Hope at the tip of Africa. But he managed to get across the Indian Ocean anyway and reach the pepper-rich port of Calicut at the tip of India. The next voyage, in 1500, managed to avoid the Cape of Good Hope and to reach India without a serious hitch.

The breakthroughs of the 1490s opened direct, long-range routes of maritime trade across the world between Europe, Asia, and Africa. Success may seem sudden, but not if we view it against the background of slow developments in European chronology and knowledge and the accelerating benefits of Atlantic exploration in the previous decade. Was there more to it than that? Was there something special about European culture that would explain why Europeans discovered the world-girdling routes, linking the Old World to the New and the Indian Ocean to the Atlantic, rather than explorers from other cultures? Some European historians have argued just that—that Europeans had something others lacked.

Such a suggestion, however, seems ill conceived. Compared to the peoples of maritime Asia, Europeans were slow to launch long-range voyages. Moreover, the breakthrough explorations were not the work of "Europe" but of people from a few communities on the Atlantic seaboard and in the Mediterranean. What distinguishes them is not that they set off with the right kind of culture, but that they set off from the right place.

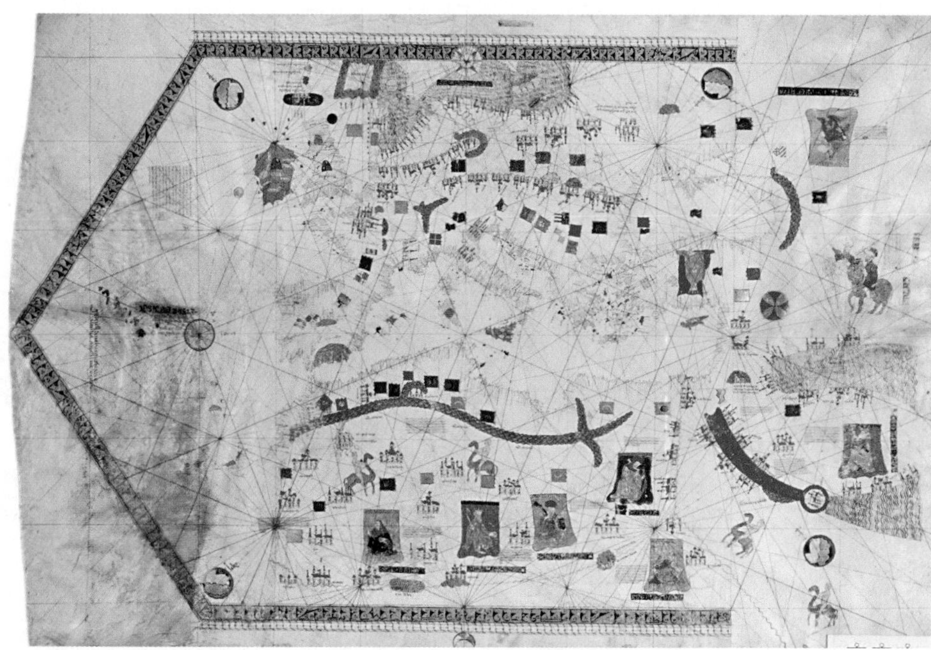

The Azores. The Atlantic voyage of Diogo de Silves of 1427 was unrecorded, except on this map, made in Majorca in 1439. The Azores, which Silves sailed around, can be seen on the extreme left, alongside the traces of a stain made when the famous French novelist, George Sand, spilled an ink pot when examining the map while on a vacation on Majorca with her lover, the composer Frédéric Chopin, in 1838–1839.

THE EUROPEAN OUTLOOK: PROBLEMS AND PROMISE

Western Europe in the fifteenth century was beset with problems. Recovery from the disasters of the fourteenth century was slow. Plagues remained frequent. Though used to the more severe climate, Western Europeans did not reoccupy the high ground and distant colonies that they had vacated in the fourteenth century. In most places, population probably had not reached levels attained before the Black Death. Food supplies were unreliable. Harvests frequently failed.

But hard times created opportunities for those with the skill or luck to exploit them. High mortality opened gaps in elites, which bureaucrats could fill, thanks, in part, to a revolution in government. To legitimize the newcomers' power, Western moralists redefined nobility as the product of virtue or education rather than ancestry.

New economic divisions appeared. The line of the Elbe and northern Danube Rivers and the lands between became a cultural fault line. To the west of this line, underpopulation boosted the value of labor. The effects were to liberate peasants and urban communities from landowners' control, split up landholdings, encourage tenancies, and convert cropland to pasture. In the east the opposite occurred. Landholders responded to the loss of manpower and revenue by clamping down on peasants' rights and forcing towns into submission. New definitions of nobility were rejected. East of the Bohemian forest, nobility was ancient blood or acquired "by martial discipline," and that was that.

Nevertheless, Western Europe showed signs of self-confidence and optimism. Scholars and artists pursued, with renewed vigor, the project of recovering the legacy of the cultural achievements of ancient Greece and Rome. The movement is commonly called "**the Renaissance**" on the grounds that the civilization of classical antiquity was reborn—but scholarship has now identified renaissances in almost every century for the previous 1,000 years. No radically new departure occurred in the fifteenth century from what had gone before—merely

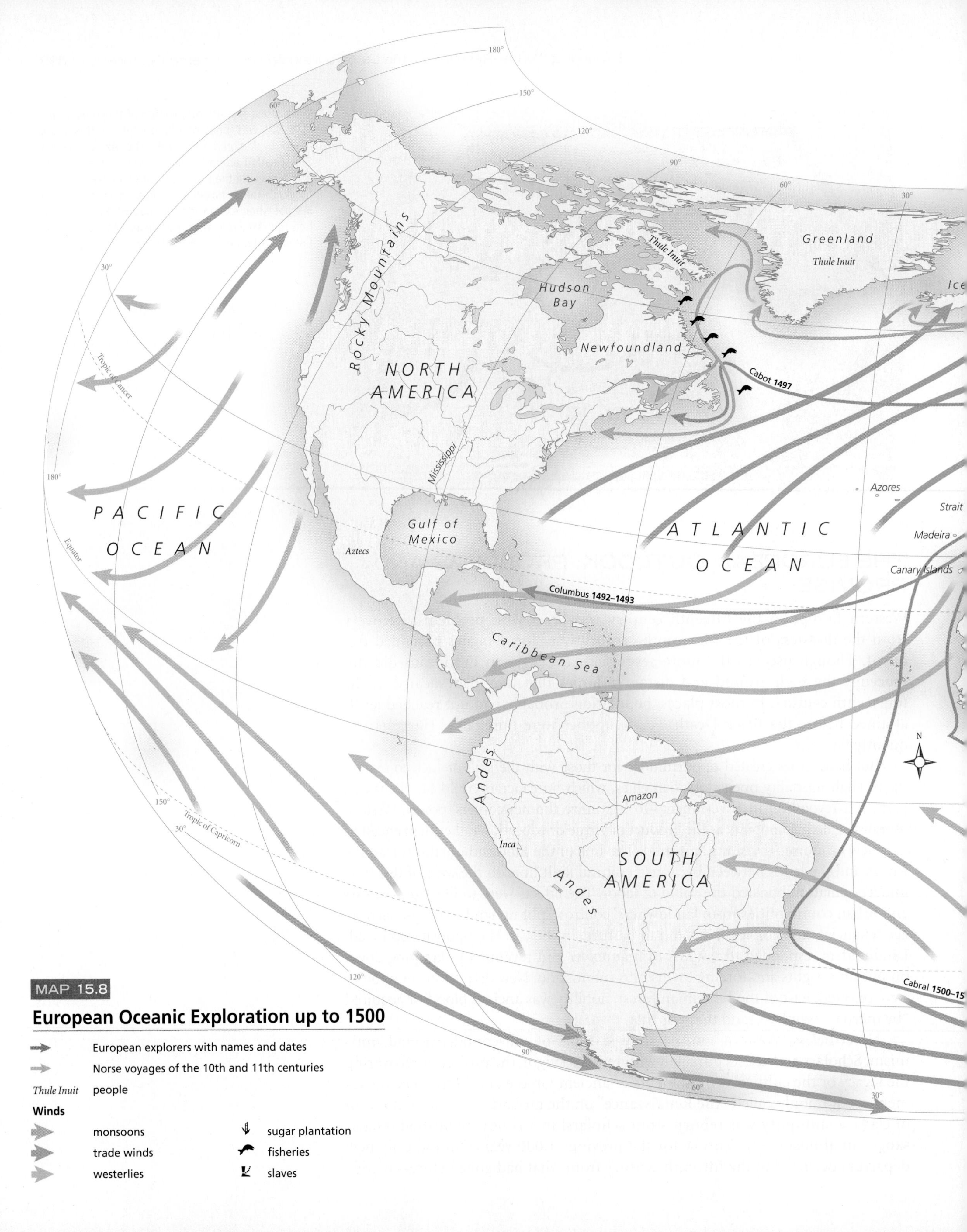

MAP 15.8

European Oceanic Exploration up to 1500

European explorers with names and dates
Norse voyages of the 10th and 11th centuries
Thule Inuit people

Winds

monsoons
trade winds
westerlies
sugar plantation
fisheries
slaves

150°
120°
90°
60°
30°
0°
E U R A S I A
RUSSIA
NORWAY
SWEDEN
Baltic Sea
LITHUANIA
Vistula
ENGLAND
HOLY ROMAN EMPIRE
Elbe
POLAND
HUNGARY
Venice
Danube
Black Sea
Caspian Sea
Volga
Genoa
Florence
ITALY
OTTOMAN EMPIRE
SPAIN
Majorca
Mediterranean Sea
Granada
Oran
Algiers
MOROCCO
Alexandria
Cairo
Jerusalem
Baghdad
Hormuz
EGYPT
Sahara
Mecca
Arabian Peninsula
Nile
Massawa
Aden
Horn of Africa
Niger
Volta
Sierra Leone
São Jorge de Mina
AFRICA
Congo
Mogadishu
Malinda
Kilwa
Sofala
Kalahari Desert
Cape Town
da Gama 1497–98
Karakorum
Beijing
Shanghai
Tropic of Cancer
PACIFIC OCEAN
Himalayas
Ganges
Macao
BURMA
Mons
Manila
Diu
Bombay
Goa
Vijayanagar
INDIA
Calicut
Bay of Bengal
Rangoon
Khmer
Bangkok
THAI KINGDOM
South China Sea
Malays
Malacca
Menado
Equator
Cabral 1500–1501
da Gama 1497–1498
INDIAN OCEAN
Tropic of Capricorn

an accentuation of long-accumulating tendencies. Humanist students adopted a predominantly secular curriculum: grammar, rhetoric, poetry, history, and moral philosophy, imbibed mainly from classical texts. The classics as well as—even, instead of—Christianity came to inform common ideas of morality, politics, and taste. Spreading, at first, from a few French and north Italian schools, **humanism** gradually became Europe's most prestigious form of learning. Political thinkers turned back to Greek and Roman history for instruction. Religious innovators modeled their ideas on evidence from early Christianity. Artists adopted realism and perspective from what they thought were Greek and Roman models.

Florence demonstrates humanism's power and limitations. In the fifteenth century, classical taste transformed the art and architecture of this Italian city. Comparisons with the Roman republic inspired its citizens to think of themselves as free and self-governing. Yet power gradually fell into the hands of a single family, the Medici, who patronized art in the classical tradition but who actually spent more on jewels and artworks that could display their wealth. When they were temporarily overthrown in 1494, after their banking business collapsed, the state that replaced them was no Roman-style republic. Rather, it was the rule of a "godly" clique, inspired by a hell-fire preacher, who preferred piety to humanism. Botticelli (1444–1510), the great artist who had painted pagan erotica for a Medici villa, turned to biblical subjects.

Still, across Europe, the rise of humanism had lasting consequences. Humanists painstakingly scrutinized the Bible and the historical traditions of the church, exposing incorrect translations and departures from the practices of early Christianity. New styles in church architecture reflected classical taste and, more deeply, arose from the desire to create a setting for the kind of devotion that humanism inspired. Open sanctuaries, brilliantly lit and approached through wide naves and aisles, allowed worshippers to see and take part in events at the altar.

The four elements. In the fourth century B.C.E., Aristotle proposed that all matter is composed of four elements—earth, water, air, and fire—and exhibits different combinations of four qualities—moist, dry, hot, and cold. Over 1,800 years later, as this fifteenth-century illustration demonstrates, people in the West still believed in this theory. The artist shows the Earth as a sphere, with one large landmass emerging from an encircling ocean. Earth, "cold and dry," is surrounded by water, "cold and moist," and air, "hot and moist." The fourth element, fire, "hot and dry," forms an outer ring.

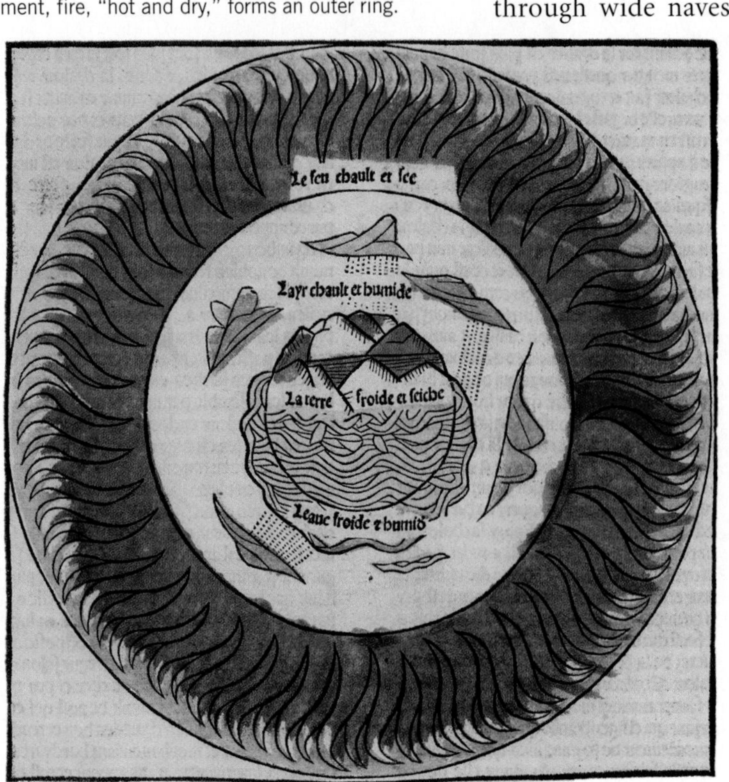

Humanism also helped arouse European interest in the wider world. In the early fifteenth century, the work of the ancient Greek scholar Ptolemy, originally written in Alexandria in the second century, invited intense speculation about geography, mapping the world, and the limits of exploration. The first-century B.C.E. work of Strabo, a Greek geographer, prompted questions about finding unknown continents. Humanists' fascination with the history of language reinforced the search for "primitive" peoples who might cast light on the question of how language originated.

Chivalry, however, was more important than humanism in stimulating overseas exploration. **Chivalry** could not, perhaps, make men good, as it was supposed to do. It could, however, win wars. In 1492, for instance, the monarchs of the Spanish kingdom of Castile extended the frontier of Christendom by conquering Granada, the last Muslim kingdom in Spain, in "a beautiful war," said the Venetian ambassador. "There was not a lord present who was not enamored of some lady," who "often handed warriors their weapons ... with a request that they show their love by their deeds." The queen of Castile died uttering prayers to the Archangel Michael as "prince of the chivalry of angels."

The typical chivalrous hero of the time took to the sea, conquered an island, married a princess, and became a ruler. Explorers—often men of humble social origins—tried to embody these fictions in real life. Adventurers in the service of the Portuguese Prince Henry (1394–1460) included former pirates and violent criminals. They indulged in chivalric rituals and gave themselves storybook names, like Lancelot and Tristram of the Island. They also colonized the Madeira Islands and parts of the Azores, and explored the coast of West Africa as far as Sierra Leone. The commercial sector that helped to back overseas adventures was looking for new opportunities—especially the Genoese, whose role in the eastern Mediterranean at this period was largely confined to high-bulk, low-profit shipping and trading. Marginal noblemen, shut out from advancement at home and imbued with chivalric ideas, were willing to take amazing risks. That, plus the availability of high-risk investment, helps to explain many early forays in Atlantic exploration.

Prince Henry himself—traditionally misrepresented as a navigator motivated by scientific curiosity—imagined himself a romantic hero, destined to win a kingdom of his own. The truth is that he never went exploring, and his desperate efforts to make enough money to pay his retainers included slave raiding and a soap monopoly. His followers included the father-in-law of Christopher Columbus, a weaver by training who reinvented himself as a "captain of cavaliers and conquests," and who took to exploration to escape the restricted social opportunities of home.

Alongside chivalry, millenarian fantasies may have influenced overseas expansion. The first king of Portugal's ruling dynasty was actually called "Messiah of Portugal." Columbus claimed that the profits of his discoveries could be used to conquer Jerusalem and help complete God's plans for a new age. Franciscan friars who supported Columbus believed that an "Age of the Holy Spirit," which would precede the end of the world, was coming soon, and some of them came to see the New World as the place where such an age might begin.

Europe's outreach into the Atlantic was probably not the result of science or strength as much as of delusion and desperation. This was a space race where it helped to come from behind. The prosperous cultures with access to the Indian Ocean felt no need to explore remote lands and seas for new resources. For cash-strapped Europe, however, the attempt to exploit the Atlantic for new products was like the efforts of underdeveloped countries today, anxiously drilling for offshore wealth from oil or natural gas. In some ways, it paid off.

IN PERSPECTIVE: Beyond Empires

The imperial habit was spreading, and new empires were forming in environments that had never experienced imperialism before. Russia, for example, extended empire to the Eurasian far north. Mwene Mutapa introduced it in sub-Saharan East Africa. The Aztecs and Incas practiced it in the Americas on an unprecedented scale. Nonetheless, most of Africa and the Americas, as well as the whole of Australia and most of the Pacific island world, as far as we know, had still not experienced anything like empire. Most of the world remained in the

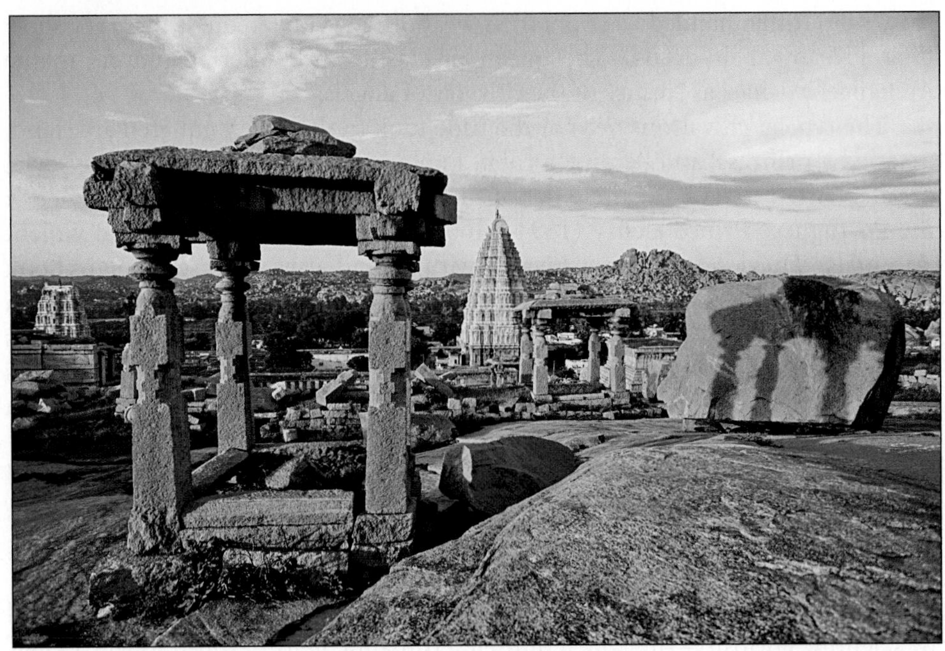

Vijayanagar. The steep, gleaming dome that dominates the ruins of Vijayanagar surmounts a shrine nearly 500 years older than the city itself, which arose in the fourteenth century as a focus of resistance against Muslim invaders from the north, on the rocky, easily defended site. By the early fifteenth century, Vijayanagar was the capital of a large state, formed by conquest and controlling much of southern India.

hands of communities with modest political ambitions—kinship networks, chiefdoms, or small states. More remarkably, perhaps, some regions with an imperial past, or under imperialist threat, shied away. Instead, they developed systems in which independent states coexisted with varying degrees of mutual hostility.

In North Africa, for instance, Mamluk Egypt was an immensely rich and productive state but remained confined to the Nile valley, unable to expand beyond the deserts that fringed it. Westward, along Africa's Mediterranean coast, lay numerous small states, founded on the profits of trade or piracy, where Mediterranean and Saharan trade routes met. At the western end of North Africa, Morocco emerged as a kingdom on the edge of the Islamic world, holding Christendom at bay.

South and southeast Asia also housed state systems. In India, the sultanate of Delhi never recovered from the setbacks of the mid–fourteenth century. Hindu states proliferated, some warlike, specifically, toward Islam. The most militaristic, perhaps, was Vijayanagar—the name means "City of Victories"—Abd-ar-Razzak's destination on his ocean voyage from Iran in 1417. Chinese expansion nibbled at the edges of southeast Asia, but China's renunciation of imperialism left the native states of the region free to try one another's strength. The Thai—founders of what is now called Thailand—certainly had expansionist ambitions. In the early fifteenth century, they created the region's largest state at the expense of the Burmese, Khmer, Mons, and Malays. Nonetheless, the region lacked a dominant empire and remained home to a state system in which a number of regional states contended with each other.

Most of Europe, too, continued to enclose a state system. East of the Vistula River, where geography favored the formation of large states, Russia, as we have seen, undertook a massive imperial enterprise. A brief union of the Polish and Lithuanian states in 1386 created what, on the map, at least, also looked like an empire from the Baltic to the Black Sea. Farther west, however, small or middling states got stronger, and the dream of reuniting them and recreating the old Roman Empire faded—or began to look unrealistic. Something like what we now call national feeling emerged where people's mutually intelligible speech and a common sense of identity, defined by birth, caused them to merge into a single community. National communities adopted patron saints. At international gatherings, such as universities and church councils, people defined themselves according to the nation to which they belonged and engaged in ferocious disputes over precedence. States increasingly asserted absolute sovereignty, rejecting any obligation to defer to such traditionally supranational authorities as the church or the Holy Roman Emperor. When, for instance, the Emperor Sigismund visited England in 1415, a knight rode into the sea to challenge him to renounce all claim to authority in England before he was allowed to disembark. Kings of France called themselves "emperors in their own realm" and those of Castile in Spain asserted "my sovereign absolute power."

Some rulers developed ideological grounds for their claims to absolute sovereignty. French kings were supposedly endowed with divine powers to heal. Richard II of England (r. 1377–1399) had himself painted attended by angels, opening his hands to receive the body of Christ from the hands of the Virgin Mary herself.

CHRONOLOGY

ca. 1325	Aztecs found city of Tenochtitlán, according to legend
1368	Beginning of Ming dynasty
1370–1406	Reign of Timur
Late fourteenth century	Ethiopia expands into surrounding regions
1405	First voyage of Zheng He
1417	Voyage of Abd-ar-Razzak to Vijayanagar (India)
1430s	Portuguese establish way stations in Azores
1440s	Portuguese begin to obtain slaves from West Africa
ca. 1450	Inca begin period of expansion and conquest
1453	Ottomans capture Constantinople
1462–1505	Reign of Ivan the Great
ca. 1475	Center of power in southern Africa shifts from Zimbabwe to Mwene Mutapa
1480s	Portuguese make contact with Kingdom of Kongo
1482	Portuguese establish trading post of São Jorge da Mina on West African coast
1484	Sugar production begins in Canary Islands
1490s	First Portuguese diplomatic missions arrive in Ethiopia
1492–1493	First voyage of Christopher Columbus; Spanish kingdom of Castile captures Granada, last Muslim kingdom in Spain
1496	John Cabot discovers direct route across North Atlantic
1497	Pilgrimage of Muhammed Touray Askia, ruler of Songhay, to Mecca; first voyage of Vasco da Gama
1500	Vasco da Gama reaches India; Aztec Empire at its peak

Meanwhile, the power of the state really did increase. One reason was improved communications. As paper replaced parchment, increasing the output of documents, royal bureaucracies reached more people in more parts of the realm. Changes in the concept of law also strengthened the state. Traditionally, the law was a body of wisdom handed down from the past. Now it came to be seen as a code that kings and parliaments could endlessly change and recreate. The state's power also expanded over vast new areas of public life and common welfare: labor relations, wages, prices, land tenure, markets, the food supply, livestock breeding, and even what people could wear.

Meanwhile, the power of the church declined. Between 1378 and 1415, rulers in Latin Christendom could not agree whom to recognize as pope. The power vacuum eroded what little unity Christendom still had. Secular states became stronger as heresies arose. Under the influence of reformers who demanded—among other changes—lay control of appointments in the church and worship in everyday language, Bohemia for a time refused to recognize papal authority. Reformers known as conciliarists argued that the church should become a kind of republic, with power transferred from Rome to bishops who would meet periodically.

How much difference did the state system make to Europe's prospects? On the one hand, the state system deprived Europeans of unified command of the sort found, for instance, in the Chinese or Ottoman Empires. On the other hand, it stimulated competition among rulers, multiplying the possible sources of patronage available to innovators. For European maritime expansion, the state system was not decisive in launching most initiatives. Explorers and would-be empire builders relied on private enterprise, with little or no state backing. Columbus, for instance, got no direct financial support from the Spanish crown—the myth that Queen Isabella of Castile pawned her jewels for him is nonsense. Prince Henry's Atlantic enterprise was a private venture. Furthermore, as the example of southeast Asia shows, a state system was not in itself sufficient to produce overseas imperialism. For that, the stimulus of coming from behind was necessary. Asian states were at the nodes of the world's richest trades. They had no need to explore new markets or conquer new centers of production, because everything came to them anyway. Europeans, on the other hand, had to expand to gain access to anything worth exploiting.

For all its hesitations and limitations, fifteenth-century expansion was new and potentially world changing. The new routes pioneered in the 1490s linked the populous central belt of Eurasia to the Americas and Africa, and Europe to Asia by sea. We can see the beginnings of a framework of an interconnected globe—a **world system** able to encompass the planet. The expanding empires of the age were reaching toward each other. Where they made contact, they became arenas of unprecedented scale for trade and for transmitting technology, ideas, sentiments, and ways of life. The consequences would transform the world of the next three centuries: worldwide encounters, commerce, conflict, contagion, and cultural and ecological exchange.

PROBLEMS AND PARALLELS

1. Why can the last half of the fifteenth century be considered an age of expansion? How did the beginnings of a world system emerge around 1500?
2. Why were African states fragile in this period?
3. What is meant by the term ecological imperialism? How did the Inca exploit the many different ecosystems of their empire? What was the role of tributary networks in the Aztec Empire?
4. How did the Russian and Turkish worlds expand in the fourteenth and fifteenth centuries?
5. Why did the Chinese turn away from maritime expansionism in the fifteenth century? Why was frontier stability more important than expansion?
6. How do the developments discussed in this chapter demonstrate the importance of winds in world history? Why did the beginnings of European oceanic imperialism have as much to do with geography as with culture?

DOCUMENTS IN GLOBAL HISTORY

- From *The Narrative of the Journey of Abd-ar-Razzak*
- Leo Africanus on Timbuktu
- The founding of Tenochtitlán
- From the *Muqaddimah* by Ibn Khaldun
- A contemporary describes Timur
- From Ma Huan, *The Overall Survey of the Ocean's Shores*

Please see the Primary Source DVD for additional sources related to this chapter.

READ ON

The material on Abd-ar-Razzak comes from R. H. Major, ed., *India in the Fifteenth Century* (1964). D. Ringrose, *Expansion and Global Interaction*, 1200–1700 (2001) gives the background.

On Ethiopia, S. C. Munro-Hay, *Ethiopia: the Unknown Land* (2002), and R. Pankhurst, *The Ethiopians: A History* (2001) are valuable general histories. W. G. Randles, *The Empire of Monomotapa* (1975) is excellent on Mwene Mutapa. On West Africa in this period, E. W. R. Bovill, *The Golden Trade of the Moors* (1995) is a readable classic. Songhay is not well served by books in English but a useful collection of sources is J. O. Hunwick, ed., *Timbuktu and the Songhay Empire: Al-Sa'di's Ta'rîkh al-Sudan Down to 1613, and Other Contemporary Documents* (1999). Anne Hilton, *The Kingdom of Kongo* (1985) is outstanding.

Of histories of the Inca and Aztecs, J. V. Murra, *The Economic Organization of the Inca State* (1980), T. N. D'Altroy, *The Incas* (2003), and M. Smith, *The Aztecs* (2002) are particularly strong on ecological aspects.

My material on the White Sea comes from R. Cormack and D. Gaze, eds., *Art of Holy Russia* (1998). J. Martin, *Treasures of the Land of Darkness* (2004) is enthralling on the economic background to Russian expansion. I. Gray, *Ivan III and the Unification of Russia* (1972) is a businesslike introduction. Ibn Khaldun's great work is *The Muqaddimah: An Introduction to History,* tr. Franz Rosenthal (1969). B. F. Manz, The Rise and Rule of Tamerlane (1999) is the outstanding work on its subject.

For the Ottomans, see H. Inalcik, *The Ottoman Empire: The Classical Age* (2001). E. L. Dreyer, Early Ming China (1982), and *Zheng He: China and the Oceans in the Early Ming Dynasty* (2006) cover the Chinese topics of this chapter admirably. L. Levathes, *When China Ruled the Seas* (1997) is readable and reliable.

On Europe C. Allmand, ed., *The New Cambridge Medieval History, VII* (2005) is comprehensive, while M. Aston, *The Prospect of Europe* (1968) offers a short introduction. On Portuguese expansion, P. E. Russell, *Henry the Navigato*r (2001) is admirable, and F. Bethencourt and D. Curto, eds., *The Portuguese Empire* (1998) provides a broad survey. P. O. Kristeller, *The Cambridge Companion to Renaissance Humanism* (1996) is an unsurpassed classic on its topic, and M. H. Keen, *Chivalry* (1986) is on the way to attaining the same status.

PART

Seven

Convergence and Divergence to ca. 1700

CHAPTER 16 Imperial Arenas: New Empires in the Sixteenth and Seventeenth Centuries 410

CHAPTER 17 The Ecological Revolution of the Sixteenth and Seventeenth Centuries 434

CHAPTER 18 Mental Revolutions: Religion and Science in the Sixteenth and Seventeenth Centuries 462

CHAPTER 19 States and Societies: Political and Social Change in the Sixteenth and Seventeenth Centuries 488

A Mixtec worldview of the fifteenth century painted on deer hide. At the center of the world the god Xiutecutli spills the life forces of fire and blood. Trees grow toward each of four directions. At the top, a sun disc, rising over temple steps, signifies east. In the west, where the sun sets, the tree is uncolored.
National Museums and Galleries on Merseyside, Liverpool, England, U.K.

ENVIRONMENT

since 1492
Columbian exchange

since 1513
Atlantic navigation–Gulf Stream mastered

CULTURE

ca.1500–1600
Portuguese maritime empire

since 1565
Pacific Navigation–Japan current mastered

since early 1600s
Dutch navigation of "roaring 40s"

since ca. 1640
Decline of steppelands

mid-16th century
Atlantic slave trade takes off

ca.1550–1650
Expansion of Asian empires

1640
Closing of Japan

1600–1700
Western Scientific Revolution

CHAPTER 16 Imperial Arenas: New Empires in the Sixteenth and Seventeenth Centuries

Portuguese, armed mainly with bows, resist the attack on Hormuz, which restored the island fortress to Persian rule in 1622. This was the first of a long series of campaigns in which indigenous powers ejected the Portuguese from their trading outposts on the coasts of Asia and East Africa.

IN THIS CHAPTER

MARITIME EMPIRES: PORTUGAL, JAPAN, AND THE DUTCH
The Portuguese Example
Asian Examples
The Dutch Connection

LAND EMPIRES: RUSSIA, CHINA, MUGHAL INDIA, AND THE OTTOMANS
China
The Mughal Example in India
The Ottomans

NEW LAND EMPIRES IN THE AMERICAS
Making the New Empires Work

THE GLOBAL BALANCE OF TRADE

IN PERSPECTIVE: The Impact of the Americas

The letter was only one page long. But in it Jeronimo de Quadros poured out his troubles to his king. In 1572, after a career spent fighting up and down the east coast of Africa and Arabia and in the Persian Gulf, he had succeeded his father as commander of a Portuguese fort on the Persian mainland, at a spot the Portuguese called Comorão, modern Kumora. By the end of the 1580s, he was concerned about the rewards for service he hoped to receive back home. All the other Portuguese garrisons in the region had fallen to native enemies. Jeronimo de Quadros's own fort was becoming indefensible. He had, he wrote, only seven Portuguese and 45 native mercenaries under his command to man the fort, control local marauders, and escort traders who might want to do business with Portugal. He had difficulty keeping his men supplied with arrows. Gunpowder and shot were far beyond his reach. Every year, he explained, he had to rebuild his fort after the rains "because it is made of mud." His most revealing problem was the want of sufficient opium to meet the needs of his men. Their task was so hopeless, in this remote and abandoned corner of an overextended empire, that they could only face it with the help of narcotics. His fort fell into enemy hands shortly afterward. Now, like all the Portuguese forts that once dotted the region, it lies in ruins. Quadros's predicament was typical of the sixteenth, seventeenth, and eighteenth centuries, when empires seemed to overreach the limits of the possible and to exceed the scope of the technology at their command.

PERSIAN GULF

• • • • •

Nowadays, *empire* has become one of the dirty words of politics. We recoil from the idea that any political community should be subject to another. But from the sixteenth century to the eighteenth, empires spread as much by collaboration as by conquest. They were not usually held together by force, because no state had enough resources for such a task. Moral effects were mixed. Some communities were victimized, subjugated, exterminated, or enslaved, while others grew rich, as markets expanded and trade routes lengthened. Above all, empires were arenas of exchange—and not solely or primarily of exchange of trade. They stimulated—and sometimes enforced—human migrations on a scale never previously undertaken, over unprecedented distances, and in unprecedented directions. Technologies, religions, political ideas, artistic tastes became interchangeable across vast distances as never before.

FOCUS questions

- HOW WERE empires the agents of change in the sixteenth and seventeenth centuries?
- WHY DID the Dutch replace the Portuguese as the main European imperial power in Asia?
- HOW WERE maritime empires different from land empires in Asia during the sixteenth and seventeenth centuries?
- WHAT ROLES did war and conquest play in the Mughal and Ottoman Empires?
- WHY WERE Native Americans so important in the Spanish conquests of the Aztec and Inca Empires?
- WHY DID the global balance of trade begin to shift during the seventeenth century?

Perhaps most importantly, **imperialism** helped to introduce a new era in evolution. Formerly, each continent had its own peculiar plant and animal life. Everything tended to be different—from human types to microbes. About 500 years ago, this long history of divergence ended. As empires crossed oceans, the continents swapped life-forms. The world we inhabit today began to take shape—in which you can find specimens of the same creatures, wherever climate permits, all over the world (see Chapter 17).

So empires offer a framework for understanding all the major long-range, long-run changes of the period. Western historians used to see the empires founded from Western Europe as the sources of the most important initiatives and even to call the period the "Age of European Expansion." But imperialism was not a peculiarly Western vice. Asian, African, and Native American peoples created and led some of the most impressive empires of the period. And the "European" empires usually depended on non-European collaborators. Indeed, the numbers of Europeans involved were normally small compared with the numbers of native peoples or of non-European migrants from elsewhere. The influences that shaped the empires and made them different from one another generally owed more to environmental or economic circumstances than to their home countries and the traditional allegiances of their ruling elites.

MARITIME EMPIRES: PORTUGAL, JAPAN, AND THE DUTCH

Until about 500 years ago, most empires were concerned with controlling large amounts of two resources: people and land. They may have had ideological or religious reasons for wanting to extend their territorial control; or they may have engaged in conquests out of hatred or insecurity. The economic purpose underlying empire, however, was usually to gain control of, or power over, the places and people that produced valuable goods.

Less commonly, imperial communities could enrich themselves by controlling trade as well as, or even instead of, production. By land, imperialism of this kind is hard to achieve without occupying vast territories, because traders tend to outflank imperialists. At sea, however, the opportunities are better. By seizing what is often a limited number of suitable ports, or by patrolling what are often limited routes of access that winds, currents, and straits shape, imperial-minded people can obtain a stranglehold on trade in some commodities within some climatic or geographical zones. Or they can colonize limited amounts of coastal territory that seaborne communications link to produce and ship commercial commodities for their own profit. As we have seen, empires of these kinds flourished in the ancient and medieval Mediterranean and maritime Asia.

From the sixteenth to the eighteenth centuries, opportunities multiplied to found and extend such empires. Technological improvements accompanied the new opportunities. European or European-designed ships began to rival, and even outclass, those of traditional Asian construction, partly thanks to borrowings from Asian technology, such as rudders, bulkheads between the

MAKING CONNECTIONS

LAND EMPIRES AND MARITIME EMPIRES COMPARED

TYPE OF EMPIRE	CHARACTERISTICS
Maritime	• Control of international trade via strategic seizure of suitable ports, control of sea-lanes • Colonization of limited coastal territory • Production and shipment of high-value commodities • Limited military confrontation and investment in imperial colonies • Exploitation of improved maritime technology • Expanded use of sea charts for exploration, control of far-flung regions • Dependence on native collaborators
Land	• Emphasis on control of large amounts of people and land • Large military investment required to staff outposts and fund armies • Land and sea access routes vulnerable unless controlled • Massive capital investment to support imperial colonies and build infrastructure • Superior technology needed to overcome resistance from natives • Expanded social and cultural contacts with imperial subjects • Dependence on native collaborators

ship's interior compartments, more streamlined hulls, and technical aids to navigation. Improved artillery and fortifications made it ever easier to defend coastal trading posts. Naval powers could control sea-lanes or exclude rival ships by aggressive policing. Meanwhile, sea charts gradually became an accepted and necessary part of nautical equipment. The expanding reach of exploration improved these nautical maps. Longitude-finding techniques also improved, although no really reliable method was devised until the late eighteenth century.

Improved technology, however, was of little use without new routes where it could be deployed. As we saw in Chapter 15, for most of history, the world's only really effective long-range, ocean-crossing routes were confined to monsoonal seas. In the sixteenth century, however, the monopoly of the Indian Ocean ended. With the discovery of the Gulf Stream in 1513, the last major element of the wind and current system of the Atlantic became known to navigators. In the Pacific, Spanish navigators explored the easterly wind corridors that link the New World to Asia, but the route back eluded them until an expedition of 1564–1565 solved the problem by exploiting the way the winds circulate in the northern Pacific, using the Japan Current to get back to the western coast of America from the Philippines. Finally, in the early seventeenth century, Dutch sailors began to exploit the fierce westerly winds that enable sailing ships to circle the globe around 40 degrees latitude south. This made it possible to link the commerce of the Atlantic, Pacific, and Indian Oceans with new speed and reliability. As explorers cracked the wind codes of the world's oceans, previously inconceivable interconnections became possible: directly between Europe and the Indian Ocean; between America and Asia; or among Europe, Africa, and the Americas.

Maritime Imperialism: Technology and Sea Routes

1513	Gulf Stream discovered
1520s–1530s	Spanish navigators explore easterly wind corridors that link the New World to Asia
1564–1565	Northern Pacific route between Asia and New World discovered
Early seventeenth century	Dutch use westerlies to circumnavigate globe

The Portuguese Example

On an unprecedented scale, Europeans could now gain access to the commerce of the Indian Ocean and maritime Asia. The main motive was simple. The economies of the region were hugely richer and more productive than those of Europe. Anyone who could get ships into the region and carry some of its trade could make money. Moreover, the region produced luxury manufactures of a quality Europeans could not produce for themselves: especially textiles from India and China and porcelain from China and Japan. Even more important were foodstuffs, drugs, and spices. Finally, eastern markets were highly exploitable. Gold was relatively cheap, in exchange for silver, in China but relatively expensive in India. Canny traders could make fortunes out of the difference.

Portugal was well placed to take advantage, partly thanks to its position on the Atlantic edge. Portuguese venturers opened direct trade with the pepper-growing region of southern India in 1500 and founded a coastal trading post nearby at Goa in 1510. They also established direct access to the trading world of the islands off southeast Asia. They began direct contact with Thailand and China in the second decade of the sixteenth century and with Japan in the 1540s.

In some ways, the Portuguese enterprise in Asia was a classic case of maritime imperialism. They used force to compel unwilling partners to trade with them, especially in the "Spice Islands" of what is now eastern Indonesia, where low-bulk, high-value spices and aromatics grew. They attacked rival shipping. They established expensive bases at the mouth of the Red Sea, on the coast of East Africa, and in the Persian Gulf—and, eventually, even on the Persian coast—in unsuccessful efforts to divert trade into their own hands and to strangle alternative routes. In 1529, they agreed with Spain to extend to the Pacific the system they had already

Goa. Jan van Linschoten's travels in the Portuguese trading posts of the East in the late sixteenth century were an intelligence-gathering mission that helped to launch Dutch overseas expansion. The engravings that illustrated the published versions of his account of his trip were based on drawings he claimed to have made from life. This one depicts the street life of Goa in Portuguese India. Note the business being recorded at the table of the public scribe and the merchants gathering around it, the unsuccessful peddler in European dress, the sale of a concubine on the left, and that characteristic institution of Portuguese colonial life, the almshouse, on the right.

agreed to observe in the Atlantic, in which each guaranteed the other's monopoly over selected routes, while denying access to other powers. In the early seventeenth century, Portugal tried to control by force the trade of Sri Lanka—the world's main source of cinnamon (see Map 16.1).

Still, Portuguese imperialism was, by the standards of native Asian empires of the day, a feeble and shallow affair—a minor irritant, causing only local or temporary disruption. The main business of the Portuguese was to participate as shippers and traders in the existing commerce of Asia along traditional routes. Three or four Portuguese ships a year carried the whole of the Indian pepper trade to Europe in the 1590s. A hundred years later, when other European trading communities had joined in the business, 400 ships left Europe for Asia, most of them destined to return with Asian goods. But direct dealing with Europe was only a secondary element. Most of Asia's Portuguese lived beyond areas of Portuguese rule, as servants, mercenaries, technicians, missionaries, or commercial agents in Asian states. They were welcome because their trading activities and their work as shippers in established trades enriched existing economies.

Typically, Portuguese blended into local society as well as local politics and regional trade by marrying or living with local women, who supported their husbands' business. African or Indian wives administered their Portuguese husbands' estates while the latter were away on trading voyages. Such marriages could be mutually beneficial. The merchant got access to valuable commercial contacts. His bride acquired substantial rights to share the profits of his business under Portuguese law. Her family was often rewarded with offices in Portuguese firms or trading posts.

Until the second half of the seventeenth century, most European involvement in Asia was of the same sort, what historians have called "trading-post empires."

MAP 16.1

Maritime Imperialism in the Indian and Pacific Oceans, 1500–1700

- ◆ Portuguese trading post with date
- ◆ Dutch trading post with date
- ◆ Spanish trading post with date
- ◆ English trading post with date
- ○ major Chinese port
- → Japanese campaigns in Korea, 1592–1598
- → Japanese expansion
- → trade routes
- → Manila galleon from Mexico

There were direct trades with Europe, chiefly in spices, principally pepper, conducted by aspiring monopolists. These monopolists were the Portuguese crown and, from the early 1600s, English and Dutch companies. A similar trade with the New World, chiefly in Chinese silks and porcelain, traveled annually in a single Spanish galleon via Spain's colonial outpost in Manila in the Philippines. But European participation in commerce between Asian countries and in shipping ventures within Asian waters eclipsed these trades in value and extent.

Asian Examples

To understand the increased opportunities for Europeans, we need to look at the context of the enormously increased activity—as merchants, colonists, and even maritime imperialists—of native Asian states and communities. At either end of maritime Asia—in Japan in the east and in Oman on the coast of Arabia and the Ottoman Empire in the west—were rulers and adventurers interested in maritime imperialism (see Map 16.1).

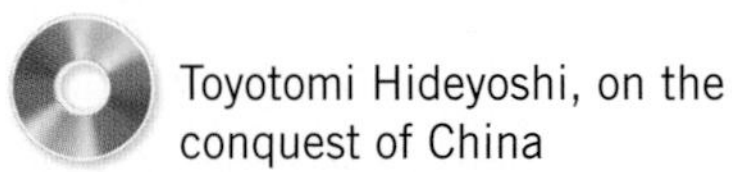
Toyotomi Hideyoshi, on the conquest of China

Toyotomi Hideyoshi, the warlord who took over Japan in 1585, is a case in point. He sent demands for submission to the kingdoms of mainland southeast Asia and to the Spanish governor in the Philippines. He vowed to ravish China "like a maiden" and "crush it like an egg." He proclaimed himself the gods' choice for mastery of the world. It sounds insane. But it was a rational strategy in the circumstances. Civil wars had militarized Japanese society. Professional warriors needed employment. Arms industries needed markets. Warlords' energies had to be redeployed. Japanese pirates had shown how vulnerable China was, raiding Chinese cities far inland and holding them to ransom.

Hideyoshi imagined his future conquests vividly. The Koreans and Chinese would "learn Japanese customs," and the Japanese emperor would be invested with the mandate of heaven. At first when the Japanese invaded in 1592, Korea seemed easily conquerable. But the Korean navy had long experience of conflict against pirates and was equipped with new technology: "turtle ships" with reinforced hulls and ship-killing cannon. In combination with the typhoon-lashed seas and the Chinese fleet, the Korean sailors made it impossible for the Japanese to supply armies in Korea. After Hideyoshi's death in September 1598, the Japanese aborted their campaigns on the mainland of Asia.

It was not, however, the end of Japanese expansion. Okinawa and the Ryukyu Islands south of Japan became, in effect, a Japanese dependency by conquest in 1609. The northern land frontier of Japan gradually expanded to fill the whole of what we now think of as the Japanese home islands, at the expense of the native Ainu people (see Chapter 19). And in the eighteenth century, Japanese expansion met that of Russia in the northern Pacific, where the two powers disputed control of the huge island of Sakhalin. Meanwhile, although the Japanese state formally renounced southward expansion and, from the 1630s, practically forbade its subjects to travel overseas, illegal migrants and "pirates" continued to take part in the new economic opportunities trade and colonization opened up in southeast Asia. Some were Christians, fleeing from persecution, like the community that a Portuguese missionary met in mid–seventeenth century Burma—close-knit, hungry for the sacraments, longing to build a church. Most Japanese migration, however, was, like that of the Chinese, economically motivated. Many surviving letters show that the Japanese authorities were only half-hearted in suppressing the migrants' movements and content to allow them to send money home to enrich the domestic economy.

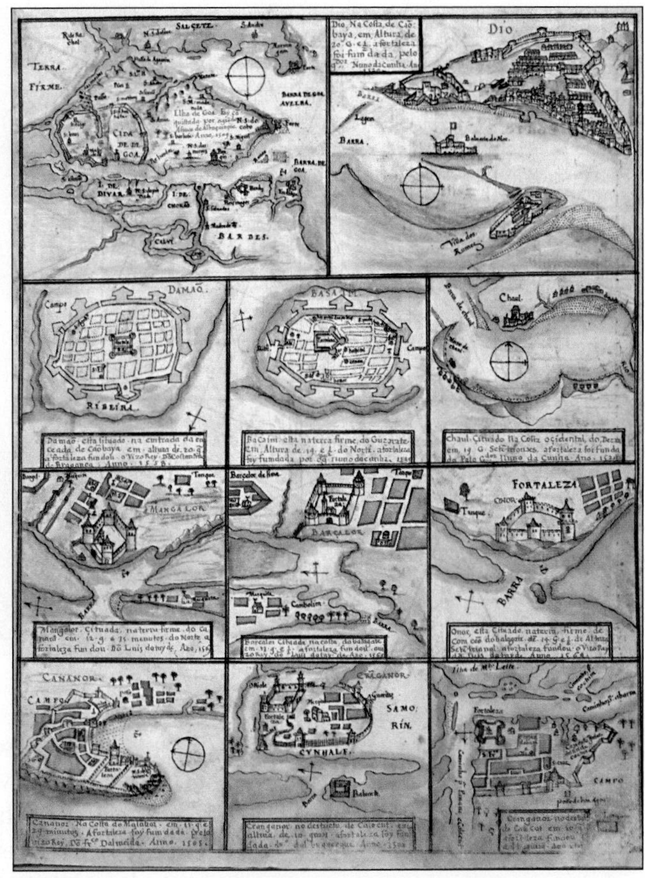

The *Estado da India*. The empire that the Portuguese called the *Estado da India* was actually a string of trading posts around the edges of the Indian Ocean and east Asia. The outposts depicted here were in India in 1630, shortly before Portugal began to withdraw from most of the region in the face of native hostility and Dutch competition. Note how lightly fortified most of these places are and how several of them include mosques—sometimes within, sometimes outside the walls. Like other European overseas expansion, that of Portugal depended on native people's willingness to collaborate with it and tolerate it.

Even greater was the outpouring of colonists from China. In many colonial outposts—in the Spanish colony of Manila, for example—though the nominal authority, the garrisons, and the guns were European or under European officers, the real colonists, who settled the towns and exploited the economy, were Chinese. Without a metropolitan government of their own committed to overseas imperialism, the migrants used Western empire builders to protect and promote their own activities.

Batavia, for example, bore the old Roman name for Holland. Its founder in 1619 was a Dutch soldier, Jan Pieterszoon Coen. Its sovereign proprietors were the directors of the Dutch East India Company, which had a government-granted monopoly on trade between Holland and Asia. But the entrepreneurs who created its economy and attracted settlers to it in its great days were Coen's two principal Chinese collaborators: Souw Beng Kong, known as Bencon—the godfather figure of the Chinese community—and the energetic labor broker whom the Dutch called Jan Con. Lanterns inscribed "The Original Founder of the Region" flanked the entrance to Bencon's country house. In Chinese eyes, the Dutch role was subordinate.

The Dutch merchant Pieter Cnoll painted in 1644 by Jacob Coeman. At one level, this seems an ordinary scene: a rich colonial trader with his elegant family and the trappings of his wealth. But the slave stealing an apple went on to become a famous bandit chief, while Cornelia, Cnoll's half-Japanese wife, became, after Cnoll's death, the richest businesswoman in the Dutch East Indies and the notorious protagonist of an agonizingly long and expensive divorce case against her second husband.

The Chinese character of the colony became even more marked after 1684, when the Chinese government relaxed controls on emigration. Thousands of Chinese residents enriched China by sending money home—as Jan Con had, feeling guilty for deserting his parents' home. Chinese shipping in Batavia's harbor normally outnumbered that of any other country by at least two and a half to one.

Overwhelmingly, the migrants were what we would now call economic refugees—escapees from poverty and contempt at home. In 1603, when the first of a long series of hate riots provoked a massacre of the local Chinese by native Filipinos in Manila, the emperor of China refused to intervene on the grounds that his murdered subjects were "scum, ungrateful to China, their land, their parents and ancestors for they had failed to return to China for so many years that such people were deemed to be of little worth." Yet the Chinese colony in the Philippines kept growing. By 1621, it had regained its premassacre level of 15,000, and it had more than doubled by the time of the next massacre in 1639.

Chinese and Japanese participated in empires and became colonists, because their home governments, in attempts to control trade, restricted their commercial opportunities. Most merchants who operated in maritime Asia and the Indian Ocean, therefore, tended to come from other parts of Asia—especially from India and Armenia. The most important single source of long-range commercial enterprise was Gujarat, in northern India. Gujaratis linked maritime trade with that of the Armenian and Indian traders dispersed throughout Central Asia and Persia. They were the biggest operators in banking and commerce in the Arabian Sea. Sometimes the same individuals engaged in both types of business. Virji Vora, reputedly the richest man in the world in the early seventeenth century, was the biggest creditor of European merchants in India. He was a capitalist in the truest sense of the word, ever reinvesting his profits in commercial enterprise, so that looters who attacked his house were disappointed not to find great riches there. European merchants felt oppressed by Gujarati power in key markets. In 1692, for instance, the Dutch East India Company had to sell a large cargo of spices at half price to a Gujarati broker, because the company's representatives feared the power of another Gujarati—Muhammad Sahid, who was trying to control the market and was willing to undercut any competitor.

Capitalism—contrary to the traditional assumptions of Western historians—was not a European speciality. Nor was it peculiar to any religious tradition. Max Weber, one of the most influential sociologists ever, first proposed in 1904 the idea that religion predisposes some communities to particular kinds of economic behavior. But in most cases, the theory does not seem to work. Jains (JAH-eens), Christians, and Muslims were all prominent in Gujarat's trading community. Despite the common belief that Hinduism regards commerce as a polluting and demeaning activity, even Hindus could engage in capitalism without losing caste. Hindus dominated the trade of Goa, although nominally this was a Portuguese-controlled city. In an auction in 1630, for instance, the local Hindu merchants outbade their Portuguese counterparts and the government itself for about half of what was on offer. In seventeenth-century Kerala, south of Goa, most bankers were Brahmins—Hindus of the highest caste—who, according to Dutch complaints, "by and large control the pepper trade."

The Dutch Connection

For over 100 years, from their arrival in the Indian Ocean in 1498, the Portuguese fitted into this Asian-dominated world, without provoking seriously disruptive conflicts. Gradually, however, from roughly the 1620s, the situation changed. Asian hosts lost patience with the presence of sovereign ports and offshore trading establishments, where Portuguese religious intolerance damaged trade by discriminating against Muslim and Hindu merchants. As Asian empires became more assertive, they eliminated key Portuguese outposts. Even after the capture of the mainland forts of which Jeronimo de Quadros was a commander, Portuguese occupation of the offshore trading post of Hormuz was tolerated until 1622, when the Portuguese were expelled from the Persian Gulf. A series of similar expulsions followed: from Hooghly—their fort in Bengal—in 1632, from Ethiopia in 1634, and from Japan in 1639. From 1640, their own attitude to their Asian interests changed. Portugal became involved in a long war against Spain that deflected Portuguese resources from the east. Atlantic priorities took over, as Portugal's Brazilian sugar plantations became increasingly profitable and the transatlantic slave trade boomed (see Chapter 20).

Moreover, Asian communities could become more choosey about their partnerships with the Portuguese because far more European buyers and shippers were now operating in maritime Asia. English, French, and Scandinavians all played increasing roles in the seventeenth century, but the contribution of the Dutch eclipsed them all.

The provinces of Holland and Zealand, in what is today the Netherlands, were, like Portugal, poor communities on Western Europe's ocean edge. Their people had a long-standing maritime vocation as fishermen, whalers, and shippers in northern seas. In the late sixteenth

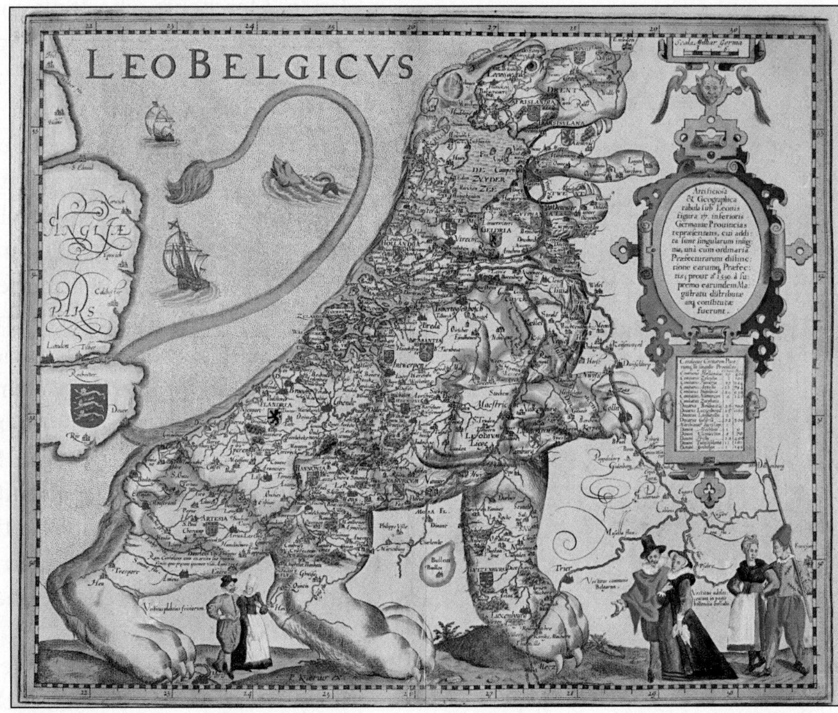

The Netherlands. Although the Netherlands were divided into 17 provinces, all determined to preserve their own separate institutions and ways of life, the inhabitants long had a sense of common identity. This map of 1550 expresses that unity by depicting the provinces as "the Belgian lion"—which was already a traditional image—strong and warlike, clawing and snapping at Germany across the Rhine, lashing the North Sea with its tail. But it also hints at the cultural differences that divided the provinces from each other by showing how the traditional dress of Holland and Belgium, shown on the right, was different from that of the province of Frisia, shown on the left. From the 1560s to 1648, religious and political conflicts heightened the differences between the northern and southern provinces of the Netherlands and shattered their sense of unity. In consequence, two separate states emerged: a Protestant-ruled republic took shape in the seven northern provinces, while the rest of the Netherlands, which eventually became modern Belgium, remained loyal to the Catholic Habsburg dynasty.

century, merchants from the Netherlands broke into the trading world of the Mediterranean. In part they were driven by necessities arising from their rebellion against their ruler—who, by a series of dynastic accidents, happened also to be king of Spain. In part, too, a civil war against the provinces to their south in what is today Belgium drove them. Netherlanders' contact with long-distance trade began because the Portuguese used Antwerp in the southern Netherlands as the clearinghouse for distributing Asian spices into northern Europe. During the war, many merchants from Antwerp migrated north to escape Spanish control. The commercial center of gravity in the Low Countries shifted with them to Holland. Meanwhile, in 1580, the king of Spain also inherited the throne of Portugal. This made Portuguese ships and possessions fair game in the eyes of Dutch rebels.

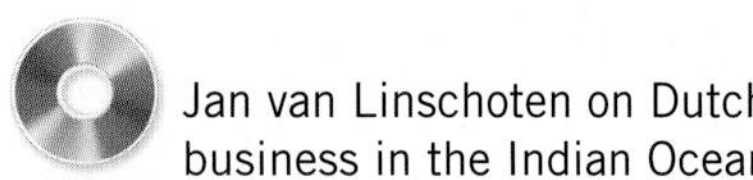
Jan van Linschoten on Dutch business in the Indian Ocean

In the 1590s, Jan van Linschoten, a Dutch servant of the Portuguese Archbishop of Goa, explored the prospects of extending Dutch business into the Indian Ocean. The publication of his findings ignited a craze. In 1602, leading merchants of the port of Amsterdam formed a **joint-stock company** to exploit, as a monopoly, trade with Asia.

Even at its height, Holland's would-be monopoly of the rarer spices—cloves, nutmeg, cinnamon, and mace—was a leaky vessel. Nevertheless, the Dutch did establish a dominant position as carriers of Europe's Asian trade in the seventeenth century, effectively replacing the Portuguese while keeping well ahead of other European rivals in all theaters and—in combination with political instability in Central Asia—helping to deflect trade from the Silk Roads. Four reasons underpinned Dutch success: the speed and efficiency of their route; the problems that harassed the Portuguese seaborne empire in the east as some indigenous states transferred their favor to the Dutch; the selectively aggressive policies that, as we shall see, gradually brought the Dutch control of more—and more valuable—production of Asian communities than any European rivals; and above all, the privileged position they established in trade with Japan.

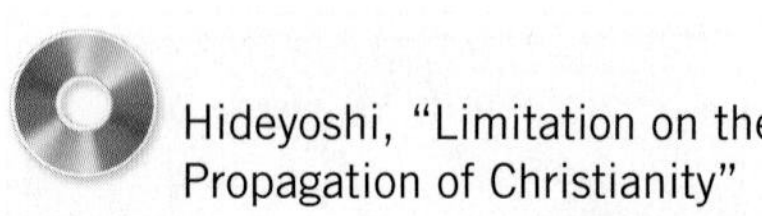
Hideyoshi, "Limitation on the Propagation of Christianity"

The most valuable trading enterprise of maritime Asia led to Japan, because Japan was the world's leading producer of silver. Silver was relatively cheap in Japan. Merchants who took goods there, or performed services for Japanese businesses or rulers, could exchange the silver on favorable terms for profitable trade goods elsewhere. They used it to buy pepper and cotton textiles in India and aromatic woods and spices from Indonesia. In China they acquired silks, porcelain, and rhubarb, which was prized as a laxative in Western medicine at this time. Increasingly they bought tea, which grew in importance as tastes changed, along with other aspects of culture, along new trade routes. Japanese silver supplied more cash for the world's markets, stimulating economic activity.

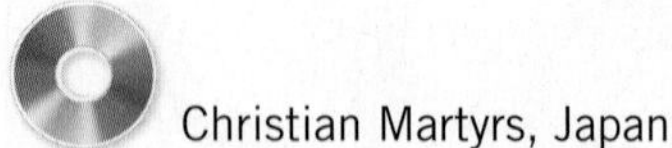
Christian Martyrs, Japan

However, Japan's willingness to participate in the spreading web of economic interconnections almost collapsed in the 1630s. The main reason for this was the success of Catholic missionaries, who had accompanied Portuguese and Spanish merchants in the country and made hundreds of thousands of converts. Fears that this alien religion would undermine traditional loyalties to the state provoked an official ban on Christianity in 1597, and the bloody martyrdom of Catholic clergy and converts until Christianity was driven underground in 1638–1639. From 1640, Dutch merchants were the only Europeans allowed in Japan. The Japanese government channeled Dutch trade through an island off the port of Nagasaki and strictly monitored the merchants' contact with Japanese subjects for more than 200 years.

Yet to be able to continue to trade in Japan at all was an enormous bonus. For the rest of the seventeenth century—until other Europeans began to build up their trade in other parts of Asia to levels at which they could generate comparable earnings—the Dutch dominated the handling of the most valuable products of China and southeast Asia for European markets. The Netherlands—formerly a poor and marginal part of Europe—experienced a "Golden Age" of wealth, art, empire-building, and military and naval power. Dutch imperialists challenged the Spanish monarchy in parts of the New World. They drove the Portuguese out of Malacca in 1641, Sri Lanka in the 1650s, and from many places in India thereafter. They fought off Spain and France in the seventeenth century. Meanwhile, they drove the English out of the Spice Islands and defeated them on the sea. Eventually, in 1688–1699 the Dutch ruler, taking advantage of internal conflicts in Britain, invaded England and became its king by deposing his English father-in-law.

The fall of Makassar, June 12, 1660, painted by Frederik Woldemar. The capture of Makassar in what is today Indonesia was part of the Dutch campaign to build an empire in the East Indies. Makassar was an independent sultanate whose ruler was supported by the Portuguese, and the painting shows a Portuguese ship that the Dutch had already taken. While the guns in the sultan's palace exchange fire with the Dutch ships, native troops march to the sultan's aid. The neutral English trading post flies the flag of St. George. The decisive moment of the encounter came when a Dutch landing party seized the stronghold.

A further consequence of the growing wealth and power of the Dutch was growing ambition in empire-building in Asia. Increasingly, from the 1660s, they aimed to control not only trade in valuable commodities, but also their production. Refugees from Dutch aggression elsewhere poured into Makassar. Malays swelled its ships' crews. Moluccans brought their know-how in growing spices. Portuguese from Malacca introduced their long-range trading contacts. Makassar became their "second and better Malacca." According to a Dominican friar who visited in 1658, it was "one of the greatest emporia of Asia" with a ruler who collected European books and scientific instruments.

In the 1650s, the Dutch began a relentless war in the East Indies. "Do you believe," sneered the sultan of Makassar, "that God has reserved for your trade alone islands which lie so far from your homeland?" The conquest took nearly 20 years. That of Bantam, on Java, with its big pepper output, followed in the early 1680s. Southeast Asia's age of trade was ending as native Asian cultivators abandoned cash crops that seemed only to attract foreign predators.

Domingo Navarrete, "Of My Stay in the Kingdom of Makassar"

Other European trading communities also began to turn from maritime imperialism, based on control of trade, to territorial imperialism, which aimed to control production. At first their efforts were modest and unsuccessful. The Portuguese expanded outward from Goa and in the 1680s conquered the passes leading toward the Deccan, acquiring a subject population of about 30,000 people. The French crown, which had opened a permanent trading establishment at Pondicherry in southeast India in 1674, contemplated taking over Thailand but had to withdraw in humiliation. The English East India Company, founded in 1600, challenged the Mughal Empire in India to war but was defeated in 1685–1688.

Gradually, however, in the eighteenth century, Europeans would take more and more production under their direct control, building up land empires in Asia that transformed the global economy. The profits Europeans made in Asian trade in the sixteenth and seventeenth centuries had modified Europe's age-old trading deficit with Asia in Europe's favor. Now it could be reversed, as Europeans not only influenced markets but also manipulated production.

European Maritime Imperialism in the Indian and Pacific Oceans, 1500–1700

1500	Portuguese begin direct trade with southern India
1510	Portuguese trading post at Goa established
1571	Spanish trading post of Manila founded
1600	English East India Company established
1602	Dutch East India Company founded
1619	Dutch found trading post of Batavia (Indonesia)
1620–1640	Portuguese expelled from trading posts in Persian Gulf and Indian Ocean
1640	Dutch merchants only Europeans allowed in Japan
1674	French establish trading post at Pondicherry (India)

LAND EMPIRES: RUSSIA, CHINA, MUGHAL INDIA, AND THE OTTOMANS

These European land empires in Asia were, however, all modest affairs until well into the eighteenth century with one exception—Russia. The conquest of Kazan in 1552 gave the **czars**—as Russian rulers were styled in allusion to "Caesar"—command of the entire length of the Volga River, which was the great corridor of commerce at the western edge of Asia, and eliminated Russia's rival for control of Siberia's fur trade. The czars' next task was to conquer Siberia and control the production of furs as well as the trade in them (see Map 16.2). In 1555, Czar Ivan IV began to call himself Lord of Siberia. Three years later, he cut a deal with a big dynasty of fur dealers, the Stroganoffs, who were prepared to pay to turn that title into reality. The language of a chroniclers' account reflects the typical mind-set of European conquerors in new worlds: the assertion that pagans have no rights; that their lands are "empty"; that they are subhuman—bestial or monstrous; that financial privileges can promote colonization; and that the work is holy.

From the 1570s, the "protection" of Russian armies "against the fighting men of Siberia" was proclaimed for native peoples who submitted and paid tribute in furs. Like other European military operations on remote frontiers, the Russians ascribed their success to technology: firearms mounted on river barges, from which the waterborne conquerors exchanged bullets for bowshots with defenders on the banks. The Siberian khan was said to be dismayed to hear that "when they shoot from their bows, then there is a flash of fire and a great smoke issues and there is a loud report like thunder in the sky. . . . and it is impossible to shield oneself from them by any trappings of war."

MAP 16.2

Eurasian Land Empires of the Sixteenth and Seventeenth Centuries

- Ottoman Empire
- China (Ming/Qing Empires)
- Russian Empire
- Mughal Empire
- Safavid Empire
- Silk Roads

Native peoples were subjected to tribute and controlled by oaths of traditional, pagan kinds. One Siberian people, the Ostyaks, were made to swear on a bearskin on which a knife, an axe, and a loaf were spread. The oath breaker would choke to death or be cut to pieces in battle with men or bears. The Yakuts had to swear by passing between the quarters of a dismembered dog. The first object of the conquest, however, was not to vanquish these "savages" who ranged the pine forests and tundra but to eliminate the only state able to challenge Russia in the region: the Mongol khanate of Sibir. Thus, the conquest was sold as a Crusade. Russians credited Khan Kuchum with a prophetic vision in October 1581: "The skies burst open and terrifying warriors with shining wings appeared. . . . They encircled Kuchum's army and cried to him, 'Depart from this land, you infidel son of the dark demon, Muhammad, because now it belongs to the Almighty.'"[1]

Russian Expansion Eastward

1552–1556	Russian conquest of Kazan
1555	Czar Ivan IV claims title of Lord of Siberia
ca. Late seventeenth century	Russian and Chinese expansion meets
1689	Treaty of Nerchinsk with China checks Russia's eastward expansion

China

By the late seventeenth century, Russian expansion in eastern Siberia met China's along the Amur River. The Treaty of Nerchinsk of 1689 formalized Chinese claims to vast unexplored lands of doubtful extent in northeast Asia, where some mapmakers imagined a huge landmass pointing to or even joining America.

Much of this territory was effectively beyond any practical frontier of settlement. Generally, however, Chinese imperialism was of an intensive kind compared with Russia's: dedicated not merely to economic exploitation and trade, but also to colonization and to spreading Chinese ways among native peoples. Before the end of the seventeenth century, Outer Mongolia had been crudely incorporated into the Chinese Empire and more than 1.5 million settlers had been lured into Sichuan (seh-chwhan) in southern China by the promise of immunities from taxation. The Xinjiang (sheen-jeeahng) frontier in western China was peopled next. By 1700, 200,000 Chinese migrants had settled there. Manchuria, homeland of the ruling dynasty, the Manchus or Qing (see Chapter 21), was normally closed to settlers, but its rich soils drew them unofficially, until the Chinese government was obliged to accept their presence. Meanwhile, the people of Manchuria were progressively converted to Chinese ways. On all fronts, the pressure of intensive new settlement provoked a cycle of conflicts and solutions familiar to students of European colonialism: tribal peoples reshuffled or penned in reservations; militarized agricultural colonies. Schools spread Chinese language and values.

The Mughal Example in India

The Russian and Chinese empires practiced large-scale colonization, with attempts at new kinds of exploitation of conquered or resettled soil. That was the pattern of most new imperialism from this period onward. But there were still old-fashioned empires, conquest states that tended to leave the political, social, demographic, and economic structures of their conquests largely intact and to exploit them indirectly by levying tribute. The Mughal Empire was the newest and fastest-growing empire of this type in the late sixteenth and seventeenth centuries. Its founder Babur (1483–1530) was an adventurer from Central Asia. His dream was to rebuild his ancestor Timur's empire (see Chapter 15) from the city of Samarkand, but after he had won and lost that city twice over, he turned to India. In 1526, he conquered Delhi in north India and made it his capital (see Map 16.2).

The assault on Chittorgarh. The Mughal Emperor Akbar (r. 1556–1605) commissioned artists to record his campaigns. This painting shows a notable moment in his siege of the supposedly impregnable fortress of Chittorgarh. A tunnel mined by Akbar's engineers exploded, killing hundreds of his own men. When the fort fell, most of the defenders were massacred.

The state Babur founded remained small and unstable until the long rule of his grandson, Akbar (r. 1556–1605). The priorities of Akbar's empire emerge vividly from the account compiled by his friend and minister, Abul Fazl Allami, who begins by describing the emperor's jewel chest, then turns to the treasury, the coinage, the mints for gold and silver, the court cuisine with its gold-laced dishes, the emperor's writing room, his arsenal, his elephants, horses, cows, and camels. When he turns to what he considers the lesser aspects of government, he deals first with protocol, before insisting on a ruler's responsibilities for spiritual welfare; then come accounts of building projects, the army, revenue raising and rites (including hunting and games), lists of great nobles and court personalities.

In short, the Mughal Empire was like a business, run for profit—an investment in power and majesty, with rich returns in the form of tribute and taxes. The heartlands it ruled directly never extended much beyond the limits of Babur's conquests in north India. Beyond this area, existing power structures and local rulers remained in place, supplying money and manpower for future conquests, and linked to the imperial court by every device of networking. The 800 wives Akbar assembled from the rulers who paid him tribute were, in effect, hostages and mediators of sometimes uneasy alliances. Religious tolerance was essential in an empire that straddled the Hindu and Muslim worlds.

The Mughal war machine was so big and costly that it was impossible to operate at a profit without a constant stream of victories. The most dramatic battle of Akbar's reign was the assault on Chittorgarh, the clifftop stronghold of a Hindu prince, in 1567–1568. Of the defending garrison of 8,000 and their 40,000 servants, 30,000 reputedly died in the last onslaught.

In some ways the Mughal Empire seems ramshackle, stumbling between victories, with no central institutions except the imperial court and army, no agreed rules of succession to the throne, and an elite divided by ethnic and religious differences and economic jealousies. The death or old age of every emperor triggered rebellion and civil war. Yet the frontier kept growing, reaching deep into south India by the time of Akbar's death in 1605, slowing during the half century that followed and again advancing rapidly under the emperor Aurangzeb (AW-rang-zahb) (r. 1656–1707) to cover almost the entire subcontinent.

The Ottomans

Abul Fazl Allami, from the *Institutes of Akbar*

West of India were states superficially similar to the Mughals, where Muslim rulers—the Safavid dynasty in Persia and the Ottomans, based in Turkey—dominated huge territories and diverse populations by mobilizing large armies equipped with up-to-date firepower. Historians call both of them empires, but the Safavids ruled a compact state, more or less corresponding to modern Iran and never managed permanently to annex much other territory. Their story belongs in Chapter 19.

The Ottomans, by contrast, were among the most effective empire builders the world had ever known. And although the areas they conquered had all been part of big empires before, the empire the Ottomans built up had no exact precedents. The diversity literally echoed around Lady Mary Wortley Montagu, an English ambassador's wife, in 1718, who heard her servants chatter in ten different languages. "I live," she went on, "in the perpetual hearing of this medley of sounds, which produces a very extraordinary effect upon the people that are born here. They learn all these languages at the same time and without knowing any of them well enough to write or read in it."

In the Ottoman world, boundless ambitions seemed possible. The Ottomans inherited three universalist traditions: one from their steppelander ancestors, whose aim was to make the limits of their empire match those of the sky; another from Islam, whose caliphs' legacy and title the Ottoman sultans claimed; a third from ancient Rome, whose legacy they claimed by conquering much former Roman imperial territory.

Mughals and Ottomans

1517	Ottomans conquer Egypt
1519	Babur founds Mughal Empire
1520–1566	Reign of Ottoman sultan Suleiman the Magnificent
1526	Babur makes Delhi his capital
1529	Ottomans besiege Vienna
1656–1707	Aurangzeb extends Mughal Empire over most of Indian subcontinent

The Ottomans could afford to invest in strategies of conquest, because the sixteenth and seventeenth centuries were an era of prosperity in Turkey unprecedented at the time and unparalleled since. Their heartlands were in the Anatolian plateau. Beyond it, the Ottoman lands were grouped around three great waterways: the eastern Mediterranean, the Black Sea, and the twin rivers of Mesopotamia. Beyond what they called Rumelia, the westernmost of the provinces they ruled directly, lay a broad frontier zone that they controlled and that reached into Central Europe. In North Africa, beyond Egypt, the sultans enjoyed nominal allegiance, at least, from the principalities of the Barbary coast, as far west as what is now Algeria. They got control of most continental transit points between Asia and Europe: the western reaches of the Silk Roads, the Persian Gulf, the Red Sea, and the main ports of Egypt and the eastern Mediterranean seaboard. New trade routes from Europe to south and southeast Asia did not deflect existing trade from Ottoman territories. On the contrary, with improved communications and expanding demand, the total volume of the spice trade grew, and more of it passed through Ottoman hands in the sixteenth century than ever before.

On the other hand, the Ottomans were, in some respects, disadvantageously placed. They had no outlets to the Atlantic or the Indian Ocean—or even to the western Mediterranean, except through narrow straits that enemies controlled. Wars frequently broke out with permanently hostile neighbors—Persians in the east, Christians in the north and west. Armies shuttled back and forth across the empire to keep Europeans and Safavid Persians at bay. Beset, as the Ottomans were, by enemies on every side, their state needed extraordinary strength to survive. Only a state of extraordinary efficiency could expand.

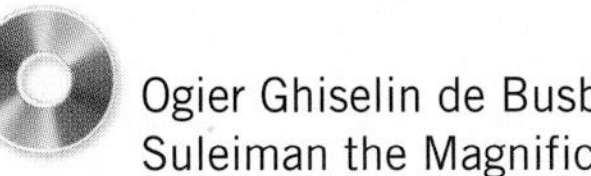
Ogier Ghiselin de Busbecq on Suleiman the Magnificent

Yet expand they did. They overran Egypt in 1517 and exploited it for huge tax surpluses that sustained campaigns elsewhere. The armies of Suleiman (soo-lay-MAHN) the Magnificent (r. 1520–1566) reached Belgrade in Serbia in the northwest Balkans in 1521 and the island of Rhodes in the Aegean in 1522. A punitive expedition against Hungary in 1525 conquered most of that country. Suleiman conquered Iraq from Persia and most of the shores of the Red Sea, while exerting lordship over much of the rest of Arabia. He extended his rule over almost the whole southern shore of the Mediterranean, where his naval commanders, the Barbarossa brothers of Algiers, organized a seaborne empire of war galleys and pirate havens (see Map 16.2). In 1529, Suleiman was called from besieging Vienna in Austria to fight the Persians in Iraq, while a Turkish fleet raided the city of Valencia in Spain. During a single campaigning season in 1538, Ottoman forces conquered Moldavia in the northeast Balkans, besieged the Portuguese stronghold of Diu in India, and wrecked a Christian fleet off the shores of Greece.

The pace of expansion slowed under Suleiman's successors, but not because the empire was running out of energy. Rather, it was because remoter conquests brought diminishing returns. The Ottoman naval effort—it is true—faltered: outgunned in the Indian Ocean by Portugal and in the central Mediterranean by Spain. But every generation brought a net gain of territory until the last years of the seventeenth century.

The degree of imperial authority could hardly be uniform in so extensive an empire, but it was felt everywhere. The younger Barbarossa, who ruled the remotest outposts on the North African coast, was called a king, even in Turkish accounts. He recruited ships and men with his own resources and won his victories by his own strength. Yet when Suleiman summoned him to Constantinople, Barbarossa did not hesitate to obey. The khans of Crimea in what is today Ukraine negotiated terms of pay—often in the form of captive slaves—for joining the sultans' campaigns, and sometimes simply disobeyed the sultan. Turks garrisoned but did not directly rule Wallachia and Moldavia (in modern Romania). Transylvania, on the western edge of the empire, was a vassal state, with low taxes and a Christian prince whom its medieval parliament elected. In Arab lands, the sultans used religion as a source of legitimacy, but—with only sporadic displays of force to back it up—they found it hard to turn that legitimacy into effective allegiance. As we shall see in Chapter 19, even the parts of their empire that the sultans ruled directly were a patchwork of different methods of rule that were hard to keep under close control.

NEW LAND EMPIRES IN THE AMERICAS

Across the Atlantic, meanwhile, European imperialism led landward. Columbus (see Chapter 15) envisaged no more than a trading setup when he first saw what he thought was Japan, the Caribbean island of Hispaniola (ess-pah-nee-O-lah) in 1492, imagining a European merchant-colony under Spanish control, trading in cotton and slaves. However, these products were unavailable in large quantities in the Caribbean. Columbus based his initial hopes on the illusion that the riches of Asia lay only a short way farther west. But he had grossly underestimated the size of the world. Instead, therefore, the Spaniards had to focus on exploiting the gold mines of the island. Columbus's war of conquest in Hispaniola of 1495–1496 was the first step toward creating a Spanish territorial empire.

Bernal Díaz del Castillo, from *The True History of the Conquest of New Spain*

The settlement of more Caribbean islands and, between 1518 and 1546, the conquests of Mexico and Peru confirmed this trend. As a result, Spaniards found themselves obeyed over huge tracts of the most densely populated territory in the Americas. Indeed, Spain—which was a relatively poor and underpopulated country—had acquired, within the space of a few years, two of the fastest-growing and most environmentally diverse empires of the age—those of the Aztecs and the Incas (see Chapter 15). This achievement was effected thousands of miles from home, with relatively primitive technology, few resources, and privately recruit bands of only a few hundred men (see Map 16.3).

How was it possible? In early colonial times, four explanations occurred to those who tried to make sense of the way the conquest had turned out. The clergy favored the view that the conquest was God-given. The conquerors, their heirs, and cronies explained it as the result of their own godlike prowess. But this was incredible and self-interested—designed to maximize rewards from a grateful crown. The Spaniards' Native American allies saw the overthrow of the Aztecs and Incas as their own work, with a little help from their Spanish friends. Finally, according to early colonial analysts, the Native American empires were victims of their own shaky morale. Hernán Cortés (1485–1547), the adventurer who led the band that conquered Mexico, spread the claim that the Aztec Emperor Moctezuma II (mok-tak-ZOO-ma) (r. 1502–1520) had surrendered power into his hands in the belief that Spanish supremacy was the fulfillment of a prophesy. This claim was almost certainly made up to head off awkward questions churchmen and lawyers in Spain raised about whether the Spaniards had any right to rule in Mexico. The aggressive,

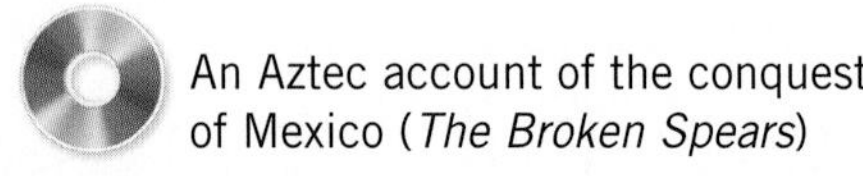
An Aztec account of the conquest of Mexico (*The Broken Spears*)

MAP 16.3
Land Empires in the Americas, ca. 1700

- Spanish possessions
- Portuguese possessions
- English possessions
- French possessions
- Dutch possessions
- *Tlaxcalteca* native peoples described on pages 554–557
- Portuguese slaving raids
- Manila galleon
- Treasure Fleet to Seville

confident, dynamic, and expanding Aztec state showed no signs of weak morale and resisted ferociously.

Historians have added other explanations. The technology gap is often assumed to have been decisive. And in some respects, Spanish war technology was important. In 1521, in the final siege of the Aztec capital Tenochtitlán, Spanish gunships patrolled the lake that surrounded the city. Spanish steel-edged weapons were probably more effective than the blades made from volcanic glass native armorers used. Crossbows could outperform any Native American missile weapons. The importance of guns and horses, however, was probably slight. Horses are of limited value in mountain warfare and street fighting—conditions in which some of the most critical episodes of the conquests occurred. It is hard to credit claims that the defenders were awestruck by these devices or inhibited by the belief that they were magical. Such claims were always linked with efforts to mock the natives' intellectual and rational powers. Native Americans quickly adapted to European styles of warfare and used horses and firearms, where these were effective, themselves.

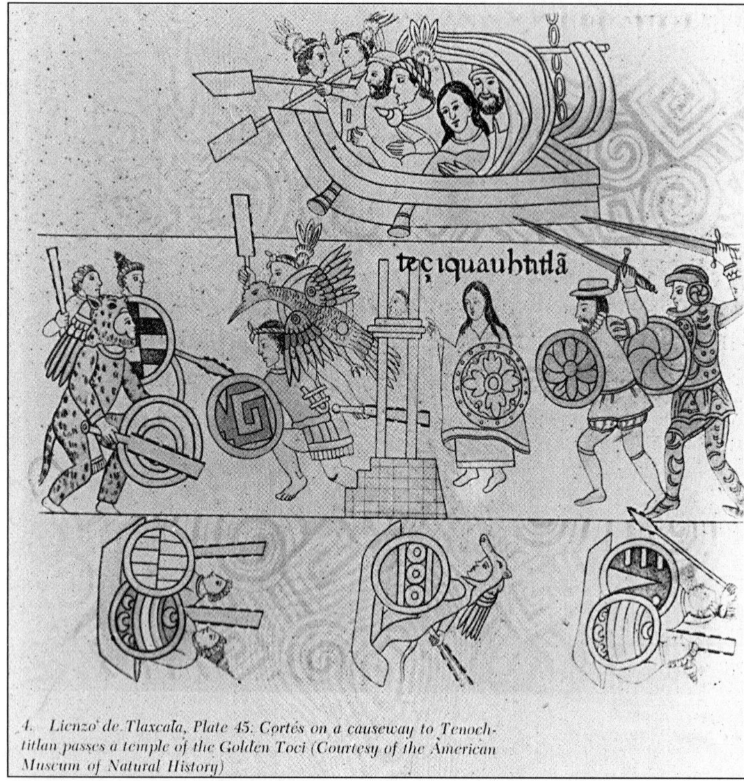

4. Lienzo de Tlaxcala, Plate 45: Cortés on a causeway to Tenochtitlan passes a temple of the Golden Toci (Courtesy of the American Museum of Natural History)

The Native American Doña Marina rather than the Spaniard Cortés directs the battle of Tenochtitlán in the Lienzo de Tlaxcala, a mid–sixteenth-century Native American portrayal of scenes from the conquest of Mexico. The same source also always shows Doña Marina center-stage negotiating alliances. Here she commands along the central causeway, where native warriors lead the attack against the Aztecs, and in the Spanish gunboat that native paddlers propel across Lake Texcoco.

As we shall see in the next chapter, disease was, in the long run, of enormous importance in thinning native numbers. It is more doubtful, however, whether it was decisive in the early stages of conquest. Maladies hard to identify, made worse by malnutrition, weakened and killed many of the defenders of the Aztec capital. By the time of the conquest of Peru in the 1530s, smallpox was devastating unimmunized populations. Spanish carriers unwittingly spread it wherever they went. Yet its effects cut both ways, harming the Spaniards' allies at least as much as their enemies, while still leaving formidable numbers of foes in the field. Spaniards themselves, after all, were also operating in unfamiliar and debilitating environments.

It is worth bearing in mind that many—perhaps most—European successes were by-products of war among Native Americans themselves. Civil war wracked the Inca Empire when the Spaniards arrived. Most of its subject peoples resented Inca rule. Even some of the Incas' former allies had grown disenchanted. The Incas' demands for forced labor, which drove many workers hundreds of miles from their homes, were acutely hated. When the empire fell, thousands of conscripted workers returned to their orignal communities.

The Aztecs' demands similarly alienated tributary peoples. The tribute system was both the strength and weakness of their state: strength, because it embodied their power to command resources from a vast area; weakness, because Tenochtitlán became dependent on tribute for basic necessities—the food and cotton the city could not produce for itself—and the luxuries from distant climates, needed to sustain the way of life of the elite: the ritual cacao and incense, the rubber for the ball game, the gold, the jade, the amber, the seashells, the exotic featherwork and ceremonial clothing. When the Spaniards' allies denied Tenochtitlán its tribute, they effectively starved the Aztec capital into submission.

The Spaniards' triumph was therefore less a battlefield victory than a diplomatic maneuver. The single most important ingredient in Spanish diplomatic success was probably their interpreter, whom they called Doña Marina. She was a native speaker of the main language of central Mexico and quickly learned Spanish. She was, at a crucial phase, the only person with the linguistic qualifications to mastermind negotiations. Native pictures of the conquest invariably show her center stage, mediating between Spaniards and Native Americans and supervising military operations.

None of these explanations, however, really matches what happened in the Americas when Europeans arrived for, usually, the transition to new kinds of European-led imperialism happened with little or no violence. Traditionally, historians have concentrated on conflicts between Europeans and their native "victims." Spanish conquests in the New World have had a bloody reputation. Terror was a common tactic, not because the Spaniards were morally different from other warriors, but because they were subject to intense strains of operating in hostile environments, surrounded by enemies whose cultures seemed savage and unintelligible. Yet considered from another aspect, the Spanish "conquest" seems remarkably peaceful. Most communities, especially within the regions previously subject to the Aztecs and Incas, offered the Spaniards little resistance or welcomed them, so eager were they to escape from their Native American overlords.

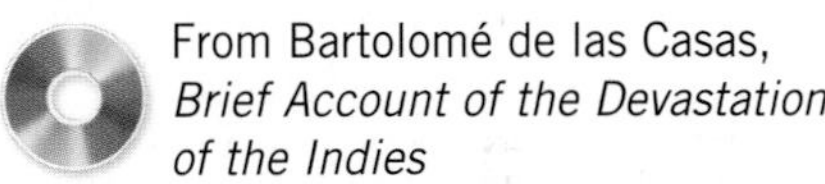

Even where no oppressive native empires existed, Native Americans were often surprisingly hospitable to European intruders, who usually seemed at first too few, vulnerable, and unused to local conditions to be much of a threat. Most European communities relied on native collaboration for food or allies or both. Sexual alliances with native women of elite rank, especially in areas of Spanish and Portuguese operations, helped the newcomers to get established and, according to native custom in many areas, conferred on the host communities a duty to help with labor and food. Spanish friars were amazingly successful in making themselves useful as holy men, healers, arbiters of disputes, and protectors against secular exploiters. In short, the reception of Europeans owed much to a remarkably widespread feature of Native American cultures: what we might call the **stranger effect**—the tendency some peoples have to esteem and defer to strangers, whose usefulness as arbitrators of disputes, dispensers of justice, and preservers of peace arises from the objectivity that their foreign origins confer.

Making the New Empires Work

The Spanish Empire preempted European rivals in regions selected precisely because they were densely populated with productive economies. In consequence Spanish policy—rarely successful in practice—was always to preserve the Native American population. This was not the case in most other parts of the Americas, where the Indians were too few, too warlike, or too unaccustomed to large-scale production to meet the colonists' labor needs. In most colonies, once reliance on native charity was no longer necessary, Native Americans seemed at best a nuisance, unless they were needed to keep trade going.

Throughout British America, for instance, the native peoples were a source of conflict between frontiersmen and the representatives of the crown, who wanted the protection of Indian buffer states and the benefit of a relatively dense pool of white labor, which frontier conquests would disperse. For most colonial subjects, however, the Native Americans merely got in the way of land grabbing. Genocide was the best means to deal with them. In 1637, an explicit attempt to exterminate an entire Native American people—the New England Pequots—was half finished in a massacre on Mystic River in Massachusetts, where, the governor reported, the victims could be seen "frying in the fire and the streams of blood quenching the same." The tribe's very name was banned. In defiance of official policy, a settler

Spanish and English Land Empires in the New World

1492	Columbus arrives in Caribbean
1495–1496	Columbus begins war of conquest in Hispaniola
1518–1546	Spanish conquests of Mexico and Peru
1675	Bacon's rebellion (Virginia)

malcontent, Nathaniel Bacon, launched war in Virginia in 1675 to destroy all Native Americans, friendly and hostile alike. This was a characteristic outrage in the late seventeenth century: a period of increasing tension—which also provoked violent clashes in areas of Spanish settlement in Florida and New Mexico—between colonies and threatened Native Americans. In areas of predominantly British colonization or "Anglo" rule, preconquest population levels for Native Americans have never revived, outside the formerly Spanish-ruled Southwest of the United States.

Some Native Americans were useful as slaves. On the fringes of the Amazon jungles, slaving became a major industry for Portuguese based in the port of São Paulo in southern Brazil. The early economy of the Carolinas depended on the slave trade with Native Americans, who raided neighbors as far inland as the Mississippi River valley. In this part of the North American South, there were more Native American slaves than black slaves until the early eighteenth century.

Generally, however, the English colonies relied on imported labor—whether enslaved or not—and so could afford to massacre their Native Americans or drive them west. They had a ready-made ideology of extermination. They were the new Israel. The Native Americans were the "uncircumcized," to be dealt with as the biblical Israel dealt with its pagan enemies: smitten hip and thigh. The English, indifferent to clerical discipline, rarely endured Spanish-style agonies of conscience about the justice of their presence in America or the morality of their wars. People who left their land underexploited or unfenced deserved to lose it. Only the line of the fence or the marks of the plow proved true tenure. Native Americans in British areas of expansion were too poor to exploit for tribute. It was more economical to replace them with white farmers or black slaves. The only colony where this reasoning was modified was early Pennsylvania. Here moral and material considerations favored a policy of friendly collaboration with the Native Americans. Thanks to the founder's Quaker high morality, supposedly just prices were paid for land purchases from the Indians, who were encouraged to stay on the frontier as buffers against hostile tribes or rival European empires. Whether expelled, exterminated, diminished by disease, or absorbed into colonial society by marrying Europeans or adopting European ways, the Native Americans retreated to the margins of colonial life wherever European colonies were founded.

Potosí in Bolivia—the world's most productive silver mine in the late sixteenth and seventeenth centuries. The "Silver Mountain" really does have an abrupt, conical outline, but all early modern representations exaggerate that shape and emphasize its dominance over the puny dwellings and almost antlike workers.

THE GLOBAL BALANCE OF TRADE

It is not generally realized that in the colonial New World precolonial patterns of exchange often remained intact. European merchants joined existing Native American trading communities, extending the reach or increasing the volume of traffic, enhancing what Indian Ocean venturers called **country trades,** which involved local or regional exchanges that never touched Europe. In North America, trade in deerskins and beaver pelts in colonial times extended precolonial practice. The French backwoodsmen slotted into an existing Native American framework that linked hunting grounds and routes of trade and tribute. The Huron, Native American farmers and traders who did not need to hunt, except to supplement their diet, were the middlemen of the early seventeenth-century fur trade, supplying French buyers in Quebec in Canada. Spanish entrepreneurs took part in a profitable canoe-borne trade in local textiles, healing plants, and dyestuffs along the coast of Venezuela in the 1590s. Similarly, the economy that sustained the Spanish conquerors of Yucatán was an extension of the age-old Maya trade with central Mexico, based largely on cacao for consumption in Mexico City.

Of course, Spanish activity was not confined to modest ventures of these kinds, along traditional grooves. The Spanish monarchy inaugurated new intra-American trade routes. New cities, founded in places never before settled on a large scale especially on the Pacific and Atlantic coasts, became magnets to supply food-stuffs, cotton textiles, and building materials. The conquest of Peru demanded a new transcontinental route from the Caribbean to the Pacific across the Isthmus of Panama in Central America, which became, like the alternative later opened from Bolivia to the Atlantic via the River Plate, a major silver-bearing artery of the Spanish Empire. Mule-train routes that the Native American civilizations, which had no horses or mules before the arrival of the Europeans, had never required, served the new mining ventures in remote hinterlands. The conquest of much of Chile in the mid–sixteenth century stimulated the creation of a new seaborne route, far into the Pacific, to overcome the Humboldt Current. Sailing ships took longer to get from Lima in Peru to Concepción in Chile than from Seville in Spain to Santo Domingo in the Caribbean.

Meanwhile, new commerce opened with the wider world. A system of convoys linked Spain to America and injected Europe's cash-starved economies with veins of gold and silver. The need for slaves led other European merchants to Spanish colonies and linked the Americas to Africa. The route of the Manila Galleon, a Spanish ship that made an annual crossing of the Pacific from the Philippines to Acapulco on the Pacific coast of Mexico, facilitated the direct exchange of Mexican silver for Chinese silk and porcelain. For the first time, trade tied the Americas, Africa, and Eurasia into a single, interconnected system.

IN PERSPECTIVE: The Impact of the Americas

Suppose Columbus had been right. Suppose the globe was small, and no Americas lay in the way of Europeans' westward approach to Asia. Europeans would still, of course, have taken part in Asia's carrying trades. They would have made money out of it and closed the wealth gap that separated them from the richer economies of maritime Asia. They would have contributed to recycling Japanese silver and helped to make the world's economy more liquid. They would probably have gone on to found the land empires that began to take shape in Asia in the late seventeenth century. The total volume of resources at their command would, however, have remained modest. The Americas were a huge

CHRONOLOGY

1492–1493	Columbus discovers routes to and from the New World
1500	Portuguese begin direct trade with southern India
1510	Portuguese trading post at Goa established
1513	Discovery of the Gulf Stream
1518–1546	Spanish conquest of Mexico and Peru
1519	Babur founds Mughal Empire
1519–1521	Spanish navigators complete first global navigation
1520–1566	Reign of Suleiman the Magnificent (Ottoman Empire)
1521	Spanish capture Tenochtitlán; end of Aztec Empire
1529	Spain and Portugal divide Pacific seaborne routes between themselves
1530s	Spanish conquest of Peru
1552–1556	Russian conquest of Kazan
1556–1605	Mughal expansion and centralization under Akbar
1564–1565	Northern Pacific sea route between New World and Asia discovered
1585–1598	Reign of Toyotomi Hideyoshi (Japan)
1600	East India Company founded (England)
1602	Dutch East India Company founded
Early 1600s	Dutch use westerlies to circumnavigate globe
1619	Dutch found Batavia (Indonesia)
1620–1640	Portuguese expelled from trading posts in Persian Gulf and Indian Ocean
1640	Dutch merchants only Europeans allowed in Japan
1656–1707	Mughal Empire covers most of Indian subcontinent under Aurangzeb
1674	French establish trading post at Pondicherry (India)
1689	Treaty of Nerchinsk with China checks Russian expansion eastward

bonanza—of land, of food and mineral resources, of opportunities for the productive deployment of labor, of new markets and manufactures. Western Europeans' privileged access to those resources made a new era in world history possible. The traditional poor relations of Eurasia—the formerly impoverished West—could now challenge previously towering economies, such as those of India and China, that had been dominant in Eurasia for thousands of years.

PROBLEMS AND PARALLELS

1. In what ways were empires agents of change in the sixteenth and seventeenth centuries?
2. How were empires created in the sixteenth and seventeenth centuries? What are the differences between land and maritime empires?
3. How did the maritime imperialism of Japan compare with Portuguese and Dutch imperial ventures?
4. What roles did native collaborators, interpreters, merchants, and middlemen play in the empires of the sixteenth and seventeenth centuries?
5. What are the differences and similarities among the Russian, Chinese, Ottoman, and Mughal Empires of this period?
6. How was Spain able to achieve such a vast empire in so short a time?
7. How did a global trade network emerge in the sixteenth century?

DOCUMENTS IN GLOBAL HISTORY

- Toyotomi Hideyoshi, on the conquest of China
- Jan van Linschoten on Dutch business in the Indian Ocean
- Hideyoshi, "Limitation on the Propagation of Christianity"
- Christian Martyrs, Japan
- Domingo Navarrete, "Of My Stay in the Kingdom of Makassar"
- Abul Fazl Allami, from the *Institutes of Akbar*
- Ogier Ghiselin de Busbecq on Suleiman the Magnificent
- Bernal Díaz del Castillo, from *The True History of the Conquest of New Spain*
- An Aztec account of the conquest of Mexico (*The Broken Spears*)
- From Bartolomé de las Casas, *Brief Account of the Devastation of the Indies*

Please see the Primary Source DVD for additional sources related to this chapter.

READ ON

The best introduction to the Portuguese maritime empire is A. J. Russell-Wood, *The Portuguese Empire, 1415–1808* (1992). See now also F. Bethencourt and D. Curto, eds., *The Portuguese Empire* (2006). P. Pérez-Mallaína, *Spain's Men of the Sea: Daily Life on the Indies Fleets in the Sixteenth Century* (trans. Carla Rahn Phillips, 1998) is a superb social history of shipboard life in the age of maritime expansion. C. R. Boxer, *The Dutch Seaborne Empire: 1600–1800* (reprint, 1991) is a slightly dated but still valuable and very readable account of the rise of Dutch colonial power. Its perspective on southeast Asia should be balanced by W. Cummings, *Making Blood White: Historical Transformations in Early Modern Makasar* (2002), a sophisticated recent study of the transition from oral to literate culture in an area of increasing Dutch influence. K. So, *Japanese Piracy in Ming China During 16th Century* (1975) explores the impact of *wako* raids around the South China Sea in the sixteenth century. M. Berry, *Hideyoshi* (2001) is a superb study of that ruler. B. Walker, *The Conquest of Ainu Lands: Ecology and Culture in Japanese Expansion, 1590–1800* (2001) is important on continuing Japanese expansion.

R. L. Edmunds, *The Northern Frontier in Qing China and Tokugawa Japan: A Comparative Study of Frontier Policy* (1985) is valuable. On Qing expansion, J. Waley-Cohen, *Exile in Mid-Qing China* (1991) is important. On Batavia, L. Blusse, *Strange Company* (1986) is outstanding. J. F. Richards, *The Mughal Empire* (1996) is a fine introduction to Mughal history, while P. M. Brand and G. D. Lowry, *Akbar's India: Art from the Mughal City of Victory* (1985) explores the cultural expressions of Mughal might and ruling style. R. Murphey, *Ottoman Warfare, 1500–1700* (1999) analyzes Ottoman military power in its social, economic, and geographic contexts. K. Chase, *Firearms: A Global History to 1700* (2003) offers an overview of the dynamics of power in Eurasia whose central thesis is simplistic but whose details on the spread of gunpowder weaponry are valuable.

My material on Russian icons comes from the Royal Academy exhibition catalog *The Art of Holy Russia: Icons from Moscow, 1440–1660* (1998). On Siberia, T. Armstrong, ed., *Yermak's Campaigns in Siberia* (1975) unites the main chronicles. J. Forsyth, *A History of the Peoples of Siberia* (1994) is the best overall study.

M. Restall, *Seven Myths of the Spanish Conquest* (2003) is essential on New World imperialism. J. H. Elliott, *Empires of the Atlantic World* (2006) compares English, later British, and Spanish experience. B. E. Mundy, *The Mapping of New Spain: Indigenous Cartography and the Maps of the Relaciones Geograficas* (2000) offers an excellent scholarly analysis of the local maps and surveys collected by the Spanish government in the late sixteenth century as part of its effort to govern its new empire more effectively. A fine edition of W. Bradford, *Of Plymouth Plantation* (1999) gives a firsthand account of the creation of the Plymouth colony. E. H. Spicer, *The American Indians* (1982), is an authoritative summary of Native American history, including relations with the expanding European presence in North America.

On global trade balances in the sixteenth and seventeenth centuries, see A. Gunder Frank, *Re-ORIENT: Global Economy in the Asian Age* (1998), a provocative study that argues forcefully for Asia, especially China, as the center of gravity of global trade right through to 1800. E. van Veen, *Decay or Defeat? An Enquiry into the Portuguese Decline in Asia* (2000) makes some important corrections, and R. Barendse, *The Arabian Seas* (2002) is extremely helpful.

CHAPTER 17 The Ecological Revolution of the Sixteenth and Seventeenth Centuries

The flavors and colors of Italy, by way of the Americas. Tomatoes, peppers, and potatoes—as well as other nonnative fruits and vegetables—entice the shopper in a market in old Naples, 1981.

IN THIS CHAPTER

THE ECOLOGICAL EXCHANGE: PLANTS AND ANIMALS
Maize, Sweet Potatoes, and Potatoes
Weeds, Grasses, and Livestock
Cane Sugar
Coffee, Tea, and Chocolate
Patterns of Ecological Exchange

THE MICROBIAL EXCHANGE
Demographic Collapse in the New World
Plague and New Diseases in Eurasia

LABOR: HUMAN TRANSPLANTATIONS

WILD FRONTIERS: ENCROACHING SETTLEMENT
Northern and Central Asia: The Waning of Steppeland Imperialism
Pastoral Imperialism in Africa and the Americas

IMPERIALISM AND SETTLEMENT IN EUROPE AND ASIA
China
India

NEW EXPLOITATION IN THE AMERICAS
The Spanish Empire
Brazil
British North America

HOME FRONTS IN EUROPE AND ASIA
New Energy Sources
Land Reclamation

FRONTIERS OF THE HUNT

IN PERSPECTIVE: Evolution Redirected

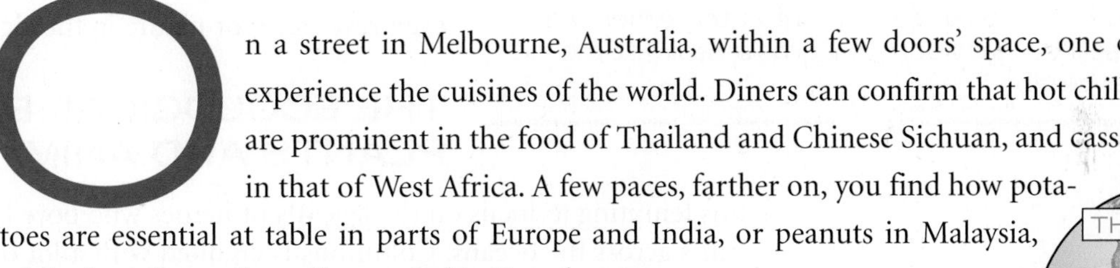

On a street in Melbourne, Australia, within a few doors' space, one can experience the cuisines of the world. Diners can confirm that hot chillies are prominent in the food of Thailand and Chinese Sichuan, and cassava in that of West Africa. A few paces, farther on, you find how potatoes are essential at table in parts of Europe and India, or peanuts in Malaysia, while chocolate and vanilla are vital in French pastry.

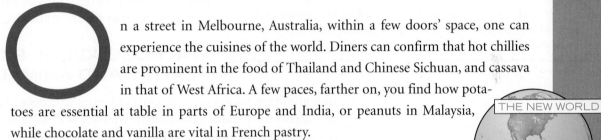

All these ingredients originated in the Americas and were unknown in Europe or Asia before the sixteenth century. Indispensable on an Italian menu are tomatoes, gnocchi, and polenta—made from native American plants. Jerusalem artichokes originated in North America, not Jerusalem. The turkey was first recorded in Mexico, not Turkey. The pineapple was unknown in Europe until Columbus described it during his first transatlantic journey.

• • • • •

The transfer of plants and animals in the opposite direction, from the Old World to the New, transformed the food of the Americas even more deeply. Imagine an Argentine restaurant without beef, or a school cafeteria in North America without milk, orange juice, or wheat bread, or Southern food without molasses, yams, or pork, or Caribbean food without rice or bananas.

Taken together, the profound ecological transformations that overtook the world of the sixteenth and seventeenth centuries (what historians now call the **Colombian Exchange**) were the biggest revolution that human agency ever made on Earth. A pattern of evolution, hundreds of millions years old, had made the life forms of the various continents ever more different from one another. About 500 years ago, that pattern was reversed. People began to swap the life forms of different continents.

Meanwhile, the human relationship with fatal pathogens underwent puzzling lurches. At one level, the period from the mid–fourteenth century to the eighteenth was an age of plagues, when lethal diseases spread over the world. On the other hand, the microorganisms responsible seem, late in the period, to have retreated, with surprising and still unexplained suddenness, from their eco-niches. A worldwide population explosion began toward the mid–eighteenth century.

FOCUS questions

- WHY WAS the Columbian Exchange so important and how did it affect nutrition in Europe and Asia?
- HOW DID the introduction of new diseases by Europeans affect population levels in the Americas?
- WHY DID the Europeans import slaves to the Americas?
- WHY DID the balance of power change between nomads and settled peoples?
- IN WHAT new ways did people around the world exploit the natural environment in the seventeenth century?
- HOW DID the European settlement in the Americas and increased contact across Eurasia redirect the course of evolution?

Human settlement invaded new ecological frontiers on an unprecedented scale: farming grasslands, felling forests, climbing slopes, reclaiming bogs, penetrating game preserves and deep-sea fisheries, expanding and founding cities, turning deserts into gardens and gardens into deserts. This was part of a drive for resources and energy sources in an increasingly populous world. Hunters ransacked previously unmolested wild zones for animal furs, fats, and proteins. Much of this hunting took place at sea, in pursuit of migrating fish and wandering whales and seals. The exploitation of new frontiers created an illusion of abundance that inspired ecological overkill. Yet imperialism also had positive environmental effects, as colonialists came, in some cases, to see themselves as custodians of tropical Edens, preparing the way for a revived respect and even reverence for nature in the eighteenth-century West.

THE ECOLOGICAL EXCHANGE: PLANTS AND ANIMALS

It is tempting to focus on the legends of heroes who bore life-changing new foodstuffs across the oceans. Columbus is credited with a lot of "firsts." From his first ocean crossing in 1492, he brought back descriptions and samples, including pineapple and cassava. In 1493, he took sugarcane to the island of Hispaniola—but let it grow wild. Pigs, sheep, cattle, chickens, and wheat made their first appearance in the New World on the same occasion. Other heroic firsts are the subjects of legends or fables. Juan Garrido, a black companion of Cortés, supposedly first planted wheat in Mexico. The story of Sir Walter Raleigh, the sixteenth-century poet, courtier, historian, and pirate, introducing potatoes to England is false but has an honored place in myth.

The real, although unwitting, heroes, however, are surely the plants and animals themselves, who survived deadly journeys and adapted to new climates, sometimes—in the case of seeds—with little human help, by accident. They traveled in the cuffs or pleats of clothing, or were caught in the fabric of bales and sacks. A few instances stand out. Out of Eurasia to new worlds in the Western and Southern Hemispheres went wheat, sugar, rice, bananas, coconuts, apples, pears, apricots, peaches, plums, cherries, olives, citrus fruits, wine grapes, and major meat-yielding and dairy livestock. Yams, okra, and collard greens were among vegetables that made the crossing from Africa (see Map 17.1). Medicinal plants crossed the ocean in the opposite direction. Quinine from Peru had enormous long-term significance, because it can control the effects of malaria and therefore equipped Europeans to survive in the tropics. Tobacco—"with which," said a Spanish reporter in the 1540s, Native Americans "perfume their mouths"—was thought to aid digestion. But the staple products—and therefore the most important gifts of the New World to the rest, because they could feed vast populations—were maize, potatoes, and sweet potatoes.

Maize, Sweet Potatoes, and Potatoes

Maize at first revolted Old World taste buds but fascinated Old World plant specialists. As the Spanish botanist Juan de Cárdenas reported in 1591, it thrives "in cold, hot, dry, or wet climates, in mountainous regions or grasslands, as a winter or summer crop, irrigated or dry-farmed," with a high yield and short land-use cycle. Turkic frontiersmen bore it as a tribute plant to China, where it was first recorded in 1555. Meanwhile, it also came by sea to Fujian, where a Spanish friar saw it cultivated in 1577. Its advantages over millet and rice—it required less labor per unit of production and could grow in eco-niches where the traditional crops could not—gradually made it popular, especially in areas of new settlement. In Europe, where it was initially welcomed only for livestock, it slowly became a human food in the eighteenth century in the Mediterranean, the Balkans, Ukraine, and southern Russia.

The sweet potato, too, had a transforming effect in parts of China. First reported in southern China near the Burmese border in the 1560s, it was favored in hill country by immigrants and settlers who were obliged to occupy land previously thought marginal. In 1594, a governor of Fujian supposedly recommended sweet potatoes when the conventional crops failed. Potatoes, which the Portuguese introduced to Asia in 1605, failed to win popular favor in Japan, Korea, or China. Yet they became an inescapable ingredient of Bengali meals and conquered northern Europe, where war spread them, because peasants favored a crop that grew concealed in the ground and so eluded plundering troops. Scholars and bureaucrats promoted the potato because of impressive nutritional qualities. If eaten in sufficient quantities, it is the only major staple that provides all the nutrients essential to human health.

Tobacco was thought to be good for the digestive system. In this seventeenth-century Dutch illustration, Cupid carries the smoker's pipe and pouch because tobacco, like lovemaking, is a fleeting pleasure that quickly goes up in smoke.

Weeds, Grasses, and Livestock

Much of the Americas became farmland and ranchland for European food. Colonization by European weeds and grasses made parts of the New World able to support sheep, cattle, and horses. Weeds from Europe made the revolution work. They bound soil together, saved it from drying out, filled eco-niches, and fed livestock.

Conscious transpositions followed. Horses and cattle came first. To Spanish cattlemen, the South American pampa and the North American prairie were the last frontiers of an enterprise that began in the Middle Ages, when they had adopted ranching to exploit the empty, conquered lands in Spain after the Muslim population had fled or been expelled. The lower levels of the central valleys of Mexico proved highly suitable for wheat, and although most of the Indians continued to rely on maize, wheat bread became a badge of urban sophistication. Within a few years of the Spanish conquest, the city council of Mexico City demanded a supply of "white, clean, well-cooked and seasoned bread."

Not all efforts to introduce wheat in the Americas were successful, at least at first. Corn bread and fish, Native American foodstuffs, were the mainstays of early colonial Florida. The first English colonists in Virginia were unable to grow food for themselves and relied on handouts from the natives. Investors and imperialists back home blamed colonists' moral deficiencies for these failures. But the problems of the mutual adaptation of Old World farming and New World environments were formidable, especially for settlers of exposed seaboards in an era of imperial competition. Colonies sited for defense, behind marshes or swamps, in difficult climates, needed generations of investment and long periods of heartbreaking rates of mortality before they could be made viable. At every stage of European colonization of new worlds, the remarkable thing is not the high rate of failure but the perseverance that led to ultimate success.

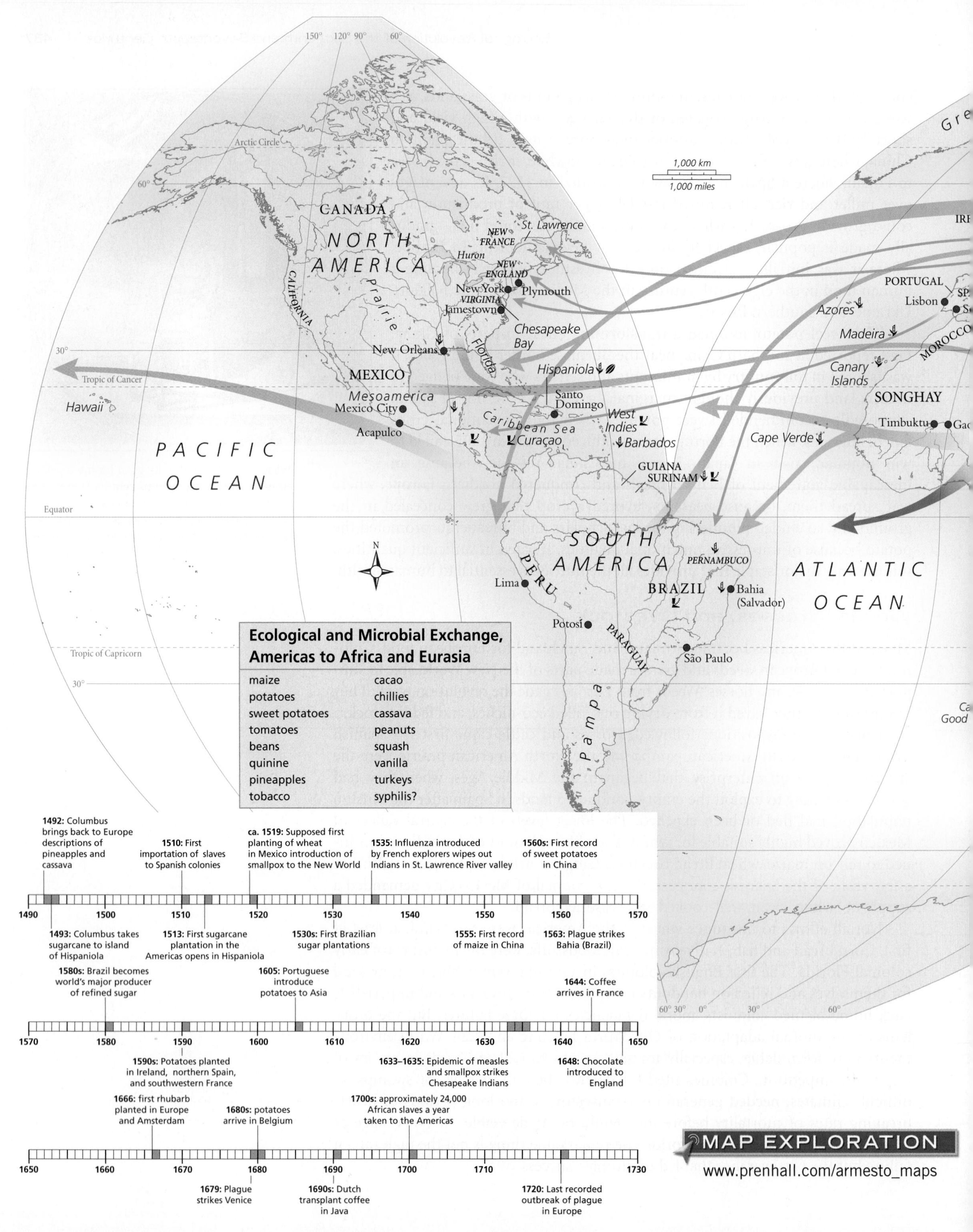

Ecological and Microbial Exchange, Americas to Africa and Eurasia

maize	cacao
potatoes	chillies
sweet potatoes	cassava
tomatoes	peanuts
beans	squash
quinine	vanilla
pineapples	turkeys
tobacco	syphilis?

1492: Columbus brings back to Europe descriptions of pineapples and cassava

1493: Columbus takes sugarcane to island of Hispaniola

1510: First importation of slaves to Spanish colonies

1513: First sugarcane plantation in the Americas opens in Hispaniola

ca. 1519: Supposed first planting of wheat in Mexico introduction of smallpox to the New World

1530s: First Brazilian sugar plantations

1535: Influenza introduced by French explorers wipes out Indians in St. Lawrence River valley

1555: First record of maize in China

1560s: First record of sweet potatoes in China

1563: Plague strikes Bahia (Brazil)

1580s: Brazil becomes world's major producer of refined sugar

1590s: Potatoes planted in Ireland, northern Spain, and southwestern France

1605: Portuguese introduce potatoes to Asia

1633–1635: Epidemic of measles and smallpox strikes Chesapeake Indians

1644: Coffee arrives in France

1648: Chocolate introduced to England

1666: first rhubarb planted in Europe and Amsterdam

1679: Plague strikes Venice

1680s: potatoes arrive in Belgium

1690s: Dutch transplant coffee in Java

1700s: approximately 24,000 African slaves a year taken to the Americas

1720: Last recorded outbreak of plague in Europe

MAP EXPLORATION

www.prenhall.com/armesto_maps

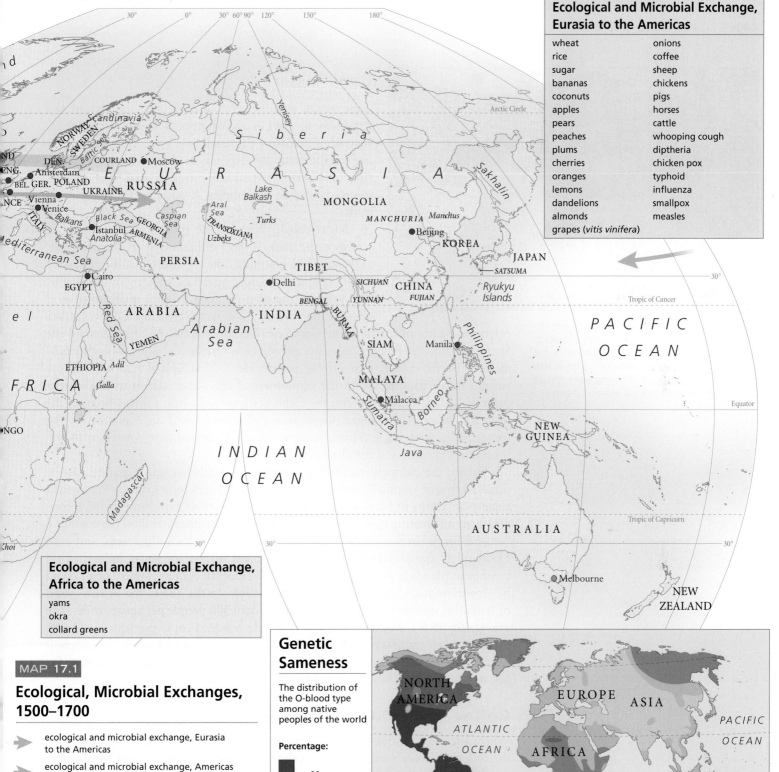

Ecological and Microbial Exchange, Eurasia to the Americas

wheat
rice
sugar
bananas
coconuts
apples
pears
peaches
plums
cherries
oranges
lemons
dandelions
almonds
grapes (*vitis vinifera*)
onions
coffee
sheep
chickens
pigs
horses
cattle
whooping cough
diptheria
chicken pox
typhoid
influenza
smallpox
measles

Ecological and Microbial Exchange, Africa to the Americas

yams
okra
collard greens

MAP 17.1

Ecological, Microbial Exchanges, 1500–1700

- ecological and microbial exchange, Eurasia to the Americas
- ecological and microbial exchange, Americas to Africa and Eurasia
- ecological and microbial exchange, Africa to the Americas
- European immigration to the Americas, 1500–1700
- forced migration of Africans to the Americas
- sugar plantation
- major importer of slaves
- coffee plantation
- modern-day city described on page 435
- *Huron* peoples

Genetic Sameness

The distribution of the O-blood type among native peoples of the world

Percentage:

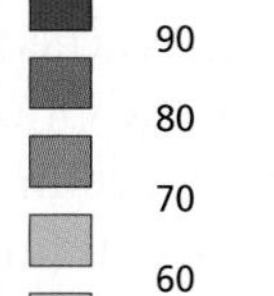

Before 1500, the distribution of the blood group O gene was far higher among the native peoples of the Americas than anywhere else in the world. This confirms, their protracted isolation from the people of the Old World which left them exposed to disease.

A water-driven sugar mill in Pernambuco during the Dutch occupation of northern Brazil, depicted here in a Dutch atlas of 1662. Slaves carry the mill owner, slung in a hammock under a rich awning in the foreground. The sugarcane arrives by oxcart, to be ground by the power of the mill.

Cane Sugar

Cane sugar was the first transplanted product in the Americas to have a major impact on world markets. Instead of following the usual laws of economics, according to which supply responds to demand, sugar was the first of a series of tropical products that were recommended by their availability. It enslaved European taste buds.

Sugar rapidly became the most important item of transoceanic trade. It was a difficult crop to plant, harvest, and refine, demanding lots of capital and specialized labor. Trading in sugar, however, was highly profitable. The value of the crop doubled or even quadrupled as it crossed the Atlantic. The sugar-growing area was never extensive—parts of Brazil, some Caribbean islands, patches of coasts around the Spanish Main, and French Louisiana around New Orleans—but it was highly productive. By the 1580s, four effects were evident. First, Brazil had become the world's major producer, and the economies of the sugar islands of the eastern Atlantic—Madeira, the Azores, the Cape Verdes—went into eclipse. Second, the need for labor in the sugar plantations and mills caused an explosion in the transatlantic slave trade. Third, sugar production created new American industries: refining sugar and distilling rum.

Finally, the competition for sugar-producing lands became a major cause of imperial rivalry among European states. Dutch invaders took over the Portuguese sugar plantations in Pernambuco in 1630, then, on their expulsion in 1654, concentrated on creating their own plantations in the Caribbean and on the coast of a "second Brazil" in Surinam. English, French, Spaniards, Scandinavians, and even Courlanders from a duchy on the Baltic coast all set up sugar industries on Caribbean islands in the second half of the seventeenth century. Where sugar could be grown, unprecedented prosperity was possible. In the 1680s, the British island of Barbados sustained a population of more than 300 people per square mile—the average figure for Western Europe at the time was 92 people per square mile. By then, the sugar trade was undergoing a further revolution that would transform it into one of the world's most popular products: the popularization of the taste for hot sugar-sweetened beverages in Europe.

Coffee, Tea, and Chocolate

Thomas Gage, on chocolate

Where sugar led, coffee—and, ultimately, tea and chocolate—followed. By 1640, the coffee of Yemen rivaled pepper as the main trading commodity of the Arabian Sea. In Persia, coffee consumption reached nearly a million pounds a year by 1700. About 17 million pounds went to the Ottoman Empire via the Red Sea and Egypt. Coffee arrived from Turkey in France in 1644, and within half a century, coffee became the West's favorite addictive stimulant.

The next stage was to transplant it to lands where Europeans could control the supply. The great coffee boom of the eighteenth and nineteenth centuries took it to Brazil, to the French islands of the Indian Ocean, and to the French colony of Saint-Domingue, which, until the black slaves there rebelled and proclaimed the independence of Haiti in 1804, was the most productive island in the world for coffee and sugar alike. One of the most enduringly successful of the new coffee lands was Java, where the Dutch introduced the plant in the 1690s, gradually expanded production during the eighteenth century, and, in the nineteenth, fought wars to boost production on ever more marginal soils.

While coffee spread across the world from the Middle East, chocolate followed, more slowly, a similar path from a starting place in Mesoamerica. In a work of 1648, credited with introducing chocolate to the English-speaking world, Thomas Gage described how colonial Mexico liked it—mixed with Old World flavors, such as cinnamon, cloves, and almonds, as well as in the traditional Mesoamerican stews of bitter chocolate and chillies. As the new drink became fashionable in Europe, the cacao from which chocolate was made was transplanted to West Africa, where Danish plantations helped supply the growing trade in the eighteenth century. Tea also contributed to the growth of global trade but not to the ecological exchange. China supplied almost the whole of world demand until the nineteenth century when the British established tea plantations in India and Sri Lanka.

Chocolate. In this canvas of about 1640—presumably intended to adorn a dining room—the Spanish painter Juan de Zurbarán (1620–1649) exalts chocolate, raising it on a silver pedestal and placing it center stage as if he were painting its portrait. In the seventeenth century, rich Europeans consumed chocolate the way the Aztec elite had—as a luxury beverage. Zurbarán here depicts a truly global experience in conspicuous consumption: Expensive chocolate imported to Spain from Mexico is to be drunk in even more costly porcelain cups imported from China.

Patterns of Ecological Exchange

The ecological exchange did not merely bounce back and forth across the oceans between the Old World and the New. Some ecological exchanges happened within the Americas. Domesticated turkeys formed no part of the first Thanksgiving meal. They were introduced to New England from Mexico later in the seventeenth century. The real maker of English economic success in Virginia was John Rolfe. He was the husband of the Indian princess Pocahontas—the forger of a kind of understanding with the natives, based on collaboration, mutual benefit, and sexual alliance that was normal in Spanish, Portuguese, and French colonies but that remained rare in English colonial practice. He introduced tobacco from the West Indies, because Europeans could not stand the taste of Virginia's native variety. It turned the colony from an unprofitable swamp into a field for settlers.

Along the routes of transmission, gardens where plants could be adapted were way stations of ecological exchange. Dutch horticulture led the way. John Maurice of Nassau grew African and Indonesian plants in his garden in Brazil and sent Chilean monkey-puzzle trees to Germany. Nicolaas Witsen, a director of the Dutch East India Company, planted the first rhubarb in Europe in Amsterdam in 1666. A fellow director made it his life's work, or folly, to try to grow oranges and lemons in cold, damp Holland. By the end of the seventeenth century, the company's gardens on the southern tip of Africa had become the meeting place of hundreds of European, African, American, and Asian plants.

The result of the ecological exchange was a better-nourished world in the eighteenth century, better equipped than before with medicinal drugs derived from plants. This presumably contributed to the population explosion that then began and has continued ever since.

Human population, however, depends not only on what people do but also on how disease-bearing microorganisms behave. In the sixteenth and seventeenth centuries, a long and hazardous period of relatively low and uncertain growth preceded the upward surge of world population. The reasons population patterns change are still poorly understood. Social structures—and marriage disciplines above all—play a big part. Nutrition is important, because it affects fertility and can keep more people alive for more of their fertile years. But we cannot even begin to understand changing world patterns of population in the sixteenth and seventeenth centuries without examining the microbial world.

THE MICROBIAL EXCHANGE

Instead of increasing population, colonization in the New World provoked the worst recorded demographic disaster in history. Smallpox, fatal to the immune systems of unaccustomed populations, was probably the most effective killer. But symptoms often baffled their beholders. Even if we assume that Native American societies were like those in the rest of the world and had suffered undocumented pestilence before the Europeans arrived, it seems incontestable that the diseases colonization brought were new and the effects unprecedented. "The breath of a Spaniard" was said to be enough to kill a Native American. The first Spanish navigators of the Amazon, in 1542, beheld cities built on stilts on the river banks, fed by aquaculture and the intensive cultivation of bitter manioc. The Spaniards only passed by, yet when the next European visitors arrived a generation later, that populous world had vanished.

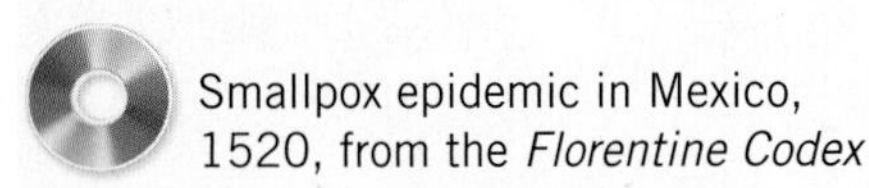
Smallpox epidemic in Mexico, 1520, from the *Florentine Codex*

Demographic Collapse in the New World

Demographers have been unable to produce convincing figures for the extent or duration of the collapse, but even at the most optimistic estimates, the Indian population of Hispaniola, where New World colonization began, was virtually wiped out. In the densely settled and highly exposed regions of Mesoamerica and the Andes, Indian populations typically fell by 90 percent before they began to recover—which they did only patchily and intermittently until well into the seventeenth century and in many places not until the eighteenth.

Benevolent attitudes by colonial authorities made no difference. No empire has ever legislated so persistently, or so ineffectually, for the benefit of its victims as Spain's in the New World. It is impossible to imagine a system more benevolent—in paternalist fashion—than that of the Jesuits in vast areas of Brazil and Paraguay, where they built model, self-sustaining Christian communities for the Native Americans. Somehow, however, this paradise got mislaid. Baptismal records show that by 1650, of the 150,000 people the Jesuits had baptized in their missions in the four most forward frontier provinces, only 40,000 survived the raids of Portuguese slavers and the visitations of plague.

The more spacious environments of North America bred equally devastating diseases. The influenza French explorers unwittingly introduced on the St. Lawrence River valley in Canada in 1535 and the nameless plague a Spanish expedition spread in the Deep South in 1538 inaugurated a history in which every attempted European settlement infected Native Americans.

Smallpox victims. A native artist drew these victims of smallpox in sixteenth-century Mexico to illustrate a history that a Spanish friar wrote in Nahuatl—the language of the Aztecs. At top left, an Aztec physician is talking to his patient, who was almost certainly doomed. Hardly any Europeans died of smallpox at the time, but the disease killed millions of Native Americans, who had had no opportunity to develop immunity to it.

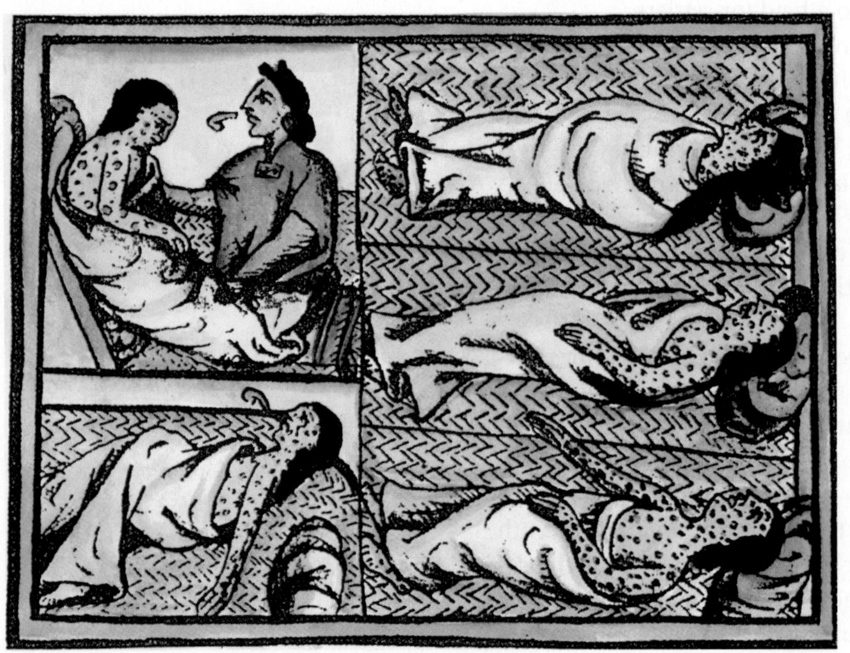

The first English settlement in Virginia spread a quick-killing disease among the Indians, "so strange that they did not know anything about it or how to cure it." The next major epidemic of 1633–1635 was recognizably of measles followed by smallpox. The Chesapeake Indians disappeared by the end of the seventeenth century. The numbers of the Huron in Canada collapsed so dramatically after contact with Europeans that one Jesuit argued desperately that it was a sign of divine favor. God was gathering his chosen to him. By the end of the seventeenth century, the Native American population in regions Europeans penetrated had fallen—according to rival estimates—by between 60 and 90 percent.

Huron demographic collapse, from *The Jesuit Relations* (1669–1670)

Plague and New Diseases in Eurasia

Some regions outside the Americas suffered comparable devastation. In parts of Siberia, unimmunized natives were equally vulnerable to unaccustomed diseases. Eighty percent of the tribespeople east of the Yenisey River perished in the 1650s. Later, European penetration of Australia and parts of the Pacific had similar effects.

So, in a sense, the "age of plague" that started in the Old World in the fourteenth century increased in virulence as disease-bearing microorganisms spread across the world. Microbial evolution, meanwhile, altered the patterns of disease in Eurasia. Leprosy diminished in range, but new diseases arose or old ones mutated. Tuberculosis does not seem to have been around in Europe on a significant scale—and certainly was not a major killer—until the sixteenth century. New strains of venereal disease developed in Europe—perhaps transferred from the New World.

Lethal sicknesses that Europeans continued vaguely to call plague remained a constant problem in parts of southern Europe. The plague of Venice of 1679 left thousands of dead lying in a ditch, smothered in quicklime "like pickled game in a barrel." Plague in Spain in 1657 inspired terrifying paintings of lives stalked by death or focused on putrefaction. In a hospital in Seville, a brotherhood of aristocrats sought to atone for their sins by burying the plague dead and tending the plague sores of the poor with their own hands. China in the 1580s and 1640s endured more epidemics of greater virulence than in the more notorious plagues of the fourteenth century. A survivor in Hunan in 1657 claimed nine of ten inhabitants were smitten, with a third of them breaking out in fever at midday to "become delirious in the evening" and dead at sunrise, "gnawed by rats".

Yet for reasons that remain poorly understood, the age of plagues gradually exhausted its virulence. The deaths of unimmunized populations left well-adapted survivors. Improved nutrition fortified increasing numbers of people. Quarantine helped. Microbes shifted their targets or mutated to become less deadly. After all, it is not necessarily efficient for microorganisms to kill off their hosts. Of course, other diseases occupied the eco-niches retreating microbes vacated or leaped into new ones that social, economic, or environmental change opened up. Cholera and yellow fever, for instance, broke out of their tropical heartlands to attack some of the fast-growing, densely populated, polluted cities and ports in the industrializing West (see Chapter 23). Dysentery and typhus throve in the unsanitary environments of rapidly growing towns. Dense concentrations of people helped tuberculosis to spread. Bubonic plague, in its modern form, may be another new disease of this period—or an old disease with new characteristics. As we saw in Chapter 14, historians' longstanding assumption that bubonic plague was the sole or main affliction of the "age of plague" in Europe is probably false. In China, there is no decisive evidence that any epidemic before the nineteenth century was of bubonic plague in its modern form.

In Yunnan province, however, on China's southwest border, where mining towns boomed, strong similarities with modern bubonic plague characterized a series of epidemics from the 1770s until the 1820s. Modern bubonic plague is endemic in particular kinds of rodents. It spreads to humans when rat fleas bite people and inject the bacillus into human bloodstreams. The Yunnan plague was incontestably associated with rats, according to observations made at the time, not only by physicians but also by a poet who wrote,

Shi Daonon, "Death of Rats"

Dead rats in the East!
Dead rats in the West!
. . . .
A few days following the death of the rats,
Men pass away like falling walls!

Still, when plague receded from Yunnan in the 1830s, it became dormant or sporadic. The next major outbreak in China did not occur until 1894. In any case, the new or spreading diseases of the eighteenth and nineteenth centuries could no longer seriously restrain the growth of world population.

For as long as the age of plague lasted, problems of severe regional labor shortages had to be faced. The gravest of these were in the last region to suffer devastating losses of population to disease: the New World. The solution lay in transplanting human labor.

LABOR: HUMAN TRANSPLANTATIONS

Even before native numbers thinned, the colonial Americas suffered from shortages of useful labor. Native Americans were, with few exceptions, ill suited to the work Europeans wanted done, such as plantation labor, domestic service, and specialist skills in mining and sugar refining. Europe, however, was unsatisfactory as an alternative labor source. Spanish schemes to introduce Spanish laborers failed in the sixteenth century. The Dutch encountered similar failure in the seventeenth. Sixteenth-century attempts to found North American colonies almost all failed. Those founded in the seventeenth century took a long time to renew their populations by sustainable birth rates. They could not rely, as most of Spain's early American conquests could, on native population levels to keep them viable. There are no reliable estimates of the size of the native population of North America when the Europeans arrived—well-informed guesses range from 2 to 7 million—but there is no doubt that the region was sparsely populated.

Immigration could not, at first, make up the deficit. Virginia was farmed mainly with a form of forced labor imported from England—"indentured" poor, escapees from social exclusion at home, who contracted with masters to serve for years at a time, on subsistence wages or payments in kind, with no hope of release. But there were never enough of them, and as the market for black slaves gradually opened up to the English, Africans replaced them. Again, the model of exploitation was found in the Spanish, Portuguese, and (by now) Dutch colonies to the south.

Until the second half of the seventeenth century, life expectancy in Virginia remained low. Few colonists lived beyond age 50. The Virginia swampland, where the first permanent settlements were founded from 1607 onward, was so unhealthy that of the first 100 or so settlers, only 38 were still alive nine months after landing. Of the first 3,000, only a couple of hundred were still alive after a bloody war with the Indians in 1622. The population did not begin to increase naturally until some 50 years after the first settlement. The breakthrough was accompanied by increased rates of immigration, which tripled from about 1650 to 1670.

New England's environment was less hostile. From early in the 1630s (Plymouth, the first New England colony, was founded in 1620), the colonists could grow enough to feed themselves, and natural increase kept the population growing. Without valuable cash products, however, the region was of little appeal to immigrants. Only 21,000 came in the whole seventeenth century, and the numbers of immigrants diminished over time—only a third of that total arrived after 1640. These were problems general to northern colonies. There were only 5,000 settlers in New Netherland when the English conquered the colony, which became New York, in 1664. New France, founded in Canada in 1608, received fewer than 4,000 immigrants in the second half of the seventeenth century. France, though densely populated by European standards, never persuaded many colonists to go to Canada.

King Alvaro VI of Kongo. In the seventeenth century, wars between rivals for the crown damaged the Kingdom of Kongo, while Portuguese and Dutch envoys and traders sought to identify and back potential winners. Here Alvaro VI (r. 1636–1662) receives Dutch visitors toward the end of his reign, shortly after the Dutch had captured Portuguese slave-trading posts in neighboring Luanda. The Dutch are acting submissively because they want the king to accept the terms of a slave-trading contract.

In the Spanish colonies, as early as 1510, the importation of slave labor began from the only source near enough and demographically buoyant enough to provide it: Africa. By the 1570s, Spanish America was importing, on average, about 2,500 African slaves a year. The average figure over the next century and a half, during which the trade to Spanish America was fairly stable, was 3,500 slaves a year. Brazil became a major importer of slaves from the 1570s. There were probably fewer than 15,000 black slaves in Brazil in 1600, but numbers soared thereafter with the growth of sugar plantations, and the colony was soon absorbing more slaves than the whole Spanish Empire put together.

For the first 150 years or so of the colonial era, Spanish naval supremacy and Portuguese control of many of the sources of slaves denied adequate supplies of this resource to the British, Dutch, and French colonies. But as demand for slaves grew, routes of supply diversified—through piracy and illicit trading at first, then increasingly by agreement of the Spanish and Portuguese authorities with slavers of other nationalities. In the 1640s, Dutch slavers turned the island of Curaçao, off the coast of Venezuela, into a huge slaving station, supplying Spanish colonies at first and, increasingly, their own. Scandinavian traders entered the market in the 1650s. From the late 1660s, French and English companies tried to break into the slave trade. In the third quarter of the seventeenth century, nearly 15,000 slaves a year left Africa on average. In the final quarter, the number increased to 24,000 a year.

After experiments with other kinds of enforced labor, slavery became the universal method to develop the plantation crops, including the rice and cotton that, in preference to tobacco, coffee, and sugar, suited some of the land the English seized in North America. The system was imitated from Spanish and Portuguese precedents in areas where Native Americans were reduced by disease or refused to do plantation work. Climate drove it, as is apparent from the failure of early antislavery laws in Georgia, which was founded in 1733 as a refuge for the British poor. Subtropical America could not be made to pay without labor from Africa. Nowhere else could supply enough workers adaptable to the climate.

The Columbian Exchange: Plants, Animals, Microbes, and People

1492	Columbus arrives in the New World, beginning process of biological exchange
1500s	Horses and cattle introduced to New World
1510	Importation of slave labor in the Spanish colonies begins
1555	First record of maize cultivation in China
1570s	Brazil becomes a major importer of slaves
1580s	Brazil becomes the world's major sugar producer
ca. 1700	Native American population in regions penetrated by Europeans declines 60 to 90 percent
1700s	Coffee becomes popular in Europe and Middle East Coffee production begins in Brazil and Indonesia

WILD FRONTIERS: ENCROACHING SETTLEMENT

The slave trade was part of the development of new ways to exploit the soil, which, in combination with the widening of trade, increased the wealth of the world. This could be called the economic dividend of imperialism: the extension of land exploited for ranching, farming, and mining, and the conversion of some land from relatively less-productive to relatively more-productive methods of exploitation.

Northern and Central Asia: The Waning of Steppeland Imperialism

In northern and Central Asia, the political background was of a shift of power, as steppeland imperialism waned and the growing strength and reach of settled empires in China, Persia, and Russia squeezed the pastoralists' domains (see Map 17.2). New attempts to galvanize the power of the steppelanders, by leaders who claimed descent from Genghis Khan or his heroic lieutenants (see Chapter 13), brought little success. At the beginning of the sixteenth century, for instance, two new enemies locked horns in southwest Asia. The pastoralist Uzbek (OOZ-behk) Empire, with its heartlands in the steppes of Transoxania, between the Aral Sea and Lake Balkhash, celebrated the identity of "men of the steppe: all our wealth consists of horses; their flesh is our favorite food. . . . Houses have we none." The Safavid Empire of Persia, which was largely based on settled agriculture, was their neighbor to the south (see Chapter 19). To judge from the previous 500 years, anyone tempted to bet on the outcome of a clash between these two states would back the steppelanders to win. But, during nearly a century of warfare, the Safavids repeatedly got the upper hand, until a final Persian victory in 1597 provoked the breakup of the Uzbek state into small khanates.

Meanwhile, at the eastern end of the steppes, the Mongols found it impossible to renew a lasting threat to China. They could not even, for much of the time, securely dominate Tibet, which in the seventeenth century became the objective of the most ambitious Mongol chiefs.

There was, however, one uncharacteristic and perhaps deceptive instance of steppeland dynamism in the period. In the 1640s, a Manchu army, which the Chinese Empire had created to help police the Mongol frontier, intervened decisively in a Chinese civil war, conquered China (see Chapter 19), and dethroned the last Ming emperor in 1644. In more or less token ways, the Manchus imposed their own values on China. One of the first commands the new regime, which survived until 1912, issued was that Chinese should signify their submission by shaving their hair in Manchu fashion. According to Confucian notions of filial piety, hair was part of the sacred legacy children inherited from their parents and therefore should not be cut off. But the Manchu commander replied to objectors, "I spared your heads and now you want to keep your hair?" In most respects, however, the new dynasty rapidly adopted Chinese ways. Indeed, the great achievement of the Qing (cheeng)—the name the Manchu dynasty adopted in China—was to reverse the direction of empire. The Qing conquered much of the steppeland and spread Chinese culture deep into Central Asia.

Disputes over Tibet eventually provoked China into sustained war against the Mongols. In the 1690s, the Kangxi (kong-shee) emperor, himself a Manchu, campaigning in person on the Mongol front, described in letters home his days of early rising, "braving the sand and the dust" with "hands all blistered from holding the

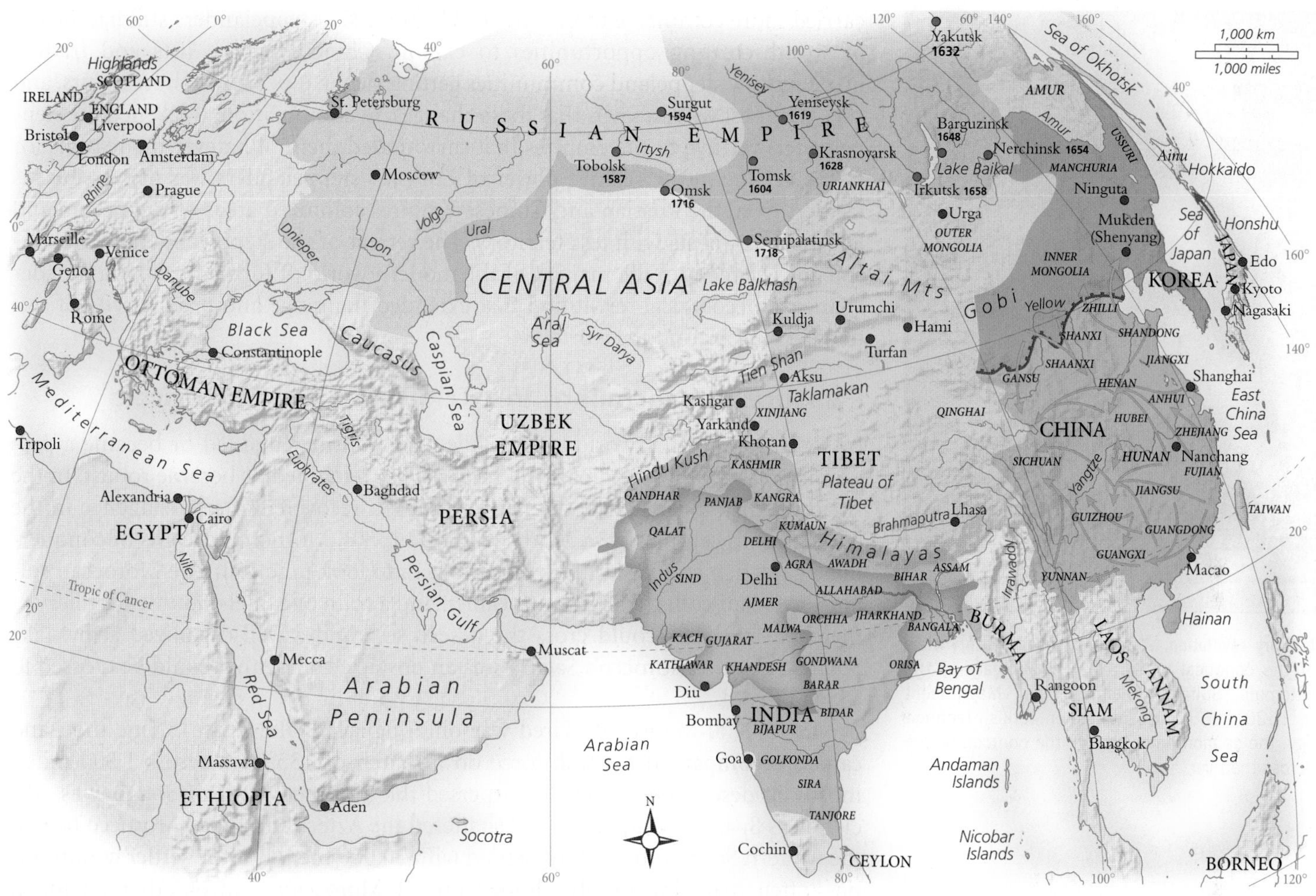

reins." By 1697, he was able to announce, with only a little exaggeration, "There is no Mongol principality that has not submitted to my rule." The historic pattern of imperialism in Central Asia was undergoing a kind of inversion. The Chinese Empire was reaching into the Mongol steppe, instead of lying at the periodic mercy of steppeland conquerors.

Why did the balance of power between settled life and pastoralism shift in favor of the former? The usual answer appeals to the so-called **military revolution** that accompanied the rise of firepower technology. Large forces of well-drilled, fire-armed infantry, with heavy artillery behind scientifically designed fortifications, made "gunpowder empires" invulnerable to steppeland cavalry. Demographic change also favored the settled peoples, whose populations grew faster than those of pastoralists. The progress of Islam and Buddhism in Central Asia supposedly eroded the ideologies of conquest that had animated earlier steppeland empires. Changes in the pattern of trade in the seventeenth century, when the role of the Silk Roads declined in relation to oceanic trade routes, cut off some of the liquid wealth that mobilized nomad war bands.

None of these explanations seems adequate. Steppelanders had adapted to new warfare technologies in the past. The Mongols, for instance, would never have been able to conquer China without incorporating infantry and siege engines into their armies (see Chapter 13). Settled neighbors had always outnumbered pastoral peoples, whose economic system, by its very nature, demands a lot of grazing land to feed relatively fewer mouths. Although many new trade routes

MAP 17.2

Imperialism and Settlement in Eurasia, 1600–1725

- Russian Empire, ca. 1600
- Russian Empire, ca. 1600–1725
- Russian cities founded 1587–1718
- Qing Empire in ca. 1644
- Qing Empire in ca. 1660
- Qing Empire by ca. 1770
- internal migration in China in the 18th century
- Mughal Empire, ca. 1700
- Mughal Empire, ca. 1605
- Japanese expansion northward
- *Ainu* people

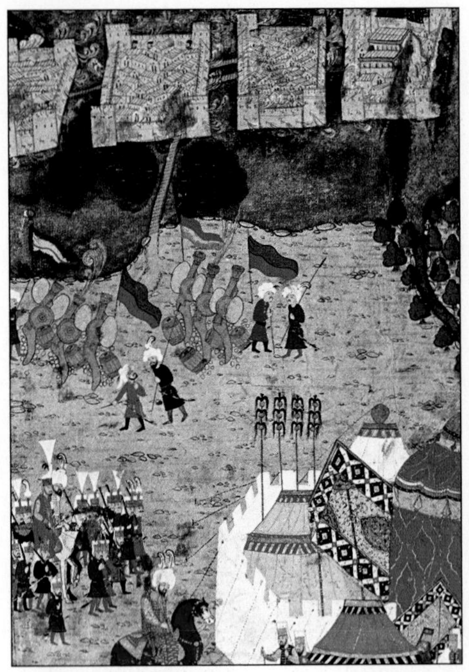

Military revolution. A late sixteenth-century view of the conquest of Szigetvár in Hungary by the Ottoman Sultan Suleiman the Magnificent (r. 1520–1566) concentrates on Turkish technology: the cannon belching fire, the pontoon bridge across the river.

carried more commerce than those of Central Asia, steppelanders still had plenty of wealth-creating opportunities to exploit. Chinese tribute lists and trading licenses show steppeland communities getting richer, especially in horses, furs, and silks. The best we can say is that these changes, in combination, weakened the steppelanders relative to the empires that surrounded them. Whatever the reasons for it, the decline in the relative power of Eurasia's steppelanders was irreversible, as farmers from the Russian and Chinese Empires colonized areas of steppeland and left the pastoralists with less territory. The retreat of the steppelanders was a conspicuous element in the making of the modern world. It formed part of a broader change: an ecological revolution that extended the range and productivity of settled farming around the world.

Pastoral Imperialism in Africa and the Americas

In some parts of the world, meanwhile, pastoralism remained or became a predominant way of life, and pastoral imperialism remained or became robust. In the African Sahel, for instance, the native tradition recovered after a challenge in the late sixteenth century from Morocco. In the 1580s, Morocco's dreams of conquering a gold-rich empire in black Africa began to look practical. The Moroccan sultan al-Mansur collected 2,500 marksmen and a train of camel-mounted artillery. If merchant caravans could cross the desert, so could a well-organized army. Like Spain's Atlantic, Morocco's Sahara was an obstacle course that could be crossed to a land of gold.

In 1588, al-Mansur declared war on Songhay (SOHN-geye). Nine thousand camels accompanied his task force on a march of 135 days across 1,500 miles, mostly of desert. The survivors dispersed the mounted hosts of Songhay as efficiently as Spanish conquerors had shattered the Aztecs and Incas. Morocco turned the western Sahel into a colony settled with 20,000 men. But the settler communities, often marrying locally, slipped out of Moroccan control. After an initial bonanza, the gold shipments dwindled, and by the 1630s, Morocco's gold reserves were running out. No outside power again attempted to conquer the Sahel until the French arrived in the nineteenth century. The supremacy of the Sahel pastoralists remained secure.

The centuries-old process of expansion of arable farming from the Ethiopian highlands went into reverse in the sixteenth century, as pagan and Muslim pastoralist invaders from the east and south seized lands and destroyed the monasteries that were the engines of Ethiopian frontier settlement. At the southern tip of Africa, herding grew in economic importance. The Cape of Good Hope had long been grazed by thousands of head of long-horned cattle, herded by pastoralists who called themselves Khoi and who had probably been driven into the region by Bantu farmers from the north. The total numbers of livestock doubled in the second half of the seventeenth century, when Dutch settlers introduced sheep following the establishment of a colony of the Dutch East India Company on the Cape in 1652. The Dutch followed Khoi strategies for selecting seasonal grazing and corralling their herds against predators. Although the Dutch also practiced arable farming, their ranching activities were incomparably greater.

In the Americas, of course, there had never been much pastoralism because there had never been large domesticable livestock herds, except for the llamas and their cousins in the Andes. In the sixteenth and seventeenth centuries, however, the introduction of horses, cattle, and sheep made new ways of life possible, raising the prospect of empires whose economy was based on herding livestock. It is tempting to see Spanish and Portuguese imperialism in parts of what are now Mexico and

Brazil as a form of pastoral imperialism imposed on sedentary Indian peoples. Sheep and cattle numbered millions by the early seventeenth century and grazed hundreds of thousands of square miles of land—much of it vacated by native farmers and hunters. But by the late eighteenth and early nineteenth centuries (see Chapter 21), horse-borne Native American empire builders threatened to dominate the prairie and the pampa.

So in parts of the world, arable farming lost acreage or yield. In other areas, methods of exploiting the soil remained limited to hunting and gathering. Although California and parts of Australia, for instance, were highly suited to arable farming, their native inhabitants were uninterested in changing methods of feeding themselves that had worked satisfactorily for thousands of years. Not until European intrusions in the eighteenth century did ranching and tillage begin fundamentally to alter their landscapes. But the main trend of the period was the extension of new forms of exploitation—especially arable farming—onto lands where it had never before been practiced. The new empires, which encouraged colonists and drove and mined for new resources, forced the pace of this change (see Map 17.2).

IMPERIALISM AND SETTLEMENT IN EUROPE AND ASIA

The Russian conquest of Kazan in the 1550s made possible the colonization of the "black earth" regions of the lower Volga River and southwest steppeland, pressing back and penning Mongol and Turkic herdsmen. By the end of the sixteenth century, a million settlers had turned a quarter of the region to grain cultivation. Although the conquest of Siberia was launched for the fur trade, the ambition to see the land colonized gradually eclipsed the original vision. The foundation of frontier cities marked the progress of colonization: Tobolsk on the Irtysh River in 1587, Tomsk in 1604, Barguzinsk in 1648, Nerchinsk in 1654. By the eighteenth century, there were 300,000 peasants, outnumbering the surviving native Siberians.

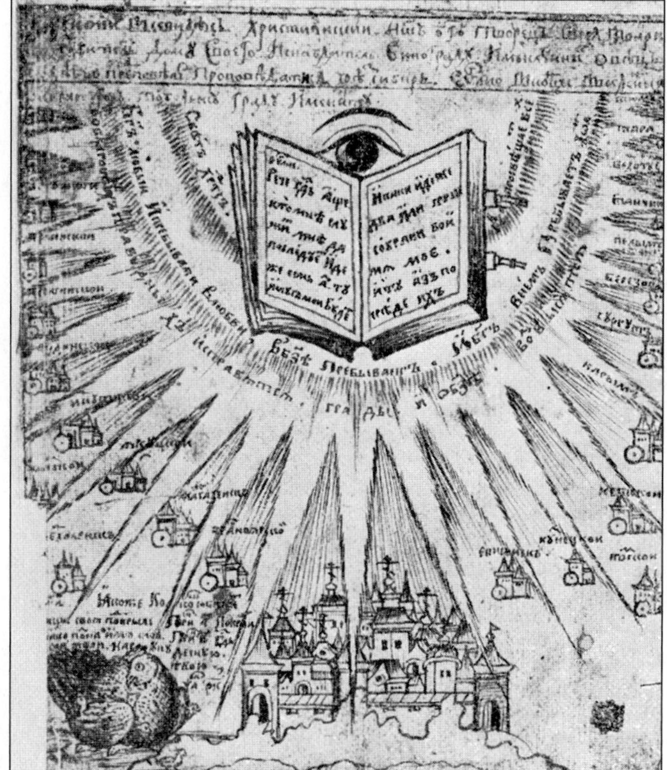

The Remezov Chronicle. Several narrative accounts document the Russian conquest of Siberia. In the Remezov Chronicle, written about 1700, and illustrated with 154 pen and ink drawings, Russian territorial expansion is depicted as an evangelizing and civilizing mission. Shown here is the title page from the Chronicle. The panel at the top of the page reads: "From the beginning of time, our Christian God, the All-Seer... decreed for the Gospels to be preached throughout Siberia to the ends of the universe and the lomit of the mountains to the famous city of Tobolsk." Tobolsk is flatteringly depicted at the bottom of the page, while rays from the Gospel spread to 21 other towns.

Similar appropriations of territory by encroaching farmers displaced traditional peoples at the extremities of Eurasia in the British Isles and Japan. The English and lowland Scots waged wars to seize land from Ireland to the Highlands and islands of Scotland. These were, from one point of view, culture wars that self-styled civilization waged against so-called savagery, by Protestants against Catholics, by English speakers against Celtic speakers, by feudalism against tribalism. They were also wars fought to convert pastoral land to arable. In Japan, after the Ainu War of 1669–1672, about half of Hokkaido was set aside for Japanese peasants to settle, at the expense of the displaced natives, whom the Japanese classed as primitive and savage, using language similar to that of English and Scots propaganda about the highlanders, islanders, and Gaelic Irish.

China

Imperial China sponsored the biggest movements of agricultural settlers in frontier regions and new conquests. Uncultivated land was wasted land. Sixteenth-century Chinese officials denounced the "laziness" of gatherers of wild reeds on land that could grow food. Manchu conquest of Sichuan in southern China eliminated—so it was said—three-quarters of the people. Yet between 1667 and 1707, tax emptions lured more than 1.5 million settlers to Sichuan. Here and on the southeast frontier, the pressure of intensive new settlement provoked conflicts. Rebellious tribes were penned in reservations. Militarized agricultural colonies grew wheat, barley, peas, and corn while keeping the natives obedient. Schools spread Chinese language and values.

The civil wars of the third quarter of the seventeenth century, which pitched the last Ming loyalists against the Manchu conquerors, drove Chinese peasants out of the densely populated provinces of Fujian and Guangdong (gwahng-dahng) into Guangzxi (gwahng-shee) and the Yangtze highlands to the tea and timber industries or to cultivate sweet potatoes or maize. Celebrating his conquests against the "half-human" natives of Guizhou (gway-joh) in the mid–seventeenth century, a Manchu general described "chiseling" through the "forests that extend beyond the horizon. . . .Every day, for our imperial court, we've developed new arable lands. . . . So these far-off wastelands and tribal domains yield us menials and serving girls."

Large-scale immigration preceded the Chinese conquest of Taiwan in the 1660s. During some four decades of Dutch rule, which preceded the Chinese conquest, Dutch colonialists rewarded Chinese migrants with land concessions, cheap seed, draft animals, and tax breaks. By the time Chinese took over the government, over 35,000 settlers had brought nearly 25,000 acres under the plow, growing mainly rice and cane sugar. When the Manchu government assumed control of the island in 1684, the "raw aboriginals" enjoyed a period of official favor. The Manchus used the native deerstalkers to repress the suspect immigrant Chinese population in an offshore province where resistance to Manchu conquest had been strong. But that did not prevent the depletion of the deer herds, as Chinese peasants encroached on land officially reserved for the native Taiwanese.

To the north of traditional China, in the borderlands of Mongolia and Manchuria, colonization proceeded on a different footing. The Kangxi emperor (r. 1661–1722) tried to stop the colonization of Manchuria on the grounds that he "wished to maintain the original equestrian and hunting ways and martial virtues of the Manchus and Mongols in their home territory, which should remain

Building a dike in seventeenth-century China. Peasant conscripts rig screws to drive piles into the mud to form the walls of the dike. Others use heavy wooden hammers to level the dike, or dig earth, which fellow-workers shift in baskets yoked by poles.

a recruiting ground for soldiers." In practice, however, the frontier of settlement could not be controlled. The cultivated zone of Manchuria grew by nearly 30,000 acres in the decade following Kangxi's decree.

The earliest colonization had a camp-life quality. In the frontier town of Ning'an (neen-ahn), in the generation after its foundation in 1660, only 400 households lived inside the ruined wall of mud. There was "no person of leisure" and the exiles' womenfolk—"descendants of the rich and honorable families of China"—slid barefoot down the icy hillside under the burden of water from the only well.

Yet anyone with scholarly pretensions—let alone degrees—was prized in Ning'an. The deference the natives accorded to the Chinese and the prosperity of the settlers impressed a visitor in 1690. The older merchants even "greeted the military governor as a younger brother": In other words, they affected superiority over him. The hierarchies of home persisted alongside new rankings the emerging society of the frontier had evolved.

India

We can detect the same trends—imperial expansion, fostering new settlement, increasing the range of farming, and exploiting new resources—in India. Forest clearance was a policy the Mughal Emperors (see Chapter 16) embraced determinedly. In Bengal, deforestation was part of a long-standing struggle to advance the frontier of settlement and of Islam by granting forested areas to Muslim holy men and communities, who planted wet rice in the cleared zones. On the edges of the Mughal heartland, deforestation was an instrument of control, uprooting the jungles where bandits and rebels sheltered, and encouraging settlement and, therefore, increasing revenues for the state. The emperor received a third of every harvest. Indian peasants generally produced two crops a year—whether of millet, rice, or wheat. Lumberjacks accompanied seventeenth-century Mughal armies. Colonists who followed them to new lands received tax concessions and cheap plows. When the Mughals conquered areas from Burma in 1665, they evicted the existing population as ruthlessly as any European imperialists and introduced hundreds of Muslim religious foundations to clear the forest and plant rice.

NEW EXPLOITATION IN THE AMERICAS

The decline of the Native American population may have led to the abandonment of vast zones that the Indians had farmed before the Europeans arrived. But colonial regimes found alternative methods to exploit the land that, in total, probably made the colonial economy as productive as the Indian system had been: mining, ranching, and plantations (see Map 17.3). The arrival of plows, which had been unknown in the Americas before the Europeans brought them, meant that heavy soils could be exploited for the first time. Horses, mules, and oxen took on burdens Native American porters formerly bore on their backs.

The Spanish Empire

The Spanish Empire in the Americas had every avenue to wealth at its disposal. Suitable environments for all the new kinds of activity were available in abundance, while traditional native economies continued to produce their time-honored crops—such as maize, beans, squash, cotton, and cacao in Mesoamerica or coca, potatoes, and sweet potatoes in the Andes—and generate tribute. The most

Great Slave Lake
Carrier
Chipewyan
Lake Athabasca
Beaver
Hudson Bay
Fort Churchill
York Factory 1682
Churchill
Nelson
Severn Factory
RUPERT'S LAND
James Bay
East Cree
Naskapi
Labrador
Saskatchewan
Cree
Lake Winnipeg
Fort Albany 1670
Eastmain
Rupert House 1668
Moose Factory 1671
Montagnais
Beothuk
Newfoundland
Gulf of St. Lawrence
Cape Breton Island
Kutenai
Rocky Mountains
Blackfoot
Gros Ventres
Assiniboine
Nez Perce
Flathead
Crow
Northern Shoshoni
Great Plains
Fort Kaministikwia
Ojibwa
Lake Superior
Ottawa
Nipissing
Algonquin
St. Lawrence River
Quebec 1608
Micmac
Halifax 1749
NOVA SCOTIA
NEW FRANCE
Montreal 1642
NEW ENGLAND
Lake Champlain
Yanktonai
Mississippi
Santee
Arikara
Teton
Dakota
Bannock
Shoshoni
Cheyenne
Michilimackinac 1697
Menomini
Lake Huron
Huron
Petun
Fort Orange 1624 (Albany 1664)
Boston 1630
Western Shoshoni
NORTH AMERICA
Yankton
Winnebago
Lake Michigan
Sauk
Fox
Mascouten
Detroit 1701
L. Ontario
Niagara
Mohican
Pequot
Narraganset
Newport
East India Trade
Iroquois
Kickapoo
L. Erie
Miami
Susquehanna
Delaware
New Amsterdam 1625 (New York 1664)
Philadelphia 1682
Powhatan
Pawnee
Iowa
Oto
Illinois
Ute
Arapaho
Arkansas
Missouri
Southern Paiute
Shawnee
Ohio
Appalachian Mountains
Richmond 1733
Jamestown 1607
ATLANTIC OCEAN
Colorado
Hopi
Navajo
Queres
Taos
Taos 1680
Santa Fe 1609
Zuni
Acoma
Pecos
Mojave
Kiowa
Kansa
Kaskaskia
The Illinois Post 1700
Osage
LOUISIANA
INDIAN TERRITORY
Yuchi
Monacan
Tutelo
Tuscarora
Pamlico
Western Apache
Cocopa
Apache
Imuris
Jocome
Jano
Mescalero Apache
Comanche
Wichita
Caddo
Quapaw
Chickasaw
Cherokee
Catawba
Charleston 1672
Coosa
Creek Confederacy
Savannah 1733
Alabama
Hitichi
Yamasee
Papago
Lower Pima
Nevome
Suma
Jumano
Concho
Opata
Lipan
Tonkawa
Tunica
Choctaw
Houma
New Orleans 1718
Chitimacha
Acolapissa
Apalachee
St. Augustine 1565
Potano
1565
Timucua
Cochimi
Tarahumara
Tubar
Mayo
Atakapa
Karankawa
Rio Grande
Toboso
Coahuilteco
Waicuri
Tropic of Cancer
Guasave
Tepehuan
Zacateco
Guachichil
Tamaulipeco
Gulf of Mexico
1567
Ais
1566
Seminole
Calusa
Tekesta
Bahamas 1629
Tropic of Cancer
Tampico
Havana 1511
Arawak
Cuba
Hispaniola
Danish Virgin Islands.
San Juan 1509
Puerto Rico
Antigua 1632
Guadeloupe 1635
Martinique 1635
St Lucia 1605
Barbados 1605
Grenada 1650
Trinidad 1577
Mérida 1542
VICEROYALTY OF NEW SPAIN
Pame
Jonaz
Tlaxcalan
Cuyute
Loco
Mexico City 1521
Veracruz 1519
Yucatan Peninsula
Yucatan Maya
SAINT-DOMINGUE
Ciboney
Santo Domingo 1497
1509–1655
1655
Jamaica
West Indies
Aztec
Zoque
BELIZE
Gulf of Honduras
Trujillo 1525
Caribbean Sea
Mixe
Chorti
Paya
Mosquito
Xinca
Cholutec
Pipil
Matagalpa
MOSQUITO COAST
Nicarao
Aruba
Bonaire
Curaçao
Caracas 1567
Cartagena 1532
PACIFIC OCEAN
Talamanca
Guymi
Panama 1519
VICEROYALTY OF NEW GRANADA
500 km
500 miles
N

MAP 17.3 **Land Exploitation in the Americas up to ca. 1725**

Cuzco, home city of the Incas, never really looked like this. Built amid mountains, its monumental palaces, temples, and fortifications, constructed of huge blocks of stone, enclosed irregular spaces. But when Georg Braun and Franz Hogenberg published their views of the world's great cities in the late sixteenth century, they imagined Cuzco as a flat grid—the supposedly ideal form of Renaissance urban planning that inspired many colonial American cities.

vivid measure of success were the cities of Spanish America, for Spanish imperialism was uncompromisingly urban minded.

Spanish colonization slotted into the framework of Native American civilizations. In the 1520s and 1530s, while the Spanish monarchy absorbed the existing great urban centers of Mesoamerica and the Andean region through conquest or diplomacy, the biggest cities of the Americas acquired new characteristics: Spanish-speaking elites, a new Native American middle class that served Spaniards' economic needs, an African-American slave class for domestic service, Spanish courts and town councils, Christian religious foundations, cathedrals, and even, in Mexico City and Lima, universities and printing presses. Similar developments followed Spanish colonization in other parts of the Americas. Spanish colonists founded cities wherever they went. The new cities rooted easily in areas where native cities and a strong urban tradition already existed. In other areas of mainland Spanish America—California, Florida, the frontier grasslands of North and South America—urbanization was harder, growing slowly from kernels that missions, military garrisons, and naval stations planted.

European styles in buildings smothered or supplemented the old angular look of Native American architectures with arches and domes. Some old Indian cities were flattened and rebuilt. Others were lightly adapted and recrafted. Some were abandoned with the collapse of the Native American population. New cities on new sites, like Lima, Peru, still perhaps the most Spanish of Spanish-American cities in looks and atmosphere, replaced some Native American capitals. Parts of Old San Juan in Puerto Rico look exactly like a Spanish city of the seventeenth and eighteenth centuries, complete with walls, sea gates, courtyard gardens, and cathedral square. The civic model of life, the city-centered model of administration, was extended into new areas. From the 1570s, the Spanish crown issued exact regulations to construct new cities, with their grid plan and classically inspired buildings and monumental scale, the exact placing of cathedrals, government buildings, hospitals, and schools. But in North America in the seventeenth and early eighteenth centuries, beyond the Spanish frontier, cities of English and French construction generally remained, in a sense, in the Iroquois tradition. They were largely built of wood and, though intended for permanent occupancy, had a gimcrack air of instant shabbiness.

Brazil

Other European empires in the Americas lacked the local labor sources that the Spanish lands could exploit. As a result, they tended at first to expand landward on only a modest scale, so that they could increase the areas of cultivation of the crops they introduced, such as sugar in the Caribbean, West Indian tobacco in Virginia, rice in South Carolina, and wheat almost everywhere. In Brazil, sugar was suitable only to coastal enclaves. It would never, on its own, have induced planters to create a large territorial domain in the hinterland. Rivalry with Spain to control the Amazon, however, turned Portuguese thoughts toward the Brazilian interior, especially after rival Spanish and Portuguese expeditions tested the navigability of the Amazon River system in the 1630s. Gold and diamonds, discovered in the Brazilian province of Minas Gerais (meaning "general mines") in the 1680s, proved the incentive for Portugal to drive its Brazilian frontier inland.

Founding Dates for Spanish Cities in the Americas

Caribbean and North America		South America	
Santo Domingo	1496	Cajamarca	1532
San Juan (Puerto Rico)	1509	Cartagena	1532
San Cristobal (Havana)	1515	Cuzco	1533
Panama City	1519	Quito	1534
Mexico City	1521	Buenos Aires	1536
Guadalajara	1531	Lima	1535
Meridá	1542	Santiago	1541
Zacatecas	1546	La Paz	1548
San Juan Bautista	1564	Mendoza	1561
San Augustín (Florida)	1565	Caracas	1567
Santa Fé (New Mexico)	1610		

British North America

Elsewhere in the Americas, major sources of gold, silver, pearls, and gems remained a Spanish monopoly. The areas left for the English and French to exploit contained only fool's gold, such as the iron pyrites Martin Frobisher found in Canada in 1576, which deceived investors into ruin and lured adventurers to their deaths. Furs were the "black gold" of the far north. South of the habitat of the beaver, deerskins represented a similar luxury product. But, like the timber and fish that also abounded in and around North America, resources of these kinds could not alone sustain permanent or populous colonies.

Except in the Caribbean, where sugar and, later, coffee would grow on islands seized from or ignored by Spain, it was hard to find crops suitable to sustain colonial life. Tobacco was the first, introduced into Virginia in 1614. Later in the century, rice made fairly large-scale settlement practical in the coastal areas of South Carolina. Independent farmers could always cultivate smallholdings for their own subsistence, as they did even in the rocky soils of New England from the 1620s.

But this form of exploitation could never be the foundation of prosperity. New England only really began to reveal its potential as a great world center of wealth and civilized life in the eighteenth century when so many of the inhabitants took to the sea. Like ancient Greece and Phoenicia (Chapter 5), New England made up for the poverty of its home soils by trade and exploiting marine resources. Three trades in particular contributed to transforming New England's economy into one of the richest, per capita, in the world by the late eighteenth century: first, the slave trade, in which New England merchants worked both as shippers and dealers; second, the export of locally produced rum and manufactured goods to the slave-producing and slave-consuming markets with which the slave trade connected the New Englanders; and finally the so-called **East India trade**—mainly with China, by way of Cape Horn on the southern tip of South America—for tea and porcelain to sell at home.

From Virginia southward, English North American colonies resembled those that Spanish, Dutch, and Portuguese investors were already exploiting in Mesoamerica and South America. They were hot and wet, with torrid lowlands that could be adapted to plant cash crops with the labor of imported slaves. The first English-run sugar industry in Barbados was copied from the Dutch enterprise in Pernambuco, with Dutch capital and know-how. The effects on settler society were predictable. Economic reliance on

Imperialism and Colonization in Europe, Asia, and the Americas

1520s–1530s	Absorption of Mesoamerican and Andean cities into Spanish Empire
1550s	Russian conquest of Kazan
ca. 1560–1650	Russian colonization of lower Volga and Siberia
1600s	Expansion, colonization, and intensive farming in Mughal India
	Outflow of Chinese and Japanese settlers to southeast Asia
	Export of African slaves, especially to the Americas
	British colonization of North America
ca. 1620s–1660s	Large-scale Chinese immigration to Taiwan
1667–1707	1.5 million settlers arrive in Sichuan
1680s	Discovery of gold and diamonds prompts further Portuguese expansion in Brazil
Late seventeenth century	Japanese peasants displace native inhabitants of Hokkaido
1700s	New England becomes a world center of trade

large-scale, capital-intensive enterprises created huge disparities of wealth. English planters in parts of North America and the Caribbean became, in effect, the lords of huge estates, more reminiscent of the Mediterranean or Brazil than of England or New England. In 1700, the top 5 percent of settlers by wealth owned half of one county in Virginia.

HOME FRONTS IN EUROPE AND ASIA

Equal efforts were under way to exploit the homelands of the empires. Governments all over the world undertook land surveys to determine the extent of production and the possibilities to increase it. In the 1570s, King Philip II of Spain ordered the most comprehensive survey of his realms that any European state had ever undertaken. It was soon extended to the New World and illustrated with maps that Native Americans made. In Japan in 1580, the shogun Hideyoshi (see Chapter 16) commanded a survey of Japan that would include the dimensions and soil quality of every rice field and the location of every irrigation channel. Villagers who withheld information would be crucified. Landowners who failed to cooperate would be executed. Driven by unpitying force, the job was finished by 1598. The Mughal regime in India achieved something similar in the late sixteenth century, including a tally of average yields and market prices, field by field. In 1663, frustrated by his inability to locate undeveloped resources in France, Jean-Baptiste Colbert, the chief minister of King Louis XIV, ordered the first scrupulously accurate map of the country to be made by the latest surveying techniques. It was not fully complete until 1789 on the eve of the French Revolution.

New Energy Sources

Efforts to explore the environment led to the discovery and release of new energy sources. Timber from deforestation made an enormous contribution, together with oil from aggressive whaling by European and Japanese seamen in previously unfrequented seas. Cottonseed oil and rapeseed oil in Japan came into use as oil-lamp fuel in the early 1600s. Extracting peat to be burned as fuel from the bogs of Holland became a major industry. In some places, people shifted to coal, mined in increasing quantities in Great Britain, Germany, and the southern Netherlands (modern Belgium, a territory of the Spanish monarchy at the time). Londoners in the mid–sixteenth century burned more than 20,000 tons of coal annually—a little less than a quarter of a ton per inhabitant. By 1700, coal imports to London totaled almost 400,000 tons for a population of about 600,000. In the late seventeenth century, miners in Kyushu, Japan, began to make a success of marketing coal: to peasants for fuel, to refiners of salt and sugar. The Japanese government, meanwhile, adopted policies to conserve and replant forests, reserving valuable timber for official purposes, excluding intruders from endangered forest zones, and rewarding tree planting. "Cherishing the mountains," for the local ruler of Tugaru in the 1660s, was essential to nurture life and reverse forest shrinkage so severe that loggers were invading the northernmost Japanese island of Hokkaido for timber. Coal remained abundant in China, but the market for it remained static. Wood and charcoal still satisfied China's energy needs.

Land Reclamation

Land reclamation complemented the struggle to expand and settle new frontiers. In Holland, after terrible losses to the encroaching sea in the sixteenth century, reclamation became a matter of survival. New windmill-pumping technology drained 57,000 acres of land in North Holland between 1610 and 1640. In all the Dutch added nearly 370,000 acres of land to the total amount available for farming during the century. A minor social revolution accompanied the transformation of the landscape, as smallholders lost access to the sea and were forced to sell out to big landowners. In England, the drainage of the fenlands, which lay just across the sea from Holland in the eastern counties, began in 1600. Enforced by military occupation, against the protests of the local inhabitants, who were dispossessed, the project brought about 480,000 acres under the plow by the early 1650s. In Japan, government-sponsored schemes drained the Yodfo River delta. The Nobi plain in northern Honshu was transformed from "a marshy plain of water birds" to an area settled with hundreds of villages. The Aka River, which once flowed through marshes, fed 12,000 acres of wet rice lands by 1650. The cultivated land area of Japan grew by 82 percent between 1600 and 1720.

Huron women. Published in 1664, the *History of Canada* by the Jesuit priest François du Creux summarized the vast output of the author's fellow missionaries on the subject and helped to spread a favorable image of the Huron among learned readers in Europe. Here the engraver shows industrious Huron women peacefully engaged in a civilized agrarian activity—maize production, in an idealized setting, while an infant's cradle alludes to sentiments and social conventions that European readers would have found comforting and familiar.

FRONTIERS OF THE HUNT

Imperialism promoted more efficient—sometimes more ruthless—exploitation of the Earth. Beyond the edges of empires, improvements in the range and effectiveness of hunting, and the extension of cultivation, were happening in other parts of the world, too. When the English arrived in Virginia, they found thousands of acres under cultivation and maize stocks "of sufficient quantity to fill the holds of several ships."

The Iroquois country of northeast North America is a case in point. Toward the end of what we think of as the Middle Ages, a form of maize was developed suitable for latitudes as far north as the Great Lakes. This zone had about 140 frost-free days a year. Increasingly in the sixteenth and seventeenth centuries, the new crop was planted in forest clearings between the upper Hudson River and Lake Erie, where ecological diversity made ambitious ways of life possible.

The very diversity of their food sources imposed a mobile way of life on the Native Americans of the region. Periodically, soil erosion and forest depletion forced them to shift the sites of their towns. Maize exhausts soil more quickly than other grains. The biggest settlement in the Great Lakes region was the Illinois town of Kaskaskia, with over 7,000 people in 1680, but villages of about 1,000 people were not unusual. To make glades for planting without hard-metal tools, Native Americans cut a ring in the trunk of a tree and set it on fire until the stump burned through. The method yielded ash for fertilizer, but left a landscape strewn with stumps. Farming under these disadvantages could never entirely replace a traditional way of life based on hunting, fishing, and tapping maple trees for syrup. But, like other forest peoples of the Americas who came into contact with colonial and overseas markets, the inhabitants improved their techniques and turnover as hunters too. They adopted firearms for the kill and steel knives to butcher game. Beavers, once hunted for their meat, were now more valuable for the pelts European fur traders demanded. Beavers were almost gone from southern Ontario by the mid-1630s and virtually disappeared from New England by the end of the seventeenth century. In southern parts of North America, deerskins for the European leather trade became an equally valuable product. They made suede breeches, book bindings, and smooth yellow gloves.

MAKING CONNECTIONS

NEW WAYS OF EXPLOITING THE NATURAL ENVIRONMENT, 1500–1700

REGION / ECOLOGICAL ZONE→	NEW FORMS OF EXPLOITATION →	RESULTS
Western Hemisphere (North and South America, Caribbean)/areas with agricultural potential	Mass importation of slaves from Africa after depopulation of Native Americans due to disease	Large areas of North, Central, and South America transformed into plantations for cultivation of sugar, cotton, rice, tobacco, and indigo; creation of large African and mixed-race populations throughout Western Hemisphere
Steppeland; mountainous regions of Asia including Mongolia and Xianjang	Chinese takeover of traditional adversaries, exploitation of natural resources	Well-trained infantry, advanced artillery, well-designed fortifications end the nomadic threat; highland and steppe regions become source for raw materials
Cape of Good Hope, South Africa, Australia	Introduction of sheep and new breeds of cattle, extensive farming by European settlers	Displacement of natives
North and South America/lowlands, high plains	Farming pampas/prairies; felling forests	Creation of large-scale agricultural complexes focusing on wheat, maize, and other commodities for human and livestock consumption for domestic use and export
Mexico, South America	Development of silver and gold mines	Boost global supply of cash
Mexico, South America, and North America	Development of extensive livestock herding	Millions of square miles of lightly populated areas claimed for cattle and sheep herding
North America	Large-scale fur trade in American Midwest, West, and Canada	Beaver, deerskins, and other furs/skins become basis for gradual penetration, settlement of western and northern North America
Eurasia	Land reclamation projects; expansion of timber harvesting, mining	National leaders attempt to solidify control, expand state revenues through systematic exploitation of resources, beginning with thorough mapping and surveying projects

IN PERSPECTIVE: Evolution Redirected

In parts of the world, the effects of the ecological revolutions were delayed until the eighteenth or nineteenth centuries. But the decisive transformations had already occurred by 1700. From China to Mesoamerica and the Andes, a single network of communications transmitted the same varieties of plants and animals. The empires that dominated the zone responded in similar ways to the problems and opportunities of the time. New crops and animals helped the great colonizing movements of the era. They enabled farmers to penetrate new environments and exploit old ones more efficiently. The results included a huge increase in the amount of food people in affected regions could grow or catch. Evolution, meanwhile, was launched on a new course. The divergent history of life forms, which had gone their separate ways, continent by continent, divided from each other by uncrossable seas, now gave way to a convergent trend that has produced the world we inhabit today, when the same germs, plants, and animals occur all over the world, wherever climate permits.

The ecological revolution was the essential precondition for some of the global changes of the next few centuries, fueling some of the major themes of the next two parts of this book: population growth, breakthroughs in exploiting resources, and the globalization of empires and trade. But such effects depended on more than the physical environment. People's mental attitudes to the world changed, too, and, like the ingredients of ecological exchange, they carried these new attitudes with them across the globe through long-range travel, trade, and empire-building. These mental revolutions are the subjects of the next chapter.

CHRONOLOGY

1492	Columbus arrives in the New World, beginning process of biological exchange
1500s	Horses and cattle introduced to New World
1510	Importation of slave labor in the Spanish colonies begins
1520s and 1530s	Absorption of Mesoamerican and Andean cities into Spanish Empire
1550s	Russian conquest of Kazan
1555	First records of maize cultivation in China
ca. 1560–1650	Russian colonization of lower Volga and Siberia
1570s	Philip II of Spain orders survey of his realms
	Brazil becomes a major importer of slaves
1580s	Brazil becomes the world's major sugar producer
1580	Shogun Hideyoshi orders a survey of Japan
1600s	British colonization of North America
	Expansion, colonization, and intensive farming in Mughal India
ca. 1620s–1660s	Large-scale Chinese immigration to Taiwan
1667–1707	1.5 million settlers arrive in Sichuan
1680s	Discovery of gold and diamonds prompts further Portuguese expansion in Brazil
Late seventeenth century	Japanese peasants displace native inhabitants of Hokkaido
ca. 1700	Native American population in regions penetrated by Europeans declines 60 to 90 percent
1700s	Popularity of coffee booms in Europe and Middle East and coffee production begins in Brazil and Indonesia
	New England becomes a world center of trade

PROBLEMS AND PARALLELS

1. Why should the Columbian Exchange be regarded as one of the biggest revolutions in human history?
2. What are some of the explanations for the "age of plagues"? Why did it suddenly end in the mid–eighteenth century?
3. How did human settlement expand its range in the sixteenth and seventeenth centuries? What were the motives behind this expansion? What effect did it have on ecological frontiers? On the way colonialists viewed the natural world?
4. What are the reasons for the massive transplantation of human labor that occurred during the sixteenth and seventeenth centuries? Why did colonial America suffer from severe labor shortages?
5. Why did the balance of power between settled life and pastoralism shift in favor of the settlers in the sixteenth and seventeenth centuries? Where did pastoralism remain a predominant way of life?
6. What made Spanish colonialism in the Americas more advantageous than the ventures of the English or French?

DOCUMENTS IN GLOBAL HISTORY

- Thomas Gage, on chocolate
- Smallpox epidemic in Mexico, 1520, from the *Florentine Codex*
- Huron demographic collapse, from *The Jesuit Relations,* (1669–1670)
- Shi Daonon, "Death of Rats"

Please see the Primary Source DVD for additional sources related to this chapter.

READ ON

The major works on the ecological exchange are A. W. Crosby, *The Columbian Exchange*, and *Ecological Imperialism* (1986). J. F. Richards, *The Unending Frontier* (2003) is a superb, if necessarily selective, environmental history of the period. Classics on particular crops include N. Deerr, *The History of Sugar* (1949); S. Mintz, *Sweetness and Power* (1986); N. Salaman, *History and Social Influence of the Potato* (1985); and A. Warman, *Corn and Capitalism* (2003). M. Elvin, *The Retreat of the Elephants* (2004) is an inspiring general history of the Chinese environment. My book, *Near a Thousand Tables* (2002), puts the exchanges in the context of the history of food. R. Grove, *Green Imperialism* (1996) is an amazingly rich work that argues that European colonialism nurtured environmentalism.

On plague in general, see the works recommended in Chapter 14. The demographic disasters of the New World are the subject of intense controversy: see D. Henige, *Numbers from Nowhere* (1998) and contrast W. M. Denevan, *The Native Population of the Americas in 1492* (1992). The most balanced general treatment is in D. N. Cook, *Born to Die* (1998), though the author's argument that demographics explain the course of "conquest" should be considered critically. On plague in China, C. Benedict, *Bubonic Plague in Nineteenth-Century China* (1996) is important.

On the Atlantic slave trade, H. Thomas, *The Slave Trade* (1999) is a lively history. R. Blackburn, *The Making of New World Slavery* (1998) is an engaging introduction. J. Thornton, *Africa and Africans in the Making of the Atlantic World* (1998) is a model of scholarship and presentation. P. D. Curtin, *The Rise and Fall of the Plantation Complex* (1998); S. W. Mintz and R. Price, *The Birth of African-American Culture* (1992); B. Solow, ed., *Slavery and the Rise of the Atlantic System* (1993); D. Eltis, *The Rise of African Slavery in the Americas* (1999) are all valuable studies of the economies and societies of slave plantations.

M. Sobel, *The World They Made Together* (1989) is important on the slave world of Virginia, and L. Ferguson, *Uncommon Ground* (1995) is full of interesting material on plantation life in the North American South generally.

C. D. Totman, *Early Modern Japan* (1995) is an account particularly strong on environmental awareness. B. Walker, *The Conquest of Ainu Lands* (2001) is admirable. R. L. Edmonds, *Northern Frontiers of Qing China and Tokugawa Japan* (1985) makes an admirable comparative introduction. On Chinese expansion, R. H. G. Lee, *The Manchurian Frontier in Ch'ing History* (1970), and J. Waley-Cohen, *Exile in mid-Qing China* (1991) are indispensable. Ping-ti Ho, *Studies on the Population of China* (1959) is a valuable broad survey of its subject.

D. Twitchett and J. K. Fairbank, eds., *The Cambridge History of China*, vii (1988) is an invaluable guide to China in the period. On the Manchu conquest of China, L. Struve, *Voices from the Ming-Qing Cataclysm* (1998) is a well-selected and structured collection of sources.

There is, as far as I know, no dedicated study in English, but there are some useful pages on al-Mansur's conquest of the Sahara in A. C. Hess, *The Forgotten Frontier* (1978), and J. O. Hunwick, *Timbuktu and the Songhay Empire* (2003) contains some useful documents.

On Russian Siberia, J. Forsyth, *A History of the Peoples of Siberia* (1994) is an impressive and masterful introduction. B. Dmitrishyn et al., eds., *Russia's Conquest of Siberia* (1986) is an enormous compendium of sources. The best edition of the chronicles is T. Armstrong, ed., *Yermak's Campaigns in Siberia* (1975). J. Martin, *Treasure of the Land of Darkness* (2004) is superb on the background of the fur trade. M. Rywkin, ed., *Russian Colonial Expansion* (1988) contains some important papers.

C. Wilson, *England's Apprenticeship* (1965) is an excellent introduction to the economic history of England in the seventeenth century. For the inland see K. Lindley, *Fenland Riots and the English Revolution* (1982). J. de Vries and A. M. van der Woude, *The First Modern Economy* (1997) is the standard work on the early modern Dutch economy.

On the Mughal frontier in Bengal, R. Eaton, *The Rise of Islam and the Bengal Frontier* (1996) is of great value and importance.

On Spanish American cities V. Fraser, *The Architecture of Conquest* (1990) is a monograph (on Peru) well crafted enough to serve as an introduction.

For Brazil, J. Hemming, *Red Gold* (1978) and *Amazon Frontier* (1987) are superb and chilling accounts of the fate of the natives at the time of European conquest and colonization. S. Schwartz, ed., *Tropical Babylons* (2004) is the most up-to-date collection on the sugar colonies. G. Freyre, *The Masters and the Slaves* (1946) is a classic of such significance in Brazilian historiography that it should still be read by anyone interested in the subject. C. R. Boxer, *The Golden Age of Brazil* (1995) is almost in the same category.

B. Trigger's magnificent *A History of the Huron People*, 2 vols. (1976), is unequaled in its field.

CHAPTER

18 Mental Revolutions: Religion and Science in the Sixteenth and Seventeenth Centuries

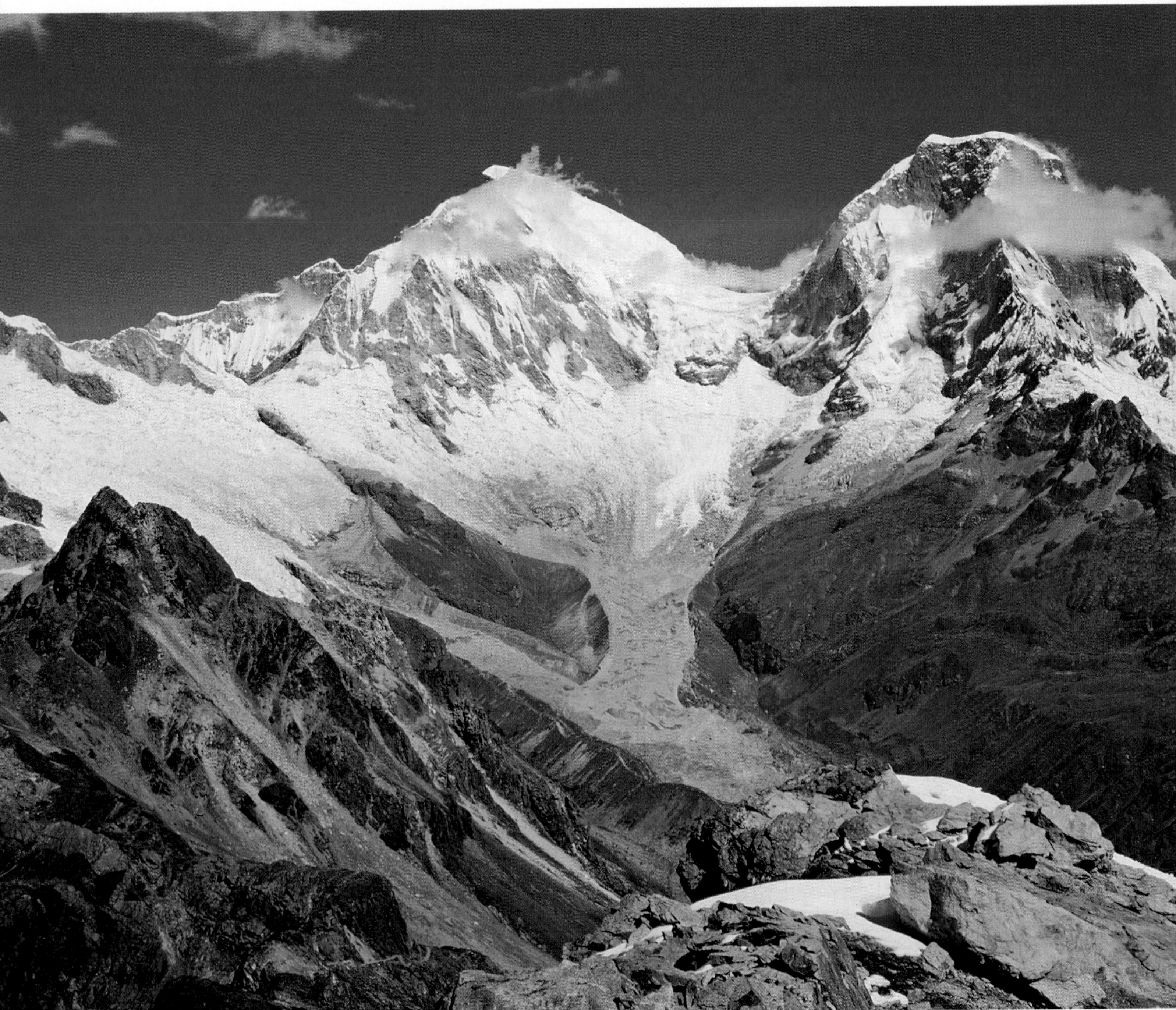

The abrupt landscape of Peru, with its high mountains and tropically hot valleys, impeded but did not deter Spanish conquerors and missionaries. Mount Huascarán, at more than 22,000 feet, was nearly twice the height of anything most Europeans had ever had an opportunity to see.

IN THIS CHAPTER

CHRISTIANITY IN CHRISTENDOM

CHRISTIANITY BEYOND CHRISTENDOM: THE LIMITS OF SUCCESS

THE MISSIONARY WORLDS OF BUDDHISM AND ISLAM
- China and Japan
- The Mongols
- Islam

THE RESULTING MIX: GLOBAL RELIGIOUS DIVERSITY—AMERICAN AND INDIAN EXAMPLES
- Black America
- White America
- India

THE RENAISSANCE "DISCOVERY OF THE WORLD"

THE RISE OF WESTERN SCIENCE

WESTERN SCIENCE IN THE EAST

IN PERSPECTIVE: The Scales of Thought

In October 1595, a young missionary set out from Andamarca in the Peruvian Andes. With an older priest for company, Nicolás de Mastrillo struggled through tracks too steep for horses. At last they reached the house of an Indian chief called Bellunti, who received them with gestures of equality, not submission—with kisses, gifts, and long speeches. Hosts and visitors sat down to dine off clay dishes of Indian food: beans, herbs, chillies, corn, and cassava. A visiting chief was suspicious. "These are not fathers," he said, but spies. Then he relented, noticing how the priests proved their goodwill by eating, without disdain, their hosts' food. The missionaries assured their audience that "we had come only to show them the way to heaven and that we did not intend to make them the slaves of Spaniards nor would we ask them for silver nor gold." Next day, priests and people began to build a chapel, and Mastrillo began to learn the local language.

The letter that tells this story never reached home. Pirates captured it en route, and it ended up in an English archive. It shows more than the precarious nature of communications across the vast distances Europeans routinely traveled in the sixteenth century. It discloses the mind and methods of Mastrillo's mission and the perils and promise of his work. Above all, it shows how human encounters initiated cultural exchanges that crossed the world.

• • • • •

Westerners primarily—but by no means exclusively—initiated the contacts. Christianity, Islam, and Buddhism all contributed to cultural exchange. The sixteenth and seventeenth centuries were an unprecedented era for the revitalization and spread of all three religions. They were also centuries of unprecedented developments in Western science and secular values. Western science reached parts of the world where, previously, it had been unknown. At the same time, encounters with non-Western cultures changed the ways people in the West thought, felt, and, in some respects, behaved.

FOCUS questions

- WHY DID European elites attempt to change Christian practice and teachings during the sixteenth century?
- HOW DID Native Americans and Africans influence Christian beliefs and worship?
- WHERE WERE Muslim and Buddhist missionaries most active in the sixteenth and seventeenth centuries?
- HOW DID the Mughal emperors deal with religious diversity?
- WHY WAS the spread of scientific thought important for the West?
- WHY WERE the Chinese so interested in astronomy?

CHRISTIANITY IN CHRISTENDOM

A new sense of mission had grown in Christendom in the late Middle Ages. Fervor to renew the dynamism of the early Church combined with a new conviction to compel right thinking and to combat heresy, unbelief, and supposedly satanic forces. People with vocations or responsibilities in the Church, or with a strong personal sense of their relationship with God, increasingly took it upon themselves to spread active, committed, Christian awareness, informed by a knowledge of dogma. Among the consequences were new religious orders, new techniques of prayer, new fashions in devotion, and increased social control (see Chapter 19).

There were still parts of society and places where Christianity had hardly reached or only superficially penetrated. In the sixteenth and seventeenth centuries, the mission-minded felt the need of a new conversion strategy, addressed to people low down the social scale: the poor; the rootless urban masses; the neglected country folk; children; the peoples of forest, bog, and mountain.

The countryside was Europe's pagan backyard. Rural communities still lived in worlds full of spirits and demons, where natural forces were personified and placated. A miller in northern Italy in the early sixteenth century could describe a remarkably coherent universe made "of cheese and worms," from which Christian traditions about creation were entirely absent. A Jesuit priest in France in 1553 was appalled to find rural people "who have never heard of mass nor of a single word of the faith." Another Jesuit in Spain in 1615 derided overseas missions "when we have so many people here who do not know whether they believe in God." In 1628, a member of England's Parliament complained of regions of the country "where God was little better known than among the Indians." In 1693, a Swedish governor of Livonia ordered the smashing of the rocks and groves people worshipped "so that not the least memorial may be left which could be used for superstition."

Campaigns like these were part of an attempt by ministers of religion to enforce a monopoly over ritual. For instance, in Spain, from the early sixteenth century, the church hierarchy ceased to validate lay people's claims to have experienced saintly visions. The universal veneration of Christ and his mother, the Virgin Mary, replaced local saints and virgins.

excerpts from the Council of Trent

Lay competition in the clergy's proper fields became subject to attempts at control or eradication, especially fortune-telling, folk healing, and magic. The Council of Trent—a series of meetings from 1545 to 1563 of bishops who acknowledged the pope's authority—ordered that "all superstition shall be removed" and the cults of saints purged of "perversion by the people...." The war on popular religion was an attempt to wean people away from a religion of survival in this world toward one of salvation in the next. Clergy of all Christian traditions strove against trials of rats and exorcisms of locusts, appeals to folk healers and wisewomen, vows to saints for worldly purposes, charms to master nature, and spells to conjure the supernatural. In the seventeenth century, Catholic clergymen were prominent in reclassifying witchcraft as a psychotic delusion, but all kinds of Christian communities remained subject, with diminishing frequency, to the fear of witches.

Public rituals affect private lives. Formal religion now intruded as never before in Europe into the most private activity: sex. In the sixteenth and seventeenth centuries in most of Europe, successful campaigns brought under the supervision of the clergy all contracts in which men and women agreed to live with each other as man and wife. Ostensibly, for instance, the Spanish Inquisition, founded in 1478, was a tribunal of faith to monitor the sincerity of former Muslims and Jews who had converted to Christianity under official pressure. In practice, most of its efforts in the second half of the sixteenth century were devoted to controlling lay people's sex lives. Bigamy and fornication were among the most common crimes the Inquisition investigated. Church leaders had never completely approved of sex, but they thought it did least harm when they themselves licensed it. Charity, as well as power lust, motivated them. It seemed vital, as a saintly campaigner claimed in 1551, "to invalidate all marriages where there is no witness" because "an infinite number of maidens have been deceived and undone...."

Witchcraft. The south German draftsman of these scenes of witchcraft turned the subject into a pretext for dark humor and social satire. Artists traditionally contrasted scenes of worldly pleasures with depictions of the pangs of hell. Here women cavort with demons in a forest clearing, where dancing hints coyly at sex, while a devil roasts meat. But the witches' executioners, stoking fires and armed with pitchforks, are almost equally demonic.

The newly self-conscious godly elites did not, however, consist entirely of clergy. On the contrary, clerical demand for more responsive congregations met lay demand for more access to the mysteries of religion: prayer, the sacraments, scripture—all the means by which the Church claimed to deliver experience or knowledge of God.

One of the most effective communicators of the Christian message to a wider public was the German theologian Martin Luther (1483–1546). He began with a conviction of his own sinfulness and of his redemption by the grace that God freely offered to all humankind. In a personal mission that he began toward the end of the second decade of the sixteenth century, he looked first to his fellow priests with patchy success. He was more successful in reaching secular rulers, whom he encouraged to take power over the Church and confiscate its wealth. He appealed to lay people over the heads of the church hierarchy, whose authority he rejected in favor of his own reading of scripture. The printing press—a medium unavailable to earlier religious reformers—spread his message and illustrated it with pictures that even illiterate people could appreciate. He devised a vivid writing style with images, for example, of his enemies whoring with Satan or defecating lies. What was more, Luther crafted his language out of various northern German dialects. It spread easily around the trading zone of the North Sea and Baltic. Here, in Scandinavia and parts of Germany, Luther's version of Christianity became the majority religion, to be carried, often in more radical forms, along the trade corridors of the Rhine, Rhone, and Danube Rivers.

Martin Luther's ninety-five theses, 1517

Within these corners and patches of Europe, Luther not only reached places and classes where Christianity had previously been superficial, but also changed the lives of individuals whose Christian awareness he touched. The poet Hans Sachs of Nuremberg in southwest Germany said simply, "Luther spoke—and all was light." In some provinces, the Church had anticipated his project. Cardinal Cisneros, for instance, who was head of the Spanish Inquisition from 1507 to 1517, had cheap editions of devotional books published in Spanish to wean readers from the pulp fiction of the day. But Luther went further, advocating reading the Bible

Martin Luther as Satan tempting Jesus (1547). Protestant propaganda during the Reformation often depicted the pope as Satan. Here Catholic propaganda turns the tables by portraying Martin Luther as the devil (note his cloven hooves and tail). Like Satan in the Bible, Luther asks Jesus to make bread out of stones, to which Jesus famously replied to Satan that human beings do not live by bread alone but according to the Word of God.

Versuchung Christi (1547), Gemalde, Bonn, Landschaftsverband Rheinland/Rheinisches Landesmuseum Bonn. Inv. Nr. 58.3.

and conducting the liturgy of the Church in languages people actually spoke, instead of in Latin.

The result was a schism within Christianity that endures to this day. National or local churches in Scandinavia, Scotland, England, and parts of Germany, France, Switzerland, Hungary, and Holland seceded from obedience to the Church of Rome, calling themselves "Evangelical," "Protestant," or "Reformed." What historians call the Counter-Reformation or the Catholic Reformation reconverted some churches to Roman obedience. Among new religious orders, the most significant for world history was the Jesuits, which Ignatius Loyola (1491–1556) founded in 1540. Loyola was an ex-soldier who brought martial virtues to the Counter-Reformation: tight discipline, comradeship, self-sacrifice, and a sense of chivalry. He was also a mystic gifted with self-transforming techniques of prayer, and a natural intellectual, who insisted on the highest standards of learning. The Jesuits became the Roman Catholic Church's most effective missionaries and educators, in Europe and in the wider world, and their schools were nurseries of science and scholarship.

Having broken the principle that the Church was indivisible, the Protestant movements split among themselves in often bitter and bloody disputes. Hostility among the different forms of Christianity led to wars justified, if not caused, by religious cant. As a result, traditional history has exaggerated differences between Protestants and Catholics. But few people understood or cared about the subtleties that divided theologians. The doctrine commonly said to define the Protestant reformers is that of "salvation by faith alone," according to which God imparts grace freely, not in return for good deeds or formal rule-keeping. Yet many Catholics stayed in the Church while sharing Protestant views on this point, and Luther himself insisted, "We should fear God because of his threat to those who transgress his law and love him for his promise of grace to those who keep it."

The missionary impulse within Europe produced no great revolution in spirituality. Most people remained as indifferent and shallow-minded as ever. But the language and imagery—the total communication—of the Christian faith were transformed. For Protestant clergy, services in the vernacular and translations of the Bible helped the laity become more involved in their faith. For Catholics, frequent communion served the same purpose, as—for women especially—did exaltation of the Virgin Mary and the founding of new teaching and nursing orders.

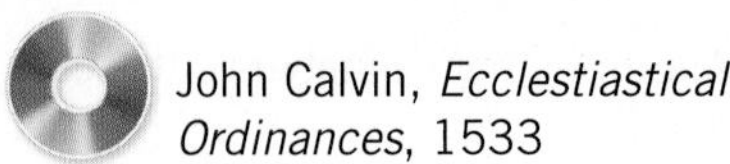

John Calvin, *Ecclestiastical Ordinances*, 1533

God became more accessible. "You seem to think that Christ was drunk," thundered Luther against subversive readings of the story of the Last Supper, "and wearied his disciples with meaningless words!" This daring joke had the virtue of treating Christ's humanity as literal and picturing him in the flesh of human weakness. By the end of the sixteenth century, an Italian painter, Caravaggio, could depict the *Last Supper*, without irreverence, as an episode of tavern low life. The German artist Matthias Grünewald in the 1520s had to hide his drawing of Jesus as a low-browed, warty-faced loser, but a century and a half later, the Spanish painter Murillo could revive the ancient tradition of depicting the Christ child as a naughty boy. Relevance to the lives of ordinary folk sanctified sacred subjects.

In Eastern Christendom, too, reform movements led to conflicts between the Christianity of the clergy and the religion of ordinary people, and ultimately to splits in the Orthodox Church. A reformation parallel to those of the West began in 1621, when the Patriarch of Constantinople, Cyril Lukaris (1572–1638) renounced what he called the "bewitchment" of tradition "and took for my guide Scripture ... and Faith alone." The Russian priest Avvakum, "though a miserable sinner," tackled popular excesses violently. He drove mummers from his village, breaking their masks and drums. In 1648, the Russian Orthodox clerical brotherhood known as the Zealots of Piety banned popular music as pagan.

Jesuit missionaries. The Jesuits' pride in the success of their overseas missions radiates from this eighteenth-century painting in which three of the order's sixteenth-century saints are prominently depicted. Flanked by personifications of the four continents in the foreground, the mythical giant Atlas presents the world to the Jesuits' founder, St. Ignatius Loyola. St. Francis Borja on the left-hand pedestal represents the order's preaching vocation; St. Francis Xavier, on the right, represents the ministry of the sacraments. Xavier also wears a Chinese-style vestment, a reminder of the Jesuits' long efforts to convert China. One of the leading Jesuit missionaries in China, Matteo Ricci, is in the background, among other Jesuit saints and heroes. Representatives of peoples the Jesuits converted kneel in prayer.

CHRISTIANITY BEYOND CHRISTENDOM: THE LIMITS OF SUCCESS

Beyond Europe, the world that exploration and imperialism disclosed was a magnet for missionaries. "Come over and help us," said the Indian on the official seal of the trading company responsible for colonizing Massachusetts. The conviction that the Algonquin Indians were a lost tribe of ancient Israel inspired John Eliot, who created "praying towns" in seventeenth-century New England where native pastors led readings from the Bible. Normally, however, only Roman Catholic religious orders had enough manpower and zeal to undertake large-scale missions, and outside areas of Spanish rule, their efforts were patchy.

Even in the Philippines, where Spanish rule built up the biggest Christian community in Asia, Christian success in direct competition with Islam was limited. In the Sulu Islands, the Muslim threat could be met by force of arms, but Christian preaching could not eradicate it. In Mindanao (mihn-dah-NOW), the Christian mission could not be sustained against Muslim intruders in the 1580s. In the late sixteenth and early seventeenth centuries, Muslim hotheads launched holy wars against the Spaniards' main base in Luzon.

For a while, Franciscans and Jesuits in Japan encountered amazing success by converting lords. Once the missionaries had a patron to make Christianity respectable, they could attract converts by displays of devotion, such as the requiem mass sung for the local ruler's wife at Kokura that attracted thousands of mourners in 1600. By the 1630s, more than 100,000 Japanese had been baptized. But the Japanese government regarded the new religion as a source of subversive political ideas and foreign influence. After sporadic persecution from the 1590s, Christianity was banned, and Christians who refused to renounce their faith were forced into exile or killed.

Hideyoshi on Christian missionaries in Japan

With no intermediate lords to serve as local flashpoints of Christian illumination, China could not be converted by similar means. But the Jesuits did make converts among the lower ranks of the scholar officials, or mandarins, some of whom passed Christianity on to their friends and families and proclaimed their faith in public. Yang Tingyun (yahng teeng-yuhn) recalled a vivid conversion experience in which one of the Jesuits' pictures of Jesus inspired him "with feelings of the presence of a great lord." After much agonizing, Yang repudiated his mistress—a more impressive test, perhaps, of Christian commitment than baptism—and went on to build a church, finance the printing of Christian works, and write books explaining Christianity.

Despite such promising instances, the Jesuits failed to convert China for three reasons. First, high-ranking Chinese were more interested in the Jesuits' scientific learning and technical skills than in their religious teaching. Second, the strategy

East meets West. This traveling altarpiece symbolizes Jesuit success in spreading Catholicism in Japan in the late sixteenth century. Imported European sacred paintings like this Madonna inspired Japanese imitators and attracted converts. The altarpiece is lacquered and gilded in Japanese style.
Photograph courtesy Peabody Essex Museum

the Jesuits adopted to convert China was a long-term one, and the revolutions of Chinese politics tended to interrupt it. No sooner had the Jesuits converted an empress than the Manchus overthrew the Ming dynasty in 1644 (see Chapter 17). Finally, the Church lost confidence in the Jesuits' methods. This was the outcome of a conflict that began with the founder of the mission, Matteo Ricci (1552–1610). He decided that Chinese converts could continue rites of reverence for their ancestors, on the ground that it was similar to veneration for saints. Missionaries split over the issue, and the effectiveness of the mission suffered when Pope Clement XI (r. 1700–1721) ruled against the veneration of ancestors.

In other parts of Asia, missionary strategists targeted potential converts at various social levels. In the seventeenth century in the Molucca Islands and Sulawesi, Protestant and Catholic missions approached sultans and local notables, with results that rarely lasted for long. In Manado, Franciscans obtained permission from an assembly of village heads at the ruler's court to launch a mission in 1619. But these notables disclaimed power over their fellow villagers' religious allegiance. Audiences shrieked to drown out the preaching, professed fidelity to their gods, and withheld food and shelter from the friars, who withdrew in 1622. Jesuits then made progress by concentrating on the ruler and his family. In the 1680s, a Protestant mission in Manado made further headway by employing converted native schoolmasters for the children of the elite. In Sri Lanka, Portuguese missionaries were more successful, but the Dutch who took over the island in 1656 were as keen to undermine Catholics as to convert Buddhists, and the long-term impact of Christianity proved slight.

In the New World, the bottom-up strategy of conversion was more usual. Franciscans baptized millions of Native Americans in the first 15 years or so of their mission in Mexico. It was an effort to re-create the

The Revitalization and Spread of Christianity

1478	Spanish Inquisition founded
1500s	Spanish Christians compete with Muslims for dominance in the Philippines
Early sixteenth century	Martin Luther initiates Protestant Reformation in Europe
Sixteenth and seventeenth centuries	Elites take on task of "re-Christianizing" Europe
1520s and 1530s	Franciscans baptize millions of Native Americans
Mid-sixteenth century	Catholic Church begins Counter-Reformation
1540	Ignatius Loyola founds Jesuits
1545–1563	Council of Trent meets
Seventeenth century	Jesuits lead Christian missionary effort in China
1621	Reformation in Eastern Orthodox Church begins
1630s	Over 100,000 Japanese baptized
1639	Christianity banned in Japan

atmosphere of the early church, when a single example of holiness could bring thousands to baptism as if by a miracle. Clearly most conversions in these circumstances cannot have been profound, life-changing experiences.

The fear of backsliding and apostasy by new converts haunted the missions. As early as 1539, clergy in Mexico worried about the multiplication of small chapels "just like those the Indians once had for their particular gods." In central Mexico, in the mid–sixteenth century, fears that new cults disguised pagan practices convulsed the church. Doubts arose even over the veneration of Our Lady of Guadalupe herself—the apparition of the Virgin Mary, supposedly to an Indian shepherd boy on the site of a pre-Christian shrine, which had demonstrated the sanctity of Mexican soil in the 1530s. In 1562, one of the worst recorded cases of missionary violence erupted in Yucatán, when the head of the Franciscan mission became convinced that some of his flock were harboring pagan idols. In the subsequent persecution, 4,500 Indians were tortured, and 150 died.

In central Peru in 1609, a parish priest was condemned for using excessive violence toward backsliders among his flock. The papers he collected include the story of a revealing trauma. Don Cristóbal Choque Casa, the son of an Indian leader, reported that, some 30 or 40 years after a Jesuit mission had nominally converted his people, he was on his way to meet his mistress at the abandoned shrine of a tribal god, when the devil in the form of a bat attacked him. He drove out the demon by reciting the Lord's Prayer in Latin, and the following morning summoned his fellow natives to warn them not to frequent the shrine on pain of being reported to the parish priest. But that same night, he dreamed that he was drawn to the accursed spot himself and compelled to make an offering to the god. The story evokes a vivid picture of the consequences of "spiritual conquest": old, neglected shrines, fit only for bats and fornication; menacing powers that still haunt dreams.

Dotrina breue muy p-
uechosa delas cosas q ptene-
cen ala fe catholica y a nra cri
stiandad en estilo llano pa co-
mu intelige̅cia. Co̅puesta por
el Reuere̅dissimo. S. do̅ fray
Jua̅ çumarraga primer obpo
d Mexico. del co̅sejo d su ma
gestad. Imp[illegible] la misma ciu-
dad d Mex[illegible] por su ma̅dado
y a su cost[illegible] año d. M.dxliij.

First book printed in the New World. "In a plain style for common understanding": The first book printed in the New World was a catechism issued by Juan de Zumárraga in Mexico City in 1543. The tasseled hat signifies that the book was published under the patronage of the archbishop of Mexico. The ornamented borders were fashionable decoration for books at the time in Europe. Zumárraga was a Franciscan friar who was committed to spreading Catholic doctrine to poor and uneducated people who knew little or nothing about the faith. The church in New Spain was not just a missionary effort directed at Native Americans, but also part of a movement active throughout the Christian world, in which the clergy and the godly tried to re-express Christian doctrine in simple terms that a wide audience could understand.

For the rest of the colonial period, the eradication of pre-Christian devotions in Peru became the work of professional "extirpators." In most of the rest of Spanish America, every generation of clergy repeated the frustrations and disillusionment of their predecessors. In the early eighteenth century, priests were still making the same complaints as their predecessors a century and a half before. Indians were attached to "idols" and to their own seers. They turned the saints into pagan deities. They accused each other of working with demons. Only with extreme caution could they be trusted to revere images of Jesus and the saints without idolatry.

Still, the New World was a rich mission field. Aided by the tendency—common in the Americas—of some cultures to welcome and defer to strangers, missionaries could establish an honored place in their host societies, learn the languages, and guide congregations to redefine themselves as Christians.

THE MISSIONARY WORLDS OF BUDDHISM AND ISLAM

Other religions paralleled Europe's mission to the infidel within.

China and Japan

In China, Zhu Hong (jew hung) (1535–1615) and Han Shan (hahn shahn) (1546–1623) presented Buddhism as a religion people could practice "at home," eliminating the priestly character that had made it seem inaccessible to lay followers. Lay devotees could worship Buddha, fast, adopt vegetarianism, and even don

The Ongons, or Ongghot, small figures of cloth or wood kept in a box or—like these, dangling from a tent pole in a pouch—are the most conspicuous feature of Mongolian shamanism. In traditional Mongol belief, the souls of the dead "become ongghot" with the power both to help and harm living people. Using the little images, the shaman, in his ecstasy, can transmit the presence and power of these spirits into himself. In the late sixteenth and seventeenth centuries, Buddhist missionaries tried with varying success to stamp out shamanism and belief in the Ongons.

the saffron robe that signified a religious vocation. In the eighteenth century, Peng Shaosheng (pahng show-shuhng) explained techniques of mental prayer, unprompted by images of gods. This emphasis on direct religious experience, unmediated through priests, resembled what was going on in Europe.

In seventeenth-century Japan, comparable movements, embracing both Buddhism and native religion, began with the reexamination of ancient texts, just as Christian reformers began by going back to the Bible. The monk Keichu (1640–1701) recovered authentic texts of the *Manyoshu*, poetic native scriptures of the eighth century, which, along with other old myths, became the basis of a born-again local religion, stripped of the additions of intervening centuries and of influences from outside Japan. Among Keichu's successors, Motoori Morinaga (1730–1801) used the *Manyoshu* as Protestants used the Gospels—to reconstruct a model of purity and denounce the degeneracy of latter days. Meanwhile, the suppression of Christianity created an opportunity for Buddhism. Wealthy lords, merchants, and peasants endowed many new Buddhist foundations.

The Mongols

The decisive initiative in reenergizing missionary Buddhism came from Mongolia in the 1570s. Altan Khan (1530–1583) ruled a swathe of territory along the northern loop of the Yellow River to Tibet. He was a pagan, who treated his gout by paddling inside the split-open body of a human-sacrifice victim. But—realizing that Buddhist help would be vital to his schemes of conquest—he invited the ruler of Tibet, known as the **Dalai Lama,** to visit Mongolia in 1576 and 1586. Tibet was a priestly Buddhist state, and the Dalai Lama was, by unalterable convention, the head of the Buddhist establishment. He guided reform of Mongol customs. Human sacrifices were forbidden, and blood sacrifices of all sorts stopped. The ongons—the felt images in which spirits resided (see Chapter 13)—were burned and replaced by Buddhist statues. The new religion was at first limited to the aristocracy. But over the next century, Buddhism spread down through society and across the Mongol dominions. The next Dalai Lama was the son of a Mongol prince. His training for his role in the 1590s took place in Mongolia, amid scholars who were translating the Buddhist scriptures into Mongolian. Young noblemen joined the priesthood. Increasingly in the late sixteenth and early seventeenth centuries, the documents Mongol chiefs issued during diplomatic exchanges contain allusions to Buddhism, and when they made alliances with pagan peoples, Buddhist and pagan language and ceremonies marked the occasions.

From the 1630s, Prince Neyici Toyin (1557–1653) took the Buddhism of Tibet into Manchuria, building the great Yellow Temple in Shenyang (shehn-yahng). Toyin worked by "miracles" of healing that may have owed something to the superiority of Tibetan and Chinese medicine over the unscientific therapies of the shamans. Manchu political power after they conquered China in 1644 reinforced the mission. The Manchu emperors perceived Buddhist missionaries as agents of imperial policy. They appointed Tibetan lamas to instruct the Mongols and reconcile them to Chinese rule.

Like Catholic missions in the New World, political conquests and violence shadowed and disfigured those of Buddhists in northern Asia. Advice to Buddhist missionaries in Mongolia in the mid–seventeenth century was, "Whoever has worshipped ongons, burn their ongons and confiscate their cattle and sheep. From those who let the shamans and shamanesses perform fumigations, take their horses, fumigate the shamans in their turn with dog dung." In practice, the old gods reemerged as Buddhist deities, just as the Native American gods survived as

Christian saints. In both Mongolia and the Americas, the old gods continued to mediate between humans and nature.

Islam

The trend to what might be called low-level strategy—missionary efforts targeted on ordinary people—also affected Islamic missions (see Map 18.1). In southeast Asia and in Africa, the two great arenas of Islamic expansion at the time, the means of conversion were fourfold: commerce, deliberate missionary effort, holy war, and

MAP 18.1

The Spread of Christianity, Islam, and Buddhism in Asia by 1750

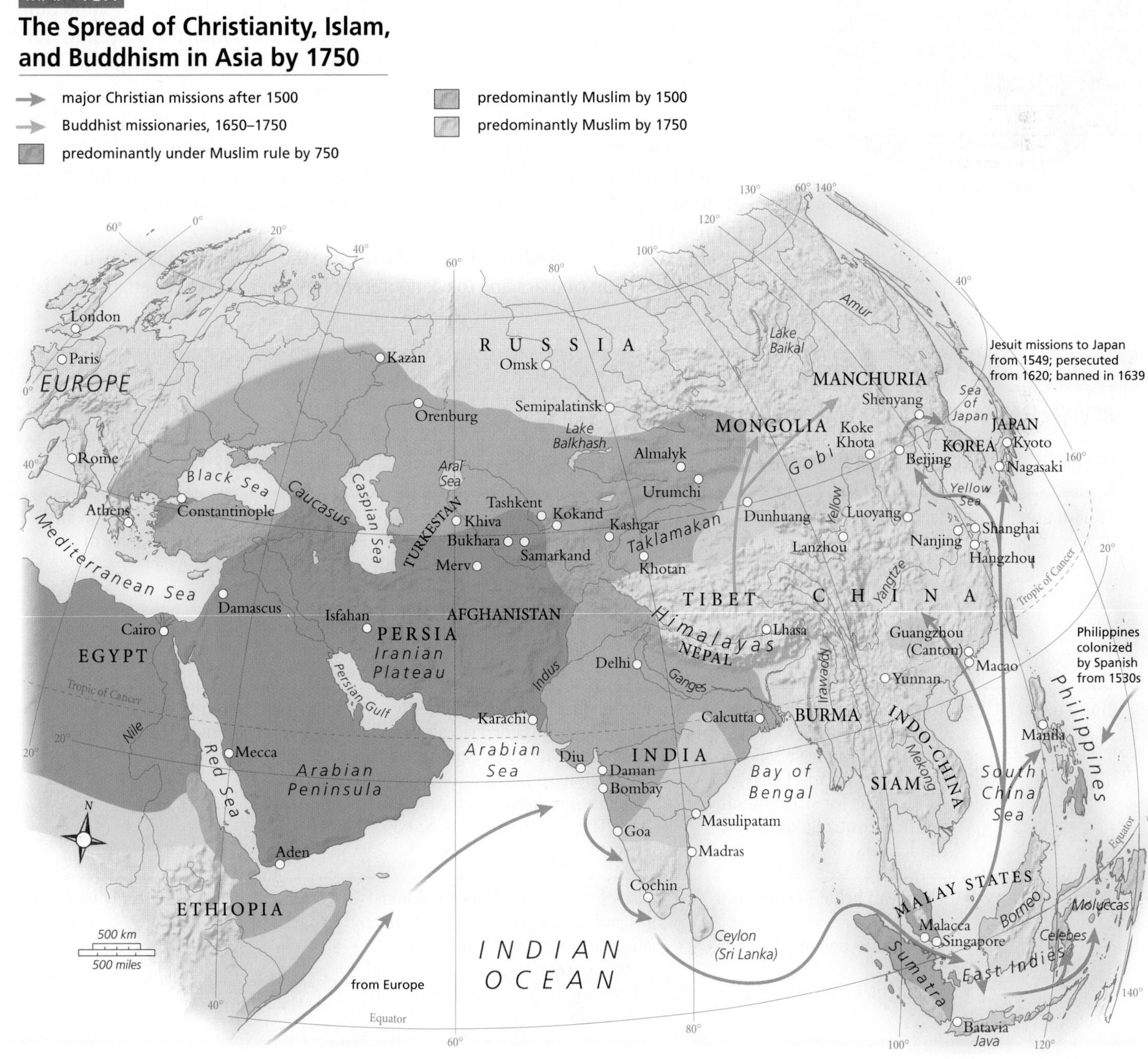

The Chronicles of Java. Islam in southeast Asia has often been mixed with elements from other religions. This illustrated manuscript tells the history of the island of Java in what is today Indonesia and the spread of Islam there by Sufi saints and rulers up to 1647. Written in Javanese, it seeks to give the Muslim rulers of the state of Mataram legitimacy by telling of how one of their ancestors had ties to three different religious traditions: He was blessed by a Muslim saint, practiced Hindu asceticism, and married the goddess of the southern ocean.

dynastic links. As in southeast Asia, on the Islamic world's African front, the arrival of Christian Europeans hardly affected the retreat of paganism. Except in the coastal toeholds of Christendom, the same combination of merchants, missionaries, and warmongers ensured the dominance of Islam.

Merchants and missionaries spread Islam together. Trade shunted pious Muslims from city to city and installed them as officials and agents to local rulers. Missionaries followed. In some areas, **Sufis** (see Chapter 9) made crucial contributions. In southeast Asia, Sufis congregated in Malacca, and after the city fell to the Portuguese in 1511, they fanned out from there through Java and Sumatra. In the late sixteenth and seventeenth centuries, the sultanate of Aceh in northwest Sumatra was a nursery of Sufi missionaries of sometimes dubious Islamic orthodoxy, such as Shams al-Din, who saw himself as a prophet of the end of the world. Even peaceful Muslim missionaries saw themselves as waging a "jihad of words." During the seventeenth century, perhaps under the goad of competition from Christianity, the "jihad of the sword" grew in importance, and the extension of the Islamic world depended increasingly on the aggression of sultans, especially from central Java.

In West Africa, merchant clans or classes, like the Saharan Arabs known as Kunta, who made a habit of marrying the daughters of holy men, were the vanguard of Islam.

MAKING CONNECTIONS

REVITALIZATION OF WORLD RELIGIONS, 1500–1700

RELIGION →	REASONS FOR REVITALIZATION →	CONSEQUENCES →	NEW ADHERENTS
Christianity	• To renew dynamism of early Church • To combat heresies, paganism, witchcraft • To engage unevangelized and underevangelized people	New religious orders; new techniques of prayer; new types of devotion; increased coercion and social control by church–state alliances; sharp restrictions on localized beliefs and rituals; emphasis on missionary efforts	Lower-class Europeans, urban and country; colonized peoples in America, Africa, Asia
Buddhism	• To popularize Buddhism in China and Japan • To adapt to native religious beliefs (China and Japan) • As a vehicle for strengthening political control (Mongolia, Manchuria)	Eliminating the need for priestly leadership; simplified rituals; emphasis on direct religious experience via meditation, ritual; creation of new systems of monasteries throughout Asia; Tibetan lamas restructured Mongol spiritual practices	Laymen, peasants, and other social classes throughout Japan, China, Central Asia
Islam	• To spread belief to southeast Asia, Africa • To adapt to native religious beliefs • To enhance Muslim spirituality	Use of merchants, Sufi missionaries, holy war (jihad), and dynastic alliances to expand Islamic influence; intermarriage as a method of advancing Islam; spread of Islamic schools increases literacy	Ordinary people, especially in southeast Asia, Africa

The black wandering scholars known as the Torokawa incited revivalism and jihad in Hausaland from the 1690s. Schools with a wide curriculum spread Islam among the Hausa, scattering pupils who attracted students of their own (see Map 18.2). A sheikh who died in 1655 was able, at school near the present border of Niger and Nigeria, to "taste to the full the Law, the interpretation of the Quran, prophetic tradition, grammar, syntax, philology, logic, study of grammatical particles, and of the name of God, Quranic recitation, and the science of meter and rhyme."

MAP 18.2

The Spread of Islam in Africa, ca. 1700

THE RESULTING MIX: GLOBAL RELIGIOUS DIVERSITY—AMERICAN AND INDIAN EXAMPLES

The forms of Catholic Christianity that became characteristic of Spanish America were, in their way, as different from the Catholic mainstream as was the Protestantism of most of the English colonies. In part, this was because of the imperfections of the "Spiritual Conquest" of Spanish America by Catholic missionaries. Missionaries were few. Cultural and linguistic obstacles impeded communication. Pre-Christian religion could not be destroyed. Latin American Catholicism is still rippled with Native American features.

Secular scholars, and Protestant critics of Catholic missionary activities, sometimes call these Native American influences **syncretic** features or pagan survivals because Christianity and paganism seemed to fuse in a new religion that was a blend of both. Yet the proper comparison for colonial religion is not—or not solely—with the religion of the Native American past but with that of Europe of the same era, where clerical bafflement at the stubborn survival of popular religion was just as great. The Christianity of the American countryside was deficient in similar ways to that of the European countryside. Anxiety about this world interfered with concern for the next. Rites to induce rain, suppress pests, elude plague, and fend off famine drove Scripture and sacraments into neglected corners of ordinary lives. As reform unfolded in Europe, clergy and educated laity acquired ever-higher standards of doctrinal awareness, ever-deeper experiences of Christian self-consciousness. Their expectations of their flocks increased accordingly—which accounts for their continual dissatisfaction.

Shamans still burn incense on the steps of the church of Saint Thomas at Chichicastenango in the Guatemala highlands, where worshippers leave offerings of flowers and rum. The steps—a mound similar to pre-Hispanic Maya temples—seem to rival the church interior as a place of devotion. Is this paganism, Christianity, or a mixture of the two? Most local shamans now serve as officials of societies dedicated to Christian saints, and the religion of Chichicastenango may be best understood as one of the many local forms of Christianity that developed in the colonial New World.

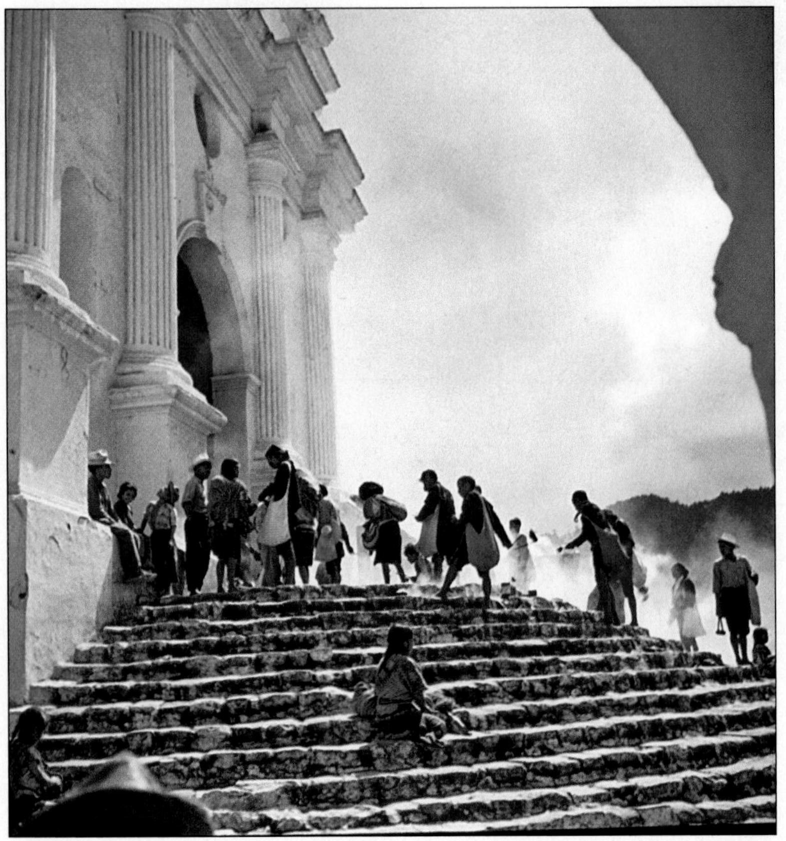

Black America

The religion of black people in the Americas—though it varied from place to place, molded into conflicting traditions by the influence of Protestantism and Catholicism respectively—was always different from the religion of white people. In colonial Brazil, black artistic vocations and religious devotion were centered on cult images and charitable associations of black Catholic laypeople. These **confraternities** melded the culturally uprooted into a coherent community, renewing their sense of identity and belonging. Confraternities comforted black people in a white world. Encouraged by the Church, the black brotherhoods were hotbeds of disorder.

Their choice of patron saints, whose statues they paraded through the streets, was sometimes defiant. St. Elesbaan, for instance, was a black emperor of Ethiopia, who led an expedition to avenge the massacre of Christians by a Jewish ruler in Yemen in 525. He was easy to reinterpret as a symbol of resistance to the many plantation owners of Portuguese–Jewish ancestry. St. Benedict of Palermo, perhaps the favorite patron of black confraternities, was born the son of Nubian slaves in Sicily in 1526. As a Franciscan lay brother, he became guardian of his friary and worked

A CLOSER LOOK

THE CULT IMAGE OF ST. ELESBAAN

Devotion to St. Elesbaan, shown here in an early eighteenth-century statue from the Confraternity of Our Lady of the Rosary, was one of a number of politically charged, socially subversive cults that attracted black worshippers in colonial Brazil.

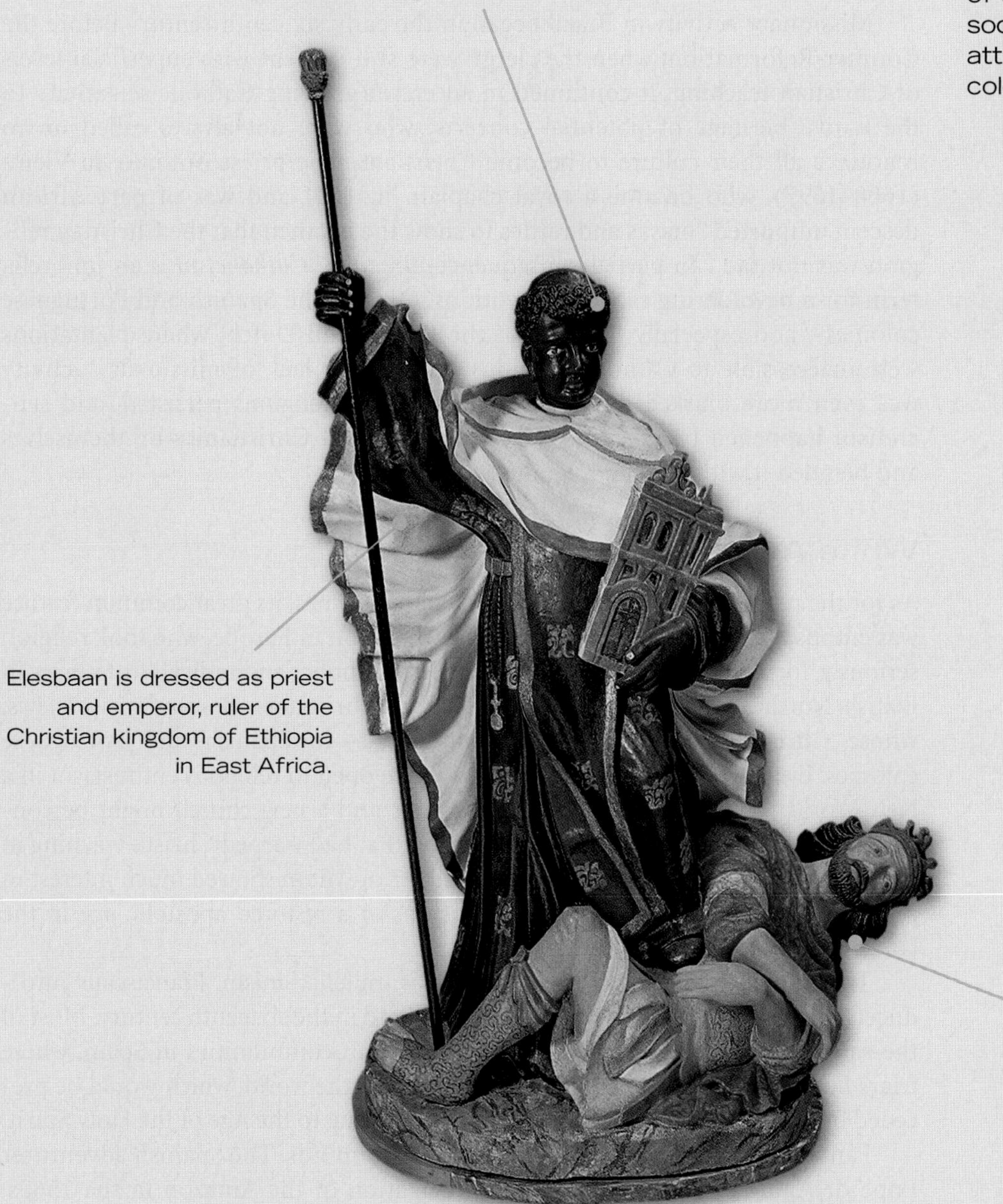

Black saints were inspiring models for the black confraternities, lay Christian brotherhoods that flourished in Brazil.

Elesbaan is dressed as priest and emperor, ruler of the Christian kingdom of Ethiopia in East Africa.

Elesbaan supposedly led an Ethiopian invasion across the Red Sea to Yemen in southern Arabia in 525 to dethrone a Jewish ruler who was persecuting Christians. The many black slaves in Brazil felt persecuted by their masters, many of whom were of Jewish or allegedly Jewish ancestry.

How does this statue show the uniqueness of black Christianity in colonial Brazil?

miracles after his death in 1583. The cult of St. Iphigenia, a legendary black virgin, who resisted the spells of her suitor's magicians with the help of 200 fellow virgins, embodied the triumph of faith over magic. But it also sanctified virginity in a slave society where women did not want to produce children who would become slaves. Black Catholicism was an excitant, not an opiate. Rather than playing the role commonly assigned to religion—keeping believers in their place—it inspired hopes of betterment in this world. A commonly depicted scene was of black tormentors torturing white Judas in hell. White people reviled black confraternities' "revolutionary pretensions, just as though they were no different from honest white people."

Missionary activity in Brazil began in the early sixteenth century before the Counter-Reformation, when the clergy were still content with superficial levels of Christian teaching. It continued in an era of growing Catholic sensitivity to the native heritage of potential converts, who were not always called on to renounce all their culture to become Christians. The priest António da Vieira (1608–1697), who became a royal chaplain in 1641 and was of part African descent, imported "masks and rattles to show the heathen that the Christian religion was not sad." In partial consequence, *Brazilian Catholicism* is an umbrella term for a bewildering range of devotions. Outside the Spanish and Portuguese colonies—and especially in those of the British and Dutch, where plantations were inaccessible to Catholic religious orders—the lack of missionary activity was even more marked. In consequence, African religions persisted, and syncretism happened because the slaves often learned Christianity by themselves and blended it with African religious beliefs.

White America

As for the religion of white Americans in colonial times, its great common feature was enthusiasm. Refugees from religious persecution in Europe, who took religion seriously, formed or infiltrated many colonies: Catholics and radical Protestants in British North America, Jews or so-called New Christians—descendants of Jews, whose Christianity Judaism deeply influenced—in Spanish and Portuguese colonies. Even hard-headed laymen could prove open to religious enthusiasm in a New World where everything seemed possible and a new church might be constructed from scratch, without the corruption that had warped Christ's teaching in the Old World. Columbus and Cortés—neither of whom showed much interest in religion in their early lives—both had visions of a restored apostolic age in the lands they explored and conquered.

The most extreme form of enthusiasm is millenarianism. Franciscans introduced Christian millenarianism to the New World in the sixteenth century. Most of the early missionaries came from a few Franciscan communities in Spain, where friars nurtured obsessions with the coming end of the world, which would be preceded by a cosmic war between good and evil leading to the Age of the Holy Spirit.

Fantasies of this kind unhinged unorthodox minds. The Spanish adventurer Lope de Aguirre, during a harrowing navigation of the Amazon in the 1560s, imagined himself the embodiment of God's wrath. His Franciscan contemporary, Francisco de la Cruz, was the self-proclaimed universal pope and emperor of the last days. The fervor of the spiritual Franciscans mingled with whatever forms of millenariansim were inherited from Native American tradition. In Mexico in 1541, an Indian chief called Don Martín Ocelotl (oss-ehl-OT-el) proclaimed the second coming of Christ, embodied in himself. In 1579, in

Paraguay, another Indian chief, Oberá the Resplendent, launched a rebellion against Spanish rule with a similar message. In Peru, so-called *Inkarrí* movements fused legends of the Inca Empire with expectations of the coming of a "Last World Emperor."

Meanwhile, North America merged similar traditions with Protestant millenarianism. Because millenarianism was generally considered heretical, it became common in America, driven there by persecution, nourished there by toleration. Anabaptism (the belief that only adults should be baptized), world's-end biblical fundamentalism, and sects invented by prophets who preached that the last days of the world were at hand have all contributed to the formation of the United States. The founders of Massachusetts saw the colony as a refuge for those God intended "to save out of general destruction." The Puritan minister John Cotton predicted the end would come in 1655. The Shakers, another Protestant sect, called themselves "The United Society of Believers in Christ's Second Coming."

India

Religious frontiers, where rival creeds and communions meet, are often places of conflict. But they can also stimulate creative thinking, as contrasting religious groups strive to understand and live with each other. Sixteenth-century India produced a new religion: **Sikhism**, which blended Hindu and Muslim tradition—or, as Sikhs say, went beyond both. Neither Hindu nor Muslim paths to God suffice, said Guru Nanak (GOO-roo NAH-nahk) (1469–1539), the Sikh founder, "so whose path should I follow? I shall follow the path of God."

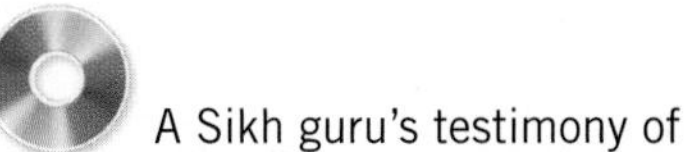
A Sikh guru's testimony of faith

Nanak was a widely traveled pilgrim of enormous learning. The Mughal Emperor Akbar (r. 1556–1605), who was illiterate and traveled mainly on military campaigns, sought to outdo him by founding a religion of his own. Like Nanak he recognized that in a religiously plural world, it made better sense—and better served the peace of his realm—to look at what religions had in common rather than at what divided them. "God should be adored with every form of adoration," he said, according to a Jesuit who lived at his court. And indeed, he exhibited broad-mindedness unparalleled in Christendom in his day. Awestruck by the realism of a European painting of the Virgin Mary, Akbar and his courtiers "could not contain their joy at seeing the infant Jesus in his mother's arms and it seemed as if they would like to play with him and talk to him." Catholic religious imagery became part of the decor of his court.

He promoted debates between teachers of rival religions in an attempt to establish a synthesis, which he called the "Faith of God." The new religion seemed like an attempt to make the Mughal state itself sacred, and Akbar came to see himself as a manifestation, even an embodiment of God. Most Muslims were repelled and resolved never to try to accommodate other religions again. Later Mughal emperors felt torn between tolerance and hostility toward non-Muslim faiths. The need to appease Hindus caused a mid–seventeenth-century revival of Akbar's efforts by Dara Shukoh, a pretender to the throne, who proposed "the mingling of the two oceans" of Muslim and Hindu teaching. But his fanatically Muslim brother, Aurangzeb (r. 1658–1707), defeated him and promoted Islam aggressively. He executed the Sikh leader, Guru Hari Rai, for blasphemy and discriminated against Hindus. The result was a backlash. When a Sikh prince seized the city of Jodhpur, for example, in 1707, he banned Islam and burned the mosques.

THE RENAISSANCE "DISCOVERY OF THE WORLD"

In the long run—according to traditional readings of world history—religious diversity, which arose from the splitting and mingling of religions in the sixteenth century, made the world more secular. People became less committed to their religions, because they had to live at peace with neighbors of different faiths. The mutual challenges of rival religions weakened all of them by comparison with godless or materialistic ways of looking at the world.

But these changes, if they happened at all, took a long time to take effect. In Europe, for instance, in the sixteenth and seventeenth centuries, most of the ideas contemporaries denounced as atheism were really challenges to traditional Christian descriptions of God. Religious subjects did become less common in art. But this may have had more to do with economics. As wealth spread, so did art patronage. The Church's dominance of the art market weakened. Religions did become more mutually tolerant, in some places where they mingled and forfeited their claims to exclusive truth. In other cases, however, the opposite occurred and, overall, on a global scale, religious warfare and persecution probably became more bitter and widespread.

In the first half of the sixteenth century, fashions in learning, art, and letters informed by the inspiration of classical Greece and Rome, leaped from Italy, where they had originated, across Europe, in a movement traditionally called the Renaissance (see Chapter 15). During his invasion of Italy in 1515, King Francis I of France saw "all the best works"; he began to collect casts of ancient sculptures and acquire the services of Italian artists, including Leonardo da Vinci (1459–1519). The sixteenth-century courts of Henry VIII of England, the Habsburg Archduchess Mary of Hungary (who ruled the Low Countries for her nephew, the Emperor Charles V), Sigmund I and II in Poland and Lithuania, and Ferdinand I and Maximilian II in Austria and Bohemia became similar centers for spreading the Renaissance. Beyond royal courts, artists, scholars, and civic patrons took the same classicizing tradition to the cities of Germany and Switzerland.

Church architects tried to create spaces for the kind of devotion that study of ancient Christian texts endorsed, with open sanctuaries, brilliantly lit and approached through wide aisles and naves. Poets who scoured the reign of the Roman Emperor Augustus (r. 27 B.C.E.–14 C.E.) for models and churchmen who looked back to the time of Christ shared the same perspective. Virgil (70–19 B.C.E.), Augustus's favorite poet, was credited with having prophesied the birth of Jesus. Christian Platonism and Christian stoicism (see Chapter 6) were fashions of the era, and the most influential thinker of the first half of the sixteenth century, Erasmus of Rotterdam (1466–1536), made "the philosophy of Christ" a current term. The Italian sculptor Benvenuto Cellini's (1500–1571) *Crucifixion* expresses serene stoicism, rather than the searing passion earlier sculptors had represented. In a series of sculptures by Michelangelo (1475–1564), "captives" in human shape

Michelangelo's "captives" are often described as unfinished. But they illustrate an idea of the ancient Greek philosopher Plato: Like captives from their bonds, or reality from the shadows, true forms emerge struggling from the rocks that enclose them.

emerge from the coarse particularity of rocks. He seems to have been trying to embody the notion that matter hides reality—which is spiritual—from our senses and that we need genius or grace to see it.

Meanwhile, the discoveries of explorers transformed how Europeans pictured the world. They confirmed the vastness of the globe and disclosed the existence of a New World in the Western Hemisphere. The discoveries also challenged European notions of what it means to be human, as encounters unfolded with a previously unsuspected range of cultures and civilizations.

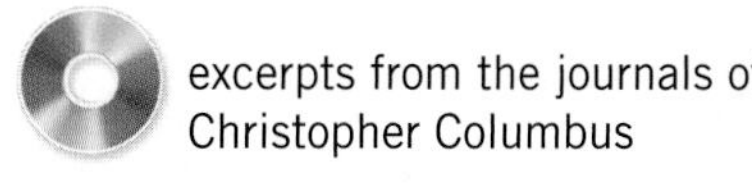
excerpts from the journals of Christopher Columbus

The most exciting moment of all occurred when Christopher Columbus first glimpsed "naked people," on Friday, October 12, 1492, on an island he called San Salvador, which most scholars identify with Watling Island in the Bahamas. The natives were probably Lucayos—a people of whom little is known, though archaeological evidence endorses Columbus's account of their material culture. His description deploys many of the categories, comparisons, and images available in his day to help Westerners understand other cultures. Many of his observations cut two ways. The natives' ignorance of warfare established their innocent credentials but also meant they would be easy to conquer. Their nakedness evoked a primitive Eden or an ideal of dependence on God, but also suggested savagery and similarity to beasts. Their lack of commercial skills showed that they were both morally uncorrupted and easily fooled. Their rational faculties made them identifiable as human and exploitable as slaves. Columbus seemed torn between conflicting ideas about the Native Americans. After all, he and his men were undergoing an experience no European had ever had before.

A long quest began to understand the diversity of humankind. Discoveries in the natural world complicated it. In the seventeenth century, as Europeans got to know the great apes and other primates, the problem of where to draw the limits of humankind grew increasingly puzzling. Discoveries about the human body kept pace with those of human cultures. Traditional ideas of human nature reeled under the impact of discoveries on every side.

Pope Paul III on the Indians of the New World, from *Sublimis Dei*

Eyes adjusted slowly to the new realities. Influenced by missionaries eager to save souls among newly encountered peoples, the Church took a positive view of their natural qualities to protect them from secular exploitation and extermination. The question of whether the Native Americans were fully human, endowed with rational souls, was settled—at least for Catholics—affirmatively by Pope Paul III in the 1530s, but their status needed frequent shoring up against slippage. Missionary scholars in the Americas built up files to demonstrate the social and political sophistication of native societies. The Aztecs, for example, posed typical problems. Cannibalism and human sacrifice tarnished the record of a people who otherwise appeared highly "civil." In evidence—painted by native artists at the court of the Spanish Viceroy of Mexico—compiled under missionary guidance in the 1540s, one can see the qualities the clergy held up for admiration. The training of an Aztec candidate for the priesthood of the pre-Christian gods is shown in gory detail, as his teachers beat his body to bleeding. But this was evidence not of barbarism but of the similarity of Aztec values to those of their Franciscan evangelists, who also practiced devotional whipping and tortured their own flesh. The Aztec state was depicted as a pyramid, symmetrically disposed to administer justice, with an emperor at the top, counselors below him, and common pleaders at the lowest level: a mirror image of the society the missionaries had left back home. The Aztecs' sense of justice was shown to conform to the standards Europeans deemed natural. An adulterous couple, stoned to death, suggested a comparison with the ancient Jews and, therefore, openness to the milder Christian message. Justice was tempered with mercy. Though drunkenness among the Aztecs was punishable by death, the aged were depicted as enjoying exemption. Mild restraint took the place of execution. When the Aztecs went to war, provocations on their enemies' part were shown to precede hostilities, which followed only after diplomatic efforts had been rebuffed. The natives, it seemed, practiced "just" war by traditional Christian standards—something that the Spanish monarchy strove to do with imperfect success. Missionaries could cite similar examples for every native community where they worked.

In the mid-sixteenth century, a Spanish bishop Bartolomé de Las Casas (1474–1566) was the loudest spokesman for broadening the definition of humankind to include Native Americans. He was a convert to conscience—an exploiter of Indian labor, who reformed when he heard a preacher's challenge: "Are the Indians not human beings, endowed with rational souls, like yourselves?" He joined the Dominicans and became the official Protector of the Indians. In effect, he was a professional lobbyist who managed to get the Spanish crown to legislate for Indian rights. Human sacrifice, according to Las Casas, should be seen rather as evidence of the misplaced piety of its practitioners, or of their pitiable state as victims of the devil, than as an infringement of natural law. His conclusion—"All the peoples of mankind are human"—sounds self-evident, but it was a message important enough to bear repetition. It was applied patchily at first. Black people hardly felt the benefits for centuries. It made possible a new view of history, according to which all peoples were created equal, but passed through universal stages of historic development. Broadly speaking, this model prevailed in educated European minds in the seventeenth and eighteenth centuries. Nicolás de Mastrillo himself—the young missionary with whom this chapter opened—was a glowing example. He went on to be head of the Jesuits in Peru.

American cannibals

THE RISE OF WESTERN SCIENCE

Partly because of privileged access to the recycled learning of classical antiquity and partly owing to the new data accumulated during the exploration of the world, Western science registered leaps in the seventeenth century that science in other parts of the world could not match.

If secularism did not displace religion to any great extent in the West, science did, in some degree, probably displace magic. Just by offering this opinion, we raise a problem: What is the difference between magic and science? Both are attempts to explain and control nature. Sixteenth- and seventeenth-century Western science grew, in part, out of magic. Renaissance writers argued that magic was good if it was used to heal or to accumulate knowledge of nature, and that some ancient magical texts were lawful reading for Christians.

The most influential text was the work supposedly written by an ancient Egyptian known as "Hermes Trismegistos" (Hermes Thrice-Blessed), but which was actually composed by an unidentified Byzantine forger. It arrived in Florence in 1460 among a consignment of books bought from the Balkans after the fall of Constantinople to the Turks in 1453 and caused a sensation. Renaissance scholars felt inspired to pursue "Egyptian" wisdom as an alternative to the austere rationalism of classical learning—a fount of older and purer knowledge than could be had from the Greeks or Romans. The distinction between magic and science as means of attempting to control nature almost vanished in the sixteenth century.

Doctor Faustus, who sold his soul to the devil in exchange for magical access to knowledge, was a fictional character, but he symbolized a real yearning. The Emperor Rudolf II (r. 1576–1612) was hailed as the new Hermes. At his castle in

Wonder chamber. In Europe in the late sixteenth and seventeenth centuries, art collection expanded to include the "curiosities" of nature and science. This seventeenth-century painting records the splendors of a Dutch gentleman's collection. Portraits of the owner and his wife preside over an array of objects that is modestly representative of the world: scenes from nature, the Bible, classical myth, and antique ruins—all the traditional sources of wisdom—are on the walls. A personification of the Tiber River—representing ancient Rome—is over the door. Wonders of nature—coral and shells—mingle with classical statues. On the tables, learned visitors contemplate the sphere of Earth and the heavens and the new wonders revealed by exploration. In the center, the artist warns against religiously inspired vandals who destroyed art and learning.

Adriaen Stalbent (1589–1662) "The Sciences and the Arts." Wood, 93 × 114 cm. Inv. 1405. Museo del Prado, Madrid, Spain. Photograph © Erich Lessing, Art Resource, NY

Prague, magicians practiced astrology, alchemy, cabbalism (the ancient mystical and magical wisdom of the Jews), and *pansophy*—the attempt to classify all knowledge and so unlock access to mastery of the universe.

None of this magic worked, but the effort to manipulate it was not wasted. Alchemy fed into chemistry, astrology into astronomy, cabbalism into mathematics, and pansophy into the classification of nature. Would-be wizards constructed "theaters of the world" in which all knowledge could be divided into compartments and displayed and "wonder chambers" where specimens of everything in nature could be gathered. The eventual outcome of this work included the methods for classifying plants, animals, and languages that we still use today. Wonder chambers developed into museums. Many of the great figures of the scientific revolution in the Western world of the sixteenth and seventeenth centuries either started with magic or maintained an interest in it. Johannes Kepler (1571–1630), who worked out the path of the planets around the sun, was one of Emperor Rudolf's favorites. Sir Isaac Newton (1642–1727) was a part-time alchemist. The philosopher and mathematician Gottfried Wilhelm Leibniz (1646–1716) studied ancient Egyptian hieroglyphs (though he could not read them) and cabbalistic notation.

But Western science gradually moved toward empirical methods, rational explanations, and verifiable facts. One of the most conspicuous examples is the abandonment of the image of the universe centered on the Earth that appeared in the Bible and was generally accepted in the ancient world. In 1543, the Polish astronomer and churchman Nicolaus Copernicus (1473–1543) proposed reclassifying the Earth as one of several planets revolving around the sun. His theory was formulated tentatively, advocated discreetly, and spread slowly. It took nearly 100 years after his death to remold people's vision of the universe. In combination with the work on the mapping of orbits around the sun published early in the seventeenth century by Johannes Kepler, the Copernican revolution expanded the limits of the observable heavens, substituted a dynamic for a static

 A Copernican view of the universe

system, and wrenched the universe into a new shape around the paths of the planets, accurately represented. This shift of focus from the Earth to the sun was a strain on eyes adjusted to an outlook that made the Earth the center of the universe. Every subsequent revelation of astronomy has reduced the relative dimensions of our dwelling place and ground its apparent significance into tinier fragments.

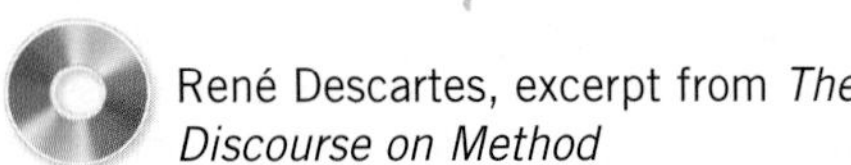

René Descartes, excerpt from *The Discourse on Method*

Scientific reasoning grew more systematic. Two particularly influential styles of thinking are illustrated—and were first fully formulated—in the work respectively of the English experimenter, Francis Bacon (1561–1626), and the French philosopher and logician, René Descartes (1596–1650). Bacon took from the Dutch scientist J. B. van Helmont (1577–1644) the motto, "Logic is useless for making scientific discoveries." He prized observation above tradition and devised the method by which scientists turn observations into general laws: the so-called **inductive method** by which a general inference is made from a series of uniform observations and is then tested. The result, if it works, is a scientific "law." Scientists can then use this to predict how natural phenomena will behave under similar circumstances.

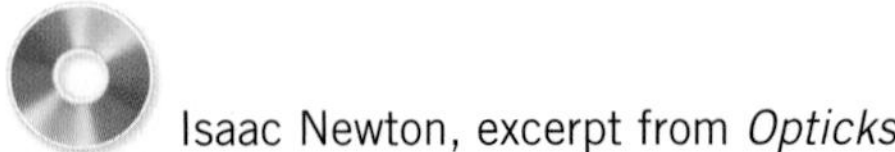

Isaac Newton, excerpt from *Opticks*

Descartes, who affected laziness and detested the restless lives of men such as Bacon (who also pursued a political career), made doubt the key to the only possible certainty. Striving to escape from the suspicion that all appearances are false, he reasoned that the reality of his mind was proved by its own self-doubts. His starting point was the age-old problem of **epistemology**: How do we know that we know? How do we distinguish truth from falsehood? Suppose, he said, "some evil genius has deployed all his energies in deceiving me." It might then be that "there is nothing in the world that is certain" except that "without doubt I exist [even] ... if he deceives me, and let him deceive me as much as he will, he will never cause me to be nothing so long as I think that I am something." This left a further problem: "What then am I? A thing which thinks. What is a thing which thinks? It is a thing which doubts, understands, conceives, affirms, denies, wills, refuses, which also imagines and feels."[1]

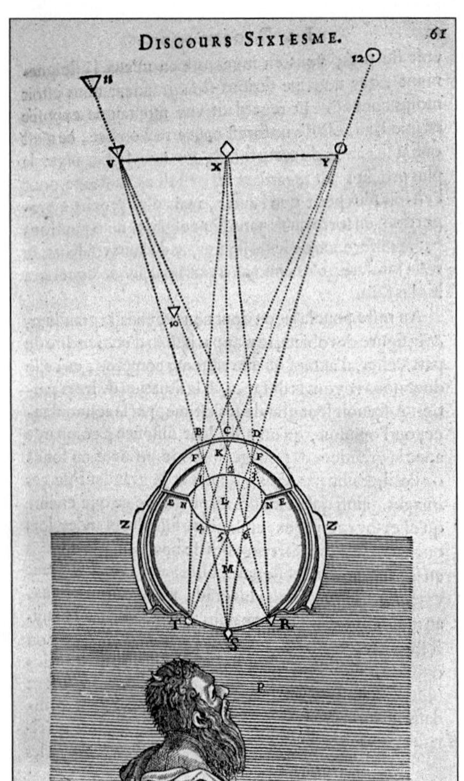

A vision of vision. The French philosopher René Descartes (1596–1650) described how we see things in his *Opticks*, which was published in 1637. Light travels—in waves, Descartes guessed—between object and eye. The eye itself works like a lens, bending the light to form an impression. Science, like magic, had the power to make humans "masters and possessors of nature."

The work of Isaac Newton typified the achievements of seventeenth-century Western science. In a bout of furious thinking and experimenting, beginning in the 1660s, he seemed to discover the underlying "secret of the universe" that had eluded the Renaissance wise men. He imagined the universe as a mechanical contrivance. It was tuned by a celestial engineer and turned and stabilized by a universal force—gravity—observable in the swing of a pendulum or the fall of an apple, as well as in the motions of moons and planets.

Newton was a traditional figure: an old-fashioned humanist, obsessed by trying to determine the chronology of the Bible. He was even, in his wilder fantasies, a dabbler in magic, hunting down the secret of a systematic universe, an alchemist seeking the Philosophers' Stone, which legend said could turn base metals into gold. He was also a representative figure of a trend in the thought of his time: **empiricism**, the doctrine, beloved in England and Scotland in his day, that reality is observable and verifiable through our senses. The universe consisted of events "cemented" by causation, of which Newton found a scientific description and exposed the laws. "Nature's Laws," according to the poet Alexander Pope, "lay hid in Night" until "God said, 'Let Newton be!' and there was Light."

It turned out to be an act of divine self-withdrawal. Newton thought gravity was God's way of holding the universe together. Many of his followers did not agree on that point. Belief in a supreme being (though not necessarily in God as Christianity describes him) throve in eighteenth-century Europe, partly because the mechanical universe could dispense with the divine "Watchmaker" after he had given it its initial winding. By the end of the eighteenth century, the French astronomer and mathematician Pierre-Simon de Laplace (1749–1827), who interpreted almost every known physical phenomenon in terms of the attraction and repulsion of atomic particles, could boast that he had reduced God to "an unnecessary hypothesis."

WESTERN SCIENCE IN THE EAST

It would be wrong, however, to speak of the rise of science at the expense of religion. There is no necessary conflict between the two, and no one in the sixteenth or seventeenth centuries, as far as we know, even suspected that there could be. Science did prove, however, in one respect, to be more powerful than any single religion. It showed more cultural flexibility, appealing more widely across the world. Christianity, Buddhism, and Islam all ran up against cultural limits. Buddhism grew mainly in Central Asia. Islam registered little appeal in Europe outside of the Turkish-controlled Balkans. Christianity was rejected in China and India and all but wiped out in Japan. Western science, however, had the power to penetrate everywhere. The cultural exchange that took Christianity to Asia also took Western science across Eurasia. Indeed, Jesuit scholars were the agents of both transfers.

In some respects, the intellectual climate in eastern Asia was unwelcoming to Western ideas. In the seventeenth century, a Confucian revival in China, Japan, and Korea impeded Western thought because it spread ancient Confucian prejudice against Western "barbarians." The Dutch, on whom, from 1639, Japan depended exclusively for information about the West, were generally regarded—said one of their few Japanese admirers—as "a sort of beast." According to the Korean Confucian scholar Yi T'oegye (1501–1570), "It is no exaggeration to liken [Westerners] to birds and beasts." Japanese scholars welcomed the Western view of the world as undermining China's claims to cultural superiority, but they hesitated to adopt Western ideas as uniquely true. The Zen monk Ishin Suden (1569–1633) used traditional language to explain the nature of Japan as a "divine land." In Confucian terms, Japan was "born of Earth and Heaven"; by Daoist thought, it was "grounded in the opposing principles of Yin and Yang"; and it was also a "Buddha-land."

In China, the change of dynasty of 1644 from the Ming to the Qing stimulated the Confucian revival. Because he did not want to serve rulers whom he considered usurpers, Wang Fuzhi (wahng foo-jih) (1619–1692) withdrew to the distant south. There he celebrated Confucian values and dreamed of "the order of heaven" restored on Earth. Gu Yanwu (goo yehn-woo) (1613–1682), similarly alienated from the new dynasty, returned to Confucian guidelines for life: "study all learning" and "have a sense of shame." Like a Renaissance scholar in Europe, he dedicated himself to "the search for antiquities." "Anything legible I copied by hand, and when I saw an inscription unseen by my predecessors I was so overjoyed that I could not sleep." He and his fellow scholars guarded the spoils of time against erosion, damage, and oblivion.

This Chinese renaissance was comparable to that of Europe's, but did not achieve the same effects. For the first time in recorded history, China slipped behind Europe in scientific achievement. On the whole, the global history of technology up to this time reflected consistent Chinese superiority. World-shaping innovations typically happened first in China. Take a few key examples. Printing and paper, the bases of modern communications until the late twentieth century, were Chinese inventions. So was paper money—without which modern capitalism

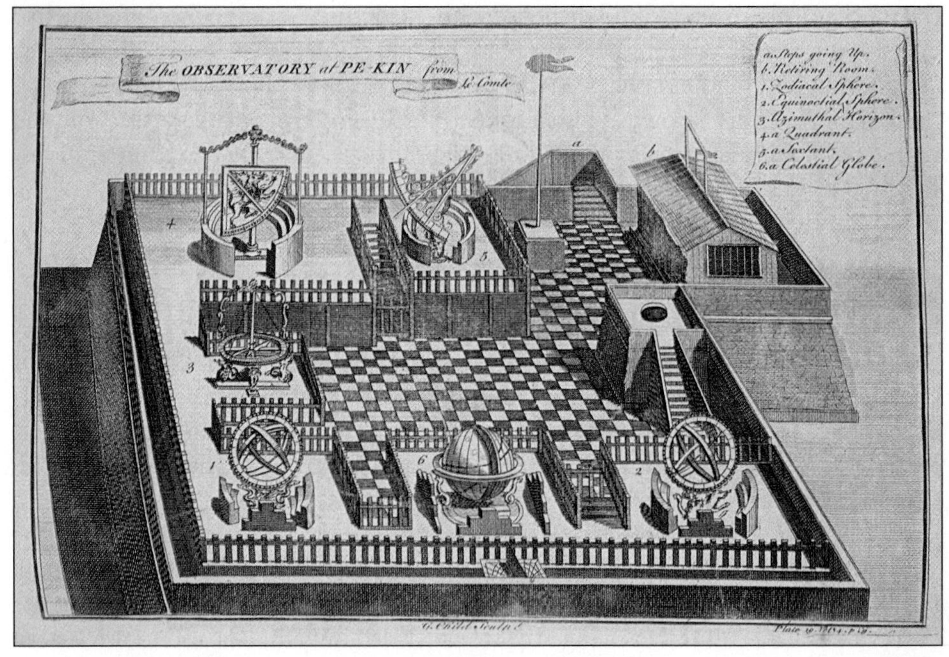

The observatory at Beijing. In 1674, the Chinese government handed over the observatory at Beijing to the Jesuits for reorganization. Among the results was a new observatory, shown in this eighteenth-century engraving, that the Jesuits set up on the roof of the imperial palace using instruments built to European specifications. Some of these instruments have survived and have only recently been removed to a museum.

would be unthinkable. So was gunpowder, the key to modern warfare. So were the rudder and the construction methods that protected the vessel against sinking by dividing the hull into separate compartments—these were vital for the development of global shipping. The blast furnace, essential for modern industrialization, came from China, too. In what we think of as the late Middle Ages, however, Western technology edged ahead in two areas: clockwork and lens making (see Chapter 13). These came together in the science of astronomy.

The impact of Western astronomy in China is visible in one of the world's most extraordinary books, *A Treatise on Astronomy,* that Manuel Dias, a young Jesuit missionary, wrote in Latin and, with native help, in Chinese in 1610—the year after the great Italian astronomer Galileo Galilei (1564–1642) first used a telescope to study the heavens. "Lately," Dias told Chinese readers, "a famous Western sage has constructed a marvelous instrument." Through the telescope, "the moon appears a thousand times larger"; Saturn's rings become visible; "Jupiter appears always surrounded by moons. . . . The day this instrument arrives in China we shall give more details of its admirable use."

Jesuit skill in astronomy was the most important of the many technical skills with which they impressed the Chinese. The Chinese Board of Astronomy, an official department of the Chinese court, existed not for the disinterested study of the heavens but to devise a ritual calendar. The ceremonies of the imperial court were attuned to the rhythms of the stars, so that earthly order should reflect heavenly harmony. To perform the rites for movable feasts and unique occasions, the stars had to be favorable. The Chinese believed that the success of imperial enterprises, the survival of the dynasty, and the life of the empire depended on it. The environment of a star-struck court stimulated scientific knowledge. Though the Board of Astronomy was young—created in the early seventeenth century—the imperial observatory had a continuous history of some 400 years behind it, and the number and quality of recorded observations available to Chinese astronomers had been unequaled anywhere in the West until well into the sixteenth century.

Yet the Jesuits' superiority over the Muslim personnel who then ran the observatory seemed so marked that the imperial court abandoned the entire native Chinese tradition and turned the practice of astronomy over to the newcomers. The Jesuit Ferdinand Verbiest took over the Board of Astronomy in 1669 and systematically reformed the calendar. In 1674, at the emperor's request, the observatory was reequipped with instruments of Jesuit design. The German mathematician, Gottfried Wilhelm Leibniz believed that China was superior to Europe in civilized values, ethics, and politics: "I almost think," he wrote, "that Chinese missionaries should be sent to us to teach us the aims and practices of natural theology, as we send missionaries to them to instruct them in revealed religion." But he thought Europe was ahead in mathematics and what we would now call physics. The reversal in the balance of technical skill in Eurasia had begun. In succeeding centuries, similar reversals in historic patterns of power and wealth would elevate the West in other respects.

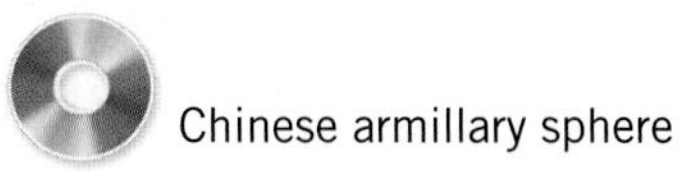

Chinese armillary sphere

IN PERSPECTIVE: The Scales of Thought

Despite the shortcomings of the missionaries or of their congregations, the enormous extension of the frontiers of Islam, Buddhism, and Christianity remains one of the most conspicuous features of the sixteenth and seventeenth centuries. Buddhism and Islam expanded into territories that bordered their existing heartlands. By overleaping the Atlantic and Pacific Oceans, Christianity registered a spectacular difference. Islam, however, had the advantage of expanding in the demographically vigorous worlds of Africa, Malaysia, and Indonesia, whereas the territories Buddhism won in northern Asia were vast but sparsely populated. As we saw in the last chapter, the millions Christianity won in the Americas quickly withered with the rapid decline of the Native American population.

In the long run, however, the sheer size of the New World counted for most. Because of the exclusion of Islam from the Western Hemisphere, Muslim predominance among world religions slipped in the eighteenth and nineteenth centuries, when the Americas made up and exceeded their lost population. In the balance of resources, Christendom acquired potentially vast extra weight.

Equally significant for the history of the world over the following centuries was the spurt of Western science and the recognition it achieved in China. Although China, the Islamic world, and India had rich scientific tradition, and although the Islamic world, like the West, had privileged access to the scientific legacy of the ancient Greeks and Romans, Westerners now pushed ahead in some respects. Of these, astronomy was of key importance in the seventeenth century because it won acceptance for Westerners in other cultures. And in the eighteenth century, Western superiority in military, naval, and industrial technologies would begin to be felt. The resulting shift in the world balance of power and resources is the subject we have to tackle next.

CHRONOLOGY

Fifteenth century	Study of classical Greece and Rome provides foundation for the rise of Italian humanism
Fifteenth and sixteenth centuries	Merchants and missionaries spread Islam
Early sixteenth century	Martin Luther initiates Protestant Reformation in Europe
1500s	Spanish Christians compete with Muslims in the Philippines
Sixteenth and seventeenth centuries	Royal courts in northern Europe spread humanism; contact with Native Americans challenges European notions of what it means to be human; elites take on task of "re-Christianizing" Europe
1520s and 1530s	Franciscans baptize millions of Native Americans
1540	Ignatius Loyola founds Jesuit Order
1543	Nicholas Copernicus proposes heliocentric theory
Mid–sixteenth century	Catholic Church begins Counter-Reformation
1545–1563	Council of Trent meets
1596–1650	René Descartes, French philosopher and proponent of deductive reasoning
1570s	Altan Khan stimulates the revival of missionary Buddhism in Mongolia
Late sixteenth century	Mughal emperor Akbar attempts to establish the "Faith of God"
Seventeenth century	Jesuits lead Christian missionary effort in China
1621	Reformation in Eastern Orthodox Church begins
1630s	Missions initiated by Prince Neyici Toyin bring Buddhism to Manchuria
1639	Christianity banned in Japan
1669	Jesuit Ferdinand Verbiest takes over the Chinese Board of Astronomy
1687	Sir Isaac Newton publishes *Principia Mathematica*

PROBLEMS AND PARALLELS

1. Why were the sixteenth and seventeenth centuries an unprecedented era in the revitalization of Buddhism, Christianity, and Islam? What role did missionaries play in this revitalization? How did the missionary strategies of these different faiths compare?
2. How successful were Christian missionaries in Asia, Africa, and the Americas? How did pre-Christian religious practices persist? What were the varieties of Christianity in the Americas? What kinds of new religious thinking emerged in India in this period?
3. How did the Renaissance "discovery of the world" impact European thinking and spirituality? How did their encounters with non-Western cultures transform the way Westerners saw the world?
4. Why were the sixteenth and seventeenth centuries significant in the development of Western science and secular values and in the transmission of Western science to other parts of the world? What was the relationship of Western science to magic? How did this relationship evolve over time?
5. How was Western science received in the East? What Western ideas were most welcome in the East and which were not? How were the Jesuits agents of cultural exchange in Asia?

DOCUMENTS IN GLOBAL HISTORY

- excerpts from the Council of Trent
- Martin Luther's ninety-five theses, 1517
- John Calvin, *Ecclestiastical Ordinances*, 1533
- Hideyoshi on Christian missionaries in Japan
- A Sikh guru's testimony of faith
- excerpts from the journals of Christopher Columbus
- Pope Paul III on the Indians of the New World, from *Sublimis Dei*
- American cannibals
- A Copernican view of the universe
- René Descartes, excerpt from *The Discourse on Method*
- Isaac Newton, excerpt from *Opticks*
- Chinese armillary sphere

Please see the Primary Source DVD for additional sources related to this chapter.

READ ON

J. D. Tracy, *Europe's Reformations* (1999) is a reliable account, but J. Bossy, *Christianity in the West* (1985) and J. Delumeau, *The Catholic Church from Luther to Voltaire* (1977) are radical and searching. My account follows F. Fernández-Armesto and D. Wilson, *Reformations* (1997). On China and Indonesia respectively, I am indebted to W. J. Peterson, *Why Did They Become Christians?* Y. T'ing-yün, L. Chih-tsao, and H. Kuang-ch'i' in J. W. O'Malley et al., eds, *The Jesuits: Cultures, Sciences and the Arts, 1540–1773*, which is an important collection generally, and A. Meersman, *The Franciscans in the Indonesian Archipelago, 1300–1775* (1967). M. C. Ricklefs, *A History of Modern Indonesia: c. 1300 to the Present* (1981) is an excellent general history that traces Islamic missionary efforts in Indonesia in the seventeenth century. On Buddhist missions, W. Heissig, *The Religions of Mongolia* (2000) is fundamental, as is M. Hodgson, *The Venture of Islam* (1977) on Islam.

R. Ricard, *The Spiritual Conquest of Mexico* (1966) is an enduring classic. P. U. Bonomi, *Under the Cope of Heaven: Religion, Society, and Politics in Colonial America* (1986) and S. Schwartz, *"A Mixed Multitude": The Struggle for Toleration in Colonial Pennsylvania* (1987) explicate the emergence of religious diversity in North America's Middle Atlantic colonies in the seventeenth century. M. Deren, *Divine Horsemen: The Living Gods of Haiti* (1985) is the best introduction to the Afro-Caribbean religion. A. Métraux, *Black Peasants and Their Religion* (1960) is an enduring classic.

J. Rubiés, *Travel and Ethnology in the Renaissance: South India through European Eyes, 1250–1625* (2000) is a brilliant analysis of European perceptions of religious diversity in India during the Renaissance. L. Jardine, *Worldly Goods: A New History of the Renaissance* (1998) reexamines the cultural achievements of the Renaissance in the context of the material and commercial world that produced them. L. Jardine and J. Brotton, *Global Interests: Renaissance Art between East and West* (2000) sets the global context.

S. Shapin, *The Scientific Revolution* (1998) examines how the world of seventeenth-century scientists shaped their understanding of nature. A. Grayling, *Descartes* (2006) is up-to-date, readable, and provocative; L. Jardine and A. Stewart, *Hostage to Fortune: the Troubled Life of Francis Bacon* (1999) is masterly. J. Waley-Cohen, "China and Western Technology in the Late Eighteenth Century," *American Historical Review* (1993) traces the reception of various Western technologies, including gunpowder, in China. M. Jacob, *Scientific Culture and the Making of the Industrial West* (1997) offers a detailed analysis of how the cultural dissemination of Newtonian mechanics affected the emergence of industrial technology, especially in Britain. L. Brockey, *Journey to the East: the Jesuit Mission to China* (2007) reveals a formerly unknown aspect of Jesuit activity in China, among peasants and artisans.

CHAPTER

19 States and Societies: Political and Social Change in the Sixteenth and Seventeenth Centuries

Queen Nzinga. In 1622, before she came to the throne of Ndongo, Nzinga made a treaty with the Portuguese. This contemporary engraving shows her conducting negotiations, seated on a slave's back to avoid standing in the presence of a white man of lower rank than herself.

IN THIS CHAPTER

POLITICAL CHANGE IN EUROPE
WESTERN POLITICAL THOUGHT
WESTERN SOCIETY
THE OTTOMANS
MUGHAL INDIA AND SAFAVID PERSIA
CHINA
Chinese Politics
Chinese Society
TOKUGAWA JAPAN
THE NEW WORLD OF THE AMERICAS
AFRICA
IN PERSPECTIVE: Centuries of Upheaval

In the 1640s, Queen Nzinga of Ndongo, in Central Africa, announced that she would "become a man." Her husbands dressed in women's clothes and slept among her maids (under pain of beheading for illicit sex). Her ladies-in-waiting became bodyguards. She led her troops into battle and could still handle weapons skillfully at the age of 80, in 1662, when an Italian visitor to her court witnessed a military parade. She had overcome challenges to her right to rule by reclassifying herself as masculine.

This was not the first transformation in Nzinga's life. She came to power as regent for her nephew, the rightful king, in 1615, but she killed him and declared herself queen. In 1622, she adopted Christianity to secure Portuguese help. She used ferocious mercenaries known as Imbalanga—private war bands that grew by kidnapping boys—to fight her battles. When they cheated her, she vowed to "become an Imbalanga" herself and lead her own war band. As this involved rituals of sacrifice, cannibalism, and child killing, she had to renounce Christianity. But she returned to the faith in the 1640s to obtain more Portuguese help.

Hers was a surprising career. It was also a representative episode of early modern politics. All Nzinga's self-transformations were strategic moves in her struggle for power—hard-fought wars, in which she repeatedly clawed her way back from defeat. That struggle was part of a longer, broader, deeper story of political change that many parts of the world echoed: the rise of strong monarchies, the subduing of aristocracies, the shift of power to royal dependants. In the 1560s, when Portuguese explorers, slavers, and missionaries first described Ndongo, it was a loosely defined kingdom, where big landowners wielded the most power and claimed the right to elect the monarch. Over the next decades, kings asserted their hereditary right to the throne and wrenched authority from aristocrats. Nzinga's first rivals in the wars she fought to secure the throne were nobles. Her effort to assert the legitimacy of female rule was successful. Women occupied the throne of Ndongo for 75 of the 100 years after her death.

Nzinga's realm was small but fiercely contested. As we look around the world of political and social change in the sixteenth and seventeenth centuries in this chapter we see similar conflicts unfold, as monarchs struggled to redistribute power to their own advantage, and new or newly empowered classes contended for a share in the growing might and resources of states.

FOCUS questions

- HOW DID European rulers strengthen their power in the sixteenth and seventeenth centuries?
- WHY WERE the Ottomans able to build such a successful and long-lasting empire?
- WHAT ROLE did Shiite Islam play in Safavid Persia?
- HOW DID Chinese society change under the Qing dynasty?
- HOW DID the Tokugawa shoguns govern Japan?
- HOW DID the "creole mentality" affect Spanish America?
- WHAT ROLES did African states play in the Atlantic slave trade?
- WHAT COMMON features affected the development of states all over the world during this period?

POLITICAL CHANGE IN EUROPE

Europe already had a state system (see Chapter 11). Events of the sixteenth and seventeenth centuries made the political reunification of Western Europe unthinkable for centuries. There were three principal reasons for this.

First, as European states solidified their political independence and exerted more control over their inhabitants, hopes of reviving the unity of the ancient Roman Empire faded. In 1519, Charles, ruler of Spain and many other lands (see Map 19.1) was elected to be head of the group of mainly German states still known as the Holy Roman Empire. Propagandists speculated that Charles or his son would be the "Last World Emperor," whose reign would inaugurate the final age of the world before the Second Coming of Christ. Naturally, however, most other states resisted this idea or tried to claim the role for their own rulers. Charles's failure to impose religious uniformity on his empire demonstrated the limits of his power. After his abdication in 1556, no one ever again convincingly reasserted the prospect of a universal state in the tradition of Rome.

Treaty of Westphalia

Second, rulers' power against rivals to their authority and states' power over their own citizens increased. In 1648, the Treaty of Westphalia gave rulers the right to impose their religions on their subjects. Though most European states experienced civil wars in the sixteenth and seventeenth centuries, monarchs usually won them. Cities and churches surrendered most of their privileges of self-government. Aristocracies became close collaborators in royal power, rather than rivals to it, as aristocrats had often been in the past. Offices under the crown became profitable additions to aristocrats' income from inherited estates. Countries that had been difficult to rule before their civil wars became easy to govern when their violent and restless elements became dependent on royal rewards and appointments. England and Scotland had been particularly hard for their monarchs to tax in the sixteenth and early seventeenth centuries. The so-called Glorious Revolution of 1688–1689, which its aristocratic leaders represented as a blow against royal tyranny, turned Britain into Europe's most fiscally efficient state. In place of a dynasty committed to peace, the revolution installed rulers who fought expensive wars. Taxation trebled under the monarchs the British revolutionaries crowned.

Finally, no power seemed able to impose unification. France spent much of the period racked by civil wars between aristocratic factions and did not fulfill its potential until the late seventeenth century, after the last of the wars was over. England, crippled by a low tax yield and religious dissent, failed to exploit its strategic position between the Atlantic and the North Sea. Germany was a geographical expression, a loose collection of semi-independent states, incapable of working together. Poland, though vast in area, had insecure frontiers and a nobility that defied royal power. Italy was a muddle of small states that no one could unify and only Spain could dominate. As a result, smaller, less naturally favored states had moments as major powers: Sweden for much of the seventeenth century, Holland in the second half of it.

Spain had the advantage of privileged access to silver from Mexico and Peru. While shipments from these mines remained regular, until the 1620s or 1630s, they gave Spanish kings better credit ratings than other rulers. In Castile, people really

MAP 19.1

The Dominions of Charles V

 Habsburg lands of Charles V

— boundaries of the Holy Roman Empire

believed that service conferred nobility on subjects of the crown. Monarchs and nobles combined in the 1520s to suppress rebellion and continued to collaborate until the 1640s, when the aristocratic spirit of service—and tax revenues—collapsed. Moreover while religious conflicts divided other parts of Western Europe, Spain's religious minorities—Jews, Muslims, the few Protestants—were subjected to forcible conversion or eradicated. Finally, in 1580, dynastic accident added the vast Portuguese empire to Spain's dominions.

In the 1580s and early 1590s, Spain seemed able to bid for the role of arbiter of Europe, or even—in the minds of Spaniards, who fantasized about conquering Cambodia, China, and Japan—of the world (see Map 19.2), while the frontiers of the Spanish monarchy continued to expand in the Americas and Asia, and Spanish armies invaded France and advanced against rebels in the Netherlands. But success proved unsustainable. The 1590s were a turning point, as the loyalty of subordinate kingdoms showed signs of strain, state revenues ebbed, and a catastrophic decline of population, which would last for most of the seventeenth century, began. By the time Philip II (r. 1556–1598) died, he had decided to leave to his heir a policy of

MAP 19.2

The Spanish Monarchy in 1600

- Dominions of the king of Spain
- → Carrera de Indias
- → Portuguese trade with maritime Asia

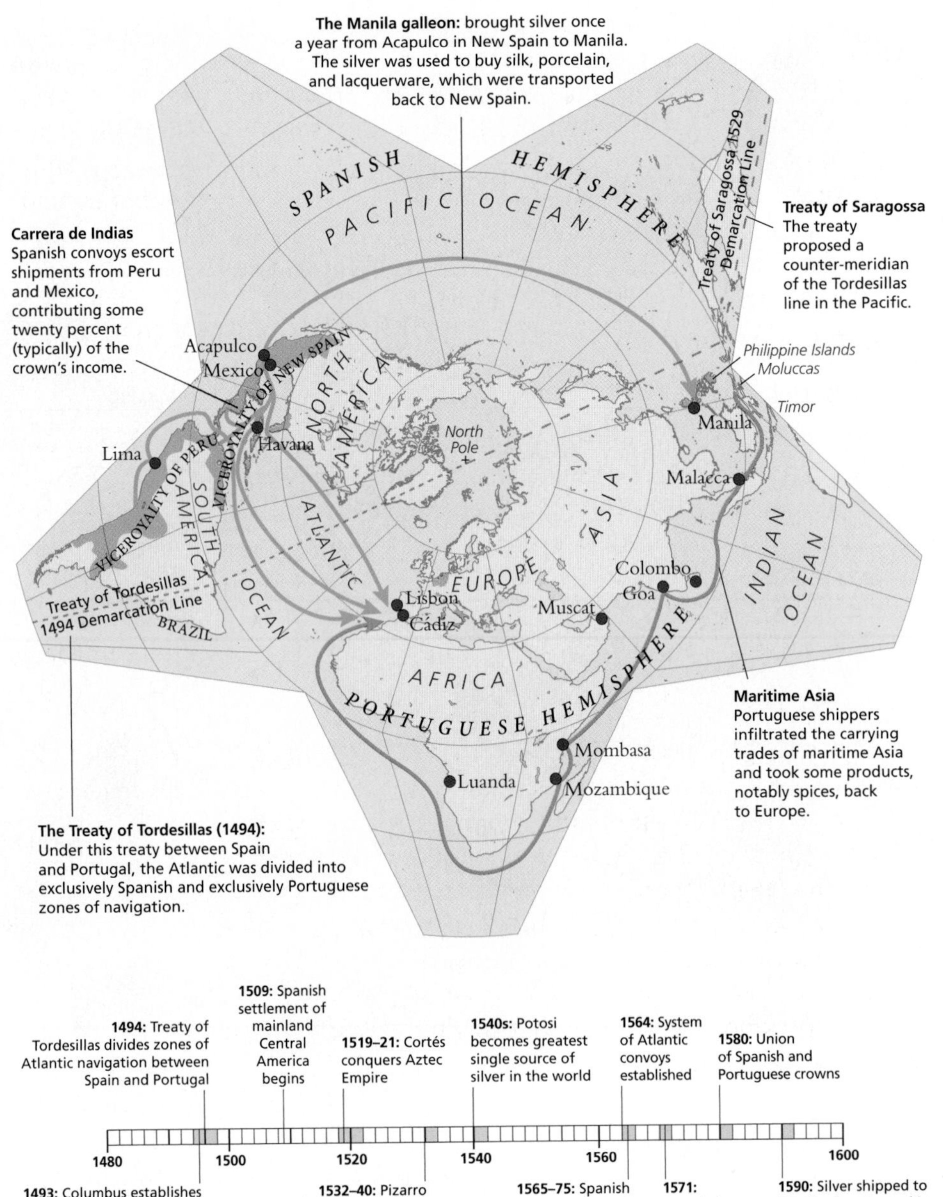

The Manila galleon: brought silver once a year from Acapulco in New Spain to Manila. The silver was used to buy silk, porcelain, and lacquerware, which were transported back to New Spain.
SPANISH HEMISPHERE
PACIFIC OCEAN
Treaty of Saragossa 1529 Demarcation Line
Treaty of Saragossa The treaty proposed a counter-meridian of the Tordesillas line in the Pacific.
Carrera de Indias Spanish convoys escort shipments from Peru and Mexico, contributing some twenty percent (typically) of the crown's income.
Acapulco
Mexico
VICEROYALTY OF NEW SPAIN
NORTH AMERICA
Havana
Lima
VICEROYALTY OF PERU
SOUTH AMERICA
North Pole
Philippine Islands
Moluccas
Timor
Manila
Malacca
ASIA
INDIAN OCEAN
ATLANTIC OCEAN
Treaty of Tordesillas 1494 Demarcation Line
BRAZIL
Lisbon
Cádiz
EUROPE
Muscat
Goa
Colombo
AFRICA
PORTUGUESE HEMISPHERE
Mombasa
Mozambique
Luanda
Maritime Asia Portuguese shippers infiltrated the carrying trades of maritime Asia and took some products, notably spices, back to Europe.
The Treaty of Tordesillas (1494): Under this treaty between Spain and Portugal, the Atlantic was divided into exclusively Spanish and exclusively Portuguese zones of navigation.
1494: Treaty of Tordesillas divides zones of Atlantic navigation between Spain and Portugal
1509: Spanish settlement of mainland Central America begins
1519–21: Cortés conquers Aztec Empire
1540s: Potosi becomes greatest single source of silver in the world
1564: System of Atlantic convoys established
1580: Union of Spanish and Portuguese crowns
1480
1500
1520
1540
1560
1600
1493: Columbus establishes first Spanish settlement in Western Hemisphere
1532–40: Pizarro conquers Inca Empire
1565–75: Spanish conquest of Philippine Islands
1571: Foundation of Manila
1590: Silver shipped to Manila almost equal in value to Atlantic trade

peace. When that peace broke down across Western Europe in the 1620s, the strain proved unbearable. Spanish naval supremacy faltered in the 1630s. In the 1640s, Spanish armies' long record of victory collapsed with major defeats by the French. Rebellions broke out in Naples and Catalonia, and Portugal recovered independence. Despite a recovery in the eighteenth century, Spain never again attempted to outclass Europe's other powers.

WESTERN POLITICAL THOUGHT

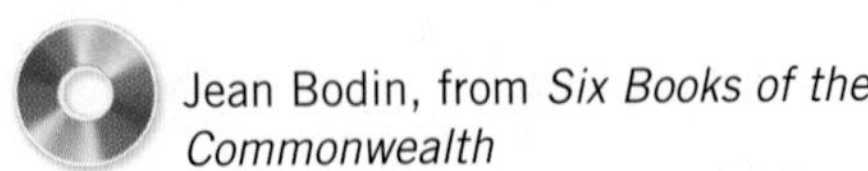
Jean Bodin, from *Six Books of the Commonwealth*

Along with the growth of state power, people came to take the sovereignty of the state for granted. The French political philosopher Jean Bodin formulated the doctrine in 1576. Sovereignty defined the state, which had the sole right to make laws and distribute justice to its subjects. Sovereignty could not be shared with the church, any sectional interest, or outside power.

More radically, in 1513, the Florentine office seeker Niccolò Machiavelli challenged the traditional assumption that the state must have a moral purpose: to increase virtue or happiness. According to *The Prince*, Machiavelli's book of rules for rulers, the only basis for decision making was the ruler's own interest, and his only responsibility was to retain power. He should keep faith only when it suits him and pretend virtue. Machiavelli's other books are strongly republican, and *The Prince* may have been ironical. Irony, however, is the hardest form of rhetoric to detect. Later thinking borrowed two influences from *The Prince*: first, the doctrine of **realpolitik**, which says that the state is not subject to moral laws and serves only itself; second, the claim that anything is permissible to ensure state security. Among moralists, *Machiavel* became a term of abuse, and the devil became "old Nick."

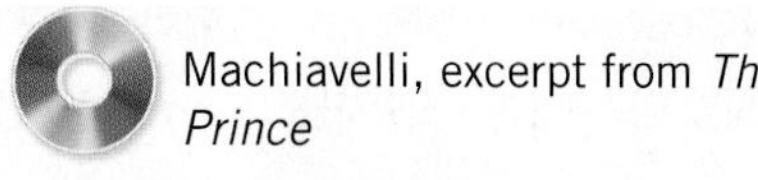
Machiavelli, excerpt from *The Prince*

In the absence of any overriding authority or mechanism for sharing sovereignty, the European state system needed international laws. When Thomas Aquinas (see Chapter 13) summarized Western thinking in the thirteenth century, he distinguished the laws of individual states from what he called the **law of nations,** which all states must obey and which governs the relationships among them. Yet he never said what this law was or how it could be codified. The Spanish Jesuit Francisco Suárez (1548–1617) solved the problem in a radical way. The law of nations "differs in an absolute sense," he said, "from natural law" and "is simply a kind of positive human law." It says whatever people agree it should say.

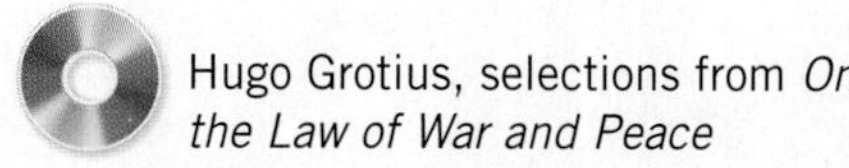
Hugo Grotius, selections from *On the Law of War and Peace*

This made it possible to construct an international order along lines first proposed by the Dominican Francisco de Vitoria, who advocated laws "created by the authority of the whole world"—not just agreements between states. In 1625, the Dutch jurist Hugo Grotius worked out the system that prevailed until the late twentieth century. Natural law obliged states to respect each other's sovereignty. Their treaties regulated relations among them with the strength of contracts, enforceable by war. This system did not need the support of any particular ideology or religion. It could embrace the world beyond Christendom. It would remain valid, Grotius said, even if God did not exist.

WESTERN SOCIETY

Modern societies are divided into horizontally stacked classes defined according to income or wealth—upper class, middle class, working class. But in the sixteenth and seventeenth centuries, classes intersected with other structures in which most people were more likely to situate themselves: vertical structures—interest groups, professions, trades, the clients of noblemen and officials, social orders, such as the nobility or the peasantry, religious sects, clans—whose members' sense of mutual belonging depended on the differences they felt between themselves and outsiders rather than on shared values, wealth, priorities, or education (see Figure 19.1). The nobility and clergy were not classes in any sense that a modern market researcher or pollster would recognize. They were communities of privilege uniting people of hugely different degrees of wealth, whose tax privileges and legal advantages marked them out. A prince-bishop ruling a semi-independent state like Cologne in Germany belonged to the same clerical estate as a penniless priest. Nobility embraced a duke with an income exceeding a king's and an impoverished rural nobleman.

(a) Modern societies

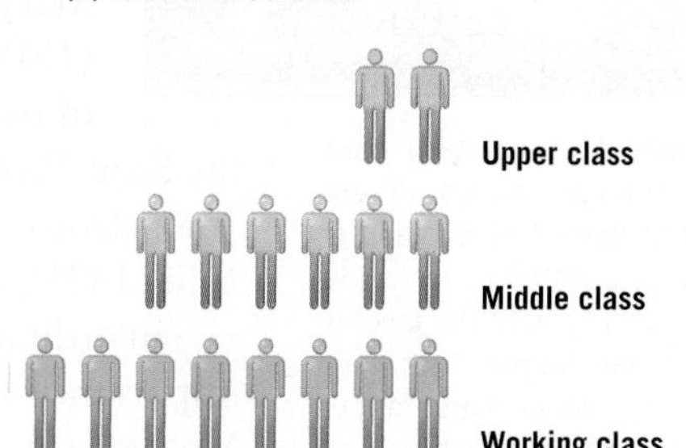

(b) Societies in sixteenth and seventeenth centuries

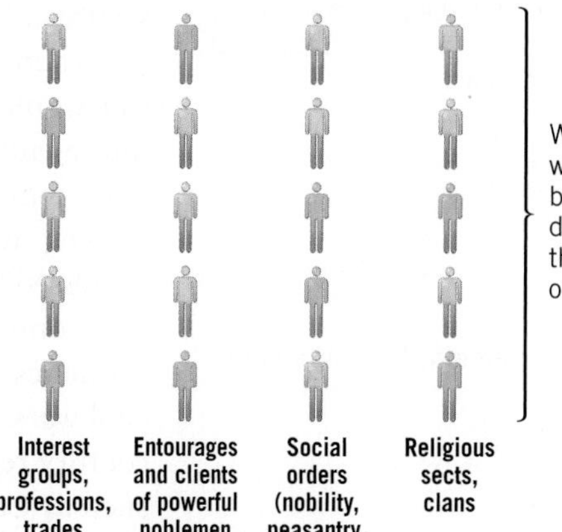

FIGURE 19.1 ORGANIZATION OF SOCIETY IN THE SIXTEENTH AND SEVENTEENTH CENTURIES COMPARED TO MODERN SOCIETIES

Queen Elizabeth I. Although it upset many men, women rulers became familiar figures in sixteenth-century Europe. Elizabeth I of England (r. 1558–1603) had her image boosted by icons like this frontispiece to a book of 1579. In the inscription that appears below her throne "her form shines to behold"; peace, "while wars fatigue neighboring peoples" and knowledge, "while blind errors afflict the world" sound themes of royal propaganda: Love embraces war, and explorers brandish scientific equipment. Yet England's real achievements at the time in science and exploration were minor, and Elizabeth, surrounded by aggressive advisors, could not keep England at peace or out of Europe's wars.

Cities formed communities of a similar kind, jealous of their jurisdiction, walled against the world, and fortified in their civic identities by the enjoyment of economic "liberties"—such as the right to hold markets or levy tolls. In most countries, Jews formed similar communities, with privileges as well as disabilities. So did the Protestant minorities in France and Poland. Noblemen's relations, tenants, servants, and other dependants gathered for festivals and sometimes lived together, eating their meals in common. The "families," as they were usually called, of urban artisans, with generations of apprentices sharing their roofs, had the same characteristics.

Vast, slow erosion changed this way of organizing society. In most of Europe, the family was redefined as an ever-smaller knot of close kin. Between the sixteenth and eighteenth centuries, aristocrats escaped from the communal great hall into family dining rooms. Court portraits of Philip IV (r. 1621–1665) of Spain and Charles I (r. 1625–1649) of England reveal nuclear families. In Protestantism, the family grew in importance because many other structures of life—religious brotherhoods, guilds, and monasteries—were abolished. The glittering courts of monarchs sucked provincial aristocracies away from their estates and hereditary followings.

Women's status was transformed. In the 1550s, the Italian anatomist Gabriele Falloppio sliced open women's cadavers and found that they worked in unsuspected ways. Women were not just nature's bungled attempts to make males, as earlier medical theory claimed. Women rulers appeared in unprecedented numbers in Europe. Some—like the flighty Mary, Queen of Scots (r. 1512–1567), or Catherine de' Medici (1519–1589), Regent of France—reenacted in their lives cautionary tales of the biblical Eve: submitting to lovers or favorites, manipulating men. To the Scots Protestant preacher John Knox (ca. 1513–1572), women in power were a "monstrous" aberration. But most women rulers, like Elizabeth I of England (r. 1558–1603), earned praise for ruling like men.

In ordinary homes, struggles between different forms of Christianity gave new importance to women's traditional domain as the guardians of household routine. Mothers transmitted simple religious faith and devotional practice from one generation to the next. Their choices ensured the survival of Catholicism or the progress of Protestantism. Women who married according to the clergies' new rules (see Chapter 18) could be better protected against male predators and more secure in keeping their property when their husbands died.

There could, however, be no corresponding increase in what feminists today call women's "options." New economic opportunities on a sufficient scale were unavailable until industrialization began in the late eighteenth century. Widowhood remained the best option for women who wanted freedom and influence. For women were still often victims: beaten by husbands, scolded by confessors, repressed by social rules, and cheated by the courts.

Glückel of Hameln, from *Memoirs*, 1690

Conflicts along class lines were rare. The so-called Wars of Religion between Catholics and Protestants in sixteenth-century France resembled old-fashioned civil wars, in which aristocrats' private armies battled each other. Other sixteenth-century rebellions were similar, or else were the protests of threatened minorities, such as Catholics in England and Ireland, or descendants of Moors in Spain. Or they were assertions of provincial identity, like those of Aragonese who rioted against Spanish royal power in 1590, or Netherlanders who rose up in 1568 against the foreign methods and officials of Philip II of Spain. The English Civil Wars of

1640–1653 used to be held up as a classic case of class revolution. But they seem better understood as a mixture of traditional rebellion, provincial revolt against intrusive central government, "ins" versus "outs," and genuine wars of religion.

Patterns of social change varied. From the fifteenth century, an economic fault line opened in Central Europe, roughly along the Elbe and upper Danube Rivers. In the west, peasants could take advantage of intense demand for labor to weaken limitations on their freedom to move and acquire property. In most of Eastern Europe, however, as the region gradually took over the Mediterranean basin's role as grain supplier to the continent, landlords restricted peasants' freedom to sell their labor. Even free towns lost rights of jurisdiction to aristocrats and rulers. In Poland, Hungary, and Bohemia, the nobility reclaimed or enforced their right to elect the king. A world of aristocratic dominance was emerging.

Demon barber. Czar Peter the Great (r. 1682–1725) enforces conformity to the religion of the state in Russia. The Old Believers, religious dissidents who split from the Russian Orthodox Church in the 1660s, believed that beards were part of the image of God and that, therefore, it was a sacrilege to shave. Peter saw beards as signs of Russia's backwardness and of resistance to his rule, and he imposed a tax on facial hair.

Despite growing differences between East and West, Peter the Great of Russia (r. 1682–1725) tugged and wrenched the frontier of Europe eastward by striving to make Russia more like Western Europe. It was an information revolution—a transfer of technology as well as fashion and taste from West to East. Preachers called Peter the sculptor and architect of Russia. He allowed women out of the home where traditional Russian practice had tried to confine them. He made two great journeys through Europe to learn Western ways. His role models were Dutch, German, and Swedish. He became an honorary Danish admiral and a member of the French Academy of Sciences. But rebels regarded him as the Antichrist or satanic.

Peter's policies and, in particular, his decision to relocate the capital of Russia on the Baltic at St. Petersburg should be considered part of the northward shift of Europe's center of gravity. The newly rising powers of the seventeenth century—the Netherlands, Sweden, England, France—were all in the north. So were some of the fastest growing cities—Amsterdam, Paris, London. The Mediterranean seemed stagnant by comparison. It was in the north that the great global trading companies and banks arose. There were undeniable advantages to being in business in northern rather than southern Europe. Inflation flowed from south to north—stimulated by new sources of gold and silver, by new forms and expanded levels of credit, and by the demand an increase of population created. This meant goods were cheaper in the north. Northerners used that price advantage to break into the Mediterranean in the late sixteenth century. Demand for their shipping helped—to import grain and to counter losses from Muslim piracy. From shipping, northerners diversified into slaving and banking, handling—and creaming off—the wealth of the cash-rich empires of Spain and Portugal, diverting the trade of Venice and the eastern Mediterranean.

Peter the Great, "Correspondence with Alexis," 1715

THE OTTOMANS

Europe's shifting axis of wealth affected the Ottoman Empire, a Mediterranean power. Yet this was a state that straddled Europe and Asia and, as we saw in Chapter 16, combined diverse traditions of political thought. The nerve center of the empire was the sultan's palace in Constantinople, the Topkapi Saray. The Topkapi was a fortress, a sanctuary, and a shrine. The bustle of the outer courts contrasted with the inner silence of the sacred spaces where the sultan was cocooned, close to his vast collection of relics of the Prophet Muhammad.

MAKING CONNECTIONS

FACTORS CONTRIBUTING TO EUROPEAN STATE-BUILDING

HISTORICAL DEVELOPMENTS →	INFLUENTIAL CONTRIBUTING FACTORS →	SOCIAL AND POLITICAL CONSEQUENCES
Renaissance: development of Western political thought	• Sovereignty becomes dominant way to identify the state • Retaining power becomes dominant political motivation • Need for international cooperation leads to commercial, maritime laws	• Machiavelli's *The Prince* becomes handbook for gaining and maintaining power • Law of nations becomes important factor in states honoring each other's sovereignty • The "ends justify the means" to ensure states' survival
Spanish dominance 1500–1600	• Access to silver mines of Mexico, Peru • Relatively unified monarchy; aristocracy ennobled by service; religious hierarchy • Developed superior military and naval forces • Dynastic connections	• First wealthy colonial superpower controls Portugal, much of Africa, Asia, Central and South America; challenges England, France; controls much of Italy, Netherlands, Germany • Economic, military decline in seventeenth century leaves opening for other European states
Social transformation of Europe	• Smaller family units become primary social unit • Intermarriage between aristocratic, royal families • Expansion of the role of women as moral exemplars	• Religious conflicts supercede class conflict • Increasing economic freedom, opportunity for urban dwellers • Traditional notions of nobility become entrenched • Western "progress" becomes a model for Peter the Great of Russia and others

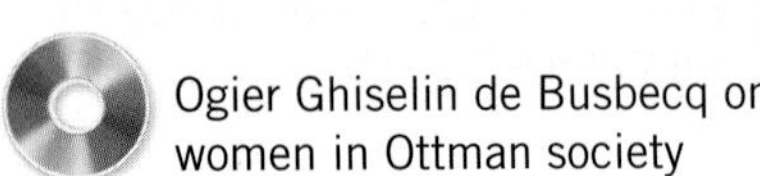
Ogier Ghiselin de Busbecq on women in Ottman society

Inside the sultan's private quarters, we can sense the hidden methods of government. Here talk was of politics: pillow talk and conversation in the baths, as well as the diplomatic encounters and the sultan's meetings with his ministers. In the absence of rules of succession to the throne, women and eunuchs manipulated the transfer of power from one sultan to the next. Sultans commonly put their brothers to death as security against rebellion or confined them in luxurious prison quarters. Access to a sultan's mother or favorite concubine was an avenue of political influence. For much of the seventeenth century, the effective chief executives of the state were queen mothers who knew little of the world beyond the harem walls, but who learned much from spies and servants, and who can be seen in paintings of court life, listening, from behind screens, to audiences with ambassadors and council meetings.

The efficiency of the Ottoman state from the fifteenth to the seventeenth centuries could rival any Western competitors, many of whose traditions it shared. Other empires of nomadic origins failed to keep up with the technology of war, but the Ottomans could float a vast navy or blow away enemies with firepower. The modernization of the army influenced social change. The traditional aristocracy, the mounted "protectors"—cavalrymen who served in war and were maintained by tribute—lost roles and revenues. Conquests in Europe gave the sultans access to huge numbers of Christian subjects, who paid discriminatory taxes and supplied a quota of their male children to serve as enslaved soldiers, called **Janissaries**, or in the administration. In the seventeenth century, the Janissaries became a hereditary corps, probably at the cost of their military efficiency, and conquests on the Christian front ceased.

To Western observers, the sultan seemed a despot. He made and unmade laws, both religious and secular, at will. Unlike Christian rulers, sultans had no need of a Reformation to curb the power of clergy. Though wary of the Islamic clerical establishment, they controlled the power structure of Sunni Islam themselves. Westerners regarded Ottoman government as disturbingly alien, but in the 1570s, the Ottoman jurist Ebu us-Suud (EH-boos SOOD) produced a justification of the ruler's power similar to Jean Bodin's theory of sovereignty in France. Still, the Ottoman system was unquestionably more autocratic than anything European "absolute" monarchs could manage. The dominions of Sultan Murad IV (moo-RAHD) (r. 1623–1640) were more tightly reined to the center than those of his counterparts in most of Europe. His Spanish contemporary, Philip IV, for instance, ruled multiple kingdoms with the aid of an up-to-date bureaucracy but without an overarching source of authority. In different places, his rule was known by different titles, legitimized by different theories, embodied in different institutions, and constrained by different laws. Not so Murad's.

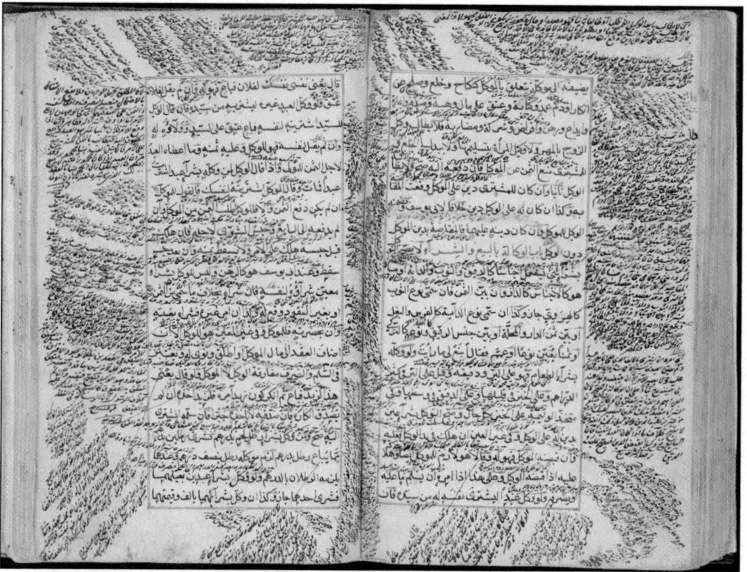

Ottoman law book. Written in Arabic in Istanbul in 1517 by Ibrahim al Halabi, the Islamic legal textbook known as *Multaqa al-Abhur (Confluence of the Currents)* remained an authoritative guide to the laws of the Ottoman Empire for 300 years. It contains rules for almost every human activity: spiritual rites, domestic relations, inheritance, commercial transactions, and crimes. The section shown here refers to buying and selling done by third parties. Various commentators made notes on this copy of the text.

In most of the Ottoman Empire, the sultan's representatives were chosen in a remarkably uniform way. It is not true, as Europeans said, that these men were all in a formal sense the sultan's slaves. The head of the civil service, the Grand Vizir was indeed a slave, but lesser officials were drawn from every class and part of the empire. Typically, in the sixteenth century, they trained as pages in the sultan's household before taking provincial commands. They rose through the administrative ranks of the provinces to which they were assigned.

Military and administrative life was the best route to wealth. Provincial governors made more out of their offices than even the richest merchants made from trade. The emphasis was not quite on plunder to the same extent as in Mughal India. Suleiman the Magnificent (r. 1520–1566; see Chapter 16) regulated the fees courts charged to litigants and practiced restraint in taxation and exploitation. Still, rational exploitation of subjects' wealth was the aim of the rulers of the empire. *Dirlik* (DEER-leek)—the term applied to provincial government—literally meant "wealth."

In the seventeenth century, the need to make the state efficient in war, in the face of the mounting costs of modern weaponry, drove changes in administrative practices. The lower ranks of the provincial administration became a career dead end, as governors came more and more from the army. The result was the rise of powerful provincial governors. When some of them rebelled in 1658, the state barely mustered the resources to beat them.

Despite the central training of the ruling elite, and its close dependence on the sultan, it is easy to overrate the degree of control the empire exercised in the provinces. The system could perhaps best be characterized as centralization tempered by chaos. Rival governors, for instance, sometimes got simultaneous letters of appointment to the same place and were left to fight it out. Banditry usurped authority—fed with manpower by deserters from the army and peasants whom immoderate tax gatherers forced into outlawry. In a typical incident in 1606, a notorious bandit chief agreed to police the Persian border with 16,000 men in exchange for lucrative governorships for himself and his kin. Many states faced problems with bandits, but most tried to deal summarily with them. The Ottomans negotiated with them and tried to manipulate them. This was typical of the Ottoman approach, which was always flexible and adaptable. There was one law, but it could always be modified to take into account local custom. The sultan derived his authority from religious principles, but these could be emphasized in different ways to suit different communities. Uniform rules, in theory, governed taxation, but in practice it was arbitrary and changeable.

Historians tend to date "decline" too early, because they know what follows. To speak of Ottoman decline in the seventeenth century seems premature, but they did cease to expand. In 1683, they failed to capture Vienna and in subsequent treaties gave up further ambitions in Europe. If they faltered, it was not so much because of imperfections in their system of government—which, after all, had proved itself in the past—as because of an unexplained stagnancy in the population of their empire. Ottoman population growth did not match that of Europe, India, China, or Japan. And in the eighteenth century, population growth slowed, relatively speaking, even more.

MUGHAL INDIA AND SAFAVID PERSIA

Like that of the Ottomans, the empire of the Mughals in India throve on the economic success of the people they ruled. Or perhaps it would be fairer to say that the Mughals and their subjects enriched each other. The Mughals' fantastic demand for revenues stimulated economic inventiveness and forced peasants to produce for urban markets. Spectacular spending on war, buildings, and luxuries recycled wealth and stimulated an economy that high taxation might otherwise have stifled.

Captive rebels arrive at the palace of the Mughal Emperor Akbar (r. 1556–1605) in 1573, wearing animal skins to symbolize the unnatural perversity and bestiality of the act of rebellion. The emperor is offstage to the right because it would diminish his dignity to depict him in the company of rebels. The painting is one of a series Akbar commissioned to commemorate the great events of his reign.

The Mughals' understanding of sovereignty was rooted in their conviction that they descended from Timur and ultimately from Genghis Khan (see Chapters 13 and 15). They ran their empire as a conquest—which, of course, it was, but it is more usual for conquerors to come to identify with the realms they rule. As we saw in Chapters 16 and 17, outside the relatively small, centrally administered core of the empire, Mughal methods of control relied on dividing tribute among a network of their relations, followers, clients, and allies. Like the Mongols and the Ottomans, they never established clear rules of succession. Every reign saw dynastic rebellions. Rivalries and alliances shifted unstably. The Mughals had always to balance the conflicting claims of rival aristocracies on whom they relied to keep their empire together and extend it.

The emperor Aurangzeb (r. 1658–1707) found the formula to keep the system going for a time: constant war to keep the aristocracies occupied, and continual conquests to multiply their rewards. A new generation of leaders arose, "born in the camp," as one of his ministers observed. New nobles, recruited from the frontier regions in south India as Aurangzeb's conquests grew, got the choicest shares of tribute and composed nearly half the upper ranks of the aristocracy by the end of the reign. Restlessness and rebellion in the heartlands and older conquests were among the results as ambitious or disaffected nobles clashed with each other and the imperial administration. Disruption and loss of revenues followed. In part, the Mughal Empire was a victim of its success. It expanded too fast to sustain the system of keeping nobles dependent by assigning them revenues. Still, when he died in 1707, Aurangzeb left a treasury stuffed with reserves.

Squeezed between the Ottomans and the Mughals, the Safavids of Persia (1501–1773) ran, in some respects, a similar state to both of them, with universalist rhetoric, a nominally all-powerful ruler, and flexible relationships between the ruler and subordinate sources of authority. Like the Ottomans, the Safavids benefited from the growth in trade across Eurasia: especially, in the Safavid case, the silk trade. Like the Ottomans, they drew on ancient traditions of kingship, as well as Muslim political thought, to legitimize their rule. The first ruler of the dynasty commissioned a lavish history of the ancient Persian kings. Their rules of succession were, like the chaotic systems of the Ottomans and Mughals, divisive and bloodily enforced. Shah Abbas I the Great (r. 1588–1629) imprisoned his sons and exterminated his remoter relations. Isfahan, his capital, resembled a great Indian or Ottoman city, full of unmistakable evidence of power, wealth, confidence, and energy. There were 273 public baths and 1,802 inns for caravans.

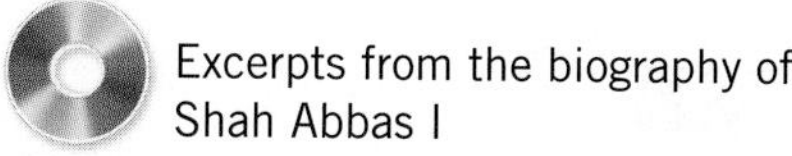

Nevertheless, Safavid rule never relied on the kind of uniform bureaucracy the Ottomans used. Practices resembling those of the Mughals kept them in power. The Safavids deployed a hereditary class of warrior horsemen, known as the Qizilbash, to enforce taxation and repress rebellion. As time went on, however, the Qizilbash tended to put down roots in the regions they ruled and became rebels themselves. To tie elite loyalties firmly into the center, the Safavids used marriage, distributing the womenfolk of the ruling house around the provinces. Where possible, rulers exterminated troublesome Qizilbash clans or replaced them with their personal representatives. But the dynasty rarely had the power to put these devices into practice.

The Safavids, however, practiced two unique policies. First, they were fiercely Shiite. They contemplated neither the religious pluralism of the Mughals nor the toleration of the Ottomans. They wanted to rule an exclusively Shiite Muslim people. Shiism was the basis of their claim to legitimacy. Religious minorities were forced to convert or were persecuted. Second, the Safavids had no nostalgia for a mythic steppelander past. On the contrary, they claimed to be enemies of the nomads, and as we saw in Chapter 17, defeated the Uzbek steppelanders (see Map 19.3).

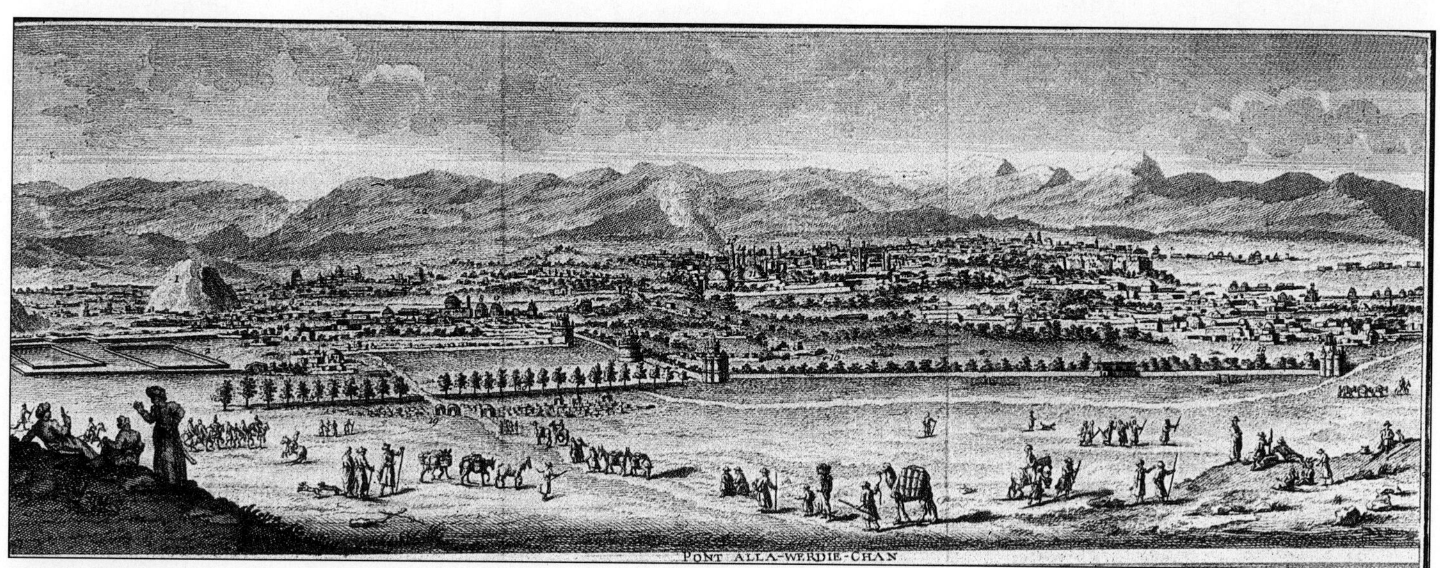

Isfahan, a vital center of trade, provides unmistakable evidence of the power, wealth, and dynamism of Safavid Persia. In this illustration, from the 1725 edition of *Voyages to Moscow, Persia, and the East Indies* by the Dutch traveler Cornelis de Brun (1652–1726), a camel caravan approaches the city.

Shah Ismail describes himself to his followers

The Safavids' religious policies are hard to understand, since—at the start of the period—most of the people they ruled were not Shiites. A desire to have a distinctive ideology, in opposition to that of the Ottomans, seems to have impelled them. Or perhaps, like Akbar in India, they wanted a religion of their own. Like so many dynasties—like Islam itself—warrior holy men, who turned tribesmen from deserts and mountains into formidable armies, founded the Safavid dynasty. The first Safavid shah, Ismail I (r. 1501–1524), was a visionary who conversed with a vision of Muhammad's nephew Ali (see Chapter 8) and who appears to have considered himself an incarnation of God. He imposed Shiism by force. But force is never enough to change emotional allegiances. In subsequent reigns, dazzling, frightening ceremonial impressed Shiism on the people's minds. In 1641, a visiting Western observer described a typical ritual, designed to commemorate the death of one of the martyrs of Shiism: a terrifying mock conflict, a melee of horses, camels, and "naked persons who struggled and screamed as if in despair, gashed with wounds, which they beat to make them spurt blood." An accompanying parade featured mourning women and children dressed in hides that were pierced with arrows and smeared with blood. Throughout such ceremonies, messages of hatred were directed against the supposed heirs of the martyr's murderers—the Sunni Ottomans.

Paradoxically, perhaps, Safavid rulers never seemed very pious—tending to exempt themselves from Islamic rules about drink and sex—until one of the last

MAP 19.3

The Safavid Empire, 1501–1736

Safavid Empire, 1722
territory under Ottoman control, 1722
Mughal Empire, 1722
easternmost limit of area contested by Ottomans to 1736
Uzbek invasion, 1587
Uzbeks people

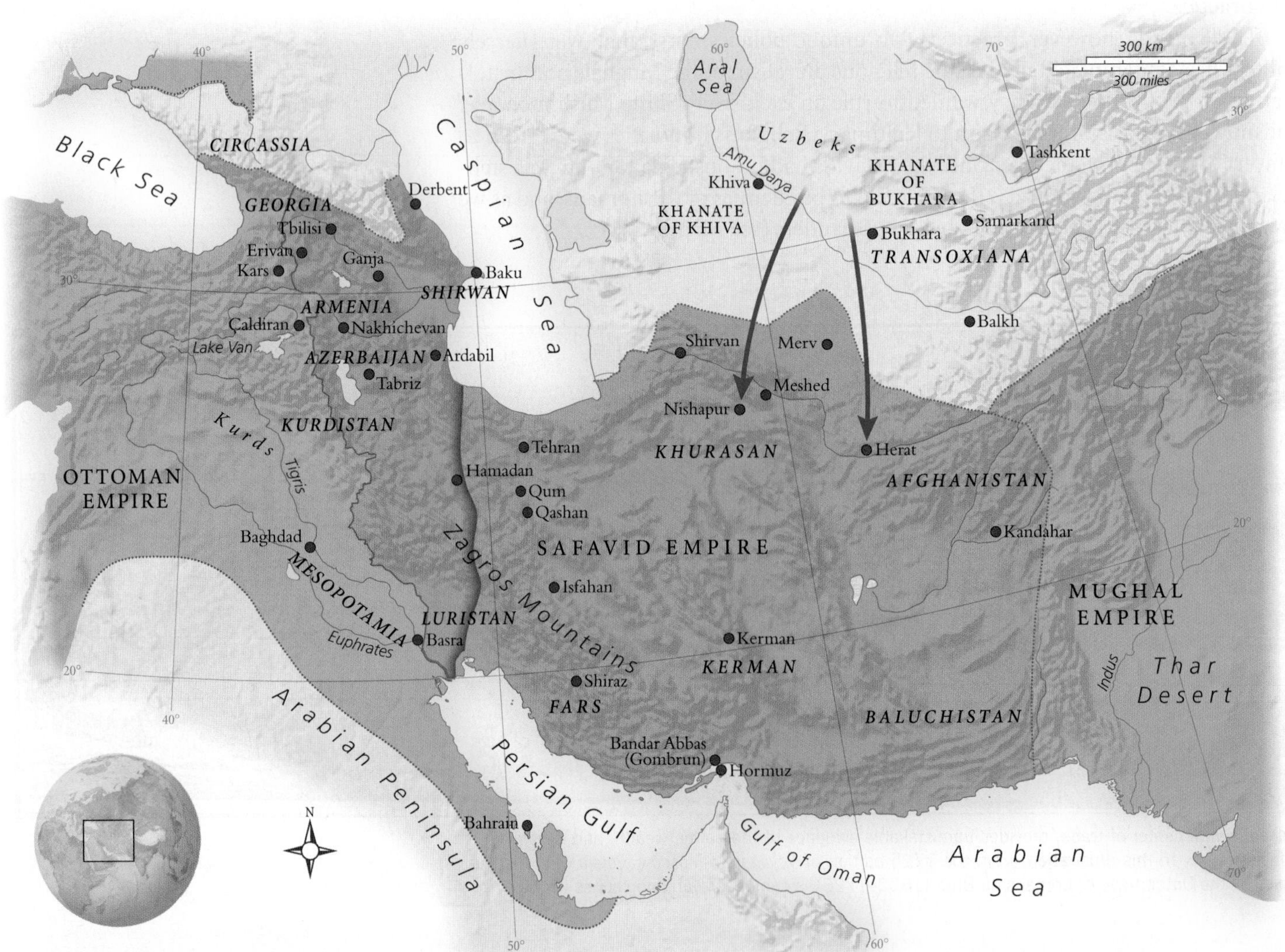

shahs of the dynasty, Husain (r. 1694–1722), smashed the 6,000 wine bottles in the imperial cellars, forbade song, dance, coffee, games, and prostitution, and banished even respectable women from appearing in the streets. These commands seem like a desperate attempt to capture the allegiance of an alienated clergy.

It is remarkable that the Safavids succeeded for so long. Whereas the Ottomans and Mughals were able to renew their strength by making new conquests, the Safavids' opportunities were limited. Ismail I thought himself invincible. When Ottoman artillery stopped his cavalry at the Battle of Chaldiran in Iraq in 1514, he flew black banners inscribed with the word *revenge*. But he never achieved that revenge. The Safavids did make some gains on the Turkish front, and their armies raided Ottoman Baghdad twice. Thousands of Georgian, Armenian, and Circassian prisoners were drafted into the slave corps that served the shahs as administrators. Portuguese intruders were turned out of the Persian Gulf. But the strength of the Ottomans to the west and of the Mughals to the east left the Safavids nowhere to expand.

Islamic Empires: The Ottomans, Safavid Persia, and Mughal India

Fifteenth and sixteenth centuries	Ottomans create an elite slave army, the Janissaries
1501–1773	Safavid dynasty in Persia
r. 1501–1524	First Safavid ruler, Shah Ismail I, imposes Shiism by force
1570s	Ottoman jurist Ebu us-Suud justifies the Sultan's power
1658	Rebellion of provincial governors against Ottoman authority
1683	Ottomans fail to capture Vienna and cease conquests on the Christian front
r. 1658–1707	Emperor Aurangzeb engages in almost constant warfare in India
r. 1694–1722	Safavid ruler, Husain, imposes strict Islamic law
ca. Eighteenth century	Mughal power begins irreversible decline
1857	End of Mughal Empire

CHINA

While Europe became ever more divided among competing states, and the Ottoman, Mughal, and Safavid Empires consolidated, the unity of China survived potentially devastating threats.

Under the Ming dynasty (1368–1644), sixteenth-century China enriched its subjects. The wealth gap between China and most of the rest of the world probably went on increasing over the next two centuries, as demand soared for goods in which China dominated world markets: porcelain, fine lacquerware, tea, ginseng, and rhubarb. By the mid–seventeenth century, China probably contained about a third of the world's population.

Chinese Politics

The emperors' authority, unlimited in theory, was restricted in practice by the power of the 20,000 or so scholar **mandarins** who ran the administration. They qualified for their jobs by passing competitive examinations in knowledge of classical Confucian texts. In consequence, most of them never questioned Confucian ideas. They wanted emperors to stick to the performance of sacred rites and administer justice. The empire, they felt, was best left in a state of peaceful balance, without aggression against its neighbors. Traditionally, emperors had escaped the control of bureaucrats by appealing to the Buddhist clergy, the court eunuchs, and the army. In the sixteenth century, however, the mandarins' supremacy appeared unshakable. The emperor was not allowed to leave the capital—ostensibly, to prevent the delegation of power into profane hands while he was away. For example, the Zhengde (jehng-duh) emperor (r. 1505–1521), who moved out of the palace and surrounded himself with eunuchs and monks, insisted on going on campaign on the Mongol frontier to escape the suffocating presence of his ministers. But he had to abandon the expeditions when the scholars, in effect, went on strike, crippling the administration.

The gravest crisis arose in 1587, when the Wanli (wahn-lee) emperor (r. 1572–1620) resolved to defy the mandarins. Evidence of widespread corruption in the civil service had undermined his confidence in them. He proposed to assert his power by altering the rules of succession, passing over his eldest son in favor of a son by his favorite concubine. Factions supporting the rivals traded accusations of witchcraft and distributed pamphlets among the people. After ten years of stalemate, in which government effectively came to a halt, the emperor backed down. Intellectual trends reflected the shift in the location of power. The philosopher Li Zhi (lee jeh) wrote a new version of Chinese history, in which emperors counted for nothing, and the heroes were mandarins. The effectiveness of Ming government was never fully restored.

The Ming Empire seemed unable to cope with ecological disasters—floods and famines—in the 1630s. The peasant rebellions that followed became civil wars as army commanders fought to control or even capture the throne. Meanwhile, from about 1590, the Ming delegated defense on the Mongol frontier to Nurhaci, a chief of a pastoral war band in Manchuria. Chinese support enabled him to unite the Manchus. He began to call himself emperor and to represent himself as the spiritual heir of Manchu ancestors who had conquered northern China in the twelfth century. In 1636, his successor, Abahai, decreed a new ideology, which he called "Qing." The name was an allusion to "pure" water, which would quench the "bright" flame of "Ming." The Manchus methodically and bloodily took over China, proclaiming the Qing dynasty. The last Ming claimant to the throne was executed in 1662. The last Ming loyalists were not rooted out from their nests on the island of Taiwan until the 1680s.

The shock of conquest by the Manchus made Chinese intellectuals rethink the whole basis of political legitimacy. The most startling result was the development of a doctrine of the sovereignty of the people, similar to that of Western Europe. Huang Zongxi (hwang dzohng-shee) (1610–1695) thought that a state of nature had once existed when "each man looked to himself" until benevolent individuals created the empire. Corruption set in, and "the ruler's self-interest took the place of the common good. . . ." Lü Liuliang (loo lee-o-lee-ahng) (1629–1683) went further: "Social order . . . originates with the people and reaches up to the ruler. . . . Heaven's order and Heaven's justice are not things rulers and ministers can take and make their own."

Yet, whereas in the West, this sort of thinking helped to justify republics and generate revolutions, nothing comparable happened in China until the twentieth century, when Western influence had done its work. Meanwhile, as throughout the Chinese past, peasant revolts aimed to renew the empire and replace the dynasty, not transfer the **mandate of heaven** from a monarch to the people. Unlike the West with the memory of ancient Greece and Rome, China had no examples of republicanism or democracy to look to in its history or idealize in myth. Still, the work of Huang, Lü, and similar theorists helped to keep radical criticism of the imperial system alive and prepare Chinese minds for the later reception of Western revolutionary ideas.

Manchu warrior. "The bandits' heads were strung together. . . . Without even combing his horse's mane, he returned to make his report." The poem about this portrait of Zhanyinbao of the Chinese imperial guard, in 1760, praises his prowess in law enforcement, but the artist shows him in hunting dress, armed with the bow that the Qianlong emperor, in the Manchu tradition, favored for the hunt. The realism and animation with which the subject's face is portrayed suggest that one of the Jesuit court artists painted this picture.

The Metropolitan Museum of Art, Purchase, The Dillon Fund Gift, 1986 (1986.206) Photograph © The Metropolitan Museum of Art

Chinese Society

China experienced a revolution in the ownership of land. Peasant revolts in the 1640s challeged landowners' privileges. Over the next few decades, the government gradually abolished limitations on peasants' freedom to sell their labor. In 1681, peasants could no longer be sold along with the land they farmed but were free to "do as they please." As a result, the landlord life became less attractive. Land was still valued as a source of prestige or security, but agriculture was despised as "the labor of fools," while peasant fierceness made rent collection "a task to be feared." China became increasingly a land of peasant smallholders. Rural investment took the form of pawnbrokering by urban loan sharks who lent money to peasants to buy seed grain. A history of hatred between city and country began that has lasted to this day.

So in China, as in Europe, economic change broke down some of the traditional structures of society. Migrations probably contributed to the effect. But the clan, or extended family that persisted from one generation to another, could not be destroyed. Ancestor worship made the clan into a religion. The administrative system perpetuated its role because Chinese clans, thousands strong, combined to select the best candidates from among their members to take the exams to enter the civil service. Rich clan members paid to educate poor relations, in order to elevate some bright young boy to influence in the state. Wives had to support the interests of their husbands' clan. There are signs that the restriction and even oppression of women got worse in seventeenth-century China. Female foot binding literally hobbled its victims and restricted their mobility (see Chapter 12). Widow suicide was encouraged. Widows who stayed alive often prospered in business but rarely remarried. In Europe, by contrast, remarriage was a standard way to cope with the effects of high mortality.

Letters of Zheng Zhilong

Elements in China's seventeenth-century experience combined to strengthen and spread Chinese identity. This may seem surprising. The disruptions caused by civil war might have weakened allegiance to the state. The vastness of the empire meant that China's new rulers had to adapt their legitimacy: as Manchus in Manchuria, as khans in Mongolia, as protectors of the Buddhist establishment in Tibet. Only on their extreme western frontier, where their subjects were Muslims, did the Qing emperors show hostility to the local culture, but everywhere their policy was to favor the adoption of Chinese ways. By the end of the eighteenth century, China's ethnic minorities had largely forfeited their traditional identities and had come to think of themselves as Chinese. Internal migrations helped. They induced minorities to leave their traditional homelands and encouraged a sense that everyone within the empire was Chinese. Meanwhile, the overseas Chinese found themselves thrust into communities composed of migrants from many parts of China. As a result they increasingly felt a sense of belonging to the same community, which they projected home in their letters.

Qing strategy was to reconcile the different Chinese elites, especially the scholar-gentry, from among whom the mandarins were mostly recruited, to Manchu rule with generous rewards and complete deference to the Confucian point of view that was deeply rooted among the Chinese elites. The Kangxi emperor (r. 1661–1722), who was the second Manchu to rule China, took lessons in the Confucian classics daily before dawn. The Qing avoided the impasse with the mandarins in which late Ming rule had been mired for three reasons. First, the scholars clung to the Qing as guarantors against disorder. Second, the dynasty and the bureaucracy had a common enemy in the warlords whose armies survived the civil wars that had brought down the Ming and who ruled vast areas with little input from the central government. The Kangxi emperor overthrew them in 1673. Finally, the Qing had their own power base in the Manchu warrior-elite. A twofold problem arose: how to perpetuate the martial readiness of Manchus, softened by adopting Chinese ways, and how to preserve a balance in the dynasty between Chinese and Manchu identities. Though the Qing emperors spoke and wrote Chinese, they kept up their knowledge of the Manchu language, favored Manchus who remained loyal to their traditional culture, and founded schools of martial virtue for Manchu sons.

Ming and Qing China: Politics and Society

1368–1644	Ming dynasty
1500s	Commercial economy booms
1587	The Wanli emperor precipitates a crisis by challenging the mandarins
1630s	Ecological disasters undermine Ming power
1640s	Peasant revolts challenge landowners' privileges
1644–1912	Qing dynasty
Seventeenth and eighteenth centuries	Mandarins reconciled to Qing power
Early eighteenth century	Last restrictions on peasant freedom eliminated

TOKUGAWA JAPAN

Compared with the diverse societies that the Qing, Ottomans, or Mughals ruled, the Japanese already had remarkably uniform notions about themselves. The only ethnic minority in the Japanese islands was the Ainu people of the far north, and most of them lived outside the boundary of the Japanese Empire in 1600. The Japanese treated those Ainu whom they did conquer with suspicion. In any case the number of Ainu was relatively small.

Nevertheless, in other respects, the dynamic features of the period affected Japan as sweepingly as any of the other newly or lately interconnected regions in Eurasia that we have been discussing. Historians have always regarded the seventeenth century as a period of deepening Japanese isolationism. And Japanese governments did try to exclude foreign culture—but only that of "barbarian" Westerners. Chinese and Korean arts and ideas remained welcome, and, indeed, Confucianism revived (see Chapter 18). Moreover, imperial expansion went on, and despite government controls, overseas trade continued to grow throughout the seventeenth and eighteenth centuries, partly through the Dutch and Chinese agents who were allowed restricted trading privileges in Japan, and partly through illegal trade that the Japanese authorities never wholly suppressed. In any case, Japan generated its own internal commercial revolution. The area under cultivation doubled in 100 years from the mid–sixteenth century. Population rose from around 12 million in 1550 to 30 million by 1721.

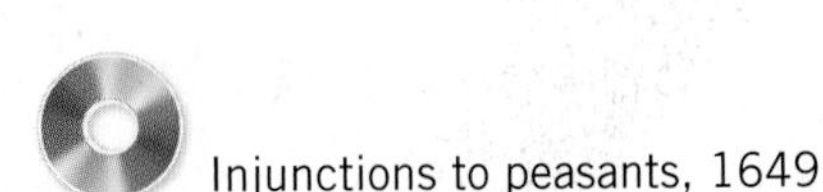
Injunctions to peasants, 1649

Peasants and merchants were the big gainers from the new prosperity, as peasants switched to surplus production to feed the growing cities, and merchants exploited the expanding markets. Edo, the old name for Tokyo, was one of the biggest cities in the world, with at least 600,000 people in 1700. A service-industry bourgeoisie of merchants, clerks, and craftsmen throve. Peasant prosperity eased the former cycle of famine and rebellion. Governments encouraged people to concentrate on getting rich. The writer of novellas, Saikaku, was the spokesman of the age. Most of his stories tell of self-enrichment by hard work or intelligence. A street scavenger becomes a chopstick-manufacturing millionaire. A desperate widow makes a fortune by raffling her house.

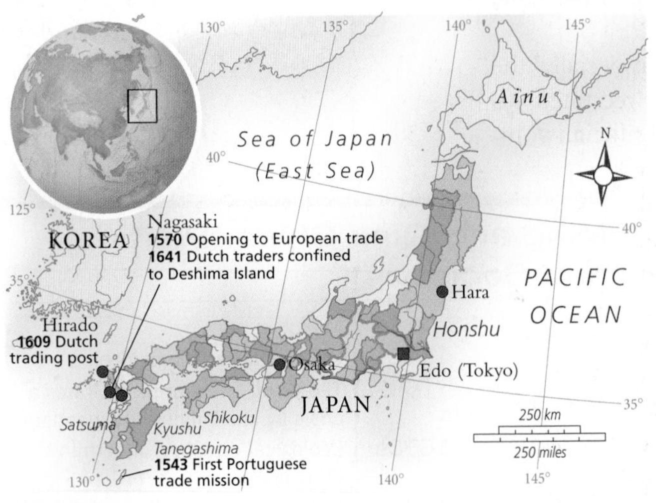

MAP 19.4

Tokugawa Japan

— *daimyo* boundaries

— Tokugawa domain from 1614

Ainu people

There were losers, too. Peace was bleak for the traditional warrior class, the samurai, who suffered from low land values, high interest rates, and stagnant pensions. Many samurai were reduced to the role of *ronin*—underemployed freelance soldiers, drifting between service to different lords, called **daimyo**, who rarely paid samurai proper salaries.

Korea experienced similar problems with impoverished members of its noble class, or *yangbans*, as they were called. Traditionally, they discharged responsibilities in war and administration and could obtain land and wealth. But those excluded from office led lives of impoverished idleness, amid low-life hangers on, satirized in popular literature and art.

For those who shared it, Japanese prosperity was founded on internal peace. A dynasty of chief ministers, the Tokugawa, ruled as **shoguns** in Edo, while the emperors remained secluded figureheads, performing sacred rites at the old capital in Kyoto. The key to stability was management of relations between the shoguns and the 260 or so daimyo who ran Japan's provinces (see Map 19.4). The daimyo came from a limited number of noble families, but the shogun appointed

MAKING CONNECTIONS

CHINA AND JAPAN: STABILITY AND CHANGE, 1500–1700

STATE AND SOURCES OF STABILITY →	CHALLENGES →	SOCIAL, CULTURAL, AND POLITICAL ADAPTATIONS
China / Confucianism; scholar mandarins run the state regardless of emperor, dynasty	• Ecological disaster—floods and famines in the 1630s • Peasant rebellions, civil wars resulting from natural disasters • Conquest by Manchus • Pressure for land reform, challenges to landowners	• Development of the doctrine of sovereignty of the people • Elimination of right to sell peasants along with land • Breakup of large estates • Continuation of clan loyalty, ancestor worship amid social, economic change
Japan / ethnic homogeneity; imperial system of rule; stable population and economic prosperity	• Christian missionaries convert many people • Disenfranchisement of traditional warrior class (samurai) • Need to maintain peace between shoguns and provincial rulers (daimyo)	• Enforced isolationism from West balanced by continuing trade with Asia • New emphasis on Confucian, Buddhist beliefs • Encouragement of commercial revolution, urbanism

and frequently transferred them, though some managed to secure hereditary succession in their chosen regions. The Shimazu lords of the huge domain of Satsuma in southern Japan, for instance, built up enough power to exercise effective autonomy (and, eventually, in the nineteenth century to challenge the shoguns). Normally, the Tokugawa obliged daimyo to maintain houses—and, in effect, leave hostages—in Edo and reside there for part of each year. Shoguns also arranged marriages between daimyo families. In these respects, the system resembled the way many European monarchs dealt with their most powerful nobles.

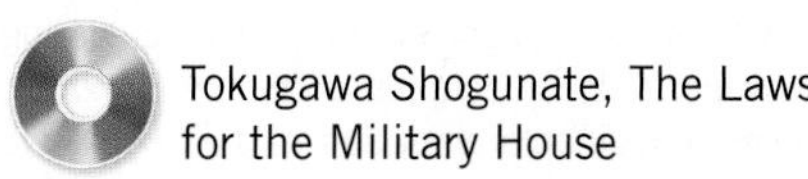

Tokugawa Shogunate, The Laws for the Military House

THE NEW WORLD OF THE AMERICAS

Historians' favorite question about European overseas colonization is whether it created frontier societies—altered by generation gaps and pioneer radicalism—or duplications of home: transplanted Old Worlds. The answer is that the colonies were both. Molded and changed by new challenges and opportunities, settler communities usually tugged at nostalgic images of a home they aped or mirrored. An early apologist for the Spanish Empire conceived it as the colonists' obligation to rebuild New Spain in the image of the old Spain. Even Puritans, who did consciously want to make something new of New England, went about it by fencing and planting to create English-style fields.

Yet colonies had to adapt to new environments and, in many cases, to new neighbors. Sectarian religious communities, democratic commonwealths, and plantation economies were all new, for instance, to the English experience. A bureaucratic state, with little delegation of authority to nobles and towns, was unfamiliar in Spain. While slaves had existed in Europe in the Middle Ages, slavery on the American scale was unprecedented. Huge mixed-race populations, of the kind that filled Spanish and Portuguese America, had never before had a chance to emerge outside the Muslim world. The new colonies were products of their environments that changed the people who lived in them.

D ESPANOL, Y MULATA
PRODUCE MORISCA.

Mixing of the races. One of the most popular subjects for painters in eighteenth-century Spanish America was the vast range of skin complexions that intermarriage among Europeans, Native Americans, and black Africans produced. Hundreds of sets like this one survive, each consisting of many portraits of couples and their children, with every imaginable gradation of skin color. No one knows exactly what these paintings were for, but Spaniards who returned to Europe brought them home as souvenirs.

The New World really was new. The Spanish experience there was one of the biggest surprises of history: the creation of the first great world empire of land and sea, and the only one, on a comparable scale, erected without the aid of industrial technology. A new political environment took shape.

Historians have searched for the origins of the "modern state," in which the authority the aristocracy exercised shrank to insignificance. The crown enforced an effective monopoly of government jurisdiction. The independence of towns withered. The church submitted to royal control. And sovereignty—formerly definable in terms of the right to pronounce justice—became increasingly identified with supreme legislative power as laws multiplied.

States in Europe developed along those lines, but only the Spanish Empire in the New World fully matched all the criteria. Great nobles were generally absent from the administration, which was staffed by professional, university-trained, royally appointed bureaucrats. Town councils were largely composed of royal nominees. Church patronage was exclusively at the disposal of the crown. With a few exceptions, feudal tenure—combining the right to try cases at law along with land ownership—was banned. Meanwhile, a stream of legislation regulated—or was supposed to regulate—the new society. The Spanish Empire was never efficient because of the vast distances royal authority had to cover. Remote administrators could and did ignore royal commands. But this was a modern state because it was a bureaucratic state and a state governed by laws.

It also threw up new microsocieties: the shipboard world of to-ing and fro-ing across the Atlantic and Pacific; the missions; the slave plantations; the little kingdoms runaway slaves called **maroons** set up; the households Spanish conquerors founded with native wives. In Spanish colonies, **creole** consciousness—identity distinct from that of the "mother country"—arose in the conquerors' first generation. Pride in mixed ancestry—especially claims to be descended from Indian nobility—was a sure sign of creole self-assertion. In the late sixteenth and early seventeenth centuries, Fernando de Alva Ixtlilxochitl's (eesh-tleel-ZOCH-eet-el) was a typically self-conscious creole voice: a historian of his community in Mexico, an interpreter of Native American language in the law courts, a government representative on municipal councils, a collector of Aztec literature. In the same period in Peru, the royal Inca blood of Garcilaso de la Vega made him highly sought after as a godparent by young families in the Spanish town where he lived.

Historians have often supposed that the trauma of conquest and the catastrophic diseases Europeans introduced shocked Native Americans into docility. In many ways, however, it is remarkable how much—and how long—their society survived. Sometimes it simply evaded the Europeans. The Inca state, for instance, withdrew in the 1530s to a new, lowland environment centered on Vilcabamba, until Spanish conquest uprooted it in 1572. Independent Native American states survived for generations and even centuries in the rain forests of Guatemala, the Mexican desert, and the Florida swamps. In other cases, Native Americans formed partnerships with Spanish religious orders as their protectors or—especially in the former Aztec and Inca subject areas—by collaborating with the Spanish monarchy and simply continuing to pay to the new elite the tribute they had formerly paid to Native American imperialists.

New elites were not just composed of Europeans but also of newly elevated Native American individuals and communities. In the Aztec world, for instance, where war and disease wiped out much of the former generation of leaders, Spaniards—especially missionaries—forged relationships with surviving youngsters in mission schools. In urban environments Native American *ladinos* learned Spanish and earned Spanish trust. Everywhere, the children of marriages between Spaniards and Indians assumed a potentially advantageous place in colonial society. Because people at the time were more sensitive to differences of class than of race, these *mestizos*, as the descendents of Europeans and Native Americans were called, had access to positions of power and opportunities of wealth.

Of all the new kinds of society the global interconnections of the period created, the most novel were surely those of "the world the slaves made" in the Americas. From Virginia to Brazil, much of Atlantic-side America became, in early colonial times, more African than European. In 1553, the viceroy of Mexico was afraid that Africans would swamp white settlers. While black people rarely were a majority in the Spanish colonies—Cuba and Santo Domingo were two exceptions – Africans were often the largest part of the population. By 1700, England's Caribbean colonies had over 120,000 black slaves and only about 15,000 white inhabitants. The slaves practiced their own religions (see Chapter 18), maintained their own household patterns, and ate their own food. They created languages of their own to bridge the communication gaps among people from so many different parts of Europe and Africa. Even in tightly controlled plantations, slave communities often created autonomous institutions. In Jamaica, the British were never able to eliminate the secret power of the *obeah-men*, whom they denounced as sorcerers, or curb the "benches" of elders, who were the self-regulating judges of the slaves. The evidence from British North America also suggests that slaves themselves seem to have evolved the social order of plantation life—the family structures, the regulation of relationships, the norms of behavior. African culture was only slowly transformed, because most owners resisted Christianizing their slaves. The Bible might give them subversive ideas about equality. Clergy might interfere with owners' abuse.

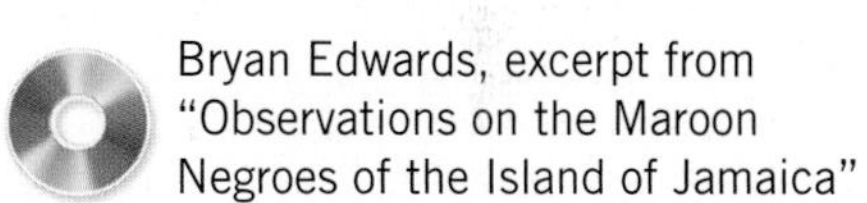
Bryan Edwards, excerpt from "Observations on the Maroon Negroes of the Island of Jamaica"

As well as African ways of life, there were African political structures in America: independent states established by runaways, sometimes in collaboration with Native Americans (see Map 19.5). Colonial authorities were forced to recognize the most successful maroon kingdoms. It was easier to establish a working relationship

Don Francisco Arove and his sons, leaders of the maroon kingdom of Esmeraldas, who submitted to the Spanish crown by treaty in 1599. A government official commissioned the painting for presentation to King Philip III. The mixed culture of this community of runaway slaves is reflected in the appearance of its leaders: their black faces, their rich clothing in the style of Spanish noblemen, the costly ear and nose ornaments borrowed from Native American tradition.

MAP 19.5

Maroon Communities in the Americas, 1500–1800

MAP EXPLORATION
www.prenhall.com/armesto_maps

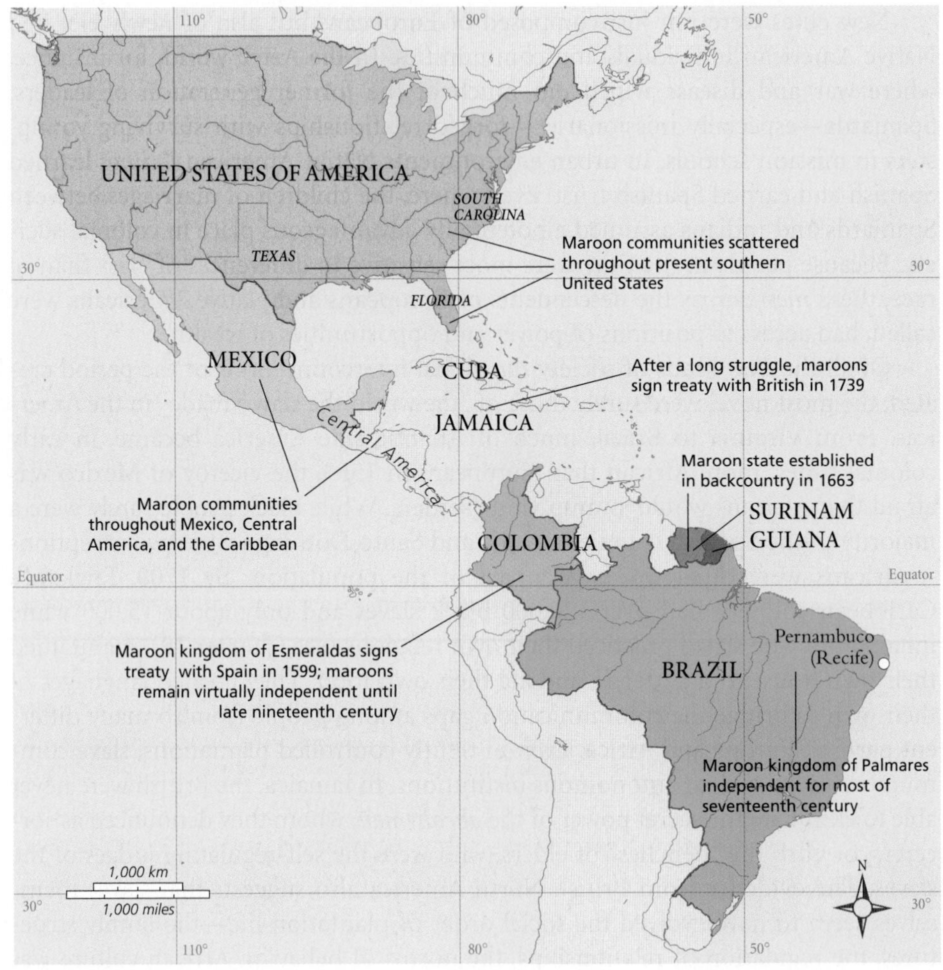

than run the risks of war and of inflaming slaves' grievances. The best-known case is that of the maroon kingdom of Esmeraldas in the hinterland of what is today Colombia, which signed a treaty with the Spanish crown in 1599.

In the seventeenth and eighteenth centuries, maroon states in South Carolina and Jamaica were also protected by agreements with the colonial authorities that guaranteed their peaceful toleration in exchange for joint regulation of the fate of new fugitives from the plantations. In the backcountry of Surinam, a maroon state was established in 1663 (the year the maroons of Jamaica received the first treaty acknowledging their autonomy), with the connivance of planters who sent their slaves there to evade the head tax. The best documented and longest lasting of the runaways' states was upcountry from Pernambuco in Brazil, where the kingdom of Palmares defended its independence from Portugal for almost the entire seventeenth century. At its height, in the late seventeenth century, it had a royal guard 5,000 strong, an elaborate court life that impressed visiting Portuguese, and a black elite rich enough to have many slaves of their own.

Europeans dealing in the slave trade convinced themselves that slavery represented a civilizing process: the recovery of one of the virtues of ancient Greece and Rome, which slave energy had fueled, and the removal of slaves from the supposedly "barbarous darkness" of Africa to the "light" of Christian European civilization. In practice, it is hard to imagine anything more barbarizing. Slavery nourished its own lies and cant: racism, which depicted black people as inherently inferior to white people, or claimed that they were better off enslaved than at home. It corrupted owners by giving them power over the lives and bodies of their slaves and encouraging them to abuse it. It corrupted shippers, who overcrowded their cargoes to maximize their profits and, in verifiable incidents, tossed live slaves overboard for the insurance ship owners could earn for dead "cargo." It kept black and white people in mutual fear and loathing, driving black rebels to horrific and despairing acts to find refuge or gain revenge, and trapping colonial governments in policies of inhuman rage and repression. It let loose predatory gangs of slavers and bounty hunters. It encouraged war in Africa between predator states that profited from the trade and their victims. The moral effects are important because every memory of inhumanity is precious in a world still riddled with vices of cruelty and greed.

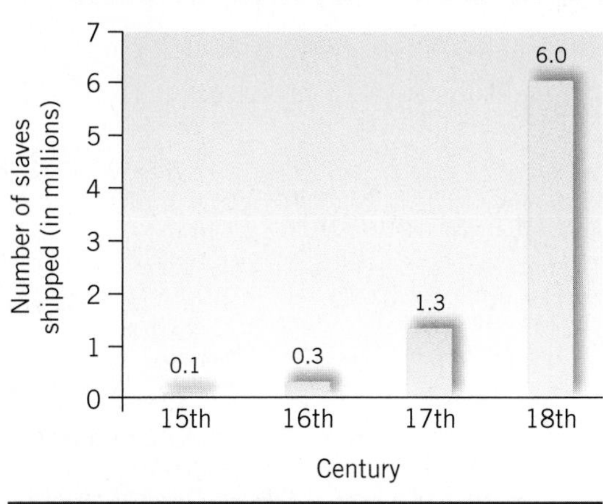

FIGURE 19.2 THE ATLANTIC SLAVE TRADE, FIFTEENTH TO EIGHTEENTH CENTURIES

From Cañizares-Esguerra, Jorge; Seeman, Eric, The Atlantic in Global History: 1500–2000, *© 2007. Electronically reproduced by permission of Pearson Education, Inc., Upper Saddle River, New Jersey.*

AFRICA

The social, political, and demographic effects of the slave trade in Africa are hard to measure. The slaves that crossed the Atlantic came especially from the West African bulge, the Congo basin, and Angola. The New World needed substantial numbers of them. Outside British North America, most slave communities in the Americas did not reproduce naturally, for reasons that historians still do not fully understand. Constant new imports were therefore required to maintain labor levels. Over 1.5 million black slaves reached the New World by 1700, and nearly 6 million more in the eighteenth century. The numbers shipped out of Africa were even larger, because many slaves died during the passage across the Atlantic. From the best available figures, almost 400,000 of those exported from Africa before 1800 never reached the Americas (see Figure 19.2).

Overwhelmingly, they were obtained through black African sellers by war and raiding that reached deep into the interior. Despite the size of the catchment area, it is hard to believe that the export of manpower on the scale demanded did not seriously affect the victim societies. For a time the Angola region seems to have developed an excess of females over males because many more men than women were shipped across the Atlantic. On the fringes of African slave-trading societies, some areas may have been depopulated.

The political effects are glaring. Dahomey illustrates them—one of many slave-trading states that sprang up or grew in West Africa during the slaving era (see Map 19.6). The kingdom arose in the interior of the present state of Benin in the early seventeenth century. Europeans already called the region the Slave Coast. Dahomey subordinated all other values to a ferocious warrior cult. Guests at the king's table dined with silver-handled forks on food European-trained cooks prepared, but they had to approach the king's palace over a path paved with skulls and were obliged to witness the human sacrifices that celebrated royal funerals and annual commemorations of former kings. Around the mid–seventeenth century, Dahomey began to accumulate muskets in exchange for slaves it obtained by raiding farther north. The 18 trading communities subject to Dahomey in the 1680s grew to over 200 within 20 years. Dahomey acquired a strip of coast—so King Agaja told European traders—to control outlets for slaves.

Africa, the Americas, and the Slave Trade

Late sixteenth century	Maroon kingdom of Esmeraldas
Seventeenth and eighteenth centuries	Slave states proliferate in West Africa; maroon states in South Carolina and Jamaica
Late seventeenth century	Black slave population of British Caribbean reaches 120,000
	Maroon kingdom of Palmares reaches its height
ca. 1700	Number of slaves shipped to New World reaches 1.5 million
ca. 1800	Number of slaves shipped to New World reaches 7.5 million

MAP 19.6 West and West-Central Africa, ca. 1750

Yet with a productive territory in an area of varied commerce, Dahomey did not depend on slaving, which accounted for perhaps 2.5 percent of its economy. Slaving apologists frequently pointed out that a war ethic motivated Dahomeyan aggression and that Dahomey prized captives more as potential human sacrifices than as slaves. White slave traders claimed that they performed a work of mercy by redeeming their victims from certain death. Dahomey's wars were not fought primarily for slaves. Indeed, only a third of the campaigns acquired enough victims to cover the costs. Still, some facts are clear. Dahomey rose and fell with the rhythms of the slave trade, and its cult of ferocity coincided with the market for captives. The economics of the slave trade obliged African suppliers to be warriors or bandits, because the prices Europeans paid made it worth raiding for slaves but not worth raising them.

Farther west, the history of Ashanti shows that state-building on an even greater scale was possible with resources other than slaves. Gold was the basis of Ashanti's spectacular rise from the 1680s to the dimensions of a great kingdom by the mid–eighteenth century, occupying 10,000 square miles of present-day Ghana and commanding a population of 750,000. The royal chest was said to be able to hold 400,000 ounces of gold. The throne was a golden stool said to have been called down from the sky. The court sheltered under ceremonial umbrellas as big as trees. For the annual yam ceremony, when the king's tributaries gathered with their followers, the capital at Kumasi housed 100,000 people. More adaptable than Dahomey, Ashanti used firepower to defeat mounted armies from the Sahel, while coping with a variety of environments and fronts. Part of its armies' success was owed to outstanding intelligence and logistics, with runners operating along cleared roads. Even Ashanti, however, relied on slaving to supplement its gold during the eighteenth century.

To the east of the Gold Coast, Akwamu was another substantial slave-stealing state. Its ruler enslaved many of his subjects by arranging phoney denunciations for adultery—a crime many African states punished by servitude—and mobilizing gangs of "smart boys" to kidnap victims. Similarly, in the other main slave-producing region—the Congo basin and Angola—the profits of slaving enabled ambitious monarchs to consolidate and centralize states. Kongo became a hereditary kingdom, whose rulers appointed the chiefs of subordinate states and who succeeded, on the whole, in preventing or at least limiting enslavement of their own subjects. Ndongo, in the interior of what is now Angola, grew similarly rich and centralized and, as we saw, under the formidable warrior queen, Nzinga, resisted Portuguese attempts at conquest for most of the seventeenth century.

IN PERSPECTIVE: Centuries of Upheaval

The upheaval of the sixteenth and seventeenth centuries affected much of the world. As we saw in Chapter 18, ecological exchanges had reversed, in a crucial respect, the course of evolution. Empires covered much of the globe. The balance of power in Eurasia had shifted definitively from pastoral to settled peoples. Migrations and exchanges of culture

CHRONOLOGY

1368–1644	Ming dynasty
Fifteenth and sixteenth centuries	Ottomans create an elite slave army, the Janissaries
Sixteenth through eighteenth centuries	Nuclear family moves to the center of European society
1500s	Chinese commercial economy booms
1501–1773	Safavid dynasty in Persia
r. 1501–1524	First Safavid ruler, Shah Ismail I, imposes Shiism by force
1513	Machiavelli writes *The Prince*
1519	Charles V becomes Holy Roman Emperor
1520s	Afghans and Persians help establish Mughal power in India
1570s	Ottoman jurist Ebu us-Suud justifies the Ottoman Sultan's power
1576	Jean Bodin formulates doctrine of sovereignty
1603–1868	Tokugawa shogunate
1630s	Ecological disasters undermine Ming power
1640s	Strain of empire precipitates decline of Spanish power
1644–1911	Qing dynasty
Seventeenth and eighteenth centuries	Mandarins reconciled to Qing power
1658	Rebellion of provincial governors against Ottoman authority
1658–1707	Emperor Aurangzeb engages in almost constant warfare
r. 1682–1725	Peter the Great attempts Westernization of Russia
1683	Ottomans fail to capture Vienna and cease conquests on the Christian front
Late seventeenth century	Maroon kingdom of Palmares reaches its height
Seventeenth and eighteenth centuries	Slave states proliferate in West Africa; Japan undergoes a "commercial revolution"
Eighteenth century	Last restrictions on freedom of Chinese peasants eliminated; Mughal power begins irreversible decline
1721	Population of Japan reaches 30 million
ca. 1800	Number of slaves shipped to New World reaches 7.5 million

crossed oceans and continents, sometimes with profoundly transforming effects. For the first time, a single system of trade encircled the Earth. Some regions were still outside this system: Australia and most of the South Pacific, parts of inland Africa, the far interiors of the Americas. But they were unlikely to be left outside it for long.

Increasing demand was caused by rising population and fueled by huge increases of cash from the silver mines of Japan and the Americas. New economic opportunities enriched new countries and new classes. A military revolution, as scholars now call it, introduced new technology to war: firearms that a peasant could handle with little training; fortifications that were proof against traditional horse-borne warriors; armies disciplined in the routines of battle rather than being trained, like knights of old, in individual combat. These changes started in Europe, but they transformed warfare in all the "gunpowder-empires" of the Old World. The military revolution loosened aristocracies' hold on one of the most basic forms of power, creating easily drilled armies of massed infantry, equipped with guns. Stronger states emerged in Europe and Africa; stronger empires in Asia; unprecedented empires in the Americas.

PROBLEMS AND PARALLELS

1. How did the power of the state grow in the sixteenth and seventeenth centuries? How did monarchs seek to redistribute power to their own advantage? Which newly empowered classes contended for a share in the growing might and resources of states?
2. Why was Spain such an unlikely superpower in the sixteenth and seventeenth centuries? What were the sources of its strength? Why did it eventually lose its preeminent position in Europe?
3. How did the way Westerners think about politics change in this period? What were the significant societal changes in Europe during this period?
4. What are the similarities and differences among the Ottoman, Mughal, and Safavid Empires during this period?
5. What economic and social changes occurred in China during the early Qing dynasty? How did these changes affect Chinese politics? How was Japan affected by the dynamic features of this period?
6. In what ways were European colonies in the Americas products of their environments? How did the colonies change the people who lived in them? In what ways was the Spanish Empire a modern state? How did slave communities in the Americas create autonomous institutions?
7. What effect did the slave trade have on African states during this period?

DOCUMENTS IN GLOBAL HISTORY

- Treaty of Westphalia
- Jean Bodin, from *Six Books of the Commonwealth*
- Machiavelli, excerpt from *The Prince*
- Hugo Grotius, selections from *On the Law of War and Peace*
- Glückel of Hameln, from *Memoirs*, 1690
- Peter the Great, "Correspondence with Alexis," 1715
- Ogier Ghiselin de Busbecq, on Women in Ottoman society
- Excerpts from the biography of Shah Abbas I
- Shah Ismail describes himself to his followers
- Letters of Zheng Zhilong
- Injunctions to peasants, 1649
- Tokugawa Shogunate, The Laws for the Military House
- Bryan Edwards, excerpt from "Observations on the Maroon Negroes of the Island of Jamaica"

Please see the Primary Source DVD for additional sources related to this chapter.

READ ON

The account of Queen Nzinga is indebted to work by J. K. Thornton, whose *Africa and Africans in the Making of the Atlantic World* (1995) is fundamental. A very readable introduction to the social transformation of early modern Europe is G. Huppert, *After the Black Death: A Social History of Early Modern Europe* (2nd ed., 1998). G. Parker, *The Military Revolution: Military Innovation and the Rise of the West, 1500–1800* (1988) is a vastly influential though technologically oriented statement of the connection between military and political change in Europe and globally. B. Downing, *The Military Revolution and Political Change* (1992) takes a closer, regionally differentiated look at political transformation. R. Carr, ed., *Spain: A History* (2000) is the best introduction to its subject. R. Harrison, *Hobbes, Locke, and Confusion's Masterpiece: An Examination of Seventeenth-Century Political Philosophy* (2002) is a masterful explication of seventeenth-century political philosophy. O. Hufton, *The Prospect Before Her* (1996) and I. Maclean, *The Renaissance Notion of Woman* (1983) are important for understanding the role of women in the West.

I. M. Kunt, *The Sultan's Servants: The Transformation of Ottoman Provincial Government* (1983) looks at the local and bottom-up forces affecting Ottoman governance, while H. Inalcik, *The Middle East and the Balkans Under the Ottoman Empire: Essays on Economy and Society* (1993) explores the mutual impact of rulers and ruled in the most ethnically and religiously diverse area of Ottoman control. K. Barkey, *Bandits and Bureaucrats: The Ottoman Route to State Centralization* (1994) studies Ottoman state formation from the perspective of the central government.

I. Gallup-Diaz, *The Door to the Seas and the Key to the Universe: Indian Politics and Imperial Rival in Darien, 1640–1750* (2002) takes an ethno-historical perspective on Indian responses and resistance to European encroachment in this period. P. Jackson and L. Lockhart, eds., *The Cambridge History of Iran: Volume 6, The Timurid and Safavid Periods* (1986) is the standard history of Persia during this period.

R. Huang, *1587: A Year of No Significance* (1982) tells the story of the crisis of that year in China. My account of the rise of the Qing is indebted to L. Struve, *Voices from the Ming-Qing Cataclysm* (1998). F. Wakeman, Jr., *The Great Enterprise* (1985) looks at the social bases of early Qing political and military power. P. Chi-won, *Tale of a Yangban* (1994) offers a story of Chinese influence in Korea. C. Totman, *Politics in the Tokugawa Bakufu* (1967) is the classic study of the political transformations of Japan after unification. S. Morillo, "Guns and Government: A Comparative Study of Europe and Japan," *Journal of World History* (1995) uses Japan as a case study in the primacy of social over military change, challenging Parker's "military revolution" thesis.

P. P. Boucher, *Cannibal Encounters: Europeans and Island Caribs, 1492–1763* (1999) traces cultural interactions in the Caribbean and demonstrates the effectiveness of Carib resistance to Europeans.

PART Eight

Global Enlightenments, 1700–1800

CHAPTER 20 Driven by Growth: The Global Economy in the Eighteenth Century 516

CHAPTER 21 The Age of Global Interaction: Expansion and Intersection of Eighteenth-Century Empires 538

CHAPTER 22 The Exchange of Enlightenments: Eighteenth-Century Thought 562

A Buddhist world map by the Japanese monk-painter Sokaku, ca. 1709. In the world-view of Buddhists and Hindus, the Earth is divided into seven island continents, each separated by an encircling sea, and each continent double the size of the preceding one. This example shows the continent of Jambudvipa, which forms the innermost circle of continents. The map incorporates European geographical knowledge, including Europe itself in the upper-left corner.

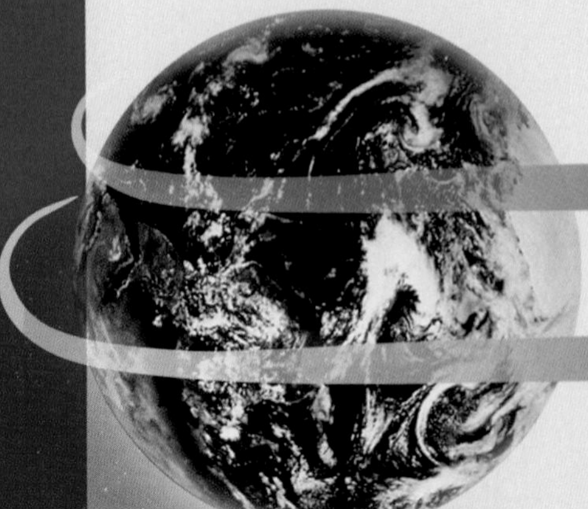

ENVIRONMENT

since ca. 1700
Global navigation and trade

since 1720s
Rise of global horticulture

CULTURE

since early 1700s
Decline of Asian empires

ca. 1720–1790
European Enlightenment

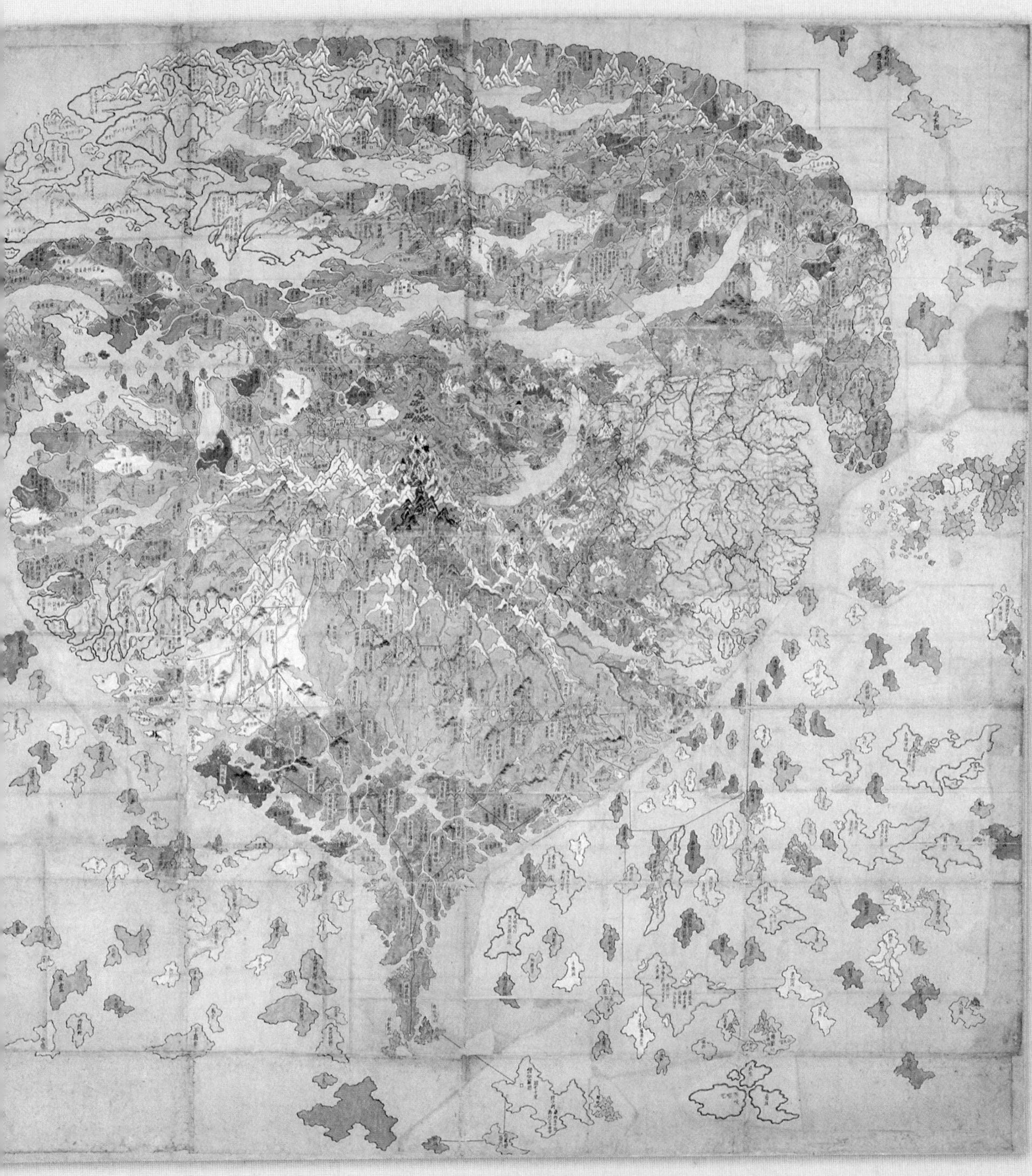

ca. 1750
Population boom starts:
Europe, China, and the Americas

since ca. 1760
British industrialization

1756–1757
British conquest of Bengal

1776–1783
American Revolution

1780–1800
Peak of Atlantic slave trade

1789–1795
French Revolution

CHAPTER 20 Driven by Growth: The Global Economy in the Eighteenth Century

Avenging angels soar through the dust-filled sky over Lisbon, Portugal, after the earthquake of 1755. The themes highlighted by the painting are echoed in the literature of the time: the revival of religion in the aftermath of horror, divine righteousness, the moral opportunity for displays of charity, the leveling effects of the disaster, which reduced the rich to the same destitution that the poor suffered.

POPULATION TRENDS
Urbanization
Explanations
Medicine
The Ecology of Disease
ECONOMIC TRENDS: CHINA, INDIA, AND THE OTTOMAN EMPIRE
China
India
The Ottoman Empire and Its Environs
THE WEST'S PRODUCTIVITY LEAP
The Scientific Background
The British Example
THE EXPANSION OF RESOURCES
Global Gardening
IN PERSPECTIVE: **New Europes, New Departures**

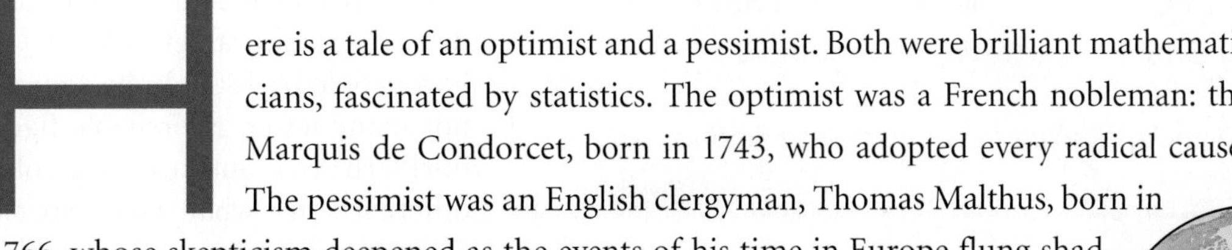

Here is a tale of an optimist and a pessimist. Both were brilliant mathematicians, fascinated by statistics. The optimist was a French nobleman: the Marquis de Condorcet, born in 1743, who adopted every radical cause. The pessimist was an English clergyman, Thomas Malthus, born in 1766, whose skepticism deepened as the events of his time in Europe flung shadows and gushed blood. Condorcet believed humankind was heading for perfection. Malthus believed it was heading for extinction.

For Condorcet, in *The Progress of the Human Mind*, published shortly after his death in 1794, one of the proofs of progress was growth of population: evidence—he thought—of happier, healthier, more fertile, longer-lived people, more willing to bring children into the world. He correctly spotted the broad population trends of his day. World population was booming. Between about 1750 and 1850, the population of China doubled, that of Europe nearly doubled, and that of the Americas doubled three times. In 1700, world population was perhaps a little over 600 million. By 1800, it had climbed to around 900 million. The global population explosion of modern times had begun.

In his *Essay on the Principle of Population* of 1798, Malthus drew the statistical basis of his thinking from Condorcet's work but refiltered it through his own pessimistic vision. He concluded that "population, when unchecked, increases in a geometrical ratio. Subsistence only increases in an arithmetical ratio." Only "natural checks"—famine, plague, war, and catastrophe—could keep numbers down to a level at which people could be fed.

● ● ● ● ●

Malthus panicked the elites of the West. His view, according to the influential English writer William Hazlitt (1778–1830), was "a ground on which to fix the levers that may move the world." But Malthusian anxieties proved false. Overpopulation is rare in history. Experience suggests that people breed less when they attain prosperity. Despite the huge increase of world population since Malthus's day to over 6 billion, food production has matched or exceeded it.

Condorcet was closer to being right. Population increase is stimulating. We cannot fully understand anything else in the history of the eighteenth century without it: the speeding up of economic activity; the extension of settlement into new lands; the huge increases in production as empires pursued resources; the drive of science to understand and exploit nature; the intellectual challenges that accompanied this ferment. On the whole, with exceptions, shifts in the balance of wealth and power also reflected demographic change. Rising

FOCUS questions

- WHY DID the world's population rise in the eighteenth century?
- WHY DID rising population stimulate economic activity in Europe?
- WHY WAS China's position as the world's richest economy threatened in the late eighteenth century?
- HOW DID British exploitation affect India's economy?
- HOW DID imperial expansion stimulate economic activity?

Thomas Malthus, from *Essay on the Principle of Population*

Marquis de Condorcet, from *Sketch for a Historical Picture of the Progress of the Human Mind*

regions, like Europe, China, and parts of North America and Africa, experienced sharp population increases, whereas areas of relatively stable population, such as the Ottoman Empire, housed stagnant or declining states (see Map 20.1).

POPULATION TRENDS

Population growth took two forms: dispersal on underexploited frontiers, and concentration in growing cities and denser agricultural settlements. China had nearly 350 million people by 1800, India some 200 million, and Europe not many fewer. No reliable figures exist for central and northern Asia, but incoming colonists made a significant difference in what were sparsely populated regions. Although figures are unavailable for Africa, evidence of restless migration suggests that the population was increasing there, too. In East Africa, for example, Oromo herdsmen (see Chapter 17) spread over much of Ethiopia. The cattle-rearing Masai of what is now Kenya expanded to fill all the land available for the kind of herding economy that suited them. In Central Africa, the Mongo people colonized the lower Kasai and Sunkuru valleys and the forest fringe. In the far south, settlers of Dutch origin spread ever farther into the interior from the Cape. It is hard to see how the relentless growth of the slave trade in the seventeenth and eighteenth centuries could have been sustained without a rising population in the West African regions the slavers most frequented. East Africa, meanwhile, supplied slaves on a lesser scale to markets in Muslim Asia and to new European plantations in the Dutch East Indies and the islands of the Indian Ocean.

In the Americas, the effects of Old World diseases had penetrated most areas by the seventeenth century. Disease still had destructive work to do in previously protected places, particularly in the American West, where smallpox and measles decimated Native Americans in the early nineteenth century. On the whole, however, a population boom replaced the Americas' era of demographic decline. In Spanish America, while Indian populations showed signs of recovery, increased numbers of settlers and slaves were moving inland. By 1800, Spain's American empire probably contained 14.5 million people. The population of British North America increased fivefold in the first half of the century, and nearly tenfold to 2.5 million in the second half. Numbers of white and black people rose, while the numbers of Native Americans dwindled, as they were driven from their lands or exposed to unaccustomed diseases (see Figure 20.1). Immigrants replenished and overflowed the space the Native Americans left behind. In the Caribbean, slaves accounted for most of the increase. The slave population in the British West Indies grew—mainly because so many new slaves were brought from Africa—during the eighteenth century from about 120,000 to nearly 750,000, who lived alongside about 100,000 white people.

FIGURE 20.1 THE AFRICAN, NATIVE AMERICAN, EUROPEAN, AND MIXED RACE POPULATION OF THE AMERICAS, 1500–1800

Colin McEvedy and Richard Jones, Atlas of World Population History*, p. 280. Reproduced with permission of Curtis Brown Group Ltd, London on behalf of the Estate of Colin McEvedy. © Copyright Colin McEvedy 1978.*

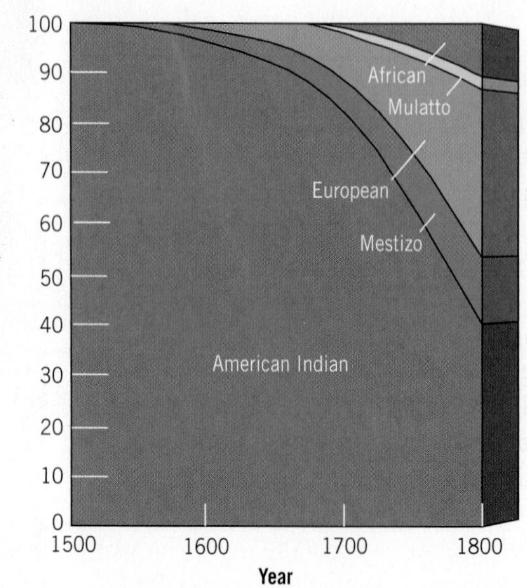

Some parts of the world lagged behind in population growth or experienced it in different ways. Japan's demographic surge ended before the mid–eighteenth century, when it had over 30 million inhabitants. Japanese censuses of 1721 and 1804 reveal hardly any change. The population was disproportionately concentrated in a small part of the country, around and between Osaka and Ise Bays, where there was perhaps genuine overpopulation or at least a sense that space was tight. Indeed, the census figures show outward movement from the heartland into the islands of Shikoku, Kyushu, and western Honshu. Japanese families seem to have practiced a variety of measures to restrain fertility, including delayed marriage, infanticide, and contraception. In Europe, the French were taking similar measures. The most populous country in Europe, France was also the first to experience a slowdown in the rate of population increase, which was already noticeable before 1800. The Ottoman and Persian Empires were the other main areas exempt from spectacular population growth. They seem, for unknown reasons, to have registered only small increases. It helps to understand the fading of the Ottoman Empire, among the great powers of the world, to know that the ratio of its population relative to that of Europe as a whole dropped from perhaps about 1:6 in 1600 to about 1:10 in 1800.

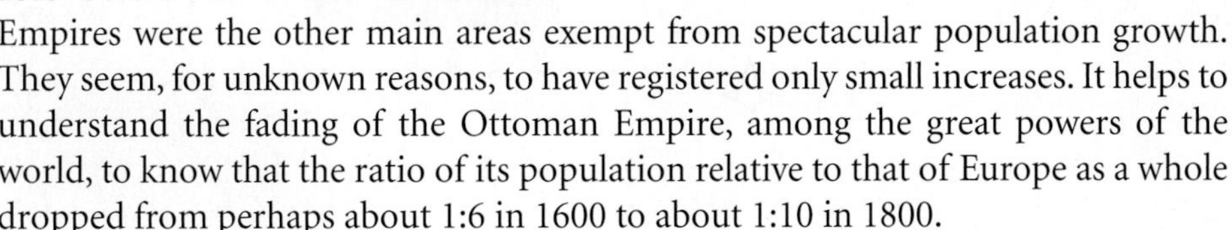

The Tokaido Highway. This scroll map depicts an aerial view of one of the most famous roads in Japan—the Tokaido Highway—as it looked from 1660 to 1736. This highway was the main land route from Edo (the old name for Tokyo) to the port of Osaka and the center of a densely populated zone. The Tokaido Highway became the route on which super-express highways and high-speed railroad lines were built in the twentieth century.

Urbanization

Irrespective of the overall trends in population, cities and towns increased over most of Eurasia and the Americas. China, India, and Japan housed the most urbanized societies. The extended metropolis of which Guangzhou (gwang-joh) in southern China was the center had as many people as all the capitals of Western Europe put together. By the best available estimates, Dacca in what is today Bangladesh, the world's greatest center of textile production, had over 200,000 people in 1800; Patna in northern India had over 300,000. In Japan, the population was, to an exceptional degree, concentrated in cities, with at least 6 percent of Japanese living in urban concentrations of over 100,000 inhabitants. The corresponding figure in Europe was only 2 percent.

But Europe also experienced intensified urbanization and, in pockets, exceeded even Japan's rate. Britain had only one big city, but it was a monster of a place. London approached a million inhabitants by 1800. Paris at the same time had over 500,000, and Naples in southern Italy not many fewer. Moscow, Vienna, and Amsterdam each exceeded 200,000, as did Russia's new capital St. Petersburg, which in 1700 did not even exist.

Urbanization was also prominent in the Americas. Nearly a third of the people in Spanish America lived in settlements officially classed as towns or cities, though urban growth seems to have slowed in many areas in the last quarter of the century. Mexico City and Lima, Peru, were colonial capitals able to compete in splendor with most cities of Europe. By the mid–eighteenth century, even British North America had towns of respectable size—15,000 people in Boston, 12,000 in Philadelphia and New York.

Explanations

Except in the New World, where the combination of arriving migrants and receding disease accounts for rising population, we cannot satisfactorily explain the demographic growth of the eighteenth century.

Improved food supply was important, but it is not a sufficient explanation on its own. Nutrition did improve over much of the world during these years, thanks to the worldwide ecological exchange of plants and animals, which increased

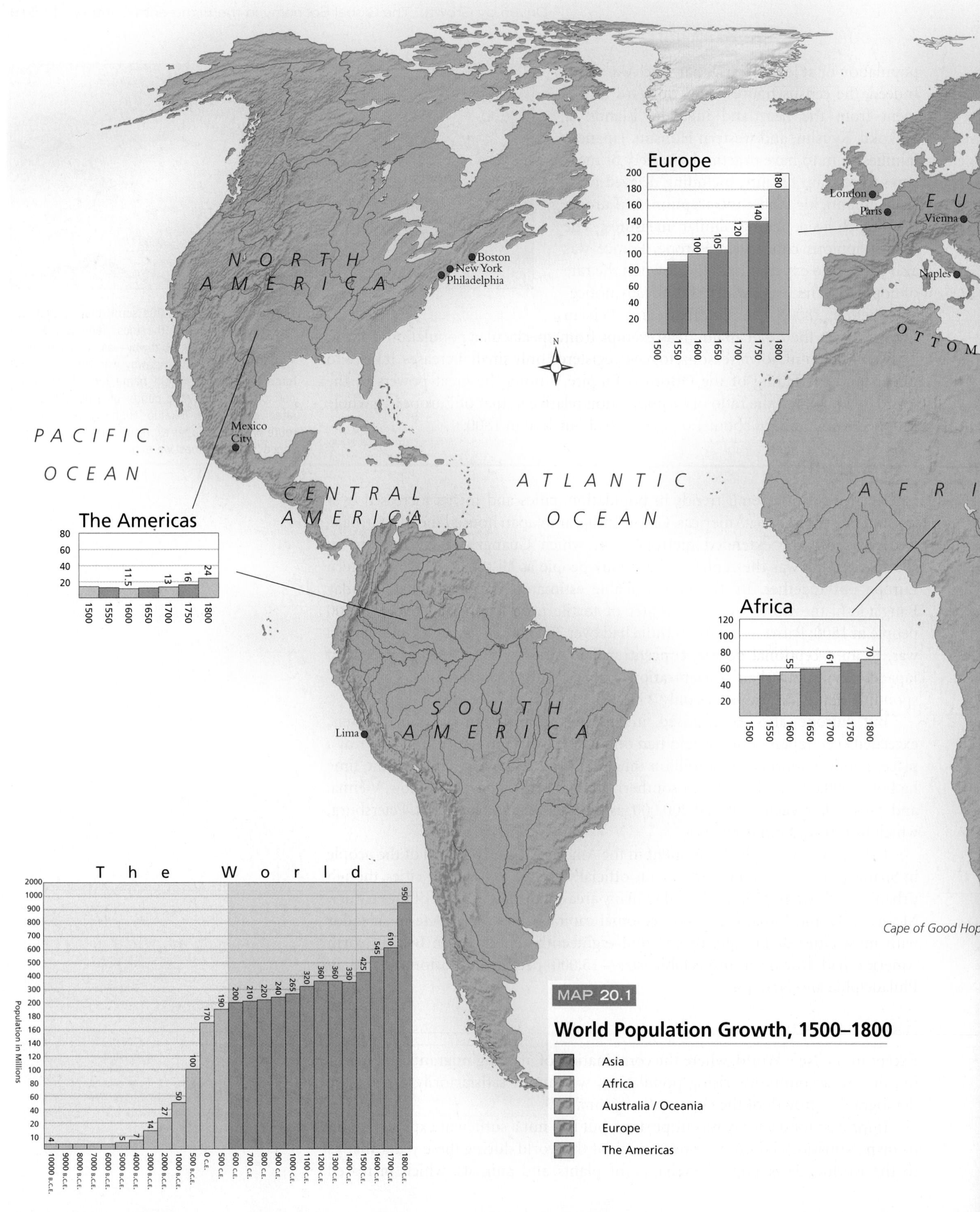

MAP 20.1

World Population Growth, 1500–1800

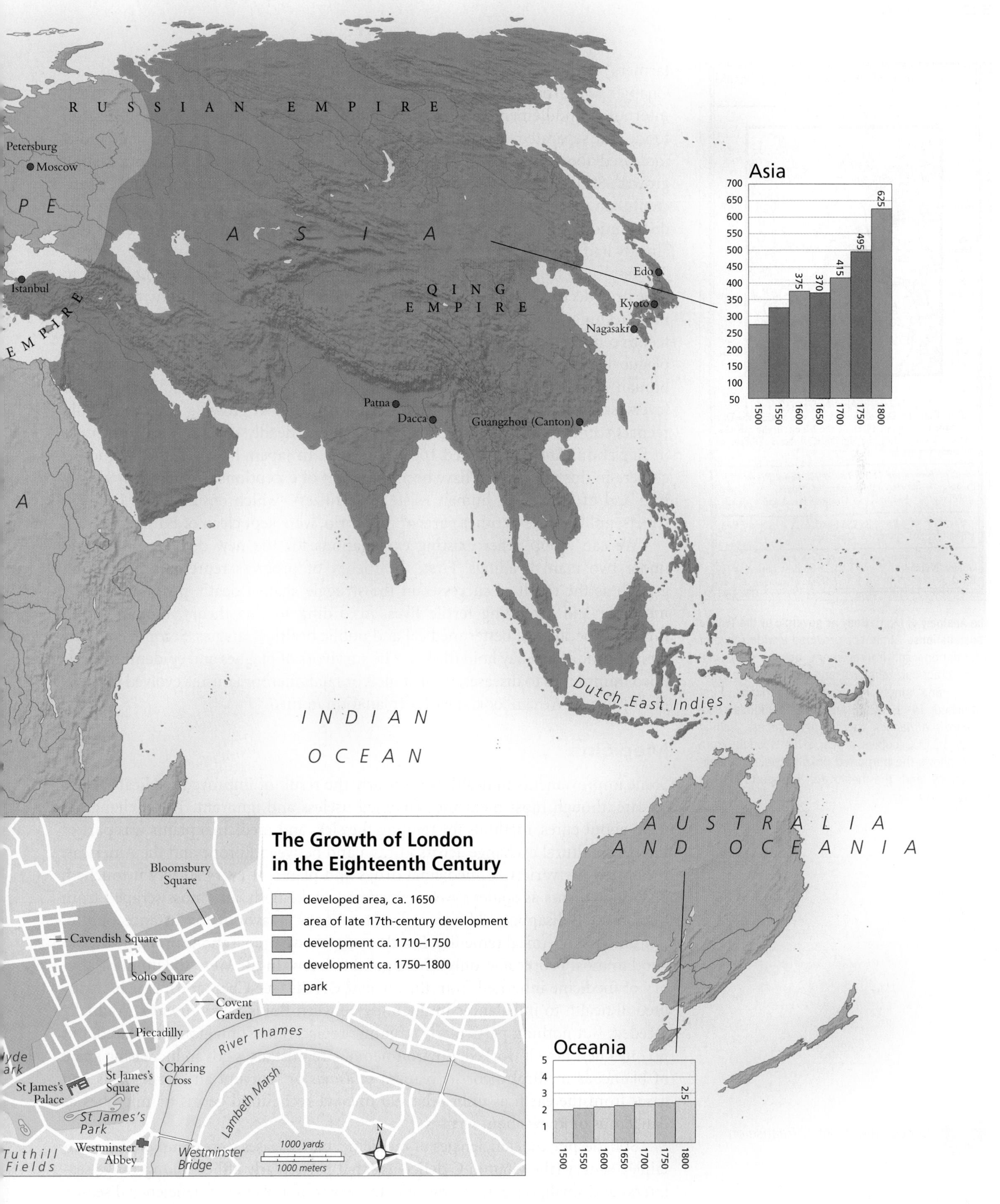

RUSSIAN EMPIRE
Petersburg
Moscow
ASIA
Istanbul
QING EMPIRE
Edo
Kyoto
Nagasaki
Patna
Dacca
Guangzhou (Canton)
Dutch East Indies
INDIAN OCEAN
AUSTRALIA AND OCEANIA
Asia
700
650
600
550
500
450
400
350
300
250
200
150
100
50
375
370
415
495
625
1500
1550
1600
1650
1700
1750
1800
Oceania
5
4
3
2
1
2.5
The Growth of London in the Eighteenth Century
developed area, ca. 1650
area of late 17th-century development
development ca. 1710–1750
development ca. 1750–1800
park
Bloomsbury Square
Cavendish Square
Soho Square
Covent Garden
Piccadilly
River Thames
Charing Cross
St James's Square
St James's Palace
St James's Park
Lambeth Marsh
Westminster Abbey
Westminster Bridge
Tuthill Fields
1000 yards
1000 meters
N

The Anatomy of Man's Body as govern'd by the Twelve Constellations. Almanacs provided a wide range of information, self-improvement advice, and wisdom—practical, religious, and scientific—to eighteenth- and nineteenth-century Americans. First published in 1732, Benjamin Franklin's *Poor Richard's Almanack* was a huge success, selling nearly 10,000 copies a year. This woodcut from 1750 shows the purported links between the constellations and the health of the parts of the human body.

farmers' options and extended the amount and yield of cultivable land (see Chapter 17). Urbanization, on the other hand, made the diet of the poor worse. It interposed middlemen between poor city dwellers and farmers, raised the cost of food, and separated consumers from fresh local produce. In China and India, increased food production does not seem to have kept pace with population growth. Still, concentrated markets for anything, including food, are more efficient than dispersed ones. Improved shipping, canals, and coastal trade made the distribution of bulk foods easier, notably in China, Japan, and Europe—areas that already had relatively good transport networks.

Improved hygiene may have helped increase populations, but it is not likely to have been decisive. Urbanization bred ever more unsanitary conditions, even in the most technically ambitious and sophisticated societies, until well into the nineteenth century (see Chapter 24). An age of typhus and cholera succeeded the age of plague because bigger cities exposed more people to water contaminated by human sewage and to the lice that spread typhus. Typhus, typhoid, and other fevers, some of tropical origin, colonized eco-niches in growing cities and could reenact scenes reminiscent of the age of plague. A deadly series of local epidemics in England in the 1720s killed 100,000 people. In Japan, however, the absence of cholera in this period may have been the result of exceptional standards of sanitation and of the use of human waste as fertilizer—which ensured that Japanese streets, unlike those in other parts of the world, were kept clean of human feces.

We can group other existing explanations for the new demographic trend under two main headings. First, the theory of progress represents population growth as the result of successes in the struggle against death, postponing early mortality and extending fertile lives. According to this theory, human health improved because of better medical and public health strategies. Second, environmental conditions may hold the key. The survivors of plagues and epidemics developed immunities to diseases, for instance, or fatal microorganisms evolved into less deadly forms. We can look at each explanation in turn.

Medicine

Some improvements in health were clearly the result of improved medical science or care, though most medicine remained useless and ignorant. The exchange of ideas about cures, methods for treating the sick, and medicinal plants was part of the great cultural exchange across Eurasia and between Europe and the Americas. It boosted the variety of medicinal drugs and plants of every society it touched. Such ingredients as spider's webs, powdered snake flesh, and moss scraped from human skulls disappeared from medical textbooks in favor of, for instance, opium, quinine, and chemical remedies. But these expensive preparations probably did no good to most people and only a little good to a few. In the West, the humoral theory of medicine inherited from the ancient Greeks (see Chapter 6), which attributed ill health to imbalances in the body between fluids called *humors*, gradually receded. But nothing particularly scientific replaced it. Contagion was feared, but no one knew how it worked. Environmental circumstances got an increasing share of blame, as medical theorists blamed *miasmas* or "corrupt air" from mists and gases from the earth as unhealthy. No one yet recognized germs or microbes as dangerous or knew about viruses.

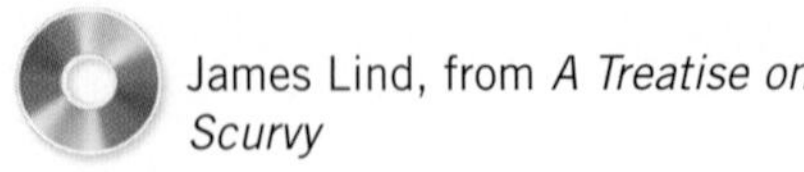
James Lind, from *A Treatise on Scurvy*

Still, despite the deficiencies of medicine, two diseases were conquered or contained: scurvy (the vitamin C deficiency that particularly afflicted long-range seafarers) and smallpox. Scurvy was only the worst of a plague of deficiency diseases, including beriberi, blindness, and "idiotism, lunacy, convulsions," that afflicted oceangoing crews. Unlike with other vitamins, the human body cannot store more vitamin C than it needs in a day, and naval rations, typically salted meat and hard bread, provided none of the vitamin. The Spanish-sponsored voyage of Alessandro Malaspina, the most ambitious scientific expedition of the eighteenth century, from 1789 to 1794 (see Chapter 22), virtually banished scurvy from the fleet with ample supplies of oranges and lemons, but there was still no way to preserve citrus at sea for long. The only effective remedy was to replenish ships with fresh supplies at every opportunity and to eat as many fruits and green vegetables as crews could find wherever a ship could land, ravaging desert islands for the barely edible weeds sailors called scurvy grass. Official resistance to new ideas meant that the issue of citrus-juice rations to English sailors did not begin until as late as 1795. Even then, of course, although doctors knew that citrus juice worked, they did not know why because vitamins had not yet been discovered.

Vaccination. When Louis Léopold Boilly painted this scene of a smallpox vaccination in 1807, the procedure still seemed curious and alarming. But it had become a routine part of doctors' domestic visits across much of Europe and the Americas.

Scurvy was not a major killer. More important, for the population statistics, was progress against smallpox—still a significant taker of young lives. China, India, and the Middle East had long known about inoculation as a means of prevention. Now the practice spread to Europe. In 1718, Lady Mary Wortley Montagu, wife of the British ambassador in Constantinople, volunteered her six-year-old son to be a guinea pig in an inoculation experiment by an "old Greek woman, who had practised this way for many years." After injection, the boy was covered in pustules, with swollen arms, dry mouth, and an urgent fever. Yet the experiment was a success, and when London was threatened with an epidemic in 1721, Lady Mary repeated it on her daughter. King George II (r. 1727–1760) had his daughters inoculated, and British high society adopted the practice. Lady Mary had achieved an ambition she conceived as a patriotic duty: "to bring this useful invention into England." Cheap, mass methods of inoculation followed. In 1796, Edward Jenner substituted cowpox for smallpox in the inoculation process. This was an improvement, since cowpox had the same immunizing effect, but carried almost no risk of harming inoculated persons.

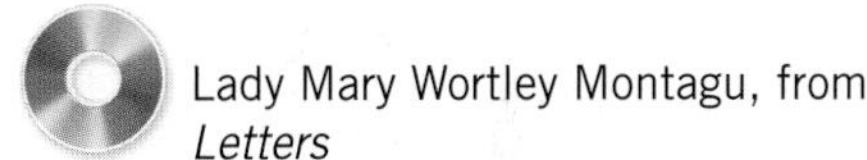

Lady Mary Wortley Montagu, from *Letters*

The Ecology of Disease

The success of this campaign against smallpox was remarkable. More remarkable still was the way the global profile of disease changed on its own without humans doing anything to affect it. Part of this was a consequence of ecological exchange: Fewer populations suffered from lack of natural immunization. Still, migrations of disease-bearing organisms remained dangerous. Yellow fever crossed the Atlantic from Africa and spread beyond the tropics, hitting cities as far north as Philadelphia repeatedly in the eighteenth century. The European cocktail of diseases that despoiled the Americas of native peoples in the sixteenth and seventeenth centuries continued to wreak havoc on new discoveries.

Yet the age of plague ended. The last European pandemic of a disease its victims called "plague" occurred from 1661 to 1669, rolling from Turkey across Europe to Amsterdam, where it killed 34,000 people in 1663–1664, and London before filling mass graves in Spain and Italy. Thereafter, Europe suffered only local visitations. The last outbreak of a level of severity characteristic of the age of plague occurred in 1711 in eastern Germany and Austria, with over 500,000 deaths. The last occurrence of any sort in Western Europe was in Marseilles in 1720. Between corpse-strewn gutters and mass plague pits, the archbishop led the population in penitential processions and prayers. Eleven of his twelve companions died at his side.

After that, plague never returned to Europe. Changes in the distribution of carrier species of rats, fleas, and lice (see Chapter 14) may have played a part. But the demise of plague could be like most other forms of species extinction: a product of evolution. We think of evolution as a slow-working process. Viruses experience it fast. Those that kill off their hosts are obviously not adaptively successful. They need to find new eco-niches to ensure their own survival, or they are self-condemned to disappear. For reasons we do not know—but which must be connected with their own evolutionary advantage—hostile microorganisms may switch their attention away from one set of victims to another. Historically, our improving health may owe less than we suppose to our own cleverness and more to the changing habits and nature of microbes.

ECONOMIC TRENDS: CHINA, INDIA, AND THE OTTOMAN EMPIRE

More population means more economic activity. That is not surprising. But eighteenth-century economic activity did mark a new departure from long-prevailing global patterns, as the gap in production and, therefore, in wealth began to narrow. The West began to catch up with China and India. The new rich among the world's economies began to emerge in Europe and America. By 1800, India went into sharp relative decline. China maintained its supremacy, but its days as the world's richest society were numbered.

China

The distribution of the world's most productive and profitable industries indicates what was going on. The most intensive concentrations of industrial activity were still in east and south Asia. Take the case of the Beneficial and Beautiful wholesaling firm, founded in the seventeenth century in Hangzhou (hahng-joh) on the coast of central China. In the early eighteenth century, the firm employed 4,000 weavers and several times that number of spinners. The dyeing and finishing were concentrated in a specialized suburb of the city in 1730, where 10,900 workers were gathered under 340 contractors and, claimed the firm's publicity, "for two hundred years now there has been no place, either north or south, that has failed to consider Beneficial and Beautiful cloth to be lovely."

Meanwhile, a porcelain center in eighteenth-century Jiangxi (jee-ahng-shee) in southern China "made the ground shake with the noise of tens of thousands of pestles." Farther south ironworks employed 2,000 to 3,000 men, and water-driven hammers pounded incense "without any expenditure of muscular effort." In the southwest provinces, similar machines for husking rice were lined up by the hundred, while water-driven papermakers hummed "like the whirr of wings." Nanjing's three imperial textile factories employed 2,500 artisans. Managers could make fortunes. One of them, Zaoyin, was a shy, modest man who pretended to read as he was carried in his litter to screen his eyes from the sight of the common people rising in respect as he passed. But his wealth "piled up like mountains or the waters of the sea."

The sheer size of China's internal market guaranteed a dynamic economy (see Map 20.2). In about 1800, over 10 percent of grain production was for sale rather than eaten by the farmers who grew it, together with more than a quarter of the raw cotton produced throughout the empire and over half the cotton cloth—amounting to 3 billion bolts of cloth a year. Nearly all the silk, tea, and salt in the empire were sold on the market.

Foreign trade, against this background, was relatively unimportant to China. It was vital, however, for the economies of much of the rest of the world. In the foreign trading posts called **factories** of Guangzhou, the world clamored for admittance at China's barely open door. All the trade of Europeans and Americans in search of Chinese tea, silk, rhubarb, and porcelain was funneled through this narrow opening. A privileged group of Chinese merchants controlled the trade. China's favorable trade balance, moreover, continued to expand, thanks to the growth of the European tea market. Dutch tea purchases in Guangzhou rose more than 1000 percent between 1729 and 1791. By that time, the British had taken over as the main customers.

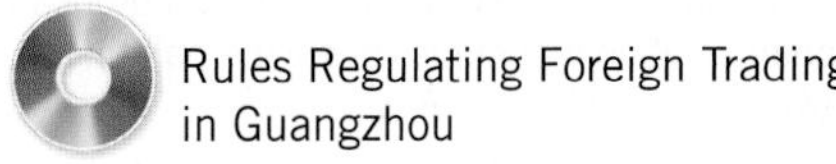
Rules Regulating Foreign Trading in Guangzhou

The "barbarians," as the Chinese called Europeans, still paid almost entirely in silver. Eventually, Western merchants found a commodity they could market in China: opium. As with the milder drug China exported in exchange—the tea that promoted wakefulness—supply seems to have led demand. When China first banned the opium trade in 1729, imports were reckoned at 200 of what the Chinese called "chests" a year. In 1767, 1,000 chests were recorded. In 1773, the British East India Company imposed a monopoly on the opium trade in India. By the early nineteenth century, 10,000 chests of opium were entering China annually. Foreigners now had, for the first time in recorded history, a chance to narrow their trade gap with China (see Chapter 25).

MAP 20.2

China in the Late Eighteenth Century

Qing Empire by 1770

Great Wall

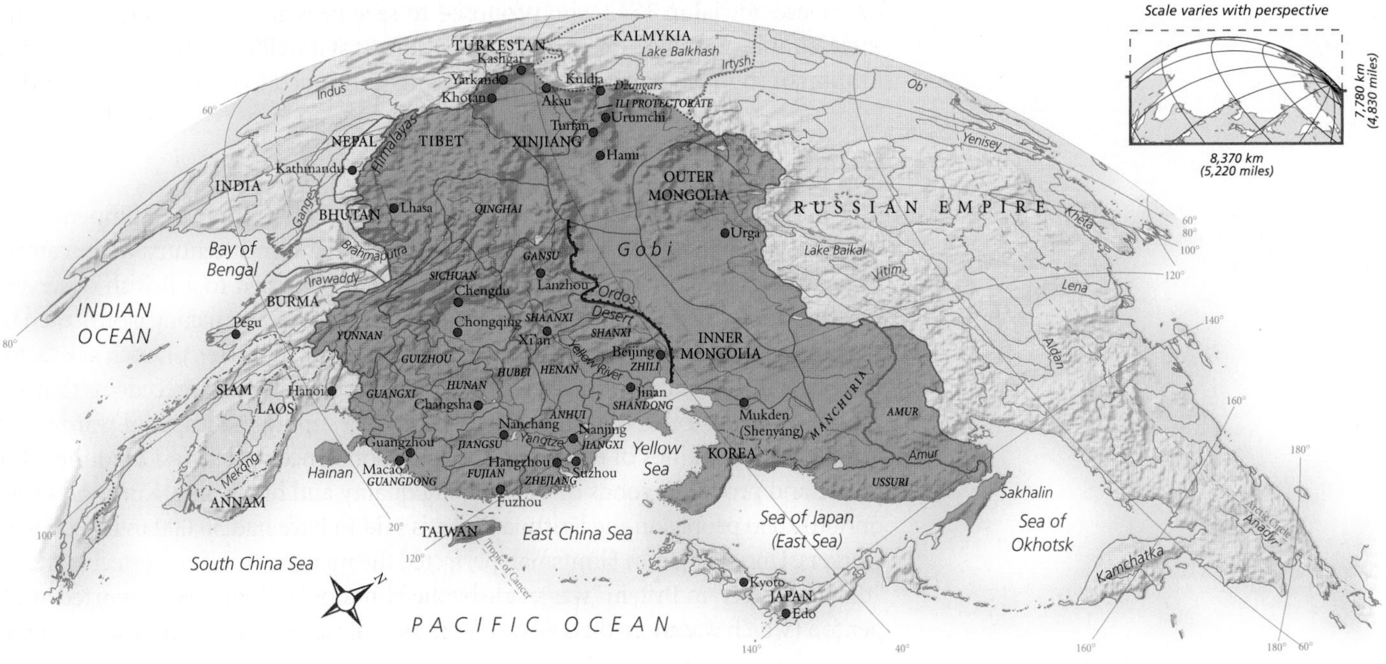

Scale varies with perspective

8,370 km (5,220 miles)

7,780 km (4,830 miles)

Guangzhou. In 1800, Guangzhou harbor still carried more international trade than any other port in the world. European traders were not allowed anywhere else in the Chinese Empire. Their residential quarters and warehouses are the white buildings in the center foreground. A European merchant probably commissioned the painting as a souvenir of his stay in China.
Photograph Courtesy Peabody Essex Museum.

China's economic supremacy had lasted a long time, but it was vulnerable to erosion in three ways. First, foreign suppliers could exploit the opium market. Second, they could make their own porcelain and silk, grow their own rhubarb, and find alternative places, such as India and Sri Lanka, to plant tea. Finally, they could outstrip Chinese production by mechanizing their industries. In the long run, the last of these changes made the greatest difference, for China could not mechanize. The empire was caught in what the historian Mark Elvin has called a "**high-level equilibrium trap.**" Industries that met huge demand with traditional technology had no scope to increase output. An economy with surplus labor had no incentive to replace muscles with machines.

Comparison with Britain illustrates the point. Starting from a low threshold, Britain tripled cotton-cloth production between the 1740s and 1770s. A similar rise in Chinese output would have glutted the world. The entire world supply of raw cotton would have been insufficient to meet it. Cheap labor is good for industrialization, but cheap capital is better. In India and China, the cost of labor relative to that of capital may have been too low for industry's good. The trap was typified by the experience of a Chinese official in 1742 who proposed to save peasants in his charge four-fifths of their labor by installing expensive copper pumps at a wellhead. Aghast at the immobilization of so much hard wealth, the peasants continued to draw water by hand.

India

The Indian economy was even more vulnerable than China's to competition from mechanizing systems. Yet Indian industries in the eighteenth century were scarcely less impressive than those of China. In Bengal, where it seemed to a British observer that "every man, woman, or child in every village was employed in making cloth," each major type of textile was the specialist product of a particular subcaste. A Dutch silk factory in Bengal, with 700 or 800 workers, was modeled less on European precedents than on the official textile factories the Mughals sponsored to supply the imperial wardrobe with fine cloth. Other kinds of economic specialization concentrated vast amounts of manpower and produced goods of outstanding quality and high value. Kurnool, a town of only 100,000 people on the Krishna River, is said to have had 30,000 to 60,000 iron ore workers. Until Benjamin Huntsman perfected the manufacture of cast steel in the 1760s, "the finest steel" in Britain "was made by the Hindoos" in India and imported at £1,000 per ton (which was more than 40 times the annual wages of a skilled British worker). By the conventional economic standards of Europe, the Mughals' tax demands—exacting perhaps 50 percent of the gross product of the empire—might seem depressing to any developing industrial spirit. But high taxation created a huge administrative class with surplus spending power (see Chapter 21). Their demand may have stimulated the concentration of production. Mughal India was almost certainly the world's most productive state in terms of manufacture for export, despite the modest technical equipment with which its industries were generally supplied.

Against this background, India's industrial collapse is astonishing. The drain of Westerners' silver into India, which had been going on since pre-Roman times (see Chapter 7), was reversed in Bengal by the 1770s, In 1807, John Crawfurd reported that "kite makers, falconers, astrologers, and snake-charmers" had replaced useful trades in Bengal. A French missionary claimed, "Europe is no longer dependent on India for anything, having learned to beat the Hindus on their own ground, even in their most characteristic manufactures and industries, for which from time immemorial *we* were dependent on *them*. In fact the roles have been reversed and this revolution threatens to ruin India completely."

How did this collapse happen? Indian industry may have been caught, like China's, in an equilibrium trap. But it was more fragile in any case: less high powered, less technically advanced. The decline of Indian industry probably started with the decline of the Mughal Empire in the eighteenth century—skewered at its heart by Persian and Afghan invaders who sacked Delhi, the Mughal capital, shredded at its edges by usurping officials and rebellions. The impoverishment of the Mughal court deprived native industry of its best market. After Persian invaders looted the imperial treasury at Delhi in 1739, the nobles could no longer buy the products of Bengal. Then, with an exactness rare in history, India's industrial debacle coincided with one of the dramatic new developments of the next chapter of this book: the establishment of British rule or influence over most of India and, in particular, over its former industrial heartlands. Between the 1760s and the 1780s, in the early years of British rule in Bengal, silver imports into India virtually ceased. Instead, the British used tax revenues they extracted from the country to

Dutch trading post. With its huge fluttering flag, formal grounds, spacious quarters, and splendid gates in the Mughal style, the Dutch trading post at Hoogly in northeast India looks like an outpost of empire. In fact, however, it represents how dependent European merchants of the seventeenth century were on the wealth of the East. The post opened for trade in 1635, so that the Dutch East India Company could acquire relatively cheap silk in India and exchange it at a handsome profit for silver in Japan.

Global Population and Economic Trends

ca. 1500	Population of Europe reaches 80 million
Eighteenth century	Urbanization increases in Europe and the Americas; most intense concentrations of industry found in east and South Asia
ca. 1750–1800	Indian industry goes into decline
	Population of China doubles; population of the Americas increases sixfold
1784–1814	British import 300 million pounds of tea from China
Late eighteenth century	Ottoman Empire loses control of its shipping industry
1794	Condorcet's *The Progress of the Human Mind* published
1796	Edward Jenner develops improved smallpox vaccine
1798	Malthus's *Essay on the Principle of Population* published
ca. 1800	Population of Europe reaches 180 million

pay for the goods they exported to it. The British East India Company and its servants shamelessly exploited their monopoly by cutting prices to suppliers and acquiring allegedly low-quality Indian goods at confiscatory prices before reselling them to Indians and Europeans at enormous profits. Nor did the British neglect the opportunity to impose high prices for primary materials on Indian manufacturers. In 1767, for instance, the company's representative sold silk yarn to weavers at double the price he paid for it.

The rapidity of the transformation of India from an economic powerhouse to a declining economy surprised contemporaries. For the Irish statesman Edmund Burke (1729–1797), it was one of the "stupendous revolutions that have happened in our age of wonders." The dual nature of India's predicament, political and commercial, decorates the ceiling of the East India Company's headquarters in London, where Britannia, enthroned, receives the riches of the East from an abject procession led by India.

The Ottoman Empire and Its Environs

Some of the same inducements and problems affected the industrial development of the Ottoman Empire. Here, too, raw materials were abundant. The vitality of the luxury market impressed European visitors. But the selectivity of Turkish talent for industry and the lack of technical inventiveness made the empire as vulnerable as India to European competition. According to a voyager in the Persian Gulf in the mid–eighteenth century, the expensive spending habits of local notables mainly benefited French importers. In the second half of the eighteenth century, the carrying trade of the Ottoman Empire passed entirely into foreign hands—mainly French, English, and Venetian. In 1775, Tunisian shippers (Tunis in North Africa was nominally part of the Ottoman Empire) abandoned a heroic effort to compete with French shippers, whose home government supported them with tax breaks and naval protection. Persian silk, previously transmitted through Ottoman territory, and Egyptian linen disappeared from the export lists of the empire, as British, French, and Italian manufacturers produced cheaper alternatives. A critical observer of the Turks in 1807 admitted that "Europe certainly cannot surpass them in several of their manufactures"—essentially fine textiles—and that "in many of the inferior trades," Turkish workmen were equal to those of France. But he added that from laziness or lack of enterprise they "have not introduced or encouraged several useful arts of later invention."

THE WEST'S PRODUCTIVITY LEAP

The overall picture is clear. In the eighteenth century, economies in northern and Western Europe were catching up with and, in some respects, surpassing the parts of Asia that had previously been enormously more productive. At first sight, **industrialization** in Europe looks like one of those great transformations of history that just happen because of impersonal forces—economic, demographic, environmental—beyond human control: necessities that mother invention. Yet an active and fruitful period in the history of Western science preceded and accompanied—though it did not cause—industrialization (see Chapter 18). Science and technical innovations were parallel results from the growing curiosity about the real world and a growing interest in tinkering with things to see how they work. It makes sense to look into the realm of ideas to try to find the origins of Europe's leap in production.

The Scientific Background

Galileo, Third Letter on Sunspots, 1612

The scientific revolution that occurred in the West during the seventeenth and eighteenth centuries disclosed previously unglimpsed realms in nature. Galileo Galilei (1564–1642) could see the moons of Jupiter through his telescope. Anton van Leeuwenhoek (1632–1723) saw microbes through his microscope. Marin Mersenne (1588–1648) measured the speed of sound. Robert Hooke (1635–1703) could sniff what he called "nitre-air" in the acrid smell of vapor from a lighted wick, before Antoine Lavoisier (1743–1794) proved the existence of oxygen by isolating it and setting it on fire. Isaac Newton (1642–1727) could wrest the rainbow from a shaft of light or feel the force that bound the cosmos in the weight of an apple (see Chapter 18). Luigi Galvani (1737–1798) could feel the thrill of electricity in his fingertips. Friedrich Mesmer (1734–1815) thought hypnotism was a kind of detectable animal magnetism. Through life-threatening demonstrations with kite and keys, Benjamin Franklin (1706–1790) claimed to show lightning is a kind of electricity.

These discoveries accustomed Europeans to the idea that barely detectable forces can have enormous power, just as the strength of the body reposes in thread-like muscles. The idea of harnessing natural energy arose unsurprisingly in the context of scientific thought. Steam, the first such power source to replace muscles, was a fairly obvious case. You can see it and feel its heat, even though it takes imagination to believe that it can work machinery and make things move. Engineers in late eighteenth-century Britain used a discovery of "pure" science—atmospheric pressure, which is invisible and only an experiment can detect—to make steam power exploitable.

Still, conditions have to be right before good ideas get applied. The principles of the steam engine had been known in ancient Rome, and the science of the West had largely been anticipated in China. But, just as conditions in China restrained industrial output in the eighteenth century, conditions in parts of Europe promoted it. Population was rising fast enough to boost demand without activating a high-level equilibrium trap. The global context favored economies that had privileged access to sea-lanes of global commerce. And, within Europe, new energy sources were being explored and released. The most conspicuous case is Britain's, where, in the second half of the eighteenth century, industrial output exhibited the most dynamic increases of any economy in the world (see Map 20.3).

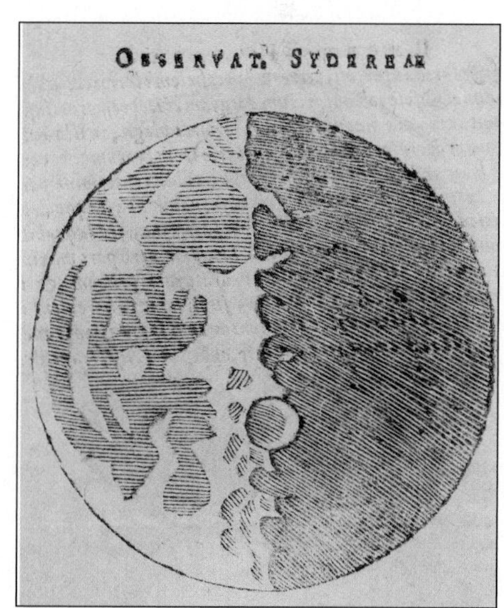

The moon. By the time Galileo published the results of his astronomical observations through a telescope in 1610, the instrument was famous throughout Europe, and a Jesuit missionary had even written a book about it in Chinese. The telescope revealed that the moon, formerly perceived as being a perfect sphere, was in fact ridged and pitted.

The British Example

With fewer than 9 million people in 1800, Britain was puny compared with the industrial giants of Asia. But Britain had unrivaled resources of untapped energy just below the surface of its soil. In the late seventeenth century, the annual output of British coal miners was less than 3 million tons. By 1800, it had reached almost 14 million tons. Steam pumps enabled miners to dig deeper, below the water table, into shafts that could be drained. In turn, the pumps got people thinking about wider applications of steam-driven technology. Britain, moreover, was an outstanding example of success in exploiting a position on the Atlantic. By the 1770s, the Atlantic world of Africa and the Americas absorbed more of Britain's exports than Europe or Asia did and almost the entire export output of the British cotton and iron industries, while the merchant marine tripled to nearly 700,000 tons. For the rest of the century, annual output grew at 1.8 percent compared with 1 percent previously. Pig-iron production doubled and then doubled again. Exports, which had more than doubled in the first three-quarters of the century to over £14 million in value, reached £22 million by the century's end.

It would be exaggerated, however, to speak—as historians used to do—of an eighteenth-century Industrial Revolution. In most industries, development was piecemeal. Methods remained traditional. In England, between 1785 and 1800, beer production rose by about a third, as did that of tallow candles. Soap manufacture rose by over 40 percent in the same period. Overwhelmingly, these industries grew without significant mechanization, and the spectacular growth of London provided their market. In the same period, sales of imported commodities, which required little processing, grew comparably or even more impressively. Tobacco sales increased by over a half; those of tea more than doubled.

The great exceptions—where transformed methods did boost production—were the textile and iron industries. Output of iron rose from 17,350 tons in 1740 to over 125,000 tons in 1796. The first iron bridge spanned the river Severn in 1779. The first iron ship sailed in 1787. In 1779, Edmund Crompton found a way to use water or steam to power a machine to weave yarn into cloth: the cost of processing raw cotton was cut by more than half in 20 years. The first steam-powered textile mill opened in 1785. Raw cotton imports, which amounted to under 3 million pounds weight in 1750, reached nearly 60 million pounds in 1800. A new way of working evolved in mechanized factories, with huge concentrations of workers, a pattern that would revolutionize the societies it affected in the next century (see Map 20.3).

Daniel Defoe, from *The Complete English Tradesman*

Historians have always wondered and often asked whether there was anything special about British values or mind-sets or "spirit" that might help to explain why Britons took up the opportunities of the age with so much enthusiasm and effectiveness. Commercial values may have occupied a relatively high priority in British culture. Certainly, people thought so at the time. Napoleon—who developed intense hatred for Britain after he became ruler of France in 1799—sneered at "a nation of shopkeepers," but Britons accepted the sneer with pride. Early in the eighteenth century, the English novelist Daniel Defoe exulted in the incalculably huge number of British tradesmen. You may as well, he said, "count the stars in the sky."

The British economist David Ricardo (1772–1823) recognized a principle of economics—that labor adds value to a product. He went further. Value, he argued, is proportional to the labor invested in it, "labor ... being the foundation of all value, and the relative quantity of labor ... almost exclusively determining the relative value of commodities." In its crude form, the theory is wrong. Goods are not always exchanged at values proportionate to the labor invested in them. Capital plays a part (and is not always just stored-up labor, since raw natural assets can be sold for cash). So does the way the goods are perceived. Rarity value—which Ricardo did recognize, citing objects of art and "wines of a peculiar quality"—is the most obvious example. Advertizing and recommendation can also add value. Still, the principle is right. Ricardo drew from it a counterintuitive conclusion. If labor makes the biggest contribution to profits, one would expect high wages to reflect this (as generally, in modern industrial societies, they do). Ricardo, however, thought that to maximize profits, capitalists would always keep wages low. "There can be no rise in the value of labor without a fall in profits." In fact, wages were static in England and rose a little in Scotland. Industrialization did not drive wages down, because the growth of population and of trade continually drove demand upward.

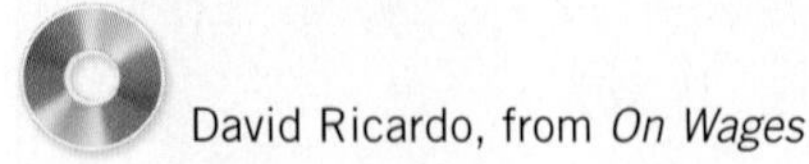
David Ricardo, from *On Wages*

In broad context, however, Britain's eighteenth-century experience seems more characteristic than extraordinary—just a more pronounced case of an effort to maximize the use of resources that was happening all over western and northern Europe. By the time of the French Revolution in 1789, for instance, similar if smaller industrial complexes were emerging in parts of France, Belgium, Germany, and Spain. This effort was most widely generalized in the case of land—universally recognized, along with labor, as the most basic resource of all. In Britain, landholdings were consolidated during the eighteenth century, with important consequences for efficiency. By 1790, over a quarter of the land in England was concentrated in estates of over 3,000 acres. In much of the highland zone of Scotland, landlords expelled or exterminated smallholders to make way for large sheep-grazing estates. Over most of the country, landowners adopted a common program: reducing labor costs, replacing inefficient farming with grazing, improving soils by draining and fertilizing, enhancing livestock by scientific stockbreeding, diversifying crops to maximize use of the earth, and, perhaps most importantly, by "enclosing" land—fencing off underexploited land that had been open to anyone in the community for their own use. French agriculturalists who called themselves "physiocrats" recommended ways to improve agriculture to enrich France. Agricultural improvement societies promoted English-style changes in Spain and Spanish America. Similar approaches spread over much of Europe.

MAP 20.3

Industrial Britain, ca. 1800

- iron works
- shipbuilding
- major urban growth
- pottery
- cutlery
- woolens/cloth/cotton
- silk
- coalfields
- turnpike road network, 1750
- Manchester 33 journey time from London, in hours

Agricultural improver. Thomas Coke of Norfolk (1752–1842), shown on the left, was an exemplary British agricultural improver, whose work with sheep was particularly influential. He boosted his flock from 800 to 2,500 without increasing the amount of grazing land the sheep needed, thanks in part to the scientific improvement he made in the South Down breed, depicted here, which produced highly prized mutton.

These European changes had parallels in east Asia beyond the reach of the equilibrium trap. In Korea and Japan, many works of popular agricultural advice were published to satisfy a passionate market for agricultural improvement. In Korea, farmers began to sow barley after the rice harvest to boost grain production. As in England, small landholdings were consolidated into huge farms for cash crops: ginseng, tobacco, and cotton. A measure of the Korean economic boom was the 1,000 new markets that sprang up in the first half of the eighteenth century. In Japan, too, agriculture became commercialized, as peasant subsistence agriculture virtually disappeared. Cotton cultivation spread from Osaka almost throughout the country. The new crops that ecological exchange made available also played their part. In 1732, for instance, a locust plague in Kyushu destroyed the grain, but people had sweet potatoes to fall back on. Famines still occurred, but now local communities could afford social-welfare schemes to mitigate their effects. Landowners paid a wealth tax to supply emergency rice stocks, make loans to new businesses, and support the elderly. The leveling off of the Japanese population looks like a classic case of prosperity restraining birthrates. In Okayama, over the century as a whole, the average size of a household declined from seven persons to five.

THE EXPANSION OF RESOURCES

The effort to coax more food from the soil was only one aspect of a worldwide search for new food resources—a search in which Western Europeans occupied a privileged place.

Global Gardening

In the late eighteenth century, the Botanical Garden of Madrid in Spain founded in 1756 was one of the grand ornaments of European science, forming the last link in a chain of such gardens in Manila in the Philippines, Lima in Peru, Mexico City, and the Canary Islands off the coast of Africa. At least in theory, samples of the plant life of every climate the Spanish monarchy occupied could be centralized in a single place of research. From Peru, for instance, in 1783, came 1,000 colored drawings and 1,500 written descriptions of plants. Perhaps the most important collections were those of Hipólito Pavón, whose expedition to Chile and Peru in 1777–1788 allowed him to indulge his personal passion—the study of the healing properties of plants—and to produce the most complete study of quinine yet attempted. Another prolific contributor was José Celestino Mutis, who presided over scientific life in one of the heroic outposts of the Spanish Empire at Bogotá, in what is today Colombia, from 1760 until his death in 1808.

At their best, empires could gather useful specimens from an astonishing diversity of climes and make their flowers bloom together in scientific proximity. The Botanical Garden in Paris performed a comparable role. The French Jesuit missionary Pierre Nicolas le Chéron d'Incarville sent rare Chinese and Japanese plants there with Russian caravans across Asia. In England, the Royal Botanical Gardens at Kew, London, and the garden of the University of Oxford had similar functions, as, in the Netherlands, did the town gardens of Amsterdam and Utrecht and the University Garden of Leiden.

The plants of the world could gather in Europe and be redistributed around European empires, because only these empires were scattered widely enough around the globe and had the environmental range to exploit the opportunities to the full. European empires became laboratories of ecological exchange. Pierre Poivre, for instance, launched one of the most breathtaking experiments in France's Indian Ocean island colonies in 1747. Until he transformed them, the islands were economically unsuccessful—wasted by deforestation and attempts to introduce plantation monocultures. Poivre smuggled 3,000 spice plants out of southeast Asia and planted them in the island of Mauritius off the east coast of Africa, where they eventually became the basis of a commercially successful operation in cloves, cinnamon, and pepper. When he eventually became governor of France's Indian Ocean colonies, he combined the policy of diversifying crops with a strategy to restore the islands' forests to maintain rainfall levels.

Similar transplantations occurred to and fro, as the ecological exchange became more systematic and planned. Coffee is a case in point. Southern Arabia had long enjoyed a world monopoly of coffee. But in 1707, the Dutch introduced it into Java as part of a system of political control in which local rulers guaranteed to deliver it at prices that exploited producers, who had to be forced to grow it. Coffee was one of the most commercially successful products of the eighteenth century. The French planted it in the island of Bourbon (modern Réunion) in the Indian Ocean and in Saint-Domingue (modern Haiti) in the Caribbean, and the Portuguese in Brazil (see Chapter 17). By midcentury, the Arabian coffee trade had ceased to grow, and the British East India Company no longer sent regular ships there. Since almost all coffee drinkers of the era took their cups heavily sweetened, the sugar and coffee trades grew together, and sugar, of course, had wider applications. The expansion of sugar lands in the seventeenth-century Atlantic was followed, in the eighteenth century, by a similar expansion around the Indian Ocean. By 1800, sugar had probably replaced pepper as southeast Asia's major export.

Even places too isolated for the global ecological exchange to affect could achieve high levels of productivity. Hawaii is a case in point, since it remained outside the range of European navigation until 1778. The earliest European accounts of Hawaii were full of praise for the native farmers. Expeditions from the late 1770s to the 1790s recorded fields outlined with irrigation ditches and neat stone walls, planted with taro, breadfruit, sweet potato, sugarcane, and coconut, and laid out in a pattern calculated to impress European readers as civilized. The roads "would have done credit to any European engineer." An engraving made on the basis of British reports from the 1790s shows a field system of a regularity that arouses one's suspicions that it was made up to present a picture attuned to European ideals. Yet the same array of farmers' geometry is visible today, under the surface of fields on the Big Island of Hawaii. Only in Hawaii, moreover, among Polynesian settlements, was fish farming fully developed. Into the grid of fields and pools, other constructions were slotted. Massive platforms of stone supported temples of exact symmetry, and the wall-building techniques were adaptable to the demands of fortifications two or three times the height of a man. Early European visitors could

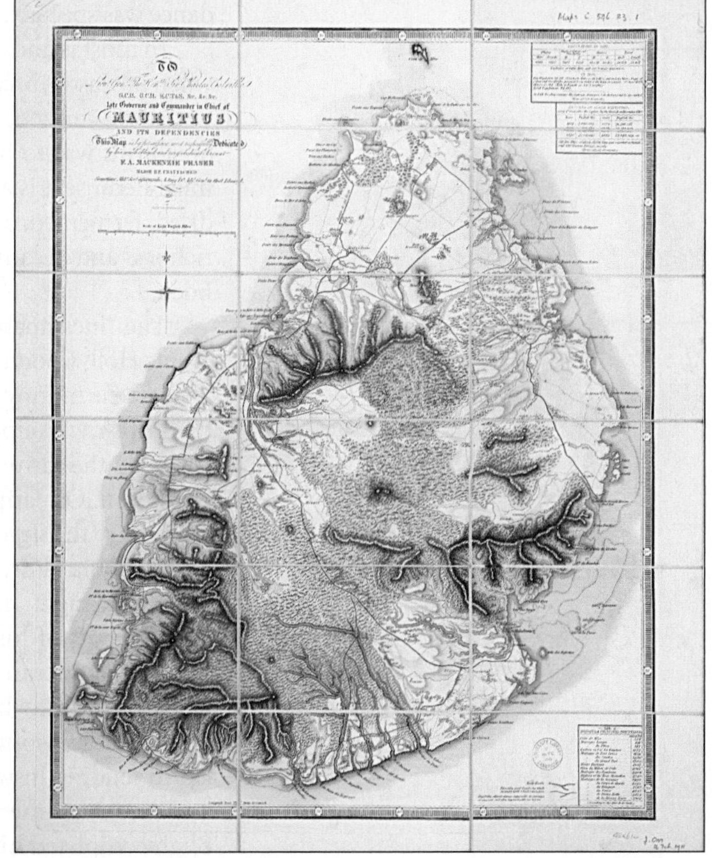

Map of Mauritius in 1835. In the eighteenth century, French administrators introduced forest conservation to the Indian Ocean island and banned colonists there from growing what were thought to be ecologically unsuitable crops, such as cotton and wheat. The map shows the surviving forests in the center and the lower left.

recognize not only institutions of statehood but also an island-wide empire in the making—a process completed in 1795, when the first king, Kamehameha I, extended his rule over all the Hawaiian islands.

Transplanting breadfruit. Thomas Gosse, the official artist of the British expedition that took breadfruit from Tahiti to Jamaica in the 1790s, gave pride of place to the Tahitians in the pictures he painted of the voyage. He depicted the British in a marginal, subordinate, and passive role. The breadfruit was supposed to provide cheap food for Jamaica's slaves, but the slaves rejected it.

The Pacific generally was a latecomer to the great ocean-borne exchange of foodstuffs. In 1774, a Spanish expedition tried to annex Tahiti. It failed, but left Spanish hogs behind, which replaced the small, long-legged, long-snouted native pigs. In consequence, Tahiti had an advantage in the pork trade that soon transformed the Pacific as a result of two developments. First, Captain James Cook (1728–1779) perfected a method to keep salt pork edible after a long sea voyage. Second, Australia became a British colony. It proved more economical for Australia to import salt pork from Tahiti than to breed its own pigs. In the first year of the trade, 1802–1803, merchants in Sydney handled 300,000 pounds of the meat. By the time the trade waned in the late 1820s, ten times that amount had changed hands. The muskets that paid for the pork stimulated civil war and turned Tahiti into a monarchy.

The breadfruit was an eye-catching part of the abundance that made the South Sea islands wonderful to eighteenth-century European sailors: places where the long-felt wants of seaboard life were supplied. Along with the sexual license of Tahitian life, ample fresh food helped to make the South Seas seem "the paradise of the world," according to a British visitor in 1787. In the lingo of modern economists, this was a world of "subsistence affluence," where there was little specialization in food production and limited trade in food products, but where, in normal times, abundance was spectacular.

In most islands, yams, taro, and plantains contributed most to the basic diet, but when in season, breadfruit was the starchy complement to the festive meats: pigs, turtles, dogs, chicken, fish, and some insects. The most widely favored way to prepare breadfruit was to bake it whole. It was also eaten in fish stews, cooked in coconut milk. Because it is a seasonal product and rots if not harvested when ripe, it was also dried, fermented, and smoked. It helped to communicate an illusion of nutritional richness and became a fixture in Europeans' mental picture of the South Sea–island Eden.

The "inestimable benefit" of "a new fruit" inspired the voyage that ended with events Hollywood turned into the most famous episode of eighteenth-century naval history: the mutiny on the *Bounty*. Captain William Bligh's mission as commander of the British warship *Bounty* in 1787 was to pluck a bit of the paradise of the South Pacific in the form of breadfruit tree seedlings and transfer it to the slave hell of the Caribbean. On Jamaica, Bryan Edwards, a planter who was always looking for ways to improve the slave economy, believed that breadfruit could energize slaves and turn his island into a hive of industry. So the British government sent Bligh to Tahiti.

He brought his single-minded, demonic energy to the task. In the South Pacific, most of his men mutinied. The captain and the loyal survivors were cast adrift in midocean and saved, after terrible deprivations, only by Bligh's ability as a navigator. Meanwhile, some of the mutineers lived in self-condemned exile with their Tahitian women on Pitcairn, an uncharted island where predictable quarrels led to feuding in which most of them were killed. The Royal Navy hunted down and executed others. After six years' bloodshed and hardship and with a new ship, Bligh completed his mission. But there was an ironic twist—the breadfruit experiment proved disastrous. Breadfruit is not a particularly useful food. It has few nutrients. It does not keep well. The slaves would not eat it.

Other food transfers were more successful. Captain James Cook, the explorer who was responsible for so many more famous initiatives in Pacific history, was also the prophet of pigs and potatoes in New Zealand. The Dutch had discovered New Zealand in 1642, but it was then forgotten. Cook rediscovered the islands in 1769. The native inhabitants of New Zealand, the Maori, who preferred their own food, resisted his first efforts to introduce new foodstuffs (see Chapter 14). But Maori in the north of New Zealand were trading potatoes by 1801 and pigs by about 1815. Other attempted introductions, such as goats, garlic, cattle, and cabbage, failed because they did not fit into traditional Maori ways of farming. Potatoes, however, proved popular in New Zealand because they were sufficiently like the kumara or sweet potatoes that had long been familiar to the Maori. who also welcomed pigs, which could be grazed and eaten.

New Zealand was an outstanding example of what Alfred Crosby called **New Europes:** lands in other hemispheres where the environment resembled Europe's enough for European migrants to thrive, European plants to take root, and a European way of life to be transplanted. Even with help from the climate, however, it was not easy to catch reflections of home in such distant mirrors. The strenuous efforts the British had to apply to adapt in the Australian colony of New South Wales are vividly documented. Take, for instance, James Ruse. He was a pardoned convict who had been a farmer in England. In 1789, he received a grant of 30 acres at Parramatta in Australia. The "middling soil," it seemed to him, was bound to fail for want of manure. He burned timber, dug in ash, hoed, clod molded the earth, dug in grass and weeds, and left the soil exposed to sun for sowing. He planted turnip seed "which will mellow and prepare it for next year" and mulched it with his own compost, made from straw rotted in pits. He and his wife did all the work themselves.

Watkin Tench, from *A Complete Account of the Settlement of Port Jackson*

Success with such untried soils depended on experimentation with varied planting strategies. Early Australia was a strange sort of new Europe at first—made with yams, pumpkins, and maize. On the warm coastal lowlands where the first settlers set up, maize did better than the rye, barley, and wheat that the founding fleet shipped from England in 1788. Firs and oaks were planted, but the food trees were more exotic: oranges, lemons, and limes grew alongside indigo, coffee, ginger, and castor nut. On the outward voyage, the fleet acquired tropical specimens, including bananas, cocoa, guava, sugarcane, and tamarind. The most successful early livestock were introduced from India and South Africa, which also supplied fruit trees.

In the long run, a European model did prevail, but it was primarily a Mediterranean one. Sir Joseph Banks (1744–1820), the British botanist who equipped the founding expedition, believed southern Australia to resemble southwest France and sent over citrus fruits, pomegranates, apricots, nectarines, and peaches. "All the vegetables of Europe" fed the colonists in the 1790s, but Mediterranean colors predominated in visitors' descriptions. The first governor had oranges in his garden, "as many fine figs as ever I tasted in Spain or Portugal," and "a thousand vines yielding three hundredweight of grapes." Watkin Tench, whose study of the soils was vital to the colony's success commended the performance of grape "vines of every sort ... That their juice will probably hereafter furnish an indispensable article of luxury at European tables has already been predicted in the vehemence of speculation." By the time of a French visit in 1802, peaches were so plentiful that they were used to fatten the hogs. The

Economic Revolution in the West

Seventeenth and eighteenth centuries	Scientific revolution
Eighteenth century	Concentration of landholdings in Britain
1756	Botanical Garden of Madrid founded
1760–1808	José Celestino Mutis leads scientific study in Colombia
1769	Captain James Cook rediscovers New Zealand
1770s	The Atlantic world absorbs more British exports than Europe or Asia
1780s	Sharp increase in Britain's national product
1800	British coal production reaches 14 million tons
1805	Merino sheep introduced to Australia

Mediterranean world also provided Australia with an exportable staple—wool. The first consignment of merino sheep, a Spanish breed, left for New South Wales in 1804. Only five rams and one old ewe survived the journey, but these were enough to begin the stocking of the country, which today has more sheep than people.

This Australian experience set the pattern for the colonial New Europes of the nineteenth century, where "the roots are European but the tree grows to a different pattern and design." The North American West, New Zealand, and to a lesser extent, the "cone" of South America—Uruguay, Argentina, and Chile—were all settled, displacing the native cultures with dynamic, outward-going, and relatively populous economies. All defied their original planners and developed their own distinctive characters—tricks that the alchemy of settlement worked in the crucible of new environments.

IN PERSPECTIVE: New Europes, New Departures

"There was never," observed Samuel Johnson (1709–1784), the English man of letters, contemplating his own era, "from the earliest ages a time in which trade so engaged the attention of mankind, or commercial gain was sought with such general emulation." The world was encircled by a cycle that was speeding up: growing population, growing demand, growing output, growing commerce, all stimulated each other. The big gainers were economies that bordered the Atlantic, where traders and shippers could participate in the increasing opportunities worldwide, for the Atlantic led to the wind systems of the world and to exploitable empires.

Overseas colonies were an unmixed blessing for the states that founded them. Colonies demanded heavy investment and paid modest returns. They drained manpower from home countries without always adding much to long-term demand. On the contrary, colonies tended to develop regional economies, "creole mentalities," and—as we shall see in the next chapter—independence movements. The biggest, most precocious, and, in terms of cash yield, richest of the empires—that of Spain—never stimulated much of a commercial or industrial revolution in Spain itself. Yet, in less obvious ways, overseas imperialism did contribute to European world dominance.

The New Europes made the West big. A culture crammed, for most of its history, into a small, remote, and beleaguered corner of Eurasia, now had much of the Western Hemisphere and important parts of the Pacific and Africa at its disposal. Even without the technical and scientific advantages the West was building up, the growing resources available to Western economies were enough to change the world.

China and Japan were also big gainers from the economic and demographic changes of the eighteenth century. But a future in which the West would be increasingly dominant was already visible. In the late eighteenth and early nineteenth centuries, the industrialization of Britain would keep rough pace with the deindustrialization of India at British bayonet point. Domination of India acquired even greater significance

CHRONOLOGY

ca. 1500	Population of Europe reaches 80 million
Seventeenth and eighteenth centuries	Scientific revolution in the West
ca. 1700	Population of Europe reaches 120 million
Eighteenth century	Urbanization increases in Europe and the Americas; concentration of landholdings in Britain; most intense concentrations of industry found in east and south Asia; economic boom in Korea and Japan
1721–1804	Population of Japan stabilizes
ca. 1750–1800	Indian industry goes into decline
1750–1850	Population of China doubles; population of the Americas increases sixfold
1756	Botanical Garden of Madrid founded
1769	Captain James Cook rediscovers New Zealand
1760–1808	José Celestino Mutis leads scientific study in Colombia
1770s	The Atlantic world absorbs more British exports than Europe or Asia
1777–1788	Hipólito Pavón's expedition to Chile and Peru
1780s	Sharp increase in Britain's national product
1784–1814	British import 300 million pounds of tea from China
1787	*Bounty* begins journey to South Pacific
Late eighteenth century	Ottoman Empire loses control of its shipping industry
1794	Condorcet's *The Progress of the Human Mind* published
1796	Edward Jenner develops improved smallpox vaccine
1798	Malthus's *Essay on the Principle of Population* published
ca. 1800	British coal production reaches 14 million tons; population of Europe reaches 180 million; 10,000 "chests" of opium imported into China annually
1805	Merino sheep introduced to Australia

in the nineteenth century when the British turned Indian land over to the production of tea and opium, which destroyed China's trade balance, and ultimately to the farming of quinine in industrial quantities, which enabled European armies to treat malaria, one of the worst hazards of tropical environments. Meanwhile, other eighteenth-century developments, which are the subjects of the next two chapters, contributed to reshaping world history: the growth, strain, instability, and—in some cases—collapse of land empires, and the increasing exchange of ideas between parts of Asia and the West.

PROBLEMS AND PARALLELS

1. What are the various explanations for the demographic growth of the eighteenth century? What was the impact of increased urbanization and health care on the demographic trends of this period?
2. How does the economic history of the eighteenth century mark a departure from prevailing global patterns? Why did the disparity in productivity and wealth between China and India and the West begin to narrow? Why did Ottoman economic activity decline?
3. How did the demographic changes and the speeding up of economic activity affect the global balance of power? Why did Europe's productivity leap in the eighteenth century? How did science contribute to European technical innovation in this period?
4. What does the term *New Europes* mean?
5. What are the social, economic, and political reasons for the rise of Britain as a world power in the eighteenth century? What factors led to its military and economic strength?

DOCUMENTS IN GLOBAL HISTORY

- Thomas Malthus, from *Essay on the Principle of Population*
- Marquis de Condorcet, from *Sketch for a Historical Picture of the Progress of the Human Mind*
- James Lind, from *A Treatise on Scurvy*
- Lady Mary Wortley Montagu, from *Letters*
- Rules Regulating Foreign Trading in Guangzhou
- Galileo, Third Letter on Sunspots, 1612
- Daniel Defoe, from *The Complete English Tradesman*
- David Ricardo, from *On Wages*
- Watkin Tench, from *A Complete Account of the Settlement of Port Jackson*

Please see the Primary Source DVD for additional sources related to this chapter.

READ ON

On the great eighteenth-century thinkers about population, see W. Godwin, *Progress, Poverty and Population: Re-Reading Condorcet, Godwin and Malthus* (1997). R. Duplessis, *Transitions to Capitalism in Early Modern Europe* (1997) contains much nuanced information on European demographics and is a good overview of the run up to industrialization, distinguishing Britain from the Continent. M. Jacob, *Scientific Culture and the Making of the Industrial West* (1997) shows the cultural conduits through which Newtonian mechanics influenced technological progress. See also J. Mokyr, *The Lever of Riches: Technological Creativity and Economic Progress* (1990), which is perhaps overly optimistic.

On China during the eighteenth century, P. Crossley, *The Manchus* (1997) is useful, as is J. Waley-Cohen, "China and Western Technology in the Late Eighteenth Century," *American Historical Review* (1993). But now fundamental are K. Pomeranz, *The Great Divergence: China, Europe, and the Making of the Modern World Economy* (2001) and A. Gunder-Frank, *ReORIENT: Global Economy in the Asian Age.* For a contrasting view, see D. Landes, *The Wealth and Poverty of Nations* (1998). H. Islamoglu-Inan, *The Ottoman Empire and the World Economy* (1987), puts the Ottoman economy in perspective. S. Alavi, ed., *The Eighteenth Century in India* (2002) collects the most significant work on the Indian economy and the impact of British commercial and political interventions.

Grove, *Green Imperialism: Colonial Expansion, Tropical Island Edens and the Origins of Environmentalism, 1600–1860* (1996) is excellent for the development of resources. *The Journals of Hipolito Ruiz: Spanish Botanist in Peru and Chile, 1777–1788*, trans. Richard Schulte et al. (1998) provides a fascinating firsthand account. Dodge, *Islands and Empires: Western Impact on the Pacific and East Asia* (1976) is useful, while A. Crosby, *Ecological Imperialism: The Biological Expansion of Europe, 900–1900* (1993) is a classic.

CHAPTER 21 The Age of Global Interaction: Expansion and Intersection of Eighteenth-Century Empires

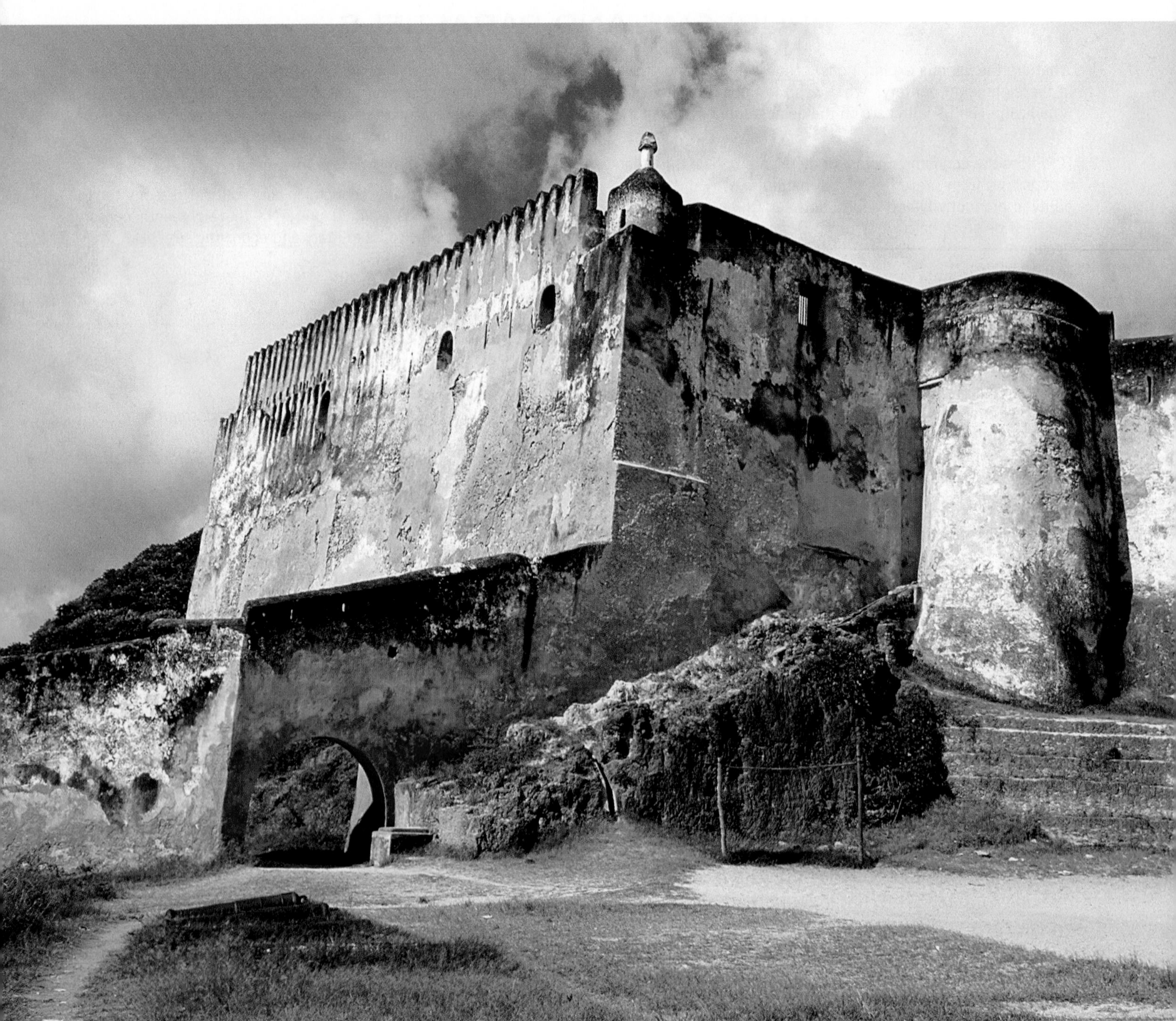

Fort Jesus, Mombasa, in what is today Kenya, was one of a string of forts the Portuguese founded around the rim of the Indian Ocean. It fell to Omani attackers in 1698—one episode in Portugal's long retreat from most of its eastern outposts in the face of hostility or competition from non-European empires.

IN THIS CHAPTER

ASIAN IMPERIALISM IN ARREST OR DECLINE: CHINA, PERSIA, AND THE OTTOMANS
China
The Asian Context
Persia and the Ottoman Empire
IMPERIAL REVERSAL IN INDIA: MUGHAL ECLIPSE AND BRITISH RISE TO POWER
THE DUTCH EAST INDIES
AFRICA, THE AMERICAS, AND THE SLAVE TRADE
LAND EMPIRES OF THE NEW WORLD
The Araucanos and the Sioux
Portugal in Brazil
Spanish America
Creole Mentalities
Toward Independence
IN PERSPECTIVE: The Rims of Empires

In September 1697, after 18 months of siege, all the defenders were dead, except a few Swahili mercenaries under a local sheikh known as Bwana Daud. Fort Jesus, at Mombasa, on the east coast of Africa, was the principal Portuguese station at the western end of the monsoon wind system of the Indian Ocean. It looked as if it was bound to fall to a seaborne empire: the Sayid dynasty of Oman, in southeast Arabia.

MOMBASA

"Loyalty counted more with me than ambition or maternal love," wrote Daud later to the King of Portugal, and he held out until reinforcements arrived. But by December 1698, the situation was again desperate. A few hours after the last defenders were cut down, a relief force from Portuguese Goa in India appeared offshore. They saw the red flag of Oman fluttering over the ramparts and turned back. Over the next three decades, Sayid imperialism mopped up all the Portuguese stations on the Swahili coast of East Africa.

It was part of an Omani strategy to control westward trade along the old monsoonal routes. Oman was an unusual state. It created an unusual empire. The Omani brand of Islam was neither Sunni nor Shiia, but maintained that the true heir of the Prophet Muhammad was whoever was best qualified to lead the people: the **imam**, as the Omanis called him. In practice, the Sayids had established a hereditary monarchy, but the principle of the imamate ensured that their people rejected the ideologies of neighboring empires: the Sunni Ottomans, Shiite Persians, and Christian Portuguese.

On the coast of East Africa, peaceful colonization by Omani merchant families preceded armed intervention. Independent city-states had dotted the region and the islands offshore since at least the twelfth century. These states had a common economic culture—commercial and maritime—a common religion in Islam, and a common language, Swahili. Portuguese incursions in the sixteenth century had disrupted East Africa, but Arabian and Indian merchants never stopped trading in the area.

FOCUS questions

- WHY DID China rely more on colonization than on conquest to expand its empire in the eighteenth century?
- WHAT INTERNAL problems and foreign foes did the Ottoman Empire face in the eighteenth century?
- HOW DID Britain become the dominant power in India?
- WHY WAS the slave trade so important for the economies of West Africa, Europe, and the Americas?
- WHY DID new Native American empires begin to arise during the eighteenth century?
- WHY DID the British and Spanish colonies in the New World come to resent imperial control from Europe?

Omanis established garrisons at Mombasa, Kilwa, Zanzibar, and Pemba. For the native East Africans, the Omanis were as foreign as the Portuguese. Rebellions followed. In Oman, the political elite split, as some of the Sayids' subjects felt that the dominance of one dynasty was a betrayal of the imamate. Oman never had enough shipping to handle all the African ivory and Indian cloth that crossed the ocean, though Omanis did dominate the East African slave trade. Political control was weak. The Omani Empire became a loose network of autonomous states, tied by a sense of kinship among Sayid clan members, like the regional branches of a family business.

Beyond the reach of Omani naval power, even more informal networks spread, as Omani migrants crossed the Indian Ocean. They were welcome, wherever Islam was practiced, as descendants of the Prophet and speakers of perfect Arabic. They became judges, royal advisers, and the husbands of rich women. They founded dynasties in Borneo and Sumatra. "They have spread everywhere throughout the Malay countries," complained a Dutch governor in Melaka in 1750, "and have revealed too much to the natives": too much, that is, about the vulnerability of European outposts.

• • • • •

In one respect, the emergence of Omani power is typical of the time—intelligible in a context of multiplying opportunities to accumulate wealth and temptations to invest it in empire. Yet the Omani network seemed an old-fashioned empire—concerned to control trade, not production, stringing maritime outposts together into the loosest kind of web—whereas the trend was for maritime empires to build up territorial conquests and centralize power.

On the whole, in the eighteenth century, Europeans were becoming more successful in encounters with enemies in other parts of the world. Though they still did not dare to tackle China or Japan, European arms gradually established their superiority against Indians and southeast Asians. At the least, European operations in Asia were no longer at the mercy of native empires, as they had been in the seventeenth century. These are related problems: the growth of land empires and the rise of Western power, wealth, and inventiveness.

ASIAN IMPERIALISM IN ARREST OR DECLINE: CHINA, PERSIA, AND THE OTTOMANS

Empires grew not only by conquest but also by colonization. In the eighteenth century, an era of colonization worldwide or, at least, world widespread, peopled the border lands of the expanding empires and lined political frontiers with settlers. Colonists began to extend the limits of the inhabited world. At the edges of the empires to which they belonged, where they reached out to touch the outposts of other expanding peoples, they helped to mesh the world together.

China

China's was the world's fastest-growing empire in the eighteenth century. It engulfed Tibet in 1720, thrust into Central Asia, and gained territory from Mongolia, Russia, Burma, and Vietnam. Chinese continued to colonize Manchuria and Taiwan (see Chapter 19). The conquest of China's "wild west" in Xinjiang was complete by 1759. When the scholar Ji Yun (chuh-y ywahn) was exiled there ten years later, he felt the awe of entering "another world"—the usual sentiment of a Chinese traveler on leaving China. Yet he soon settled down on a frontier that was being tamed with remarkable speed. The town of Urumqi (oo-room-chee), where he made his new home, had bookshops selling classical Chinese texts. His neighbors grew Chinese peonies and peaches.

By 1800, at least 200,000 Chinese immigrants had settled in Xinjiang. Plenty of them were criminals and political undesirables, but many others were volunteers. For merchants the opportunities in Xinjiang were so profitable that they were punished for wrongdoing by being sent back home. The government offered legitimate migrants subsidies and land. Market towns mushroomed. The frontier absorbed everything the lead and iron mines of Urumqi produced.

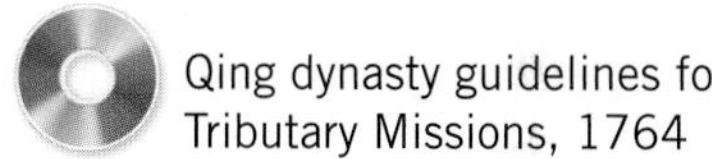
Qing dynasty guidelines for Tributary Missions, 1764

For the ruling Manchu Qing dynasty, colonization of the frontier was too important to be left to the Chinese. In a reshuffling of tribal peoples, reminiscent of the defense strategies of the late Roman Empire (see Chapter 8), the Qing moved Mongol bands about like knights on a chessboard, shifting some between weak points in the borderlands, inducing others into the empire.

Meanwhile, Chinese continued to migrate by sea. They became miners in Malaya and farmers in the Philippines. Some of them made fortunes as businessmen and brokers. In Manila, the capital of the Philippines, in 1729, the archbishop and other leading citizens complained that they had tried to obtain for a Spaniard the contract to supply the city with bread but were unable to wrest the concession from the Chinese. Immigrants went on repeopling Chinese quarters in Manila and Batavia, the capital of the Dutch East Indies, despite the periodic massacres inflicted by native Filipinos and Javanese who feared the Chinese would "swamp" them. The migrants flowed in, in defiance of the efforts of the Chinese government

Tribute. The Qianlong emperor of China (r. 1735–1796) loved horses, as a good Manchu should. Here, in a painting probably produced by Chinese and Jesuit painters at the emperor's court, he receives some of the famed horses of Central Asia from Mongol envoys. The background to this scene was the expansion of the Chinese Empire and the emperor's efforts to bring nomadic peoples under imperial discipline.
The Tartar envoys presenting their horses to Emperor Qianlong. 1757. 45 × 257 cm. Musée du Louvre/RMN Réunion des Musées Nationaux, France. SCALA/Art Resource, NY.

to stop them—or, at least, to persecute those who returned home. A famous case was that of Zhen Yilao, who made a fortune in the Dutch East Indies. He returned to southern China in 1749 to, he said, "fulfill his filial duty of looking after his aging mother." His punishment was the seizure of his fortune and exile—this time, inside the borders of the empire. Chinese traders benefited, as trade in southeast Asia slipped out of the control of states and large companies. In 1732, Chinese controlled 62 percent of the shipping into Batavia from other parts of southeast Asia.

View of Batavia, 1764

Content with profit, they rarely made bids for power. A rebellion by the Chinese quarter of Batavia in 1740 was for self-defense. In Batavia, according to the rebels, "the Dutch dare to treat the Chinese so harshly and oppress them so unjustly that it cannot be tolerated. The Chinese nation is forced to unite and declare war against the Dutch."[1] In Manila, the growing sense of common identity among the Chinese overcame the usual Chinese emphasis on clan or family lineage, especially as the Chinese became entangled in local marriages. A Chinese had to woo his intended bride's family and placate them with gifts. Traditionally, Filipino women remained part of their parents' families, which their husbands joined. But the Chinese lived in exclusively Chinese neighborhoods. So mixed marriages, unlike those between two Filipinos, took a bride away from her parents' home. The structure was neither wholly Filipino nor particularly Chinese, but something new.

Some overseas Chinese took power for the sake of trade. For instance, after trouble with European advisers and French envoys in the late seventeenth century, Thailand underwent a revulsion against European influence. But the Thai court had a long tradition of installing foreign favorites. So from 1700, Chinese occupied the position of royal favorite and purchased most of the other principal offices in the kingdom. Chinese concubines surrounded King Thaisa (r. 1709–1733). But the Thai became jealous of the Chinese community's profits and afraid of its growing numbers. When a new Thai king, Borommakot, suspended the pro-Chinese policy in 1733–1734, the Chinese, who by now numbered 20,000, fell under suspicion of plotting to oust him. Expected vengeance from China did not materialize. Overseas adventures remained private initiatives in which the Chinese state was uninterested.

Back in mainland China, tax returns showed the economic dynamism of the empire. Revenues rose by about two-thirds in the eighteenth century, despite substantial tax reductions, especially the abolition of the poll tax in 1712. The increase in the revenue was the result of rising population, rising production, and rising trade. The Qianlong emperor (r. 1735–1796) enjoyed an annual surplus of 8 to 9 million silver dollars and left 400 million silver dollars in his treasury at his abdication—probably more than twice as much as the Mughal Empire in India amassed at its height. By the emperor's last years, however, China had reached the limits of expansion with the technology at its disposal and had little wish or will to make new conquests, adopt new technologies, or undertake new initiatives. The giant, as Napoleon noticed, had "fallen asleep."

The Asian Context

It is tempting to see this as part of an Asian general crisis of the late eighteenth century. Most of the other great Asian empires—Ottoman, Mughal, Persian, Japanese, Thai—lost impetus during the eighteenth century. The large states in southeast Asia stopped expanding or broke up. Burma first shrank, then collapsed in 1752, after civil wars between provincial rulers. Partial recovery directed Burmese energies against the neighboring Thai Empire in what the Burmese represented as holy wars on behalf of

Buddhism. This was a crisis for which an era of internal peace from 1709 to 1758 had left the Thai ill prepared. Burmese invaders effectively wiped out the Thai capital at Ayutthaya in 1767. The Thai Empire shattered among five small states. Vietnam also fell apart in the chaos of peasant rebellions between 1771 and 1778.

Persia and the Ottoman Empire

In southwest Asia, static population levels held back the Persian and Ottoman worlds. The Safavid Empire in Persia fell in 1722. Like Humpty Dumpty, no one seemed able to put it back together. Although Safavid shahs regained the throne at intervals until 1773, the dynasty had lost the allegiance of its subjects (see Chapter 19). Ironically, the Safavid emperors, who had forced their Shiite Islam on their people, found themselves condemned for their own lack of piety. Between 1719 and 1730, Persia was the playground of invading Afghan warlords. The former bandit chief Nadir Shah, who drove them out tried to end internal strife by turning Persian ambitions outward and to discipline the Shiite clergy by privileging Sunni Islam. He sought to bring the Afghan chiefs into line by reviving the old Afghan practice of raiding India. He even sacked the Mughal court in Delhi and stole its treasure in 1739. He bought English warships to regain control of trade in the Caspian Sea and the Persian Gulf. But he could never escape from rebellions. After his assassination in 1747, state institutions were neglected. The navy rotted away.

The Ottoman Empire—the Safavids' neighbor and longtime enemy—was more robust, but encountered difficulties that seemed crippling. The check to Ottoman expansion toward the end of the seventeenth century (see Chapter 19) shocked the elite, who embarked on long and inconclusive self-examination. The efficiency of the state declined, as hereditary officeholders took over the administration. The numbers of slave-bureaucrats, who tended to strengthen central control because they depended on the sultan's patronage, dwindled. Sultans relied on the Muslim clergy to keep the administration going. But clerics were hard to manage because, unlike the Sultan's slave-bureaucrats, they did not depend on his patronage.

As a result of the economic changes described in Chapter 20, trade revenues fell. The French, for instance—formerly the Turks' best customers—took only 5 percent of their imports from Turkey by the late eighteenth century, compared with about 16 percent in 1700. Imports from Turkey had accounted for 10 percent of Britain's trade in the mid–seventeenth century. The total fell to less than 1 percent by 1800. The end of the coffee monopoly of southern Arabia, as coffee production grew in the East and West Indies, hurt the Ottoman economy.

The balance of power between the empire and its neighbors, which, for so many centuries, had favored the Ottomans, was shifting. A series of border wars with Russia led in 1774 to the Treaty of Küçük Kaynarca, in which the Ottomans ceded control of the north shore of the Black Sea. This was a serious setback, for not only did the Ottomans lose control of important trade routes, but they also conceded sovereignty over a Muslim population to a Christian power. This undermined the sultans' traditional status as protectors of Islam. Further Russian campaigns bit into the Caucasus. In 1798, France invaded Egypt and Syria. The French soon withdrew to fight more urgent wars in Europe, but henceforth, the empire's North African provinces, which, in addition to Egypt, included Algeria, Tunisia, and Libya, became virtually autonomous.

Trends in Asian Imperialism

Eighteenth century	China is world's fastest-growing empire; Persia and Ottoman populations static; Ottoman government goes into prolonged decline
1720	China conquers Tibet
1722	Safavid Empire collapses
1759	Chinese conquest of Xinjiang complete
1767	Burmese invasion leads to disintegration of Thailand
1771–1778	Vietnam collapses under strain of peasant rebellions
1774	Ottomans cede land to Russia in the Treaty of Küçük Kaynarca

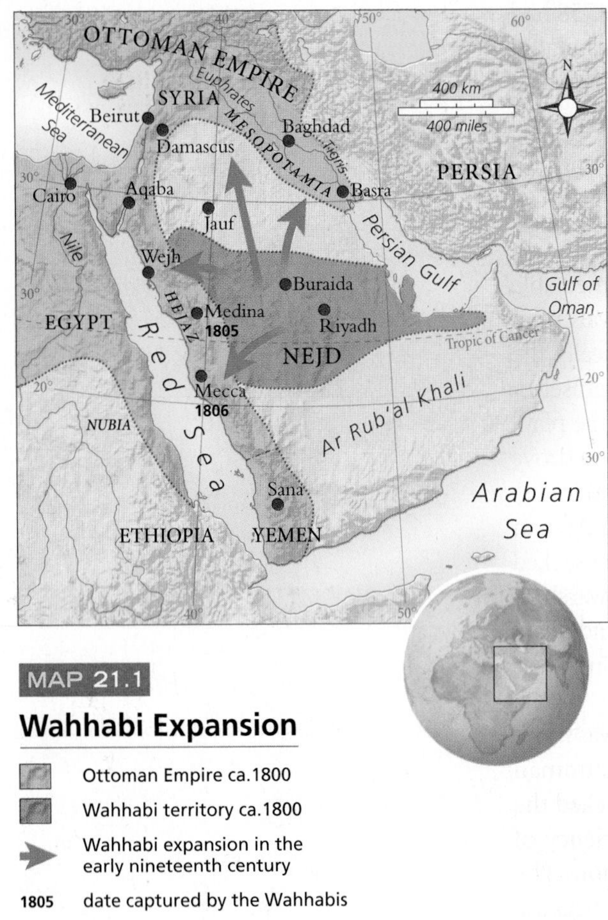

MAP 21.1

Wahhabi Expansion

Ottoman Empire ca.1800

Wahhabi territory ca.1800

Wahhabi expansion in the early nineteenth century

1805 date captured by the Wahhabis

Control of other outlying areas weakened. In the Balkans, many Christian communities withdrew into hill regions, where they planted maize on upper slopes, beyond reach of the Turkish tax collectors. In what is today Romania, the empire conceded autonomy to local inhabitants. The Arabian provinces—never a secure part of the Ottoman dominions—seceded in a religious rebellion. Muhammad ibn Abd al-Wahhab (1703–1787) launched a religious reform movement named **Wahhabism** after him, calling for a return to Quranic purity, and rejecting the legitimacy of the Ottomans' claims to the caliphate. The Wahhabites conquered Arabia and pressed on the borders of Ottoman-controlled Iraq (see Map 21.1).

The Ottomans' difficulties can be measured in their loss of prestige. Europeans began to eye the sultans' possessions like greedy creditors around a rich man's deathbed.

IMPERIAL REVERSAL IN INDIA: MUGHAL ECLIPSE AND BRITISH RISE TO POWER

The most dramatic reversal of fortune—and the one with the most profound implications for the future—happened in India. The Emperor Aurangzeb (r. 1658–1707) had driven the frontiers of the Mughal state southward (see Chapter 19). But after his death, the empire exhibited signs of the strains that arise from success. Widened borders enclosed ever more-diverse cultures, religions, political systems, and ethnic identities. Sikhs and Hindus were hard to accommodate in the fiercely Muslim ideology that Aurangzeb had imposed. The Emperor Muhammad Shah (r. 1719–1748) attempted to take control of the Muslim clergy by claiming the privilege of judging between rival schools of Islamic law. He appealed to the Shiite minority by calling himself "heir of Ali," the Prophet Muhammad's son-in-law who had been murdered in the seventh century, and gave himself the title of "Shadow of God on Earth." But these measures only alienated him further from most religious communities in the realm.

The Mughals had always made money out of war in the past. But empire was a capital-intensive business, subject to diminishing returns. The tax burden necessary to sustain Aurangzeb's policy provoked frequent peasant rebellions. Accommodations with conquered elites became increasingly generous—triggering the anger of the Mughal's old comrades and supporters, who resented the privileges granted to the elites in recently conquered lands. The growing importance of merchants to whom the government farmed out the collection of taxes and from whom it borrowed large sums made this resentment worse. In the remoter parts of the empire, the Mughals, in effect, delegated power to local elites.

The danger of this policy became obvious in a dramatic sequence of events, beginning in 1719–1720. The emperor made spectacular concessions to petty Hindu princes, called the **Marathas** (mah-RAH-tahs), whom their Muslim neighbors despised as bandits. The Nizam al-Mulk who governed for the Mughals on the frontier with the Marathas, responded by defying Mughal authority. In 1725, he conquered Hyderabad in central India and established it as an effectively independent Muslim state (see Map 21.2). He paid no tribute to the Mughal emperor in Delhi. He handed out offices and rewards without reference to the emperor. He took three-quarters of the tribute due to the Mughals and left the remaining quarter to buy peace with his Hindu neighbors. The Mughal Empire still claimed "lordship of the universe" and monopolized reverence and religious rituals. Prayers for the emperor were still offered in mosques throughout India, but it was becoming clear that the Mughal state was in decay and that India was up for grabs.

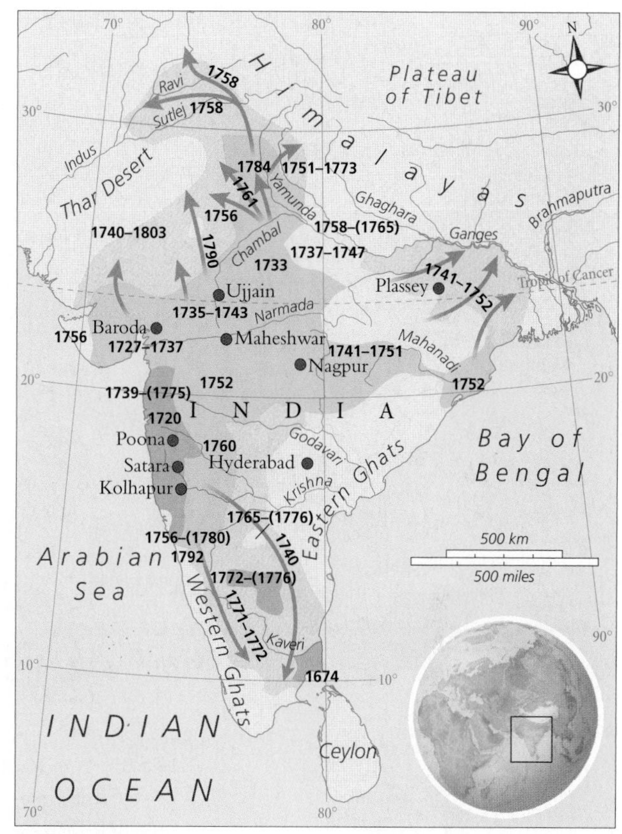

MAP 21.2

The Marathas

- Core territories
- Maratha's expansion, 1708–1800
- Maratha's subject states
- areas of irregular tribute
- **1739** date of acquisition by Marathas
- **(–75)** date of subsequent loss by Marathas to ca. 1800
- → Maratha campaigns into neighboring territory, with date

Native princes contemplated replacing the empire or seizing control of what remained of it. Or else they simply ceased to obey the emperor. But tradition still counted. Regional or local rulers could not challenge the empire without calling into question their own legitimacy, which emperors conferred. Traditionally, conquerors or reunifiers of India had always come from outside, as had the Mughals themselves, who originated in Afghanistan. It was easier for Indians to accept a foreign conqueror than one from inside the empire. Huns, Afghans, Mongols, Turks, and Persians had all played this role in the past. Now, because of the huge shifts of power that had overtaken the world, the successors of the Mughals would be British.

As late as 1750, the British East India Company, which had been founded in 1600, insisted that its officials think of themselves as the "agents of merchants" rather than as a military colony. Violent competition with French rivals in India, however, was already forcing the company's men to rethink their roles. Young Robert Clive (1725–1774), for instance, was a clerk in the Indian port of Madras. But he spent his leisure reading military history, and when fighting broke out, he found soldiering to be his true vocation.

In 1756, Clive turned what was to have been a punitive expedition into a campaign of conquest. Bengal in northeast India was the most important trading area in India for European commerce. In the 1730s, for instance, nearly half of Holland's imports from Asia, and as much as two-thirds of all Asian exports to England, originated in Bengal. The Nawab (nah-WAHB), the local ruler, alienated the British by allying with France, seizing the British port of Calcutta, and allegedly allowing the mistreatment and murder of British women and children. Bengal was full of internal dissent: Hindu resentment of Muslim rule, warlord rivalry with the Nawab, popular resentment of taxation, military unrest at overdue pay.

Clive blundered into this tense arena with an army of about 1,000 Europeans and 2,000 Indian trainees, outnumbered in the field by over 12 to 1. But Clive aimed to destroy the enemy by dividing them. He succeeded by putting together a coalition that ousted the Nawab at Plassey in 1757 by what was in effect a battlefield coup. Traditionally, historians have represented the battle as the result of British superiority, whereas it showed only the superiority of some Bengali factions over others. Confronted by a conspiracy among his followers, the Nawab fled after little more than exchanges of cannon and skirmisher fire.

Bengal was easily the richest of the fragments into which the Mughal Empire dissolved. Clive looted it—"astonished," he said, "at my own moderation." Booty never dulls the appetite it feeds. Clive's men almost mutinied at dissatisfaction with their share of the plunder even though it had made them all rich. Yet Bengal was the biggest prize of any pirate since Pizarro seized Peru for Spain in the 1520s (see Chapter 16). The East India Company raised £2 million in 1761–1764 and almost £7.5 million in 1766–1767. The riches of Bengal paid for the conquest of other Indian principalities. By 1782, the East India Company, whose motto had once been "trade, not war," was keeping an army of 115,000 men in India.

MAP 21.3

European Expansion in South and Southeast Asia, ca. 1800

- area under British rule, ca. 1800
- area under Dutch control and possessions, 1765
- Spanish possessions
- French possessions
- area under Portuguese control and possessions, 1765
- Danish possessions
- petty tribal polities
- other states
- frontiers, ca. 1765

The parallel with the Spanish conquerors in the Americas is striking. The British first installed a puppet ruler in Bengal, then used the profits of confiscatory policies to conquer the Ganges River valley and the shore of the Bay of Bengal, just as the Spaniards had used the wealth and manpower of the formerly Aztec-dominated highlands of Mexico to conquer the surrounding regions. As in Mexico and Peru, the speed of the conquerors' triumph gave it the illusion of inevitability. Once the growth of a land empire had begun, it had to continue. Security always demanded control of the next frontier. The existing setup in India, in which native princes bargained with rival Western buyers and shippers, became intolerable to the British once they realized they could enforce a monopoly. With Bengal in their power, the British extended their control over the spice-rich south (see Map 21.3).

Under cover of the next European war in the 1790s, which again neutralized the French threat, Britain put together a coalition of Indian clients and mercenaries to defeat piecemeal the only regional powers capable of reversing the trend. Tipu Sultan, ruler of Mysore in south India, posed the biggest threat. He spurned the Mughals, took imperial trappings for himself, and looked to the distant Ottomans to legitimate his claims. In the 1780s, while the Mughal emperor swallowed his pride and sought Maratha protection, Tipu confronted the British for supremacy in India. Political realism, idealized as holy war, underpinned his anti-British policy. He realized that Indians could no longer deal with the British in the traditional frameworks of commerce and politics. They had to be expelled or obeyed.

Tipu's neighbors, however, preferred to back the British rather than to support him. They preferred to have rulers far away in London rather than dangerously close in Mysore. Hopelessly besieged in 1799, Tipu died in the fighting. The Maratha states accepted British overlordship in 1806.

British supremacy was only the latest variant on an old theme of Indian history: dominance by foreign military elites. But in a crucial sense, the phenomenon was new. Britain's India was the first big European empire on the mainland of Asia. The British could now seize or clear much of India to grow products that suited them. They could smother the potential competition of Indian industries, shifting the balance of the world's resources in favor of the West (see Chapter 20). Britain's Indian Empire was the last of the old adventurer conquests, achieved with native collaboration and without conspicuous technical advantages, and the forerunner of the new industrial conquests, by which Europeans would extend their empires in the next century. There were, as yet, no machine guns or ironclad ships or quinine pills to give Westerners technical advantages. Steam power and rifles were in their infancy. But British industry affected the conquest of India. By the 1790s, British artillery was so superior to the Indian product that Tipu's finely decorated cannon were good to the British only for their value as scrap metal.

THE DUTCH EAST INDIES

Events in India illustrated the way European imperialism in Asia was turning to territorial conquest. The Spanish continued to build up their empire in the Philippines, crushing a rebellion after the British briefly seized Manila in 1762. The Portuguese, despite being expelled from their East African outposts by the Omanis, hesitantly expanded their frontiers around Goa on the southwest Indian coast. The Dutch built up a land empire on Java, dividing authority among rival Javanese clients called regents. Sheikhs in Arabia accused these puppet rulers of being "the devil's kings," taunting, "Shall the Europeans be more powerful than Allah?" But the regents depended on the Dutch just as the Dutch depended on them, and the relationship benefited both sides.

In the end, the landward turn did the Dutch little good. Their strength was in their shipping, and a seaborne, piratical empire suited their talents and technology. Their weakness was a shortage of manpower. Territorial acquisitions overstretched and exhausted them. The Dutch could only pay for war by enforcing high prices. As they devastated rivals' lands, uprooted surplus crops, and destroyed competitors' ships, they risked ruining the entire region and being left profitless, as one of their leaders warned, "in depopulated lands and empty seas."

Mughal Decline

1600	East India Company (EIC) founded
Eighteenth century	Spanish, Dutch, and Portuguese expand holdings in southeast Asia
1707	Death of Aurangzeb and the end of Mughal expansion
1725	Nazim al-Mulk conquers Hyderabad
1756–1757	Robert Clive leads EIC conquest of Bengal
Late eighteenth century	Marathas offer only nominal obedience to the Mughals
1761–1764	EIC revenues: £2 million
1766–1767	EIC revenues: £7.5 million
1806	Maratha states accept British overlordship

Yet what choice did the Dutch have? Unlike the Spaniards and Portuguese, they had little access to marketable assets, such as gold and silver mines or sources of slaves. They could finance their inroads into eastern markets only by the profits of intra-Asian trade and shipping or by growing their own cash crops. By opting for the latter strategy, they committed themselves to seizing the spices and, in the end, the land the spices grew on, by force. They ended up with an empire, the Dutch East Indies, whose costs exceeded its profits until they forced much of Java to grow coffee.

AFRICA, THE AMERICAS, AND THE SLAVE TRADE

Olaudah Equiano, excerpt from *The Interesting Narrative*

Equaling or exceeding the vast movements of internal colonization in Asia was the shift of people across the Atlantic. Most of them were black Africans, forced into slavery and transported to the New World. In the eighteenth century, nearly 400,000 were imported into English North America, nearly 1 million into Spanish colonies, over 1 million into the Caribbean, and some 3 million into Brazil. The structures of the trade were the same as in the previous century (see Chapter 19), but its scale grew (see Map 21.4).

Our traditional image of the horrors of the Atlantic crossing comes from slave memoirs and the writings of abolitionists who sought to do away with the slave trade. Skeptics have wondered whether shippers can really have been so careless of their cargo as to tolerate—and even invite—heavy losses of life en route. Yet such evidence as the deck plan of the British slave-ship *Brookes* in 1783 is decisive. Slaves were stacked "like books on a shelf," in spaces little more than five feet high by four feet wide. The ship's surgeon watched their "laborious and anxious efforts for life," which resembled those "we observe on expiring animals subjected by experiment to bad air." The *Brookes* lost 60 slaves out of 600 on the crossing.

Yet, strictly from the point of view of profits, the slavers knew what they were doing. In a telltale case, a captain from the British port of Liverpool in 1781 had 130 slaves thrown overboard to claim the insurance for lost cargo. It was a horrifying instance, but it was normal to dispose of sick or mutinous slaves in the same way.

The slave ship *Brookes*. Over 600 slaves were crammed into a space on the *Brookes* designed to carry no more than 450 persons. The extent of the inhumanity and inefficiency in the slave trade is shocking.

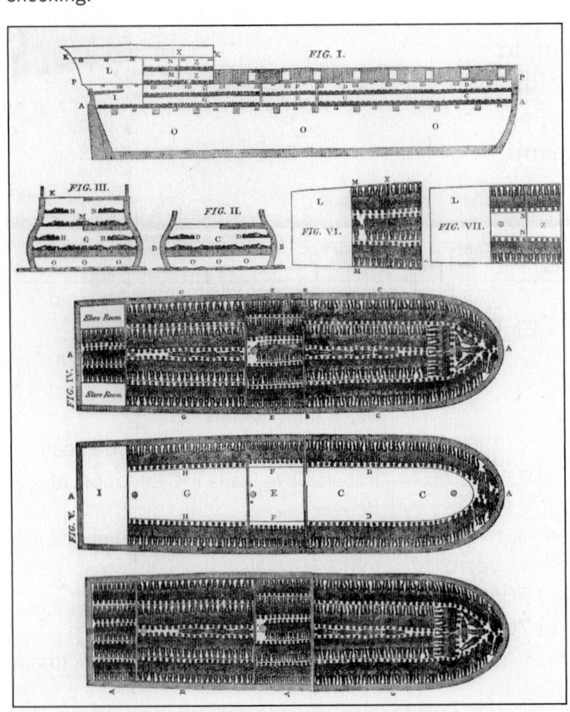

The economics of slavery are hard to understand. Forced labor, according to economic theory, is never efficient, and the difficulty of managing slaves to maximize production is one of the few conclusions on which all observers of slave plantations in the eighteenth century agreed. Yet slavery was just one form of forced labor, on which most eighteenth-century economies relied. Indentured workers, peasants tied to the land, unpaid apprenticeships, and convict workers all made compulsion seem normal. Traditional forms of employment gave employers—masters, as they were commonly called—enormous power over their workers' lives: where the workers lived, how they spent their leisure, whom and when they married. So until economic thought began to challenge such practices in the late eighteenth century (see Chapter 22), it is not surprising that people tolerated the savageries and inefficiencies of the slave plantations. And demand for slave-grown commodities was such that plantations managed to make profits. Sometimes planters could enjoy spectacular results in a small space. France's colony of Saint-Domingue in the eighteenth century occupied only one-third of the island of Hispaniola. It was hardly much of a land empire, but Saint-Domingue was what we would now call an economic miracle—a source of enormous wealth, the world's major producer of coffee and sugar, with important sidelines in indigo and cacao.

Depictions of black societies in the Americas range from the idealized through the colorful and the satirical to the horrific. But the crack of the lash can be heard between the lines even of idealized accounts—like the Englishman William Beckford's of Jamaica, where he was a slave owner in 1788. He claimed that "the situation of a good negro under a kind owner . . . is very superior (the idea of indiscriminate punishment excepted) to those of the generality of labouring poor in England." More typical was his contemporary Edward Long, who justified slavery in 1774 on the grounds that black Africans were so unlike other peoples—among other reasons, because of a "narrow intellect" and "bestial smell"—that they were almost a different species.

Yet within the constraints of plantation life, black people retained a degree of initiative that allowed them to craft their own social worlds, domestic practices, values, and norms of behavior. To some extent, the white men's laws reflected these values. In the 1780s, the Spanish and French crowns enacted codes guaranteeing slaves' rights to marriage, to the inseparability of husbands and wives, and, in the French case, to the inseparability of children from parents before puberty. Spanish, French, and Portuguese colonies had many local laws against sexual abuse of slaves by owners, removing slave children from their parents' care, and denying conjugal rights to married slaves. In practice, this worked against slave marriage, because owners tended to discourage or prevent their slaves from marrying to escape the consequences of the laws. As a result, neither Church nor state recognized most sexual alliances between slaves, but those unions were often stable, nonetheless.

Quadroon woman. John Stedman fought as a mercenary against rebellious black slaves in the late eighteenth century, but his sympathetic account of them helped the antislavery cause. He particularly admired the so-called quadroon looks typical of women, like the one shown here, who had one white and three black grandparents. Even in Surinam, where laws regulating slaves were particularly repressive, black women could achieve wealth and high status by marrying white men.
Dagli Orti (A)/Picture Desk, Inc./Kobal Collection

In most of the colonies that depended on slave labor, marriage between black and white threatened the social order. The only universally tolerable kind of sex between people of different color was between white men and black women, where the power relationship was clear. In early eighteenth-century Surinam, a Dutch colony on the northeast coast of South America, for instance, white women were flogged, branded, and banished for fornication with black men. Their male black partners were liable to the death penalty. In 1764, when a rich, free, black widow wanted to marry a white man 30 years her junior, the local government ruled it "repugnant and loathsome," because it would reverse the normal relations of power.

Yet there was nothing to stop a white master in Surinam from taking a black mistress, or—indeed—marrying her (although slave-holding colonies in British North America outlawed interracial marriages). In Spanish colonies, the moral power of the Church had some influence. Spanish clergy pressured white masters to marry slave concubines and owners to grant dowries to female slaves on marriage. Some owners were canny enough to realize that it was cheaper to get slaves to breed than to purchase new ones. In general, however, the traditions of African societies, not the Church, molded slaves' attitudes to marriage. Transportation on the same ship, or membership in the same group of runaways, or association in the same religious brotherhoods (see Chapter 19) became forms of ritual kinship, within which marriage was taboo.

The Code Noir (France)

Phyllis Wheatley, "To The Right Honorable William, Earl of Dartmouth ..."

Some mainland colonies—those far from the main markets where slaves were relatively expensive to buy—found that it made sense not to jeopardize their investments by wasteful ill use. Better conditions of life for the slaves were the key to improved security and natural increase of population. In Virginia, Delaware, and Maryland, for instance, most of the slave population was born locally from about 1750. In most of the New World, however, the slaves' most effective form of resistance was to refuse to

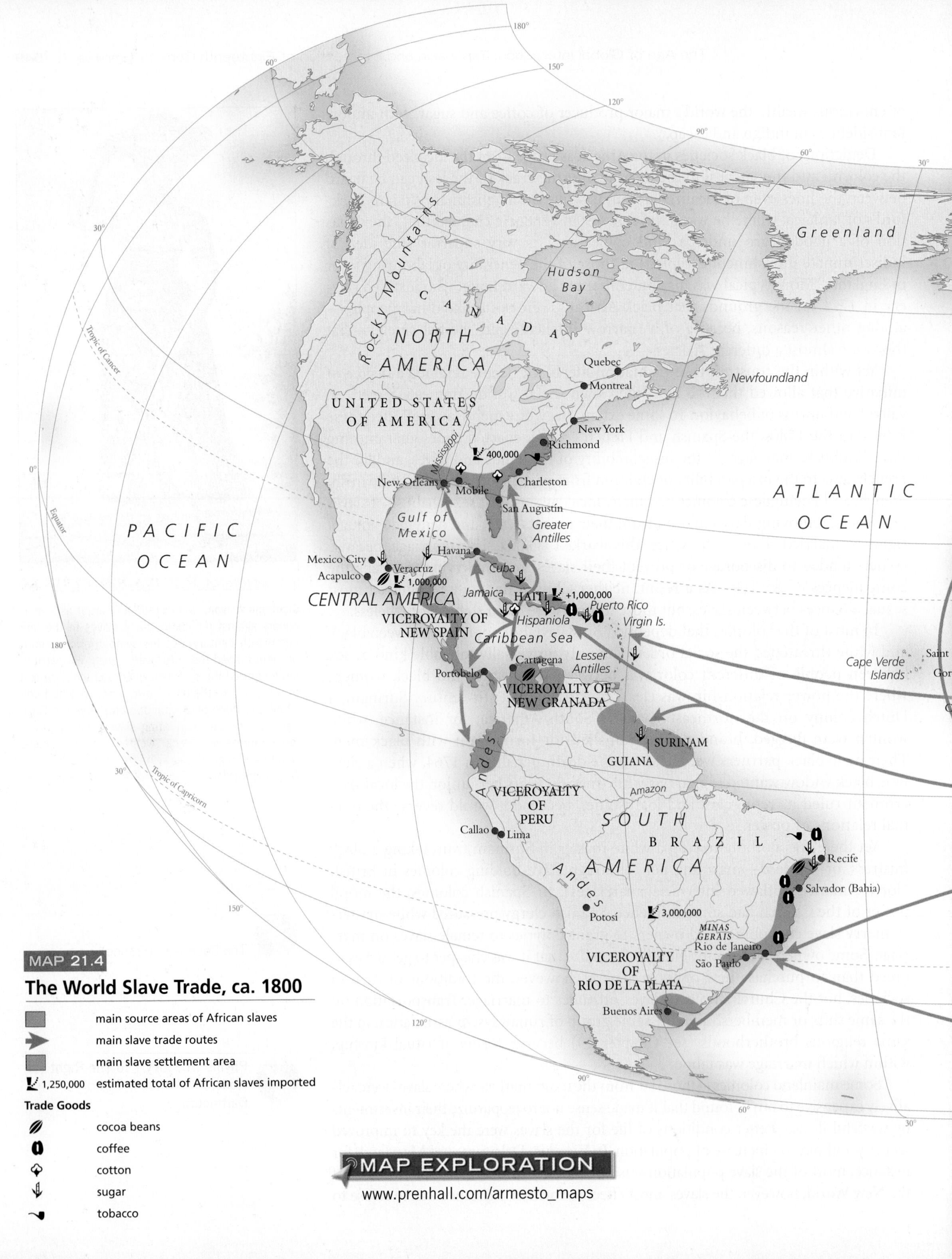

MAP 21.4

The World Slave Trade, ca. 1800

- main source areas of African slaves
- main slave trade routes
- main slave settlement area
- 1,250,000 estimated total of African slaves imported

Trade Goods

- cocoa beans
- coffee
- cotton
- sugar
- tobacco

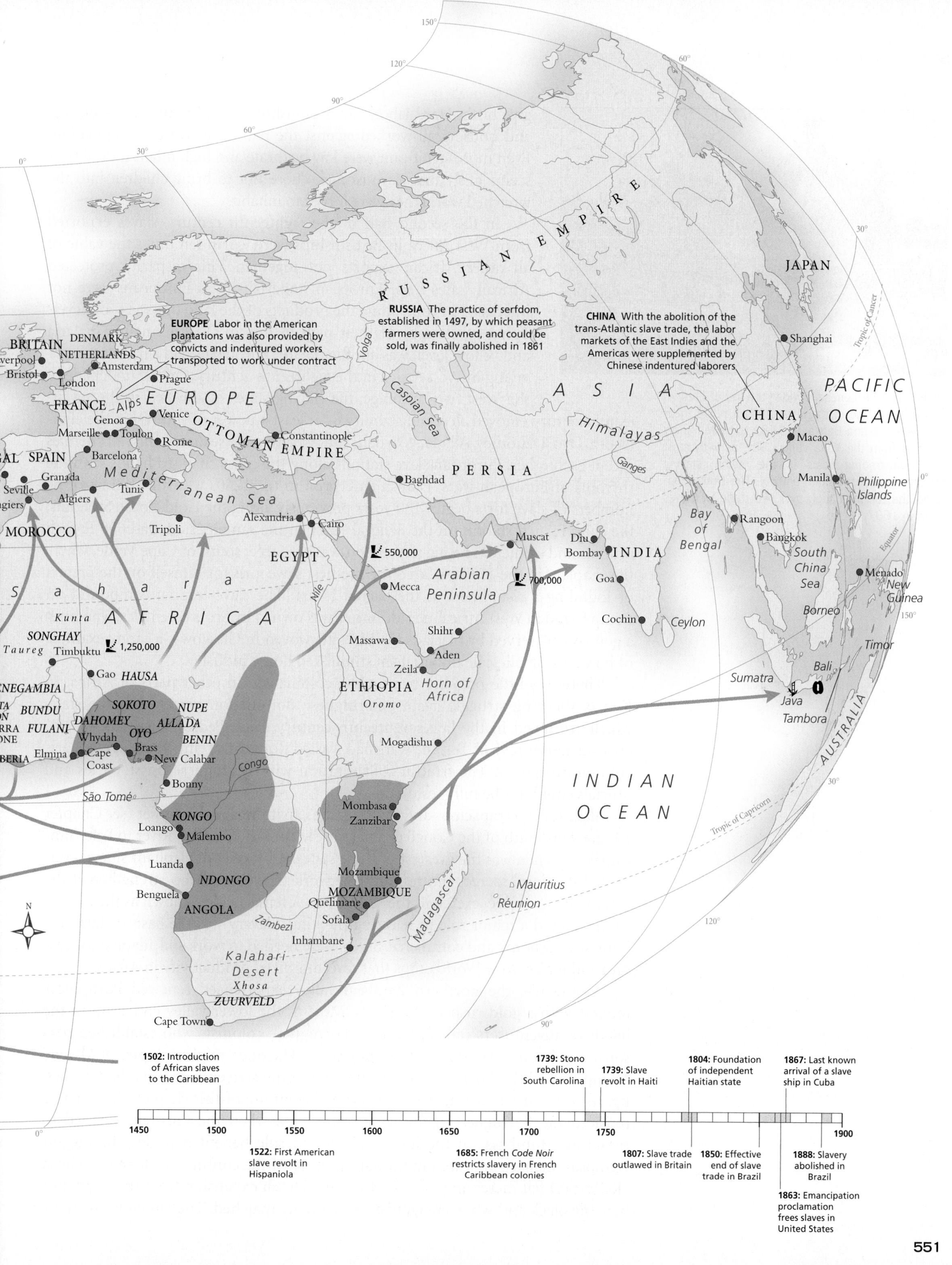

RUSSIAN EMPIRE
RUSSIA The practice of serfdom, established in 1497, by which peasant farmers were owned, and could be sold, was finally abolished in 1861
EUROPE Labor in the American plantations was also provided by convicts and indentured workers transported to work under contract
CHINA With the abolition of the trans-Atlantic slave trade, the labor markets of the East Indies and the Americas were supplemented by Chinese indentured laborers
JAPAN
Shanghai
BRITAIN
DENMARK
NETHERLANDS
Amsterdam
Liverpool
Bristol
London
Prague
FRANCE
Alps
EUROPE
Genoa
Venice
Marseille
Toulon
Rome
Barcelona
SPAIN
Granada
Seville
Algiers
Tunis
Tripoli
MOROCCO
OTTOMAN EMPIRE
Constantinople
Mediterranean Sea
Alexandria
Cairo
EGYPT
Nile
Volga
Caspian Sea
ASIA
Himalayas
Ganges
PERSIA
Baghdad
550,000
Mecca
Arabian Peninsula
Muscat
700,000
Diu
Bombay
INDIA
Goa
Cochin
Ceylon
Bay of Bengal
CHINA
Macao
PACIFIC OCEAN
Manila
Philippine Islands
Rangoon
Bangkok
South China Sea
Menado
New Guinea
Borneo
Timor
Bali
Sumatra
Java
Tambora
AUSTRALIA
Sahara
AFRICA
Kunta
SONGHAY
Taureg
Timbuktu
1,250,000
Gao
HAUSA
SENEGAMBIA
BUNDU
FULANI
SOKOTO
NUPE
DAHOMEY
ALLADA
OYO
BENIN
Whydah
Elmina
Cape Coast
Brass
New Calabar
LIBERIA
Congo
Bonny
São Tomé
KONGO
Loango
Malembo
Luanda
NDONGO
Benguela
ANGOLA
Massawa
Shihr
Aden
Zeila
ETHIOPIA
Oromo
Horn of Africa
Mogadishu
Mombasa
Zanzibar
Mozambique
MOZAMBIQUE
Quelimane
Sofala
Zambezi
Inhambane
Madagascar
Mauritius
Réunion
Kalahari Desert
Xhosa
ZUURVELD
Cape Town
INDIAN OCEAN
Tropic of Cancer
Equator
Tropic of Capricorn
N
1502: Introduction of African slaves to the Caribbean
1522: First American slave revolt in Hispaniola
1685: French Code Noir restricts slavery in French Caribbean colonies
1739: Stono rebellion in South Carolina
1739: Slave revolt in Haiti
1804: Foundation of independent Haitian state
1807: Slave trade outlawed in Britain
1850: Effective end of slave trade in Brazil
1863: Emancipation proclamation frees slaves in United States
1867: Last known arrival of a slave ship in Cuba
1888: Slavery abolished in Brazil
1450
1500
1550
1600
1650
1700
1750
1900

Elmina. The Portuguese founded the fort of Elmina, on the underside of the West African bulge, near the rivers Pra and Benya, in 1482 to trade mainly for gold from the Volta valley. But, as with most European trading posts in the region, slaving rapidly became the main activity. The Dutch captured the fort and took over the trade in slaves there in 1637.

give birth. Hard labor, harsh punishment, and poor food, clothing, and housing all worked against the natural increase of population. Even more significant were low birthrate and high infant mortality. It seems likely that slave women chose not to bring children into the wretched world they were forced to inhabit.

In the second half of the eighteenth century, slaves exported from West Africa in British ships were worth ten times the value of all other African exports put together. This disparity protected African states from European imperialism, as Europeans were not interested in controlling the products of the land or—yet—of developing plantations of their own in Africa. Disease, mainly malaria and yellow fever, was another factor. Europeans had a hard time surviving in West Africa in the eighteenth century. On the underside of the West African bulge, the slaving states established in the seventeenth century enjoyed a certain stability or at least a power of survival in the eighteenth. Oyo, Dahomey, Allada, Whydah, and Ashanti were secure against all enemies except each other. European slave stations along the coast changed hands with the rhythms of European wars. Danish enterprise in the 1780s was still adding to the numbers of slave forts begun 100 years previously along the Gold Coast. St. Louis, the chief French station on the Senegal River in the same period, had 600 French officials and soldiers. The biggest station was at Gorée, south of Cape Verde, where the chaplain in the 1780s secured the prettiest slave girls for himself on the pretext of founding a sisterhood of the Sacred Heart. The slave-trading compound on Bence Island in West Africa in midcentury was owned by Scots eccentrics, who built a golf course, served by black caddies in kilts woven in Glasgow—a canny example of how even small-scale imperialism stimulated home industry.

There was little pressure from white colonialism in other parts of Africa. In Kongo, the long struggle against Portuguese domination wore down the state, which crumbled in the late seventeenth century. King Pedro IV (r. 1695–1709) effected a brief revival. But the wars had wasted Kongo and ruined its former agricultural prosperity. The fruitful collaboration with Portuguese missionaries and officials could not be fully restored.

Slave states as rapacious and militaristic as anything known earlier (see Chapter 19) grew up south of the Congo drainage area, from the Kwango River to Lake Tanganyika. Luanda was the greatest of these states. A bracelet of elephant sinews confirmed its kings' sacred nature. But a network of women, who strengthened the dynasty by marriage, exercised the real power. A female elder, known as the *Lukonkashia*, played a major role in selecting the king. Slavery was the basis of Luanda's domestic economy and commerce. Slaves were needed to work soil adapted for cassava and maize, New World crops that revolutionized productivity in Africa.

Meanwhile, the northern Zambezi valley experienced renewed Portuguese interest with a gold rush in the 1740s. Most of the lower valley ended up in the hands of adventurers called *prazeros*—Portuguese colonists who established personal dominance over the native populations. The once-mighty empire of Mwene Mutapa, which had defeated the Portuguese in the sixteenth century, had broken up. In coastal East Africa, as we saw at the beginning of this chapter, the Omanis replaced the Portuguese definitively from 1729, when the Portuguese failed to recapture Mombasa. In the long run, Omani rule benefited trade. The biggest European menace appeared in the southern tip of the continent, where the Xhosa (KOH-sah) felt increasing pressure from the Dutch expansion from the Cape. But here the black and white antagonists were evenly matched. The Dutch farmers (or

"Boers") halted at the edge of the Zuurveld in wars that ended in 1795. By that time the Boers had fallen out among themselves, and the British had seized the Cape Colony from the Dutch East India Company.

The really big threats to African states came not from European imperialism but from within Africa. Ethiopia failed to contain Oromo migrations. Early in the eighteenth century, the Oromo began to organize states of their own and to become Muslims. Oromo became high officials and commanders inside what was left of Ethiopia and rulers of effectively independent provinces. A siege mentality took over the Ethiopian elite, with rival factions and sects squabbling over a diminishing powerbase. In the 1760s, the most powerful provincial governor, Mika'el Suhul, built up a well-trained army equipped with firearms and took government into his own hands. Ethiopia's "Era of Princes" began, in which the emperor was a pawn or puppet of warlords.

In West Africa, meanwhile, the continuing expansion of the Islamic world put relentless pressure on local African states. Senegambia fell to Muslim-led revolutions that displaced native dynasties. Bundu fell in 1690, Futa Jallon in 1725, and Futa Toro in 1776. Muslim Tuareg (too-AH-rehg) warriors and Kunta holy men proved, in combination, an irresistible force along the middle Niger River. The process gathered pace. In 1794, a holy man in the Sahel, Usuman da Fodio, had a vision in which he was "girded with the Sword of Truth, to unsheathe it against the enemies of God." The strict Islamic Wahhabite movement from Arabia inspired him. He saw himself as the forerunner of the **Mahdi** (MAH-dee), a Muslim messiah, whose coming would inaugurate a cosmic struggle, preceding the end of the world.

Usuman attracted a fervent following among the Fulani, traditional herdsmen of the Sahel. Their empire was a combination of three traditions: another pastoralist attempt to exploit the Sahel's potential for long-range grazing of flocks; another frustrated step to unify the area politically; and another Islamic holy war. By 1820, Usuman's followers had conquered an empire that stretched from Bornu to beyond the Niger, with a capital of sunbaked clay buildings at Sokoto (see Map 21.5). This was the world's last great pastoralist empire. It lasted until British conquest in 1906.

Usuman da Fodio declares a jihad

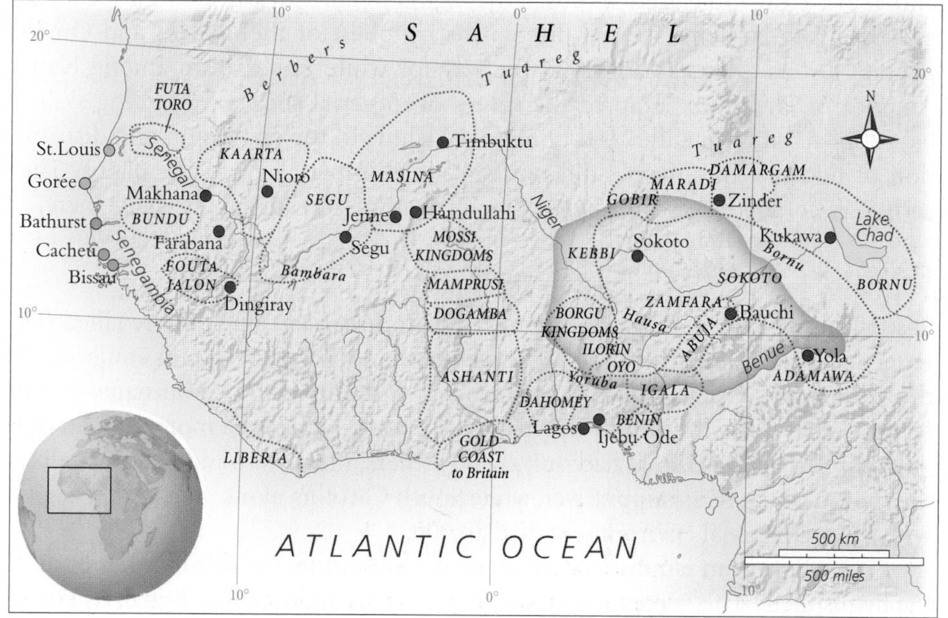

MAP 21.5
The Sokoto Fulani Kingdom, ca. 1820

- Sokoto Fulani Kingdom, ca. 1820
- British possession
- French possession
- Portuguese possession
- borders, ca. 1820
- *Hausa* people

LAND EMPIRES OF THE NEW WORLD

The Fulani Empire had parallels in the Americas. By the eighteenth century, horse-borne hunting made the South American pampa and North American prairie desirable places to live. Intrusions of farmers and city dwellers on the edges enhanced the new economic opportunities horses, cattle, and sheep offered.

The Araucanos and the Sioux

Pastoralism and mining enabled native peoples of the pampa in what is today Argentina to open new trade with Chile and to absorb lessons in large-scale chieftaincy from the Araucanos—the impressive warriors of the South American southwest, who maintained effective independence beyond the frontiers of the Spanish Empire. By the mid–eighteenth century, chieftains on the rivers Negro and Colorado, such as Cacapol and his son Cangapol, could turn the elective position of war chief into hereditary rule. They could organize lucrative trade in furs, assemble harems of a size to mark their status, impress a Jesuit visitor as "monarchs over all the rest," raise thousands of warriors, and threaten the city of Buenos Aires.

A similar transformation began to affect the North American prairie. Huge kills of buffalo for their hides generated a trading surplus, which in turn introduced maize to Native American hunters' diets, whiskey to their religious rites, and guns to their armories. Even before white men disputed control of them, the prairies became an arena of competition between ever-growing numbers of immigrant Native American peoples—many driven, as much as drawn, from east of the Missouri River by the pressure of white empire building. All tended to become herders of horses as well as hunters of buffalo—which forced them into unstable contact with each other on shared trails and pastures. The Sioux were converts to nomadism. Numbering 25,000 by 1790, they were a potentially imperial people who became the terror of a settled Native American world on the upper Missouri River.

Even when they had adopted a horse-borne way of life and an economy based on the slaughter of bison, the Sioux kept an interest in their traditional forest economy. Even when their conquests covered the plains, they extended them into new forests farther west, where deer hunting conferred prestige. The Black Hills in South Dakota were their "meat store," which they seized from Kiowa, Cheyenne, and Crow. Meanwhile, trade exposed the region to killer diseases of European origin. Smallpox epidemics eased the Sioux's conquest of the Arikara and Omaha peoples just as diseases had paved the way for white imperialism among Native Americans. The Sioux adopted the values of imperial society, rewarding skill in battle above other qualities and tying social status to the possession and distribution of booty. White people did not introduce imperialism to the plains. They arrived as competitors with a Sioux Empire that was already taking shape there.

Portugal in Brazil

East of this region, France's attempt to create an American land empire failed. The French, despite the density of their home population, were reluctant emigrants in the eighteenth century. Before France ceded it to Spain in 1763, Louisiana—a vast territory that took in most of the Mississippi valley—was little more than an outline on the map. In 1746, it had only 3,300 settlers, mostly around New Orleans at the mouth of the Mississippi River, while South Carolina alone, in a poorer region with a less congenial environment, had 20,000.

Other European empires, however, made substantial inroads in other parts of the hemisphere. The Portuguese developed a vast, rich domain in Brazil. As Portugal withdrew from or lost most of its outposts in Asia and East Africa, Brazil became the jewel in the crown of a now compact empire.

In the "golden century" from the 1690s, gold and diamonds replaced sugar as Brazil's cash crops. Some cash went on British service industries and manufactured goods, stimulating industrialization in Britain. Some of it ended up in India and China, funding the West's persistent balance of payments deficit with the East. Much of it funded the creativity of sculptors and painters, like Aleijadinho, the crippled, black genius whose sculptures are among the wonders of the churches in Minas Gerais. By the 1760s, the Portuguese had pushed Spanish outposts back roughly to the line of the present linguistic boundary between Spanish and Portuguese in South America. Although Spain's New World land empire was bigger, Portugal's was in some ways more impressive: carved out of hostile jungle environments. Brazil had little useful Native American manpower, and most of what there was had to be enslaved to work the mines and plantations.

The black Brazilian sculptor Aleijadinho (ca. 1730–1804) carved this statue of the prophet Ezekiel for the church of Nosso Senhor do Bom Jesus de Matosinho, in the province of Minas Gerais. Because Aleijadinho's hands were crippled, he would not have been able to depict the animation, emotion, and decorative detail displayed here if he had not been carving in soapstone, which is soft when freshly quarried but hardens on exposure to air.

Spanish America

Spanish expansion happened more modestly. The experience of the seventeenth century showed that the Spanish Empire could triumph by force only on exceptionally well-settled frontiers, like New Mexico, which the Spanish reconquered from Native American rebels in the 1690s. Instead, in the eighteenth century, Spanish strategy switched to a method that proved surprisingly successful: attracting peoples into the monarchy through negotiations, on equal terms. Communities that accepted Spanish rule moved into the supposed security and prosperity of rationally planned settlements.

In the second half of the century, the Spanish persuaded Indians to settle in 80 new towns on the Argentine and Chilean frontiers, and in many more settlements in what is now the southwest United States. Similar means drew runaway slaves back into the empire. At San Antonio in Texas, black settlers had the right to exclude white colonists, except for a priest. By 1779, San Antonio had nearly 1,500 citizens.

In California, 21 new missions extended Spain's reach beyond its remotest garrisons. From 1769 to his death in 1784, the Franciscan missionary Brother Junípero Serra founded a string of mission stations along the coast of upper California, where the arrival of an annual ship was the only contact with the rest of the Spanish monarchy. Here he converted the environment as well as its inhabitants, wrenching the natives out of nomadism, producing new crops—wheat, grapes, citrus, almonds, figs, olives—from the soil. His foundations stretched from San Diego to San Francisco, to keep the wilderness, paganism, and rival empires—British and Russian—at bay. The missions worked economically, too. They had 427 head of cattle in 1775 and at least 95,000 by 1805. But prosperity did not help the Native Americans survive the unfamiliar diseases that contact with Europeans brought. The Indians, as a missionary observed, "fattened and sickened."

Plan of San Antonio, Texas, 1780

At the other end of the empire, where the Jesuits tended the southeast frontier in Paraguay until the Spanish government expelled them in 1768, dozens of mission churches mark the boundaries. Even on Spain's most troublesome frontier, in what is now southern Chile, progress was made in the 1770s and 1780s, when previously hostile Indian peoples joined the Spanish monarchy, and even the Mapuche, whom the Spanish could not conquer, allowed them to build a road and missions.

Creole Mentalities

Colonies laboriously created, carefully built in the image of Europe, gradually grew away from home. Some settlers came to the Americas to escape their mother

Aztec calendar stone. Just after European scholars had proclaimed the natural inferiority of the New World, spectacular archaeological finds in Mexico seemed to vindicate pre-Columbian America's claim to house great civilizations. This "Aztec calendar," unearthed in 1790, appeared to demonstrate mathematical proficiency, elevating the knowledge its makers had from "superstition" to "science." The glyphs on the carving surround an image of the god Tonatiuh who is crowned with a sunbeam and arrayed with images of a jaguar's head and claws, a sky serpent, a feathered shield with an emblem of the sun, and a basketful of the remains of human sacrifice.

countries. Others, determined to remold the frontier in the image of home, were nonetheless seduced by the novelties of the New World, striking inland and seeking a new identity. By the eighteenth century, creolism was a strong Spanish-American ideology. Creole science responded to European scholars' contempt for America by arguing that American nature was superior to that of the Old World. The elite of Peru affected Inca dress and collected Inca artifacts. In Mexico, from the 1770s, discoveries of impressive Maya and Aztec antiquities boosted creole pride.

These movements had parallels in British colonies. Until independence in 1776, most of the leaders of the colonies that became the United States still thought of themselves as Englishmen, but the sense of being American was beginning to take shape. Americans were founding a new society, Thomas Jefferson thought, just as their Saxon ancestors had done when they left their native Germany for Britain. After the Revolutionary War, in the 1780s, the French traveler Michel-Guillaume Jean de Crèvecoeur, who had believed that American freedom was an overseas version of England's "national genius," revised his opinion. Americans, he thought, were "neither Europeans nor the descendants of Europeans" but "a new race of men."

Toward Independence

The America that broke away from Britain in the war of 1775–1783 was in many ways a new society. Immigrants' numbers had soared by a factor of ten within three generations. On the eve of the Revolution, the total population was probably over 2.5 million (see Figure 21.1). This astonishing increase had no parallel elsewhere in the New World. Between the mid–eighteenth century and the outbreak of the Revolution in 1775, the number of towns founded in New England tripled each year, as—roughly—did the populations of Georgia and South Carolina. In the 1760s, the population of New York rose by nearly 40 percent and Virginia's more than doubled.

From about 1760, a rush of settlers scaled the Appalachian Mountains to found a biblical "land of Canaan" between the Susquehanna and the Ohio Rivers. By 1771, 10,000 families were living on this frontier. The migrants came with alienated loyalties. Those from England were almost all young. More came from Scotland, mostly from the Highlands and Islands—regions subject to vicious political and religious persecution. Many of the hearts and minds in which the Revolution was conceived were those of newcomers, gripped by exciting possibilities. Independent America was, to a great extent, a nation of latecomers.

New Englanders could never fully participate in the landward turn. Mountains and the boundaries of rival states cut the maritime colonies off from the interior. The impoverished hinterland of New England drove work and wealth creation seaward, to the cod and whale fisheries and long-range trade.

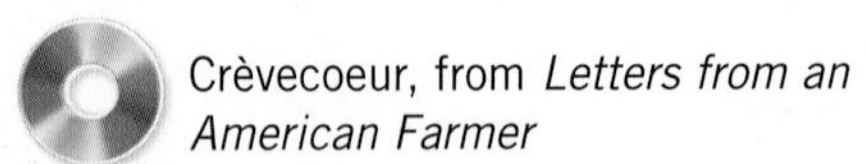

Crèvecoeur, from *Letters from an American Farmer*

In a sense, these were the wages of success. In the eighteenth century, New England's population outgrew its capacity to grow food. A trading vocation replaced the farming vocation with which the founding fathers had arrived. But the regulations of empire were a disadvantage for a trading people. New England's quarrels with Britain focused on barriers to trade and the freedom of the seas: disputes over what goods were legal to trade and what taxes merchants and consumers had to pay on those goods. The great symbolic acts of resistance that preceded the Revolutionary War happened offshore and made these issues explicit in acts of civil disobedience: the Boston Tea Party in 1773 and the seizure of the small British piracy-control *Gaspée* in Narragansett Bay, Rhode Island, in 1772.

Meanwhile, under the stress of war with France in the 1750s and 1760s and in the flush of victory that followed the end of France's American empire in 1763, Britain's attitude to America became more centralizing and interventionist. The British colonies had their own institutions and liberties that got in the way of some of the most crucial functions of government, especially housing troops and levying taxes. The new demands of the pre-Revolutionary years came not so much from the colonists as from a Britain anxious to exact efficiency from its empire. The threat to the colonies' habits of effective self-rule and cheap government provoked confrontation.

Moreover, British rule threatened two vital colonial interests. First, in 1772, a British judge declared slavery illegal on English soil, in a judgment that aroused premature anticipation among black Americans. It seemed only a matter of time before colonial slave owners clashed with an increasingly abolitionist elite in Britain. Second, the British government was determined to keep the peace on the "Indian" frontier and to preserve Native American buffer states between the British and Spanish Empires in the interior of North America. This was precisely where American colonists were looking to expand.

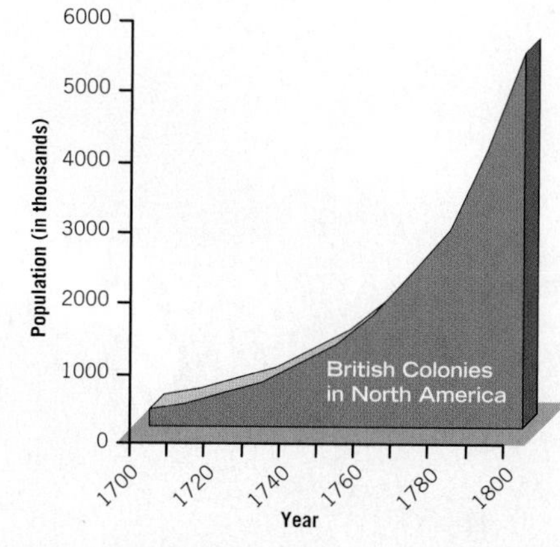

FIGURE 21.1 POPULATION GROWTH IN BRITISH NORTH AMERICA, 1700–1800
Historical Statistics of the United States (Washington, DC: Government Printing Office, 1976), 1168.

Increasing interventionism from Europe and increasing friction with colonial elites had parallels in the Spanish monarchy, where reformist governments also took increasingly burdensome measures in a similar spirit: reasserting controls, reorganizing defense, eliminating traditional colonial customs, maximizing the power and fiscal reach of the crown. In both empires, home governments encouraged militarization—mobilization and training for defense. These measures were a rational response to the problems of security in vast territories with ill-defined frontiers, but they created potential reservoirs of armed revolutionaries.

The Seven Years' War, which began in 1756 and ended in 1763, removed the French threat to the colonists' security with the British conquest of Canada and the French cession of Louisiana to Spain. The colonies were now free to challenge their rulers in England. By imposing high costs on imperial defense, the war encouraged Britain to seek new ways to tax America, with all the familiar consequences. It trained American fighters in the skills they would need if they were ever to challenge British forces. Military collaboration between American militias and British regulars exposed cultural differences. The floggings and other brutalities of discipline that troops in the British army were subject to repelled the volunteers in the colonial militias, while the British attacked colonial resistance to stationing troops in private houses, which was the usual practice in the British Empire, as "neglect of humanity" and "depravity of nature." The colonists saw themselves as true-born Englishmen but were shocked to find that their fellow countrymen from across the Atlantic did not share their self-perception. Mutual alienation led to violence.

Historians used to depict the uprising in 13 of the English mainland colonies in the 1770s as a peculiarly English affair—the inevitable outcome of traditions of freedom that colonists took with them from deep in the English past. On the contrary, current scholarship tells us, it was an improvised solution to short-term problems, a typical convulsion of a colonial world that was full of rebellions in the late eighteenth century: against the British government in the north of Ireland, against Spain in Colombia and Peru. The war was in one sense an English civil war, pitting self-styled free-born Englishmen against an intrusive government, recycling the rhetoric of seventeenth-century conflicts in Britain itself in which the "commonwealth" had fought the crown. At another level, it was an American civil war, in which at least 20 percent of the white population, and most of the black people and Native Americans, sided with the British. Increasingly, it also became an international conflict. After the first three years' campaigns, when the raw American forces proved surprisingly effective, France in 1778 joined by Spain in 1779 saw the opportunity to defeat the British. French intervention proved decisive, and the colonies that now began to call themselves the United States of America were the main beneficiaries (see Map 21.6).

British defeat. John Trumbull (1756–1843) painted the surrender of British to American forces at Yorktown in Virginia in 1781 in symbolic fashion. American General Benjamin Lincoln accepts the surrender on a horse with a raised forepaw—a traditional symbol of triumph, under a darkening sky that suggests the shadowing power of divine providence. Only the Americans are shown victorious in the painting, whereas the war against the British was brought to this conclusion thanks to French and Spanish help. A large French army participated in the siege of Yorktown, and the French fleet forced the surrender by preventing the British from escaping by sea.
John Trumbull (American 1756–1843), The Surrender of Lord Cornwallis at Yorktown, *19 October 1781, 1787-c. 1828. Oil on canvas, 53.3 × 77.8 × 1.9 cm (21 × 30 5/8 × 3/4 in.) Yale University Art Gallery, Trumbull Collection.*

The Spanish colonies, with their longer, stronger tradition of creole consciousness, were likely to follow the example of the northern revolutionaries. Indeed, rebellions and conspiracies multiplied in Spanish America during the 1770s and 1780s. Soon after the emergence of the independent United States, Alessandro Malaspina—one of the new scientifically trained Spanish naval officers—prepared an official fact-finding voyage across the Hispanic world: the most ambitious survey of the Americas and the Pacific ever undertaken. The results were dazzling—the product of the efforts of an enlightened government. Malaspina and the scholars who accompanied him gathered hundreds of thousands of samples, drawings, maps, and reports about plants, animals, native peoples, geology, climate, and the oceans.

Yet Malaspina was also responsible for reporting on the political state of the empire and the best measures of reform. Spanish America was poised between two possible futures. On the one hand, as Malaspina envisioned, Spain could delegate authority into provincial hands, slash defense costs, and open trade to universal competition. On the other, the monarchy could continue to attempt to enforce centralization, regulate trade to benefit Spain not the colonies, spend heavily for defense, and risk provoking the kind of revolution that had shattered Britain's American empire. Unfortunately, Malaspina's voyage outlasted the moment when the Spanish government might have embraced reform. By the time he returned to Spain in the 1790s, the French Revolution was under way, and the Spanish government was in no mood to embrace reform. Malaspina was disgraced, and the vast feedback of information from his scientific team was locked up in state archives. In America, two decades later, when French invaders immobilized the Spanish state, local elements, in both Spain and America, fell back on the old Spanish tradition of setting up local councils, or juntas, to handle emergencies. The American juntas saw little reason to accept a return to Spanish control, even after the French were driven from Spain in 1814.

The independence revolutions had similar causes across the Americas but differing outcomes. The Caribbean saw only one successful revolution: that of Haiti from 1791 to 1802 (see Chapter 19). Canada remained loyal to the British crown. Brazil was ruled until 1889 by emperors descended from the royal house of Portugal. This was understandable, since the Portuguese royal family chose exile in Brazil when France overran Portugal in 1807. Brazilian independence came almost bloodlessly in 1822 when a Portuguese prince was proclaimed Emperor Pedro I (see Map 21.6).

In the United States, foreign help shortened the war for independence, and the fighting, though traumatic, lasted barely eight years, from 1775 to 1783. The Spanish colonies had no such luck. Most of them were condemned to nearly two decades of merciless violence against Spanish armies. The wars of independence also ruined the economies of the Spanish colonies, whereas the United States, enjoying the protection of the French and Spanish navies, actually gained new trading partners and multiplied its shipping during its struggle against the British.

Slavery and Empire in the New World

1690s	Gold and diamonds replace sugar as Brazil's main revenue source
Eighteenth century	Imports of black slaves: English North America: approx. 400,000; Spanish colonies: approx. 1 million; Caribbean: approx. 1 million; Brazil: approx. 3 million; European expansion into South American pampa and North American prairie
1756–1763	Seven Years' War
1775–1783	American colonies gain independence from Britain
Late eighteenth century	Slaves are West Africa's most valuable export
1791–1802	Haiti gains independence from France
1822	Brazil proclaims independence from Portugal

IN PERSPECTIVE: The Rims of Empires

It was not only in the Americas that the rights of empires were questioned. When the French navigator Louis de Bougainville left Tahiti in the South Pacific in 1768, he set up a plaque with the words, "This land

is ours." A French satirist, Denis Diderot, who was also one of the most influential intellectuals of the mid–eighteenth century (see Chapter 22), had a fictional Tahitian reply: "If a Tahitian landed one day on your shores, and scratched on one of your rocks or the bark of your trees, 'This country belongs to the people of Tahiti,' what would you think?" Diderot went further: "Every colony, whose authority rests in one country and whose obedience is in another, is in principle a vicious establishment." Much of the European elite applauded the independence of the former colonies.

There was little revulsion of feeling between the mother countries and their rebellious children. The independence of most of the Americas might have split the

CHRONOLOGY

1690s	Gold and diamonds replace sugar as Brazil's main revenue source crop
Eighteenth century	China is world's fastest-growing empire; Chinese tax revenues increase by two-thirds; Persia and Ottoman populations static; Ottoman government goes into prolonged decline; Spanish, Dutch, and Portuguese expand holdings in southeast Asia; European expansion into South American pampa and North American prairie; scale of Atlantic slave trade increases
1707	Death of Aurangzeb and the end of Mughal expansion
1720	China conquers Tibet
1722	Safavid Empire collapses
1756–1757	Robert Clive leads East India Company (EIC) conquest of Bengal
1756–1763	Seven Years' War
1759	Chinese conquest of Xinjiang complete
1761–1764	EIC revenues: £2 million
1766–1767	EIC revenues: £7.5 million
1767	Burmese invasion leads to disintegration of Thailand
1771–1778	Vietnam collapses under strain of peasant rebellions
1774	Ottomans cede land to Russia in the Treaty of Küçük Kaynarca
1775–1783	American colonies gain independence from Britain
Late eighteenth century	Marathas offer only nominal obedience to the Mughals; slaves become West Africa's most valuable export
1780s	Spanish and French laws protect the rights of slaves
1789	French Revolution begins
1791–1802	Haiti gains independence from France
1799	British conquer Mysore
ca. 1800	200,000 Chinese immigrants settled in Xinjiang
1806	Maratha states accept British overlordship
1822	Brazil proclaims independence from Portugal

Atlantic world that had grown up in the previous three centuries. On the contrary, Atlantic trade continued to grow after the independence of most of the Americas, as did migration from Europe. Nor did conflict interrupt the exchange of ideas. Independence did, however, make a difference. The independent colonies had the prospect of becoming empires in their own right by expanding in their own hinterlands. For the United States, the outlook was particularly encouraging. The circumstances in which it achieved independence left the new country strong and wealthy, and the states had enormous, underexploited resources in nearby lands.

The exploitation of colonial frontiers had hardly begun. No recorded crossing of North America from the Atlantic to the Pacific was made until 1793. The interior of the hemisphere was so ill recorded that patriots in Washington, D.C., in the early 1800s were unsure where the Rocky Mountains were. Scholars in Europe did not know that the Amazon and the Orinoco Rivers in South America were connected until Baron von Humboldt—one of the world's most adventurous scientists—made the journey between them in 1800. Only a beginning had been made. Yet what had been achieved did matter.

Empire-building initiatives had become—for a while—almost a European monopoly. Native Asian empires had crumbled, or their expansion had largely halted. The nineteenth century saw few if any reversals comparable to those the Omanis had inflicted on the Portuguese, for instance. From now on, successful empire builders would need continually to update their war-making technology with industrially produced guns and ships. For most of the nineteenth century, only a few powers—European, for the most part, and the United States—had access to such technology.

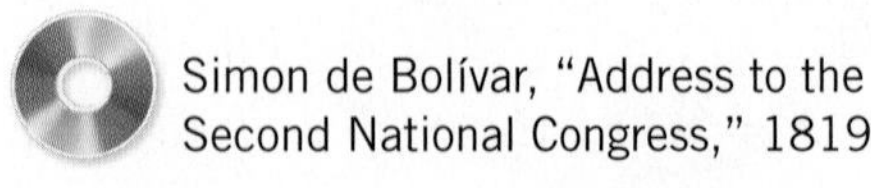

Simon de Bolívar, "Address to the Second National Congress," 1819

Though most of the world remained outside the rule of the empires of the age, imperialism had bridged some of the world's great chasms of communication. There were touch points of empire, at which the colonialism of rival powers met, in some of the most impenetrable places of the globe. In the late eighteenth century, Chinese and Japanese agents vied to collect tribute from native chiefs in Sakhalin Island, north of Japan, where Russia was also beginning to cast covetous looks. In the depths of Brazil, Portuguese soldiers wiped out the Jesuit missions in 1755, with Spanish permission, in a murderous rationalization of a previously vague frontier. In 1759, at Quebec tiny British and French armies of 2,000 or 3,000 men settled the fate of Canada in a battle the British won. In 1762–1763, the British occupied Spanish Manila in the Philippines, on the edge of the South China Sea, where the purely commercial maritime expansion of China had met the rival, armed imperialisms of Portugal, Holland, England, and Spain. In 1788, a French expedition anchored off Botany Bay in Australia only to find that a British colonizing venture—using convict exiles—had just beaten them to it.

In 1790, Britain and Spain almost went to war when Spanish forces seized British ships, dispatched from Sydney in Australia, at Nootka Sound, on the northwest coast of America, where British, Spanish, and Russian expansion converged. In 1796, the Spanish crown's glib Welsh agent, John Evans, persuaded the Mandan Indians of the upper Missouri to hoist the Spanish flag, defining a new frontier with the British Empire, represented by the formerly French fort of La Souris, two weeks' march away. The hand of empire may have lain lightly on some lands, but it stretched long fingertips over the world.

PROBLEMS AND PARALLELS

1. Where were the touch points of empire in the eighteenth century? Why did land empires expand in this period?
2. How did China use colonization and settlement to expand its territory? What impact did Chinese immigration have on southeast Asia?
3. How did the Ottoman, Mughal, Persian, Japanese, and Thai Empires lose impetus in this period?
4. Why did the British gain ascendancy in India? What are the parallels between British imperialism in India and the Spanish conquest of the Americas?
5. Why did the slave trade last so long in the Americas? What was the economic rationale for slavery?
6. How did black people in the Americas craft their own social customs and norms of behavior? Why were laws enacted to prevent marriage between blacks and whites?
7. How did ecological change and the presence of Europeans strengthen certain Native American peoples in the eighteenth century?
8. How did the growth of national identity affect relations between European mother countries and their colonies? Why did conflict between empires and the colonies have little impact on trade and the exchange of ideas?

DOCUMENTS IN GLOBAL HISTORY

- Qing dynasty guidelines for Tributary Missions, 1764
- View of Batavia, 1764
- Olaudah Equiano, excerpt from *The Interesting Narrative*
- The Code Noir (France)
- Phyllis Wheatley, "To The Right Honorable William, Earl of Dartmouth ..."
- Usuman da Fodio declares a jihad
- Plan of San Antonio, Texas, 1780
- Crèvecoeur, from *Letters from an American Farmer*
- Simon de Bolívar, "Address to the Second National Congress," 1819

Please see the Primary Source DVD for additional sources related to this chapter.

READ ON

On Mughal decline and the rise of British influence, J. Gommans, *Mughal Warfare: Indian Frontiers and Highroads to Empire 1500–1700* (2003) provides important background, and M., Hodgson, *The Venture of Islam, Volume 3: The Gunpower Empires and Modern Times* (1977) is a classic that also covers the Ottoman and Persian experiences in this age. D. Kolff, *Naukar, Rajput, and Sepoy: The Ethnohistory of the Military Labour Market of Hindustan, 1450–1850* (2002) shows the complexity of the political and military interaction between Indian and European powers. E. Rawski, *The Last Emperors* (1999) covers China and the slowing of Qing imperialism.

J. Cañizares-Esguerra and E. Seeman, eds., *The Atlantic in Global History: 1500–2000* (2006) is a broad-ranging introduction to the contours of Atlantic history, including the slave trade. H. Thomas, *The Slave Trade: The Story of the Atlantic Slave Trade, 1440–1870* (1999) is massively detailed and comprehensive. The classic firsthand account of Olaudah Equiano is readily available in *The Interesting Narrative and Other Writings* (2003).

Fascinating work is being done on the dynamics of American land empires in the late colonial period. See J. Canizares-Esguerra, *How to Write the History of the New World: Histories, Epistemologies, and Identities in the Eighteenth-Century Atlantic World* (2001), which is brilliant on creolism, while T. Burnard, *Creole Gentlemen: The Maryland Elite, 1691–1776* (2002) is excellent on the same phenomenon in North America. R. Price, ed., *Maroon Societies: Rebel Slave Communities in the Americas* (1996) collects important work on Atlantic slave rebellions. *The Malaspina Expedition, 1789 to 1794: Journal of the Voyage by Alejandro Malaspina: Cadiz to Panama,* ed. A. D. David, et al. (2002) provides a fascinating firsthand account of the Spanish crown's attempt to improve its knowledge of its American colonies, fix frontiers, improve scientific and geographical knowledge, and generate maps.

CHAPTER 22 The Exchange of Enlightenments: Eighteenth-Century Thought

As a portrait painter, the British artist Henry Perronet Briggs made a specialty of theatrical subjects. His study of Raja Rammohan Roy (1774–1833) seems romantic and dramatic, giving the Indian sage a visionary stare and a strange, vaguely oriental outfit, in a setting that seems to recall the Mughal Empire.

IN THIS CHAPTER

THE CHARACTER OF THE ENLIGHTENMENT

THE ENLIGHTENMENT IN GLOBAL CONTEXT
The Chinese Example
Japan
India
The Islamic World

THE ENLIGHTENMENT'S EFFECTS IN ASIA
The Enlightenment and China
Western Science in Japan
Korea and Southeast Asia
The Ottomans

THE ENLIGHTENMENT IN EUROPE
The Belief in Progress
New Economic Thought
Social Equality
Anticlericalism

THE CRISIS OF THE ENLIGHTENMENT: RELIGION AND ROMANTICISM
Religious Revival
The Cult of Nature and Romanticism
Rousseau and the General Will
Pacific Discoveries
Wild Children
The Huron as Noble Savage

THE FRENCH REVOLUTION AND NAPOLEON
Background to the Revolution
Revolutionary Radicalism
Napoleon

IN PERSPECTIVE: The Afterglow of Enlightenment

In 1829, a rumor reached the English Bishop of Calcutta. India's most respected thinker, Raja Rammohan Roy (1774–1833), had turned to Christianity. Roy had spent most of his life in Bengal under British rule, except for a period of study in London. He had become an admirer of Western ways, a master of Western languages, a scholar of Western science. As a teacher, he introduced his pupils to the writings of Western philosophers. He translated Western literature into Indian languages. He led movements to abolish female infanticide and the custom that required widows to burn themselves to death on their husband's funeral pyres. He argued for freedom for women.

In short, many observers saw Rammohan as representative of a new phase of global history: the slow but unstoppable triumph, from the late eighteenth century onward, of Western ideas, as Western power spread them around the world. Indeed, there is truth in that image. But it does not do justice to the complexity of Rammohan's thought or to the diversity of the traditions he inherited. He was a scholar of the Veda and of classical Persian literature long before he became a student of Western learning. His liberal, radical, humane, and skeptical notions were confirmed, not created, by Western influence. He sought not to turn India into an Eastern version of the West, but to use Western help to restore what he saw as a golden age of reason from India's own past. He rejected superstition and social abuses, whether they were Indian or Western.

The Western authors Rammohan loved and taught were those connected with the innovative movement of eighteenth-century European thought that we call the **Enlightenment**—writers who elevated reason, science, and practical utility, challenged conventional religion, and sought to expose cant. When the bishop of Calcutta congratulated him on his supposed conversion to Christianity, Rammohan denied it with the kind of irreverent wit he had picked up from European writers: "My Lord, I assure you, I did not abandon one superstition merely in order to take up another." The Enlightenment, indeed, was the source of the most powerful influences that spread from Europe over the world of the nineteenth and twentieth centuries. Even before the eighteenth century was over, the Enlightenment made a home in the Americas, with some modifications, and gripped fingerholds in Asia.

FOCUS questions

- WHAT WAS the Enlightenment and how did it influence Western social, political, and economic thinking?
- HOW DID China and Japan view Europe in the eighteenth century?
- WHY WERE the ideas of Rousseau so influential?
- WHY WAS there a reaction against the cult of reason, and what forms did it take?
- HOW DID Enlightenment ideas influence the course of the French Revolution and Napoleon's policies?
- WHAT INTELLECTUAL trends did Europe, the Americas, Islam, and east Asia have in common in the eighteenth century?

Moreover, the Englightenment was global in its inspiration as well as its effects. Historians have debated about where in northern or Western Europe the Enlightenment started. But this debate misses the fundamental contribution made by the interaction of Western European thought with ideas from overseas, and, in particular, from China.

The best way to approach the Enlightenment may be by first telling a story that expresses its character better than any attempt at a dictionary-style definition. We can then look at the global exchange of influences that surrounded enlightened ideas, the key texts that encoded them in Europe, and the changes that overtook and transformed the Enlightenment during the eighteenth century.

THE CHARACTER OF THE ENLIGHTENMENT

To understand what the Enlightenment was like, a good place to start is Kittis in northern Finland, near the Arctic Circle, where a French scientist, Pierre Louis Moreau de Maupertuis, pitched camp in August 1736. Maupertuis was engaged in the most elaborate and expensive scientific experiment ever conducted up to that time. Traditionally, Western scientists had assumed that the Earth was perfectly spherical. Seventeenth-century theorists, however, led by Isaac Newton in England, argued that it must be distended at the equator and flattened at the poles, owing to centrifugal force (the thrust or sense of thrust you get on the edge of a circle in motion, which tends, for instance, to fling you off a merry-go-round). Meanwhile, mapmakers working on the survey of France had made a series of observations that suggested the contrary. The world seemed to be elongated toward the poles. To resolve the debate, the French Royal Academy of Science sent expeditions—of which Maupertuis's was one—to measure the length of one degree along the surface of the circumference of the Earth. If measurements at the Arctic Circle matched those at the equator, the globe was spherical. Any difference between them either way would indicate where the world bulged (see Map 22.1).

Pierre Louis de Maupertuis (1698–1759), on his return from the Arctic in 1737, seems to flatten the globe in this portrait by the French artist Robert Lervac-Tournières. The hero points the way forward. A map of the area he surveyed in Finland is on the table, with the Laplanders' fur-lined cap he wore on his expedition.

In December 1736, Maupertuis began his measurements with rods made of fir, because it was least likely to shrink from the cold. His readings helped to convince the world that the planet was indeed squashed at the poles and bulging at the equator. On the front page of his collected works, he appears in a fur cap and collar over a eulogy that reads, "It was his destiny to determine the shape of the world."

Like many scientific explorers seared by experience, Maupertuis eventually became disillusioned by science but inspired by nature. He set off believing that every truth was quantifiable and that every fact could be sensed. By the time he died in 1759, he had become something of a mystic. "You cannot chase God in the immensity of the heavens," he concluded, "or the depths of the oceans or the chasms of the Earth. Maybe it is not yet time to understand the world systematically—time only to behold it and be amazed." Perhaps, he speculated, only God exists, and perceptions are illusions of a mind "alone in the universe."

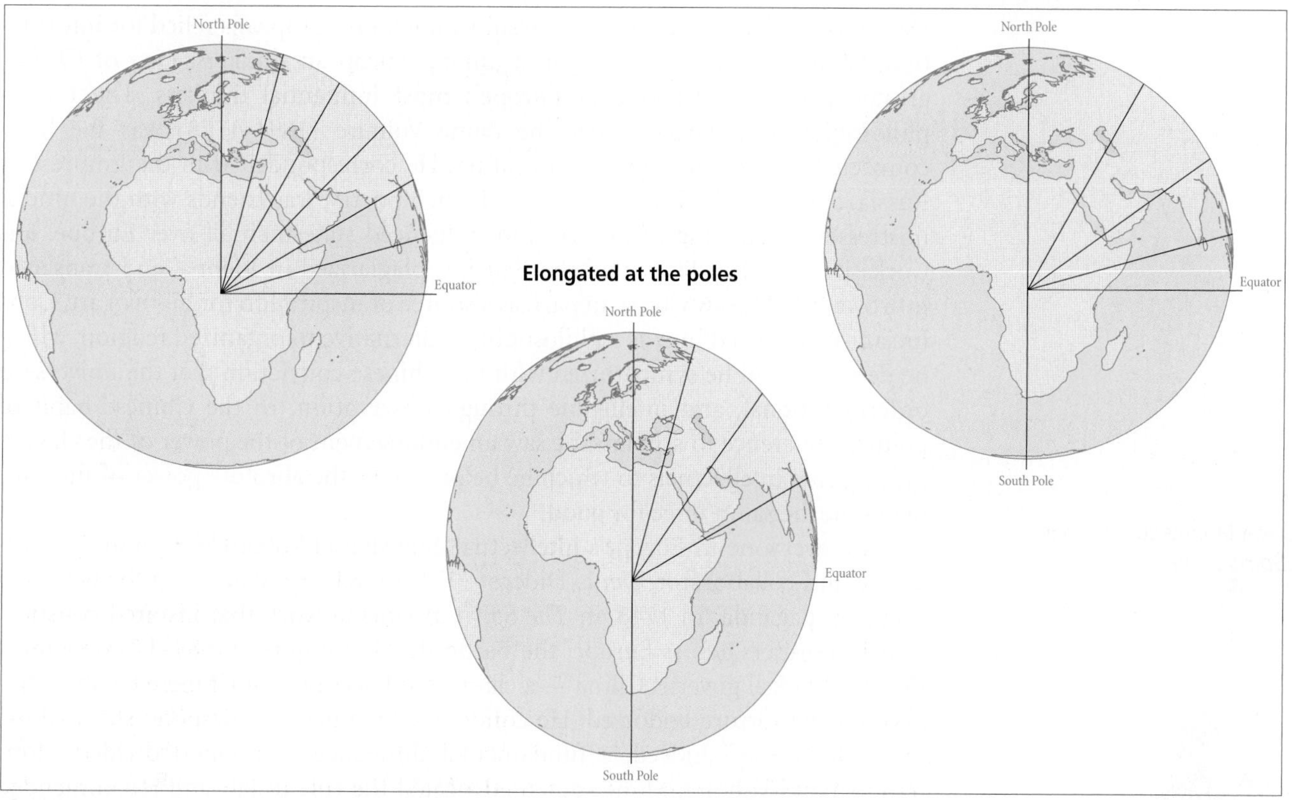

MAP 22.1 **The Shape of the Earth**

Maupertuis's mental pilgrimage between certainty and doubt, science and speculation, rationalism and religious revelation reproduced in miniature the history of European thought in the eighteenth century. First, in a surge of optimism, the perfectibility of humankind, the infallibility of reason, the reality of the observed world, and the sufficiency of science became common assumptions. In the second half of the century, the Enlightenment flickered as intellectuals rediscovered the power of feelings over reason and sensations over thoughts. Then revolutionary bloodshed and warfare, in which the century ended, seemed to extinguish the torch completely. But embers remained: enduring faith that freedom can energize human goodness, that happiness is worth pursuing in this life, and that science and reason—despite their limitations—can unlock progress and enhance lives.

THE ENLIGHTENMENT IN GLOBAL CONTEXT

During the eighteenth century, despite the long reach of some European empires, China's was, as we saw in Chapter 21, still the fastest-growing empire in the world. China also looked more modern than any society you could find in the West. It was a better-educated society, with over a million graduates from a demanding educational system, and a more entrepreneurial society, with bigger businesses and bigger clusters of mercantile and industrial capital than you could find anywhere else. It was a more industrialized society, with higher levels of production in more specialized concentrations, and a more urbanized society, with denser distributions of population. China's was even—for adult males—a more egalitarian society, in which the hereditary landed gentry had to defer to scholar-bureaucrats who were drawn from every level of rank and wealth.

The Chinese Example

Described with admiration by the Jesuits on whom Europeans relied for information, China excited positive interest among European thinkers. One of China's greatest fans was also one of Europe's most influential thinkers. The French philosopher who wrote under the name Voltaire (1694–1778) was the best-connected man of the eighteenth century. He corresponded with the Empress of Russia, corrected the King of Prussia's French poetry, was friends with the official mistresses of the king of France, and influenced statesmen all over Europe. His works were read in Sicily and the Balkans, plagiarized in Vienna, and translated into Swedish. He saw China, in part, as a source of inspiration for his own art. Confucianism attracted him as a philosophical alternative to organized religion, which he detested. And he sympathized with the Chinese conviction that the universe is orderly, rational, and intelligible through observation. In the Chinese habit of political deference to scholars, he saw an endorsement of the power of the class of professional intellectuals to which he belonged. In the absolute power of the Chinese state, he saw a force for good.

Baron de Montesquieu, from *The Spirit of the Laws*

Not everyone in Europe's intellectual elite shared Voltaire's opinion. His colleague and collaborator, Denis Diderot (1713–1784), ridiculed him for believing Jesuit propaganda. In 1748, in *The Spirit of Laws*, a work that inspired constitutional reformers across Europe, the Baron de Montesquieu (1689–1755) claimed that "the cudgel governs China"—a claim Jesuit accounts of Chinese harsh justice and judicial torture endorsed. He condemned China as "a despotic state, whose principle is fear." Indeed, a fundamental difference of opinion divided Montesquieu and Voltaire. Montesquieu advocated the rule of law and recommended that constitutional safeguards should limit governments. Voltaire never really trusted the people and felt that strong, well-advised governments could best judge the people's interests. Montesquieu, moreover, developed an influential theory, according to which Western political traditions were benign, and tended toward liberty, whereas Asian states were despotic and concentrated power in the hands of tyrants. "This," he wrote, "is the grand reason of the weakness of Asia, and of the strength of Europe; of the liberty of Europe and of the slavery of Asia." *Oriental despotism* became a term of abuse in Western political writing. François Quesnay (1694–1774), Voltaire's colleague, who echoed the idealization of China, countered that "enlightened despotism" would favor the people rather than elites. He even persuaded the heir to the French throne to imitate a Chinese imperial rite by plowing land in person as an example to agrarian improvers.

Voltaire. When Voltaire died in 1778, the sculptor Jean-Antoine Houdon (1741–1828) used the great writer's death mask (a plaster cast of the face made just after a person died) to represent him realistically. But this sculpture remains highly charged with symbolic meaning. Voltaire is robed like an ancient philosopher-sage; his hands are wrinkled with useful toil; a sardonic smile represents his use of irony and humor to challenge the institutions of church and state.

One way or another, whether you favored China or rejected its examples, Chinese models seemed to be shaping European political thought. By the 1760s, a satirist in England could complain that busts of Confucius were replacing those of Plato and Aristotle and that instead of relying on the classics, "we take our learning from the wise Chinese." The dramatist Oliver Goldsmith (1728–1774) composed fictional *Letters of a Chinese Philosopher* to express disapproval of English society.

Meanwhile, Chinese influence was changing elite taste in Europe. Until the eighteenth century, China exercised its artistic influence on the West almost entirely through porcelain, lacquers, and textiles. Now Chinese wallpaper became accessible to a rich elite, and European furniture and dishes were decorated with Chinese themes. The French painter Jean-Antoine Watteau's (1684–1721) designs of Chinese scenes to decorate an apartment for King Louis XIV inaugurated a taste for Chinese-style schemes. It spread through the palaces of the Bourbon dynasty, which ruled France, Spain, and Naples, and was connected by marriage with many of Europe's other royal families. From Bourbon courts, the Chinese look radiated through Europe. In England, the king's son, the Duke of Cumberland, sailed on a fake Chinese pleasure boat. William Halfpenny's *Chinese and Gothic Architecture* (1752) was the first of many books to treat Chinese art as equivalent to Europe's. The fashionable British architect Sir Willim Chambers designed a pagoda for Kew Gardens in London and Chinese furniture for aristocratic homes, while "Chinese" Thomas Chippendale, England's leading cabinetmaker, popularized Chinese themes for furniture. By midcentury, engravings of Chinese scenes hung even in middle-class French and Dutch homes.

Japan

Enthusiasm embraced Japan as well as China. Jesuits, of course, did not praise Japan, whose rulers had expelled them in the 1630s. Since then, Japanese governments had persecuted Christianity. The Japanese policy of excluding foreigners kept Europe ignorant of Japanese life. But the Dutch East India Company's trade with Japan opened a window. Engelbert Kaempfer, a company envoy, published the most influential account of Japan in 1729. His portrait of a people in "slavery and submission" fed into European ideas for centuries to come, but he was also frank about the peace, order, and prosperity he observed. Opinion about Japan in Europe split as it did over China. Montesquieu saw Japan as an oriental despotism. Voltaire saw it as the embodiment of "the laws of nature in the laws of a state."

India

Voltaire found an even better model in India. In 1756, he published *Dialogue Between a Brahman and a Jesuit*. The Brahman speaks with Voltaire's voice. He wants, above all, "a state in which the laws are obeyed." Voltaire's work on India was more profound than his assertions about China and Japan, because he recognized how much Western thought owed to Indian civilization. "It is probable," he averred, "that the Brahmins were the first legislators of the earth, the first philosophers, the first theologians." The study in the West of Asian languages strengthened this contention. The Collège Royal in France introduced Chinese studies in the 1730s, but Jesuit work on Indian languages, especially Sanskrit, facilitated the most remarkable disclosure. In 1786, the English scholar Sir William Jones realized that Sanskrit—the language of the Indian classics—was related to Latin and Greek and probably shared with them a common root.

The Islamic World

Muslim Turkey and Persia, too, influenced Western minds in the eighteenth century, mainly as sources of exotic imagery, and also, in Turkey's case, as a model of good and bad government. Montesquieu added objectivity and credibility to his critiques of Western society in his *Persian Letters* (1721) by pretending that they were the work of a Persian sage. Playwrights favored Turkish settings and characters for social satire. In 1782, Mozart's comic opera, *The Abduction from the Seraglio*, showed Turks outfoxing Europeans and exceeding them in generosity. Turkey was often cited as a model for hygiene, education, charitable institutions, and what a late seventeenth-century traveler praised as "order, ... economy and the regulation of provisions." In 1774, Simon-Nicolas-Henri Linguet pointed out that in Turkey and Persia the Quran protected liberty by restraining the power of rulers. Well-informed observers commended the Ottomans for religious toleration,

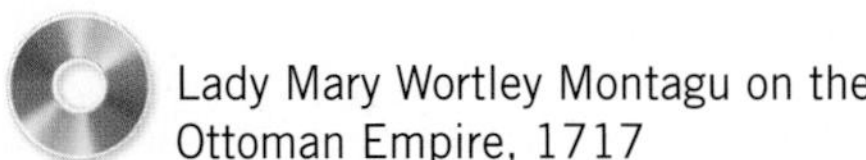
Lady Mary Wortley Montagu on the Ottoman Empire, 1717

Concubine. In the eighteenth century, Chinese emperors inaugurated a fashion at the imperial court for having one's portrait painted in Western dress. Here the favorite concubine of the Qianlong emperor (r. 1735–1796) wears a Western suit of armor. The artist, Giuseppe Castiglione, was a member of the Jesuit mission in China from 1730 until 1768. He also helped design the gardens of the imperial summer palace, with their complicated series of fountains that constituted a feat of hydraulic engineering.

respect for laws, customs, and property rights, and benevolence toward minorities—the very virtues that some Enlightenment thinkers thought that Europe lacked.

Nonetheless, during the eighteenth century, European critics of Ottoman life and customs became increasingly strident. Features of government formerly praised as evidence of strength and wisdom—the lack of a governing aristocracy, for instance, the docility of the sultan's subjects, the vulnerability of high officeholders to the sultan's mood—came to be seen as arbitrary and despotic. Turkey, even more than China, became a reference point for denunciations of oriental despotism. "In such distressful regions," wrote a follower of Montesquieu, "man is seen to kiss his chains, without any certainty as to fortune and property; he adores his tyrant; and without any knowledge of humanity or reason, is reduced to have no other virtue but fear."

THE ENLIGHTENMENT'S EFFECTS IN ASIA

European interest in Asia transformed Europe but changed Asia only a little.

The Enlightenment and China

Historians have generally regarded the Chinese attitude to European ideas at the time as arrogant, unrealistic, and restricted by outmoded traditions. But Westerners had always had more to learn from China than the other way round. Even in the eighteenth century, the inferiority of the West was only beginning to be reversed. So it is not surprising that the Chinese were still selective in their receptivity to Western ideas. At the beginning of the century, when Jesuits were already installed as the emperors' favorite astronomers, mapmakers, and technicians (see Chapter 18), one of them, Father Chavagnac, complained that the Chinese still "cannot be persuaded that anything which is not of China deserves to be regarded." Chavagnac found it particularly distressing that Chinese scholars still expressed skepticism when he showed them his map of the world. "They all cried out, 'So where is China?' 'It is this small spot of land,' said I. 'It seems very little,'" was their reply.

Nevertheless, the Jesuits extended their activities at court. "Every day," they claimed in letters home during the reign of the Kangxi emperor (r. 1661–1722), "from two hours before noon to two hours after noon, we were at the emperor's side, lecturing on Euclid's geometry, or on physics, astronomy, etc." The emperor commissioned Jesuits to map inner Asia and commanded the translation of Western mathematical works and all the texts Jesuits recommended on the calendar. The Yongzheng (yung-jheng) emperor (r. 1722–1735) restricted missionaries' freedom to make converts but had himself painted in a Western curled wig and coat. For the Qianlong emperor (r. 1735–1796), European artists painted his favorite concubine dressed in Western armor. Other Jesuits designed his gardens and engineered its fountains and mechanical statues.

Western technology made its biggest impact, perhaps, on war. In 1673, the emperor threatened to expel all Christians from China unless the Jesuits consented to design and manufacture artillery for him. The priests' designs continued in use until the mid–nineteenth century. They supervised gunnery practice, under compulsion, insisting that they were men of peace. In the mid-1780s, when news of hot-air balloons in the West reached the Chinese court, the Chinese immediately inquired about its possible military applications. Nonetheless, Westerners still seemed just clever barbarians to the Chinese, useful in their place, dangerous when they aimed higher.

Western Science in Japan

Admiration for the West penetrated deeper—though still not very deep—in Japan. The shogun Yoshimune (r. 1716–1745) took an interest in science and technology comparable to Kangxi's. From 1720, he allowed Chinese translations of Western books to circulate in Japan. The Japanese scholar Miura Baien (1723–1789) recognized that Western astronomy had revolutionized knowledge of the universe. Like many Western philosophers of the time, he advocated practical utility and technical efficiency above traditional values. "A tiny lantern that lights humble homes," he wrote, "is worth more than gems." Yet it was hard to find ways to promote Western knowledge. Japan's seventeenth-century experience (see Chapter 19) still made its government determined to exclude Christianity and limit foreign access to the country. Since the representatives of the Dutch East India Company were the only Europeans allowed in Japan—and even then only under tight restrictions—access to scientific information was haphazard. Japanese scholars had no way to judge what information was accurate or up to date. The interpreters who negotiated with the Dutch worked exclusively in Portuguese, the traditional language of Western commerce in east Asia. To read Western books, Japanese scholars had to teach themselves Dutch from scratch.

The case of Rembert Dodens's *Crudetboeck*, a Dutch study of plants published in 1554, is instructive. In 1659, a Dutch embassy presented an edition of 1618 to the shogun. Hidden away in the palace library, it was extracted at Yoshimune's command in 1717, in the belief that it might contain useful medical knowledge. It was handed over to a translator, who eventually produced his translation in 1750. The work was by then nearly 200 years out of date. The same translator worked on another supposed guide to plants for 24 years before realizing that it was a zoological work that had no medical information.

title page from a Japanese anatomy text, 1775

A breakthrough came only in 1771, when the dissection of a corpse demonstrated the accuracy of European books of anatomy. A group of enthusiastic beginners in "Dutch studies" started meeting six or seven times a month to puzzle over the meaning of Western books. "After about a year," wrote one of them, "we became capable of reading as much as ten or more lines of text per day if the particular passage was not too difficult."

So China remained the dominant intellectual influence in Japan, and Confucianism remained the foundation of Japanese thought. Most new developments came not from the West but from Japanese reactions against Confucianism. Independently, Japanese thinkers discovered principles similar to those philosophical radicals in Europe and America advocated: the virtues, especially, of universal reason—*ri*, the Japanese called it—approached scientifically, through observation. Ogyu Sorai (1666–1728) advocated experience in place of speculation as the key to truth. "History," he declared, "is ultimate knowledge." Tominaga Nakamoto (1715–1746) went further, doubting the possibility of any universally valid statements because experience seemed too diverse. In 1713, Kaibara Ekken argued that nature was in constant flux and so could only be understood by observation, not by the grand generalizations of Confucian theory. Some radicals embraced an egalitarian theory of human nature. Ishida Baigan (1685–1744), an advocate of reason as the unique means to truth, was one of many teachers who opened their classes to people of modest social backgrounds, in the belief that commoners had the same mental powers as the gentry.

A CLOSER LOOK

A MEETING OF CHINA, JAPAN, AND THE WEST

Eastern and Western Enlightenments meet in this late eighteenth-century Japanese painting on silk.

In the background, firefighting teams from Japan, China, and Holland tackle the same blaze with their respective techniques. The Dutch seem to be most effective.

The Japanese man, who seems the dominant presence, in this discussion group, is perhaps a self-portrait of the artist, Shiba Kokan, who played a big part in promoting "Dutch learning" in Japan. His position near the European suggests his admiration for Western science.

The unidentified Dutchman displays a book of anatomy—one of the sciences in which the Japanese acknowledged Western superiority. The closeness of the Dutch and Japanese figures is emphasized, while the Chinese participant sits somewhat apart, listening critically.

How does this painting illustrate the global exchange of ideas in the eighteenth century?

Korea and Southeast Asia

In Korea and Vietnam, too, national revulsions from Confucianism and Chinese cultural dominance stimulated new thinking. In Korea, the movement called "practical learning" started as a reaction against Confucianism but acquired knowledge of Western technology by way of China. A design for a Western crane, copied from a Chinese book, helped to build a castle. Koreans began to model world maps on Western examples. In the mid–eighteenth century, Yi Ik began a systematic study of Western learning in Chinese books. In the 1780s, Korean intellectuals founded a society to introduce Catholicism into the country. In Vietnam, meanwhile, the most remarkable echo of new ideas from the West appeared in the work of the poet Ho Xuang Huong. "Down with husband-sharing!" she exclaimed when her husband took a second wife. "One [wife] rolls in warm blankets, the other freezes. . . . I've turned into a half-servant, an unpaid maid! Had I known, I would have stayed single."

Other Asian cultures were even less hospitable to Western thought. In Thailand, an exchange of embassies with France in the 1680s stimulated, at first, enormous interest in both countries. For the French, Thailand offered a model of the exotic. For the Thai, the French presented an insight into the Western technical proficiency already admired in China. Kosa Pan, the Thai envoy to France, took home a large collection of European maps, and the French mission to Thailand established an observatory in the royal palace. The king attended lectures by Jesuit astronomers. But Western influence in Thailand receded after a palace revolution there in 1688.

The Ottomans

Inhibited by Muslim religious scruples, the Turks and Persians, too, were slow to open up to the worldwide exchange of ideas. The first printing press in Turkey was only set up in 1729. When the authorities closed it down in 1742, it had produced

MAKING CONNECTIONS

ENLIGHTENMENT INFLUENCES IN ASIA

COUNTRY/REGION →	EXAMPLES OF INFLUENTIAL IDEAS →	SOURCES →	SOCIAL/POLITICAL/ECONOMIC CONSEQUENCES
China	Western astronomy, mathematics, scientific methods, technology	Jesuit missionaries; European diplomats	Imperial leaders collect Western mechanical devices; use Western-designed artillery
Japan	Western astronomy, mathematics, scientific methods, technology; Japanese concepts of universal reason, scientific observation	Dutch diplomats, merchants; Japanese thinkers (Sorai, Nakamoto, Ekken)	Restrictions on trade and interaction limit exposure to Western ideas, technology; Japanese ideas spread more rapidly as reaction against Confucianism
Korea, Vietnam	Korea: "practical learning"	Korea: reaction against Confucianism and interest in Western technology, religious inspiration	Korea: development of new technology aids in construction, mapmaking; Catholicism introduced by intellectuals
	Vietnam: interest in women's rights	Vietnam: Ho Xuang Huong (writer)	Vietnam: critique of traditional marriage practices

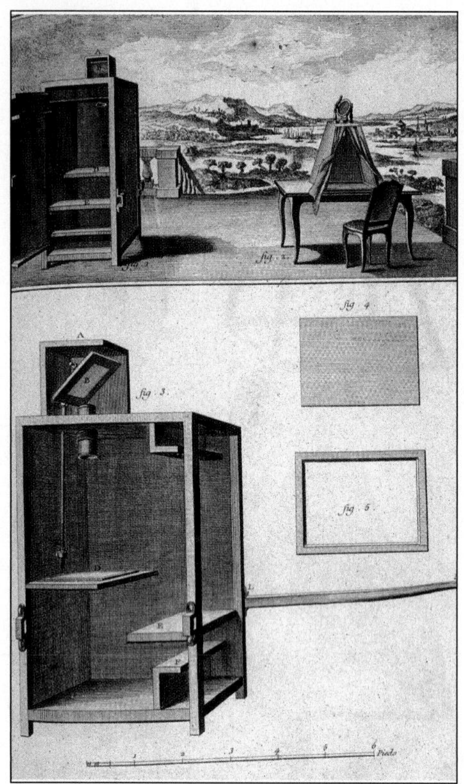

Camera obscura. Denis Diderot's *Encyclopedia* promoted technology and "useful" knowledge—in this case, the construction of a camera obscura, which was the forerunner of modern photography. The camera obscura captured an image by projecting rays of light from an object through a pinprick opening onto the inner wall of a chamber. Painters used this technique to ensure realism in their art.

only 17 titles. In 1798, French armies invaded Egypt and Syria, leaving—after their early withdrawal—seeds of Western thinking. Here, as in India, aspects of Western thought were only enthusiastically embraced in the nineteenth century after unmistakable demonstrations of Western military strength (see Chapter 25).

THE ENLIGHTENMENT IN EUROPE

Even in Europe, new thinking met distrust, censorship, and persecution. To understand why—and to identify the defining themes of the thought of the time—the best source is the French *Encyclopedia*, subtitled *Reasoned Dictionary of the Sciences, Arts and Trades*, which appeared in 17 volumes of texts and 11 volumes of illustrations between 1751 and 1772. By 1779, about 25,000 sets had been sold throughout Europe, in the teeth of condemnation by reactionary governments and established churches. This may not seem many, but the ideas the *Encyclopedia* contained reached the entire European elite, one way or another, and circulated in countless spinoff works. Diderot, who masterminded the project, wanted a comprehensive work that would "start from and return to Man," while covering every intellectual discipline along the way. The *Encyclopedia*, he announced, would "assemble the knowledge scattered over the face of the Earth ... that we may not die without having deserved well of mankind."

Of course, the book had a slant. First, its values were practical. It emphasized utility, engineering, mechanics, technology. There was, according to Diderot, "more intelligence, wisdom, and consequence in a machine for making stockings" than "in a system of metaphysics." Second, the writers advocated reason and science as means to truth. Third, although the contributors by no means agreed among themselves on questions of political philosophy, the *Encyclopedia* was generally critical of Europe's monarchies and aristocracies. Drawing on the English thinker, John Locke (1632–1704), most contributors on political questions favored constitutional guarantees of the liberty of the citizen against the state. Many insisted on the "natural equality" of all men. Finally, the work was uniformly hostile to organized religion.

The Belief in Progress

Only optimists could have undertaken such an ambitious project. To make progress credible, someone had to think up a way to understand evil, and explain away the woes of the world. Theologians had never satisfactorily answered the atheists' challenge, "If God is good, why is there evil?" In the seventeenth century, the growth of atheism made the task seem urgent. In 1710, the German philosopher Leibniz (1646–1716) did so. He was the most wide-ranging thinker of his day, combining philosophy, theology, mathematics, linguistics, physics, and law with his role as a courtier in Hanover. He started from a truth witnessed in everyday experience: Good and evil are inseparable, because each is meaningless without the other. Freedom, for example, is good, but must include freedom to do evil. Altruism is good only if selfishness is an option. But of all logically conceivable worlds, ours has, by divine decree, the greatest possible surplus of good over evil. So—in the phrase Voltaire used to mock this theory—"All is for the best in the best of all possible worlds." Even then, believers in progress feared that it was merely a phase, enjoyed by their own times, but exceptional by the standards of history in general. The Marquis de Condorcet (see Chapter 21), for instance, thought he could see "the human race ... advancing with a sure step along the path of truth, virtue, and happiness" only because political and intellectual revolutions had subverted the crippling effects of religion and tyranny. The human spirit was now at last "emancipated from its shackles" and "released from the empire of fate."

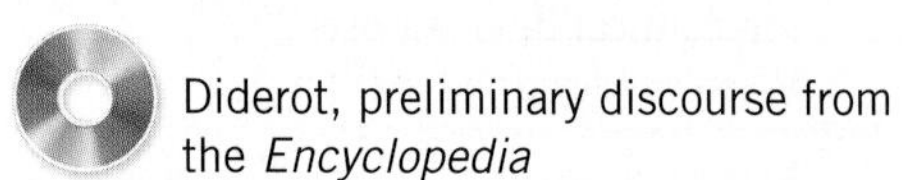

Diderot, preliminary discourse from the *Encyclopedia*

New Economic Thought

If you believe in human goodness, you believe in freedom. Pessimists about human nature favor strong, even repressive governments to keep destructive instincts in check. Optimists hope to liberate people to do good. Montesquieu and the authors of the *Encyclopedia* were particularly concerned to recommend political freedom, but economic freedom was an equally important theme.

Free trade was a new doctrine. Long experience of an unfavorable trade balance with Asia had induced two obsessions in Western economic thought: Bullion—gold and silver—is the basis of wealth; and to grow rich, an economy must sell more than it buys. According to the Spanish moralist Tomás de Mercado, what "destroys this abundance and causes poverty is the export of money." All European governments believed this. To evade impoverishment they hoarded bullion, trapping cash inside the realm, limiting imports and exports, regulating prices, defying laws of supply and demand, and founding empires to create markets for their goods.

The consequences were woeful. Overseas investment was restricted, except in imperial ventures. The protection of trade nourished inefficiency and squandered resources. Competition for protected markets caused wars. Money drained out of circulation. These conditions, which inhibited economic growth, were much criticized from the late seventeenth century onward. The eighteenth-century French school of economists known as the physiocrats devised the slogan **laissez-faire** to mean "leave the market to itself." The British economist David Ricardo (see Chapter 21) agreed. "Wages," he recommended, "should be left to the fair and free competition of the market, and should never be controlled by the interference of the legislature." The decisive moment in the shift toward economic freedom came in 1776, when the Scots professor of moral philosophy, Adam Smith, published *The Wealth of Nations*.

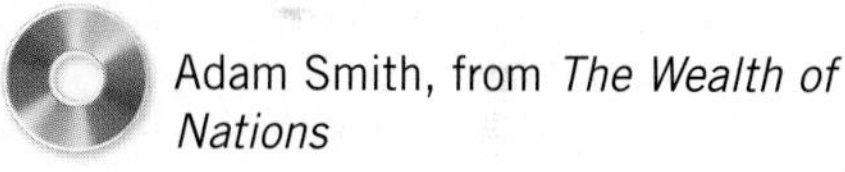
Adam Smith, from *The Wealth of Nations*

Smith had a lofty view of the law of supply and demand, believing that it affected more than the market. "The natural effort of every individual to better his own condition" was the foundation of all political, economic, and moral systems. Self-interest could be left to serve the common good. "It is not from the benevolence of the butcher, the brewer or the baker that we expect our dinner, but from their regard to their own interest." The rich, Smith declared, "in spite of their natural selfishness and rapacity, are led by an invisible hand to make nearly the same distribution of the necessaries of life which would have been made, had the earth been divided into equal portions among all its inhabitants."

The Wealth of Nations appeared in the same year as the Declaration of Independence and should be counted among the United States' founding documents. It encouraged the American Revolution, for Smith said that government regulations limiting the freedom of colonies to engage in manufacture or trade were "a manifest violation of the most sacred rights of mankind." The United States has remained the homeland of economic liberalism ever since.

Social Equality

Smith claimed that freedom would deliver equality. This is not necessarily true, but it was characteristic of the time. Reason suggested that all men are naturally equal. So what about women? Montesquieu saw no reason to exclude them. The ideas we now call **feminism**—that women collectively constituted a class of society, historically oppressed and deserving emancipation—appeared in two works of 1792, the *Declaration of the Rights of Woman and of the Female Citizen* by Marie-Olympes de

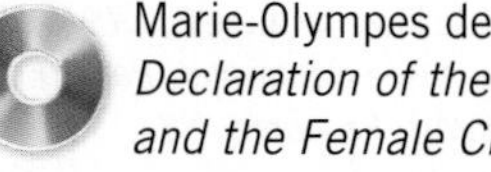
Marie-Olympes de Gouges, *Declaration of the Rights of Woman and the Female Citizen*

Mary Wollstonecraft, *A Vindication of the Rights of Woman*

Gouges and *A Vindication of the Rights of Woman* by Mary Wollstonecraft. Both authors had to struggle to earn their living. Both died tragically. Wollstonecraft died in childbirth in 1797 at the age of 38. De Gouges was guillotined in 1793 during the French Revolution for defending the king and queen of France. Both writers rejected the previous tradition of female championship, which praised women for their domestic and maternal virtues. Instead, they admitted women's vices and blamed male oppression.

Anticlericalism

For most of the philosophers who worked on the *Encyclopedia*, the great obstacle to progress was the Church. They catalogued the crimes of the Church—inquisitions, persecutions, clerical abuses of power. The article on cannibalism referred to articles on the Eucharist, Communion, altar, and such. "We must show that we are better than Christians," wrote Diderot, "and that science makes more good men than grace." Voltaire erected his own temple to "the architect of the universe, the great geometrician" but regarded Christianity as an "infamous superstition to be eradicated—I do not say among the rabble, who are not worthy of being enlightened and who are apt for every yoke, but among the civilized and those who wish to think." Many people in France ceased to mention God and the saints in their wills. Donations to religious foundations dwindled. King Louis XV (r. 1715–1774) abandoned the traditional rites of laying supposedly healing royal hands on the sick, because he found belief in miracles embarrassing.

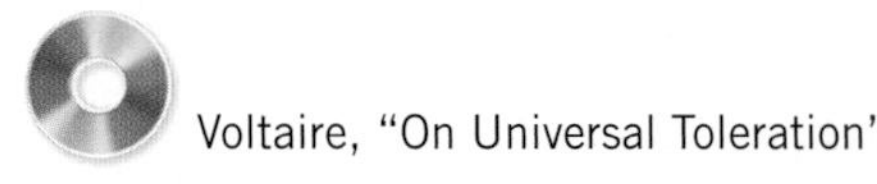

Voltaire, "On Universal Toleration"

We can measure the progress of the Enlightenment in anticlerical acts. In 1759, Portugal expelled the Jesuits and confiscated their property. In 1762, Catherine the Great of Russia secularized a great portfolio of church property. Between 1764 and 1773, the Jesuit Order was abolished in most of the rest of the West. In the 1780s, governments in parts of Europe confiscated church lands and forced 38,000 monks and nuns into lay life. In 1790, the King of Prussia proclaimed absolute authority over clergy in his realm, both Protestant and Catholic. Meanwhile, among the European elite, the cult of reason was taking on the characteristics of an alternative religion. In the secret ceremonies of freemasonry, a profane hierarchy celebrated

"The cult of reason was taking on the characteristics of an alternative religion." For Catholicism, reason is a gift of God and can enlighten faith, but eighteenth-century critics in France denounced the Church for smothering reason and encouraging superstition. They also hated the Church for wasting—as they thought—economic resources and supporting an oppressive political order. Many of them advocated deism—belief in God, without the supposed irrational doctrines of Christianity. In 1794, this "cult of the Supreme Being" briefly replaced Catholicism as the official religion of France, in a gaudy ceremony presided over by the head of a group of fanatics who had seized power during the Revolution.

Pierre-Antoine Demachy, Festival of the Supreme Being at the Champ de Mars on June 8, 1794. *Musée de la Ville de Paris, Musée Carnavalet, Paris, France. Bridgeman-Giraudon/Art. Resource, NY*

the purity of its own wisdom, brilliantly portrayed in Mozart's opera *The Magic Flute*, first performed in 1791. In 1794, the French revolutionary government tried to replace Christianity with the cult of the Supreme Being.

To some extent, the success of science encouraged mistrust of religion. From John Locke, eighteenth-century radicals inherited the conviction that it was "fiddling" to waste time thinking about what, if anything, lay beyond the scientifically observed world. The evidence of our senses was all true and—with certain exceptions about sound and color that experiments could confirm—it was all caused by the real objects our senses seemed to disclose to us: The jangling is proof of the bell, the heat of the fire, the stink of the gas. "Freethinking" atheism got a boost from the microbial world, with its apparent evidence of spontaneous generation. The very existence of God—or at least, the validity of claims about God's unique power to create life—was at stake.

John Locke, *Essay Concerning Human Understanding,* 1689

THE CRISIS OF THE ENLIGHTENMENT: RELIGION AND ROMANTICISM

This attitude, however, which we would now call *scientism*, did not satisfy all its practitioners. The Scottish philosopher David Hume (1711–1776) pointed out that sensations are not really evidence of anything except themselves—that objects cause them is just an unverifiable assumption. Many scientists, like Maupertuis, drifted back from atheism toward religion or speculated about truths beyond the reach of science. In 1799, with the aid of a powerful microscope, Lorenzo Spallanzani observed fission—cells reproducing by splitting. He demonstrated that if heating killed bacteria they could not reappear in a sealed environment. He concluded that living organisms did not appear from nowhere. They could only germinate in an environment where they were already present. No known case of spontaneous generation of life was left in the world.

Religious Revival

The churches, moreover, knew how to defeat unbelievers. Censorship did not work. But appeals, over the intellectuals' heads, to ordinary people did. Despite the hostility of the Enlightenment, the eighteenth century was a time of religious revival in the West. Christianity reached a new public. In 1722, Nicolas Ludwig, Count Zinzendorff built the village of Herrnhut (meaning "the Lord's keeping") on his estate in Germany to be a refuge for persecuted Christians. It became a center from which evangelical fervor—or "enthusiasm," as they called it—radiated over the world. Zinzendorff's was only one of innumerable movements to offer ordinary people an affective, unintellectual solution to the problems of life: proof that, in their way, feelings are stronger than reason, and that religion—for most people—is more satisfying than science. As one of the great Christian revivalists, Jonathan Edwards (1703–1758) of Massachusetts, said, "Our people do not so much need to have their heads stored, as to have their hearts touched." His meetings, characteristically, were occasions for congregations to purge their emotions in ways intellectuals found repellent. "There was a great moaning and crying through the whole house," observed a witness to one of Edwards's sermons, "the shrieks and cries were piercing and amazing."

Preaching was the information technology of these movements. Between 1740 and his death in 1758, George Whitfield (or Whitefield—he spelled it both ways) was always on the move, all over Britain and across the American colonies.

Addressing a congregation composed of almost the entire population of Boston, he made the town seem "the gate of heaven. Many wept enthusiastically and cried out under the Word." In 1738, with a "heart strangely warmed," John Wesley (1703–1791) began a mission to the workers of England and Wales, traveling 8,000 miles a year and preaching to thousands at a time. He communicated a mood rather than a message—a sense of how Jesus can change lives by imparting feelings of love. Catholic evangelism was equally stirring and targeted the same enemies—materialism, rationalism, apathy, and formalized religion. One observer compared Alfonso Maria Liguori's (1696–1787) mission among the poor in Naples to the preaching of a biblical prophet. In 1765, the pope authorized devotion to the Sacred Heart of Jesus—a bleeding symbol of divine love.

Music contributed to the mood. In the eighteenth century, God seemed to have all the best tunes—from the hymns that Wesley's brother, Charles, wrote to the stirring settings of Christ's passion by Johann Sebastian Bach (1685–1750). In 1741, George Friedrich Handel wrote *Messiah*, telling the life of Jesus in music so sublime that when the first London performance approached its climax, King George II rose to his feet and heard the "Hallelujah Chorus" standing. The scriptures Handel set made an effective reply to skeptics: "I know that my Redeemer liveth, and though worms destroy this body, yet in my flesh shall I see God." Mozart's music, too, ultimately served the Church better than the Masonic movement. He died in 1791 while writing his great *Requiem Mass*—his own triumph over death.

Cynically, some European monarchs used religious revival to distract people from politics and strengthened churches as institutions of social control. Frederick the Great of Prussia (r. 1740–1786) was a freethinker who liked the company of philosophers at dinner. He employed, for a while, both Maupertuis and Voltaire. But he favored religion for his people and his troops, founding military chaplaincies and requiring religious teaching in schools. He was applying a principle Voltaire uttered: "If God did not exist, it would be necessary to invent him."

The Cult of Nature and Romanticism

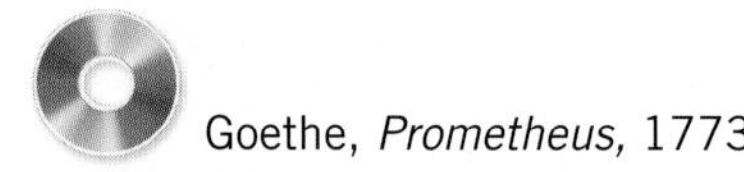
Goethe, *Prometheus,* 1773

The cult of nature was something Christians and their enemies could agree on. Nature seemed both more beautiful and more terrible than any construction of the human intellect. In 1755, an earthquake centered at Lisbon, Portugal, shook even Voltaire's faith in progress. One of Europe's greatest cities, home to nearly 200,000 people, was reduced to ruins. It was the worst natural disaster on record in European history. As an alternative to the return to God, radical philosophers responded to the call, "Return to Nature," which one contributor to the *Encyclopedia*, Baron d'Holbach, uttered in 1770: "She will console you, drive out from your heart the fears that hobble you ... the hatreds that separate you from Man, whom you ought to love." "Sensibility" became a buzzword for responsiveness to the power of feelings, which were valued even more than reason. Romantic values included imagination, intuition, emotion, inspiration, and even passion, alongside—or in extreme cases, ahead of—reason and scientific knowledge as guides to truth and conduct. Romantics professed to prefer nature to human works, or, at least, wanted art to demonstrate sympathy with nature.

Exploration in the eighteenth century was constantly revealing new marvels of nature. The influence of American landscapes on romantic minds began with the drawings that two young Spaniards, Jorge Juan and Antonio de Ulloa, made during a scientific expedition to the equator. In work published in 1752, they combined scientific diagrams with images of awestruck reverence for untamed nature. Their drawing, for instance, of the volcanic Mount Cotopaxi erupting in Ecuador, with, in the background, arcs of light in the sky, combines precision with rugged romance. The Andean settings they recorded remained the source of the most powerful romantic images of America. Cotopaxi became a favorite subject of American landscape painters.

Cult of the unattainable. Alexander von Humboldt stoops to pluck a botanical specimen near the foot of Mount Chimborazo. His account of his climb to the top of Chimborazo is a poignant litany of the cult of the unattainable so characteristic of romanticism.

The merging of science and romance is apparent in the work of one of the greatest scientists of the age, Baron Alexander von Humboldt (1769–1859). In the 1790s, he began a series of journeys of scientific exploration in America: "to see Nature in all her variety of grandeur and splendour." The high point of his endeavors came in 1802, when he tried to climb Mount Chimborazo—Cotopaxi's twin peak. Chimborazo was thought to be the highest mountain in the world—the untouched summit of creation. Sickened by altitude, racked by cold, bleeding from nose and lips, Humboldt had almost reached the top when he was forced to turn back. His story of suffering and frustration was just the sort of subject romantic writers were beginning to celebrate in Europe. The cult of the unattainable—an unfulfillable yearning—lay at the heart of romanticism.

Romantics also valued the supposedly natural feelings of uneducated people. Their poetry, said the English poet William Wordsworth (1770–1850), was "the language of ordinary men." The music of romanticism ransacked traditional songs for melodies. Its theater and opera borrowed from the antics of street performers. Its prophet was Johann Gottfried Herder (1744–1803), who praised the moral power of the "true poetry" of "those whom we call savages." Its philosopher was Jean-Jacques Rousseau (1712–1778), who taught the superiority of natural passions over cultivated refinement. Its portrait paintings showed society ladies in peasant dress in gardens landscaped to look natural, reinvaded by romance. "The people" had arrived in European history as a creative force.

von Humboldt, from *Personal Narrative of a Journey to the Equinoctal Regions of the New Continent,* 1773

Rousseau and the General Will

Of the thinkers who broke with the outlook of the *Encyclopedia*, Rousseau was the most influential. He was a restless supertramp with a taste for low life. He changed his formal religious allegiance twice without once appearing sincere. He betrayed all his mistresses, quarreled with all his friends, and abandoned all his children. Addiction to his own sensibilities became the guideline of his life. In 1750, in the prize-winning essay that made his name, he repudiated one of the most sacred principles of the Enlightenment—"that the Arts and Sciences have benefited Mankind." The fact that the topic could be proposed at all shows how far disillusionment with enlightened optimism had gone. Rousseau's assertion of the natural goodness of humankind in its primitive state made Voltaire want "to walk on all fours," like an animal.

Nonetheless, Rousseau's political thinking helped shape the politics of his day and has remained influential. Rousseau regarded the state as a sort of organism, in which the individual identities of the citizens are submerged. At a previous, unknown stage of history, the act occurred "by which people become a people, ... the real foundation of society." "The people becomes one single being.... Each of us puts his person and all his power in common under the supreme direction of the general will." Citizenship is fraternity— equivalent to the blood bond between brothers. The commands of the general will are perfect freedom—social or civil freedom, Rousseau called it—and anyone constrained to obey them is simply being "forced to be free." "Whoever refuses to obey the general will shall be compelled to do so by the whole body."

Rousseau was vague about the moral justification for this dangerous doctrine. The German philosopher Immanuel Kant (1724–1804) provided one. By setting aside one's individual will or interests and exercising reason instead, one can identify goals of a merit everyone can see. Submission to the general will limits one's own freedom in deference to the freedom of others. In practice, however, the general will just meant the tyranny of the majority. Rousseau admitted that "the votes of the greatest number always bind the rest." In Rousseau's utopia, political parties are outlawed because "there should be no partial society within the state." The same logic would forbid trade unions, religious communions, and reformist movements. Yet the passion with which Rousseau invoked freedom made it hard for many of his readers to see how illiberal his thought was. Revolutionaries adopted the opening words of his essay of 1762: "Man is born free and everywhere he is in chains!"

Pacific Discoveries

Underlying the elevation of the common man and woman to be fit for participation in government were influences from surprising directions: the Pacific and the Americas. The Pacific in the eighteenth century stretched between myths: an unknown continent called *Terra Australis*, supposedly awaiting discovery in the south, and the rumored sea passage around America in the northwest. Investigation of those myths became the objective of the English navigator Captain James Cook (see Chapter 19). In 1769, he was ordered to Tahiti in the South Pacific to observe the transit of the planet Venus and returned with a burning vocation to sail "as far as I think it possible for man to go."

from *Captain Cook's Journal During His First Voyage Round the World*

In three voyages of Pacific exploration, he charted New Zealand, the west coast of Alaska, and the east coast of Australia. He also filled in most of the Pacific's remaining gaps on the map. He brought a new precision to mapmaking, using the latest technology for finding longitude—the exquisitely accurate chronometer the English inventor John Harrison (1693–1776) had developed. He exploded the myth of Terra Australis, or at least pushed its possible location into latitudes "doomed to lie forever buried under everlasting snow and ice." His ships brought back sketches and specimens of plants and beasts unknown in Europe.

Cook was the spearhead of a scientific invasion of the Pacific by expeditions from Britain, Spain, France, Russia, and the new United States. Another "new world" became available for Western imperialism to exploit, and another treasury of natural resources was open to enrich Western economies. For intellectual history, the most important discoveries Western explorers made in the Pacific were of its peoples.

Observers dismissed some of them as intellectually insignificant. William Dampier, who published the first description of the aborigines of Australia in 1697, found them "nasty" and repellent. Early painters of the aborigines commonly depicted them crawling on the earth or scampering in the trees like monkeys.

From other parts of the Pacific, however, explorers brought home specimens of manhood, whom admirers instantly classed as **noble savages**—"proof" that to be morally admirable you did not need to be white, Western, Christian, or educated in ways that Europeans recognized as "civilized." In 1774, English society lionized

Omai, who had been a restless misfit in his native Polynesia. Lee Boo, from Micronesia, was another "prince of nature." Visitors to the Pacific found a sensual paradise. Romantic primitivism became inseparable from sexual opportunity. Images of Tahiti as the ravishing home of nymphs filled Westerners' imaginations. Diderot focused on sex to highlight the mutual incomprehension of a Tahitian girl and a French chaplain: "Honest stranger, do not refuse me. Make me a mother."

Omai—the restless young Tahitian who sailed to England with Captain Cook in the 1770s—became the darling of London society. He is shown here painted by Sir Joshua Reynolds, the most fashionable portrait painter of the day, in heroic fashion, in misplaced oriental attire, and bare feet, against a majestic backdrop. In Western eyes, Omai embodied the idea that the untutored, "natural" man could be effortlessly noble.

Wild Children

The disappointments of previous centuries had not put to rest the quest for "natural" man. On the contrary, interest in the origins of language and of political and social life, and the moral effects of civilization was acute, and scholars were anxious to examine specimens of primitive humanity untouched by civilized society. "Wolf children" seemed to supply the raw material for analysis. Carolus Linnaeus (1707–1778)—the Swedish botanist who devised the modern method of classifying species—thought that wild children were a separate species of human beings. Plucked from the woods, wrenched from the wolves and foxes that suckled them, they became experiments in efforts to teach them language and manners.

But all the experiments to "civilize" these children failed. Boys, whom bears supposedly raised in Poland, continued to prefer the company of bears. "Peter the Wild Boy" whom rival members of the English royal family struggled to possess as a pet in the 1720s, hated clothes and beds and never learned to talk. The "savage girl" kidnapped from the woods in France in 1731 preferred raw frogs to food from the kitchen, and for a long time, she imitated birdsong better than she spoke French. The most famous case was the "Wild Boy of Aveyron." Abandoned in infancy in the forests of southwest France, he survived by his own wits for years until he was kidnapped for civilization in 1798. He learned to wear clothes and to dine elegantly, but never to speak or to like what had happened to him.

The Huron as Noble Savage

The most influential source of ideas about the nobility of savagery were the Native American Huron of the Great Lakes (see Chapter 19). Secular philosophers filtered cautionary tales out of missionary accounts of the Hurons' way of life until only an idealized Huron remained. This became easier as real Hurons literally disappeared—virtually destroyed by the diseases to which European contagion exposed them.

The great secularizer of legends about the Huron was Louis-Armand de Lom de l'Arce, who called himself by the title his family had sold for cash, Sieur de Lahontan. Lahontan left France for Canada in the 1680s and set himself up as an expert on its curiosities. The mouthpiece for his freethinking anticlericalism was an invented Huron called Adario, with whom Lahontan discussed the imperfections of the Bible, republicanism, and free love.

Huron women, from the *History of Canada,* 1664

The intoxicating potential of the Huron myth was distilled in a comedy, performed in Paris in 1768, in which a Huron excels in all the virtues of noble savagery as huntsman, lover, and warrior. When urged to adopt French dress, he

The Enlightenment

r. 1661–1722	Kangxi, Chinese emperor, tutored by Jesuit scholars
1680s	Louis-Armand de Lom de l'Arce leaves France for Canada
1685–1750	Johann Sebastian Bach, composer
1689–1755	Baron de Montesquieu, author of *The Spirit of the Laws* and *Persian Letters*
1694–1778	François Marie Arouet (Voltaire), leading philosopher and admirer of China
1703–1791	John Wesley, founder of Methodism
1712–1778	Jean-Jacques Rousseau, author of the *Social Contract*
1713–1784	Denis Diderot, publisher of the *Encyclopedia*
1720	Chinese translations of Western books allowed to circulate in Japan
1736	Maupertuis's expedition to the Arctic Circle
1740–1758	Preaching career of George Whitfield, emotional preacher
1771	Japanese "Dutch studies" group begins study of Western books

denounces imitation as fashion "among monkeys but not among men." "If he lacks enlightenment by great minds," comments an observer, "he has abundant sentiments, which I esteem more highly. And I fear that in becoming civilized he will be the poorer." Unhappy in love, the Huron urges the mob to breach the prison fortress of Paris, the Bastille, to rescue his imprisoned lover. He is therefore arrested for sedition.

THE FRENCH REVOLUTION AND NAPOLEON

Believers in the nobility of the savage found it easy to believe in the wisdom of the common man. The Bastille was a symbol of oppression. Seized copies of the *Encyclopedia* were kept there. Voltaire had been briefly and comfortably imprisoned there. Urban myth insisted that hundreds of prisoners of conscience suffered there. In fact, like most organs of the French state, it was rickety, and like the government's treasury, virtually empty. Rebels who broke into it in search of arms on July 14, 1789, found only a handful of inmates.

Background to the Revolution

Historians have looked deep into the pre-Revolutionary old regime in France for explanations of the causes for the revolution that broke out on that day. Yet like most political upheavals, the French Revolution arose suddenly in the particular circumstances of the time and unrolled rapidly in ways previously unforeseeable. The costs of French participation in the American Revolutionary War, which ended in 1783 and added to the state's debts, left the monarchy desperate to increase taxes. By summoning the Estates General, the medieval assembly of the realm, for the first time since 1614 to meet the crisis, royal ministers took a risk. Many deputies arrived resentful, having sat on consultative bodies whose advice the government had dismissed. Most belonged to the literate minority the Enlightenment had affected. They had strong inclinations toward constitutionalism in politics and anticlericalism in religion. All had read the gutter press of the day: scandal sheets about alleged sexual and financial shenanigans at court.

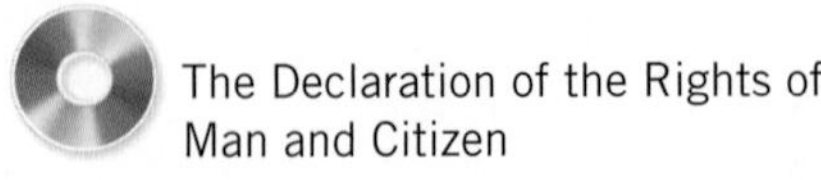

The Declaration of the Rights of Man and Citizen

Local assemblies elected the deputies. "Public opinion," King Louis XVI (r. 1774–1792) wrote in one of his schoolbooks, "is never wrong." The regulations for electing the assembly emphasized that "His Majesty wishes that everyone, from the extremities of his realm and from the most remote dwelling places, may be assured that his desires and claims will reach him." As a result, the deputies arrived with "books of grievances," full of the complaints of peasants hungry after bad harvests, venting their rage on big landowners. Most of them demanded lower taxes and relief from traditional obligations of peasants and the traditional privileges of lords—to hunt game, evade taxes, hold markets, mobilize forced labor. In June, the Estates General gave itself the title of National Assembly with the right to "interpret the General Will of the nation." In August, it enacted the Declaration of the Rights of Man and Citizen. "Men are born free and remain equal in rights," this document proclaimed. Sovereignty, said the Declaration, rested not with the king but with the whole people. As in all revolutions, radicals exploited the mood in favor of change to agitate for more change than most people wanted.

Revolutionary Radicalism

The Fall of the Bastille by the French artist Jean-Pierre Houel (1735–1813). Houel's paintings contributed to the myth that the Bastille, a medieval fortress in the heart of Paris, was a terrifying, cruel, and secretive prison, in which a repressive monarchy tortured its many victims. But when a citizen army captured the castle on July 14, 1789, they found only a small, demoralized garrison and a handful of privileged inmates lodged in comfortable cells, not chained in dungeons. This did not stop Houel from romanticizing the event. Each time he painted a different version of the fall of the Bastille, he enlarged the crowds, increased the flames, and exaggerated the scale of the struggle.

In 1790, the revolutionaries enacted a "civil constitution of the clergy" that turned priests into public servants and nationalized church property. The pope rejected it. So did the king, who had never supported radical reform. Once his opposition became known, the king became a virtual prisoner of the assembly. Opponents of the Revolution fled. Foreign powers feared the Revolution might be exported. In March 1792, war broke out, and Austria and Prussia invaded France.

In wartime, anything can happen, and only harsh measures can give governments control over events. In August 1792, the monarchy was overthrown. In 1793, the royal family was executed. Aristocrats, priests, and officials were massacred in urban riots and peasant rebellions. Ruthless revolutionary factions seized power over what remained of the state, while committees of militants and self-appointed "people's tribunals" imposed revolutionary terror. In the bloodiest spell, during June and July 1794, 1,584 heads were chopped off in Paris, and thousands of peasants and workers were killed in the provinces. "It was not," admitted a member of the government, "a question of principles. It was about killing."

So many crimes committed in the name of liberty destroyed the idealism that had launched the Revolution. Take the example of a leading revolutionary propagandist, the Marquis de Sade (1740–1814), who called himself Citizen Sade after the revolutionaries liberated him in 1789 from the Bastille, where his family had begged the government to confine him. His private correspondence exposes his revolutionary enthusiasm as a sham. In contrast to the enlightened idealism he claimed to profess, he had a record of depravity unsurpassed among eighteenth-century sexual athletes. He gave his name—*sadism*—to morbid forms of sexual cruelty. He ejaculated over a crucifix; tortured, imprisoned, and poisoned prostitutes; and—so he claimed—"proved that God does not exist" by inserting consecrated communion wafers in the rectums of people with whom he was going to have anal intercourse. His sexual antics were a distortion of liberty, his egotism a warped version of individualism, his violence a caricature of revolutionary injustice. As if in parody of Rousseau, de Sade thought no instincts could be immoral because all are natural. And as if in parody of Pierre Laplace's elimination of God from science (see Chapter 20), he thought no passions should be condemned because all are governed by chemical forces in the body. In his brief career as a revolutionary spokesman—he ended his days in an insane asylum—he tried to combine extreme individualism with the social solidarity the Revolution demanded.

Napoleon

When revolutions unleash chaos, people often turn to a "strong man." In 1799, a military coup made France's best general a dictator. Napoleon Bonaparte (1769–1821) called himself First Consul of the Republic, then, from 1804, after more victories, Emperor of the French. His military genius and the strength of his armies turned Europe into a playground for his political experiments. French power extended at its height from Spain, and Portugal to Poland and Croatia.

French armies carried revolutionary ideas into Russia, Egypt, and Syria (see Map 22.2). The wars were the nearest thing to world war that the world had yet seen, igniting conflicts in India, where the British seized the opportunity to extend their conquests, and in the Americas, where British armies attacked Buenos Aires in Argentina and burned the White House in Washington. Colonies changed hands in the Caribbean, North America, the Indian Ocean, and South Africa. Haiti achieved independence (see Chapter 21).

Napoleon—until his final defeat in 1815—was one of the most inventive rationalizers of states. He imposed a uniform law code on his conquests, which still forms the basis of the laws of much of Europe, Latin America, and Africa. He abolished ancient states, created new ones, and imposed constitutional government where it had never existed before. He subordinated the Church and created new

MAP 22.2
Napoleon's Empire, ca. 1799–1815

elites. He cultivated a romantic image of himself as a meteor that changed the fate of a continent. To the poor, he fulfilled the French Revolution. To the rich, he tamed it. In some ways, he ruled a barbarian empire, descended as much from that of Charlemagne as from Rome. Sometimes he had himself painted as a Roman emperor. Sometimes he was depicted among ancient Germanic gods. Historians have detected opportunism and lack of any general principles in his behavior. A police state operated wherever he ruled.

To the disappointment of idealists who advocated "liberty, equality, and fraternity," the French Revolution had failed to change the world. The wars the Revolution started were the real anvil of change, and Napoleon was their smith and hammer. Henceforth, no form of political legitimacy would be beyond challenge.

The French Revolution

1783	End of the American Revolutionary War
1789	Convening of the Estates General
June 1789	Estates General becomes the National Assembly
July 14, 1789	Storming of the Bastille
March 1792	Invasion of France by Austria and Prussia
January 1793	Louis XVI executed
1799	Napoleon overthrows Directorate

IN PERSPECTIVE: The Afterglow of Enlightenment

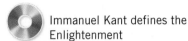

Immanuel Kant defines the Enlightenment

The French Revolution opened with noble cries—for the rights of man and the sovereignty of the people. It ended with the sickening scream that forms the last line of the "Marseillaise," calling for troughs full of the "impure" blood of aristocrats, traitors, and foreigners.

In Britain, the statesman and philosopher Edmund Burke was so appalled by the Revolution's excesses that he reached for the comforts of conservatism. In Spain, in the black paintings of Goya, and in Germany, in the private darkness of Beethoven's late music, we can sense another response: retreat into hag-ridden disillusionment. In the *Critique of Pure Reason* of 1781, Kant proposed a rickety, human-scale world of "crooked timber" in place of the grand ruined structures of the Age of Reason.

The Enlightenment was streaked with shadows. In Paris in 1798, Etienne Robert Gaspard displayed a light show in which monstrous shapes loomed at the audience from a screen or flickered eerily across clouds of smoke. In other demonstrations of the wonders of electricity, the real-life forerunners of Frankenstein made corpses twitch to thrill an audience. It was not the sleep of reason that produced these monsters. They were creations of its most watchful hours—the hideous issue of scientific experimentation, the brutal images of minds tortured by revulsion at revolutionary crimes.

The Enlightenment survived in America. The United States' Constitution of 1787 embodied some of the dearest political principles of Montesquieu and the authors of the *Encyclopedia*, substituting the sovereign people for a sovereign government, switching powers from the executive to the legislature, creating constitutional guarantees of freedom, outlawing any "establishment of religion," and expressing confidence in the people's fitness to decide their own fate. Assumptions about human equality—though they did not extend to black people, Native Americans, or women—typified American society. No formal aristocracy was acknowledged. Servants treated employers with a familiarity that shocked Europeans. Money became a more powerful indicator of social distinction than birth. To the surprise of much of the world—and of some Americans—the United States avoided becoming a military dictatorship, unlike so many other supposedly republican and egalitarian revolutions.

Even in Europe, the idea of progress survived. In the nineteenth century, it strengthened on the "march of improvement"—the history

An image of war. Francisco Goya's art began to desert the conventional subjects demanded by his early patrons in the 1790s. Under the dark and bloody impact of the French Revolution, he produced scenes of witchcraft and torture. It was the Spanish War of Independence against Napoleon in 1808–1814, however, that released from his imagination colossal monsters like this: an image of war wading through the land and overshadowing the wreckage of lives.

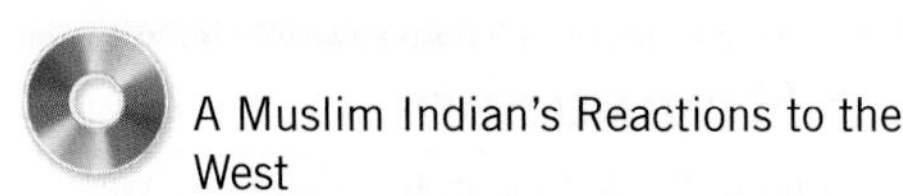
A Muslim Indian's Reactions to the West

of industrialization, the multiplication of wealth, the victories of constitutionalism against tyranny. It became possible to believe that progress was irreversible. Evolution programmed it into nature. It took the horrors of the twentieth century—a catalogue of famines, failures, inhumanities, and genocide—to make people question whether progress was inevitable or even real.

Europeans and the inhabitants of European colonies in the Americas felt growing confidence as a result of their sense that their societies were making scientific and technical progress. Rivals in Asia seemed stagnant by comparison. Western visitors to Turkey in the 1790s felt that the Ottomans had slipped into inferiority through neglect of science, "too stupid to comprehend," an English observer averred, "or too proud to learn." Even China seemed to have sacrificed former advantages. A Dutch envoy in 1794 declared that despite their sometime superiority, the Chinese remained in their " primitive state, without their even seeking, like the Europeans, to make further progress, or to bring their discoveries to perfection. . . . We have consequently so far surpassed them." The former greatness of Asia—it was alleged—had shifted to Europe.

Yet the Enlightenment rippled over the world. Rammohan Roy was not alone in trying to appropriate the scientific learning of the Enlightenment for Indians' use. Indians joined the scientific societies that the British founded in India and founded others of their own. Bal Shastri Jambedkar, a professor of mathematics who collaborated closely with English scientists in Calcutta in the 1830s, published his work in Indian languages and translated useful texts. In the same period, the work of surveying India began increasingly to rely on Indian, not British, experts. Where Western scientific impact led, the influence of Western political, economic, and philosophical thinking followed.

India had privileged access to Western ideas because of the vast number of Westerners whom British imperialism introduced to that country. Other European empires had similar effects in areas they colonized. And, increasingly in the nineteenth century, missionaries and technicians carried the effects of Western intellectual movements beyond the reach of imperialism. Jesuits were instrumental in China. Dutch merchants and ambassadors penetrated Japan. Books communicated Western ideas to parts of the world Westerners in person could hardly hope to remold. The consequences are apparent in most of the rest of this book. Up to this point in our story, the exchanges of culture we have chronicled have been mutually influential or have tended to be dominated by influences exerted on Europe from outside. From this point onward, global history becomes increasingly a story of Western influence.

CHRONOLOGY

r. 1661–1722	Kangxi, Chinese emperor, tutored by Jesuit scholars
1680s	Louis-Armand de Lom de l'Arce leaves France for Canada
1685–1750	Johann Sebastian Bach, composer
1689–1755	Baron de Montesquieu, author of *The Spirit of the Laws* and *Persian Letters*
1694–1778	François Marie Arouet (Voltaire), leading philosopher and admirer of China
1703–1758	Jonathan Edwards, New England preacher
1703–1791	John Wesley, founder of Methodism
1712–1778	Jean-Jacques Rousseau, author of the *Social Contract*
1713–1784	Denis Diderot, publisher of the *Encyclopedia*
1720	Chinese translations of Western books allowed to circulate in Japan
1736	Maupertuis's expedition to the Arctic Circle
1740–1758	George Whitfield, emotional preacher
1771	Japanese "Dutch studies" group begins study of Western books
1752	Publication of Maupertuis's *Letters on the Progress of Science*
1776	Publication of Adam Smith's *The Wealth of Nations;* United States Declaration of Independence
1783	End of the American Revolutionary War
1789	Convening of the Estates General; Estates General becomes the National Assembly
Late 1700s and early 1800s	Romantic movement
July 14, 1789	Storming of the Bastille
1792	Invasion of France by Austria and Prussia; publication of Mary Wollstonecraft's *A Vindication of the Rights of Woman*
1793	Louis XVI executed
1799	Napoleon comes to power in a military coup
1804	Napoleon crowns himself Emperor of the French
1815	Napoleon's final defeat

PROBLEMS AND PARALLELS

1. How was the Enlightenment global in its inspiration, as well as in its effects? How did ideas from overseas, particularly from China, influence the Enlightenment? How did Asian cultures influence writers like Voltaire, Diderot, and Montesquieu?
2. What role did religion play in the development of the Enlightenment? How was preaching the "information technology" of religious revivals in the West?
3. How did Diderot's *Encyclopedia* serve as a vehicle for advancing Enlightenment thinking in eighteenth-century Europe? Why was Romanticism often seen as antithetical to the Enlightenment?
4. How did influences from the Pacific and the Americas shape the elevation of the "common man"? What does the term *noble savages* mean?
5. Did Napoleon fulfill the Enlightenment or undermine its ideals?

DOCUMENTS IN GLOBAL HISTORY

- Baron de Montesquieu, from *The Spirit of the Laws*
- Lady Mary Wortley Montagu on the Ottoman Empire, 1717
- title page from a Japanese anatomy text, 1775
- Diderot, preliminary discourse from the *Encyclopedia*
- Adam Smith, from *The Wealth of Nations*
- Marie-Olympes de Gouges, *Declaration of the Rights of Woman and the Female Citizen*
- Mary Wollstonecraft, *A Vindication of the Rights of Woman*
- John Locke, *Essay Concerning Human Understanding,* 1689
- Goethe, *Prometheus,* 1773
- von Humboldt, from *Personal Narrative of a Journey to the Equinoctal Regions of the New Continent,* 1773
- From *Captain Cook's Journal During His First Voyage Round the World*
- Huron women, from the *History of Canada,* 1664
- The Declaration of the Rights of Man and Citizen
- Immanuel Kant defines the Enlightenment
- A Muslim Indian's Reactions to the West

Please see the Primary Source DVD for additional sources related to this chapter.

READ ON

S. Cromwell, Crawford *Raja Rammohun Roy and Progressive Movements in India: A Selection from Records, 1775–1845* (1983) is useful. Maupertuis is best approached through his own writings, but there are useful studies by D. Beeson, *Maupertuis* (1992), and M. Terrall, *The Man Who Flattened the Earth* (2002).

On the Enlightenment in general, P. Gay, *The Enlightenment* (1995), is a classic that is still stimulating. J. Israel, *Radical Enlightenment: Philosophy and the Making of Modernity* (2001) is a superb study that emphasizes the Dutch contribution. O. Gunn, *First Globalization* (2003) is a useful introduction to the global context.

A. Çirakman, *From the "Terror of the World" to the "Sick Man of Europe"* (2002) traces changes in the image of the Ottomans in the West. Li Yan and Du Shiran, *Chinese Mathematics: A Concise History* (1987) is fundamental. J. Waley-Cohen, *The Sextants of Beiking* (1999) is a broad survey of Chinese science, with special attention to interchange with the West. F. Wakeman, *The Great Enterprise* (1986) is a good introduction to China in the period.

For the context of Dutch studies, L. Blussé et al., *Bridging the Divide* (2001) is enthralling. J. B. Bury, *The Idea of Progress* (1982) is an unsurpassed classic.

T. Ellingson, *The Myth of the Noble Savage* (2001) is an important revisionist work. M. Newton, *Savage Girls and Wild Boys: A History of Feral Children* (2003) is a fascinating overview of its subject. A. Pagden, *European Encounters with the New World from Renaissance to Romanticism* (1994) is indispensable.

C. L. Johnson, ed., *The Cambridge Companion to Mary Wollstonecraft* (2002) is a mine of information and a valuable guide to work on early feminism.

J. C. Beaglehole's classic *The Life of Captain James Cook* (1992) is still the best biography.

S. Schama, *Citizens* (1991) tells the story of the French Revolution with vision and verve. C. Jones, *The Great Nation* (2003) is excellent on the background of eighteenth-century France. There are so many books about Napoleon: P. Geyl, *Napoleon: For and Against* (1967) is a magisterial survey of the literature.

PART Nine

The Frustrations of Progress to ca. 1900

CHAPTER 23 Replacing Muscle: The Energy Revolutions 588

CHAPTER 24 The Social Mold: Work and Society in the Nineteenth Century 614

CHAPTER 25 Western Dominance in the Nineteenth Century: The Westward Shift of Power and the Rise of Global Empires 638

CHAPTER 26 The Changing State: Political Developments in the Nineteenth Century 664

Ottoman world map. In 1803, the Turkish Military Engineering School published this world map—the first Ottoman map based on Mercator's projection—in an atlas using European geographical knowledge and map-making techniques.

ENVIRONMENT

since 1800
Global population boom

since ca. 1800
Coal and steam power

CULTURE

1800–1880
Decline of slavery

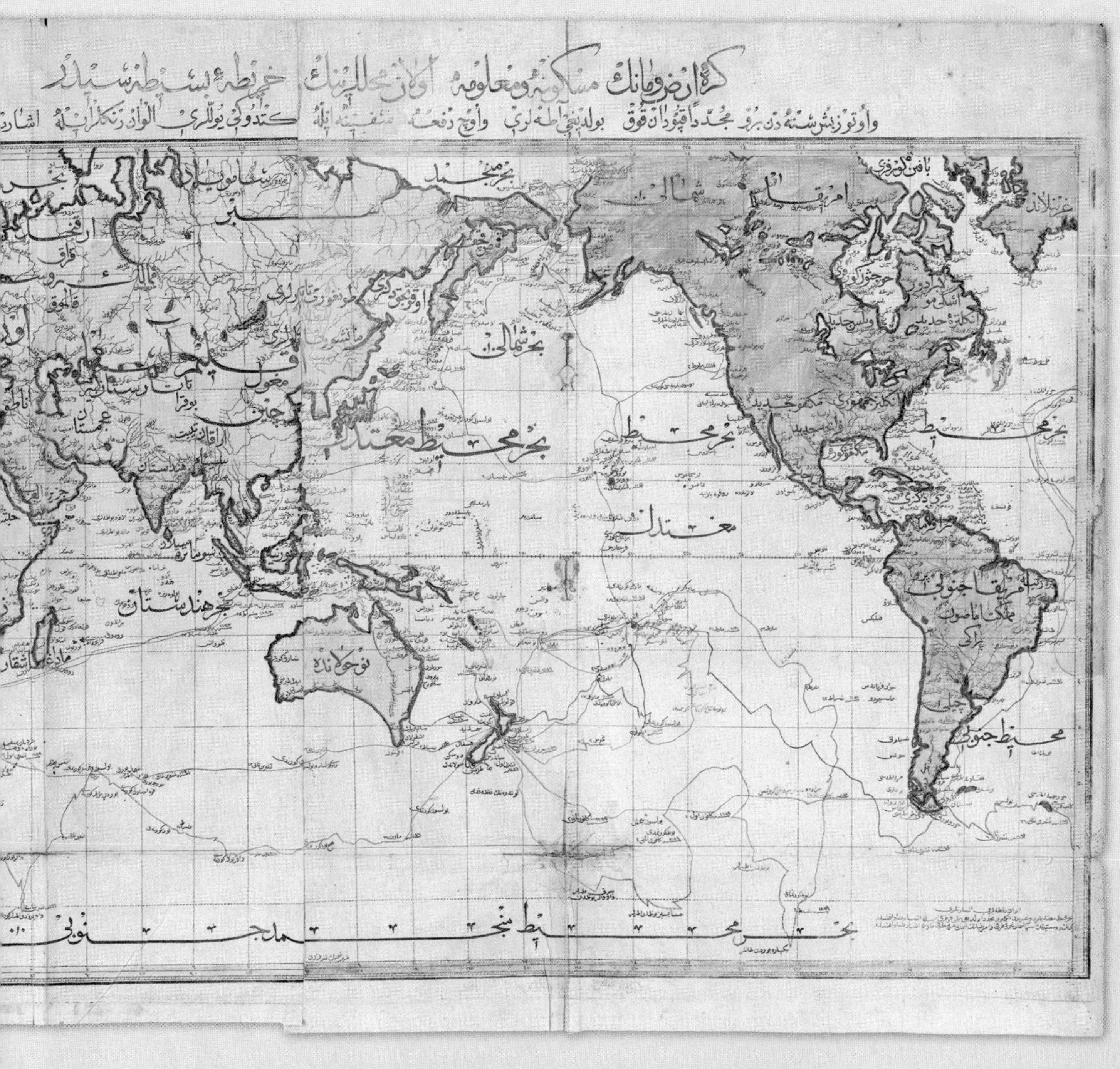

since 1850
Industrialization of food production

ca. 1850
Electricity

1870–1900
Famine and drought worldwide

1840s–1860s
Opium Wars, China

1860s–1910
Mass migrations

1870–1871
Franco-Prussian War

1885
Berlin Conference–Partition of Africa

CHAPTER 23

Replacing Muscle: The Energy Revolutions

Ambroise-Louis Garneray (1783–1857) was among the artists whose heroic whaling scenes helped to inspire Herman Melville's novel *Moby-Dick*. Garneray's depiction of whalers at work in the North Atlantic in 1836 emphasizes the solitary combat between the heroic harpooner and the great, black sea beast, and shows other dangers—the fragile boat, its frantic crew, the spurt of blood from the wounded whale, the foaming sea. In the background, the ship is calm—with fires ready to render the whale's blubber.
Photograph courtesy of the Peabody Essex Museum

IN THIS CHAPTER
GLOBAL DEMOGRAPHICS: THE WORLD'S POPULATION RISES
FOOD: TRANSITION TO ABUNDANCE
ENERGY FOR POWER: MILITARIZATION AND INDUSTRIALIZATION
Militarization
Industrialization
INDUSTRIALIZING EUROPE
INDUSTRY IN THE AMERICAS
JAPAN INDUSTRIALIZES
CHINA AND INDUSTRIALIZATION
INDIA AND EGYPT
IN PERSPECTIVE: Why the West?

THE WORLD

Moby Dick is a tale of monsters, the saga of a seaman's revenge against a huge white whale that snapped off his leg: a monstrous man, a monstrous beast, a monstrous obsession. When Herman Melville wrote it in 1851, whalers still hunted in open boats that a whale could crush or smash. Harpoonists had to worry and bleed the whale to death. The crew knelt between decks in blood and blubber to chop and melt the fat before it turned putrid. For the fat was precious: whaling was the world's main source of oil. The world was facing a fat crisis—a shortage of lipids and lubricants. Within a few years, however, a series of innovations solved the problem. In 1859, drilling began to release fossil oil from the depths of the earth. In 1865, the first fully industrial whaling ship was launched in Norway, with explosive harpoons and a steam engine that could tow dead whales into port for quick processing. Even the gigantic blue whale—which previous hunting techniques could not touch—now became prey.

Meanwhile, the search was on for other sources of fat. Intensive methods to produce feed supported more livestock and boosted supplies of animal fat. New grazing areas opened up. Demand for edible fat drove European powers into tropical colonies to produce palm, peanut, and coconut oil.

Fat made the nineteenth-century world work. It supplied calories for human consumers. It greased the machines of industrialization. It induced empire-building. But the fat crisis was part of a bigger picture: a revolution in energy sources. How people responded to the crisis is the subject of this chapter: industrialization—new ways to release energy and new uses for it. The following three chapters cover the consequences: new forms of imperialism and the effects of industrialization on society and politics.

GLOBAL DEMOGRAPHICS: THE WORLD'S POPULATION RISES

Population growth meant rising demand, which made new sources of energy necessary. In 1800, there were about 950 million people in the world. By 1900, there were about 1.6 billion people (see Map 23.1). Around 1800, only four large areas in the world could be called densely settled—with, say, more than four people per square mile: East Asia, southeast Asia, the Indian subcontinent, and Western Europe. By 1900, parts of Africa and the Americas, especially along the coasts, had comparable densities.

FOCUS questions

- WHY DID the world's population begin to rise rapidly during the nineteenth century?
- WHY DID industrialization increase the world's food supply?
- HOW WAS industrialization related to the growth of military power?
- WHY DID the economies of the United States and Latin America develop in different ways?
- WHY DID Japan and China pursue different policies toward industrialization?
- HOW DID British imperialism affect the economic development of India and Egypt?

In some ways, demographic buoyancy seemed surprising. Improvements in long-range communications made it easier for disease to spread. As people got more crowded together, new eco-niches opened for disease. Growing cities were poorly equipped with drainage and sanitation. Polluted and nutritionally inadequate food was a major problem. Urban epidemics multiplied, culminating in 1917–1919, when an influenza pandemic killed at least 30 million people worldwide. But by then, the rate of population increase was so quick that the disaster hardly made a dent in the world's population.

Nor were rural populations exempt from ecological disasters. Although food production soared in global terms, it was unevenly distributed, and famine killed more people in the nineteenth century than at any other period in recorded history. Political neglect worsened the effects, especially in large empires under distant or indifferent rulers. The most successful crops of the period—the most prolific, the most nutritious—ensnared consumers in overreliance. When fungal disease ruined potatoes in Ireland, for instance, in 1845–1859, or in Belgium and Finland in 1867–1868, millions starved or fled. Famine killed at least 4.3 to 7 million people in India in 1876–1878. Famine in China at the same time was "the most terrible disaster in twenty-one dynasties." In the 1890s, droughts associated with an unusual concentration of El Niño events caused 12 million deaths in India and 20 million in China. Famines triggered plagues. A cholera epidemic killed half the population of Guntur in eastern India after the crops failed in 1833. Smallpox and cholera also followed the great Indian famine of 1896. Nonetheless, population growth recovered from every catastrophe.

Slum life. Social reformers of the late nineteenth century listed sanitation, children's welfare, and animal abuse as some of the most pressing problems associated with urban conditions. This snapshot, taken around 1900 in New York City, captures all three issues: The ragged children play in a filthy gutter while a dead horse, presumably used to pull a cart or a trolley car, rots just a few yards away.

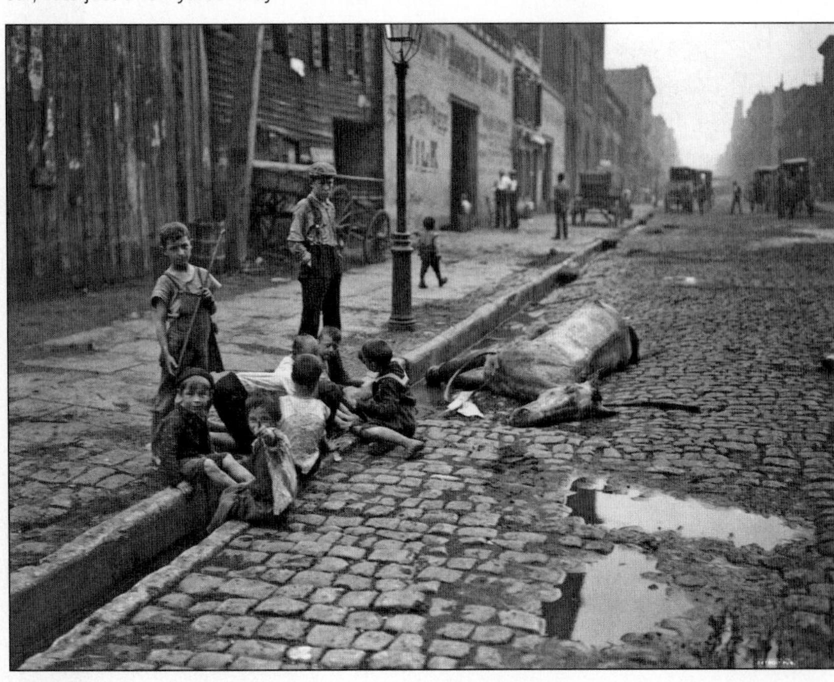

FOOD: TRANSITION TO ABUNDANCE

In view of the way famine and disease accompanied population growth, it is tempting to see Malthusian logic (see Chapter 20) linking demographic increase to ecological disaster. But population increase did not conform to Malthus's prophesies. In all parts of the world for which we have data, people practiced forms of population control. In France, they used contraception. In India, they idealized celibacy and restricted remarriage of widows. In Japan and most of Europe, they postponed marriage. Moreover, for unknown reasons, Japanese women began to delay having children until their mid-twenties, some five years later than was normal in Europe at the time. Most households had only one childbearing couple.

New ways to produce food outstripped population growth. In this respect, Malthus's critics, who expected "progress" to prevent disaster, were right. Food production soared, partly because more land was devoted to it and partly because of more efficient methods of exploitation. In the Philippines and Java, for instance, where population growth had long been static, rates of increase rose to 1 percent a year, largely because women started marrying at under 20 years of age. But this was an adjustment to new conditions that boosted food stocks and generated wealth. Large-scale deforestation released land for food production. Marginal soil was exploited to grow coconuts, not necessarily for food but for their fiber, which was used for matting, and for coconut oil, which was used in everything from cooking to making soap.

Sometimes food production rose simply because farmers applied traditional methods more systematically. For example, in Japan, agrarian output rose without significant increase in the amount of farmed land. In Egypt, wheat and barley production nearly doubled from 1880 to 1900, while the acreage under cultivation increased by less than half. Elsewhere, natural growth occurred, with little or no human effort, adding almost 600 square miles, for instance, to the fertile Yellow River delta in China in the second half of the century. Or human agency intervened. The Netherlands, for instance, reclaimed 11,000 acres from sea and wasteland during the nineteenth century. Partly in consequence, in the second half of the century, the number of Dutch cattle doubled, and pigs increased fourfold.

Rice cultivation in Japan. Hiroshige (1797–1858) specialized in painting comforting images of traditional Japan. Here bent-backed peasants labor virtuously under enriching rain in regularly patterned rice fields, surrounded by benign landscape. In the 100 years after the artist's death, enhanced efficiency enabled the Japanese to harvest more rice without extending the area under cultivation.

Beyond question, the greatest extension of the frontier of food production happened in the vast open lands of Argentina, Brazil, Uruguay, Australia, and North America. The incorporation of the North American prairie to raise cattle and grow grain was the most conspicuous large-scale adaptation of the environment for human purposes ever recorded. In 1827, when James Fenimore Cooper wrote *The Prairie*, the region seemed desolate: "A vast country incapable of sustaining a dense population." People called it the Great American Desert. Except in a few patches, the soil was too tough to plow without industrial technology.

The extension of grazing was the first stage in the region's transformation. This was the common experience of previously underexploited grasslands in the period. Much of southeast Australia and New Zealand became sheep-rearing country, though at first more for wool than for meat. Argentina became a major exporter of beef and mutton. But the North American prairie exceeded other areas in productivity, partly because railway construction concentrated large, though temporary, labor forces in parts of the region. When the railways were built, big markets in the Mississippi River valley and along the seaboards of North America became accessible to the products of the prairie.

James Fenimore Cooper, from *The Praire*

Grains soon became more important than meat, as wheat and maize replaced native prairie grasses. The change could not have happened without industrial technologies. Steel plows turned the sod of the prairie. Railways transported grain across what would otherwise be uneconomic distances. Houses built from precision-milled lumber and cheap nails spread cities in a region where most construction materials were unavailable. Repeating rifles destroyed vital links in the earlier ecosystem: the buffalo herds and their human hunters, the Native Americans. Grain elevators appeared in 1850. Machinery enabled a few hands to reap large harvests. Wire enclosed farmland against buffalo and cattle. Giant mills processed the grain into foodstuffs.

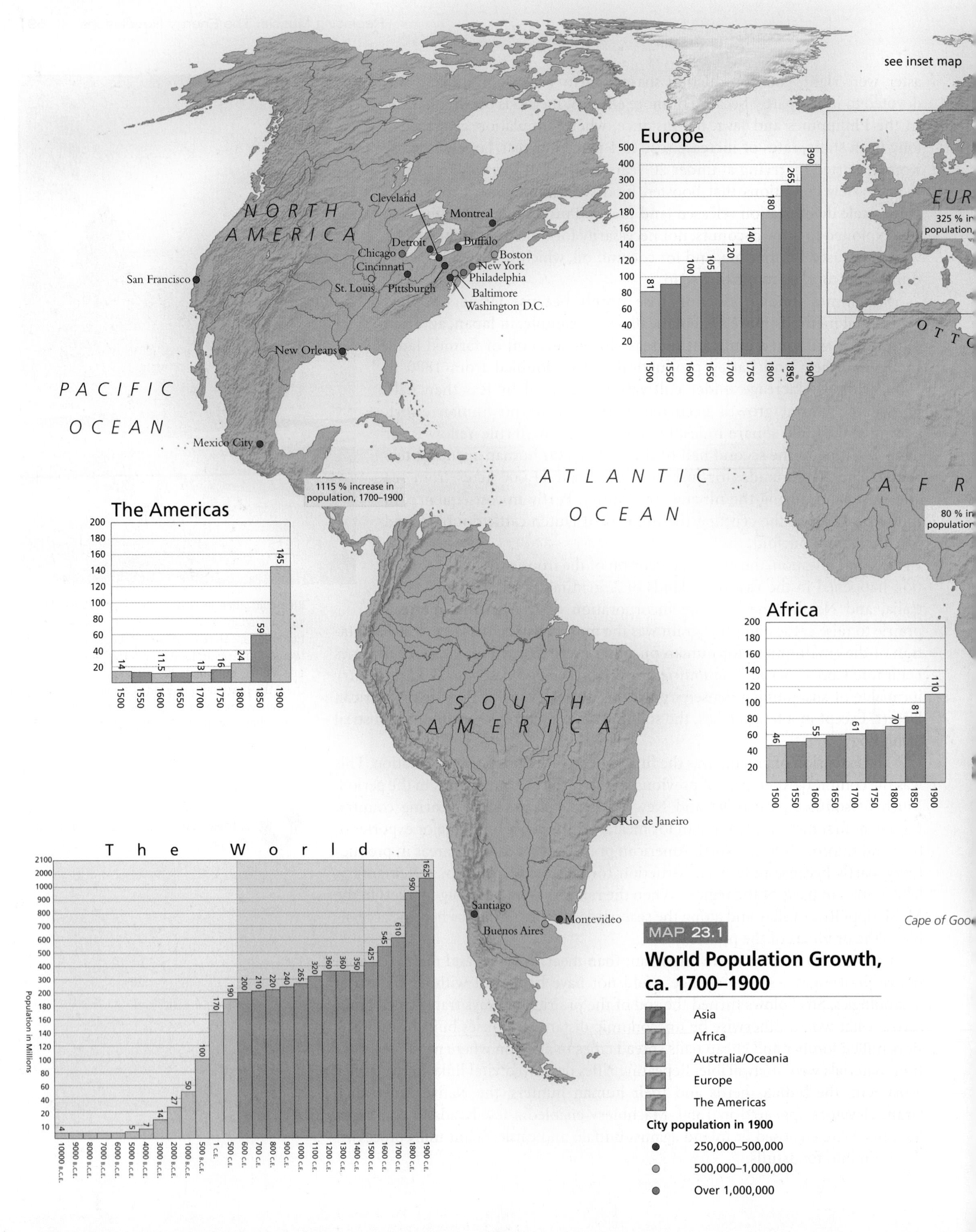

Europe (population in millions)

1500	1550	1600	1650	1700	1750	1800	1850	1900
81		100	105	120	140	180	265	390

The Americas (population in millions)

1500	1550	1600	1650	1700	1750	1800	1850	1900
14		11.5		13	16	24	59	145

Africa (population in millions)

1500	1550	1600	1650	1700	1750	1800	1850	1900
46		55		61		70	81	110

The World (population in millions)

10000 B.C.E.	4
9000 B.C.E.	
8000 B.C.E.	
7000 B.C.E.	
6000 B.C.E.	
5000 B.C.E.	5
4000 B.C.E.	7
3000 B.C.E.	14
2000 B.C.E.	27
1000 B.C.E.	50
500 B.C.E.	100
1 C.E.	170
500 C.E.	190
600 C.E.	200
700 C.E.	210
800 C.E.	220
900 C.E.	240
1000 C.E.	265
1100 C.E.	320
1200 C.E.	360
1300 C.E.	360
1400 C.E.	350
1500 C.E.	425
1600 C.E.	545
1700 C.E.	610
1800 C.E.	950
1900 C.E.	1625

MAP 23.1

World Population Growth, ca. 1700–1900

Asia
Africa
Australia/Oceania
Europe
The Americas

City population in 1900

250,000–500,000
500,000–1,000,000
Over 1,000,000

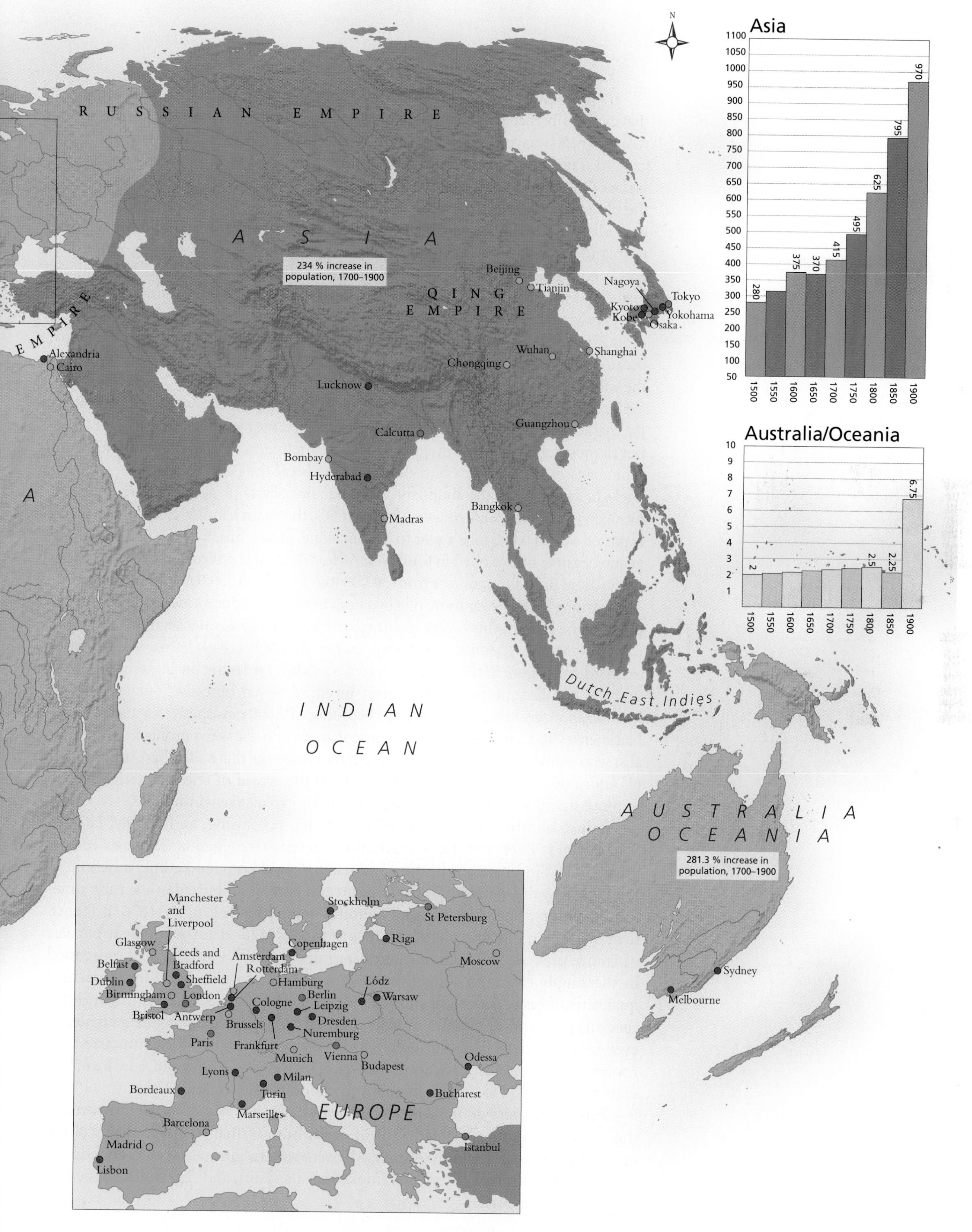

RUSSIAN EMPIRE
ASIA
234 % increase in population, 1700–1900
EMPIRE
QING EMPIRE
Beijing
Tianjin
Nagoya
Tokyo
Kyoto
Kobe
Yokohama
Osaka
Shanghai
Wuhan
Chongqing
Alexandria
Cairo
Lucknow
Calcutta
Guangzhou
Bombay
Hyderabad
Bangkok
Madras
A
Dutch East Indies
INDIAN OCEAN
AUSTRALIA OCEANIA
281.3 % increase in population, 1700–1900
Sydney
Melbourne
Asia
1100
1050
1000
950
900
850
800
750
700
650
600
550
500
450
400
350
300
250
200
150
100
50
280
375
370
415
495
625
795
970
1500
1550
1600
1650
1700
1750
1800
1850
1900
Australia/Oceania
10
9
8
7
6
5
4
3
2
1
2
2.5
2.25
6.75
1500
1550
1600
1650
1700
1750
1800
1850
1900
Manchester and Liverpool
Stockholm
St Petersburg
Glasgow
Leeds and Bradford
Copenhagen
Riga
Amsterdam
Moscow
Belfast
Rotterdam
Sheffield
Dublin
Hamburg
Lódz
Birmingham
London
Berlin
Warsaw
Cologne
Leipzig
Bristol
Antwerp
Brussels
Dresden
Nuremburg
Paris
Frankfurt
Munich
Vienna
Budapest
Odessa
Lyons
Milan
Bordeaux
Turin
Bucharest
Marseilles
EUROPE
Barcelona
Istanbul
Madrid
Lisbon

In 1861, Anthony Trollope saw the results: concentrations of food resources that had no precedent or parallel. Trollope was "grieved by the loose manner in which wheat was treated" in Minneapolis—"bags of it upset and left upon the ground. The labor of collecting it was more than it was worth." In Buffalo, he saw some of the 60 million bushels of grain that passed through the city every year. But the transformation of the prairie was only beginning. In 1862, the Homestead Act made land in the West available at nominal prices. By 1900, 500 million acres of farmland had been added. Similar changes occurred in other grasslands. Argentina had been a net importer of grain in the 1860s. By 1900, it exported 100 million bushels of wheat and maize a year. Canada also became a major grain exporter.

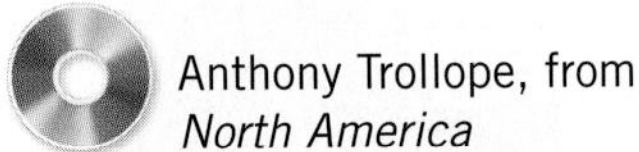
Anthony Trollope, from *North America*

Fertilizers increased productivity, too. In Europe, farmers kept their fields constantly productive, alternating beets or turnips with clover or alfalfa, which renew the soil because they recycle nitrogen. Turnips, rutabagas, and potatoes kept cattle alive during the winter, generating more manure. In 1860, British farms still got 60 percent of their fertilizers from animal waste. But the system increasingly needed supplements because the market demanded more and more meat. Turnips, moreover, demand a lot of fertilizer in most soils. The first consequence was the midcentury guano boom, mined from mountains of nitrogen-rich bird-dung on islands off the Peruvian coast, where huge flocks of birds fed on the abundant fish. The normally rainless climate preserved the nitrogen from being washed away. In the 1850s, the main handler of Peruvian guano exported over 200,000 tons a year to Britain alone. Meanwhile, in 1843, new sources of guano began to be exploited in southwest Africa. The first chemical fertilizers came into production: British output rose from 30,000 tons in 1854 to 250,000 tons in 1866.

Farming became ever more of a business, in which producers looked to boost production and make farms bigger to cut relative costs. In consequence, more and more capital went into scientific agronomy. Luther Burbank (1849–1926) was the most extraordinary figure in the field. He started a market-gardening business in California in 1875 and became the world's most inventive—even obsessive—practitioner of hybridization, grafting, and breeding. He produced 1,000 new species, including white blackberries and a fruit that was half apricot, half plum. He was a profligate sensationalist who would destroy hundreds of plants to create one that suited his purposes. But his enormous commercial success encouraged the spread of scientific techniques to improve strains and develop new plants for newly exploited environments.

Industrialization revolutionized preserving, processing, and supply. Lazzaro Spallanzani's (1729–1799) observations of bacteria (see Chapter 22) revealed new possibilities. Simultaneous heating and sealing could keep food edible indefinitely. Stimulated by the demands of the large armies Europe mobilized in the early nineteenth century, huge bottling and canning operations began. By 1836, a French firm was selling 100,000 cans of sardines a year. By 1880, factories on the west coast of France produced 50 million cans of sardines annually. Canning kept more food in the supply chain for longer. It made it possible to transport unprecedented quantities of easily perishable food in bulk over long distances, facilitating regional specialization and economies of scale. In the 1870s, Australian engineers made an even more dramatic breakthrough in preservation techniques: the compressed-gas cooler. Meat from Australia, South America, or New Zealand could now be refrigerated and shipped to Europe at relatively modest cost (see Map 23.2).

Food no longer had to be produced near to where it was eaten. In industrializing areas, agriculture declined. British agriculture virtually collapsed in the last generation of the nineteenth century. All over Western Europe, farmers abandoned growing wheat for dairy products, smoked meats, fruits, and vegetables, in the face of long-range imports.

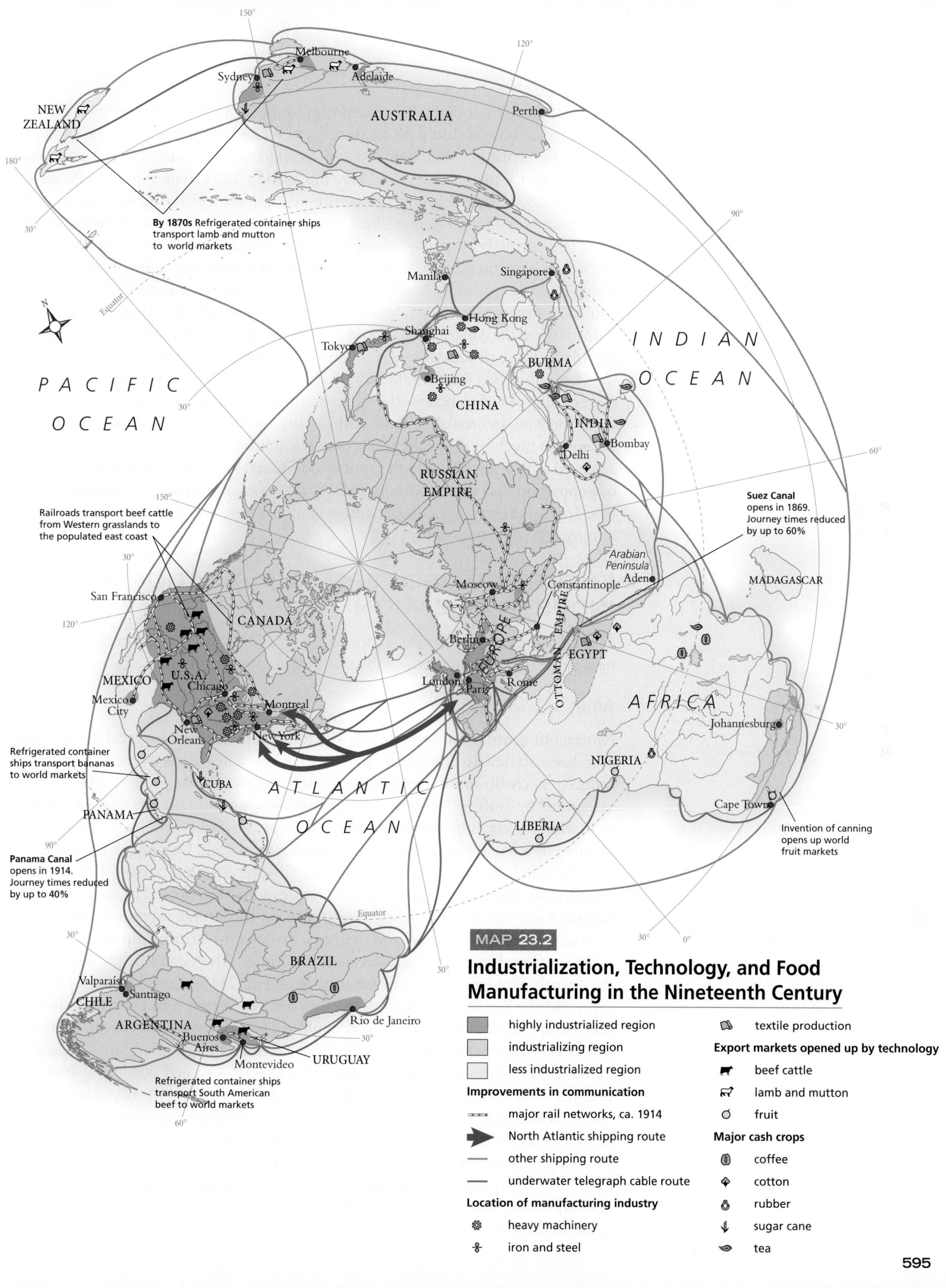

MAP 23.2

Industrialization, Technology, and Food Manufacturing in the Nineteenth Century

- highly industrialized region
- industrializing region
- less industrialized region

Improvements in communication

- major rail networks, ca. 1914
- North Atlantic shipping route
- other shipping route
- underwater telegraph cable route

Location of manufacturing industry

- heavy machinery
- iron and steel
- textile production

Export markets opened up by technology

- beef cattle
- lamb and mutton
- fruit

Major cash crops

- coffee
- cotton
- rubber
- sugar cane
- tea

Manufacturers took on more and more processing, until they were delivering some foods, mass produced on a vast scale, in forms in which consumers could eat them without further preparation. Cookies and crackers, once artisanal products, became factory-made items. In 1859, the world's three major producers, all in Britain, made 6 million pounds of cookies. By the late 1870s, the same firms were producing 37 million pounds. Other industries created new foodstuffs. In the 1840s, chocolate, formerly a luxury beverage, became a cheap food in Western Europe. In 1865, the German chemist Baron Justus von Liebig perfected cubes of beef extract, which could be made into broth by adding water. Moral crusaders sought a low-protein food that would reduce "passion" and promote chastity. They thought they found it when the American Reverend Sylvester Graham invented breakfast cereals in the 1830s. These products were suitable for industrial production methods and, by the 1890s, absorbed much of the world's increased output of grain.

For all its inefficiencies—the scars of famine, the failures of distribution—the huge increase in available food had an unprecedented impact on the world. Because so much of it was the result of new kinds of science and technology, it was achieved with a relatively small input of additional labor. Part of the vast increase of population that the food boom fed was free to engage in other economic activities. Trade, industry, agriculture, and urbanization were linked in a mutually sustaining cycle of expansion.

ENERGY FOR POWER: MILITARIZATION AND INDUSTRIALIZATION

Militarization and industrialization were linked to the midcentury fat crisis, because armies and industries consumed large amounts of fat.

Militarization

Nineteenth-century armies were big. The trend to make them bigger than they had ever been started in Europe in the 1790s when fear of the French Revolution induced a coalition of conservative countries to invade France. The French responded by drafting a citizen army or "nation in arms." This was not intended to militarize society. On the contrary, it was an old-fashioned ideal, supposedly inspired by ancient Greek and Roman republican models. During the Renaissance, classical scholars, such as Machiavelli (see Chapter 18), had argued that citizens would fight more effectively than paid professional warriors. The same idea lay behind American revolutionaries' insistence on the moral superiority of citizen militias over the professional and mercenary troops the British employed.

Karl von Clausewitz, from *On War*

The effect, however, was to create mass armies. The Grand Army with which the French Emperor Napoleon invaded Russia in 1812 numbered over 600,000 men, and the Russian forces opposing him were even larger. In the second half of the century, many European powers could mobilize armies numbering millions. The effects on warfare were enormous. The German theorist Karl von Clausewitz (1780–1831) formulated the doctrine of "total war"—waged not just against the enemy's armed forces but also against the entire population of a hostile country (see Chapter 26). The results made war worse—multiplying victims, spreading destruction, and encouraging preemptive attacks. Mass armies transformed society by taking young men from their homes, gathering them in barracks, drilling them in military discipline, and teaching them loyalty to the state. "Peasants," it was said, "became Frenchmen" through service in the army. Armies became forges of national identities.

The economic consequences of militarization were, perhaps, even more significant. Wartime logistics generated innovations in production, supply, and communications. Huge production lines, for instance, first appeared in state bakeries that produced dry bread for navies. These bakeries inspired the factory system of production that was necessary for large-scale industrialization. Armies concentrated huge numbers of men, straining food supplies and transport resources. Navies consumed unprecedented amounts of iron and steel for shipbuilding and of coal to keep the ships going. Every serviceman had to be fed. Margarine was invented for the French navy. Canning was a response to war. Canned milk was developed in the American Civil War (1861–1865). Massive armed forces demanded unprecedented quantities of mass-produced munitions. Every gun and cartridge had to be greased. In 1857, the issue of cartridges supposedly greased with pig and beef fat sparked a major rebellion among the native troops of Britain's Indian army. To the Muslims, pigs were unclean. To the Hindus, cows were sacred. (In fact, the cartridges were greased with vegetable oil.)

An early Union ironclad on the Mississippi River during the Civil War. Although the British and French navies already had ships built entirely of iron by 1860, U.S. naval experts were reluctant to believe that these vessels could be effective. But the Union navy put iron plates on wooden ships and began building iron-hulled vessels in 1862, in response to Confederate plans to launch similar ships and buy others from Britain.

Industrialization

Fossil fuels fired industrialization. Peat and coal were extracted from the ground on an unprecedented scale. Oil followed (and in the twentieth century, natural gas). In effect, mining and drilling for coal and oil released buried sunlight, accumulated millions of years ago when plants and creatures—which store energy from the sun in the carbons that form their bodies—were buried and crushed. A few pounds of coal can produce as much heat as an acre of timber. So the first effect of the release of coal from the ground was to liberate woodland for farming. The second was to provide energy for new forms of power.

Coal and steam were inextricably linked. Steam powered the pumps that drained the mines. Coal fueled the furnaces that produced the steam. Iron and steel were inescapably part of the picture. They were the materials from which the machinery was made to convert coal to energy and steam to power—the rods and the pistons, the cogs and casings of the engines. Coal produced the heat that fused the ores and forged the metals. The metals in their turn enclosed the spaces in which the coal burned.

Fuel consumption and production leaped. Japanese coal production had always been modest, but it rose from 390,000 tons in 1860 to 5 million tons in 1900. Increases of a similar order of magnitude occurred in Belgian and Spanish coal mines over the same period. The most productive coalfield in the world was already that of South Wales in Britain. Here, in the same period, output soared from 11.4 million to 35.1 million tons a year. German coal was of problematic quality, but nineteenth-century developments made its exploitation worthwhile. Over 100 million tons were being mined annually by 1900.

But what was all this extra energy for? Statistics seem to dominate the story of industrialization whenever historians tell it. Economic historians like to measure industrial change in terms of productivity figures. These are sometimes suggestive, sometimes spectacularly revealing. Machinery in Britain by the 1830s, for instance, could produce in 135 hours the same amount of cotton that took 50,000 hours to spin by hand. This helps to explain the appeal of industrialization. But it also

Power to rival nature's. Philippe-Jacques de Loutherbourg, born in France in 1740, made his career as a painter in England, where his work as a stage designer helped to add a showy, theatrical quality to his art. His painting of the great iron-works of Coalbrookdale in the English Midlands shows the rural setting typical of early industrial sites and displays the "sublime," "picturesque," and "romantic" qualities for which he became famous. The smoke and flames from the forge are more on the scale of a volcano than of a factory.

points to a paradox. In an age of increasing population, more muscle power was becoming available worldwide. So why bother to mechanize?

In part, the explanation lies in the geography of industrialization. On the whole, it happened earliest and fastest in regions where labor was relatively expensive: in areas such as Europe and Japan, where the size of the workforce was relatively modest compared with, say, China and India; or in the United States, which, despite the huge increase in its population, was still underpopulated in the nineteenth century. Second, industrialization was a function of demand. Population increase accounted in part for increasing demand, but so did the multiplication of sources of wealth—the new resources unlocked from the soil, the enormous expansion of financial institutions, the growth in the money supply as governments took on increasing responsibilities and minted cash to pay for them. The growth in the money supply worldwide would have been hugely inflationary if production and trade had not increased proportionately and absorbed its effects. Although mechanization stripped workers of employment in traditional industries and in unindustrialized parts of the world, it generated new wealth and, therefore, new employment opportunities in other activities and other areas. Trade and capital were essential extra spokes in the cycle that linked food, population, and industry. They provided incentives to mechanize and money to invest in mechanization.

Economic circumstances alone, however, cannot explain industrialization. It was more than an economic phenomenon. For contemporaries who took part in it, the appeal of industry was a form of enchantment. Like magic, it multiplied power and effected dazzling transformations. A passenger aboard the first commercially viable locomotive train—George Stevenson's *Rocket* in Britain, which achieved a speed of 35 miles per hour in 1829—called it a "magical machine with its flying white breath and rhythmical unvarying pace. When I closed my eyes the sensation of flying was delightful." A witness of the unveiling of one of the century's most impressive technologies—Sir Henry Bessemer's process for turning iron into steel in 1856—described the event with the slack-jawed awe of a sorcerer's apprentice: "Out came a volcanic eruption of such dazzling coruscations as had never been seen before. When combustion had expended all its fury, most wonderful of all, the result was steel!"

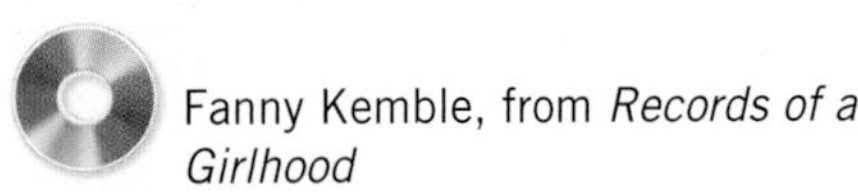

Fanny Kemble, from *Records of a Girlhood*

Industrial technology represented, for its early witnesses, the triumph of imagination over nature. Admirers of mechanization saw it as romantic—a perspective we have lost today. The English artist Turner (1775–1851) painted the speed of the locomotive. The German composer Mendelssohn (1809–1847) turned the noises of steam navigation into music. The British author Samuel Smiles (1812–1904), who convinced the English-speaking world of the virtues of industrialization, called the steam engine "the noblest machine ever invented by man." Engineers became heroes. Smiles wrote their lives in the style of romances of chivalry or even of fairy tales.

Indian railway. When it began to operate in 1881, the Darjeeling Railway in northwest India ran 55 miles from the port of Calcutta, mounting steep slopes to reach the tea-growing regions. This loop, photographed in the late nineteenth or early twentieth century, shows one of the devices the British engineers who built the railway used to conquer the sharp ascent. The tea the trains carried eventually went to England, supplying a cheap stimulant for the workforce of British industry.

There were martyrs as well as heroes. One hundred workers died digging two miles of a railway tunnel I. K. Brunel (1806–1859) designed in Britain. And, of course, industrialization had its enemies. It threatened livelihoods in traditional crafts. Moralists condemned techniques that forced workers into soulless rhythms of work in the backbreaking, disease-breeding environments of factories and mines, and as we shall see in Chapter 24, their laments were justified. For some people, railways desecrated the countryside or damaged and stole the land. Nostalgia for the fate of the land inspired artists, novelists, and reactionary social movements (see Chapter 26) wherever industrialization occurred.

Even industrialists often seemed uncommitted to what we should now call entrepreneurial spirit. In England, "captains of industry" typically devoted wealth to buying country estates and building huge country houses in imitation of traditional landed aristocrats. Their managers, who could not afford country estates, imitated the longed-for way of life in so-called garden suburbs. French industrialists commonly affected scorn for entrepreneurship. In 1836, a member of a great textiles dynasty of northern France went on a pilgrimage "to obtain illumination from the Holy Ghost, so that we should never undertake anything in business above our strength, lest we should be troubled by hazardous speculations." François Wendel died a multimillionaire in 1825, having become, he said, an iron master and owner of profitable businesses "against my will." Another French magnate, Jules Siegfried, engraved "To work is to act" on his cufflinks, but retired from manufacturing textiles at the age of 44. In Japan (as we shall see), entrepreneurs insisted that they worked for honor or patriotism rather than profit. Again, they sought to imitate the warrior aristocracy. Even in the United States, Cornelius Vanderbilt (1794–1877), the owner of steamships and railroads, liked to see himself as a "knight of industry" and had himself depicted in a church window dressed in medieval armor. In the southern states, manufacturers aped planters' lifestyles. Industrialization, in short, succeeded only where people could reconcile it with traditional values.

Even regions with few or no factories or mechanized production methods, such as China, India, and South America, got railways, steamships, and electric telegraphs. The first successful experiment in steam locomotion was carried out in 1804, when Richard Trevithick carried ten tons of iron along nine miles of tracks in Britain. The local paper predicted "a thousand instances" of uses "not yet thought of." Trevithick's designs were too slow and cumbersome to be commercially useful, but viable railways soon spread around the world with amazing speed. Although the web of railways was densest in industrial regions, the rails also stretched across vast distances of the unindustrialized world, delivering to ports and factories ingredients for machines to turn into saleable goods, and food and drugs to keep the workers at their tasks. The first line across the American continent opened in 1869. By 1900, the United States had nearly 170,000 miles of track. Most of the network linked regions of primary products to centers of industrial processing and consumption.

Among the most intensive scenes of railway building in the mid–nineteenth century were India and Cuba—colonial lands where the ruling powers discouraged manufactures and exploited their basic products to serve industries in Britain and Spain, the "home countries." India's case is especially spectacular. Railway construction began in 1852. Fifty years later, India had nearly 42,000 miles of track—more than all the rest of Asia put together. One hundred fifty million pounds of British capital made the enterprise possible. In terms of labor, however, this was a genuinely Indian enterprise, with over 370,000 Indians a year working on the lines by the 1890s. Indian contractors, who supplied workers and, in most cases, supervised the work, made the biggest fortunes in railway construction. Jamsetji Dorabji Naegamwalla (1804–1882) was the most successful of all. He was an illiterate carpenter in a British-run dockyard when, in 1850, he realized the potential of the railways. He employed thousands of Indians and a handful of European engineers, ensuring the smooth running of the operations the government confided to him. When a viaduct he built collapsed in 1855, he bullied the authorities to let him rebuild it at extra cost and waive their usual demand for cash securities in advance. Unlike most British contractors who worked on railway construction, he made money and retired in 1870 to enjoy his wealth.

The development of steam-powered shipping kept pace with that of the railways. In 1807, the first commercial steamboat, built by Robert Fulton, navigated the Hudson River, traveling 150 miles upriver from New York City to Albany in 32 hours. The first regular transatlantic steam service began in 1838. Ten or 12 days instead of 6 weeks became the normal length of an Atlantic crossing between Western Europe and North America.

Intersecting rail and shipping lines was the scaffolding of the world, along which trade and travelers could clamber to every part of it. James Hill, who built the cathedral of St. Paul, Minnesota, founded a steamship line that linked the great food-producing and consuming belt of the world, from Vladivostock to Vancouver on Canada's Pacific coast. The railways made a startling difference. They wrenched trade in new directions. They made it possible for land-based systems of communications to carry freight on a scale previously possible only by sea. The world's great hinterlands, far from seas and ports and even navigable rivers, in the innermost parts of the continents, could be integrated into an increasingly global economy.

Electricity began to rival steam power. In the 1830s and 1840s, the English amateur physicist Michael Faraday demonstrated the possibilities of electric lighting. The biggest contribution arose from one of his first gadgets: an electromagnetic induction machine made in 1831. The following year, the American Samuel Morse used Faraday's discovery to transmit messages. The first long-range telegraph line linked Washington, D.C., to Baltimore, Maryland, in 1844. Submarine cables to transmit telegraph messages crossed the Atlantic in 1869, shrinking the ocean to the dimensions of a pond. An electric age was

Population, Food, and Energy

1780–1831	Karl von Clausewitz, developer of theory of "total war"
ca. 1800	Global population: 950 million; areas with regions in excess of four people per square mile: East Asia, southeast Asia, India, Western Europe
1804	First successful railroad locomotion
1807	First commercial steamboat
1850s	British imports of guano reach 200,000 tons per year
1850–1900	500 million acres added to U.S. farmland
1860–1900	Japanese coal production rises from 390,000 to 5 million tons; British coal production rises from 11.4 million to 35.1 million
1866	British output of chemical fertilizers reaches 250,000 tons
1869	First transcontinental railroad in United States; first telegraph messages cross the Atlantic
1870s	Australian engineers develop compressed-gas cooler
ca. 1900	German coal production reaches 100 million tons annually
	Argentina exports 100 million bushels of wheat per year; global population: 1.6 billion; new areas with regions in excess of four people per square mile: Americas, Africa

MAKING CONNECTIONS

INDUSTRIALIZATION AND MILITARIZATION

INDUSTRIAL DEVELOPMENT →	MILITARY ADAPTATION →	EFFECTS
Food technology: preservation, production, innovation	To supply massive armies of nation-states: canning of food, beverages; automated production lines for baked goods; new products like margarine to supply naval personnel	Extension of ability to provision large-scale armies/navies across continents and oceans; projecting military power; ability to manage colonies more effectively
New energy sources: fossil fuels	Coal-generated energy and steam power fuel industrialized production of weapons, ammunition	Largest industrial nations (Europe, U.S.) develop massive armies, navies equipped with weapons and ammunition that are more deadly
Transportation technology	Railroads, steamships used to transport troops and supplies rapidly across oceans, continents	Tighter control of homelands, colonies through technologically advanced military forces
Electrical technology	First practical application focuses on communication—telegraphy, used by military forces to coordinate troop movements	Ability to maintain control of large-scale armies on battlefields or across continents and oceans via telegraph messages

about to succeed the age of steam. The gasoline-fueled internal combustion engine, invented in the 1890s, also pointed the way to a further stage of locomotion without rail tracks. It would have as transforming an impact on the twentieth century as the steam engine had on the nineteenth.

INDUSTRIALIZING EUROPE

One way to measure the spread of industrialization is to map the distribution of steam-powered businesses. By these standards, Europe developed early and mightily. In the first half of the nineteenth century, Britain, Spain, Italy, and Belgium all doubled their steam-driven industrial capacity. France and Russia tripled theirs. In what is now the Czech Republic (but what was then part of the Austrian Empire), capacity grew fivefold, and Germany's capacity multiplied by six.

Industries transcended traditional national boundaries. In 1830, the Englishman John Cockerill's core business was manufacturing textiles in Belgium. He set up a factory in Liège to manufacture his own equipment. He diversified into weaving in Germany and Russian-ruled Poland and into producing cotton yarn in Spain. He went into mining in various European countries to obtain raw materials for his engineering factories and into international banking to finance his operations. He even had a sugar plantation in the Dutch colony of Surinam in South America. When his empire collapsed in 1837, he built railways in Russia.

From 1815 to 1914, city growth came to exceed army growth as the motor of change in Europe. Industrialization helped shape what remains, on the map, a conspicuous feature of the modern world: a zone of densely clustered industrial cities from Belfast in Northern Ireland and Bilbao in northwest Spain to Rostov and St. Petersburg in Russia (see Map 23.3). By 1900, nine European cities had more than a million people. Most of the population of Britain and Belgium had forsaken agriculture for industry and rural life for the cities. The rest of industrializing Europe

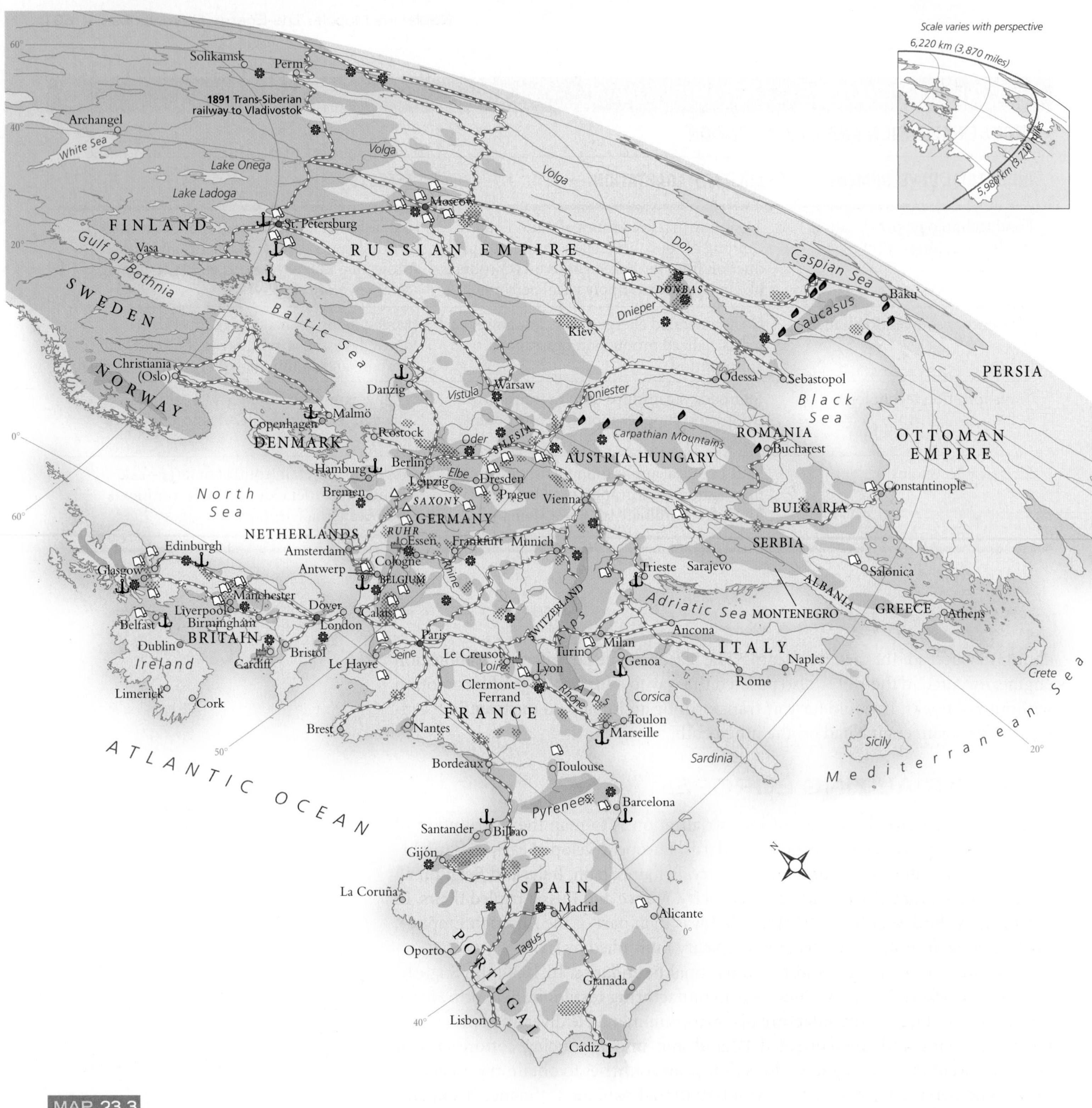

MAP 23.3

The Industrialization of Europe by 1914

Land use 1914

- mountainous area/wasteland
- agriculture and stock rearing
- forest
- industrial area

Resources

- coalfield
- oil
- potash

Manufacturing industry

- textiles
- iron smelting
- machinery
- shipbuilding

Population growth

- city with population over 500,000 in 1850
- city with population over 500,000 in 1914
- city with population under 500,000 in 1914
- principal railways 1914

showed the same drift to the towns. The Russian Empire remained an overwhelmingly peasant country, but two-thirds of the inhabitants of St. Petersburg, Russia's capital, were former peasants.

Still, European industrialization tended to be concentrated in particular areas. Only little Belgium was a fully industrialized country in the sense of having industry evenly scattered throughout its territory. Southern Britain actually lost industrial capacity, which became concentrated in northern and central England and along the river Clyde in Scotland. In France, the northeast had most of the country's industry. In Switzerland, it was in the north. In Germany, most industry was located in two regions: the Ruhr in the west and in Silesia and Saxony in the east. Italy's industries were concentrated in the north in Piedmont and Lombardy and focused on the cities of Turin and Milan. In Russia, the two favored areas were in St. Petersburg and in the Donets Basin to the north of the Black Sea. In Spain, only the Basque Country and Catalonia were industrialized.

To try to understand why neighboring areas responded differently to the opportunity to industrialize, the Low Countries are a good place to look. If Britain was, as is commonly said, the first industrial nation, Belgium was the second. Belgian entrepreneurs concentrated on iron and steel production, for which Belgium was well supplied with raw materials. By 1870, Belgian furnaces were producing on average a third more iron than those of Britain, over half as much again as those of Germany, and more than double those of France. Zinc and glass were other Belgian specialties. Belgium was also well served by railways. Its 1,800 miles of track in 1870 constituted a substantial network for such a small country.

The Netherlands, meanwhile, remained overwhelmingly agricultural. Its industrial sector was dedicated to food processing, especially to making candy, using the cane sugar from Dutch colonies in the Caribbean and the Dutch East Indies and the beet sugar Dutch farmers produced. Dutch firms supplied 80 percent of the British market for condensed and powdered milk by 1900 and the Netherlands was Europe's biggest manufacturer of margarine. Despite the traditional importance of shipbuilding, Dutch iron and steel production only began to catch up with European averages in the 1890s.

So why were the two countries, which had similar histories and cultural profiles, so different? If anything, the Netherlands had historic advantages: a large colonial empire and a tradition of overseas trade—both of which, according to economic theorists in the nineteenth century, should have stimulated industrial development. Dutch coal was mainly anthracite and hard to mine—but similar limitations did not restrain industry in Germany. If there is such a thing as an industrial or capitalist spirit, it is unlikely that it should have been prevalent in one country and not in its neighbor. Indeed, when global conditions changed in the late nineteenth and twentieth centuries, the Netherlands did turn to industrialization.

In the nineteenth century, however, the two countries' economies were complementary: Belgium specialized in heavy industries, while the Netherlands specialized in producing and processing food for industrializing markets, including those of Belgium. The patchiness of industrialization, in short, was essential to industrialization's success. It was part of a pattern of specialization in which some regions supplied food and raw materials while others concentrated on manufacturing. If some places had comparative advantage in resources, others had comparative advantage in finance and access to markets, or a relatively disciplined or suitably educated labor force. The system was reproduced at a global level, as large areas of the world became suppliers of primary produce to industrializing economies.

Ankle-deep in coffee on a plantation in Brazil in the early twentieth century. The freshly harvested beans are tipped into troughs to be washed. Business imperialism continued to promote long-range ecological exchange as global trade increased, making South American coffee a major product alongside coffee from southeast Asia, and sending Brazilian rubber trees to southeast Asia.

INDUSTRY IN THE AMERICAS

The United States was a surprising industrializer, with a long history of supplying raw materials—pelts and skins, whaling products—for other people's industries. The southern states produced raw cotton for mills in Britain, and tobacco and sugar, which contributed to the world economy mainly as mild drugs to make workers' dreary lives more bearable. The Midwest had, by the mid–nineteenth century, an obvious future as a source of food for the world. The rest of the American interior had vast stocks of lumber, agricultural land, and mineral deposits. The states' main manufactures in the eighteenth century had specialized in the partial processing of raw products, such as turning sugar into molasses and rum.

Still, in other ways, the United States was a suitable arena for industry. High per capita incomes meant money for investment. A large merchant marine connected with global markets. Mechanization could make up for the shortage of labor. Slavery, lawful in almost half the country until 1865, tied down a lot of labor unproductively, raising labor costs elsewhere. Nor did the abolition of slavery do much for this problem, because most former slaves remained in the South as sharecroppers or subsistence farmers. On the other hand, high immigration rates from Europe (see Chapter 24) supplied enough manpower to make factory systems viable and ensured growing domestic demand for industrial products. There was plenty of coal and iron. High tariffs were designed to shut out European products and protect native industry. By the 1890s, factories in the United States produced twice as much as those of Britain and half as much again as the whole of Europe.

Nothing like this industrialization happened in the rest of the Americas. Canada became an agricultural country, thanks to the domestication of its prairie, but not an industrial one. Fewer than 500,000 Canadians, out of some 7 million, worked in industry in 1900, and a third of those processed timber and food.

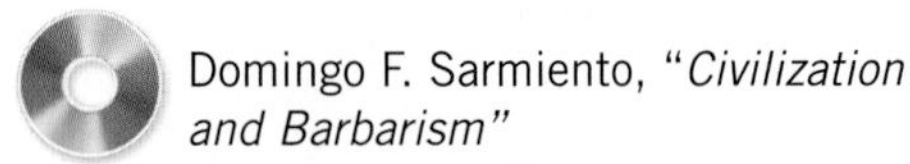

Domingo F. Sarmiento, *"Civilization and Barbarism"*

Most of Latin America was even less industrialized. The wars of independence left much of Latin America exhausted and divided (see Chapter 22). The newly independent nations, after spending heavily to fight Spain, had to maintain big armies in wariness of each other and to suppress domestic discontent. They lacked the north's incentive to mechanize. Latin America had plenty of ex-slaves, Indians, and illiterate laborers. In a sense, the region never fully emerged from colonial-style exploitation. Its elites became the exploiters of their own peasants, whereas until the emancipation of the slaves, the United States hardly had any dependent peasants, and none of them lived in the areas that industrialized. In North America, small farmers were their own bosses. Big North American ranchers used the mobile labor of "cowboys."

Free trade, which most of the independent Latin American states practiced, favored industrializing economies that could produce cheap goods and condemned Latin American economies to underdevelopment. Having fought Spanish monopolists under the banner of free trade, the new countries were unable to protect their native industries, such as they were, against European imports. They became locked into a role as producers of primary products: the ore, timber, and rubber that supplied the factories of Europe and the United States; the foods and fertilizers that fed the workforces; the tobacco and coffee that provided the stimulants that fought workers' need for sleep; the sweets that kept their blood sugar up. The grasslands of South America never followed the grain-rich, city-sprinkled model of the North American prairie, not even in Argentina, which had plenty of prairie-like land—the pampa—that still remains ranching country. The pampa was too far from most centers of population. The success of the United States became a standing reproach to the economically frustrated countries to its south.

Much of Latin America became a continent of disillusioned hopes. In 1857, Carlos Barroilhet, who did more than anyone else to explain the merits of guano to the world, prophesied that Peru was destined to be "at once the richest and happiest nation on Earth," but by the 1880s, guano—much depeleted by overexploitation—was considered a "curse." Competition from African guano and chemical superphosphates undermined a monopoly on which governments had staked all their economic plans. Brazil, similarly, lost its rubber monopoly when British businessmen smuggled out some plants and replanted them in Malaya. Late nineteenth-century Brazil relied more on coffee—another asset subject to increasing global competition—than rubber. Mexico lost its potentially most valuable territories—unmined gold and silver, untapped oil—in war with the United States in 1846–1848. In 1900, Argentina seemed still—in some ways, more than ever—a land of promise. Frozen meat exports and a meat-extract processing industry made the dominance of ranching in the pampa seem like a wise strategy. According to an "oath to the flag" that educational reformers introduced in 1909, Argentina was simply "the best land in the world," which would know "no history without a triumph." But its economy remained at the mercy of foreign investment and precarious global markets, and its promise was never fulfilled.

JAPAN INDUSTRIALIZES

Commodore Perry sailed into Tokyo Bay on July 8, 1853. His mission was to persuade or oblige the Japanese to open their ports to trade with the United States. He meant business in every sense of the word. He had four heavily armed ships with him. "The universal Yankee nation," wrote the expedition's interpreter, Samuel Williams, had arrived to end Japan's "apathy and long ignorance" with the example of "a higher civilization." Nevertheless, what Williams actually saw in Japan conformed only in part to the stereotype of a country consigned to backwardness by isolation. Japan's modernization had already begun, and the country was well poised to invest in innovative technologies: rich, urban, with a long history of commercial growth and a large middle class.

Japanese views of American naval technology

The project for the elites of late nineteenth-century Japan was to create an industrial economy like those in Europe and the United States. Japan would become the "floating wharf of the Pacific." "We need industry to attain the goal of becoming a rich nation," declared the government in 1868.

At first, unfair terms of trade held Japan back. Western powers imposed "unequal treaties" that allowed them to sell products in Japan cheaply and exempted their nationals from having to obey Japanese laws or be judged in Japanese courts. The trade balance remained adverse—Japan imported more than it sold abroad—until the 1880s. In 1884, only 176 nongovernment factories employed more than 50 people, and only 72 were steam powered. By 1899, however, Japan was able to break out of the unequal relationship and revise the terms of trade with the West, while imposing terms on China after defeating that country in 1895. Japan's total foreign trade increased tenfold between 1877 and 1900. The emperor

The Tokyo terminus of the new Tokyo-Yokohama railway line, built in 1872 with the aid of foreign engineers. From a series of prints called "Famous Places on the Tokaido: A Record of the Process of Reform," it was published only seven years after the Meiji Restoration opened Japan to foreign trade and ideas in 1868.

presided at the opening of the first long-distance railway in 1872. Nearly 5,000 miles were added by 1900. At the century's end, 50 cities had telephone exchanges, handling 45 million calls a year.

There were surprising successes. Buttons, previously unknown in Japan, became a major export by 1896. The textile-producing area of Britain inspired Japanese entrepreneurs to reorganize their country's cotton production. Cotton yarn production swelled more than sixfold to 250 million pounds—25 percent of Japan's total industrial output—by 1900. This was a remarkable achievement, because cotton textiles were one of the world's most competitive sectors. But women's labor kept costs down.

Two strategies were essential: first, expanding traditional economic activities and reinvesting the profits in new industries; and second, heavy investment by the state to kick-start industrial enterprises. Exports of traditional Japanese products, especially raw silk and tea, paid for industrialization, taking up what would otherwise have been China's expanding markets. By 1900, Japan exported practically as much silk as China.

Meanwhile, the strategy of involving state finance in the establishment of industry began to pay off at the cost of huge losses for the treasury. In the 1880s, state enterprises sold off mining interests and textile centers to private companies. Shipyards, established to build warships in the 1850s and 1860s, diversified into civil engineering and the production of iron and steel for industry. The foundations of wealth were available at cut price. Great corporations, of the kind that still dominate Japanese economic life, such as Mitsui and Mitsubishi, were able to take advantage, thanks to connections with the government and to the wealth they had accumulated during under the Tokugawa shoguns (1603–1868).

Japan's was industrialization Japanese style—not a copy of that of the West. Japanese responded to the West by trying to adapt rather than ape, equal rather than imitate. Western theorists of the merits of private enterprise and enlightened self-interest were well known in Japan, but the Japanese preferred to see business as a form of service to the community and the state. They knew the laws of supply and demand, but preferred to regulate consumption for moral reasons. Industrialists claimed to have patriotic motives. Fukuzawa Yukichi (1835–1901) convinced samurai of the merit of trade "for profit and for Japan." His books and pamphlets sold 10 million copies in Japan in his lifetime. Eiichi Shibusawa, who spent a long time as the government minister responsible for industrial development, confessed that he began by thinking that only the military and political classes were honorable. "Then," he wrote, "I realized that the real force of progress lay in business."

These mental habits and convictions made collaboration between the state and the private sector easy. The Western division between the state and private enterprise did not apply. Industrialists collaborated with government to restrain domestic demand and prioritize strength for war. Governments responded with contracts and concessions. In part this was because influential Japanese misunderstood Western models. Okuba Toshimichi, who visited manufacturing cities in Britain in the 1870s, reported that there was "no instance" in Europe where "a country's productive power was increased without the patronage and encouragement of its officials." This was not a false observation, but the inference he drew was misleading. The engine of Western capitalism—unless you count Russia as Western—did not need the state to stoke it, only to keep hands off the damper.

Nonetheless, the overall achievement of industrialization in Japan was remarkable. Compared with the beginning of the nineteenth century, Japan's national output of manufactured goods, raw materials, and agricultural products had quadrupled, and the proportion contributed by industry had at least doubled.

CHINA AND INDUSTRIALIZATION

As so often in Chinese history, peasant rebellion, rather than foreign example, was the spur to change. Western industrialization should have alarmed Chinese officials and intellectuals in the first half of the nineteenth century. It eroded Chinese domination of the global economy and reversed the military balance of power—with effects that China painfully felt, as we shall see in the next chapter. But influential Chinese did not develop their response until 1861. They called it "**self-strengthening.**"

In 1860, two events brought on a sense of crisis. First, huge areas fell into the hands of peasant revolutionaries, notably the Taipings, who mounted a serious threat to the Qing dynasty from 1852 to 1864. Second, an Anglo-French army occupied Beijing. The immediate pretext for this invasion was an apparently trivial matter of diplomatic procedure, but the background included a series of incidents that convinced the Westerners that they had to humble China to secure freedom of action for Western merchants and missionaries (see Chapter 25).

While smarting under their humiliations, China's elites took comfort from the outcome. The Western barbarians had no intention of trying to wrest the mandate of heaven from the Qing. Their aims were commercial, and the Chinese could buy their goodwill with trade. Barbarian skills could be employed to strengthen China. As an official memorandum of early 1861 put it, China had the chance "to snatch good fortune out of disaster, to transform weak to strong...." Civil servants reporting to the emperor insisted that the technology that gave the barbarians a present advantage was all of Chinese origin, anyway. They were largely right.

China would have to relearn its old skills from the foreigners. Shipbuilding and munitions manufacture were technologies China could adopt from Europe. "Now that we know what they depend on for victory," agreed Prince Gong, the emperor's chief minister, "we should try to master it."

Because European soldiers of fortune and merchants helped the Chinese government suppress the Taiping rebellion, General Li Hongzhang could inspect Western munitions closely. "If China were to pay attention to these matters," he concluded, "she would be able to stand on her own a hundred years from now." He called for a revolution in values that would elevate technicians and engineers above scholars and writers. "Seek machines that make machines and men who make machines."

As in Japan, the early impact of mechanization was confined to munitions. The Jiangnan arsenal opened in 1865 to manufacture guns and ships. It also had a translation department charged with keeping up to date with Western knowledge in armaments. But it never managed to produce rifles that were as good or as cheap as imported models. Its ships cost twice as much as those available from competitors abroad. A naval yard inaugurated in 1866 built 40 ships, none of which performed well.

Li Hongzhang (1823–1901). The Chinese statesman and general Li Hongzhang was the chief negotiator of the treaty that ended the first Sino-Japanese War in 1895. In 1896, he also negotiated a treaty that granted Russia the right to build the Trans-Siberian railroad across northern Manchuria.

Zeng Guofan (dzung gwoh-fahn), the model administrator responsible for modernizing China, went on insisting that imperial rule and rites were perfect. "Propriety and righteousness" came above "expediency and ingenuity." After his death in 1872, the focus of self-strengthening switched to civilian industries, the infrastructure, and the economic basis of a strong state: civil steamships, mechanization of coal mining and textile manufacture, and the telegraph system. A railway-building boom, paid for with foreign capital, followed in the 1880s, linking coal mines and agricultural hinterlands to the ports. Yet China remained a preindustrial power. Private investment was channeled through state-run monopolies in all these fields.

In war against Japan over who would dominate Korea in 1894–1895, the difference between the belligerents showed. On paper the Chinese navy, which had cost more than Japan's, looked more formidable—bigger and more heavily armed —than the Japanese navy. But when battle began, the Chinese guns had only three rounds of ammunition each. Most of their ships avoided action. The Japanese captured or sank those that did fight.

China and the West were mutually blinded by perceptions of each other's barbarism. From 1840, the Opium Wars (see Chapter 25) exposed China's weakness and dispelled the Western respect for the empire and its people that had featured so prominently during the Enlightenment (see Chapter 22). In China, it was heresy to acknowledge the West as civilized. For Westerners, the Chinese were Asiatic barbarians to be treated with contempt. For most of the Chinese elite, the big problems were those of longest standing: the peasant uprisings; the unrest of Muslim minorities, whose rebellions the Qing repressed with difficulty; the erosion of state power to provincial bosses. Carefully measured deference to selective Western superiority seemed the best course. "Chinese essence, Western practice" became the government's slogan after the humiliating defeat in the Sino-Japanese war of 1894–1895.

In the 1880s, the tea trade shrank in the face of Indian competition. Although Chinese silk exports remained significant, new exports from China were geared to an industrializing world: primary foodstuffs intended for processing abroad, skins and straw, hog bristles and timber, coal and iron ore. Much of the trade supplied Japanese industries that were outstripping those of China. The era of dominance for China through its luxury products was largely over.

INDIA AND EGYPT

In the nineteenth century, India deindustrialized. India's traditional industries, particularly cotton textile weaving, began to collapse in the 1820s. The disappearance of the great courts and armies of the Mughal era (see Chapter 21) left India without the motors of demand that once drove its economy. Indians had to turn back to the land.

The British made matters worse. They bureaucratized tax collection—cutting out native Indian capitalists. From an industrial giant, India became a producer of raw materials for the British Empire: tea, coffee, quinine, opium, jute, cotton. Early in the century, while the balance of trade with China was still unfavorable, Britain's trade drained cash from India's economy. Industrialization elsewhere lowered prices for Indian products. Millions of Indian laborers emigrated in the second half of the century, most to work on construction projects or plantations elsewhere in the British Empire. India still had a favorable trading balance with its Asian trading partners, but not with Britain. The machinery of British cotton mills pulverized Indian manufactures. By the end of the nineteenth century, British-made textiles accounted for over a third of India's total imports. India bought two-fifths of Britain's cotton exports (see Map 23.4). The British set the tariffs to favor their own exports. British firms effectively monopolized India's shipping, insurance, and international banking.

The British built a new economic infrastructure in India: dams, bridges, tunnels, roads, harbor installations, and, above all, railways. But the railways moved troops, administrators, travelers, and the primary goods the empire demanded. They did not contribute, as they did in Europe or North America, to industrialization.

In most of the rest of the world, industrial models of development had little appeal. Rulers wanted to get their hands on modern munitions—generally by buying them from the West—and to hire Western technicians to train their armies. Elsewhere, rulers or elites welcomed Western investment to build railways and bridges, but rarely tried to compete with Western manufactures.

The big exception was Egypt. Its population had grown rapidly from 2.5 million inhabitants in 1800 to 6.8 million in 1882. The passage of French Revolutionary armies through the country in 1798–1799 was an experience Egypt shared with much of Europe. While they were in Egypt, French officials opened factories for guns, gunpowder, food, and beer. After they departed, Mehmet Ali (1769–1849)—who, from 1805, was nominally the viceroy or khedive (heh-DEEV) for the Ottoman Empire but was, in effect, an independent monarch and the founder of a dynasty that ruled Egypt until 1953—brought in the services of Western, mostly French, experts to reproduce the activities already characteristic of industrializing Britain: cotton mills, munitions factories, steelworks, shipyards, a printing press. One of his French hired hands, Louis-Alexis Jumel, introduced a new strain of cotton that proved amazingly successful as the basis of fine textiles. In 1826, Mehmet Ali imported 500 steam-powered looms from Britain. About ten years later, Egypt was producing 1,200,000 bolts of cotton cloth a year. The industry was a state monopoly. In 1839, however, Britain forced Egypt to abandon protective tariffs when they blocked Mehemet Ali's attempt to overthrow the Ottoman Empire with

MAP 23.4

The Politics of Cotton

- raw cotton from U.S. to Britain
- cotton textiles to India
- raw cotton from India to Britain
- cotton-producing region
- textile town
- major cotton-producing states

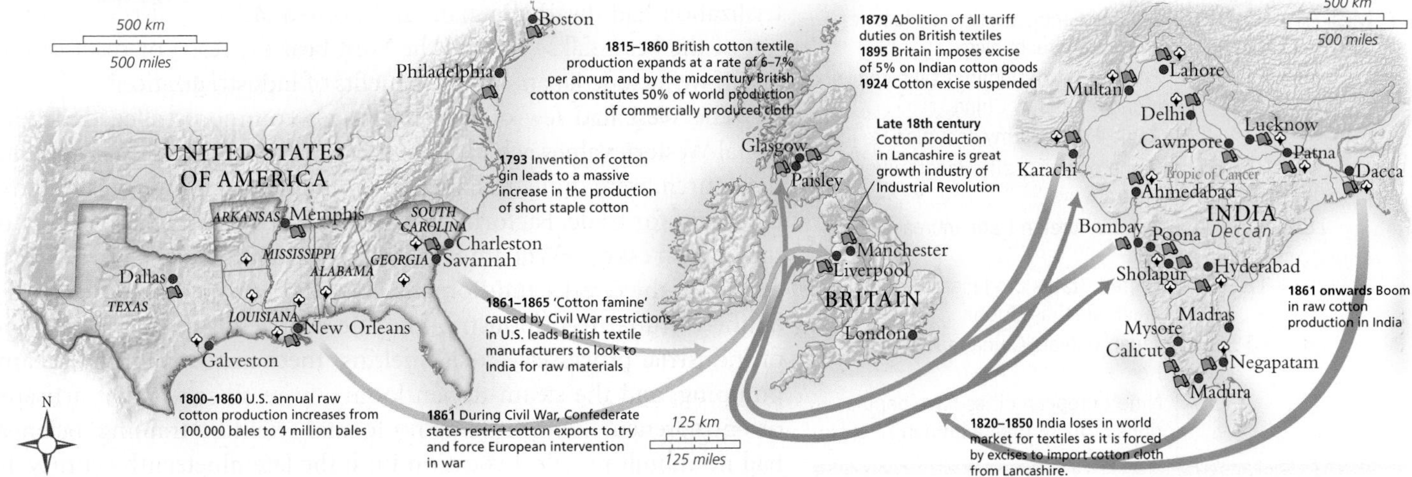

The Suez Canal. The French artist Edouard Rion (1833–1900) went to Suez to record Egyptian life for the French illustrated press just before the opening of the canal. Engravings of many of his paintings—including this bustling interpretation of the inaugural procession of ships through the canal in November 1869—appeared as illustrations to the account of the canal's construction written by Ferdinand de Lesseps, the canal's promoter and chief engineer.

French support. As a result, the Egyptian cotton industry dwindled, and Egypt, like the American South, became a major exporter of cash crops—sugarcane and raw cotton. Continuous irrigation was required to force the extra output needed to support the military and government facade of a modern state from the land. The peasants were impoverished and overburdened, and the opportunity to modernize on the Western European model slipped from Egypt's grasp.

Egyptian intellectuals remained faithful to Western models of development, and Khedive Ismail (r. 1863–1879), Mehemet Ali's grandson, tried to revive his grandfather's program. Ismail proclaimed Egypt part of Europe. Borrowing money at outrageous interest from European bankers, he built docks, sugar mills, an opera house in Cairo, and a school for girls. He had the Suez Canal driven across Egypt using French engineers and French capital. The canal opened in 1869 and, by connecting the Mediterranean to the Red Sea, reduced the sailing time from Europe to India and the Far East from months to weeks. But his extravagances bankrupted the state. In 1875, Britain purchased Ismail's shares in the canal. In 1879, his European creditors forced him to abdicate. Much of Egypt's revenue was assigned to repay foreign debts, and 1,300 foreign bureaucrats arrived to manage the country's finances and armed forces. In September 1881, the handful of native Egyptian officers still left in high ranks rebelled under the slogan "Egypt for the Egyptians."

Britain responded by occupying the country "to save," as a British official claimed, "Egypt from anarchy, and all European nations interested in Egypt from incalculable losses in blood and treasure." Egypt became a British dependency with a puppet government and a large British garrison until after the Second World War.

Industrialization in Global Context

1798–1799	French armies occupy Egypt
Nineteenth century	India deindustrializes
1800–1850	Dramatic increase in steam-driven industrial capacity in Europe
1805–1849	Rule of Mehmet Ali in Egypt, proponent of industrialization
1839	Britain forces Egypt to end protection of cotton industry
July 8, 1853	Commodore Perry sails into Tokyo Bay
Mid-nineteenth century	Japanese industrialization focuses on military technology
1860	Peasant revolutionaries take control of large parts of China Anglo-French army occupies Beijing
1861	China begins "self-strengthening" program
1877–1900	Japan's foreign trade increases tenfold
1890s	United States produces twice as much steel as Britain
1895	Japan defeats China in war over Korea
1900	Nine European cities have populations of more than a million

IN PERSPECTIVE: Why the West?

In 1800, China was probably about eight times as productive as Britain. By 1900, Britain produced about three times as much as China. In 1800, Britain and Germany combined contributed less than 5 percent of global industrial production. By 1900, those two countries alone accounted for nearly a third of that output. China's share in the same period fell from over a third to barely 6 percent (see Figure 23.1). Industrialization had dwarfed a giant and hoisted jacks-of-all-trades to the top of the beanstalk. Why did the West beat the rest—or most of the rest, if we include Japan—to the benefits of industrialization?

The West had few of the advantages commonly alleged. Traditional Western values, which were those of the landed aristocracy and the church, were industrialization's antibodies, training elites to have contempt for trade. Factories went up in a world where, according to the English essayist William Hazlitt (1778–1830), "people were always talking of the Greeks and Romans." Nor did Europe's supposedly scientific culture breed industry. The late eighteenth-century inventors of industrial processes—coke smelting, mechanized spinning, steam pumping, and the steam-driven loom—were all self-taught artisans or entrepreneurs with little or no formal scientific training. Science had no inbuilt practical vocation until the late nineteenth century. It would be fairer to say that industry hijacked European science—bought it for useful research, diverted it to social responsibility. Nor is it enough—though it is important—to say that the distribution of coal and iron privileged some economies for industrialization. In some places outside the West and beyond Western control, coal and iron reserves were left unexploited. In others, such as New England and parts of northern Spain and Italy, industrializers found ways to compensate for the lack of them.

Share of World Manufacturing Output, 1750–1900

	1750	1800	1830	1860	1880	1900
Europe	23.1	28.0	34.1	53.6	62.0	63.0
China	32.8	33.3	29.8	19.7	12.5	6.2
India	24.5	19.7	17.6	8.6	2.8	1.7

FIGURE 23.1 SHARE OF WORLD MANUFACTURING OUTPUT, 1750–1900

Derived from B. R. Tomlinson, "Economics: The Periphery," in Andrew Porter (ed.), The Oxford History of the British Empire: The Nineteenth Century, *Oxford 1990, p. 69 (Table 3.8).*

The West's real advantage was commercial. Commerce makes specialization possible. Without extensive systems of long-range trade, large concentrations of labor dedicated to manufacturing particular items or producing particular primary products are impossible. In the eighteenth and nineteenth centuries, Western Europe and North America were excellent environments for banking and what would now be called financial services industries, thanks to the climate of economic liberalism, and the commitment of states to foster commerce. Europe was not unique in this respect. Capitalism and commercial entrepreneurship were also ingrained in many communities and ruling elites in Asia. In China, however, commerce did not enjoy the same level of support from the state. Moreover, China was slow to change this attitude in the nineteenth century.

The pace of commerce is a function of the size of the market. European populations experienced exceptionally high growth rates in the nineteenth century. The population of Europe more than doubled to over 400 million in 1900. The populations of Belgium, Britain, and Germany all rose faster than the average. The United States had 76 million people by 1900—making it the most populous state in the Western world. Taken together, the demographic trends of the nineteenth century represented a shift in the global balance of resources in favor of the West. The continent, which had about a fifth of the world's population at the start of the century, had about a quarter by its end. The traditional pattern of global history, in which the hugely populous and productive societies of East and South Asia predominated, was ending or over. In some ways, the population figures mask an even greater shift: The extra people that Europe and the United States acquired produced hugely disproportionate increases in wealth, thanks to giant strides in the output of food and manufactures.

Westerners, finally, came from behind. That is where innovation usually comes from, because leaders in any field have little interest in promoting

CHRONOLOGY

1780–1831	Karl von Clausewitz, developer of theory of "total war"
1798–1799	French armies occupy Egypt
Nineteenth century	India deindustrializes
ca. 1800	Global population: 950 million; areas with regions in excess of four people per square mile: East Asia, southeast Asia, India, Western Europe
1800–1850	Increase in steam-driven industrial capacity: Britain, Spain, Italy, Belgium doubled; France, Russia tripled; Czech Republic increased fivefold; Germany increased sixfold
1804	First successful railroad locomotion
1805–1849	Reign of Mehmet Ali in Egypt, proponent of industrialization
1807	First commercial steamboat
1839	Britain forces Egypt to end protection of cotton industry
Mid-nineteenth century	Japanese industrialization focuses on military technology
1850–1900	500 million acres added to United States farmland
1850s	British imports of guano reach 200,000 tons per year
July 8, 1853	Commodore Perry sails into Tokyo Bay
1860	Peasant revolutionaries take control of large parts of China; Anglo-French army occupies Beijing
1860–1900	Japanese coal production rises from 390,000 to 5 million tons; British coal production in South Wales rises from 11.4 million to 35.1 million
1861–1865	American Civil War
1861	China begins "self-strengthening" program
1866	British output of chemical fertilizers reaches 250,000 tons
1869	First transcontinental railroad in United States
1870s	Australian engineers develop compressed-gas cooler; Belgium leads world in iron- and steel-making equipment
1877–1900	Japan's foreign trade increases tenfold
1890s	United States produces twice as much steel as Britain
1895	Japan defeats China in war over Korea
Late nineteenth century	Belgium and Netherlands develop increasingly complementary economies
1900	German coal production reaches 100 million tons annually; Argentina exports 100 million bushels of wheat per year; global population: 1.6 billion; nine European cities have populations of more than a million

change. Economies like those of India and China, which had productive traditional industries and enormous reserves of labor, felt no call to mechanize.

Industrialization was disastrous for many who took it up. Like the ancient adoption of farming, it had adverse consequences for nutrition, health, and what we would now call quality of life. It nourished oppression and tyranny. So why did people accept it—why, indeed, did they relish it so much that almost every community that has had the chance to industrialize over the last 200 years has opted to do so?

Industrialization had one obvious benefit—it released land for food production. It was no longer necessary, for instance, to maintain forests to provide wood for fuel. Forests in England halved between 1800 and 1900. The conservation policies of eighteenth-century Japan (see Chapter 20) were abandoned. In the nineteenth century, the carefully husbanded woodlands that formerly covered much of the islands of Honshu, Kyushu, and Shikoku largely vanished as coal replaced wood as a source of fuel, and Japan devoted more land to agriculture. The opposite happened in much of New England, where the rock-ribbed soil, which had largely been under the plow in 1800, began to revert to forest as food production shifted westward in the 1820s and 1830s.

Second, as we shall see in Chapter 24, the long-term consequences of industrialization tended to spread the benefits widely. In its early stages, mechanization increased the burden of labor for the workers who operated the machines. But it was labor saving for others. And technical improvements gradually liberated even the machine workers to enjoy increased leisure.

Finally, it is worth dwelling for a moment on the example of agrarianization. As readers of earlier parts of this book know, early farming communities adopted new production methods despite adverse short-term effects. In part, this was because most people—especially those most likely to suffer, because they were poor and powerless—had no say in decision making. Industrialization, like farming, was an elite option. It appealed to people whose power it increased. It enabled the controllers of industrial wealth to join or replace existing elites, and it empowered industrialized and industrializing communities to dominate the rest of the world and extort or exploit its resources.

PROBLEMS AND PARALLELS

1. How did fat—oil from animals, plants, and minerals—make the world of the nineteenth century work? What other sources of energy were exploited in the nineteenth century?
2. How did the population explosion of the nineteenth century lead to new ways to exploit and use the Earth's resources? Why did population increase not conform to Malthusian logic?
3. Why was the incorporation of the vast, open lands of Argentina, Brazil, Australia, and North America so important?
4. How did industrialization revolutionize the world's food supply?
5. How did militarization and industrialization put intense pressure on the world's energy sources in the nineteenth century?
6. What are the explanations for nineteenth-century industrialization? Why did industrialization have social consequences?
7. Why did Japan industrialize more rapidly than China? How did industrialization affect India and Egypt?

DOCUMENTS IN GLOBAL HISTORY

- James Fenimore Cooper, from *The Praire*
- Anthony Trollope, from *North America*
- Karl von Clausewitz, from *On War*
- Fanny Kemble, from *Records of a Girlhood*
- Domingo F. Sarmiento, "*Civilization and Barbarism*"
- Japanse Views of American naval technology

Please see the Primary Source DVD for additional sources related to this chapter.

READ ON

C. A. Bayly, *The Birth of the Modern World* (2004) is an insuperable survey of global history in the nineteenth century. E. A. Wrigley, *Peoples, Cities and Wealth: The Transition of Traditional Society* (1989) provides an overview of some of the most conspicuous issues. P. N. Stearns, *The Industrial Revolution in World History* (1998) is an introductory essay.

On food, F. Fernández-Armesto, *Near a Thousand Tables* (2003) is a short, general history. J. Burnett, *Plenty and Want* (1988) surveys the topic for Britain. J. Goody, *Cooking, Cuisine and Class* (1982) is an ingenious, anthropologically informed work that opens up comparative perspectives. P. N. Stearns, *Fat History* (2002) studies attitudes to fat in France and the United States. On famine, M. Davis, *Late Victorian Holocausts* (2002) is important and challenging.

On the domestication of the prairie, W. Cronon, *Nature's Metropolis* (1991) is essential reading. R W. Paul, *The Far West and the Great Plains in Transition* (1998) is an excellent study. W. Cronon et al., eds., *Under an Open Sky* (1993) includes some important essays. On fertilizers W. M. Mathew, *The House of Gibbs and the Peruvian Guano Monopoly* (1981) is a most helpful monograph. On Burbank, F. W. Clampett, *Luther Burbank* (1926) provides a rather uncritical outline.

On the militarization of society, E. Weber, *Peasants into Frenchmen* (1979) is a classic study. P. Paret, *Clausewitz and the State* (1985) is a useful study of Clausewitz's work in social and political perspective.

G. R. Taylor, *The Transportation Revolution* (1951) is an old but still authoritative study of the infrastructure of industrialization. On the industrialization of Europe, T. Kemp, *Industrialization in Nineteenth-century Europe* (1969) provides an overview. D. Landes, *The Unbound Prometheus* (1969) is a classic survey. P. N. Stearns, *Lives of Labor* (1975) takes a comparative approach focused on workers' experience.

On Britain and France, P. O'Brien and R. Quainault, eds., *The Industrial Revolution and British Society* (1993), and P. O'Brien and C. Keyder, *Economic Growth in Britain and France* (1978) are in some respects correctives of the still important classic study, P. Mathias, *The First Industrial Nation* (1969). T. Zeldin, *France 1848–1945*, 2 vols. (1973) is a wonderful book: sensitive and stimulating with an impressively original method. For Germany, T. Pierenkemper and R. Tilly, *The German Economy during the Nineteenth Century* (2005) is a good brief introduction. J. Mokyr, *Industrialization in the Low Countries* (1976) is basic. E. H. Kossmann, *The Low Countries 1798–1914* (1978), and J. C. H. Blom and E. Lamberts, eds., *History of the Low Countries* (1998) provide useful overviews. J. L. Van Zanden, *The Economic Development of the Netherlands since 1870* (1996) includes a brief history of Dutch industrialization. J. de Vries and A. van de Woude, *The First Modern Economy* (1997) is an influential survey of pre–nineteenth-century Dutch economic history. Spain is superbly covered by D. Ringrose, *Madrid and the Spanish Economy* (1983), and N. Sanchez-Albornoz, ed., *The Economic Modernization of Spain* (1987). For Italy, J. Cohen and G. Federico, *The Growth of the Italian Economy* (2001) is an efficient introduction. D. C. North, *The Economic Growth of the United States* (1966) is a venerable and reliable work. G. J. Kornblith, ed., *The Industrial Revolution in America* (1998) contains some stimulating essays. M. Girouard, *The Return to Camelot* (1981), and D. C. Lieven, *The Aristocracy in Europe 1815–1914* (1993), are helpful on the survival of an aristocratic ethos in the industrializing West.

J. Batou, ed., *Between Development and Underdevelopment* (1991) is an important collection on attempts at industrialization in the extra-Western world in the nineteenth century.

R. Bin Wong, *China Transformed: Historical Change and the Limits of European Experience* (2002) is of fundamental importance; L. Aiguo, *China and the Global Economy since 1840* (1999) is a helpful introductory work. India is covered in D. Kumar, ed., *The Cambridge Economic History of India, II* (2005), and I. J. Ker, *Building the Railways of the Raj* (1998). M. B. Jansen, ed., *The Cambridge History of Japan* V (1995), and S. Sugiyama, *Japan's Industrialization in the World Economy* (1988) deal with Japan; S. Hanley and K. Yamamura, *Economic and Demographic Change in Preindustrial Japan* (1967) is valuable on the background and takes a critically acute approach to controversial issues in historical demography. On the Middle East, R. Owen, *Cotton and the Egyptian Economy* (1969), and *The Middle East and the World Economy* (1993). C. Issawi, ed., *The Fertile Crescent, 1800–1914* (1988) is a useful economic overview of the Middle East with many documents. P. J. Vatikiotis, *The History of Modern Egypt* (1991) is an outstanding survey.

Debate on the reasons for the West's great leap forward is mainly conducted in K. Pomeranz, *The Great Divergence* (2001); A. Gunder Frank, *ReOrient*; D. Landes, *The Wealth and Poverty of Nations* (1999); and J. Goody, *The East in the West* (1996).

CHAPTER 24

The Social Mold: Work and Society in the Nineteenth Century

Akira Kurosawa's epic movie of 1954, *The Seven Samurai*, was set in the Japan of the sixteenth century, but it depicted the predicament of the samurai in modern times. By the nineteenth century, the samurai had become an obsolete class, whose prestige and wealth had been diminished by social, economic, and political changes. But in their own eyes, and in those of most Japanese, they still embodied timeless values of honor and courage. In the movie, the seven find work as mercenaries, defending villagers from bandits. In the process, they teach the peasants the art of war, thus rendering themselves—and by extension, all samurai—useless.

IN THIS CHAPTER

THE INDUSTRIALIZED ENVIRONMENT
Palaces of Work: The Rise of Factories
Critics of Industrialization: Gold from the Sewers
URBANIZATION
BEYOND INDUSTRY: AGRICULTURE AND MINING
CHANGING LABOR REGIMES
Slavery and the Slave Trade
Female and Child Labor
Free Migrants
HUNTERS AND PASTORALISTS
ELITES TRANSFORMED
IN PERSPECTIVE: Cultural Exchange—Enhanced Pace, New Directions

As the police closed in, four rebels struggled in bitter March cold through mountains south of Osaka, Japan. When the first one faltered, his companions cut off his head. The second hanged himself. Only Oshio Heihachiro and his son were left. When the police caught up with them, Oshio's son wanted to flee, but, screaming, "Coward! Coward!" Oshio stabbed him to death, set fire to the house where they were hiding, slashed his own throat, and perished amid the flames on May 1, 1837.

In Japan, Oshio has always been regarded as a hero, despite, or perhaps because of, his horrific suicide. He was a member of the hereditary warrior caste—a proud samurai—who had grown up believing that nobles' obligations to the poor were more important than their privileges over them. As a magistrate, he rooted out secret practitioners of Christianity—which still had followers 200 years after Japan banned it—and exposed scandals in the administration. He then retired, after a mystical vision, to found a small school.

JAPAN

His was a new kind of revolt in Japanese history. For the first time, samurai made common cause with the poor against the middle class. As had happened before in Japan, and in every society dependent on one staple crop, the 1830s was a decade of rice failures and famine. In 1837, as people died of starvation in Osaka, the state granaries were well stocked, and the officials who ran them got rich by shipping rice to the capital. Oshio petitioned local officials to open the warehouses, but they threatened him with prosecution for meddling where he had no official status.

He bought firearms and hired an artillery expert to train his men in their use. He then issued a summons to revolt, promising to "visit Heaven's vengeance" on the officials and merchants, and calling on peasants to burn the tax records on which the authorities relied. He stressed, sincerely, that he did not aim to seize power, only to right injustice.

Oshio's call was echoed in surprising places. In Bengal in India, for instance, a landlords' agent, Titu Mir, led a peasant revolt against moneylenders, tax collectors, and rent gougers in 1831. In England, at about the same time, conservative aristocrats saw workers and landowners as natural allies in a struggle to save the old economy of the land against the new economy of capital. In North America, some slave owners appealed to their slaves to fight alongside them against would-be liberators who wanted to subordinate the states to the federal government. In Latin America, aristocratic rebels recruited peasants to fight in civil wars. In France, middle-class intellectuals dreamed of leading the masses to progress. In the Ottoman Empire, Butrus Bustani, a Western-influenced aristocrat, spoke up for rebellious peasants in Lebanon. In Russia the great novelist Count Leo Tolstoy (1828–1910), renounced his wealth and adopted a peasant's way of life.

New wealth from commerce and industry threatened traditional society, diminishing aristocracies, elevating bourgeoisies, ruining peasants, creating industrial working classes, and eliminating traditional forms of labor such as slavery and serfdom. Traditional resentments—of merchants by aristocrats, of profiteers by peasants—grew. Global wealth gaps gaped ever more widely, turning some regions and peoples into suppliers of staple products for consumers thousands of miles away.

FOCUS questions

- HOW DID industrialization change society and the economy?
- WHY WAS Marx wrong in predicting that industrialization would lead to violent revolution?
- WHY WERE the slave trade and slavery abolished in the nineteenth century?
- WHY WERE some aristocracies able to adapt to the changes industrialization brought?

Even in unindustrialized societies, economic status rivaled age-old ways of determining people's place in society—parentage, ancestry, birthplace, learning, strength, sanctity. Where industry flourished, social change was even more convulsive. Instead of identifying with communities that embraced people at all levels of rank and prosperity—neighborhoods, cities, provinces, sects, families, clans, big households, ethnic groups—people, uprooted and regrouped in industrial centers, came to define themselves in terms of wealth or what they increasingly called class. Nineteenth-century observers in the West believed that the world was being redrawn on class lines. Some governments even adopted class as a way to categorize people as nobles, bourgeois, peasants, or workers. Karl Marx (1818–1883) championed a new theory of history: that all change was part and product of inevitable **class struggles** that pitted the rich against those whom they exploited. This chapter is about the spaces people occupied in this changing world: the way their work altered and shifted, the new relationships they developed, the shaken kaleidoscope of class and rank.

THE INDUSTRIALIZED ENVIRONMENT

Machines created unprecedented differences of power and wealth: between regions and countries, of course, but also, within industrializing regions, between classes, sexes, and generations.

Palaces of Work: The Rise of Factories

Work moved from country to city, from outdoors indoors, from homes and small workshops into factories and mines, from relatively healthy to relatively unhealthy environments that were often deafening, exhausting, and alienating. In the past, small groups of workers had shared intimate surroundings: workshops in which a few equals or near equals collaborated, or households in which a master craftsman marshaled apprentices who lived together like a large family. Now seismic social upheavals raised factories, like "smoking volcanoes" (as contemporaries said), burying the world of artisans and flattening traditional social hierarchies.

Factories reorganized work and reordered life. For their admirers, factories represented proof of progress, a magical extension of human power over nature, a romantic adventure. In 1802–1803, for instance, the German artist, C. A. G. Goede, traveling through industrializing landscapes between the cities of Birmingham and Shrewsbury in England, marveled at "mountain and valley in flames" for miles around, "beautifully lit by the gleaming glow of coal." Mechanization made people feel godlike. The ways early nineteenth-century artists painted factories are full of echoes of volcanic imagery.

Early depictions, moreover, show factories in harmony with nature, sited in the countryside for convenient access to raw materials. Philippe-Jacques de Loutherbourg painted Coalbrookdale in England in 1801, with furnaces ablaze in a cozy pastoral setting. In 1830, Karl Schurz painted steelworks, near Cologne in Germany, in the style of a farmyard scene against a background of rolling hills.

Factories were creations of the imagination. Architects sought models from the ancient world and fiction, raising fantasy buildings, bristling with turrets, battle-

Unthreatening industry. William Ibbitt's engraving of industrial Sheffield, in northern England, in the mid–nineteenth century, depicts the towering factories that rival the city's churches, the outpouring smoke, and the huge sprawl of the growing city. But, nestling in nature, industry seems at ease with the environment, and traditional rural life is undisturbed in the foreground.

ments, spires, and domes, to be what contemporaries called cathedrals of work or castles of industry. "These palaces house no pharaohs, no orgies, but are a means of life for hundreds of families," said a Spanish newspaper in 1855. The words express belief in the nobility of work and reveal the power-hunger of industrialists who based their claims on merit rather than wealth. **Paternalism** leaps from the page.

One of the problems for historians of industrialization is to explain why people left the land for factories. Most probably had no choice. The mechanization of agriculture reduced the amount of work available. Economies of scale concentrated more land in fewer hands. Global specialization shifted food production and industrial raw materials out of the industrializing world, leaving some rural workforces unemployed. Factory owners had to compete with one another for labor, as industries multiplied and businesses crowded the marketplace.

Some entrepreneurs had vision or vocation, religious or charitable. Samuel Smiles spoke of the spirit of industry as "the gospel of work." Henry Heinz (1844–1919) of Pittsburgh epitomized that spirit. His early ambition was to be a Lutheran minister. When he made a fortune from his canned and bottled food business, Heinz chose a famous slogan: "57 Varieties," not because there were really 57 of them—there were soon many more—but because the number came to him in a vision. His vast factory in Pittsburgh resembled a church.

Samuel Smiles, from *Self-Help*

His employees worked hard. In 1888, entry-level employees got five cents an hour for a ten-and-one-half-hour day—lower wages than many other local employers paid. But Heinz provided generous benefits. His workers, for instance, got free uniforms, medical and dental care, and, if they handled food, a daily manicure. There were hot showers, a gymnasium, a roof garden, and a reading room. Heinz had carriages to take workers for rides in the park and hired trains for outings. He provided lectures, concerts, and free courses. There were four dances a year and a Christmas party, where Mr. Heinz welcomed Santa Claus. Critics branded this style of management as paternalist and self-serving, but Heinz's methods had a genuinely benevolent message: Capital and labor were not enemies but natural allies. Management—not exploitation and profiteering—was the key to success.

Critics of Industrialization: Gold from the Sewers

Philanthropic industrialization showed that industry could spread the benefits of prosperity widely and increase leisure for workers as well as bosses. Most bosses, however, did not share Heinz's devotion to good works. And with the rush to industrialize came evils. Outside the few exemplary factories and model industrial towns, in the streets and slums that the concentration of labor created, the effort to erect a romantic environment for industrial society was a horrible failure.

Industrialization uprooted lives, disrupted families, and imposed bleak working conditions in cities rife with filth and disease. Visiting the British city of Manchester in 1835, Alexis de Tocqueville, considered the greatest social analyst of his time, recoiled from factories that "keep air and light out of the human habitations which they dominate; they envelop them in perpetual fog; here is the slave, there is the master; there is the wealth of some, here the poverty of most." Yet she wrote, "from this filthy sewer, pure gold flows."

Karl Marx and Frederich Engels, from *The Communist Manifesto*

Karl Marx foretold that industrialization would worsen class warfare. At first, in the 1830s and 1840s, it looked as if he must be right. Workers, Marx thought, must soon discover their power, realize that their labor was the source of society's wealth, and demand their share of prosperity. The result would be a bloody revolution, in which the working class, or **proletariat,** would overthrow the bourgeoisie. "Workers of the world arise," he proclaimed in 1848, "you have nothing to lose but your chains!" Riots, if not rebellions, were commonplace in industrializing cities.

Yet, in the world's most industrialized societies, Marx's warnings went unfulfilled. Workers soon had more than chains to lose. Increasingly, they had a stake in their societies. In the second half of the nineteenth century, reformers responded with a new concept: "public health"—sewers and clean water provided by municipal authorities. Town planning showed the power of industrial capitalism to "improve." The uniformity of the grid plan for city streets evoked an ideal of social equality. Governments stepped up their services to citizens, especially by regulating health, education, and food supply.

Meanwhile, moral restraint, Christian good works, and "enlightened self-interest" blunted the fangs of industrial capitalism and helped to ensure that workers benefited from the wealth industries created. Warned, perhaps, by prophets like Marx and the social movements he helped inspire, or driven by the energy of the market, employers raised wages and improved working conditions. Cheap food, better pay, and declining disease smothered or diminished revolutionary inclinations. Prosperity bought out proletarian rage. As William Cobbett (1763–1835), a leading English reformer, observed, "You can't agitate a man on a full stomach."

Businesses and governments were not purely benevolent. States wanted to be able to recruit large, effective armies. Employers realized that good wages and healthy workforces enhanced production and increased demand for their products. Churches championed workers to forestall revolution.

The United States is the most remarkable case, because Marx expected revolution to start there. Instead, socialists in America were the first to sell out to capitalism. Rather than leading the world into socialism, America led the world in revulsion from it. Industry soaked up all the new labor that immigration and population rise created. The frontier (see Chapter 23) sucked rebels and malcontents out of industrializing areas. Cheap land in the West enabled even poor settlers to achieve prosperity. The American dream became a nightmare for socialists, diverting the hopes of the poor from revolution to self-enrichment.

Socialists yearned for a better future. Other critics of industrialization yearned for a lost past. Artisans smashed machinery to defend their jobs. Romantics deplored a world that the English priest and poet Gerard Manley Hopkins (1844–1889) described as "seared with trade, bleared, smeared with toil." Ironically, escapees from industrialization were often also its beneficiaries. G. Poldi-Pezzoli, an Italian industrialist, collected medieval art. In Barcelona, the architect Antoni Gaudí (1852–1926) created fantasy buildings for captains of industry. The machine age enabled the rich to live out their romantic fantasies in comfort.

Instant metropolis. In the second half of the nineteenth century, exploitation of the North American prairie and the development of commerce on the Great Lakes turned Chicago from a small fort and trading post into a vast city. This image was made in 1892, when the city shaped its World's Fair to mark the 400th anniversary of the European discovery of the New World.
Dagli Orti (A)/Picture Desk, Inc./Kobal Collection

When factory workers got home, however, they would often find the "loathsome wretchedness" that Dr. Philip Kay described in Manchester in 1832 in houses "dilapidated, badly drained, damp." Or the worker might be confined to one of the cellar dwellings swilling with filth from the street and from underground. Disease got trapped in the bad ventilation.

Reformers stressed the effects of an industrial environment on workers' morale. In Barcelona, Jaume Balmes thought workers worse off than ancient slaves. Moral criticism reflected the values of the critics, and workers did not necessarily share it. Philip Kay watched the tenants of vile housing "wallow in the unrestrained licence of animal appetite." For workers, the vices he cited were rational survival strategies. Gambling was a form of investment for people with no spare cash to save. Alcohol was a lubricant for dreary lives. Popular songs—the genuine utterances of the working classes—mocked middle-class prudery and praised pleasures that moralists attacked, including drink, gambling, idleness, and sex.

Bosses—according to critics of industrialization—were in moral danger, too. A Barcelona newspaper warned owners that "the mechanics in your factories ... must not be confused with the machines you have in your workshops." This mixture of conscience and common sense was typical of the Catholic response to industrialization. Pope Leo XIII (r. 1878–1903) tried to save workers from seduction by socialism. He would not undermine a social hierarchy in which the church had a strong vested interest, but he encouraged Catholics to found their own trade unions. He could not endorse socialism, but he condemned naked individualism.

There had been gigantic concentrations of people before, especially in China, but never had so much population, in so many places, been gathered together in big cities.

In the industrializing world, this was hardly surprising. Owners needed to concentrate labor and communications. Steam power and improved transport moved production nearer to markets, making cities even bigger. The result was a new way to organize life around specialized production processes. Former villages, such as Manchester and Birmingham in Britain and Essen in the Rhineland, became great cities.

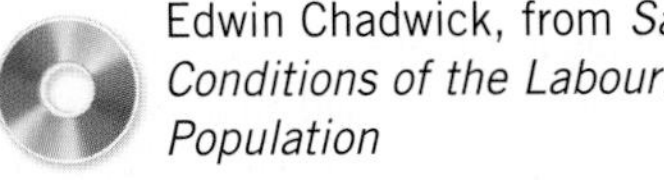
Edwin Chadwick, from *Sanitary Conditions of the Labouring Population*

At first, industrialization created flimsy cities that bred disease and disorder. In the 1840s, works such as Edwin Chadwick's *Sanitary Conditions of the Labouring Population* in Manchester, or Jaume Salarich's survey of working-class health in Barcelona in the 1850s, described the effects of the textile mills: labored breath, profuse sweat, exhaustion, gastric trouble, poor circulation, mental weariness,

MAP 24.1

The Growth of Manchester, England, 1840–1900

- railway
- railway station
- park
- built-up area 1840
- growth of city 1840–1900

nervous prostration, corrosion of the lungs, poisoning from machine oils and dyes. Slums clung to city centers. Shanties spread around city edges (see map 24.1).

Food is an even more basic index of the standard of living than hygiene and housing. Growing towns make fresh foods relatively expensive and hard to obtain. As late as 1899, R. Seebohm Rowntree found that most working families in northern England were inadequately fed. Their normal diet was monotonous, with only occasional treats of meat and fish. Unlike their rural counterparts, they could not grow vegetables or keep a pig. Some lived almost entirely on oatmeal.

URBANIZATION

Madcap urbanization also happened in parts of the world that played only a minor or marginal role in industrialization. Mining, for instance, created mushroom-growth towns, such as San Francisco and Kimberley and Johannesburg in South Africa. In 1871, diamonds were found on a farm at Kimberley. By 1900, 100,000 miners worked there. Gold turned Melbourne, on Australia's farthest Pacific edge, from a village in 1837, the year Queen Victoria came to the throne, into the third largest city in the British Empire, with over 800,000 people, by the time she died in 1901.

Trade, meanwhile, stimulated ports all over the world. The most conspicuous examples were where industrialization was taking off. New York, for instance, grew from 60,000 inhabitants in 1800 to nearly 3.5 million by 1900. But outside the industrializing world, ports from which primary produce was shipped overseas also grew. Cotton trade boosted Alexandria on Egypt's Mediterranean coast from only a few thousand people in 1800 to about 250,000 by 1900. Lagos in Nigeria boomed in the late nineteenth century because of palm oil and cocoa. Buenos Aires grew rapidly thanks to the refrigerated meat trade. Calcutta, a small settlement in 1800, had more than 750,000 people in 1900, because of its role in exporting the dyes and coarse fibers of Bengal. In the 1850s Shanghai became the port of choice for European merchants in China. Thanks to its role in exporting opium, the population of Izmir on the Mediterranean coast of Turkey grew at a rate of 2 percent a year from the 1840s, to house more than 200,000 people by the 1880s. Izmir illustrates how a new kind of cultural life became possible. It had French-built boulevards and British gas lighting. There were 5 newspapers, 17 printing houses, a large public library, and one of the first theaters in the Ottoman Empire.

Most Populous Cities in 1900

Name	Population
1. London, United Kingdom	6,480,000
2. New York, United States	3,437,000
3. Paris, France	3,330,000
4. Berlin, Germany	2,707,000
5. Chicago, United States	1,717,000
6. Vienna, Austria	1,698,000
7. Tokyo, Japan	1,497,000
8. St. Petersburg, Russia	1,439,000
9. Manchester, United Kingdom	1,435,000
10. Philadelphia, United States	1,418,000

United Nations; United States Census Bureau

Earlier cities were fearsome places, heavily policed, filled with rootless populations, and stalked by diseases. Now they acquired facilities for recreation, education, and welfare that are only possible where many people congregate and large resources concentrate. Towns were remodeled or enlarged on new principles of urban planning. Paris and Vienna acquired the boulevards familiar today. Grids of rationally planned streets were added to Madrid and Manhattan. In Cairo and Alexandria, new quarters enveloped the chaotic old cities in networks of straight streets. Opera houses arose in places as remote as Cairo and Manaus, the center of the rubber-producing region in Brazil. New roads, sewerage, water-supply systems, public baths, large stores, street lighting, cafes and clubs, sporting facilities, and trolleys and buses multiplied. New kinds of public spaces arose on cast-iron arches: so-called crystal palaces—glass-covered markets, railway stations, greenhouses, shopping arcades. London's Crystal Palace, scene of the first great

Universal Exposition of 1851, housed a display of the world's industrial arts. Madrid's main market, built in 1870, enclosed more than 100 acres in a pyramid of glass.

New urban spaces permitted new kinds of social activity. Mass education was a remarkable development. In some places investment by the state spurred education, partly because states wanted to train people for soldiering. In Japan in 1880, 35 percent of girls—and 70 percent of boys—went to school. Compulsory universal education, introduced in many European countries and the United States during the nineteenth century, was in one respect the most remarkable development of all, for it defied two cherished beliefs: the doctrines of parental responsibility for children and individual freedom.

Opera in the jungle. The nineteenth-century rubber boom turned Manaus, in the Brazilian rain forest, into a grand, rich city, with this enormous opera house that attracted famous singers and musicians from Europe. But Manaus was ruined toward the end of the century when rubber production shifted to the British colonies in Malaya.

BEYOND INDUSTRY: AGRICULTURE AND MINING

But the spread of industry and the growth of towns skipped huge areas of the globe, which remained largely a world of peasants, even in the West. Yet even unindustrialized and deindustrialized regions experienced pressures for social change.

MAKING CONNECTIONS

INDUSTRIAL TRANSFORMATIONS IN THE NINETEENTH CENTURY

ECONOMIC / POLITICAL TRANFORMATIONS →	SOCIAL CHANGES →	CHANGES IN DAILY LIFE
Development of industrial/factory-based employment	Urbanization, increased population density; increased labor specialization, formal division of work and leisure time	Work moves from country to city, outdoors to indoors; from homes and small workshops to factories and mines; large, impersonal work environments, bleak working conditions
Salary-based labor system	Shift from proprietorship to large-scale enterprises where power is concentrated in small number of factory and mine owners	Plentiful workers relatively powerless to negotiate unless organized; strict organization of daily routines
Urbanization and mixture of factory–residential districts	Proximity of work offset by increase in air and water pollution; grimy surroundings, lack of public sanitation in high-density cities	Increased exposure to epidemics of cholera, dysentery, and chronic diseases such as tuberculosis
Increased power of municipal, national governments to regulate	Development of idea of "public health" to stem disease, child mortality rates, epidemics, etc.	Increased town planning, public sanitation by 1900 lead to longer life spans, increased livability of cities
Growth of global trade	Increased movement of goods and traders in port cities all over the world; generation of wealth	Foreign goods and luxury items as well as technological innovations spread rapidly in industrialized countries

Peasants from Adjara. The region of Adjara, in present-day Georgia, straddles the southeastern shore of the Black Sea and was contested by the Ottoman and Russian empires throughout the nineteenth century, with Russia gaining the upper hand in 1878. Soon thereafter, the port of Batumi was developed into a major seaport and rail terminus, and commercial agriculture quickly transformed the lives of the peasantry. Farmers, like the ones shown here on their way to market, produced crops, such as tea, for consumption throughout the Russian Empire, and crops, such as corn, for both local markets and export abroad.

In the country, work in ever-larger fields, employing ever-less labor, displaced traditional agriculture, with its communal habits, companionship, and shared rituals. Revolutions in tenure arose as the brokers or middlemen who sold peasants' crops to merchants began to invest in land themselves, using their control of credit to obtain holdings cheaply. Agriculture, like industry, became increasingly a specialized activity, with particular crops concentrated in favored regions.

The American Midwest, Australia, and Argentina could produce meat and grain with methods that involved relatively little labor, thanks to mechanized harvesting and, for ranching, small, specialized, and free-spirited workforces—cowboys or, in Argentina and Uruguay, *gauchos*. Elsewhere, however, peasants had to be induced or compelled into growing labor-intensive crops. In the East Indies, for instance, the Dutch, in collaboration with native elites, forced peasants to grow coffee, whether their land was suitable for it or not. In Egypt, too, world demand for cotton forced peasants to provide a product they could not eat, at prices they could not influence. Peasant landholdings tended to split under the strain. By the end of the century, Egypt had some 2 million landless peasants, who were subject to forced labor in the irrigation works and conscription into the army.

The Ottoman Empire became a net exporter of crops for the first time in history, thanks to the grapes and opium of western Anatolia, where exports increased by more than 500 percent between 1845 and 1876. Private owners took over state landholdings, while much land passed from the hands of peasants into those of tribal or local chiefs, city merchants, moneylenders, and officials. Sixty percent of the soil of Ottoman Syria—once a peasant land—was officially reclassified as large estates in the early twentieth century. Many estate owners were outsiders—Armenians, Greeks, and Jews.

In West Africa, palm-oil production, formerly the work of gatherers of wild plants, became, from the 1840s, a focus of systematic farming. Harvesting palm fruits, pounding the nuts to extract the oil, and getting the product to market were labor intensive. Typically, a group of independent farmers would combine under an elected leader. In Nigeria, families could operate small palm-oil farms. But as time went on, merchants grabbed land and started slave-operated plantations. Much of the profit went into private armies to fight for power or seize more slaves. Labor was wrenched out of food production to keep up the flow of oil. Transporting and marketing the oil enriched a growing commercial class.

In southern Bengal, indigo planting was the big new opportunity. But it required capital investment, which forced peasants to borrow. Getting a loan—said a magistrate in 1830—reduced the borrower to "little better than a bond slave to the factory." In the second half of the century, jute—a cheap fiber for making rope and bags—became dominant. Peasants abandoned rice to grow jute on plots of an acre or two. But reliance on a single export crop left them at the mercy of the market and led to impoverishment and high levels of debt, incurred to tide them over hard times.

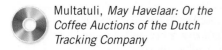

Multatuli, *May Havelaar: Or the Coffee Auctions of the Dutch Tracking Company*

The **caste system** gripped India more tightly than ever, as the British imposed forms of discrimination that were supposedly traditional because they were enshrined in ancient texts, but that people had not practiced much. In southern India, especially, British policy favored the concentration of the best agricultural land in the hands of a few dominant families, reducing many peasants to abject poverty. Western immigrants could also end up joining the losers in the global marketplace. In the mid–nineteenth century, the Portuguese government began settling poor white farmers in Angola to extend Portuguese control of the native Africans. Most of these settlers abandoned export crops and struggled to feed their families, living in hovels, and dressing in rags. The fate of black peasants in Angola was even worse: dispossession and enslavement. In the 1870s, Portugal officially abolished slavery, but not until the early twentieth century did the authorities make serious efforts to stop the illegal export of slaves.

The erosion of independence and of local prosperity was a common—but not universal—consequence of specialization. In the second half of the century, Thailand, formerly a self-sufficient country, began to specialize in a few exportable commodities: rice, tin, and teak. The Thai stayed on the land, increasing output by extending the amount of land under cultivation. They left commerce to Chinese immigrants. The amount of capital investment required for growing rice was modest, and, among foreigners, Chinese supplied most of it. Thailand never succumbed to foreign "business imperialists" (see Chapter 25). Relative to other staple foods, rice earned good profits for the people who grew it. Only about 50 percent of the export price went to the middleman, miller, and shipper.

The face of Africa, scarred and pitted by colonial exploitation. Open-cast diamond mining in the "blue earth" at Kimberley, South Africa, in 1872. At that early stage—not much more than a year after the first diamond was discovered on the De Beers's farm—the diggings were checkered with the square plots of individual prospectors. The inability to dig deep enough to find diamonds on small plots led to the consolidation of these shallow digs into bigger holdings and to the formation of the De Beers Mining Company in 1874. By 1914, the Kimberley pit had become the largest man-made crater ever dug.

As well as the fruits of increasingly specialized agriculture, the unindustrialized world also supplied raw minerals in ever-larger quantities. The local impact was often intense. The Kimberley diamond mines in South Africa were a good example. "Every foot of the blue ground," said Cecil Rhodes (1853–1902), one of the big early investors in the enterprise and a champion of the British Empire in Africa, "means so much power." Mines meant power to their owners. To workers, they signified the destruction of traditional life. As soon as diamonds were discovered, black African workers wrenched from agrarian and pastoral communities poured in, struggling to re-create the layouts and routines of their home villages in the squalid, lawless vicinity of the mines. Black mine workers were forbidden to acquire licenses to establish their own diggings. Though nominally not slaves, they could be fined or flogged for desertion of employment, and their wages were never more than a fifth of what white miners earned for similar work.

Although miners in Europe and North America were better treated, mines could wreak comparable havoc in the industrializing world. The Río Tinto copper mines in Spain recruited thousands of Spanish and Portuguese workers in the 1870s and 1880s. The company aimed to practice the sort of productive benevolence associated with the best factories. But decent housing and modest health care and schooling did little to ease the feelings of alienation understandable in uprooted communities or the impatience workers felt at the company's paternalism. Living conditions were always overcrowded, because the building program could not keep up with the demand for labor. The environment was literally poisonous, as sulphurous fumes hung over the area whenever the wind fell. Most of the British staff—the management and most of the top technicians were Britons—were housed in what would now be called a gated community, where ordinary workers and local people were forbidden to enter.

Industrialization, Mechanization, and Urbanization

Nineteenth century	Factories in the United States and Western Europe reorganize work and reorder workers' lives
1842	Poor living conditions in Manchester detailed in Edwin Chadwick's *The Sanitary Condition of the Labouring Population*
1844–1919	Henry J. Heinz, industrialist and proponent of paternalist management
1845–1876	Ottoman agricultural exports increase fivefold
1848	Publication of Marx's and Engels's *The Communist Manifesto*
1851	London's Universal Exposition held at Crystal Palace
1870	New central market built in Madrid
r. 1878–1903	Pope Leo XIII, advocate of social reform
ca. 1900	Cotton cultivation in Egypt contributes to the creation of 2 million landless peasants
	Population: Izmir, 200,000; Alexandria, 250,000; Calcutta, more than 750,000; Melbourne, 800,000; New York, 3.4 million, London, 6.5 million

CHANGING LABOR REGIMES

The virtual disappearance of slavery—and the total disappearance of plantation slavery in the Americas—was perhaps the most surprising episode of the nineteenth century. Almost every pre-industrial society we know about has considered slavery normal and legitimate—a suitable status for supposedly inferior people, for captives, or for those unable to survive except as a master's chattel. Nineteenth-century Western science produced strong, new justifications for slavery: Certain races were inferior to others. Black people were, according to some anthropologists, more like apes than Europeans.

Slavery and the Slave Trade

On the other hand, slavery repelled believers in three doctrines of growing appeal in the world, especially in the West: evangelical Christianity, egalitarianism, and economic liberalism. According to evangelical Christians, Jesus' message of universal love outlawed slavery. According to egalitarians, all people were equal, and it was nonsense for anyone to be born into slavery. For economic liberals, and especially for those who believed in free trade, slavery was irrational, because people worked better when they did so freely and for wages.

Impeccable in theory, the free-trade doctrine did not seem to be borne out in reality. On the contrary, the world economy relied, as it had relied for centuries, on compulsion to work. In much of Africa, slaves were both a vital labor force and a major export product. In the tropical and subtropical latitudes of the Atlantic-side New World, they were the only labor force available. Trade in slaves sustained shipping in Europe and America. In Liverpool, Britain's leading port, a quarter of the ships were engaged in the slave trade around 1800. Cotton manufacture in Europe, the rum industry of New England, and the arms trade to Africa would all be jeopardized without slavery. In the long run, mechanization might make slavery out of date. But no one could foresee this in the early nineteenth century. On the contrary, the kind of plantation environment in which slavery was entrenched seemed unsuitable for mechanization. In any case, in slave-owning societies, slavery was part of culture and tradition. People practiced it not because it was profitable but because it was part of the fabric of life. So it was not just economics that eliminated slavery. The rise of a new morality changed cultural assumptions. Reformers dismantled the system despite the dictates of tradition, ideology, economics, and what passed for science.

They started with the slave trade. This was an easier target than slavery, because it did not involve problems of how to compensate slave owners or dispose of liberated slaves. In the 1790s, in Europe and America, a wave of sentiment against the slave trade broke against the fears and obstacles that vested interests raised. But in 1803, Denmark outlawed the trade. Britain and the United States followed. The abolition of the slave trade became a British national crusade. Indeed, it became a way to justify British imperialism and inspired wars, in which thousands of native slave-traders and their families, who thought they were engaged in a traditional and lawful activity, died. Meanwhile, Britain paid rulers in Africa and the Indian Ocean to stop dealing in slaves.

Reformers expected the abolition of the slave trade to lead to the disappearance of slavery. Demographic trends suggested this possibility. As we saw in Chapter 20, plantation slave populations in the eighteenth century normally had high death rates and low birthrates. But abolition had two unforeseen effects that combined to frustrate the abolitionists' predictions.

First, abolition made slaves more expensive and, therefore, gave new life to the slave trade. The total number of slaves shipped across the Atlantic from Africa to the Americas in the nineteenth century was about 3.3 million. Slavers made great fortunes, charging premiums for the risks they faced in running the gauntlet of the British Navy's patrols. By the 1830s, Pedro Blanco of Cadiz in Spain reckoned that if he could save one vessel in three from capture he could make a profit. At his slave-holding camp in West Africa, he could keep 5,000 slaves at a time. He permanently employed a lawyer, 5 accountants, 2 cashiers, 10 copyists, and a harem of 50 African slave girls.

Second, abolition of the slave trade made slave owners more careful of their slaves. As a result, numbers of slaves began to grow through natural reproduction. When Spain ended the slave trade in 1818, it allowed owners a period of grace during which they could import slave women of fertile years, so that "by propagating the species, the abolition of the commerce in slaves should be less noticeable in future." Meanwhile, in the southern United States, the number of slaves multiplied from under 1 million at the start of the century to almost 4 million by 1860. The upward trend was unstoppable. Even when federal law banned the trade after 1808, world demand for cotton drove the rise of slavery in the South.

Slaves played surprisingly little part in their own liberation. Though rebellions were frequent, plantation societies learned to live with them, absorbing the costs of suppression or confining the runaways to roles that were troublesome rather than fatal to planter control. The big exception was Haiti, the French colony called Saint-Domingue where rebellious slaves seized power in the 1790s. The French Revolution, igniting expectations about "the rights of man" (see Chapter 22), provided Haitian slaves with an ideology of liberation. Yet controversy in Haiti early in the Revolution focused not on whether slavery was right or wrong but on whether free black and mixed-race people should have the right to vote. The slave revolt that began in 1791 seems to have started outside revolutionary circles—with rumors that the king of France had freed the slaves, with voodoo ceremonies, and with a slave leadership barely connected with free black people, some of whom also rebelled against white rule.

In 1792, a new phase began, when Léger-Félicité Southonax arrived as the representative of the French Republic with orders to pacify the colony. The following year, impelled by revolutionary fervor and the worsening security situation, with the British poised to invade, he freed the slaves of the northern province—creating at a stroke, he said, "200,000 new soldiers for the republic." He promoted the most talented black officer, Toussaint L'Ouverture (1746–1803), who, in effect, seized power in 1797.

After the French captured L'Ouverture in 1802, Haitian resistance became desperate. In 1804, L'Ouverture's successor, Jean-Jacques Dessalines, proclaimed "Independence or Death." In a remarkable reversal of the white man's usual rhetoric, he denounced the French as barbarians:

> What have we in common with that bloody-minded people? Their cruelties compared to our moderation—their color to ours—the extension of seas that separate us—our avenging climate—all plainly tell us they are not our brethren. . . . Let them shudder . . . at the terrible resolution we are going to make—to do to death any native of France who shall defile, with his sacrilegious footstep, this land of liberty.

The Haitians officially won their liberty in 1825 at the cost of agreeing to pay a crippling indemnity to compensate French property

Slavery in the Nineteenth Century

1790s	Abolitionist sentiment on the rise in Britain and the United States
1791–1803	Haitian Revolution
1800	1 million slaves in the United States
1800–1900	3.3 million slaves shipped from Africa to the Americas
1803	Denmark outlaws slave trade
1807	Britain outlaws slave trade
1808	Importation of slaves banned in United States
1823	Spain outlaws slavery
1825	Haiti wins official independence
1834	Slavery abolished in the British Empire
1848	France outlaws slavery
1860	4 million slaves in the United States
1863	Emancipation Proclamation (United States)
1885	Egypt outlaws slavery
1886	Cuba outlaws slavery
1888	Brazil outlaws slavery

owners. They excluded white colonists, depriving their country of capital investment and technical expertise. They also sent tremors of fear through other planter societies.

Even without the Haitian example, emancipation of slaves was likely to follow the abolition of the slave trade. In the 1820s and 1830s, some Spanish-American republics led the way, not because they were peculiarly virtuous, but because slavery played a relatively small part in their economies. The British Empire as a whole did not ban slavery until 1834. It took the Civil War (1861–1865) to free the slaves of the southern United States—and even then the federal government's Emancipation Proclamation in 1863 was more a practical response to war conditions than an act of morality. Spain freed its slaves—but not those of its colonies—in 1823. France decreed emancipation in 1848 and the Netherlands in 1863. The Spanish colony of Cuba held out until 1886 and the Empire of Brazil until 1888. Outside the world of plantations, slavery survived longer. Persia signed an anti-slave-trade treaty with Britain in 1882 but never enforced its terms. Egypt made slavery illegal in 1885. Formal laws against the slave trade were proclaimed in the Ottoman Empire in 1889 and in Zanzibar in 1897—which, as part of an Omani trading empire that had ousted the Portuguese from much of East Africa (see Chapter 21), throve as a slave-trading center.

Slavery was not the only form of forced labor to dwindle in the nineteenth century. There was also serfdom in which peasants were tied to the land they worked and could be sold along with, but not apart from, it. In Europe, wars in the aftermath of the French Revolution shifted the frontiers of serfdom eastward, forcing the emancipation of the peasants of central and eastern Germany. The Habsburg monarchy finally granted all former serfs freedom and land in 1853–1854. In Thailand, almost the entire male population was bound by forced labor laws, which the government abolished bit by bit throughout the century.

Even Russia, where most people were still serfs, joined the trend. Peasant violence in the 1840s and, in 1855, defeat in the Crimean War by Turkey, France, and Britain helped to concentrate minds in favor of reform. Russia also felt the pressure of a European model of economic change: recognition that the empire had to enter the railway age and reorganize for industrialization. The Czar proclaimed emancipation of the serfs in 1861.

In Japan, meanwhile, peasants became participants in an enlarged marketplace as communications improved and cities grew. Individual farms tended to replace the traditional village collectives in which all the village families had worked the land in common and shared the harvests. There were crosscurrents. New regulations favored landowners, especially by limiting traditional tenants' rights in common land. But the peasants' lot generally improved. In 1868, the government promised, "the common people, no less than the civil and military officials, shall be allowed to pursue their own individual callings so that there may be no discontent." In the 1870s, government decree freed the dependent peasants and workers of Japan. In 1877, when disaffected samurai attempted a rebellion of the type Oshio Heicharo had tried to launch in 1837, the peasants were on the other side, drafted into the government's army, armed with guns, and drilled in obedience.

In some parts of the world, convicts became a substitute for slave labor. "Hard labor" became a way to exploit criminals' potential for work and to exact retribution from them on behalf of society. In Japan, criminals worked in the notorious Ashio copper mine. Governments in Europe deported hundreds of thousands of convicts—often for minor crimes—to remote, previously uncultivated lands. Australia alone, for instance, absorbed over 150,000 British convicts between 1788 and

TIPPOO TIB

Tippu Tip, "the biggest slaver of them all," whose activities on behalf of Sultan Barghash of Zanzibar (see Chapter 25) almost succeeded in preempting European imperialism, before he became a collaborator in the empire-building efforts of King Leopold II of the Belgians. In the opinion of Jerome Becker, one of Leopold's agents in the Congo in the 1880s, "From his [Tippu's] immense plantations, cultivated by thousands of slaves, all blindly devoted to their master, and from his ivory trade, of which he has the monopoly, he has in his duplex character of conqueror and trader, succeeded in creating for himself in the heart of Africa a veritable empire."

1868. Some Pacific Islands, Siberia, former slave-holding states in the United States after the Civil War, and French Guiana in northwest South America relied on convict labor to sustain their economies.

The slaves' main successors worldwide, however, were millions of **coolies:** laborers, mainly from poor communities in India and China, conned or coerced at miserable wages as contracted or indentured workers for some of the era's most demanding work on sugar plantations, tropical mines, and colonial railway-building projects (see Map 24.2). Technically, the Chinese government required that every recruit from Chinese jurisdiction should enter "freely and voluntarily" into his agreement with his employers and shippers. In practice, officials connived in what were effectively deportations or abductions. In the 1860s and 1870s, French recruiters shipped some 50,000 laborers from India to the Caribbean, where, Indian government officials complained, the French "tried everything they could to keep Indians in perpetual servitude." A British report of 1871 characterized the condition of Chinese and Indian laborers in British Guiana in South America as the new slavery. A Chinese government inquiry in 1873 found that "the lawless method by which the Chinese were—in most cases—introduced into Cuba, the contempt there shown for them, the disregard of contracts, the indifference about working conditions, and the unrestrained infliction of wrong, constitute a treatment which is that of a slave, not of a man who has consented to be bound by a contract." After Spain abolished slavery in Cuba in 1886, slave catchers stayed in business—hunting down runaway Chinese workers. There were perhaps 25,000

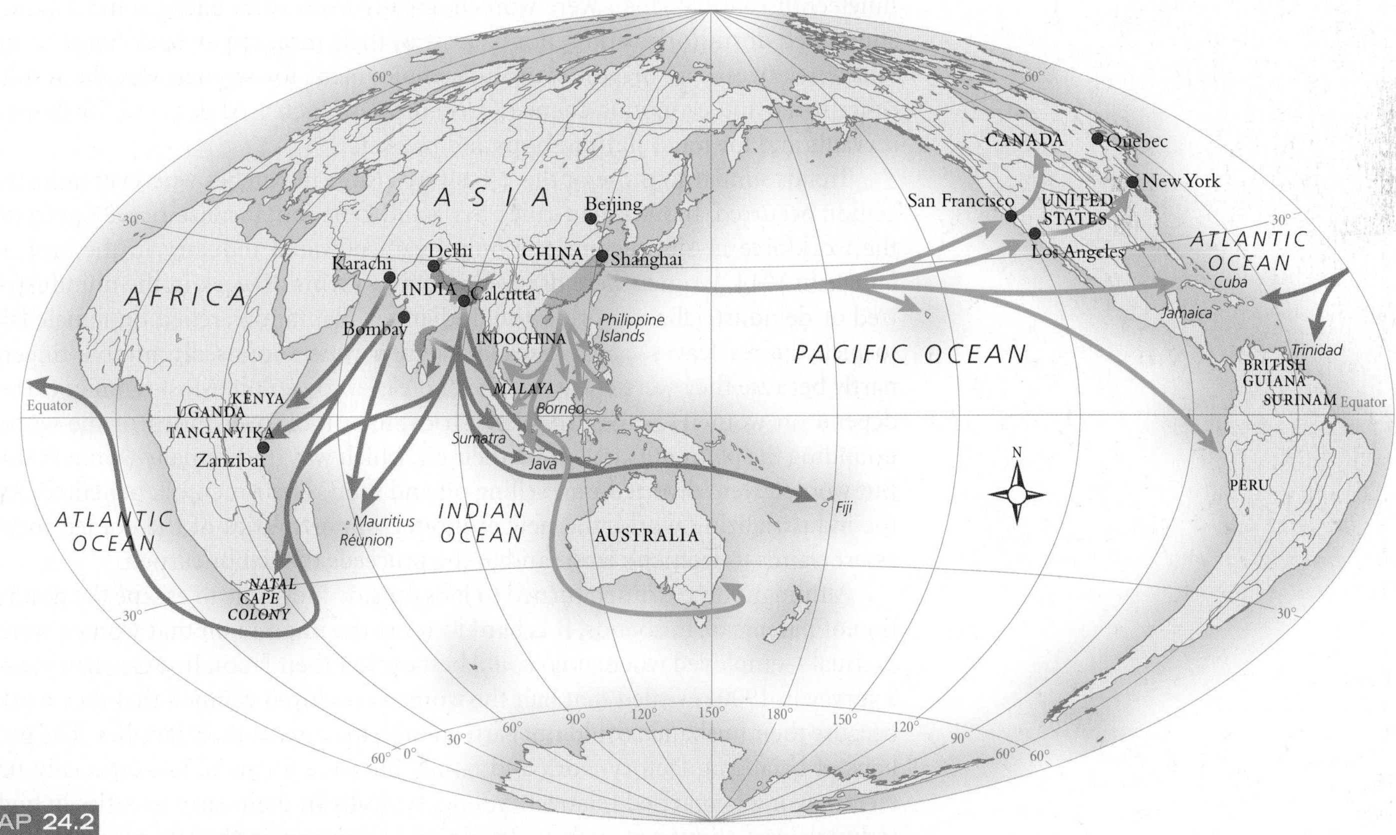

MAP 24.2

The Movement of Indentured Labor in the Late Nineteenth Century

Chinese in California in the 1850s. The Central Pacific Railroad employed 10,000 of them. From 1868, by agreement with China, 16,000 arrived annually. Many went to factories in San Francisco, where "Little China" had nearly 50,000 residents by 1875. Violence and immigration controls followed.

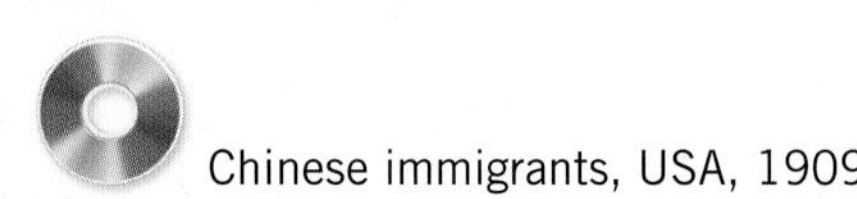

From 1834, when the British Empire abolished slavery, until the eve of the First World War in 1914, 4 million workers, mainly from India and China, kept the empire supplied with cheap labor. France conquered Indochina from the 1850s to the 1880s in part to solve the problems of a labor shortage elsewhere in the French Empire.

Female and Child Labor

So although slavery was abolished in most places and formal serfdom disappeared from Europe, other forms of forced and dependent labor survived and spread. In industrializing economies, it is doubtful how far wage labor was morally superior to slavery. Unlike the masters of slaves, factory owners did not have the right to sell their workers or, at least in theory, sexually abuse them. But work in the factories and mines of the West and its colonies was highly disciplined, unless and until governments allowed workers to organize in trade unions and bargain collectively for their wages. Women and children joined the workforce. Child labor was, of course, entirely forced labor, as was much of the work that women did. Both categories contributed to the success of industrialization. In Germany in 1895, nearly 700,000 workers were under 16 years of age. In France in the 1890s, 32 percent of the manufacturing workforce were women. Well over half the industrial workforce in late nineteenth-century Japan were women, mostly from rural backgrounds, living in supervised dormitories and sending most of their meager pay back home to their village relatives. The biggest source of employment for women was the result of other social and economic changes. Urbanization increased demand for domestic servants and for retail staff in shops and markets.

Trends similar to those of the West were visible in patches wherever industrialization occurred. In Ottoman-ruled Syria and Lebanon, for instance, 85 percent of the workforce in silk reeling, the only steam-powered industry in the area, was female in 1914. Women were dragged into new forms of work in the unindustrialized or deindustrialized worlds, too. Indian tea plantations relied on female labor to pick the tea leaves, partly because women were supposedly nimble fingered, partly because they were cheap to hire and easier to exploit. Most families came to depend on women's wages. In West Africa, men took over much of the work of pounding the palm nuts to extract their oil, which was traditionally women's work. But women were diverted into selling oil and food. Their menfolk benefited. As in the industrializing world, the new economic opportunities of the era led men to assert claims to women's labor and to the proceeds that labor earned.

Although some women turned to jobs outside the home to escape the domination of parents or husbands, it is hard to resist the impression that women were—as usual—employed where men could best exploit their labor. In a German factory, a survey in 1900 revealed that half the women employed claimed that they worked because their husbands could not earn enough to support their families. The problems of balancing factory work and family life were formidable—especially since factory workers married relatively young, typically in their early twenties in highly industrialized countries, such as Britain and Germany, in the late nineteenth century. Even women who stayed at home worked harder, as factories and mines sucked in their menfolk and deprived wives of their husbands' help at home. In the cities, prostitution boomed, often employing, in effect, enslaved women.

In the long run, industrialization led Westerners to reevaluate womanhood and childhood. Women and children were perceived as ideal for certain industrial tasks but were also treated as marginally efficient workers. Gradually, mechanization took them out of the labor market. Society rationalized the process by representing it as a form of liberation and even of elevating the status of women and children. Womanhood was placed on a pedestal. Children were treated as a distinct rank of society whereas formerly they had often been seen as little adults, or as "enemies" who needed discipline, or simply as negligible, even expendable, given the high rates of child mortality.

These were uniquely Western cults, barely intelligible in cultures where women and children were still men's partners in production. The status looked enviable in artists' and advertisers' images of delicate femininity or angelic childhood. But there were disadvantages. Societies that freed children from the workplace tried to pen them inside schools. For many children, and for parents who needed their children's wages, compulsory education was a form of tyranny. The romantic ideal of childhood was more often forced than coaxed into being. Schools were repressive and designed to mold pupils according to adult agendas.

Tea picker. Tea was an imperial beverage in the nineteenth century. First, Britain encouraged mass production of tea in India to undermine Chinese exports. Then the British introduced the crop to Sri Lanka, where this harvester is shown at work in a photograph from the 1890s. This "Ceylon tea" is now prized, but it was originally a cheap, inferior beverage to help keep British industrial workers alert.

Henrik Ibsen, from *A Doll's House*

Women liberated from work were assigned a role and rights that resembled, in some respects, those of children. Stiflingly male dominated, middle-class homes confined women. Henrik Ibsen (1828–1906) brilliantly captured the atmosphere in 1879 in his play, *A Doll's House*, which depicts the married household as an oppressive pen from which a woman must struggle to escape. For middle-class women, the fall from the pedestal could be bruising. In 1858, the British artist Augustus Egg painted an adulteress in three terrible stages of decline and destitution. Great composers devoted operas to sexually promiscuous heroines who came to a bad or a sad end—Verdi's *La Traviata* (1851), Bizet's *Carmen* (1875), and Puccini's *Manon Lescaut* (1891), and *La Bohème* (1896). The fallen woman became the favorite villain or victim of the age.

For peoples formerly enslaved, only a modified form of freedom emerged. Even in Haiti, the army kept slaves at work. In areas of previously slave-staffed plantations, a labor crisis followed emancipation. It was met by enforcing new sources of labor and going back to an older pattern of tenure with peasants, renting the land and sharecropping, forced to give landlords a percentage of their harvests. Liberated slaves were too numerous to command much power in a free labor market. In the British West Indies, they made up 80 percent of the population. In the French and Dutch Caribbean, the proportions were 60 and 70 percent respectively. Poor European immigrants supplied the labor that industry needed in the United States, while Indian and Chinese coolies in the Caribbean kept labor there relatively cheap. For most black people in the United States, part of the consequence of emancipation was economic misery and subjection to "color bars": In many states white people excluded them not just from the right to vote and equal opportunities in employment but also from supposedly public spaces and services. Black Americans were subjected to the petty humiliations, enforced by violence if necessary, of exclusion from white churches, schools, restaurants, hotels, athletic and recreational facilities, hospitals, and even streetcars, railroad cars, drinking fountains, cemeteries, and park benches.

Free Migrants

Massive migration of free labor was the final feature that helped to reshape the world's labor force. Population increase combined with improved, cheap, long-range communications to make unprecedented migration rates possible.

Russian and Chinese migration into northern Asia—Siberia and Manchuria—illustrates this well. Russia's population exceeded 167 million in 1900—an increase

New Labor Patterns

1788–1868	150,000 convicts shipped from Britain to Australia
1850s	25,000 Chinese live and work in California
1853–1854	Serfs in Habsburg Empire emancipated
1860s and 1870s	French ship 50,000 Indian laborers to the Caribbean
1861	Serfs in Russia emancipated
1870s	Japanese workers and peasants freed by official decree
1880s	5.25 million immigrants arrive in the United States
1890s	32 percent of French work force is female; 1 million settlers move to Siberia; 14 million people emigrate from China
1890–1920	Migration adds 18.2 million people to U.S. population
1895	700,000 German workers under 16 years of age
1914	30 percent of the population of Argentina is foreign born

of nearly 20 million since 1880. Siberia relied on convict labor until the 1870s, but by the end of the century, almost all the migrants there were free. Nearly 1 million settlers entered Siberia during the 1890s while the Trans-Siberian Railway was under construction (see Chapter 23). About 5 million followed early in the twentieth century, when the railway was complete. Chinese colonization of Manchuria increased after 1860 when the Qing relaxed the rules restricting it. China, indeed, was still the world's most prolific source of long-range colonists. The age-old Chinese diaspora in southeast Asia gathered pace, rising to a total of almost 14 million in the 1890s, and leaping further in the years before the First World War.

Meanwhile, the steamship trade, which also facilitated coolie migration, helped to populate under-exploited frontiers in the Southern Hemisphere and the North American West, and to provide labor for American industrialization. Europe, because of its exceptional rise in population, was the main source of free migrants. "New Europes," areas with similar climates and environments to those the migrants left behind, were the most attractive destinations. There were areas of this kind in North America, the southern cone of the Americas—Brazil, Argentina, Chile, and Uruguay—Australia, New Zealand, and South Africa.

Most transatlantic migrants headed for the United States, which gained more than 128,000 migrants in the 1820s, and over 500,000 in the 1830s. Numbers tripled in the next decade, mostly from Germany, Britain, and Ireland. A further leap in the 1880s brought the total to over 5.25 million, from all over Europe and especially from Scandinavia, Italy, Central Europe, and the Russian Empire. This was the manpower that fueled continental expansion and industrialization.

Italian immigrants. The photographs Lewis Hine (1874–1940) took of immigrants arriving at Ellis Island in New York City in 1904–1905 launched his career as one of the most socially influential photographers in U.S. history. This shot of an Italian mother and her children, which Hine hand colored, typifies his talent for capturing the dignity and promise of the poor and oppressed.

From 1890 to 1920, migration brought a net gain of 18.2 million people to the United States—more than in the entire previous history of the country (see Map 24.3). In combination with industrialization, this turned the United States into a major world power. After 1892, the United States subjected immigrants to quotas and questioned them for suitability. Political undesirables and the morally suspect were excluded, as were those suffering from infectious diseases, such as syphilis and tuberculosis. Canada and some South American countries, especially Argentina, also made huge gains. By 1914, when 13 percent of the population of the United States was foreign born, the corresponding figure in Argentina was 30 percent. Nearly half Argentina's immigrants came from Italy and nearly a third from Spain. Most of the rest were Eastern Europeans.

HUNTERS AND PASTORALISTS

When the pattern of world population settled after the shake-up, former parts of it had vanished or shrunk. After slaves, the numbers of pastoral and foraging peoples diminished the most. In some places, mechanized agriculture wiped them out or penned them in reservations where they were doomed to decline. In others, they were converted to settled ways of life. Alternatively, the unfamiliar diseases that contact with outsiders introduced diminished or destroyed them. They survived only in environments too unappealing for better-armed peoples to contest, such as the harsh Kalahari, where San hunters of southern Africa fled to elude their black and white persecutors, or in the vast but merciless Australian interior, where aboriginals retreated from white settlers, or in the Arctic. Occasionally, the hesitations of potential enemies saved them: inhibitions that were sometimes romantic, sometimes practical, sometimes a bit of both. In 1884, for instance, when the Swedish government was considering the fate of the Sami—the reindeer herders of the far north—some theorists argued that the pastoralists were relics of an inferior race, whom the laws of nature doomed to extinction. Opponents countered that Sami culture was "the only one suited to expansive regions of the country." The "small peoples of the north," as Russians called them, benefited from the perceptions of romantics who saw them as embodiments of the ideal of the noble savage (see Chapter 22) or as survivors from an earlier phase of their own peoples' past.

An Auracano chief in native dress with the Andes behind him, painted in 1853. The native peoples of the extreme southern cone of the Americas fought off Spanish conquistadores and resisted the Chilean and Argentine republics until industrially produced machine guns defeated them in the late nineteenth century.

Most pastoralists and foragers, however, lacked such protectors. Railways carved up the lands of the hunter peoples of the North American West. Reservations broke up their communities. Phoney treaties shifted them onto marginal lands where survival was hard. Massacres harassed them into submission. Rifles and machine guns enabled generals to exterminate native peoples "like maniacs or wild beasts." Free rations of cattle bought off the survivors of wars. In 1872, an American army officer reported of the Shoshone of the Great Plains: "Their hunting grounds have been spoiled, their favorite valleys are occupied by settlers and they are compelled to scatter in small bands to obtain subsistence." He described the same depths of demoralization and beggary to which other Native American peoples of the mid- and far west had plunged.

Similar ruthlessness solved the problem of what to do with foragers in the grasslands of South America. In the 1840s, an Argentine president decided that white competition doomed his country's Indians "to disappear from the face of the Earth." In the 1880s, machine guns fulfilled his prophesy when the discovery of gold in the far south of Argentina turned the remotest limits of the American hemisphere into contested territory. Professional manhunters charged around five dollars for every Indian they killed. At the opposite end of the hemisphere, in the Aleutian Islands off the coast of Alaska, missionaries and bureaucrats saved the native fishing communities from extermination by Russian conquerors but could not mitigate the effects of diseases to which the inhabitants had no resistance. An epidemic in 1838–1839 wiped out half the population. When Russia sold Alaska to the United States in 1867, another wave of looters arrived, with another alien culture, imposed by force.

Less dramatically, but equally effectively, governments in the Old World induced nomads to change their way of life. Mehmet Ali, the khedive of Egypt (see Chapter 23), turned nomadic Arab tribal leaders into landowners, mobilized the desert warriors, and seized their horses. The former nomads shifted to the towns or became "lost among the peasants." Russian governments forced Muslim Khazaks and Kirgiz nomads in Central Asia into agriculture by confining them to land grants too small for them to graze their flocks.

ELITES TRANSFORMED

Industrialization created proletariats. The dwindling of slavery, serfdom, and foraging transformed rural lives and work patterns. Migration and new forms of social control shook up the role and distribution of the world's labor. At the top end of society, the changes of the period were almost as traumatic for those they touched. While peasantries and working classes suffered, the era of industrialization transformed aristocracies or, at least, severely tested them. They survived by diversifying from an emphasis on landed estates into new economic activities. When they failed to adapt, they perished.

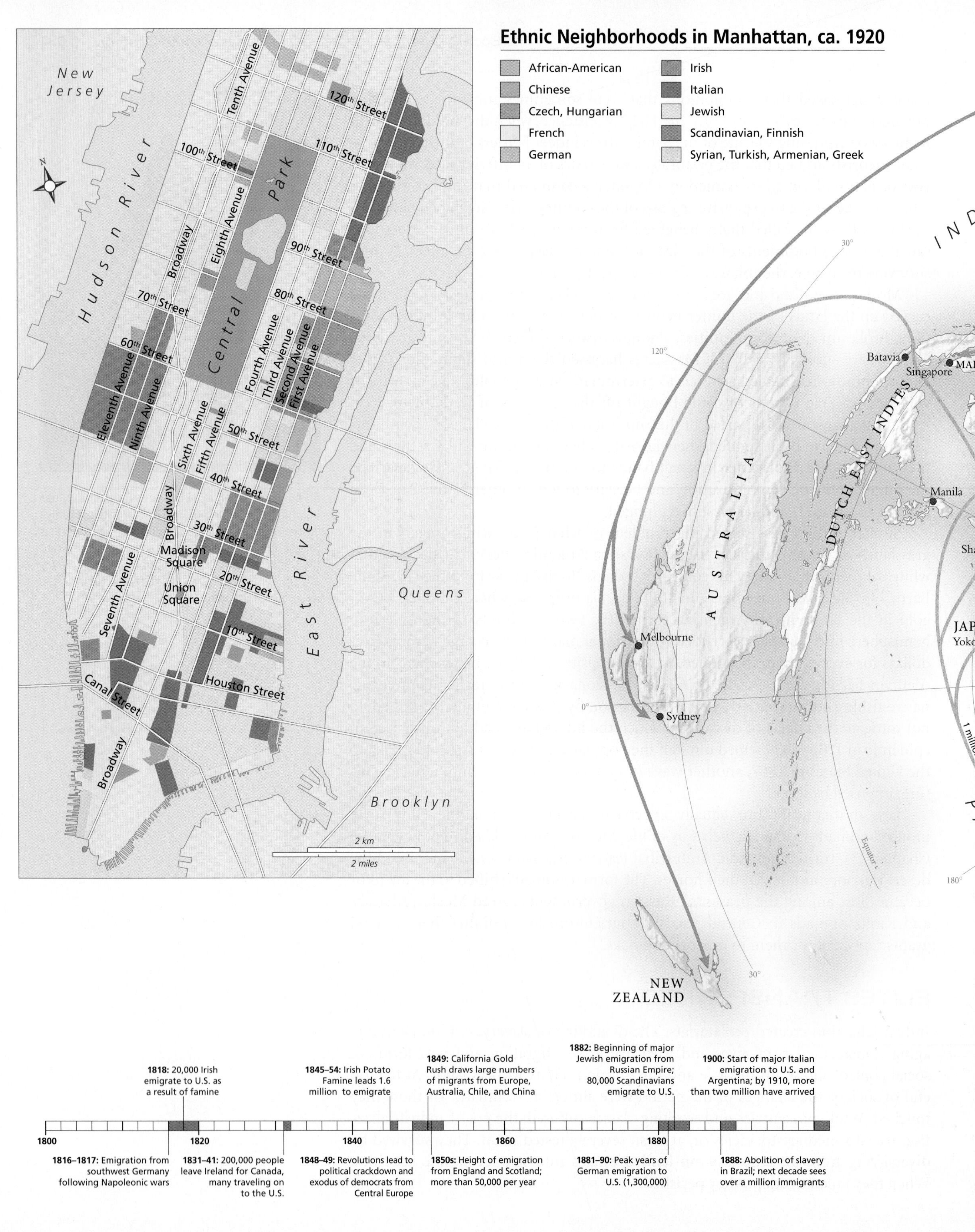

Ethnic Neighborhoods in Manhattan, ca. 1920
African-American
Chinese
Czech, Hungarian
French
German
Irish
Italian
Jewish
Scandinavian, Finnish
Syrian, Turkish, Armenian, Greek
New Jersey
Hudson River
Central Park
East River
Queens
Brooklyn
Tenth Avenue
120th Street
110th Street
100th Street
90th Street
80th Street
70th Street
60th Street
50th Street
40th Street
30th Street
20th Street
10th Street
Houston Street
Canal Street
Broadway
Eighth Avenue
Eleventh Avenue
Ninth Avenue
Sixth Avenue
Fifth Avenue
Fourth Avenue
Third Avenue
Second Avenue
First Avenue
Seventh Avenue
Madison Square
Union Square
2 km
2 miles
AUSTRALIA
DUTCH EAST INDIES
Batavia
Singapore
MAL
Manila
Melbourne
Sydney
NEW ZEALAND
JAPA
Yokol
Shar
1 million
30°
120°
0°
Equator
180°
1818: 20,000 Irish emigrate to U.S. as a result of famine
1845–54: Irish Potato Famine leads 1.6 million to emigrate
1849: California Gold Rush draws large numbers of migrants from Europe, Australia, Chile, and China
1882: Beginning of major Jewish emigration from Russian Empire; 80,000 Scandinavians emigrate to U.S.
1900: Start of major Italian emigration to U.S. and Argentina; by 1910, more than two million have arrived
1800
1820
1840
1860
1880
1816–1817: Emigration from southwest Germany following Napoleonic wars
1831–41: 200,000 people leave Ireland for Canada, many traveling on to the U.S.
1848–49: Revolutions lead to political crackdown and exodus of democrats from Central Europe
1850s: Height of emigration from England and Scotland; more than 50,000 per year
1881–90: Peak years of German emigration to U.S. (1,300,000)
1888: Abolition of slavery in Brazil; next decade sees over a million immigrants

MAP 24.3
World Migration, ca. 1860–1920
Transatlantic migration
to North America
to South America and the Caribbean
to Europe from the Americas
Other European migration
to Australia and New Zealand
to North Africa
Asian migration
to the Americas and Australia
Russian migration into Siberia
Indian migration within British Empire
transcontinental railroad
major exporters of people
major importers of people
MADAGASCAR
SOUTH AFRICA
Cape Town
Lake Nyasa
Mombasa
Lake Victoria
Mogadishu
Lake Tanganyika
Congo
AFRICA
Nile
Suez Canal 1869
Lagos
Niger
Dakar
ATLANTIC OCEAN
CEYLON
Bombay
INDIA
Calcutta
Tashkent
Baku
OTTOMAN EMPIRE
Constantinople
Odesa
AUSTRIA-HUNGARY
Naples
ITALY
Genoa
Marseille
CHINA
ASIA
Novosibirsk
Moscow
EUROPE
Beijing
Trans-Siberian Railway
Ob
St. Petersburg
GERMANY
Hamburg
Antwerp
SPAIN
Amsterdam
PORTUGAL
Southampton
Liverpool
BRITAIN
IRELAND
RUSSIAN EMPIRE
Yenisey
6 million
4 million
1.5 million
3 million (2.5 million British)
7 million returnees
8 million
24.1 million
ARCTIC OCEAN
OCEAN
Halifax
Quebec
Boston
New York
see inset map
CANADA
Canadian Pacific
Vancouver
Northern Pacific
Central Pacific
UNITED STATES
San Francisco
Los Angeles
NORTH AMERICA
New Orleans
CUBA
JAMAICA
Panama Canal 1914
PUERTO RICO
MEXICO
Mexico City
Rio de Janeiro
Belém
BRAZIL
Amazon
SOUTH AMERICA
URUGUAY
Montevideo
Buenos Aires
ARGENTINA
PERU
Lima
CHILE
Valparaíso
Equator
MAP EXPLORATION
www.prenhall.com/armesto_maps

Elite uniforms. The Freemason's Lodge of Freetown, in Sierra Leone in West Africa, presents an address to the Duke of Connaught, a son of Queen Victoria, on December 15, 1910. The white ladies, in their tea dresses under the canopy, and the top brass with ceremonial swords and pith helmets, look positively informal by the standards of the black dignitaries, who wear what appears to be full court dress in the heat of the tropical day. It would be hard to find a more telling image of determination to defy the environment.

In Japan, the government abolished samurai privileges in the 1870s. A military draft for all able-bodied men in 1873 eliminated the main legal distinction—the right to bear arms—between samurai and commoners. Japan now had no warrior caste. Many samurai benefited from the abolition of distinctions within their own class. Lower samurai were now free to accumulate wealth and honor. Professions that had formerly been considered socially beneath them, such as merchants and civil servants, opened up to the gentry, and many of them became dependents of the government. They also served as officials and as officers in the new European-trained army and navy or invested in new industries. Others merged into the ranks of the commoners.

Traditionally, in China merit had been the means to attain high social rank. But rich families had an advantage because they could afford good schooling for their sons and tended to monopolize access to the scholar elite in the nineteenth century. "The gentry are at the head of the common people," said imperial instructions to magistrates, "and to them the villagers look up." The impoverished landowners of China shook off the ties of extended kin and the traditional social obligations of their status. Thanks to their efforts to find new sources of wealth, by engaging in trade, or by exploiting the labor of poor neighbors and tenants on their land, they found themselves demonized as "evil gentry."

The British aristocracy survived the collapse of land prices by diversifying into commerce, by marrying American heiresses, and by absorbing into its ranks the "beerage"—the new class of wealthy entrepreneurs, such as those who owned the massive, mechanized breweries that supplied the workers' beer.

The sons of the **new rich** acquired the habits, friends, and tastes of gentlemen at the numerous new and expensive schools—called "public" in Britain only because they sought to be of public importance—and the growing universities. Old blood allied with new money. Industrialization shifted the balance of power and wealth away from landed estates and into cities. But landowners could also benefit by mining coal and iron ore on their estates or by leasing or selling the land on which to build towns and docks. The third Marquess of Bute (1847–1901) did all these things and left an estate equivalent to several hundred million dollars today. As early as the 1840s, about a sixth of England's landed gentry earned a significant part of their wealth in business, mainly through manufacturing, banking, and railways. Aristocracies were becoming middle class while the middle class was adopting aristocratic tastes.

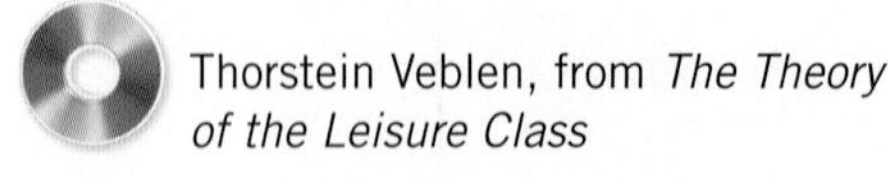

Thorstein Veblen, from *The Theory of the Leisure Class*

Every industrializing economy had its new rich and its declining aristocracies. In Spain, Pérez Galdós satirized the decline of old money in one of his best novels, *Mercy* (1897), about hard times for an aristocratic family, who were maintained by their maid's talents as a beggar. In Russia, Chekhov's play *The Cherry Orchard* (1904) features an old landed family compelled to sell its estate, and the upwardly mobile entrepreneur who buys them out, after enduring years of their contempt.

In the United States, "old" money, which was in truth not very old, was more vulnerable to intrusion by the new rich because the country had no landed aristocracy and no titled nobility. Nonetheless, in 1899, Thorstein Veblen proposed in *The*

Theory of the Leisure Class that America had acquired an elite basd on inherited wealth. In the 1870s and 1880s, Samuel Ward McAllister attempted to create high society, based on the admission of supposedly suitable people to entertainments given by socially exclusive hostesses in New York City—exclusive, that is, according to McAllister himself. "We want the money power," he explained in 1872, "but not to be controlled by it." In effect he was admitting that the American aristocracy was open to new money, and indeed, merchants and railroad men's sons and daughters got into McAllister's list of America's "First Four Hundred."

Cultural exchange. The fashion for Japanese art and taste in the late nineteenth-century West extended to women's clothing. Paintings of Westerners in Japanese kimonos—like these American women painted in San Francisco around 1880—demonstrate the fashionable appeal of Japan. Note the view of Mount Fuji in the background on the left-hand panel.
Photograph courtesy of the Peabody Essex Museum

Outside the West, westernization made the rise of a new class easier by spreading values and tastes distinct from those of traditional aristocracies. In the 1870s, one Angolan chief looted his own people to build a medieval-looking castle. In the 1890s, another hired an ex-slave who had worked for the Portuguese as a maid to teach him European etiquette. Almost everywhere, Western dress became the uniform of the world's elite—at least for men. Formal suits with top hats were the uniform of male power, whether among well-to-do of West Africa or the Maori chiefs of New Zealand. The self-reinvented samurai who staffed the Japanese government chopped off the topknots from their hair and clamped shiny top hats to their heads.

IN PERSPECTIVE: Cultural Exchange—Enhanced Pace, New Directions

Industrialization restored a kind of uniformity to Western society. A gap opened between the developed and underdeveloped worlds. The technology gap became a wealth gap between the regions that supplied commodities and those that turned them into manufactured goods. These worldwide inequalities were bigger, and would prove more enduring, than the internal class differences that divided industrializing societies.

Meanwhile, exchanges of culture crossed the world with greater intensity and speed than ever before. No example was more obviously attuned to the pace of industrialization than the standardization of time. Until the nineteenth century, every place determined its own time of day according to the sun and set its clocks accordingly. But the railway made it impossible to maintain this "natural" time. People could move too fast. The railway schedules became too complex. In 1852, an electric telegraph system was set up to transmit the time at the Royal Observatory in Greenwich across Britain. In 1880, Greenwich time became the official standard time for the whole country. In 1884, the same standard became the basis for a sequence of time zones covering the globe. Cultural exchange got faster and more complicated than ever, in part because people could travel farther and more frequently than formerly. The world's first travel agent, Thomas Cook and Company, was founded in Britain in 1841. By 1900, Cook's was selling 3 million travel packages a year, mostly to working- and middle-class tourists within Britain. But Cook's also took luxury travelers, big-game hunters, businesspeople, and even officials of the British Empire across the world.

Japanese impressions of American culture, 1860

Cultural exchange, however, was not one-way Westernization. What Europeans considered exotic became fashionable in the West. The Japanese-inspired style that

CHRONOLOGY

1791–1803	Haitian Revolution
1800	1 million slaves in the United States
1800–1900	3.3. million slaves shipped from Africa to the Americas
1807	Britain outlaws slave trade
1808	United States bans importation of slaves
1825	Haiti wins official independence
1834	Slavery abolished in the British Empire
1838–1839	Epidemic wipes out half of the native population of the Aleutian Islands
1842	Edwin Chadwick's *The Sanitary Condition of the Labouring Population*
1845–1876	Ottoman agricultural exports increase fivefold
1848	France outlaws slavery; publication of Marx's and Engels's *The Communist Manifesto*
1850s	25,000 Chinese live and work in California
1853–1854	Serfs in Habsburg Empire emancipated
1860s and 1870s	French ship 50,000 Indian laborers to the Caribbean
1861	Serfs in Russia emancipated
1863	Emancipation Proclamation (United States)
1870s	Japanese workers and peasants freed by official decree; samurai privileges abolished
1880s	5.25 million immigrants arrive in the United States; bounty offered for killing Indians in Argentina
1885	Egypt outlaws slavery
1886	Cuba outlaws slavery
1888	Brazil outlaws slavery
1890s	32 percent of French work force is female; 14 million people migrate from China
1890–1920	Immigration adds 18.2 million people to U.S. population
ca. 1900	Cotton cultivation in Egypt contributes to the creation of 2 million landless peasants
	Population: Izmir, 200,000; Alexandria, 250,000; Calcutta, more than 750,00; Melbourne, 800,000; New York, 3.4 million; London, 6.5 million
1914	30 percent of the population of Argentina is foreign born

Western designers called "Japonisme" was the most striking case. Monet (1860–1926) portrayed his wife in a kimono. Puccini, the leading operatic composer in 1900, put Japanese, Chinese, and even Native American music in his operas. These exchanges took in wider influences, too. In the 1890s, Dvorák was among the first European composers to draw on African-American music. European painters and sculptors began to discover what they called primitive art from Africa and the South Seas. Some exchanges bypassed the West altogether. In the 1890s, Chief Mataka of the Yao—deep in the East African interior—made his people don Arab dress, launched Arab-style ships on Lake Nyasa, planted coconut groves and mangoes, and rebuilt his palace in the mixed Arab–African Swahili style (see Chapter 21). "Ah!" he exclaimed, "now I have changed Yao to be like the coast!"

Although cultural transmissions increasingly crisscrossed the world, one route the big new influences came from was the United States, heralding trends that would dominate the twentieth century. This was new. North America had previously followed European and Latin American cultural leadership. In politics, as we shall see, the United States launched, nurtured, or revised some ideas of enormous and growing influence in the world—including, notably, democracy and socialism—but no significant movement in the arts, literature, science, or philosophy started in the United States before the 1890s. Then, however, the flood began, as European composers discovered American ragtime. It was a small beginning, but it was the herald of the dawn of an "American century" in which the United States was increasingly to be the source of worldwide trends in popular culture, entertainment, the arts, taste, food, technology, and ideas.

PROBLEMS AND PARALLELS

1. What were the advantages and disadvantages of modernization and industrialization in Japan and Europe in the nineteenth century? Who were the winners and losers from this process?
2. How did industrialization change daily life for the average urban dweller? Did these changes improve life or make it more difficult? What does the term *paternalism* mean? Why did Karl Marx's prediction of a workers' revolution not come to pass?
3. How did large-scale urbanization transform social, economic, political, and cultural life in the nineteenth century? What types of organizational structures, architecture, and municipal systems developed to cope with highly concentrated populations? How did machines change the way people viewed the environment?
4. What forms of labor replaced slavery in the nineteenth century? How did industrialization change women's and children's lives?
5. How did massive migration of free labor reshape the world's labor force?

DOCUMENTS IN GLOBAL HISTORY

- Samuel Smiles, from *Self-Help*
- Karl Marx and Frederich Engels, from *The Communist Manifesto*
- Edwin Chadwick, from *Sanitary Conditions of the Labouring Population*
- Chinese immigrants, USA, 1909
- Multatuli, *May Havelaar: Or the Coffee Auctions of the Dutch Tracking Company*
- Cotton plantation, USA
- Henrik Ibsen, from *A Doll's House*
- Thorstein Veblen, from *The Theory of the Leisure Class*
- Japanese impressions of American culture, 1860

Please see the Primary Source DVD for additional sources related to this chapter.

READ ON

My version of the story of Oshio Heicharo is based on I. Morris, *The Nobility of Failure* (1988).The best general survey of the nineteenth-century world is C. A. Bayly, *The Birth of the Modern World* (2003).

T. Hunt, *Building Jerusalem* (2004), and A. Briggs, *Victorian Cities* (1993) deal with urbanization in the British state and empire. J. Merriman, ed., *French Cities in the Nineteenth Century* (1981) is a good survey of France; C. Chant and D. Goodman et al., eds., *European Cities and Technology: Industrial to Post-industrial City* (1999) is a valuable six-volume collection of essays and documents. Peter Hall, *Cities in Civilisation* (1998) is particularly good on urban culture. On the effects on health, D. Brunton, *Health, Disease, and Society in Europe* (2004) is a highly useful collection of documents. R. J. Evans, *Death in Hamburg* (1987) is an impressive case study.

On working conditions in the industrializing world, P. Stearns, *Lives of Labor* (1975) is particularly good. J. Burnett, ed., *Useful Toil* (1994) is a valuable collection of English working-class autobiographical materials. A. Kelly, *The German Worker* (1987) does a similar job for Germany. R. C. Alberts, *The Good Provider* (1973) is a lively biography of Heinz. G. Marks and S. M. Lipset, *It Didn't Happen Here* (2000) is a useful attempt to explain the failure of socialism in the United States.

M. Lynch, *Mining in World History* (2004) is a magisterial survey, with emphasis on technological aspects. S. Kanfer, *The Last Empire* (1995) is an enjoyable history of De Beers. D. Avery, *Not on Queen Victoria's Birthday* (1974) studies the Río Tinto case.

On rural conditions in the unindustrializing world, S. Bose, *Peasant Labour and Colonial Capital* (1993) is an outstanding study of Bengal; for Thailand, J. C. Ingram, *Economic Change in Thailand* (1971) is excellent. On Africa, M. Lynn, *Commerce and Economic Change in West Africa* (2002), and W. G. Clarence-Smith, *Slaves, Peasants, and Capitalists in Southern Angola* (1979) are important. J. McCann, *Green Land, Brown Land, Black Land* (1999) surveys sub-Saharan Africa with emphasis on the ecological effects of economic development. C. Issawi has published a series of invaluable works, rich in documents, on the Middle East, notably *The Economic History of the Middle East* (1966) and *An Economic History of Turkey* (1980), which can be supplemented with R. Kasaba, *The Ottoman Empire and the World Economy*; P. Richardson, *Economic Change in China* (1999) is a good introductory survey on that country.

For changes in labor regimes, H. Thomas, *The Slave Trade* (1999) and D. Northrup, *Indentured Labor in the Age of Imperialism* (1995) are fundamental. The eight volumes of P. J. Kitson and D. Lee et al., eds., *Slavery, Abolition, and Emancipation* (1999) make an invaluable collection of mainly literary and theoretical source materials. S. Miers and R. Roberts, eds., *The End of Slavery in Africa* (1988) and P. C. Emmer and M. Morner, eds., *European Expansion and Migration* (1992) are useful collections. P. Kolchin, *Unfree Labor* (1990) compares America and Russia.

CHAPTER 25 Western Dominance in the Nineteenth Century: The Westward Shift of Power and the Rise of Global Empires

Unequal combat in the Opium Wars. The British ironclad *Nemesis* blows Chinese war junks to smithereens with impunity, on January 17, 1841, off Guangzhou. The print was circulated at the British shipbuilders' and arms-makers' expense, partly to advertise their wares.

IN THIS CHAPTER

THE OPIUM WARS
THE WHITE EMPIRES: RISE AND RESISTANCE
METHODS OF IMPERIAL RULE
BUSINESS IMPERIALISM
IMPERIALISM IN THE "NEW EUROPES"
EMPIRES ELSEWHERE: JAPAN, RUSSIA, AND THE UNITED STATES
RATIONALES OF EMPIRE
Doctrines of Superiority
The Civilizing Mission
IN PERSPECTIVE: The Reach of Empires

On February 10, 1842—Chinese New Year's Day—General Yijing (yee-jing) consulted the oracles in the Temple of the War God. China was at war with Britain. Yijing could succeed, the oracle warned, only if "you are hailed by humans with the heads of tigers." A few days later, a band of aboriginal recruits arrived dressed in tiger-skin caps. The general was delighted and distributed similar caps throughout the army. All his ways to secure victory had a touch of desperation. He contemplated attacking the British ships with monkeys strapped with firecrackers to their backs. But the monkeys died of starvation.

The campaign was chaotic. Chinese troops mistook and fought their own men. The supply department failed, inflicting unendurable hunger on the army. Commanders received rewards for writing reports on nonexistent victories. Embezzlers raided the war chest. Only a fraction of the army arrived in time for the battle. They faced, moreover, a new kind of "barbarian." The British forces had state-of-the-art munitions—products of early industrialization—and steam-powered gunboats. They could recruit men—"black devils," as the Chinese called them—from India, where Britain was building up an empire. The Chinese could not stop the invasion.

At first glance, the outcome looks like a triumph for modernity. Ancient methods and magic failed in the face of professional forces equipped with industrially produced equipment. The dynamic out-thrust of a go-ahead Western nation shattered an inward-looking, self-satisfied empire.

● ● ● ● ●

Such conclusions would be unfair. Chinese respect for omens did not usually cloud rational judgment or obstruct military efficiency. The deficiencies of organization and generalship in Yijing's command were not unique to, or typical of, Chinese warfare. The Chinese government was negotiating with France to buy the latest Western military and naval technology, but the war broke out before the Chinese could acquire it.

Nevertheless, the conflict revealed how much the balance of power in the world had shifted. For most of recorded history, China had been the source of world-shaping technological innovations, the "central country," with the strength to influence or dictate politics far from its own borders and shores. Britain had spent most of history on the edge of Eurasia—literally, a marginal part of the world—absorbing influences from outside rather than radiating its own influence to the rest of the world. Now the positions were reversed. Thanks in part to the substitution of machine power for manpower, a small country like Britain could defeat a giant such as China. Thanks to the exploration of the wind systems of the world and the development of technologies of long-range communications, a position on the edge of the West had turned from a disadvantage into an advantage. From the shores of the Atlantic, powers in Western Europe and North America could use seaborne communications to mesh together ambitious and vast territorial domains. The broader context of General Yijing's failures reveals a further vast shift in global history: an economic shift—upheaval in the traditional balance of wealth and reversal in the traditional structures of trade.

FOCUS questions

- WHY DID China cease to be the world's richest nation in the nineteenth century?
- WHY WAS the West able to subjugate so much of the world?
- HOW DID African states resist Western imperialism?
- WHAT WAS business imperialism?
- WHERE WERE the "New Europes"?
- WAS THE United States an empire in the nineteenth century?
- HOW DID social Darwinism justify imperial rule?

THE OPIUM WARS

A trade dispute, indeed, had provoked the war of which Yijing's campaign formed part. At the center of the dispute was opium. The opium trade represented a breakthrough into a market in which, previously, most foreigners had virtually nothing to sell. Because narcotics are addictive, they create their own captive markets and command high prices. This makes them ideal commodities for relatively poor producer economies seeking outlets in rich economies.

The annual value of the opium that reached China rose fivefold in the 20 years preceding the mid-1830s. As the trade increased, it caused alarm in China, much as today's global traffic in heroin and cocaine alarms the West.

Chinese statesmen blamed opium for demoralizing, enfeebling, and impoverishing large numbers of Chinese. The drain of revenues also threatened one of China's historic sources of strength: its favorable balance of trade with the rest of the world. The situation became acute in the 1830s, because Britain abolished trading monopolies among its own subjects and opened free trade with China. The Chinese emperor, therefore, appointed Commissioner Lin to end the opium trade.

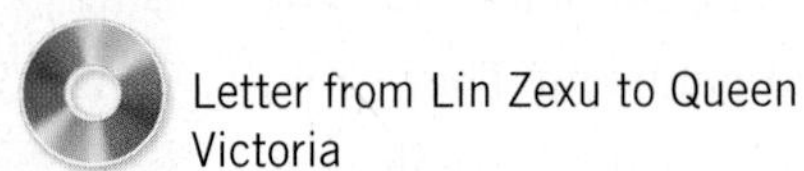

Letter from Lin Zexu to Queen Victoria

In February 1839, Lin drafted a summary of Chinese thinking for British readers. "Our great, unified Manchu Empire," Lin wrote, "regards itself as responsible for the habits and morals of its people and cannot rest content to see any of them become victims to a deadly poison. For this reason we have decided to inflict very severe penalties on opium dealers and opium smokers.... What it is here forbidden to consume, your dependencies must be forbidden to manufacture. When that is done, not only will the Chinese be rid of this evil, but your people too will be safe. For so long as your subjects make opium, who knows but they will not sooner or later take to smoking it?" Lin also appealed to something the British understood: commercial considerations. "The laws against the consumption of opium are now so strict in China that if you continue to make it, you will find that no one buys it and no more fortunes will be made. Rather than waste your efforts on a hopeless endeavour, would it not be better to devise some other form of trade?"

In the spring and summer of 1839, Lin flushed all the opium he could find into the sea. He was unable, however, to secure promises from the British merchants that they would withdraw from the trade, and in January 1840, the imperial court suspended trade with Britain. The British acknowledged that China could punish its own subjects for smoking opium. But to ban the trade itself was unlawful interference in the freedom of commerce and to confiscate opium from British merchants was an outrage against private property. In the summer of 1840, a British expeditionary force blockaded China's ports, reopening trade by force. The following year, British warships, with opium vessels in their wake, sacked China's coastal and river towns. The British hardly noticed General Yijing's counterattack of 1842.

The Treaty of Nanjing

In the Treaty of Nanjing, which ended the war, China ceded Hong Kong to Britain, opened five other ports to British trade, and paid an indemnity of 21 million silver dollars (equivalent in purchasing power today to around $2 billion). Henceforth, British officials, not Chinese, would settle disputes between British and Chinese subjects. Britain would have what we now call "most favored nation" rights in China. British subjects would automatically enjoy any privileges and immunities that China conceded in future to other foreigners. The United States, France, and Sweden soon persuaded or forced the Chinese to grant them similar treaties.

To the Westerners' surprise, the subsequent growth of trade still favored the Chinese, at least until the late 1860s. Tea was a more valuable drug in the West than opium was in China, and the market for it was bigger and faster growing. Britain's official deficit with China rose from under $20 million in 1842 to nearly $55 million in 1857. It took more British incursions and invasions from 1856 onward to wrest from China terms of trade weighted in Westerners' favor. In 1860, the Taiping rebellion virtually paralyzed the Chinese state. A French and British task force found it easy to march to Beijing, burn the imperial summer palace, and exact the terms the Westerners wanted from the Chinese government (see Chapter 23).

Destroying opium. Commissioner Lin destroyed the opium he confiscated from Western—chiefly British—merchants at Guangzhou in 1839 by mixing it with lime and flushing it into the sea or, in the example here, setting it on fire.

Henceforth, foreigners dominated China's trade and bought up the best real estate in the major trading centers (see Map 25.1). In 1880, for instance, two British steamship companies handled 80 percent of China's shipping business. The effects of the wars partly account for this leap to Western ascendancy. In the background, other influences piled up. First, industrialization in the West compensated for China's size and enabled Western economies to overtake China's in wealth. Second, imperialism in other parts of the world increased the resources available to Western powers.

The rise of the West to economic superiority over China—and of some Western powers to economic dominance within China—was one of the major reversals of history. Since then, the world has experienced an abnormal situation, in which—until the last few years, at least—China has been stagnant and, by the technical standards of Western powers, backward or underdeveloped, while historical initiative—the capacity for some groups in the world to influence others—has been concentrated in the West. Whereas for centuries China had been the only country to occupy the position of a *superpower*—a state exceeding in strength that of all rivals combined—Western states have been the main contenders for that role. Britain exercised it briefly in the nineteenth century, and the United States has enjoyed it—briefly again, so far—in the late twentieth and early twenty-first centuries.

THE WHITE EMPIRES: RISE AND RESISTANCE

The change occurred in the context of a new feature of global history in the nineteenth century: the rise—beginning, like industrialization, in Western Europe and rapidly including Russia, the United States, and Japan—of enormous empires that virtually carved up the world among them. Previously, most of the big empire-building initiatives in the world had originated in Asia, and the empires expanded by land into territories that bordered on those of the conquerors. Such was the nature of the empires of the Persians, Arabs, Chinese, Indians, and Mongols whose stories have dominated much of this book. Chinese rulers had never sent fleets beyond the Indian Ocean or armies beyond Central Asia (see Chapter 15).

Alongside the great empires, smaller imperial ventures had also set out to control trade rather than production, to dominate sea-lanes and harbors rather than

MAP 25.1

Foreign Imperialism in East and Southeast Asia, 1840–1910

Area of control or influence

- Russian
- Japanese
- French
- British
- Dutch
- American
- Portuguese
- German

1898 date of acquisition by foreign power

Leased territory	Treaty ports
◆ Japanese	● Japanese
◆ French	● French
◆ British	● British
◆ Portuguese	● American
◆ German	● open port

Qing Empire at its greatest extent ca. 1850

Foreign attacks on China

- → British (Opium War 1840–1842)
- → Anglo-French campaigns 1858–1860
- → French 1883–1885

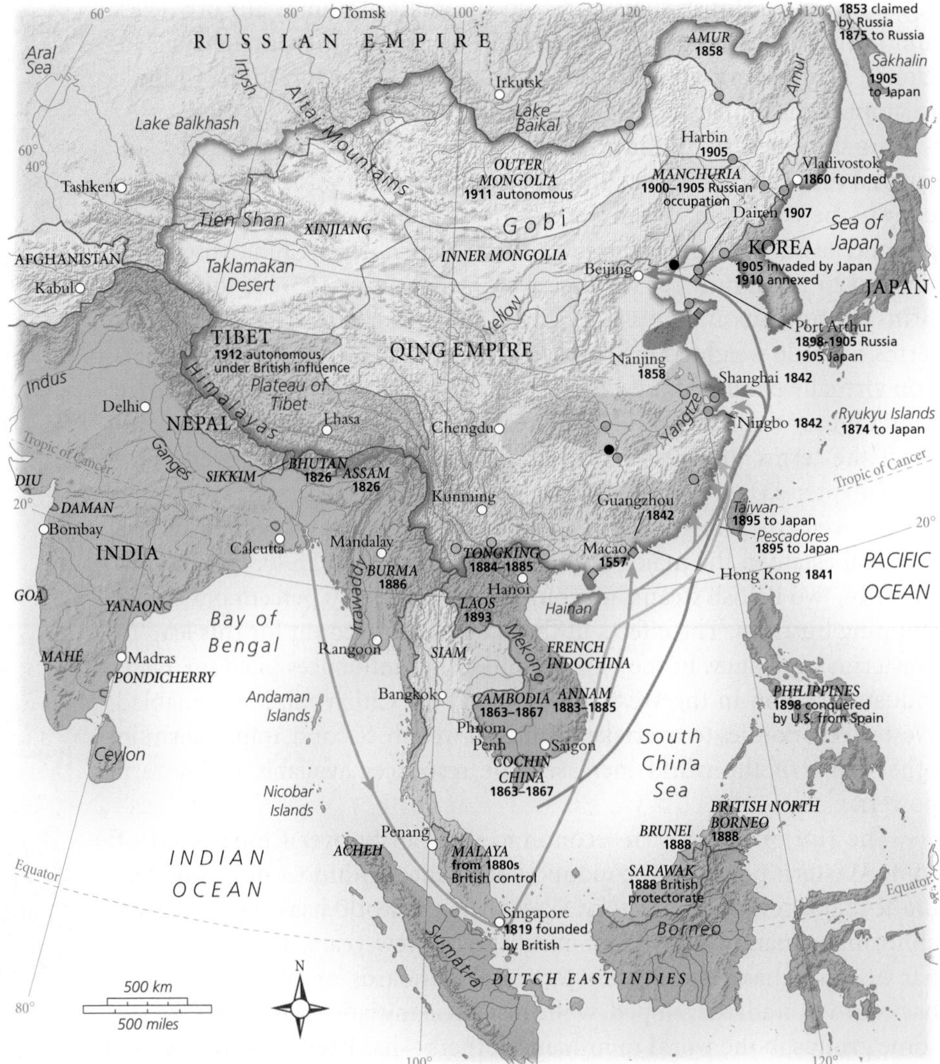

large stretches of land. Most European imperialism had been of this character. Until the eighteenth century, as we saw in Chapter 21, no empire except Spain's had been able to combine these roles on a large scale. Europeans overseas had generally depended on local collaborators in existing economic systems. Now their relationship with the world they had entered changed, as they exploited the advantages of industrially equipped armies and navies to control the production of the key commodities of global trade. The combination of land and sea empires became commonplace.

As in industrialization, Britain established an early lead in imperialism. The first world war—different, of course, from the First World War of 1914–1918—began during the French Revolution in the 1790s (see Chapter 22) and ended with the final defeat of Napoleon in 1815. The British government had already begun to think globally, locating colonies in strategic positions along the world's trade routes. While continental European powers fought each other, Britain wrested colonies from France, Spain, and Holland and seized stations to control global communications by sea, including Malta and other Mediterranean islands, South Africa, parts of the Dutch East Indies, French islands in the Indian Ocean, and islands and coastal positions in and around the Caribbean.

Other governments had, as yet, no such vision. China was self-absorbed, barely aware of events in the wider world. Japan was still proudly ignorant of global events—content to rely on Dutch informants. Even the French closed windows to the world in the early nineteenth century. First, France withdrew from Egypt, then abandoned the effort to reconquer Haiti from rebellious slaves, then, in 1803, sold to the United States its claims to the vast territory known as Louisiana. The British could consolidate the conquests they had already made, thanks to a long period of peace with other European countries that lasted for almost 40 years after the fall of Napoleon.

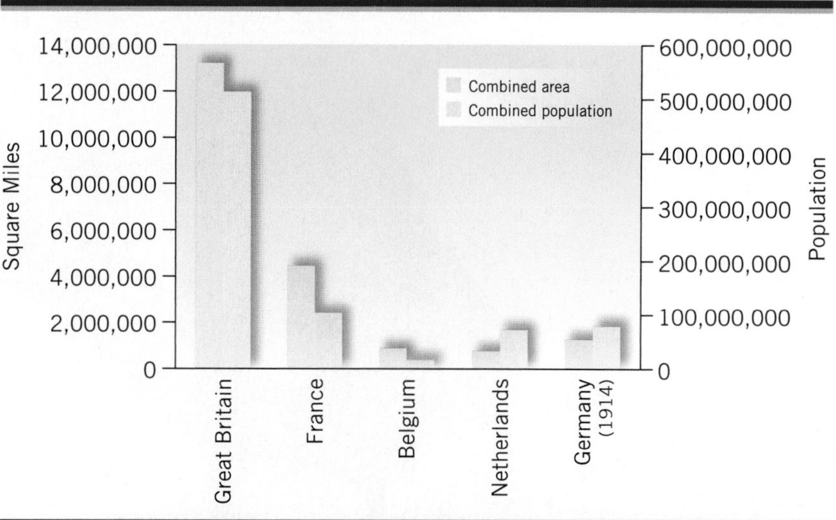

FIGURE 25.1 EUROPEAN EMPIRES: AREA AND POPULATION, CA. 1939

Niall Ferguson, Empire: The Rise and Demise of the British World Order and the Lessons for Global Power, *New York: Basic Books, © 2003, p. 242.* Reprinted by permission of Basic Books, a member of Perseus Books Groups.

For other powers, the empire-building process really took off in the second half of the century (see Map 25.2). In Africa, seven European powers colluded to seize 10 million square miles of territory. The Pacific was sliced up in similar fashion. In southeast Asia, only Thailand eluded European, Japanese, or American imperialism. Even in parts of the world largely exempt from the rule of these empires—Latin America, and east and southwest Asia—local governments had to accept economic domination and political interference.

Existing empires enlarged. The extent of land under French rule doubled between 1878 and 1913. The total territory of all European empires more than doubled to more than 20 million square miles over the same period, while the total population of their empires increased from a little over 300 million to over 550 million people (see Figure 25.1). New empires emerged: those of Germany, Italy, and Belgium. These were new countries, outcomes of European rebellions and wars: Belgium only came into being in 1830, while Italy and Germany were forged by the unification of many smaller states in the 1860s. Italy's empire was built up by a state with no direct access to the Atlantic. Italy used the Mediterranean as a route to expand into North Africa and the Levant, and the new Suez Canal, which opened in 1869, as a means of access to conquests in East Africa. Portugal acquired a "third" African empire in Angola and Mozambique to replace those it had lost in the Indian Ocean and Brazil. The Netherlands withdrew from West Africa to consolidate a huge empire in Indonesia. Some parts of Europe took little part: the Scandinavian powers and Spain engaged in the outreach of this period only modestly, while the Habsburg Empire, centered in Austria and Hungary, with limited access to the sea, showed no interest in overseas expansion. Russia's vast land empire left it little scope and energy for maritime adventures (see Chapter 21). With these exceptions, however, it is fair to speak generally of "European" global imperialism.

In part, we need to understand European expansion against the background of demographic change. Over the eighteenth and nineteenth centuries as a whole, despite big rises in population in parts of Asia, Europe's share of world population rose from around a fifth to over a quarter, whereas Africa's share of world population dropped to little more than 8 percent by 1850. The reasons for this are unknown. It seems, however, that while plague (see Chapter 14) receded from Europe, sub-Saharan Africa's killer diseases—malaria, sleeping sickness, yellow fever—remained rampant, and in North Africa plague lingered until at least the 1830s. The decrease of population in Africa altered its role in the world.

MAP 25.2

The Imperial World, 1900

- Ottoman Empire
- Britain and possessions
- France and possessions
- Denmark and possessions
- Spain and possessions
- Portugal and possessions
- Netherlands and possessions
- German Empire and possessions
- Russian Empire and possessions
- Japan and possessions
- Italy and possessions
- United States and possessions

RUSSIAN EMPIRE
Siberia
Yenisey
Lena
Ob'
Volga
Moscow
AUSTRO-HUNGARIAN EMPIRE
Black Sea
Istanbul
Caspian Sea
BUKHARA
AFGHANISTAN
Tehran
PERSIA
KUWAIT
BAHRAIN
Tigris
Euphrates
Suez Canal
Cairo
Red Sea
Nile
Arabian Peninsula
OMAN
HADHRAMAUT
Aden
ERITREA
ANGLO-EGYPTIAN SUDAN
FRENCH SOMALILAND
BRITISH SOMALILAND
ITALIAN SOMALILAND
Addis Ababa
ETHIOPIA
BRITISH EAST AFRICA
GERMAN EAST AFRICA
Zanzibar
BRITISH CENTRAL AFRICA
PORTUGUESE EAST AFRICA
SOUTHERN RHODESIA
Zambezi
SOUTH AFRICAN REPUBLIC
ORANGE FREE STATE
NATAL
BASUTOLAND
MADAGASCAR
Socotra
Seychelles
Amirante Islands
Comoro Islands
Mauritius
Réunion
Chagos Islands
MALDIVE ISLANDS
INDIAN OCEAN
Gobi
QING EMPIRE
Yellow River
Yangtze
Beijing
Port Arthur
Jiaozhou
Nanjing
Shanghai
KOREA
JAPAN
Tokyo
Amur
Himalayas
NEPAL
BHUTAN
Indus
Ganges
Delhi
INDIA
Chandernagore
Diu
Damão
Bombay
Yanaon
Goa
Madras
Pondicherry
Karikal
Mahé
CEYLON
Burma
Taiwan
Macao
Hong Kong
Guangzhouwan
SIAM
Mekong
Bangkok
FRENCH INDOCHINA
Saigon
PHILIPPINE ISLANDS
Manila
BRITISH NORTH BORNEO
BRUNEI
MALAYA
SARAWAK
Singapore
Borneo
Sumatra
DUTCH EAST INDIES
Batavia
Java
PORTUGUESE TIMOR
Christmas Island
Cocos Islands
KAISER WILHELM'S LAND
New Guinea
PAPUA
BISMARCK ARCHIPELAGO
Mariana Islands
Guam
Marshall Islands
Caroline Islands
PACIFIC OCEAN
Gilbert Islands
Solomon Islands
Ellice Islands
Santa Cruz Islands
Fiji
New Caledonia
AUSTRALIAN COLONIES
Darling
Sydney
Lord Howe Island
NEW ZEALAND
N
Percentage of Earth's Land Surface Controlled by Colonial Empires in 1914
Independent: 29.8%
Chinese: 6%
Ottoman: 1.5%
Russian: 15%
Portuguese: 1%
Spanish: 1%
French: 7.7%
Belgian: 1.6%
Italian: 1.8%
German: 1.6%
Japanese: 0.4%
United States: 7.6%
Danish: 1.5%
Dutch: 1.4%
British: 21.5%

The Battle of Omdurman. "Whatever happens, we have got the Maxim gun and they have not," wrote a British cynic about combat between modern Western armies, armed with machine guns, repeating rifles, and heavy artillery, and their non-Western foes who still fought with spears, swords, and shields. This contemporary commemorative panorama of the British victory over the Sudanese at the Battle of Omdurman revels in the slaughter wrought by irresistible technical superiority. Almost 11,000 Sudanese were killed and at least 16,000 wounded in this battle, at a cost of 48 British lives—half of which were lost when a British colonel insisted on fighting one anachronism with another by launching a cavalry charge.

For European intruders, it came to make more sense to take over African soil and exploit its products and potential directly, instead of milking the continent for slave labor.

Europe still did not have enough manpower to dominate the world. Industrial technology, however, made up much of the shortfall. Victim-peoples of Western imperialism found it hard to resist invaders borne on steamboats, fortified by quinine, and armed with steel guns. In the last quarter of the century, machine guns, especially the Maxim gun, patented in 1884, made a huge difference because unlike heavy artillery, they could be easily transported almost anywhere. In 1880, General Roca machine-gunned his way through the Native American defenders of the pampa in Argentina. In 1881, a similar campaign of extermination began against the Yaqui Indians in northwest Mexico. The government expropriated their lands, giving 1 million acres to a frontier rancher and over 1.2 million acres to a U.S. construction company. In 1884, French guns silenced opposition to their takeover of Indochina. British gunships blasted the southeast Asian kingdom of Burma out of existence in 1885. In 1893, white settlers in what is now Zimbabwe in southern Africa shot the spear-armed Ndebele warriors to pieces. In a typical gesture of despair in 1895, Ngoni priests in Mozambique in East Africa threw away their bone oracles after defeat by invincibly well-armed Portuguese. In 1898, at the battle of Omdurman, the British mowed down the forces of a Sudanese leader. The Sudanese lost 11,000 dead and 16,000 wounded. British losses are usually put at 48 killed, 382 wounded. Like all technological advantages, the West's military superiority could not be permanent, but it was vital while it lasted.

Still, it would be a mistake to attribute the empires' dominance to technology alone, any more than to demographics alone. Despite medical advances, disease could still defeat white armies in tropical climes throughout the century. In South Africa in 1879, it killed twice as many British soldiers as were lost in combat to the Zulus. In Cuba in 1898, during the Spanish-American War, three times as many Americans fell to disease as to enemy action. Partly because of the ravages of disease, it took France 13 years of brutal warfare, from 1882, to conquer Vietnam, even with an army of 35,000 men. Nor did Western armies always have things all their own way on the battlefield. During wars against the Sikhs of northwest India in the 1840s, the British found that the defenders could almost match their firepower. In 1876, an alliance of Sioux and Cheyenne almost annihilated a cavalry force at the Little Bighorn. In 1879, a Zulu army surprised a British force at Isandlhwana in South Africa. Of 1,800 British troops, only about 350 escaped alive.

Underequipped native defenders on colonial frontiers could prolong the wars with guerrilla tactics, keeping the British out of Afghanistan in the 1840s and 1870s and harassing the French in Algeria. In the East Indies, the Dutch lost 15,000 men subduing resistance in Java in the 1820s. It later took them 30 years, from 1873, to bring the sultanate of Aceh in northern Sumatra under control, thanks to fierce native guerrillas and killer diseases.

Two cases illustrate the possibilities of successful native resistance in conventional warfare. The Maori wars in New Zealand lasted from 1845 to 1872, on and off. Maoris repeatedly got the better of the British by devising tactical and technical responses to the invaders' superior firepower, copying the volley-firing discipline of European troops. Indeed, the Maori were among the most effective users of muskets. In the 1830s, musket-armed Maori conquered the Chatham Islands, southeast of New Zealand, dispossessing and slaughtering the native fisher folk.

A European view of the battle of Adowa. In contrast to the Ethiopian version of the battle depicted on the Closer Look on page 649, the European press managed to invest the Italian defeat with the heroic quality of a last stand against overwhelming odds. In this typical example from a British newspaper, *The Graphic*, the light is falling on the Italians' gleaming uniforms, which convey an impression of civilization and almost of sanctity, in contrast to the demonic savagery of their Ethiopian attackers. The Italian troops are surrounded by spent cartridge cases. The kneeling soldier on the right, with his transfixed look and prayerful posture, is trying to reload despite a mortal wound. Outlined against the gunsmoke, on a rearing horse, General Baratieri, the Italian commander, raises his helmet in a last salute to rally his doomed troops.

Ethiopia proved to be even more robust. Emperor Menelik II (r. 1889–1913) came to the throne as a passionate modernizer with a love of gadgets. He used revenues from expanding trade to buy Western arms. By the mid-1890s, he had 100,000 modern rifles. He also reformed the army's supply services, while upholding the traditional methods of recruiting soldiers, via the warrior aristocracy and local chiefs, and the traditional ideology of crusade. He proved that an African state could compete with European empires in the scramble for Africa.

Menelik conquered an empire of his own in the south and along the upper Nile to the west. He scattered garrisons in conquered territory, imposed Christianity on pagan communities, and introduced the customs of his native province of Shoa. In 1896, Italy attempted to take over his empire. At the battle of Adowa, the Italian army crumbled in the face of Ethiopian firepower. The Italians lost a third of their 18,000 men killed, plus a further 1,500 wounded and 1,800 captured. Ethiopia emerged from the scramble for Africa as the only enlarged native African state.

Ethiopia is a reminder that even in the nineteenth century imperial expansion was not a white privilege. Other native African states tried it but succumbed to conquest by Europeans. Khedive Ismail of Egypt (r. 1863–1879), for instance, was, for a time, one of Africa's most successful native imperialists. He realized that steam power could open up the African interior and that he could exploit Western sympathies to help him create an empire among the remotest reaches of the Blue and White Niles. Posing as the policeman of slave-trading routes, he would raise finance for empire-building among antislavery philanthropists in Britain and France. He employed Europeans to lead armies and administrators into what he called the "province of Equatoria," in Central Africa. But the difficult environment and vast distances defeated him. His armies were overwhelmed or isolated. Along the Red Sea and Blue Nile, he encountered invincible resistance from the native states. Meanwhile, his ambitions bankrupted Egypt, and his westernizing ways helped provoke a nationalist rebellion. In 1882, Britain took control of the Egyptian government (see Chapter 23). What remained of Ismail's conquests became the Anglo-Egyptian Sudan—in effect, an unruly part of the British Empire.

In northwest Africa, meanwhile, the sultan of Morocco, Mulay Hassan (r. 1873–1894) tried to preempt European imperialism by claiming dominion over the Sahara, as ruler of "all the tribes not subject to another sovereign" and of "the land of all the tribes who mention the sultan in their prayers." These were unrealistic pretensions. The desert peoples acknowledged "no other chief than Allah and Muhammad." After Mulay Hassan's death, rebellious sheikhs and jealous European powers weakened his empire until, in 1904, France and Spain partitioned Morocco between them.

MAKING CONNECTIONS

TECHNOLOGY AND IMPERIALISM

TOOLS AND TECHNOLOGY →	REGION OF DEVELOPMENT/DATE OF INVENTION →	EFFECTS
Invention of chronometer	Britain / 1770s	Allowed for precise location of longitude, increasing security of long-range navigation; effective planning of voyages
Steelmaking technology	Britain and Western Europe / 1730s–1800s	Increased productivity in steelmaking creates more products; more effective small arms and artillery
Rifles and breach-loading artillery	Britain and Western Europe / 1840s–1900	Combined with better materials (see above) to improve weaponry
Tropical-weight clothing	Britain and Western Europe / 1850s–1900	Allowed more mobility, comfort in tropical zones for colonial military and officials
Quinine pills, powders, and other medicines	Europe (1750); large-scale use by 1850	Used to stave off effects of malaria; helped increase mobility of European colonial officials and soldiers in Africa/Asia
Steam power	Britain / 1769–1900 (continuously improved)	Powering ships, railroads, vastly increased speed over wind-propelled sails or horsepower on land
Machine guns	Europe / 1860s–1900 (continuously improved)	Allowed for annihilation of native resisters of colonialism in Latin America, Central America, Indochina, Africa, and Burma

The sort of empire Mulay Hassan imagined in North Africa, Said Barghash (r. 1870–1888), sultan of the island of Zanzibar in East Africa, dreamed of in the heart of the continent. "Chosen," he claimed "by Providence to found a great African kingdom which will extend from the coast to the great lakes and beyond to the west," he realized that he needed to conciliate European powers. He therefore posed as a foe of the slave trade—but, along with ivory, slaves were the wealth of the region he claimed. Instead of relying, like Khedive Ismail, on European officers, Barghash employed African and Arab agents to represent him in the African interior. They were often implicated in slaving, which was a provocation to the Europeans. Barghash's system was doomed. By the time he died, Britain and Germany had dismembered and shared out his territories. Zanzibar became a British protectorate in 1890.

METHODS OF IMPERIAL RULE

White imperialism relied almost everywhere on native collaborators. Far from being passive playthings of white superiority, native Asian, African, and Pacific states were participants in the process and native peoples were its exploiters and manipulators, as well as its victims. Without native help in policing and administration, the Western colonial empires could never have functioned.

India, for instance, had fewer than 1,000 British administrators in the 1890s in a country of 300 million people. European observers considered Java, with 300 Dutch administrators for 30 million people "overgoverned." British troops in India never numbered more than 90,000 men—0.03 percent of the population. The rest of the Indian army, more than 200,000 men, was made up of Indian troops under British officers. Though empires sometimes shipped large armies to their colonies for conquests or to repress rebellions, they could never afford to keep such forces in place for long.

A CLOSER LOOK

AN ETHIOPIAN VIEW OF THE BATTLE OF ADOWA

In the Battle of Adowa in 1896, the Ethiopians under the command of Emperor Menelik II (r. 1889–1913) annihilated an invading Italian army. An Ethiopian painting from early in the twentieth century shows the victors in a more positive light than in the European version of the same battle on page 647.

Menelik calmly directs his troops. He is dressed in imperial regalia and accompanied by officials and holy men who survey the action from underneath umbrellas that signify their rank. The umbrellas are dark colored as a sign of mourning that Christian blood was being shed by both sides.

Astride a white horse, and protected by a halo painted in the national colors of Ethiopia, St. George leads Menelik's army.

Ethiopian firepower includes cannon, machine guns, and repeating rifles.

Legendary Ethiopian heroes, clad in traditional dress, slash the Italian infantry with swords.

With his horse facing backward, the Italian commander, General Baratieri, appears ready to order a retreat.

How does this painting provide a different perspective on nineteenth-century imperialism from the version that most Westerners believed in at the time?

The most common device for harnessing native cooperation was what the British called **indirect rule** (or *dual role* as the Dutch called it, or *association* to use the term the French applied in Indochina). "The keynote of British colonial method," said Frederick Lugard (1858–1945), the official largely responsible for developing the system of indirect rule in Africa, was "to rule through and by the natives." As a British parliamentary committee recommended in 1898, "Adopt the native government already existing; be content with controlling their excesses and maintaining peace between them."

Lugard exaggerated in claiming that this was a uniquely British method, which "has made us welcomed by tribes and peoples in Africa." On the contrary, it was how most empires succeed and have succeeded throughout history. Europeans were welcome in many places that became regions of indirect rule because of the *stranger effect* (see Chapter 16). Some cultures are disposed to grant what may seem surprising power to outsiders—sometimes because of the high esteem accorded to the exotic and strange, and sometimes because of a shrewd calculation: The foreigner is useful, because outsiders can be—or appear to be—objective. So, as long as they retained local power, many native elites were willing to grant the topmost level of authority to European intruders and pay them to exercise it.

Indirect rule worked particularly well in British colonies because British administrators, even though they were usually middle class, had an aristocratic outlook and education and came from an old monarchy. They could sympathize with traditional elites and aristocracies and could even sense that they had more in common with them than with many of their fellow Britons. Especially after 1877, when Queen Victoria officially took the title of Empress of India, British administrators sought to link the traditional Indian elite to the crown with aristocratic trinkets: coats of arms, lavish ceremonies, knighthoods, and other titles. Indirect rule was more than a charade, however. Local, regional, and subordinate native rulers retained real power. More than one-third of India was divided among states ruled by Indian princes, and native sultans ruled virtually the whole of Malaya.

Friendly native chiefs administered parts of German East Africa (modern Namibia). Traditional local rulers and autonomous sultanates survived in the Dutch East Indies. Even the French republic ruled through native monarchs in Cambodia, Laos, and Vietnam, while Morocco and Tunisia were French *protectorates* under puppet Arab monarchs. In their tropical African possessions, the French delegated awkward jobs, such as tax collecting, to native chiefs.

The British far preferred to rely on traditional aristocracies rather than on the "educated natives" whom the French favored. But educated natives, especially interpreters, were indispensable. Even though most colonial regimes privileged some particular set of laws—usually those of their own mother country—in practice many competing systems of traditional and customary law applied in vast territories inhabited by many different historic communities. Locals, who knew their way around the native cultures, were vital guides. In the 1860s, 4,000 of them served in the administration of the British-ruled parts of India. Twenty years later, Indians occupied nearly two-thirds of the jobs.

An alternative strategy to indirect rule or reliance on native administrators was to ship collaborators in from far away. When Frederick Lugard marched into Uganda in East Africa in 1890, his forces included many African Muslims. When Henry Morton Stanley claimed the lower Congo in Central Africa for King Leopold II of the Belgians in 1880, he found a French outpost commanded by a black Senegalese sergeant, dressed "in dirty African rags," who declared "in all seriousness that, being the only White man there, he was glad to see others arrive to keep him company." In Sierra Leone in West Africa, Britain established a colony of freed slaves from the Caribbean, who created an imitation of England in their capital at Freetown, with garden parties, lecture circuits, concerts, and a temperance union to combat alcoholism. Sawyer's bookshop in Freetown sold such English middle-class manuals of behavior as *The Ballroom Guide* and *Etiquette and the Perfect Lady*.

In other places, local allies enabled the Europeans to rule. The British fought the Zulus with the help of other peoples of South Africa and recruited Hausa gunners from Nigeria to keep order in West Africa. The French conquerors of Tukolor on the Niger River in West Africa in 1889 incorporated thousands of other Africans into their army. Then, when their native soldiers rebelled, the French enlisted the conquered Tukoloros against them. In the 1890s, the British Empire nurtured the Kingdom of Lozi in southern Africa while pulverizing the neighboring Ndebele people into submission. The Lozi king acquired a portrait of Queen Victoria, visited London to great acclaim, and became a satisfied client of white imperialism.

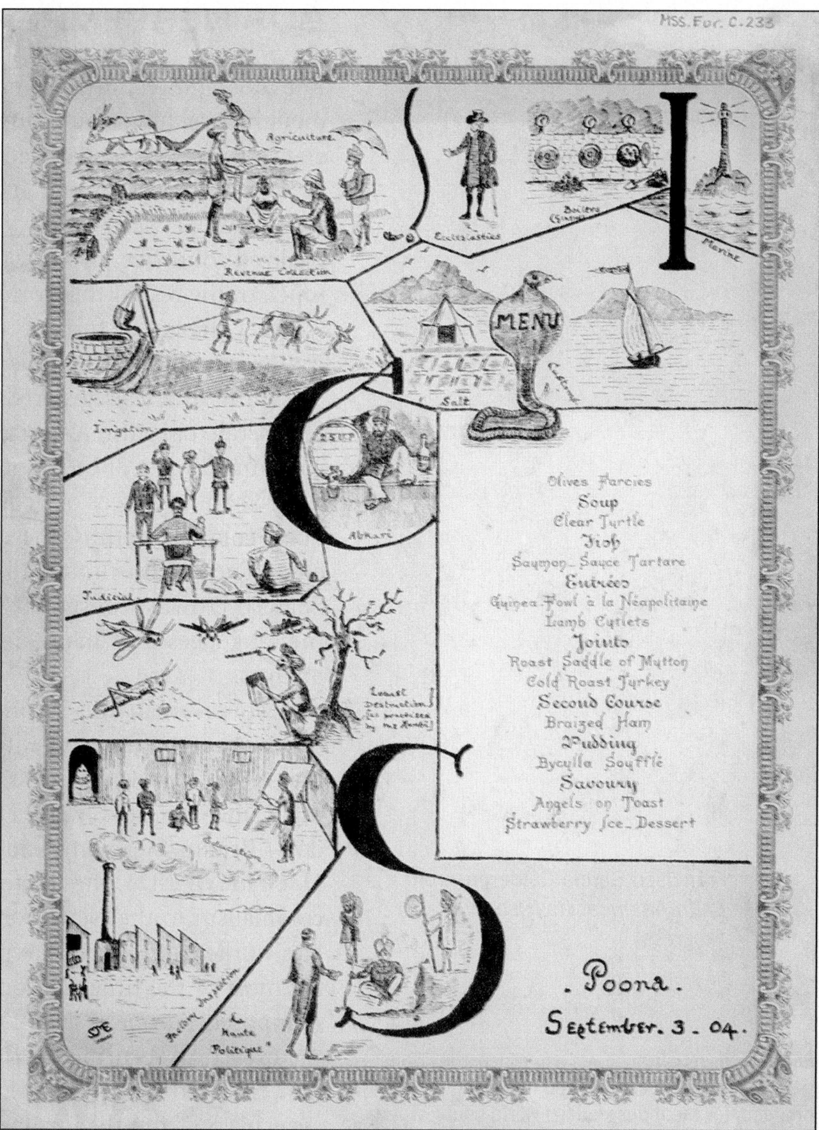

White Man's Burden. The Indian Civil Service (ICS) was the highly paid, professional bureaucracy that governed Britain's Indian Empire. Until the 1920s, its members were overwhelmingly British. This dinner menu for members of the ICS in 1904 looks lavish and self-indulgent at first but reveals much about the difficulties of governing distant empires: the range of activities for which the civil servants felt responsible; the differences in development in the largely rural India of the day; nostalgia for the tastes of home; and the self-mocking humor that helped English administrators cope with their jobs.

© The Trustees of the British Museum

Women were among the most important native collaborators. "White" women were in short supply in the European colonial territories in the first half of the nineteenth century, but relations between European men and native women could be advantageous to both parties, opening useful local links for the colonizers and, for local groups, exploitable channels of communication with the incoming elite. The future British field marshal Sir Garnet Wolseley (1833–1913) wrote as a young officer to his mother from India that with a native concubine he could supply "all the purposes of a wife without any of the bother." Concubinage, however, virtually ceased in India after native soldiers rebelled against British rule in 1857, which panicked the British into distancing themselves further from native society. Female emigration from Europe also increased in the late nineteenth century. In the Dutch East Indies, less than a quarter of the European settler population was female in 1860. The proportion had risen to well over a third by the end of the century. India saw a similar rise in the numbers of British women. In former times, the children of sexual alliances between natives and newcomers had often cemented the alliances on which empires relied. In the nineteenth century, that became harder, because racism classed "half-breeds" as inferior and kept them on the margins of the communities from which they sprang.

BUSINESS IMPERIALISM

The most indirect form of imperial rule was economic control, which left government in local hands but bought up resources, skimmed off wealth, introduced foreign business elites, reduced economies to dependency, and diverted wealth and political influence abroad. Industrialization made business imperialism possible. A wealth gap between primary and secondary producers gave the rich of the industrialized countries surplus capital with which to buy up the productive capacity of much of the rest of the world. Though the evidence is insufficient, scholars debate whether large-scale foreign enterprises frustrated economic growth and industrialization in regions where business imperialism was rife.

Latin America registered the most obvious effects. In a sense, colonialism never really ended in Latin America. Native communities, or "indios," as they were called, constituted most of the population in most of the region, but they never exercised a fair share of power or acquired a fair share of wealth. Instead, they became the quasi-colonial victims, the exploited human "resources" of their countries' own elites. These elites, though they drove out the representatives of the Portuguese and Spanish crowns, continued themselves to represent European culture—to speak the languages and maintain the customs and privileges of the European conquerors.

Moreover, in the second half of the nineteenth century, foreign investors became a powerful extra elite tier in much of Latin America. A new form of colonial-type dependency arose, this time on international big business. Overwhelmingly, the investors were Europeans, from the major imperial powers of the day—Britain, Germany, and France—and from the United States. In the **Monroe Doctrine** of 1823, the United States had unilaterally decreed a ban on European colonialism in the New World. Thanks in large part to European agreement, the ban worked, and European powers stayed out of most of mainland Latin America for most of the time. But business imperialism almost became the forerunner of reimposed European rule. In 1864, France installed a puppet ruler in Mexico, on the pretext of securing Mexican debts owed to European creditors. Popular rebellion, the need for troops in Europe, and United States' diplomacy drove the French away in 1867, but the involvement of foreign business in the Latin American economy kept growing.

Francisco García Calderón, from *Latin America: Its Rise and Progress*

British investments in Latin America rose from $425 million in 1870 to $3,785 million by 1913. This added up to two-thirds of the total foreign investment in the region. British companies controlled over half the shipping in Argentina and Brazil and most of South America's railways. By 1884, Europeans owned two-thirds of Chile's nitrates—the valuable new fertilizers of the period (see Chapter 23). Argentina's foreign trade almost trebled in the last three decades of the century. Foreign capital led the boom. Similar developments occurred throughout Latin America. Like other forms of imperialism, business imperialism was a collaborative project between locals and strangers: local elites and foreign capitalists. In 1870, a British firm opened for business in Rosario, Argentina's second largest city, to provide water and drainage. The local authorities demanded high levels of investment and a high share of the yield for themselves. In Brazil, British power in the coffee market aroused many complaints, but Brazilians owned or acquired most plantations, and the government accepted underdevelopment and economic inferiority to foreigners as inevitable.

Business imperialism. Even countries that "business imperialism" condemned to produce primary products for the industrialized world could experience industrialization of their own. Some cotton-growing countries, for example, sought to become textile manufacturers. This early twentieth-century photograph of a factory in Ecuador shows automated spinning under way on the right and cylinders full of carded cotton on the left.

Hostility to foreigners was rarely effective. A pattern emerged: Local interests attracted foreign investment. This led to foreign control of key technologies for producing and transporting primary commodities. The consequence was dependence on foreign markets and financiers and, often, political control by foreign businessmen. In 1870, for instance, Costa Rica contracted out its railway-building program to an engineer from the United States. A few years later, his nephew began using the railway to ship bananas to North America. His firm eventually grew into the United Fruit Company—a conglomerate so rich and monopolistic that it became more powerful in the early twentieth century than any government in Central America. The United States itself, meanwhile, was an important arena for European businessmen, who invested massively in industry and construction projects.

The scale and success of business imperialism raise a further question: Was all imperialism really economic? Imperialism was the result of capitalism and industry: a drive for markets. Between 1850 and 1859, the value of world trade increased by 80 percent. During the last quarter of the century, world trade roughly doubled in volume and increased in value by a third. Between 1870 and 1900, world industrial production roughly quadrupled. World shipping nearly doubled to about 30 million tons.

Jules Ferry, from *Le Tonkin et la Mere-Patrie*, 1890

The New European Imperialism: Africa and Asia

Nineteenth century	European population explosion fuels economy and creates surplus population for global migration; Africa's population declines
ca. 1815–1835	Value of opium exported to China increases fivefold
Summer 1840	British blockade Chinese ports in response to Chinese suspension of
1842	Treaty of Nanjing ends Opium War
1850–1859	Value of world trade increases by 80 percent
1857	End of Mughal rule in India
1860–1861	Anglo-French force occupies Beijing
1863–1879	Khedive Ismail attempts to build an Egyptian Empire
1869	Suez Canal opens
1870–1900	World industrial production quadruples; world shipping doubles; world trade doubles in volume
1870s	French face increased guerrilla warfare in Algeria
1877	Queen Victoria takes title of Empress of India
1878–1913	Total territory of European empires doubles to 20 million square miles; population of European empires expands from 300 million to 550 million
1880–1914	Most of Africa brought under European control
1884	Maxim machine gun patented
r. 1889–1913	Emperor Menelik modernizes Ethiopian army and expands empire in Africa
1890s	300 Dutch administrators oversee the government of 30 million Indonesians on Java
1896	Battle of Adowa
1898	Battle of Omdurman

There were cases of profitable imperialism. Between 1831 and 1877, revenues from the Dutch East Indies covered a quarter of Dutch state expenditure. Phosphates in Morocco, diamonds in South Africa, and gems, ivory, and rubber in the Congo enriched, respectively, France, Britain, and the king of the Belgians. It used to be thought that the Portuguese Empire in Africa was a silly extravagance for such a poor country, but it seems to have been acquired as an act of economic calculation. Russia's expansion into Central Asia was—in part at least—directed toward lands that could grow cotton for Russia's textile industries. Indochina yielded coal, zinc, and tin for French industry.

Few parts of Africa with exploitable resources were left out of the global economy. Traditional traders were exterminated or became extinct. Some suffered because they were slavers, others because they got in the way of armed greed. King Leopold II proclaimed war on slave traders in the Congo. But his real aim was to cloak his ruthless ivory and rubber grabbing in moral rhetoric. The native palm-oil traders of the Niger delta in West Africa were innocent of slaving, but British merchants impoverished them. Driven into rebellion in 1895, the natives apologized for their attack on the representatives of the British Niger Company, "particularly in the killing and eating of parts of its employees.... We now throw ourselves entirely at the mercy of the good old Queen [Victoria], knowing her to be a most kind, tenderhearted and sympathetic old mother." The face of Africa was scarred and pitted with roads, railways, and mines, or scratched and scrubbed for plantations and new crops. The scramble for Africa was, in part, a scramble for resources (see Map 25.3).

It is tempting to see greed as the spur to empire-building. But political competition drove imperialism, too. Patriotic pride and the pursuit of glory inspired imperialists who were indifferent to economics. Like other external wars, imperial adventures were ways to export unrest. In Britain, the empire rewarded otherwise potentially rebellious groups. The Scots and Irish, who tended to

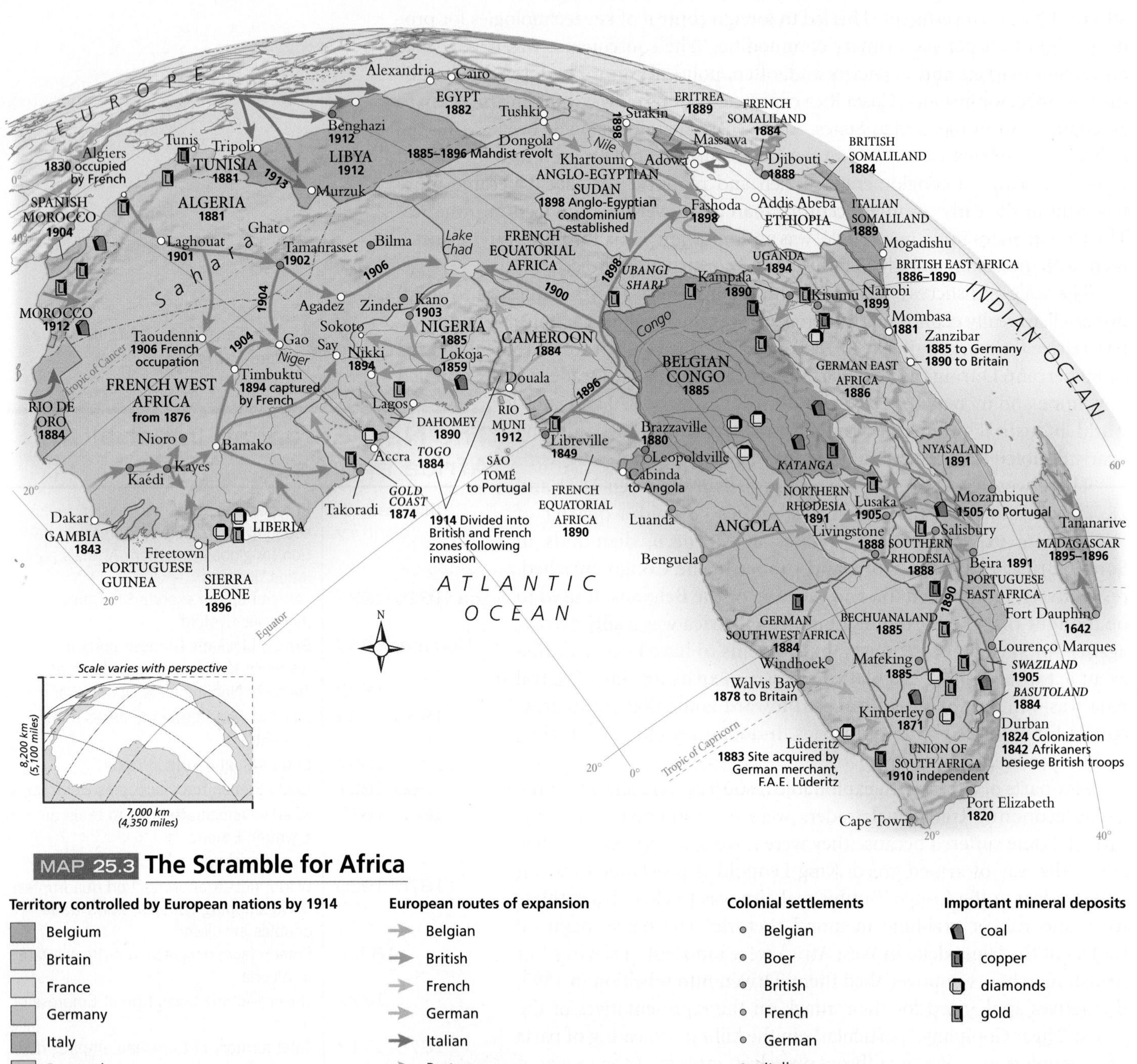

MAP 25.3 The Scramble for Africa

resent English rule, were disproportionately represented in the ranks of British colonial officials and merchants. The empire gratified the working class, and popular culture celebrated it. "C is for colonies," trumpeted *An ABC for Baby Patriots*, "Rightly we boast/That of all great countries/Great Britain has the most." The "Great Game"—Anglo-Russian rivalry in Central Asia—drew Russia deeper into Asia to forestall the expansion of British India. Rivalries among European powers prompted the scramble for Africa.

In some ways, however, competition among the great powers did more to frustrate empires than promote them. Iran and Afghanistan stayed independent, partly by playing off the British against the Russians. Thailand staved off colonialism by balancing French and British power. China was so weakened by the end of the century that it seemed ripe for partition among European powers and Japan, but they could not agree on how to divide it.

IMPERIALISM IN THE "NEW EUROPES"

Some lands were subjected to empire because they were **"New Europes"**—regions similar in climate to much of Europe and, therefore, exploitable for European colonization. Most of these regions—in South Africa, Canada, New Zealand, and Australia—belonged to the British Empire or, like Chile and Argentina, were influenced by British business imperialism.

South Africa had already become a New Europe. In some ways, it was less oppressive than those elsewhere in the world, for here, at least, the European settlers allowed the native peoples to survive, so that they could exploit their labor. In most other regions of similar climate—in the South American cone of Argentina, Chile, and Uruguay, the North American West, Australia, and, with less success, in New Zealand—white settlers waged wars of extermination against the native inhabitants. Australia and New Zealand were exploited at first mainly for sheep raising. But refrigeration enabled both countries to export meat and dairy products to Britain. Gold rushes, meanwhile, attracted huge investment and coaxed large cities into being in Australia, California, and South Africa.

Canada was exemplary among the New Europes. During the century that followed the end of the War of 1812, in which the Canadian colonies repelled attacks from the United States, the population grew—modestly by the standards of other parts of the Americas—tenfold to about 8 million people. The vast territorial expansion across the continent to the Pacific included much unproductive territory. The Canadian prairies produced grain but never as much as those of the United States. A railway crossed the continent on Canadian territory, but it carried less freight and fewer passengers than the parallel railways in the United States. Yet merely to survive, alongside a United States that frequently seemed to be threatening to annex it, was an achievement for Canada. Even though the Atlantic-side Canadian provinces, with their English-speaking inhabitants, had little in common, commercially or culturally, with the mainly French settlements in Quebec, all of them combined in a confederation in 1867. Canada incorporated the Pacific coast in 1871 and created a state with potential for social welfare, cultural pluralism, constitutional flexibility, prosperity, and peace. The main casualties were the native peoples. Ignored in the constitution, brushed aside in the westward drive, by the early twentieth century, they had declined at a rate similar to that of most Native Americans of the United States, to a total of around 100,000 people.

Sydney. New Europes rapidly came to look like old Europe. George Street, Sydney, Australia, photographed in 1899, looks like a commercial street in a prosperous English provincial city of the same era.

The system Britain had established in Canada was really a variant of indirect rule, with elected colonial leaders exercising direct power instead of native chiefs and traditional aristocracies. Demographics, combined with improved communications, made this possible. Toward the end of the nineteenth century, Britain's other colonies of white settlers in Australia and New Zealand were approaching population thresholds—about 4 million and about 750,000, respectively—that enabled them to have the same status as Canada in the British Empire. South Africa, the last of Britain's New Europes, was more of a problem. Unlike the other colonies, it still had a native majority. It had even more mineral wealth than Australia—by the end of the century, South Africa was the world's main supplier of gold and diamonds. It also had a sizable community called *Boers*, white citizens, mainly of Dutch ancestry, who had to be forced into collaboration with the British in a series of wars, ending in 1902. Effectively, Britain bought their loyalty by giving them power over black South Africans. As one of the Boer leaders wrote, rejecting British desire to grant civil liberties to "every civilized man" regardless of color, "I sympathize profoundly with the Native races of South Africa, whose land it was long before we came here to force a policy of dispossession on them. . . . But I don't believe in politics for them."

French imperial planners imagined Algeria in North Africa as a New Europe, too, or a sort of Old World America, where France could encourage American levels of input and achievement among the colonists, while penning the native races—Arabs and Berbers—in doomed desert reservations. Algeria was a "promised land," to be farmed "with gun in hand," as Alexis de Tocqueville (1805–1859) put it. Algiers would become like a town in the American Midwest—"Cincinnati in Africa." Tocqueville believed that Algeria, with its rich coastlands along the Mediterranean and its untapped resources, would play a crucial role in the future of France. The best the natives could hope for was to be absorbed by their conquerors. In 1850, 130,000 Europeans lived in Algeria. There were more than 500,000 by 1900.

EMPIRES ELSEWHERE: JAPAN, RUSSIA, AND THE UNITED STATES

Japan, Russia, and the United States lagged only slightly behind Western Europe in imperialism as in industrialization.

Japanese intellectuals began to envy European empires in the late eighteenth century, when Honda Toshiaki, a leading Japanese scholar of Western literature, argued that Japan needed long-range shipping, munitions, and an empire of its own. Colonies could be stripped of resources and their populations exploited for labor. Overseas empires were like unified nationhood, parliamentary constitutions, codified laws, industrial economies, trousers, and bow ties: signs of modernization, qualifications for admission to the circle of the great powers.

The era of Japanese adventures overseas coincided almost exactly with the great age of Western imperialism. A sense of urgency drove Japan to compete for the diminishing living space that rival empires claimed. Japan's population began to grow in the late nineteenth century. Soldiers and businessmen allied to advocate empire. For samurai who had lost their social privileges, external wars were a means of discipline, a purifying ritual for a society polluted by change at home. Victory in the war of 1894–1895 against China (see Chapter 24) equipped Japan with the foundations of an empire: possession of Taiwan and the Pescadores Islands, semicontrol of Korea, and a springboard for further expansion at Russian and Chinese expense (see Map 25.4).

MAP 25.4 Russian and Japanese Expansion, 1868–1918

Russian Empire, ca. 1855	**1868** date of foundation or acquisition	Japanese attacks in Sino-Japanese War, 1894–1895
acquisitions 1856–1876	Trans-Siberian Railway, built 1891–1917	Japanese attacks in Russo-Japanese War, 1904–1905
acquisitions 1877–1914	Japanese Empire, 1870	borders 1914
temporary acquisition, with dates	Japanese, 1874–1895	*Chechens* people
Russian sphere of influence, 1914	Japanese, 1905–1910	

In Siberia, Russians, of course, already had an empire. They continued to build up their land empire in Europe on their western and southern frontiers. Russian imperialism took a huge leap in the Napoleonic Wars (1799–1815), with the annexation of Finland from Sweden in 1809 and the consolidation of Russia's hold on Poland and the Baltic states. The colonization of "New Russia"—southern

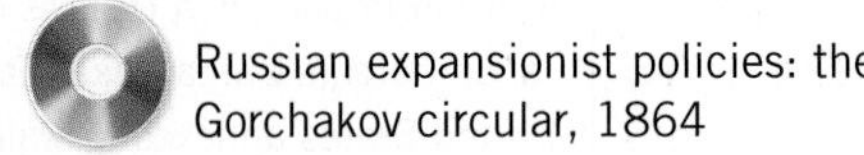
Russian expansionist policies: the Gorchakov circular, 1864

The first satirical Muslim journal in the Russian Empire was published from 1905 to 1917 in Tbilisi, Georgia, the administrative capital of Russian Transcaucasia. Although the Russian Empire had many Muslim subjects, they were divided into competing and often mutually hostile national groups. This journal targeted educated Azerbaijani readers, many of whom had more in common with Shiite Iran than with the Sunni Islam practiced by other Muslims in the Caucasus. The cover page of the November 22, 1909, issue shows the Russian bear growling menacingly while the symbol of Turkish wisdom, the legendary popular philosopher Mullah Nasreddin, sleeps unaware.

Ukraine—followed. In 1853–1856, in the Crimean War, Britain and France halted the Russian advance into the Balkans at Ottoman expense. Meanwhile, the fantasy of a seaborne empire on the Pacific, reaching to the Antarctic, haunted Russian imaginations. Not much came of it. In 1867, Russia sold Alaska to the United States and withdrew from the North American mainland. But the Aleutian Islands off the coast of Alaska remained a maritime frontier, divided between Russia and the United States (see Map 25.4).

Retreat from Alaska and the Balkans made Russia focus even more on Central Asia. From 1868, sparing only a few places, which were left to particularly powerful or obedient native dynasties, Russian armies enforced a new system of direct rule and direct taxation beyond the Oxus. In 1891, a new law limited landholding in the steppes of what is now Kazakstan to 40 acres per person—far less than a nomad needed to survive. Russia, meanwhile, ruled Chechnya in the Caucasus by terror, on the grounds, as a Russian viceroy put it, that "One execution saved hundreds of Russians from destruction and thousands of Muslims from treason." Finally, in the 1890s, Russian imperialism concentrated on the Far East, where it met Japanese empire-building, with grave consequences for the future.

The United States was also an empire. Americans were perfectly frank about it and proud of expanding their territory at other people's expense. They called this America's "manifest destiny." The United States absorbed Mexicans, Canadians, and Native Americans by force or the threat of it. The United States' great leap across the continent began in earnest in the 1830s, with attempts to sweep all the native peoples of the Midwest and Southeast into what is today the state of Oklahoma. It was a genocidal act that the Cherokees called the Trail of Tears, in which thousands died from disease, exposure, and starvation. Many United States planners hoped that it would kill off most Native Americans. Indeed, by 1900, the total Native American population of the United States was recorded as 237,196—a decline of probably 50 percent during the nineteenth century. Only in the Southwest did Indians escape eclipse. Meanwhile, in the 1840s, conquests gobbled up Mexican territory north of the Rio Grande.

Toward the century's end, American imperialism spilled into the oceans. In the Pacific, the Hawaiian kings had fended off European predators for years. But traders from the United States overthrew the Hawaiian monarchy in 1893 with American military and diplomatic support. Annexation followed in 1898. Meanwhile, the United States also annexed American Samoa in the South Pacific and seized the Philippines, Guam, and Puerto Rico, after defeating Spain in 1898. Cuba became a virtual protectorate, and the United States also acquired the Canal Zone in 1904 after enabling Panama to secede from Colombia. The whole American hemisphere became "Uncle Sam's backyard."

The Imperial Ambitions of Japan, Russia, and the United States

1803	Louisiana Purchase transfers vast territory from France to the United States
1809	Russia annexes Finland
1823	United States issues the Monroe Doctrine
1830–1860	Russians struggle to conquer Chechens
1867	Purchase of Alaska from Russia by the United States
1890s	Russian imperialism focuses on the Far East
1894–1895	Japan defeats China, takes Taiwan
1898	United States annexes Hawaii, seizes Philippines, Guam, and Puerto Rico after defeating Spain
1904	United States acquires Panama Canal

RATIONALES OF EMPIRE

How did imperialists justify their activities? Two rationales were overwhelmingly popular: what imperialists called their **civilizing mission**, and the doctrine that they were naturally superior.

Doctrines of Superiority

The most influential doctrine originated in the search for a scientific way to explain the diversity of nature. A theory originally conceived to apply to biology got wrenched out of its original background and applied to society.

In 1800, Haydn's "Creation Oratorio" proclaimed in ravishing music the biblical account of how the planet got filled with so many different plants and creatures. God had created the world and everything in it in six days. It was a metaphor, designed to reveal more than literal truth. Most people who thought about it knew that the planet was immensely old—fossils discovered in the eighteenth century had proved that—and that life developed slowly, growing in complexity, from simple, primitive forms. What remained unknown—the "mystery of mysteries," as Charles Darwin (1809-1882) remarked in the 1830s—was how those life-forms changed, or how God changed them, into the amazing variety visible in nature.

Darwin's earliest scientific interests were in sponges and beetles— life-forms regarded as primitive. In 1839, he got a chance to extend his observations when he accepted a post as the resident scientist on a round-the-world mission by the British navy. In Tierra del Fuego at the southern tip of South America, he was shocked to see how little material culture or intellectual or spiritual life the natives had. "Man in his natural state," Darwin reported, was "so beastly, so vile." He was surprised that the inhabitants could endure the freezing climate in virtual nakedness. He guessed that their bodies must have adapted to the environment. He began to see humans for what they are—well-adapted animals.

Later in the voyage, further revelations occurred off the northwest coast of South America, in the Galápagos Islands, where the diversity of species, and the differences among species from island to island, seemed almost inexplicable. "I never dreamed," he wrote, "that islands would be so differently tenanted. Temples filled with the varied productions of God and Nature ... filled me with wonder." Clearly, conditions from island to island must have encouraged life-forms to develop in different ways. When Darwin got home, two circumstances crystallized his thinking.

A Fuegian on the frontispiece of Robert Fitzroy's *Narrative of the Surveying Voyage of HMS Adventure and Beagle* (1839). "Nothing," wrote Darwin in his *Beagle* journal, "is more likely to create astonishment than the first sight in his native state of a barbarian—of man in his lowest and most savage state. One's mind hurries back over past centuries, and asks, could our progenitors have been men like these, men who do not appear to boast of human reason. I do not believe it is possible to describe or paint the difference between savage and civilized man.... It is greater than between a wild and domesticated animal." The remarkable environmental adaptation that made the Native American inhabitants of Tierra del Fuego, at the tip of South America, able to withstand the cold was one of the observations that influenced Darwin's thinking about a theory of evolution.

First, he devoted himself to the study of domestication: how farmers, stockbreeders, and pigeon fanciers, for instance, select to ensure that the offspring of their animals will inherit favored characteristics. Maybe nature functioned in the same way, favoring characteristics suitable to particular environments. Ill-adapted specimens of plants or animals would tend to die earlier and have a shorter fertile life span than more successful specimens. The fittest would survive longest and breed most.

Second, Darwin's personal circumstances affected his theories. He had married his cousin and their children were sickly. When his favorite daughter died, it became "impossible," he said, "for me ever to feel joy again." He began to hate God. In his later years, he ceased to go to church and subscribed to an atheist organization. He thought his own family demonstrated that nature was "clumsy, wasteful, blundering, low, and horribly cruel," or rather, indifferent to sentiment. Nature would allow only strong, well-adapted specimens to survive and pass on their characteristics to their offspring. He held the struggle for life in awe, partly because his own children were victims of it. "From the war of nature, from famine and death," he wrote, "the production of higher animals directly follows."

Darwin published that opinion in *The Origin of Species* in 1859. As his theory became accepted, other thinkers proposed terrible refinements that came to be known as **Social Darwinism**. Nature decreed "the survival of the fittest" and the extinction of the weak. Conflict is natural and, therefore, good. Nature decrees the rule of more evolved races and individuals over "degenerate" people—what we would now call the underclass—who represented throwbacks to some more primitive stage of evolution. It would be unfair to blame Darwin for the consequences. He advocated the unity of humankind and denounced slavery.

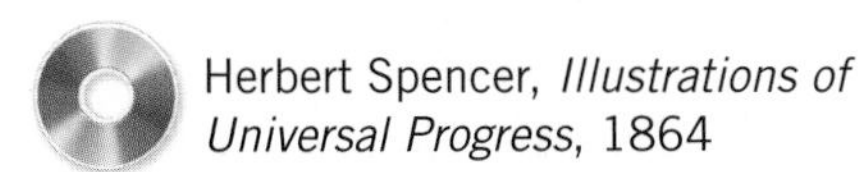

Herbert Spencer, *Illustrations of Universal Progress*, 1864

Nevertheless, no clear line divided social Darwinism from scientific Darwinism. Darwin was the father of both. As early as 1839, he claimed that "When two races of men meet, they act precisely like two species of animals. They fight, eat

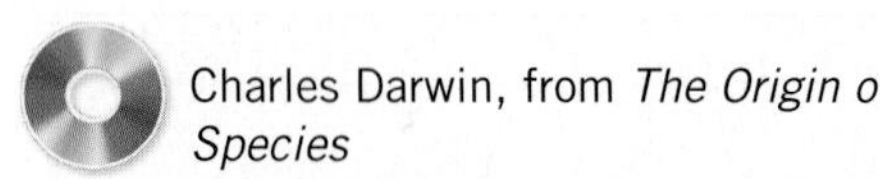

each other. . . . But then comes the more deadly struggle, namely: which have the best fitted organization or instincts (i.e., intellect in man) to gain the day?" Black people, Darwin speculated, would have evolved into a distinct species had European imperialism not ended their isolation. As it was, he thought, black people were doomed to extinction. Many people used Darwin's theories to justify the inequalities of their day: a world stacked in order of race.

A French anthropologist, the Count de Gobineau (1816–1882), arrayed humankind in order of excellence, with white people at the top, black people at the bottom, and others in between. Craniologists proved to their own satisfaction that the skulls of black people resembled those of apes. "No full-blooded Negro," stated the *Encyclopedia Britannica* in 1884, "has ever been distinguished as a man of science, a poet, or an artist, and the fundamental equality claimed for him by ignorant philanthropists is belied by the whole history of the race." The governor of the Dutch East Indies in 1850 thought "the right of rule" was "a characteristic of the pure white race." Some black Africans and Eskimos in Europe and the United States were actually displayed in zoos and exhibitions.

The Civilizing Mission

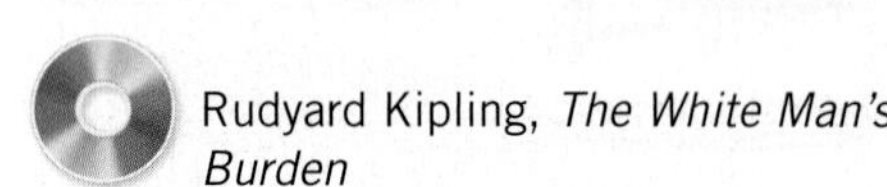

Alternatively, "the basic legitimization of conquest over native peoples," a French administrator insisted, "is the conviction of our superiority, not merely our mechanical, economic, and military superiority, but our moral superiority." Sir Francis Younghusband, who led a British military expedition to Tibet in 1902, claimed to have witnessed evidence of European superiority over Asian and African peoples due to "that higher moral nature to which we have attained."

A British administrator in South Africa was surely right when he observed "how thin is the crust that keeps our Christian civilization from the old-fashioned savagery—machine guns and modern rifles against knob sticks and spears ... do not add much to the glory of the superior races." But Europeans, white North Americans, and Japanese seemed determined to seize other people's land and wealth. To some extent, this was a reaction to historic positions of inferiority—Europe's with respect to Asia, Japan's with respect to China and Korea, that of the United States to most of the rest of the world.

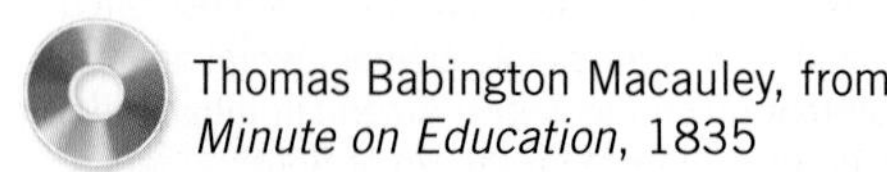

The civilizing mission seemed inapplicable to much of the colonial world, and especially to India, whose civilization was older and, arguably, richer than that of Europe. But in 1835, the British historian and legislator Thomas Macaulay dismissed Indian civilization as "absurd history, absurd metaphysics, absurd physics, absurd theology." A single shelf of a good European library, he claimed, "is worth the whole native literature of India and Arabia." The English, he predicted, would be to the Indians as the Romans, in their day, had been to the ancient Britons. English would be the new Latin. "Indians in blood and color" would become "English in tastes, in opinions, in morals and in intellect."

Civilization was undeniably a property of Chinese and Japanese societies. Western admiration for China never died out entirely, though the Opium Wars did much to subvert it. Japan's potential to catch up was obvious from the 1870s onward (see Chapter 24). For Westerners, therefore, China and Japan were potential rivals, who could be recruited or resisted. Many Europeans adopted a defensive attitude to what they called "the Yellow Peril." In 1900, the German Emperor Wilhelm II (r. 1888–1918) exhorted German members of an international task force sent to Beijing to rescue European residents from Chinese rebels, "You should give the name of German such a cause to be remembered in China that for a thousand years no Chinaman shall dare look a German in the face."

On the whole, it is hard to assess imperialists' claims to have governed for the benefit of their victims. Under the grasping rule of King Leopold II of the Belgians, 10 million people in the Congo died in massacres or from callous neglect. Native peoples who perished to make room for white empires in the Americas and Australia had no opportunity to count blessings. The British Empire spent much blood and treasure in suppressing the slave trade (see Chapter 24). But even this was not an exclusively benign business. In 1879, in southern Sudan, General Charles Gordon, who was in charge of antislaving operations there, was sickened by the skulls and skeletons his men's work left: slavers' women slaughtered to stop them breeding, thousands of slaves abandoned to starve when caravans were destroyed.

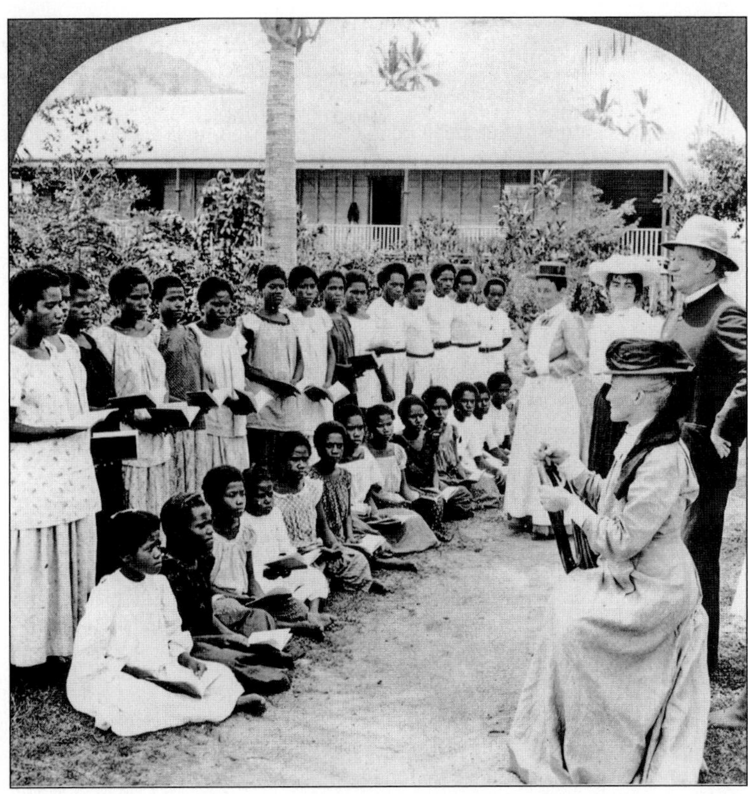

The civilizing mission, New Guinea, 1919. The British missionary stands in a position of authority, on the right. The white women are relaxed and wear hats. The New Guineans are presumably receiving instruction, but it might as well be orders. Almost everything in the scene is mysterious. Is a class or a religious service taking place? Why do only females, not males, hold books? Why is the lady in the black hat seated facing the back of her chair?

For those who suffered from it, imperialism was often a path to hell paved with the good intentions of white people who stumbled under the burdens of their self-imposed imperial responsibilities. Outside Europe, North America, and a few other lucky locations, the last three decades of the nineteenth century were an age of famine, exceeding all others up to that time for mortality and perhaps for every other kind of measurable severity. Thirty million people may have died in India and an equal number in China. In some respects, imperialism helped people find food for survival. Cheap iron plows from Europe increased food production in West Africa. It is hard, however, to exempt European imperialism from some of the blame for mismanaging the consequences of famine. Humanitarian sentiment, like food, was plentiful in their countries, but they found no way to turn their surplus of either to practical use.

Earlier, native states had handled famine relatively well. China coped with protracted crop failure in 1743–1744. In India in 1661, the Mughal Emperor Aurangzeb (see Chapter 21) "opened his treasury" and saved millions of lives. Western countries—with the exception of the Russian Empire, where crop failures killed millions around the middle Volga and in Ukraine in 1878–1881—seemed able to save people from famine in the late nineteenth century if they so wished. The American Midwest suffered as badly as almost any other part of the world from drought in 1889–1890, but relief was well organized, and deaths were few.

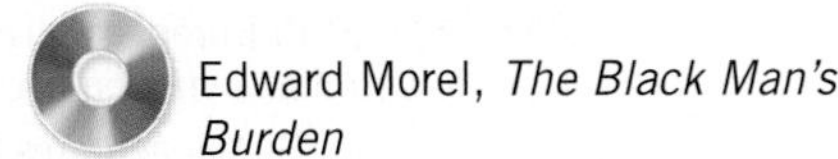

Edward Morel, *The Black Man's Burden*

IN PERSPECTIVE: The Reach of Empires

At the start of the nineteenth century, the English poet and artist William Blake could still draw Europe as one of the Graces among equals in the dance of the continents. But during the century, unprecedented demographic, industrial, and technological strides transformed Europe's place in the world. The result was European dominance. By 1900, European powers ruled much of the world, and European political influence and business imperialism controlled much of the rest.

It was, by the standards of world history, a brief phenomenon. By 1900, Japan and the United States had overtaken many European countries in industrial strength and in their capacity for war. In the twentieth century, European empires would collapse as spectacularly and as quickly as they had arisen (see Chapter 28). Meanwhile, even under imperialism, people continued to make their own history,

CHRONOLOGY

Nineteenth century	European population explosion fuels economy and creates surplus population for global migration; Africa's population declines
1803	Louisiana Purchase transfers vast territory from France to the United States
1809	Russia annexes Finland
1812–1814	War of 1812
1823	United States issues the Monroe Doctrine
1830s–1860s	Russians struggle to conquer Chechens
1839	Charles Darwin begins around-the-world expedition
1842	Treaty of Nanjing ends Opium War
1845–1872	Maori Wars in New Zealand
1850	130,000 Europeans live in Algeria
1850–1859	Value of world trade increases by 80 percent
1857	End of Mughal rule in India
1863–1879	Khedive Ismail attempts to build an Egyptian Empire
1867	Purchase of Alaska from Russia by the United States; Canadian Confederation is formed
1869	Suez Canal opens
1870–1900	World industrial production quadruples; world shipping doubles; world trade doubles in volume
1877	Queen Victoria takes title of Empress of India
1878–1913	Total territory of European empires doubles to 20 million square miles; total population of European empires expands from 300 million to 550 million
1880–1914	Most of Africa brought under European control
1884	Maxim machine gun patented
r. 1889–1913	Emperor Menelik modernizes Ethiopian army and expands empire in Africa
1890s	Russian imperialism focuses on the Far East
1894–1895	Japan defeats China
1898	Battle of Omdurman; United States annexes Hawaii and seizes Philippines, Guam, and Puerto Rico from Spain
1899–1902	Boer War
1900	500,000 Europeans live in Algeria, 4 million live in Australia, 1 million live in New Zealand
1904	United States acquires Panama Canal

thanks to systems of indirect rule and the empires' reliance on collaborators. Still, the nineteenth remains a century of a "European miracle": the sudden, startling climax of long, faltering commercial outthrust, imperial initiatives, and scientific progress.

Despite their defects, the empires were of immense importance in global history as arenas of cultural exchange. As we saw in Chapter 23, imperial commerce followed the lines laid down by the effects of industrialization, dividing the world into specialized areas of primary production and manufacturing, encircling the Earth with steamship routes and railroads. As Chapter 24 made clear, these arteries carried culture as well as commerce. Empires intensified the process of exchange. Like distorting mirrors, the colonies reflected imperfect images of Europe around the world.

Cultural exchange happened despite climate and distance. Indian thinkers and writers gave a discriminating welcome to Western influence. The first great Indian advocate of Western ideas, Raja Rammohan Roy (1772–1833), was a child of the Enlightenment (see Chapter 22). Yet the roots of his rationalism and liberalism came from Islamic and Persian traditions. The next great figure in Roy's tradition, Isvarcandra Vidyasagar (1820–1891), did not learn English until he was on the verge of middle age. When he argued for the remarriage of widows or against polygamy, or when he advocated relaxing caste discrimination in the schools, he found ancient Indian texts to support his arguments. But he dismissed the claims of pious Brahmans who insisted that every Western idea had an Indian origin. He resigned as secretary of the Sanskrit College of Calcutta in 1846 because of opposition to his program to include "the science and civilization of the West" in its curriculum. "If the students be made familiar with English literature," he claimed, "they will prove the best and ablest contributors to an enlightened Bengali renaissance." And, indeed, Indian writers did inject Western influences into their work with revitalizing effect. The British in India were like many foreign, "barbarian" conquerors before them, adding a layer of culture to the long-accumulated sediments of the subcontinent's past.

Today, what were once British colonies still have legislatures and law courts modeled on those of England, universities copied from Scotland, and sports that colonists from England's public schools spread. The French Empire spread French culture, Parisian cuisine, and the Code Napoleon (see Chapter 22). Africa became the great growth land of Christianity, thanks to the missionaries who followed or carried the flags of European empires. In much of the ex-colonial world, European languages—English, Spanish, Portuguese, French, Russian—remain the language of first choice. The colonial worlds reciprocated the exchange. Mughal style adorned nineteenth-century British buildings. The industrialists of Paisley in Scotland copied Indian patterns for their textiles. Curry from India has become virtually an English national dish, as has Indonesian rijstafel in Holland and North African couscous in France.

From the end of the nineteenth century, images and works of art looted from empires affected European imaginations and gave artists new models to follow. Despite the barriers to understanding that pseudoscientific racism erected, far frontiers kept increasing the white world's stock of examples of noble savagery (see Chapter 22). In the twentieth century, as we shall see, social scientists found, among the subject peoples of empire, disturbing new perceptions: new ways to see not only the "primitives" and "savages" but also themselves and the nature of human societies.

PROBLEMS AND PARALLELS

1. Why did the British and other foreign powers gain significant control of the Chinese economy by the late nineteenth century?
2. Why were European powers able to control so much of Asia, Africa, the Pacific, and the Middle East in the nineteenth century?
3. How did the Maori and Emperor Menelik of Ethiopia resist European imperialism?
4. What methods did Europeans use to govern native peoples in their colonial possessions? What does the term *business imperialism* mean? How did Europeans justify imperialism?
5. What were the imperial ambitions of Japan, Russia, and the United States in the nineteenth century?

DOCUMENTS IN GLOBAL HISTORY

- Letter from Lin Zexu to Queen Victoria
- The Treaty of Nanjing
- Francisco García Calderón, from *Latin America: Its Rise and Progress*
- Jules Ferry, from *Le Tonkin et la Mére-Patrie*, 1890
- Russian expansionist policies: the Gorchakov circular, 1864
- Herbert Spencer, *Illustrations of Universal Progress*, 1864
- Charles Darwin, from *The Origin of Species*
- Rudyard Kipling, *The White Man's Burden*
- Thomas Babington Macauley, from *Minute on Education*, 1835
- Edward Morel, *The Black Man's Burden*

Please see the Primary Source DVD for additional sources related to this chapter

READ ON

On the Opium War, A. Waley, *The Opium War Through Chinese Eyes* (1979) is a lively collection of sources. J. Y. Wong, *Deadly Dreams: Opium, Imperialism, and the Arrow War (1856–1860) in China* (1998) is excellent on the consequences and on the second Opium War.

J. Darwin, *After Tamerlaine* (2007) is a brillant essay in the global history of empires. H. L. Wesseling, ed., *Expansion and Reaction* (1978) contains groundbreaking papers on imperialism. H. L. Wesseling, *The European Colonial Empires* (2004) is the best overall survey. The same author's *Divide and Rule: The Partition of Africa* (1996) and T. Pakenham, *The Scramble for Africa* (1991) are outstanding in different ways—the first for impeccable judgement, the second for thrilling vividity. On Britain, W. R. Louis, ed., *The Oxford History of the British Empire*, vol. iii (2001), ed. by A. Porter, is sweeping in its coverage. D. R. Headrick, *Tools of Empire* (1981) is important on the technology of imperialism. A. Knight, *The Mexican Revolution*, vol. i (1990) is a model work from which I drew the details on the Yaqui. J. Belich, *The New Zealand War* (1998) is a brilliant work that reset the agenda of the study of colonial warfare.

On Africa, *The UNESCO History of Africa*, vol. vii (1990) and *The Cambridge History of Africa*, vol. vi (1985) offer expert general surveys. G. Prins, *The Hidden Hippopotamus* (1980) is a sensitive, anthropologically informed study of Lozi history. N. R. Bennett, *Arab Versus European: Diplomacy and War in Nineteenth-Century Central Africa* (1986) is useful, especially on Zanzibar. The details on Ma el-Ainin come from J. Mercer, *Spanish Sahara* (1976).

On Johor, J. Gullick, *Malay Society in the Late Nineteenth Century* (1987) is invaluable. Many novels of Bankimcandra Chattopadhyaya are available in English, as are those of Jorge Mármol. On business imperialism, D. C. M. Platt, *Business Imperialism* (1977) is the indispensable introduction. A. de Tocqueville, *Writings on Slavery* is the source of the material on that writer. On the Russian Empire, D. Lieven, *Empire* (xxx), is the best survey.

On Darwin, the best books are the provocative A. Desmond and J. Moore, *Darwin* (1994), and E. J. Brown, *Charles Darwin* (1996) of which two volumes have appeared so far. M. Bates and P. S. Humphrey, eds., *The Darwin Reader* (1956) is a good introduction to Darwin's writings.

CHAPTER 26 The Changing State: Political Developments in the Nineteenth Century

Nene, leader of Maori in Hokianga in northern New Zealand, took the name Tamati Waka after Thomas Walker, his British godfather, when he was baptized a Christian in 1839. Nene sought to befriend and, if possible, exploit the British. He sided with them in the Maori wars of the 1840s, achieving fame as the Maori "who did more than any other to establish the queen's authority," meaning Queen Victoria of England.

IN THIS CHAPTER

NATIONALISM
Nationalism in Europe
The Case of the Jews
Nationalism Beyond Europe

CONSTITUTIONALISM

CENTRALIZATION, MILITARIZATION, AND BUREAUCRATIZATION
In and Around the Industrializing World
Beyond the Industrializing World

RELIGION AND POLITICS

NEW FORMS OF POLITICAL RADICALISM
Steps Toward Democracy
The Expansion of the Public Sphere

WESTERN SOCIAL THOUGHT

IN PERSPECTIVE: Global State-Building

In 1882, a British visitor wandered into an ill-mapped area in New Zealand's North Island. James Kerry-Nicholls thought he was still in the British Empire. Instead, he found an "extensive region ruled over by the Maori king" where "an absolute monarch ... defied our laws" and "ignored our institutions." The region is still known as the King Country. In the early 1880s, it occupied over a fifth of the North Island and had a population of some 7,000, who simply ignored British orders. Invited to parley with the British in the year of Kerry-Nicholls's visit, King Tawhiao listened patiently to their proposal to give up his independence in exchange for land. "I will remain," said the king, "in the place where my ancestors and my fathers trod. . . . You can remain on your side, and administer affairs, and I will remain on my side."

NEW ZEALAND

The King Country was the last stronghold of a movement that had originated in the 1850s to unify the Maori into a single state to confront British aggression and stop chiefs from ceding Maori land. Twenty-six Maori tribal groups had come together in 1858, numbering in all perhaps 25,000 or 30,000 souls, to elect a king. The groups had no ties of kinship or traditional alliances with each other. "Do not be concerned for your own village," said one native prophet to his people. "No, be concerned for the whole land." In 1861–1863, the British tried to destroy this new state, sending in armies up to 14,000 strong, with mortars and cannon. But after defeats and inconclusive engagements (see Chapter 25), they gave up. The King Country settled into uneasy coexistence with the British Empire.

Presumably, the Maori got the idea of a unitary state by imitation from the British. Their purpose, as one Maori leader explained, was "that they should become united, ... like the Pakehas," as they called the white men. The idea of switching from armed to peaceful resistance was attributed to native prophets, but perhaps it owes something to Christian missionaries and the model of Jesus' kingdom (which was, as the Bible says, "not of this world"), or maybe even to the secular notion of civil disobedience that some Western intellectuals at the time advocated to effect peaceful change.

● ● ● ● ●

The political inventiveness of the Maori illustrates general features of the way nineteenth-century states grew and changed. New states emerged out of traditional groupings, such as chiefdoms and tribes. Old states made themselves more systematic by eliminating political anomalies, devising constitutions, codifying laws, rationalizing institutions, breaking the power of rival sources of authority (clergies, aristocracies, city councils, or heads of tribes or clans), and imposing centralization or, at least, increasingly consistent methods of administration, on their subjects. *Modernization* is, strictly speaking, a meaningless word, since every era produces its own modernity, but we can use it as a label for these processes because they produced states similar to those that prevail in today's world.

FOCUS questions

- WHY WAS Westernization often equated with modernization in the nineteenth century?
- WHY WAS nationalism so potentially disruptive?
- WHY DID some African and Asian states succeed in resisting Western imperialism?
- HOW DID the growth of armies and bureaucracies increase the power of states?
- WHAT ROLES did nineteenth-century socialists want government to play?
- WHY DID organized religion and the state come into conflict in the nineteenth century?

Some models of state development or refashioning began in Europe and North America and spread through the world during the "white man's" outreach—by example or the power of imperialism. The process did not end where white rule ended, and some instances probably happened independently of white initiative. Examples we have already met illustrate this: the reforging of Japan and Egypt in response to European industrialization and imperialism, the success of Ethiopia in the scramble for Africa, and the Sioux's efforts to create an empire in the North American prairie. As we shall see in this chapter, some states modernized far from the frontiers of European empires or the reach of European influence.

Nevertheless, the story of state modernization and of how and why it happened must begin in the West, partly because some features of modern states emerged there first. For much of the world, modernization really was *Westernization*, the conscious imitation of the world's most powerful, most prosperous states: Britain, France, Germany, and the United States. From the West, models of state development unfolded and were imitated around the world. Here theories about politics and society were formulated that achieved global importance and global impact. From this point in the story of the world, Westernization is a conspicuous global theme.

We will look at its clearest manifestations—nationalism, constitutionalism, militarization, centralization, and bureaucratization—before turning at the end of the chapter to some of the other influential but, for the time being, frustrated political movements of the period—religiously inspired utopianisms, democracy, and other forms of political radicalism that radiated from the West.

NATIONALISM

Nationalists claimed that a people who shared the same language, historic experience, and sense of identity made up a nation, an indissoluble unit, linked (to quote a Finnish nationalist) by "ties of mind and soul mightier and firmer than every external bond." Nationalists believed that everyone must belong to a nation of this kind and that every nation had to assert its identity, pursue its destiny, and defend its rights. "The voice of God" told Giuseppe Mazzini (1805–1872), the republican fighter for Italian unification, that the nation was the essential framework in which individuals could achieve moral perfection.

Odd as this notion seems, many people believed it. In the nineteenth century, nationalism triumphed in the West. The American and French Revolutions stimulated it. So did the Napoleonic Wars. Belligerants who wanted their people to fight encouraged it. Nationalism spread from the West to touch or transform much of the world.

Nationalism in Europe

Almost all European states contained more than one nation. Many European nations straddled the borders of states. **Nationalism** was therefore potentially disruptive. German nationalists yearned to unite all German-speaking people in a single state. French nationalists wanted to meld France's historic communities into a unified force and secure France's "natural frontiers" by incorporating all the land west of the Rhine and north of the Alps. Spain remained a "bundle" of nations—notably, Castilians, Catalans,

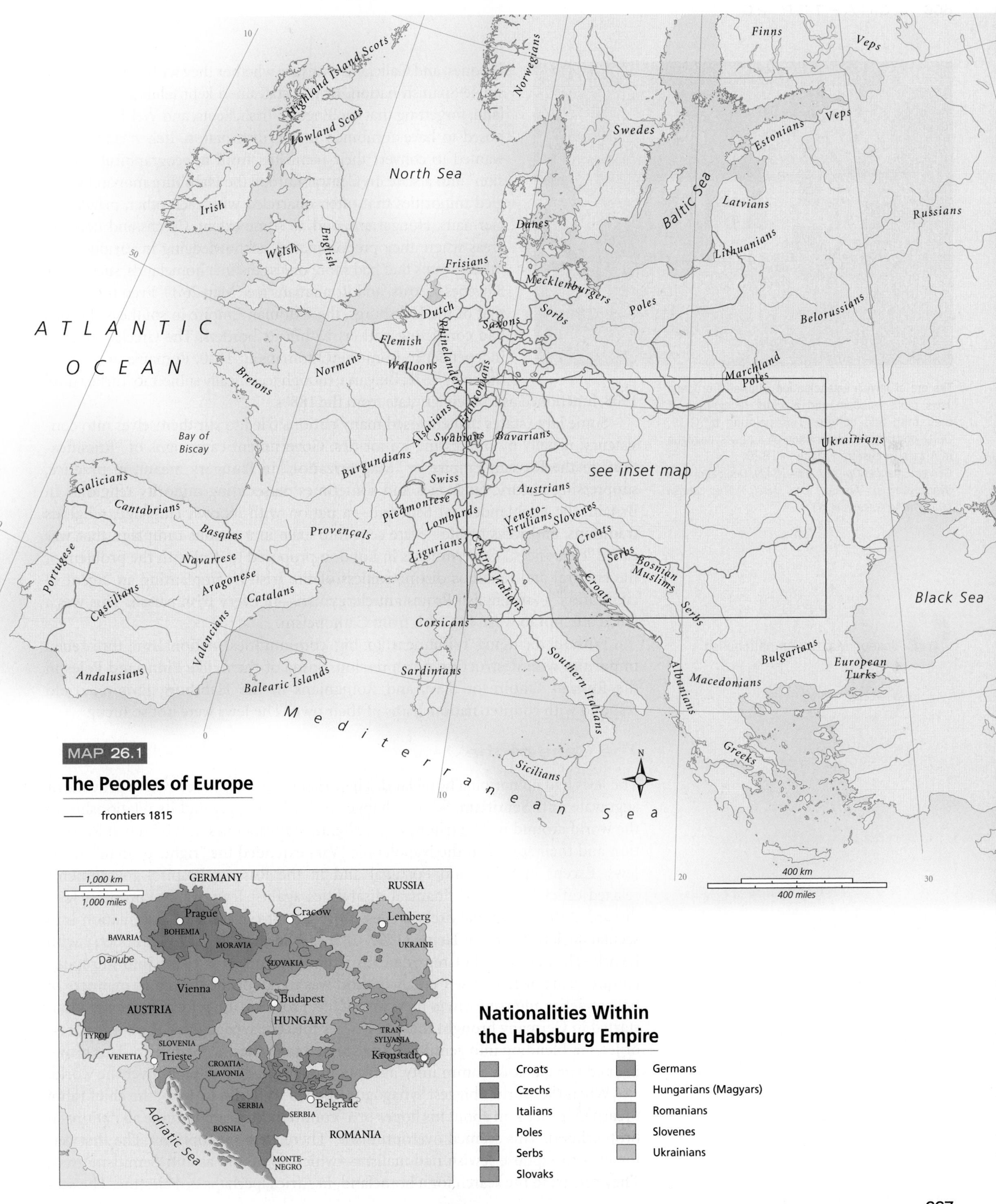

ATLANTIC OCEAN
North Sea
Baltic Sea
Bay of Biscay
Black Sea
Mediterranean Sea
Highland Island Scots
Lowland Scots
Irish
Welsh
English
Norwegians
Swedes
Finns
Veps
Estonians
Latvians
Lithuanians
Russians
Danes
Frisians
Mecklenburgers
Dutch
Flemish
Walloons
Rhinelanders
Saxons
Sorbs
Poles
Belorussians
Marchland Poles
Ukrainians
Normans
Bretons
Alsatians
Franconians
Swabians
Bavarians
Burgundians
Swiss
Austrians
see inset map
Galicians
Cantabrians
Basques
Piedmontese
Lombards
Veneto-Frulians
Slovenes
Croats
Serbs
Bosnian Muslims
Provençals
Ligurians
Central Italians
Portuguese
Navarrese
Aragonese
Castilians
Catalans
Valencians
Andalusians
Balearic Islands
Corsicans
Sardinians
Southern Italians
Sicilians
Albanians
Macedonians
Bulgarians
European Turks
Greeks
N
400 km
400 miles
MAP 26.1
The Peoples of Europe
frontiers 1815
1,000 km
1,000 miles
GERMANY
RUSSIA
Prague
Cracow
Lemberg
BOHEMIA
BAVARIA
MORAVIA
UKRAINE
Danube
SLOVAKIA
Vienna
Budapest
AUSTRIA
HUNGARY
TYROL
SLOVENIA
TRAN-SYLVANIA
VENETIA
Trieste
CROATIA-SLAVONIA
Kronstadt
Belgrade
SERBIA
SERBIA
BOSNIA
ROMANIA
Adriatic Sea
MONTE-NEGRO
Nationalities Within the Habsburg Empire
Croats
Czechs
Italians
Poles
Serbs
Slovaks
Germans
Hungarians (Magyars)
Romanians
Slovenes
Ukrainians

The era of Jewish emancipation allowed European Jews more freedom and a wider recognition of their faith and culture. This painting by G. E. Opitz portrays the dedication of a new synagogue in Alsace in eastern France in 1820.
George Emanuel Opitz (1775–1841), Dedication of a Synagogue in Alsace, *ca. 1820. The Jewish Museum/Art Resource, NY.*

Basques, and Galicians—unsure whether they wished to become a single Spanish nation. British statesmen kept talking about England, forgetting that the English, Irish, Scots, and Welsh were supposed to have combined in a British nation. Italian nationalists wanted to convert their peninsula from a "geographical expression" into a state. In Central Europe the Habsburg monarchy juggled minorities that often quarreled with each other, privileging Germans, Hungarians, and, to some extent, Czechs and Poles, in areas where they predominated, acknowledging in various ways other groups that had more or less distinct homelands, such as the Slovenes, Croats, and Romanians (see Map 26.1). Even more than that of the Habsburgs, the Ottoman Empire in southeast Europe had conflicting nations within its borders. The Greeks achieved independence from the Ottomans in 1830, Romania and Serbia did so by 1878. Bulgaria, though technically subject to Turkey until 1908, functioned as a sovereign state from the 1880s.

Some large states that enclosed many nations tried to stir themselves into consistency, usually by oppressing minorities. Government campaigns of "Russification" in the Russian Empire or "Magyarization" in Hungary meant, in practice, suppressing historic languages and sometimes persecuting minority religions. In Britain, the Highlanders of Scotland—a nation with its own language, religious traditions, and ways of life—were sent into exile in a vicious campaign that was called "clearances." Governments in London proposed to deal with the problem of the cultural and religious distinctiveness of the Irish by implanting an "agent of civilization"—an English Protestant clergyman—in every Irish parish. This was a failed attempt to wean the Irish from Catholicism.

Joseph Mazzini on nationalism

Without bringing fulfillment to big communities, nationalism threatened minorities with destruction or repression. Some of them, like Finns and Poles in the Russian Empire or Slavs and Romanians in the Habsburg Empire, could respond with counter-nationalisms of their own. The Jews were not so lucky.

The Case of the Jews

The Jews had no national homeland. Their rising population seemed to provoke or aggravate **anti-Semitism**. So did changes in Jewish society and its relationship to the world around it. The triumph of enlightened principles in the French Revolution and their spread in the Napoleonic Wars extended the "rights of man" to the Jews. Except in Spain and Portugal and in the Russian Empire, governments relaxed official legal and financial disabilities against Jews. Many European Jews discarded the traditional exclusiveness of the ghetto in favor of assimilation into secular society. Heinrich Heine (1797–1856), a German Jew, filled his poetry with Jewish self-awareness but regarded Christian baptism as "a ticket into European culture." Part of Jewish self-emancipation was to adopt the dress and manners of host societies and conform to their way of life. From 1810, a reform movement that started in Germany brought these new ways into the synagogues. The very success of Jews in blending into gentile society seemed to excite anti-Semitism. This growing and conspicuous community, anti-Semites claimed, might take over the world.

When the world's biggest synagogue opened in Berlin in 1866, the chief rabbi preached in German about his hopes of a "common Messiah" to unite all nations in brotherhood. This seemed overoptimistic. There were two options. The first was for Jews to espouse Jewish nationalism—which some did as anti-Semitism grew. They turned to the search for a homeland, in Africa, perhaps or Palestine. The second possibility, which most Jews embraced, was to join in the nationalism of the country in which they lived. The young Walter Rathenau (1867–1922), whose family owned the largest electricity-producing firm in Germany, believed that German Jews could help Germany achieve world supremacy.

Assimilation, however, was always risky for unconverted Jews, unless they were immensely rich. In the prayer book of French Jews in the 1890s, France was praised as the country "preferred by God," and the French, according to the country's chief rabbi, were "the chosen race of modern times." None of this prevented French anti-Semitism, as became all too clear in the case of a Jewish officer in the French army accused of spying for the Germans in 1893. Captain Alfred Dreyfus was obviously innocent, but the French gutter press bayed for his blood, in effect because he was Jewish. He was led into imprisonment crying, "Long live France!" and after his innocence was proved, he won medals fighting in the French army.

Nationalism Beyond Europe

Beyond Europe, nineteenth-century nationalism is hard to distinguish from resistance against European imperialism (see Map 26.2). But by 1900, many independence movements in European empires overseas had adopted nationalism as their

MAP 26.2

Examples of Resistance to European and United States Imperialism, 1880–1920

Anti-colonial uprisings and incidents

- anti-British
- anti-Dutch
- anti-French
- anti-German
- anti-Italian
- anti-Portuguese
- anti-Russian
- anti-Spanish
- anti-American
- boundary at 1914

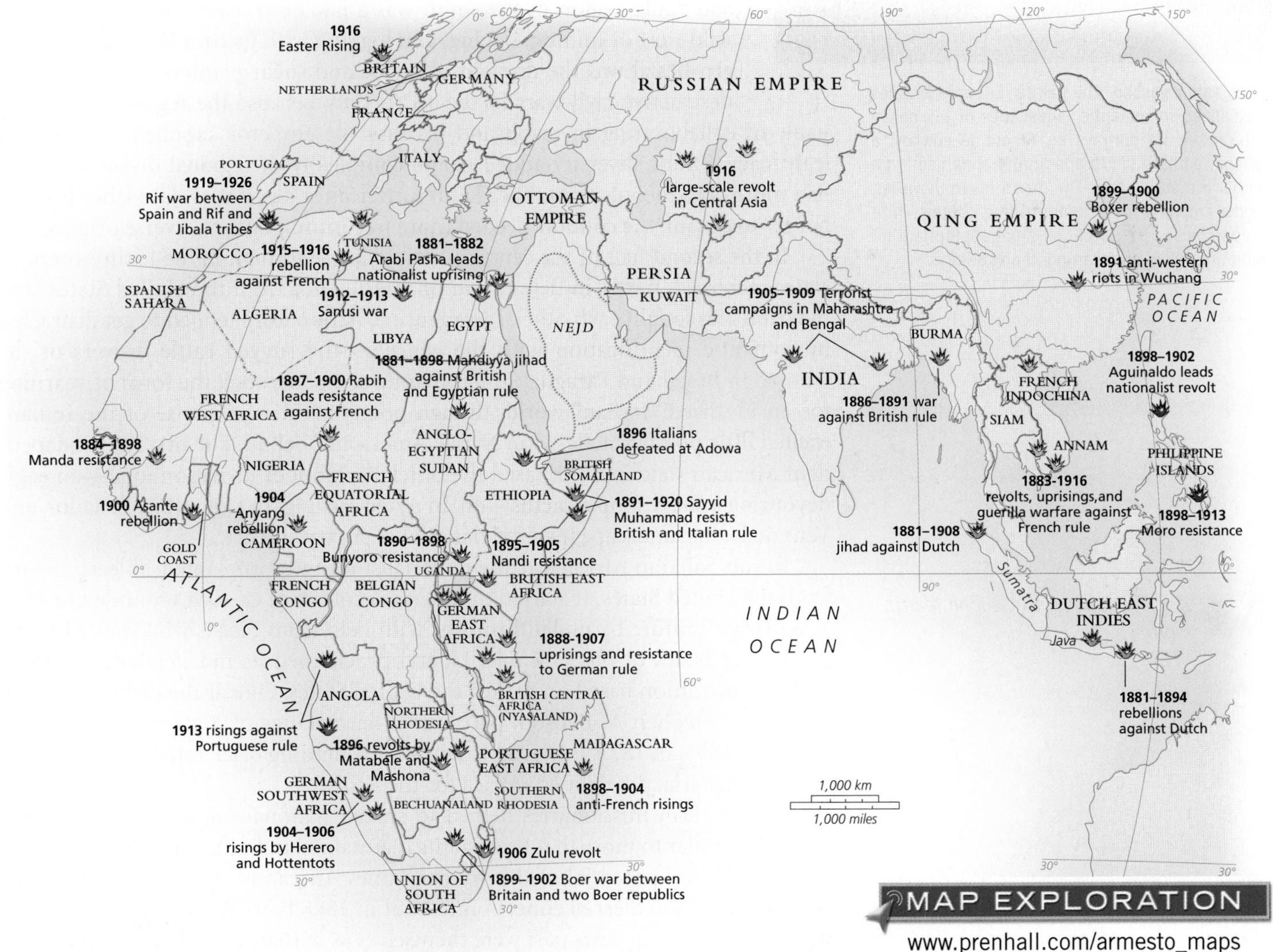

MAP EXPLORATION
www.prenhall.com/armesto_maps

An Argentine gaucho. The painter Eduardo Morales specialized in romantic landscapes of his native Cuba. Here he portrays an Argentine cowboy, a gaucho, and the landscape of Argentina itself in a similar romantic style. The man's horse, however, seems groomed for a formal riding contest, with forepaw raised in a tradition more appropriate for depicting rulers and warriors than cowboys.

own ideology. Rebels proclaimed as "nations" countries, such as "the Philippines," "Indonesia," "Algeria," and "India," that had never existed and that housed many different historic nations.

This phenomenon started in the Americas. Though the Creole elites shared a common identity as "Americans," their desire to exercise power in states of their own creation exceeded their willingness to remain united. Spanish-American unity was a Humpty Dumpty, smashed by its fall in struggles against Spanish rule between 1810 and the 1820s. Paraguay and Uruguay fought to stay apart from Argentina and Brazil. Bolivia and Ecuador rejected union with Peru. In the 1830s, large states that had emerged from the independence wars dissolved into small ones. Gran Colombia split into Colombia and Venezuela. The United Provinces of Central America crumbled into Guatemala, Honduras, Nicaragua, Costa Rica, and El Salvador. The fissures continued to spread, detaching Texas and California from Mexico and almost detaching Yucatán as well in the 1840s.

Brazil, meanwhile, like the United States, emerged formally united but, unlike the United States, was fragile in the short term (see Chapter 21). Offshore currents in the South Atlantic divided coastal Brazil into two zones, between which it was hard to communicate. The ranch-rich São Paulo region in the south was a law unto itself. The interior was a wild west of mining, slaving, and logging with its own boss class. Northern Brazil was the domain of coffee and sugar planters. Unity survived destructive civil wars in the 1830s only because the regions were incapable of collaborating in revolt and because the emperor supplied a symbol of legitimacy. Ethnic diversity added to the complexity of regional divisions. Brazil had more black people than other Latin American states, but as slave labor became harder to obtain, the country needed more free immigrants of diverse origins.

In the second half of the century, nationalist sentiment in the Latin American states increased, partly in detestation of interference from the United States, and the countries fought each other. In Argentina, nationalism tended to get distracted by romantic identification with the *gauchos*—the rugged cattle drovers of the pampa. In Brazil and Paraguay, the romantic sympathy took the form of yearning for an idealized "Indian" world, though poetry written in praise of the Indians excited little political activity on Native Americans' behalf. The first fully independent Mexican state in 1822 based the official symbol of its nationhood—an eagle devouring a snake atop a cactus—on an Aztec carving. In Colombia, Ecuador, and Venezuela, the landscape inspired nationalist poetry and art.

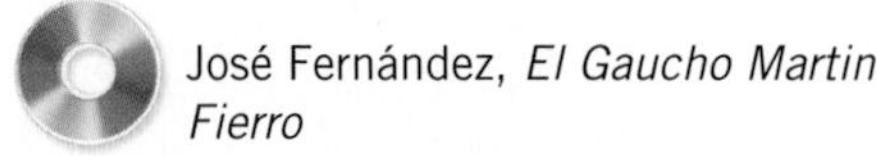

José Fernández, *El Gaucho Martin Fierro*

In sub-Saharan Africa, too, the nationalist idea was implanted, at least in part, from the United States. It started in Liberia, a colony of ex-slaves founded in 1821 as a private venture by philanthropists, with help from racists who wanted to rid the United States of black people. Liberia proclaimed its independence in 1847, with a constitution based on that of the United States. One of the earliest Liberian presidents, Stephen A. Benson, perceived "the makings of a great nation" in the colony in 1856. In 1872, Edward Blyden, an outstanding black intellectual who had settled in Liberia, proclaimed "Africa for the African."

West African missionaries helped to spread nationalism, imagining national churches similar to those that Protestants maintained in Europe. Black intellectuals saw the political potential of this model. James Africanus Horton, for instance, a black doctor from Sierra Leone, pointed out in 1868 that "We have seen European nations who in long years past were themselves as barbarous and unenlightened as the negro Africans are at present, and who have exhibited wonderful improvement within the last century. This should urge the Africans to increased exertions, so that their race may, in course of time, take its proper stand in the world's history." Talk of nationalism began to have real political effects in West Africa. In 1871, Fanti chiefs in what is now Ghana founded a confederation "to advance the interest of the whole Fanti nation."[11]

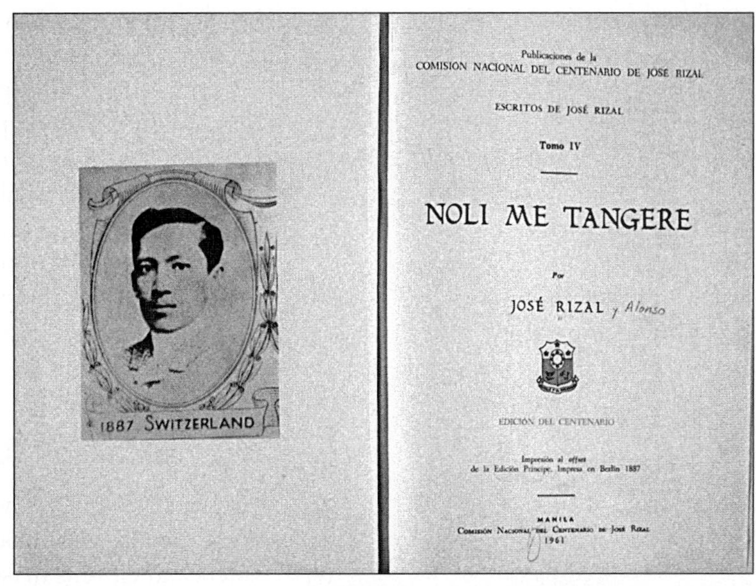

José Rizal. In 1887, José Rizal published, in the form of a novel, what he called "the first impartial and bold account" of the Filipino independence movement and the injustice that inspired it. "Felicity," Rizal wrote, "is proportional to liberty." He compared Spanish rule to a wooden bridge—vulnerable to wind and rot.

North of the Sahara, meanwhile, nationalism emerged as the Ottoman Empire retreated and European imperialism threatened. In the second half of the nineteenth century, Egyptian intellectuals began to give the Arabic word *watan*—which originally meant something like "birthplace"—the sense of the European term *nation*, with the same romantic associations. One of the most influential of them was Ali Mubarak Pasha (see Chapter 23), who published a nationalist novel in 1882, the year when opponents of British and French influence rose up with the cry, "Egypt for the Egyptians!"

To some extent, Western empires encouraged nationalism around the world, regarding its spread as evidence of successful Westernization and of the fulfillment of Westerners' supposedly civilizing mission. In the early 1850s, a British statesman, Lord Grey, believed that by bringing the chiefs of Ghana together, Britain had turned "barbarous tribes. . . . into a nation." British administrators in Canada assumed that nation making was an obligation of empire. Even without official collaboration, Western empires tended to have this effect. In colonial settings, budding nationalists could read and learn about what was going on in Europe. Many of them went to Europe to study or attended European-style schools at home. To them, nationalism seemed a way to confront traditional elites allied with or controlled by outsiders.

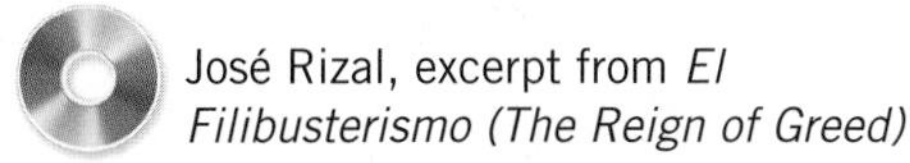
José Rizal, excerpt from *El Filibusterismo (The Reign of Greed)*

José Rizal (1861–1896), for instance, the great spokesman of Filipino nationalism in the late nineteenth century, crammed his writings with allusions to classical, Spanish, English, and German literature, but he also searched for inspiration in the poetic traditions of his homeland. Spanish observers noticed Rizal's patriotic poetry as early as 1879 and identified him as "a man who bears watching, a rare and new kind of man. . . . for whom the mother country is the Philippines, not Spain." He spent his last years in exile, charged with conspiring with other nationalists to make the Philippines independent. When he returned to Manila and was shot by the Spaniards as a rebel, he struck out the words "Chinese half-breed" on his death warrant and wrote "pure native" instead.

Rizal's subversive novels showed how literature could help forge nationalism in colonial environments. Equally powerful were the novels that another culturally ambiguous figure whom we met in the last chapter, Bankimcandra Chattopadhyaya in India, wrote. Bankim often chose politically inflammatory themes for his fiction while serving the British as a deputy magistrate. This was typical of the nationalists who formed the Indian National Congress in 1885. Most of the founder members and early recruits belonged to the civil service or the legal profession. Most of the leading figures were graduates of British-style universities in Calcutta, Bombay, and Madras.

Western models promoted the growth of nationalism worldwide. Nevertheless, other influences were also at work. Japan became a model for Asian nationalists because its success demonstrated that Asian nations could rival or surpass Western powers. Vietnamese nationalism fed on memories of age-old resistance to the Chinese as well as on opposition to the French in the nineteenth century. To some extent, nationalism happened independently wherever big empires provoked subject-peoples to react or rebel. The Russian, Habsburg, Chinese, and Ottoman Empires all faced similar problems. Chinese nationalism was itself an expression against the ruling Qing dynasty, even though the emperors' Manchu origins were now 200 years in the past (see Chapter 21). Opponents of the regime appealed to Chinese "purity." The first rebellion of the movement that called itself "nationalist," in Guangzhou in 1895, was an attempt to found a Chinese state free of Manchu domination.

CONSTITUTIONALISM

Nationalism was one way to justify the new structures of power or challenge old ones. **Constitutionalism**—the doctrine that the state is founded on rules that rulers and citizens make together and are bound to respect—was another.

Constitutionalism was not confined to Europe, but Europe was its great battleground. After the French Revolutionary Wars, most European states tried to prevent another such explosion by sanctifying existing frontiers and outlawing or restricting constitutional reforms. By mutual agreement, they intervened to repress each other's revolutions. The system worked well, and revolutionaries achieved freedom to act only when the European powers fell out among themselves. The nineteenth century was, therefore, a great age for monarchies. All the new European states of the period—Belgium, Greece, Romania, Serbia, Bulgaria—were kingdoms or principalities. Republics that fell during the Napoleonic Wars—in Venice, Genoa, and the Netherlands—were not restored. Even in Latin America, some states toyed with plans for monarchical systems. Mexico and Haiti had monarchs for a time. Brazil's monarchy survived until 1889.

Most European monarchies, however, eventually granted or accepted constitutions, or enlarged the numbers and nature of those of their subjects admitted to the political process. Constitutionalism not only redistributed power; it also changed how people thought about the state—no longer the domain of the ruler, but of the rule of law, to which the monarch and government were themselves subject. Constitutionalism did not necessarily embody the idea that the people were sovereign, but it at least implied that more than one person and more than one class shared sovereignty. In Britain, for instance, though no written constitution was ever granted, a series of Reform Acts turned parliament from an enclave of the aristocracy and gentry into an assembly that was also representative of the middle class and even, from 1867, of the more prosperous workers.

On the fringes of Europe, the Ottoman and Russian Empires staved off constitutionalism with difficulty. In 1864, the Russian monarchy permitted district assemblies with representatives from all classes to meet, while judges became at least nominally independent of the government. The Ottoman court convened an assembly of provincial representatives in 1845, but the sultan quickly abandoned this experiment in constitutionalism. In 1876, a constitutional revolt made the executive responsible to the legislature. "All Ottoman subjects," the new constitution decreed, "regardless of whether they possess property or fortune, shall have the right to vote." Religious liberty and equality before the law were enshrined. The constitution lasted only a few months before the sultan reimposed his authority, but resentment festered among the educated classes.

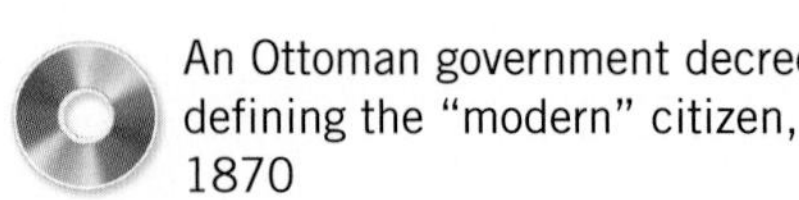
An Ottoman government decree defining the "modern" citizen, 1870

Constitutionalism spread, along with other Western ways, to Japan, where in 1882, the decision to draw up a constitution was based on the results of a fact-finding mission to Europe. Because Japan was now industrializing, the framers of the constitution thought that they had to accommodate the middle classes. Sovereignty remained the prerogative of the "sacred and inviolable" emperor, who would govern "with the consent" of a representative assembly, elected by a franchise restricted to those rich enough to pay property taxes. The constitution also enshrined what we now call civil and human rights—to hold and transfer property, to speak and associate freely, to practice religion without hindrance, and to be tried under the law. The emperor, however, could suspend these rights in emergencies. Political parties had a role in running the assembly but not the country. Because it was considered vital for the emperor to remain "above politics," he appointed ministers, on the advice of senior statesmen without reference to party.

In other parts of the world, constitutionalism rarely achieved power. Copycat constitutions accompanied the independence of all the new Latin American states, but they were usually mere formalities that disguised the rule of military strongmen, dictators, and oligarchies. The same can be said of Liberia's constitution. Nonetheless, there were attempts to create effective constitutions. In the North American Southeast, under the influence of German missionaries, and the inspiration of their chief, Sequoia (1770–1843), the Cherokee people established their own republic alongside the United States, with representative institutions and laws codified in a written version of their own language. The Cherokee state flourished until the United States crushed it and expelled its people in the 1830s. The Fanti confederacy in West Africa, as James Africanus Horton described it, was "the pivot of national unity, headed by intelligent men, to whom a great deal of the powers of the kings and chiefs are delegated.... Through it the whole of the Fantee race can ... boast of a national assembly." The chiefs elected a king-president. Education and road maintenance were among the government's responsibilities.

Although constitutionalism was Western inspired, traditional societies often had similar systems or conceptions of government of their own that limited rulers' power or subjected them to control by aristocratic or popular assemblies. When, for instance, the war leader Atiba reconstructed the Kingdom of Oyo in central Nigeria in the 1850s, he looked back to his people's traditions, restoring the rites of ancient gods and instituting worship of royal ancestors, even though he and most of his people were nominally Muslims. He enjoyed such grandiose titles as Owner of the World and of Life and Companion of the Gods. But the king could not act without the support of the council of representatives of noble families, who nominated officials and had the right to demand his self-sacrifice by ritual suicide. In Ghana, the king of the Asante was known as "He Who Speaks Last" because, although he made policy decisions, he listened first to the views of the chiefs.

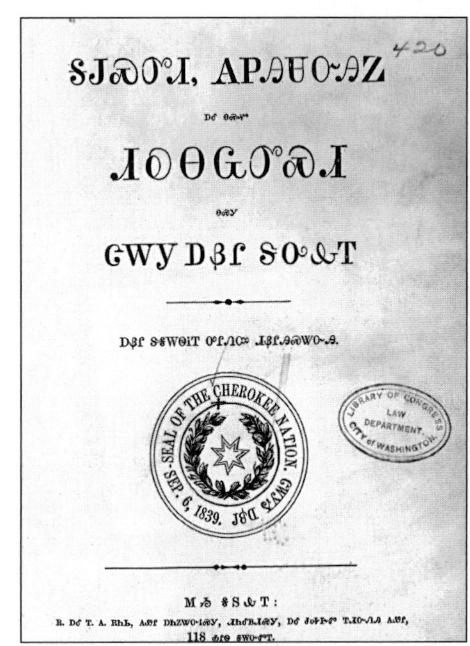

Constitution of the Cherokee Nation. Sequoia (ca. 1770–1843) developed a writing system for the Cherokee language in 1809, in which each of 85 symbols stands for a syllable. In 1839, a Cherokee assembly used it to write the Constitution of the Cherokee Nation, which provided for all land to be common property and for a chieftain, legislature, and judiciary to be elected by all males over 25 years old, descended from "Cherokee men by free women." Black people and Cherokee men who were part black, however, were explicitly denied a vote.

The Constitution of the Empire of Japan, 1889

CENTRALIZATION, MILITARIZATION, AND BUREAUCRATIZATION

Whether monarchical or republican, constitutional or absolutist, nineteenth-century states tended to become more centralized, as industrialization and militarization boosted the power of governments.

In and Around the Industrializing World

In the Ottoman Empire, for instance, Sultan Mahmud II (r. 1808–1839) reorganized the army on European lines in 1826 and used his new troops to wipe out the

Janissaries, the old, politically unreliable military corps. The army became the spearhead of movements of political reform and the guardian of what increasingly—as the multinational empire shrank—felt like a Turkish nation-state. Under the next sultan, a new bureaucracy took over tax collecting, which the state had farmed out to local agents. Muhammad Ali in Egypt (see Chapter 23) had launched a similar program as early as 1820, conscripting peasants into an army he called the New Order. To recruit and pay for the army, he overhauled the administration, dividing Egypt into 24 provinces and creating layers of bureaucracy that reached from the capital into every village. Rulers in Libya, Tunisia, and Morocco created similar bureaucracies that functioned alongside traditional authorities.

In the industrializing world, the most spectacular cases of restructured state power were those of Germany, Italy, the United States, and Japan. In the 1860s, all of these countries experienced unifying wars won by industrialized regions. Germany and Italy had long been divided among many different states. Japan had a long history as a unitary state, but the central government had lost control of remote provinces. The United States was still a new state, but its constitution had never really settled a crucial issue: whether the separate states had permanently and irrevocably renounced their sovereignty in favor of the federal government. When some of the slave-holding states seceded from the Union, the federal government contested it.

China underwent a "restoration" in the 1860s after old-fashioned rebellions—Muslim risings on the edges of the empire, peasant revolutions at its heart—and the invasions by Britain and France recounted in Chapter 25 (see Map 26.3). The restoration did not involve the radical recrafting that circumstances really required, and decentralization continued in defiance of the trend in the industrializing world. The Chinese government sold offices—wrecking the ancient examination system as a method for filling official positions by merit. Partly to maximize sales, the government appointed magistrates for short terms, so local administration tended to fall into the hands of petty officials who, once appointed as magistrates' underlings, remained in their jobs indefinitely.

Centralization did not always or even primarily mean extending the power of central institutions. It was also a matter of overcoming traditional provincial, regional, and communal loyalties with a common sense of allegiance to the state. Governments used universal military service (see Chapter 23) to create a statewide sense of political community, usually in combination with efforts to spread nationalist feelings. Japan's army, typically, became a nursery for reeducating young men in a new version of samurai values, focused on obedience to the emperor and self-sacrifice for the state.

"Honored dead." The reality of the field of Gettysburg was litter-strewn and squalid, with gaping, crumpled corpses. Photography helped to take romance out of depictions of war.

The Japanese army, in consequence, felt no loyalty to the civil government and remained, in effect, outside and above the constitution. A similar pattern can be discerned in Spain and Latin America, where the wars of the early nineteenth century militarized huge proportions of the populations. Armies became the agents of independence and in some cases of modernization, the guardians of the state and, therefore, the arbiters of constitutional conflicts. All countries that used their armed forces to mobilize the entire society risked suffering, or did suffer, similar consequences: Militarized societies produced politicized armies. The United States was fortunate that by the time of its Civil War (1861–1865) its civil institutions and traditions were strong enough to survive the trauma. Civil conflict in the United States never led, as it has done in most countries, to military dictatorship. Britain, too, escaped the danger by keeping its army small and avoiding conscription until 1916 during the First World War.

As well as bringing armies into politics, militarization made wars worse. The Prussian military theorist Carl von Clausewitz (1780–1831) thought the only rational way to wage war was "to the utmost. . . . He who uses force unsparingly, without reference to the bloodshed involved, must obtain a superiority." The ultimate objective was to disarm the enemy permanently. This encouraged belligerents to fight for unconditional surrender when they were winning, to resist it obstinately when they were losing, and to impose harsh terms in victory.

In combination, the improved technology of war, the doctrines of militarism, and the transformation of society into a battleground all made the horrors of war worse. Photographers and chroniclers of the American Civil War and the Franco-Prussian War of 1870–1871 introduced a new awareness of war's consequences. The novels of Emile Zola (1840–1902) depicted bloody hospitals, decaying dead,

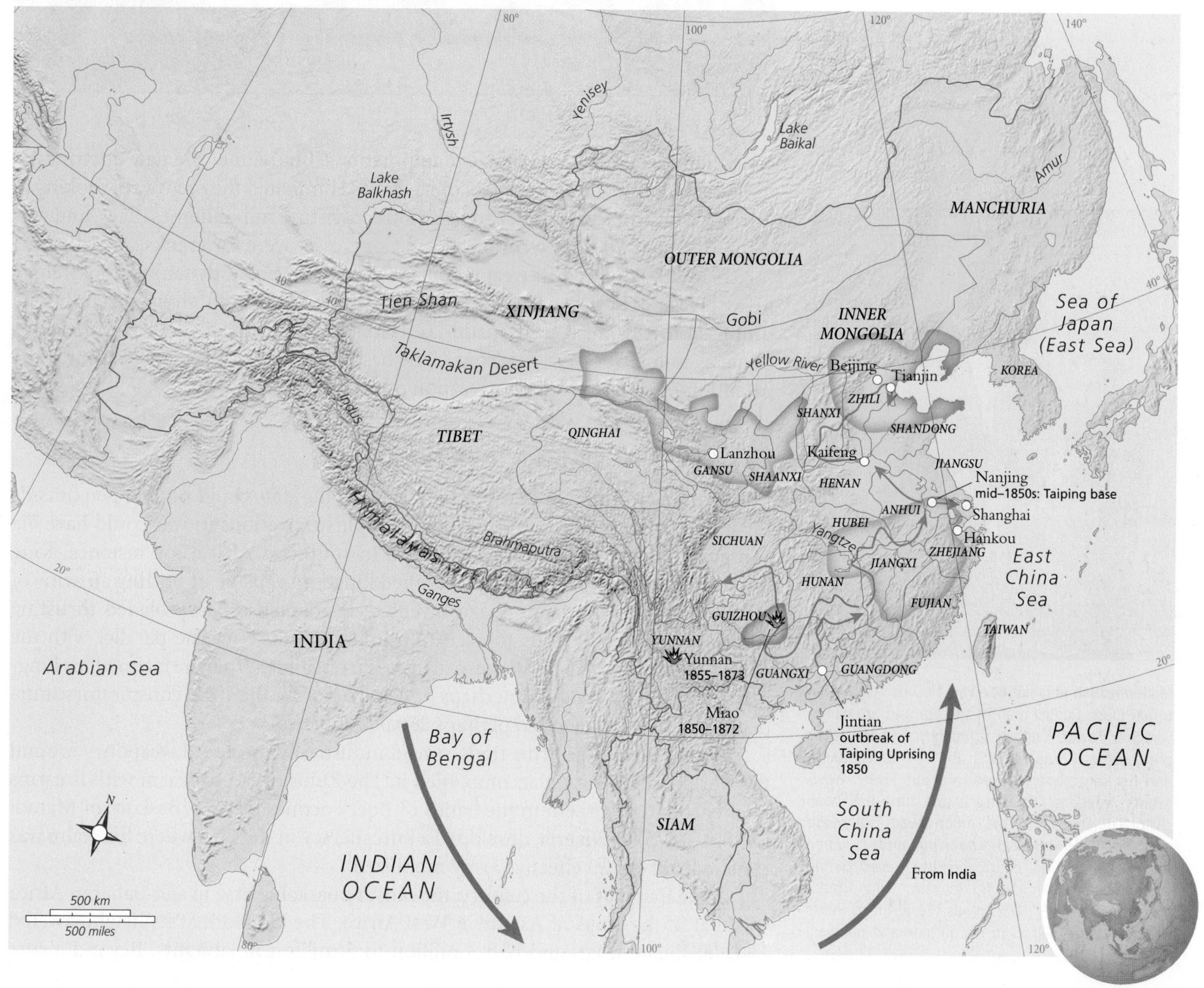

MAP 26.3

Revolts in the Qing Empire, 1850–1901

- Qing Empire
- tribal risings
- Muslim revolts
- area of Northwestern Muslim rising 1863–1873
- area controlled by Taiping rebels 1853–1863
- Taiping rebellion
- area of Boxer uprising 1900–1901
- Guizhou Muslim uprising 1854–1872
- opium trade

Asante King. Reminiscences of the greatness of the Asante kings persisted after defeat by the British in the late nineteenth century. In this photograph of the 1890s, King Agyeman Prempeh I, borne by slaves, sits on his litter under the royal umbrella, surrounded by drummers and praise singers. Shortly after the photograph was taken, the British arrested and exiled him and provoked a further—and, for the Asante, disastrous—war by demanding custody of the Asante's sacred golden stool.

gangrenous wounded, and frenzied amputations. But neither the new doctrines of militarism nor the new awareness of its effects eliminated the old way of looking at war as a chivalrous, romantic, and glorious adventure full of heroes, flags, and colorful uniforms. So wars went on. Peace Congresses were for cranks. Alfred Nobel (1831–1896), the Swedish weapons magnate who invented dynamite, took refuge in extravagant projects for world peace. War would "stop short instantly," he promised in 1890, if it were made "as death-dealing to the civilian population at home as to the troops at the front." The best hope he could see for peace was the invention of germ warfare or a weapon of mass destruction.

Modernization personified. The clothes suggest an upper-class Englishman of the era and an expensively educated English schoolboy. But the faces are those of Chulalongkorn, the king of Thailand, and his son, photographed in about 1890. Westerners' image of Thailand at the time has been distorted, thanks to the much-loved Hollywood and Broadway musical *The King and I*, which depicts an exotic court, presided over by an unbending patriarch king. In fact, King Chulalongkorn (r. 1868–1910), was Westernized in his sentiments as well as in his outlook and policies. See p. 678.

Beyond the Industrializing World

It is tempting to suppose that similar effects on the state could not happen outside the industrializing world. But relatively simple innovations in war could have big consequences in pre-industrial societies. In southeast Africa, for instance, King Shaka reorganized the Zulus into a unified kingdom capable of putting an army of 50,000 men into the field. Shaka invented or adapted a heavy-bladed thrusting spear and developed drills to accustom infantry to use it. The parallel with the effects of firearms drill on Western armies is irresistible. When he claimed his kingdom in 1816, his clan had perhaps 350 warriors. By the time conspirators murdered him in 1828, he ruled perhaps 250,000 subjects.

In any case, as the arms trade spread industrially produced weaponry around the world, militarization accompanied it. The Zulus began to rearm with firearms after encountering them in the hands of Boer enemies in 1838. Baskore of Maradi (r. 1854–1875) in Nigeria, developed a bureaucracy in Katsina, where his realm was centered, to keep an effective army mobilized.

In the first half of the century, the most remarkable case in sub-Saharan Africa was that of the kings of Asante in West Africa. The kingdom at its height covered 150,000 square miles and had 3 million to 5 million inhabitants. Beyond a core area around the capital, Kumasi, where the ruler's war companions ruled their own followers without much interference from the court, a central treasury that also ran the kings' own commercial transactions—mining, slave trading, and hunting for ivory—regulated tribute, taxes, and tolls. Early in the century, the kings adopted Arabic as a language of record keeping, which thereafter was done on paper instead of in the old form of piles of shells and coins. The Asante usually redesignated traditional rulers of conquered peoples as captains of the Asante king and placed agents alongside them to keep them in order. Bureaucrats were at the disposal of the king. "We are willing to prove to your majesty," ran the declaration of office of the highest treasury official, "our devotion to your person by receiving your foot on our necks, and taking the sacred oath that we will perform all your commands. Our gold, our slaves and our lives are yours, and are ready to be delivered up to your command."

But Ethiopia was the most successful case of political modernization in sub-Saharan Africa. In the third quarter of the century, Ethiopia emerged from a long period of internal war and weak leadership. The emperors never enjoyed

MAKING CONNECTIONS

STATE MODERNIZATION IN THE NINETEENTH CENTURY

TYPE OF DEVELOPMENT/IDEOLOGY →	CORE IDEA/PURPOSE →	SCOPE AND RESULTS
Nationalism	Uniting people who shared same language, historic experience, and sense of identity into a cohesive state	Worldwide; positive effects include increased self-government, popular sovereignty; negative effects include repression of minorities (ethnic, religious, racial) within larger states; promotion of assimilation
Constitutionalism	Belief that state is founded on rules that rulers and citizens create and are bound to obey within a legal framework	Worldwide; beginning in Britain, United States, and Europe; vigorously opposed because of the implication that sovereignty was shared by more than one person/one class; threatened divine right of monarchy and aristocracy; eventual spread to Middle East and Asia
Centralization	Overcoming traditional provincial, regional, communal loyalties by fostering allegiance to the state; often extending power of central institutions	Worldwide, especially in quickly developing regions; often propelled by civil wars (United States, Japan, Germany, Italy) and in areas threatened with fragmentation
Militarization	Use of armed forces to mobilize populations; boosts power of governments to tax and spend on a large scale	Worldwide, especially in industrializing regions and colonial territories; use of larger armies, advanced technology expands warfare to civilian population, increases military and civilian casualties; arms race for improved technologies
Bureaucratization	Systemizing tax collecting, census taking, and regulation; often relying on regional governors to exercise local authority	Worldwide, in old empires (Ottoman), new industrial states (United States, Germany, Britain), and regions with progressive rulers (Ethiopia, Thailand, Asante kingdom); improved ability to harness economic systems to government goals

Nationalism, Constitutionalism, Militarization, Centralization, and Bureaucratization in the Nineteenth Century

ca. 1800–1850	Asante kings centralize and bureaucratize their kingdom
1805–1872	Giuseppe Mazzini, Italian nationalist
1810	Beginning of Jewish reform movement
ca. 1810–1820s	Wars of independence from Spain fought in Latin America
1820	King Shaka controls most of southeast Africa
1821	Founding of Liberia
1822	First fully independent Mexican state
1830	Greece gains independence from Ottoman Empire
1830s	Large Latin American states dissolve into smaller ones
1832	Great Reform Act becomes law in Britain
1839	Constitution of the Cherokee Nation
1845	Ottoman sultan convenes an assembly of provincial representatives
1861–1896	José Rizal, Filipino nationalist
1864	Creation of district assemblies in Russia
1870s–1880s	King Chulalongkorn of Thailand (Siam) modernizes his state
1878	Romania and Serbia gain independence from Ottoman Empire
1889	Japanese constitution created by imperial decree
1893	French Captain Alfred Dreyfus accused of spying for the Germans
1895	Nationalist rebellion in Guangzhou region of China
Late nineteenth century	Ethiopia undergoes political modernization

uncontested legitimacy or universal obedience, but at least they had credible programs of reunification. The system of government was loosely federal, with regional rulers exercising authority without reference to the center, except for paying tribute and defending the country from invaders.

In the 1870s, as a result of victories against Egyptian invaders, Emperor Yohannes IV (r. 1872–1889) began to build up a huge supply of captured modern weapons and to reorganize the army so that it had a professional core. When Menelik II (r. 1889–1813) became emperor, he concentrated on creating a militarily efficient state, armed with the best guns he could buy from Europe. He established garrisons in remote parts of the empire, dominating the country, stimulating markets, and spreading Christianity. At his death, the empire had postal, telegraph, and telephone services and a rail link to the Red Sea. The emperors imported technical know-how from Europe. Alred Ilg, a Swiss engineer, was Menelik's chief aide, attending to everything from the palace plumbing to foreign policy. Menelik also used Italian technical advice and arms shipments before the outbreak of conflict with Italy in 1896. As a result of all these changes, Ethiopia, uniquely among native African states in the late nineteenth century, not only repulsed European invasion but also participated in imperial expansion on its own account alongside European powers (see Chapter 24).

Thailand was a southeast Asian state that modernized even more thoroughly than Ethiopia and also achieved the distinction, unique in its region, of avoiding European conquest. In the 1830s, Prince Mongkut, who already had a reputation as an outstanding Buddhist scholar and reformer, came into contact with French Catholic and American Protestant missionaries and immediately appreciated that Thailand had a lot of catching up to do if it were to survive in a Western-dominated future. When he became king in 1851, he began reforms, inaugurating a government newspaper, printing laws, and—in a break with a tradition—allowing his face to be seen in public. He permitted his subjects to petition him, gave women rights to choose marriage partners, and educated his successor, Chulalongkorn, in a Western as well as a traditional curriculum.

Chulalongkorn (r. 1868–1910) inherited a bigger empire than any that southeast Asia had ever seen. But it was decentralized: a tributary empire at its edges, with hundreds of traditional communities, all with their own peculiar relationships to the throne. Chulalongkorn placed royal princes in charge of government departments, bypassing the old customs by which ministers succeeded by hereditary right. In the 1870s and 1880s, royal commissioners brought outlying autonomous regions of the Thai Empire under control of the central administration. In 1897, the king went to Europe and professed himself "convinced that there exists no incompatibility" between the acquisition of Western know-how "and the maintenance of our individuality as an independent Asiatic nation." Although Western examples inspired his reforms, he presented them as triumphs of Buddhist morality.

Bureaucratic centralization occurred in every continent. Until the British invasions of the 1840s, the Sikh state in the Punjab in northern India was creating a bureaucracy, surveying the territory it occupied, and introducing a consistent scheme of taxation. In the Central African highlands, King Mutesa (r. 1857–1884) of Buganda in what is now Uganda imported European weapons to equip his own servants and clients and Christian missionaries to strengthen his bureaucracy. He was able to concentrate unprecedented power in his own hands. In West Africa, the empire of Sokoto survived throughout the nineteenth century, in part because it created a bureaucracy to replace the local power of chiefs. The kingdoms of Fouta Toro and Fouta Jalon became elective monarchies, relying on Muslim clergy as servants of the state (see Map 26.4). Tawhiao, the proud Maori who alarmed James Kerry-Nicholls in New Zealand, had counterparts in state creation all over the world.

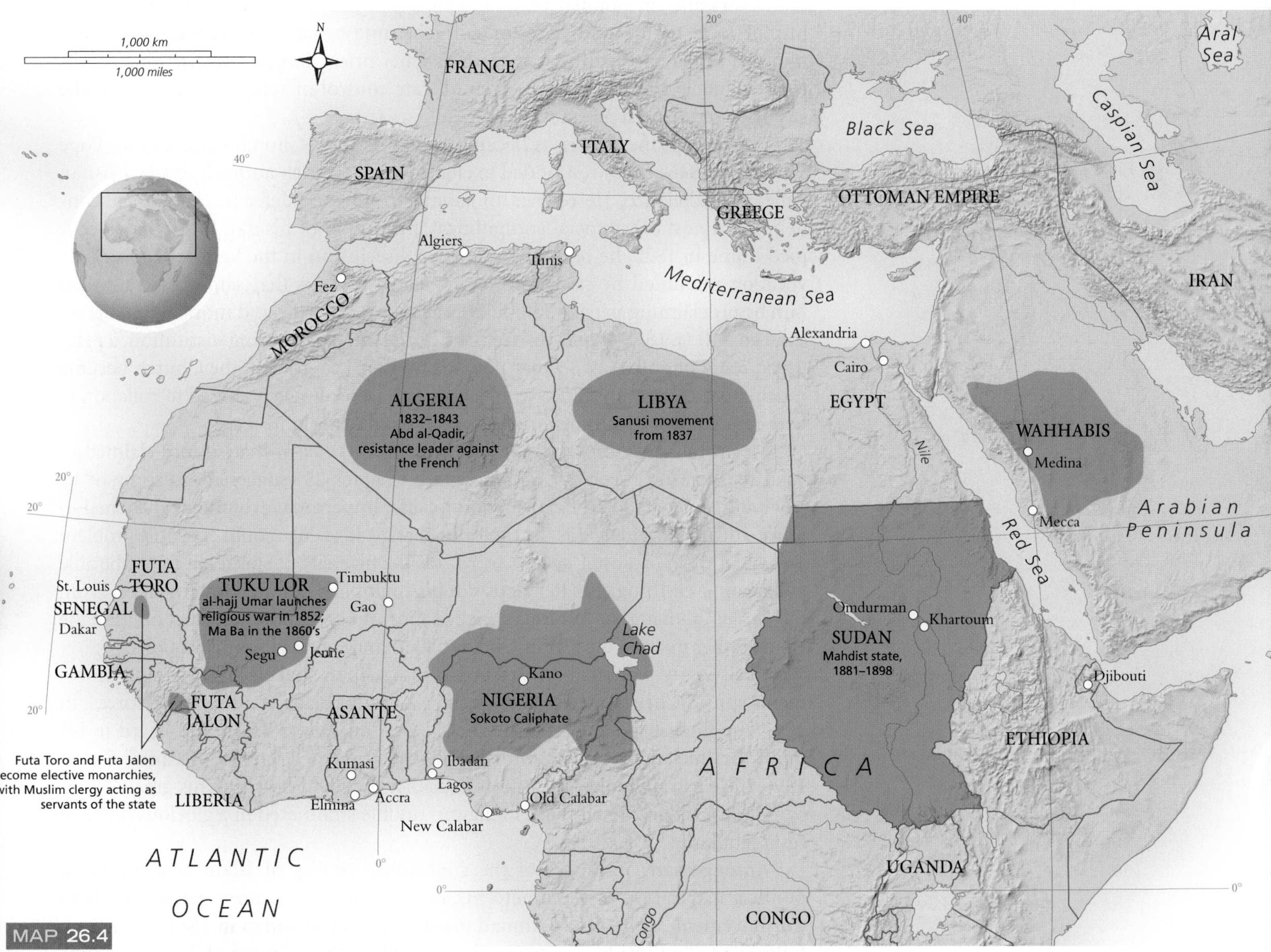

MAP 26.4

Muslim Reform Movements in Africa and Arabia in the Nineteenth Century

Islamic reform movement

RELIGION AND POLITICS

State power mopped up rivals. Nationalism, militarization, and centralization eclipsed other traditional allegiances. Aristocracies, as we have seen, were on the wane anyway in most places (see Chapter 24). Religion, however, was more problematic. In the nineteenth century, morality, family life, and the spaces in which social relationships were forged—the household, educational institutions, and the workplace—became arenas fiercely contested between religious institutions and states. In the West, civil marriage was the state's most important intrusion. Most countries with codified law made provision for it. Education was another battleground, usually resolved by compromise, because clergy were too cheap and too valuable as teachers to eliminate from schools. States that had not already done so, in some cases, even took over existing religions, funding them and appointing clerics. Japan's ancient popular religion, Shintoism, which had always been a chaotic mix of local nature and ancestor cults, became a national organization under imperial leadership with the emperor as chief priest, largely because nineteenth-century intellectuals in Japan perceived state control of religion to be one of the strengths of Western powers.

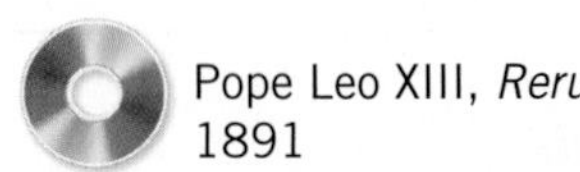
Pope Leo XIII, *Rerum Novarum*, 1891

Europe and the Americas became arenas of state–Church competition. Pope Pius IX (r. 1846–1878) responded to challenges to Church authority and Christian belief with defiance. He refused to submit to force or defer to change. He condemned almost every social and political innovation of his day. When Italy occupied Rome in 1870, he retreated into virtual seclusion in the Vatican. For a godly vocation undiluted by compromise, his fellow bishops that same year rewarded him by proclaiming papal infallibility in religious doctrine and morals. His successor, Leo XIII (r. 1878–1903) turned the Church into a reforming institution, a privileged critic of abuses of secular power. But after Leo's death, the Church became much more conservative. Clergy in every faith were always prepared to collaborate with repression and authoritarianism on the political right.

Meanwhile, religion resisted a challenge from atheism that science claimed to validate. Darwin's theory of evolution (see Chapter 25) suggested, to some of its advocates, a new God-free explanation for life. Impersonal evolution threatened to replace divine Providence as the motor of change. If science could explain a problem as "mysterious"—to use Darwin's word—as the diversity of species, it might be able to explain everything else. Religious doubts multiplied among Western elites. From the 1870s, "humane" or "ethical" societies aimed to base moral conduct on humane values rather than on the fear of God or the dogmas of religious institutions.

Christianity was stirred in response rather than shaken. Evangelizing movements spread Christian awareness in the new industrialized, urban workforces. In 1867, the English poet Matthew Arnold stood on Dover Beach and heard in his mind the "melancholy, long, withdrawing roar" of the "the Sea of Faith." But in 1896, the Austrian composer Anton Bruckner died while writing his great "Ninth Symphony," a dark document of religious doubts smothered in a glorious finale of resurgent faith.

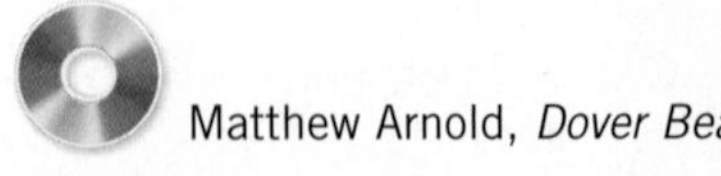
Matthew Arnold, *Dover Beach*

Among many instances of the continuing vitality of Islam as a source of political inspiration in the nineteenth century, none was more spectacular than the movement Muhammad Ahmad proclaimed in the Sudan in 1881. Calling on followers to "put aside everything that resembles the customs of Turks and infidels," he came to see himself as the *Mahdi*—the successor of the Prophet Muhammad, the restorer of the faith, whose coming would herald the end of time. His typical follower was, as the British admitted (in lines by the great poet of the British Empire, Rudyard Kipling [1865–1936]) "a pore benighted 'eathen, but a first-class fightin' man." The Mahdi himself had a different explanation for his success: "Every intelligent person must know that Allah rules. If ... you persist in denying my divine calling, ... you are to be killed." The Egyptian and British governments were unable to suppress the movement until 1898, when a crushingly well-armed British force slaughtered the Mahdists at the Battle of Omdurman (see Chapter 25).

Religion remained a revolutionary force in the world. In 1847, a conflict known as the Caste War broke out in Yucatán in Mexico. Maya rebels threatened to kill all white people. Government supporters retorted with threats to exterminate the Maya. The rebels' rallying point was the so-called Talking Cross of the shrine of Chan Santa Cruz—an oracle proclaiming divine sanction and success for the rebel cause. In the 1850s and 1860s, holy men launched religious wars in West Africa. In 1860, for instance, Muslim preachers roused the peasants of Sine against their king, who said he wanted to do with subject-peoples "as we have always done. These people are my slaves. . . . I will take their property, their children and their millet." In Ethiopia, Emperor Tewodros II (r. 1855–1868) appealed to Christians as a Messiah, and to Muslims as a Mahdi, before behaving like a Western modernizer and secularizing church property.

In Japan in the 1860s, a woman who claimed to be divine inspired thousands of peasants to rebel. She preached equality and peasant solidarity. In China at around the same time, a failed examination candidate, who came to see himself as a "brother of Jesus," led a rebellion that, as we saw in Chapter 25, almost overthrew the Qing Empire. In 1866, a woman who called herself the Virgin of the Rosary led a rebellion in Bolivia. In the North American plains, meanwhile, the Ghost Dance was a Native American ritual to bring the dead back to life. In the 1880s, prophets associated it first with a project to bring on the end of the world, then with a plan to invoke divine help against the white invaders. Most Ghost Dancers never intended violent resistance, but settlers called in the United States' cavalry who massacred Sioux Ghost Dancers at Wounded Knee in 1890.

On the whole, despite the vigor of religiously inspired politics, religion lost out in its conflicts with secular states. The charms religious zealots such as the Mahdi issued did not work against the machine gun. Sacred notions of political authority succumbed to new kinds of legitimacy that nationalists, constitutionalists, and bureaucrats advocated.

NEW FORMS OF POLITICAL RADICALISM

Popular revolutionary movements of religious inspiration were not new. But more subversive ways of thinking about the state were building up strength for the future.

Steps Toward Democracy

In the West, enthusiasm for democracy became a major force for change independent of any sect. The United States—perhaps because men steeped in reverence for both the classics and Christianity founded it—was the laboratory of democracy for the nineteenth-century world. Democracy as we understand it today—with a representative legislature, elected on a wide suffrage, and political parties—was, in effect, an American invention. Despite major imperfections—slaves, Native Americans, and women were excluded—democracy developed early in the new republic. By the early 1840s, almost all adult, white, free males could vote.

Stump Speaking. George Caleb Bingham (1811–1879) chronicled the life of the Missouri valley in the mid–nineteenth century in his accomplished, well-observed paintings. He was also active in politics on behalf of Andrew Jackson, which gives his political scenes an edge of personal commitment. Typically, as here in *Stump Speaking* (1853–1854), a politician's passion contrasts with the attitudes of his audiences—variously cool, critical, idly curious, sneering, bored, or depraved.

George Caleb Bingham (American, 1811–1879), Stump Speaking, *1853–54. Oil on canvas, 42 1/2 × 58 in. The Saint Louis Art Museum, Gift of Bank of America. Photo © The Saint Louis Art Museum.*

In Europe, however, democracy seemed at first to be one of America's "peculiar institutions," like slavery, that it would be best to avoid. Why should elites share power with poorly educated masses who tended to vote for demagogues and charlatans? The bloodshed of the French Revolution seemed to show that the "common man" was untrustworthy. In consequence, the first half of the nineteenth century was a time of democratic retreat in most of Europe, as rulers withdrew or diluted constitutions that they had conceded in the crises of the Napoleonic Wars. The new constitutions that did emerge in Europe at this time were designed to create alliances among monarchs, aristocrats, churches, and the middle classes and, thus, to defend traditional privileges by enlarging support for them. Whenever possible, the birth of working-class organizations was aborted, radical presses censored, demonstrators shot. In Britain, the Reform Act of 1832, often hailed as a first step toward democratic progress, actually disenfranchised working-class voters.

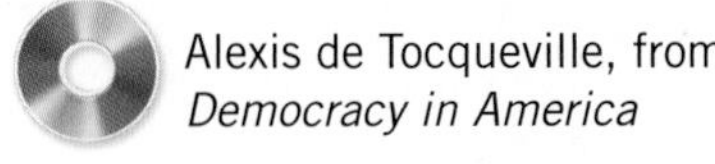

Alexis de Tocqueville, from *Democracy in America*

Nevertheless, the model of the United States became increasingly attractive as the young country proved itself. European radicals who visited America returned enthused. The first influential apologist for American democracy was a German, Karl Postl, who in 1828 recommended a "system which unites the population for the common good." Between 1835 and 1840, Alexis de Tocqueville published *Democracy in America*. His aristocratic self-confidence in the face of popular sovereignty helped reconcile Europeans to democratic change. While most Europeans of his class felt the menace of the revolutionary mob, Tocqueville saw "the same democracy ... advancing rapidly toward power in Europe." Properly managed, the result would be "a society which all men, regarding the law as their work, would acknowledge without demur." Where rights were guaranteed, he wrote, democracy would "shelter the state" from tyranny, on the one hand, and lawlessness, on the other. Democracy became the first American cultural product to conquer Europe—even before jazz, rock music, casual manners, fast food, and tight jeans. In the late nineteenth century, most European countries modified their constitutions in a democratic direction and enlarged the franchise. Though France,

Switzerland, and Spain were beacons of universal male suffrage, the most conspicuous concentration of states with democratic franchises was in the former Ottoman dominions in the Balkans. In Greece, Bulgaria, Serbia, and Romania, the right to vote was more widely shared than in Britain or Scandinavia. This was understandable. The newest states, repudiating the empires that preceded them, had the least historic baggage to discard in adopting democracy.

There was, however, no uniform march of progress toward practical democracy in most of Europe. On the contrary, democracy remained marginal throughout the century, for effective democracy is not just a matter of how many people have the right to vote. Everywhere small groups tried to manipulate mass electorates. In Romania, the constitution was often suspended or ignored. In Britain, the biggest single extension of the franchise in 1884–1885 was accompanied by a redistribution of parliamentary seats to preserve the existing parties' shares of power. Constitutional reform in Europe never completely pried open the world of the dominant political caste and its recruits. The aristocracy retained formal power. When Germany introduced universal male suffrage in 1871, it was only for elections for one chamber of the national legislature, the Reichstag, whose power was limited.

The Expansion of the Public Sphere

Even where there was little or no democracy, more people got involved in what historians and sociologists now like to call the **public sphere**: in clubs, institutions, and associations outside the home, in arenas of debate in cafes and bars, and in places of worship. Public readings of newspapers made even illiterate people politically informed. In Cuba, this was the normal entertainment for workers in factories while they rolled cigars. In Barcelona in 1852, a friar found factory workers listening to children reading aloud from "political journals which generally spread subversive doctrines, mocked holy things ... spoke ill of the proprietors and government, and preached socialism and communism." Catholic clergy provided reading material for factories to deflect workers from hearing too much inflammatory or revolutionary propaganda.

The public sphere was widest and most developed in North America and parts of Europe. That is why democracy got a foothold in those regions. But there were outposts and echoes elsewhere in the world. Although the number of people who took part in political life in Latin America was relatively small, they contested power with great commitment and sustained ferocious debates in the press. In Brazil, the proliferation of political clubs, newspapers, and rallies preceded the abolition of slavery in 1888 and the proclamation of the republic in 1889. In the late nineteenth century, most Argentine intellectuals regarded their country as a democracy.

In Japan, the spread of education (see Chapter 24) enlarged the public sphere. Examinations replaced samurai privileges as a means to recruit state officials. Even in China, the political class expanded, thanks in part to the creation of hundreds of provincial academies to train officials. On the whole, the Qing responded to crisis by resisting social or political change and clinging to the notion that the inherited order of society was sacred. The terms of public debate, however, were enlarged. At the height of the crisis caused by rebellion and Anglo-French invasion in the 1860s, Feng Guifen (fung gway-fun) (1809–1874), director of one of the largest provincial academies, advocated the professionalization of the civil service and popular election of village headmen. The government, however, shelved his proposals.

Feng Guifen on Western strength

WESTERN SOCIAL THOUGHT

The clash of political visions in the nineteenth-century West was part of a worldwide tension between secularism and religiosity in everyday conceptions of life and the world. Were men apes or angels? Would the goodness inside them emerge in freedom or was it corroded with evil that had to be controlled? In 1816, the English writer Thomas Love Peacock gathered fictional philosophers in the setting of his comic novel, *Headlong Hall.* "Mr. Forster, the perfectibilian," expected "gradual advancement towards a state of unlimited perfection," while "Mr. Escot, the deteriorationist," foresaw, with gloomy satisfaction, "that the whole species must at length be exterminated by its own imbecility and violence." These extremes of optimism and pessimism echoed real debates. In France, for instance, Louis Blanc (1811–1882) believed that the state could eliminate human wickedness, while his contemporary, Alphonse Karr, thought that attempted reforms only made things worse. The politics of fear and hope pitted rival kinds of radicalism—reformist philosophies that claimed to get to the root of the world's problems—against each other.

Robert Owen, *Address to the Workers of New Lanark,* 1816

Socialism was an extreme form of optimism. Socialists advocated the ideals of equality and fraternity that those Enlightenment thinkers who believed in the perfectibility of human nature had proclaimed (see Chapter 22). Early socialist communities in Europe and America practiced sharing and cooperating. Charles Fourier (1772–1837) planned a settlement called New Harmony, where even sexual orgies would be organized on egalitarian principles. In Texas in 1849, Étienne Cabet (1788–1856) founded a town he called Icaria, where abolishing property and forbidding rivalry would prevent envy, crime, anger, and lust.

These experiments and others failed, but the idea of reforming society as a whole on socialist lines appealed to people unrewarded or outraged by the unequal distribution of wealth in the industrializing world. Economic theorists maintained that since workers' labor added the greater part of the value of most commodities (see Chapter 24), the workers should get the lion's share of the profits—or so some socialists inferred. This was a capitalist's kind of socialism, in which ideals carried a price tag. Louis Blanc convinced most socialists that the state could impose their ideals on society. John Ruskin (1819–1900) echoed these arguments in England. For him "the first duty of a state is to see that every child born therein shall be well housed, clothed, fed and educated," and he relished the prospect of increased state power to accomplish it.

Meanwhile, Karl Marx (1818–1883) predicted the inevitability of socialism's triumph through class conflict. As economic power passed from capital to labor, so workers—degraded and inflamed by exploitative employers—would seize power in the state. "Not only," he announced, "has the bourgeoisie forged the weapons that bring death to itself. It has also called into existence the men who are to wield those weapons—the modern working class, the proletarians." The transition, he believed, would be violent. The ruling class would try to hold on to power, while the rising class struggled to gain it. So he tended to agree with the thinkers of his day who saw violence as conducive to progress. In part, the effect was to inspire revolutionary violence, which sometimes succeeded in changing society, but never seemed to bring the communist utopia into being or even into sight. All Marx's predictions, so far, have proved false. Yet the brilliance of his analysis of history ensured that he would have millions of readers and millions of followers.

While mainstream socialists put their faith in a strong, regulatory state to realize revolutionary ambitions or sought to capture the state by mobilizing the masses, revolutionary violence sidetracked others. Some of these "anarchists," as they called themselves, turned to the bloodstained ravings of Johann Most

Noble workers. Giuseppe Pelizza's painting *Il Quarto Stato,* completed between 1899 and 1901 expresses the grandeur and grind at the heart of Socialism. The workers advance heroically united, but with the look of automation, with individuality suppressed. Pelizza was convinced that artists were workers who had a social responsibility to educate, elevate, and inspire other workers.
G. Pellizza da Volpedo, The Fourth Estate. *Milano, Galleria Civica D'Arte Moderna. © Canali Photobank.*

(1846–1896), the first great ideologue of terror. The entire elite—including their families, servants, and all who did business with them—were, for Most, legitimate targets of armed struggle, to be killed at every opportunity. Anyone caught in the crossfire was a sacrifice in a good cause. In 1884, he published a handbook on how to explode bombs in churches, ballrooms, and public places, where the "reptile brood" of aristocrats, priests, and capitalists might gather. He also advocated exterminating policemen on the grounds that these "pigs" were not fully human. The bombs of terrorism exploded in elite ears. Social outcasts and the chronically disaffected formed pacts to assassinate rulers, provoke revolutions, fight the state, and defy the repressive realities of politics and economics.

In most European countries in the late nineteenth century, socialists built up mass organizations for political and industrial action. They believed their triumph was determined by history. The questions that divided them were whether that triumph should be triggered violently, pursued democratically, or engineered by industrial action.

Opponents of socialism included philosophical pessimists, who believed humans could not be reformed, and that only law and order could redeem their wickedness. Between extreme optimism and extreme pessimism, centrist political thinking developed. In the nineteenth century, the English philosopher Jeremy Bentham (1748–1832) devised the most influential form of centrist thinking, called **utilitarianism**. Bentham proposed a new way to evaluate social institutions without reference or deference to their antiquity or authority or past record of success. He thought good could be defined as a surplus of happiness over unhappiness

Religion, Utopianism, Democracy, and Political Radicalism in the Nineteenth Century

1748–1832	Jeremy Bentham, proponent of utilitarianism
1772–1837	Charles Fourier, created planned community of New Harmony based on egalitarian ideals
1788–1856	Étienne Cabet, founded utopian community of Icaria
1806–1873	John Stuart Mill, combined individualism with social reform
1811–1882	Louis Blanc, argued that the state could eliminate human wickedness
1818–1883	Karl Marx, predicted socialism's inevitable triumph
1835–1840	Publication of Alexis de Tocqueville's *Democracy in America*
ca. 1840	Almost all adult white males can vote in the United States
1844–1900	Friedrich Nietzsche, rejected liberalism and religion
r. 1846–1878	Pope Pius IX, opponent of social and political innovation
1847	Caste War begins in southeast Mexico
1881	Muhammad Ahmad calls on Muslims in the Sudan to join his reform movement

and that the aim of the state was "the greatest happiness of the greatest number." For Bentham, social utility was more important than individual liberty. His doctrine was thoroughly secular. Bentham's standard of happiness was pleasure, and his index of evil was pain. His views, therefore, appealed to the irreligious. But the greatest happiness of the greatest number means sacrifices for some. It is strictly incompatible with human rights, because the interest of the "greatest number" will always tend to leave some individuals without benefits.

Modifying, then rejecting utilitarianism, Bentham's disciple, John Stuart Mill (1806–1873), adopted a scale of values with freedom at the top. Liberty, he thought, is absolute, except where it interferes with others. "The only purpose," he wrote, "for which power can be rightfully exercised over any member of a civilised community, against his will, is to prevent harm to others," not to make him happier. For Bentham's "greatest number," Mill substituted the individual. "Over himself, over his own body and mind, the individual is sovereign." Mill's individualism, however, never excluded social priorities. "For the protection of society," the citizen "owes a return for the benefit." He can be made to respect others' rights and to contribute a reasonable share of taxes and services to the state. Freedom and social priorities, however, did not commend themselves to everybody. Philosophical opponents of liberalism—the most eloquent of whom was Nietzsche (1844–1900)—favored "heroes" and "supermen" to solve social problems. Dictators in the next century would adopt these ideas.

Meanwhile, Benthamism was amazingly influential. The British state was reorganized along lines Bentham recommended. The penal code was reformed to minimize unhelpful pain. The government bureaucracy was restaffed with administrators who had passed competitive exams. Capitalist and libertarian prejudices could never quite exclude public interest from legislators' priorities, even under nominally right-wing governments. Benthamism made social welfare seem like the job of the state. In promoting social welfare, Germany led the way, introducing pensions, health services, and education for all in the 1880s. The German policy is often seen as an attempt to preempt the appeal of socialism—as indeed it was. But it was also the outcome of a trend, begun during the Enlightenment, of philosophical respect for the common man. Australia and New Zealand copied German initiatives in an attempt to create a common identity for settlers—an identity, moreover, distinct from those of the snobbish and class-ridden society that migrants from Britain had left behind. A worldwide consensus in favor of a socially responsible state gradually emerged. The main disagreements, which would be bloodily fought out in the following century, were over how far that responsibility extended.

John Stuart Mill, from *On Liberty*

IN PERSPECTIVE: Global State-Building

All the transformations of nineteenth-century states need to be understood against a common background: the declining credibility of traditional forms of authority, as conflicts overthrew old supremacies and economic change enriched new aspirants to power. During the changes that followed, the sphere of the state enlarged. States had still not penetrated vast areas of the globe, but these regions were now the exception—underpopulated and relatively inaccessible environments. In most of the rest of the world, the state had arrived: imposed from outside by imperialist invasions, or created from within by monarchs or elites, usually in imitation of Western powers. In parts of the world with long experience of states, such as Japan, Egypt, and Thailand, governments had extended their reach. States took on new responsibilities as their power increased. Education, as we have seen, received a boost from militarization. States interfered more and more in religion and family life. It even became increasingly accepted that the state was responsible for the total well-being of its citizens.

After all the wars, reforms, constitutional conflicts, radical thinking, and administrative tinkering, how strong were the states and empires that covered most of the world by 1900? Had they reformed for survival? Or were they, as socialists thought, doomed to disappear? Old rivals of the state—religious institutions and allegiances—had proved remarkably strong. And although local, regional, and tribal loyalties were in retreat, they had only been checked, not destroyed. As we shall see, they would often reemerge in the twentieth and twenty-first centuries. In 1900, it looked as if some states, such as Japan, the United States, and the British Empire, had met the challenges of the century successfully and recast themselves in lasting form. Others, such as the Ottoman Empire and China, looked vulnerable. In between were superficially strong states, such as the German, Russian, and Habsburg Empires, which were to prove surprisingly fragile when tested in the twentieth century. While white empires continued to grow, the days of their supremacy were numbered. Their power was founded on technological superiority, which was a wasting asset. Nonwhite powers in Asia and Africa had already demonstrated that they could copy the trick, either by buying European technology, as Ethiopia had, or, like Japan, launching their own industrialization programs.

CHRONOLOGY

1748–1832	Jeremy Bentham, proponent of utilitarianism
1772–1837	Charles Fourier, created planned community of New Harmony based on egalitarian ideals
ca. 1800–1850	Asante kings centralize and bureaucratize their kingdom
1805–1872	Giuseppe Mazzini, Italian nationalist
1806–1873	John Stuart Mill, combined individualism with social reform
ca. 1810–1820s	Wars of Independence from Spain fought in Latin America
1811–1882	Louis Blanc, argued that the state could eliminate human wickedness
1818–1883	Karl Marx, predicted socialism's inevitable triumph
1820	King Shaka gains control of most of southeast Africa
1821	Founding of Liberia
1822	First fully independent Mexican state
1830	Greece gains independence from Ottoman Empire
1830s	Large Latin American states dissolve into smaller ones
1832	Great Reform Act becomes law in Britain
1835–1840	Publication of Alexis de Tocqueville's *Democracy in America*
1844–1900	Friedrich Nietzsche, rejected liberalism and religion
1845	Ottoman sultan convenes an assembly of provincial representatives
r. 1846–1878	Pope Pius IX, opponent of social and political innovation
1847	Caste War begins in southeast Mexico
1861–1896	José Rizal, Filipino nationalist
1870s–1880s	King Chulalongkorn of Thailand modernizes his state
1873–1901	British conquest of Kingdom of Asante
1878	Romania and Serbia gain independence from Ottoman Empire
1881	Muhammad Ahmad calls on Muslims in the Sudan to join his reform movement
1889	Japanese constitution created by imperial decree
1893	French Captain Alfred Dreyfus accused of spying for the Germans
1895	Nationalist rebellion in Guangzhou region of China
1896	Battle of Adowa
Late nineteenth century	Ethiopia undergoes political modernization

To maintain its power in the world, Europe needed peace at home. Only brief wars broke that peace in the nineteenth century. For almost 40 years after the defeat of Napoleon in 1815, no major war flared on Europe's home ground. The wars of the midcentury to 1870 were short and did not overstrain the belligerents. After 1870, short-term military service became the universal fashion in the West—with the major exceptions of Britain and the United States but including almost all of Latin America—and Japan, as states sought to give more male citizens experience of military service. Armies therefore had to make up in technology what they lacked in professional ability, because most recruits did not serve long enough to become skilled soldiers. Ever more efficient means of mobilizing armies were called on, as railways linked front lines to barracks and bases all over Europe. Ever more accurate and long-range weapons were required to compensate for soldiers' lack of expertise in firing them. The result was an arms race that made peace precarious and an atmosphere of anxiety among the powers to mobilize rapidly should a new war threaten: a recipe, in short, for rupturing peace. Still, until the end of the nineteenth century, enough powers were sufficiently evenly matched to keep the peace for most of the time.

By then, however, the fear of revolution had so diminished, and the habit of short wars had become so familiar, that neither the fragility of peace nor the fear of war excited much alarm in Europe. The balance of power, on which peace depended, was beginning to tilt toward war because of the uneven distribution of heavy industry. By 1900, Germany produced vastly more coal, iron, and steel than all the other European powers combined. The Russian Empire, with its huge population, was beginning to show signs of being able to catch up. This fact—little noticed outside Germany—made a trial of strength seem urgent. In the arena of Europe, the sand that the changes of the nineteenth century kicked up was raked into new patterns of alliance, made with war in mind rather than to contain change or maintain the balance of power. The arena was ready for the gladiators.

PROBLEMS AND PARALLELS

1. What were the differences between European nationalism and nationalist movements outside Europe? What was the relationship between constitutionalism and modernization in the nineteenth century?
2. How did new states emerge in the nineteenth century? What roles did nationalism, constitutionalism, militarization, and bureaucratization play in state development?
3. Why did many nineteenth-century states emphasize centralization? Who benefited from centralization? Which groups lost power?
4. Why did religion and politics clash in the nineteenth century? Why did some clergy oppose the theory of revolution? Why was religion a "revolutionary force in the world" during the nineteenth century?
5. How did democracy become more widespread in the nineteenth century? What does the term *public sphere* mean? Why did new forms of political radicalism emerge in the nineteenth century?

DOCUMENTS IN GLOBAL HISTORY

- Joseph Mazzini on nationalism
- José Fernández, *El Gaucho Martin Fierro*
- José Rizal, excerpt from *El Filibusterismo (The Reign of Greed)*
- An Ottoman government decree defining the "modern" citizen, 1870
- The Constitution of the Empire of Japan, 1889
- Pope Leo XIII, *Rerum Novarum*, 1891
- Matthew Arnold, *Dover Beach*
- Alexis de Tocqueville, from *Democracy in America*
- Feng Guifen on Western strength
- Robert Owen, *Address to the Workers of New Lanark,* 1816
- Mikhail Bakunin, "Principles and Organization of the International Brotherhood, " 1866
- John Stuart Mill, from *On Liberty*

Please see the Primary Source DVD for additional sources related to this chapter.

READ ON

The opening story comes from J. H. Kerry-Nicholls, *The King Country* (1974). J. Belich, *The New Zealand Wars* (1988), and *Making Peoples* (1996) are gripping revisionist studies of New Zealand. B. Anderson, *Imagined Communities: Reflections on the Origin and Spread of Nationalism* (1991) is the fundamental starting point for contemporary thinking about nationalism. G. Wawro, *Warfare and Society in Europe, 1792–1914* (2000) is a solid introduction to the impact of militarization on European states and society. Lord Durham's *Report on the Affairs of British North America*, ed. by C. Lucas (1970), shows the thinking that went into the emerging political structure of the British Empire.

Nationalism and state-building beyond Europe is beginning to receive more attention in the literature. Among the many books by B. Lewis, *The Middle East* (1997) is a good introduction to the politics of the Arab world. F. R. Hunter, *Egypt Under the Khedives, 1805–1879: From Household Government to Modern Bureaucracy* (1984) is the foundational work on the emergence of the modern Egyptian state. H. S. Wilson, *Origins of West African Nationalism* (1969) analyzes the impact of colonial rule on the emergence of African nationalisms, while *West African Kingdoms in the Nineteenth Century*, ed. by D. Forde and P. M. Karberry (1967), studies the range of successes in indigenous African state-building. B. Farwell, *Prisoners of the Mahdi* (1967) recounts the story of three Western prisoners of the Mahdi in the Sudan and explores this religiously inspired revolt against colonial encroachment. M. A. Klein, *Islam and Imperialism in Senegal, 1847–1914* (1968) provides a more analytical account of the interaction of religion and imperial pressure. *José Rizal and the Asian Renaissance* (1996) sets a very broad context. His novels and many of Bankim's are available in English translations.

C. A. Bayly, *The Birth of the Modern World, 1780–1914* (2004) is indispensable for understanding the nineteenth-century state in global dimensions. D. Ralston, *Importing the European Army: The Introduction of European Military Techniques and Institutions in the Extra-European World, 1600–1914* (1996) studies several key examples of non-European states attempting to the new world of militarized centralization. D. Wyatt, *A Short History of Thailand* (1984) explores one of the few cases of successful Asian resistance to imperial pressures. R. Scheina, *Latin American Wars: Volume I, The Age of Caudillos, 1791–1899* (2003) gives a detailed military narrative that reveals the reasons behind the failures of Latin American state building. K. Pomeranz, *The Great Divergence: China, Europe, and the Making of the Modern World Economy* (2001) is excellent on the different paths taken by Britain and China after 1800, linking political regimes to economic development in unexpected ways.

PART

Ten

Chaos and Complexity: The World in the Twentieth Century

CHAPTER 27 The Twentieth-Century Mind: Western Science and the World 692

CHAPTER 28 World Order and Disorder: Global Politics in the Twentieth Century 718

CHAPTER 29 The Pursuit of Utopia: Civil Society in the Twentieth Century 748

CHAPTER 30 The Embattled Biosphere: The Twentieth-Century Environment 774

Cyberspace. This map of the Internet looks a lot like the Milky Way. But each of the wispy strands represents millions of computer networks that crisscross the planet like a lattice. The reddish wisps indicate networks in East Asia and the Pacific. Europe, Africa, the Middle East, and Central and South Asia are green. North America's heavily wired landscape is evident in the predominance of blue, while the relatively few yellow fibers suggest the scarcity of connections in Latin America and the Caribbean. Sectors of the Internet that have yet to be mapped shimmer in white like distant galaxies.

ENVIRONMENT

since 1905, 1918, 1930
Relativity—Quantum machanics

CULTURE

1914–1918
World War I

1929–1939
Great Depression

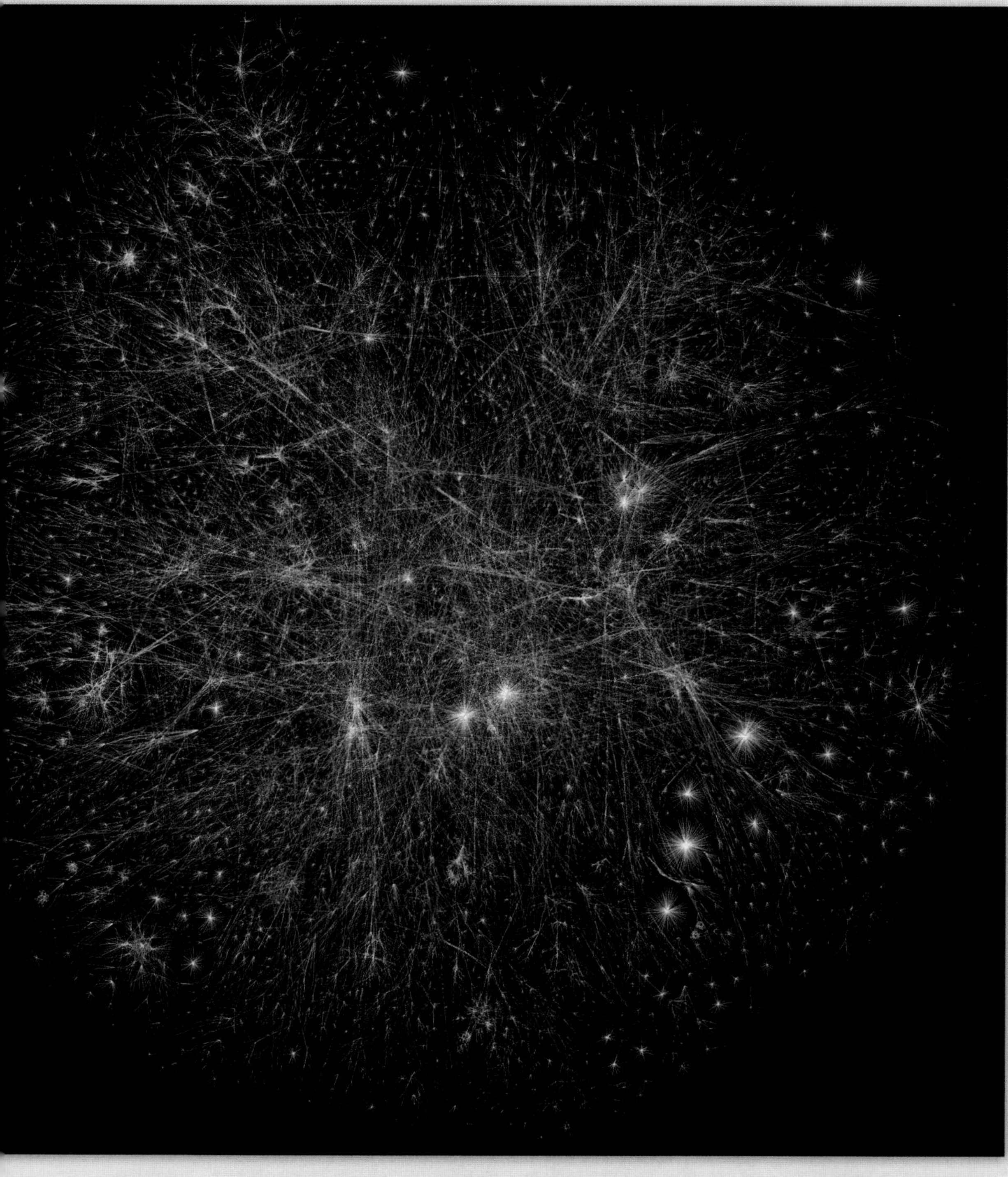

since 1950s
Global warming

since 1960s
Intensive deforestation

since mid-1980s
AIDS epidemic

since 1990s
Genetically modified crops

1936–1945
World War II

1945–1989
Cold War

since early 1950s
Television

since mid-1990s
Internet

CHAPTER 27 The Twentieth-Century Mind: Western Science and the World

Dr. Edward H. Hume taking a patient's pulse at the Yale-Hunan Clinic. Dr. Hume founded the clinic in the city of Changsha, in Hunan, China, in 1914 and was its dean until 1927. The presence of guards shows that this photograph was taken after the clinic began to attract socially elevated patients.

IN THIS CHAPTER

WESTERN SCIENCE ASCENDANT
China
India
The Wider World

THE TRANSFORMATION OF WESTERN SCIENCE
Physics
Human Sciences
Anthropology and Psychology
Philosophy and Linguistics

THE MIRROR OF SCIENCE: ART

THE TURN OF THE WORLD

IN PERSPECTIVE: **Science, Challenging and Challenged**

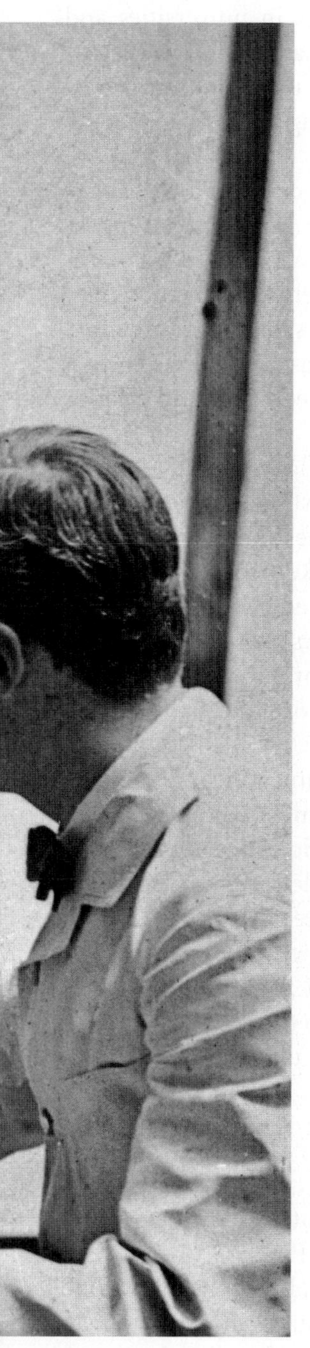

Edward H. Hume's heart sank when he saw the gateway to the city where he was to begin his new life. He arrived in China in 1905 from Yale University to start a clinic in Changsha, in remote Hunan province, where the Chinese government admitted foreigners as part of its policy to develop the interior. The city gate had been symbolically bricked up at the orders of the local gentry, who resented having foreign barbarians in their midst.

CHINA

The notables of the town shunned him. For the poor, however, Hume's services were attractive. With backing from Yale alumni, he could afford to treat them for nominal sums. So they frequented his clinic, as well as visiting the shops of his Chinese rivals—an astrologer, a fortune-teller, a physiognomist who diagnosed illnesses by scrutinizing the faces of the sick, and an old soldier who had become a folk pediatrician.

For nearly three years, Hume had no patients from among the mandarins, the scholar-elite who monopolized authority in China. Then one morning, he heard harsh voices outside his clinic. "Stand aside, you brats! This is a mandarin's chair!" Apprehensive at first, the newcomer seemed pleased when Hume began to check his pulse. But when Hume dropped his patient's wrist and shoved a thermometer into his mouth, the mandarin was enraged. "Why," he said to the attendant who accompanied him, "did you let this foreigner put this strange, hard thing inside my mouth? Can't you see that he knows nothing of medicine?" Only subsequently did Hume learn how he had offended his patient. He had read his pulse by taking his left wrist, but Chinese tradition dictated that a doctor must also check pulse points on the right arm. By proceeding straight to taking the patient's temperature, Hume had exposed himself, in his patient's eyes, as an ignoramus.

It took years of painstaking work before Hume retrieved official confidence. His struggle was an episode in a long, slow, and fitful story of the assimilation of Western medicine in China, which was itself part of the spread of Western science—led by medicine and military technology, but extending to every kind of science and to scientific habits of thought—across the world. In no area was the rise of the West to world dominance more apparent.

FOCUS questions

- WHY DID Western science dominate the world during the first half of the twentieth century?
- WHAT FORMER certainties about the cosmos and human nature did science undermine during the twentieth century?
- WHY DID many people turn away from science in the late twentieth century?
- HOW DID styles in the arts mirror developments in science?
- WHY HAVE many people in the West come to rely on non-Western forms of medical treatment?

In the twentieth century, science set the agenda for the world. Whereas previously scientists had tended to respond to the demands of society, now science drove other kinds of change. In Europe and the Americas, a scientific counterrevolution exploded certainties inherited from seventeenth- and eighteenth-century science. Revolutions in psychology and social anthropology made people rethink cultural values and social relationships. A new philosophical climate challenged traditional ideas about language, reality, and the links between them. Ever larger and costlier scientific establishments in universities and research institutes served their paymasters—governments and big business—or pursued their own programs. New theories shocked people into revising their image of the world and their place in it.

Yet the lessons of Western science proved equivocal. New technologies raised as many problems as they solved: moral questions, as science expanded human power over life and death; practical questions, as technologies multiplied for exploiting the Earth. In the twentieth century, ordinary people and nonscientific intellectuals lost confidence in science. Uncertainty corroded the hard facts with which science was formerly associated. Faith that science could solve the world's problems and reveal the secrets of the cosmos evaporated.

In part, this was the result of practical failures. Though science achieved wonders, especially in medicine and communications, consumers never seemed satisfied. Every advance unleashed side effects. Machines fought wars and destroyed or degraded environments but could only make people happier in modest ways and did nothing to make them good. Even medical improvements brought equivocal effects. The costs of treatment sometimes exceeded the benefits. Health became a purchasable commodity. Medical provision buckled, in prosperous countries, under the weight of public expectations and the intensity of public demand.

As the power of science grew, more and more people came to fear and resent it and react against it. Science stoked disillusionment, even as it spread. It disclosed a chaotic cosmos, in which effects were hard to predict, and interventions went wrong. A century dominated by Western science ended with the recovery of alternative traditions that Western influence had displaced or eclipsed.

The stories of these changes fill this chapter—starting with the global diffusion of Western science, then turning back to the West to see how science changed from within, and how art mirrored the changes. In the remaining chapters, we can look at the effects of the changes on politics, culture generally, and the environment.

WESTERN SCIENCE ASCENDANT

The early twentieth-century world seethed with discontent at Western hegemony. Yet the allure of Western science (see Map 27.1) was twofold. First, it worked. Western military technology won wars. Western industrial technology multiplied food and wealth. Information systems devised in the West revolutionized communications, business, leisure, education, and methods of social and political control. Western medical science saved lives. Second, Western science offered infallibility:

knowledge that matched observation, fulfilled predictions, and withstood tests. Chinese revolutionaries called science a faith and represented "scientism" as an alternative to Confucianism.

China

The Chinese reception of Western science began in a continuous and systematic fashion in the 1860s, at the start of the "self-strengthening" movement (see Chapter 23). In 1866, Beijing's Foreign Language Institute opened a department "for the use of logical reasoning, methods of manufacturing and being practical. . . . This is the path to strengthening China." It was a promising beginning, but, as we have seen, Chinese self-strengthening was patchy in the nineteenth century, and the absorption of Western ideas was slow and subject to the mistrust of foreigners, whom Chinese often continued to see as barbaric or demonic.

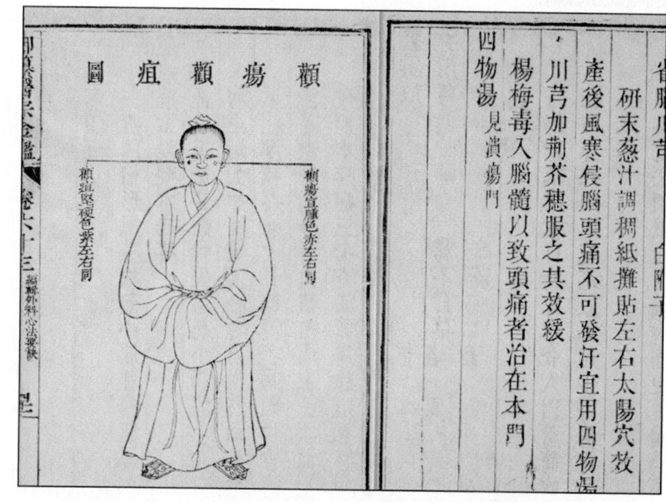

Chinese herbal medicine. In 1869, the emperor of China, Tongzhi, presented the U.S. government with 933 volumes of materials on Chinese herbal medicine and ancient Chinese agricultural techniques. This illustrated volume from the *Complete Survey of Medical Knowledge* demonstrates the proper usage of pertinent Chinese herbal medicine for illness.

Nor was the pace of change uniform in all the sciences. At first, medicine lagged behind mathematics and military and industrial technology. In 1876, for instance, a comparative study by Chinese physicians upheld the superiority of ancient Chinese methods over Western medicine. In 1883, however, the Beijing School of Medicine launched a Western-style curriculum. Chinese students began to go abroad to study medicine. By 1906 there were 15,000 Chinese students studying science abroad—13,000 of them in Japan, where the Western scientific curriculum was triumphant. Western doctors, meanwhile, acquired Chinese assistants and took advantage of Chinese interest in Western methods to move to China to practice. Dr. Hume was one of about 100 Western physicians in China in his day. In 1903, the University of Beijing acquired a medical department. Meanwhile, in essays published from 1895 onward, Yan Fu (yen foo) introduced Darwin's theory of evolution to China (see Chapter 25), and 20 or 30 Western scientific books were being translated into Chinese each year, with more reaching China via Japan.

The revolution of 1911, which made China a republic, brought intellectuals indebted to the West for many of their political ideas to power. They proclaimed what they called New Culture, in which science would play a prominent part, to modernize and "save" the country from Western and Japanese competition. In 1914, Chinese students in America met at Cornell University to found the Science Society of China. When they returned home, it became one of the most influential organizations in the country, dedicated to popularizing Western-style science and promoting scientific education. Science as Westerners understood it became part of the general curriculum, as well as the core of professional training. By 1947, for instance, China had 34,600 medical practitioners trained according to Western methods. By 2000, all Chinese physicians had at least some Western-style training.

In China, Western science had to rely chiefly on its inherent appeal. While the Qing had ceded a few small urban areas to foreign custody or control, in most of the country Western power was exercised only indirectly. Westerners had to buy or bribe their way into positions of influence. Yet Western science still exercised an irresistible fascination, even where it could not be forced on people. In parts of the world under direct Western rule the uptake was even greater, for European empires spread Western science. India, for instance, had a colonial government committed to promoting science and a native intelligentsia anxious to learn.

MAP 27.1

Spread of Western Scientific Learning, 1866–1961

NORTH AMERICA
UNITED STATES OF AMERICA
1914 Science Society of China founded by Chinese students at Cornell University
SOUTH AMERICA
Albert Schweizer spea
Western medicine in
West Africa in the e
mid-twentieth c

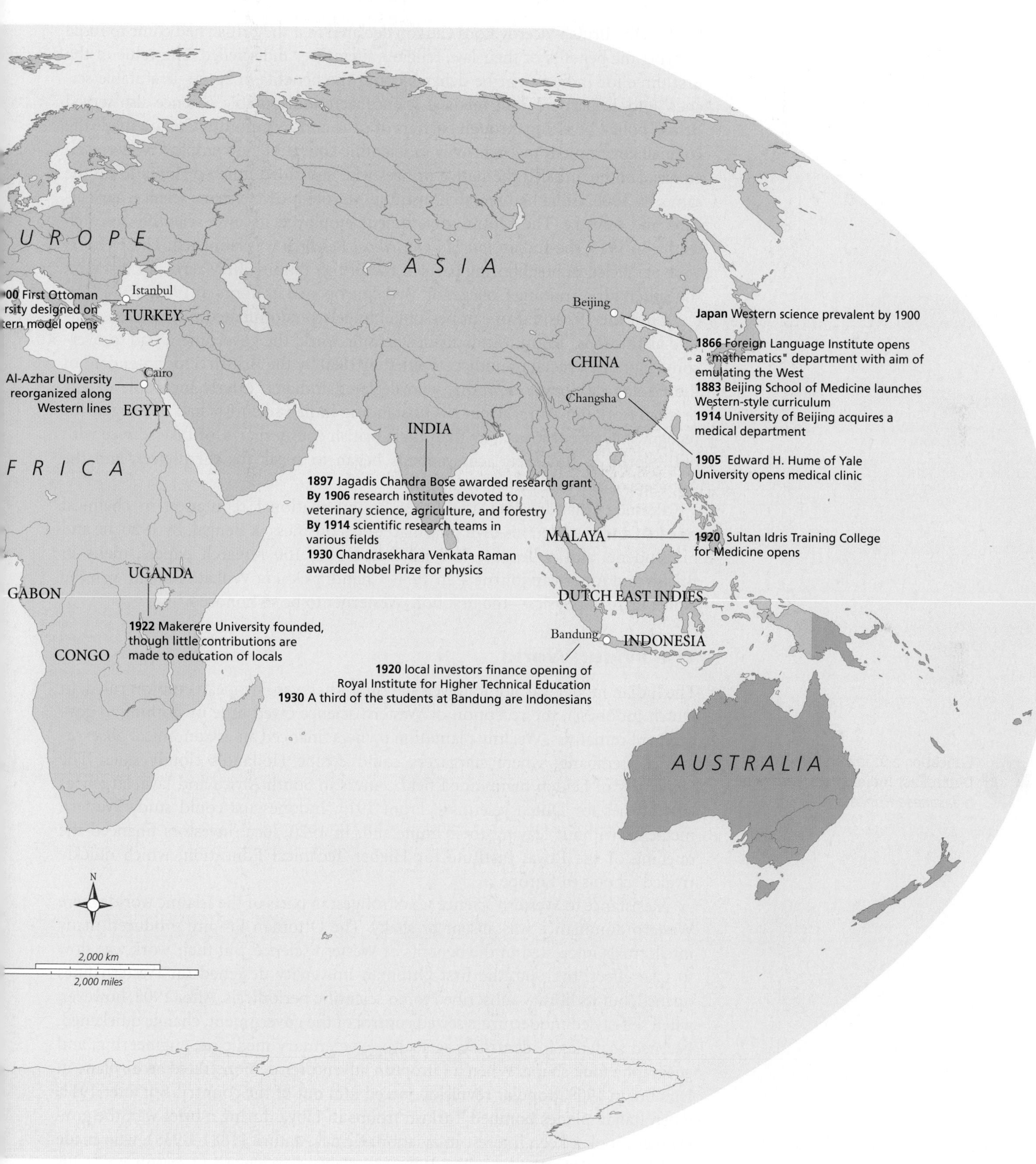
U R O P E
A S I A
00 First Ottoman
rsity designed on
tern model opens
Istanbul
TURKEY
Beijing
Japan Western science prevalent by 1900
1866 Foreign Language Institute opens a "mathematics" department with aim of emulating the West
1883 Beijing School of Medicine launches Western-style curriculum
1914 University of Beijing acquires a medical department
CHINA
Al-Azhar University reorganized along Western lines
Cairo
EGYPT
Changsha
INDIA
1905 Edward H. Hume of Yale University opens medical clinic
F R I C A
1897 Jagadis Chandra Bose awarded research grant
By 1906 research institutes devoted to veterinary science, agriculture, and forestry
By 1914 scientific research teams in various fields
1930 Chandrasekhara Venkata Raman awarded Nobel Prize for physics
MALAYA
1920 Sultan Idris Training College for Medicine opens
UGANDA
GABON
DUTCH EAST INDIES
1922 Makerere University founded, though little contributions are made to education of locals
CONGO
Bandung
INDONESIA
1920 local investors finance opening of Royal Institute for Higher Technical Education
1930 A third of the students at Bandung are Indonesians
AUSTRALIA
N
2,000 km
2,000 miles

India

In 1899, the British viceroy Lord Curzon declared that the British had come to India to bring the benefits of their law, religion, literature, and science. The value of the first three for India might be debatable, but the benefits of "pure, irrefutable science" and, in particular, of medical science were indisputable. Science also served British policy, breaking through barriers of caste and community. Curzon made the colonial government invest heavily in scientific education and employ Western scientists, and he induced the native princes who still ruled much of India to do the same. By 1906, India had research institutes devoted to veterinary science, agriculture, and forestry. The central government employed its own scientific research teams. In 1913, the Indian *Journal of Medical Research* was launched. These efforts were paralleled in neighboring parts of the British Empire. In Malaya, for instance, the Sultan Idris Training College for Medicine opened its doors in 1920.

Until the 1920s, European personnel hugely predominated in the new scientific institutions. To train Indians in scientific work, the government had to overcome ingrained racial prejudice, typified in 1880 by the British Superintendent of the Geological Survey of India, who declared Indians "utterly incapable of any original work in natural science." Outstanding Indian scientists had to struggle for recognition, accept lower pay than their British counterparts, or take service with native princes. But their achievements began to speak for themselves, and the numbers of native scientists multiplied.

Prafulla Chandra Ray established an international reputation in chemical research and founded his own pharmaceutical business in Bengal. By 1920, he and his students and colleagues had published over 100 research papers, many in British and American journals. In 1930, Chandrasekhara Venkata Raman won the Nobel Prize in physics—the first non-Westerner to be so honored.

The Wider World

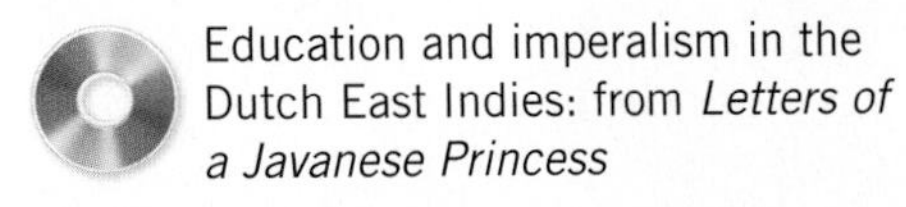
Education and imperalism in the Dutch East Indies: from *Letters of a Javanese Princess*

The Indian model was not followed slavishly wherever European empires ruled. In Dutch Indonesia, the reception of Western science owed little or nothing to government initiatives. Wealthy plantation owners financed an astronomical observatory at Lembang, where stargazers could escape Holland's cloudy skies. The University of Leiden maintained field centers in South Africa and Java, largely as laboratories for Dutch scientists. From 1913, Indonesians could study Western medicine without leaving their homeland. In 1920, local investors financed the opening of the Royal Institute for Higher Technical Education, which quickly rivaled schools in Europe.

Resistance to Western science was strongest in parts of the Islamic world where Western dominance was absent or shaky. The Ottoman Empire produced many intellectuals interested in the benefits of Western science, but their work was slow to take effect. In 1900, the first Ottoman university designed on Western lines opened, but its library subscribed to no scientific periodicals. After 1908, however, when self-styled modernizers seized control of the government, change quickened. Learned societies in dentistry, agriculture, veterinary medicine, engineering, and geography took shape. When a European adventurer demonstrated an airplane in Istanbul in 1909, popular revulsion forced him out of the country. But after 1911, when Italian planes bombed Turkish troops in Libya during a brief war, the government took a keen interest in aviation. Kemal Ataturk (1881–1938), who made Turkey a secular republic in the 1920s, proclaimed "science and reason" to be his legacy.

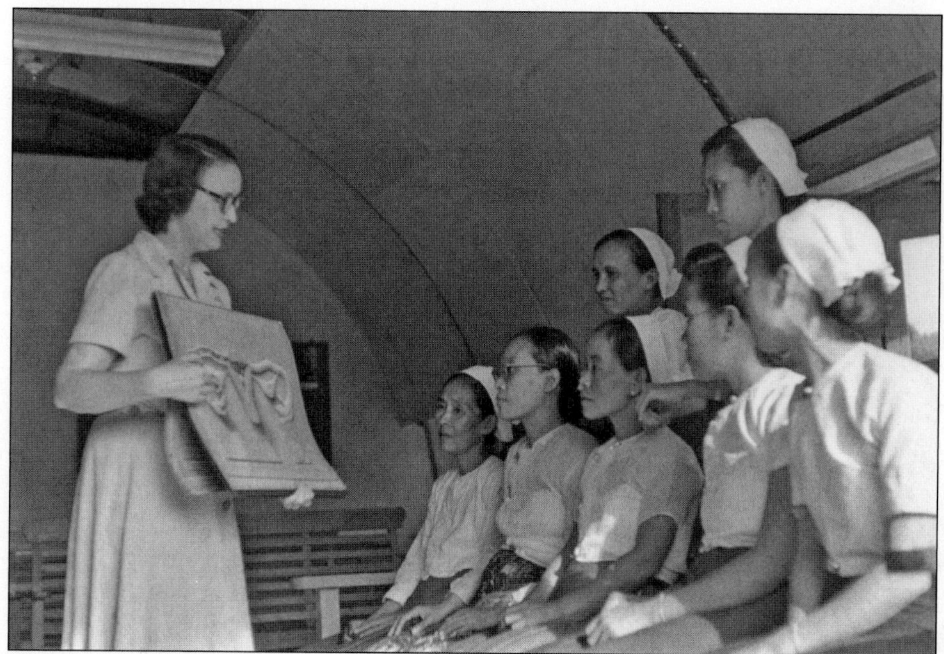

Colonial science. A British midwife instructs Burmese nurses in midwifery in the 1950s. The picture is posed to suggest Western superiority. The students—some older and presumably wiser than their teacher—are in Western-style uniforms, submissively listening to a lesson reinforced by simple diagrams.

On the fringes of the Ottoman Empire, and outside areas of Ottoman control, Muslim modernizers praised science as a proper occupation for a Muslim. One of the most influential modernizers, Jamal al-Dinal-Afghani, denounced religious establishments—Christian and Muslim alike—for hostility to science. The Lebanese Shiite scholar Husayn al-Jisr, who died in 1909, was the first great apologist for Darwin in the Islamic world. The Egyptian Ismail Mazhir (1891–1962) continued his work in a series of translations of Darwin, beginning in the 1920s. Scientific interpretation of the Quran was, at that time, one of the most popular types of literature in the Muslim world.

Al-Afghani on faith and reason

A survey of scientific research in the Middle East, conducted during the Second World War (1939–1945), found only a handful of Muslim scientists to consult. In 1952, a survey in Egypt counted 1,392 individual practitioners of science. By 1973, Egypt had 10,655 scientists. In 1961, the great Muslim educational center of Cairo, known as al-Azhar, was reorganized along the lines of a Western university. Similar changes were under way throughout the Arab world. Over the following two decades, at least 6 million Arabs studied Western-style science at universities.

In sub-Saharan Africa, meanwhile, Western science spread more slowly and selectively. While European empires lasted, racist assumptions inhibited colonial authorities from training African scientific elites. For most of the first half of the century, therefore, black Africans were the passive recipients of Western science, especially of medicine. Albert Schweizer (1875–1965), a Swiss theologian and doctor who devoted himself to the care of the sick in French West Africa for nearly 30 years, typified the spirit of the medical missionary, transforming the life expectancy of his patients not so much by his medical skill, which was never advanced, as by his efficient hospital buildings, emphasis on hygiene, and ability to dispense Western medicine. Thousands of idealistic Westerners followed similar vocations. From the 1930s until the 1980s, new pharmaceuticals, which were invented at a dizzying pace, slashed death rates and helped bring a population explosion to Africa. Medicine everywhere was the banner bearer of Western science.

THE TRANSFORMATION OF WESTERN SCIENCE

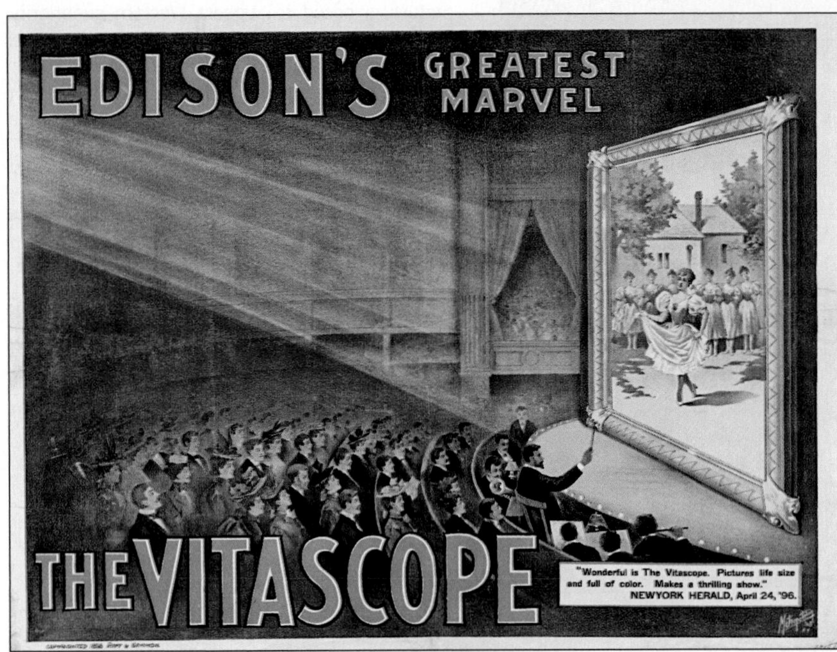

The vitascope was an early device for projecting cinematic images, displayed here showing the ballet *Giselle* in an advertisement of 1896. The gilt frame, prominent orchestra, and choice of theme all evoke the marketing context: a tasteful art form for the middle class.

Even while it achieved enormous influence and registered enormous effects across the world, conflicts changed Western science from within. Conventionally, historians represent the first decade or so of the twentieth century as a spell of inertia, a golden afterglow of the romantic age, which the real agent of change, the First World War, would turn blood red. But even before the war broke out in 1914, the worlds of thought and feeling were already alive with new colors. Technology hurtled into a new phase. The twentieth century would be an electric age, much as the nineteenth had been an age of steam. In 1901, Guglielmo Marconi broadcast by wireless radio across the Atlantic. In 1903, the Wright brothers took flight in North Carolina. Plastic was invented in 1907. The curiosities of late-nineteenth-century inventiveness, such as the telephone, the car, and the typewriter, all became commonplace. Other essentials of technologically fulfilled twentieth-century lives—the atom smasher, the steel–concrete skyscraper frame, even the hamburger—were all in place before 1914.

On the other hand, when the century opened, the scientific world was in a state of self-questioning, confused by rogue results. In the 1890s, X-rays and electrons were discovered or posited, while puzzling anomalies became observable in the behavior of light. In 1902, Henri Poincaré questioned the basic assumption of scientific method: the link between hypothesis and evidence. Any number of hypotheses, he said, could fit the results of experiments. Scientists chose among them by convention—or even according to "the idiosyncrasies of the individual." He compared the physicist to "an embarrassed theologian, ... chained" to contradictory propositions. Science usually affects society less by what it does or says than by how it is misunderstood. Readers misinterpreted Poincaré to mean that science could not disclose truths.

Physics

Thanks to the way Poincaré shook up perceptions, people became more willing to listen to radical theories. In 1905, Albert Einstein (1879–1955) emerged from obscurity to explode most educated people's image of the cosmos. According to traditional physics, the speed of a body ought to affect the speed of the light it reflects or projects, rather as a ball gains speed from the vigor with which it is thrown. Yet experimental data seemed to show that the speed of light never varied. Most people assumed an error in the measurements. Einstein proposed, instead, that the invariability of the speed of light was a scientific law and that the apparent effects of motion on speed were illusions. Rather, time and space change with motion. Mass increases with velocity, whereas time slows down.

Einstein's work broke on the world with the shock of genius: the sensation of seeing something obvious that no one had ever noticed before. The implications of a cosmos in which time was unfixed took getting used to. In Einstein's universe, mass and energy could be changed into each other. Twins aged at different rates.

Parallel lines met. The curvature of the trajectory of light literally warped the universe. Scientists hungered for an explanation that would resolve the apparent contradictions. Nonscientists were confused. "The spirit of unrest," the *New York Times* said in 1919, "invaded science."

While Einstein proposed a restructured universe, other scientists repictured the tiniest particles, or *quanta* of which the universe is composed. Ernest Rutherford's work in 1911 proved that atoms consist of masses and electric charges, including a *nucleus* surrounded by *electrons*. The basic structure of matter, it seemed, was being laid bare. But ever smaller particles, ever more elusive charges continued to come to light. Between 1911 and 1913, work on atomic structures revealed that electrons appear to slide erratically between orbits around a nucleus. Findings that followed from the attempt to track the untrappable particles of subatomic matter were expressed in a new field of study called **quantum mechanics.**

The terms of this new science were paradoxical—like those employed by Niels Bohr (1885–1962), who described light as consisting, simultaneously, of both waves and particles. By the mid-1920s, more contradictions piled up. When the motion of subatomic particles was plotted, their positions seemed irreconcilable with their momentum. They seemed to move at rates different from their measurable speed and to end up where it was impossible for them to be. Working in collaborative tension, Bohr and Werner Heisenberg (1901–1976) proposed a principle they called uncertainty or indeterminacy. Their debate provoked a revolution in thought. Interpreters made a reasonable inference—observers are part of every observation, and their findings can never be objective.

Major Inventions, 1850–1914

1852	Gyroscope
1853	Passenger elevator
1856	Celluloid
	Bessemer converter
	Bunsen burner
1858	Refrigerator
	Washing machine
1859	Internal combustion engine
1862	Rapid-fire gun
1866	Dynamite
1876	Telephone
1877	Phonograph
1879	Incandescent lamp
1885	Motorcycle
	Electric transformer
	Vacuum flask
1887	Motorcar engine
1888	Pneumatic tire
	Kodak camera
1895	Wireless radio
	X-rays
1897	Diesel engine
1902	Radio-telephone
1903	Airplane
1911	Combine harvester

This was of enormous importance because other scholars—historians, anthropologists, sociologists, linguists, and even students of literature—were seeking to class their own work as scientific, precisely because they wanted to escape from subjectivity. It turned out that what they had in common with scientists, strictly so-called, was the opposite of what they had hoped—they were all implicated in their own findings.

Maybe it was still possible to pick a way back to certainty by following mathematics and logic. These systems, at least, seemed infallible, and they guaranteed each other. Mathematics was reliable because it was logical and logical because it was mathematical—or so people thought, until 1931, when Kurt Gödel severed mathematics from logic and showed that both systems, ultimately, must yield contradictory results.

Werner Heisenberg, "Uncertainty," 1927

Gödel inspired an unintended effect. He thought, like earlier philosophers, that we can reliably grasp numbers, but he helped make others doubt it. He believed that numbers really exist, objectively, independently of thought, but he provided encouragement to skeptics who dismissed them as merely conventional. The effect of Gödel's demonstrations on the way the world thinks, was comparable to that of termites in a ship that the passengers had thought was watertight. If mathematics and logic leaked, science would sink.

Meanwhile, practical discoveries and empirical observations upset the old picture of the cosmos. In 1929, thanks to a powerful telescope operated by Edwin Hubble, the universe was found to be expanding. It seemed so strange a finding that some physicists sought to explain it away for 50 years. By the 1970s, however,

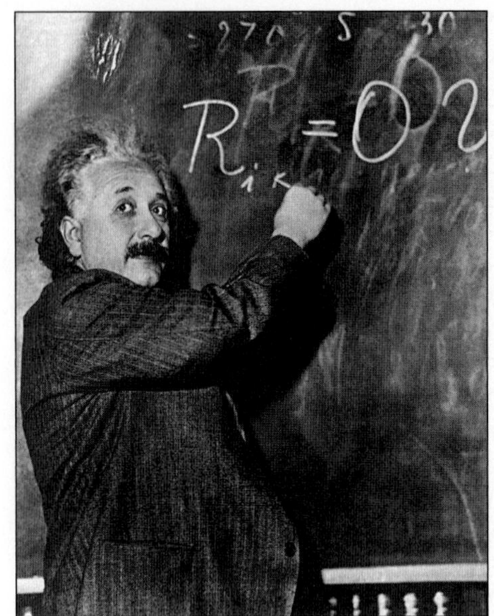

Theoretical physicist Albert Einstein writes an equation on a blackboard while turning to his audience at the California Institute of Technology, ca. 1931. Einstein's distinctive looks—the ever-alert eyes, the deliberately disordered hair—became the universal image of a "typical," perhaps ideal, scientist.

most cosmologists took the view that expansion started with a **big bang,** an explosion of almost infinitesimally compressed matter that is still going on. For some interpreters, this was evidence of divine creation, or a description of how God did it. For others, it was a naturalistic explanation of change in the universe that made divine intervention an unnecessary hypothesis.

Contributions later in the century only seemed to put more space between science and certainty. In 1960, Thomas Kuhn argued that scientific revolutions were the result not of new discoveries about reality but of what he called paradigm shifts, changing ways of looking at the world, and new ways of expressing them. Most people drew an inference Kuhn repudiated—that the findings of science depended not on the objective facts but on the mind-set of the inquirer.

In the 1980s, **chaos theory** made the world seem hopelessly unpredictable. The idea emerged in meteorology as a result of the dawning awareness that weather systems are so complex that, ultimately, causes and effects are untraceable. A butterfly flapping its wings, according to a popular way to sum up the theory, can work up a storm. There is still, according to this way of thinking, some deep order in nature, some chain of cause and effect in which the whole of experience is linked—but we cannot see it whole.

Throughout these shake-ups, workers in theoretical physics never abandoned the search for a comprehensive way to explain the cosmos—a "theory of everything" that would resolve the contradictions of relativity theory and quantum mechanics. The way matter behaves—at least, the way it behaves when we observe it—is riddled with paradoxes that subtle thinking has to reconcile. By 2000, cosmologists were proposing terms for understanding the universe that described nothing anyone had ever experienced or could easily imagine: infinite dimensions, superstrings, supersymmetry, supergravity. No experiment validated any of these models of how the universe is structured.

Human Sciences

In some respects science did deliver measurable progress. Medicine registered spectacular advances. Doctors could control diseases ever more effectively by imitating the body's natural hormones and adjusting their balance. In 1922, they isolated insulin, which controls diabetes. Since the discovery of penicillin in 1931, doctors used *antibiotics* to kill microorganisms that cause disease. Inoculation programs and health education gradually became available almost everywhere.

Other advances in biology challenged people to rethink human nature. In 1925, in Tennessee, in the Scopes "monkey" trial an American court upheld the right of school boards to ban Darwin from the curriculum, on the grounds that evolution was incompatible with the Bible. Belief in creation and belief in evolution are not necessarily contradictory. Evolution, which is the most convincing description we have of how and why species change, could, to a religious mind, be part of God's creation and plan. But people on both sides of the debate kept picking fights with one another. Evolution became more controversial as its proponents' claims became more strident. Some late twentieth-century Darwinians claimed to have found an evolutionary explanation for morality, for instance, and even to be able to explain cultural change in evolutionary terms. These claims got headlines but left most people unconvinced.

While disputes about evolution rumbled, the new science of genetics posed even more searching problems. Beginning in 1908, T. H. Morgan at Columbia University demonstrated how genes transmit some characteristics. In 1944, Erwin

Schrödinger predicted that a gene would resemble a chain of basic units, connected like the elements of a code. A few years later, scientists in England built up the picture of what DNA (deoxyribonucleic acid) was really like. It soon emerged that genes in individual genetic codes were responsible for some diseases and perhaps for behavior that changing the code could regulate. The codes of other species could be modified to obtain results that suit humans: producing bigger plant foods, for instance, or animals designed to be more beneficial.

This discovery shed new light on an old controversy—the **nature versus nurture** debate. On one side are those who believe that "social engineering" cannot improve character and capability, which inherited genes determine. Their opponents believe that experience—nurture—produces these qualities and that social change can, therefore, improve us. Genetic research seemed to confirm that we inherit more of our makeup than we have traditionally supposed. Meanwhile, sociobiology, a new synthesis devised by Edward O. Wilson, created a scientific constituency for the theory that evolutionary necessities determine differences between societies and that we can rank societies accordingly. Two fundamental convictions survived in most people's minds: that individuals make themselves, and that society is worth improving. Nevertheless, genes seemed to limit our freedom. Genetic and sociobiological claims inhibited reform and encouraged a mood we shall examine in the next two chapters: the prevailing conservatism of the late twentieth and early twenty-first centuries.

By the 1990s, genetically modified plants promised to solve the world's food-supply problems. The potentially adverse economic and ecological consequences, as we shall see in Chapter 30, evoked a chorus of protest. Modification of human genes promised to eliminate genetically transmitted disease and enable infertile couples to have children. But it posed terrifying moral questions, best illustrated by the controversy over cloning of human embryos. This meant breeding human embryos to extract useful cells from them. A woman could produce as many embryos as she might wish and pick the specimens she most preferred. The rest would have to be discarded. In effect, this meant destroying human beings, since embryos, whatever their status in other respects, are human.

Less morally troubling methods of treatment would soon replace cloning to deal with infertility and treat inherited disease. But the prospect of "designer babies" selected for particular features of character or appearance was even more troubling. Children might be engineered with fashionable looks or exploitable talents, or along the lines once prescribed by eugenics—improving the human species through controlled breeding. Governments could legislate supposedly undesirable personality genes out of existence. States could enforce normality at the expense, for instance, of genes supposed to dispose people to be criminal or homosexual or just uncooperative. Morally dubious visionaries foresaw societies without disease or deviancy. In a world recrafted, as if by Frankenstein, humans could now make their biggest intervention in evolution yet: selecting according to what they happen to want at the moment. In 1995, a coalition of self-styled religious leaders in the United States signed a declaration opposing the patenting of genes on the grounds that they were the property of their real creator: God. The World Health Organization, UNESCO, and the European Parliament all condemned human cloning as unethical. Many countries banned it.

Meanwhile, the genetic revolution nudged people toward a materialist understanding of human nature. It became harder to find room for nonmaterial ingredients, such as mind and soul. Neurological research showed that thought is an

The Electronic Numerical Integrator and Computer. One of the first electronic digital computers in the United States was commissioned by the U.S. Army and installed, at first, at the University of Pennsylvania in Philadelphia. The choice of female programmers was presumably dictated by the public relations objectives of this photograph.

electrochemical process in which synapses fire and proteins are released. These results made it possible to claim that everything traditionally classed as a function of mind might take place within the brain.

Artificial intelligence (AI) research reinforced this claim—or tried to—with a new version of an old hope or fear: that minds may be mechanical. Pablo Picasso (1881–1973) painted a machine in love in 1917. In the second half of the century, computers proved so dextrous, first in making calculations, then in responding to their environments, that they seemed capable of settling the debate over whether mind was different from brain. But people on either side were really talking about different things. Proponents of AI were not concerned with building machines with creative, artistic imaginations, or with intuitive properties, or with the ability to feel love or hatred—qualities that opponents of AI valued as indicators of a truly human mind.

Meanwhile, primatology and paleoanthropology also challenged human self-perception. Paleoanthropologists discovered, among remains of humans' nonhuman ancestors and related primates, features formerly thought unique to *Homo sapiens*. Neanderthal burials demonstrated that Neanderthals had ritual lives and moral practices, including care of the elderly and reverence for the dead. This evidence proved that nonhuman species have existed who were morally indistinguishable from human beings. The question was important because, as we shall see in Chapter 29, it emerged at a time when the notion of **human rights** became current—a notion based in part on the assumption that being human constitutes a meaningful moral category that excludes nonhumans.

Animal rights movements challenged that assumption. So did improved knowledge of apes and monkeys. First, scientists working with macaque monkeys in Japan realized that these creatures, though modestly endowed with brains, have culture. They can learn and transmit what they learn across generations. The breakthrough discovery came in 1952, when a monkey was observed teaching her community how to wash the dirt off sweet potatoes. The tribe took up the technique and continued to practice it, even when supplied with ready-washed potatoes, showing that washing had become a cultural rite, not a practical measure.

In subsequent decades, primatologists, led by Jane Goodall, found that chimpanzees have, albeit to a much smaller extent than humans, all the features of culture that were formerly thought to be peculiarly human, including toolmaking, language, war, rules for distributing food, and political habits. Further studies of other social animals—beginning with other great apes, such as gorillas and orangutans—showed similar results, suggesting that culture is only uniquely human as a matter of degree. Many observations and experiments cast doubt on the belief that humans have unique cognitive properties. Apes, for example, proved to be self-aware and showed sensibilities hard to distinguish in practice from the senses of morality and transcendence formerly thought to be human peculiarities. By the end of the twentieth century, some ethicists were campaigning for animal rights or for redefining the moral community to embrace great apes.

The discoveries of primatologists and comparative zoologists belonged in a broader context of scientific change: the rise of ecology, the study of the interconnectedness of all life and its interdependence with the physical environment. Ecologists' exposure of a vast range of new practical problems arising from human overexploitation of the environment became a major influence in the late twentieth century. We discuss them in Chapter 30.

Anthropology and Psychology

In anthropology, as in science, the early twentieth century was decisive. Among the West's supposedly scientific certainties was that some peoples and societies were evolutionarily superior to others: an image of the world stacked in order of race. Westerners used this picture to justify their rule over other peoples (see Chapter 25). But Franz Boas (1858–1942) showed that no race was superior to any other in brainpower. Societies could not be ranked in terms of a developmental model of thought. People, he concluded, think differently in different cultures not because some have superior mental equipment but because thought reflects the traditions to which it is heir, the society that surrounds it, and the environment in which it exists. Fieldwork piled up data to bury the crude hierarchical schemes of the nineteenth century.

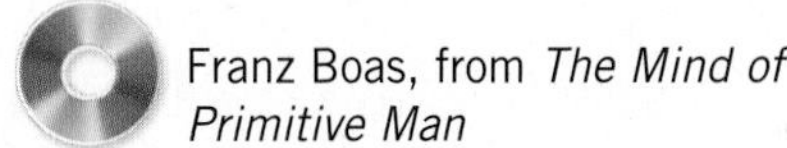
Franz Boas, from *The Mind of Primitive Man*

The result was **cultural relativism**: the doctrine that we cannot rank cultures in order of merit but must judge each on its own terms. As we shall see in Chapter 30, this proved problematic. Should cannibals be judged on their own terms? Or cultures that licensed slavery or the subjection of women? Or those that practiced infanticide, head-hunting, or other abominations? Or even those that condoned milder offenses against values the West cherished—such as torture or female circumcision? Cultural relativism had to have limits, but anthropology compelled educated people to examine their prejudices and question their own convictions of superiority. "Primitive cultures" and "advanced civilizations" came to be labeled "elementary structures" and "complex structures." The long-standing justification for Western imperialism—the civilizing mission—lapsed, because conquerors could no longer feel enough self-confidence to impose their own standards of civilization on their victims.

Psychology was even more subversive than anthropology, because it challenged the notions individuals had about themselves. In particular, the claim, first advanced by Sigmund Freud (1856–1939), that much human motivation is subconscious, challenged traditional notions about responsibility, identity, personality, conscience, and mentality. In 1896, Freud exposed his own *Oedipus complex*, as he called it: a supposed, suppressed desire—that he believed all male children had—to supplant his father. In succeeding years, he developed a technique he called **psychoanalysis** to make patients aware of their subconscious desires. Hypnosis or, as Freud preferred, free association could retrieve repressed feelings and ease nervous symptoms. Many patients who rose from his couch walked more freely than before.

Freud seemed able to illuminate the human condition. He claimed that every child experienced before puberty the same phases of sexual development. Every adult repressed similar fantasies or experiences. Women who previously would have been dismissed as hysterical malingerers became, in Freud's work, case studies from whose example almost everyone could learn. This contributed to the reevaluation of women's role in society (see Chapter 29). Freud's science, however, failed to pass the most rigorous tests. When Karl Popper asked how to distinguish someone who did not have an Oedipus complex from someone who did, the psychoanalytic fraternity had no answer. Nevertheless, for some patients, psychoanalysis worked.

Veterans of twentieth-century wars became patients of psychiatry. The nightmares of trench survivors in the First World War (see Chapter 28) were too hideous to share with loved ones. The guilt of those who missed the war echoed the shell-shock of those who fought it. Introspection—formerly regarded as self-indulgence—became routine in the West. Repression became the modern demon and the analyst an exorcist. The "feel-good society," which bans guilt, shame, self-doubt, and self-reproach, was among the results. So was sexual candor. So was the fashion of treating metabolic or chemical imbalances in the brain as if they were deep-rooted mental disorders. The good and evil that flowed from Freud's theory are nicely balanced and objectively incalculable. Psychoanalysis and other schools of therapy helped millions and tortured millions—releasing some people from repressions, condemning others to illusions or futile treatments.

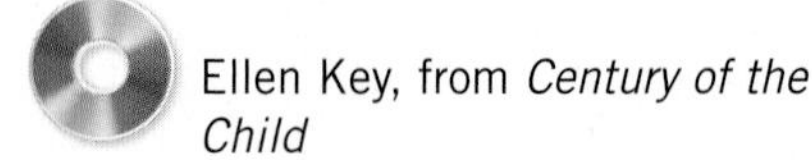

The most profound influence psychology exercised was not, however, on the treatment of mental disorder but on how children were raised. In 1909, the feminist Ellen Key proclaimed the rediscovery of childhood. Children were different from adults. This was, in effect, a summary of the idea of childhood as it had developed in the nineteenth-century West (see Chapter 24). It was, perhaps, a valid observation. But it had questionable consequences. Children who were not treated as adults in childhood "never grew up," like the tragic hero of J. M. Barrie's play of 1911, *Peter Pan*, who withdrew into Neverland. Generations raised on the assumption that they could not face adult realities found themselves deprived of truths about their own lives and became fodder for the new therapies of psychiatry. Generational "hang-ups" became a new curse for Western children. People outside the West, where the new image of childhood arrived patchily and late, had fewer such troubles.

In the West, better treatment for childhood disease enabled more children to lead longer lives. So children became more suitable objects in whom to invest time, emotion, and study. Working on Freud's insights, educational psychologists in the West built up a picture of mental development in predictable, universal stages. School curricula changed in the 1950s and 1960s to match the supposed patterns of childhood development. Schoolchildren were deprived of challenging tasks because child psychology said they were incapable of them. While formal education got longer and longer, most children emerged from it with no experience of traditional elements of the curriculum that were now thought unsuitably difficult, such as calculus, foreign languages, sophisticated vocabulary, ancient authors, even grammar. Other developments, which belong in Chapter 29, stimulated this trend, including the economic changes that made vocational qualifications seem disproportionately important in education and the social pressures that made for "dumbing down."

Philosophy and Linguistics

To scientific uncertainty and cultural relativism, the opening decade of the century added philosophical unease. In combination with Einstein's disquieting revelations about the nature of time, the theories of Henri Bergson (1859–1941) proved both unsettling and inspiring. He formulated a concept he called "duration"—the new sense of time we get when consciousness "abstains from establishing a separation between present states and the preceding states." This difficult idea fortified educated people's faith in free will. Time is not a constraint that nature imposes on us, but a concept that we impose on nature. Bergson coined the term *élan vital* to express the freedom we retain to make a future different from the one that science predicts—a spiritual force with the power to reorder matter. Time, the way Bergson saw it, became not a sequence of atomized events, but a product of memory, which is different from perception and, therefore, "a power independent of matter."

Bergson's thinking infuriated scientists and inspired artists. Novels written in the **stream of consciousness** were among the results. He argued that evolution was not a scientific law but an expression of the creative will of living entities, which change because they want to change. Critics accused Bergson of irrationalism on the grounds that he was attacking science and representing objective realities as purely mental concepts. Indeed, consistent with his principles, he never tried to demonstrate the validity of his ideas by logical exposition or scientific evidence. This did not diminish their attractiveness or their effectiveness in liberating people who felt inhibited by the supposedly scientific determinism of the early twentieth century. Bergson reassured those who doubted whether, for example, history really led inevitably to the revolutions Marx predicted, or to the white supremacy "scientific" racism preached, or to the destruction the laws of thermodynamics predicted. Nature was unorganized. The chaos that made scientific minds despair offered hope to Bergson's readers.

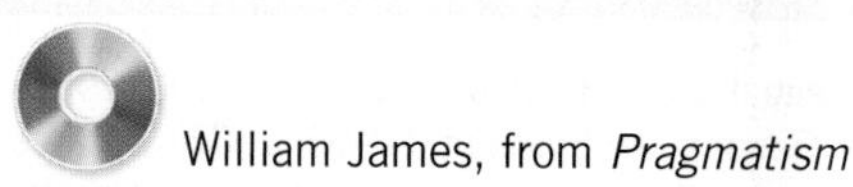
William James, from *Pragmatism*

Bergson's followers hailed him as the philosopher for the twentieth century. His first great rival for that status was William James (1842–1910). James wanted a distinctively American philosophy, reflecting the values of business and hustle. Seeking to make people share his belief in God, he argued in1907 that "if the hypothesis of God works satisfactorily in the widest sense of the word, it is true." He called this doctrine **pragmatism.** But what one individual or group finds useful, another may find useless. James's claim that truth is not what is real but is whatever serves a particular purpose was one of the most subversive claims a philosopher ever made. James had set out as an apologist for Christianity, but by relativizing truth, he undermined it.

Linguistics produced similar doubts about the reality of truth and whether language could express it. Ferdinand de Saussure's lectures, published by his students after his death in 1913, contained a revolutionary idea: the distinction between social speech, the *parole* addressed to others, and subjective language, the *langue* known only to thought. Saussure seemed to say of language what Poincaré seemed to say of science—any language we use refers only to itself and cannot disclose remoter realities.

Mainstream philosophers were reluctant to pursue the implications of this idea. The dominant philosophy of the 1920s and 1930s, the years between the First and Second World Wars, was *positivism*, which asserted that what the human

Final passage from *Ulysses* (1922) by James Joyce, perhaps the most famous stream of consciousness novel in the twentieth centary.

. . . serene with his lamp and O that awful deepdown torrent O and the sea the sea crimson sometimes like fire and the glorious sunsets and the figtrees in the Alameda gardens yes and all the queer little streets and pink and blue and yellow houses and the rosegardens and the jessamine and geraniums and cactuses and Gibraltar as a girl where I was a Flower of the mountain yes when I put the rose in my hair like the Andalusian girls used or shall I wear a red yes and how he kissed me under the Moorish wall and I thought well as well him as another and then I asked him with my eyes to ask again yes and then he asked me would I yes to say yes my mountain flower and first I put my arms around him yes and drew him down to me so he could feel my breasts all perfume yes and his heart was going like mad and yes I said yes I will Yes.

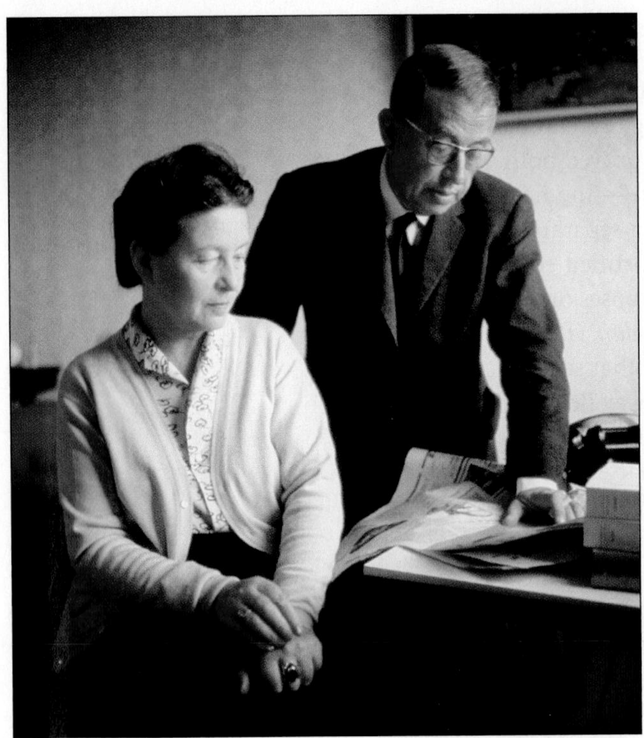

Existentialists. Jean-Paul Sartre (1905–1980) and Simone de Beauvoir (1908–1986) became icons of radicalism—she for her feminist classic, *The Second Sex,* he for the influence of his philosophy on postwar Western youth. At home in Paris, however, they seem like a model middle-class couple, stiffly sharing a newspaper in their underdecorated apartment.

senses perceived was real and that reason could prove that what our senses perceive is true. But developments in science and logic were undermining such confidence. In 1953, in *Philosophical Investigations,* Ludwig Wittgenstein argued that we understand language not because it corresponds to reality but because it obeys rules of usage. Therefore, we do not necessarily know what language refers to, except its own terms.

Equally disturbing, because of what it implied about human nature, was the work Noam Chomsky published in 1957. Chomsky was impressed at how easily children learn speech. They can, in particular, combine words in ways they have never actually heard. He also found it remarkable that the differences between languages appear superficial compared with the "deep structures"—the parts of speech, the relationships between terms that we call *grammar* and *syntax*—that are common to all of them. Chomsky suggested a link between the structures of language and the brain. We learn languages fast because their structure is already part of how we think. This suggestion was revolutionary. Experience and heredity, nurture and nature, it implied, do not make us the whole of what we are. Part of our nature is hardwired and unchangeable. As Chomsky saw it, at least at first, this "language instinct" or "language faculty" was untouchable—and, therefore, perhaps not produced—by evolution. Chomsky's views resonated in minds worried about the problems of using language and science to access reality.

Chomsky also argued that our language prowess, which some people claim is a uniquely human achievement, is like the special skills of other species: that of cheetahs in speed, for instance. "It is the richness and specificity of instinct of animals," he said, "that accounts for their remarkable achievements in some domains and lack of ability in others, so the argument runs, whereas humans, lacking such . . . instinctual structure, are free to think, speak and discover. ... Both the logic of the problem and what we are now coming to understand suggest that this is not the correct way to identify the position of humans in the world." This chimed in with the disarming discoveries of primatology and paleoanthropology.[1]

By the time Chomsky entered the academic arena, unease and pessimism were rampant, especially in Europe and parts of Asia, where the destruction of the Second World War had been most keenly felt. The most widely accepted response to the war had emerged from a group of German philosophers known as the Frankfurt School. They defined what they called alienation as the central problem of modern society. Economic rivalries and short-sighted materialism divided individuals and wrecked common pursuits. People felt dissatisfied and rootless. Martin Heidegger proposed a strategy to cope with this. We should accept our existence between conception and death as the only unchangeable thing about us and tackle life as a project of self-realization, of "becoming"—who we are changes as the project unfolds. This **existentialism** represented the retreat of intellectuals into the security of self-contemplation in revulsion from an ugly world.

Heidegger was discredited because he collaborated with the Nazis. In France, however, Jean-Paul Sartre (1905–1980) relaunched existentialism as a creed for the postwar era. "Man," he said, "is ... nothing else but what he makes of himself." For Sartre, self-modeling was more than an individual responsibility. Every individual action is an exemplary act, a statement about humankind, about the sort of species you want to belong to. Yet there is no objective way to put meaning into such a statement. God does not exist. Everything is permissible, and "as a result man is forlorn, without anything to cling to." "There is," he wrote, "no explaining things away by reference to a fixed ... human nature. In other words, there is no determinism, man is free, man is freedom."

In the 1950s and 1960s, Sartre's version of existentialism was used to justify every form of self-indulgence. Sexual promiscuity, revolutionary violence, indifference to manners, defiance of the law, and drug abuse could all be part of becoming oneself. The 1960s, to which we shall return in Chapter 29, would have been unthinkable without existentialism: beat culture and permissiveness—ways of life millions adopted or imitated—as well, perhaps, as the late twentieth-century's libertarian reaction against social planning. Existentialism was, briefly, the philosophical consensus of the West. But it never caught on in the rest of the world, and Westerners who saw more urgent problems than shaping one's personal future detested it. By the 1970s, a global reaction was in the making: conservative in politics, mistrustful of materialism, inclined to religion, anxious to recover tradition and rebuild social solidarity—especially through the family. It was particularly powerful in the Americas, while in Asia and Africa, revulsion from Western-dominated thinking strengthened the trend.

The Diffusion and Transformation of Western Science

1842–1910	William James, American philosopher, developed the doctrine of pragmatism
1856–1939	Sigmund Freud, developer of psychoanalysis
1860s	China's "self-strengthening" program begins
1875–1965	Albert Schweizer, medical missionary to Africa
1879–1955	Albert Einstein, developer of the theory of relativity
1881–1938	Kemal Ataturk, founder of modern Turkey and proponent of secularism and Western science
1883	Western-style curriculum at Beijing School of Medicine
1885–1962	Niels Bohr, won Nobel Prize in 1922 for work on the structure of the atom
1891–1962	Ismail Mazhir, translator of Charles Darwin's work into Arabic
1901–1976	Werner Heisenberg, developed uncertainty principle
1902	Henri Poincaré questions the link between hypothesis and evidence
1903	Powered flight
1905–1980	Jean-Paul Sartre, French philosopher associated with existentialism
1907	Plastic invented
1912	Overthrow of the Qing dynasty increases pace of Westernization in China
1913	Indian *Journal of Medical Research* launched
1914	Science Society of China founded by Chinese students at Cornell University
1920	Royal Institute for Higher Technical Education founded in Indonesia
1931	Penicillin discovered
1944	Erwin Schrödinger predicts structure of the gene
1953	Ludwig Wittgenstein's *Philosophical Investigations* and Simone de Beauvoir's *The Second Sex* published

THE MIRROR OF SCIENCE: ART

Never more than in the twentieth century, artists represented the world not as they saw it directly but as science and philosophy displayed it for their inspection. The revolutions of twentieth-century art exactly match the jolts and shocks science and philosophy administered.

In 1909, Emilio Filippo Marinetti (1876–1944) proclaimed what he called **futurism.** At the time, most artists professed modernism: the doctrine that the new was superior to the old. Marinetti believed that what was traditional had not only to be surpassed but also repudiated and wrecked. He rejected coherence, harmony, freedom, conventional morals, and conventional language because they were familiar. Comfort was artistically sterile. Instead, futurism glorified war, power, chaos, and destruction, which would shove humankind into novelty. Marinetti and his followers celebrated the beauty of machines, the morals of might, and the syntax of babble. Sensitivity, kindness, and fragility were old-fashioned. Futurists preferred ruthlessness, candor, strength.

Painters inspired by Marinetti's lectures painted "lines of force"—symbols of coercion. The excitement of speed—attained by the new internal combustion engine—represented for Marinetti the spirit of the age, speeding away from the past. His movement united adherents of the most radical politics of the twentieth century: fascists, for whom the state should serve the strong, and communists, who hoped to incinerate tradition in revolution. They hated each other. But they agreed that the function of progress was to destroy the past.

Emilio Filippo Marinetti, "Futurist Manifesto"

Marinetti seems prophetic. The deepening destructiveness of wars and the quickening power of machines did indeed dominate the future. The speeding machines turned the world into a global village where every place was within, at most, a few hours' travel of every other place, and where information was accessible

MAKING CONNECTIONS

TRANSFORMATIONS OF WESTERN SCIENCE AND THOUGHT IN THE TWENTIETH CENTURY

DISCIPLINE →	NEW THEORIES →	EFFECTS ON SOCIETY
Physics/Mathematics	Henri Poincaré: notes the elastic connection between hypothesis and evidence and how multiple hypotheses can fit results of experiments Albert Einstein: proposes and proves speed of light is a constant and time and space change with motion (theory of relativity) Ernest Rutherford: establishes basis of subatomic world Niels Bohr: light described as both waves and particles; links to Heisenberg's indeterminacy principle (uncertainty principle)	By mid–twentieth century, physics helped unleash the power of charged subatomic particles in practical technology including weapons (atomic bombs), communications (transistors, microprocessors, integrated circuits) The "new physics" also revolutionizes astronomy, chemistry, other physical sciences
Astronomy	Edwin Hubble: with large-scale telescopes, discovers that universe is expanding Development of radio telescopes, infrared and other means of examining distant stars	Combined with the "new physics" and jet propulsion, astronomical findings set the stage for exploration of solar system; they also challenge or confirm religious beliefs depending on religious standpoint; also raise new possibilities of extraterrestrial life
Biology	T. H. Morgan: demonstrates that genetic transmission influences physical characteristics Neuroscience demonstrates how mental functions operate within the brain	Advances in human biology lead to medical developments: controlling infections through use of antibiotics; controlling diabetes and developing large-scale preventive medical programs (inoculations, health education)

everywhere, instantly. The machines also achieved dazzling power to destroy. Toward midcentury, people devised massive gas chambers and incinerators that killed millions and disposed of their bodies economically and efficiently. Bombs obliterated thousands at a time and spread deadly radiation capable of killing millions more.

Other artists, meanwhile, preferred a vision that atomic theory suggested of an elusive, ill-ordered, uncontrollable world. In 1907, an artistic style called **cubism** began to hold up to the world images of itself reflected as if in a distorting mirror, shivered into fragments. Pablo Picasso and Georges Braque, the originators of the movement, denied they had ever heard of Einstein. But scientific vulgarizations reached them through the press. As painters of an elusive reality from many different perspectives, they were reflecting the science and philosophy of their decade. Marcel Duchamp (1887–1968) tried to represent Einstein's world. He called his painting *Nude Descending a Staircase,* of 1912, an expression of "time and space through the abstract presentation of motion." His notes on his sculpture *Large Glass* revealed how closely he had studied relativity. Meanwhile, in 1911, Vasily Kandinsky (1866–1944) had read Rutherford's description of the atom "with frightful force, as if the end of the world had come." After that, his paintings suppressed every reminder of real objects. The tradition he launched of entirely "abstract" art, which depicted objects unrecognizably or not at all, became dominant for most of the century. The new rhythmic beat of jazz and the noises of atonal music, developed in

DISCIPLINE →	NEW THEORIES →	EFFECTS ON SOCIETY
Genetics	Search for genetic codes begins in 1944, to establish basic building blocks of life in the 1950s, DNA is discovered and awareness follows that genetic codes could help solve medical problems	Fifty years of study leads to ability to manipulate genes of plants and animals to produce more beneficial results; more controversial is the focus on cloning and genetic engineering to develop most desirable humans
Primatology and paleoanthropology	Primatology: discovery that animals also have shared culture, language, toolmaking skills Paleoanthropology: discovery of features originally thought uniquely human (rituals, morality) among nonhuman ancestors	Widened research efforts in both disciplines; reinforced connection between all humans and led to deeper understanding of ecology, the study of interconnectedness of all life
Anthropology	Franz Boas: comparative study of societies shows that no race is superior to any other in brainpower, development of thought	New doctrine of cultural relativism focuses on studying communities in context of their traditions; widened appreciation for non-Western, native cultures (Native American, Samoan, etc.)
Psychology	Sigmund Freud: uncovered role of human subconscious in motivating actions; developed psychoanalysis to expose subconscious feelings, thoughts Development of new theories on child raising and education by Sigmund Freud and Ellen Key emphasizing childhood as a separate phase of life	Transformation of school curricula, child raising to conform with ideas of stages of child development; belief in subconscious strata of human mind leads to widespread interest in popular psychology including psychoanalysis and dream analysis
Philosophy and Linguistics	Henri Bergson and others reconceptualize time and causation as part of human-determined memory and experience F. de Saussure and others deconstruct language as human-constructed medium that cannot convey objective reality	New understandings of deep structures of language furthered by experiments of Noam Chomsky showing that language, speech, grammar, and syntax are linked to the brain, and are hardwired—debate widens on the usefulness of language and the accessibility of truth.

Vienna by Arnold Schoenberg from 1908 onward, subverted the harmonies of the past as surely as quantum mechanics began to challenge its ideas of order.

In art, the effects of the new anthropology were even clearer than those of the new physics. Picasso, Braque, and members of Kandinsky's circle copied "primitive" Pacific and African sculptures from museums of natural history, while artists in the Americas and Australia rediscovered the art of native peoples. As in science and philosophy, Asian traditions made a big impact in the West in the last four decades of the century, especially in music, architecture, and stage design. The vogue for primitivism ensured that craftsmen outside Europe had a market for their traditional arts. Yet whenever innovations occurred in art, as in science, Western initiatives predominated globally throughout the century.

As in so many areas of modernization, Japanese artists led the way in assimilating Western influences. Outstanding painters, such as Kuroda Seiki and Wada Eisaku, were already studying in Europe in the 1890s and the early 1900s. In China, influence radiated chiefly from Russia, especially from the late 1940s, as Russian-inspired Communists became all-powerful. Their characteristic subjects were stocky, heroic peasants and workers in poster-art style. This still dominated the art of Wang Guangyi (wahng gwang-yee) in the late twentieth century. Meanwhile, however, China had opened up to every kind of Western influence. The outstanding

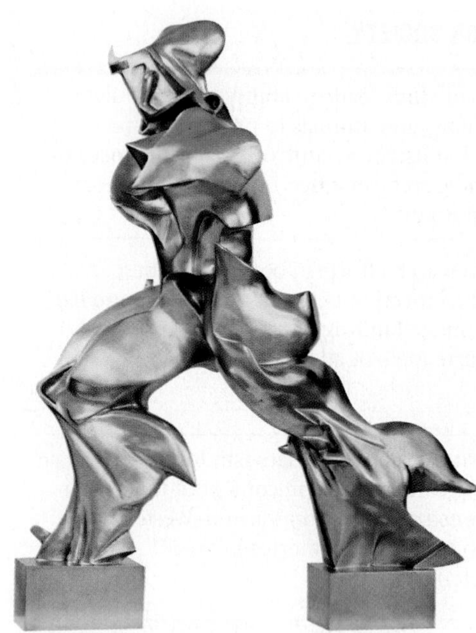

Man as machine, speeding and striding into the future. The Italian artist Umberto Boccioni (1882–1916) captured the spirit of futurism in this sculpture of 1913. "Our straight line will be alive and palpitating," he wrote, aiming to "embed" the math and geometry of machines "in the muscular lines of a body."
Umberto Boccioni, Unique Form of Continuity in Space, *1913 (cast 1931). Bronze, 43 7/8 × 34 7/8" × 15 3/4" (111.4 × 88.6 × 40 cm). Acquired through the Lillie P. Bliss Bequest. The Museum of Modern Art/Licensed by Scala-Art Resource, NY*

young artist of the 1990s, Zhou Chunya (joe chwun-yah), was reported as saying, "Even though Western art dominates my painting style, I would say I am a Chinese painter ... because I maintain a Chinese lifestyle within myself." For painters working in the shadow of Western influence, this sentiment was typical.

Among artists who resisted or filtered Western influences, those from India were most conspicuous. At the end of the nineteenth century, Abindranath Tagore rejected his Western-style training as a painter to find inspiration in Mughal art (Chapter 19). His followers and successors—notably Nandalal Bose (1882–1966)—made anticolonialism part of the message of their work. Many artists around the world also turned to folk art to supply new styles. But even painters who loudly rejected the West could not escape altogether the magnetism of Western techniques, materials, and models.

The novel, modeled on the Western tradition, became a universal genre. Cinema, a new medium of Western origin, became the most popular art form in the world, and, although different cultures evolved their own schools of cinema, the "Hollywood" style dominated the global market. New initiatives in sculpture and architecture, and new genres, such as video art and computer-generated art, depended on technologies the West invented.

Paradoxically, it was in the West that the influence of Western art during the twentieth century declined. Though governments patronized conventional artists, the characteristic art of the First World War and its aftermath was **dada**—externalized disillusionment, deliberately brutal, ugly, and meaningless. The "Dada Manifesto" of 1918 celebrated World War I as the "great work of destruction." In Germany, Kurt Schwitters (1887–1948) scraped collages together from bits of smashed machines and ruined buildings. Max Ernst (1891–1976) exposed post war nightmares, often using hostile materials—barbed wire, rough wood. The artists who called themselves surrealists continued this trend in the 1920s and 1930s, reflecting psychology by creating paintings and films in which they aimed to externalize subconscious neuroses and desires. Their project overlapped with a school that established a more enduring tradition: Expressionists, most of whom were more concerned with color and texture than with form, reached inside themselves and their subjects to represent emotion and mood.

After that, art seemed to lose some of its power to make people see the world afresh. Plenty of great artists challenged onlookers' world picture, but none succeeded in changing it. In part, this was because propaganda seduced art, especially the most powerful new art of the twentieth century, cinema. Most of the great movie directors and music composers of the 1930s and 1940s in Europe, America, and Russia got caught up in the ideological conflicts of the time. Governments—even in democracies—victimized artists whose messages they disliked. More treacherously, art, like so much else in the twentieth-century West, became fodder for consumerism, commercialism, celebrity, and fashion. Artists escaped from political control by appealing to the mass market and to rich collectors. Salvador Dalí (1904–1989) was probably the most technically accomplished painter of the age. His paintings, film–set designs, and the marketing of his images in poster form communicated the spirit of surrealism to a worldwide public. But many of his fellow artists hated him for his dedication to self-promotion to boost the prices of his works. Picasso became the richest artist of the century by exhibiting uncanny business sense and becoming a celebrity, famous for being famous almost as much as for his art.

Art lost influence, too, because taste splintered. From the 1930s onward, the market lurched among fashions. Every school of artists had to repudiate every other school to attract buyers. Technology multiplied media exponentially from the 1960s onward, and the market responded by huddling in niches. From the 1960s, artists influenced by the new theories in philosophy and linguistics lost belief in the power of symbols generally. Images, some of them came to feel, like words, have no direct relation to reality.

Painting and sculpture yielded popularity to film and to mass entertainment. Arts suited to the new media—cinema, radio, photography, and the gramophone at first, television later, computers and video toward the century's end—spread secondhand experiences, received wisdom and hand-me-down values. The artists who really touched people were cartoonists. Walt Disney (1901–1966) became, perhaps, the world's most influential artist ever because his cartoon movies depicted the most commonplace emotions, morals, and character types in ways that people of all ages in all cultures could immediately grasp. Musical theater, sacrificing sophistication for melody, displaced opera. Pop music was to art what factory products were to crafts: cheap to make and capable of generating huge profits. In the second half of the century, when—for reasons we shall discuss in Chapter 29—masses of young people in the West acquired unprecedented spending power, the record industry became the home of the most socially revolutionary and subversive arts, a role writers had once filled. Now rock bands issued messages of political protest and sexual liberation. These messages proved less saleable, in the long run, than escapism.

Bollywood. Few aspects of Indian life demonstrate the appropriation of Western culture so deeply as the Bombay (Mumbai) film industry, which has created its own imagery and values from a distant Hollywood model.

By 2000, the most commercially successful genre was fantasy—the depiction of worlds that magic regulated or transformed, which suited computer-generated imagery. It seemed an ironic end to a century dominated by science, but it was symptomatic of the impatience with or revulsion from science that characterized popular responses. Meanwhile, the art form that attracted the most investment and, therefore, attained the highest technical standards was television advertising. Advertising jingles and images became the common artistic culture of the time—the only things you could rely on just about everyone to recognize. Sport, especially soccer, was the only rival—largely because it was broadcast all over the world.

Architecture ought to be the most popular art of all because people who never enter an art gallery live in some form of architecture. Indeed, after the Second World War, architecture replaced painting and rivaled cinema as the most socially powerful of the arts. The world had to be rebuilt after the destruction of the war and the neglect of colonialism. However, doctrines that proved hostile to most people such as functionalism and rationalism, which favored machinelike buildings, fashioned by necessity, stripped to their most elementary forms, angular, and unrelated to human scale, dominated the architecture of the period. So much had to be built so quickly that officialdom decided what and how to build, without giving much thought to the needs and feelings of the people who had to live in the huge apartment blocks, work in the offices, factories, and schools of the era, and recover or die in the hospitals. Only in the 1970s did

"Modern" Art

1866–1944	Vasily Kandinsky, Russian artist, launched tradition of entirely abstract art
1876–1944	Emilio Filippo Marinetti, proponent of futurism
1881–1973	Pablo Picasso, cofounder of cubism
1882–1966	Nandalal Bose, Indian artist, incorporated anticolonialism in his work
1887–1968	Marcel Duchamp, French artist influenced by Einstein's theory of relativity
Early twentieth century	Karoda Seiki and Wada Eisaku, Japanese painters, create works that assimilated Western influences
1918	Proclamation of the "Dada Manifesto"
1920s and 1930s	Emergence of surrealist and expressionist movements

architects and urban planners begin to heed popular demands, tear down some of the worst excesses of functionalism, and start again on a smaller scale and along more traditional lines.

THE TURN OF THE WORLD

In the second half of the twentieth century, a reaction set in. The West rediscovered "Eastern wisdom," alternative medicine, and the traditional science of non-Western peoples. Other cultures renewed their confidence in their own traditions. In the 1940s, J. Robert Oppenheimer, the American physicist who led the research team that developed the A-bomb, was one of many Western scientists who turned to the ancient Indian texts, the Upanishads, for consolation and insights, in a West disillusioned by war (see Chapter 28).

Then in 1956, Joseph Needham began to publish one of the momentous works of the twentieth century, *Science and Civilisation in China*, in which he showed that China had a scientific tradition of its own, from which the West had learned the basis of most of its progress in technology until the seventeenth century. Indian scientists, meanwhile, had made similar claims for the antiquity of scientific thinking in their own country. In the 1960s, India became a favored destination for young Westerners in search of values different from those of their own cultures. Zen Buddhism (Chapter 14) and Daoist descriptions of nature provided some Westerners with models to interpret the universe that seemed to match scientific discoveries.

Even in medicine, non-Western traditions gained ground. Westerners often came to respect and learn from the healers they met far afield. Edward Hume himself learned much from traditional Chinese herbalists during his years in Changsha. But it took a long time for such respect to become general in the West. In the 1980s, the World Health Organization began to realize the value of traditional healers in delivering health care to disadvantaged people in Africa. Nigeria, South Africa, and other African countries introduced alternative medicine to health-care centers.

Meanwhile, in the West, traditional healing arts of non-Western peoples attracted big followings. Researchers discovered the healing plants of Amazonian forest dwellers, Chinese peasants, and Himalayan shamans. Scientists began to appreciate that so-called primitive peoples had a cornucopia of useful drugs unknown to Western medicine. Traditional medicine had never died out in India and China. In a remarkable reversal of the direction of influence in the late twentieth century, Western patients seeking alternative medicines turned to Indian herbalism and Chinese acupuncture, along with other forms of traditional medicine in both countries. Westerners began to travel to China and India to study herbal treatments, just as Asian students had headed to the West for medical learning at the beginning of the century. Western demand for alternative medicine became an economic opportunity for Chinese and Indian physicians in the West. The world had come full circle since Edward Hume's day.

IN PERSPECTIVE: Science, Challenging and Challenged

In the first half of the twentieth century, the intellectual hegemony of science was linked with the global dominance of the West. All the major new scientific initiatives came from Europe and America. The rest of the world could only endure this supremacy or imitate it. In the 1960s, however, the pattern began to shift. Western scientists began to turn to non-Western, and especially to Asian, traditions of thought to help interpret some of the conflicting data their observations accumulated. These contradictions seemed, especially to nonscientists, to expose the imperfections of science as a system of knowledge that could explain the universe. Non-Western countries, especially in Asia, imitated Western technologies so well that they could afford their own scientific institutions.

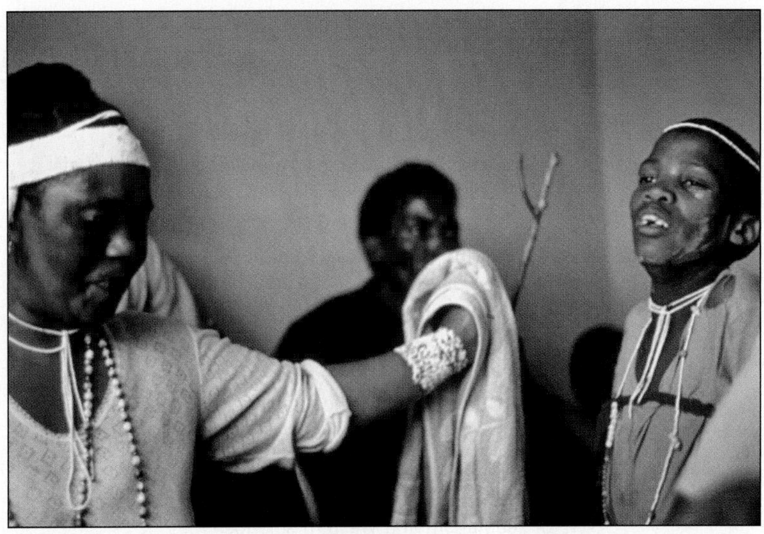

African healing cult. In Cape Town, South Africa, a ritual of initiation into Ngoma—a shamanistic cult widespread in Africa. Practitioners use music and dance to attain a trance-like state in which they communicate with spirits, usually to access powers of healing.

Meanwhile, revulsion from science increased prestige for what came to be known as alternative methods. Some people, especially professional scientists, remained convinced of the all-sufficiency of science and scorned these trends. Their critics called them "scientistic." Toward the end of the century, divisions—sometimes called culture wars—opened between apologists of science and advocates of alternatives.

The search for the underlying or overarching order of the cosmos seemed only to lead to chaos. "Life is scientific," says Piggy, the doomed hero of William Golding's novel of 1959, *Lord of the Flies*. Other characters prove him wrong by killing him and reverting to instinct and savagery. Golding's novel seemed to be an allegory of its times. Science—in most people's judgment—soared and failed. It sought to penetrate the heavens and ended by contaminating the Earth. Among its most influential inventions were bombs and pollutants. The expansion of knowledge added nothing to wisdom. Science did not make people better. Rather it increased their ability to behave worse than ever. Instead of a universal benefit to humanity, science was a symptom or cause of disproportionate Western power. Under the influence of these feelings, and in response to the undermining of science by skepticism, an antiscientific reaction set in. It generated conflict between those who stuck to Piggy's opinion and the vast global majority who—as we shall see in Chapter 29—turned back to religion or even magic to help them cope with the bewildering world of rapid change and elusive understanding.

The revival of unscientific ways to picture reality surprised most observers. But by making the cosmos rationally unintelligible to most people, science stimulated religious revival. Motions we cannot measure, events we cannot track, causes we cannot trace, and effects we cannot predict all became familiar and seemed to license metaphysical and even supernatural explanations. Modern Japan is a land of high-tech Shinto, where spirits infest computers and an office tower of steel and plate glass can be topped off with a shrine to the fox-god. Some medical practitioners collaborate with faith healers. Even religious fundamentalism—one of the most powerful movements in the late twentieth century—mimicked science in seeking certainty.

The last wave of revulsion from science—or, at least, from scientism—in the twentieth century was a form of humanism: a reaction in favor of humane values. Science seemed to blur the boundaries between humans and other animals, or even between humans and machines. It seemed to take the soul out of people and substitute genes for it. It seemed to make freedom impossible and reduce moral choices to evolutionary accidents or genetically determined options. It turned human beings into subjects of experimentation. Ruthless regimes abused biology to justify racism and psychiatry to imprison dissidents. Extreme scientism denied all nonscientific values and became, in its own way, as dogmatic as any religion. The "new humanism" was much more, however, than an antiscientistic reaction. It

CHRONOLOGY

1856–1939	Sigmund Freud, developer of psychoanalysis
1858–1942	Franz Boas, anthropologist, proved that races are of equal intelligence
1860s	China's "self-strengthening" program begins
1866–1944	Vasily Kandinsky, Russian artist, launched tradition of entirely abstract art
1883	Western-style curriculum at Beijing School of Medicine
1871–1937	Ernest Rutherford, postulated concept of the atomic nucleus
1875–1965	Albert Schweizer, medical missionary to Africa
1876–1944	Emilio Filippo Marinetti, proponent of futurism
1879–1955	Albert Einstein, developer of the theory of relativity
1881–1938	Kemal Ataturk, founder of modern Turkey and proponent of secularism and Western science
1881–1973	Pablo Picasso, cofounder of cubism
1882–1966	Nandalal Bose, Indian artist, incorporated anticolonialism in his work
1885–1962	Niels Bohr, won Nobel Prize in 1922 for work on the structure of the atom
1891–1962	Ismail Mazhir, translator of Charles Darwin's work into Arabic
1901–1976	Werner Heisenberg, developed uncertainty principle
1902	Henri Poincaré questions the link between hypothesis and evidence
1903	Powered flight
1905–1980	Jean-Paul Sartre, French philosopher associated with existentialism
1906	15,000 Chinese study science abroad
1907	Plastic invented
1913	Indian *Journal of Medical Research* launched
1914	Science Society of China founded by Chinese students at Cornell University
1920s and 1930s	Emergence of surrealist and expressionist movements
1920	Royal Institute for Higher Technical Education founded in Indonesia
1925	Scopes "Monkey" Trial
1931	Penicillin discovered
1944	Erwin Schödinger predicts structure of the gene
1953	Ludwig Wittgenstein's *Philosophical Investigations* published
1956	Publication of Joseph Needham's *Science and Civilisation in China*

tended to blame religion—or, at least, religious conflicts—as much as science for the failures of history, and its thinkers and practitioners sought a morality based on universal values. More than either science or religion, the barbarities of the violent political history of the twentieth century stimulated the new humanism.

The story of politics in the twentieth century matched that of science. In politics, too, the new century opened with new departures. The world's first full democracies—in the sense that women had equal political rights with men—took shape in Norway and New Zealand. In 1904–1905, Japanese victories in a war with Russia foreshadowed the end of white supremacy. Independence movements arose in Europe's overseas empires. In 1911, the first great "rebellions of the masses" began. Contrary to the expectations of Karl Marx, these were not launched by urban workers but by peasant revolutionaries in Mexico and disaffected intellectuals and soldiers in China. In Mexico, the effect was to end the power of the two elements of society that had been dominant since colonial times: the church and the big landowners. In China, the Qing dynasty, which had reigned since 1644, was overthrown, the mandate of heaven abolished, and a republic proclaimed. This was an extraordinary reversal for a system that had survived so many convulsions for more than 2,200 years, and a sign that no form of political stability, however long-standing, could now be taken for granted. Both revolutions soured, turning into civil wars, breeding dictators. This too was an omen of the future. Most of the many violent regime changes of the twentieth century had similar consequences.

The future that the radicals of the nineteenth century imagined never happened. Ordinary people never really got power over their own lives or over the societies they formed—even in states founded in revolutions or regulated by democratic institutions. The progress people hoped for in the early years of the twentieth century dissolved in the bloodiest wars ever experienced. And just as Western science receded in the second half of the century, so did Western empires. To those stories we must now turn.

PROBLEMS AND PARALLELS

1. How did science come to set the agenda for the world in the twentieth century? How did Western empires affect the spread of Western science? How was Western science received in China, India, and the Islamic world?
2. How was Western science transformed in the twentieth century? What effects did uncertainty have on human self-perception and religious values?
3. Why is twentieth-century Western art a mirror of twentieth-century science? How did the revolutions in twentieth-century art match the jolts and shocks of science and philosophy?
4. Why did a reaction against Western science take hold in the second half of the twentieth century?

DOCUMENTS IN GLOBAL HISTORY

- Education and imperialism in the Dutch East Indies: from *Letters of a Javanese Princess*
- Al-Afghani on faith and reason
- Werner Heisenberg, "Uncertainty," 1927
- Franz Boas, from *The Mind of Primitive Man*
- Ellen Key, from *Century of the Child*
- William Jones, from *Pragmatism*
- Emilio Filippo Marinetti, "Futurist Manifesto"

Please see the Primary Source DVD for additional sources related to this chapter.

READ ON

T. Dantzig, *Henri Poincaré, Critic of Crisis: Reflections on His Universe of Discourse* (1954) is still the fundamental study of the thought of one of the founders of modern science, whose own philosophy of science is available in Henri Poincaré, *The Foundations of Science* (1946). Also valuable for the emergence of modern physics, and more recent, is G. J. Holton, *Einstein and the Cultural Roots of Modern Science* (1997).

On the history of psychology, see the very readable book by C. P. Bankart, *Talking Cures: A History of Western and Eastern Psychotherapies* (1996), which sets the different traditions in their cultural contexts. A good study of one of the founders of modern psychology is R. B. Perry, *Thought and Character of William James* (1935). The key work by a founder of modern anthropology is F. Boas, *Mind of Primitive Man* (1911), while a foundational work of modern linguistics is available as *Saussure's First Course of Lectures on General Linguistics (1907): From the Notebooks of Albert Riedlinger*, eds. E. Komatsu and G. Wolf (1996). For those willing to tackle one of the hardest of twentieth-century philosophers, L. Wittgenstein, *Philosophical Investigations*, translated by G. E. M. Anscombe (1953) is accessible. The quotation on page 708 is from N. Chomsky, *Knowledge of Language* (1986).

On the influence of Western science beyond the West, a number of fine works are available. E. H. Hume, *Doctors East, Doctors West: An American Physician's Life in China* (1949) is a first-hand account of the meeting of medical cultures, from which the story that opens the chapter comes. Li Yan and Du Shiran, *Chinese Mathematics: A Concise History* (1987), trans. by J. N. Crossley and A. W. C. Lun, and L. A. Orleans, ed., *Science in Contemporary China* (1980) both illuminate the influence of Western science in China, while J. Reardon-Anderson, *The Study of Change: Chemistry in China, 1840–1949* (1991) examines the crucial transitional period of Chinese contact with Western learning. D. Arnold, *Science, Technology, and Medicine in Colonial India* (2000) does the same for the subcontinent, as does L. Pyenson, *Empire of Reason: Exact Science in Indonesia, 1840–1940* (1997) for southeast Asia. E. Ihsanoglu, *Science, Technology, and Learning in the Ottoman Empire: Western Influence, Local Institutions, and the Transfer of Knowledge* (2004) traces in detail the routes and methods of the transmission of Western science into the Ottoman world. A. B. Zahlan, *Science and Science Policy in the Arab World* (1980) brings elements of that story into recent times. *The Political Economy of Health in Africa* (1991), eds. T. Falola and D. Ityavyar, brings us into sub-Saharan Africa and back to medicine as a crucial vector of the spread of Western science globally.

P. Conrad, *Modern Times, Modern Places* (1999) is a sophisticated analysis of modern art globally as a reflection of changing social and cultural trends. The iconoclastic J. Waller, *Fabulous Science* (2002) debunks many scientific myths. W. Hung, ed., *Chinese Art at the Crossroads* (1991), examines the challenges posed by modernity to historical artistic traditions, with specific attention to China. D. Edgerton, *The Shock of the Old* (2006) is brilliantly revisionist on technology. T. Judt, *Postwar* (2006) helps explain the context of the new humanism.

CHAPTER 28

World Order and Disorder: Global Politics in the Twentieth Century

Ministry of War Tokyo Stop Chinese bandits have blown up Shanghai-Nanking rail-way ...

Not significant! We'll soon see about that...

This is Radio Tokyo!...The effrontery of Chines guer-illas knows no bounds! News just in details a treacherous attack on the Shanghai-Nanking railway ...

...Reports tell of many killed trying to defend them-selves.

Twelve Japan-ese died. After the attack...

...the bandits, numbering more than a hundred, fled with their loot.

Tokyo Express!...Special!... Special!... Chinese bandits attack passenger train!... Many dead...Read all about it!

...Japan must
the guardian
in the Far
soldiers who
defend this

1931: News of the Manchurian Incident flashes around the globe, as imagined by the brilliant Belgian cartoonist Hergé. The Japanese propaganda version of the incident was false. Rogue Japanese agents, not Chinese "bandits," had blown up the railway track, and there were no casualties. The cartoon strip's boy hero, Tintin, discovers the truth and becomes entangled in the Japanese invasion of China for which the incident was a pretext. © Hergé/Moulinsant 2006

IN THIS CHAPTER

THE WORLD WAR ERA, 1914–1945
The First World War
Postwar Disillusionment
The Shift to Ideological Conflicts
The Second World War
THE COLD WAR ERA, 1945–1991
Superpower Confrontation
DECOLONIZATION
THE NEW WORLD ORDER
The European Union
IN PERSPECTIVE: The Anvil of War

In Manchuria in the 1920s and 1930s, the brothels in the city of Harbin resembled clubs, where the regular clients became friends and met each other. On September 19, 1931, the Russian journalist Aleksandr Pernikoff arrived at his favorite haunt, Tayama's. The door was opened by a scholarly looking Japanese man with gold-rimmed glasses. As he shook hands with his friends, Pernikoff became aware of the tension in the atmosphere:

MANCHURIA

...stopped the train and attacked the innocent passengers...

"What's all this about?" Pernikoff asked in a whisper.

"Didn't you hear?" replied one of the men. During the night, the Japanese had invaded Manchuria, claiming that the Chinese "tried to blow up a Japanese train."

"Did they blow it up?" asked Pernikoff.

"No," answered the man, with a half-smile. "The mine went off after the train had passed. But the Japanese troops were ready and waiting."

A Japanese client of the brothel read out the official Japanese report of the incident. Miraculously, "by divine intervention," although thrust "up into the air" with the force of the explosion, the train descended back onto the rails, resumed its journey, and reached its destination without loss. "All of us in the room," wrote Pernikoff, "felt uneasy at hearing this childish account."

"What will happen now?" he asked.

"War."[1]

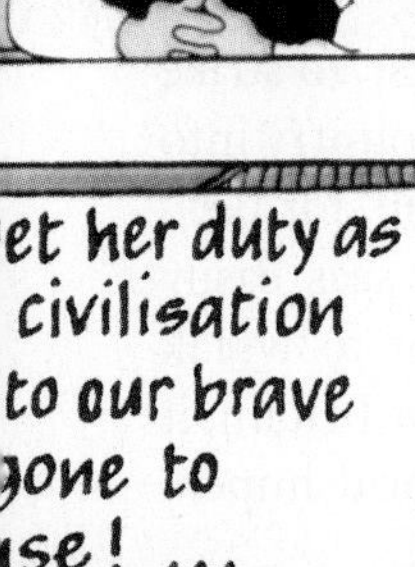

et her duty as
civilisation
to our brave

This episode, known as the **Manchurian Incident,** was the first in a series of crises that Japanese militants manufactured over the next six years—not always with the knowledge or approval of their own government. The first results were to convert Manchuria into a Japanese puppet monarchy. Then, in 1937, a tenacious Japanese attempt to conquer China began. It dragged on until 1945, merging with other struggles, in which all the world's potential superpowers—Japan, China, the United States, Russia, and Germany—were locked, together with the British, French, and Dutch Empires and most of the other sovereign states that then existed.

The war was part of a long series of global conflicts. Catastrophic warfare punctuated the first half of the century. A **cold war** between ideological antagonists dominated most of the second half, waged in local or regional outbreaks and in economic and diplomatic competition.

We can follow the story of politics in the twentieth century along a path picked between these conflicts. To make space for the cultural and environmental history of the century, we need to try to tell the political story briefly rather than dwelling, as textbooks usually do, on all the many twists and turns, and all the forgettable statesmen and generals whose legacy has not lasted. In the pages that follow, we divide the century roughly into three periods: first, that of the world wars, which ended in 1945; then, the era of superpower confrontation that began as world war ended. Finally, toward the end of the century, a "new world order" arose, as the United States outgunned or outlasted rivals.

FOCUS questions

- HOW DID the world wars weaken Europe's global dominance?
- WHY WERE totalitarian and authoritarian regimes so widespread during the twentieth century?
- HOW DID the United States become the world's only superpower?
- WHY DID the Cold War lead to the collapse of the Soviet Union?
- HOW DID decolonization affect Asia and Africa?
- WHY DID democracy spread around the world in the late twentieth century?
- ARE THE European Union and China likely to become superpowers in the twenty-first century?

THE WORLD WAR ERA, 1914–1945

One way to understand Japan's conflict with China is as a sort of civil war within a single civilization. Japanese usually represented the conflict as a decisive struggle to determine which country would be the "big brother" and which the "little brother" in a common empire or, as Japanese propagandists said, the Great East Asia Co-prosperity Sphere.

The European conflicts that merged with this intra-Asian war, and that overspilled Europe itself to become a global war, had similar characteristics. At first, in the episode known as the First World War, from 1914 to 1918, national and imperial rivalries triggered hostilities. The European powers disagreed about little except how to distribute power and territory among themselves. After the war had begun, to the great question of which country would dominate Europe, another greater question was added: Which ideology would dominate Europe? Would the common culture of European peoples in the future be religious or secular, liberal or authoritarian, capitalist or socialist, individual or collective?

The First World War

When the struggles began, all the belligerent states had more or less the same ideology. Except for France, they were all monarchies. Although most were not democratic, they all aspired to mobilize the allegiance of their peoples with the same rhetoric of chivalry, idealism, and crusade.

For Germany, the war was an attempt to resolve two obsessions: first, to strike a preemptive blow against Russia, before industrialization turned that country into a superpower; second, to break out of maritime containment by Britain, for Germany had no access to the ocean highways except through narrow seas easily policed by British naval power. For France, the war was an attempt to wreak revenge on Germany for humiliation in their last war in 1870–1871. For Britain, it was an exercise in traditional British grand strategy: pinning down a world-imperial rival—Germany—in a continental war.

Soldiers' accounts of battle

For the Habsburg Empire of Austria-Hungary, striving to contain restless and violent national minorities, war was a desperate act of impatience with Serbian subversion, which threatened to detach the empire's southern Slavic provinces. For Italy, the objective was frontier snatching at Austria's expense. For the Ottoman Empire, fearing Russian expansion, it was a gamble to survive. For the Russian czar, war in defense of fellow Slavs in the Balkans was an obligation of honor. His ministers also feared that Germany had "a gigantic plan of world domination."

For all the belligerents, the war went wrong. On the Western Front, armies stuck in the mud in trenches from the English Channel to the Alps. In the east, Germans, Austrians, and Turks collided blunderingly with Russians in the vast terrain. In the Alps, Italians hurled themselves against Austrians who occupied the higher ground. The elites who had started the war could not control its course or its costs.

Russia dropped out in revolution and disorder toward the end of 1917—the first major belligerent to collapse. Germany could therefore switch its main effort to the west. The balance of forces, however, was already shifting against the Germans, for in April 1917 the United States joined the fray.

This was a surprising development. It made sense for Americans to take the profits peace offered. This policy, known as **isolationism,** however, gradually became impractical, as "Uncle Sam," in the slang of the British press, had become "Brother Jonathan, a power among the powers."

America might have favored the Germans. There were millions of German immigrants in the United States. Many Americans viewed the British Empire with distaste. But Britain was America's biggest creditor and trading partner. Germany, meanwhile, offended against two of America's pet values: peaceful problem solving and freedom of the seas. Squeezed between France and Russia, the Germans practiced militarism partly as a survival technique. Once war in Europe broke out, Germany had to resort to submarine warfare—which, being sneaky and secretive, offended American sensibilities—to damage British commerce. In 1917, Germany announced that its submarines would sink any ships—hostile or neutral—in British waters. By then, the United States was already looking for a pretext to join the war against Germany. Its intervention was decisive because no belligerent could match America's power. American industrial output equalled that of the whole of Europe combined.

The United States entered the war to meet an American agenda: to crush militarism, free the seas, weaken European empires, lift American debts, consolidate America's growing superiority in wealth, liberate the Eastern European homelands of millions of American citizens, and make the world safe for democracy. But the war was a unifying experience for the powers that faced each other across the Atlantic. Three of the world's most powerful, resourceful, and predatory states—the United States, Britain, and France—were now in partnership. The rest of the world faced a source of cultural influence of peculiar force.

The First World War was a crucible, in which the world seemed to dissolve. It destroyed elites, empires, and traditional ways of life. Almost 10 million men died

A trench with wounded and dead, June 1915, on the western front in northern France during World War I. The apparently unposed photograph is shocking because of the standing soldiers' apathetic acceptance of the plight of their wounded comrade in the foul, brutalizing environment of the trenches.

Total Casualties in the First World War

Country	Dead	Wounded	Total Killed as a Percentage of Population
France	1,398,000	2,000,000	3.4
Belgium	38,000	44,700	0.5
Italy	578,000	947,000	1.6
British Empire	921,000	2,090,000	1.7
Romania	250,000	120,000	3.3
Serbia	278,000	133,000	5.7
Greece	26,000	21,000	0.5
Russia	1,811,000	1,450,000	1.1
Bulgaria	88,000	152,000	1.9
Germany	2,037,000	4,207,000	3.0
Austria-Hungary	1,100,000	3,620,000	1.9
Turkey	804,000	400,000	3.7
United States	114,000	206,000	0.1

Niall Ferguson, The Pity of War (New York: Basic Books, 1998).

in action. There were 25 million casualties in all. The war wiped out a generation of the natural leaders of Europe and provoked political revolution or transformation wherever its armies marched. Twelve new sovereign, or virtually sovereign, states emerged in Europe or on its borders (see Map 28.1). The Russian, German, Austro-Hungarian, and Ottoman Empires were felled at a stroke. Even the United Kingdom lost a limb, when revolution and civil war in Ireland ended with, in effect, independence for most of the island. Huge migrations redistributed peoples. After the war, more than 1 million Turks and Greeks shunted to safety across the new borders of their mutually hostile states.

MAP 28.1

Europe, the Middle East, and North Africa in 1914 and 1923

Europe, the Middle East, and North Africa, 1914

Europe, the Middle East, and North Africa, 1923

President Woodrow Wilson (1856–1924) appreciated the opportunity to recraft the world. He denounced imperialism. His country bought its last permanent acquisitions of territory (three of the Virgin Islands in the Caribbean) in 1917 from Denmark. Wilson did his best to discourage the imperialism of his allies and insisted, within Europe, on "self-determination." New nations sprang into being or reemerged at the rhythm of a State Department typewriter: first, what Wilson called "Czecho-slovakia," then "Jugo-slavia," Poland, Finland, Estonia, Latvia, and Lithuania.

On the other hand, the claims of Ukraine, Georgia, Armenia, Belarus, the Kurds, and the Muslim peoples of the Russian Empire were ignored. In Africa, the belligerents swapped colonies with no thought for self-determination. The aspirations of the Arab subjects of the Ottoman Empire were patchily treated. A leader of anti-Ottoman resistance in Arabia, Sharif Husayn (1856–1931), proclaimed himself King of the Arabs in 1917, with popular support, but the British and French divided his territory between them, leaving only what are now Jordan and Iraq to his heirs, and allowing an Islamist chieftain, Ibn Saud (1880–1953), to conquer what is now Saudi Arabia in 1924–1925. Meanwhile, in Libya, rebels against the Italians who had seized the country from the Ottomans in 1911–1912 proclaimed an Arab republic in 1918, but Italy suppressed them shortly afterward. From 1917, the British outraged Arabs by permitting—albeit halfheartedly—the creation in Palestine of what they called a "national homeland" for the Jews of Europe.

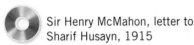

Sir Henry McMahon, letter to Sharif Husayn, 1915

For Turkey itself, the loss of empire seemed a relief. The new, secular Turkish republic, founded by Mustafa Kemal in 1923 (he took the surname Atatürk, meaning "Father of the Turks"), had universal male suffrage in 1924 and women's right to vote from 1934. Atatürk made Friday, the Muslim Sabbath, a workday, imposed the Roman alphabet on a language formerly written in Arabic characters, and founded an opera, a university, and a symphony orchestra. His success inspired other Muslim secular nationalists. In Iran, for instance, an army strongman, Riza Khan, proclaimed himself shah in 1925 and imitated Atatürk's secularizing policies, abolishing the veil for women and banning Islamic religious schools.

Covenant of the League of Nations

Finally, President Wilson proposed the **League of Nations** as a forum to resolve international disputes peacefully. But the United States Senate rejected Wilson's vision. Americans had no taste for world leadership. The costs of the Great War had been enough. When America refused to take part in the League and retreated into isolation, the new world order was doomed.

Or perhaps it was doomed anyway. The treaties the Allies imposed left too many dissatisfied states. Germany had been barely defeated, but the victors treated it with contempt: subject to massive reparations and loss of territory, with humiliating restrictions on the right to rearm. Italy remained discontented with its modest territorial gains. Japan, which had joined the Allies in 1914 expecting a free hand in East Asia, felt let down. Russia, stripped of its influence over Eastern Europe, was excluded from the postwar settlement and looked for ways to unpick it. Most of the new nation states included large, restive minorities. Faced with these resentments, the League was useless, its representatives—in the words of an English comedian—turning up for meetings "in taxis that were empty."

But the war changed expectations for the future. It was an experience of unmatched horror. The men who marched away expected another war like those of nineteenth-century Europe: short and glorious. What they got was more than four years of suffering. Soldiers on the Western Front lived in filthy trenches, contending with rats, lice, mud, and poison gas. While they cowered

Gassed. Poison gas was ineffective on the battlefield during World War I, but it symbolized the nature of technologically "advanced" weaponry: inhuman and undiscriminating. Except in the U.S. cinema, wartime artists almost entirely abandoned heroic images in favor of scenes of horror. Blindness and blundering—as here in John Singer Sargent's painting *Gassed*—became metaphors for the misconduct and incompetence of political and military leaders.
John Singer Sargent (1856–1925), "Gassed, an Oil Study." 1918–19. Oil on canvas. Private collection. Imperial War Museum, Negative Number Q1460

underground, massive artillery barrages pounded their dugouts. When they charged, they faced machine guns and died, or watched their comrades die, in millions. Experiences too terrible to confide to loved ones back home became secret neuroses. Shell shock plagued the demobilized. The battlefield became soulless, desolate, a blackened, barbed-wired Golgotha. Tanks displaced cavalry. Machines crushed life out of the landscape and chivalry out of war. The war destroyed "even the survivors" of battle, said the German writer Erich-Maria Remarque (1898–1970) in *All Quiet on the Western Front*, the most influential of the war-born novels and memoirs.

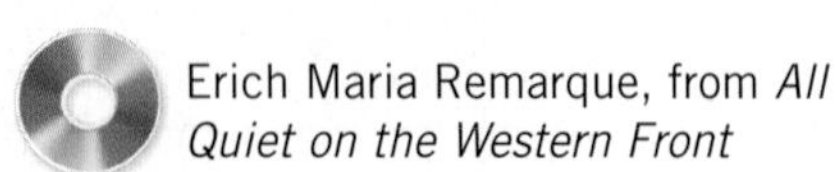

Erich Maria Remarque, from *All Quiet on the Western Front*

Postwar Disillusionment

Optimism, however, survived in other places—especially where people resented European empires. The war was a collective humiliation for Europe. The United States was revealed as the world's leading power. Japan mopped up formerly German-owned islands in the Pacific and bases in China. Almost before the smoke cleared, nationalist movements got under way in the colonial empires. In Dutch-controlled Indonesia in 1916, the group known as Sarekat Islam mobilized a mass movement for self-government. In 1919, the Pan-African Congress demanded that Africans share in governing their own countries. In the same year, the Egyptian Wafd or Nationalist Party was founded to pressure the British into leaving.

In India in 1919, amid riots against the continuation of wartime measures, the British suspended civil liberties. Mohandas Gandhi (1869–1948) launched a movement he called **satyagraha**— "the force of truth"—relying on "passive disobedience": strikes, fasts, boycotts, and demonstrations. Other protesters derailed trains, battled police, and cut telegraph wires. The British responded nervously. In Amritsar, troops fired on demonstrators "to teach," their commander said, "a moral lesson": 379 unarmed people were killed and 1,200 wounded. Britain's hold—such as it was—on popular sentiment in India deteriorated rapidly. Much of the Indian intelligentsia was looking forward to dismantling Western hegemony and dismembering Western empires.

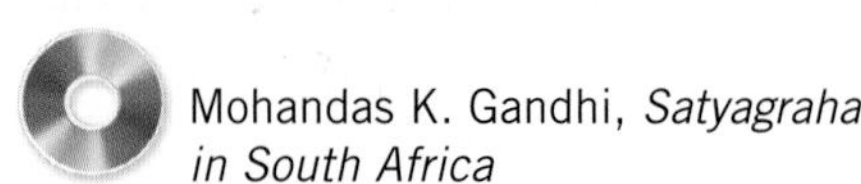

Mohandas K. Gandhi, *Satyagraha in South Africa*

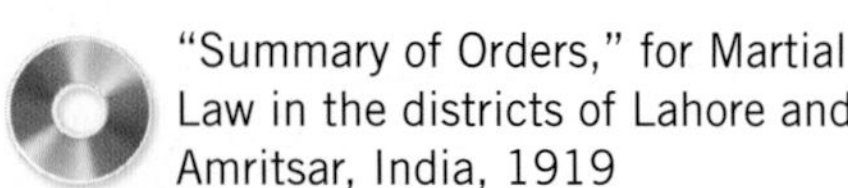

"Summary of Orders," for Martial Law in the districts of Lahore and Amritsar, India, 1919

In the euphoria of peace, even some Western politicians were free with optimistic rhetoric. The war would "end all wars." Its survivors would return to "homes fit for heroes." Progress would resume.

In America, where no fighting took place, this was believable, at first. But war-scarred Europe found it hard to match this mood. Europeans were already becoming convinced of the imminent "decline of the West"—the title of the German historian Oswald Spengler's postwar blockbuster. For those who could afford it, the 1920s in Europe was an age of desperate pleasure seeking. For the rest, it was a time to try to salvage something from disillusionment. The results included labor unrest, extremist politics, economic failures, and impoverishing inflation.

Disillusionment hit America later. The war made the United States' economy boom. In "seven fat years" from 1922 to 1929, a spiraling stock market seemed to promise universal riches. In 1924, 282 million shares of stock changed hands on Wall Street. In 1929, that figure was 1.824 billion. That same year, the crash came. In three weeks, beginning on October 24, American stocks fell in value by $30 billion (almost $400 billion in today's money). The effects bounced the economy into recession, bounded across the Atlantic, and set off a string of bank failures. Meanwhile, ecological disaster struck farms in the American West. "Brother, can you spare a dime?" sang crooners in the character of a war hero down on his luck.

Gandhi as he wished to be seen. He squats in a traditional position for Indian mystics, working calmly in a scholarly, reflective manner. His gaunt body, modest loincloth, and simply furnished home proclaim his selflessness and asceticism. He adopted a spinning wheel as the symbol of his movement for Indian independence to signify tradition, patience, constructiveness, self-sufficiency, and peace.

Disillusionment afflicted Latin America particularly deeply, because expectations there were so enormous. Argentina, Chile, Uruguay, Mexico, and Brazil were all self-styled lands of promise. In the early twentieth century, Argentina was the world's most desired destination for migrants. But Latin America's economies, after booming in the First World War, went into dramatic reversal after the war when demand for raw materials plummeted. Violent changes of government ensued. In 1930, in Argentina, Peru, and Brazil, army officers seized power or installed "emergency" governments with dictatorial powers. Guatemala, Honduras, Nicaragua, the Dominican Republic, and El Salvador soon followed suit.

The economic disasters of Europe and the Americas in the 1920s and 1930s seemed to show that the West was wormwood. It was an age of faultfinding with Western civilization. Some of the things people blamed were so fantastic as to be rationally incredible—yet miserable millions believed the rabble-rousers' claims and were susceptible to the appeal of "noisy little men" proposing easy and even "final" solutions. Anti-Semites, for instance, claimed that Jews controlled the world's economies and exploited gentiles. Advocates of eugenics claimed that unscientific breeding weakened society by encouraging inferior classes and races and degenerate individuals.

Marx's predictions seemed to be coming true. The poor were getting poorer. The failures of capitalism would drive them to revolution. Democracy was a disaster. Only authoritarian governments could force people to collaborate for the common good. Perhaps only totalitarian governments, extending their responsibility over every department of life, could deliver justice.

J. M. Keynes, from *The End of Laissez-Faire*

People who still believed in democracy and capitalism thought the system could be reformed from within. J. M. Keynes (1883–1946) advocated the most persuasive program. Governments could redistribute wealth through taxation and public spending, without weakening enterprise or infringing freedom. Well-judged interventions of this sort would stimulate the economy without stoking inflation (see Chapter 29). Britain, France, and Scandinavia adopted this solution to economic depression. So did President Franklin D. Roosevelt (1887–1945) in the United States.

Workers' demonstration. The Spanish painter Ramon Casas (1866–1932) specialized in meticulously painted scenes of bourgeois life of his native Barcelona, but he could also play the role of a social commentator. In 1902 he exhibited this scene of police dispersing a crowd of striking workers against a backdrop of gaunt factories. In the sky, there is gold beyond the industrial smog and perhaps a patch of hope.

The Shift to Ideological Conflicts

The alternatives were authoritarian or totalitarian. The right-wing or *corporatist* solution was to preserve private enterprise, but only on the understanding that individual rights, freedoms, and property were not to be allowed to exist for their own sake, but were at the disposal of the state. The state would force all citizens to collaborate and coerce or exterminate any groups thought to resist the common pursuit. Left-wing versions proposed to collectivize virtually all economic activity, seizing private property and eliminating "class enemies." This would have a morally, as well as economically, improving effect. The other main difference between Right and Left was that the Right was unashamedly nationalist, whereas the Left proclaimed internationalism, at least in its rhetoric. The Left was divided between those—usually called *anarchists*—who wanted collectives of workers to run economic activities, and *communists,* who wanted the state to own and control production, distribution, and exchange.

Long-accumulating class hatreds underlay ideological differences. Before the war, European elites talked themselves into expecting a showdown with the working class. Workers' demonstrations kindled fear and provoked massacres. On the eve of war in 1914, the British Foreign Secretary Sir Edward Grey predicted, "There will be socialist governments everywhere after this."

Such predictions were exaggerated. The first and, for a long time, the only successful revolution was hardly a workers' triumph. The Bolshevik uprising in Russia of October 1917 was a well-planned coup, which elevated the Communist Party to the role of an aristocracy and charismatic dictators—first Vladimir Ilyich Lenin (1870–1924), then Joseph Stalin (1879–1953)—to greater power than the czars'. What was left of the Russian Empire was renamed the "Soviet [meaning collective] Union." Copycat revolutions were defeated in Finland, Germany, Hungary, Bulgaria, and Italy. Socialists compromised with bourgeois rulers as the price of sharing power. But left-wing militancy kept up the struggle. Moscow encouraged and financed international communism.

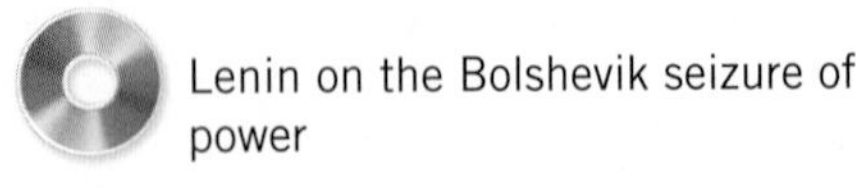

Lenin on the Bolshevik seizure of power

Communists often attached more importance to suppressing left-wing splinter groups than to overthrowing capitalist regimes. It may seem odd that leftists fought each other under the guns of their common enemies, but it is worth remembering that most of them accepted the Marxist dogma that revolution was inevitable. For the communists it was more important to ensure their own leadership of the revolution than to provoke it prematurely.

In some places beyond Europe, in the 1920s and 1930s, conflicts over power were increasingly seen as clashes of classes or ideological showdowns. In China, for instance, the main contending parties called themselves Nationalist and Communist. Their conflict escalated in the 1930s, despite the menace of Japanese invasion. In parts of the British, French, and Dutch Empires, rebels and malcontents identified with socialism. They saw a similarity between the plight of their own peoples, oppressed by imperialism, and the worker-victims of capitalism, whom they got to know when they worked or studied in the metropolitan centers of the empires to which they, unwillingly, belonged. Ho Chih Minh (1890–1969), for instance, who later led a communist revolution in Vietnam, worked as a waiter in Paris after the First World War. Tan Malaka, leader of Indonesian communists, learned communism in the Netherlands. Thus, the West exported its ideological conflicts, along with so many other aspects of its culture.

Indonesian communists. In 1925, when this photograph was taken in Batavia (now Jakarta), the Indonesian communist party had just launched a new policy of armed insurrection, after a series of unsuccessful strikes and a growing sense of desperation, as the Dutch authorities expelled its leaders. The three languages of the placard tell a story. Chinese immigrants were prominent in the movement. Malay—written here in Arabic script rather than the Roman alphabet currently preferred—was the language of the masses. The elite who ran the party, however, used Dutch. The rebellion launched the following year was another failure.

Whether **fascism**—an extreme and violent corporatist movement—was another splinter ideology of socialism, an independently evolved doctrine, or a state of mind in search of a doctrine has been passionately debated. Stubbornly undefinable, its symbols best expressed its nature. In ancient Rome, the *fascis* was a bundle of rods with an axe through the middle of it, carried before magistrates as an emblem of their power to scourge or behead wrongdoers. Italian fascists adopted these bloodstained images of law enforcement as what we would call their logo. They appealed to a system of values that put the group before the individual, cohesion before diversity, revenge before reconciliation, retribution before compassion, the supremacy of the strong before the defense of the weak. They justified the enforcement of order by violence and the obliteration of misfits, subversives, deviants, and dissenters.

Ho Chih Minh, "Equality!" 1922

Communists tended to be as ruthless as fascists. Communists persecuted and massacred class enemies. Fascists victimized or exterminated "inferior" communities and races. The Nazis put more than 6 million people to death because they were Jews or Gypsies. In the Soviet Union, Stalin exterminated millions of peasants and ethnic minorities. Both sets of extremists believed in the omnipotence of the state. Fascism had, perhaps, wider appeal. Advocating policies that could be summarized as socialism without the abolition of private property, fascists could mobilize small property owners from among the inflation-impoverished bourgeoisie. The cults of violence were equally characteristic of the militants of both Left and Right. Both extremes recruited their street armies from the victims of economic slump and social dislocation. The same ideals of fraternal community kept parties at both extremes together.

Individuals moved between fascism and militant socialism as if through connecting doors. Benito Mussolini (1883–1945) who, as leader of the first successful Fascist Party—he coined the word *fascist*—seized power in Italy in 1922, began his political life as a socialist. The German Nazi Party—whose program was essentially fascist, with an anti-Semitic driving force—was officially called the National Socialist German Workers' Party. Britain's failed "man of destiny," Colonel Juan Perón (1895–1974), who took over Argentina in 1946 and founded a movement that remains influential there, promised employers that with "workers organized by the state, revolutionary currents endangering capitalist society can be neutralized." But he also used socialist demagoguery. His wife Eva (1919–1952), a former radio diva, became a proletarian goddess, "the faithful voice of the shirtless masses."

Excerpts from the speeches of Juan Perón

By 1933, when the Nazis took power in Germany, it was clear that in European politics, ideological defiance transcended national hatreds. But the conflicts that followed were not straightforward struggles of Left and Right. Old hatreds crisscrossed the killing grounds. Between 1936 and 1939, for instance, civil war in Spain seemed to project to the rest of the world images of a dress rehearsal for a global struggle of Left against Right. In reality, however, the fighting was between broad coalitions pursuing domestic Spanish agendas. The right-wing coalition partnered virtual fascists with awkward allies: traditional Catholics, who were defending the Church; old-fashioned liberal centralists, who were equally numerous on the other side; romantic reactionaries who yearned to reinstate a long-excluded branch of the royal house; constitutional monarchists, who wanted to return to the cozy, corrupt parliamentary system of the previous generation; worshippers of "the sacred unity of Spain," who thought they were fighting to hold the country together. On the other side, along with the mutually warring sects of the Left, were conservative republicans, liberal anticlericals, admirers of French and British democratic standards, and right-wing regionalists, who supported the republicans as the lesser evil.

Adolf Hitler, excerpt from *Mein Kampf*

The World War Era, 1914–1945

1914	United States industrial production equal to whole of Europe combined
August 1914	World War I begins
1915	Mohandas K. Gandhi, leader of Indian independence movement, returns to India from South Africa
1916	Sarekat Islam mobilizes mass movement for independence of Indonesia
1917	Russian Revolution begins; United States enters World War I
November 1918	World War I ends
1919	First meeting of Pan-African Congress
1919–1920	Paris peace conference
1922	Benito Mussolini's Fascist Party takes power in Italy
1923	Turkish Republic founded
1924	Vladimir Lenin, leader of Russian Revolution dies; Joseph Stalin emerges as new Soviet leader
1929	U.S. stock market crash
1930–1931	Army officers seize power in Argentina, Peru, Brazil, Guatemala, El Salvador, and the Dominican Republic
1931	Japan invades Manchuria
1933	Nazis take power in Germany
1936–1939	Spanish Civil War
1939	Germany invades Poland; World War II begins
1939–1945	Nazis carry out genocide of Europe's Jews
1941	Germany invades Soviet Union; Japan attacks Pearl Harbor
June 1944	Allied liberation of France begins
August 1945	United States drops atomic bombs on Hiroshima and Nagasaki; World War II ends

Ideology, in any case, could still be sacrificed to national interest. The Nazi dictator, Adolf Hitler (1889–1945), regarded Jews and communists as his main enemies, but one of his chief aims was to crush Russia and conquer an empire of "living-space" and slave labor for Germany in Eastern Europe. In 1939, he made a nonaggression pact with his Soviet counterpart, Joseph Stalin. For both dictators, the pact was a temporary expedient. Hitler wanted to clear the ground for a knock-out war against France and Britain to free himself to deal with Russia in the future. Stalin wanted to get his hands on the resources of Finland, Romania, the Baltic states, and eastern Poland.

The pact wrecked the Western democracies' strategy for containing Hitler. Britain and France had attempted to buy time by conceding Hitler's demands and ignoring his provocations. Beginning in 1934, Hitler built up a massive military regime and reoccupied demilitarized parts of Germany. Then he forced German-Austrian unification and seized most of Czechoslovakia after trumping up a dispute over that country's German minority. The French and British hoped that Russia would keep him in check. The pact between Hitler and Stalin crushed those hopes and made war inevitable. The French and British had gambled that they could restrain Hitler by guaranteeing the integrity of his next target, Poland, even though geography made it impossible for them to offer Poland effective assistance. The German invasion of Poland, launched in September 1939, plunged them into a war that they had never wanted to fight and for which they were not ready.

The Second World War

In Europe, the Second World War (1939–1945) reran aspects of the First World War. This time, however, France crumbled, not Russia, and it was on their eastern front, rather than in the west, that the Germans became stuck. Hitler attacked Russia prematurely in June 1941, without first knocking Britain out of the war. Aided by "Generals January and February," and by Hitler's strategic blunders, Russia proved unconquerable. The decisive element was again American intervention—again procured despite American isolationism. Hitler made America's decision himself, declaring war in December 1941 in support of his ally, Japan.

Japanese society had become consecrated to war in the struggle to conquer China. The conflict escalated. Japan realized that it would have to procure the supplies its armies needed by conquering Dutch and British oilfields in southeast Asia. This was bound to become a global conflict. If Japan were to succeed, the United States would have to be intimidated into standing aside. In December 1941, Japan launched a preemptive strike against the American Pacific Fleet at Pearl Harbor in Hawaii. The attack was a success, but the strategy was miscalculated. The Americans were knocked out for long enough for Japanese forces to occupy French Indochina, overrun Dutch Indonesia and British Hong Kong, Malaya, and Burma, drive the United States from the Philippines and Guam, and fan out over the western Pacific. But a war of attrition began, in which the Americans, with help from Britain, Australia, and New Zealand and from the Chinese refusal to give up, gradually thrust the Japanese back (see Map 28.2).

Hiroshima, Japan, after the explosion of the atomic bomb. In August 1945, Japan's defeat was already manifest, but rather than negotiate a conditional surrender or sacrifice thousands of American lives by invading the Japanese islands, President Truman (1884–1972) decided on a terrible alternative: the incineration of the Japanese cities of Hiroshima and Nagasaki with atom bombs.

MAKING CONNECTIONS

THE WORLD WAR ERA, 1914–1945

BELLIGERENTS →	CONFLICT →	CAUSES →	OUTCOMES
Germany, Austria-Hungary, Ottoman Empire versus Great Britain, France, Russia, Italy, other European powers	World War I, 1914–1918	Imperial and national rivalries	Defeat of Germany: dismantling of Austria-Hungary and Ottoman Empires; Bolshevik Revolution in Russia; Britain and France victorious but empires weakened and discredited; United States emerges as richest nation in the world; League of Nations formed; postwar disillusionment pervades Europe
Japan versus China	Second Sino-Japanese War, 1937–1945	Various incidents instigated by Japan lead to full-scale war in 1937 in an attempt to turn China into a subject territory	Japanese invade China and turn Manchuria into a puppet state (Manchukuo); conflict merges with World War II
Allies (Great Britain, United States, Soviet Union, other powers) versus Axis (Germany, Italy, Japan, other powers)	World War II, 1939–1945	Clash between different ideologies and forms of government (fascism, communism, democracy), and national/imperial interests	Germany, Italy, and Japan defeated; Eastern Europe falls under Soviet domination; Germany divided; Holocaust and forced migrations transform European society; Japanese Empire dismantled; European powers begin to decolonize; formation of United Nations; United States and Soviet Union emerge as nuclear superpowers

MAP 28.2

World War II

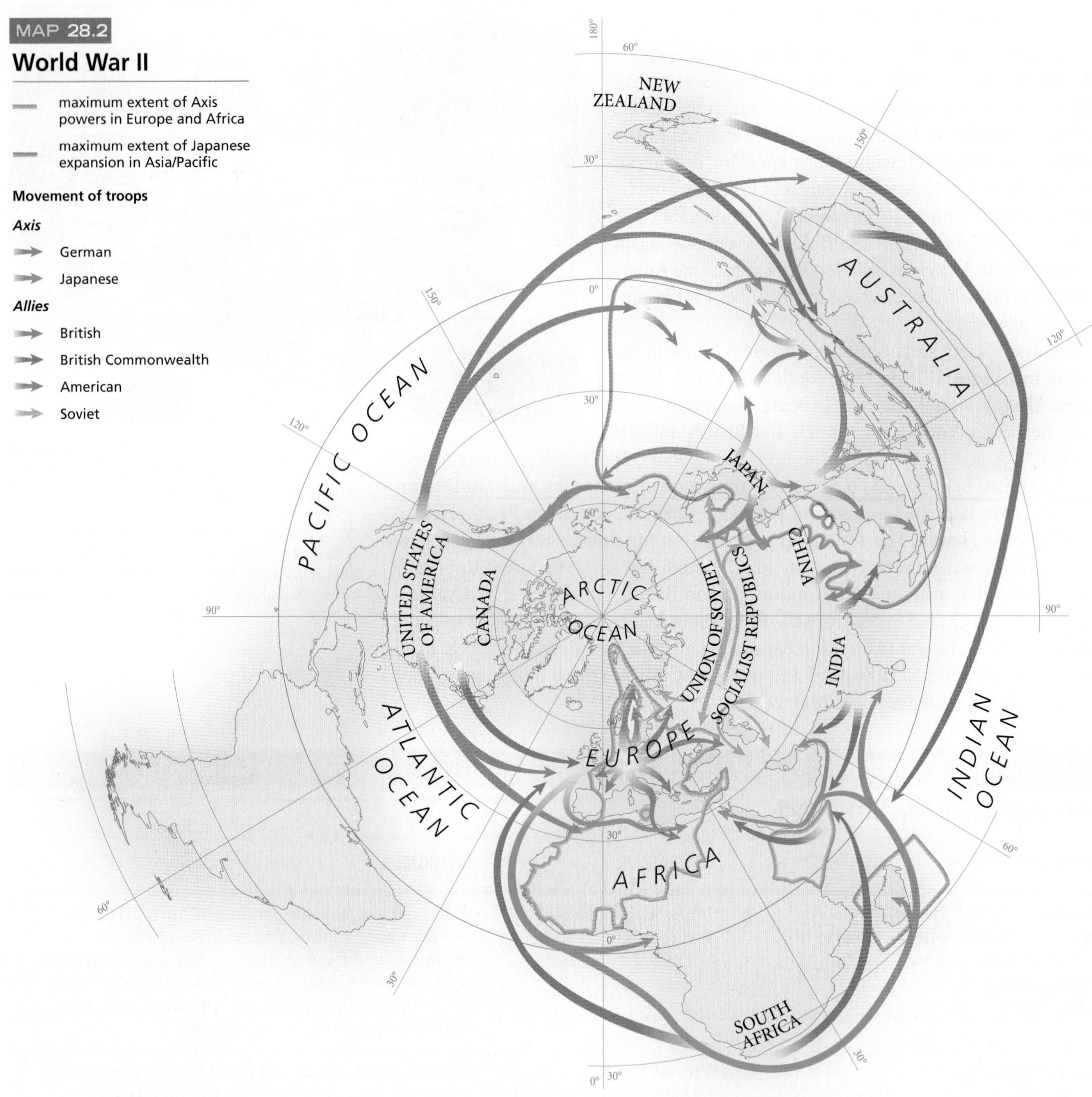

America and Britain constructed a vast coalition—known informally as the Allies and officially as the United Nations—to fight the war. In 1940, Italy joined Germany in what became known as the Axis. But Italians felt little enthusiasm for war. German troops became overcommitted pursuing Italian adventures in North Africa, where the British forces triumphed in 1943, and the Balkans. Meanwhile, the Russian campaign ground down the German armies. With the invasion and liberation of France that began in June 1944, Allied victory in Europe became irreversible. The Germans launched terrifying rocket bombs against Britain toward the end of the war, but these weapons made little difference. Germany was crushed between Russians from the east and the Allied forces from the west. By the time Hitler killed himself on April 30, 1945, aerial bombing had pulverized Germany, its armed forces were collapsing, and the Russians were in Berlin.

There was never any real likelihood of Japanese victory. Japanese leaders were aware of this. Their naval command compared war with the United States to a risky operation that might kill a critically ill patient. The Japanese ended up with too many enemies and overextended lines. Even so, Japan fought on, recoiling from surrender, which, in Japanese culture, was considered shameful. The end came only because the war stimulated research into devastating new technology. In August 1945, American planes dropped atom bombs on Hiroshima and Nagasaki, killing over 120,000 people and poisoning the survivors with radiation. The Japanese, who had no such bombs, surrendered.

THE COLD WAR ERA, 1945–1991

The peace was harder to win than the war. Franklin Roosevelt, like Wilson before him, had a vision of a new world order. In Roosevelt's version, Britain, Russia, and China would, in effect, divide the world among them and collaborate to police peace. But protracted conflict threatened from three sources: civil wars in "liberated" countries, the ambitions of international communism, and Russia's desire for security or power along its borders. Stalin seized or garrisoned much of Eastern Europe. In March 1946, Winston Churchill (1874–1965), who had led the British government for most of the war years, announced the descent of an "Iron Curtain" from the Baltic to the Adriatic, dividing Soviet-dominated Eastern Europe from the West.

Winston Churchill, the "Iron Curtain" speech

George C. Marshall, "The Marshall Plan," 1947

Superpower Confrontation

In 1947, America tried one of the most generous foreign aid programs ever, the **Marshall Plan** (named after Secretary of State George C. Marshall [1880–1959]), to seduce former enemies into dependence on the United States and "create the social and political conditions in which free institutions can exist." American taxpayers paid for European reconstruction, and Western Europe began to recover. But by choice, Russian occupation, or communist coups, the states east of the Iron Curtain became Soviet satellites. At Stalin's orders, they turned down Marshall aid. A ring of American client states faced a heavily fenced Soviet Empire.

So another opportunity to reconstruct world order had been lost. However, democracy did take root in countries American forces occupied. Japan was transformed into a demilitarized, democratic state and a staunch American ally. Italy also democratized without difficulty. Germany had to be partitioned. The Soviet zone in the east became a rigid dictatorship, but the American-, British-, and French-occupied zones in the west were combined to form another model democracy, the Federal Republic of Germany.

The world shivered under a nuclear cloud. British experimenters had noted the explosive properties of nuclear fission as early as 1911. In 1935, Frédéric Joliot, in his speech receiving the Nobel Prize for work on nuclear energy, warned that an atomic chain reaction could destroy the world. By 1939, European scientists had nearly overcome the technical obstacles to the manufacture of a bomb, but the more immediate

Bomb shelter. A U.S. public-information campaign photograph of the 1950s makes the "shadow of the bomb" seem almost comfortable with a family posed earnestly together around a radio in their well-stocked bomb shelter. But this reassuring propaganda was a sham. Only the elite had shelters, and if their shelters had survived an atomic bomb, these people would have emerged into a deadly, poisoned environment.

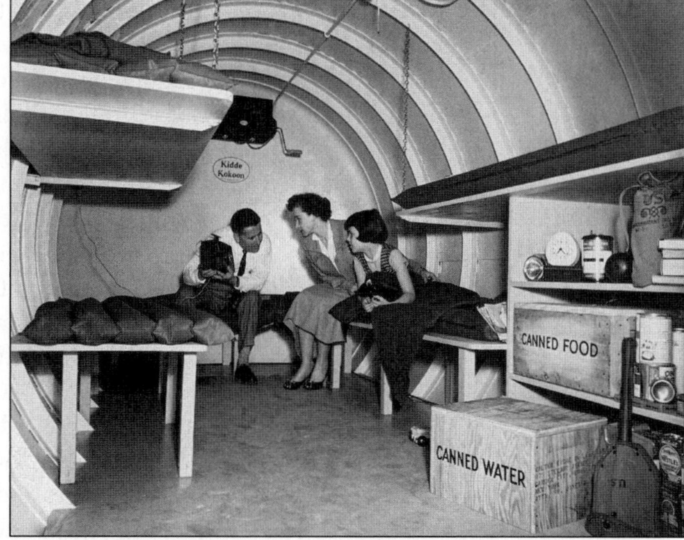

demands of the war effort distracted British researchers. Nazi conquest dispersed Joliot's team in France. In Germany, Werner Heisenberg (see Chapter 27) was unwilling or unable to put a bomb in Hitler's hands.

So the first bombs were made in America. Had the United States kept its monopoly of the weapon, it would have been permanently secure in the role of world arbiter. But Russia produced its own "A-bomb" in 1949.

Nuclear equivalency with the United States guaranteed Russia's free hand in territories it had already conquered or coerced. Yugoslavia broke free of Russian hegemony in 1947–1948 before the completion of the Soviet bomb. Afterwards, other East European satellite states tried to do the same and failed. Within a few years, technical improvements brought Russian and American firepower to the level of "mutually assured destruction." The balance of terror kept the peace between them.

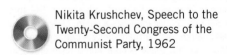

Harry S Truman, The Truman Doctrine, 1947

Soviet and Western blocs confronted one another in a cold war that never quite reached boiling point. The Western allies ringed the Soviet world with alliances of anticommunist states in Europe, the Middle East, and Asia. The Soviet Union nurtured revolutionary allies among the poor countries of the world (see Map 28.3).

Depending on one's point of view, the conquests of international communism were battering rams pointing at Western Europe and the rest of the world, or giant buffers projecting the natural caution of a Russia that had barely survived the Second World War. Russian leaders' rhetoric wavered between defensive anxiety and aggressive bravado, reflecting struggles for supremacy within the Soviet elite. Stalin's eventual successor, Nikita Khrushchev (1894–1971), hammered loudly on the table at international conferences to distract attention from his weakness and practiced "brinkmanship"—periodically scaring the world with the threat of nuclear war—to deter the West from aggression. One of these crises—in 1962, over the housing of Soviet missiles in Cuba—nearly led to nuclear conflict. But both sides backed down. The Russians removed their missiles from Cuba, the Americans removed theirs from Turkey. Both powers recognized the need for co-existence, at least between themselves.

Nikita Krushchev, Speech to the Twenty-Second Congress of the Communist Party, 1962

In retrospect, the Soviet phenomenon was bound to fail. Russia's postwar power reflected its natural endowments: a larger population than most of its neighbors, vast resources, and a heartland too big for enemies to conquer. On the other hand, the Soviet Empire was ramshackle, no more able than that of the czars to contain the national and religious identities of its subject-peoples. State-run economies tend to inefficiency. The Soviet elite compounded the problem by bad policies: collectivization of agriculture, which deprived farmers of any stake in the land; repression of the free market for goods and services, which led to nightmares of central planning and a chronic shortage of basic consumer goods; suppression of traditional cultures, which created festering resentment; and a horrific disregard for the environment, which wasted resources and polluted the landscape. The survival of the Soviet system to 1991 is more surprising than its collapse.

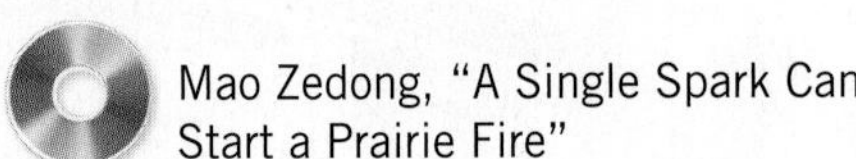

Mao Zedong, "A Single Spark Can Start a Prairie Fire"

For a long time, however, it looked as if communism would win the ideological struggle and the Soviets would get most of the world on their side. In 1949, for instance, China appeared to join the Soviet camp when the Chinese communists defeated the nationalists. Since the overthrow of the Qing dynasty in 1911 (see Chapter 27), no Chinese government had been able to replace the legitimacy of the old imperial order or hold the country together. The Chinese communists succeeded where others had failed: mobilizing popular enthusiasm, unifying the country, creating a new elite—the Party—to replace the old mandarinate. Mao Zedong (mao dzeh-dohng) (1893–1976) was the most effective leader the Chinese

MAP 28.3

The Alliances of the Cold War

Communist Party had, organizing its weak forces into an army that could never be defeated because it could never be pinned down.

At first China's revolution seemed a great addition to Soviet power. The United States struggled against communist encroachments in Korea. The country had been divided in 1945 because Soviet troops had occupied its northern half while

Atrocity. This 1973 Pulitzer Prize winning photo shows South Vietnamese forces casually walking behind terrified children, including Kim Phuc, center, as they head down a highway after a plane dropped napalm on suspected communist guerrilla hiding places. The terrified girl had ripped off her burning clothes while fleeing.

American forces had garrisoned the south. Supposedly, North and South Korea would be reunited after elections, but the rulers Russia installed in the north and those the United States backed in the south never held the elections. In June 1950, the north invaded the south. America stepped in, with military support from Britain and Australia. Despite Chinese intervention on the other side, the Americans and their allies drove the invaders back to the north. Korea remains divided.

In Vietnam, however, a similar situation led to a disaster for the United States. In the 1950s, after French imperialism in Indochina collapsed, a partition of Vietnam between communist and anticommunist regimes led to civil war. American troops poured into South Vietnam from 1961. The war of containment the Americans tried to fight proved impracticable against Vietnamese guerillas. The United States got trapped in rising costs, mounting casualties, plunging morale. American opinion would neither approve perseverance nor admit defeat. America entered a 12-year agony that dominated the world's media. No war had ever been so ruthlessly exposed on television and in the newspapers. Daily images of dead and wounded soldiers, atrocities, and ineptitude disturbed domestic audiences.

In response, peace movements spread across the West. "Flower power" celebrated "love, not war." Young men sought to evade serving in the military. In 1968, massive street demonstrations across Europe and America toppled some governments and shook others. The would-be revolutionaries mostly talked themselves into inertia or outgrew rebelliousness. Protest ebbed with the war. But the collapse of South Vietnam in 1975 wrecked American prestige and undermined America's moral authority. The insurgents' success encouraged America's enemies. Americans recoiled from responsibility for other people's liberty. The newly independent countries of the era were disinclined to take America's side. Communist takeover in Cambodia and Laos in the 1970s made the American rout seem worse. Cambodia's regime was one of the most brutal in a savage century, but its communism proved unique and demented. Pol Pot (1926–1998) proposed a return to a purely agrarian state, such as had supposedly prevailed in Cambodia's medieval golden age, by massacring the bourgeoisie, wrecking industry, and depopulating the cities.

As if these political setbacks were not enough, the West also seemed to be losing in the economic and scientific stakes against the Soviet system. In 1957, Russia launched the first successful spacecraft, *Sputnik I,* and in 1961 put the first man in space. Space exploration was expensive and brought virtually no useful economic or scientific returns. But America, in danger of forfeiting world prestige, was forced to play catch-up, which it did, putting the first man on the moon in 1969. Meanwhile Russia seemed ahead in the struggle to forge what a British prime minister called the "white heat" of technology.

However, the Soviet economy was not as strong as propaganda painted it. "Socialism is management," Lenin once said. But no Russian government managed the economy well. In 1954, for instance, Khrushchev launched a disastrous initiative known as the Virgin Lands scheme. He intended to turn vast areas of steppe into farmland—the way the great ecological revolution of the nineteenth century had transformed the North American prairie (see Chapter 23). In this case, however, intensive farming soon exhausted the soil of the grasslands the Russians plowed up. In all, an area greater than that of the entire farmland of Canada was lost.

In most respects, however, the era of Soviet economic success lasted until the world oil crisis of 1973, when oil-exporting countries, by hiking the price of fuel, triggered massive global inflation. The economies of Russia's satellite regimes in Eastern Europe slipped out of economic dependence on Moscow, which could not afford to subsidize them as lavishly as before, and into indebtedness to Western bankers who loaned them vast sums. Then, in the 1980s, after sending troops into Afghanistan to replace a ruler who was becoming too independent with a more pro-Moscow puppet government, Russia found itself embroiled in a hopeless war against fanatical Islamic guerrillas who were financed by conservative Arab regimes and armed by the United States. The costs in blood and cash were greater than Russians were willing to bear. President Ronald Reagan (1911–2004) stepped up the arms race, outstripping Russia's paying power. The Chicago economists (see Chapter 29) on whom Reagan relied for advice convinced the world that private enterprise made for prosperity and that economics was too important to be left to the state. The thinker who worked along ide them, the Austrian F. A. von Hayek (1899–1992), became the source of the era's fashionable idea: order in the service of freedom.

The pope helped dissolve Soviet power. In 1978, a Polish cardinal, Karel Wojtyla (d. 2005), became Pope John Paul II. He used his wide range of acquaintances among Catholics in Eastern Europe to build up resistance to Soviet domination. The Polish trade union Solidarity launched a series of strikes and demonstrations

"Each day of labor—a step toward communism!" Russian communists adopted the hammer and sickle emblem to symbolize the alliance of peasants and workers. In practice, however, landowning peasants remained hard to convince. Joseph Stalin had millions of them massacred and exiled in the 1920s and 1930s for refusing to join collective farms. As late as 1968, however, propaganda still featured images of steel and grain—the privileged products of Soviet economic planning.

A CLOSER LOOK

REPORTING OUR HARVEST TO CHAIRMAN MAO

Mao Zedong's "Great Cultural Revolution" was meant to remake society by forcing the privileged to share the lives of peasants and workers. But by victimizing the educated and the enterprising, Mao wrecked the economy and impoverished China. Propaganda strove to conceal the truth—not least from Mao himself.

The bystanders and the little girl nestled protectively in Mao's arm represent peasants and youth—the groups Mao tried to mobilize against professionals and intellectuals, whom he saw as enemies.

Mao, godlike in stature and simple in dress, recites his "Thoughts" to implausibly smiling adorers.

The girl on the left wears the badge of the communist party on her peasant's wide straw hat. Under Mao, the party became the country's only permitted elite.

Peasants bring agricultural abundance to Mao—like tribute-bearers to a traditional emperor or worshippers to a god. In reality, there was no abundance of food or anything else in China. Mao's policies undermined productivity in agriculture as well as industry.

How does this painting differ from historians' accounts of China under Mao?

from 1980 onward, first against economic mismanagement by Poland's communist regime and then against the regime itself.

From 1985, the Soviet Union floated off the shoals and into the wake of the West, under a leadership that had ceased to believe in socialist rhetoric. Mikhail Gorbachev (b. 1931) dismantled the command economy, freed the market, introduced accountable government, and, eventually, submitted to demands for democracy and for self-determination by the Soviet Union's ethnic minorities. Moscow manipulated or permitted similar revolutions in the satellite states—the last act of a dying supremacy. Dissidents took over. Satellite states zoomed out of the Soviet orbit. The two European communist supranational states—the Soviet Union and the Yugoslav federation—splintered.

China, meanwhile, had become an enemy to both sides in the Cold War. Mao disappointed Moscow almost from the moment he took power. He admired the bandit heroes of Chinese romance more than he did Lenin or Stalin. He was a peasant by birth and developed his own theory of peasant revolution. "He doesn't understand the most elementary Marxist truths," said Stalin, who hated Mao. Under his rule, China remained as aloof from the Soviet Union as from the West. Mao denounced America for imperialism and the Russians for "bourgeois deviationism"—turning the Communist Party into a new kind of middle class. He competed with both for the friendship of the successor states of dismantled empires, while pursuing an aggressive policy toward neighbors. China overran Tibet, intervened in the Korean War, provoked confrontations on the Indian, Vietnamese, and Russian borders, and encouraged insurgents in Nepal.

Mao's domestic policies arrested China's development. He caused famine by communalizing agriculture and environmental disaster by absurd schemes of industrialization. He launched campaigns of mass destruction against a sequence of irrationally selected enemies: dogs, sparrows, rightists, leftists—even, at one point, grass and flowers. He outlawed romantic love as bourgeois and, proclaiming that vice was hereditary, reduced the descendants of ancient elites—scholars, landowners, officials—to the ranks of an underclass. In 1966, his regime proclaimed a **Cultural Revolution.** In practice, this meant forcing professionals—including teachers, scientists, doctors, and technicians, on whom the country relied—into manual labor or degrading them with humiliating punishments. For more than three years, intellectuals were brutalized, antiquities smashed, books burned, beauty despised, study subverted, work stopped. China's economy reverted to chaos.

Cultural Revolution: violence at Qinghua University, 1968

The long-term outcome of Mao's moral and economic failures was the reconversion of China to capitalist economics. Between 1969 and 1972, President Richard Nixon (1913–1994) abandoned America's traditional hostility, accepting China into the United Nations and opening American trade with it. It was an attempt to wedge Russia and China further apart, while mopping up some of the spoilage from the Vietnam War. Nixon's strategy worked, especially after Mao's death.

Deng Xiaoping on capitalism

Mao's successor, Deng Xiaoping (1904–1997), recommended Chinese "to get rich"—which neither Mao nor Confucius would ever have approved. After making trade agreements with America and Japan, Deng freed up the Chinese economy, gradually returning more and more production and finance to the private sector. In 1986, Vietnam, too, adopted a policy of market liberalization. By the 1990s, China's was the fastest-growing economy in the world. Early in the new century, Chinese demand was driving up the prices of energy and commodities worldwide. North Korea was the only state in the region, in the world, really, that remained inward looking, isolated, and hostile to economic freedoms.

DECOLONIZATION

Before the Cold War could end, the world had to endure the agonies of decolonization—the breakup of the old European empires in Asia and Africa (see Map 28.4). Between 1941 and 1945, Japan drove white rulers out of southeast Asia. After the war, the United States conceded independence to the Philippines. In other parts of Asia, nationalist resistance forced the colonialists to surrender power.

The Dutch "police operation" in the East Indies (1945–1949) was really a brutal war that ended in Dutch retreat and the independent Republic of Indonesia. The French suffered ignominious defeat in Indochina in 1954. The British managed to defeat communist insurgents in Malaya, but colonial rule ended there in 1957.

Frantz Fanon, from *The Wretched of the Earth*

Meanwhile, in 1947, the British pulled out of India in haste, escaping horrific problems of famine control and ethnic and religious conflict. Partition of Britain's Indian Empire between Hindu and Muslim states—India and Pakistan, respectively—claimed at least 500,000 lives. The British bullied or blackmailed native princes into joining either India or Pakistan. Eventually the maharajahs were stripped of their powers.

European decolonization dismantled more than empire. In many places, colonial powers felt forced to abandon or sideline old elites—European settlers and native aristocracies—in favor of upstart leaders from the rising native middle classes. Usually the newcomers had been educated in Europe or mission schools at home. Once the colonial armies left, the new men, who commanded popular support, revolutionary armies, or help from abroad, stepped into leading roles, cutting out traditional elites or reducing the old aristocracies and monarchies to purely ceremonial functions. In India, which became the world's most populous democracy, the process worked exceptionally well. Pakistan was less successful and more typical. After about a generation of independence, it was defeated in two wars against India, partitioned to accommodate secessionists in what became known as Bangladesh, and subjected to long periods of military rule.

Guerrilas, not rebels. In line with U.S. policy, which favored Indonesian independence and the end of Dutch colonialism in southeast Asia, the caption for this Associated Press photograph, in July 1947, identified these fighters not as rebels against Dutch colonialism, but as "non-uniformed combat guerrillas" of "supporting units to the regular military forces" of the "Republic of Indonesia." After bitter fighting, the Dutch finally ceded Indonesian independence in 1949.

Most Westerners assumed that Africa would take longer to decolonize than Asia, but the winds of change blew up a storm in that continent, too. Because sub-Saharan Africa largely escaped the Second World War, some forms of production—especially of rubber and food—were relocated there. As a result, an ambitious African middle class developed. Meanwhile, modern medicine produced a population boom. Uncontrollable numbers of needy people made empires unprofitable. Rather than shoulder escalating costs, it became cheaper for European powers to grant independence and foreign aid.

Egypt played the role in Africa that the Japanese played in Asia—uncovering the weakness of European empires and hastening their downfall. Britain and France, the two main colonial powers, were humiliated in a showdown with Gamal Abdel Nasser (1918–1970), an Egyptian nationalist whom an officers' coup elevated to power. When he seized the Suez Canal Company in 1956, Britain and France, joined opportunistically by Israel, invaded. For reasons of its own, the United States repudiated the Franco-British operation and, in effect, forced its allies to accept Egypt's case. A flight of colonial powers from Africa followed.

Nasser, speech on the Suez Canal crisis

The cracks spread outward from Egypt. In the year of Suez, Britain evacuated Sudan, and France left Tunisia and Morocco. Algeria was more problematic. Although the vast interior of the country was a French colony, the parts of Algeria on the Mediterranean were considered an integral part of France, with over 1 million European settlers by the 1950s, many of whom were prepared to fight France, if necessary, to remain French. A savage war that broke out in 1954 between the French army and Muslim rebels settled the question in favor of independence by 1962, but not before mutinous generals and enraged settlers threatened to topple the government of France itself. Meanwhile, in 1957, Ghana in West Africa became the first sub-Saharan African state to gain independence. After that, the skirts of empire were lifted with indecent haste. In 1960, 14 new states came into being in Africa. Again, newcomers, schooled in resistance, replaced old elites. In Ghana, for instance, the independence leader Kwame Nkrumah (1909–1972) had "PG" for prison graduate embroidered on his cap. In Kenya, the first president, Jomo Kenyatta (1889–1978), had probably been the secret leader of the terrorists who had slaughtered white settlers and African loyalists under British colonial rule in the 1950s.

Kwame Nkrumah, from *I Speak of Freedom: A Statement of African Ideology*

Postcolonial rulers in Africa adopted or affected secular programs, usually heavily influenced by socialism, and flirted with Moscow or Beijing, either out of ideological conviction or to maximize their freedom of maneuver and opportunities for graft or aid. The ease with which many of them slid into despotic habits, and reduced their countries to dictatorships and destitution, dismayed Western liberals who had hoped that decolonization would bring freedom and prosperity.

Jomo Kenyatta, from *Facing Mt. Kenya*

Leader cults filled the gaps that the extinction or subversion of traditional loyalties left open. Nkrumah, who called himself the Redeemer, became prey to messianic delusions, as his troops sang, "Nkrumah never dies." Jean-Bedel Bokassa (1921–1996) declared the Central African Republic an "empire" and crowned himself its emperor in imitation of Napoleon. Idi Amin (1925–2003) used terror as a method of government and plunged Uganda into chaos. In Sierra Leone, Siaka Stevens (1905–1988) became preoccupied with justifying polygamy. In Congo, Joseph Mobutu (1930–1997) milked the economy of billions of dollars. Francisco Macías Nguema in Equatorial Guinea—executed by his own nephew after a coup in 1979—and Robert Mugabe (b. 1924) in Zimbabwe impoverished their countries and deployed armed gangs to terrorize opponents.

Decolonization left lands staggering under terrible burdens. Their populations were normally growing at an unprecedented pace, for which the colonial regimes had not prepared them. They were usually encumbered with irrational, indefensible borders that the departing colonialists had hastily outlined. The principle of national self-determination, which had guided, however imperfectly, the dismantling of imperialism inside Europe after the First World War, was ignored in the wider world. Colonial regimes crammed historically hostile communities into single states, or forced them into unstable "federal" superstates, or imposed borders between newly independent states that neither side found acceptable. International law treated postcolonial borders as inviolable, even where they were oppressive or unworkable.

MAP 28.4

Decolonization Since World War II

before 1950

1950–1956

after 1956

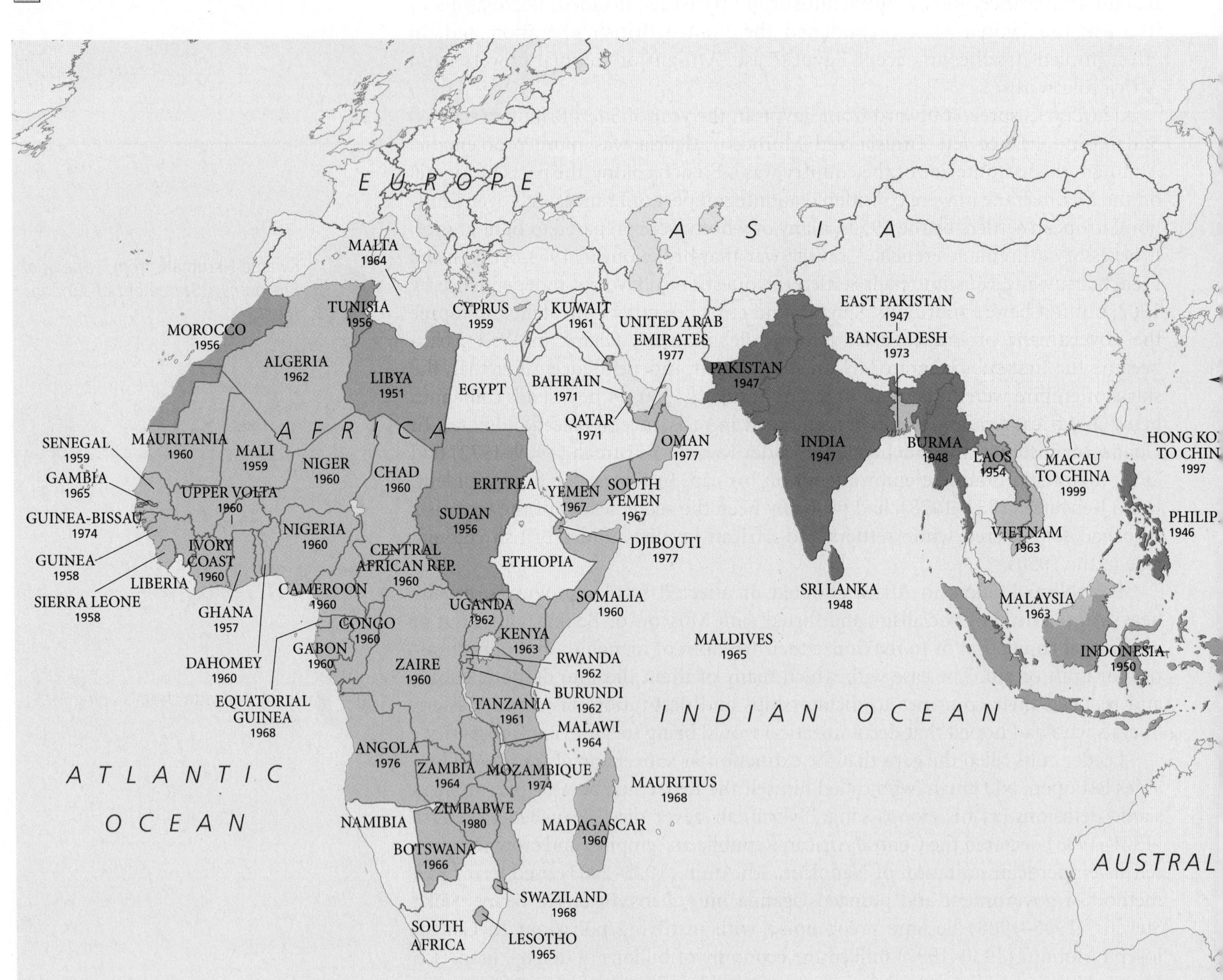

So civil wars commonly accompanied or followed decolonization, and disputes over the divisions of territory often remained unresolved into the twenty-first century: between new states, such as India and Pakistan; between Catholics and Protestants in Ireland; Jews and Arabs in Israel and Palestine; Turks and Greeks in Cyprus; Christians and Muslims in Nigeria, Sudan, Ivory Coast, and the Philippines; Tamils and Singhalese in Sri Lanka; centralists and secessionists in Congo, western Sahara, and Uganda; rivals for resources in Angola and Mozambique; and traditional elites and historically underprivileged groups in Liberia, Sierra Leone, Rwanda, Burundi, and other new countries in Africa and Asia.

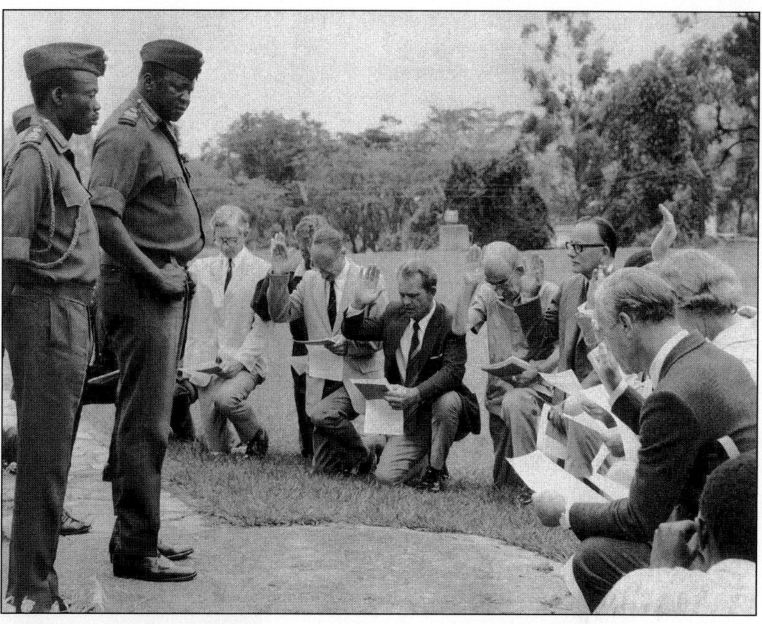

Leader cult. When colonial powers rushed ill prepared to disengage from Africa in the 1960s, they left dysfunctional states behind, prey to ruthless dictators, sprung from the new elites that Europeans promoted to offset the power of traditional leaders. Idi Amin, for instance, of Uganda, who seized power there in 1971, had been a sergeant under the British. This photograph from 1975 captures an incident of his increasingly unbalanced behavior as ruler of his country, when he forced white subjects and employees into taking bizarre and humiliating oaths of allegiance to him, drafting them into the armed services, so that they would be under military discipline, and exacting vows to fight against the white-dominated South African regime.

All the ensuing wars multiplied the sufferings of the people who endured them, but the Palestinian conflict had the worst long-term effects on global history. In 1948, the British, who had occupied the country since the collapse of the Ottoman Empire in 1918, left in the face of murderous conflict between Jews and Arabs. What swiftly emerged was a division of Palestine into a Jewish state and Arab enclaves. The Jews, who called their state Israel, were victorious in subsequent wars that left them in control not only of territory the British and the United Nations had assigned to the Arabs of Palestine, but also of land that Arab states had previously occupied. In the early twenty-first century, despite fitful progress, the resulting problems remained. Israel agreed in principle to recognize a Palestinian state, but its boundaries and nature were undetermined. Guarantees for Israeli security remained unsatisfactory. By choosing in effect to guarantee Israel's survival, the United States stoked Arab rage and alienated international opinion, especially in the Muslim world.

Palestinian Declaration of Independence, 1988

Meanwhile, the economic problems of decolonized lands mounted. In the 1970s and 1980s, the value of many primary products on the world market collapsed. This was the result of two so-called revolutions: the first, known as the green revolution, glutted the world with cheap grains (see Chapter 30). Simultaneously, an information revolution replaced many traditional industries and bore the West into a postindustrial age, in which services and information replaced manufacture as the main source of employment. The gap in wealth between the ex-imperialists and their former subjects became an abyss. Business imperialism was not easily thrown off. Even after colonies achieved political independence, their economic dependence frequently continued, often on the Soviet Union or the United States—the Cold War contenders whom newly independent governments sought to play off against one another. Cuba—always smarting under American economic control—played the game with some success after 1959, when revolutionaries, under Fidel Castro (b. 1927), threw out a dictatorship that had enjoyed Washington's support. Castro nationalized businesses—especially those Americans owned—and established an egalitarian welfare system. The United States took both offense and fright, and Castro became a client of the Soviet Union, while imposing authoritarian controls on Cuba. He even sent troops to Africa where the Soviets wanted to shore up regimes that favored them. The collapse of his Soviet ally in 1991 and the changing conditions of global trade obliged Castro to relax economic controls, but Cuba remained perhaps the only example of sustained socialism in the world.

Fidel Castro, *History Will Absolve Me*, 1953

Hamas supporters. A series of wars from 1948 to 1974 left Israelis in occupation of lands with a large and resentful Palestinian population, many of whom, rejecting the very existence of the State of Israel, resorted to resistance by terrorism. Even peaceful demonstrations—like this one in 2005 by supporters of the radical party Hamas—became exercises in martial discipline. Disputes over the distribution of land, water, jobs, and financial aid, and the exclusion by Israel of some Palestinian refugees from their former homes, inflamed the situation. Hamas won democratic elections—against rivals who favored accommodation with Israel—in 2006.

THE NEW WORLD ORDER

At the end of the Cold War, the United States had no rival and could set the world's agenda. Most of the world willingly adopted the democratic principles long associated with America. In 1974, only 36 states could reasonably be called democracies. By 2000, 139 states were democracies. Democracy was the only political ideology universally praised, albeit often insincerely.

Authoritarian government disappeared from southern Europe. Between 1974 and 1978, Greece, Portugal, and Spain all made the transition to democracy. In much of Latin America, military dictatorships seized power in the 1970s, often with the connivance of U.S. administrations. By the 1990s, however, democracy was restored—shakily in some countries—in almost the whole of the continent. The Philippines experienced a democratic revolution in 1986, In 1994, South Africa embraced democracy. The white parliament dissolved itself, and the first democratic elections brought Nelson Mandela (b. 1918) to the presidency (see Chapter 29).

Nelson Mandela, from "The Struggle Is My Life" from *Freedom, Justice and Dignity for All South Africa*

While much of the world democratized, most countries adopted **human rights** into their laws. These rights included guarantees of life, personal liberty, and dignity; freedom of expression, of religion, of education, and of equality under the law; and minimal standards of nourishment, health, and housing. The Helsinki Agreement of 1975, which pledged its signers to respect human rights, was particularly significant, because the Soviet Union signed it, along with most other European countries, Canada, and the United States. Dissident groups throughout the communist world were enormously encouraged. It was easier, however, to get assent in principle to the concept of human rights than to implement them. In practice, states ignored such rights whenever they wished. Even the United States found ways around its obligations in dealing with people accused of terrorist acts or of collaboration with the enemy during wars in Afghanistan and Iraq in the early twenty-first century. Some detainees captured in these wars were interned offshore in an attempt to exclude them from the protection of United States' laws. Others were subjected to torture by executive dispensation in defiance of the law or handed over to governments, such as those in Syria, Egypt, and Saudi Arabia, that abused prisoners.

Democratization made little impact in some states—especially in Africa and the Muslim world. Some post-Soviet republics fell into the hands of authoritarian leaders. Under Vladimir Putin, who became president in 1999, Russia itself attracted fears that democracy was in jeopardy. In South Asia, India and Sri Lanka preserved democracy, despite a secessionist war by the Tamil minority in Sri Lanka, while Pakistan and Bangladesh were often under military rule. In southeast Asia, a fault line divided nondemocratic Myanmar, Laos, and Vietnam from the more or less democratic states in the rest of the region.

In Latin America, Cuba remained a dictatorship, while some new democracies seemed fragile. Elected presidents of authoritarian inclinations—Hugo Chávez (b. 1954) in Venezuela, for instance—showed scant respect for democratic institutions. Most disturbingly, China continued to repress democratic opposition.

United Nations Declaration of Human Rights, 1948

If there was an opportunity to fashion a more democratic, just, and peaceful world, the United States did not take it. American leaders from the 1980s onward lacked what President George H. W. Bush (b. 1924) called "the vision thing." They made no attempt to create international institutions to preserve world peace. They declined to accept the jurisdiction of an International Criminal Court. They kept aloof from efforts to establish a global environmental policy. They bypassed the United Nations when it suited them to do so. They intervened militarily on their own say-so in foreign countries. They exhibited what much of the world condemned as bias toward the Middle East.

In pursuit of its own national interests, the United States often sponsored antidemocratic regimes, especially in the Arab world. Nor were America's own democratic credentials perfect. Two presidents—John F. Kennedy in 1960 and George W. Bush in 2000—almost certainly came to power as a result of electoral malpractice. In 1974, President Nixon had to resign after revelations that he had attempted to obstruct justice by subverting investigations into a break-in in 1972 at Democratic Party headquarters. Elections have been bought with millions of dollars and abandoned by millions of voters.

Most Americans wanted America to be a benevolent superpower, but the United States had cast itself in the role of world policeman, and the American taxpayer had to pick up the tab. This pleased no one. American governments, however, proved unwilling or unable to spread the burden, share power, or provide for a future in which America could no longer take care of the world.

"Freedom for Bush." Graffiti in Baghdad in June 2004 satirize President George W. Bush's claim to have made war in Iraq to promote freedom. One graffito clothes the Statue of Liberty in the garb of violent U.S. racists; the other shows a tortured Iraqi. American soldiers had been caught photographing each other torturing and sexually humiliating Iraqi prisoners, including innocent noncombatants. Soon after, the U.S. government admitted that it had authorized other instances of torture beyond the jurisdiction of U.S. courts.

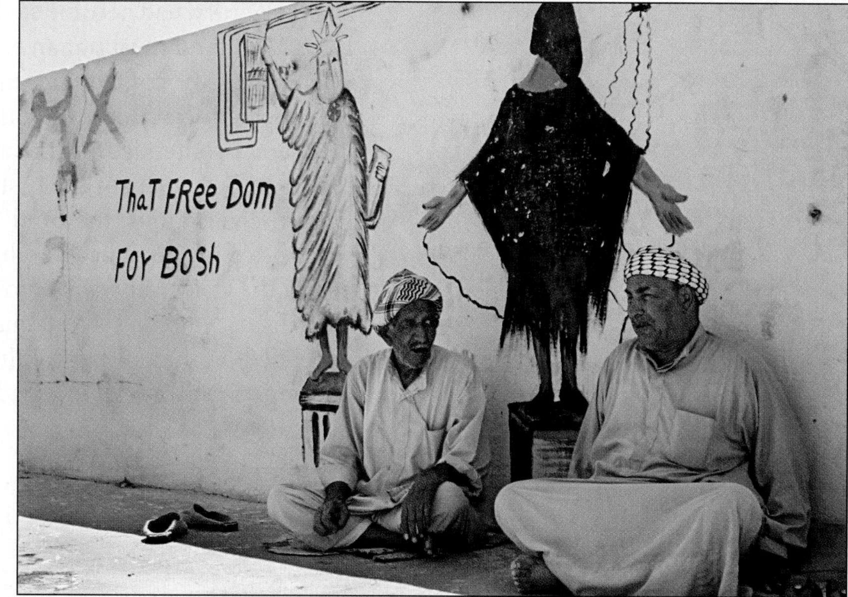

The European Union

China was the most likely successor to the United States in the role of global hegemon. Although leaders talked of Pan-Arab or Pan-African unity, nothing meaningful ever came of it. But a chance to build loyalties across European frontiers arose from the ruins of the

Decolonization and the Post–Cold War World

1941–1945	Japanese occupation sets stage for postwar decolonization of southeast Asia
1947	Indian independence and partition into India and Pakistan
1948	State of Israel established
1950s and 1960s	Decolonization of most of Africa
1956	Suez Crisis
1959	Fidel Castro takes power in Cuba
1970s	Military dictatorships take power in much of Latin America
1970s and 1980s	Value of many commodities on world market collapses
1974	36 states have a democratic franchise
1975	Helsinki Agreement
1986	Democratic revolution in the Philippines
1990s	Under Deng Xiaoping China becomes world's fastest-growing economy
1994	Nelson Mandela becomes president of South Africa
1997	Hong Kong returns to Chinese control
1999	Vladimir Putin becomes president of Russia
2000	139 states are classifiable as democracies
2004	European Union enlarged to include 25 states

Treaty on European Union, 1992

Second World War. France, West Germany, Italy, Belgium, the Netherlands, and Luxembourg combined in the European Coal and Steel Community in 1952. The Messina Declaration in June 1955 proclaimed the goal of "... a united Europe, through the development of common institutions, ... the creation of a common market, and the gradual harmonization of social policies."

At every step, however, Europeans dragged their feet, partly because governments were jealous of their sovereignty and partly because peoples were protective of their national identities. The Council of Ministers that ran the **European Union (EU)** was deliberately an international rather than a supranational body.

The economic success of the EU complicated the problems, as the community enlarged from the 6 original member states to 25 in 2004. With each enlargement, consensus became more difficult. Some countries opted out of key initiatives, including the single European currency, the Euro, introduced in 2002. Divisions opened between countries, typified by Britain, that wanted power to stay with the member states and those that wanted a centralized European superstate. Reluctance to admit Muslim states—Turkey and Bosnia—was also obvious. Yet Europe needed to show that the EU could accommodate Muslims, if only because, as we shall see in the next chapter, Muslim minorities were growing rapidly throughout Western Europe.

IN PERSPECTIVE: The Anvil of War

War can almost be said to have determined global politics in the twentieth century. War strained the empires that Europeans had constructed in the nineteenth century. In the first half of the twentieth century, those empires barely endured, and in the second half, they collapsed. Decolonization was usually violent and economically disruptive. Much of the decolonized world, especially in Africa, was left impoverished and racked by instability. Only the United States emerged from global conflict richer and stronger.

Meanwhile, war stimulated the development of new military technologies that, by midcentury, had become so destructive that as President John F. Kennedy said in 1961, "Mankind must put an end to war, or war will put an end to mankind."

At one level, contending superpowers dominated the story of global politics in the twentieth century. At another, it was a tale of ideological conflicts, in which democracy contended with rival kinds of authoritarianism and totalitarianism.

If the great wars of the first half of the century were civil wars of Western and Eastern civilizations, the Cold War was the conflict of an increasingly globalized world—a struggle to decide what the common culture of the world would be. The end of the Cold War was part of a more general climax that spread democracy and capitalism. Yet efforts to establish a peaceful world order failed. By 2000, the world depended on the only remaining superpower, the United States, to act as a global policeman. No one would find this satisfactory for long. The chances increased that rivals would contest superpower status, as the European Union began to function and as China recovered, after a long period of unfulfilled potential. The prospect revived that global history would again unfold from the east as the era of Chinese disintegration and weakness ended.

In retrospect, the long-term significance of the Sino-Japanese war whose opening Aleksandr Persikoff witnessed, was boundless. Dominance in East Asia and the Pacific was at stake; over the twentieth century as a whole, this seems to have been the strategic area of greatest importance. For, as we shall see in the next chapters, during the twentieth century, the great shift of the balance of population, wealth, and power westward from Asia into European and North American hands—the dominant trend of global history in the nineteenth century—began to ease. The Pacific replaced the Atlantic as the world's foremost arena of long-range trade.

Americans, meanwhile, may have relished their country's role but did not choose it. They suffered resentment and hatred in return. In part, this was because the United States' exercise of global responsibilities seemed to many people to be unreasonable and unjust. On the one hand, the importance of the United States for the peace of the world was illustrated in 1990, when Iraq invaded Kuwait, and American-led forces restored the status quo. Some interventions, on the other hand, seemed poorly chosen. Under President Bill Clinton (1993–2001), military action in Somalia, Sudan, and Serbia seemed weakly justified and ill targeted. In 2002 and 2003, President George W. Bush's invasions of Afghanistan and Iraq appeared, to most of the rest of the world, to have little justification in the Afghan case and none at all in that of Iraq. Both adventures committed America to long-term interventions, without clear exit strategies. American power alone was not enough to preserve peace indefinitely. American administrations did little to build international institutions to share the burdens or take over the task.

It was not, however, solely American might that made the twentieth century "the American century." The magnetism of the United States was more a matter of what political scientists call *soft power:* cultural influence and the appeal of American institutions and ways of life. But for every admirer of American culture, others detested or despised it. To understand the context of these reactions, we have to turn to the social and cultural history of the twentieth century.

CHRONOLOGY

1914–1918	World War I
1917	Russian Revolution begins
April 1917	United States enters World War I
1919–1920	Paris peace conference
1922	Benito Mussolini's Fascist Party takes power in Italy
1929	U.S. stock market crash
1930–1931	Army officers seize power across Latin America
1931	Japan invades Manchuria
1933	Nazis take power in Germany
1936–1939	Spanish Civil War
1939–1945	Nazis carry out genocide of Europe's Jews; World War II
1941	Germany invades Soviet Union; Japan attacks Pearl Harbor
August 1945	United States drops atomic bombs on Hiroshima and Nagasaki
1947	Indian independence and partition
1948	State of Israel established; Soviet blockade of Berlin begins; Marshall Plan initiated
1949	North Atlantic Treaty Organization (NATO) formed; Soviet Union produces atomic bomb; communists take power in China
1950s and 1960s	Decolonization of most of Africa
1950–1953	Korean War
1955	Warsaw Pact formed
1959	Fidel Castro takes power in Cuba
1961–1973	U.S. involvement in Vietnam War
1966	Mao launches Cultural Revolution in China
1970s	Military dictatorships in much of Latin America
1973	World oil crisis triggers global inflation
1974	36 states have democratic franchises
1985	Mikhail Gorbachev takes power in Soviet Union
1989–1991	Collapse of Soviet control of Eastern Europe and of the Soviet Union itself
1990s	Under Deng Xiaoping China becomes world's fastest-growing economy
1994	Nelson Mandela becomes president of South Africa
2000	139 states are classifiable as democracies

PROBLEMS AND PARALLELS

1. Why can Japan's conflicts with China in the first half of the twentieth century and the European conflict of World War I be viewed as civil wars?
2. Why did the non-Western world view World War I as an opportunity to challenge European colonial control?
3. How did the United States emerge as the world's leading power after World War I? What effect did postwar disillusionment have on European society?
4. Why were conflicts over power in the 1920s and 1930s increasingly seen as ideological conflicts?
5. What effect did nuclear armaments have on world politics? How did the Cold War dominate world affairs from the late 1940s to the late 1980s?
6. What were the effects of colonization on decolonized lands? On former empires?

DOCUMENTS IN GLOBAL HISTORY

- Soldiers' accounts of battle
- Sir Henry McMahon, letter to Sharif Husayn, 1915
- Covenant of the League of Nations
- Erich Maria Remarque, from *All Quiet on the Western Front*
- Mohandas K. Gandhi, *Satyagraha in South Africa*
- "Summary of Orders," for Martial Law in the districts of Lahore and Amritsar, India 1919
- J. M. Keynes, from *The End of Laissez-Faire*
- Lenin on the Bolshevik seizure of power
- Ho Chih Minh, "Equality!" 1922
- Excerpts from the speeches of Juan Perón
- Adolf Hitler, excerpt from *Mein Kampf*
- Winston Churchill, the "Iron Curtain" speech
- George C. Marshall, "The Marshall Plan," 1947
- Harry S Truman, The Truman Doctrine, 1947
- Nikita Krushchev, Speech to the Twenty-Second Congress of the Communist Party, 1962
- Mao Zedong, "A Single Spark Can Start a Prairie Fire"
- Cultural Revolution: violence at Qinghua University, 1968
- Deng Xiaoping on capitalism
- Frantz Fanon, from *The Wretched of the Earth*
- Nasser, speach on the Suez Canal crisis
- Kwame Nkrumah, from *I Speak of Freedom: A Statement of African Ideology*
- Jomo Kenyatta, from *Facing Mt. Kenya*
- Palestinian Declaration of Independence, 1988
- Fidel Castro, *History Will Absolve Me*, 1953
- Nelson Mandela, from "The Struggle Is My Life" from *Freedom, Justice and Dignity for All South Africa*
- United Nations Delaration of Human Rights, 1948
- Treaty on European Union, 1992

Please see the Primary Source DVD for additional sources related to this chapter.

READ ON

The opening story comes from O. A. J. Pennikoff, *Bushido: The Anatomy of Terror* (1973). Good starting points for World War I include I. Beckett, *The Great War, 1914–1918* (2001), an overview of the military, political, social, economic, and cultural aspects of the conflict; M. Gilbert, *First World War* (1996); N. Ferguson, *The Pity of War: Explaining World War I* (2000), a controversial revisionist account of the war; and P. Fussell, *The Great War and Modern Memory* (2000), a cultural history of the Western reaction to the struggle and to its legacy. Probably the best introduction to World War II is W. Murray and A. R. Millet, *A War to Be Won: Fighting the Second World War, 1937–1945* (2000). Also solid is G. Weinberg, *A World at Arms: A Global History of World War II* (1995).

I drew on F. L. Allen's *The Lords of Creation* (1996) for the background to the Depression. S. L. Engermann and R. E. Gallman, eds., *The Cambridge Economic History of the United States,* vol. III (1996) is searching and comprehensive.

The historiography of the Cold War has not surprisingly proven ideologically contentious. J. L. Gaddis, *The Cold War: A New History* (2005) is a reasonably balanced and well-written overview that emphasizes the relationship between the superpowers, the United States and the Soviet Union. O. A. Westad, *The Global Cold War: Third World Interventions and the Making of Our Times* (2005), focuses instead on the global and Third World dimensions of the conflict and their complicated connections to decolonization. I found H. Thomas, *Armed Truce* (1986) helpful. A convenient introduction to decolonization itself is D. Rothermund, *The Routledge Companion to Decolonization* (2006), which presents both a detailed chronology and narrative and thematic analysis. P. Duara, *Decolonization (Rewriting Histories)* (2004) provides significant excerpts from the writings of major leaders of decolonization movements and presents the process from the perspective of the colonized.

Books on "The New World Order" tend to range from the partisan to the paranoid, but A. Slaughter, *A New World Order* (2005) is an original if dense reconceptualization. On the European Union, see J. McCormick, *Understanding the European Union: A Concise Introduction* (3rd., 2005). For a broad examination of the role of war and military power in shaping world orders, see J. Black, *War and the World: Military Power and the Fate of Continents, 1450–2000* (2000).

CHAPTER

29 The Pursuit of Utopia: Civil Society in the Twentieth Century

In war, atrocities breed atrocities. Chinese nationalist soldiers execute fellow countrymen accused of collaboration with the Japanese after the "Rape of Nanjing" in 1937.

IN THIS CHAPTER

THE CONTEXT OF ATROCITIES
THE ENCROACHING STATE
UNPLANNING UTOPIA: THE TURN TOWARD INDIVIDUALISM
COUNTER-COLONIZATION AND SOCIAL CHANGE
GLOBALIZATION AND THE WORLD ECONOMY
CULTURE AND GLOBALIZATION
SECULARISM AND RELIGIOUS REVIVAL
IN PERSPECTIVE: The Century of Paradox

A few days before Christmas 1937, John Rabe found women and children, "their eyes big with terror," huddled in his garden in Nanjing. "Their one hope is that I, 'the foreign devil,' will drive the evil spirits away." Rotting corpses were piling up in the streets—torched or hacked to death, with a ferocity Rabe found impossible to understand. The victims of the atrocities could not believe their assailants were fellow human beings. But the perpetrators were Japanese soldiers, not evil spirits. Within a few weeks, more than 250,000 fugitives filled the Safety Zone that Rabe and his European friends—missionaries and businessmen—had set up to protect noncombatants from torture, rape, assault, and murder. The Japanese authorities, while nominally respecting the zone, were "content," Rabe wrote, "to let the refugees starve to death." He had witnessed one of the most intense massacres in history. Japanese soldiers who took part in the slaughter—such as Nagatomi Hakudo, who remembered "smiling proudly as I ... began killing people"—subsequently found their own behavior impossible to understand. But the **Rape of Nanjing**, as the episode was called, was by no means unusual. The most terrifying paradox of the twentieth century was that the advances of the era—in science, in technology, in the spread of education and knowledge, in the increased availability of information, and in progress toward worldwide prosperity—did nothing to avert moral catastrophe.

CHINA

The paradox does, however, make a kind of hideous, warped sense. For people who experienced the unprecedented rate of progress in the twentieth century, **utopia** seemed attainable. A world improved or perfected seemed within reach. Massacre was just one way to get there: creating a world without enemies. The social history of the twentieth century is largely a story of failed utopian projects, as chaos overpowered progress.

THE CONTEXT OF ATROCITIES

The twentieth century was a century of atrocities, partly because it was a century of war. War is morally brutalizing. Propaganda, which portrays atrocities as excesses of the other side, often conceals that fact from the public. War blinds people to their enemies' humanity. As we saw in Chapter 28, when the Sino-Japanese War started in 1931, the belligerent peoples were inclined to be prejudiced in each other's favor—to see themselves as fraternally linked. But by the time of the Nanjing outrages, Chinese called the Japanese "evil spirits," while Japanese called the Chinese "insects," "pigs" or—in the case of women enslaved for military brothels—"public urinals." Japanese soldiers, according to their own later accounts, were taught to regard a Chinese victim as "something of rather less value than a dog or a cat."

FOCUS questions

- HOW WERE the atrocities of the twentieth century related to the attempts to create ideal societies or utopias?
- WHY DID the influence of the state increase and then decrease in the twentieth century?
- HOW IS globalization shifting the global patterns of wealth and power?
- HOW HAS migration from former colonies and underdeveloped regions affected social change in the West?
- WHY DID religion become more vigorous in the late twentieth century?

Transcript from the Rape of Nanjing sentencing, 1947

Eyewitness account of genocide in Armenia, 1915

Along with war, ideological and intercommunal hatreds stimulated inhuman behavior, which war conditions made worse. During the Second World War, Nazis consciously set out to exterminate groups they blamed for the ills of society: Gypsies, homosexuals, and, above all, Jews. Once they had perfected systematic, industrialized methods of genocide, the killers herded millions of Jews into death camps where they gassed them to death. The Nazi vision of utopia also demanded a world from which the physically weak or mentally sick had been gutted out and discarded. No case of genocide matched the Nazi campaign against the Jews, but comparable attempts to exterminate whole peoples continued throughout the century (see Map 29.1). Among attempts to eradicate political and economic communities, Stalin's dictatorship in Russia massacred independent peasants on a scale that equaled or excelled the Nazis', and Mao Zedong in China and Pol Pot in Cambodia also killed millions (see Chapter 28).

No level of civilization, education, or military discipline immunized people against barbarism, whenever war or fear ignited hatred and numbed compassion. During the Second World War, for instance, thousands of normally decent Germans, who prided themselves on their civilized attainments—including artists and intellectuals—helped massacre Jews and other alleged enemies, "deviants," and "subversives" without apparently realizing that they were doing anything wrong. On a lesser scale, soldiers who were raised in democracies and educated in humane values became corrupted. In the Vietnam War, for instance, in March 1968, nice, homey American boys massacred noncombatant peasants, women, and children in the village of Mai Lai, under the influence of fear-induced adrenalin. During war in Iraq in 2004, pictures of American soldiers of both sexes amusing themselves by torturing and sexually abusing Iraqi prisoners, almost all of whom proved to be innocent noncombatants, shocked the world. The perpetrators of these outrages did not even have the excuse of being depraved by combat. They were prison guards. Like some of the Japanese in Nanjing, they actually posed for souvenir photographs, smiling as they performed vicious and degrading acts.

The Holocaust. At the Nordhausen concentration camp, the Nazis spent nothing to build and operate the gas chambers they used in other camps. The inmates at Nordhausen—cataloged as too weak or ill to be useful as slave labor—were left to starve to death. In an attempt, apparently, to leave no witnesses, guards massacred the survivors when U.S. troops approached the camp in April 1945. This photograph shows some of the more than 3,000 corpses the Americans found, but a few of the inmates were still alive.
Art Archive/Picture Desk, Inc./Kobal Collection

THE ENCROACHING STATE

For most of the century, states seemed to be the likely agents of utopia, because they controlled more power and resources than ever before. Even in the liberal West, which had inherited from the Enlightenment the doctrine of social and economic laissez-faire (see Chapter 22), states took on ever more responsibility, for education, health, and welfare.

Social policy had to regulate increasingly complex and unwieldy societies. Planning—which meant, in effect, a huge surrender of individual liberty to public power and an extension of state interference into private life—seemed an irresistible cure-all. The example of the United States, where federal initiatives helped to dispel the misery of the Great Depression of the 1930s, was encouraging. The influence of John Maynard Keynes (1883–1946), who argued for the "end of laissez-faire," was, for some governments, decisive (see Chapter 28).

The Second World War (1939–1945) also encouraged regimentation and collectivism. The war accustomed citizens to take orders, produce by command, and accept rationing. Canada and Britain acquired command economies almost as heavily regulated as those under fascism and communism. Peace eased but did not end these conditions. In most of Europe, governments nationalized major industries on which the economic infrastructure depended, such as transport, communications, and energy supply. Even noncommunist states applied such measures.

Medicine and schooling illustrate the politicization of social issues. Compulsory, state-funded immunization ended the rapacious diseases that had regularly killed children, including polio, measles, mumps, and rubella. Health education, combined with fiscal measures, changed people's habits. Smoking—a universal relaxation in the early twentieth century—became a pariah activity in many Western countries by 2000. Addictive stimulants and narcotics increased in popularity as they became relatively cheap—including, especially, marijuana and coca-derived substances. But governments took tough countermeasures. Toward the end of the century, public health campaigns targeted alcohol and fatty foods.

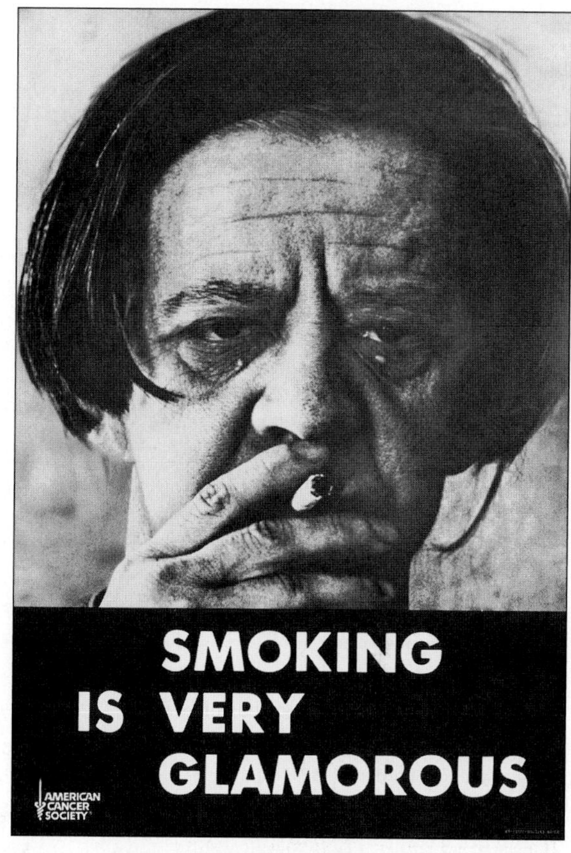
SMOKING
IS VERY
GLAMOROUS
AMERICAN CANCER SOCIETY

When antismoking campaigns began in the West in the 1970s, they were often privately funded and directed against the tobacco industry's own messages. Increasingly, as evidence accumulated that smoking undermined health, governments took over, combating smoking first with taxation and public health campaigns, then with outright prohibitions on smoking in public. In the mid–twentieth century, smoking was an almost universal indulgence. By the early twenty-first century in the United States, Canada, and parts of Western Europe, smokers had become a persecuted minority, forced to practice their habit furtively and in shame.
Reprinted by the permission of the American Cancer Society, Inc. All Rights Reserved.

States paid doctors and ran hospitals. Except for the United States, all rich countries acquired huge public health establishments. Millions of poor people were liberated from fear of neglect. Life, for the seriously sick, ceased to be a privilege confined only to those who could pay for treatment. But as the costs of medical care spiraled out of control, states struggled to pay the bills.

Meanwhile, education changed. Governments' priorities for schools were concerned with solid citizenship and economic efficiency. Like democracy, education was the cure-all of a former age—transforming dangerous masses into easily influenced, collaborative patriots. Theorists and practitioners in elite institutions pursued grander projects—such as enhancing the pleasure students take in life, acquainting them with their cultural heritage, and stimulating their critical responses. For most children, these remained postponed ideals. In the twentieth century, coarser objectives replaced them: curbing unemployment, manning technology, and keeping young criminals off the streets. More people got more education at greater cost than ever, yet almost everywhere parents and employers complained about the results. In practice, out-of-school education took up the slack: universities, in-work training, and continuing-education programs that enabled people to return to college during their working life.

No part of the world was exempt from "big government," but the United States experienced the phenomenon less than most other countries. The reasons are clear. The world wars left America unscarred. The American economy never suffered from the division of the world into primary and secondary producers. The United States always managed to perform both functions in a big way. Although budgets and bureaucracy grew as the federal government inaugurated public welfare programs, Americans took seriously their perception of their country as the land of the free. This was important in a world that looked increasingly to the United States for models to follow.

For a while, however, the Scandinavian countries were more widely admired, and the system they shared looked like it was becoming the model for the world. Scandinavians favored liberal law-and-order policies with a welfare state and a

MAP 29.1

Genocides and Atrocities, 1900–Present*

location and date with approximate number of people killed

political borders, 2007

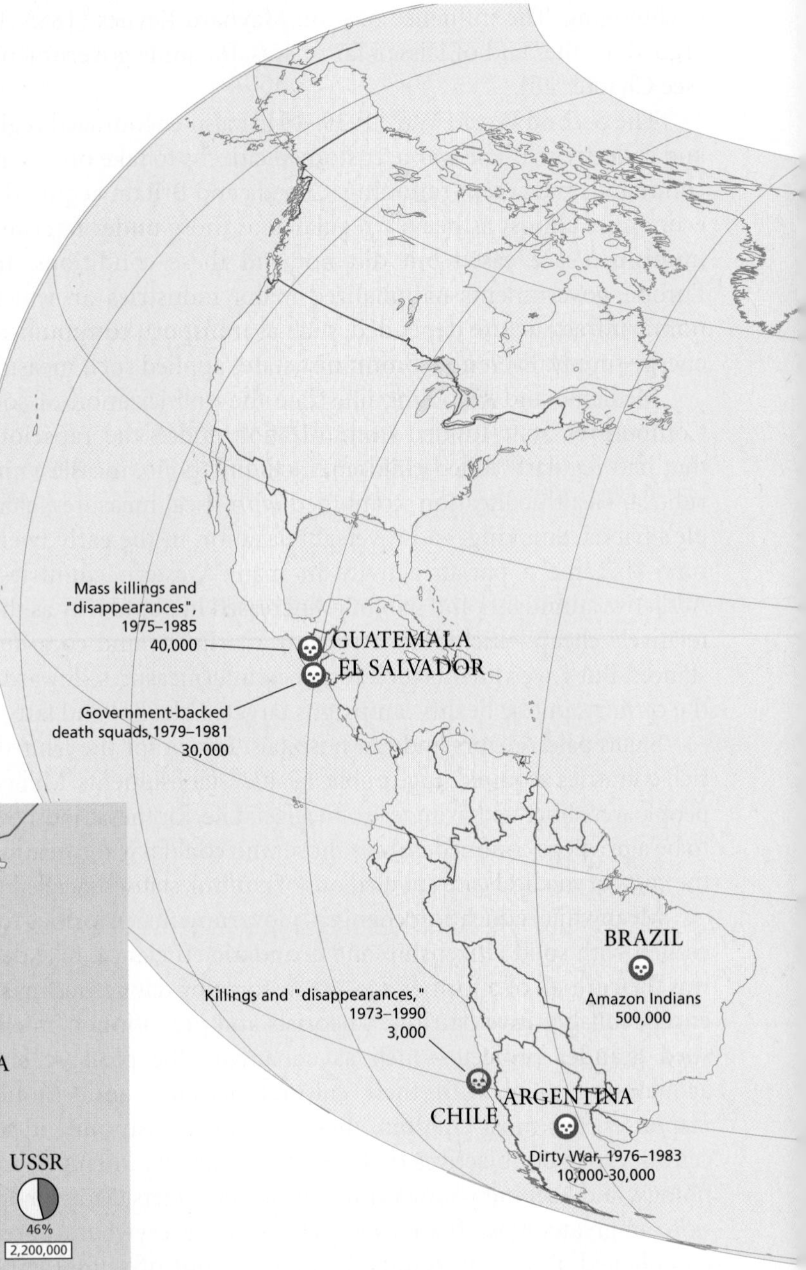

Mass killings and "disappearances", 1975–1985 40,000

GUATEMALA

EL SALVADOR

Government-backed death squads, 1979–1981 30,000

BRAZIL

Amazon Indians 500,000

Killings and "disappearances," 1973–1990 3,000

CHILE

ARGENTINA

Dirty War, 1976–1983 10,000-30,000

The Holocaust

extent of German Reich, 1942

under German occupation, 1942

concentration camp

60,000 estimated number of Jews murdered in Holocaust

percentage of total population of Jews murdered in Holocaust

political borders, 1939

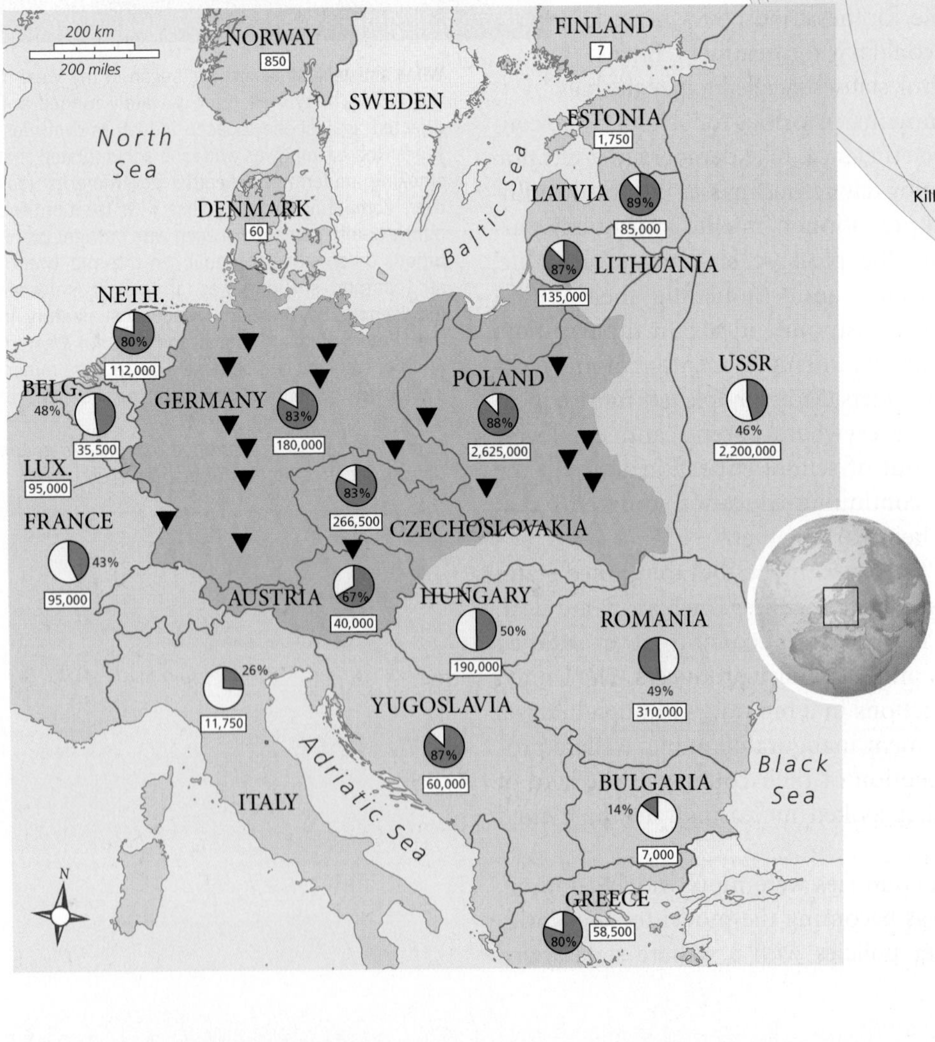

200 km

200 miles

NORWAY 850

FINLAND 7

SWEDEN

North Sea

ESTONIA 1,750

Baltic Sea

LATVIA 89% 85,000

DENMARK 60

LITHUANIA 87% 135,000

NETH. 80% 112,000

BELG. 48% 35,500

GERMANY 83% 180,000

POLAND 88% 2,625,000

USSR 46% 2,200,000

LUX. 95,000

83% 266,500 CZECHOSLOVAKIA

FRANCE 43% 95,000

AUSTRIA 67% 40,000

HUNGARY 50% 190,000

ROMANIA 49% 310,000

26% 11,750

YUGOSLAVIA 87% 60,000

Adriatic Sea

ITALY

BULGARIA 14% 7,000

Black Sea

GREECE 80% 58,500

N

*This map does not purport to be comprehensive, but to convey the global nature of genocides and other atrocities in the twentieth century.

mixed economy, heavily regulated and centrally planned. But the defects included "Scandisclerosis"—business restrained by regulation—where bureaucracy stifled initiative, and welfare provision cut the risk and zest out of life. Social engineering, however benevolent, did not deliver happiness. In the tawdry utopias modern architecture created (see Chapter 27), citizens recoiled from the dreariness of over-planned societies. By the 1980s, it became apparent to people all over the world that America's relatively underregulated economy was better at delivering prosperity.

Planning failed, not only because human beings love liberty but also because planners' assumptions were naïve. Societies and economies are chaotic systems, where unpredictable effects disrupt expectations. So the four- and five-year plans that were produced almost everywhere at some time up to the 1970s were almost

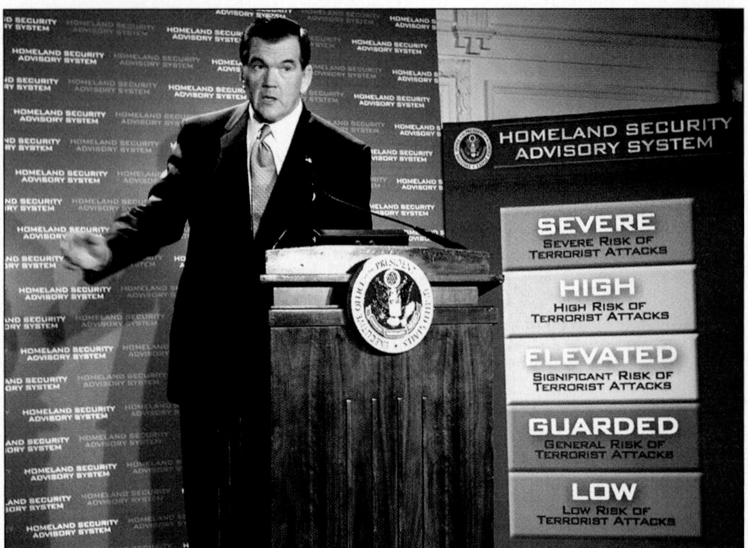

Terror alert. Secretary of Homeland Security Tom Ridge unveils a color-coded terrorism warning system on March 12, 2002, in Washington, D.C. Ridge said the nation was on yellow alert. The five-level system was in response to public complaints that broad terror alerts issued by the government since the September 11, 2001, attacks raised alarm without providing useful guidance. The vague categories—menacing without being informative—and the scary, angular graphics were part of the U.S. government's proclaimed "War on Terror," which justified the president in assuming, for an indefinite period, exceptional wartime powers of detention and surveillance that violated American traditions of civil liberties.

Excerpt from the 9/11 Commission Report

everywhere discarded. In the 1980s and 1990s, governments—even those nominally socialist—shed nationalized industries and made peace with market forces. The perfectly planned urban projects of the 1960s, which represented the fulfillment of the ideals of rationalist architects—creating functional, egalitarian, technically proficient environments—proved practically uninhabitable. After a generation or so, they had to be demolished. At about the same time, the mixed economies and command economies favored in the postwar period were dismantled, deregulated, and restored to private enterprise. By the mid-1990s, private enterprise was responsible for more than 50 percent of output in Europe, even in formerly communist states. This was a change that swept the world. By 2000, only North Korea remained implacably hostile to the private sector.

This did not mean that bureaucracies ceased to grow. The balance between the public and private sectors seemed impossible to get right. Whenever governments shifted responsibilities to the private sector, some communities and groups got left out of the benefits. Poverty gaps widened. Underclasses bred crime and rebellion. More government spending had to help pay for the consequences. More state welfare agencies appeared to try to remedy the effects. Toward the end of the century, most governments faced rising crime rates. Western governments exploited the threat by exaggerating it. In the early twenty-first century, terrorist-induced alarmism attained new heights, thanks to an entirely exceptional terrorist success that demolished the World Trade Center towers in New York and damaged the Pentagon in Washington, D.C. This was an unrepeatable attack, achieved with minimal weaponry—using razor blades to hijack aircraft that the terrorists employed, in effect, as missiles. Meanwhile, terrorism took its place alongside the hazards of modern life that demanded to be policed at the expense and inconvenience of the public—along with crime, drunkenness, drug addiction, and other antisocial behavior.

In consequence, even after the Cold War had ended, defense and internal security demanded more funds and more personnel. Public spending accounted for 25 percent of gross domestic product (GDP) in the world's seven richest countries in 1965, and 37 percent by 2000. The encroaching state pressed upon civil liberties, as police multiplied and surveillance became intrusive. Nor could governments shed welfare responsibilities, once they had undertaken them, without alienating voters and leaving citizens' health or welfare exposed. State-funded workers' pensions became barely affordable for many countries, because, as we shall see in the next chapter, life expectancy rose sharply in the late twentieth century. But somehow governments had to find ways to pay.

UNPLANNING UTOPIA: THE TURN TOWARD INDIVIDUALISM

In the last quarter or so of the century, the world turned away from social and economic planning, first toward a rival kind of utopianism, represented by confidence in **individualism** and freedom, then—when that seemed to fail, too—toward a search for a third way that would deliver both prosperity and social solidarity.

Marxists' explanations for the shift are worth hearing with respect, because Marxists have a profound need to explain the forms of radicalism with which they are out of sympathy. For them, the shift was economically determined. Like all rev-

MAKING CONNECTIONS

THE ENCROACHING STATE

AREA OF CONCERN →	STATE ACTIONS →	CONSEQUENCES
Medicine	Compulsory state-funded immunization programs; health education; public-health campaigns focusing on smoking, food, drugs; establishment of hospitals, medical care paid for by government	Control and elimination of once virulent diseases (polio, measles, mumps, rubella, etc.); decline of smoking; increase in life expectancy; health care becomes available to poor, elderly, and previously neglected groups
Education	Public funding of education through high school and new emphasis on college education and continuing education through grants, funding	Higher rates of literacy, increased science and technology education leads to innovations, social transformations; unemployment declines as education increases
Welfare	Assistance for children and poor via direct payments, education, and health programs	Increased life expectancy, educational achievement, and employment rates among poor; improved standard of living
National Insurance	Financing of retirement by compulsory contributions from employers, employees	Improved standard of living for elderly; drastic drop in poverty levels compared to pre-1940 era, better health care through specialized medical programs for elderly (e.g., Medicare in United States)

olutions, it accompanied a transition from one means of production to another: from industrial to postindustrial economies, from the energy age to the information age. It is true that the rise of information technology created a major new source of wealth and empowered a new class of businesspeople. At about the same time, growing prosperity increased demand for service industries, which displaced manufacturing as the big money spinners in the global economy, and especially in the richest countries and communities. Individualism, therefore, according to the Marxist argument, arose again as the ideology of a new "knowledge class," which now ran the world: the manipulators of information, who had replaced the puppeteers of production and the manipulators of the state.

The global turn toward conservatism may also have been connected with inflation. Inflation was a marked feature of the twentieth century. At times, it galloped uncontrollably, attaining rates of several thousand percent a year in Germany in 1923, for example, when the central bank deliberately printed as much money as it could. But, at historically unprecedented levels, it was a constant feature of life wherever money circulated. This fact is inseparable from the huge expansion of both resources and demand, which is part of the subject of the next chapter. If, however, one single influence drove prices upward more than anything else, it was governments' spending. As the number of governments grew, thanks to decolonization, and utopian projects gobbled up cash, global money supply got out of control. The situation became intolerable in the 1970s. In October 1973, oil-exporting countries attempted to influence American foreign policy by raising their prices. This triggered unprecedented worldwide inflation. Governments only succeeded in controlling it by curtailing their ambitions, cutting expenditure, reducing borrowing, and reining in the money supply.

Deeper, longer-term influences were also at work. Wartime solidarity was an emergency response for most of the societies that experienced it. It was bound to disappear into the generation gap that opened up in the 1950s and 1960s. As young people grew up without shared memories of wartime, they turned to libertarianism, existentialism, or mere self-indulgence. When postwar economic recovery created well-paid work, the young spent in ways calculated to offend elders and express independence: on fashions, for instance, that were first extrovert, then psychedelic. The growth of the generation gap was measurable in the 1960s. Pop bands discarded their uniforms and grew their hair. Health statistics began to register the effects of sexual permissiveness, with epidemics of sexually transmitted disease and cervical cancer. The contribution or response of the Catholic Church—the world's biggest and most influential Christian communion—is not often acknowledged. But in the Second Vatican Council, which convened in the 1960s, the Church relaxed its rules in favor of freedom. If the Church could not resist individualism, the state would not be able to either.

In extreme cases young rebels in the West turned to violence. Urban guerrilla movements were never numerically strong but they hoped that bombing, kidnapping, and shooting would spread terror, incite repression, and excite revolution. In Europe, they mounted spectacular operations against politicians, celebrities, businessmen, policemen, and service personnel, without provoking the intended reactions. They were most successful in Latin America. In Argentina in the 1970s, they provoked the authorities into horrifying countermeasures, involving at least 15,000 victims of abduction, torture, and murder by the army and police. In Brazil, from 1969 to 1973, the government waged war against a movement that specialized in kidnapping foreign diplomats. Uruguay's almost unbroken democratic tradition was suspended while the army broke the urban guerrillas. Even in these countries, however, outraged youth only succeeded in provoking reaction, never in launching revolution.

The generation gap opened almost as wide in communist countries as in the West. The failed revolutions that marked the coming-of-age of postwar youth in 1968 came nearest to success in Paris and Prague. Student revolutionaries on one side of the Iron Curtain denounced the crisis of capitalism, while those on the other called for a postcommunist "spring" or "thaw." In China, the ruling clique deflected youth rage into the Cultural Revolution (see Chapter 28). The revolutionaries' failures were part of a series of disillusioning experiences. In Russia, China, and other communist countries, no relief followed for the sufferings of ordinary people, no end to the tyranny of small elites. In the rest of the world, capitalism was spreading prosperity, fomenting democracy, winning the approval of working-class voters. The Left switched to soft targets: sexism, racism, elitism, the remnants of colonialism, traditional morality.

China: a Farmer's perspective, 2002

The trends of the next generation, when voters swung right, hair got shorter, fashion rebuttoned, and "moral majorities" found voice, were widely perceived as a reaction against "60s permissiveness." In reality, they represented the continuation in maturity of the projects of the young of the previous decade. Demands for personal freedom, sexual liberation, and existential self-fulfillment when one is young transform themselves naturally, when one acquires economic responsibility and family obligations, into policies of economic laissez-faire and less government. To "roll back the frontiers of the state" became the common project of those who rose to power in the West in the 1980s. Individual gratification—or *fulfillment*—replaced broader codes of conduct and dominated many people's decision making over whether to marry, to divorce, or procreate, or how to occupy one's time.

The triumph of liberation became inseparable from sex in Western minds. The development of reliable methods of contraception, and of fairly reliable methods of protection against sexually transmitted diseases, equipped people to lead undisciplined sex lives. Freedom to choose and change sexual partners proved incompatible, however, with the instinctive human tendency to feel sexual jealousy. Permissive sex

Warped Westernization? Brides and grooms standing in lines as the Unification Church weds 790 couples in a single mass ceremony in the 1970s in Seoul, South Korea. The sect, founded by Sun Myung Moon, and popularly called "the Moonies," was among the most successful new religious cults of the day. Its Christian roots were, at best, remote. Moon, not Jesus, was its messiah, and his followers believed him to be divine. The Unification Church exploited the appeal of Western fashion but suppressed individualism.

subverted some of the collective loyalties on which Western society traditionally relied. Families scrambled by sexual betrayal or boredom became typical. Even in the small nuclear families characteristic of Western society, individualism had a dissolving effect, as family activities diminished, and family members began to eat separately and scatter for entertainment to personal video monitors, computer screens, or friendships outside the household. In the United States, fewer than one child in five was born outside wedlock in 1980. By 2000, the number had risen to a third, and two-fifths of American marriages ended in divorce. What had once been normal—parents and children sharing the same household—became exceptional. Less than a quarter of households in the United States conformed to this pattern by 2000.

In the rapidly urbanizing environments of the world, family stability could not thrive as it had done in the rural communities from which the new town dwellers came. Street children crowded the streets of the developing world, becoming fodder for journalism and films, and the recruits of criminal gangs, warlords' armies, insurgents, guerrillas, and terrorists. The influence of Western lifestyles that movies, music, and broadcasting spread around the world created generation gaps everywhere. In Japan, commentators called the rootless young "new humans"—so profound was their rejection of traditional values and behavior. But the same sort of phenomenon could be observed everywhere. In the Muslim world, the young expected more freedom to choose marriage partners and careers. In Korea and parts of Africa and the Americas, millions joined new religions and cults. Of course, every change set off reactions and, while gaps opened between generations, chasms opened within them.

COUNTER-COLONIZATION AND SOCIAL CHANGE

The world shrank. Ever-cheaper, faster transport technologies meant that long-range migration became possible for many of the poor of the world. The huge and growing disparities in wealth between the West and the rest drew migrants. Wars, tyrannies, and political instability drove them. In the second half of the twentieth century, the population boom in colonial and ex-colonial territories reversed the demographic trends of the past. The long flow of migration from Europe to other parts of the

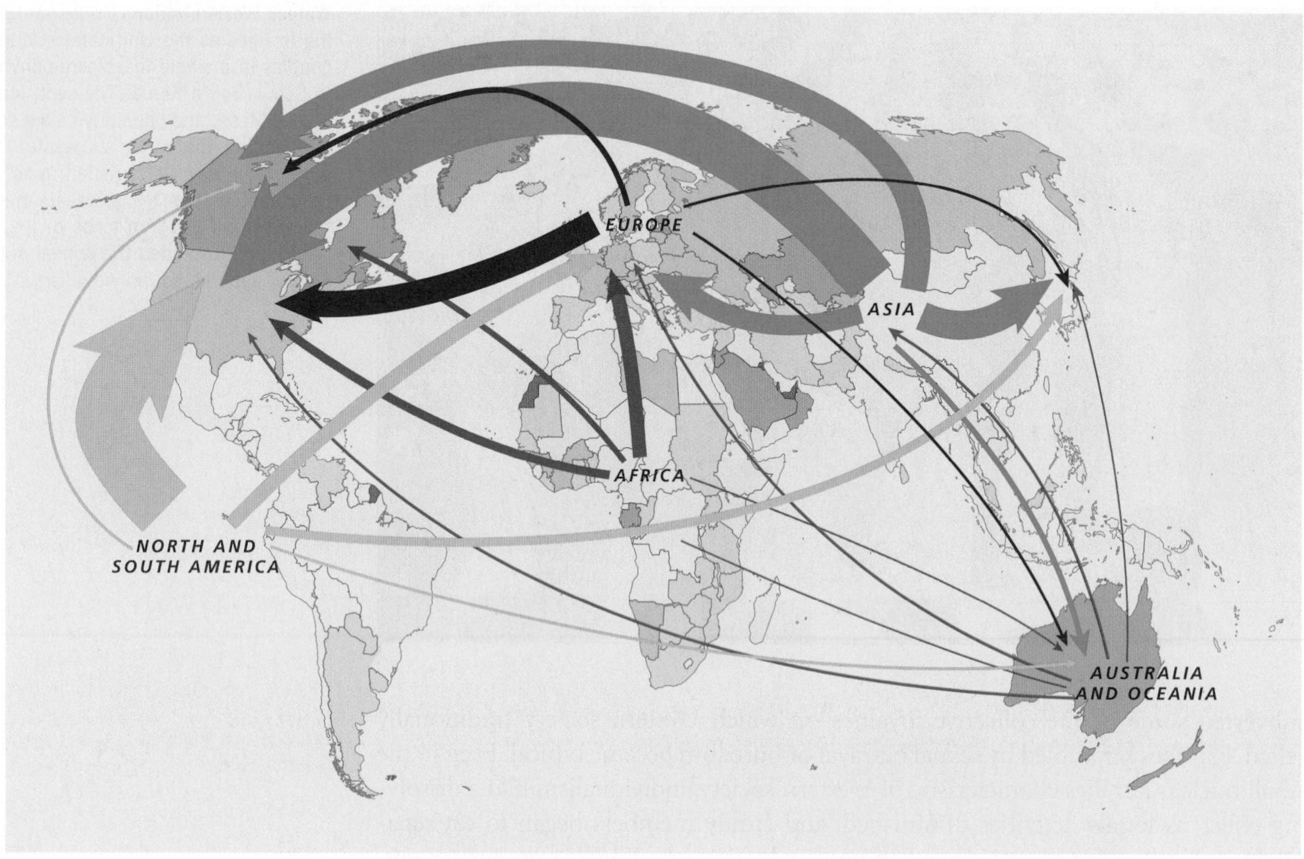

MAP 29.2

Percentage of Noncitizen Population, ca. 2005

- greater than 40%
- 18%–40%
- 8%–17%
- 2%–7%
- less than 2%

International migration trend since 1990 (arrow width reflects number of migrants)

- North and South American immigration
- European immigration
- Asian immigration
- African immigration
- Australia and Oceania immigration

world ended. Instead, **counter-colonization** began. Birth rates in the former imperial "mother countries" declined. Labor from the rest of the world filled the gap.

It happened quickly, in step with decolonization (see Chapter 28). In 1948, the first black Jamaicans to arrive in Britain were astonished to see white men doing menial work. Immigrants to Britain from the West Indies numbered tens of thousands by 1954. Those from India reached the same number the following year, and those from Pakistan two years later. By the end of the century, Britain had more than 2 million Muslims, and France had more than 4 million.

The exchange of population was most intense, at first, between former colonies and their European mother countries, but it soon became more general, as migrants shifted from relatively poor, overpopulated parts of the world to relatively rich, underpopulated regions (see Map 29.2). Migrants from Latin America and Puerto Rico became the largest minority in the United States—over 36 million strong by the early twenty-first century. This was a form of counter-colonization, since the United States had seized the territories most affected, California and the Southwest, from Mexico during its empire-building in the nineteenth century (see Chapter 25) and had exercised informal empire over much of Latin America for most of the twentieth century. In other places, the link between imperialist pasts and present immigration patterns was barely discernible. In Italy, Spain, and Scandinavia, most of the immigrants came from outside the old imperial territories. In the Netherlands, the numbers of Moroccans and Turks equaled or exceeded those of immigrants from former Dutch colonies. In Germany, whose overseas empire had disappeared in 1918, and Switzerland, which had never had an empire, Turks formed the biggest category of guest workers. The Philippines had been an American colony but supplied labor—much of it illegal—for many European countries.

Intercommunal tensions took on a new form, as communities of widely differing culture adapted to life alongside each other. One of the most remarkable changes of the late twentieth century was the way racism became socially and politically unacceptable in the West. This was, perhaps, another outcome of the Second World War. The Nazis had been racists, who regarded black people and Jews, in particular, as among the "subhuman" groups suitable for exploitation or extermination. The defeat of Nazism was, therefore, a victory for pluralism. The black and Asian soldiers who fought for Britain, France, and the United States demonstrated their credentials for equality. The decline of racism was also a consequence of scientific progress. The pseudoscience that justified nineteenth-century racism was discredited in the twentieth.

Immigrant community. A woman leaves a Turkish clothing shop in Berlin's Kreuzberg district, which has been called "little Istanbul." In 1961, the governments of West Germany and Turkey signed an agreement that allowed Turks to come to Germany as guest laborers. Many put down roots and never left. Today, Germany's Turkish community numbers over 2.5 million—the biggest minority group in the country.

Nevertheless, it took a long time to convince prejudiced people to accept and respect new circumstances and new science. The United States was the critical battleground, partly because it came to lead the world in just about everything, and partly because, with its huge black minority, it typified the problems. Many of the states had a history of exploiting and persecuting black people, and, in the mid–twentieth century, anti-black prejudice was still widespread. Beginning in the 1940s, African Americans fought a long series of legal cases, backed by political movements that organized demonstrations—especially those Martin Luther King, Jr. (1929–1968), led—and influenced voters to enshrine the principle of equality in the law. Only in the 1960s, thanks to pressure from the federal courts and Presidents Kennedy (1917–1963) and Johnson (1908–1973), did major breakthroughs occur. The federal government obliged reluctant and resisting states to desegregate schools and public amenities and enforce black people's right to vote. By the end of the century, it was still not clear that efforts to redress racial inequalities had gone far enough. Urban ghettoes, pockets of rural poverty, and inequalities in education remained.

Martin Luther King, Jr., *Letter from Birmingham Jail*, 1963

Abolition in 1961 of the "white Australia" policy, which had restricted immigration to Australia to persons of European descent, was another landmark. Migration to the country became open to people of every hue. South Africa, meanwhile, was a sticking point. Its ruling class was white, and most white South Africans, isolated from the intellectual changes that had discredited racism in most of the rest of the world, clung to a conviction that black and white people should be consigned to exclusive spheres of *separate development*, which in practice supported white privilege. Increasingly, however, it became apparent that it was wiser for white South Africans to conserve their wealth and sacrifice their political power, rather than risk both in a catastrophic revolution. In the early 1990s, South Africa abandoned the policy of separate development. Black people were admitted to equality of rights, and a largely black political party assumed power peacefully, without either victimizing white South Africans or causing economic dislocation.

In response to unresolved tensions, people fell back on a reworked sense of their own identity. New forms of black identity were, perhaps, the most conspicuous example. Early in the twentieth century, Afro-Cuban scholars in newly independent Cuba began to treat black languages, literature, art, and religion on terms of equality with white culture. Coincidentally, white musicians discovered jazz, and

Black consciousness. In November 1970, four "Bush Negro" chiefs from Surinam—direct descendants of maroon communities established in South America in the sixteenth and seventeenth centuries (see Chapter 19)—toured West Africa to great acclaim. Here they are being received as dignitaries by Chief Apétor II of Togo. "The same wind that drove us against our will from Africa," one Bush Negro chief observed during the trip, "has now helped us to find the way back."

white primitivist artists began to imitate African "tribal" art. In 1916, in the United States, the Jamaican immigrant Marcus Garvey launched the slogan, "Africa for the black peoples of the world." The idea that black culture embodied values superior to those of white culture emerged during the 1920s and spread wherever black people lived. In French West Africa in the 1930s, Aimé Césaire and Léon Damas became brilliant spokesmen for the black self-pride they called **Négritude**.

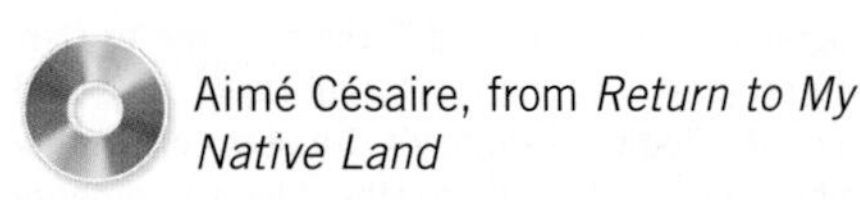

Aimé Césaire, from *Return to My Native Land*

Leopold Senghor on Négritude

Counter-colonization changed the prevailing direction of cultural exchange. By the 1990s, in Leicester—the midmost city in England— people could listen to 40 hours a week of broadcasts in Gujerati, an Indian language. Australian public broadcasting services operated in 78 languages. Vietnamese and North African restaurants abounded in Paris. Indian and Indonesian dishes had joined the national cuisines of Britain and Holland, respectively.

But the spread of Asian influences in Westerners' tastes and thoughts also owed a lot to Western self-reevaluations. Under the weight of guilt about imperialism, postcolonial Westerners felt their own need for liberation from the legacy of the past. In the 1960s, travel to India became a compulsive fashion for Western intellectuals, along with Indian philosophy, mystical practices, music, and food. Political protesters in European and American streets in the same decade brandished copies of "little red books" containing thoughts of Mao Zedong. These fads waned, but Japanese, Chinese, and Indian art and thought became more important in the West. Zen became a widely revered intellectual tradition in the West. Buddhism, which had never attained the breadth of appeal of Christianity and Islam, began to attract converts in every clime. Black music and art, which had begun to influence the cultural mainstream in America and Europe in the earliest years of the century, captured the admiration of the white world.

The prevailing values of the late twentieth century were appropriate to a postcolonial, multicultural, pluralistic era. The fragility of life in a crowded, shrinking world and a global village encouraged or demanded multiple perspectives, as neighbors adopted or sampled each other's points of view. Hierarchies of value had to be avoided, not because they are false but because they led to conflict. Relativism—the doctrine that each culture and even individuals, can choose appropriate norms and, therefore, that no single set of norms is universally applicable (see Chapter 27)—displaced Westerners' confidence in their own superiority.

This doctrine, however, made it hard to argue for the universality of human rights. It also caused tension between cultural relativism and social norms. Conflicts arose when migrants brought with them cultural practices and values that conflicted with the laws of their new homelands. In Islamic countries increasingly influenced by Sharia, or Islamic law, for instance, Westerners found that they could be prosecuted for using alcohol or for not respecting traditional codes of dress and comportment for women. In the West, immigrants could not be allowed to continue traditional practices, such as female circumcision among African communities, or polygamy, or the marriage of minors. "Asian values" justified the use of the criminal law in, for example, Malaysia and Singapore, against practices the West tolerated, such as homosexuality and recreational drugs.

Equality before the law was so ingrained in the West that it would have been unthinkable to allow people of different cultural backgrounds to be treated separately in the courts or to be assigned separate jurisdictions, as had been usual, for instance, in the Middle Ages or under the Ottoman Empire. Most countries legislated for everyone to share the same civil rights, regardless of cultural background. Yet in practice, there were always cases of discrimination.

The status of women provoked some of the deepest difficulties. In 1900, no one expected different cultures to treat women the same. In the West, attention was riveted on the right to vote. In the Islamic world, controversy centered on the rights of women in the home: to choose their husbands, for instance, or to equality with men under marriage law and in property rights. The First World War (1914–1918), however, launched a profound revolution in the role of women in Western society. In practice, women were left to take command of their lives while so many men were away fighting. The dead of the war left gaps that societies were refashioned to fill. Meritocracies replaced hereditary aristocracies in power. Women replaced men in the workplace. Before the war, only a few marginal countries gave women the vote. After it, Russia, Germany, the United States, Britain, and most other Western countries enfranchised women. So did Japan and Turkey.

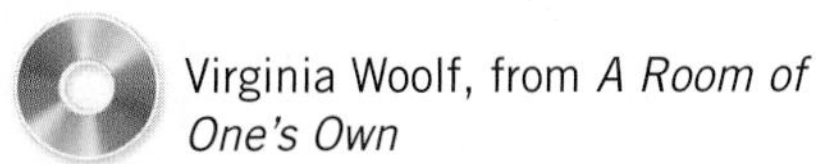
Virginia Woolf, from *A Room of One's Own*

Women had to want to break out of domesticity, but it was not necessarily in their interests to do so. Many of those who competed with men suffered for it. To succeed, they had either to be *superwomen*—the term became current in the 1980s for a professional or working woman who managed her life so well that she could work outside the home and also discharge the traditional roles of wife and mother within it—or accept subordination. Although legislation to equalize opportunities became normal in the West, it was never fully effective. Many women accepted lower wages or worse contractual terms than men in corresponding jobs, so that they could move in and out of work as their family responsibilities demanded. Some workplaces, especially in traditional male preserves, such as the armed forces, the police, the construction industry, and industrial and financial boardrooms, had jock cultures that made it hard for women to fit. Nevertheless, the cause of equality for women became one to which all Western governments committed, at least in theory.

The first woman to be elected an African head of state, President Ellen Johnston-Sirleaf of Liberia, photographed in November 2005 just after her victory. Johnston gave a new twist to feminist arguments in favor of political empowerment for women by suggesting that women had special nurturing and peacemaking talents that made them more suited to leadership in the modern world than men.

Westerners expected people in other cultures to reevaluate women's roles in the same way. This did not seem unattainable: Israel, India, Sri Lanka, the Philippines, Nicaragua, Dominica, Argentina, and even Muslim countries—Pakistan, Turkey, Indonesia, Bangladesh—all had female presidents or prime ministers between 1960 and 2000. But these were exceptional cases, and restraints on women's freedom or status remained in much of the world. China did not allow women to marry until they were 20 years old, and the growing preponderance of male over female children in China suggests that more infant girls than boys were

Timeline of Women's Suffrage

New Zealand	1893
Australia	1902
Finland	1906
Norway	1913
Denmark, Iceland	1915
Soviet Union	1917
Canada, Germany, Austria	1918
Poland, Czechoslovakia	1919
United States, Hungary	1920
Mongolia	1924
United Kingdom	1928
Turkey	1930
Spain	1931
Brazil	1932
Indonesia	1941
France	1944
Italy	1945
China, India	1949
Mexico	1953
Kenya	1963
Switzerland	1971
South Africa	1994
Kuwait	2005

http://www.nzhistory.net.nz/politics/suffrage-worldtimeline

killed or aborted. It is hard to imagine fiercer discrimination than that. Opponents in Morocco and Iran interpreted government programs to establish female equality of employment and rights of freedom of marriage as infringements of parental rights and threats to the stability of home life. Female circumcision, a tradition in many African cultures, offended Western sensibilities. Women's educational opportunities remained restricted in much of the world outside the West, especially in rural areas. In India 87 percent of rural women were classed as illiterate in 2000. The corresponding figure for Bangladesh was 97 percent.

Problems associated with the status of women became acute with the mingling of cultures that accompanied the global migrations of the late twentieth century. Conflicts arose over arranged marriages and the rights of divorcees. In awarding custody of children, for example, Western courts tended to favor mothers, Islamic courts fathers. The disputes that best illustrate the difficulty of resolving conflicts between normative laws and cultural diversity concerned the issue of appropriate dress for women and girls. In some Muslim cultures, traditions of modesty enjoined garments for women that concealed most of the body and the whole of the face from male eyes. To some Westerners, these rules seemed to be male-imposed infringements on female liberty—although many women supported them. The potential for conflict with Western laws arose in schools, where these traditional Muslim dress codes conflicted with school regulations. In France, in the early twenty-first century, the courts banned Muslim girls from wearing headscarves over their heads, on the grounds that such scarves were religious symbols, incompatible with the secular nature of the French Republic.

Such disputes raised fundamental questions about the future of the world. The new multiracial societies in the West posed unprecedented problems. Existing populations became prey to alarmism about the adulteration of their identities or their cultures. Debate raged over whether integration in the host society—adopting its values, language, dress, manners, food, and even, perhaps, religion—best served new immigrants; or whether **multiculturalism** could work, in which people of divergent cultures agreed on a few core values, such as allegiance to the state and deference to democracy. Both responses had their disadvantages. Integration imposed on people's freedom. Multiculturalism, according to its opponents, created ghettoes and opened dangerous gaps in mutual understanding between neighboring communities. As the numbers of migrants began to reach critical thresholds, most Western governments began to encourage integration and tightened immigration controls as they lost confidence that multiculturalism could keep the peace. The Netherlands required immigrants to learn Dutch and submit to citizenship tests. Britain introduced allegiance tests. In the twenty-first century, multiculturalism was beginning to look like another utopian dream in danger of being discarded.

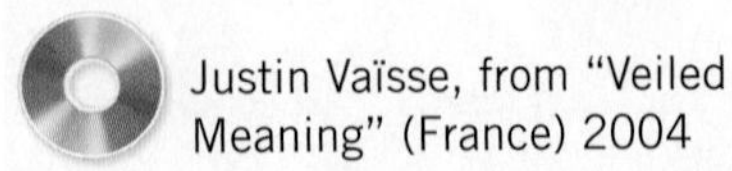
Justin Vaïsse, from "Veiled Meaning" (France) 2004

GLOBALIZATION AND THE WORLD ECONOMY

Not only were cultures getting more intermingled, but so were economies. In the last quarter of the century, in line with the worldwide withdrawal of the state from economic regulation, and the relaxation of controls on cross-border trade, businesses were able to operate internationally with greater freedom than ever before.

The growing interdependence of regional and national economies promoted peace, increased prosperity, and stimulated cultural exchange. The benefits of this **globalization**, however, were unevenly distributed. Relatively few vast business corporations, most of them centered in the United States, handled a disproportionate amount of the world's economic activity, shunting assets around the world, evading regulation by individual governments (see Map 29.3). Powerful countries—the United States above all—were able to demand free trade where it suited them but retain protective tariffs or subsidies for businesses they favored. To some extent, globalization perpetuated the old colonial pattern of the world economy—peasants and sweated labor in poor countries supplied rich ones with cheap goods, twisting the poverty gap into a poverty spiral.

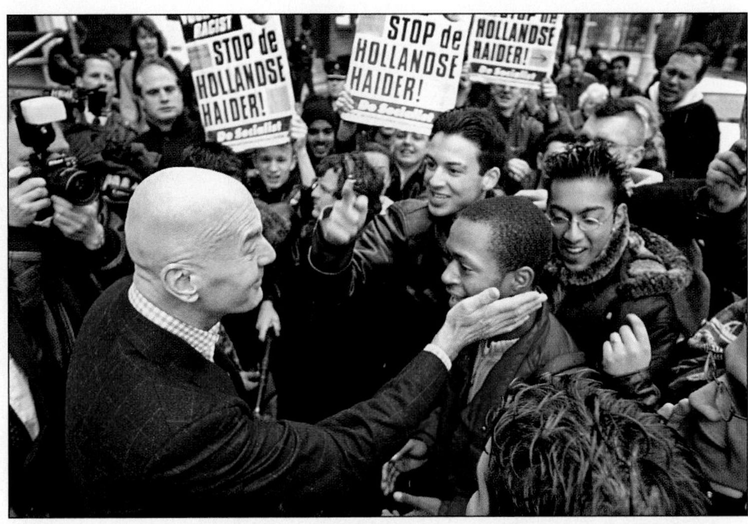

Confrontation. Pim Fortuyn (1948–2002) confronts protestors in Rotterdam during elections for the Dutch parliament. Fortuyn's Livable Netherlands Party had a distinctly anti-immigration agenda. Fortuyn was assassinated by a white Dutch environmentalist in May 2002, shortly after this photo was taken. The slogan, "Stop the Dutch Haider," alludes to Jurgen Haider of Austria, another populist politician who successfully campaigned for tough immigration controls. The way Fortuyn caresses the demonstrator was part of his public image. He was a homosexual who appeared on campaign with Moroccan boys as evidence that his opposition to immigration was not based on racial discrimination.

Such defects, however, could probably be fixed. Some countries in Asia demonstrated that well-run communities could achieve prosperity and that globalization could make them as rich as the West.

Japan's was the exemplary case. After its defeat in 1945, Japan was ready for a makeover. No other country endured the A-bomb. But the Japanese, who live over seismic faults on typhoon-lashed coasts, are used to rebuilding after disaster. The psychological problems were harder to cope with. Japanese felt the shame of defeat more deeply than people of other cultures. Never before had their country surrendered or submitted to occupation. The emperor renounced his divinity. The people disclaimed superiority over other races and meekly accepted an American formula to remake their country into a democracy.

The abandonment of militarism helped conserve investment for industry. The big corporations—which the Americans had abolished—returned in the 1950s and 1960s. Workers sacrificed an independent social life and became infused with corporate loyalty. This was not Western-style capitalism, but it worked. In 1969, Japan overtook Germany to become the world's second biggest national economy. In the 1970s, despite the high price of oil, Japan caught up with the average European gross national product per capita. In 1985, Japan became the world's biggest foreign investor. Growth faltered toward the end of the century, but Japan remained in the premier league of world economic powers, with the highest per capita income in the world.

Other economies in Asia followed Japan toward European or North American levels of prosperity. In South Korea in the 1960s, collaboration between governments and huge corporations launched spectacular economic growth: 9 percent a year, on average, over the following three decades. The country became one of the world's major manufacturers of cars and electronic gadgets. South Koreans demonstrated that a country could industrialize itself out of poverty. By 2000, Japan and South Korea together—countries with only 3 percent of the world's population—accounted for 15 percent of its income and 10 percent of its trade.

Other "tiger" economies leaped in the same direction. The mid to late 1960s and early 1970s were bonanza years in southeast Asia because American military involvement in Vietnam created a huge demand for supplies, leisure facilities for troops, and all the infrastructure of a wartime baseline. Not everyone benefited. Cambodia, on Vietnam's flank, got sucked into the conflict and began a long, destructive civil war. But other neighbors were drenched in American investment. The biggest gainers were the already industrialized or industrializing economies of

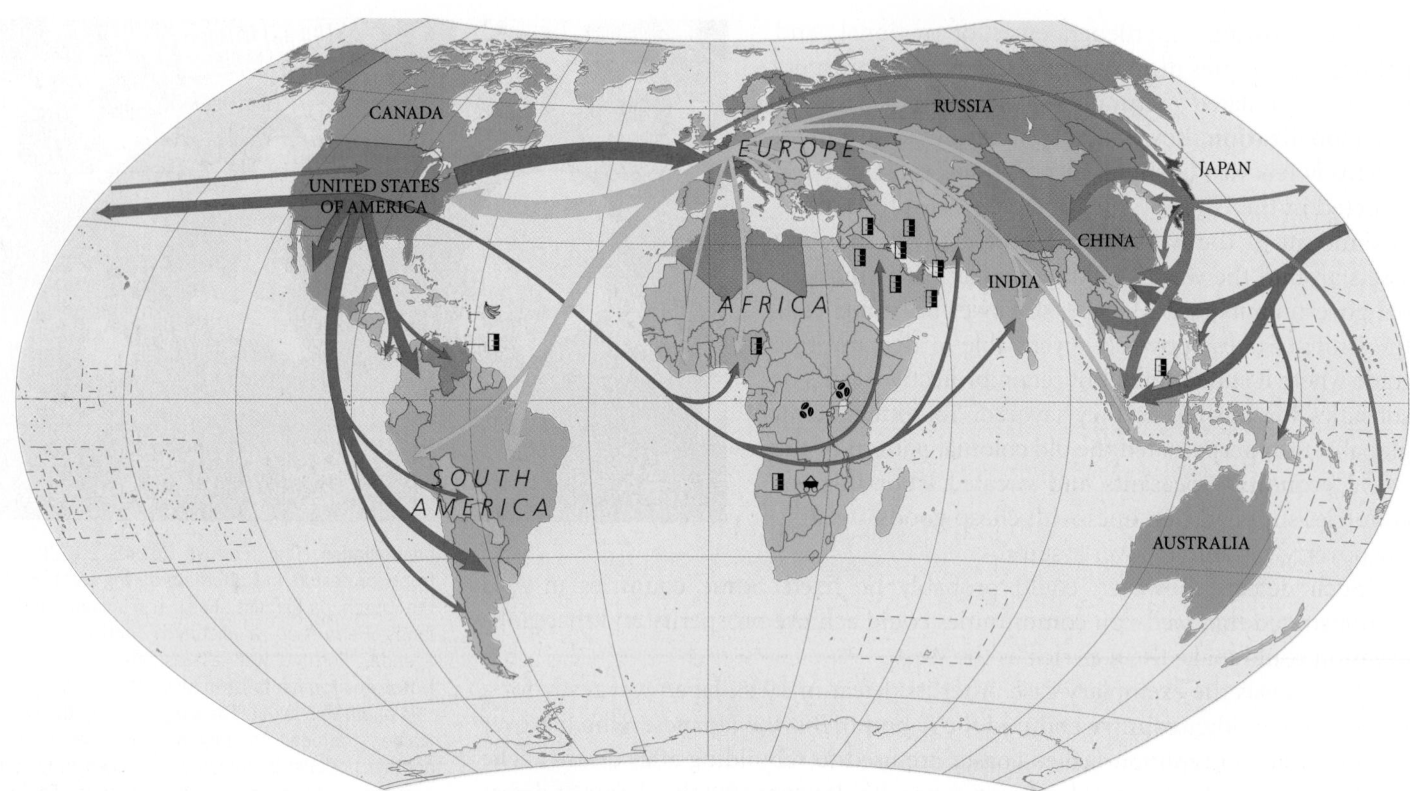

MAP 29.3

International Trade Flows, ca. 2004

Direct investment
(arrow width reflects level of investment)

from USA
from Europe
from Japan

Examples of countries reliant on a single export

bananas
coffee
oil/petroleum
copper

Balance of trade (millions US$)

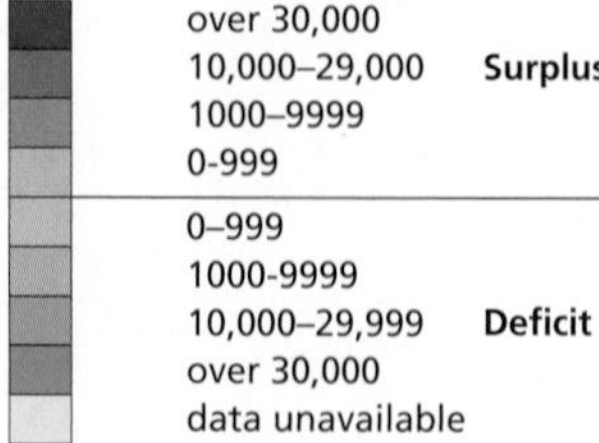

over 30,000
10,000–29,000 **Surplus**
1000–9999
0-999

0–999
1000-9999
10,000–29,999 **Deficit**
over 30,000
data unavailable

MAP EXPLORATION
www.prenhall.com/armesto_maps

Japan, South Korea, Hong Kong, and Taiwan. In the mid-1960s, Singapore followed the same path. The accelerating trade of these tiger economies generated potential for investment all around the world. Most of their surplus money, however, went on projects around the shores of the Pacific. By 1987, the Pacific had displaced the Atlantic as the world's major arena of commerce. Communities and investments moved around the Pacific's shores with increasing ease and freedom.

Meanwhile, Latin American countries struggled to play catch-up with the rest of the West. The game began after the global economic crisis of the 1930s, when governments in Mexico, Argentina, and Brazil saw selective industrialization as a solution to the collapse of markets for their primary produce. As these policies spread through the continent, their effects proved mixed. Native industries continued to rely on machinery imported from North America and Europe. The falling prices of basic commodities made it hard for Latin American economies to accumulate capital to reinvest in industry. Mechanization increased unemployment. In the 1960s and 1970s, partly in response to these problems, authoritarian regimes took over most of the region. In most cases, authoritarian rule only protracted the economic disappointments, straining some countries' relations with trading partners elsewhere in the world, subjecting others to new forms of dependency on United States and European corporate allies and creditors. The military junta that took over Argentina in 1976, for instance, proclaimed Argentina's commitment to "the Western and Christian world" but alienated allies by repression at home and military adventurism abroad. For most Latin Americans, the period was impoverishing. Between 1980 and 1987, average personal income fell in 22 countries in the region. In Peru and Argentina, people were poorer on average in 1986 than they had been in 1970. Even Mexico, which stayed ostensibly democratic and avoided the worst of the region's economic problems, only survived by incurring massive debts—and defaulting on them in 1982.

Shanghai in the early twenty-first century emblemized China's promise and perils. Skyscrapers symbolized the stunning growth rates that enabled China to aim for superpower status and potentially resume its normal place as the world's richest country. The price was pollution and gaping disparities in wealth.

Still, the more enmeshed the global economy got, the more opportunities multiplied. More countries, more people were able to squeeze a share of the benefits. China's was the most spectacular case. The Chinese economy registered annual growth rates of nearly 10 percent in the 1990s and the early twenty-first century—enough, if those rates could be sustained, to enable China's economy to overtake that of the United States as the world's biggest by 2020. By 2004, more than 400 of the world's 500 biggest companies had branches or subsidiaries in China, overwhelmingly concentrated in regions bordering the Pacific. India became a leading player in high-tech industries, where many multinational companies located centers of computer manufacture and telecommunications services. In the 1980s, a dose of Chicago-style economics—the doctrine, advocated by economists at the University of Chicago, that low taxes and light regulation could unleash economic success—turned the Chile of the military dictator Augusto Pinochet into a prosperous country with a large middle class. Integration in the global economy shored up South Africa's delicate new democracy in the 1990s and helped to provide a capital-starved economy with the wealth the country needed to start rebuilding after centuries of injustice. Brazil, meanwhile, which had already become a major manufacturing economy with a lively high-tech sector, achieved, in the early twenty-first century, levels of growth not far short of China's. Even some economies that remained tied to primary production generated huge profits that their governments could invest in global markets. The oil-exporting countries on the Arabian shore of the Persian Gulf became major players in the global economy.

China: "A Harmonious Society," 2006

Even economists who acknowledged the benefits of globalization were prey to doubts about its stability. Some systems theorists argued that the more complex the world economy grew, the more fragile it would become, because, in an interdependent system, a local failure could cause widespread disruption. In fact the opposite happened. Early in the twentieth century, a local economic failure, such as the American stock market crash of 1929, could plunge much of the world into depression. In the 1980s and 1990s, markets reacted nervously to similar collapses of major stock markets in 1987, of the British currency in 1992, of the banking system in Argentina in 1999, and of the oil-pricing system and major commodity markets at irregular intervals. But none of these disasters had uncontrollable repercussions. Perhaps the greatest panic of all ensued in 2001, when terrorists destroyed the

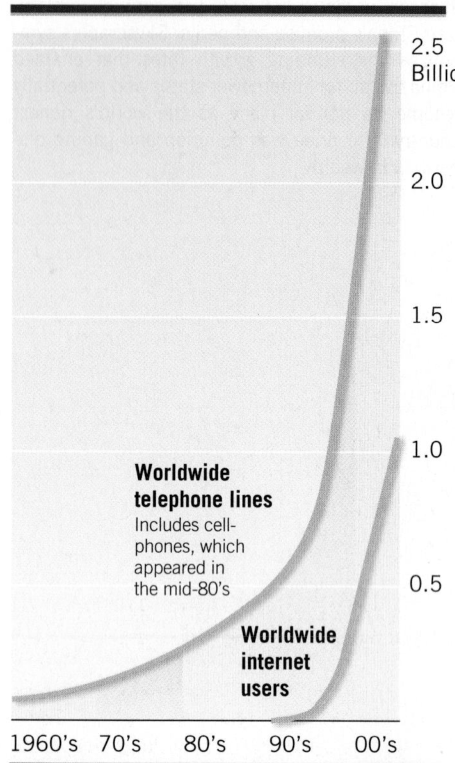

FIGURE 29.1 TELEPHONE LINES AND INTERNET USERS, CA. 1960–2000
Worldwatch Institute, www.worldwatch.org

World Trade Center in New York. The economic consequences were slight. Even the firms worst hit by the attack were back at work within days. In practice, the globalized economy could endure terrible dislocations. Complexity made the system more robust, because multiple interconnections enabled it to bypass failures.

CULTURE AND GLOBALIZATION

Information traveled globally with even more freedom than trade. In 1971, the world's first microprocessor appeared. In combination with radio transmission, it made virtually every item of information from every part of the world universally accessible. There were over 2.5 billion telephones in the world by 2000 and over 500 million computers (see Figure 29.1).

The way people handled information changed. Miniaturization boosted individualism and enabled the like-minded to form cyberspace communities. The trend was unstoppable. China, for instance, tried to control Internet access, especially after demonstrators coordinated their activities by computer in what almost turned into a revolution in 1989. But China had 30 million Internet users by 2000. Worldwide censorship became difficult—at least for a while. But major servers have begun to impose filters.

The surfeit of data drove some consumers into narrow-minded retreat. Some cyber communities became cyber ghettoes, in which people spent their time with minds closed to the rest of the Web. Increasing information did not necessarily increase knowledge. Wider literacy helped. By 2000, just about everyone in the world was familiar with writing, and probably about 85 percent of them could make at least some use of it. But most consumers used the new technology for trivial entertainments rather than self-education. Professional intellectuals succumbed to specialization, partly in response to the proliferation of information. Students became reliant on data culled from the Internet, which changed constantly and was beyond verification. Cutting and pasting became a new form of literary activity, in which no text was stable and no work genuinely original. **Virtual reality** excited fears it would spawn a generation of "nerds"—introverted sociopaths who communed only with their computers.

Still, the Internet promoted globalization in the strongest sense of the word: the global spread of uniform culture. In a plural world, this was not a threat to cultural diversity, though people often perceived it as such. If there ever were to be a global culture, it would probably not replace diversity, but supplement it. What people really feared was global Americanization, the triumph of American popular culture, commonly called "McDonaldization" and "Coca-Cola colonialism" after two of the prevalent products of American industry. Hamburgers and sodas symbolized American cultural influence, because the world associated American lifestyles with what became the nearest thing to a common culture the world possessed: consumerism.

Pope John Paul II on consumerism, from *Centesimus Annus*

Consumerism is best defined as a system of values that puts the consumption and possession of consumer goods at or near the top of social values—as high as or higher than social obligations, spiritual fulfillment, or moral qualities. The best index of the growing importance of consumerism in the twentieth century is the sheer scale of consumption, which is among the subjects of Chapter 30. As we shall see, the late twentieth-century world was a battleground of consumerism against environmentalism. Consumerism nearly always won the battles. Products that best measure consumerism are those that can fairly be described as a waste of money. Consumption of tobacco, alcohol, and more addictive drugs makes the case. First on grounds of morality, then—as the century wore on and morality became unfashionable—on grounds of health, governments struggled to contain these extreme forms of consumerism. Nonetheless, by 2000, the alcohol industry worldwide turned over $252 billion annually, tobacco $204 billion. The term *drugs* is harder to define and the statistics fuzzier, but by the most widely respected estimates, the drug trade was worth about $150 billion by 2000, of which about $60 billion was spent in the United States.

Even those who condemned American cultural influence as trivial, trashy, and corrosive of traditional cultures found it hard to resist. American businesses dominated the major new media—cinema, television, and the Internet. So American images proliferated around the world (although the Indian film industry was beginning to shape up as a potential rival). Often those onlookers became admirers. The magnetism of American higher education was an important ingredient of America's soft power. American institutions educated a disproportionate number of the world's elites.

The most pervasive index of the global appeal of American culture was the adoption of American English as the universal language of business, politics, science, and study. This was a major reversal in the history of culture. While imperial, sacred, or trading languages had sometimes displaced or extinguished other tongues, never before had a single language achieved the role of a global common tongue. Mandarin Chinese, Spanish, and Portuguese also showed some potential. The extinction of minority languages became a conservation problem.

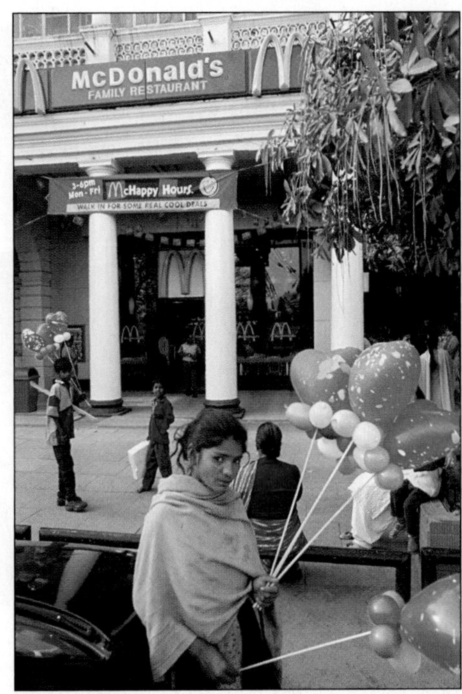

Selling dreams. Garish signs of Western economic takeover and cultural invasion deface a traditional building on a prime commercial site in New Delhi, while child workers hope to make a few pennies by selling balloons to kids rich enough to feast on the fatty carbohydrates associated (in India) with U.S. fast-food businesses.

SECULARISM AND RELIGIOUS REVIVAL

Most of the really powerful utopian visions of the twentieth century were irreligious, even antireligious. Utopians who put their faith in the state often did so in conscious revulsion from religious establishments, which had failed to enhance virtue or spread welfare or justice. Communists usually regarded atheism as part of their own creed. Nazis wanted to sweep away the Church. Social planning relied for its appeal on a scientistic notion: that human agency alone could change societies like chemicals in a lab, and achieve predictable results, with no need for appeals to Providence or grace. The world—from these perspectives—would be better off without religion, which had caused wars, retarded science, and stifled reason with dogma. Religion was one of the first casualties of the skepticism that, as we saw in Chapter 27, was a major twentieth-century theme.

For most of the century, the demise of religion was widely forecast. The decline of churchgoing in the West, which lasted in America until the 1960s and still prevails in Western Europe and Canada, seemed to suggest that prosperity would erode faith. Religion had to face serious challenges and sometimes ferocious persecution from hostile political ideologies.

In response to secularism, however, people with religious identities felt them more fiercely. In Egypt, for instance, the number of mosques increased nearly twice as fast as the population under the secular-minded rulers of the second half of the twentieth century. The most striking case occurred in Iran, where Shah Mohammad Reza Pahlavi (r. 1941–1979) imposed secularization on a reluctant country in the 1960s. He claimed to be ruling people who "resembled

Globalization

1950s	Japan spends 2 percent of GDP on defense
1950s and 1960s	Big corporations return to Japanese economy
1960–1967	Japanese incomes double
1960s	Asian "tigers" (Japan, South Korea, Hong Kong, and Singapore) begin rapid economic ascent
1971	World's first microprocessor
1980–1987	Incomes fall in most Latin American nations
1982	Mexico defaults on national debt
1985	Japan becomes world's biggest foreign investor
1989	Tiananmen Square protests in China
1990s	China's economy grows at annual rate of almost 10 percent
Late 1990s	Economies of India and Brazil grow at rapid rate
1995	World Trade Organization (WTO) created
2000	30 million Internet users in China
2001	Terrorist attack on World Trade Center and Pentagon

Revolution's patron saint. After his death in 1989, Ayatollah Ruhollah Khomeini continued to influence Iranian politics. His shrine outside Tehran became a place of pilgrimage for followers who wanted to perpetuate Islamic revolution, like the women photographed here in 2001 on the twelfth anniversary of his death. His cult helped to mobilize voters for his unusual combination of agendas—communitarian, religious, populist, nationalist—and helped slow down and, at times, halt Iran's hesitant return to secular priorities and normal relations with the rest of the world.

Americans" in the "France of Asia." He ignored the Muslim clergy. He seized religious endowments without compensation to redistribute the land among peasants. He also made himself unpopular in other ways—especially by spending on the armed services rather than on social welfare—but he lost his throne by alientating religious sensibilities.

A Shiite cleric, Ayatollah Ruhollah Khomeini (1900–1989) gradually emerged as the voice of outraged Islam. Broadcasting from exile, he attracted millions of followers by his incorruptibility and self-righteousness. The Shah's regime was, he proclaimed, literally the work of the devil and must be destroyed. Khomeini called for an Islamic republic—a welfare state that would enrich all its faithful and in which all the necessities of life would be free. In 1979, he inspired a revolution. His followers filled the streets, deserted the army, and paralyzed the government. The Shah went into exile. An Islamic republic dominated by Shiite clergy replaced the ancient Iranian monarchy. The Iranian experiment, which followed an Islamist experiment in Pakistan in 1977, encouraged similar movements all over the Islamic world.

Religion did decline in Western Europe. But in much of the rest of the world, traditional religion proved ineradicable, surviving, strengthened by persecution, after all the hostile ideologies collapsed. Far from outbidding religion, prosperity made spirituality marketable. In the United States, the world's richest country, people sought relief from materialism in religion. Yet religion never lost its appeal to the victims of poverty, for whom rewards in the next world compensated for being underprivileged here and now. Christian and Muslim propagandists found huge audiences in sub-Saharan Africa.

Abu'l 'Ala Mawdudi, on the scope and purpose of the Islamic state

Traditional religions, especially Roman Catholicism, Islam, radical forms of Christianity, and Lamaist Buddhism, self-reformed successfully to confront secularism and widen their global appeal. The main challenge to traditional religions came not from atheism or secularism but from new religions. Most of these could be characterized as cults or folksy superstitions, or as personal religions concocted by individuals who did not see themselves as belonging in any particular communion but who picked and mixed from various traditions to create a menu of their own choice, like an Internet-surfing student plagiarizing a paper with the cut-and-paste facility.

Twentieth-century conditions favored cults in cities full of rootless, spiritually uneducated constituencies with excited expectations. Some fashions in belief were weird. Astrology was the starting point of the New Age movement, which, beginning in the 1960s, proclaimed the "dawning of the Age of Aquarius"—the doctrine that the astral prominence of the constellation Pisces is gradually being replaced, after about 2,000 years, with world-transforming effects. It is hard to believe that anyone could have taken such a doctrine seriously—but its success indicated how uneasy people felt. Toward the end of the century, sects predicting the end of the world achieved a brief vogue—even though the year 2000 had no particular significance, since our system of numbering years is purely arbitrary. Surprisingly, skepticism favored the proliferation of weird beliefs because, as the English writer G. K. Chesterton (1874–1936) reputedly said, "When people cease to believe in something, they do not believe in nothing; they believe in anything."

The biggest growth point was the kind of religion called **fundamentalist**. It started in a Protestant seminary in Princeton, New Jersey, in the early twentieth century in reaction to critical readings of the Bible. The idea was that the Bible contains fundamental truths that cannot be questioned by critical inquiry or scientific evidence. The name "fundamentalism" has been applied retrospectively to a similar doctrine, traditional in Islam, about the Quran. It can arise in the context of any religion that has a founding text or holy scripture. Karen Armstrong—one of the foremost authorities on the subject—sees fundamentalism as modern: scientific or pseudoscientific because it reduces religion to matters of undeniable fact. Apart from the bleakness of modernity, fundamentalism's other parent is fear: that the end of the world is imminent, of *Great Satans* (Iranian clerics' term for the United States and the West), of chaos, and above all, of the unfamiliar. To fundamentalists, all difference is subversive. These facts help to explain why fundamentalism arose in the modern world and has never lost its appeal. By 2000, fundamentalisms in Islam and Christianity, taken together, constituted the biggest movement in the world.

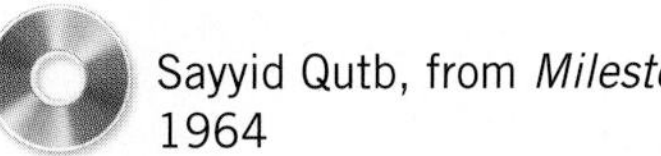
Sayyid Qutb, from *Milestones*, 1964

All fundamentalist movements are different but can be identified by the features they share: militancy, hostility to pluralism, and a determination to confuse politics with religion. Fundamentalists are self-cast as warriors against secularism. Yet, in practice, most fundamentalists are pleasant, ordinary people, who make their compromises with the world and leave their religion—as most people do—at the door of their church or mosque. The militant minorities among them, meanwhile, cause trouble by declaring war on society. Some sects, with their crushing effects on individual identity, their ethic of obedience, their paranoid habits, and their campaigns of hatred or violence, behaved in frightening ways like the early fascist cells.

When they got power, fundamentalists tended to treat people of other traditions with hostility. Bahais, Christians, Sunni Muslims, and Jews all suffered discrimination and persecution in Khomeini's Iran. In Afghanistan in the 1990s, the Islamic Taliban regime vandalized Buddhist monuments, smashed ancient art in the museums, suppressed Christian worship, ordered women out of school, and slaughtered homosexuals—of whom there were many since homosexual practice was a long-standing Afghan tradition. Saudi Arabia"s "religious police" imposed a rigid and uncompromising form of Islamic law even on non-Muslims. When a Christian fundamentalist general took power in Guatemala in 1982, the army persecuted Catholic churchmen and women for supposedly helping Native American rebels. Where Islamic fundamentalists took power nationally or locally, they usually imposed interpretations of Islamic law that often had dire consequences for women, whose freedoms were restricted, and for people who led supposedly irregular sex lives, who were liable to be put to death. Christian fundamentalists in the United States advocated laws to ban practices they considered objectionable on religious grounds, including homosexuality, the teaching of evolution, sex education in public schools, contraception, and abortion. Religious fundamentalism rarely managed to retain power for long, or to remain unseduced by the need for political compromise, but it continued to grow as a social movement, even when its political aspirations were frustrated or diluted.

Fundamentalism was one form of the religious response to secularism. Another was to imitate the secularists—to beat them at their own game. Traditional religions could do this by showing that they could make a difference to lives in the here and now, as well as in the hereafter, by organizing social services for worshippers and aid programs for the poor. New religions could try an alternative strategy. In developed countries, a lot of the new religion of the late twentieth century looked suspiciously like secularism—or even consumerism—in disguise. In South Korea, the Full Gospel Church promised its followers health and prosperity: bounding riches and bouncing bodies. In Japan, Soka Gakkai was a Buddhist prosperity cult that founded its own political party and spread to Europe and America. American churches increased their congregations by imitating the familiar world of trivial, middle-class lives, with coffee parties, muzak, casual clothes, and undemanding moral prescriptions. In Orange County, California, worshippers in the Crystal Cathedral believed that business success was a mark of divine election.

Vaclav Havel, "The Need for Transcendence in the Postmodern World"

Some new religions were essentially healing ministries—offering a form of alternative therapy for a health-obsessed age in which, in the absence of shared moral values, health was the only commonly acknowledged good. Other new religious movements of the period were more political. The supposedly Buddhist Aum Shinrikyo cult in Japan waged war on the rest of society. A fashionable cult known as Scientology, which called itself a church, was instead classed as a political organization or as a business in many countries. The **Liberation Theology** movement in Latin America was concerned with justice for the poor and oppressed, arguing that sin was not just individual moral failure but also a structural feature of capitalist society.

IN PERSPECTIVE: The Century of Paradox

Traditions had to struggle to survive the quickening pace of change, which made social and political relationships unrecognizable to successive generations and bewildering to those whose lives spanned the transformations. Science drove change, inspiring new technology, reforging how people saw the world. The relentless growth of global population, which wars did not interrupt, increased the pressure on the world's resources. But, even more than population growth, spiraling desire—consumerism, as it came to be called, lust for abundance, impatience to enjoy the rewards of economic growth—made people exploit the planet with increasing ruthlessness.

An execution by guillotine in France in 1929. Revolutionary France began executing people by guillotine in 1792. The guillotine was supposed to be an efficient and humane death-machine because it killed quickly with a single blow without torture. But during the Revolution, it made a horrible spectacle of mass executions and became a symbol not of the Enlightenment but of barbarity. France continued to guillotine condemned criminals until 1977. Today, the laws of France, like those of almost every Western country, acknowledge that even criminals have basic human rights, of which the most fundamental is the right to live.

Most of history had favored unitary states, with one religion, ethnicity, and identity. Large empires have always been multicultural, but they have usually had a dominant culture, alongside which others are, at best, tolerated. In the twentieth century, this would no longer do. The aftermath of the era of global empires, the range and intensity of migrations, the progress of ideas of racial equality, the multiplication of religions, and the large-scale redrawing of state boundaries made the toleration of diversity essential to the peace of most states. Those states that rejected toleration faced traumatic periods of "ethnic cleansing."

What was true of individual states was true of the entire world. "Shrinkage" brought peoples and cultures into unprecedented proximity. The peace and future prosperity of the world at the end of the century demanded an effort to accommodate religions, languages, ethnicities, communal identities, versions of history, and value systems in a single global community. Isaiah Berlin (1909–1997) explained, "There is a plurality of values which men can and do seek. . . . And . . . if a man pursues one of these values, I, who do not, am able to understand why he pursues it or what it would be like, in his circumstances, for me to be induced to pursue it. Hence the possibility of human understanding." Pluralism differs from cultural relativism. It does not say, for instance, that all cultures can be accommodated. One might exclude Nazism, say, or cannibalism. It leaves open the possibility of peaceful argument about which culture, if any, is best. It claims, in Berlin's words, "that the multiple values are objective, part of the essence of humanity, rather than arbitrary creations of men's subjective fancies." In a world where globalization made most historic communities defensive about their own cultures, it has been difficult to persuade them to coexist peacefully with the contrasting cultures of their neighbors. Still, pluralism is the only truly uniform interest that all the world's peoples have in common.

Human rights provided the key test of whether universal values could thrive in a plural world. Even in the United States, where public advocacy of human rights was as strong as anywhere, presidents seemed willing to ignore or circumvent them (see Chapter 28).

The problems went even deeper. The experiences of the century made human rights a lively issue but did not dispel moral confusion about the value of life. Almost everyone, for instance, by 2000, paid lip service to the rights to life and to equality of respect, but these values were more honored in theory than in practice. Many countries outlawed capital punishment. But this did not mean that they treated human life as inviolable. In some places, the lives of some criminals continued to be regarded as dispensable, even in most states of the United States. Many jurisdictions exempted unborn babies from the principle of inviolability of human life. The decriminalization of abortion in most of the West served humane ends: freeing women who felt obliged to have abortions, and those who helped them, from prosecution under the law. But the effects were morally questionable. Euthanasia became another focus of concern over the limits of human rights. Did the moribund and the vegetative have them? Did the incurably dying have a moral right to choose to end their sufferings by physician-assisted suicide?

CHRONOLOGY

1933–1935	Restrictions placed on German Jews
December 1937	Rape of Nanjing
1939–1945	World War II
1939–1945	Holocaust
1950s	Japans spends 2 percent of GDP on defense
1950s and 1960s	Big corporations return to Japanese economy; generation gap emerges; civil rights movement in the United States
1960s	Second Vatican Council; Asian "tigers" (Japan, South Korea, Hong Kong, and Singapore) begin rapid economic ascent
1960–1967	Japanese incomes double
1961–1973	U.S. involvement in Vietnam War
1965	Public spending accounts for 25 percent of GDP of world's seven wealthiest nations
March 1968	Mai Lai massacre in Vietnam
1968	Prague Spring
1971	World's first microprocessor
1979	Islamic revolution in Iran
1980s and 1990s	Governments around the world move away from nationalized economies
1980–1987	Incomes fall in most Latin American nations
1982	Mexico defaults on national debt
1985	Japan becomes world's biggest foreign investor
1990s	China's economy grows at annual rate of almost 10 percent
Late 1990s	Economies of Brazil and India grow at rapid rate
Late twentieth century	Christian and Islamic fundamentalism on the rise; 30 million Internet users in China; public spending accounts for 37 percent of GDP of world's seven wealthiest nations; Muslim population: Britain, 2 million; France, 4 million; migrants from Latin America largest minority group in the United States
2001	Terrorist attack on United States

By 2000, the world seemed to have tried everything. The "final solutions" and "inevitable" revolutions that extremists of Right and Left proposed had failed. Social planning went wrong. But the return to individualism failed to restrain the growth of government, widened the poverty gap, and bred terrorism and crime. The world was left looking for a "third way" between capitalism and socialism, in which freedom and order would coexist, governments would make society more equal without choking differences, and individual enterprise would thrive at the service of a wider community. These objectives were easier to state than to deliver.

The twentieth century was a century of paradox. Frustrated hopes coincided with unprecedented progress. Uncontrolled change left much of the world mired in stagnancy. Utopias nourished moral sickness, suicide, and crime. The century of democracy was the century of dictators. The century of war was also the century of pacifism. Rule by the aged survived the empowerment of the young. Globalization broke down some states and communities but encouraged others to recover historic identities. Science and secularism revived faith. As we shall see in Chapter 30, the twentieth century could also be called the century of ecology, but it was peculiarly destructive of nature.

PROBLEMS AND PARALLELS

1. Why did science, technology, education, and prosperity fail to avert moral catastrophes in the twentieth century?
2. The nation-state was the central actor in reorganizing societies after the economic disasters and wars of the twentieth century. Nation-states, however, were also the most efficient killers of tens of millions of people through war and misguided policies. What are the reasons for this paradox?
3. How did individualism manifest itself in both conservative and counterconservative ways?
4. How did the demands for personal freedom, sexual liberation, and existential self-fulfillment affect Western societies? Family structures? The status of women?
5. How did globalization affect economies and cultures in the late twentieth and early twenty-first centuries?
6. What does the term *counter-colonization* mean? How did people redefine the sense of their own identities in the twentieth century? Why did it take so long to dismantle the legacy of racism?
7. How did traditional as well as new religions respond to secularism? What features do fundamentalist movements have in common around the world?

DOCUMENTS IN GLOBAL HISTORY

- Transcript from the Rape of Nanjing sentencing, 1947
- Eyewitness account of genocide in Armenia, 1915
- Excerpt from the 9/11 Commission Report
- China: a farmer's perspective, 2002
- Martin Luther King, Jr., *Letter from Birmingham Jail*, 1963
- Aimé Césaire, from *Return to My Native Land*
- Leopold Senghor on Négritude
- Virginia Woolf, from *A Room of One's Own*
- Justin Vaïsse, from "Veiled Meaning," (France) 2004
- China: "A Harmonious Society," 2006
- Pope John Paul II on consumerism, from *Centesimus Annus*
- Sayyid Qutb, from *Milestones*, 1964
- Abu'l 'Ala Mawdudi, on the scope and purpose of the Islamic state
- Vaclav Havel, "The Need for Transcendence in the Postmodern World"

Please see the Primary Source DVD for additional sources related to this chapter.

READ ON

The study of wartime atrocities is ably represented by I. Chang, *The Rape of Nanking: The Forgotten Holocaust of World War II* (1997), which shows how Nanjing served as a training ground for further Japanese slaughter of civilians. *Good Man of Nanking: The Diaries of J. Rabe*, ed. by E. Wickert, translated from the German by J. E. Woods (1998) offers a firsthand account of the massacre by a German businessman who organized refuge for Chinese civilians.

D. Bell, *The Coming of Post-Industrial Society* (1976), predicted the coming of the Information Age and the social and cultural transformations it has wrought. It should be read in conjunction with F. Jameson, *Postmodernism or the Cultural Logic of Late Capitalism* (1991), a densely written but very sophisticated analysis of postmodernism as the artistic expression of its material milieu. The same author's *Marxism and Form* (1971) remains the basic manifesto of modern Marxist cultural analysis. J. Tomlinson, *Globalization and Culture* (1999) explores similar themes from a different perspective.

A. Musallam, *From Secularism to Jihad: Sayyid Qutb and the Foundations of Radical Islamism* (2005) is an insightful examination of the founder of modern Islamic political fundamentalism. T. Madan, *Modern Myths, Locked Minds: Secularism and Fundamentalism in India* (1997) looks at the intersection of secularism, religion, and politics for India's major faiths. S. Jacoby, *Freethinkers: A History of American Secularism* (2004) examines the paradox of the secular foundations of the United States very religiously tinged democratic culture.

N. Woods, ed., *The Political Economy of Globalization* (2000), explores key economic and political problems associated with globalization. R. Compton, *East Asian Democratization: Impact of Globalization, Culture, and Economy* (2000) uses detailed case studies of various East Asian countries to compare the political and cultural impact of globalizing economies.

CHAPTER
30 The Embattled Biosphere: The Twentieth-Century Environment

The World Health Organization has checked the spread of river blindness in Burkina Faso, but the problems of soil degradation and the ruin of villages continue.

IN THIS CHAPTER

FUEL RESOURCES
FOOD OUTPUT
URBANIZATION
THE CRISIS OF CONSERVATION
THE UNMANAGEABLE ENVIRONMENT: CLIMATE AND DISEASE
IN PERSPECTIVE: The Environmental Dilemma

"Why do you travel such a long distance with this load of wood and your baby on your back?" the environmental worker asked.

"What a question!" said the woman, whose name was Rasmata. The conversation, reported in 1991, began after a long drought in Burkina Faso, just south of the Sahara. "My baby is ill. I nursed her with traditional medicine but the illness went on.... With the takings from the wood, I will be able to buy ... modern medicine...."

"Don't you know that it is the excessive culling of trees that is causing the advance of the desert into our country?"

"What can we do? When I was a girl, there were many fruits to be gathered. We kept a third for ourselves to eat, and sold the remainder in town.... Now these trees are rare.... We used to collect firewood from trees that had died naturally. Now there aren't any. We have to go a long way, to cut living shrub and leave it to dry out for days or weeks before we can use it for our fires. It is for lack of other produce that I sell wood...."

Some of Burkina Faso's problems are part of the inescapable geography of the region. The Sahara has been drying and growing for thousands of years. Winds powder the land beyond the desert with infertile soil. Most of the country has, on average, only a little over two inches of rain in a good year. In the late twentieth century, droughts became routine.

BURKINA FASO

Scientific interventions have improved life in some respects. For instance, 10 percent of the population used to suffer from river blindness—sight-destroying lesions, caused by a tiny worm that gets into the skin when black fly bite. The internationally funded program that checked the disease in the 1980s cost less than a dollar for each person it helped.

But Burkina Faso, like neighboring countries on the desert edge, suffers from human-made environmental problems. Its population doubled to 10 million in the 20 years from 1975. It was a medical triumph, but it strained the country's resources, forcing people to farm so intensively that the soil became enfeebled or to increase their herds of livestock. By 2000, the number of cattle in Burkina Faso was growing at a rate of 2 percent a year and those of sheep and goats at 3 percent a year. Overgrazing is as bad for soil as overcropping. What is more, the herdsmen occupied ever more land, spreading ahead of the advancing desert, from the north of the country. Between 1980 and 1993, drought and overexploitation of the kind Rasmata mentioned destroyed more than 3 million acres of forest in Burkina Faso.

FOCUS questions

- HOW HAS the increased consumption of fossil fuels affected the world's atmosphere?
- WHAT WAS the green revolution?
- WHAT WERE the successes and failures of twentieth-century food production?
- HOW DID the pattern of human settlement and population growth change in the twentieth century?
- HOW HAVE the world's rising population and demand for resources put pressure on the natural environment?
- HOW DID the pattern of disease change in the twentieth century?
- CAN HUMAN beings influence climate change?

Well-intentioned interventions in the environment by governments and international agencies often made the problems worse. To help combat river blindness, for instance, in the mid-1970s, foreign agencies insisted on resettling farmers. By the late 1980s, many of the new settlements were unsustainable. To feed the increased population, farmers ceased to leave fields fallow. As a result, soils could not recover their natural fertility. The rising costs of fertilizer and insecticides hugely exceeded the increase in the value of the farmers' cotton. Families moved in ways the planners had not been able to foresee—many, for instance, in search of irrigation water, flocking to Burkina Faso's extreme southeast, where a new hydroelectric dam was being built.

Fluctuations in government policy and economic fashion could have devastating effects. Development strategies came and went with bewildering speed. International agencies suspended aid if projects failed to produce quick results—three- or five-year terms were normal for funding reviews. In 1983, a military coup in Burkina Faso brought in a government the West denounced as communist. Peasants were promised the right to use any land they cleared, with terrible consequences for the forests. In 2000, the government began to encourage big, supposedly efficient farms. This was contrary to the traditions of a country of small family enterprises, typically of 7 to 15 acres.

Meanwhile, international market conditions tended to impoverish these peasants, obliging them to grow cheap cash crops—mainly cotton and peanuts—for rich consumer countries. From the 1980s, there was a world glut of the cheap grains the farmers were encouraged to grow to feed themselves.

We can trace the combination of natural and man-made effects in the dust to which so much of the soil of Burkina Faso turned. In 1988, more than half the land in the country was officially classed as biologically degraded. By 2000, over two-thirds of the soil of the northern, central, and eastern provinces was affected. Food economists now think that Burkina Faso can no longer support its population.

Though Burkina Faso is particularly badly off, the problems it suffers from are global problems, intelligible and containable—if at all—only in a global context. In 1900, the population of the world was 1,630 million. In 2000, it was 6.1 billion. Global population doubled in the last 40 years of the century. This was not as fast as the growth rate in Burkina Faso—but it was still hard to cope with. Even before we take other factors into account, population explosion has put unprecedented pressure on the world's resources of energy, stressing and stretching our means of providing enough food and fuel to keep humankind going (see Map 30.1).

Demand for resources, moreover, has outstripped population growth. Not only are there more people in the world than ever before, but they also demand, on average, vastly more food and goods and consume vastly more energy. If the population-growth figures seem astonishing, the output figures are even more startlingly disproportionate. Between 1900 and 1950, the total value of the goods people consumed rose, at 2003 prices, from $2 trillion to $5 trillion. Between 1950 and 2000, the total soared to $39 trillion. In other words, while the population of the world less than quadrupled, consumption rose more than nineteenfold.

Why did consumption leap ahead? It is hard to separate cause and effect. New technologies enabled industries to unlock energy resources with a consequent rise in prosperity. Abundance, it seems, is there to be exhausted. "Spiraling desire"—an instinct, or maybe a pathology—makes people want whatever is available or envy whatever others have. In the twentieth century, the world economy grew, on average, by about 1.5 percent a year—about two and a half times as fast as in the nineteenth century, when growth rates seemed dazzlingly high. Greed grows from growth. In 1991, an average American used up between 30 and 50 times as much copper, tin, and aluminum as a citizen of India, 43 times as much petroleum, and 184 times as much natural gas. When prosperity leaps, people's expectations explode. Demand and supply feed off each other. The world got hooked on prosperity, locked into dependence on economic growth (see Map 30.2). Electorates wanted more food, goods, energy. So governments encouraged, or at least allowed, environmental overexploitation.

Fast economic development always outstrips environmental restraints. China, where real average incomes virtually quadrupled in the late twentieth century, demonstrates the possibilities and the dangers. By the mid-1990s, of the ten cities with the most acute air-pollution problems in the world, five were in China, where pollution-related diseases were estimated to cause 1 million deaths a year—including poisoning by fluorides and arsenic that industries released into the food chain. China emitted more deadly sulphur dioxide into the atmosphere than any other country, causing acid rain to fall on much of its own land and on that of its neighbors. Overgrazing is turning the northern steppe to desert. The Gobi Desert is advancing from Central Asia toward the Yellow River valley. And desert dust from China blows across the Pacific, mixed with sulphur dioxide, over Japan and North America. The Chinese government hardly began to tackle these problems until the late 1990s, when it tried to reduce sulphur dioxide emissions to "only" double those United Nations guidelines considered safe.

We can understand the problems better, though maybe not solve them, if we look first at the way humans treated energy resources in the twentieth century, then at the effects in urban and other habitats, before turning to dangers beyond human agency or control.

MAP 30.1

World Population, 2003

Country Area Roughly Proportional to Population

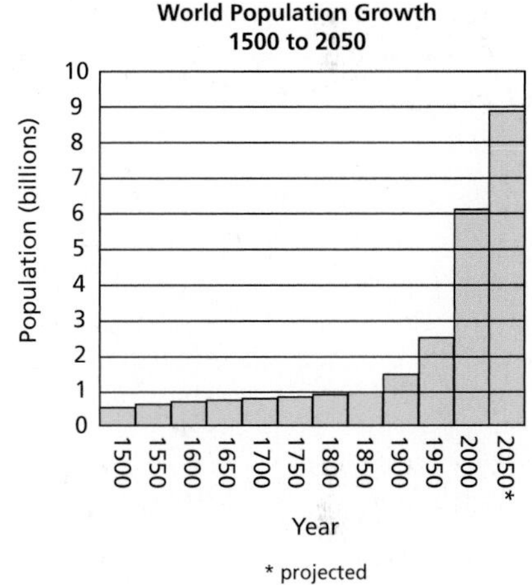

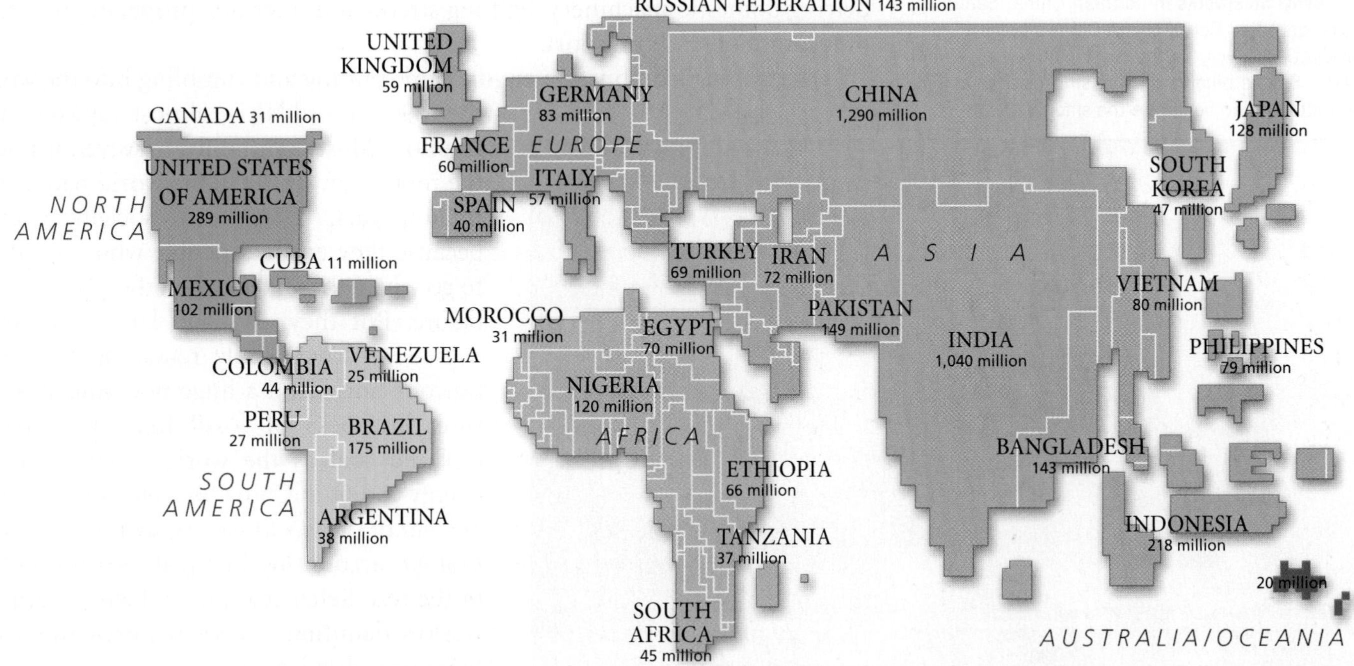

MAP 30.2

Comparative World Wealth, ca. 2004

- high income (over $25,000 per year)
- upper-middle income ($10,000-$25,000 per year)
- lower-middle income ($5,000-$10,00 per year)
- low income (less than $5,000 per year)
- data unavailable

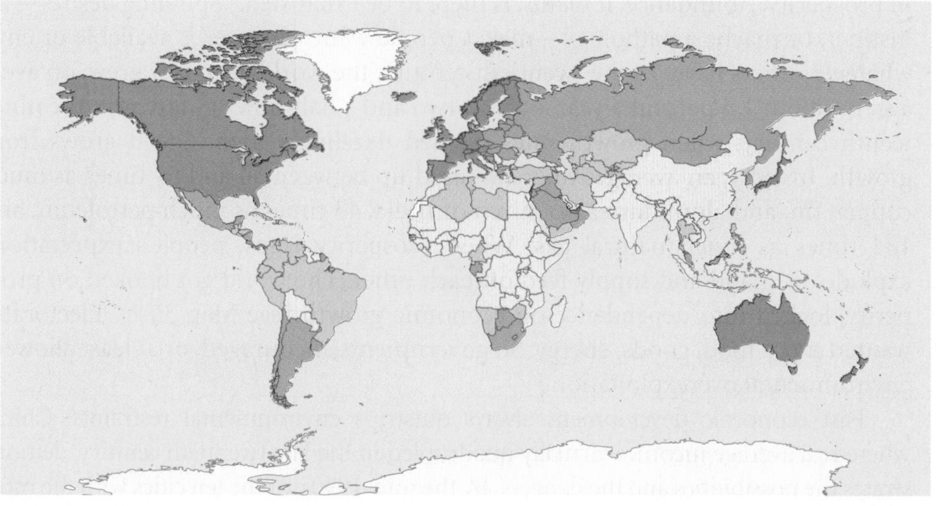

FUEL RESOURCES

Just as steam power transformed the nineteenth century, electricity and the internal combustion engine transformed the twentieth century. Electricity replaced gas for lighting and steam for power for most purposes. The battery and the local generator harnessed electric power way beyond the industrial world. Electricity facilitated long-range communication and seemingly infinite means of managing information. In 1901, Guglielmo Marconi transmitted the first wireless telegraph message across the Atlantic. Radio waves soon linked every part of the world, communicating messages at the speed of light. In the 1960s, it became possible to engrave battery-operated computers on silicon microchips .0394 of an inch in diameter. These were the most spectacular applications of electricity, but they required relatively little power. More pervasive and effective in changing the world were the ways electricity penetrated everyday life: powering factories and farms, driving domestic machinery, lighting streets and interiors, propelling the engines of locomotion and transport.

The internal combustion engine came puffing and rumbling into the world in the 1890s. It could drive almost any kind of contraption. Most commonly, however, it powered the motor car. By 2000, the world had over 600 million cars. They were socially liberating because they enabled people who owned them to go where they liked, when they liked, as never before. But they also had lamentable effects: aggressive drivers, ugly roads, noxious fumes, raucous noise, and a huge new source of pressure on stocks of fossil fuels. Oil gradually replaced coal as the world's major source of energy except in China. By 2000, oil supplied 40 percent of the world's energy, with coal and natural gas accounting in equal measure for most of the rest. Reliance on fossil fuels to supply the world's daunting energy requirements carried two major disadvantages.

The Benxi Steelworks in northern China. Satellites have identified Benxi, one of China's biggest steel production towns, as the most polluted place on Earth. Smoke billows up from smokestacks as the sun attempts to penetrate the smog.

First, fossil fuels are a limited resource. Exploration kept pace with demand for oil, but people kept worrying that stocks would run out. Competition for oil caused or exacerbated wars. Countries with major oil fields combined to control the price of fuel. In 1973, for instance, the Organization of Petroleum Exporting Countries (OPEC), an alliance of major oil producers, hiked the price and plunged the world into crisis. When price stability resumed, so did high levels of production and consumption.

Second, fossil fuels release carbon gases into the atmosphere. In the Ice Age that began about 150,000 years ago, there were 200 parts of carbon dioxide per million in the air around the Earth. In the 1800s, there were 280. Today, there are 370 parts per million (see Figure 30.1). Most of this increase is the result of human agency: the recirculation of carbon formerly locked in forests or buried underground for millions of years as coal, oil, and gas.

FIGURE 30.1 LEVEL OF CARBON DIOXIDE IN THE ATMOSPHERE, 1750–PRESENT

Carbon in the atmosphere intensifies the effects of the rays of the sun, boosting temperatures, killing the plankton on which marine life depends for food, melting the icecaps, raising sea levels, and—if sustained for long enough—modifying the flow of ocean currents and the pattern of the winds. Popular science calls this phenomenon the **greenhouse effect.** We do not know what the consequences would be if the world's wind and current system were to change permanently, but the periodic disasters caused by the temporary oscillations observable at intervals are alarming (see Chapter 14).

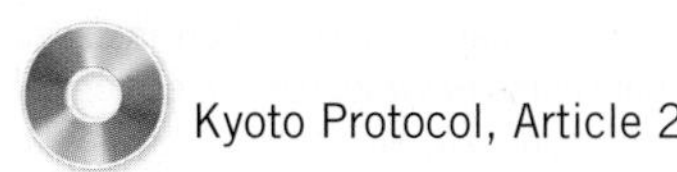
Kyoto Protocol, Article 2

In view of the problems fossil fuels posed, energy consumers in the late twentieth century invested heavily in alternative sources of power. The idea of hydroelectricity was simple. As water cascades from a higher to a lower level, it can turn turbines that would generate electricity. But hydroelectricity needed big rivers that could be dammed to concentrate and regulate the flow of water. Moreover, as we shall see, dams nearly always harmed agriculture.

Other possibilities were problematic. Nuclear power was cost-efficient but used an exhaustible resource: uranium, some types of which are constructed of atoms that release tremendous amounts of energy when split. Moreover, nuclear power left lethal waste products. As early as 1874, Jules Verne (1828–1905) imagined a hydrogen-powered world. But hydrogen motors need frequent refueling. There will be no mass switch to hydrogen cars until the service stations are in place, and no stations until drivers have hydrogen cars. Ethanol from grain could replace fossil oil. But the plants would have to be genetically modified to yield enough output without exhausting available land.

In the late twentieth century, the search for fossil-fuel substitutes switched to **renewable energy.** The sun, however, is unreliable, and its rays are unevenly distributed around the globe. Wind power required vast numbers of intrusive windmills to generate relatively modest output. Technology to

Winds of change. Even renewable energy sources have ecological costs. Wind exploitation demands the concentrations of thousands of turbines that disfigure landscapes—as here, in the California desert—and demand maintenance.

Aswan High Dam. Four monstrous, cavernous hydraulic tunnels lie under the unfinished Aswan High Dam during the dam's construction in Egypt in 1964. The dam came to symbolize the ecological irresponsibility of high-cost, high-prestige hydraulic projects. It displaced population, swamped precious archaeological sites, exposed valuable water to evaporation, impoverished soils, and sped pollutants down the Nile, extinguishing much marine life in the eastern Mediterranean.

harness magnetism on a large scale has eluded researchers. Planetary and cosmic forces are, so far, beyond our grasp. Nevertheless, enough had been accomplished to encourage further work.

FOOD OUTPUT

The world needed more food than ever before. Meanwhile dwellings, cities, and industries took up space that might grow food, and the spread of deserts put more pressure on existing land. The spread of the Sahara in Africa, for instance, has been one of the most continuous, relentless processes observable on our planet since the last Ice Age ended 20,000 years ago. Human agency has aggravated the loss of cultivable land.

In some places, for instance, in the twentieth century, as so often before—only now on a bigger scale—overexploitation wasted soils and exhausted irrigation resources. In 1932, unrestrained overcropping helped to turn much of Oklahoma and other parts of the North American west into a "Dust Bowl." Marginal land all over the world became ever less productive as the result of a vicious circle of cause and effect. Much of the world is still trapped in this cycle, especially in Africa and Asia. Population growth raises food needs. Farmers resort to overcropping to meet them. This impoverishes the land. Food output falls, and hunger—or, more commonly, dependence on foreign aid—spreads.

Two traditional responses are irrigation and fertilization. In the second half of the twentieth century, huge dams—usually combining irrigation schemes with efforts to generate hydroelectric power—made desertification worse. Dams usually have to be backed by reservoirs, which speed up evaporation by exposing more water to the sun. Meanwhile, the reservoirs absorb water from tributaries in the vicinity. This increases the salt content of the soil, because streams no longer dilute the salt. So the dams actually leach fertility from the soil.

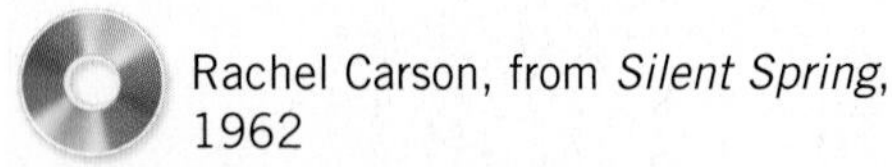

Rachel Carson, from *Silent Spring*, 1962

Yet from the 1930s, when the world's first great dams blocked the Volga and the Colorado in the American West, until the late 1960s, when the effects of damming became intolerable, dams were showpiece projects, like the temples and pyramids of antiquity. A classic example occurred in Egypt. Built with Soviet aid during the Cold War, the Aswan Dam stretched across the Nile in the 1960s. It generated massive amounts of electricity and made it possible to regulate irrigation in Egypt with great precision. But it also trapped the silt that the Nile had carried since time immemorial to enrich Egypt's fields, shrinking the Nile delta, raising salt levels in the lower river, and choking off the flow of nutrients on which much Mediterranean marine life had formerly depended. Perhaps the single most disastrous project was the diversion in the 1950s of the two great rivers of Central Asia—the Oxus and Jaxartes (or Amu Darya and Syr Darya)—in what was then the Soviet Union. Soviet planners hoped to irrigate a vast plain for cotton production. Instead, they dried up the Aral, a huge inland sea, wrecked its fishing industry, and exposed deadly salt flats that turned the landscape barren.

Though the fashion for dams declined, some monster projects continued, like dinosaurs escaping extinction. Between 1975 and 1991, Brazil and Paraguay collaborated to build a series of dams nearly five miles long across the river Paraná. The system generates more electricity than any other development in the world. In 2003, China opened an even bigger dam across the Yangtze—one of Mao Zedong's pet projects, completed after nearly half a century of planning, debate, and construction. This Three Gorges Dam will eventually flood so much space that 2 million people will have to be resettled. At the time of its inauguration, more than two-thirds of the river waters of the world passed through dams, and China continued to plan more massive hydroelectric projects (see Figure 30.2).

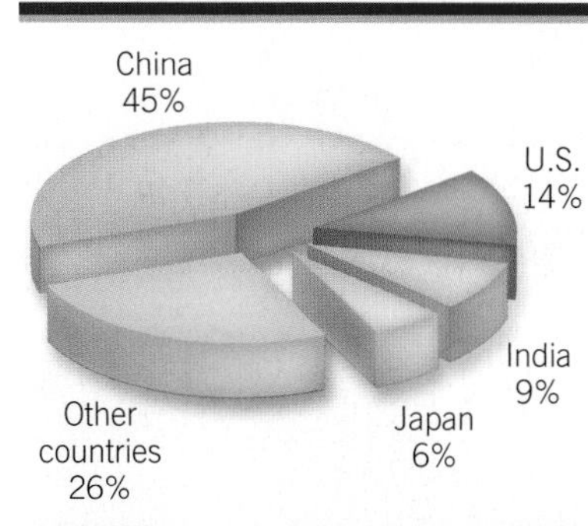

FIGURE 30.2 THE SHARE OF THE WORLD'S DAMS
Reprinted by permission of the Pacific Institute. www.worldwater.org

By 2000, 40 percent of the world's food was grown on irrigated land. Most irrigation water is pumped from below ground, where huge lakes and freshwater seas lie. But this water is an exhaustible resource. The Ogallala Aquifer underlies the North American prairie. But 150,000 pumps are sucking it dry. In 1970, farmers in Kansas were told there was enough water left for 300 years. By the 1990s, the estimate had been revised to perhaps 20 or 30 years. The water table under the Sahara falls year by year. Unchecked consumption of irrigation resources in California, the Indian Punjab, the Murray-Darling river system in Australia, and the Cochabamba valley in Bolivia has had similar effects on the water table.

Fertilization, meanwhile, proved as mixed in its effects as irrigation. In 1909, Fritz Haber discovered how to extract nitrogen from the atmosphere and use it to manufacture commercial fertilizer. It was like plucking food from the air. No other single invention did more to feed the growing population in the second half of the century. In 1940, the world used some 4 million tons of artificial fertilizer. By 1990, it was using about 150 million tons. Phosphate mining provided another source of fertilizers. Agrochemicals manufacturers double-dosed the soil with chemicals to stimulate crops and kill weeds.

The practice had a startling effect. Insects lost their weedy habitats. The birds, reptiles, and mammals that fed off the insects lost their food supply. By the 1960s, the effects were so marked that Rachel Carson, a former United States' government agronomist, published *Silent Spring*, in which she predicted an America without birdsong. An ecological movement mobilized millions of people, especially in Europe and America, to defend the environment against pollution and overexploitation. The satirist Tom Lehrer warned listeners to beware of two things: "don't drink the water and don't breathe the air." Norman E. Borlaug, the Nobel Prize–winning agronomist who helped to develop fertilizer-friendly crops, denounced "vicious, hysterical propaganda" against agrochemicals by "scientific halfwits," but he could not stem the tide of environmentalism at a popular level. Only the resistance of governments and big business could check it.

DDT. In the 1950s, DDT (dichloro-diphenyl-trichloroethane) was a "wonder-insecticide" credited with controlling the mosquitoes that transmit malaria. "U.S. monoplanes daily swoop over Korea's capital," proclaimed the proud caption to this U.S. propaganda photo, "in the battle against disease and insects," spraying the city with DDT. In 1962, in the revolutionary environmentalist manifesto *Silent Spring*, Rachel Carson denounced DDT for causing cancer and killing birds and other animals.

In any case, the arguments were not as decisively imbalanced as Rachel Carson and her followers claimed. Humankind at that moment needed agrochemicals. Population growth was outstripping farmers' capacity to feed the world. Even when used together, irrigation and fertilization could not meet the growing demand for food.

In theory, the world could have got by in other ways. Farmers could cut down on production of less nutritious foods and increase more efficient forms of output. Livestock raising, for instance, is an inefficient way to use edible grain. Yet more than 70 percent of the grain grown in the United States in 2000, and some 40 percent of the world's grain, was devoted to animal feed. More nutrition could be wrested from less land if people were willing to live on diets of soybeans, high-lysine maize, insects, plankton, algae, and edible bacteria. But by and large, they are not. In the global food market, the hungry are powerless, and farmers are not going to switch from more profitable to less profitable markets. Nor can they afford to do so.

As fears of global food shortages became acute, there was therefore only one way out: make plant foods more productive. Agronomists had to develop fast-growing, high-yielding, disease-resistant varieties of nutritious staples for a range of different environments. In the 1950s, research concentrated on some of the traditionally most successful and adaptable grains, especially wheat, rice, and maize. The big breakthrough came with the adaptation of dwarf varieties of wheat from Japan and of rice from Taiwan and Indonesia. These crops were stunted in stature and so could be sprayed with fertilizers without toppling them over. Experiments in Mexico and Washington State produced successful hybrids. By 1980, the world's average wheat yield per acre was double that of 1950. Under experimental conditions, the most successful new varieties yielded ten times as much again as older ones. The new crops covered three-quarters of the world's grain-growing areas by the early 1990s. Meanwhile, in 1970, the UN Food and Agriculture Organization reversed its predictions of widespread famine and estimated that the world could grow enough food to feed 157 billion people.

The **green revolution**—as people called it at the time—saved millions of lives. Even with the huge increase in global food output, failures of distribution contributed to many famines in the third quarter of the century. Without the new varieties the green revolution nurtured, the death toll would have been much higher. Nevertheless, the agronomists' successes came at a price. The new varieties were heavily dependent on chemical fertilizers and pesticides. So, as the green revolution spread, the world was—in effect—doused with poisons and pollutants. By 1985, according to the World Health Organization, pesticides had caused 1 million deaths, mostly among agricultural workers. Meanwhile, the new wonder crops crowded out traditional, local staples. Peasant farmers in poor regions of the world produced ever-increasing quantities of cheap grains for survival and had little or no produce that they could sell at fair prices to rich consumers. Global poverty was becoming institutionalized.

In the late twentieth century, some scientists proposed to remedy the problems of the green revolution by switching to **genetically modified (GM) crops.** It became possible to modify the genes of food crops to make them resistant to insects, for example, without needing insecticides, or to deliver high yields with relatively little irrigation. The GM strategy, however, was rather like buying a rattlesnake to kill a rat—the solution might be worse than the problem. The new strategy might have undesirable ecological side effects of its own. Outside the United States, most governments were reluctant to encourage it, in case GM crops displaced or cross-pollinated with existing varieties and caused further losses of biodiversity. Nor would GM crops liberate farmers from reliance on chemical fertilizers (see Figure 30.3).

FIGURE 30.3 COUNTRIES LEADING IN GENETICALLY MODIFIED (GM) AGRICULTURE.

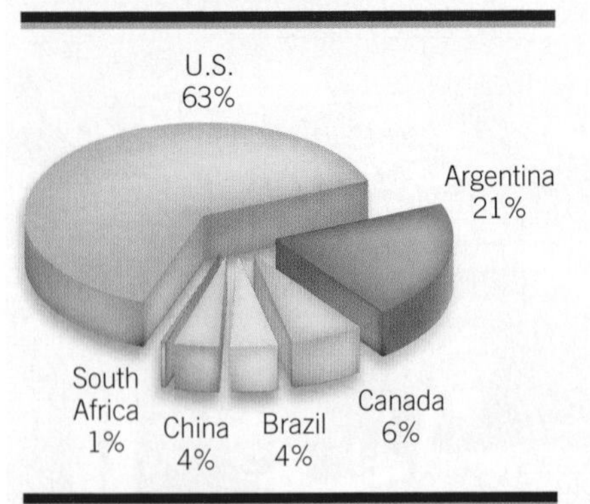

Reprinted with permission of the Food and Agricultural Organization of the United Nations

Moreover, GM technology demanded high investment in the form of development capital. A few companies dominated the market for GM seeds. With the U.S. government's blessing, the big bankrollers patented genes, excluded competition, and produced seed that would not reproduce naturally—in effect, compelling farmers to buy new seed every year. If widely adopted, GM would perhaps guarantee cheap food for the world for the future. But this would condemn food producers, including most of the world's peasants, to poverty as part of a system of overproduction, depriving them—should they become dependent on GM crops—of the opportunity to specialize in the supply of rare and expensive food to rich markets. In short, GM would make the poor poorer by forcing them to buy seed to produce goods they could not sell.

Cheap food was a by-product of the success of the green revolution. In 1900, an average American family spent about 35 percent of its income on food. By 2000, the corresponding figure had fallen to less than 15 percent—and that money bought a lot more to eat. Abundance of choice grew with abundance of quantity. Big multinational companies made the most of the situation. Cheap, mass-produced foods, with low unit profits, could make fantastic fortunes for the companies that sold them if they marketed them on a large enough scale. McDonald's became a globally recognizable example of this sort of strategy. It began as a no-frills drive-in restaurant in San Bernardino, California, in 1937. By 2000 McDonald's had thousands of outlets in 120 countries. Global urbanization favored the trend. In booming cities, migrants from the countryside were cut off from the sort of food they formerly ate: painstakingly grown plant foods, freshly harvested and locally prepared. A massive switch to mass-produced food occurred in just about every major urbanizing environment—not just in the industrialized West. Paradoxically, while prosperity grew and food became abundant, many people's diets deteriorated.

Basic Resources: Fuel and Food

1890s	Development of internal combustion engines
1930s	World's first great dams constructed
1932	Dust Bowl emerges in central and western United States
1940–1990	Use of artificial fertilizer increases from 4 to 150 million tons
1950–1980	Wheat yields per acre double
1950–2000	Land under irrigation increases from 247 to 644 million acres
1962	Publication of Rachel Carson's *Silent Spring*
1973	Organization of Petroleum Exporting Countries (OPEC) oil embargo against the United States, Western Europe, and Japan
Late twentieth century	Acceleration of use of genetically modified crops; search for alternative fuels intensifies
ca. 2000	600 million cars worldwide; fossil fuels account for most of world's energy consumption; carbon dioxide levels in the atmosphere reach 370 parts per million

At the same time, the science of dietetics failed. In the last 40 years of the twentieth century, on dieticians' advice, Western governments promoted massive health campaigns in favor of high-carbohydrate diets, recommending breads, potatoes, pasta, rice. Cheap foods, laden with carbohydrates, especially in the form of sugar, glutted the market. In combination with the problems of distribution that urbanization created, the result was a pandemic of obesity. It started in the West, especially in the United States. In 1950, 5 percent of Americans were classified as clinically obese. By 2001, the figure rose to 26 percent. Particularly alarming was the rate of increase among the young. Well over a third of under-19-year-olds qualified as obese. Though the United States weighed in at the top of the fat stakes, the same trend was detectable throughout the West. It was also beginning to be noticeable even in countries where obesity was virtually unknown—including China, India, and even Japan, which registered the world's steepest increase in clinical obesity in the 1990s.

Remarkably, late twentieth-century obesity was particularly a problem of the poor. This was a stunning reversal of what had been, almost universally, the historical pattern up to this time. In just about every previous period, in most societies, the rich were fat and the poor were thin. Now, it was the other way round. Formerly, only the rich could afford to be fat. When cheap food became abundantly available to the poor, the rich—at least, those who were fashion conscious—fled from fatness into dieting. In the twentieth-century West, wealth could buy you a thin physique by way of expensive "health foods," plastic surgery, personal trainers, and gym fees. "You can never be too rich or too thin," Wallis Simpson (1896–1986) said. She was a waif-thin socialite, whom King Edward VIII of Britain renounced his throne in 1936 to marry. Meanwhile, the poor consoled themselves with calories in quantities they could never before afford.

The rise of obesity panicked health agencies. One of the most remarkable facts about late twentieth-century obesity is how little harm it did. Nonetheless, the dramatically deadly new illnesses of the period included two major killers to which the corpulent are particularly prone: heart diseases and type-2 diabetes. More than 60 percent of type-2 diabetes cases in America, according to a study done at Harvard University in 2001, were attributed to excessive weight. For the many people prone

Obesity in China. Patients, all of them young, perform aerobics at the Aimi Fat Reduction Hospital in Tianjin, China, in March 2005. The hospital, which attracts obese people from several Asian countries, uses acupuncture, diet, and intensive exercise to help patients shed weight.

to the effect, fat in the bloodstream coated and clotted their arteries, inducing high blood pressure, strokes, and heart attacks. In short, twentieth-century food strategies succeeded in fighting famine and feeding the world. But they failed in just about every other important respect: overproducing abundance, increasing poverty, diminishing biodiversity, and undermining health.

URBANIZATION

Agriculture was becoming, under the pressure of economies of scale, a vast business for huge corporations. It got harder to be a peasant. A few rich countries, such as Germany and France, subsidized small farmers. In most of the rest of the world, peasants abandoned the land and followed the roads and railway lines toward cities and a promise of prosperity that often remained unfulfilled. This was one of the most dramatic new departures ever in how people live. For 10,000 years, most people had lived in agricultural settlements. Now centers of industrial manufacturing and services took over. Towns and cities became the normal environments for people to live in. By 2000, half the world lived in settlements with populations of 20,000 or more (see Map 30.3). Cities grew even in countries where agriculture remained the economically dominant way of life. In Nigeria, typical for regions struggling to escape from a role as primary producers for other people's industries, a fifth of the population lived in towns in 1963. By 1991, the proportion had shot up to a third.

Urbanization came at a high short-term cost in living standards. The world hardly seemed to have learned from the degradation of urban life in the industrializing cities of the nineteenth century (see Chapter 24). Towns grew like fungus: profusely and unhealthily. The Brazilian town of Cubatão, which sprang suddenly from the mangrove swamps at the foot of the Serra do Mar mountains in the 1960s, typifies the horrors. Within 20 years, Cubatão became Brazil's major center for producing steel and fertilizers. In 1980, when 35 percent of infants there died before their first birthday, people who breathed toxic smog under acid rain called their home town the "valley of death."

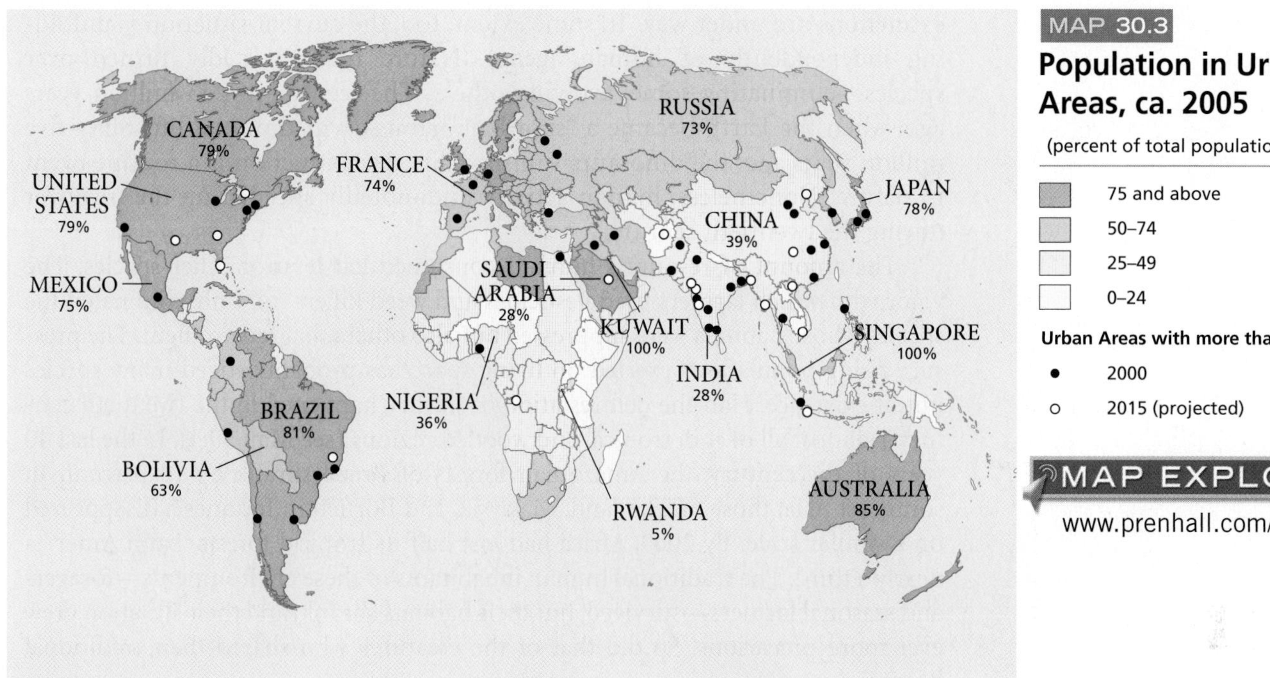

MAP 30.3

Population in Urban Areas, ca. 2005

(percent of total population)

75 and above

50–74

25–49

0–24

Urban Areas with more than 5 Million People

• 2000

○ 2015 (projected)

MAP EXPLORATION

www.prenhall.com/armesto_maps

Cleanups eased these problems in Cubatão, but the pattern kept being repeated elsewhere. In 1980, half the world's city dwellers had no access to treated water. Over the twentieth century as a whole, air pollution probably killed as many people as war. Shanties enveloped many of the great or growing cities of the world. In India in the 1990s, 1.5 million people lived on the streets of the cities, not out of poverty but because of the lack of housing. Nonrecyclable waste piled up. Newcomers to city life found themselves at the mercy of suppliers of the cheap, high-energy fast foods that were filling and satisfying but rarely nutritious. This is why mass obesity rapidly outgrew its origins as a disease of the newly affluent in North America and Europe and became a worldwide urban scourge. Meanwhile, rootless populations with unanchored loyalties bred criminal gangs and private armies for the civil wars that disturbed Africa, Asia, and Latin America.

By 2000 urbanization was easing. São Paulo and Mexico City—overgrown giants with populations approaching 20 million each by some counts—began to shrink. The rise of markets for rare, traditional, and exotic foods promised to restore the rural economy in parts of the world. The trend suggested that cities of 100,000 to 1 million people would remain normal and that megacities of over 10 million people would shrink.

THE CRISIS OF CONSERVATION

In the twentieth century, the human domain expanded. One result was predictable—other species could not compete. As well as crowding out some life-forms, humans blasted others into oblivion, disrupting their ecosystems, hunting them to extinction, exterminating them with pest controls, depriving them of habitats or food. The world faced the loss of more species than at any time since the end of the last Ice Age. One percent of recorded species of birds and mammals disappeared in the twentieth century. Invertebrate species, which are less well documented, are likely to have suffered far more. To some extent, current alarm may be a trick of the evidence. We are aware of more extinctions, so we suppose more extinctions are under way. To some extent, too, the current situation is unfolding independently of human agency. Nature has repeatedly turned over species—eliminating some, evolving others. The Ice Age of 245 million years ago, when the Earth became a "snowball," almost wiped out all life. Sixty-five million years ago, the dinosaurs vanished. Species extinction is a routine event in nature. Nonetheless, human activity undoubtedly speeded up the turnover during the twentieth century.

The amount of resources humans consumed left less for other species. The vigor with which farmers used pesticides and weed killers not only eliminated the species whose habitats were suppressed but also others that fed on them. The pressure rising populations exerted on living space has probably edged many species out of existence. Half the deforestation of history happened in the twentieth century—almost all of it in tropical and wooded regions (see Map 30.4). In the last 40 years of the century, the Amazonian forests of Brazil shrank by 10 percent. In southeast Asia, those of Thailand, Malaysia, and Borneo in Indonesia disappeared on a similar scale. By 2000, Africa had lost half its tropical forests, Latin America nearly a third. The traditional human inhabitants of these environments—foragers and seasonal farmers—survived, but their habitats shrank, and their situation grew ever more precarious. So did that of the creatures who shared their traditional homes.

The bleakest story of species depletion is a sea story. In the twentieth century, fish as a foodstuff leaped in popularity, like a salmon jumping the rapids. Historians debate why. In the second half of the century, after the beneficial health effects of fish oils became known (they boost nutrition, reduce cholesterol, and help prevent heart attacks), health concerns may have played a part. A romantic longing for wild, unfarmed food may have been influential, too. Fish is still largely a product of the hunt. Though industrial trawlers now make the catch, they still have to track the fish in the wild.

Whatever the reasons, the amount of fish that fisheries handled worldwide grew fortyfold in the twentieth century. Over that period, according to historian John McNeill, the world consumed 3 billion tons of fish. If McNeill's calculations are right, that exceeds the whole catch landed during the entire previous history of the world. Some varieties were fished to near extinction. At the end of the century, Atlantic cod stocks stood, according to common calculations, at only 10 percent of their historic

MAP 30.4

Deforestation Worldwide, ca. 2005

- frontier forest
- degraded forest
- frontier forest 8,000 years ago

MAP EXPLORATION
www.prenhall.com/armesto_maps

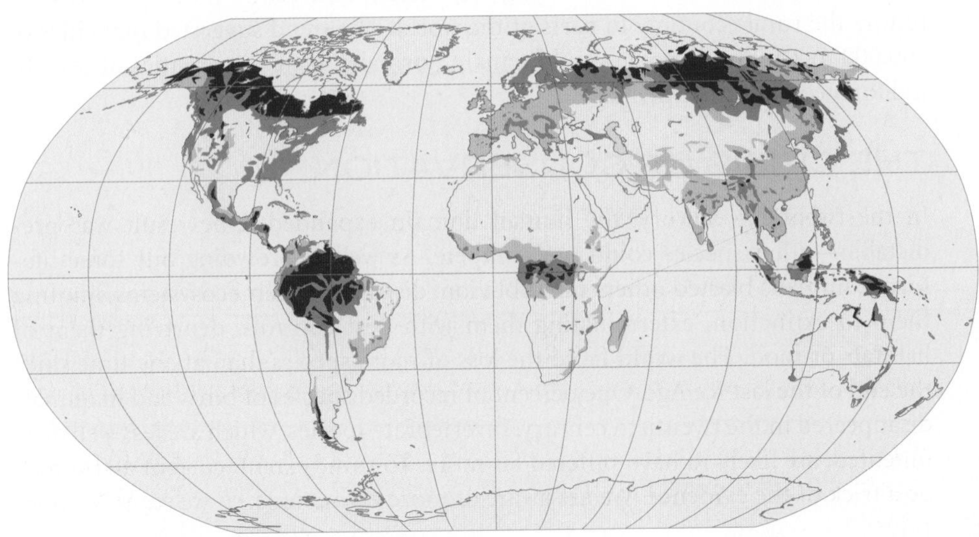

average. California sardines became rarities. North Sea herrings—once a staple food in Europe—are now a costly treat. The Japanese sardine fishery was the most abundant in the world in the 1930s but had virtually collapsed by the mid-1990s. Off Namibia in southern Africa, fishermen caught millions of tons of sardines in the 1960s. By 1980, none were left. By 2000, the predicament of the Chilean sea bass, which has become a trendy dish in the United States and Western Europe, precipitated a crisis. Profit-conscious Chilean fishermen pleaded with clients to go on eating the species, while ecological enthusiasts tried to persuade restaurateurs to ban it.

If fish stocks are permanently lost, the results will be catastrophic. The use of fishmeal in fertilizers and animal feeds makes fish a vital food source for the world, way beyond the tonnage humans directly consume. But was the apparent depletion of the world's fishing stocks in the twentieth century an irreversible disaster or a temporary blip? Fish migration patterns change, and the fact that we have lost sight of traditional stocks of some species in the vastness of the ocean does not necessarily mean that they have disappeared forever. Some extraordinary recuperations have been recorded. The supply of Maine lobsters, for instance, waxed and waned almost regularly during the twentieth century. Some oyster beds, once thought to have been exhausted, are now plentiful again. The recovery of populations of whales and harbor seals showed that marine conservation programs could work. In 2005, successful conservation policies attracted blame for an increase in the incidence of shark attacks on people in Australian waters. Fish conservation methods seem to be working for Atlantic cod and haddock. Fishermen now concentrate on each species in turn, allowing the other to recover.

Still, many authorities have concluded that the future lies with fish farming. Fish farms produced 5 million tons of food worldwide in 1980, and 25 million tons by 2000. China accounted for more than half the total. Fish farming is an effective method of food production. Farmed salmon yield 15 times more nutrition per acre than beef cattle. The sea bass grows twice as fast under farmed conditions as in the wild. In the wild, it takes a million eggs to produce a fish. By the early twenty-first century, farmers were regularly turning 60 percent of eggs into fish. Meanwhile, techniques of fish farming improved. What was formerly a freshwater and coast-bound activity began to be possible in the deep ocean. So, despite the losses from overfishing, the world's stocks of edible fish probably were and are secure for the foreseeable future. Again, of course, we will have to pay an environmental cost. Fish farms are eco-niches for marine plagues. Farmed species will inevitably escape into the wild and crowd out others by infection and crossbreeding.

THE UNMANAGEABLE ENVIRONMENT: CLIMATE AND DISEASE

Ecological alarmism has become a trend of our times—a modern, secular form of millenarianism. We scare ourselves into expecting the apocalypse, the end of the world, or at least the end of civilization as we know it. Our fears could well come true. Civilizations have collapsed because they failed to get their relationship with the environment right. Overexploitation is a constant temptation. We still succumb to it. No period can match our own for the sheer wasteful carelessness with which we pollute our planet and consume its resources. But the ecological problems of our times do not start or stop with our self-inflicted difficulties. Bigger dangers are worrying precisely because they are not of our making. If we caused them, we could control them. But we do not cause them. They are beyond our control.

The power of nature. The center of Hurricane Katrina's rotation at 9:15 A.M. EST on August 29, 2005, over southeast Louisiana. Winds over 135 mph and accompanying floods effectively destroyed much of the city of New Orleans and emptied all but the highest ground of population, causing billions of dollars of damage, costing many lives, and provoking a crisis of conscience in the United States. Despite long-standing predictions of disaster, many parts of New Orleans and surrounding communities had been left without adequate defenses or relief.

The Earth is still in its infancy. The planet has, at a reasonable guess, several billion years to go before it sizzles or freezes into lifelessness. By supposing that we could destroy our planet, we are guilty of a kind of arrogance. The Earth is hugely bigger than anything we have power to wreck. Nature will surely outlast our species. Trees that were here before humans existed will go on growing after humans have gone. So will microbes and—probably—insects, reptiles, birds, and marine species vastly older than humankind. When the planet perishes, it will be nothing to do with us. It will happen long after we are gone. And the cause will rest with cosmic forces that we are aware of but have no power to influence.

These considerations are worth bearing in mind, because if we kid ourselves into thinking that all ecological problems are our own fault, we shall be deluded into supposing that we can fix them all. It is worth remembering that we have hardly scratched the surface of the planet we inhabit. Our deepest oil wells are only thousands of feet deep. Most species have never been cataloged and are perhaps unknown. The oceans, a habitat we have not yet begun to colonize and have still done little to exploit, make up 90 percent of the planet.

So despite our self-inflicted disasters, a lot of nature still threatens us without being threatened in return. In 2005, a hurricane devastated New Orleans, provoking President George W. Bush to acknowledge that Nature was "the world's greatest superpower." Some of the dangers prophets invoke are close to the edges of science fiction. Asteroid bombardment, for instance, is unlikely to happen, but the threat of it demonstrates the perplexities we face in confronting natural forces outside human control. The U.S. government is popularly supposed to have plans to deflect or explode an approaching asteroid with nuclear missiles, but such a defense would have unpredictable and incalculable consequences.

We face more immediate dangers. Two of the most powerful sources in nature remain barely understood and beyond our power to manage: disease-bearing microorganisms and climate. Either or both could destroy humankind with no help from us. Take climate first. For all our accumulated cunning, we cannot control climate change or reverse its effects. At best, we seem able only to edge it in directions in which we do not want it to go: speeding up global warming, reducing rainfall, intensifying desertification. As we have seen, for most of the period this book covers, from the waning of the last great Ice Age some 20,000 years ago, the world has been experiencing a protracted warming phase. From about the fourteenth century C.E. to about the eighteenth, warming went into a temporary eclipse. Allowing for many ups and downs, temperatures declined slightly but significantly over much of the world (see Chapter 14). Around the mid–nineteenth century, however, warming seems to have intensified. Despite a wavering in the third quarter of the twentieth century, when falling temperatures excited prophesies of a new Ice Age, global temperatures by 2000 recovered or exceeded levels last reached some 800 years ago (see Figure 30.4). If this continues, rising sea levels could swamp much of the

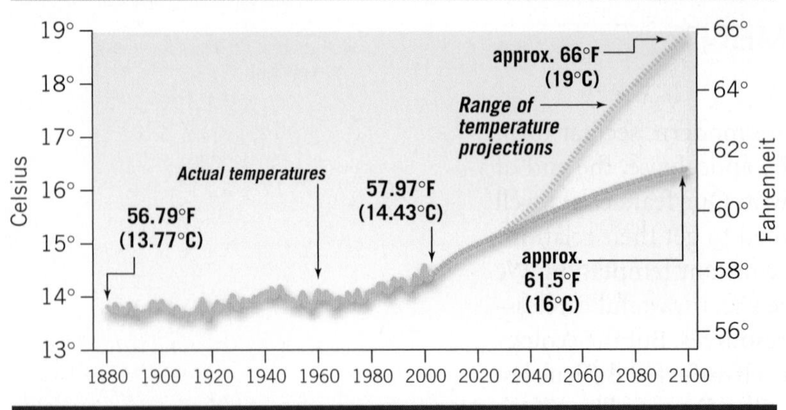

FIGURE 30.4 GLOBAL ANNUAL AVERAGE TEMPERATURES AND PROJECTIONS, 1880–2100

MAKING CONNECTIONS

GLOBAL ENVIRONMENTAL CHALLENGES

AREA OF HUMAN ACTIVITY →	ENVIRONMENTAL AND SOCIAL EFFECTS
Fuel resources: human dependence on electricity, internal combustion engine, and fossil fuels	Electricity permeates everyday life and economic activity; dependence on internal combustion engine to power transport and link suburban residential districts; oil wars; increased carbon dioxide levels and global warming
Food resources: need to supply over 6 billion humans	Increased dependence on agrochemicals and large dams and irrigation projects; reliance on hybrid and genetically modified staple crops; depletion of fisheries, increased availability of cheap, mass-produced food leads to deterioration of human diets and overreliance on carbohydrates, fats (obesity)
Housing: increased urbanization/suburbanization	Widespread substandard housing and urban air, water pollution; increased nonrecyclable waste; dependence on automobiles for transportation; favorable environment for criminal organizations; gangs
Swapping plants and animals around the world to increase yields	Displacement of indigenous plant/animal species from native environments; disappearance of thousands of species of plants/animals, adding to decline in biodiversity

world. Crops could succumb to heat. Areas, for instance, devoted now to cool-temperature varieties of rice will have to switch to some other, currently unknown staple or be abandoned.

We do not yet know how to cope with global warming if the planet continues to heat up. Some of our efforts to deflect it seem feeble: cutting the rates of increase of carbon emissions, often by relying on trivial measures, such as recycling refrigerators (which are cooled by carbon-based gases) and banning aerosol sprays. On the other hand, a new Ice Age may occur. We do not at present know how to prepare for it. The future, it seems, will be fire or ice.

Or disease will dominate it—a recurrent age of plagues (see Chapter 14). Despite the achievements of medical science, humans still do not control—or even adequately understand—the microbial world in which much disease originates. The spectacular victories of the twentieth century include the defeat of polio, smallpox, and a range of illnesses formerly responsible for heartbreaking levels of infant mortality. Treatments almost eliminated tuberculosis, though it revived in the late twentieth century. New remedies spared the lives of diabetics, though the disease is acquiring new victims. Surgery made organ transplants possible. Medicine made a big contribution to the rising life-expectancy figures. Sanitation and public health care probably did even more. In Western Europe, Canada, Australia, New Zealand, and the United States, average life expectancy at the end of the century was in the mid-seventies for men and the low eighties for women. Fears multiplied of a future in which the workforce would be too small to support an increasingly elderly population. In Japan, the trend was similar, with 16 percent of the population aged over 65 in 1998. Japan, faced with the world's biggest increase of over-70-year-olds in the population, began to subsidize old people to resettle overseas. In China, by 2000, most people could expect to live into their late sixties. In India, life expectancy rose to an average of 63 years of age.

The massive increase of world population in the late twentieth century was, above all, a triumph of what we might call death control. The great population growth of the eighteenth century was probably the result of adjustments in the microbial world (see Chapter 20). That of the twentieth, by contrast, arose from human agency: medical remedies and the preventive measures of public health policy.

But scientific self-congratulation over these successes masked worrying, persistent problems. Medical advances were unfairly distributed. Life expectancy in many African countries in 2000 remained stuck at an average in the mid- to low forties. At 112 deaths per thousand in Nigeria and 90 in Ivory Coast, sub-Saharan infant mortality rates were three or four times worse than those of most of East and southeast Asia and immeasurably worse than those of Western Europe (see Map 30.5).

Moreover, and inseparably, medical advances were costly. Health care costs in America left many of the poor out of the loop. In Europe, where state-run national health services ensured a fairer distribution of benefits, taxpayers struggled to keep pace with the costs. In Britain, for instance, the National Health Service (NHS) cost £400 million to run in 1951, about £32 billion a half-century later. The cost more than doubled over the following two years, while inflation generally rose at less than 2 percent a year. By that time, NHS was absorbing 6.6 percent of the nation's income. The leap in life expectancy made health care costs worse. People lived longer, contributed less to national wealth as they got older, and consumed more of that wealth in health care. By the early 1990s, health care costs absorbed between 7 and 10 percent of the gross domestic product of most developed countries and over 14 percent in the United States.

Furthermore, although medicine eliminated old diseases, new ones—or new forms of old ones—arose to torment humanity. The effects of pollution, drug abuse, undiscriminating sex habits, and affluence—which condemned the unwary to overindulgence and inertia—were major killers. Far more lethal, however, was the rapid evolution of viruses. Some killers, such as Ebola, Lassa fever, and the immune-destroying virus known as HIV, leaped from the econiches in which they had formerly been contained and began to attack humans.

MAP 30.5

Life Expectancy, ca. 2005

(years)

- 70 and above
- 60–69
- 50–59
- 40–49
- less than 40

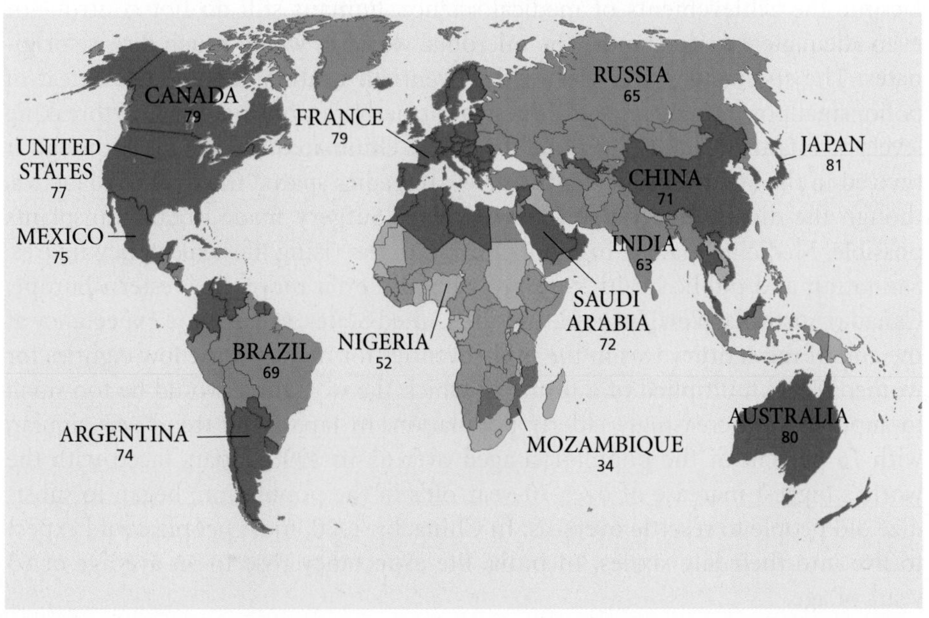

New forms of influenza appeared regularly, though none attained the virulence of the pandemic of 1918–1919, which claimed an estimated 30 million lives worldwide. A new strain of tuberculosis resists every known drug and kills half the people it infects. Bubonic plague has returned to India. New strains of cholera and malaria have emerged. Malaria cases in India rose a hundredfold to 10 million between 1965 and 1977. In sub-Saharan Africa, malaria kills 1 million children a year. Yellow fever—which had almost been eradicated by the midcentury—killed 200,000 people a year in Africa in the 1990s. Measles, a disease that immunization was expected to eradicate, was still killing 1 million people a year in 2000. New viruses can defeat antibiotics and other drugs, which decline in effectiveness from overuse.

Other new diseases arose in man-made eco-niches: Legionnaire's disease, which breeds in the dampness of air-conditioning systems, was the prime example. Intensive farming created breeding conditions for salmonella in chickens and accumulated toxins in the food chain. Human-variant CJD, or "mad cow disease," is a brain-killing disease, apparently caused by intensive cattle-farming methods—recycling dead sheep and cattle as fodder—and was transmitted to at least some of its victims in tainted food. Twentieth-century interventions in the environment opened many new eco-niches for disease in over fertilized soil stripped of insect life; in polluted waterways; and in the disturbed depths of the sea, where bacteria multiply in searing hot vents that humans have only lately begun to penetrate. In an increasingly interconnected world, human carriers took diseases way beyond accustomed environments. In the 1990s, West Nile virus from Africa turned up in New York City. Influenza from China caused widespread deaths, especially in Canada. Dengue fever from Asia has become endemic in the Caribbean.

Broadly speaking, infectious diseases ceased to be major killers, though old ones constantly threatened to reemerge and new ones to develop. Chronic diseases, meanwhile, replaced infections as the major menace. Cancer and heart diseases grew spectacularly, especially in rich countries, without anyone knowing why. By the 1980s in the United States, one death in every four was blamed on cancer. In Britain, one death in three was ascribed to heart disease, which caused 10 million deaths a year worldwide by 2000. Some forms of cancer were "lifestyle diseases." Cervical cancer, for instance, was thought to be connected to sexual promiscuity or adolescent sexual intercourse, while smoking caused lung, throat, and mouth cancers and contributed to heart disease and stroke. Obesity and its related disorders, as discussed earlier, owed their prevalence, in part, to bad eating habits. In the second half of the twentieth century, evidence began to accumulate that some medical treatments were actually contributing to the disease environment. Doctors prescribed drugs so widely that people were becoming dependent on them, while many viruses and strains of bacteria were developing immunity to them. Even where physical health improved, mental health seemed to get worse. The highly competitive capitalist societies of the West became prey to neurotic disorders collectively known as stress. Worriers "medicalized" their anxieties and feelings of malaise, classifying them in their own minds as medical problems and taking them to the doctor. Hard-pressed medical services became overburdened.

Two new diseases demonstrated the microbial world's destructive potential. The first was the influenza of 1918–1919, the second, the scourge of AIDS, which lashed into prominence in the 1980s. AIDS

Bird flu. In 2005, bird flu became one in a long series of new diseases feared as the potential "next plague." Health workers culled tens of millions of poultry wherever the infection appeared. The photograph shows such an operation in progress in Turkey. Farmers lost livelihoods. Governments spent fortunes. Fear of bird flu has thus far proved exaggerated. The disease has not spread easily to humans. But mounting health scares showed growing awareness of the world's vulnerability to unfamiliar viruses.

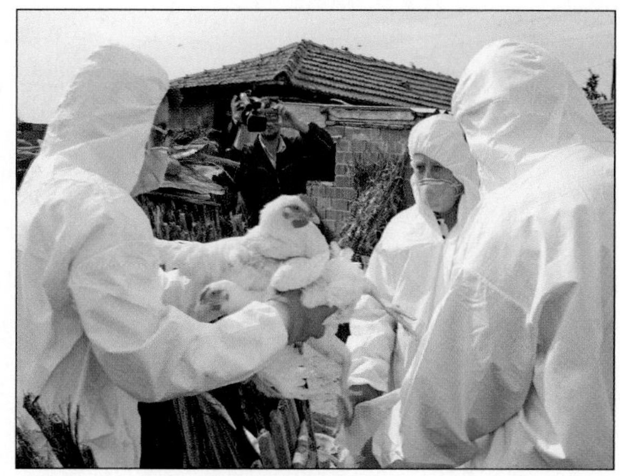

started in Africa as a sexually communicated syndrome between men and women. It then broke out in the West, where, at first, it was particularly virulent among homosexuals. Eventually it spread around the world as a result of the transfusion of infected blood or the transmission—usually through sex—of other bodily fluids. By 2000, the virus generally held to be responsible for AIDS, a condition in which the patient's immunity to all kinds of disease is progressively destroyed, had killed 27 million people and infected some 80 million worldwide. Although the disease seemed to be under control in most of Europe and the Americas, it was rampant in Africa and Asia, where, for cultural and economic reasons, governments were less committed to fighting it. Toward the end of the century, doctors in South Africa reckoned that AIDS accounted for 40 percent of deaths among sexually active people (see Map 30.6).

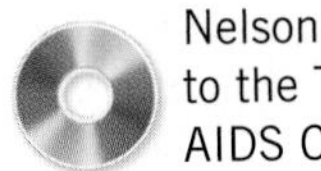

Nelson Mandela, Closing Address to the Thirteenth International AIDS Conference, 2000

IN PERSPECTIVE: The Environmental Dilemma

We can monitor the environmental transformations of the twentieth century on the map. The surface of the Earth has become a gridwork of routes laid out by human hands. Instead of the physical features—rivers, mountains, forests, deserts—that used to be the markers travelers relied on, roads, rails, air routes, and shipping lanes now connect or, in their absence, isolate locations.

The results were not evenly spread across the world. On the contrary, a development gap widened between regions of growing prosperity, which produced and consumed immeasurably more than other regions, and underdeveloped parts of the world, where most people got little chance to share in the increased wealth. In

MAP 30.6

HIV in Africa

HIV Prevalance Rates in African Adults (15-49 Years of Age) as of the end of 2005

- 0.0%–1.9%
- 2%–4.9%
- 5%–9.9%
- 10%–19.9%
- 20% or greater

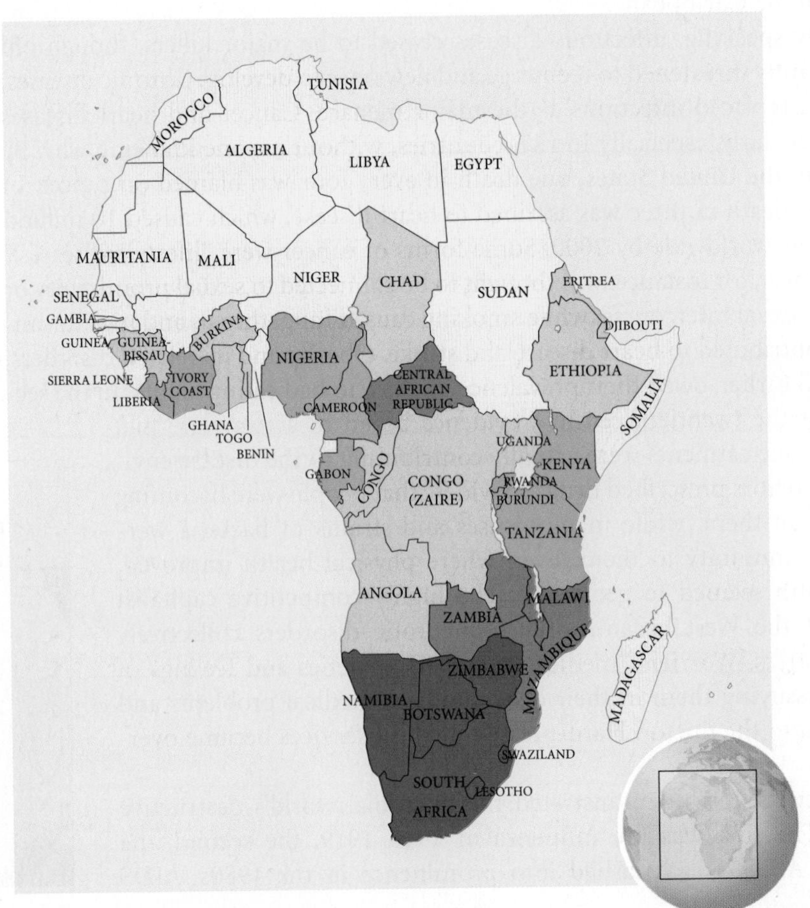

2000, the average income of people in the poorer half of the world was less than 5 percent of that of citizens of the top 20 richest countries.

In the late twentieth century, prosperity seemed to be the best contraceptive. In rich, industrialized communities, population growth slowed or reversed. Where poverty reigned, children were too valuable a resource to forgo. As a result, the world's wealth gaps widened. Growing populations strained resources in the regions that could least afford to feed and care for them, while the relative wealth of the developed world multiplied. This should not surprise anyone. Human reproduction resembles, in some respects, the production of commodities. It operates according to laws of supply and demand. Birthrates fall as income rises, because in mechanizing societies, manpower loses value and people, therefore, produce fewer babies. Economic progress promotes a further kind of change that also holds down population. Women's "liberation" encourages women to switch from having children to other productive activities.

Migration from poor, overpopulated areas in Africa, Asia, and Latin America into rich areas that have a shortage of labor was an inevitable consequence with huge social, political, and cultural effects (see Chapter 29). Industrialized nations invited guest workers in, while struggling to regulate their numbers. It then proved hard to prevent the erosion of traditional cultures or intercommunal violence.

By 2000, however, there were signs that the regions of the world were on a convergent course. In most of Latin America and Asia, population growth slowed down. Demographers began to predict that world population would peak in the early twenty-first century and then begin to fall, probably between 2020 and 2050.

On the far side of that peak in population, the world will look different. A big shift has occurred across the world in the demographic balance between old and young, north and south, east and west. While population continued to soar in Africa and the Americas, Europe was demographically stagnant. The population of much of Eastern Europe—especially of Russia, Latvia, and Ukraine—fell in the 1990s. Political and economic dislocation (see Chapter 28) contributed to the effect. In Western Europe, the overall population levels would also have fallen if immigrants had not helped keep the numbers up. Declining birthrates and declining male fertility—the causes of which are unknown—combined with increased life expectancy to boost the relative numbers of the elderly and inactive and reduce those of the young.

China suffered from a similar problem because the regime, alarmed at the pace of population growth, began to penalize families who had more than one child. The government imposed compulsory abortions, sterilization, and fines on offenders.

CHRONOLOGY

1890s	Development of internal combustion engines
1900–2000	1 percent of recorded bird and mammal species goes extinct; amount of fish handled by world's fisheries increases 40-fold
1918–1919	Worldwide influenza epidemic
1930s	World's first great dams constructed
1932	Dust Bowl emerges in central and western United States
1940–1990	Use of artificial fertilizer increases from 4 to 150 million tons
1950	Global population 2.5 billion
1950–1980	Wheat yields per acre double
1950–2000	Land under irrigation increases from 247 to 644 million acres
1962	Publication of Rachel Carson's *Silent Spring*
1970	Global population 3.7 billion
1973	OPEC oil embargo against the United States, Western Europe, and Japan
1978	First known cases of AIDS
1980	50 percent of world's urban population has no access to treated drinking water
1980–2000	Fish-farm production increases from 5 to 25 million tons
1990	Global population 5.3 billion
Early 1990s	Health-care costs absorb 14 percent of GDP in the United States
Late twentieth century	Acceleration of use of genetically modified crops; search for alternative fuels intensifies
ca. 2000	50 percent of world's population lives in settlements larger than 20,000 people; world's four largest cities: Tokyo, 28 million; Mexico City, 18 million; Mumbai (Bombay), 18 million; São Paulo, 17 million
ca. 2000	600 million cars worldwide; fossil fuels account for most of world's energy consumption; carbon dioxide levels in the atmosphere reach 370 parts per million
August 29, 2005	Hurricane Katrina destroys coast of southeastern United States
2010	Global population 6.9 billion (est.)
2020	Global population 7.6 billion (est.)

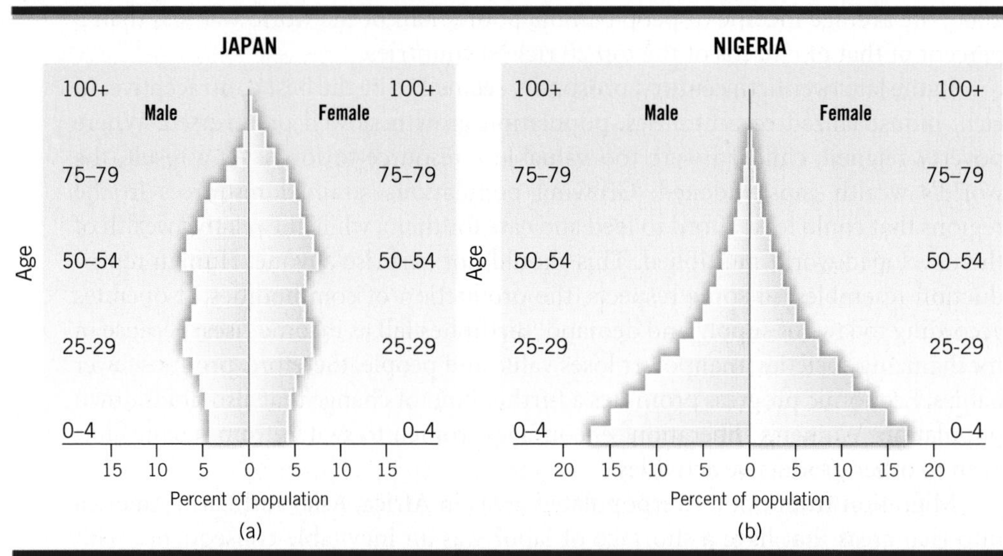

FIGURE 30.5 THE POPULATIONS OF JAPAN AND NIGERIA COMPARED
Reprinted by permission of the Reference Bureau.

The result is that China faces a population imbalance comparable to that of Europe, with a large aging population and a relative dearth of young labor. Indian governments encouraged birth control programs but never imposed policies as severe as those of China. India's growth rate fell to about 2 percent a year by 2000 but it was still vigorous enough to ensure that the size of its population would continue to rank second in the world—and might even overtake China's. By 2000, birthrates in Thailand, Indonesia, Mauritius, and much of Latin America were not much higher than in Europe. The pattern for the future looked increasingly like one of stabilizing population worldwide.

Meanwhile, in Africa and most of the Islamic world, especially the Muslim countries on the edges of the Indian subcontinent, populations were increasing rapidly. In these regions, and in parts of Latin America that are still in the early stages of a transition to European- or Japanese-style demographics, the ratios of old and young are reversed. There are huge numbers of young people, not enough for them to do, and, typically, not enough locally produced food for them to eat (see Figure 30.5).

The twentieth century was a period of intense and frequently violent competition between ideologies. Adherents of different kinds of political totalitarianisms fought wars against each other and against democracy. Religions conflicted with atheism and secularism as well as with each other. Battle lines formed around incompatible understandings of human rights and responsibilities. Economic systems collided. Whole civilizations threatened to clash. It seems surprising, on the face of it, that amid all this friction and frenzy environmentalism should have found the space to express itself and emerge as a contender to be the world's most widely shared consensus. One way to measure this is to count the increase in the number of international environmental organizations. There were 20 when the Second World War started in 1939 and about 40 in the late 1940s. By 1990, there were 340. Such an increase would have been impossible had the century not also witnessed unprecedented human impact on our planet. As the century wore on, the changes humans wrought—and the damage they inflicted—became glaringly visible and measurable, provoking the movement that we now usually call environmentalism: a deepening and spreading conviction that humans are part of the web of the natural world; that our relationship with our environment is the inescapable framework for everything we do; and that, in consequence, care of the environment is our essential priority, whether as a self-interested strategy or as a moral or religious duty that we owe to other forms of life.

In the early twenty-first century, much of the world is experiencing growth fatigue—the feeling people have in some rich communities that we do not want a world winding into the stratosphere of spiraling desire, at ever more irresponsible levels of consumption, production, and resource depletion. Rationally, we do not need to grow richer. Instead, those of us who enjoy the privilege of relative prosperity in an unequal world need to safeguard our riches by redistributing them more fairly. The opposite argument says that capitalism works—at least, it works less badly than any other economic system ever devised in human history, because it is attuned to human nature. People are always going to want to better themselves economically. We can no more renounce the pursuit of material "happiness" than stop the world in its orbit. So it is best to try to make a virtue of this trait and find environmentally sustainable ways to increase the world's wealth and free markets to distribute it more evenly.

We can best understand the eco-history of recent times in the context of changing notions about the place of humankind in nature—the results of the new science described in Chapter 27. We know too much about our common ancestry with other animals, the limits of our peculiarities compared with other social and cultural creatures, the moral overlap between *Homo sapiens* and other species, and our ties to a complex, interconnected ecosystem to go on thinking of humans as apart or distinct from the rest of nature. The future of our relationship with the rest of nature is best considered in the light of evidence dispersed throughout this book. Many of the failed civilizations of the past weakened or wrecked themselves by overexploiting their environments. What are we going to do with our world? It is, so far, the only one we have to live in.

PROBLEMS AND PARALLELS

1. How has population explosion put unprecedented pressure on the world's energy resources and food supply?
2. What are the drawbacks of fossil fuels? How do they contribute to the greenhouse effect? What are the advantages and disadvantages of alternate sources of power?
3. What costs were associated with the green revolution? What are the drawbacks of genetically modified crops?
4. Why did obesity increase in countries such as China, India, and Japan where it had previously been rare?
5. How did twentieth-century urbanization affect human societies? What pressures do megacities put on the environment?
6. How significant is the "crisis of conservation"? Is the outlook bleak?
7. What threats do disease and climate pose to humans in the early twenty-first century?

DOCUMENTS IN GLOBAL HISTORY

- Kyoto Protocol, Article 2
- Rachel Carson, from *Silent Spring*, 1962
- Nelson Mandela, Closing Address to the Thirteenth International AIDS Conference, 2000

Please see the Primary Source DVD for additional sources related to this chapter.

READ ON

The story of Rasmata comes from O. Bennett, ed., *Greenwar: Environment and Conflict* (1991). On Burkina Faso, D. E. McMillan, *Sahel Visions: Planned Settlement and River Blindness Control in Burkina Faso* (1995) is a fascinating, personally engaged anthropologist's account of one development project. There is little else of book length available in English, but important pamphlets include B. Paaru-Laarsen, *The Concept of Drought and Local Social and Economic Strategies in the Northern Burkina Faso*, and M. Ou draogo, *Land Tenure and Rural Development in Burkina Faso* (2002). The context is covered in M. Mortimore, *Roots in the African Dust: Sustaining the Sub-Saharan Drylands* (1998).

J. E. McNeill, *Something New Under the Sun* (2001) is a superb global history of the twentieth-century environment. D. Worster, *Nature's Economy* (1985), and A. Bramwell, *Ecology in the Twentieth Century* (1989) are excellent surveys of environmentalism with contrasting arguments. F. Harris, ed., *Global Environmental Issues* (2004) is a useful and comprehensive overview. On the idea of spiraling desire, M. Girard, *Violence and the Sacred* (1979) is fundamental. D. Worster, *Dust Bowl* (1982) is an outstanding case study of degradation.

On energy, J. Twidell and T. Weir, *Renewable Energy Resources* (2005) is a good introduction to renewables. D. Yergin, *The Prize* (1993) is the classic account of oil. M. Klare, *Blood and Oil* (2004) is both scholarly and shocking. J. Rifkin, *The Hydrogen Economy* (2003) sketches the possible hydrogen-dependent future. On China, V. Smil, *China's Environmental Crisis* (1993) is perhaps the best study.

On biodiversity, K. J. Gaston and I. J. Spicer, *Biodiversity* (2004) is a sober introduction. R. Leakey and R. Lewin, *The Sixth Extinction* (1996) is vigorous, challenging, and controversial. T. M. Swanson, ed., *The Economics and Ecology of Biodiversity Decline* (1998) is a helpful collection, which demonstrates the difficulties clearly. W. D. Ean, *With Broadax and Firebrand* (1997) narrates the destruction of the Amazonian forest. L. Lear, *Rachel Carson* (1998) is a useful life of the great environmentalist.

On food, K. Blaxter and N. Robertson, *From Dearth to Plenty* (1995) sets the context well. D. Goodman and M. J. Watts, eds., *Globalising Food* (1997) is important and wide-ranging. E. Sclosser, *Fast Food Nation* (2001) is an influential study of U.S. excess. G. Critser, *Fat Land* (2004) is journalistic and sensationalist but full of data. H. Levenstein, *Revolution at the Table* (2003) takes a longer-term view of changes in the American diet. M. Goran, *The Story of Fritz Haber* (1967) is a good biography of the pioneer of modern fertilizers.

J. Hardoy, D. Mitlin, and D. Satterthwaite, *Environmental Problems in an Urbanizing World* (2001) is a good introduction to twentieth-century urbanization.

L. D. D. Harvey, *Global Warming: The Hard Science* (1999) is clear and minatory about climate. L. Garrett, *The Coming Plague* (1994) is a page-turner on disease, though much criticized for exaggerating the problems. S. Levy, *The Antibiotic Paradox* (2002) is useful for understanding the limitations of some twentieth-century therapies. A. Macfarlane, *The Savage Wars of Peace* (2003) is a wonderful study of the impact of public health policies, with special reference to Britain and Japan. I. Illich, *Limits to Medicine: The Expropriation of Health* (1999) is a classic study of the modern social history of health issues, on which L. Payer, *Medicine and Culture* (1996), and P. Starr, *The Social Transformation of American Medicine* (1984) are also important.

Abolitionism Belief that slavery and the slave trade are immoral and should be abolished.

Aborigine A member of the indigenous or earliest-known population of a region.

Aborigines Indigenous people of Australia.

Afrikaans An official language of South Africa, spoken mostly by the Boers. It is derived from seventeenth-century Dutch.

Age of Plague Term for the spread of lethal diseases from the fourteenth through the eighteenth centuries.

Ahriman The chief spirit of darkness and evil in Zoroastrianism, the enemy of Ahura Mazda.

Ahura Mazda The chief deity of Zoroastrianism, the creator of the world, the source of light, and the embodiment of good.

Al-Andalus Arabic name for the Iberian Peninsula (Spain and Portugal).

Alluvial plains Flat lands where mud from rivers or lakes renews the topsoil. If people can control the flooding that is common in such conditions, alluvial plains are excellent for settled agriculture.

Almoravids Muslim dynasty of Berber warriors that flourished from 1049 to 1145 and that established political dominance over northwest Africa and Spain.

Alternative energy Energy sources that usually produce less pollution than does the burning of fossil fuels, and are renewable in some cases.

Alternative medicine Medicines, treatments, and techniques not advocated by the mainstream medical establishment in the West.

Americanization The process by which other cultures, to a greater or lesser degree, adopt American fashions, culture, and ways of life.

Anarchists Believers in the theory that all forms of government are oppressive and undesirable and should be opposed and abolished.

Animal rights Movement that asserts that animals have fundamental rights that human beings have a moral obligation to respect.

Anti-Semitism Hostility or prejudice against Jews or Judaism.

Arthasastra Ancient Indian study of economics and politics that influenced the Emperor Asoka. The *Arthasastra* expresses an ideology of universal rule and emphasizes the supremacy of "the king's law" and the importance of uniform justice.

Artificial intelligence The creation of a machine or computer program that exhibits the characteristics of human intelligence.

Arts and Crafts Movement Nineteenth-century artists and intellectuals who argued that the products produced by individual craftsmen were more attractive than and morally superior to the mass, uniform goods produced by industry.

Assassins A secret order of Muslims in what is today Syria and Lebanon who terrorized and killed its opponents, both Christian and Muslim. The Assassins were active from the eleventh to the thirteenth centuries.

Atlantic Slave Trade Trade in African slaves who were bought, primarily in West Africa, by Europeans and white Americans and transported across the Atlantic, usually in horrific conditions, to satisfy the demand for labor in the plantations and mines of the Americas.

Atomic theory The theory that matter is not a continuous whole, but is composed of tiny, discrete particles.

Australopithecine ("southern ape-like creatures") Species of hominids that occurred earlier than those classed under the heading "homo." Most anthropologists date australopithecines to 5 million years ago.

Axial Age A pivotal age in the history of world civilization, lasting for roughly 500 years up to the beginning of the Christian era, in which critical intellectual and cultural ideas arose in and were transmitted across the Mediterranean world, India, Iran, and East Asia.

Axial zone The densely populated central belt of world population, communication, and cultural exchange in Eurasia that stretches from Japan and China to Western Europe and North Africa.

Aztecs People of central Mexico whose civilization and empire were at their height at the time of the Spanish conquest in the early sixteenth century.

Balance of trade The relative value of goods traded between two or more nations or states. Each trading partner strives to have a favorable balance of trade, that is, to sell more to its trading partners than it buys from them.

Bantu African people sharing a common linguistic ancestry who originated in West Africa and whose early agriculture centered on the cultivation of yams and oil palms in swamplands.

Big bang theory Theory that the universe began with an explosion of almost infinitesimally compressed matter, the effects of which are still going on.

Black Death Term for a lethal disease or diseases that struck large parts of Eurasia and North Africa in the 1300s and killed millions of people.

Boers Dutch settlers and their descendents in southern Africa. The first Boers arrived in South Africa in the seventeenth century.

Bon Religion that was Buddhism's main rival in Tibet for several centuries in the late first millennium C.E.

Brahman A member of the highest, priestly caste of traditional Indian society.

British East India Company British trading company founded in 1600 that played a key role in the colonization of India. It ruled much of the subcontinent until 1857.

Bureaucratization The process by which government increasingly operates through a body of trained officials who follow a set of regular rules and procedures.

Business Imperialism Economic domination and exploitation of poorer and weaker countries by richer and stronger states.

Byzantine Empire Term for the Greek-speaking, eastern portion of the former Roman Empire, centered on Constantinople. It lasted until 1453, when it was conquered by the Ottoman Turks.

Cahokia Most spectacular existent site of Mississippi Valley Native American civilization, located near modern St. Louis.

Caliph The supreme Islamic political and religious authority, literally, the "successor" of the Prophet Muhammad.

Canyon cultures Indigenous peoples of the North American Southwest. The canyon cultures flourished beween about 850 and 1250 C.E.

Capitalism An economic system in which the means of production and distribution are privately or corporately owned.

Caste system A social system in which people's places in society, how they live and work, and with whom they can marry are determined by heredity. The Indian caste system has been intertwined with India's religious and economic systems.

Centralization The concentration of power in the hands of a central government.

Chaos theory Theory that some systems are so complex that their causes and effects are untraceable.

Chicago economics The economic theory associated with economists who taught at the University of Chicago that holds that low taxes and light government regulation will lead to economic prosperity.

Chimú Civilization centered on the Pacific coast of Peru that was conquered by the Inca in the fifteenth century.

Chinese Board of Astronomy Official department of the Chinese imperial court created in the early seventeenth century that was responsible for devising the ritual calendar.

GLOSSARY

Chinese diaspora The migration of Chinese immigrants around the world between the seventeenth and nineteenth centuries.

Chivalry The qualities idealized by the medieval European aristocracy and associated with knighthood, such as bravery, courtesy, honor, and gallantry.

Chola Expansive kingdom in southern India that had important connections with merchant communities on the coast. Chola reached its height around 1050 C.E.

Christendom Term referring to the European states in which Christianity was the dominant or only religion.

Cistercians Christian monastic order that built monasteries in places where habitation was sparse and nature hostile. Cistercians practiced a more ascetic and rigorous form of the Benedictine rule.

Citizen army The mass army the French created during the Revolution by imposing mandatory military service on the entire active adult male population. The army was created in response to the threat of invasion by an alliance of anti-Revolutionary countries in the early 1790s.

Civilization A way of life based on radically modifiying the environment.

Civilizing mission The belief that imperialism and colonialism are justified because imperial powers have a duty to bring the benefits of "civilization" to, or impose them on, the "backward" people they ruled or conquered.

Clan A social group made up of a number of families that claim descent from a common ancestor and follow a hereditary chieftain.

Class struggle Conflict between competing social classes that, in Karl Marx's view, was responsible for all important historical change.

Climacteric A period of critical change in a society that is poised between different possible outcomes.

Code Napoleon Civil code promulgated by Napoleon in 1804 and spread by his armies across Europe. It still forms the basis for the legal code for many European, Latin American, and African countries.

Cold war Post–World War II rivalry between the United States and its allies and the Soviet Union and its allies. The cold war ended in 1990–1991 with the end of the Soviet Empire in Eastern Europe and the collapse of the Soviet Union itself.

Columbian Exchange Biological exchange of plants, animals, microbes, and human beings between the Americas and the rest of the world.

Commune Collective name for the citizen body of a medieval and Renaissance Italian town.

Communism A system of government in which the state plans and controls the economy, and private property and class distinctions are abolished.

Confraternities Lay Catholic charitable brotherhoods.

Confucianism Chinese doctrine founded by Confucius emphasizing learning and the fulfillment of obligations among family members, citizens, and the state.

Constitutionalism The doctrine that the state is founded on a set of fundamental laws that rulers and citizens make together and are bound to respect.

Consumerism A system of values that exalts the consumption and possession of consumer goods as both a social good and as an end in themselves.

Coolies Poor laborers from China and India who left their homelands to do hard manual and agricultural work in other parts of the world in the nineteenth and early twentieth centuries.

Copernican revolution Development of a heliocentric model of the solar system begun in 1543 by Nicholas Copernicus, a Polish churchman and astronomer.

Council of Trent A series of meetings from 1545 to 1563 to direct the response of the Roman Catholic Church to Protestantism. The council defined Catholic dogma and reformed church discipline.

Counter Reformation The Catholic effort to combat the spread of Protestantism in the sixteenth and seventeenth centuries.

Countercolonization The flow of immigrants out of former colonies to the "home countries" that used to rule them.

Country trades Commerce involving local or regional exchanges of goods from one Asian destination to another that, while often handled by European merchants, never touched Europe.

Covenant In the Bible, God's promise to the human race.

Creoles People of at least part-European descent born in the West Indies, French Louisiana, or Spanish America.

Crusades Any of the military expeditions undertaken by European Christians from the late eleventh to the thirteenth centuries to recover the Holy Land from the Muslims.

Cubism Artistic style developed by Pablo Picasso and Georges Braque in the early twentieth century, characterized by the reduction and fragmentation of natural forms into abstract, often geometric structures.

Cultural relativism The doctrine that cultures cannot be ranked in any order of merit. No culture is superior to another, and each culture must be judged on its own terms.

Cultural Revolution Campaign launched by Mao Zedong in 1965–1966 against the bureaucrats of the Chinese Communist Party. In lasted until 1976 and involved widespread disorder, violence, killings, and the persecution of intellectuals and the educated elite.

Culture Socially transmitted behavior, beliefs, institutions, and technologies that a given group of people or peoples share.

Cuneiform Mesopotamian writing system that was inscribed on clay tablets with wedge-shaped markers.

Czars (Trans.) "Caesar." Title of the emperors who ruled Russia until the revolution of 1917.

Dada An early twentieth-century European artistic and literary movement that flouted conventional and traditional aesthetic and cultural values by producing works marked by nonsense, travesty, and incongruity.

Dahomey West African slave-trading state that began to be prominent in the sixteenth century.

Daimyo Japanese feudal lord who ruled a province and was subject to the shoguns.

Daoism Chinese doctrine founded by Laozi that identified detachment from the world with the pursuit of immortality.

"Declaration of the Rights of Man and Citizen" Declaration of basic principles adopted by the French National Assembly in August 1789, at the start of the French Revolution.

Decolonization The process by which the nineteenth-century colonial empires in Asia, Africa, the Caribbean, and the Pacific were dismantled after World War II.

Deforestation The process by which trees are eliminated from an ecosystem.

Democracy Government by the people, exercised either directly or through elected representatives.

Demokratia Greek word signifying a state where supreme power belonged to an assembly of citizens (only privileged males were citizens).

Devsirme Quota of male children supplied by Christian subjects as tribute to the Ottoman Sultan. Many of the boys were drafted into the janissaries.

Dharma In the teachings of Buddha, moral law or duty.

Diffusion The spread of a practice, belief, culture, or technology within a community or between communities.

Dirlik (Trans.) "Wealth." The term applied to provincial government in the Ottoman Empire.

Divine love God's ongoing love for and interest in human beings.

Dominicans Order of preaching friars established in 1216 by Saint Dominic.

Druze Lebanese sect that regards the caliph al-Hakim as a manifestation of God. Other Muslims regard the Druze as heretics.

Dualism Perception of the world as an arena of conflict between opposing principles of good and evil.

Dutch East India Company Dutch company founded in 1602 that enjoyed a government-granted monopoly on trade between Holland and Asia. The company eventually established a territorial empire in what is today Indonesia.

Dutch East Indies Dutch colonies in Asia centered on present-day Indonesia.

The Encyclopedia Twenty-eight volume compendium of Enlightenment thought published in French and edited by Denis Diderot. The first volume appeared in 1751.

East India Trade Maritime trade between Western Europe and New England and Asia (predominantly India and China) between 1600 and 1800. Westerners paid cash for items from Asia, such as porcelain, tea, silk, cotton textiles, and spices.

Easterlies Winds coming from the east.

Ecological exchange The exchange of plants and animals between ecosystems.

Ecological imperialism Term historians use for the sweeping environmental changes European and other imperialists introduced in regions they colonized.

Ecology of civilization The interaction of people with their environment.

Economic liberalism Belief that government interference in and regulation of the economy should be kept to a minimum.

Edo Former name of Tokyo when it was the center of government for the Tokugawa shoguns.

El Niño A periodic reversal of the normal flow of Pacific currents that alters weather patterns and affects the number and location of fish in the ocean.

Elan vital The "vital force" hypothesized by the French philosopher Henri Bergson as a source of efficient causation and evolution in nature.

Empirical Derived from or guided by experience or experiment.

Empiricism The view that experience, especially of the senses, is the only source of knowledge.

Emporium trading Commerce that takes place in fixed market places or trading posts.

Enlightened despotism Reforms instituted by powerful monarchs in eighteenth-century Europe who were inspired by the principles of the Enlightenment.

Enlightenment Movement of eighteenth-century European thought championed by the *philosophes*, thinkers who held that change and reform were desirable and could be achieved by the application of reason and science. Most Enlightenment thinkers were hostile to conventional religion.

Enthusiasm "Religion" of English romantics who believed that emotion and passion were positive qualities.

Epistemology The branch of philosophy that studies the nature of knowledge.

Equilibrium trap Term coined by the historian Mark Elvin to refer to China in the eighteenth century, when industries were meeting demand with traditional technologies and had no scope to increase output.

Eugenics The theory that the human race can be improved mentally and physically by controlled selective breeding and that the state and society have a duty to encourage "superior" persons to have offspring and prevent "inferior" persons from reproducing.

Eunuchs Castrated male servants valued because they could not produce heirs or have sexual relations with women. In Byzantium, China, and the Islamic world, eunuchs could rise to high office in the state and the military.

European Union (EU) Loose economic and political federation that succeeded the European Economic Community (EEC) in 1993. It has expanded to include most of the states in Western and Eastern Europe.

Evolution Change in the genetic composition of a population over successive generations, as a result of natural selection acting on the genetic variation among individuals.

Examination system System for selecting Chinese officials and bureaucrats according to merit through a series of competitive, written examinations that, in theory, any Chinese young man could take. Success in the exams required years of intense study in classical Chinese literature. The examination system was not abolished until the early twentieth century.

Existentialism Philosophy that regards human existence as unexplainable, and stresses freedom of choice and accepting responsibility for the consequences of one's acts.

Factories Foreign trading posts in China and other parts of Asia. The chief representative of a factory was known as a "factor." Though the earliest trading posts were established by the Portuguese in the sixteenth century, the number of factories grew rapidly in the eighteenth and nineteenth centuries, with European and American merchants trading for silk, rhubarb, tea, and porcelain.

Fascism A system of government marked by centralization of authority under a dictator, stringent socioeconomic controls, and suppression of the opposition through terror and censorship.

Fatimids Muslim dynasty that ruled parts of North Africa and Egypt (909–1171).

Feminism The belief that women collectively constitute a class of society that has been historically oppressed and deserves to be set free.

Final Solution Nazi plan to murder all European Jews.

Fixed-wind systems Wind system in which the prevailing winds do not change direction for long periods of time.

Fossil fuels Fuels including peat, coal, natural gas, and oil.

Franciscans Religious order founded by Francis of Assisi in 1209 and dedicated to the virtues of humility, poverty, and charitable work among the poor.

Free trade The notion that maximum economic efficiency is achieved when barriers to trade, especially taxes on imports and exports, are eliminated.

French Revolution Political, intellectual, and social upheaval that began in France in 1789. It resulted in the overthrow of the monarchy and the establishment of a republic.

Fulani Traditional herdsmen of the Sahel in West Africa.

Fundamentalism Strict adherence to a set of basic ideas or principles.

Futurism Artistic vision articulated by Emilio Filippo Marinetti in 1909. He believed that all traditional art and ideas should be repudiated, destroyed, and replaced by the new. Futurists glorified speed, technology, progress, and violence.

Gauchos Argentine cowboys.

General will Jean-Jacques Rousseau's concept of the collective will of the population. He believed that the purpose of government was to express the general will.

Genetic revolution Revolution in the understanding of human biology produced by advances in genetic research.

Genocide The systematic and planned extermination of an entire national, racial, political, or ethnic group.

Ghana A medieval West African kingdom in what are now eastern Senegal, southwest Mali, and southern Mauritania.

Global gardening The collecting in botanical gardens of plants from around the world for cultivation and study.

Globalization The process through which uniform or similar ways of life are spread across the planet.

Glyph A form of writing that uses symbolic figures that are usually engraved or incised, such as Egyptian hieroglyphics.

GM Crops that have been *genetically modified* to produce certain desired characteristics.

Golden Horde Term for Mongols who ruled much of Russia from the steppes of the lower Volga River from the thirteenth to the fifteenth century.

Grand Vizier The chief minister of state in the Ottoman Empire.

Greater East Asia Co-Prosperity Sphere Bloc of Asian nations under Japanese economic and political control during World War II.

Green revolution Improvements in twentieth-century agriculture that substantially increased food production by developing new strains of crops and agricultural techniques.

Greenhouse effect The increase in temperature caused by the trapping of carbon in the Earth's atmosphere.

Guardians Self-elected class of philosopher-rulers found in Plato's *Republic*.

Guomindang (GMD) Nationalist Chinese political party founded in 1912 by Sun Yat-Sen. The Guomindang took power in China in 1928 but was defeated by the Chinese Communists in 1949.

Habsburgs An Austro-German imperial family that reached the height of their power in the sixteenth century under Charles V of Spain when the Habsburgs ruled much of Europe and the Americas. The Habsburgs continued to rule a multinational empire based in Vienna until 1918.

Haj The pilgrimage to Mecca that all faithful Muslims are required to complete at least once in their lifetime if they are able.

Han Dynasty that ruled China from ca. 206 B.C.E. to ca. 220 C.E. This was the period when the fundamental identity and culture of China were formed. Chinese people still refer to themselves as "Han."

Hanseatic League Founded in 1356, the Hanseatic League was a powerful network of allied ports along the North Sea and Baltic coasts that collaborated to promote trade.

Harem The quarters reserved for the female members of a Muslim household.

Herders Agriculturalists who emphasize the raising of animals, rather than plants, for food and products, such as wool and hides.

High-level equilibrium trap A situation in which an economy that is meeting high levels of demand with traditional technology finds that it has little scope to increase its output.

Hinduism Indian polytheistic religion that developed out of Brahmanism and in response to Buddhism. It remains the majority religion in India today.

Hispaniola Modern Haiti and the Dominican Republic.

Hohokam People Native American culture that flourished from about the third century B.C.E. to the mid–fifteenth century C.E. in south-central Arizona.

Holocaust Term for the murder of millions of Jews by the Nazi regime during World War II.

Holy Roman Empire A loose federation of states under an elected emperor that consisted primarily of Germany and northern Italy. It endured in various forms from 800 to 1806.

Homo erectus (Trans.) "Standing upright." Humanlike tool-using species that lived about 1.5 million years ago. At one time, Homo erectus was thought to be the first "human."

Homo ergaster (Trans.) "Workman." Humanlike species that lived 800,000 years ago and stacked the bones of its dead.

Homo habilis (Trans.) "Handy." Humanlike species that lived about 2.5 million years ago and made stone hand axes.

Homo sapiens (Trans.) "Wise." The species to which contemporary humans belong.

Human rights Notion of inherent rights that all human beings share. Based in part on the assumption that being human constitutes in itself a meaningful moral category that excludes nonhuman creatures.

Humanism Cultural and intellectual movement of the Renaissance centered on the study of the literature, art, and civilization of ancient Greece and Rome.

Hurons A Native American confederacy of eastern Canada. The Huron flourished immediately prior to contact with Europeans, but declined rapidly as a result of European diseases such as smallpox. They were allied with the French in wars against the British, the Dutch, and other Native Americans.

Husbandry The practice of cultivating crops and breeding and raising livestock; agriculture.

Ice-Age affluence Relative prosperity of Ice-Age society as the result of abundant game and wild, edible plants.

Icon A representation or picture of a Christian saint or sacred event. Icons have been traditionally venerated in the Eastern, or Orthodox, Church.

Il-Khanate A branch of the Mongol Empire, centered in present-day Iran. Its rulers, the Il-Khans, converted to Islam and adopted Persian culture.

Il-khans ("subordinate rulers") Viceroys of the Mongols who ruled Persia and environs in the thirteenth and early fourteenth centuries.

Imam A Muslim religious teacher. Also the title of Muslim political and religious rulers in Yemen and Oman.

Imperator A Latin term that originally meant an army commander under the Roman Republic and evolved into the term *emperor*.

Imperialism The policy of extending a nation's authority and influence by conquest or by establishing economic and political hegemony over other nations.

Incas Peoples of highland Peru who established an empire from northern Ecuador to central Chile before the Spanish conquest in the 1530s.

Indian National Congress Political organization created in 1885 that played a leading role in the Indian independence movement.

Indirect rule Rule by a colonial power through local elites.

Individualism Belief in the primary importance of the individual and in the virtues of self-reliance and personal independence.

Indo-European languages Language family that originated in Asia and from which most of Europe's present languages evolved.

Inductive method Method by which scientists turn individual observations and experiments into general laws.

Industrial Revolution The complex set of economic, demographic, and technological events that began in Western Europe and resulted in the advent of an industrial economy.

Industrialization The process by which an industrial economy is developed.

Information technology Technology, such as printing presses and computers, that facilitates the spread of information.

Inquisition A tribunal of the Roman Catholic Church that was charged with suppressing heresy and immorality.

Iroquois Native American confederacy based in northern New York State, originally composed of the Mohawk, Oneida, Onondaga, Cayuga, and Seneca peoples, known as the Five Nations. The confederation created a constitution sometime between the mid-1400s and the early 1600s.

Isolationism Belief that, unless directly challenged, a country should concentrate on domestic issues and avoid foreign conflicts or active participation in foreign affairs.

Jainism A way of life that arose in India designed to free the soul from evil by ascetic practices: chastity, detachment, truth, selflessness, and strict vegetarianism.

Janissaries Soldiers in an elite Ottoman infantry formation that was first organized in the fourteenth century. Originally drafted from among the sons of the sultan's Christian subjects, the janissaries had become a hereditary and militarily obsolete caste by the early nineteenth century.

Jesuits Order of regular clergy strongly committed to education, scholarship, and missionary work. Founded by Ignatius of Loyola in 1534.

Jihad Arabic word meaning "striving." Muhammad used the word to refer to the inner struggle all Muslims must wage against evil, and the real wars fought against the enemies of Islam.

Joint-stock company A business whose capital is held in transferable shares of stock by its joint owners. The Dutch East India Company, founded in 1602, was the first joint-stock company.

Kaaba The holiest place in Islam. Formerly a pagan shrine, the Kaaba is a massive cube-shaped structure in Mecca toward which Muslims turn to pray.

Keynesianism Economic policy advocated by J. M. Keynes, based on the premise that governments could adjust the distribution of wealth and regulate the functioning of the economy through taxation and public spending, without seriously weakening free enterprise or infringing freedom.

Khan A ruler of a Mongol, Tartar, or Turkish tribe.

Khedive Title held by the hereditary viceroys of Egypt in the nineteenth century. Although nominally subject to the Ottoman sultans, the khedives were, in effect, sovereign princes.

Khmer Agrarian kingdom of Cambodia, built on the wealth produced by enormous rice surpluses.

Kongo Kingdom located in west central Africa along the Congo River, founded in the fourteenth century. The Portuguese converted its rulers and elite to Catholicism in the fifteenth century.

Kulturkampf (Trans.) "The struggle for culture." Name given to the conflict between the Roman Catholic Church and the imperial German government under Chancellor Otto von Bismarck in the 1870s.

Laissez-faire An economic policy that emphasizes the minimization of government regulation and involvement in the economy.

Latin Church Dominant Christian church in Western Europe.

Latitude The angular distance north or south of the Earth's equator, measured in degrees along a meridian.

Law of nations Political theory that serves as the foundation for international law, first theorized by Thomas Aquinas in the thirteenth century and further developed by the Spanish theologion Francisco Suarez (1548–1617).

League of Nations International political organization created after World War I to resolve disputes between states peacefully and create a more just international order.

Legalism Chinese philosophical school that argued that a strong state was necessary in order to have a good society.

Levant The countries bordering on the eastern Mediterranean from Turkey to Egypt.

Liberation theology Religious movement in Latin America, primarily among Roman Catholics, concerned with justice for the poor and oppressed. Its adherents argue that sin is the result not just of individual moral failure but of the oppressive and exploitative way in which capitalist society is organized and functions.

Little Ice Age Protracted period of relative cold from the fourteenth to the early nineteenth centuries.

Logograms A system of writing in which stylized pictures represent a word or phrase.

Longitude An imaginary great circle on the surface of the Earth passing through the north and south poles at right angles to the equator.

Lotus Sutra The most famous of Buddhist scriptures.

Low Countries A region of northwest Europe comprising what is today Belgium, the Netherlands, and Luxembourg.

Magyars Steppeland people who invaded Eastern Europe in the tenth century and were eventually converted to Catholic Christianity. The Magyars are the majority ethnic group in present-day Hungary.

Mahayana One of the major schools of Buddhism. It emphasizes the Buddha's infinite compassion for all human beings, social concern, and universal salvation. It is the dominant branch of Buddhism in East Asia.

Mahdi A Muslim messiah, whose coming would inaugurate a cosmic struggle, preceding the end of the world.

Maize The grain that modern Americans call "corn." It was first cultivated in ancient Mesoamerica.

Mali Powerful West African state that flourished in the fourteenth century.

Malthusian Ideas inspired by Thomas Malthus's theory that population growth would always outpace growth in food supply.

Mamluks Egyptian Muslim slave army. The mamluks provided Egypt's rulers from 1390 to 1517.

Mana According to the Polynesians, a supernatural force that regulates everything in the world. For example, the mana of a net makes it catch a fish, and the mana of an herb gives it its healing powers.

Manchurian Incident Japanese invasion of Manchuria in 1931, justified by the alleged effort of the Chinese to blow up a Japanese train. In fact, Japanese agents deliberately triggered the explosion to provide a pretext for war.

Manchus A people native to Manchuria who ruled China during the Qing dynasty.

Mandarins A high public official of the Chinese empire.

Mandate of heaven The source of divine legitimacy for Chinese emperors. According to the mandate of heaven, emperors were chosen by the gods and retained their favor as long as the emperors acted in righteous ways. Emperors and dynasties that lost the mandate of heaven could be deposed or overthrown.

Manichaeanism A dualistic philosophy dividing the world between the two opposed principles of good and evil.

Manifest destiny Nineteenth-century belief that the United States was destined to expand across all of North America from the Atlantic to the Pacific, including Canada and Mexico.

Manila Galleons Spanish galleons that sailed each year between the Philippines and Mexico with a cargo of silk, porcelain, and other Asian luxury goods that were paid for with Mexican silver.

Maori Indigenous Polynesian people of New Zealand.

GLOSSARY

Marathas Petty Hindu princes who ruled in Maharashtra in southern India in the eighteenth century.

Maritime empires Empires based on trade and naval power that flourished in the sixteenth and seventeenth centuries.

Maroons Runaway slaves in the Americas who formed autonomous communities, and even states, between 1500 and 1800.

Marshall Plan Foreign-aid program for Western Europe after World War II, named after U.S. Secretary of State George C. Marshall.

Marxism The political and economic philosophy of Karl Marx and Friedrich Engels in which the concept of class struggle is the determining principle in social and historical change.

Material culture Concrete objects that people create.

Matrilineal A society that traces ancestry through the maternal line.

Maya Major civilization of Mesoamerica. The earliest evidence connected to Maya civilization dates from about 1000 B.C.E. Maya civilization reached its peak between 250 and 900 C.E. Maya cultural and political practices were a major influence on other Mesoamericans.

Mercantilism An economic theory that emphasized close government control of the economy to maximize a country's exports and to earn as much bullion as possible.

Mesoamerica A region stretching from central Mexico to Central America. Mesoamerica was home to the Olmec, the Maya, the Aztecs, and other Native American peoples.

Messiah The anticipated savior of the Jews. Christians identified Jesus as the Messiah.

Mestizos The descendents of Europeans and Native Americans.

Microbial exchange The exchange of microbes between ecosystems.

Militarization The trend toward larger and more powerful armed forces and the organization of society and the economy to achieve that goal.

Military revolution Change in warfare in the sixteenth and seventeenth centuries that accompanied the rise of fire-power technology.

Millenarianism Belief that the end of the world is about to occur, as foretold in the biblical Book of Revelation.

Minas Gerais (Trans.) "General Mines." Region of Brazil rich in mineral resources that experienced a gold rush in the early eighteenth century.

Ming Dynasty Chinese dynasty (1368–1644) noted for its flourishing foreign trade and achievements in scholarship and the arts.

Mongol peace A period of history, from about 1240 C.E. to about 1340 C.E., when peace and order, imposed by the Mongols, fostered trade, communication, and cultural exchange across the Eurasian steppes.

Mongols Nomadic people whose homeland was in Mongolia. In the twelfth and thirteenth centuries, they conquered most of Eurasia from China to Eastern Europe.

Monocultures The cultivation of a single dominant food crop, such as potatoes or rice. Societies that practiced monoculture were vulnerable to famine if bad weather or disease caused their single food crop to fail.

Monroe Doctrine The policy enunciated by President James Monroe in 1823 that the United States would oppose further European colonization in the Americas.

Monsoons A wind from the southwest or south that brings heavy rainfall each summer to southern Asia.

Mound agriculture Form of agriculture found in pre-Columbian North America.

Mughals Muslim dynasty founded by Babur that ruled India, at least nominally, from the mid–1500s until 1857.

Multiculturalism The belief that different cultures can coexist peacefully and equitably in a single country.

Napoleonic Wars Wars waged between France under Napoleon and its European enemies from 1799 to 1815. The fighting spilled over into the Middle East and sparked conflicts in North America and India and independence movements in the Spanish and Portuguese colonies in the Americas.

Nationalism Belief that a people who share the same language, historic experience, and sense of identity make up a nation and that every nation has the right to assert its identity, pursue its destiny, defend its rights, and be the primary focus of its people's loyalty.

Natural selection The process by which only the organisms best adapted to their environment pass on their genetic material to subsequent generations.

Nature versus nurture Debate over the relative importance of inherited characteristics and environmental factors in determining human development.

Nazis Members of the National Socialist German Workers' Party, founded in Germany in 1919 and brought to power in 1933 under Adolf Hitler.

Neanderthal Humanlike species, evidence for whose existence was found in the Neander River valley in northern Germany in the mid–nineteenth century. Neanderthals disappeared from the evolutionary record about 30,000 years ago.

Negritude The affirmation of the distinctive nature, quality, and validity of black culture.

Nestorianism The Christian theological doctrine that within Jesus are two distinct and separate persons, divine and human, rather than a single divine person. Orthodox Christians classed Nestorianism as a heresy, but it spread across Central Asia along the Silk Roads.

New Europes Lands in other hemispheres where the environment resembled that of Europe and where immigrants could successfully transplant a European way of life and European culture.

New Rich Rich people whose wealth was acquired in the recent past, often in industry or commerce.

New World Term Europeans applied to the Americas.

Nirvana The spiritual goal of Buddhism, when a person ends the cycle of birth and rebirth and achieves enlightenment and freedom from any attachment to material things.

Noble savage Idealized vision that some people in the West held about certain non-Europeans, especially some Native Americans and Polynesians. It was based on the notions that civilization was a corrupting force and that these peoples lived lives more in tune with nature.

Northwest Passage Water route from the Atlantic to the Pacific through the Arctic archipelago of northern Canada and along the northern coast of Alaska. For centuries, Europeans sought in vain for a more accessible route to the Pacific farther south in North America.

Obsidian Volcanic glass used to make tools, weapons, and mirrors.

Old regime Term for the social, economic, and political institutions that existed in France and the rest of Europe before the French Revolution.

Old World Term for the regions of the world—Europe, parts of Africa and Asia—that were known to Europeans before the discovery of the Americas.

Ongons Tibetan images in which spirits are thought to reside. Shamans claimed to communicate with the ongons.

OPEC The Organization of Petroleum Exporting Countries, an alliance of the world's major oil producers.

Oracle A person or group that claims to be able to have access to knowledge of the future by consulting a god. Ancient rulers often consulted oracles.

Oriental despotism Arbitrary and corrupt rule. Eighteenth-century Europeans saw it as characteristic of Asian or Islamic rulers.

Orthodox Church Dominant Christian church in the Byzantine Empire, the Balkans, and Russia.

Ottoman Empire Islamic empire based in present-day Turkey, with its capital at Istanbul. At its height in the sixteenth century, the Ottoman Empire stretched from Iraq across North Africa to the borders of Morocco and included almost all the Balkans and most of Hungary. The empire gradually declined, but endured until it was dismembered after World War I.

Pampas A vast plain of south-central South America that supports huge herds of cattle and other livestock.

Pan-African Congress A series of five meetings held between 1919 and 1945 that claimed to represent all black Africans and demanded an end to colonial rule.

Pangaea A hypothetical prehistoric supercontinent that included all the landmasses of the Earth.

Partition of India The division in 1947 along ethnic and religious lines of the British Indian Empire into two independent states: India, which was largely Hindu, and Pakistan, which was largely Muslim. The division involved widespread violence in which at least 500,000 people were killed.

Paternalism A social or economic relationship that resembles the dependency that exists between a father and his child.

Patrilineal A society that traces ancestry through the paternal line.

Philosopher's stone A substance that was believed to have the power to change base metals into gold.

Physiocrats Eighteenth-century French political economists who argued that agriculture was the foundation of any country's wealth and recommended agricultural improvements.

Plantation system System of commercial agriculture based on large landholdings, often worked by forced labor.

Polestar Bright star used for navigation.

Positivism Doctrine that asserts the undeniability of human sense perception and the power of reason to prove that what our senses perceive is true.

Pragmatism Philosophy advocated by William James that holds that the standard for evaluating the truth or validity of a theory or concept depends on how well it works and on the results that arise from holding it.

Proletariat The working class, which according to Karl Marx, would overthrow the bourgeoisie.

Protectorate A country or region that, although nominally independent and not a colony, is in fact controlled militarily, politically, and economically by a more powerful foreign state.

Protestantism The theological system of any of the churches of Western Christendom that separated from the Roman Catholic Church during the Reformation. The advent of Protestantism is usually associated with Martin Luther's break from the Catholic Church in the 1520s.

Psychoanalysis Technique developed by Sigmund Freud to treat patients suffering from emotional or psychological disorders by making them aware of their subconscious conflicts, motivations, and desires.

Public sphere Sites for the public discussion of political, social, economic, and cultural issues.

Qing dynasty Last imperial Chinese dynasty (1644–1912), founded when the Manchus, a steppeland people from Manchuria, conquered China. It was succeeded by a republic.

Quantum mechanics Mechanics based on the principle that matter and energy have the properties of both particles and waves.

Quran The sacred text of Islam dictated from God to the Prophet Muhammad by the Archangel Gabriel. Considered by Muslims to contain the final revelations of God to humanity.

Rape of Nanjing Atrocities committed by the Japanese during their occupation of the city of Nanjing, China, in 1937.

Rastafarianism A religious and political movement that began among black people in Jamaica in the 1930s. Its adherents believe that former Emperor Haile Selassie of Ethiopia (r. 1930–1974) was divine and the Messiah whose coming was foretold in the Bible.

Rationalism The doctrine that reason by itself can determine truth and solve the world's problems.

Realpolitik Political doctrine that says that the state is not subject to moral laws and has the right to do whatever safeguards it and advances its interests.

Reformation The Protestant break from the Roman Catholic Church in the sixteenth century.

Renaissance Humanistic revival of classical art, architecture, literature, and learning that originated in Italy in the fourteenth century and spread throughout Europe.

Renewable energy Energy that is not derived from a finite resource such as oil or coal.

Rig Veda A collection of hymns and poems created by a sedentary people living in the area north of the Indus valley where northern India and Pakistan meet. The *Rig Veda* provides evidence for the theory that invaders destroyed Harappan civilization.

Romanticism Intellectual and artistic movement that arose in reaction to the Enlightenment's emphasis on reason. Romantics had a heightened interest in nature and religion, and emphasized emotion and imagination.

Rus A Slavic-Scandinavian people who created the first Russian state and converted to Orthodox Christianity.

Safavids Shiite dynasty that ruled Persia between 1501 and 1722.

Sahel A semiarid region of north Central Africa south of the Sahara Desert.

Saint Domingue A French colony on Hispaniola that flourished in the eighteenth century by cultivating sugar and coffee with slave labor. It became the modern republic of Haiti after a protracted struggle that began in the 1790s.

Samurai The hereditary Japanese feudal-military aristocracy.

Sati In Hinduism, the burning of a widow on her husband's funeral pyre.

Satyagraha (Trans.) "The force of truth." Nonviolent movement launched by Mohandas K. Gandhi, with the goal of achieving Indian independence.

Savanna (or "Savannah") A flat grassland of tropical or subtropical regions.

Scientific revolution The sweeping change in the investigation of nature and the view of the universe that took place in Europe in the sixteenth and seventeenth centuries.

Scientism The belief that science and the scientific method can explain everything in the universe and that no other form of inquiry is valid.

Scramble for Africa Late nineteenth-century competition among European powers to acquire colonies in Africa.

Sea Peoples Unknown seafaring people that contributed to the instability of the eastern Mediterranean in the twelfth century B.C.E., attacking Egypt, Palestine, Mesopotamia, Anatolia, and Syria.

Second Vatican Council Council of the Roman Catholic Church that convened at intervals in the 1960s and led to major changes in church liturgy and discipline.

Secularism Belief that religious considerations should be excluded from civil affairs or public education.

Self-determination Principle that a given people or nationality has the right to determine their own political status.

Self-strengthening Mid–nineteenth-century Chinese reform movement initiated in response to Western incursions.

Seljuks A Turkish dynasty ruling in Central and western Asia from the eleventh to the thirteenth centuries.

Serf Agricultural laborer attached to the land owned by a lord and required to perform labor in return for certain legal or customary rights. Unlike slaves, serfs could not usually be sold away from the land.

Shaman A person who acts as an intermediary between humans and spirits or gods. Such a person functions as the medium though which spirits talk to humans.

Sharia Islamic law. The word *sharia* derives from the verb *shara'a*, which is connected to the concepts of "spiritual law" and "system of divine law."

Shiites Members of the most important minority tradition in the Islamic world. Shiites believe that the caliphate is the prerogative of Muhammad's nephew, Ali, and his heirs. Shiism has been the state religion in Iran since the sixteenth century.

Shinto A religion native to Japan, characterized by veneration of nature spirits and ancestors and by a lack of formal dogma.

Shogun A hereditary military ruler of Japan who exercised real power in the name of the emperor, who was usually powerless and relegated to purely ceremonial roles. The last shogun was removed from office in 1868.

Sikhism Indian religion founded by Nanak Guru in the early sixteenth century that blends elements of the Hindu and Muslim traditions.

Silk Roads Key overland trade routes that connected eastern and western Eurasia. The route first began to function in the aftermath of Alexander the Great's expansion into Central Asia at the end of the fourth century B.C.E.

Sioux A nomadic Native American people of central North America who, with the benefit of horses introduced to the Americas by the Spanish, formed a pastoralist empire in the late eighteenth and mid–nineteenth centuries.

Social Darwinism The misapplication of Darwin's biological theories to human societies, often to justify claims of racial superiority and rule by the strong over the weak.

Socialism Any of various theories or systems in which the means of producing and distributing goods is owned collectively or by a centralized government.

Socialist realism An artistic doctrine embraced by many communist and leftist regimes that the sole legitimate purpose of the arts was to glorify the ideals of the state by portraying workers, peasants, and the masses in a strictly representational, nonabstract style.

Sociobiology The study of the biological determinants of social behavior.

Solidarity Polish trade union founded in 1980 that played a key role in bringing down Poland's communist regime.

Solomids Dynasty that seized power in Ethiopia in 1270 C.E. and claimed descent from the Biblical King Solomon.

Song dynasty Dynasty (960–1279) under which China achieved one of its highest levels of culture and prosperity.

Songhay An ancient empire of West Africa in the present-day country of Mali. It reached the height of its power around 1500 C.E.

Soninke West African kingdom on the upper Niger River.

Soviet Russian term for a workers' collective.

State system Organization of early modern Europe into competing nation-states.

Steppe A vast semiarid, grass-covered plain, extending across northern Eurasia and central North America.

Stoicism Philosophy founded on the belief that nature is morally neutral and that the wise person, therefore, achieves happiness by accepting misfortune and practicing self-control.

Stranger effect The tendency some peoples have to esteem and defer to strangers.

Stream of consciousness A literary technique that presents the thoughts and feelings of a character in a novel or story as they arise in the character's mind.

Subsidiarity Doctrine that decisions should always be made at the level closest to the people whom the decisions most affect.

Suez Canal Canal linking the Mediterranean and the Red Sea. It was built by French engineers with European capital and opened in 1869.

Sufis Members of Islamic groups that cultivate mystical beliefs and practices. Sufis have often been instrumental in spreading Islam, but Muslim authorities have often distrusted them.

Sundiata Legendary hero said to have founded the kingdom of Mali in West Africa.

Sunnis Members of the dominant tradition in the Islamic world. Sunnis believe that any member of Muhammad's tribe could be designated caliph.

Surrealism Literary and artistic movement that attempts to express the workings of the subconscious.

Syllogisms A form of argument in which we can infer a necessary conclusion from two premises that prior demonstration or agreement has established to be true.

Syncretic Characterized by the reconciliation or fusion of differing systems of belief.

Taiping Rebellion Rebellion (1852–1864) against the Qing Empire that resulted in tens of millions of deaths and widespread destruction in southern China.

Tang dynasty Chinese dynasty (618–907) famous for its wealth and encouragement of the arts and literature.

Taro a fibrous root indigenous to New Guinea, first cultivated 9,000 years ago in swamplands.

Tengri "Ruler of the sky." The supreme deity of the Mongols and other steppeland peoples.

The Mongol Peace Era in the thirteenth and fourteenth centuries when Mongol rule created order and stability in Central Asia and enabled goods and ideas to flow along the Silk Roads.

Theory of value The theory that the value of goods is not inherent, but rather determined by supply and demand.

Theravada A conservative branch of Buddhism that adheres to the nontheistic ideal of self-purification to nirvana. Theravada Buddhism emphasizes the monastic ideal and is dominant in present-day Sri Lanka and southeast Asia.

Third Rome Term Russians used for Moscow and Russian Orthodox Christianity. It expressed the belief that the Russian czars were the divinely chosen heirs of the Roman and Byzantine emperors.

Thule Inuit Indigenous Native American people who crossed the Arctic and arrived in Greenland around 1000 C.E.

Tillers Agriculturalists who emphasize the cultivation of plants for food and products, such as timber and cotton.

Tokugawa A family of shoguns that ruled Japan in the name of the emperors from 1603 to 1868.

Trading-post empires Term for the networks of imperial forts and trading posts that Europeans established in Asia in the seventeenth century.

Treasure Fleets Spanish fleets that sailed from the Caribbean each year to bring gold and silver from mines in the Americas back to Europe.

Tundra A treeless area between the ice cap and the tree line of Arctic regions.

Turks A member of any of the Turkic-speaking, nomadic peoples who originated in Central Asia. The Turks eventually converted to Islam and dominated the Middle East.

Uncertainty principle Niels Bohr and Werner Heisenberg's theory that because observers are part of every observation their findings can never be objective.

United Nations International political organization created after World War II to prevent armed conflict, settle international disputes peacefully, and provide cultural, economic, and technological aid. It was the successor to the League of Nations, which had proved to be ineffectual.

Universal love Love between all people, regardless of status, nationality, or family ties.

Upanishads The theoretical sections of the Veda (the literature of the sages of the Ganges civilization). The Upanishads were written down as early as 800 B.C.E.

Urbanization The process by which urban areas develop and expand.

Utilitarianism System of thought devised by Jeremy Bentham, based on the notion that the goal of the state was to create the greatest happiness for the greatest number of people.

Utopianism Belief in a system or ideology aimed at producing a perfect or ideal society.

Vaccination Inoculation with a vaccine to produce immunity to a particular disease.

Vernacular languages The languages that people actually spoke, as opposed to Latin, which was the language used by the Roman Catholic Church and was, for a long time, the language of scholarship, the law, and diplomacy in much of Europe.

Virtual reality A computer simulation of a real or imaginary system.

Wahhabbism Muslim sect founded by Abdul Wahhab (1703–1792), known for its strict observance of the Quran. It is the dominant form of Islam in Saudi Arabia.

Westerlies Winds coming from the west.

Westernization The process by which other cultures adopt Western styles or ways of life.

World system The system of interconnections among the world's population.

World War I Global war (1914–1918) sparked by the assassination of Archduke Francis Ferdinand of Austria by a Serb terrorist in June 1914.

World War II Global conflict that lasted from 1939 to 1945 and ended with the defeat and occupation of Fascist Italy, Nazi Germany, and Japan.

Zen A school of Mahayana Buddhism that asserts that a person can attain enlightenment through meditation, self-contemplation, and intuition.

Ziggurat A tall, tapering Mesopotamian temple. Ziggurats were the physical and cultural centers of Mesopotamian cities.

Zimbabwes Stone-built administrative centers for rulers and the elite in southern Africa. The zimbabwes flourished in the fifteenth century.

Zoroastrianism Iranian religious system founded by Zoroaster that posited a universal struggle between the forces of light (the good) and of darkness (evil).

A NOTE ON DATES AND SPELLINGS

In keeping with common practice among historians of global history, we have used B.C.E. (before the common era) and C.E. (common era) to date events. For developments deep in the past, we have employed the phrase "years ago" to convey to the reader a clear sense of time. Specific dates are given only when necessary and when doing so improves the context of the narrative.

Recognizing that almost every non-English word can be transliterated in any number of ways, we have adopted the most widely used and simplest systems for spelling names and terms. The *pinyin* system of Chinese spelling is used for all Chinese words with the exceptions of *Hong Kong* and *Yangtze*, which are still widely referred to in their Wade-Giles form. Following common usage, we have avoided using apostrophes in the spelling of Arabic and Persian words, as well as words from other languages—thus, *Quran* and *Kaaba* instead of *Qu'ran* and *Ka'ba*, and *Tbilisi* instead of *T'bilisi*. Diacritical marks, accents, and other specialized symbols are used only if the most common variant of a name or term employs such devices (such as *Çatalhüyük*), if they are part of a personal noun (such as *Nicolás*), or if the inclusion of such markings in the spelling of a word makes pronouncing it easier (*Teotihuacán*).

Throughout the text the first appearance of important non-English words whose pronunciation may be unclear for the reader is followed by phonetic spellings in parentheses, with the syllable that is stressed spelled in capital letters. So, for example *Ugarit* is spelled phonetically as "OO-gah-riht." Chinese words are not stressed, so each syllable is spelled in lowercase letters. Thus, the city of Hangzhou in China is rendered phonetically as "hahng-joh." For monosyllabic words, the phonetic spelling is in lowercase letters. So *Rus* is spelled as "roos." The table below provides a guide for how the vowel sounds in *The World: A Brief History* are represented phonetically.

a	as in *cat, bat*
ah	as in *car, father*
aw	as in *law, paw*
ay	as in *fate, same*
eh	as in *bet, met*
ee	as in *beet, ease*
eye	as in *dine, mine*
ih	as in *if, sniff*
o	as in *more, door*
oh	as in row, slow
oo	as in *loop, moo*
ow	as in *cow, mouse*
uh	as in *but, rut*

CHAPTER 2

1. J. L. Harlan, *Crops and Man* (1992), p. 27.

2. Charles Darwin, *The Variation of Plants and Animals under Domestication*, 2 vols (1868), i, pp. 309–310.

CHAPTER 11

1. G. Coédès, *Angor: An Introduction* (1963), pp 104–105.

2. G. Coédès, *Angor: An Introduction* p. 96.

3. Patrologia Latina, cli, col. 0572; William of Malmesbury, *Chronicle of the Kings of England*, 68 IV, ch. 2 (ed. J. A. Giles [1857], p. 360).

CHAPTER 12

1. J. T. C. Liu, *Reform in Sung China: Wang An-Shih and His New Policies* (Cambridge, MA: Harvard University Press, 1957), p. 54.

CHAPTER 13

1. P. Jackson, ed., *The Travels of Friar Willam of Rubruck* (London, 1981), pp. 113–114.

2. R. Latham, ed., *The Travels of Marco Polo* (Harmondsworth, 1972), p. 85.

3. J. Fennell, *The Crisis of Medieval Russia* (Longman Publishing Group, 1983), p. 88.

CHAPTER 14

1. R. Horrox, *The Black Death* (Manchester University Press, 1994), p. 16.

2. N. Cantor, *In the Wake of the Plague* (New York: Perennial/Harper Collins, 2002), p. 199.

3. D. Hall in *Cambridge History of Southeast Asia*, ed. N. Tarling (Cambridge University Press, 1992), i, 218.

4. F. Rosenthal ed. *The Muqaddimah*, 3 vols. (New York: Pantheon Books, 1958), i, 64–65.

CHAPTER 16

1. T. Armstrong, ed., *Yermak's Campaign in Siberia* (London, 1975), pp. 38–50, 59–69, 108, 163; B. Bobrick, *East of the Sun: The Epic Conquest and Tragic History of Siberia* (London, 1993), p. 43.

CHAPTER 18

1. *Principes de la philosophie,* Bk I, 8,7; Discours sur la méthode, ch 4.

CHAPTER 26

1. H. S. Wilson, *Origins of West Africa Nationalism* (London, 1969), p. 167.

CHAPTER 27

1. N. Chomsky, *Knowledge of Language* (Wesport, CT: 1986), p. 14.

CHAPTER 28

1. D. A. J. Pernikoff, *Bushido: The Anatomy of Terror* (1943).

CHAPTER 29

1. I. Berlin "My Intellectual Path", *New York Review of Books*, 14 May (1998); *The Power of Ideas*, ed. H. Hardy (Princeton, 2002), p.12.

CREDITS

CHAPTER 1: p. 4 Francisco Goya y Lucientes, Spanish, 1746-1828. Boy Staring at an Apparition (1824-1825) Carbon Black and watercolor on ivory (Black wash heightened with vermilion and brown) 6.03 x 6.03cm (2 3/8 x 2 3/8 in.) Museum of Fine Arts, Boston. Gift of Eleanor; **p. 7** © The Natural History Museum, London; **p. 8** Howard S. Friedman/Pearson Education/PH College; **p. 12** The Jane Goodall Institute, www.janegoodall.org; **p. 16** Charles & Josette Lenars/ © Charles & Josette Lenars/CORBIS All Rights Reserved; **p. 17** Michael & Patricia Fogden/ © Michael & Patricia Fogden/CORBIS All Rights Reserved; **p. 18** Peter/Georgina Bowater/Creative Eye/MIRA.com; **p. 19** Novosti/Photo Researchers, Inc.; **p. 22** AKG Images/Jurgen Sorges.

CHAPTER 2: p. 26 © Kevin Flemming/CORBIS All Rights Reserved; **p. 28** Rostislav Ageev /Shutterstock; **p. 30** Theya Molleson, Natural History Museum of London; **p. 32** © Joe McDonlad/CORBIS All Rights Reserved; **p. 36** © Caroline Penn/CORBIS All Rights Reserved; **p. 37** Ashmolean Museum, Oxford, England, U.K.; **p. 39** Hittite Museum, Ankara, Turkey/ET Archive, London/SuperStock; **p. 43** © Michael Holford; **p. 44** Andrew McRobb © Dorling Kindersley

CHAPTER 3: p. 50 © Copyright The British Museum; **p. 54** M. Andrews/Ancient Art & Architecture Collection Ltd.; **p. 57 TOP** Erich Lessing/Art Resource, NY; **p. 57 BOTTOM** 57 bottom Werner Forman Archive; **p. 58** Giraudon/Bridgeman Art Library; **p. 62** Borromeo/Dancing girl. Bronze statuette from Mohenjo Daro. Indus Valley Civilization. National Museum, New Delhi, India. Borromeo/Art Resource, NY; **p. 65** Michael Holford; **p. 66** Royal Museums of Art and History, Brussels, Belgium. Copyright IRPA-KIK, Brussels, Belgium; **p. 67** Lowell Georgia/Corbis/Bettmann; **p. 71** Courtesy of the Library of Congress.

CHAPTER 4: p. 74 © CM Dixon/ HIP/The Image Works; **p. 77** The Art Archive/Dagli Orti; **p. 82** The Art Archive/Heraklion Museum/Dagli Orti; **p. 84** © Erich Lessing/Art Resource, NY; **p. 87** Eric Lessing/Art Resource, N.Y.; **p. 88** The Art Archive/Dagli Orti; **p. 91** Werner Forman/Art Resource, NY.

CHAPTER 5: p. 96 The Art Archive/Dagli Orti; **p. 99** "Human-headed winged bull and winged lion (lamassu). Alabaster (ypsum); Gateway support from the Palace of AshurnasirpalII (ruled 883-859 BCE). Limestone. H: 10' 3/1/2". L: 9' 1". W: 2" 1/2". The Metropolitan Museum of Art, Gift of John D. Rockefeller, J; **p. 104** Ronald Sheridan/ © Ronald Sheridan/Ancient Art & Architecture Collection Ltd; **p. 105** The Art Archive/Museo Di Villa Giulia Rome/ Dagli Art; **p. 107** The Art Archive/Archaeological Museum Sofia/Dagli Orti; **p. 108** Lewandowski/Ojeda/Sarcophagus of a married couple on a funeral bed. Etruscan, from Cerveteri, 6th BCE. Terracotta. Lewandowski/Ojeda. Musee Louvre, Paris France. RMN Reunion Des Musees Nationeaux/Art Resource, NY; **p. 109** AGE Fotostock America, Inc.; **p. 116** 116 Michael Holford.

CHAPTER 6: p. 124 Courtesy of the Freer Gallery of Art, Smithsonian Institution, Washington, D.C.; **p. 127** © Tim Page/ CORBIS All Rights Reserved; **p. 130** Erich Lessing/Relief, Israel, 10th-6th Century: Judean exiles carrying provisions. Detail of the Assyrian conquest of the Jewish fortified town of Lachish (battle 701 BC). Part of a relief from the palace of Sennacherib at Niniveh, Mesopotamia (Iraq). British Museum; **p. 132** Courtesy of the Library of Congress; **p. 134** "THE GOOD SHEPHERD", marble, Height: as restored cm 99, as preserved cm 55, head cm 15.5. Late 3rd century A. D. Vatican Musuems, Pio-Christian Museum, Inv. 28590. Courtesy of the Vatican Museums; **p. 136** www.photos.com/Jupiter Images; **p. 139** Christopher and Sally Gable © Dorling Kindersley; **p. 141** Mark de Fraeye/Photo Researchers, Inc.; **p. 144** Erich Lessing/Art Resource, N.Y.

CHAPTER 7: p. 150 Robert Clark/Robert Clark Photography; **p. 157** The Art Archive/Picture Desk, Inc./Kobal Collection; **p. 159** Bridgeman Art Library; **p. 164** Romisch-Germanisches Museum der Stadt Koln/Rheinisches Bildarchiv; **p. 165** © The Detroit Institute of Arts, USA/Bridgeman Art Library; **p. 166** © Archivo Iconografico, S.A./CORBIS All Rights Reserved; **p. 168** Adam Woolfitt/Robert Harding; **p. 170** © Keren Su/DanitaDelimont.com; **p. 172** Werner Forman Archive Ltd; **p. 175** F9photos/Dreamstime.

CHAPTER 8: p. 180 © Justin Kerr; **p. 184** Canali Photobank; **p. 188** R. Sheridan/Ancient Art & Architecture Collection Ltd.; **p. 189** Werner Forman Archive; **p. 192** © Ancient Art & Architecture/DanitaDelimont.com; **p. 193** © Gallo Images/CORBIS All Rights Reserved; **p. 195** The Art Archive/Dagli Orti; **p. 197** Art Archive; **p. 202** Dagli Orti/Picture Desk, Inc./Kobal Collection; **p. 204** China Tourism Press. Wang, Jian Jun/Getty Images Inc.-Image Bank.

CHAPTER 9: p. 210 Fujita Museum Of Art; **p. 215** The Art Archive/British Museum; **p. 216** James Stanfield/NGS Image Collection; **p. 217** © Michael Holford; **p. 219** Natia Chakvetadze; **p. 220** Picture Desk, Inc./Kobal Collection; **p. 221** © Chris Lisle/CORBIS All Rights Reserved; **p. 226** Scala/Art Resource, N.Y.; **p. 229** Courtesy of the Library of Congress; **p. 232** Reuters America LLC/ © Reuters/CORBIS.

CHAPTER 10: p. 236 © Carmen Redondo/CORBIS All Rights Reserved; **p. 242** Sachsische Landesbibliothek **p. 243** © Erich Lessing/Art Resource; **p. 245** Werner Forman Archive Ltd; **p. 248** Christopher Rennie/Robert Harding World Imagery; **p. 253** © Luca Tettoni/Robert Harding; **p. 254** Library of Congress; **p. 256** National Museum of Ireland.

CHAPTER 11: p. 262 Kanai Morio/Tokyo National Museum/DNP Archives; **p. 266** © Staffan Widstrand/CORBIS All Rights Reserved; **p. 269** Courtesy of the Library of Congress; **p. 271** © Kazuyoshi Nomachi/HAGA/ The Image Works; **p. 272** Andrew Gunners/Getty Images-Digital Vision; **p. 276** Japan Society; **p. 278** Courtesy of the Library of Congress; **p. 279** Bayerische Staatsbibliothek; **p. 282** By permission of The British Library; **p. 283** Rheinisches Bildarchiv, Museen Der Stadt Koln.

CHAPTER 12: p. 286 Library of the Topkapi Palace Museum; **p. 288** Bibliotheque Nationale, Paris, France/Bridgeman Art Library; **p. 289** By permission of The British Library; **p. 293** Monasterio de El Escorial, El Escorial, Spain/Index/Bridgeman Art Library; **p. 294** H. Lewandowski/Musee du Louvre/RMN Reunion des Musees Nationaux, France. Art Resource, NY; **p. 297** Bridgeman Art Library; **p. 300** Paul H. Kuiper/CORBIS-NY; **p. 302** V & A Picture Library; **p. 307** The Art Archive/Freer Gallery of Art; **p. 308** The National Palace Museum.

CHAPTER 13: p. 314 © The Trustees of the British Museum; **p. 317** The Bridgeman Art Library International/Bibliotheque Nationale, Paris, France/ The Bridgeman Art Library; **p. 320** Akg-Images/VISIOARS/AKA-IMAGES; **p. 321** Copyright Museum of Imperial Collections, Sonnomaru Shozo Kan; **p. 323** The Metropolitan Museum of Art, Purchase, Bequest of Dorothy Graham Bennet, 1993 (1993.256) Photograph © The Metropolitan Museum of Art; **p. 324** Linwendy/Dreamstime; **p. 325** The Art Archive/Bibliotheque Nationale, Paris; **p. 328** National Palace Museum, Taipei, Taiwan/ The Bridgeman Art Library; **p. 329** Library of the Topkapi Palace Museum; **p. 330** © George G. Schmid/Corbis All rights reserved; **p. 333** Dallas and John Heaton/The Stock Connection; **p. 335** Canali Photobank; **p. 336** © National Maritime Museum Picture Library, London, England Neg. #E5555-3.

CHAPTER 14: p. 342 © Josef Polleross/The Image Works; **p. 354** Museum of London; **p. 349** © Bildarchiv Preussischer Kulturbesitz/Art Resource, NY; **p. 351** Aka-Images/AKA-IMAGES; **p. 354** Bibliotheque Nationale, Paris/Bridgeman Art Library; **p. 360** SEF/Art Resource, NY; **p. 362** © 1991 The Metropolitan Museum of Art; **p. 365** The Granger Collection; **p. 366** Frank Khoury/Museum purchase 86-12-2. Photograph by Frank Khoury. National Museum of African Art, Smithsonian Institution; **p. 367** Dallas and John Heaton/The Stock Connection, **p. 368** © Charles & Josette Lenars/Corbis All rights reserved.

CHAPTER 15: p. 374 Courtesy of the Harvard Map Collection, Harvard College Library; **p. 376** Courtesy of the Library of Congress; **p. 378** National Archives of South Africa; **p. 379** Photograph © 1984 The Metropolitan Museum of Art; **p. 382** Bodleian Library, University of Oxford; **p. 390** Library of the Topkapi Palace Museum; **p. 391** Courtesy of the Library of Congress; **p. 399** Instituto Amatller de Arte Hispanico, Barcelona, Spain; **p. 402** Courtesy of the Library of Congress; **p. 404** © Michael Freeman/CORBIS All Rights Reserved.

CHAPTER 16: p. 410 By permission of The British Library; **p. 414** By permission of The British Library; **p. 417** Courtesy of the Library of Congress; **p. 418** Copyright Rijksmuseum Amsterdam; **p. 419** Courtesy of the Library of Congress; **p. 421** Bibliotheque Nationale de France; **p. 424** V&A Images/Victoria and Albert Museum; **p. 428** Courtesy of the Library of Congress; **p. 430** The Hispanic Society of America/Hispanic Society of America.

CHAPTER 17: p. 434 © Jonathan Blair/CORBIS All Rights Reserved; **p. 437** Koninklijke Bibliothek, The Hague, The Netherlands; **p. 440** Courtesy of the John Carter Brown Library at Brown University; **p. 441** Musee des Beaux-Arts et d'Archeologie, Besancon, France/ Lauros/Giraudon/ The Bridgeman Art Library; **p. 442** The Granger Collection, New York; **p. 445** Courtesy of the Library of Congress; **p. 448** Library of the Topkapi Palace Museum; **p. 449** Charles Cavaliere; **p. 450** The Art Archive/Mus[eacute]e Guimet Paris; **p. 454** Courtesy of the Library of Congress; **p. 457** Library and Archives of Canada website, www.collectionscanada.ca.

CHAPTER 18: p. 462 © Richard List/CORBIS All Rights Reserved; **p. 465** Bildarchiv Preubischer Kulturbesitz; **p. 466** Versucung Christi (1547), Gemalde, Bonn, Landschaftsverband Rheinland/Rheinisches Landesmuseum Bonn. Inv. Nr. 58.3; **p. 467** Courtesy of the Library of Congress; **p. 468** Jeffery Dykes/Photograph courtesy Peabody Essex Museum; **p. 469** Courtesy of the Library of Congress; **p. 470** © The National Museum of Denmark, Ethnographic Collection; **p. 472** of the Library of Congress; **p. 474** Courtesy of the Library of Congress; **p. 475** Jerry Hardman-Jones/Art Quarterly; **p. 478** The Bridgeman Art Library International; **p. 481** © Erich Lessing, Art Resource, NY; **p. 482** Courtesy of the Library of Congress; **p. 484** Courtesy of the Library of Congress.

CHAPTER 19: p. 488 By permission of The British Library; **p. 494** Courtesy of the Library of Congress. Rare Book and Special Collections Divisoin; **p. 495** Archiv fur Kunst und Geschichte, Berlin; **p. 497** Courtesy of the Library of Congress; **p. 498** V&A Images/Victoria and Albert Museum; **p. 499** Courtesy of the Library of Congress; **p. 502** 502 © The Metropolitan Museum of Art; **p. 506** Breamore House, Hampshire, England; **p. 507** Museo De America.

CHAPTER 20: p. 516 The Art Archive/Museo de Arte Antiga Lisbon/Dagli Orti; **p. 519** Courtesy of the Library of Congress; **p. 522** Courtesy of the Library of Congress; **p. 523** Private Collection/ Agnew's, London, UK/ The Bridgeman Art Library; **p. 526** Photograph courtesy Peabody Essex Museum; **p. 527** Rijksmuseum,

Amsterdam; **p. 529** Courtesy of the Library of Congress; **p. 532** © The Bridgeman Art Library; **p. 533** The Master and Fellows of Cambridge University Library; **p. 534** National Library of Australia, Canberra, Australia/ The Bridgeman Art Library.

CHAPTER 21: **p. 538** © Wolfgang Kaehler/CORBIS All Rights Reserved; **p. 541** Musee du Louvre/RMN Reunion des Musees Nationaux, France. SCALA/Art Resource, NY; **p. 548** Library of Congress; **p. 549** Dagli Orti (A); **p. 552** Douglas Waugh/Peter Arnold, Inc.; **p. 555** Robertstock/Classicstock.com; **p. 556** Andy Crawford © Dorling Kindersley, Courtesy of the University Museum of Archaeology and Anthropology, Cambridge; **p. 558** John Trumbull (American 1756-1843),"The Surrender of Lord Cornwallis at Yorktown, 19 October 1781", 1787-c. 1828. Oil on canvas, 53.3 x 77.8 x 1.9 cm (21 x 30 5/8 x 3/4 in.) Yale University Art Gallery, Trumbull Collection.

CHAPTER 22: **p. 562** Bristol City Museum and Art Gallery, UK/ The Bridgeman Art Library; **p. 564** Musees de Saint-Malo; **p. 566** Musee Lambinet, Versailles/Giraudon/Art Resource, N.Y.; **p. 568** Collection of the National Palace Museum. Taiwan, Republic of China; **p. 570** Ruth and Sherman Lee Institute for Japanese Art at the Clark Center, Hanford. CA; **p. 572** Courtesy of the Library of Congress; **p. 574** Giraudon/Pierre-Antoine Demachy, "Festival of the Supreme Being at the Champ de Mars on June 8, 1794." Obligatory mention: Musee de la Ville de Paris, Musee Carnavalet, Paris, France. Bridgeman-Giraudon/Art. Resource, NY; **p. 577** Royal Geographical Society, London, UK/ The Bridgeman Art Library; **p. 579** Sotheby's Picture Library/London; **p. 581** Gianni Dagli Orti/Corbis/Bettmann; **p. 583** Prado, Madrid, Spain/ The Bridgeman Art Library.

CHAPTER 23: **p. 588** Photograph courtesy Peabody Essex Museum; **p. 590** Courtesy of the Library of Congress; **p. 591** The Art Archive/Oriental Art Museum Genoa/Dagli Orti (A); **p. 597** Courtesy of the Library of Congress; **p. 598** Science Museum London/ Bridgeman Art Library; **p. 599** © British Empire and Commonwealth Museum, Bristol, UK/ Bridgeman Art Library; **p. 604** Courtesy of the Library of Congress; **p. 606** Asian Art & Archaeology, Ic./Corbis; **p. 608** © CORBIS All Rights Reserved; **p. 610** image Works/Mary Evans Picture Library Ltd.

CHAPTER 24: **p. 614** Toho/The Kobal Collection; **p. 617** Sheffield Galleries & Museum Trust; **p. 619** Dagli Orti (A)/Picture Desk, Inc./Kobal Collection; **p. 621** © Wolfgang Kaehler/CORBIS All Rights Reserved; **p. 622** Courtesy of the Library of Congress; **p. 623** National Archives of South Africa; **p. 626** Image Works/Mary Evans Picture Library Ltd; **p. 629** Courtesy of the Library of Congress; **p. 630** Corbis/Bettmann; **p. 631** Courtesy of the Library of Congress; **p. 634** The Master and Fellows of Cambridge University Library; **p. 635** Photograph courtesy Peabody Essex Museum.

CHAPTER 25: **p. 638** The Art Archive/Eileen Tweedy; **p. 641** Courtesy of the Library of Congress; **p. 646** Picture Desk, Inc./Kobal Collection; **p. 647** Mary Evans Picture Library; **p. 649** Private Collection/Archives Charmet/The Bridgeman Art Library; **p. 651** © The Trustees of the British Museum; **p. 652** Courtesy of the Library of Congress; **p. 655** Courtesy of the Library of Congress; **p. 658** 658 Courtesy of the Library of Congress; **p. 659** Picture Desk, Inc./Kobal Collection; **p. 661** Library of Congress.

CHAPTER 26: **p. 664** Auckland City Art Gallery, New Zealand/Bridgeman Art Library; **p. 668** The Jewish Museum/George Emanuel Opitz (1775-1841), "Dedication of a Synagogue in Alsace," c. 1820. The Jewish Museum/Art Resource, N.Y.; **p. 670** © Judith Miller/Dorling Kindersley/Sloan's; **p. 671** Courtesy of the Library of Congress; **p. 673** Courtesy of the Library of Congress; **p. 674** © CORBIS; **p. 676** top Michael Graham-Stewart/Private Collection/The Bridgeman Art Library; **p. 676** bottom W. & D. Downey/Getty Images; **p. 682** Caleb Bingham (American, 1811-1879), "Stump Speaking," 1853-54. Oil on canvas, 42 1/2 x 58 in. Saint Louis Art Museum, Gift of Bank of America; **p. 685** G. Pellizza da Volpedo "The Fourth Estate". Milano, Galleria Civica D'Arte Moderna. © Canali Photobank.

CHAPTER 27: **p. 692** Manuscripts and Archives, Yale University Library; **p. 695** Courtesy of the Library of Congress; **p. 699** Courtesy of the Library of Congress; **p. 700** Courtesy of the Library of Congress; **p. 702** ALBERT EINSTEIN and related rights TM/© of The Hebrew University of Jerusalem, used under license. Represented exclusively by Corbis Corporation; **p. 704** © CORBIS; **p. 708** Gisele Freund/Photo Researchers, Inc.; **p. 712** Umberto Boccioni, "Unique Forma of Continuity in Space". 1913 (cast 1931). Bronze, 43 7/8" x 34 7/8" x 15 3/4" (111.4 x 88.6 x 40 cm). Acquired through the Lillie P. Bliss Bequest. The Museum of Modern Art/Licensed by Scala-Art Resource, N.Y.; **p. 713** Robert Holmes/Corbis/Bettmann; **p. 715** J.M. Janzen/The University of Kansas.

CHAPTER 28: **p. 718** © Herge'/Moulinsart 2008; **p. 721** French School, (20th century)/Private Collection/The Bridgeman Art Library; **p. 724** Imperial War Museum, Negative Number Q1460; **p. 725** Margaret Bourke-White/Getty Images/Time Life Pictures; **p. 726** Museo Nacional Centro de Arte Reina Sofia; **p. 727** © Topham/The Image Works; **p. 729** Corbis/Bettmann; **p. 731** Courtesy of the Library of Congress; **p. 734** Nick Ut/AP Wide World Photos; **p. 735** © Swim Ink 2, LLC/CORBIS; **p. 736** Private Collection/ The Bridgeman Art Library; **p. 738** Courtesy of the Library of Congress; **p. 741** © Bettmann/CORBIS All Rights Reserved; **p. 742** ©Ali/CORBIS All Rights Reserved; **p. 743** AP Wide World Photos.

CHAPTER 29: **p. 748** Courtesy of the Library of Congress; **p. 750** The Art Archive/ Picture Desk, Inc./Kobal Collection; **p. 751** Reprinted by the permission of the American Cancer Society, Inc. All Rights Reserved; **p. 754** AP Wide World Photos; **p. 757** Corbis/Bettmann; **p. 759** © Reuters NewMedia Inc./CORBIS; **p. 760** Dr. Silvia W. de Groot; **p. 761** Luc Gnago/Corbis/Reuters America LLC; **p. 763** © Robert Vos/ANP/epa/Corbis; **p. 765** © Liu Liqun/CORBIS All Rights Reserved; **p. 767** MARK EDWARDS/Peter Arnold, Inc.; **p. 768** Damir Sagolj/ © Reuters/CORBIS; **p. 770** Courtesy of the Library of Congress.

CHAPTER 30: **p. 774** David Reed © David Reed/CORBIS All Rights Reserved; **p. 778** Peter/Georgina Bowater/Creative Eye/MIRA.com; **p. 779** Simon Harris/Robert Harding World Imagery; **p. 780** Getty Images Inc. - Hulton Archive Photos; **p. 781** Courtesy of the Library of Congress; **p. 784** Mark Ralston/Corbis/Reuters America LLC/ © Mark Ralston/Reuters/Corbis; **p. 788** National Oceanic and Atmospheric Administration NOAA; **p. 791** World Wide Photos.

PART OPENER **p. 3** Image supplied courtesy of Prof. Chris Henshilwood, University of Bergen, Norway; **p. 49** William L. Clements Library, University of Michigan; **p. 123** British Museum, London, UK/Bridgeman Art Library;; **p. 179** By permission of The British Library; **p. 260** By permission of The British Library; **p. 313** Ryukoku University Library; **p. 409** World Museum Liverpool, National Museums Liverpool; **p. 515** Kobe City Museum/DNP Archives; **p. 587** National Library of Australia; **p. 691** Barrett Lyon.

A

Abahai, 502
Abbas I the Great, 499
Abbot Suger, 278, 283
ABC for Baby Patriots, An, 654
Abd al-Malik, caliph, *226*
Abd al-Rahman, 248
Abd-ar-Razzak, 375, 404
Abduction from the Seraglio, The (Mozart), 567
Abel, 309
Abelard, 283
Abolitionism, 548, G–1
Aborigine, 578, 630, G–1
  and rejection of agriculture, 28
Abortion, 771
Abrahamic religions, 133, *133*
Absolute sovereignty, 405
Abstract art, 710
Abu Simbel, 64, 93
Abul Fazl Allami, 424
Abundance theory and farming, 42–43
Academy of Athens, 144, *144*
Aceh, 646
Acupuncture, 714
Adam (Biblical), 135, *178–179*
Adam of Bremen, 266
Adario, 579
Adelard of Bath, 283
Adjara, *622*
Adowa, battle of, 647, *647, 649*
Adrianople, battle of, 185
Adulis, 237
Adultery, 511
Advertising, television, 713
Aegean civilization, 81–84
Afghanistan, 646, 655, 735, 742, 745, 769
Africa, 338. *See also* East Africa, North Africa, South Africa, West Africa
  chronology, *118, 119*
  civilization of, *118*
  climate change in the fourteenth century, *348*
  cultural exchange, 113
  decolonization in twentieth century, 739–740
  developments in ancient, 116–118
  empires in fifteenth century, 377–380
  environmental problems, 775–776
  evolution of human species, 7–13
  in fifteenth century, *384*
  foreign imperialism, 653, *653, 654*
  in fourteenth century, *365*
  geographic obstacles, *254*
  geography impeding communications, 238, *239*
  HIV, map of, *792*
  imperialism, 643, 651
  invasion by Almoravids, 283
  and Islam, 216, 331, 471
  life expectancy, 790
  map of, *239, 510*
    ancient, *117*
    fourteenth century states, *380*
    spread of Islam, *473*
    in twentieth century, *722*
  modernization, 677–678
  Muslim reform movements, *679*
  nationalism, 670
  and nomads, 309–310
  pastoral imperialism, 448
  population, 643, 646, 794
    in eighteenth century, *518*
  slaves/slave trade, 444–445, *509,* 509–511, 548–553
    chronology, *509*
  spread of agriculture in, 42
  in thirteenth century, 338
  and Western science, *715*
African Americans, 759
African bulge, 379
Africans
  as slaves, 444
Afrikaans, G–1
Afterlife, Egyptian, 64–65, *65*
Agaja, king, 509
Age of Plague, 522, G–1
Age of the Holy Spirit, 403
Agilulf, king, 195–196
Agrarianization, 612
Agriculture. *See also* farming
  by accident, 44
  in Africa, 42
  in the Americas, 38, 448–449
  in Asia, 38
  in China, 61–62, 250–253, 449–451
  chronology, *45*
  cult, 43, *43*
  domestication of animals, 659
  effect of climate change on, 345
  in Egypt, 56–58
  in eighteenth century, 531–536, *532, 533, 534*
  in eleventh century China, 307, *307*
  in eleventh century Europe, 279
  in Ethiopia, 193, 448
  in Europe, 38
  in fourteenth century Japan, 363
  in fourteenth century New Zealand, 367
  herding, *26*
  intensified, 54–55
  in Islamic world, 246–248, *247*
  in Japan, 248–249
  land reclamation, 456–457
  mechanization of, 622–623, *623*
  native Americans, 457, *457*
  in nineteenth century, 590–596, 621–623, *622*
  in North American Southwest, 266–268
  in the Pacific Islands, 42, 253–255
  in Persia/Persian empire, 158
  plow technology, 451
  preagricultural settlements, 29–30
  prehistoric, 12
  problems of, 28–30
  rejection by Aborigines, 28
  in sixteenth century, 435–436
  in Southeast Asia, 250–253
  spread of, 38–42, *40–41*
    chronology, *42*
  in Tibet, 203
Agrochemicals, 781
Aguirre, Lope de, 476
Agyeman Prempeh I, *676*
Ahar, 315
Ahriman, 127, G–1
Ahura Mazda, 126, G–1
AIDS, 791–702
Aimi Fat Reduction Hospital, *784*
Ain Jalut, battle of, 331
Ainu, 417, 504
Ainu War, 449
Air pollution, 785
Aka River, 457
Akbar, 424, *424,* 477, *498,* 500
Akkad/Akkadians, 65, 70, 92, 157
Akrotiri, 82
Akwamu, 511
Al Biruni, 273
Alamut, 287
al-Andalus, 292, G–1
Alaska, 658
al-Azhar, 699
Alchemy, 481
Alcoholism, 619
Alejiadinho, 555, *555*
Aleutian Islands, 631, 658
Alexander the Great, *107,* 142, 143, 156, 160–163, 166, 175, 191, 387
  hegemony of, 160
  map of empire, *161*
Alexandria, 162
  and industrialization, 620
Alexius IV, 302
Alfonso X, king, *293*
Alfred the Great, 214, *225,* 256
Algeria, 656, 739
al-Ghazali, 296
Algiers, 656
Algonquin Indians, 467
al-Hajj Umar, 226, *679*
al-Hajjaj, 226
al-Hakim, caliph, 287
al-Hallaj, 296
al-Hariri, *288, 354*
Ali, 200, 329, 500
Ali Mubarak Pasha, 671
Ali Pasha Mubarak, 671
Al-Idrisi, *260–261*
Alientation, 708
al-Istakhri, *277, 278*
All Quiet on the Western Front (Remarque), 724
Allies, 730
Alluvial plains, 33, G–1
  agriculture of, 37–38
Almanac, *522*
  Mayan, *242*
al-Mansur, 448
Almanzor, 293
al-Maqrizi, 349
Almohads, 293, 309
  chronology, *293*
  map of, *295*
Almoravids, 293, 309, G–1
  chronology, *293*
  map of, *295*
al-Mutawakkil, caliph, 225
Alp Arslan, 300
Alpha males, 12
Alphabet
  Greek, 104
  Phoenician, 99
al-Sarraj, *335*
Altai Shan, 322, 326
Altan Khan, 470
Alternative energy, 779–780, G–1
Alternative medicine, 714, G–1
Altigin, 224, *225*
Alvaro VI, king, *445*
Amarna, 64
Amarna Letters, *64*
Amazon, 455
America, colonial, independence, 556–558
American Indians. *See* Native Americans
American Samoa, 658
American Southwest
  climate change in the fourteenth century, *348*
  contending with isolationism, *280*
Americanization, 556, 766, G–1
Americas
  chronology, *92, 244, 458*
    of slave trade, *509*
  colonialism, 652–653
  empires, 426–429
    chronology, *431*
    map of, *427*
  expansion in eleventh and twelfth centuries, 264–270
  in fifteenth century, 381–385
  geography, 239
  imperialism
    chronology, *455*
  industrialization, 604–605
  land exploitation, 451–456, *452–453*
  map of, *559*
  nationalism, 670
  pastoral imperialism, 448–449
  population in eighteenth century, 517, *518*
  in sixteenth and seventeenth centuries, 505–509
  social classes/society, 507
  Spain, 549
  spread of agriculture in, 38
  state building, 88–92, *90, 92*
  in thirteenth century, 337
  urbanization, 519
Amin, Idi, 739, *741*
Amitabha Buddha, *228*
Ammianus Marcellinus, 185
Amritsar, 724
Amsterdam, 420, 519
Amu Darya, 780
Amun, 97
Amur River, 423
An Lushan, 203
An Lushan's rebellion, 203, 251
Anabaptism, 477
Anak, 192
Anarchists, 684, 726, G–1
Anatolia, 77, 297, 370
  trade, 77, *78–79*
Anatolian plateau, 79
Ancestor worship, *118,* 503
Andean civilization, *88,* 88–89
  art, *91*
Andes, 241, 442
  agriculture of, 35
  climate of, *381*
  expansion of, *246*
  map of, *240*
  in thirteenth century, 338
Andex, 35, 89
Angel of Death, 223
Angkor, 251, 271
Angkor Wat, 271–272, *272*
Anglo-Egyptian Sudan, 647
Angola, 509, 622
Animal husbandry, 30–31
Animal rights, 704, G–1
Animals, exchange among countries, 436–442
Anitta, king, 77
Ankara, *370*
Anna Comnena, 300–301, 303
Anselm, archbishop of Canterbury, 283
Anthropology, 705, *711*
Antibiotic, 702
Anticlericalism, 574–575
Antimenes Painter, *104*
Antiscientific reaction in the twentieth century, 714–715
Anti-Semitism, 356–357, 668–669, 725, 728, G–1
Anti-smoking campaign, 751, *751*
Antwerp, 420
Anubis, 65
Anuradhapura, *96,* 112
Anuruddha, king, 214, *225*
Apes, 705
  humanlike features, 5
Apétor II, *760*
Aphrodite (goddess), 104
Apollo (god), 227
Apollo of Miletus, 104
Appeasement policy, 171–172

Aquaculture, 442
Aqueduct, 241, *248*
Aquinas, Thomas, 333, 493
Arabia, 118, 193
  chronology, *118, 119*
  civilization of, *118*
  Muslim reform movements, *679*
Arabs, 309, 656, 741
  invasion of Roman Empire, 196–197
  against Persia and Rome, 197
  in World War I, 723
Aragon, 494
Aragonese, 494
Aral, 780
Araucanos, 554
Archimedes, 140, 334
Architecture, 713–714
  in the Americas, 454
  Christian, 478
  of early civilization, 56
  Greece, ancient, *144*
  Hittites, 77
  India, *333*
  Islam/Islamic, *236*
  Khmer kingdom, 271–272, *272*
  of Roman Empire, 164
  Tibet/Tibetans, *204*
Arctic
  climate change in the fourteenth century, 345, *348*
  contending with isolationism, *280*
  expansion in eleventh and twelfth centuries, 264–266
Arctic Circle, 564
Arganthonios, king, 109
Argentina, 622, 652, 655, 670, 683, 756, 764
  and agriculture, 594
  industrialization, 605
  post World War I, 725
Aristocracy, 188, 356, 490, 495, 631, 634–635
  British, 634, 650
Aristotle, 105, 131, 134, 135, 136, 138, 140, 142, 143, 144, *146,* 161, 283, 303, *402,* 566
Arkona, 196
Armenia, 218, 224, 418
  and Basil II, 298
Armenians, 215
Armstrong, Karen, 769
Arnhem Land, 28
Arnold, Matthew, 680
Arouet, Francois-Marie. *See* Voltaire
Arove, Don Francisco, *507*
Art, *2–3*
  abstract, 710
  American, *588*
  of the Americas, *506,* 576–577
  of ancient river valley civilizations, *62,* 63
  Andean civilization, *91*
  Assyrian, *99*
  Brazilian, *555*
  British, *532, 534, 562, 598, 646*
  Buddhist, *124, 210,* 215, *215*
  Byzantine Empire, *302,* 302–303
  in Catalhüyü, 37
  cave, *16,* 16–17, *17, 71*
  Celtic, *166*
  Cerro Sechín, *88*
  Chinese, *157, 170,* 308, *308, 325, 391, 450, 502, 526, 541,* 566–567, *568,* 712
  Chinese women, *202*
  Christian, *130, 132, 134, 256, 465, 467, 468, 475*
  Christianity, *293*
  Cretan, 82, *82*
  Cuban, *670*
  depicting industrialization, 616–617, *617*
  Dutch, *417, 564*
  early American, *682*
  Egyptian, *50, 57,* 65, *65*
  in eleventh and twelfth centuries, *282,* 282–283
  eleventh century Europe, *279*
  Ethiopian, *193*
  Etruscan, *108*
  expressionism, 712
  fifteenth century, *402*
  Franciscan, 334–335, *335*
  French, *564, 581, 598*
  German, *279, 465*
  Greek, ancient, *104*
  Harappan, *58,* 59, *62,* 63, 68
  Hittites, *74*
  Hungarian, *297*
  Ice Age, *16,* 16–17, *17*
  Il-Khanate, 329, *329*
  Indian, 712
  Japanese, *321, 591, 635,* 711
  Java, *253*
  Korean, *192, 220*
  Kushanese, *124*
  Mayan, *180, 242, 243*
  Mesoamerican, *269*
  Middle Ages, *286*
  modern, *713*
  Mongolian, *314, 320, 321*
  morality, *626*
  Mughals, *424, 498*
  Muslim, *288*
  naval, *597*
  Nazca, 241
  Nigerian, *116*
  Olmec, *91*
  Ottoman Empire, *424, 448, 498*
  Persian, *159*
  Peru, *368*
  post World War I, *724*
  prehistoric, *48–49*
  primitive, 636
  religious, *210, 282, 283*
  Revolutionary War, *674*
  rock, *39*
  Roman, *164, 166, 188, 189, 195, 197, 217*
  Romanesque, *283*
  Russian, 710–711, *726*
  Sarmatian, *172,* 172–173
  Scythian, *171,* 171–172
  seventeenth century, *417, 481*
  in sixteenth and seventeenth century, 478, *478*
  Song empire, 308, *308*
  Spanish, *4,5,* 91, *91, 441, 516*
  surrealism, 712
  Teotihuacán, 174
  Thracian, *107*
  in twentieth century, 709–714
  Vietnam, *87*
  West African, *379*
Artemis (goddess), 147
Arthasastra, 166, 167, G–1
Arthaveda, 141
Artificial intelligence, 704, G–1
Artisans, 616
Arts and Crafts Movement, G–1
Asante, 672, *676,* 676–677
Asceticism, 226
Ashanti, 511
Ashikaga shogunate, 362
  chronology of, *363*
Ashikaga Takauji, 362, *362*
Ashio copper mines, 626
Ashur, 62, 63, 76, 77, 84
Ashurbanipal, king, 99, 102
Ashurbanipal II, king, *99*
Asia
  climate change in the fourteenth century, *348*
  Enlightenment, 568–572, *570*
  exploitation of environment, *459*
  foreign imperialism, *642,* 642–643, 653, *653*
  imperialism, 449–451, 540–544
    chronology, *455*
  and imperialistic Portugal, 414–416
  and map of spread of religion, *471*
  and maritime imperialism, 416–419
  science, 714–715
  spread of agriculture in, 38
  and western science, 483–485
Asian values, 761
Asoka, 166–167, 174, 191, 214, *225*
  emperor, 166, 167, *168,* 168–169
    chronology, *169*
    map of reign, *167*
Aspero, 53–54, 89
Assassins, 287, G–1
Association (imperialism), 650
Assur (god), 84, 97, 98, 99
Assyria/Assyrians, 99–102, 157, 158
  Babylonian exile, 130, *130*
  chronology, *102*
  revival of, *103*
Asteroid, 788
Astrakhan, 326
Astrolabe, *335*
Astrology, 481, 768
Astronomy, 244, *335,* 336, 481–482, *484,* 484–495, *529,* 569, 698, *710*
Asturias, 256
Aswan High Dam, 780, *780*
Ataturk, Kemal, 698, 723
Athawulf, king, 188
Atheism, 478, 572, 680, 768
Athens, 103, 105, 160
Atiba, 672
Atlantic Ocean
  map of European exploration, *400–401*
  navigation of, 376
  wind systems of, 395–398
Atlantic slave trade, 420, 440, G–1
Atomic bomb, *729,* 731, 732
Atomic theory, 142, 147, 710, G–1
Augurers, 66
Augustus, 151, 164, 165, 478
Aum Shinrikyo, 770
Auracano, *631*
Aurangzeb, 477, 498, 544
  emperor, 424, 661
Australia, 534, 535–536, 578, 591, 622, 655, 656
  aborigines in, 28
  convict labor, 626
  exploitation of environment, *459*
  Homo sapiens migration, 9
  racism, 759
  socialism, 686
Australopithecine, 6, G–1
Avars, 255
Aviation, 698
Avicenna, *141*
Avvakum, 467
Axial Age, 122–149, G–1
  aftermath of, 174–175
  chronology, *141, 146, 147, 175*
  definition of, 125–126
  map of, *127–128*
  math, 137–138
  medicine, *141,* 141–142
  political thinking, 134–137
  reason, 138–139
  religious thinking, 132–134
  science, 139–141
  skepticism, 142–143
  structures of, 143–146
  thinkers of, 126–131, *146*
  thoughts of, 131–143, *146*
Axial zone, 237, G–1
Axis, 730
Axum, 193, 218, 271
Ayacucho, 241
Ayurvedic medicine, *141*
Ayutthaya, 543
Azerbaijan, 315, *658*
Azores, 395, *399,* 440
Aztec calendar stone, *556*
Aztecs, *382,* 382–385, 403, 426, *428,* 428–429, *442,* 556, *556,* G–1
  chronology, *382*
  in fifteenth century, *383, 384*
  social nature of, 479–480

B

Baal (god), 98
Babur, 423–424
Babylon/Babylonians, 99
  chronology, *102*
  map of, *122–123*
  revival of, 102–103, *103*
Bach, Johann Sebastian, 576
Bacon, Francis, 482
Bacon, Nathaniel, 430
Bacon, Roger, 334
Bacteria, 594
Bactria, 158, 162
Baghdad, 248, 286, 287, 288, *743*
  siege of by Mongols, *320*
Bahais, 769
Bahía, *438*
Bahrain, 116
Bakeries, 597
Balance of trade, 157, G–1
Balearic islands, 333
Bali, *28*
Balkans, 480, 483, 544, 566, 658
Ballroom Guide, The, 651
Balmes, Jaume, 619
Banditry, 303
Bangladesh, 738, 743
Bankim, 671
Bankimcandra Chattopadhyaya, 671
Banks, Joseph, 535
Bantam, 421
Bantu, 34, G–1
Bantu languages, 42, 116
Baratieri, general, *647, 649*
Barbados, 440, 455
Barbarian invasions
  of China, 189–191
  chronology, *206*
  effects of, 206–207
  in Egypt, 84–85
  and fall of Roman Empire, 184–185, 188–189
  of India, 191–192
  of Roman Empire, 195–196
Barbarian West, 188–189
  map of, *190*
Barbarians
  and Byzantine Empire, 296–297
  invading China, 303–308
  map of, *190*
  and Roman Empire, *163,* 164
Barbarossa brothers, 425–426
Barcelona, 350, 619, 683
Barghash of Zanzibar, *626,* 648
Barguzinsk, 449

INDEX

Barley, 36, 61, 203
in Greece, 103
Barrie, J.M., 706
Barroilhet, Carlos, 605
Basil II, emperor, 297–298
Baskore of Maradi, 676
Basra, 247
Bastille, fall of, 580, *581*
Batavia, 417–419, 541, 542, *727*
Battle of Little Bighorn, 646
Battle of Minato River, 362
Batumi, *622*
Baybars, 331
Beans, 35
Beatus of Liébana, *178–180*, 277
Beauvoir, Simone de, *708*
Beavers, 457
Becker, Jerome, *626*
Beckford, William, 549
Beef as food, 787
Beerage, 634
Beer-making, *57*
Beethoven, Ludwig van, 583
Beijing, 317, 392, *484*, 607, 641
Beijing School of Medicine, 695
Belgium
imperialism, 643
industrialization, 601, 603
Belgrade, 425
Belief in progress, 572
Bellerophon, *302*
Belllunti, 463
Bence Island, 552
Bencon, 417
Benedict, St., 226–227
Beneficial and Beautiful Company, 524
Bengal, 332, 393, 451, 526, 527, 545–546, 620, 622
Benin, 379, *379*, 509
Benjamin of Tudela, 301, 355
Benson, Stephen A., 670
Bentham, Jeremy, 685–686
Benthamism, 686
Benxi, *778*
Benxi steelworks, *778*
Berbers, 196, 214, 292, 656
Bergson, Henri, 707, *711*
Beriberi, 522
Bering Strait, crossing of, 19, 21
Berlin, Isaiah, 770–771
Bessemer, Henry, 598
Bessemer converter, *701*
Big bang theory, 702, G–1
Bigamy, 465
Bingham, George Caleb, *682*
Biology, *710*
Bird flu, *791*
Bird symbols, *245*
Birth control, 590, 793–794
Bishops, 188
Bitter manioc, 34
Bizet, Georges, 629
Black America religion, 474–476
Black Bone Yi, 306
Black consciousness, *760*
Black culture, 759–760
Black Death, *342*, 343, 348, *349, 351, 354*, 369–371, 386, 444, G–1
map of, *352–353*
moral and social effects, 351–358
Black Hills, 554
Black Land, 56
Blake, William, *132*, 661
Blanc, Louis, 684
Blanco of Cadiz, Pedro, 624
Blast furnace, invention of, 333, 484
Bligh, William, 534
Blood, drinking of, *32*
Bloodletting, 242, *243*, 244
Blyden, Edward, 670
Board game, 66
Boas, Franz, 705, *711*
Boccioni, Umberto, *712*
Bodhisattva, *215, 228*
Bodin, Jean, 492, 497
Boers, 553, 656, G–1
Boethius, 189
Bohème, La (Puccini), 629
Bohemia, 405, 478
in fourteenth century, 370
Bohr, Niels, 701, *710*
Boilly, Louis Léopold, *523*
Bokassa, Jean-Bedel, 739
Bolivia, 241, *430*, 670, 681
Bollywood, *713*
Bolsheviks, 726
Bomb shelter, *731*
Bombay film industry, *713*
Bon, 222, 232, G–1
Boniface, 255
Bonobos, 12
Bon-po, 222
Boris, tsar, 256
Borlaug, Norman E., 781
Borneo, 540
Bornu, 339
Borobodur, 252, *253*
Borommakot, king, 542
Bose, Nandalal, 712
Bosnia, 744
Boston, 519
Boston Tea Party, 556
Botanical Garden in Paris, 532
Botanical Garden of Madrid, 532
Botany Bay, 559, 560
Botticelli, 402
Bougainville, Louis de, 558
Bounty (ship), 534
Bourbon, 533
Bourbon dynasty, 566
Bourgeois, 726, *726*
Bow and arrow technology, 16
Boy Staring at an Apparition (Goya), *4–5*
Brahman, 111–112, 127, 132, 222, 662, G–1
Brahmanism, 127, 133
Brahmins, 419, 567
Braque, Georges, 710, 711
Brattahlid, 266
Braun, Georg, *454*
Brazil, 442, 533, 670, 683, 756, 765
in the Americas, 454–455
art, *555*
and black religion, 474–476
coffee production, 440, 604, *604*
conquest by Portugal, 554–555
dams, 780
emancipation of slaves, 626
independence, 558
missionary activity in, 476
nationalism, 670
and slaves/slave trade, 445
and sugarcane, 440, *440*
Brazilian Catholicism, 476
Breadfruit, *534*, 534–535
Bread-making, *57*
Breeding of animals, 44–45
Bride, St., 232
Briggs, Henry Perronet, *562*
Brigid, 232
Britain, 490. *See also* England
commerce with India, 608–609
constitutionalism, 672
decolonization in twentieth century, 738–739
empire, *644*
imperialism, 642, 668
in India, 648, 650
in India, 678
industrialization, 529–532, 597
map of, *531*
in Latin America, 652
and Maoris, *664*, 665
nationalism, 668
Opium Wars, *638*, 640–641
politics, 683
and Roman culture, 164
rule in Canada, 557, 656
social classes, 634
urbanization, 519
war with American colonies, 556–557
war with China, 639
war with Maoris, 647
World War I, 720, 723
World War II, 729–731
British East India Company, 525, 528, 533, 545, G–1
British Guiana, 627
British Niger Company, 653
British North America, 455–456
Bronze Age, 73
Bronze making, 79, 87, *87*
Brookes (ship), 548, *548*
Brother Jonathan, 721
Brothers of the Sword, 330
Bruckner, Anton, 680
Brun, Cornelis de, *499*
Brunel, I.K., 599
Bubonic plague, 349, 443–444, 791
Buddha/Buddhism, 112, *124, 127*, 127–130, 133, 134, 143, 144, 147, 153, 157, *168*, 212, *215*, 358, 361, 447, 678, 760
art, *210*, 215, *215, 253*
and Asoka, 168–169
in China, 200, 219, 392, 469–470
chronology, *221*
conflict and conversion, 214
in India, 222
in Japan, 204, 220–221, 469–479
in Korea, 192, 219–220
Mahayana, 221, *228*, 233
map of, *231, 471*
and Mongols, *470*, 470–471
monks, 227–228, *262*
persecution of, 192
and politics, 219
religious communities, *228*, 228–229
revitalization of, *472*
in Southeast Asia, 272–273
spread of, *225*, 229, 232–233
chronology, *471*
Theravada, 221, 233
in Tibet, 221–222
world view of, *514–515*
Zen, 362, 714
Buddhist, 167, *167*
Buddhist clergy, 168
Buenos Aires, *455*
and industrialization, 620
Buffalo, 554
Buganda, 679
Bulgaria, 668
and Basil II, 298
intensified settlements of, 54
Bulgars, 196, 223, 256, 289
and Basil II, 298
Bull of Heaven, *66*
Bulliet, Richard W., 226
Bullion, 573
Bundu, 553
Burbank, Luther, 594
Bure, 365
Bureaucratization, 673–679, *677*, G–1
chronology, *678*
Burgundians, 188
Burke, Edmund, 528, 583
Burkina Faso, *774*, 775–776
Burma, 417, 451, 542–543, 646
and Western science, *699*
Bursa, *372*
Bush, George H.W., 743
Bush, George W., 743, *743*, 745, 788
Bush Negro, *760*
Bushmen of Africa, *17*, 22, *22*
Business imperialism, *652*, 652–655, G–1
Bustani, Butrus, 615
Buttons, 606
Byblos, 97, 98
Byzantine Empire, 194–195, 206, 223–224, 296–303, 332–333, *370*, 390, G–1
art and learning, *302*, 302–303
chronology, *302*
and the crusaders, 300–302
map of, *299*
Byzantium. *See* Byzantine Empire

C

Cabbalism, 481
Cabet, étienne, 684
Cabot, John, 398
Cacao, 244, 384, 431, 441
Cacapol, 554
Cadiz, 98
Caere, 108
Cahokia, 268, G–1
Cain, 309
Cairo, 287, 331, *342*, 343, 354, 620, 699
Calcutta, 620
Calendar, *2–3*
Ice-Age, *2*, 18
Calendar stone, *556*
Calicut, 398
California, 449, 454, 628
in eighteenth century, 555
Caliph, 199–200, 332, G–1
Cambodia, *274*, 734, 750, 763
Camel caravans, *216*
Camera obscura, *572*
Cameroon, 34
Canada, 558
formation of nation, 655
and French, 557
Canal workers in China, 392
Canal Zone, 658
Cañaris, 381
Canary Islands, 398, 532
Cancer, 791
Canda
and industrialization, 604
Candra Gupta, 191
Candragupta, 166
Cane sugar, 440, *440*
Cangapol, 554
Cannibalism, 479, 574
Canning of food, 594, 597
Canon of Medicine, The (Avicenna), *141*
'Cantiga' of Alfonso X 'the Wise,' 293
Canton. *See* Guangzhou
Canyon culture, 266–268, G–1
Cape of Good Hope, 398, 448
exploitation of environment, *459*
Cape Verdes, 440
Capital punishment, 771
Capitalism, 419, 618, 684, 725, 727, 756, G–1
Capitoline Hill, 184
Captives (Michelangelo), *478*

Caravaggio, 466
Carbon dioxide emissions, 779, *779*
Carbon in the environment, 779
Carchemish, *74*
Caribbean, 440, 723
  exploitation of environment, *459*
Caribbean Islands, 426
Carmen (Bizet), 629
Caroline Islands, 253
Cars, 778
Carson, Rachel, 781, *781*
Carthage, 98–99, 162
Cartography, *260–261, 374,* 564
  Buddhist, *514–515*
  of world, 277, *277*
Cartoonists, 713
Casa, Don Cristóbal Choque, 469
Casa Grande, 345, 348
Casas, Ramon, *726*
Casimir the Great, 370
Cassava, 35, 436
Cassia, 153
Caste system, 167, 192, 222, 622, G–1
Caste War, 681
Castiglione, Giuseppe, *568*
Castile, 333, 402–403, 490
Castilians, 666
Castro, Fidel, 741
Catalan Atlas, 363–364, *364*
Catechism, *469*
Catherine the Great, empress of Russia, 574
Catholic Church, 212, 756. *See also* Catholicism
Catholic Reformation, 466
Catholicism, 463, 464–466, 728. *See also* Catholic Church; Christianity
  black, 474–476
  Brazilian, 476
  Enlightenment, 571, 574, *574*
  in Korea, 571
  missionaries in America, 474
  missionaries in Japan, 420
  persecution of, 415, 467
  response to industrialization, 619
  revival in eighteenth century, 576
  and Wars of Religion, 494
  in White America, 476–477
Cattle, in the Americas, 437
Caucasus, 543
Caucasus Mountains, 159
Cave art, *16,* 16–17, *17, 71*
Cellini, Benvenuto, 478
Celtic, art, *166*
Celts, 166
Census, 456
Central African Republic, 739
Central Pacific Railroad, 628
Centralization, 673–679, *677,* G–1
  chronology, *678*
Cerro Sechín, 88, *88*
Certainty and science, 701–702
Cervical cancer, 791
Césaire, Aimé, 760
Ceylon, 111
Ceylon tea, *629*
Chabi, *320,* 327
Chaco Canyon, 265
Chadwick, Edwin, 619
Chak Tok Ich'aak, 182
Chaldiran, battle of, 501
Cham kingdom, 251
Chambers, William, 567
Chan Chan, *368,* 368–369
Chan Santa Cruz, 681
Chang Chueh, 190–191
Chang'an, 191, 303
Changchun, 321
Changsha, *692,* 693
Changsu, king, 219
Changzhao, battle at, 327–328
Chaos theory, 702, G–1
·Charaka, 141–142
Charlemagne, 214, *225,* 255
Charles, king of Spain, 490
Charles I, king of England, 494
Charles the Great, 370
Charles V, 478
  map of dominion, *491*
Chatham Islands, 254, 647
Chaucer, Geoffrey, *357*
Chavagnac, Father, 568
Chávez, Hugo, 743
Chavín de Huantar, 89, *90, 91*
Checa, 381
Chechnya, 658
Chekhov, Anton, 634
Chen-la, 251
Cheops, 70
Cherokee, 658, 672, *672*
Cherry Orchard, The (Chekhov), 634
Chesapeake Indians, 443
Chesterton, G.K., 768
Cheyenne, 646
Chicago, *619*
Chicago economics, 765, G–1
Chichén Itzá, 270
Chichicastenango, *474*
Chiefdoms, 52
Children, *734,* 793
  as laborers, 628
  perception of, 629, 706
Chile, 431, 555, 652, 655, 765
Chimborazo, Mount, 577, *577*
Chimpanzees, *8,* 705
  humanlike features, 5
  male domination, 12
  warfare among, 12, *12*
Chimú, *43, 368,* 368–369, 381, G–1
China, 257, 655, 743
  agriculture, 61–62, 250–253, 307, *307*
  ancient chronology, *88*
  ancient civilization, 61–62, *110*
  ancient government, 67–68
  ancient politics, *69*
  art, *157, 308, 325, 391, 450, 526,* 709, 712
  barbarian invasions of, 206
  birth control, 793–794
  and Buddhism, *215,* 469–470
  centralization, 674
  and Christianity, *467*
  chronology, *157, 251, 310*
  chronology of dynasties, *191*
  cities of ancient, 61–62
  civilizing, 660
  climate change in the fourteenth century, 345, *348*
  in Cold War era, *736,* 737
  communism, 727, 732
  comparison with Rome, *191*
  conquest by Manchus, 423
  conquest by Mongols, 326–329
  conquest of Taiwan, 450
  Cultural Revolution, 756
  dams, 781
  decline of ancient civilization, 86–88, 92
  ecology of civilization, *61, 63*
  economy, 765, *765*
  economy in eighteenth century, 524–526, 536, 537
  emigration, 417–418
  empires of, 423
  energy sources, 456
  Enlightenment, 566–567, *570, 571*
  environmental problems, 777, *778*
  epidemics, 443
  expansion of, 250–251
  expansion of ancient, 62, 70–71
  expansion since 1949, 737
  fish farming, 787
  in fourteenth century, 371
  government, 189–191
    in sixteenth and seventeenth centuries, 501–502
  herbal medicine, 714
  Homo sapiens migration, 9
  imperialism, 169–172, 391–394, 404, 446–451, 541–542
  indentured labor, 627
  industrialization, 607–608
  influence on Europe, 566–567
  introduction of maize, 437
  introduction of sweet potato, 437
  invasion of, 189–191
  Legalism, 135
  Manchurian Incident, 719
  map of, *110, 252*
  map of ancient, *61*
  map of in eighteenth century, *525*
  and maritime imperialism, 423
  migration of labor, 628
  Ming, *393*
  nationalism, 672
  in ninth and tenth centuries, 303–308
  obesity in, *784*
  Opium Wars, *638,* 640–641
  origins of medicine, 141
  origins of science, 140–141
  philosophers, *145*
  plague in, 343, 349, 350, 351, 443
  political parties, 727
  population, 789, 793–794
  population in eighteenth century, 517
  public sphere, 683
  recovery chronology, *203*
  recovery of ancient civilization, 91
  recovery of empire, 200–203
  relations with Japan, 204, 277
  religion, 130, 681
  science, 140, 714, 716
  in sixteenth and seventeenth centuries, 501–503
  social classes, 634
  social classes/society, 502–503
  spread of Buddhism, 219
  spread of Christianity, 467–468
  stability and change, *505*
  and Steppelanders, 171–172, 189–191, 289
  tea trade, 608
  trade routes, 156–157
  trade with Mongols, *323*
  war atrocities, *748*
  war with Britain, 639
  war with Japan, 605, *748,* 749–750
  and western science, 483–484, 695–697
  writing, 71
China, Tang, map of, *201*
Chinese, as laborers in America, 627–628
Chinese and Gothic Architecture (Halfpenny), 567
Chinese Board of Astronomy, 484–485, G–1
Chinese Communist Party, 732–733
Chinese diaspora, 630, G–2
Chingú, 182
Chippendale, Thomas, 567
Chittorgarh, 424, *424*
Chivalry, 282, 402–403, 676, G–2
Chocolate, 441, *441,* 596
Ch'oe Sungno, 220
Chola Kingdom, 275, 284, G–2
  chronology, *275*
  contending with isolationism, *280*
Cholera, 443, 522, 590, 791
Chomsky, Noam, 708, *711*
Chonae, 297
Chopin, Frédéric, *399*
Christendom, 214, 222–223, 281, 289, 388, 464–467, G–2
Christianity, 147, 256, 463, 768. *See also* Catholicism; Latin Christendom
  art, *130, 132, 134, 256, 282, 282–283, 293, 379, 467, 468*
  Byzantine Empire, 298–300
  and chivalry, 402–403
  chronology of conversions, *219*
  chronology of spread, *219, 224*
  and commerce, 419
  conflict and conversion, 214
  conversion of monarchs, 216–218
  development of, 133
  division of, into Eastern (Byzantine) and Western (Roman Catholic), 298–300
  early, 184
  in early Western Europe, 278
  in eleventh and twelfth centuries, 281–282
  Enlightenment, 574
  expansion chronology, *257*
  expansion of, 255–256, 467–469
  in fifteenth century, 402, 405
  in Ireland, *256*
  in Japan, 420, 567
  map of, *230, 471*
  missionaries, *457*
  monks, 226–228
  and Muslim relations, 291–292, *293*
  and Native American influence, 476
  in the New World, 442
  in nineteenth century, 680
  persecution of, 467
  and philosophy, 478
  relations with Muslims, 198
  religious communities, 226–229
  revitalization of, *468, 472*
  revival in Christendom, 464–467
  revival in eighteenth century, 575–576
  and the Rus, 223–224
  in Russia, 388
  in Scandinavia, *337*
  schism, 466
  in Scotland, 231
  on the Silk Roads, 215
  spread of, 217–218, 222–225, *225, 231,* 232–233
  in thirteenth century, 333–336
  view of plague, *354*
Chronicles of Java, 472
Chronometer, *648*
Chu, 145
Chukchi hunters, 18
Chulalongkorn, king, *676,* 678
Church of the Holy Sepulchre, *226*
Churchill, Winston, 731
Cinema, 712, *712, 713*
Cisneros, Cardinal, 465
Cistercians, 278, G–2
Cities/towns, 519, 601, 620–621
  in the Americas, 454
  ancient Greece, 104
  growth of, prehistoric, 52
  in Italy, 281

Cities/towns, *(cont.)*
population of, *620*
Thrace/Thracians, 106
in twentieth century, 784–785
Citizen army, G–2
City-states, 280
Mayan, 182–183
Mesopotamian, 65–66
Civil rights, 761
Civil War, 626, 674–675
Civilization, G–2
chronology of great river valley, *68*
definition of, 31
early, 6–16
ecology of, 55–56, *63*
use of term, 56
Civilizing mission, 660–661, *661,* G–2
Clan, 616, 665, G–2
Class conflict, 684
Class struggles, 615–616, G–2
Clausewitz, Carl von, 596, 675
Clearances, 668
Clement VI, pope, 354
Clement XI, pope, 468
Clergy, 420, 464
Climacteric, 45, G–2
Climate, 787–789
in Andes, *381*
in fourteenth century, 343–348
map of, *346–347*
instability, 43
Clinton, Bill, 745
Clive, Robert, 545
Clockmaking, 336
Cloning of human embryos, 703
Clothing, *648*
Clovis people, 19, 222
Cnoll, Cornelia, *418*
Cnoll, Pieter, *418*
Coal production, 456, 529–530, 597
Coalbrookdale, *598,* 616
Cobbett, William, 618
Coca-Cola colonialism, 766
Cochabamba valley, 781
Cockerill, John, 601
Cocom, 270
Code Napoleon, 582, 662, G–2
Code of Hammurabi. *See* Hammurabi, Code of
Codex Mendoza, *382*
Coeman, Jacob, 417
Coen, Jan Pieterszoon, 417
Coffee, 440–441, *441,* 622, 652
industry, 533, 604, *604*
Coinage, 164, *314*
Coke, Thomas, *532*
Colbert, Jean-Baptiste, 456
Cold War, 719, 731–738, G–2
alliances, *733*
Collège Royal (France), 567
Cologne, 354
Colombia, 658, 670
Columba, 255
Columbian Exchange, 435–442, G–2
chronology, *445*
Columbus, Christopher, 398, 403, 406, 426, 431, 436, 476
and Native Americans, 479
Commentary on the Apocalypse (Beatus of Liébana), 277
Commerce, 151–157, 611, 620. *See also* Economy; Imperialism
cane sugar, 440
chocolate, 441, *441*
chronology, *216*
chronology of in eleventh and twelfth centuries, *284*
coffee, 440–441
in colonial New World, 430–431
of eleventh and twelfth century India, 273–274
in Eurasia, 152–156, 274–276
in Indian Ocean, 152–156
and industrialization, *621*
international flow, *764*
and Islam/Islamic, 216
Japan, 277
land routes, 156–157, *158*
Portugal, 414–416
and religion, 419
in Roman Empire, 164–165
sea routes, *158*
slave trade, 417
and spread of religion, 212–216
tea, 441, 641
in thirteenth century, *337*
Western Europe, 277–282
Western superiority over China, 641
Commune, G–2
in eleventh and twelfth centuries, 281
Communications, 337–338
Communism, 683, 726–727, *727,* 732, *736,* 756, G–2
collapse of, 735, 737
Communist Party, 726, 732
Communists, 726, *727, 735*
Communities, growth of, prehistoric, 52–55
Comorão, 411
Compass, invention of, 333
Compendium of Chronicles (Rashid al-Din), *317*
Complete Survey of Medical Knowledge, 695
Compostela, 256
Compressed-gas cooler, 594
Computers, *704*
Con, Jan, 417–418
Conciliarists, 405
Concubinage, 568, *568,* 651
Condorcet, Marquis de, 517, 572
Conficius, *146*
Confraternities, 474, *475,* G–2
Confraternity of Our Lady of the Rosary, *475*
Confucianism, 135, 139–140, 144–145, 170, 192, 200, 250, 308, 392, 483, 501, 503, 504, 566, 569, 571, G–2
in China, 304, 394
Confucius, 56, 125, 131, 134, 135, 138, 139, 143, 144–145, 191, 320
Congo, *378,* 509, 650, 653, 739
Conimbriga, 164–165
Conquistadores, *631*
Conservation of resources, 785–787
Conservatism, 755
Consolation of Philosophy, The (Boethius), 189
Constantine, 185
Constantine IX Monomachus, *300*
Constantine the Great, 224, *225*
religious conversion to Christianity, 217–218
Constantine VII, 223, 297
Constantinian model, 222
Constantinople, 185, 188, 194, 255, 296–298, 300, 301, 332, 386, 391
Constitution of the Cherokee Nation, 672, *672*
Constitution (U.S.), 583
Constitutionalism, 672–673, *677,* G–2
chronology, *678*
Consuls, 165, 281
Consumerism, 766–767, G–2
Contraception, 9, 590, 756, 769
Convict labor, 626–627
Cook, James, 27, 534, 535, 578, *579*
Cook Islands, 255
Cookie production, 596
Cooking with fire, 9
Coolies, 627, G–2
Cooper, James Fenimore, 591
Copán, 242
Copernican revolution, 481, G–2
Copernicus, Nicolaus, 481
Cordova, 248
Corinth, 103
Corporatist, 726
Cortés, Hernán, 426, 476
Cosmos, 702
Costa Rica, 653, 670
Cotopaxi, Mount, 577
Cotton
commerce of, 606, 608, *609,* 620
production, 369, 525–526, 532, *642*
Cotton, John, 477
Cottonseed oil as energy source, 456
Council of Ministers, 744
Council of Trent, 464, G–2
Counter Reformation, 466, G–2
Counter-colonization, 757–762, G–2
Country trades, 430–431, G–2
Covenant, G–2
in Jewish tradition, 131, 133
Crane catching, 316
Crawfurd, John, 527
Creation, *132*
Creation Oratorio (song), 659
Creation stories, 132
Mixtec, *269*
Creation theory, 702
Creoles, 506, 670, G–2
Creolism, 555–556
Cresques Abraham, *325,* 364, 365
Crete/Cretans, 81, 82, *83*
art, 82, *82*
chronology, *84*
decline of, *93*
Creux, Francois du, *457*
Crèvecoeur, Michel-Guillaume Jean de, 556
Crimea, 172, 426
Crimean War, 626, 658
Criminals as source of labor, 626–627
Critique of Pure Reason (Kant), 583
Crompton, Edmund, 530
Crosby, Alfred, 381, 535
Croton, 104
Crown of Reccesvinth, 233
Crown of St. Stephen, 298
Crucifixion (Cellini), 478
Crudetboeck (Dodens), 569
Crusades, 289–292, *291, 292,* 423, G–2
First, 301
Fourth, 302
invasion of Byzantine Empire, 300–302
Cruz, Francisco de la, 476
Crystal Cathedral of the Reverend Robert Schuller, 770
Crystal Palace (London), 620
Cuba, *374,* 507, 600, 658, 683, 741, 743, 759
emancipation of slaves, 626, 627
Cuban missile crisis, 732
Cubans, black, 759
Cubatão, 784–785
Cubism, 710, G–2
Cult agriculture, 43, *43*
Cult of everyday abundance, 57
Cult of nature, 576–577
Cult of the Supreme Being, *574,* 575
Cult worship, 184
Cults, *757*
Cultural exchange, 112–113, *114–115,* 635–636, 662
Cultural relativism, 705, G–2
Cultural Revolution, 756, G–2
Culture, *22,* G–2
of ancient river valley civilizations, 71–72
of animals, 705
in eleventh and twelfth centuries, 281–283
exchange of, 106–109, 635–636, 760–761
and globalization, 766–767
of Ice Age, 17–19
of India in eleventh and twelfth centuries, 273–274
and maritime imperialism, 375–376
material, 17–18
of Roman Empire, 164–165
Culture wars, 715
Cumberland, duke of, 567
Cuneiform, 71, *71,* G–2
Cupisnique, 89
Curacao, 445
Curled Dragon Town, 62
Curzon, Lord, 698
Cuzco, 381, *454*
Cyrus the Great, 158, 159
Czars, 422, G–2
Czech Republic, 601
Czechoslovakia, 728

D

da Gama, Vasco, 398
da Vinci, Leonardo, 478
Dacca, 519
Dacia, 164, 256
Dada, 712, G–2
Dada Manifesto, 712
Dahomey, 509–511, G–2
Daimyo, 504, 505, G–2
Dairy products diet, 32, *32*
Dalai Lama, 470
Dalí, Salvador, 712
Damas, Léon, 760
Damascus, 351
Dampier, William, 578
Dams, *780,* 780–781, *781*
Daoism, 130, 138, 139, 140–141, 192, 232, 483, 714, G–2
Dara Shukoh, 477
Darius I, 153
Darjeeling Railway, *599*
Darwin, Charles, 44, *659,* 659–660, 680, 699, 702
Daud, Bwana, 539
Daulatabad, *360*
David, *314,* 315
DDT, *781*
De Beers Mining Company, *623*
de Cárdenas, Juan, 436
De Gouges, Marie-Olympes, 573–574
de la Vega, Garcilaso, 506
de Quadros, Jeronimo, 411, 419
de Sade, Marquis, 581
Death/burial customs, 57, *57, 192, 354, 442*
in Americas, 53–54, 116, 241, *245,* 245–246
ancient Chinese, 68
in Bulgaria, *54*
Cahokia, 268–269
Egyptian, 64–65, *65,* 164–165, *165*
Etruscan, 108, *108*
Greek, ancient, 105

Homo ergaster, 6
Homo neaderthalensis, 7
in Ice Age, *18,* 18–19, *19*
at Jericho, 37, *37*
Mesoamerica, 174
Neanderthal, 704
Peru, 241
Roman, *165*
Debra Hayq, 271
Debra Libanos, 271
Declaration of the Rights of Man and the Citizen, 580, G–2
Declaration of the Rights of Woman and of the Female Citizen (De Gouges), 573
Decolonization, G–2
chronology, *744*
in twentieth century, 738–741, *740*
Deficiency diseases, 522
Defoe, Daniel, 530
Deforestation, 38, 451, 533, 786, G–2
map of, *786*
Deism, *574*
Delhi, 331, 423, 527, *527,* 543
Delhi Sultanate, 331–332, *332*
Delhi sultans, 359–360
Delphi oracle, 104, *139,* 160
Democracy, 681–683, 742–743, G–2
after World War II, 731
chronology, *686*
Greek, ancient, 105, 135–136
post World War I, 725
Democracy in America (Tocqueville), 682
Democritus, 139, 147
Demokrateia, 105, G–2
Demon Master, 306
Deng Xiaoping, 737
Dengue fever, 791
Depression of 1929, 725
Descartes, René, 482, *482*
Desegregation, 759
Desertification, 780
Designer babies, 703
Dessalines, Jean-Jacques, 625
Devsirme, G–2
Dharma, 214, G–2
d'Holbach, Baron, 576
Diabetes, 702, 789
type-II, 783
Dialogue Between a Brahman and a Jesuit (Voltaire), 567
Diamond, Jared, 6
Diamond mining, 455, 620, 623, *623*
Dias, Manuel, 484
Diaspora, 130, 630
Dibble tool, 33
Dictators, 165
Diderot, Denis, 558, 566, 572, *572,* 574, 579
Diffusion, 38, G–3
Diffusionist theory of civilization, 92
Dike building, *450*
d'Incarville, Pierre Nicole le Chéron, 532
Diogo de Silves, *399*
Direct rule, 204, 658
Dirlik, 497, G–3
Diseases, 789–792
in the Americas, 506
and children, 703
deficiency, 522
ecology of (migration), 523–524
in Eurasia, 443–444
and health, 590
and Native Americans, 428, *442,* 442–443, 506, 518
during warfare, 646
Disney, Walt, 713
Diu, 425
Divination. *See* Oracles
Divine love, 134, *134,* G–3
Diviners, 80–81
Divorce in ancient river civilizations, 63
DNA, 703
Doctor Faustus, 480
Doctrines of superiority, 658–660
Dodens, Rembert, 569
Doll's House, A (Ibsen), 629
Dome of the Rock, *226*
Domestication of animals, 659
Domingo de la Calzada, 279
Dominicans, 480, G–3
Doña Marina, *428,* 428–429
Dong Shou, 192
Dorset culture, 113
Dream of the Eastern Capital's Splendor (Master Meng), 307
Dresden Codex, *242*
Dreyfus, Alfred, 669
Drinking, 104
Drought of 1876–1878, 661
Drugs
illegal, 767
medicinal in eighteenth century, 522
Druze, 287, G–3
Dual role, 650
Dualism, *146,* 215, G–3
Duchamp, Marcel, 710
Duke of Connaught, *634*
Dunhuang, 156, 157, 215, *215,* 227
Duration concept, 707
Durum wheat, 248
Dust Bowl, 780
Dutch
conquest of Aceh, 646
in East Indies, 547–548
Dutch East India Company, 417, 418, *418,* 441, 448, *527,* 553, 567, 569, G–3
Dutch East Indies, 547–548, 651, 653, G–3
Dutch Indonesia and Western science, 698
Dvorák, Anton, 636
Dysentery, 443

E

Earth
and Ice Age, 13
revolution of, 481–482
shape of, 564–565, *565*
East, foreign imperialism, *642,* 642–643
East Africa, 403. *See also* Africa
contending with isolationism, *280*
in eighteenth century, 539–540
expansion of in eleventh and twelfth centuries, 270–271
in fifteenth century, 377, *384*
population in eighteenth century, 518
East India trade, 455, G–3
East Indies, 738
relations with Netherlands, 421
Easter Island, 254, 366–367, *367*
Easterlies, 413, G–3
Eastern Christendom, 466
Eastern Mediterranean, 84–85
chronology, *85*
map of, *83*
Eastern Orthodox Christians, 300
Ebla, 77, *77*
Ebola, 790
Ebu us-Suud, 497
Ecological alarmism, 787–788
Ecological exchange, 436–442, *438–439,* 533, G–3
patterns of, 441–442
Ecological imperialism, 381–385, G–3
Ecology, 705
Ecology of civilization, 55–56, G–3
Economic liberalism, 624, G–3
Economic refugees, 418
Economy. *See also* Commerce; Imperialism
of Africans, 116, 118
of ancient Middle East, 98–103
chronology, *535, 536*
in eighteenth century, 524–537
chronology, *528*
Enlightenment, 573
global, 762–766
Hittites, 77–79, *78*
Japanese, 605–606
map of in Anatolia and Mesopotamia, *78–79*
of Phoenicians, 98–99
post World War I, 725
Song empire, 306–307
South American, 627
Ecuador, *642,* 670
Edessa, battle of, *197*
Edo, 504, 505, *519,* G–3
Education, 680, 751, *755*
Greece, ancient, 144
in nineteenth century, 629
Edward VIII, king of England, 783
Edwards, Bryan, 534
Edwards, Jonathan, 575
Egalitarianism, 358, 624
Egg, Augustus, 620
Eggplant, 248
Egypt, 97, 162, 296, 425, 622
ancient civilization, *50,* 56–58, 62–63
ancient government, 64–65
ancient politics, *69*
centralization, 674
cities of ancient, 62–63
conquest by Britain, 647
decline of, 92–93, *93*
decline of ancient, 84–85
decolonization in twentieth century, 739
ecology of ancient, 56–58, *58*
ecology of civilization, *63*
effect of plague, 357
emancipation of slaves, 626
expansion of ancient, 69–70
imperialism, 609–610
industrialization, 609–610
invasion by Ottomans, 425
map of ancient, *58*
nationalism, 671
plague in, *349*
religion, 767
survival of ancient, 92–93
in thirteenth century, 330–331
and Western science, 480, 699
writing, 71
Egyptian Book of Instructions, 63
Egyptian Wafd, 724
Eight-Deer Tiger-Claw, 270
Einkorn, 44, *44*
Einstein, Albert, 700–701, *702, 710*
Eisaku, Wada, 711
El Niño, 89, 241, 344, 369, 590, G–3
El Salvador, 670
élan vital, 707, G–3
Electrical technology, *601*
Electricity, 600, 778
Electromagnetic induction machine, 600
Electronic Numerical Integrator and Computer, *704*
Eliot, John, 467
Elites, 18, 23, 51, 52, *53,* 65, 68, 72, 76, 82, 83, 106, 136, 143, 165, 174, 181, 182, 192, 194, 198, 206, 216, 220, 225, 271, 298, 303, 308, 328, 356, 357, 360, 368, 392, 394, 451, 465, 497, 503, 507, 540, 544, 547, 557, 583, 604, 605, 607, 608, 611, 631, 634–635, 652, 685, 720, 767
Elizabeth I, queen of England, 494, *494*
Ellis Island, *630*
Elmina, fort, *552*
Elvin, Mark, 343, 526
Emancipation Proclamation (1863), 626
Embryos, 703
Emishi, 249
Emmer, 44
Emperor worship, *217,* 217–218
Empires
in the Americas, 426–429
chronology, *431, 558*
chronology, *172, 560*
dynamics of, 151–152, *153*
effect of, 411–412
land, *413*
map of American, *427*
maritime, 412–421, *413*
in the New World, 554–558
in sixteenth and seventeenth century, map of, *422*
trading-post, 415
transformation of, *199*
Empirical, 333, 701, G–3
Empiricism, 333, 482, G–3
Employment, 598
and industrialization, *621*
Emporium trading, *158,* G–3
Encyclopeida (Reasoned Dictionary of the Sciences, Arts and Trades) (Diderot), 572, *572,* 660, G–8
Energy, 456
chronology, *600*
demand for, 589
and industrialization, 597
renewable, 779
Engineering
in eleventh century Europe, 277–278
in Roman Empire, 164
England, 490. *See also* Britain
in the Americas, 455–456
chronology, *430*
art, *532, 534*
colonies in North America, 505–509
imperialism, 449
in India, 544–547
industrial revolution, 529–531
land reclamation, 457
plague in, 350
relations with Netherlands, 421
and Revolutionary War, 556
English Civil Wars (1640-1653), 494–495
English East India Company, 421
English language, 767
Enki (god), 60
Enlightened despotism, 566, G–3
Enlightenment, 562–585, G–3
in Asia, 568–572
chronology, 580, *584*
in Europe, 572–575
religion and Romanticism, 575–580
Enlil (god), 70
Enthusiasm, 476, 530, G–3

Entrepreneurship, 599
Environment, *254,* 8, 13, 22, *22,* *32,* 32–38, 43–45, *45,* *63,* 86–87, 240, 243, 245–246, *246,* *247,* 248, 345–348, *348,* 437, *459,* 775–795
Environmental disasters, 343–372
Ephesus, 147
Epic of Gilgamesh, 66, 71
Epicurus, 142, 143–144, *146*
Epidemics, 522
Epistemology, 482, G–3
Equatoria, province of, 647
Equatorial Guinea, 739
Equiano, Olaudah, *548*
Equilibrium trap, 526, G–3
Erasmus of Rotterdam, 478
Eratosthenes, 140, *140*
Ernst, Max, 712
Erythraean Sea, 156
Esarhaddon, king, *99*
Esmeraldas, *507,* 508
Essay on the Principle of Population (Malthus), 517
Estado da India, 417
Estates General, 580
Ethics, 143
Ethiopia, 36, *193,* 218, 225, 257, 270, *274,* 385, 419, 448, *475,* 553, 647, *647,* 666, 677–678, 681
  chronology, *193,* *377*
  contending with isolationism, *280*
  decline of, 237
  development of, *205*
  in fifteenth century, 377, 379, *384*
  rise of, 193–194
Ethne, *118*
Ethnicity, *632*
Etiquette and the Perfect Lady, 651
Etruscans, 108–109
Euboea, 103
Eucherius, *188*
Eugenics, 703, 725, G–3
Eunuchs, 189–191, G–3
Euphrates River, 37, 55, 59
Eurasia
  chronology of empires, *172*
  commerce, 153–156
  cultural exchange, 112–113, *114–115*
  empires in fifteenth century, 385–391
  expansion of in eleventh and twelfth centuries, 275–284
  exploitation of environment, *459*
  imperialism, map of, *447*
  intensified settlements of, 54–55, *55*
  plagues of, 348–358, 443–444
  trade routes, *154–155*
Euro, 744
Europe
  chronology of sixteenth and seventeenth centuries, *492*
  chronology of technology and growth, *281*
  climate change in the fourteenth century, *348*
  democracy, 682–683
  Enlightenment, 562–585
  expansion in South and Southeast Asia, *546*
  imperialism, 411–412, 449–451
    chronology, *405,* *455*
    resistance to, *669*
  industrialization, 601–603, *602*
  map of in twentieth century, *722*
  map of oceanic explorations, *400–401*
  nationalism, 666–668, *667*
  political change in, 490–492
  political extremism, 727
  social transformation of, 493–498, *496*
  spread of agriculture in, 38
  in thirteenth century, 332–336, *337*
  unification in sixteenth and seventeenth centuries, 490–492
European Coal and Steel Community, 744
European Union (EU), 743–745, G–3
Eusebius, 224
Euthanasia, 771
Evangelical Christianity, 576, 624
Evangelical Protestants, 466
Evans, John, 561
Eve (African), 7–8
Eve (biblical), *178–179*
Evolution, 5–7, G–3
  in Africa, 7–13
  early migration, 9–13
    map of, *10–11*
  theory of, 6
Evolution, theory of, 659, *659,* 680, 695, 702–703
Examination system, 308, 674, G–3
Execution, *770*
Existentialism, *708,* 708–709, G–3
Exodus (Bible), *349*
Expressionism, 712
Extinction of animals, 785–787
Ezana, king, 218, *225*
Ezekiel, 98, *555*

F

Factories, 616–617, 628, G–3
  in eighteenth century, 525
Faith of God, 477
"Fall of Makassar" (Woldemar), *421*
Fallopio, Gabriele, 494
Family
  in ancient Greece, 105
  in China, 503
  in eleventh century, 298
  in sixteenth and seventeenth centuries, 494
  in twentieth century, 757
Famine, 590, 661, 782
Fantasy novel, 713
Fanti, 671, 672
Faraday, Michael, 600
Farmers, violence with herders, 33–34
Farming. *See also* Agriculture; Tilling/tillers
  compared to foraging, *31*
  disadvantages of, 30
  origin of, 42–45
Fars, 157, 158, 197
Fascism, 727–728, G–3
Fascists, 727
Fast food, 783
Fat
  in prehistorical society, 16
  supply of, 589
Fatimid caliphate, 290
Fatimids, 287–288, 309, G–3
Fat-tailed sheep, 310
Faxian, 192
Fayyum portraits, *165*
Feasting, 43
Federal Republic of Germany, 731
Feminism, 573–574, G–3
Feng Guifen, 683
Fenlands, 457
Ferdinand I, 478
Ferghana, 157
Fertility goddess, *39*
Fertilization of land, 781
Fertilizer, 594
Feudal tenure, 506
Fezzan, 108
Fifteenth century, chronology of, *405*
Film industry, 713
Final Cause (Aristotle), 142
Final Solution, 725, 771, G–3
Finland, 657
Firepower technology, 424
First Crusade, 301
Fish, depletion of, 786
Fish farming, 22, 533, 787
Fitzroy, Robert, *659*
Fixed-wind systems, 156, G–3
Flagellants, *351,* 354
Flintstones, The (television series), 16
Floodplains in ancient civilizations, 56–62
Florence, 349
  in fifteenth century, 402
Florida, colony, 430, 437, 454
Floris V, count, 278
Food
  chronology, *600*
  exchange among countries, 435–436
  production, 590–596
  production in eighteenth century, 519, 522
  production in nineteenth century, 594–596, *595*
  production in twentieth century, 780–784
  resources, 23, *783,* *789*
  shortages, 57–58, 776–777
  technology, *601*
  and urbanization, 620
Foot binding, 503
Foragers, 9, 21–22, 28–30
  dates of settlements, *30*
Foraging, 31
  compared to farming, *31*
Foreign Language Institute (Beijing), 695
Forests, 612, 786
Fornication, 465
Fort Jesus, *538,* 539
Fortuyn, Pim, *763*
Fossil fuels, 597, *601,* 778–779, G–3
Fourier, Charles, 684
Fourteenth century, chronology of, *372*
Fourth Crusade, 302
Fouta Jalon, 679
Fouta Toro, 679
France, 490. *See also* French Revolution
  in British North America, 557
  in Canada, 557
  conquest of Indochina, 646
  decolonization in twentieth century, 738–739
  emancipation of slaves, 626
  imperialism, 643
  imperialism in Indochina, 628
  industrialization, 596, 603
  in Mexico, 652
  nationalism, 669
  in North America, 554
  plague in, 50
  population in eighteenth century, 519
  and Revolutionary War, 557, *558*
  Seven Years' War (1756-1763), 557
  and territorial imperialism, 421
  World War I, 720
  World War II, 729
Francis Borja, St., *467*
Francis I, king of France, 478
Francis of Assisi, St., 334–335, *336*
Francis Xavier, St., *467*
Franciscans, 335, 358, 392, 403, 467, 468, *469,* G–3
  art, 335, *336*
  and millenarianism, 476–477
Franco-Prussian War (1870-1871), 675
Frankfurt School, 708
Franklin, Benjamin, *522,* 529
Franks, 188, 222, 255
Fraticelli, 392
Frederick the Great, king of Prussia, 576
Free association, 706
Free trade, 573, 604, 624, G–3
Free will, 707
Freemasonry, 574
Freemason's Lodge of Freetown, *634*
Freetown, *634,* 651
French Revolution, 531, 580–583, 596, 625, 642, 682, G–3. *See also* France
  Bastille, fall of, 580, *581*
  chronology, *583*
  Declaration of the Rights of Man and the Citizen, 580
French Royal Academy of Science, 564
Freud, Sigmund, 705–706, *711*
Frisia, *419*
Frobisher, Martin, 455
"Frozen Thames, The," *345*
Fudo Myo-o, *362*
Fuel resources, 778–780, *783,* *789*
Fujian, 437, 450
Fujiwara, 205
Fujiwara no Michizane, 276
Fulani, 553, *553,* G–3
Full Gospel Church, 770
Fulton, Robert, 600
Funan, 193
  development of, *205*
Fundamentalism, 769–770, G–3
Fur trade, 455, 457
  in the Americas, 431
  in Russia, 386, 422
Futa Jallon, 553
Futa Toro, 553
Futurism, 709, G–3

G

Gabriel (Archangel), 197
Gabriele de' Mussis, 354
Gage, Thomas, 441
Galápagos Islands, 659
Galdós, Pérez, 634
Galilei, Galileo, 484, 529, *529*
Galvani, Luigi, 529
Gambling, 619
Gandhara, 162
Gandhi, Mohandas, 724, *725*
Ganges Valley, 111–112, 166, 332
  chronology, *119*
  civilization of, *118*
Gansu, 171
Gao, 238, 378
Garamantes, 108, 116
Gardar, 266
Garden of Eden, *178–179*
Garden suburbs, 599
Gardening, global, 532–536
Garneray, Ambroise-Louis, *588*
Garrido, Juan, 436
Garum, 165
Garvey, Marcus, 760
Gaspard, Etienne Robert, 583
Gaspée (ship), 556
Gassed (painting) (Sargent), *724*

Gauchos, 622, 670, *670*, G–3
Gaudi, Antoni, 619
Gaul, 222
Gautama Siddharta, 127, *146*
Gaza, 99
Gembo, 221
Gender. *See* Male dominance; Women
General will, 577–578, G–3
Generation gap, 756
Genes, 703
Genesis (Biblical), 135
Genetic engineering, 6
Genetic revolution, 782, G–3
Genetically modification, 702–703
Genetically modified crops, 782, *782*
See also GM
Genetics, 702, *711*
Genghis Khan, 316, *317*, 317–318, 320, 328, 329, 331–332, 387, 446, 498
Genji, 283
Genoa, 279, 333
Genocide, 429, 750, G–4
map of, *752–753*
Genoese, 403
Gentile of Foligno, 354
Genus, 5
Geoffrey of Monmouth, 283
Geography
in fifteenth century, *376*, 402
in thirteenth century, 337
Geography (Ptolemy), *376*
Geometry, 138
George II, king of England, 523, 576
Georgia, 445
Georgia (country), 218, *314*, 315, 319
Georgians, 218, *219*
Gerald of Wales, 279–280
Gerbert of Aurillac, 283
German Reich, *752*
Germanic tribes, 164
and fall of Roman Empire, 184–185
Lombards, 195
Ostrogoths, 189
Visigoths, 155, 188, 206
Germany, 490
centralization, 674
democracy, 683
imperialism, 643
industrialization, 603
mob violence, 354
nationalism, 666
partitioning, 731
socialism, 686
World War I, 720–721, 723
World War II, 729–731
Gero of Cologne, archbishop, 283, *283*
Gerrha, 153
Gettysburg, *674*
Geza I, king, *297*
Ghana, 238, 257, 293, 671, 672, 739, G–4
Ghazna, 331
Ghazni, 224
Ghost Dance, 681
Ghurids, 331
Gilani, 296
Gilgamesh, *66*, 66–67, 70
Giotto, *336*
Giraffe in China, 293
Giselle (ballet), *700*
Gisho, *262*
Glacier growth in fourth century, 344–345
Glass making, 336
Global gardening, 532–536, G–4
Global trade, *604*
Global warming, 43, 788–789
Globalization, G–4
chronology, *767*
and culture, 17, 766–767
and global economy, 762–766
Glorious Revolution, 490
Glyph, 174, G–4
GM, 782, *782*, G–4
Goa, 419, 420, 421
Gõberkli Tepe, 30
Gobi Desert, 777
Gobineau, Count de, 660
Gobnet, St., 232
God
belief in, 564, 702–703
monotheistic, 132–133
Godaigo, emperor, 362
Gõdel, Kurt, 701
Goede, C.A.G., 616
Goibhnin, 232
Gojam, 377
Gold, 365, 620
technology, 89
in West Africa, 398, 511
Gold rushes, 655
Golden Gate, *289*
Golden Horde, 329, G–4
Golden Number, 137
Golding, William, 715
Goldsmith, Oliver, 566
Goodall, Jane, 12, *12*, 705
Gorbachev, Mikhail, 737
Gordon, Charles, 661
Gorée, 552
Gorillas, 5–6
Gosse, Thomas, *534*
Government, 751
absolute sovereignty, 405
ancient Egypt, 64–65
autocratic, 497
Byzantine Empire, 296–297
city-states, 106, 280
democracy, 742–743
despotism, 566
early Chinese, 190–191
in eleventh and twelfth centuries, 281
Enlightenment, 566, 577–578
imperialism, 166–172
and industrialization, *621*
Mesopotamia, 65–66
monarchy, 165, 188, *496*, 555, 650
Persian, 159–160
post World War I, 725
Roman Empire, 165, 184, 188, 189
in sixteenth and seventeenth centuries China, 501–503
sovereignty, 506, 580, 673
state system, 490, 492–493, *496*
in twentieth century, 712
Goya, Francisco, *4*, *5*, 583, *583*
Graham, Sylvester, 596
Graham cracker, 596
Grain elevators, 591
Grains, 64, 591
Grammar, 708
Gran Colombia, 670
Granada, 402
Grand Army, 596
Grand Canal (China), 200–201, 392
Grand Vizier, 497, G–4
Grapes, 436
Graphic, The (newspaper), 647
Grasses, in the Americas, 437
Grasslands, map of, *339*
Gravity, 482
Great Cultural Revolution (China), *736*, 737
Great Depression (1930s), 750
Great Drowning (1362), 345
Great East Asia Co-Prosperity Sphere, 720, G–4
Great Jaguar Paw, 182
Great River Valley civilizations, 50–73
chronology, *68*, *72*
ecology of civilization, 55–56
great floodplains, 56–62
growing communities, 52–55
map of, *55*
society/social classes, 62–72
Great Satans, 769
Great Wall of China, *136*, 170
Great Zimbabwe, 377, *377*, *378*
in fifteenth century, *384*
Greece
ancient
art, *104*
chronology, *108*, *119*
civilization of, *118*
colonialism, 104–105
democracy, 135–136
education, 144
environment, 103–104
literature, 104–105
medicine, 141
origins of science, 139–140
purity, 106
society/social classes, *105*, 105–106
war with Persia, 159–161
and Basil II, 298
and democracy, 683
nationalism, 668
Greek purity concept, 106
Green revolution, 741, 782, G–4
Greenhouse effect, 779, G–4
Greenland, 265–266, 345, 369–370
contending with isolationism, *280*
expansion in eleventh and twelfth centuries, 264–266
Gregorian Reform, 282
Gregory the Great, pope, 226
Gregory the Illuminator, 218
Gregory VII, pope, 282
Grey, Edward, 726
Grey, Lord, 671
Gross domestic product (GDP), 754
Grotius, Hugo, 493
Grünewald, Matthias, 466
Gu Hongzhong, *308*
Gu Yanwu, 483
Guadalquivir River, 248
Guam, 658
Guanaco, 35
Guangdong, 450
Guangzhou, 519, 525, *638*, *641*, 672
Guangzhou massacre, 216
Guangzxi, 450
Guano, 594, 605
Guanzhou, *526*
Guardians, 135, G–4
Guatemala, *246*, *474*, 670, 769
Guillotine, *770*
Guizhou, 450
Gujarat, 418
Gujerati, 760
Gulf Stream, 413
Gunpowder, 390, 447, 484
invention of, 333
Guntur, 590
Guomindang (GMD), G–4
Gupta dynasty, 191–192, 250
transformation of, *199*
Gyerspungs, 222
Gyoki, 249

H

Haber, Fritz, 781
Habsburg dynasty, *419*
Habsburg Empire, 626, 720
imperialism, 643
nationalism, *667*, 668
Habsburgs, 668, G–4
Hagia Sophia, 223, *300*
Haider, Jurgen, *763*
Haiti, 440, 629
rebellion, 625
revolution, 558
Haj, *372*, G–4
Hajj, *232*
Hakudo, Nagatomi, 749
Halfpenny, William, 567
Hamadan, 157
Hamas, *742*
Hammurabi, 66
Hammurabi, Code of, 66
Han, 170–171, G–4
Han China, 170–171
Han dynasty, *157*, 170–171, 172, 189, 191
chronology, *171*
transformation of, *199*
Han Feizi, 144, *146*
Han Shan, 469
Han Wudi, 170
Handel, George Fredrich, 576
Hangzhou, 524
Hanseatic League, 279, G–4
Harappa, 58, 62
ancient politics, *69*
decline of, *93*, 111
Harappan civilization, 58–59
ancient government, 68–69
decline of, 85–86, *86*, 111
map of, *59*
writing, *59*, 71
Harbin, 719
Hard labor, 627
Harem, 80, G–4
Hari Rai, 477
Harkhuf, 92–93
Harlan, Jack L., 30
Harold Bluetooth, 223
Harrison, John, 578
Harsha, 194
Harun al-Rashid, caliph, 225
Hasan al-Basri, 228
Hastayar, 75
Hatshepsut, Queen, 57
Hatti, 76
Hattusa, 80
Hattusili, 75–76
Hausa, 473, 651
Hausaland, 473
Hawaii, 254, 658
in eighteenth century, 533
Hayan Wuruk, 361
Hayden, Joseph, 659
Hayek, F.A. von, 735
Hazlitt, William, 517, 610
Headlong Hall (Peacock), 684
Healing cult, *715*
Health care, 751
Health education, 751
Heart diseases, 783, 791
Hebei, 203
Hebrew Art of the Covenant, 133
Hegemony, 160, 694, 714
Heian, *276*
Heidegger, Martin, 708
Heine, Heinrich, 668
Heinz, Henry, 617, 618
Heisenberg, Werner, 701, 732
Helen of Troy, *302*
"Hell's mouth," *282*
Helmont, J.B. van, 482
Helsinki Agreement (1975), 742

Henotheism, 132
Henry of Finland, 333
Henry VIII, king of England, 478
Hera of Samos, 104
Heraclitus, 147
Herbal medicine, *695,* 714
Herbalism, 714
Herder, Johann Gottfried, 577
Herding/herders, 3–33, *26,* 27–28, 448, G-4
compared with tilling/tillers, *34*
map of environment, *29*
violence with farmers, 33–34
Heresies, 281–282
Hergé, *718*
Hermes Trismegistos (Hermes Thrice-Blessed), 480
Herodotus, 172
Herrnhut, 575
Herto, 8
Hesiod, 104
Hideyoshi, Toyotomi, 416–417, 456
Hieroglyphs, 71, *71*
Highlanders of Scotland, 668
High-level equilibrium trap, 526, 529, G-4
Hilda of Merschede, abbess, 229, 283
Hildebrand, 185
Hildebrandslied, 185
Hill, James, 600
Hindu/Hinduism, 222, 232, 271, 272, 360, 361, 388, 544, G-4
in Chola Kingdom, 275
and commerce, 419
in India, 331, 477
Hine, Lewis, *630*
Hino Meishi, 362
Hippocrates, 141, 142
Hippocratics, 141
Hippolytus, *302*
Hiroshige, *591*
Hiroshima, *729,* 731
Hiru, 253
Hispaniola, *374,* 426, 436, 442, G-4
History of Canada (Creux), *457*
Hitler, Adolf, 728, 729–731
Hittites, 76–93
art, *74*
chronology, *81*
decline of, *93*
military/weaponry, 80
politics, 79–81
society, 79–81
trade, 77–79, *78*
HIV, 790, *792*
Ho Chih Minh, 727
Ho Xuang Huong, 571
Hogenberg, Franz, *454*
Hohokam People, 345, 348, G-4
Hokkaido, 449, 456
Holland, 417, 419, 490
agriculture, 441
land reclamation, 456–457
Hollywood, 712, *713*
Holocaust, 750, *750,* G-4
Holy Roman Empire, 490, G-4
Holy Sepulcher, *289*
Holy war, 212, 289
Homeland Security, *754*
Homer, 104, 283, 303
Homestead Act (1862), 594
Homo erectus, 6, G-4
migration of, *10*
Homo ergaster, 6, G-4
Homo floresiensis, 7, *10*
Homo habilis, 6, G-4
Homo neanderthalensis, 7
Homo sapiens, 6, 7, 704, G-4
evolution from Africa, 8–13
migration of, *10*
Homo species, 6–7
Honda Toshiaki, 656
Honduras, 670
Hong Kong, 640
Hongxi emperor, 394
Honshu, 457
Honshu island, 30, 249
Hooghly, 419
Hoogly, *527*
Hooke, Robert, 529
Hopkins, Gerard Manley, 619
Horace, 151, 162
Hormuz, *410,* 419
Horses, 337
in the Americas, 428
in art, *157*
domestication of, 54
in Mongolian society, 324
Horton, James Africanus, 670, 672
Houdon, Jean-Antoine, *566*
Houel, Jean-Pierre, *581*
Housing, *789*
Huaca de los Reyes, 89
Huaca del Dragón, *368*
Huai River, 70, 250, 304
Huai valley, 350
Huang Chao, 303
Huang Zongxi, 502
Huari, 241
Hubble, Edwin, 701, *710*
Hubei, 62
Hui Shi, 143, 145
Hui Shih, 138
Hui-te-Rangiora, 255
Hülegü, *320*
Human, diversity of, 479–480
Human cloning, 703
Human nature, 134, 569
Human rights, 704, 742–743, 761, 771, G-4
Human sacrifice, 88, *88,* 470, 479, 510
Human sciences, 702–705
Human species, 5
chronology, *23*
dates of early migration, *8*
evolution of, 5–7
first, 6–9
Homo erectus, 6, *10*
Homo ergaster, 6
Homo floresiensis, 7, *10*
Homo habilis, 6
Homo neanderthalensis, 7
Homo sapiens, 6–13
map of early migration, *10–11*
Humanism, 402, 715–716, G-4
Humbert, Cardinal, 300
Humboldt, Alexander von, 577, *577*
Humboldt, Baron von, 560
Humboldt Current, 431
Hume, David, 575
Hume, Edward H., *692,* 693, 695, 714
Humoral theory of medicine, 522
Hunan, 443
Hunan-Yale Medical College, 693
Hungary, 425, 478
art, *297*
in fourteenth century, 370
invasion by Ottomans, 425, *446*
nationalism, 668
Huns, 185, 189, 222
invasion of India, 191–192
Hunters, 630–631
in Ice Age, 16
Hunters-gatherers, 245
Hunting, 457
and male dominance, 12
Huntsman, Benjamin, 526
Hurons, 430–431, 443, *457,* 579–580, G-4
Hurricane Katrina, 788, *788*
Husain, 501
Husayn al-Jisr, 699
Husbandry, 27–28, 30–31, G-4. *See also* Animal husbandry; Plant husbandry
geographic diffusion of, 30–38
Hybrid human, 6
Hyderabad, 544
Hydroelectric projects, 779
Hydroelectricity, 779
Hydrogen as energy source, 779
Hyeyong, 220
Hygiene in eighteenth century, 522
Hyksos, 84, 93
Hypnosis, 529, 706

I

Ibbitt, William, *616*
Iberia, 219
Ibn Battuta, *342,* 343, 351, 359–360, 365
map of travels, *353*
Ibn Hwqal, 248
Ibn Khaldun, 309, 364, *366,* 369, 386
Ibn Khatib, 354
Ibn Saud, 723
Ibn Tughluq, 359–360, *360*
Ibn Wahab, 211, 232
Ibrahim al Halabi, *497*
Ibsen, Henrik, 629
Icaria, 684
Ice Age, 13–21, 786, 788
affluence, 16
art in, *16,* 16–17, *17*
culture and society, 17–19
dates of, *17*
hunters, 16
life in, 16, *16,* 17–19, *19*
map of, *14–15*
writing, 18
Ice-Age affluence, 16, G-4
Iceland, 222
I-ching, 251
Icon, *494,* G-4
Ife, 379
Igel, 165
Il Quarto Stato (Pelizza), *685*
Ilg, Alred, 678
Iliad (Homer), 104–105
Il-Khan, 325, 329, *329,* 370, G-4
art, 329, *329*
Il-Khan art, 329, *329*
Il-Khan Ghazan, 329
Il-Khanate, 329, G-4
Illusion, challenging, 137
Illyria/Illyrians, 106
Iltutmish, 331, 332
Imam, 287, 539, G-4
Imbalanga, 489
Immigration, 450, 630, *630,* 757–762, *759*
to the Americas, 444–445
and industrialization, 604
Immunization, 751
Imperator, 165, G-4
Imperialism, 411–412, 704, 723, 734, 737, G-4. *See also* Commerce
in Africa, *653*
in Asia, 540–544, *653*
chronology, *543*
business, *652,* 652–655
in China, 169–172, 391–394, 404
chronology, *455,* 535, *658, 662*
ecological, 381–385
in Europe and Asia, 449–451
foreign in East and Southeast Asia, *642,* 642–643
in India, 166–169, 275, 404, 451, 544–547
Japan, 449, 656, *657, 658*
map of, *546*
map of in Eurasia, *447*
maritime, chronology, *405, 421*
methods of ruling, 648–651
in the New Europes, 655–656
in New World, 554–561
oceanic, 395–398
chronology, *398*
pastoral, 448–449
rationales for, 658–661
resistance, *669*
Russia, 657–658, *658*
steppeland, 390, 446–448
and technology, *648*
United States, 658, *658*
white, 641–648
world map of, *644–645*
Imperialists, 623, 653
Inca Empire, 381–385, *454*
in fifteenth century, *383, 384*
Incas, 403, 426, 429, 506, 556, G-4
chronology, *382*
Incest, 80
Indentured labor, 444, 626–628, *627*
Indeterminacy principle, 701
India, 418, 738, 743, 762
ancient civilization, 111–112
architecture, *333*
art, 712
barbarian invasions of, 206
as British colony, 651
census, 456
chronology, *112*
chronology of dynasties, *191*
civilizing, 660, *661*
commerce, 153–159
contending with isolationism, *280*
decolonization, 738
dynasties, *191*
economy, 765
economy and culture, 273–274
economy in eighteenth century, 526–528, *527,* 536–537
Enlightenment, 567, 584
expansion of in eleventh and twelfth centuries, 273–275, 284
in fourteenth century, *369*
government, 167–168
imperialism, 166–169, 404, 451, 544–547, 648, 650
indentured labor, 627
industrialization, 608–609
and invaders, 289
invasion of, 191–192
life expectancy, 789
and maritime imperialism, 414–415
medicine, 141
missionary effects in, 477
Mughals, 423–424, 498
Muslim, 331–332
origins of medicine, 141
and plague, 359–360
population, 794
and Portugal's trading posts, *417*
post World War I, 724
railways, 599, *599,* 600
religion, 127, 477
science, 714
spread of agriculture, 42
and spread of Buddhism, 222
Western science in, 698
Indian Civil Service, *651*
Indian National Congress, 671, G-4
Indian Ocean, 270, 284, 375, *376,* 395
expansion around, 270–275
map of, *274*

map of maritime imperialism, *416*
trade routes, 152–153, *154–155,* 156
Indigo planting, 622
Indios, 652
Indirect rule, 650–651, *651,* 656, G–4
Individual gratification, 756
Individualism, 686, 754–755, G–4
Indochina, *648,* 650, 653, 738
expansion of, 251
and France, 628, 646
Indo-European languages, 38, G–4
Indonesia, 643, 724, *738*
communists, *727*
Indra (god), 86
Inductive method, 482, G–4
Indus, 55, 111
Indus River, 37, 58, 86
Indus Valley, 55–56, 58–59, 86
ecology of civilization, *63*
Industrial Revolution, 530, G–4
Industrialization, 526, 528–532, *621,* G–4
and agriculture, 594–596, *595*
Americas, 604–605
Canada, 604
China, 607–608
chronology, *610, 611, 623*
effect on environment, 615–620
Egypt, 609–610
in eleventh and twelfth centuries, *281*
Europe, 601–603, *602*
India, 608–609
Japan, 605–607
Latin America, 604–605
in nineteenth century, 597–601
philanthropic, 616–620
United States, 604
Infanticide, 563
Inflation, 755
Influenza, 349, 442, 791
pandemic, 590
Information age, 755
Information revolution, 741
Information technology, 766, G–4
Ingvary Ingvarevitch, 330
Inkarrí movements, 477
Inquisition, 465, G–5
Insulin, 702
Intensified settlements, 54–55, *55*
Internal combustion engine, 601, 778
International Criminal Court, 743
Internet, *690–691,* 766
users, 766, *766*
Introspection, 706
Inuit, 21–22, 23, 32
contending with isolationism, *280*
Inventions, 700
chronology, *701*
in eleventh century Europe, 279
Iran, 288, 655, 723, 767, *768. See also* Persia/Persian Empire
religion, 126–127
and spread of Islam/Islamic, 226
Iraq, 425, 742, 745, 750
invasion by Ottomans, 425
Irawaddy, 251
Ireland, 449, 722
nationalism, 668
potato famine, 590
Irene (empress), 255
Irish cross, *255*
Iron Age, 73
Iron Bridge, 530
Iron Curtain, 731
Iron industry, 529–530
Iron making, 77, 79, 116, 598
Iron pyrites, 455
Iroquois, 457, G–5
Irrigation, 64, 780
Isaac II Angelus, 301
Isabella, queen of Spain, 406
Isaiah (prophet), 159
Isandlhwana, 646
Isfahan, 157, 499, *499*
Ishida Baigan, 569
Ishin Suden, 483
Isidore of Seville, 226
Islam/Islamic, 131, 147, 196–197, 206, 212, 257, 425, 769. *See also* Muslims
and agriculture, 246–248, *247*
architecture, *236*
art, *242*
in Asia, 447
and Christianity relations, 291–292, *293*
chronology of expansion, *200*
conflict and conversion, 212–214, 216
and Crusades, 289–292
in Egypt, 331
Enlightenment Age, 567–568
in fifteenth century, 386–391
food, 246
in fourteenth century, 360
in India, 477
map of, *231, 471*
map of in Africa, *473*
monks, 227–228
and neighbors, 287–295
in nineteenth century, 680
religious communities, 227–228, *228*
revitalization of, *472*
and Sahara invaders, 291–295
in Southeast Asia, 447
spread of, 224–225, *225,* 232–233, 471–473
and steepelanders, 288–289
on trade routes, 216
and Turks, 224
in West Africa, 378–379, 472–473
and Western science, 699
Island of Dr. Moreau, The (Wells), 6
Ismail I, 500, 501
Ismail Mazhir, 699
Isolationism, 263, *280,* 366, 721, G–5
Israel, 130
conflict with Palestine, 741, *742*
Istanbul, *497*
Isthmus of Panama, 431
Isvarcandra Vidyasagar, 662
Italica, 164
Italy, *434,* 490
centralization, 674
city-states, 281
democracy, 731
fascism, 727
imperialism, 643
industrialization, 603
nationalism, 666
war with Ethiopia, 647, *647*
World War I, 720
World War II, 730
Itzamnaaj B'alam, *243*
Ivan IV, czar, 422
Ivan the Great, 386
Ivory Coast, 741, 790
Ixtilxochitl, Fernando de Alva, 506
Izmir, 620

J

Jabel Sahaba, battle of, 12
Jackson, Andrew, *682*
Jainism, 127, 144, G–5
Jains, 127, 134, 137
and commerce, 419
Jamaica, 507, 534, 549
Jamal al-Dinal-Afghani, 699
Jambedkar, Bal Shastri, 584
Jambudvipa, 514–515
James, William, 707
James of Vitry, 315
James the Great, 256
Jamshid, 153
Janissaries, 390, 496–497, 674, G–5
Japan, 204–205, 419, 770
agriculture, 248–249, 532, 591
art, *321, 591,* 711
and Buddhism, 469–470
census, 518
centralization, 674
chronology, *171*
introduction of Buddhism, *221*
isolationism, *277*
civilizing, 660
commerce, 277, 420
constitutionalism, 673
contending with isolationism, *280*
democracy, 731
development of, *205*
economy in eighteenth century, 536
emancipation of slaves, 626
Enlightenment, 567, 569, *570, 571*
expansion of, 257
expansion of in eleventh and twelfth centuries, 276–277
fashion, *635,* 635–636
in fourteenth century, 362–363, *369*
fourteenth century art, *362*
geographic obstacles, *254*
imperialism, 449, 656, *657, 658*
industrialization, 605–607
invasion of Korea, 417
isolationism, 283
land reclamation, 457
Manchurian Incident, 719
map of, *201*
fourteenth century, *363*
and maritime imperialism, 416
migration, 263
militarization, 674
nationalism, 671–672
population, 789
population in eighteenth century, 518–519
post World War II, 763
public sphere, 683
railway system, *606*
relations with China, 204, 277
and religion, 467, 681
rice cultivation, *591*
in sixteenth and seventeenth centuries, 504–505, *505*
social classes, 634
spread of Buddhism, 220–221
spread of Christianity, 467, *467*
stability and change, *505*
study of Dutch language, 569, *569*
trade with Korea, 277
unification of, 172
war relations with China, *748,* 749–750
and western science, 483, 569
World War II, *729,* 729–731
Japan Current, 413
Japonisme, 636
Jasaw Chan Kaui'il, 242
Jatakas, 153
Java, 194, 252, 360–361, 393, 441, 472, *472,* 533, 591, 646
art, *253*
imperialism, 648
invasion by Mongols, 320
Jaxartes, 780
Jayavarman II, king, 251
Jayavarman VII, king, 272–273
Jefferson, Thomas, 556
Jenne-Jeno, 238
Jenner, Edward, 523
Jericho, 37, *37*
Jerusalem, 102, 130, *225*
pilgrimages to, 289, *289*
rebuilding of temple, 159
Jesuits, 464, 466, *467,* 467–468, 555, 567, 574, G–5
in China, *484,* 484–485, 566, 568
in India, 477
in the New World, 442–443
Jesus, 131, 133, 137, 144, *146,* 198, 199, 215, 228, 233, 464
Jews/Judaism, 134, 137, *146,* 198, 725, 728, 741
in ancient civilization, 130
blame for the plague, 354–356
and Crusades, 291–292
development of, 130
emancipation, *668,* 668–669
exile of, 130, *130*
Holocaust, 750, *750*
map of in Medieval Europe and Middle East, *355*
monotheism, 133
nationalism, 668–669
social structure, 494
in White America, 476
Ji Yun, 541
Jiangnan, 607
Jiangxi, 524
Jiddah, 393
Jihad, 212, 216, *225,* 290, 291, G–5
Jihad of the sword, 472
Jihad of words, 472
Jin dynasty, 191
Jodhpur, 477
Johannesburg (South Africa), 620
Johansen, Dan, 6
John (apostle), 132
John of Piano Carpini, 321
John Paul II, pope, 735
John the Baptist, 227
Johnson, Lyndon B., 759
Johnson, Samuel, 536
Johnston-Sirleaf, Ellen, *761*
Joint-stock company, 420, G–5
Joliot, Frédéric, 731–732
Jomon, 30
Jones, William, 567
Jordan Valley, 37
Jordanes, 185
Jorge de Mina, 379
Jornada de la Muerte, 268
Joseph (Biblical), 64
Journal of Medical Research (Indian), 698
Joyce, James, *707*
Juan, Jorge, 576
Judah, 130
Julius Caesar, 163
Jumel, Louis-Alexis, 609
Juntas, 558
Jupiter (god), 227
Jurchen, 304–305
Justinian, emperor, 194–195, *195,* 200, 223, 296
Jute, 622
Jvari, *219*

K

Kaaba, 232, *232,* G–5
Kaempfer, Engelbert, 567
Kaibara Ekken, 569
Kaifeng, 307
Kalahari, 630

Kalahari Desert, 22
Kaleb, king, 193
Kalidasa, 191
Kalinga, 169
Kaliyuga, 191
Kamehameha I, 534
Kamikaze winds, 320, *321*
Kandinsky, Vasily, 710
Kanem, 339
Kanes, 77
Kangaroos, 28
Kangnido, *312–313*
Kangxi emperor, 446–447, 450–451, 503, 568, 569
Kaniska, king, 214, *225*
Kant, Immanuel, 578, 583
Karakhanids, 224
Karakorum, 32, 321
Karnataka, 274
Karr, Alphonse, 684
Kasai, 518
Kashgaria, 329
Kashmir, 194
Kaska, 81
Kaskaskia, 457
Katsina, 676
Kava, 253
Kay, Philip, 619
Kazakstan, 658
Kazan, 422, 449
Keichu, 470
Kemal, Mustafa, 723
Kennedy, John F., 743, 744, 759
Kenniff art, 17
Kenya, 739
Kenyatta, Jomo, 739
Kepler, Johannes, 481
Kerala, 419
Kerry-Nicholls, James, 665, 679
Kertanagara, 361
Key, Ellen, 706
Keynes, John Maynard, 725, 751
Keynesianism, 725, 751, G–5
Khan, *313*, 316, G–5
Khan Kuchum, 423
Khazaks, 631
Khazars, 219
Khedive, 609, G–5
Khedive Ismail, 610, 647, 648
Khitans, 304
Khmer, 251, 271–273, G–5
Khmer Kingdom
  contending with isolationism, *280*
Khoi, 448
Khomeini, Ayatollah Ruhollah, 768, *768*
Khrushchev, Nikita, 732, 735
Kiev, 223, 330
Kimberley (South Africa), 620, 623, *623*
Kimonos, *635*, 635–636
King, Martin Luther Jr., 759
King and I, The (musical), *676*
King Country, 665
King David, *314*, 315
King of Wei, 145
Kipling, Rudyard, 681
Kirgiz nomads, 631
Kittis, 564
Knossos, 82
Knowledge class, 755
Knox, John, 494
Kochi, 263
Koguryo, 172, 192, 219
  development of, *205*
Kokura, 467
Kong Fuzi, 125
Kongo Kingdom, 379, 398, *445*, 511, 552, G–5
  in fifteenth century, *384*
Konya, 288
Korea, 192–193, 504, 532, 656, 733–734
  art, *192, 220*
  chronology
    introduction of Buddhism, *221*
  Enlightenment, 571, *571*
  invasion by Japan, 417
  relations with China, 204–205
  relations with Japan, 204–205
  in sixteenth and seventeenth centuries, *504*
  and society/social class, 504–505
  and spread of Buddhism, 219–220
  trade with Japan, 277
  unification of, 172
  world map, *312–313*
Korean War, 737
Kosa Pan, 571
Kosala, 147
Kosrae Island, 253
Kremlin, 281
Kubilai Khan, 320, *320, 323*, 324, 329, 361
Kücük Kaynarca, treaty, 543
Kuhn, Thomas, 702
Kuk swamp, 33
Kukai, 249
Kulottung I, king, 275
Kulturkampf, G–5
Kumarajiva, 228
Kumasi, 511, 677
Kumbi-Saleh, 238, 293, *363*
Kunta, 472, 553
Kupe, 255
Kur Valley of Fars, 157, 197
Kurdistan, 287
Kurnool, 526
Kurosawa, Akira, *614*
Kush, 93
Kushanese art, *124*
Kussara, 75, 79
Kuwait, 745
Kwanggaet'o, king, 192, 219
KwaZulu-Natal, 377
Kyoto, 358, 503, 504
Kyushu, 456, 519, 532

L

La Venta, 91
Labor
  in the Americas, 444–445
  in ancient river valley civilizations, 62–63
  child, 628
  chronology, *630*
  criminals as source, 626–627
  in eighteenth century, 530
  female, 628–629
  forced, 548
  and industrialization, *621*
  migration of, *627*, 629–631
Lachish, *130*
Lactose tolerance and dairy consumption, 32
Ladinos, 507
Lady of Elche, 109, *109*
Lagash, 70
Lagos, and industrialization, 620
Lahontan, Sieur de, 579
Laissez-faire, 573, 750, 751, G–5
Lake Chad, 339, 345
Lake Titicaca, 35, 241
Lalibela, king, 270–271, *271*
Lamaist Buddhism, 768
Lament of Lady Qin, 303
Lancelot, 403
Land
  exploitation in Americas, 451–456, *452–453*
  overexploitation of, 780–781
  reclamation, 456–457
Land empires, *413*, 422–431
Landholding
  in eighteenth century, 531
  in eleventh century Europe, 279
Language faculty, 707
Language(s), 402, 584, 707–708
  Bantu, 42, 116, 238
  Latin, 296
  Phoenicians, 99
  Sanskrit, 557
  Slav, 297
  sociology of, 707–708
  Swahili, 539–540
Laos, 734, 743
Laozi, 130, 143, *146*
Laplace, Pierre-Simon de, 483, 581
l'Arce, Louis-Armand de Lom de, 579
Large Glass (sculpture) (Duchamp), 710
Larsa, 64
Las Casas, Bartolomé, 480
Lassa fever, 790
Last Supper (Caravaggio), 466
Latin, 296, 567
Latin America, 742. *See also* Spain in the Americas
  and business imperialism, 652–653
  constitutionalism, 672
  democracy, 743
  economy, 764
  foreign imperialism, 643
  and industrialization, 604–605
  nationalism, 670
  population, 785
  post World War I, 725
Latin Christendom, 277, 278, 283, 332–333, 405. *See also* Christianity
  map of, *334*
Latin Church, 281, G–5
Latitude, *335*, G–5
Lavoisier, Antoine, 529
Law
  during Axial Age, 135
  in fifteenth century, 405
  Mesopotamian, 66
  Ottoman Empire, *497*
  Sharia, 198
Law of nations, 493, G–5
Lazica, 219
Leader cult, *740*
League of Nations, 723, G–5
Leaseholding, 372
Lebanon, 628
Lee Bo, 579
Leeuwenhoek, Anton van, 529
Legalists/Legalism, 135, 144, 169–170, 200, G–5
Legionnaire's disease, 791
Lehrer, Tom, 781
Leibniz, Gottfried Wilhelm, 481, 485, 572
Leicester, 760
Lembang, 698
Lenin, Vladimir Ilyich, 726, 735
Leo XIII, pope, 619, 680
Leopold II, king of the Belgians, *626*, 650–651, 653, 661
Lepers, 356
Leprosy, 443
Lervac-Tournières, Robert, 564
Lesseps, Ferdinand de, *610*
Letters of a Chinese Philosopher (Goldsmith), 566
Leutard, 281–282
Levant, 131, 289, G–5
Lhasa, 204, *204*
Li, king, 110
Li family, 202
Li Hongzhang, 607, *608*
Li Longmian, 307, 308
Li Qingzhao, 306
Li Yuan, 202
Li Zhi, 502
Liao, 304
Liberalism, 686
Liberation theology, 770, G–5
Liberia, 670, 672, 741
Libya, 674, 723
Liebig, Justus von, 596
Lienzo de Tlaxcala, 428
Liezi, 142
Life expectancy, 444–445, 789–790, *790*
Life of an Ant, The (Montgomery), 12
Lifestyle diseases, 791
Ligouri, Alfonso Maria, 576
Lima, 454, 519
Limpopo River, 377
Limschoten, Jan van, *415*
Lin, commissioner, 640, *641*
Lincoln, Benjamin, *558*
Lind, James, *522*
Linguet, Simon-Nicolas-Henri, 567
Linguistics, 707–708, *711*
Linnaeus, Carolus, 579
Linschoten, Jan van, 420
Lipit-Ishtar, King, 65
Lisbon, *516*
Literature
  Byzantine Empire, 302–303
  Christian, *449*
  Greek, ancient, 86
  Japanese, 276
  novel, 707
  Philippian, 671
  Song empire, 308
Lithuania/Lithuanians, 370, 404
Little Bighorn, battle of, 646
Little China, 628
Little Ice Age, 345, G–5
Little Istanbul, *759*
Liu Bang, 170
Liu Guandao, *320*
Livable Netherlands Party, *763*
Liverpool, 624
Livestock, in the Americas, 437, 448
Livonia, 333, 464
Llamas, 369
Locke, John, 572, 575
Locomotive, 598
Loess, 63
Logic, 138
Logograms, 71, *71*, 99, G–5
Lombard cross, 196
Lombards, 195
London, 164
  population in eighteenth century, 519, *521*
Long, Edward, 549
Longitude, G–5
Lord of Hosts, 214, 217
Lord of the Flies (Golding), 715
Lotus Sutra, 228, *228*, G–5
Louis IX, king of France, 333
Louis the Great, 370
Louis XIV, king of France, 456, 566
Louis XV, king of France, 574
Louis XVI, king of France, 580
Louisiana, 554, 643
Loutherbourg, Philippe-Jacques de, *598*, 616
L'Ouverture, Toussaint, 625
Love, universal, 131–134

Loving cups, 87
Low Countries, 603, G–5
Lower Egypt, 70
Loyola, Ignatius, 466, *467*
Lozi, 651
Lü Liuliang, 502
Luanda, 552
Lübeck, 279
Lucayos, 479
Lucy (australopithecine), 6, *7*
Ludwig, Nicolas, 575
Lugal Zagesi, 70
Lugard, Frederick, 650
Lu-igisa, 64
Lukaris, Cyril, 466–467
Lukon-kashia, 552
Luther, Martin, 465–466, *466*
Luzon, 467

M

Ma Huan, 394
Macaque monkeys, 704
Macaulay, Thomas, 660
Macaw dynasty, 242
Macedon/Macedonians, 106, 161–162
Machiavel, 493
Machiavelli, Niccolò, 493, 596
Machine guns, 646, *648*
Machine-age imagery, 709–710
Mad cow disease, 791
Madagascar, 362
Madeira, 370, 440
Madinat al-Zahra, *293*
Madonna, *468*
Madrid, 620, 621
Maecenas, 151
Maes Howe, 54
Magadha, 147
Maghada, 191
Magic, 250
  and science, 480
Magic Flute, The (Mozart), 574–575
Magnetism, 780
Magyarization, 668
Magyars, 289, G–5
Maharajah, 251
Mahavamsa, 112
Mahavira, 127, 144, *146,* 147
Mahayana Buddhism, 221, *228,* 233, G–5
Mahdi, 553, 680–681, G–5
Mahmud, 331
Mahmud II, 673
Mahmud of Ghazni, 288
Mahreb, 218
Mai Lai, 750
Maitreya, 392
Maize, 35, *36,* 38, 91, 436–437, 457, G–5
  cultivation of, 245–246
  in North America, 116
Majapahit, 361
Majorca, *399*
Makassar, 421, *421*
Makerere University, *696*
Malacca, 393, 421, 472
Malaka, Tan, 727
Malal, 215
Malaria, 86, 537, 552, 643, 791
Malaspina, Alessandro, 523, 558
Malay, *727*
Malaya, 275, 698, 738
Maldives, 275
Male dominance
  in ancient river valley civilizations, 63
  in Greece, ancient, 105–106
  Hittites, 80
  in prehistorical society, 12
Mali, 363–366, 378–379, G–5
  map of, *364*
Malta, 54, *55,* 98
Malthus, Thomas, 517–518, 590
Malthusian, 517, 590, G–5
Mamluk Egypt, 330–331, 404
Mamluk sultan, 365
Mamluks, 330–331, *342,* G–5
  chronology, *331*
Mana, 253, G–5
Manado, 468
Manaus, 620, *621*
Manchester (England), 618, *620*
Manchu Qing dynasty, 541
Manchuria, 423, 450–451, 470, 503, 541, 629–630, 719
Manchurian Incident, *718,* 719, G–5
Manchus, 423, 446, 450, 468, 502, *502,* 503, 672, G–5
Mandan Indians, 561
Mandarins, 501–502, 503, G–5
Mandate of heaven, 71, 88, 109, 304, 305, 316, 328, 502, 607, G–5
Mandela, Nelson, 742
Manhattan, 620
  map of ethnicity, *632*
Mani, 215
Manichaeanism, 215, 232, G–5
Manifest destiny, 71, 658, G–5
Manila, 416, 417, 418, 541, 542, 560
Manila Galleon, 431, *492,* G–5
Manon Lascaut (Puccini), 629
Mansa Musa, 365, *365,* 378, 379
Mansas, 365, *365,* 366
Manufacturing output, *611*
Manyoshu, 470
Manzikert, battle of, 300
Mao Zedong, 732–733, *736,* 737, 750, 760
Maori, 535, 635, 647, *664,* 665, G–5
Maori Wars, 647
Mapmaking, *254,* 255, 578, *586–587*
Mapuche, 555
Maqamat (Scales of Harmony) (al-Hariri), *288, 354*
Maragha, 326
Marajó Island, 246
Marathas, 544–545, *545,* 547, G–6
Marcellinus Ammianus, 185
Marcia Procula, *164*
Marco Polo, 320, 321, *323,* 324, 325
Marconi, Guglielmo, 700, 778
Marcus Aurelius, 184
Marcus Valerius Celerinus, *164*
Margarine, 597, 603
Mari, 77
Marib, 118–119, 194
Marinetti, Emilio Filippo, 709
Maritime empires, 412–421, *413,* G–6
Maritime imperialism
  and Asia, 416–419
  chronology, *413, 421*
  map of, *416*
  and Portugal, *410,* 414–419
Maritime navigation, *252,* 253–254, 419–421
  by Europeans, 395, 398
  in fifteenth century, 375–376
Maritime technology, 333, 412–413
Maroons, 506, *507,* 507–508, G–6
  map of in the Americas, *508*
Marquess of Bute, 634
Marriage, 680
  ancient Greece, 105
  ancient river valley civilizations, 63
  in China, 503
  in fourteenth century, 362–363
  in imperialistic Portugal, 415
  interracial, 549
  in nineteenth century, 590
  in sixteenth and seventeenth centuries, 506, *506*
  of slaves, 549
Marseillaise, 583
Marseilles, 524, 574
Marshall, George C., 731
Marshall Plan, 731, G–6
Martilineal, G–6
Martin, St., 227
Marx, Karl, 616, 618, 684, 707, 716, 725
Marxism, 726, 754, G–6
Mary, Mother of God, *293*
Mary, Queen of Scots, 494
Mary of Hungary, archduchess, 478
Masai, *32,* 518
Massachusetts, 477
Massacres, 418
Massaweh, 377
Master Meng, 307
Mastrillo, Nicolás de, 463
Mataka, chief, 636
Mataram, *472*
Material culture, 17–18, G–6
Mathematics, 701, *710*
  in Axial Age, 137–138
Maui, 255
Maupertuis, Pierre Louis de, *564,* 564–565, 575, 576
Maurice, John, 441
Mauritius, 533, *533*
Mauryan Empire, 169
Maxim gun, 646, *646*
Maximilian II, 478
Maya/Mayans, 181–182, 241–244, 257, 269–270, 556, 681, G–6
  art, *242, 243*
  contending with isolationism, *280*
  expansion of, *246*
  map of, *183*
  trade, 431
  writing system, *243,* 244
Mazhir, Ismail, 699
Mazzini, Giuseppe, 666
McAllister, Samuel Ward, 635
McDonaldization, 766
McDonald's, *767,* 783
McNeil, John, 786
Mead, Margaret, 12
Meadowcroft, 21
Measles, 443, 518, 791
Meat processing industry, 594
Mecca, 232, 263
  pilgrimages, *232,* 365
Mechanization, chronology, *623*
Medici, Catherine de', 494
Medici family, 402
Medicine, *648,* 695, 698–699, *755*
  alternative, 714
  in Axial Age, *141,* 141–142
  in China, 695
  chronology, *141*
  in eighteenth century, 522–523
  Middle East, 714
  in twentieth century, 751
  Western, 702–703
    map of spread, *696–697*
Meditations (Marcus Aurelius), 184
Mediterranean
  chronology, *108*
  map of in eleventh and twelfth centuries, *290–291*
  trade routes, *154–155*
Mehmet Ali, 609, 631
Mehmet II, 391
Meiji Restoration, 606
Mekong River, 37, 251
Melaka, 540
Melbourne, 435, 620
Melville, Herman, *588,* 589
Memphis (Egypt), 57, 70
Mencius, 136, 143, 145
Mendelssohn, Felix, 599
Menelik, 647, *649*
Menelik II, emperor, 647, *649,* 678
Menes, 69–70
Mental health, 791
Mercado, Tomás de, 573
Mercantilism, *205,* 565, G–6
Mercator, *586–587*
Mercy (Galdós), 634
Meroe, 116
Mersenne, Marin, 529
Meru, 271
Mesoamerica, 116, 442, G–6
  agriculture, 35
  ancient civilization, 89–92
  art, *269*
  chronology, *268*
  contending with isolationism, *280*
  decline of ancient civilization, 98
  empire building, 173–174
  expansion in eleventh and twelfth centuries, 269–270
  expansion of, *246*
  in fifteenth century, 381–385, *384*
  growth of settlements, 53
  map of, *240*
  map of in twelfth century, *267*
  in thirteenth century, 338
Mesopotamia, 56, 59–61
  ancient government, 66
  ancient politics, *69*
  ecology of civilization, *63*
  expansion of ancient, 69–70
  map of, *60*
  trade, *78–79*
  writing, 71
Messiah, 131, G–6
Messiah (Handel), 576
Messiah of Portugal, 403
Messina Declaration (1955), 744
Mestizos, 507, G–6
Metallurgy, 53, 54
Mexico, 764
  and Christianity, 469
  conquest by Spain, 426
  exploitation of environment, *459*
  industrialization, 605
Mexico City, 437, 454, 519, 785
Mi Fei, 307, 308
Miasmas, 522
Michael (archangel), *282,* 297, 403
Michael IV, *300*
Michael VII, 333
Michelangelo, *478,* 478–479
Microbial exchange, *438–439,* 442–444, G–6
Micronesia, 253
Middle East
  map of in eleventh and twelfth centuries, *290–291*
  map of in twentieth century, *722*
  preagricultural settlements, 29–30
    map of, *29*
  trade and recovery, 99–103
  and Western science, 699
Midwifery, *699*
Mieszko, 223
Migration
  in eleventh and twelfth centuries, 264–266
  of *Homo* species, 8–13
  map of early, *10–11*
  map of world, *633*

Migration, (*cont.*)
  to New World, 19, *20,* 21–22
  in twentieth century, 721–722, 758
Migration of labor, 629–631
Mika'el Suhul, 553
Miletus, 160
Militarism, 721
Militarization, 673–679, *677,* G–6
  chronology, *678*
Military revolution, 447, *448,* G–6
Military/weaponry, 496, *648,* 674–676
  bombs, 731, 732
  British, 646, *646*
  Chinese, 171, 568
  Hittites, 80
  justification of, 495
  musket, 647
  of Native Americans, 428
  naval, *597*
  in nineteenth century, 596–597
  poison gas, *724*
  revolution, 447, *448*
  Roman, 162
  Steppelanders, 189, *189*
  submarine, 721
  World War I, 724
Mill, John Stuart, 686
Millenarianism, 357–358, 476–477, G–6
Millet, 36, 62
Milpas, 242, 244
Milvian Bridge, 217
Minamoto clan, 277
Minas Gerais, 455, 555, G–6
Mindanao, 467
Mineral phosphates, 604
Ming, 219, *225*
Ming China, *393*
Ming Dynasty, 356, 371, *391,* 392, 446, 450, 468, 483, 501–502, G–6
  chronology, *394, 503*
Mining, 620, 621–623
Minoans, 81
Mir, Titu, 615
Miracles, 127
Missionaries, 216, 297, 463, *467*
  in Brazil, 475–476
  in California, 555
  Christian, 420, *467,* 467–469
Mississippi region, 266–268
  contending with isolationism, *280*
Mitsubishi, 606
Mitsui, 606
Miura Baien, 569
Mixtec, *269,* 270, *408–409*
Moa, 367
Moais, 366–367, *367*
Mobutu, Joseph, 739
Moby Dick (Melville), *588,* 589
Moche, 239, 241, 368
  expansion of, *246*
Moctezuma II, 426
Modern art, *713*
Modernism, 709
Modernization, 665
  in nineteenth century, *676*
Mogador, 98
Mogodishu, 270
Mohenjodaro, 62, *62,* 68–69
  decline of, *93*
Mohists, 144
Mojmir I, 256
Moldavia, 425
Mollusks, 45
Molucca Islands, 468
Mombasa, *538,* 539
Monarchs, religious conversions, 216–224
Monarchy, 135–136, 165, 490, 650
Monasteries, 219, 221, *221,* 250
Monasticism, 226–229
  chronology, *229*
Monet, Claude, 636
Mongaku, 277
Mōngke Khan, 324
Mongkut, prince, 678
Mongo, 518
Mongol Peace, 321, G–6
Mongolia, 316, 450
  exploitation of environment, *459*
Mongolian Peace
  travelers during, *326*
Mongols, 370, 386–388, 446–447, G–6
  art, *314, 320, 321*
  and Buddhism, *470,* 470–471
  in China, 326–329
  chronology, *317, 340*
  conquest of China, 326–329
  conquest of Persia, 329
  conquest of Russia, 329–330
  and Egypt, 330–331
  infected by plague, 350, 351, 356
  invasion of, 315–325
  map of campaigns, *318–319*
  map of European travelers, *322*
  peaceful period, 321–324
  religion of, 470
  in Russia, 329–330
  trade with China, *323*
  uniqueness of, 336–339
Monks, 226–228, *262*
  in Russia, 330, *330*
Monocultures, 533, G–6
Monopolies, 416
Monotheism, 132–133
Monroe Doctrine, 652, G–6
Monsoons, 113, 153, 156, G–6
  and maritime navigation, 375
Montagu, Mary Wortley, 424, 523
Monte Albán, 174, *175*
  map of, *173*
Monte Cassino, 227
Monte Verde, 21
Montesquieu, 566, 567, 568, 573
Montgomery, Bernard, 12
Moonies, *757*
Moral meterology, 343
Moral superiority, 659–660
Morales, Eduardo, *670*
Morgan, T.H., 702, *710*
Morinaga, Motoori, 470
Morning Star, *242*
Morocco, 351, 404, 448, 647, 674, 739
Morse, Samuel, 600
Moscow, 386, 519
Moses, *349*
Most, Johann, 684–685
Mound agriculture, 33, G–6
Mound clusters, 267–268
Mount Huascarán, *462*
Mount Parnassus, *139*
Mozambique, 377
Mozart, Wolfgang Amadeus, 567, 574, 576
Mozi, 131, 134, 142–145, *146*
Mugabe, Robert, 739
Mughal emperors, 456
Mughals, 421, 423–424, 477, 526–527, 544–545, G–6
  chronology, *425, 547*
  in India, 451, 498
    chronology, *501*
Muhammad, 131, 133, 196–197, 198, 206, 212, 216, *226,* 228, *232,* 237, 247, 287, 296, 329, *329,* 500, 539, 680
Muhammad Ahmad, 680
Muhammad Ali, 674
Muhammad ibn Abd al-Wahhab, 544
Muhammad Shah, emperor, 544
Muhammad Touray Askia, 378–379
Mulay Hassan, 647, 648
Mullah Nasreddin, *658*
Multaqa al-Abhur (Confluence of the Currents) (Ibrahim al Halabi), *497*
Multiculturalism, 762, G–6
Mundigak, 69
Munjon, king, 277
Muqaddimah, 386
Murad IV, 497
Murillo, 466
Murray-Darling river, 781
Mursili II, 81
Muscovy, 386
Musi, 251
Music
  in eighteenth century, 576
  pop, 713
Musical theater, 713
Musket, 647
Muslims, 197–200, 214, 216, 225–226, 229, 277, 287–288, 314–316, 386, 424, 451, 477, 544, 567, 681, 762. *See also* Islam/Islamic
  art, *288*
  and commerce, 419
  in East Africa, 270
  in fifteenth century, 379
  map of, *198, 231*
  migration, 263
  and missionaries, 467
  reform movements, *679*
  in Russia, *658*
  and sufism, 296
  in thirteenth century India, 331–332
  view of plague, *354*
  in West Africa, 553
  and Western science, 699
Mussolini, Benito, 727
Mutesa, king, 679
Mutis, José Celestino, 532
Muye, 87
Mwene Mutapa, 377, 379, 385, 403, 552
Myanmar, 743
Mycenae/Mycenaens, 81, *83,* 83–84, 99
  chronology, *84*
  decline of, *93*
Mysore, 547
Mysticism, 302

N

Nabopolasar, 102
Nabta Playa, 30
Nadir Shah, 543
Naegamwalla, Jamsetji Dorabji, 600
Nagasaki, 420, *729,* 731
Nahuatl, *442*
Namibia art, 17
Nanak, 477
Nanjing, 524, 749
Nanjing, treaty of, 640
Napata, 116
Naples, *434,* 519
Napoleon Bonaparte, 530, 581–583, *583,* 596, 642, 687
  map of empire, *582*
Napoleonic Wars (1799-1815), 657, 666, 668, 672, 682, G–6
Naqia, 102
Narrative of the Surveying Voyage of HMS Adventure and Beagle (Fitzroy), *659*
Nasser, Gaml Abdel, 739
National Assemby, 580
National Health Service (Britain), 790
National insurance, *755*
National Socialist German Workers' Party, 727. *See also* Nazis
Nationalism, 404–405, 666–672, *677,* G–6
  beyond Europe, 669–672
  chronology, *678*
  in Europe, 666–668
Nationalist Party (Egypt), 724
Nationalists, 723, 726–727
Native Americans, *631*
  in Brazil, 555
  and Catholic missionaries, 468–469
  and Columbus, 479
  conquest by Spain, 426, 428–429
  contending with isolationism, *280*
  and diseases, 428–429, 506, 518
  elimination in the United States, 429–430, 658
  human nature of, 479–480
  hunting, 457
  and New England colonists, 429–430
  population in eighteenth century, *518*
  reactions to Europeans, 428–429
  and religion, 474, 769
  as slaves, 430
  and smallpox, 428, *442*
Natural selection, 27, G–6
Nature, cult of, 576–577
Nature *versus* nurture, 703, G–6
Nature worship, 139
Naucratis, 104
Nautical maps, 413
Naval technology, *597*
Naval warfare, 597, *597*
Nawab, 545
Nazca, 239, 241, 245, 249
  expansion of, *246*
Nazis, 708, 727, 728, 750, *750,* 759, G–6. *See also* National Socialist German Workers' Party
Ndebele, 646, 651
Ndongo, *488,* 489, 511
Neanderthal, 7, 704, G–6
Neanderthal Valley, *10*
Neapolis, 172
Nebamun, 56
Nebaun, *50*
Nebuchadnezzar II, 102–103
Needham, Joseph, 714
Négritude, 760, G–6
Nemesis (ship), *638*
Nene, *664*
Nenets, 23
Nepal, 194, 204
Nerchinsk, 449
  treaty of (1689), 423
Nestorianism, 329, G–6
Nestorians, 215, *225,* 233, 326
Nestorius, bishop, 215
Netherlands, 483, 494, 758
  1550 map of, *419*
  in the Americas, 444, *445*
  decolonization in twentieth century, 738, *738*
  emancipation of slaves, 626
  horticultural exchange, 441
  imperialism, 643
  industrialization, 603
  and maritime imperialism, 419–421
  and maritime navigation, 413, 419–421

relations with East Indies, 421
relations with England, 421
relations with India, *527*
relations with Portugal, 421
in South Africa, 448
Neuroscience, *710*
New age movement, 768
New Christians, in white America, 476
New Conquests, 541
New Culture (China), 695
New Delhi, *767*
New England, 556
in the seventeenth and eighteenth centuries, 455–456
in the sixteenth and seventeenth centuries, 445
New Europes, 535, 630, G–6
imperialism, 655–656
New France, 445
New Guinea
and agriculture, 33–34
civilizing, *661*
New Harmony (town), 684
New Hebrides, 253
New Israel, 430
New Jerusalem, 271, *271*
New Mexico, 430, 555
New Order, 674
New Orleans, 554, 788, *788*
New Rich, 634, G–6
New Russia, 657
New South Wales, 535
New Spain, *469*
New World, 505–509, G–6
demographic collapse, 442–444
early migration to, 19, 21–22
map, *20*
map of, *374*
in sixteenth and seventeenth centuries, 505–509
spread of Christianity, 468–469
New York, 445
New York City, 519, *590, 630*
and industrialization, 620
New Zealand, 253, 535–536, 578, 591, 655, 656, 665
democracy, 716
in eighteenth century, 535
in fourteenth century, 367–368
Maori wars, 647
socialism, 686
Newfoundland, 266, *374*
Newspapers, 683
Newton, Isaac, 481, 482, 529, 564
Newton's laws, 482
Neyici Toyin, 470
Ngoni priests, 646
Nguema, Macías, 739
Ni Bozhuang, 328
Nicaea, 333
Nicaragua, 670
Nietzsche, Friedrich, 686
Niger, 653
Niger River, 116, 379
Niger Valley, 238
Nigeria, 331, 622, 672, 714, 784
art, *116*
population, *777*
Night Revels of Han Xizai, The (Gu Hongzhong), *308*
Nihongi, 249
Nile River, 37, 55–57, 69–70, *376*
Nile Valley, 42
Nineveh, 99
Ning-an, 451
Nino, St., 218, *219*
Nintu (goddess), 60
Nirvana, 127, G–6
Nitrates, 652
Nixon, Richard, 737, 743
Nizam al-Mulk, 544
Nkrmah, Kwame, 739
Nobel, Alfred, 676
Nobi plain, 457
Nobility, 490, 491, 493, 496
Noble savage, 578–580, G–6
Nomadism, *309,* 309–310, 554, 631
See also Pastoralists
Nootka Sound, 560
Nordhausen concentration camp, *750*
Normans, in eleventh century, 300
Norse, 368–370, 395
chronology, *265*
contending with isolationism, *280*
migration, map of, *265*
migration of, 265–266
North Africa, 404, 425, 543
and Islam/Islamic, 293
map of in twentieth century, *722*
plague in, 351
World War II, 730
North America
chronology, *113, 119, 268*
civilization of, *118*
climate change in fourteenth century, 345
developments in ancient, 113–116
expansion of, *246*
exploitation of environment, *459*
fur trade, 431
geographic obstacles, *254*
map of in twelfth century, *267*
North American Southwest, 266–267
North Atlantic, climate change in the fourteenth century, *348*
North Island, 665
North Korea, 734
North Vietnam, 734
Northern Kingdom, 304
Northmen. *See* Norse
Northwest Passage, *265,* G–6
Norway, 214, 223
democracy, 716
Nosso Senhor do Born Jesus de Matosinho, *555*
Novel, 671, 707
Novgorod, 256, 281, 330, *330*
Nubia, 58, 92–93, 116, 218, 331
Nüchunyu, 202
Nuclear fission, 731
Nuclear power, 779
"Nude Descending a Staircase" (Duchamp), 710
Nüjie, 202
Numancia, 166
Nunneries, 229
Nuns, 229
Nurhaci, 502
Nutrition and human population, 442
Nyaya, 131
Nyaya School, 138–139, *146*
Nzinga of Ndongo, queen, *488,* 489, 511

O

Oaxaca, 174
Ob River, 386
Obeah-men, 507
Oberá the Resplendent, 477
Obesity, 783, *784,* 791
Obs, *379*
Observatory, *484*
Obsidian, 182, G–6
Ocean of Death, 67
Oceanic imperialism, 395–398
chronology, *398*
Ocelotl, Don Martín, 476
Ocher, *2–3*
Ochre, 17, 18
Odyssey (Homer), 105
Oedipus complex, 705–706
Ogallala Aquifer, 781
Ogyu Sorai, 569
Oil as energy source, 456, 597, 778–779
Oil crisis, 735
Okayama, 532
Okinawa, 417
Oklahoma, 658
Olaf, *225*
king of Norway, 214
Old Believers, *495*
Old regime, 580, G–6
Old San Juan, 454
Old World, G–6
agriculture of, 36
Olive growing industry, 103–104, *104*
Olive oil, 103, *104*
Olmec civilization, 35, 89, *90,* 91–92
Olof Skōtkunung
king of Sweden, 223
Omai, 579, *579*
Oman/Omanis, 116, 416, 539–540, 560
Omdurman, battle of, 646, *646,* 681
Ongghot, *470*
Ongons, 470, *470,* G–6
OPEC, 755, 779, G–6
Opera houses, 620, *621*
Opitz, G.E., *668*
Opium, 525–526, 620, 640–641, *641*
Opium Wars, 608, *638,* 640–641, 660
Oppenheimer, J. Robert, 714
Opticks (Descartes), *482*
Oracle bones, 67, *67*
Oracles, 66–67, *67,* 87–88, G–7
Greek, 104
Orangutans, 6
Organ transplants, 789
Organization of Petroleum Exporting Countries. *See* OPEC
Oriental despotism, 566, 568, G–7
Origin of Species by Means of Natural Species (Darwin), 659
Orkney Islands, 54
Oromo, 518, 553
Orontes River, *248*
Orthodox Church, 466, G–7
Osaka, *519,* 532
Oshio Heicharo, 626
Osiris, 65
Ostrogoths, 189
Ostyaks, 423
Otto I, emperor, 278
Otto III, emperor, 278, *279,* 283
Otto of Freising, 281
Ottoman Empire, 386–391, 424–426, 440, 622, 671, G–7
centralization, 673–674
chronology, *501*
constitutionalism, 672
democracy, 683
economy in eighteenth century, 528
emancipation of slaves, 626
Enlightenment, 571–572
imperialism, 416, 543–544
laws of, *497*
map of, *388–389, 586–587*
nationalism, 668
population in eighteenth century, 519
in sixteenth and seventeenth centuries, 495–498
and Western science, 698
World War I, 720
Ottoman State, map of, *370*
Ottomans, 370, *370, 390*
art, *448, 498*
chronology, *425*
Enlightenment, 567–568
Our Lady of Guadalupe, 469
Outer Mongolia, 423
Ouyang Xiu, 305–306, 308
Overall Survey of the Ocean's Shore, The (Huan), 394
Overconsumption, 766
Overpopulation, 517–518, 758
Oviedo Cathedral, 256
Oxus, 658, 780
Oxus River, 85
Oyo, kingdom, 672
Ozette, 367–368

P

Pacal, king, 242
Pachamachay, 35
Pacific
colonization of, 253–255
in the eighteenth century, 578–579
in fourteenth century, 366–369, *369*
geographic obstacles, *254*
map of fourteenth century societies, *368*
Pacific Islands, spread of agriculture in, 42
Pacific Ocean
map of maritime imperialism, *416*
Paekche, 172, 192, 204, 220
development of, *205*
Paganism, 217, *217,* 220, 232, 469
Pahlavi, Mohammad Reza, 766–767
Painting, 709–712
Byzantine Empire, 302–303
Chinese, 307, *307, 308*
cubism, 710
Dutch, *417*
Japanese, *570*
Mongolian, *316*
seventeenth century, *481*
Spanish, *4, 5*
Paisley, 662
Paizi, *323*
Pakehas, 665
Pakistan, 738, 741
Palas dynasty, 222
Palembang, 251, 361
Palenque, 242
Paleoanthropologists, 6, 7, *8*
Paleoanthropology, 704, *711*
Palestine, 162, 723
conflict with Israel, 741, *742*
Palmares, 508
Palm-oil production, 622
Pamir Mountains, 156
Pampa de Caña Cruz, 89
Pampas, 32, 431, 605, G–7
Pan-African Congress, 724, G–7
Panama, 431, 658
Pangea, G–7
Panlongcheng, 62
Pansophy, 481
Pánuco River, 382
Papago Native Americans, 44
Papal infallibility, 680
Paper, invention of, 333, 483
Paquimé, 345
Paradigm shifts, 702
Paraguay, 442, 670
dams, 780
Paraná, 780
Paranthropoi, 6

Paraquay, 555
Paris, 519, 620, 756
Paris, Matthew, 317
Paris Peace Conference (1919–1920), *728, 745*
Parliament, 672
Parmenides, 138, *146*
Parramatta, 535
Parthian shot, *189*
Parthia/Parthians, 162, *189*
Partition of India, 738, G–7
Passport, Mongolian, *323*
Pastoral imperialism, 448–449
Pastoralism, 171, 288–289, 446–447, 448
Pastoralists, 324, 630–631
Paternalism, 623, G–7
during industrialization, 616–618
Patna, 519
Patriarch of Constantinople, 466
Patrilineal, G–7
Patriotism, 653
Paul, Apostle, 214, 218
Paul III, pope, 479
Pavón, Hipólito, 532
Peacock, Thomas Love, 684
Pearl Harbor, 729
Peasants, 281–282, 493, 784
in China, 502–503
in fifteenth century China, 392
in fourteenth century Japan, 363
in nineteenth century, 622, *622*
and plague affecting land ownership, 357–358
revolts, 626
in fifteenth century China, 392
in nineteenth century China, 607
in sixteenth and seventeenth centuries, 493–495
in sixteenth and seventeenth century Japan, 504
Peat as energy source, 456, 597
Pedra Pintada, 22
Pedro I, king, 558
Pedro IV, king, 552
Pelizza, Giuseppe, *685*
Peloponnese, 81
Pencillin, 702
Peng Shaosheng, 470
Pennsylvania and Native Americans, 430
Pentagon, 754
Pepi, 93
Pepper as spice, 416, 421
Pequot War, 429
Pergamum, 162
Perm River, 386
Pernambuco, 440, *440,* 455, 508
Pernikoff, Aleksandr, 719
Perón, Eva, 728
Perón, Juan, 727–728
Perry, Matthew C., 605
Persepolis, 159, *159*
Perses, 104
Persian Letters (Montesquieu), 567
Persian-Greek Wars, 159–161
Persia/Persian empire, 147, 153, 157–162, 370, 424, 440. *See also* Iran
Arab invasion, 197
art, *159*
chronology, *160*
conquest by Mongols, 329
Enlightenment, 567–568
government, 159–160
imperialism, 543
map of, *161*
population in eighteenth century, 519
religion, 132
Safavids, 499–501
chronology, *501*
transformation of, *199*
war with Greece, 159–161
Persikoff, Aleksandr, 745
Peru, 239, 241, 426, *462,* 605, 670, 725, 766
agriculture of, 35
art, *368*
conquest of, 428, 431
ecology in eighteenth century, 436
independence, 556
and pre-Christian devotions, 469
Perun (god), 224
Pescadores Islands, 656
Peshawar, 214
Petals Palace, *204*
Peter Pan (Barrie), 706
Peter the Great, czar of Russia, 495, *495*
Peter the Wild Boy, 579
Petrarch, 354
Phagspa, *323*
Pharaohs, 64, 69, 93
Philadelphia, 519
Philip, king of Macedon, 161
Philip II, king of Spain, 456, 491, 494
Philip III, king of Spain, *507*
Philip IV, king of Spain, 494, 497
Philippines, 418, 467, 541, 591, 658, 738, 758–759
democracy, 742
map of Catholic missions, *471*
nationalism, 671
Philosopher's Stone, 482, G–7
Philosophical Investigations (Wittgenstein), 708
Philosophy, 142–143, 707
ancient Greece, 106
in Axial Age, 131
Chinese, *145*
and Christianity, 478
of eleventh and twelfth centuries, 283
Enlightenment, 572
in fifteenth century, 385, 402
Japanese, 569
map of schools, *145*
nineteenth century, 684–686
Song empire, 308
Philosophy of Christ, 478
Phocaea, 109
Phoenicia/Phoenicians, 98–99
chronology, *99*
map of civilization, *100–101*
revival of, *103*
Phosphate, 781
Photography, *572*
Phuc, Kim, *734*
Phyongrgyas, 204
Physics, 700–701, *710*
Physiocrats, 531, 573, G–7
Picasso, Pablo, 704, 710, 711, 712
Pig, 535
Pig-iron production, 530
Pilgrim ship, *262*
Pilgrimages, *262,* 263, *288*
to Jerusalem, 289, *289*
Pineapple, 436
Pinochet, Augusto, 765
Pisces, 768
Pitcairn, 534
Pithecanthropoi, 6
Piux IX, pope, 680
Plague, 194, *342,* 348–358, *349,* 369–371, 435, 442, 523, 590, 789
in Africa, 643
in China, 392
chronology, *372*
course and impact of, 350–351
in Eurasia, 443–444
moral and social effects, 351–358
treating, *351*
Plant husbandry, 30–31, 703
Plantation system, 445, 507, 549, 624, G–7
Plants, exchange among countries, 436–442
Plassey, battle, 545
Plastic, invention of, 700
Plato, 106, 131, 132, 135, 137, 143, 144, *146,* 303, *478*
Platonism, 478
Pliny, 157
Plow technology, 249, 451
Pluralism, 759
Plymouth, 445
Pneumonic plague, 349
Pocahontas, 441
Pohnpei, 253
Poincaré, Henri, 700, 707, *710*
Poison gas, *724*
Poivre, Pierre, 533
Poland, 404, 490, 728, 735
in fourteenth century, 370
Poldi-Pezzoli, G., 619
Poleis, Greek, 118
Polestar, G–7
Polio, 751, 789
Political optimism, 135–137
Political pessimism, 135
Political radicalism, 681–683
chronology, *686*
Politicization of social issues, 751
Politics. *See also* Government
in ancient river valley civilizations, 64
of Axial Age, 134–137
and Buddhism, 219
chronology, *687, 745*
extremism in Europe, 724–725
and farming, 43
Hittites, 79–81
and religion, 680–681
in thirteenth century, *337*
in twentieth century, *664,* 665–689, *761*
Western Europe, 277–282
Zhou dynasty, 87–88
Pollution, *778*
air, 785
Polo, Marco, *322*
Polynesia/Polynesians, 253–255, 263, 366–367
chronology, *255*
Polytheism, 133
Pondicherry, 421
Poor Richard's Alamack (Franklin), *522*
Pop music, 713
Pope, Alexander, 482
Pophung, king, 192, 220
Popper, Karl, 706
Population, 376, 775–777
in 1900, *620*
in the Americas, 441–442
ancient China, 171
in ancient river valley civilizations, 62–63
in British North America, 556, *557*
in China, *257*
chronology, *528, 600*
and climate change in fourteenth century, 345
control, 9
decline in the Americas, 441–442
early growth of, 9, 12, *13*
in eighteenth century, 517–524, *518, 520, 521*
of eleventh century Europe, 279
of European empires, *643*
expansion during Song empire, 305
and farming, 42
foragers and farmers, *31*
in fourteenth century, 371, *371*
increase in world, *520,* 589–590, *592–593*
map of, *785*
in Mesoamerica, 182
migration, *630,* 730, 757–758
in nineteenth century, 655
nineteenth century increase, 611
noncitizen, *758*
and nutrition, 442
trends and migration of *Homo sapiens,* 9
in twentieth century, 789–790, 793
world, 776, *777*
Porcelain, Chinese, 524
Pork industry, 534
Portugal, 333, 492
in Africa, *538,* 539–540, *552*
in the Americas, 436, 444, *445,* 508
in Angola, 622–623
in Asia, 414–416
in Brazil, 554–555
democracy, 742
in Egypt, *538*
exploration of Atlantic, 395, 398
in Goa, *414,* 414–415, 547
imperialism, 643
in India, *417*
introduction of potatoes, 437
and maritime imperialism, *410,* 414–419
in New World, 411
relations with Netherlands, 419, 421
and territorial imperialism, 421
in West Africa, *378,* 378–379
Positivism, 707–708, G–7
Possession Island, 27
Postl, Karl, 682
Pot, Pol, 734, 750
Potala Palace, *204*
Potato, 436, 437, 535
domestication, 35
famine in Ireland, 590
Potosi, *430*
Pottery, 71, *104*
Poverty Point, 113, 116
Power, alternative sources of, 779–780
Practical learning, 571
Pragmatism, 707, G–7
Prague, 756
Pragvata family, 274
Prairie, The (Cooper), 591
Prairies in North America, 437, 554, 591
Praying towns, 467
Prazeros, 552
Preagricultural settlements, 29–30
map of, *29*
Primatology, 704, *711*
Primitivism, 711
Prince, The (Machiavelli), 493
Prince Gong, 607
Prince Henry, 403, 406
Princeps, 165
Printing, *469,* 483, 571
press, 465
Procurement and agriculture production, 44–45
Progress of the Human Mind, The (Condorcet), 517
Proletarians, 684

Proletariats, 618, 631, 684, G–7
Propaganda, *734, 736,* 749
Prostitution, *62,* 628
Protectorate, 650, G–7
Protestantism, 477, G–7
Protestants, 466
and black America, 476
social structure, 494
and Wars of Religion, 494
in White America, 476
Prussia, 581, 675
Psellus, Michael, 303
Pskov, 281
Psychiatry, 706
Psychoanalysis, 706, G–7
Psychology, 705–706, *711*
Ptolemy, Claudius, *260, 376,* 402
Public health, 618
Public sphere, 683, G–7
Puccini, Giacomo, 629, 636
Puduhepa, 81
Pueblo Bonito, *267*
Puerto Rico, 658
Pump technology, 529
Punic Wars, 162
Punjab, 86, 194, 678
Punt, 57, *57*
Puritans, 505
Putin, Vladimir, 743
Pylos, 83
Pyrrho of Elis, 142
Pythagoras, 137, *146*

Q

Qianlong emperor, *502, 541,* 542, 568, *568*
Qin dynasty, 145, 169, *170*
chronology, *171*
Qing dynasty, 423, 446, 483, 502, 607, 608, 630, 672, 681, 683, 695, 716, 732, G–7
chronology, *503*
map of revolts, *675*
Qizilbash, 499
Quadroon, *549*
Quakers, 430
Quantum mechanics, 701, G–7
Quebec, 560, 655
Queen mothers, 498
Queen of Sheba, 118, 271
Quesnay, Francois, 566
Qufu, 394
Quinine, 436, 646, *648*
Quinoa, 35
Quito, 382
Quran, 197, 212, 216, 228, 287, 390, 473, 567, 699, 769, G–7
Qusayr Amra, *236*
Qutb Minar, *332*

R

Rabban Bar Sauma, 326, *327*
Rabia al-Adawiyya, 228, 229
Racial intermarriage, *506*
Racism, 508–509, 629, 651, 715, 759
scientific, 707
Radicalism, 581
Radio, 778
Radiyya, 332
Ragae, 157
Railway industry, *599,* 599–600, 631, 635
in Japan, *606*
Rajasthan, 273
Raleigh, Walter, 436
Ralpachen, king, 222
Raman, Chandrasekhara Venkata, 698
Ramiro I, 256
Ramses II, 93
Ramses III, 84, *84*
Rape, John, 749
Rape of Nanjing, *748,* 749, G–7
Rapeseed oil as energy source, 456
Raratonga, 255
Rarity value, 530
Rashid al-Din, *317*
Rastafarianism, G–7
Rathenau, Walter, 669
Rationalism, 138–139, G–7
Ravenna, 189, 195, *195*
Ray, Prafulla Chandra, 698
Reagan, Ronald, 735
Realpolitik, 493, G–7
Reasoning, 138–139
Reccesvinth, king, 233
Recession (economic), 725
Record industry, 713
Reform Act (1832), 682
Reform Acts, 672
Reformation, 466, G–7
Regents, 202, *220,* 276, 494, 546
Reichstag, 683
Relativism, 705
Religion. *See also* Specific types of religion
art, *210*
Axial Age, 131–134
Black America, 474–476
Buddhism, 126–130
in Catalhüyük, 37, *38*
chronology, *216, 233*
in sixteenth and seventeenth centuries, *485*
conversions, 218–219
cult agriculture, 43, *43*
Daoism, 130
in eleventh and twelfth centuries, 281–283
and Enlightenment, 575–580
fertility, 16, *39*
forcible conversion, 212–216
Hittites, 80
in Ice Age, 17–18
Islam, 131, 196–197
Judaism, 130
Mesopotamian, 66–67
in nineteenth century, 680–681, *686*
Persian, 159
and politics, 680–681
revitalization of, *472*
revival, 354, 767–770
in eighteenth century, 575–576
rise of, *210, 213*
in Russia, *495*
in sixteenth and seventeenth centuries, 462–287
syncretic features of, 474
in thirteenth century, *337*
tolerance of in Ottoman Empire, 388
and trade, 214–215
white America, 476–477
Zoroastrians, 126–127
Religious communities, 225–229, *228–229*
Religious fundamentalism, 715
Religious map of Europe, *471*
Religious orders, 464, 466
Remarque, Erich-Maria, 724
Remezov Chronicle, *449*
Renaissance, 399, 402, 478–480, *496,* 596, G–7
Renewable energy, 779, G–7
Requiem Mass (Mozart), 576
Resettlement, 776
Revolutionary War, 556, 580
Reynolds, Joshua, *579*
Rhine River, 188
Rhodes, 425
Rhodes, Cecil, 623
Rhubarb, 420, 441
Rhyming Chronicle, 333
Ri, 569
Ricardo, David, 530, 573
Ricci, Matteo, *467,* 468
Rice, 33, *247,* 249, 623
in the Americas, 455
cultivation of, 33, 62, 271, *272,* 307, *307, 591*
famine in Japan, 615
Richard II, king of England, 405
Ridge, Tom, *754*
Rig Veda, 86, G–7
Right to vote, 683, 761
Rindos, David, 45
Río Tinto, 109, 623
Rion, Edouard, *610*
River blindness, *774,* 775–776
River Plate, 431
Riza Khan, 723
Rizal, José, 671, *671*
Roca, general, 646
Rocket (Stevenson), 598
Rolfe, John, 441
Roman Catholicism, 768
conflict with state, 680–681
Roman Empire, 295, 490
architecture/art, 164–165
art, *164, 166, 188, 217*
barbarian invasions of, 184–185, 188–189, 195–196, 206
changes within, 185, 188
chronology, *165*
commerce, 157, 164–165
conquest of Celts, 166
culture, 164–165
eastern, 194–195
government, 136, 165, 188
invasion of Carthage, 99, 162
map of, *163, 189*
invaders, *186–187*
rise of, 162–166
transformation of, *199*
western, 184–188
Romanesque art, *283*
Romania, 668, 672
democracy, 683
nationalism, 668
Romanticism, 575–580, 576–577, 619, G–7
Romanus IV Diogenes, 300
Rome, 184, 187, 425
Arab invasion, 197
comparison with China, *191*
rise of, 162
and Steppelanders, 189
Ronin, 504
Roosevelt, Franklin D., 725, 731
Rooster in Islam, *329*
Rosario, 652
Rosary, 335
Rousseau, Jean-Jacques, 577–578
Rowntree, R. Seebohm, 620
Roy, Rajah Rammohan, *562,* 563, 584, 662
Royal Botanical Gardens, 532
Royal Institute for Higher Technical Education, 698
Royal Navy, 534
Royal Observatory, 635
Rudna Glava, 54
Rudolf II, emperor, 480–481
Rum, 455
Rumelia, 425
Rural capitalism, 358
Rus, 223–224, G–7
Ruse, James, 535
Ruskin, John, 684
Russia, 403, 404, 716, 743
art, 710–711, *726*
in Asia, 652, 654
communism, 726
conquest by Mongols, 329–330
constitutionalism, 672
emancipation of slaves, 626
empire in fifteenth century, 385–386
expansion chronology, *423*
in fifteenth century, 385–386
in fourteenth century, 358
genocide, 750
imperialism, 417, 449, *449,* 522–523, 643, *657,* 657–658, *658*
industrialization, 603
map of, *387*
migration of labor, 629–630
modernization of, 495
nationalism, 672
and Ottoman Empire, 543
plague in, 351
population in eighteenth century, 519
religion in, *495*
states, 370
technology and growth, 281
World War I, 720, 723
World War II, 729
Russian Orthodox Church, 467, *495*
Russification, 668
Rusudan, queen, *314,* 315
Rutherford, Ernest, 701, *710*
Ryazan, 330
Rye, 36
Ryukyu, 417

S

Saba/Sabaeans, 118–119
Sachs, Hans, 465
Sacred Heart of Jesus, 576
Sacrifices, human, 241–242, *243*
Sadism, 581
Safavid empire, 424, 446, *499,* 499–501, 543
map of, *500*
Safavid Persia, *498,* 498–501
chronology, *501*
Safavids, 446, 499–501, G–7
Safflower, *247*
Sages, 126, 143–146, *146*
Sahara, 42, *216,* 292–293, 448, 647, 775, 780
Sahel, 32, 238, 337–339, 448, G–7
Sahid, Muhammad, 419
Said Barghash, 648
Saikaku, 504
Sailendra dynasty, 252–253
Saint Symeon the New Theologian, 302
Saint-Domingue, 440, 533, 548, 625, G–7
Saints, patron, 471
Sakhalin, 417, 560
Saladin, 290, 291, 330
Salarich, Jaume, 619
Salmonella, 791
Salt, *379*
Salvation by faith alone, 466
Samarkand, 423
Sami, 23, 32, 631
Sammuramat, 102
Samoa, 253
Samoyeds, 23, 32
Samurai, 504, *614,* 615, 626, 634, 635, 656, G–7
rebellion, 626

Samye monastery, *221*
San (African), *17*, 22, *22*
San Antonio, 555
San Francisco, 620
San hunters, 630
San Ignacio, 182
San José de Moro, 241
San Juan Bautista, *455*
San Lorenzo, 91
San Pedro Mártir, 181
San Salvador, 479, 670, 725
San Vitale, 195, *195*
Sanchi, *168*
Sand, George, *399*
Sanitary Conditions of the Labouring Population (Chadwick), 619
Sanskrit, 567
Sanskrit College of Calcutta, 662
Santo Domingo, 507
São Jorge da Mina, 379, 398
São Paulo, 430, 670, 785
Saraswati River, 55, 58, 86
Saray, 330
Sardines, 594
Sardinia, 98
Sarekat Islam, 724
Sargent, John Singer, *724*
Sargon of Akkad, 70, 159
Sarmatians, 172
  art, *172*, 172–173
Sartre, Jean-Paul, *708*, 708–709
Sasanians, *197*
  transformation of, *199*
Sati, 222, G–7
Satsuma, 505
Satyagraha, 724, G–7
Saudi Arabia, 723, 769
Saussure, Ferdinand de, 707, *711*
Savanna, 62, G–7
Sawad, 248
Saxons, 255
Saxony, 255–256
Sayids, 539–540
Scandiclerosis, 753
Scandinavia/Scandinavians, 83, 751, 753
  imperialism, 643
  migration, map of, *265*
  migration of, 265–266
Schism, 466
Schoenberg, Arnold, 711
Schrödinger, Erwin, 702–703
Schurz, Karl, 616
Schweizer, Albert, 699
Schwitters, Kurt, 712
Science
  in Axial Age, 139–141
  chronology, *141*
  in the East, 483–485
  Indian, 714
  painting, *481*
  religion, 140, 714, 716
  rise of Western, 333, 480–483
  in sixteenth and seventeenth centuries, 462–487
  in thirteenth century, *337*
  Western, 694–709
    map of, *696–697*
    transformation, 700–709
Science, Western
  chronology, *485*, *709*, *716*
  in the East, 483–485
  transformation of, *710*
Science and Civilisation in China (Needham), 714
Science Society of China, 695
Scientific racism, 707
Scientific revolution, 335, 529, G–7
Scientism, 575, 695, 715, G–7
Scientology, 770
Scopes "Monkey Trial," 702
Scotland, 448, 531
  monarchy of, 490
  nationalism, 668
Scramble for Africa, 654, *654*, G–7
Sculpture, *116*, *555*, *566*, *712*
Scurvy, 522
Scythians, 32, 172
  art, *171*, 171–172
Sea charts, 413, *413*
Sea of Butter, 153
Sea of Milk, 153
Sea Peoples, *84*, 84–85, G–7
Seacraft, Inuit, *266*
Sechín Alto, 88
Second Sex, The (Beauvoir), *708*
Second Vatican Council, 756, G–7
Second World War. *See* World War II
Secularism, 681, 767–770, G–7
Sedentary peoples, *30*, *31*, 33, *44*, 84, 86, 164, 173, 203, 309, *309*, 316–317, 449
Sehetep-ib-Re, 64–65
Seiki, Kuroda, 711
Self-determination, 723, 740, G–8
Self-strengthening, 607–608, 695, G–8
Seljuk Turks, 288, 315
Seljuks, 224, *225*, G–8
Senate, Roman, 165
Senegambia, 239, 379, 553
Sénghor, Leopold, *760*
Sennacherib, *99*, 102
Separate development system, 759
Septicemic plague, 349
Sequoia, 672, *672*
Serbia, 668, 720, 745
Serf, 626, G–8
Serfdom, 626
Serra, Junípero, 555
Service industries, 755
Seth (god), 84
Settlement of land
  in ancient river valley civilizations, 62–63
  in eleventh century Western Europe, 277
Seven Samurai, The (movie), *614*
Seven Years' War (1756-1763), 557
Seville, 443
Sextus Empiricus, 142
Sexual economic specialization, 13
Sexuality
  candor, 706
  Hittites, 80
  in sixteenth and seventeenth centuries, 465
  in twentieth century, 756–757, *757*
Shaanxi, 61, 171, 250
Shaka, king, 676
Shaka dynasty, 192
Shakers, 477
Shaman, 18, *18*, 67, *67*, 91, *91*, 127, 324, *474*, G–8
Shamanism, *470*
Shams al-Din, 472
Shang dynasty, 62, 67, 68, 70, 71, 87, 110
  decline of, *93*
Shanghai, *765*
  and industrialization, 620
Shapur I, *197*
Sharia, 198, 761, G–8
Sharif Husayn, 723
Sheep, 655
  in Australia, 536
Sheffield, *616*
Shelian Africa, 379
Shell shock, 724
Shen Xu, 139
Shen-rab, 222
Shenyang, 470
Shi Huangdi, 169–170, *170*
Shi Jing, 62
Shia, 200
Shiba Kokan, *570*
Shibusawa, Eiichi, 606
Shield Jaguar, *243*
Shiism, 233, 329, 499–500
Shiite, 287, 290, 543, 544, G–8
Shikibu, Murasaki, 276
Shimazu, 505
Shinto, 220, 221, 232, 715, G–8
Shintoism, 680
Shipping, steam-powered, 600
Ships, ironclad, *597*
Shoa, 377, 647
Shoguns, 277, 362, *362*, 504, 505, G–8
Shoshone, 631
Shotoko, prince, *225*
Shotoku
  empress, 221, 229
  prince, 220, *220*
Shrines, map of, *290*
Shun Ti, emperor, 345
Siberia, 422, 443, 449, *449*, 629–630, 657
Sibir, 423
Sic et Non (Yes and No) (Abelard), 283
Sichuan, 306, 307, 450
Sichun, 423
Siegfried, Jules, 599
Sierra Leone, *634*, 651, 670, 739
Sigismund, emperor, 405
Sigmund I, 478
Sigmund II, 478
Sikhism, 477, G–8
Sikhs, 646, 678
Silent Spring (Carson), 781, *781*
Silk, 499, 606
  and commerce, 156–157
  reeling, 628
Silk Roads, *150*, 156–157, *157*, 171, 215, *215*, *225*, 304, 325, *325*, 386, 447, G–8
  chronology, *157*
Silla, 172, *192*, 192–193, 219–220
  development of, *205*
Silver mining, *430*
  and Spain, 490
Silver Mountain, *430*
Silver trade, 420
Simpson, Wallis, 783
Sinai, 58
Sine, 681
Singapore, 764
Sinhalese, 112
Sino-Japanese War, 608, *608*, *729*, 745, 749
Sioux, 554, 646, 666, 681, G–8
Sitalkes, king, 106
Siyaj K'ak, 181–182, 206
Skateholm settlement, 21
Skeletons, *30*
Skepticism
  in Axial Age, 142–143
  chronology, *143*
Skull decorating, *37*
Slave Coast, 509
Slaves/slave trade, 390, *549*, 615, 647–648
  abolishing, 623, 624
  African trade, *509*, 509–511
  in the Americas, 444–445, 451, 505, 507–509, 548–552
  in ancient Egypt, 330–331
  in ancient Rome, 105
  Atlantic passes, description of, 548, *548*
  and black Catholicism, 474–476
  chronology, *558*, *625*
  chronology of trade, *509*
  in colonial America, 604
  in East Africa, 271
  emancipation, 626–628
  and imperialism, 624, 653
  and industrialization, 604
  map of, *550–551*
  Native Americans, 430
  in New England, 455
  in nineteenth century, 624–628
  and population in eighteenth century, 518
  and Portugal, 379, 623
  revolts, 555, 625
  trade and sugar cane commerce, 440, *440*
Slavs, 196, 223–224
Sleeping sickness, 643
Slovakia, 723
Slums, *590*
Smallpox, 349, 428, 518, 522, 523, *523*, 554, 590, 789
  and Native Americans, 442, *442*
Smiles, Samuel, 599, 617
Smith, Adam, 573
Smoking, 751, *751*
Snails, 45
Soapstone lamp, 21, 113
Soccer, 713
Social classes/society
  in the Americas, 454, 507
  aristocracies, 490–491
  art, *282*
  caste system, 167
  categories of, 53, *53*
  China, 502–503
  chronology, *503*, *636*
  configurations of, 62–73
  division of classes, 53, *53*
  farming, 22
  foragers and farmers, 21–22, *22*
  Greece, ancient, *105*, 105–106
  growth of, prehistoric, 53, *53*
  Hittites, 79–81
  in Ice Age, 17–19
  in Japan, 362–363, 504–505
  in Korea, 504
  in nineteenth century, 615–616
  peasants in fourteenth century Japan, 363
  and plague, 356
  in sixteenth and seventeenth centuries, *493*, 493–495
  social equality, 573–574
  working class, 726
Social Darwinism, 659, G–8
Social engineering, 703
Social equality, 573–574
Social speech, 707
Socialism, 616, 618, 684–686, *685*, 726–727, G–8
Socialist regime, 726, G–8
Socialists, 726
Sociobiology, 703, G–8
Socrates, 143, 144
Soft power, 745, 767
Soga clan, 220
Sogdiana, 162
Soka Gakkai, 770
Sokaku, *514–515*
Sokoto, 553, 679
Sokoto Fulani kingdom, map of, *553*
Solar energy, 779

Solidarity, 735, G–8
Solomids, *284,* G–8
Solomon, king, 118, 271
Solomon Islands, 253
Solon, 104, *104*
Somalia, *26,* 745
Son of Heaven, 171
Song, king, 220, *225*
Song dynasty, 392, G–8
Song empire, 304–306
art, 308, *308*
economy, 306–307
map of, *305*
Songhay, 378–379, 385, 448, G–8
in fifteenth century, *384*
Songtsen Gampo, 203–204, 221
Soninke, 216, 238, G–8
Soothsayer, 76, 87
Soothsaying, 75
Sophists, 143–144
South Africa, 653, 759, 765
democracy, 742
exploitation of environment, *459*
imperialism, 655, 656
South America
expansion of, *246*
exploitation of environment, *459*
in fifteenth century, *384*
in fourteenth century, 368
geographic obstacles, *254*
South Asia
map of, *110*
in fourteenth century, *359*
recovery of ancient civilization, 111
South Carolina, 554
South Korea, 734, 770
economy, 763
South Sea islands, 156, 534
South Vietnam, 734
South Wales, 597
Southeast Asia, 763
agriculture, 250–253
contending with isolationism, *280*
Enlightenment, 571
expansion of, *252*
in eleventh and twelfth centuries, 271–273
foreign imperialism, *642,* 643–648
in fourteenth century, 360–361, *369*
and Islam/Islamic, 471–472
map of, *252*
in fourteenth century, *359*
Southern Kingdom, 304
Southonax, Léger-Félicité, 625
Souw Beng Kong, 417
Sovereignty, 506, 580, 673
Soviet, 726, G–8
Soviet Union, 726, 727
Cold War era, 731–733
decline of, 735, 737
Space exploration, 735
Spain, 333, 490, 536
in the Americas, 426–429, 442, 444–445, 451, 454, 506, 555
chronology, *430, 455*
ancient civilization, 108–109
art, *441, 516*
Christian missionaries, 464
civil war, 728
commerce in the Americas, 426
democracy, 683
dominance of in sixteenth and seventeenth centuries, 490–492, *492, 496*
emancipation of slaves, 626
government during eleventh and twelfth centuries, 281
imperialism, 643
industrialization, 603
invasion by Almoravids, 293
and maritime navigation, 413
monarchy of, 490–492, *492*
Muslim influence, *293*
nationalism, 666, 668
in the Philippines, 541
plague of, 443
in Spanish America, 578
urbanization, 281
Spallanzani, Lorenzo, 575, 594
Spanish America, independence from Spanish rule, 558
Spanish Inquisition, 465
Spanish tobacco, 441
Spanish War of Independence, *583*
Spanish-American war, 646
Sparta, 105
Species extinction, 786–787
Spengler, Oswald, 724
Spice Islands, 414, 421
Spice trade, 414
Spirit of Laws, The (Diderot), 566
Spiritual Conquest of Spanish America, 469
Spots, 713
Sputnik I, 735
Squash, 35
Sri Lanka, 112, 275, *376,* 393, 415, 421, 468, 743
chronology, *112, 119*
civilization of, *118*
Srivijaya, 251–252, 275
St. Benedict, 474
St. Elesban, 474–476, *475*
St. George, *421, 649*
St. Iphigenia, 476
St. Lawrence River, 442
St. Paraskeva, 281
St. Petersburg, 495, 519, 603
St. Sophia cathedral, *330*
St. Stephen, 298
St. Thomas, *474*
Stalin, Joseph, 726, 727, 728, 731, *735,* 737, 750
Stanley, Henry Morton, 650
State, conflicts with Roman Catholicism, 680–681
State of Israel, *742*
State system, 172, 278, 404–406, G–8
States
effect on society, 750–754
in government, 490, 492–493, *496*
society, 65–66
Statue of Liberty, *743*
Steam power, 529, 597, 600, 601, *648*
Steamship trade, 600, 630
Stedman, John, *549*
Steel production, 526, 598, *648*
Stela of Axum, *193*
Stephen of Hungary, 223
Steppe, 152, 156, 171–174, G–8
Steppeland, 18, 32, 71, 339
exploitation of environment, *459*
imperialism, 390, 446–448
invasion of China, 171–172
Mongolian, 321–324
in thirteenth century, 337
Steppelanders, 171, *189,* 189–192, 206, *286,* 288–289
invasion of India, 191–192
invasion of Roman Empire, 185
map of, *190*
Stess, 791
Stevens, Siaka, 739
Stevenson, George, 598
Stock market crash (1922), 725
Stoicism, 143, 478, G–8
chronology, *143*
Strabo, 103, 402
Strait of Gibraltar, 279
Stranger effect, 429, 650, G–8
Stream of consciousness, 707, *707,* G–8
Stress theory and farming, 42
Stroganoffs, 422
Stump speaking (painting), *682*
Stupa of Sanchi, *168*
Su Dongpo, 308
Suárez, Francisco, 493
Subconscious, 705
Subjective language, 707
Submarine warfare, 721
Sub-Saharan Africa, 257, 699
civilization of, *118*
in fourteenth century, *369*
geographic obstacles, *254*
geography of, 238, *239*
Subsidiarity, G–8
Sudan, 680, 739
Sudanese, 646, *646*
Suez Canal, 610, *610,* 643, G–8
Suez Canal Company, 739
Suffrage, 683, 723, 762
timeline, *762*
Sufis, 229, 332, 472, *472,* G–8
Sufism, 228–229, 296
Sugar, 455
cane, 248, 440, *440*
industry, 533
production of, 398
Suger of Saint-Denis, abbot, 278, 283
Suicidal utopias, 749–750
Sulawesi, 468
Suleiman the Magnificant, *390,* 425, 426, *446,* 497
Sultan Idris Training College for Medicine, 698
Sultanate of Aceh, 472
Sultanate of Delhi, 331–332, *332,* 404
Sultaniyyah tomb, *342*
Sultans, 495–497
Sulu Islands, 467
Sumatra, 194, 252, 393, 472, 540
expansion of, 251
Sumer/Sumerians, 65, *68,* 70, *71,* 72, 92
Sumpweed, 38
Sun Myung Moon, *757*
Sun Pyramid, 174
Sundiata, 364, G–8
Sunflowers, 38
Sunghir, *19*
Sun-god, 64–65
Sunkuru, 518
Sunni/Sunnism, 200, 233, 287, 290, 296, 497, 543, 768, G–8
Supe Valley, 53
Superpower, 641
Superstring theory, 702
Superwoman, 761
Surinam, 440, 508, 549, *549,* 601, *760*
Surrealism, 712, G–8
Survival of the fittest theory, 659
Suryavarman II, king, 271–272, *272*
Susa, 157
Susa-no-o (god), 249
Susutra, 141
Swahili, 539–540
Swampland for tilling, 33–35
Sweden, 223, 490
Sweet potato, 35, 42, 436–437, 532
Switzerland, industrialization, 603
Sydney, 534, *655*
Syllogisms, 138, G–8
Sylvanus, Bernardus, *374*
Synagogue, 668, *668*
Syncretic, 474, G–8
Syncretism, 476
Syntax, 708
Syr Darya, 780
Syria, 162, 543, 628
Szigetvár, *446*

T

Tabasco, *90*
Tagore, Abindranath, 712
Tagus valley, 293
Tahiti, 534, 558, 559, 578, 579
Taiping Rebellion, 607, 641, G–8
Taipings, 607
Taira, 277
Taira clan, *280*
Taiwan, 656
conquest of, 450
Taizong, 202
Taizu Emperor, 306
Takla Haymanyot, 270
Taklamakan Desert, 157, 325
Tale of Genji, The (Shikibu), 276, *276*
Taliban regime, 769
Talking Cross, 681
Tamati Waka, *664*
Tamil, 743
Tamkaru, 77
Tana, 326
Tan-fu, 67
Tang China, map of, *201*
Tang dynasty, 202–203, 250, 303–304, G–8
Tanit (god), 98
Tanjore, 275
Taro, 366, G–8
cultivation of, 33
Tartaria, 54
Tartessos, 109
Tasmania, 28
Tawhiao, 679
king, 665
Tayama's, 719
Tbilisi, *658*
Tea, 420, 441, 641
industry, *599,* 628, *629*
Technology
and imperialism, *648*
in nineteenth century, 700
Teff, 36, *36*
Telegraph, transatlantic, 600
Tel-Eilat Ghasuul, *48–49*
Telephone lines, *766*
Telescope, 484, *529,* 701
Television, 713
Temperature changes, *344, 788,* 788–789
Temple of Artemis, 147
Temple of Solomon, *289*
Temujin, 316
Tench, Watkin, 535
Tengri, G–8
Tenochtitlán, 382, *382,* 385, 428, *428*
Teosinte, 35, *36*
Teotihuacán, 174, 181–184, 206, 245, 385
art, 174
map of, *173, 183*
transformation of, *199*
Teotihuacáno, 181–183
Terra Australis, 578
Territorial imperialism, 421
Terror alert, *754*
Terrorism, *754*
Teutonic Knights, 330
Teutonic Orders, 370
Tewodros II, 681
Textile industry, 529–530, 619, *642*

Thailand, 623, 655, 678
in eighteenth century, 542
Enlightenment, 571
and imperialism, 404, 643
modernization, *676*
relations with China, 542
Thaisa, king, 542
Thaj, 153
Thames River, *345*
Thanesar, 194
Thar Desert, 86
The Mongol Peace, 321, G–8
Theaters of the world, 481
Thebes, 69
Theodora, empress, 195, *195,* 298
Theodoric, king, 189
Theodosius, 224
Theophilus, 217
Theory of progress, 522
Theory of the Leisure Class, The (Veblen), 635
Theory of value, G–8
Thera, 82
Theravada Buddhism, 221, 233, G–8
Third Rome, 386, G–8
Tholos, *139*
Thomas Cook and Company, 635
Thorgeirr Thorkelsson, 222–223
Thrace/Thracians, 106, *107*
Three Gorges Dam, 781
Thule Inuit, 370, G–8
chronology, *265*
migration, 264–265, *265*
migration, map of, *265*
Tiahuanaco, 241, 244, 257, 385
Tian Shan, 326
Tibet/Tibetans, 203–204, *204,* 446, 470, 541, 737
chronology, *204*
development of, *205*
map of, *201*
and spread of Buddhism, 221–222
Tierra del Fuego, 659, *659*
Tigris River, 37, 55, 59
Tikal, 181–182, 242
Tilling/tillers, 30–31, G–9. *See also* Farming
compared with herding/herders, *34*
environment of, 33–38
Timber as energy source, 456
Time
measurement of, 635
perception of, 707
Timur, 423, 498
map of, *388–389*
Timur the Lame, 387
Timurids, 386–389
Tintin, *718*
Tippu Tip, *626*
Tipu Sultan, 547
Tisza, 54
Tlaxcala, *428*
Tobacco, 436, *437*
in the Americas, 441, 455
Tobolsk, 449, *449*
Tocqueville, Alexis de, 618, 656, 682
Tokaido Highway, *519*
Tokugawa, *504,* 504–505, 606, G–9
Tokyo-Yokohama railway line, *606*
Tolstoy, Leo, 615
Tominaga Nakamoto, 569
Tomsk, 449
Tonatiuh, *556*
Tonga, 253
Tongzhi, *695*
Tonle Sap, 251
Tool-making technologies, *8*
Topkapi Saray, 495–496
Torokawa, 473
Tosa Lady, 263, 277
Toshimichi, Okuba, 606
Total war, 596
Toulon, *390*
Trade. *See* Commerce; Economy
Trading-post empires, 415, G–9
Trail of Tears, 658
Trajan, emperor, 256
Transoxania, 322, 446
Transportation, 522, *601*
in early civilization, 54
Trans-Siberian railway, *608,* 630
Transylvania, 426
Traviata, La (Verdi), 629
Trdat, king, 218, *225*
Treasure Fleets, *427,* G–9
Treatise on Astronomy, A (Dias), 484
Trebizond, 315
Trent, Council of, 464
Trevithick, Richard, 599
Tribunes, 165
Tribute system, 382, *382,* 384–385, 422–423, 428
Trisong Detsen, 221, *221, 225*
Tristram, 403
Trollope, Anthony, 594
Truman, Harry, *729*
Trumbull, John, *558*
Trundholm, *83*
Tsu Jia, 67
Tuareg, 553
Tuberculosis, 443, 789, 791
Tudhaliya IV, 81
Tugaru, 456
Tukolor, 651
Tula, 182, 245, 257, 385
expansion of, *246*
Tundra, 16, G–9
Tunis, 351, 528
Tunisia, 650, 674, 739
Turkestan, 329
Turkey, 424, 440, 543, 698, 723, 744
Enlightenment, 567
Turkeys, 441
Turkish Military Engineering School, *586–587*
Turkmenia, 85
Turkmenistan, 38
Turks, 288–289, 300, 360, G–9
in Germany, 758, *759*
invasion of Balkans, 425
Seljuk, 288
and spread of Islam/Islamic, 224
Turner, Joseph, 599
Turnips, 594
Turtle ships, 417
Tut-mose I, 93
Twentieth century, chronology, *745, 771, 793*
Type-II diabetes, 783
Typhus, 349, 443, 522
Tyre, 98

U

Uganda, 739, *741*
Ugarit, 77, 85
Uighurs, 215, 303, 320
Ukraine, 54
Ulloa, Antonio de, 576
Ulysses (Joyce), *707*
Umar I, caliph, 225
Umar II, caliph, 225
Umma, 70
Uncertainty principle, 701, G–9
Uncle Sam, 721
Unification Church, *757*
United Fruit Company, 653
United Nations, 730, G–9
United Provinces of Central America, 670
United Society of Believers in Christ's Second Coming, 477
United States
business imperialism, 652–653
centralization, 674
Civil War, 597, *597*
democracy, 681–682
immigration, 630, *630*
imperialism, 658, *658*
resistance to, *669*
industrialization, 600, 604
militarization, 674
nationalism, 670, 673
post World War I, 725
as superpower, 743
World War I, 720–721, 723
Universal Exposition, 621
Universal love, 131–134, G–9
Universe, view of, 481–482
University Garden of Leiden, 532
University of Beijing, 695
University of Chicago, 765
University of Dunedin, 532
University of Leiden, 698
University of Paris, 333, 334
University of Pennsylvania, *704*
Upanishads, 111–112, 127, 132, 139, 144, 714, G–9
Uplands for tilling, 35–36
Upper Egypt, 70
Ur, 62, 70
codes of, 65
Uranium, 779
Urban guerrilla, 756
Urban II, pope, 278, 289
Urban planning, 620
Urban projects, 751, 753–754
Urbanization, 454, *620,* 784–785, G–9
chronology, *623*
in eighteenth century, 519
in eleventh and twelfth centuries, 279
map of, *602, 785*
in nineteenth century, social effects, 620–621
and spread of disease, 590, *590*
Uruguay, 655, 670, 756
Uruk, 66, *66*
Urumqi, 541
Usuman da Fodio, 553
Utilitarianism, 685, G–9
Utopia, 750
Utopianism, *686,* G–9
Uzbek Empire, 351, 446, 499

V

Vaccination, *523,* G–9
Vakatakas, 192
Valencia, 425
Valerian, emperor, 197, *197*
Valley of Mexico, *383*
Vandal Stilicho, *188*
Vandals, 188
Vanderbilt, Cornelius, 599
Vardhaana Jnatrputra, 127
Vattagamani, king, 214
Veblen, Thorstein, 634–635
Veda, 127, 147, 232, 563
Velleius, 164
Veneral disease, 443
Venezuela, 431, 670, 743
Venice
and Byzantium, 301–302
plague of, 443
Venus, *242,* 255
Venus of Laussel, 16, *16*
Venus of Willendorf, 16
Verbiest, Ferdinand, 485
Verdi, Giuseppe, 629
Vernacular languages, 466, G–9
Vernes, Jules, 779
Veroli casket, *302*
Viceroy, 507
Victoria, queen of England, 620, 650, 651, 653, *664*
Vicuñas, 35
Videha, 147
Vidyasagar, Isvarcandra, 662
Vieira, António da, 476
Vienna, 498, 519, 620
Vienna Codex, *269*
Viet kingdom, 251
Vietnam, 646, *734,* 734–735, 743
art, *87*
in eighteenth century, 543
Enlightenment, 571, *571*
invasion by Mongols, 320
nationalism, 672
Vietnam War, *734,* 734–735, 750
Vijayanagar, 360, 375, 404, *404*
Vilcabamba, 506
Villani, Matteo, 350
Vindication of the Rights of Woman, A (Wollstonecraft), 574
Virgil, 164, 478
Virgin Lands, 735
Virgin Mary, *293,* 464, 466, 477
Virgin of the Rosary, 681
Virginia, colony, 437, 442, 444
Virtual reality, 766, G–9
Viruses, 790–791, *791*
Visigoths, 185, 188, 206
art, *236*
Vision, *482*
Vitamin C, 523
Vitascope, *700*
Vitis vinifera, *439*
Vitoria, Francisco de, 493
Vladimir, *225*
Vladimir of Kiev, 223–224
Vladivostock, 600
Volga River, 386, 422
Volta River, 238
Voltaire, 566, *566,* 567, 572, 574, 576, 580
Vora, Virji, 418
Voyages to Moscow, Persia, and the East Indies (Brun), *499*
Vulci, *105*

W

Wahhabbism, 544, *544,* 553, G–9
Walcher of Malvern, 283
Walid I, caliph, *236*
Walker, Thomas, *664*
Wall Strett, 725
Wallachia, 426
Wang Anshi, 308
Wang Fuzhi, 483
Wang Guangyi, 711
Wangchong, 142
Wanli emperor, 501–502
War atrocities, *748,* 749–750
War of 1812, 655
War on Terror, *754*
Warfare, *674. See also* Military/weaponry
Almoravids, 293
chronology, *216*
and Islam, 212–213
Mongols, 316–320
in nineteenth century, 674–675
origin of, 12
submarine, 721
Warring States, 118, 130, 170

Wars of Religion, 494
Watan, 671
Watermill technology, *248*
Watling Island, 479
Watteau, Jean-Antoine, 566
Wealth of Nations, The (Smith), 573
Wealth of world, 776–777, *778*
Weather
 in Andes, 381, *381*
 change in fourteenth century, 344–348
Weaving, 52
Weber, Max, 419
Weeds, in the Americas, 437
Wei, king, 145
Welfare, *755*
Wells, H.G., 6
Wenamun, 97
Wendel, Francois, 599
Were-jaguars, 89
Wesley, Charles, 576
Wesley, John, 576
West Africa, *364,* 398, 441, 622, 628
 See also Africa
 art, *379*
 conquest by Muslims, 553
 in fifteenth century, 378–379, *384*
 in fourteenth century, 363–364
 and Islam/Islamic, 472–473
 nationalism, 671
 slave trade, 552, *552*
West Germany and Turkish immigrants, *759*
West Indies, 629
West Nile virus, 791
Westerlies, *154,* G–9
Western Europe
 chronology, *284*
 contending with isolationism, *280*
 economics and politics, 277–282
 in fifteenth century, 399–403
 map of pilgrim routes and shrines, *231*
 religion and culture, 281–283
Western Front, *721,* 723–724
Western science, 694–709
 in China, 695
 chronology, *485, 709, 716*
 in India, 698
 map of spread, *696–697*
 rise of, 480–483
 transformation, 700–709, *710*
Westernization, 634–635, 666, G–9
Westphalia, Treaty of, 490
Whaling industry, *588,* 589
Wheat, 36, 37, 38, 42, 44, 782
 in the Americas, 436–437
White America religion, 476–477
White Australia policy, 759
Whitfield, George, 575–576
Widow suicide, 503, 563
Widowhood, 494
"Wife of Bath," *357*
Wild Boy of Aveyron, 579
Wild children, 579
Wilfrid the Hairy, 256
Wilhelm II, emperor of Germany, 660
William of Conches, 283
William of Rubruck, 321–324, *323, 324*
William of Tyre, 301
Williams, Samuel, 605
Wilson, Edward O., 703
Wilson, Woodrow, 723
Wind, 111, 113, *114–115,* 153, *154–155,* 156, 328, 375, *396–397,* 400–401, 413, 779, *779*
Wind energy, 779, *779*
Wind map, *396–397*
Windmill-pumping technology, 456–457
Witchcraft, 464, *465*
Witsen, Nicholaas, 441
Wittgenstein, Ludwig, 708
Wojtyla, Karel, 735
Woldemar, Frederik, *421*
Wolf children, 579
Wollstonecraft, Mary, 574
Wolseley, Garnet, 651
Women
 Almoravids, 293
 in ancient Greece, *105,* 105–106, *108*
 in ancient India, 167–168
 in ancient river valley civilizations, 62–63
 in art, *202*
 in China, 202, 307, 503
 in eleventh century, 298
 Enlightenment, 573–574
 equal rights, 716
 Etruscan, 108
 feminism, 573–574
 in fourteenth century, 356–357
 in fourteenth century Japan, 362–363
 and Freud, 706
 Greece, ancient, *105*
 Hittites, 80–81
 and imperialism, 651
 Islamic, 332
 in Japan, 205
 labor in nineteenth century, 628–629, *629*
 in Mongolian society, 324
 Muslim, 198
 Persian, 159–160
 in prehistorical society, 12–13
 religious, 229
 right to vote, 723, 761
 role in twentieth century society, 761–762
 as rulers, *488,* 489, 494, *494,* 552
 in Russia, 495
 in sixteenth and seventeenth centuries, 494
 spreading Christianity, 216–217
Wonder chambers, 481, *481*
Won'gwang, 220
Wool industry, *532,* 536
Wordsworth, William, 577
World
 creation of, 334–335
 geography, 140
 map of, *586–587*
 map of migration, *633*
World Health Organization, 714, *774,* 782
World system, 406, G–9
World Trade Center attack, *754,* 765–766
World War I, 642, 675, 700, 712, 720–724, *721, 729,* 761, G–9
 casualties, *721,* 721–722
 chronology, *728*
World War II, *729,* 729–731, 750, G–9
 chronology, *728*
 debt reparations, 723
 map of, *730*
 postwar disillusionment, 724–725
 postwar settlements, 723
Wounded Knee, 681
Wright brothers, 700
Writing, *71*
 Cherokee, *672*
 of Great River Valleys, *71,* 71–72
 Greek, 105–106
 Harappan, *58*
 in Ice Age, 18
 Mayan, *243,* 244
 Mesoamerica, 174
 Phoenician, 99
Wu, empress, 202, 229
Wu Ding dynasty, 67
Wu Zhao, 202
Wudi, 157
Wuwei, *157*
Wuyang, 71

X

Xhosa, 552
Xia, 304
Xia dynasty, 68
Xianbei, 191, 192
Xianjang and exploitation of environment, *459*
Xing, 87
Xinjiang, 423, 541
Xiongnu dynasty, 171–172, 185
 chronology, *171*
Xiutecutli, *408–409*
X-rays, 700
Xuan, 110
Xuantong, 303
Xuanzang, *210,* 222, *225*
Xunzi, 134, 141, 144, *146*

Y

Yahweh, 133
Yahya ibn Khalid, 248
Yakuts, 423
Yale-Hunan Clinic, *692,* 693
Yamatai, 172
Yamato, 204
Yams, 28, 34
Yan Fu, 695
Yang Jian, 200, 219
Yang Tingyun, 467
Yangbans, 504
Yangdi, 200
Yangtze River, 70, 171, 200, 250, 450, 781
Yangtze valley, 306, 350
Yao, 636
Yaqui Indians, 646
Yaxchilán, *243*
Yayoi, 172
Yellow Emperor, 68
Yellow fever, 443, 523, 552, 643, 791
Yellow Peril, 660
Yellow River, 55, 61–62, *62,* 70, 86–88, 200
 map of, *391*
Yellow Temple, 470
Yemen, 116, 247, 440
Yi, 140–141
Yi Ik, 571
Yi Tinggao, 328
Yi T'oegye, 483
Yijing, general, 639, 640
Yodfo River, 457
Yohannes IV, 678
Yongle emperor, 392
Yongzheng emperor, 568
Yorktown, *558*
Yoruba, 238
Yoshimune, 569
Younghusband, Francis, 660
Yu the Great, 67, 201
Yucatán, 242, 257, 269, 431, 469, 681
 contending with isolationism, *280*
Yucca, 35
Yugoslavia, 732
Yukichi, Fukuzaw, 606
Yunnan plague, 444
Yurt, *324*

Z

Zaghawa, 238
Zagros Mountains, 38, 157
Zagwe, 271
Zakros, 82, *82*
Zambezi valley, 377, *378,* 552
 in fifteenth century, *384*
Zangi, 290, 291
Zanzibar, 270, 393, 648
 emancipation of slaves, 626
Zaoyin, 524
Zayinda Rud, 157
Zaynab al-Nafzawiya, 293
Zealand, 419
Zealots of Piety, 467
Zeker Baal, 97
Zen, 362, G–9
Zen Buddhism, 714, 760
Zeng Guofan, 608
Zeno of Citium, 143, 144, *146*
Zeno of Elea, 138
Zhang Qian, 156
Zhang Zeduan, 307
Zhanyinbao, *502*
Zhao, prince, 145
Zhen Ji, *307*
Zhen Yilao, 542
Zheng He, *393,* 393–394
Zhengde emperor, 501
Zhou Chunya, 712
Zhou dynasty, 71, 87–88, 92
 chronology, *88, 119*
 civilization of, *118*
 decline of, *93,* 109–110, *110*
Zhoukhoudian, *11*
Zhu Hong, 469
Zhu Shixing, 227–228
Zhu Wen, 303
Zhu Xi, 308
Zhu Yuanzhang, 392
Zhuangzi, 143
Ziggurats, 56, *60,* G–9
Zimbabwes, 377, 646, 739, G–9
Zinzendorff, Count, 575
Zoe, empress, 298, *300*
Zola, Emile, 675
Zoroaster, 126–127, *146,* 147
Zoroastrianism, 126–127, 147, 174, 214, 215, 232, *329,* G–9
Zoroastrians, 126, *127,* 198, 225
Zulus, 646, 651, 676
Zumárraga, Juan de, *469*
Zurbarán, Juan de, *441*
Zuurveld, 553

New Sources are in **Bold**

PART 1 Foragers and Farmers, to 5000 B.C.E

1. Out of the Ice: Peopling the Earth

Text Sources
Marshall Sahlins, "The Original Affluent Society," from *Stone Age Economics*
Margaret Mead, from "Warfare is Only an Invention—Not a Biological Necessity"
Jane Goodall, from "The Challenge Lies in All of Us"

Visual Souces
Chauvet Cave—bison
Chauvet cave—horses
Chauvet cave—red dots
Chauvet cave—close up of horses
Lascaux—bull
Hominid tools

2. Out of the Mud: Farming and Herding After the Ice Age

Text Sources
James Cook, from *Captain Cook's Journal During his First Voyage Round the World*
Jack Harlan, *from Crops and Man*
David Rindos, from "Symbiosis, Instability, and the Origins and Spread of Agriculture: A New Model"
Charles Darwin, "Cultivated Plants: Cereal and Culinary Plants," from *The Variation of Animals and Plants under Domestication*

Visual Sources
Indians planting corn
The Dolmen of Kerhan

PART 2 Farmers and Builders, 5000–500 B.C.E

3. The Great River Valleys: Accelerating Change and Developing States

Text Sources
The Code of Hammurabi
Sumerian Law Code: *The Code of Lipit-Ishtar*
Excerpts from *The Epic of Gilgamesh*
Egyptian Diplomatic Correspondence: excerpts from *The Amarna Letters*
Workings of Ma'at: "The Tale of the Eloquent Peasant"
Ptahhotep, from the *Egyptian Book of Instructions*
Praise of the Scribe's Profession: Egyptian Letter
Early Criminal Justice: The Nippur Murder Trial and the "Silent Wife"
Ancestor Worship: from the *Shi Jing*

Visual Sources
Stonehenge, Salisbury, England
The Standard of Ur
Shang royal tomb
Egyptian obelisks
Cuneiform tablet

4. A Succession of Civilizations: Ambition and Instability

Text Sources
Liu the Duke and Tan-Fu the Duke, from the *Shi Jing*
Hou-Ji, from the *Shi Jing*
Hittite Law Code: excerpts from *The Code of the Nesilim*
Ancient Egyptian and Hittite Voices: (a) letter from the Pharaoh to Harkhuf the explorer; (b) Ramses III, "The War Against the Sea Peoples;" (c) Hittite soldiers' oath
Hittite Land Deed

Visual Sources
Abu Simbel
Horse and Sun Chariot from Trundholm, Denmark, circa 1800–1600 BCE

5. Rebuilding the World: Recoveries, New Initiatives, and Their Limits

Text Sources
Mission to Byblos: *The Report of Wenamun*
The Babylonian Chronicles, "The Fall of Nineveh Chronicle"
Syrian Government Documents: *The Archives of Ebla*
Hesiod, excerpt from *Works and Days*
Aristophanes, excerpt from *The Birds*
Homer, Debate Among the Greeks, from *The Odyssey*
Plutarch, from *Life of Lycurgus: Education and Family in Sparta*
Aristotle, *The Creation of the Democracy in Athens*
Sophocles, from *Antigone*
Thucydides, *Pericles Funeral Oration*
Procopius of Caesarea, History of the Wars, c. 550 CE
The Selection of Aspalta as King of Kush, c. 600 B.C.E

Visual Sources
The Parthenon
Assyrian winged bull
Assyrian warriors
Assyrian king list
Greek athletics

PART 3 The Axial Age, from 500 B.C.E to 100 C.E.

6. The Great Schools

Text Sources
The Book of Job and Jewish Literature
Vardhamana Mahariva, selections from *Akaranga-sutra*, "Jain Doctrines and Practices of Nonviolence"
Siddhartha Gautama: "Identity and Non-identity"
Selections from the *Rig Veda*
Excerpt from the *Upanishads*
The Nyaya School, "Explanation of the Sutra"
Plato, *The Republic*, "The Philosopher-King"
Plato, *The Republic*, "On Shadows and Realities in Education"
Liu An, excerpt from *Huan Nan Tzu*
Legalism: selections from the writings of Han Fei
Laozi, from *Tao Te Ching*, "The Unvarying Way"
Confucius, selections from the *Analects*
Confucian political philosophy: an excerpt from *Mencius*
Aristotle, excerpts from *Physics* and *Posterior Analytics*

Visual Sources
The opening words of Genesis
Albrecht Dürer, *Adam and Eve*
Detail of a statue from Delphi
Nine Hindu planets
Hindu Gods
Illustration of a paradox of Zeno and Elea
Daoist scroll
Confucius
Archimedes' mirror
The Book of Adam

Jain cosmographical map

7. The Great Empires

Text Sources
From the Periplus of the Erythraean Sea: Travel and Trade in the Indian Ocean
Horace, "Dulce et Decorum est Pro Patria Mori"
Livy, The Rape of Lucretia and the Origins of the Republic
Slaves in the Roman Countryside
Augustus' Moral Legislation: Family Values
Juvenal, A Satirical View of Women
Zhang Quian, *Han Shu*, "Descriptions of the Western Regions"
Sima Qian, *The Life of Meng Tian, Builder of the Great Wall*
Kautilya, from *Arthashastra*, "The Duties of Government Superintendents"

Greece and Persia: The Treaty of Antalcides, 387 BCE
Excerpts from *The Questions of King Milinda*
Emperor Asoka, from *The Edicts of Asoka*
Agatharchides of Cnidos describes Saba
The "Cyrus Cylinder": The First Declaration of Religious Freedom
Emperor Wudi, Dunhunag, China

Visual Sources
Tombstone of a Roman soldier
Teotihuacán
Thucydides and Herodotus
The Great Wall of China
Statue of Caesar Augustus
Roman Forum
Roman aqueduct
Pyramid at Tikal
Pyramid at Teotihuacán
Han Chinese house
Elephanta Water Cave, India

PART 4 Fitful Transitions, from the Third Century to Tenth Century

8. Postimperial Worlds: Problems of Empires in Eurasia and Africa, ca. 200 C.E. to ca. 700 C.E.
Marcus Aurelius, *The Meditations*, Book Two (167 CE)
Ammianus Marcellinus on the Huns
Prologue of the *Corpus Juris Civilis*
Pliny the Elder, from *The Natural History*
Treaty between Tibet and China, 821–822
Sidonius Apollinaris, *Rome's Decay* and *A Glimpse of the New Order*
Jordanes, *The Origin and Deeds of the Goths*, Book twenty-six
Faxien, *Record of Buddhist Countries*, chapter sixteen
Excerpts from the *Hildebrandslied*
Chinese description of the Tibetans
Arabic Poetry: "The Poem of Antar"
Excerpts from the Quran
Tang Daizong on the art of government

Visual Sources
The interior of Hagia Sophia
Norse ship
Cihuatán clay figure
Quran's first chapter

9. The Rise of World Religions: Christianity, Islam, and Buddhism

Text Sources:
Buddhism: excerpts from the *Dhammapada*
Xuanzang, from *Buddhist Records of the Western World*
St. Benedict's Rules for Monks
From *The Conversion of Kartli* (the life of St. Nino)
Rabi'a al-'Adawiyya, "Brothers, my peace is in my aloneness."
Ali: Instructions to Malik al-Ashtar, Governor of Egypt
Al-Tabari: Muhammad's Call to Prophecy
Al-Tabari and Ibn Hisham, from "The Founding of the Caliphate"
A selection from Muhammad's "Orations"
St. Augustine of Hippo, Theory of the "Just War"
Pope Leo I on Bishop Hilary of Aries
Pliny the Younger, *Epistulae Letters*
Paulus Orosius, from *Seven Books of History Against the Pagans*
Bishop Synesius of Cyrene, Letter to his brother
The Acts of the Apostles: Paul Pronounces the "Good News" in Greece
Gnostic Teachings of Jesus, According to Irenaeus
Perpetua, *The Autobiography of a Christian Martyr*
The Confession of Saint Patrick
Eusebius of Caesarea, selections from *Life of Constantine*
Abi Yaqubi, excerpt from *Tarikh*
Ibn Wahab: an Arab merchant visits Tang China
Ibn Fadlan's Account of the Rus

Visual Sources
The Lotus Sutra
Sutra of 1000 Buddhas
The baptism of Clovis
The Dome of the Rock
Mosque of al-Azhar
Medina
Mecca
Al Quibla schematic map
The Gelati Tondo of St. Mamai
T-O Map from Isidore of Seville
St. John the Evangelist from a twelfth-century manuscript
Jvari Monastery, Georgia
Eleventh-century illuminated Gospel manuscript
Armenian Monastery

10. Remaking the World: Innovation and Renewal on Environmental Frontiers in the Late First Millenium

Text Sources:
Indian Land Grants, 753 CE
Excerpts from the *Taika Reform Edicts*
Baghdad: City of Wonders
Harun al-Rashid and the Zenith of the Caliphate
Al-Farabi, from *Al-Farabi on the Perfect State*
Selection from *Nihongi*, "The Age of the Gods"
Nineteenth-century European descriptions of the Pacific island of Lelu
Nestor, *The Russian Primary Chronicle*
Einhard, Preface to *The Life of Charlemagne*
Buddhism in Japan: The Taika Reform Edicts

Visual Souces
Polynesian reed map
Venus calendar from the Dresden Codex

PART 5 Contacts and Conflicts, 1000 C.E. to 1200 C.E.

11. Contending with Isolation: ca. 1000–1200

Text Sources
The Magna Carta, 1215
Nineteenth-century description of Cahokia
Peter Abelard, "Sic et Non"
Murasaki Shikibu, selections from *The Tale of Genji*
Ki no Tsurayaki, excerpt from *The Tosa Diary*
Speculum Principi, "The Animal Life of Greenland and the Character of the Land in Those Regions."

Visual Sources
Shinto creation myth
Mixtec creation myth
Extract from the Domesday Book
Canyon de Chelly, Arizona
Angkor Wat, Cambodia
Wells Cathedral, England

12. The Nomadic Frontiers: The Islamic World, Byzantium, and China: ca. 1000–1200

Text Sources
Al-Ghazali, "On the Separation of Mathematics and Religion"
Al-Ghazali, excerpt from *Confessions*
Anna Comnena, from *The Alexiad*
Lu You, excerpt from "Diary of a Journey to Sichuan"
Liutprand of Cremona, excerpt from *Report of His Mission to Constantinople*
Benjamin of Tudela, selection from *Book of Travels*
A Muslim View of the Crusades: Behâ-ed-Din, Richard I Massacres Prisoners after Taking Acre, 1191
al-Tha'alibi, *Recollections of Bukhara*

The Book of Dede Korkut, "The Story of Bugach Khan"
Al Ghazali, excerpt from *Confessions*

Visual Sources
Islamic science and alchemy: page from "The Lanterns of Wisdom and the Keys of Mercy"
Islamic astronomy and astrology: illustration of Rami
Vardzia monastery complex, Georgia
Song dynasty map of China
Early Korean woodblock printing: *The Tripitaka Koreana*
Illustrated Byzantine manuscript showing Byzantines fighting the Bulgarians
View of Acre
Saladdin
Medieval Islamic map of the world
Islamic world map

PART 6 The Crucible: The Eurasian Crisis of the Thirteenth and Fourteenth Centuries

13. The World the Mongols Made

Text Sources
The Mongols: An excerpt from the *Novgorod Chronicle*, 1315
Marco Polo, excerpt from *The Travels of Marco Polo*
Excerpts from *The History of the Life and Travels of Rabban Bar Sawma*
Excerpt from William of Rubruck's *Account of the Mongols*
Francesco Balducci Pegolotti, a fourteenth-century Italian Guide for Merchants
Giovanni Di Piano Carpini on the Mongols
Thomas Aquinas, *Summa Theologica*, "Of Human Law"
Saint Francis of Assisi, selection from his *Admonitions*
Roger Bacon, "On Experimental Science", 1268
Sufi poetry: Hafez, from the *Diwan*

Visual Sources
Tamar, king of Georgia
Mongol "ger"
Medieval world view: The Book of Nature
Medieval medicine
Medieval medical manuscript
Illustration from *The Life of Christ*
Illustration from *Die Proprietatibus Rerum*

14. The Revenge of Nature: Plague, Cold, and the Limits of Disaster in the Fourteenth Century

Text Sources
Winada Prapanca, *Nagara Kertagama*
Marchione di Coppo Stefani, *The Florentine Chronicle*, "Concerning a Mortality in the City of Florence in which Many People Died"
Ibn Battuta, *The Travels of Ibn Battuta*, "Ibn Battuta in Mali"
Al-Umari describes Mansa Musa of Mali
Ibn Khaldun, from the *Muqaddimah*
University of Paris Medical Faculty, Writings on the Plague
John Ball's Sermon
Ibn Battuta, selections from the *Rihla*

Visual Sources
Ozette whale fin
The First Horseman of the Apocalypse
The Black Death: a plague victim
Wheel of Fortune
Medieval depiction of Adam & Eve: from the *Latin Book of Hours*

15. Expanding World: Recovery in the Late Fourteenth and Fifteenth Centuries

Text Sources
An essay question from the Chinese imperial examination system
Selection from *Narrative of the Journey of Abd-er Razzak*
Ma Huan, excerpt from *The Overall Survey of the Ocean's Shores*
Descriptions of the cities of Zanj
Lorenzo Valla Skewers the Supposed "Donation of Constantine"
Leo Africanus Describes Timbuktu
A Contemporary Describes Timur
Excerpts from the journal of Christopher Columbus, 1492
Excerpt from the travel journal of Vasco da Gama

Visual Sources
Great Zimbabwe
French customary laws I
French customary laws II
French customary laws III
French customary laws IV
Book of Kings: Illustrations from the *Shahnamah*
Sixteenth-century portolan from Majorca
Illustrations from *The Travels of Sir John of Mandeville*
Woodcut by Albrecht Dürer showing perspective
Sketches by Leonardo da Vinci for fortifying cities
Leonardo da Vinci's *Vitruvian Man*
Drawing from Leonardo da Vinci's *Codice Atlantico*
Ptolemaic world map
Image of the universe, from the *Nuremberg Chronicle*
Illustration from *The Properties of Things*
First printed medical text with illustrations
Cupola of Santa Maria del Fiore Church, Florence
Map of the Yellow River

PART 7 Convergence and Divergence to ca. 1700

16. Imperial Arenas: New Empires in the Sixteenth and Seventeenth Centuries

Text Sources
Ogier Ghiselin de Busbecq, "Süleyman the Lawgiver"
Excerpts from the Biography of Emperor Akbar of India
Abu'l-Fadl 'Allami's *Ain-i-Akbari*
Excerpt from the memoirs of Babur
Toyotomi Hideyoshi, on the Conquest of China
Japan Encounters the West
Jan van Linschoten, on Dutch business in the Indian Ocean
Hans Mayr, Account of Francisco d'Almeida's attack on Kilwa and Mombasa
Gaspar Correa, excerpt from his journal, 1502
Excerpt from *The Broken Spears*, an Indian account of the conquest of Mexico
Duarte Barbosa, accounts of his journeys to Africa and India
Domingo Navarrete, "Of My Stay in the Kingdom of Macasar"
Bernal Diaz del Castillo, from the *True History of the Conquest of New Spain*
Bartolomé de las Casas, from *Brief Account of the Devastation of the Indies*

Visual Sources
Founding of Tenochtitlan
The mausoleum of Akbar the Great
Ottoman naval attack on the island of Gerbi
View of Tenochtitlan
View of Kilwa
View of Hormuz
Vespucci's encounter with Indians
Sixteenth-century portolan
Seventeenth-century Portuguese trading posts in the Indian Ocean
Russian views of "People of the Empire"
Illustration of Powatan from John Smith's account
Pocahontas
John Smith and Opechancanough, from John Smith's account
Illustration from de Sahagun's "History of the Conquest of New Spain"
Francis Drake's encounter with Indians
Verardi's illustration of Columbus's encounter with the Indians
Chinese map of Central Asia
Sixteenth-century world map
Sixteenth-century map of the Atlantic
Seventeenth-century Portuguese map of the Indian Ocean
Portuguese map of the Caribbean and South Atlantic

17. The Ecological Revolution of the Sixteenth and Seventeenth Centuries

Text Sources

Shi Daonon, "Death of Rats"
Thomas Gage, Writings on chocolate
Thomas Dudey, Letter to Lady Bridget, Countess of Lincoln, 1631
Smallpox epidemic in Mexico, 1520, from Bernardino de Sahagún, *Florentine Codex: General History of the Things of New Spain*, 1585
Smallpox epidemic in New England, William Bradford, from *History of Plymouth Plantation*, 1633–1634
Charles Albanel, *Jesuit Relation* of 1669–1670

Visual Sources

First Dutch national atlas
View of Cuzco
Samuel de Champlain's map of eastern North America
Illustrations from Jacques Le Moyne and Theodore de Bry of Indians I
Illustrations from Jacques Le Moyne and Theodore de Bry of Indians II
Illustrations from Jacques Le Moyne and Theodore de Bry of Indians III
Illustrations from Jacques Le Moyne and Theodore de Bry of Indians IV
Huron women grinding corn
View of Loango
Sugar plantation, Brazil
Map of Greenland
King Philip's War
House in Benin
Gold coast dress
Early European depiction of the banana
Don Alvaro of Kongo
Cod fishing, Newfoundland, eighteenth century
Illustrations from *Voyages and Travels* by Thomas Astley I
Illustrations from *Voyages and Travels* by Thomas Astley II
Illustrations from *Voyages and Travels* by Thomas Astley III
Map of Virginia
Map of Kongo, Angola to Benguela

18. Mental Revolutions: Religion and Science in the Sixteenth and Seventeenth Centuries

Text Sources

Erasmus, "Pope Julius Excluded from Heaven," 1513
Martin Luther, "Ninety-Five Theses" (Holy Roman Empire), 1517
John Calvin, *Ecclesiastical Ordinances* (Geneva, Switzerland), 1533
The Act of Supremacy (England), 1534
The Edict of Nantes (France), 1598
The Council of Trent (Italian states), 1545–1563
Matteo Ricci, Selection from his Journals
William Bradford, excerpt from *Of Plymouth Plantation*
Saint Francis Xavier on conversion of the Indians
Pope Paul III, *Sublimus Dei*, "On the Enslavement and Evangelization of Indians in the New World"
Cotton Mather, from *Magnalia Christi Americana*
Christopher Columbus, journal excerpt and letter
William Harvey, Address to the Royal College of Physicians, 1628
René Descartes, *The Discourse on Method* and "I Think, Therefore I Am"
Nicolaus Copernicus, excerpt from *On the Revolutions of the Heavenly Spheres*
Isaac Newton, from *Opticks*
Francis Bacon, from *Novum Organum*
Galileo, "Third Letter on Sunspots" (Italian States) 1612
A Sikh guru's testimony of faith

Visual Sources

St. Francis Xavier and other Jesuit missionaries
Printers and booksellers I
Printers and booksellers III
Printers and booksellers III
Johann Tetzel selling indulgences
Illustration from 1540, *The Emperor's Astronomy*
Heretic burning at the stake
Frontspiece from the first national atlas of England
The Taj Mahal
Islamic calligraphy
Illustration from the *Chronicles of Java*
The Peking observatory
Chinese Armillary sphere
Ongons (Mongolia)
Seal of Connecticut
Jesuit martyrs in Japan
Jesuit baptizing an Indian
Hispania slaying Leviathan
First book printed in the New World
American cannibals
Title page from Vico, *Principii di una Scienza Nuova*
Title page from Francis Bacon, *Novum Organum*
The Copernican solar system
Sixteenth-century anatomical drawings, I
Sixteenth-century anatomical drawings, II
Principles of magnetism: Illustration by William Gilbert, 1600
Illustration from Pascal's *Traitez*
Illustration from Newton's *Opticks*
Illustration showing a vacuum experiment
Descartes, illustration from *Optics*
Visit of Queen Anne of England to Anton von Leeuwenhoek, 1698
Frontspiece from Maimonides's *Guide for the Perplexed*
Torah scroll: The Washington Megillah
Descartes's view of the universe
Armenian missal
Armenian creation myth

19. States and Societies: Political and Social Change in the Sixteenth and Seventeenth Centuries

Text Sources

Niccolo Machiavelli, excerpts from *The Prince*
Jean Bodin, *Six Books of the Commonwealth*, "The True Attributes of Sovereignty"
Hugo Grotius, selections from *On the Law of War and Peace*
Sunni versus Shi'ite: Letter from Selim I to Ismail I
Paul Rycaut, on the State of the Ottoman Empire, 1668
Ogier Ghiselin de Busbecq, excerpt from "Women in Ottoman Society"
Fathers Simon and Vincent Report on Shah Abbas I, the Safavid Ruler of Persia
Excerpts from the Biography of Shah Abbas I
Portrait of an Ottoman Gentleman
Shah Isma'il Describes Himself to His Followers
Tokugawa Shogunate, The Laws for the Military House, 1615
Taisuke Mitamura, excerpt from *Chinese Eunuchs: The Structure of Intimate Politics*
Letters of Zheng Zhilong
Sumptuary Laws, Tokugawa Shogunate, 1640
Injunctions to Peasants, Tokugawa Shogunate, 1649
Willem Bosman, from *A New and Accurate Description of the Coast of Guinea Divided into the Gold, the Slave, and the Ivory Coasts*
Bryan Edwards, excerpt from "Observations on the ... Maroon Negroes of the Island of Jamaica"
Jean Domat, on social order and absolutist monarchy
The Marquis de Mirabeau: *The Friend of Men*, or *Treatise on Population* (1756)
Peter the Great, "Correspondence with Alexis" (Russia), 1715
Glückel of Hameln, *Memoirs* (The Holy Roman Empire) 1690
Louis Sebastien Mercier, from *Tableau de Paris*, vol. 1, "The Saint-Marcel Neighborhood"
The Peace of Westphalia, 1648
Lady Mary Wortley Montagu, Letters: (a) on Constantinople; (b) on Smallpox; (c) on Vaccination in Turkey (see Chapter 22)

Visual Sources
Frontispiece from Andreas Vesalius, *On the Fabric of the Human Body*
Eighteenth-century European engraving of Isfahan
Safavid battle tunic
Persian miniature painting: Layla and Majnun
Ottoman law book
Buddhist world map
Illustration of Pirate attack on Panama City
Illustrations from Adam Olearius, *Voyages*
Seventeenth-century Dutch illustration of buccaneers
View of the Guinea coast
Hobbes, *Leviathan* I
Hobbes, *Leviathan* II
A *casta* painting

PART 8 Global Enlightenments, 1700–1800

20. Driven by Growth: The Global Economy in the Eighteenth Century

Text Sources
King Louis XIV, "The Code Noir" (French), 1685
Marquis de Condorcet, passage from from *Sketch for a Historical Picture of the Progress of the Human Mind*
James Lind, from *A Treatise of the Scurvy*, 1753
Daniel Defoe, selection from *The Complete English Tradesman*
Thomas Malthus, excerpt from *Essay on the Principle of Population*
David Ricardo, excerpt from *Principles of Political Economy and Taxation*
David Ricardo, "The Iron Law of Wages"
Adam Smith, *The Wealth of Nations* (Great Britain), 1776
Johnathan Swift, "A Description on a City Shower" (Great Britain), 1710
Watkin Tench, from *A Complete Account of the Settlement at Port Jackson*
Lady Mary Wortley Montagu, Letters: (a) on Constantinople; (b) on Small-pox; (c) on Vaccination in Turkey (see Chapter 22)

Visual Sources
View of Nanjing
View of Guangzhou (Canton)
The Tokaido Road in Japan
View of Cape Town
Carolus Allard, engraving of the New York fur trade
Boston harbor
New England primer
Captain Cook in the Sandwich Islands, 1779
American magnolia tree, 1731
Eighteenth-century powderhorn
Galileo's telescopic drawing of the moon
Map of Mauritius, nineteenth century

21. The Age of Global Interaction: Expansion and Intersection of Eighteenth-Century Empires

Text Sources
Uthman dan Fodio Declares a Jihad, 1754-1817
Guidelines for Tributary Missions, Qing dynasty, 1764
Lady Mary Wortley Montagu, *Letters* (see Chapter 22)
Lord McCartney's observation on the state of China, 1792
Phillis Wheatley, "To the Right Honourable William, Earl of Dartmouth..."
Olaudah Equiano, excerpt from *The Interesting Narrative of the Life of Olaudah Equiano*
Five African American spirituals
Edmund Burke, Speech on policy in India, 1783
Crevecoeur, from *Letters from an American Farmer*, "What Is an America"
Crevecoeur, from *Letters from an American Farmer*
Jose Morelos, *Sentiments of the Nation* (Mexico), 1813
Simon de Bolívar, "Address to Second National Congress" (Venezuela), 1819

Visual Sources
European views of the Chinese
European views of Tartars and Chinese
Diagram of the slave ship *Brookes*
Portrait of Olaudah Equiano
Illustration from *American Magazine*, 1758
Advertisement for a slave auction
Illustrations from *Voyages and Travels*
View of St. Petersburg from the first Russian newspaper, *Vedomosti*
View of Gibraltar
View of Cape Town
Russian charter granted to the nobility
Revolutionary ladies, North Carolina
Prussian soldiers
Plan of San Antonio, Texas
Ohio River Valley
Boston Tea Party Revolution
Battle of Yorktown
1755 Battle between British and Indians
"Tea-Tax Tempest" by Carl Guttenberg
View of Batavia, 1764
Ottoman compass points, 1729
Islamic bookbinding
Engravings showing the military victories of the Emperor Quianlong I
Chinese acupuncturist

22. The Exchange of Enlightenments: Eighteenth-Century Thought

Text Sources
Emperor Qianlong, Mandate to King George III
Voltaire, *On Universal Toleration*
Mary Wollstonecraft, Introduction to *A Vindication of the Rights of Woman*
Lady Mary Wortley Montagu, Letters: (a) on Constantinople; (b) on Small-pox; (c) on Vaccination in Turkey
Immanuel Kant defines the Enlightenment, 1784
James Burney, on contact with the Maori of New Zealand
James Cook, from *Captain Cook's Journal During his First Voyage Round the World* (see Chapter 2)
Cesare Beccaria, from *An Essay on Crimes and Punishments*
Abu Taleb Khan, A Muslim Indian's Reactions to the West
John Locke, *Essay Concerning Human Understanding* (Great Britain), 1689
Denis Diderot, Preliminary Discourse from *The Encyclopedia* (France), 1751
Voltaire, *Letters on England* (France) 1733
Johann Wolfgang von Goethe, *Prometheus*, 1773
Revolutionary France: *The Declaration of the Rights of Man and of the Citizen*, 1789-1791
Olympe de Gouges, *Declaration of the Rights of Woman and the Female Citizen*
Baron de Montesquieu, excerpt from *The Spirit of the Laws*
Voltaire: On Social Conditions in Eighteenth-century France
The *Encyclopédie*, "Bakers (Boulanger)" (France) 1763
French Peasants, *Cahiers de doléances* (Grievances) (France), 1789
Robespierre, "Speech to National Convention: The Terror Justified" (France), 1794
Edmund Burke, *Reflections on the Revolution in France*, (Great Britain) 1790
Qianlong emperor, letter to George III
Alexander von Humboldt, from a *Personal Narrative of a Journey to the Equinoctial Regions of the New Continent*

Visual Sources
Shinto temple
Profiles of Asian peoples
Northern Tartary women
Mandarins
Chinese jade book
The Jagas
Title page from a Japanese anatomy text c. 1775
Study of the Aztec calendar stone

Jewish medical text by Tobias Cohen
Illustration from *Poor Richard's Almanack*
Blake's image of the creation
Birds of America by John Audubon I
Birds of America by John Audubon II
Aztec calendar wheel
A Beethoven sonata manuscript
Origins of the French monarchy
Illustration of the execution of King Louis XVI, 1793
Illustration of the murder of Jean-Paul Marat, 1793
"Cult of the Supreme Being," French Revolution
Eighteenth-century Japanese painting, "A Meeting of China, Japan, and the West"
Map of the country of Georgia

PART 9 The Frustrations of Progress, to ca. 1900

23. Replacing Muscle: The Energy Revolution

Text Sources

William Hazlitt, selections from *The Spirit of the Age*
Parliamentary report on English female miners, 1842
Fanny Kemble, excerpt from *Records of a Girlhood*
Benjamin Disraeli, excerpt from *Sybil, or The Two Nations*
Anthony Trollope, excerpt from *North America*
Andrew Ure, from *The Philosophy of Manufactures*
Carl von Clauswitz, *On War*, "Arming the Nation"
James Fenimore Cooper, Author's Introduction to *The Prairie*
Commodore Perry's Views of the Japanese, 1853

Visual Sources

Nineteenth-century globe
View of Charleston, ca. 1870
Unloading coffee in Brazil
Tashkent textile mill
Singer sewing machine advertisement
Port of Valparaiso, Chile
Nineteenth-century whale chart
Mill on the Brandywine
Logging in Minnesota, 1893
Kimberley mine, South Africa
Illinois Central Railroad poster
Excelsior Iron Works
Nicaraguan woman sorting coffee beans, ca. 1900
Ironclad warship
Quito textile factory, circa 1910
Machine exhibit, 1904 Worlds Fair
Japanese views of Commodore Perry's mission, 1853, I
Japanese views of Commodore Perry's mission, 1853, II
Japanese views of Commodore Perry's mission, 1853, III
Japanese views of Commodore Perry's mission, 1853, IV
Japanese views of Commodore Perry's mission, 1853, V
Japanese views of Commodore Perry's mission, 1853, VI
Map of the western United States
Map of East Indies

24. The Social Mold: Work and Society in the Nineteenth Century

Text Sources

Alexander Telfair, Instructions to an Overseer in a Cotton Plantation
Pope Leo XIII, *Rerum Novarum* (Of New Things) 1891
Multatuli, *Max Havelaar: Or the Coffee Auctions of the Dutch Trading Company*
Auguste Comte, "Course of Positive Philosophy" (France) 1830–1842
"The Sadler Report: Child Labor in the United Kingdom," 1832
Frederick Winslow Taylor, "A Piece Rate System," 1896
Edwin Chadwick, Summary from the Poor Law Commissioners
Chartist Movement: The People's Petition of 1838
A Luddite pamphlet
Karl Marx and Fredrich Engels, from the *Communist Manifesto*
Henrik Ibsen, from *A Doll's House*, Act Three
Emile Zola, *Nana* (France), 1880
Friedrich Nietzsche, *Beyond Good and Evil* (Germany), 1886
Samuel Smiles, excerpt from *Self Help, with Illustrations of Character and Conduct*
African American Emancipation Songs: (a) "Many Thousands Gone;" (b) "Kingdom Coming"
Abraham Lincoln, "The Emancipation Proclamation"
Domingo F. Sarmiento, "Civilization and Barbarism," 1845
Lafcadio Hearn on Japanese geisha: from *Glimpses of Unfamiliar Japan*
George Eliot, "Review: Margaret Fuller and Mary Wollstonecraft" (Great Britain), 1855
Richard Freiherr von Krafft-Ebing, *Psychopathia Sexualia* (Germany), 1886

Visual Sources

Street scenes, Germany
Slaves carrying cotton and picking cotton II
Slaves carrying cotton and picking cotton I
Slave shackles
Moneylender's house, India
Italian immigrants in USA
Immigrants sailing to USA
Georgian (Caucasus) peasants
Advertisement for gas-smoothing iron
Filipino slaves
Slum Life: Dead horse in New York street
Cotton plantation, United States of America
Chinese immigrants in USA
Child textile worker
Ceylonese tea picker
Calcutta water dispenser
Bolivian child laborers
Architectural iron works catalog
Uncle Tom's Cabin advertisement
Frontispiece from Martin Chuzzlewit
Pinel's skull types
Muybridge photos
French engraving of profession in Cairo, Egypt
Ancient Egyptian statues
de Ovi Mamalian, by Karl von Baer
The "New Europes": Sydney
The "New Europes": New York City
The "New Europes": Johannesburg
The "New Europes": Detroit
The "New Europes": Cape Town
San Francisco earthquake
Indian School, Pennsylvania
A Peruvian couple, ca. 1860
Immigrant Hotel, Buenos Aires, ca. 1900
Photograph of an Uzbek woman from the *Turkestanskii Albom*
Inuit family, 1918
Howkan Indian village, Alaska
A Kuaba doll

25. Western Dominance in the Nineteenth Century: The Westward Shift of Power and the Rise of Global Empires

Text Sources

Peters, "A Manifesto for German Colonization" (Germany and Africa), 1884
Theodore Christlieb, *Protestant Foreign Missions: Their Present State*, 1879
Prince Aleksandr Gorchakov, "The Gorchakov Circular," (Russia) 1864
Thomas Babington Macaulay, from *Minute on Education*, 1835
Charles Darwin, from *The Origin of the Species*
Herbet Spencer, *Illustrations of Universal Progress*, 1865
Karl Marx, "The British Rule in India," 1853

Karl Pearson, "Social Darwinism and Imperialism"
Mary Kingsley, *Travels in West Africa* (Great Britain and Africa), 1893 and 1895
The Scramble for Africa
Rudyard Kipling, "The White Man's Burden"
Robert Louis Stevenson, passage from *In the South Seas*
President Millard Fillmore, Letter to the Emperor of Japan, 1852
Lord William Bentinck, on the Suppression of *Sati,* 1829
Jules Ferry, *Le Tonkin et la Mere-Patrie*
Fustel de Coulanges, Letter to German Historian Theodor Mommsen, 1870
Mary Seacole, *Wonderful Adventures of Mrs. Seacole in Many Lands*
Liliuokalani, *Hawaii's Story*
The Treaty of Nanking, 1842
Russo-Japanese War: Imperial Rescript, 1904
Long Yu, The Abdication Decree, 1912
Lin Zexu, Letter to Queen Victoria, 1839
Francisco García Calderón, excerpt from *Latin America: Its Rise and Progress*
Emperor Meiji, The Constitution of the Empire of Japan
Edward D. Morel, *The Black Man's Burden*
Letter of Plan Chu Trinh to the French Governor-General, 1906
William Hunter, "Description of European Factories in Guangzhou," 1824
China: Rules Regulating Foreign Trading in Guangzhou
Joseph Conrad, *An Outpost of Progress*, 1898
Huda Shaarawi, "Europe on the Eve of War" (Egypt), 1914
The Iranian and Turkish Constitutional Revolutions of 1906 and 1908
Kartini, Letters of a Javanese Princess (Dutch East Indies, Java) 1899–1904
The Platt Amendment

Visual Sources
Wagon train crossing the Sierra Nevada
Homestead steel mill
Tbilisi in the late nineteenth century
Portrait of Sequoyah, inventor of the Cherokee alphabet
Pygmies, 1904 World's Fair
Pears' soap advertisement
Mandan Sioux offering
Georgian musicians
US field hospital in the Philippines, Philippine-American War
Early churches in Hawaii I
Early churches in Hawaii II
Dinizulu, king of the Zulus
Christian missionaries in Africa, late nineteenth century
Chinese pavilion, 1904 Worlds Fair
K. I. Keppen, Battle of Kinburn, 1855
J. M. Stanley, Araucanian chief
Apache Indian prinsoners, 1886
Ainu woman
Afrikaner guerrillas, Second Boer War
Africans being baptized, South Africa, nineteenth century
Grigorii Chernetsov, "Parade on Tsarina's Meadow," 1831
Freemasons from Sierra Leone addressing the Duke of Connaught, December 1910.
Christian missionary in China, circa 1900
Theodore Roosevelt building the Panama Canal, 1906
Tattooed Polynesian warrior
Tattooed native of Nukahiwa
Polynesian mask
Pancho Villa
Emperor Meiji
Frontspiece from *al-Muqtataf*
Filipino insurgents, 1900
Lin Zexu destroying opium
Caucasian warriors wearing chain mail
Americans in Yokohama, 1855
A Muslim view of the Russian Empire
Harvesting sisal leaves, British East Africa, early twentieth century
Harvesting cocoa beans, British West Africa, early twentieth century
carved African footstool
Map of Africa from the Cedid Atlas

26. The Changing State: Political Development in the Nineteenth Century

Text Sources
Amrita Lal Roy, English Rule in India (1886)
A British traveler's Report on the Sokoto Caliphate
Joseph Mazzini, *Life and Writings of Joseph Mazzini,* 1805–1872
Robert Owen, excerpt from *Address to the Workers of New Lanark*, 1816
Eliza Bishee Duffey, from *No Sex in Education; or, an Equal Chance for Both Girls and Boys*, 1874
Dadabhai Naoroji, *The Benefits of British Rule in India* (1871)
Thorstein Veblen, excerpt from *The Theory of Leisure Class*
Matthew Arnold, excerpt from *Dover Beach*
John Stuart Mill, excerpts from *On Liberty*
Francisco Bilbao, *America in Danger* (1862)
Friederich Hassaurek, *How to Conduct a Latin American Revolution* (1865)
Mikhail Bakunin, "Principles and Organization of the International Brotherhood," 1866
Serbian Society of National Defense, Program for Nationalism
Alexis de Tocqueville, excerpt from *Democracy in America*
José Fernández, *El Gaucho Martín Fierro*
W.E.B. Du Bois, *Souls of Black Folk*, "Of Mr. Booker T. Washington and Others"
José Rizal, excerpt from *The Reign of Greed*
Feng Guifen, on Western Strength
Booker T. Washington, "Industrial Education for the Negro"
An Ottoman Government Decree Defines the Official Notion of the "Modern" Citizen, June 19, 1870
José Rizal, *Noli Me Tangere* (The Social Cancer)
Orishatuke Faduma, "African Negro Education," 1918
Nguyen Van Vinh's View of the Vietnamese, 1913
The Views of Ii Naosuke, 1853
The Views of Tokugawa Nariaki, 1841
Japanese impressions of American culture, 1860.
Japan: The Imperial Rescript on Education, 1890
"An Appeal to the Members of the Imperial Parliament and Public of Great Britain," petition from the South African Native National Congress, 1914.
Arthur James Balfour, "Problems with Which We Have to Deal in Egypt," 1910
China: Questions and Topics of the 1903-1904 Jinshi Degree Examination
Jiang Jieshi on the Chinese Communist Party and Japan, 1933

Visual Sources
Women suffrage parade
Reconstruction in the American South
North-South reconciliation through the Spanish-American war, 1898
Lincoln remembrance
Cherokee Constitution
Black soldier, United States Civil War
An Argentine gaucho, ca. 1870
Signing of the Treaty of Portsmouth, 1905
Portrait of Jose Rizal

PART 10 Chaos and Complexity: The World in the Twentieth Century

27. The Twentieth-Century Mind: Western Science and the World

Text Sources
William James, from *Pragmatism*, 1907
Franz Boas, from *The Mind of Primitive Man*, 1911
Filippo Tommaso Marinetti, "Futuristic Manifesto"
Ellen Key, from *The Century of the Child*
Al-Afghani on faith and reason, 1883